THE OXFORD HANDBOOK OF

# THE ECONOMICS OF THE PACIFIC RIM

THE OXFORD HANDBOOK OF

# THE ECONOMICS OF THE PACIFIC RIM

*Edited by*

INDERJIT KAUR
AND
NIRVIKAR SINGH

OXFORD
UNIVERSITY PRESS

OXFORD
UNIVERSITY PRESS

Oxford University Press is a department of the University of Oxford.
It furthers the University's objective of excellence in research, scholarship,
and education by publishing worldwide.

Oxford New York
Auckland Cape Town Dar es Salaam Hong Kong Karachi
Kuala Lumpur Madrid Melbourne Mexico City Nairobi
New Delhi Shanghai Taipei Toronto

With offices in
Argentina Austria Brazil Chile Czech Republic France Greece
Guatemala Hungary Italy Japan Poland Portugal Singapore
South Korea Switzerland Thailand Turkey Ukraine Vietnam



Published in the United States of America by
Oxford University Press
198 Madison Avenue, New York, NY 10016



Library of Congress Cataloging-in-Publication Data

The Oxford handbook of the economics of the Pacific Rim / edited by
Inderjit N. Kaur and Nirvikar Singh.
pages cm
Includes bibliographical references.
Summary: "A survey of the economy of the Pacific
Rim region"— Provided by publisher.
ISBN 978-0-19-975199-0 (alk. paper)
1. Pacific Area—Economic conditions. 2. Pacific Area—Economic integration.
3. Asia—Economic conditions. 4. Asia—Economic integration. I. Kaur, Inderjit N.,
editor of compilation. II. Singh, Nirvikar, editor of compilation.
HC681.O94 2013
330.9182'3—dc23
2013004669

1 3 5 7 9 8 6 4 2
Printed in the United States of America
on acid-free paper

# Contents

## PART III PERSPECTIVES ON ECONOMIC GROWTH AND DEVELOPMENT



## PART IV REGIONAL GOVERNANCE AND TRADE LINKAGES



## PART V INDUSTRY, POLICY, AND INNOVATION

## PART VI MACROECONOMICS AND FINANCE

# Acknowledgments

THE conceptualization of the Pacific Rim as an economic entity has emerged only in the past few decades, but the importance of this way of looking at the world will only increase. Therefore, we think this volume has great potential significance, and that underlies our acknowledgment of the hard work of many people who together made this possible. The scope and sweep of the Pacific Rim as a region made the project a long and challenging one, as we sought to cover a wide range of important issues and include diverse perspectives from a range of influential scholars.

We wish to first thank the consulting editors of the Oxford Handbook series, Michael Szenberg and Lall Ramrattan, as well as OUP Executive Editor Terry Vaughn, for the opportunity to undertake this important project. We are grateful to Catherine Rae, formerly of OUP, for her initial help, and most of all we are indebted to Cathryn Vaulman for stepping in and helping us bring this effort to fruition with great patience and care. We also wish to acknowledge the project manager of the production team, Bharathy Surya Prakash, as well as her team members, for their patient work on getting the volume into its final form.

Inderjit Kaur would like to acknowledge the rich intellectual environment of the University of San Francisco Center for the Pacific Rim, where she held a Research Fellowship of the Kiriyama Chair for Pacific Rim Studies. In particular, she is indebted to the then-Executive Director of the Center, Barbara Bundy, for many valuable conversations. She also acknowledges the consistent support of the Center's Associate Director at the time, Ken Kopp, and of the Kiriyama Chair for Pacific Rim Studies.

Nirvikar Singh would like to acknowledge his former and current colleagues at UC Santa Cruz, some of whom have contributed to this volume, for many interactions that have expanded his understanding of the economics of the Pacific Rim, and the global economy more generally: Joshua Aizenman, Yin-Wong Cheung, Menzie Chinn, Michael Dooley, K.C. Fung, Michael Hutchison and Phillip McCalman. Michael Hutchison, in particular, has been a valued collaborator on a range of projects, and he, Menzie and K.C. joined Nirvikar in founding the Santa Cruz Center for International Economics, which became an important intellectual hub for work on the global economy, including much on the Pacific Rim. Nirvikar would also like to acknowledge learning from many collaborators on various past Pacific Rim research projects: K. P. Kalirajan, Terrie Carolan, Gaofeng Han, Jesse Mora, Cyrus Talati and Hung Trieu. Much of that collaborative work was funded by the University of California Pacific Rim Research Program, and their support is gratefully acknowledged as well.

Most of all we would like to acknowledge and thank the authors who contributed to this volume. They have produced an outstanding set of pieces, which we think will be influential in guiding future thinking about the economics of the Pacific Rim. It has been a pleasure to work with them on this project, and we cannot thank them enough for their participation, cooperation and wonderful hard work. We believe that work will have a lasting impact.

# List of Contributors

**Joshua Aizenman** is Dockson Chair in Economics and International Relations at the University of Southern California and Research Associate at the NBER.

**Prema-Chandra Athukorala** is Professor of Economics at the Crawford School of Public Policy at Australian National University.

**Barry Bosworth** is Senior Fellow of Economic Research at the Brookings Institution.

**Yin-Wong Cheung** is Head & Chair Professor of Department of Economics and Finance at City University of Hong Kong, Hong Kong.

**Menzie D. Chinn** is Professor of Public Affairs and Economics at the University of Wisconsin, Madison.

**Susan M. Collins** is Joan and Sanford Weill Dean of Public Policy at the Gerald R. Ford School of Public Policy and Professor of Economics in the College of Literature, Science, and the Arts at the University of Michigan, as well as Senior Fellow of Economic Research at the Brookings Institution.

**Hinh T. Dinh** is Lead Economist in the Office of the Senior Vice President and Chief Economist of the World Bank.

**Wendy Dobson** is Co-Director of the Rotman Institute for International Business and Adjunct Professor of Business Economics at Rotman School of Management, University of Toronto.

**Reuven Glick** is Group Vice President of International Research of the Federal Reserve Bank of San Francisco.

**Maria Socorro Gochoco-Bautista** is Senior Economic Advisor at the Economics and Research Department, Asian Development Bank and Bangko Sentral ng Pilipinas Sterling Chair in Monetary Economics in the School of Economics at University of the Philippines.

**Anne Goujon** is Research Scientist of Population Dynamics and Forecasting at the Vienna Institute of Demography, Austrian Academy of Sciences.

**Deng-Shing Huang** is Researcher at the Institute of Economics at Academia Sinica.

**Michael Hutchison** is Professor of Economics at the University of California, Santa Cruz, and Co-Director of the Santa Cruz Center for International Economics.

**Hiro Ito** is Associate Professor of Economics at Portland State University.

**Eric Jones** is Professorial Fellow in Economic History at the University of Melbourne Business School.

**Devesh Kapur** is Director of the Center for the Advanced Study of India at the University of Pennsylvania.

**Inderjit Kaur** is Research Associate at the University of California, Santa Cruz.

**Anne O. Krueger** is Professor of International Economics in the School for Advanced International Studies at Johns Hopkins University.

**Manmohan Singh Kumar** is Assistant Director in the Finance Department and Chief of General Resources and SDR Policies Division at the International Monetary Fund.

**Justin Yifu Lin** is Director of the China Center for Economic Research at Peking University. He was formerly World Bank Chief Economist and Senior Vice President of Development Economics.

**Philip Martin** is Professor of Agricultural and Resource Economics, Chair of the UC Comparative Immigration & Integration Program, and Editor of *Migration News* and *Rural Migration News* at the University of California, Davis.

**Hui Miao** is China and Hong Kong Equity Strategist and Director at Deutsche Bank.

**Chikafumi Nakamura** is Assistant Professor of Economic Systems Analaysis at Kyushu University.

**Ilan Noy** is Associate Professor of Economics at Victoria Business School, New Zealand and the University of Hawai'i, Manoa.

**Eiji Ogawa** is Professor of International Finance at Hitotsubashi University, Graduate School of Commerce and Management.

**Naohiro Ogawa** is Professor of Human Development Science at Nihon University.

**Howard Pack** is Professor of Business Economics and Public Policy in the Wharton School of Business at the University of Pennsylvania.

**Peter A. Petri** is the Carl Shapiro Professor of International Finance at Brandeis University.

**John Ravenhill** is Director of the Balsillie School of International Affairs, Waterloo, Canada.

**David Roland-Holst** is Adjunct Professor in the Department of Agricultural and Resource Economics and the Department of Economics at the University of California, Berkeley.

**Nirvikar Singh** is Professor of Economics at the University of California, Santa Cruz, and Director, Center for Analytical Finance.

**Noli R. Sotocinal** is Senior Economist at the Asian Development Bank.

**Manik Suri** is a J.D. candidate at Harvard Law School, Visiting Fellow at the University of Pennsylvania's Center for the Advanced Study of India, and a Truman Security Fellow.

**F. Ted Tschang** is Associate Professor of Strategic Management in the Lee Kong Chian School of Business at Singapore Management University.

**Kar-Yiu Wong** is Professor of Economics at the University of Washington, Director of the Research Center for International Economics (RCIE), and President of the Asia-Pacific Economic Association (APEA).

**Jaejoon Woo** is Associate Professor of Economics at DePaul University and Senior Economist at the International Monetary Fund.

**Tzu-Han Yang** is Professor in the Department of Public Finance at National Taipei University.

**Shahid Yusuf** is Chief Economist of The Growth Dialogue at George Washington University.

# INTRODUCTION

INDERJIT KAUR AND NIRVIKAR SINGH

THE Pacific Rim as a geographic entity has existed for eons, but its economic salience has emerged only in the past few decades, beginning with Japan's achievement of the status of a major economic power. Japan's development heralded the start of an "East Asian Miracle" that also saw economies such as South Korea and Taiwan register rates of growth that had hitherto been unprecedented for any sustained period. More recently, China's economic trajectory and its size have given new weight to the term "Pacific Rim." The region now encompasses the three largest economies in the world, the United States, China, and Japan, as well as other major economies such as Russia and Indonesia. At the other extreme, it also includes a dozen or more small island nations. In all, over four dozen nations and territories can be considered part of the Pacific Rim, using a literal geographic designation.

The size and diversity of the geographic Pacific Rim initially made it less obvious to consider the region as an economic unit, although trade and migration throughout the southwestern side of the Rim (i.e., Southeast Asia) had been important for centuries. First the Mediterranean, and then the Atlantic, were the two major "oceanic" economies of history. Southeast Asia had significant economic connections with India, outside the Pacific Rim, but China and Japan both tried to close themselves off to the rest of the world in different ways. Trans-Pacific interactions were not the most major aspect of the global economy. The post-World-War-II political alignment, coupled with technological change and falling transportation costs, played important roles in making the Pacific a locus of economic activity and attention.

From a geostrategic perspective, the two economic giants on either side of the Pacific, the United States and China, have the potential to shape the evolution of the global economy over the next few decades. Their bilateral economic relations, reflected in trade and investment flows, and in asset holdings, have loomed large in the last decade, and the issue of global imbalances can often be reduced to the economic accounts of the United States and China. However, none of this makes the rest of the region irrelevant: natural resources, manufacturing capabilities, and human capital are spread throughout the Pacific Rim, and even city states like Singapore play important roles as trade and finance hubs. India, as a large, economically dynamic nation just slightly removed from the literal (or littoral) Pacific Rim, will also be part of the region's economic trajectory.

What are the key issues that deserve attention in thinking about the economies and economics of the Pacific Rim? Many of these key issues are not unique to the region, but their manifestations are obviously region-specific. We have noted some of the dimensions of interaction between the United States and China. This bilateral relationship has many spillovers, into patterns of trade and investment in the region. Varied attempts at regional cooperation or coordination in trade, finance, regulatory standards, and macroeconomic policies are all influenced to some extent by the regional presence of China and the United States. These regional efforts will inevitably receive increasing attention in the next few years. Issues such as the management of climate change and its impacts, as well as of other kinds of risks associated with natural disasters, will also become more important in regional efforts to coordinate institutional structures and strategies for preparation and response. The economic crisis of 2008, following on the Asian crisis of 1997, has heightened concerns about managing the large volumes of globally mobile capital that can swamp individual economies and their governments' response capabilities. Differences in regulations and policy stances across economies can exacerbate the potential problems.

Of the larger economies of the Pacific Rim, only the United States and Japan have income levels that qualify them as "advanced economies," though South Korea is coming closer, and Singapore, as a small city state, has matched them. Therefore, the problem of economic development still looms large for many of the economies of the region. How will China, Malaysia, and other economies that have a good past record of growth avoid a "middle-income trap?" How will relatively poorer nations such as Indonesia, Laos, or Cambodia even achieve middle-income status in a global economic environment that seems to be subject to increasing risks? One important issue is the configuration of global production networks and the ability of developing nations to find successful niches in these networks. Another—long debated but still unsettled—issue is the role of government policies in fostering industrial development or, more broadly, structural economic change. At the same time, governments' fiscal capacity to support whatever policies are needed—whether enabling or more activist—may come up against difficult demographic realities of aging populations. Given the important place held by innovation in economists' theoretical understanding of processes of long-run economic growth, the capacity of the developing economies of the region to innovate, or just to catch up to the technology frontier, will also be a significant issue in the coming years. In this context, the development of the capabilities of the region's people, their human capital, and their opportunities to use their skills where they are most valuable, will also be important issues.

Given the broader issues and concerns we have summarized above, for this volume we strove to collect as wide a set of specific perspectives as we possibly could, on the economies and economics of the Pacific Rim. We wanted historical perspectives, discussions of future trends, considerations of people and ideas as well as goods and money, and perspectives on politics and governance as it shapes the economics of the region. We also wanted the contributors to come from all around the region, to provide a diversity of voices and insights. To a large extent, we think this collection reflects our objectives. Authors have treated a wide variety of topics, ranging from biology and geophysics to modern financial integration. In keeping with the aim of the *Handbook*, we gave authors considerable flexibility to define the scope of their pieces. In many cases, authors chose proper subsets of the region, inevitable and even desirable given the size and heterogeneity of the Pacific Rim. In one or two cases, authors chose to include some consideration of India, which is not literally in the region, but seeks to connect more with the region's economies, and is seen by some as a future counterweight to China's economic influence. We were not able to get as much focused attention as we would have liked on the Latin American part of the region, as well as on Canada and Mexico in North America. Several chapters do consider economies on the eastern side of the Pacific Ocean, but they do not receive the same attention as the economies of the Asian Pacific Rim.

No single volume can cover every aspect of the region's economies, and this *Handbook* is no exception to that constraint. However, we believe that this volume still represents a fresh and innovative collection of pieces by an important group of economists, featuring leading experts on the region, from all over the region. We think it will be valuable not just in summarizing what we know about many aspects of the economies of the Pacific Rim, but also in raising issues for future investigation and debate. The remainder of this introduction provides a summary of all the contributions to the *Handbook*, giving the reader a bird's-eye view of the volume's scope and content.

## The Natural World: History, Climate, and Risks

Eric Jones, in chapter 1, provides a fascinating and far-reaching account of biological exploitation on the Pacific Rim. He makes the point that renewable and non-renewable resources often get lumped together, and that world history has often made Europe and the Atlantic the center of attention. Jones provides a corrective to the relative neglect of the Pacific Rim as a region in the context of the economic use of its biological resources, with a sweeping historical overview. Initially, the size and more recent discovery of the Pacific by the rising Western powers suggested that the region's resources were boundless, but, as Jones documents, the impacts on the Pacific of exploitation such as unchecked fishing were felt not too long after similar effects in the Atlantic. Going back further in time, Jones points out that cross-Pacific trade had enormously important impacts on domestic economies, well before the modern period. Transfers of crops from the Americas to China had a tremendous effect on China's agriculture and its population size and distribution, even at a time when it was viewed as conventionally "closed" to foreign economic influence.

Jones goes on to describe and document the ecological impacts of European intrusion on East Asian and other Pacific Rim landscapes. The spread of agriculture, displacing hunter gatherers, was dramatic in this period, as were impacts such as species extinction. The balance of flora and fauna was altered dramatically with the introduction of many alien species. Jones traces the development of "neo-Europes" in countries such as Australia and New Zealand, and the development of new patterns of international trade in commodities such as wool and timber. The European intrusion dramatically expanded the world's agricultural supply in several dimensions.

Irrespective of the impact of Europe, the growth of the economies on the western rim of the Pacific Ocean has started to have significant effects on the global ecosystem, including greenhouse gas emissions and changes in local ecosystems. Japan and China's ecological shadows have been very visible in their impacts on resources such as forests and marine life. A further striking aspect of the Asian Pacific Rim's growth, according to Jones, has been the demand for various body parts of animals, including many endangered species, for food, for ornamentation, and often for mythical health benefits. The rapid growth of incomes has expanded the demand for these items, as cultural norms have not adapted to economic development.[1]

The chapter goes on to discuss the positives as well as the negatives of current patterns of resource use—the positives including increased agricultural yields and overall economic progress. In considering future mitigation options, Jones provides a useful brief account of historical conservation efforts in countries such as Japan. He also offers historical perspectives on new remedies such as ecotourism. The analysis concludes with a discussion of possible future equilibria, including the outward-looking resource strategies of countries such as China. Viewing the rich sweep of the Pacific Rim's ecological history, Jones expects the region's ecosystem to continue being shaped by more and more intensive resource use by its human inhabitants. Indeed, this resource use will have increasingly global impacts, as the chapter clearly documents with historical experience.

In chapter 2, David Roland-Holst begins by noting that average temperatures in the Earth's atmosphere have begun an upward trend that is largely irreversible over the next century, regardless of climate policy options currently under discussion. He makes the point that, with large coastal populations and extensive reliance on tropical and snow-fed agrifood systems, the Pacific Rim faces momentous challenges from climate risk. His chapter reviews conceptual issues, evidence, and policy options for addressing regional climate risk.

Roland-Holst begins by distinguishing between mitigation and adaptation. The former includes approaches to limiting greenhouse gas emissions and other anthropogenic contributions to climate change. Mitigation requires cooperation, all the way up to the local level. On the other hand, adaptation is more local, and the causality is reversed from mitigation, going from effects of climate change to behavioral responses. Both mitigation and adaptation are complicated by the geographic and economic diversity of the Pacific Rim countries. The chapter focuses on adaptation, and uncertainties associated with adaptation in the realms of economic impacts and institutional capacities for response. Roland-Holst provides an excellent overview of issues with respect to valuing or pricing risks associated with climate change, as well as the costs of mitigation and adaptation. He discusses institutions, incentives, and difficulties of appropriate discounting of the future. These are all generic challenges for formulating policies in the face of climate change.

In turning to issues specific to the region, Roland-Holst begins by noting that the two largest national sources of greenhouse gas emissions are in the Pacific Rim, namely, the United States and China. He notes that economic growth will exacerbate the problem, and that this region contains several fast-growing economies. The potential growth of automobile use in the region is particularly challenging for mitigation of greenhouse gas emissions. Changing patterns of food consumption associated with income growth will also accelerate energy use in this dynamic region. The chapter also considers implications for water availability and use, and the potential impacts of sea-level rise associated with climate change.

One of the conclusions of the chapter is that there are going to be potentially high costs of adaptation to climate change, requiring large capital investments. These will need strong public institutions, at both the national and supranational levels. Roland-Holst offers some optimism in terms of the possibility of dramatic innovation in anticipation of climate change, but the overall message of the chapter is a sobering one for the region, which encapsulates some of the most challenging issues of global climate change. If these issues are not addressed in a timely fashion, as part of regional growth strategies, the Pacific Rim growth miracle that began in the late twentieth century may be short-circuited or reversed as soon as the middle of the twenty-first century.

Ilan Noy, in chapter 3, provides an excellent overview and introduction to the relatively new field of the economics of natural disasters, specifically in the context of the Pacific Rim. The region is a key source of data for this topic, since it is prone to earthquakes, associated tsunamis, and large numbers of tropical storms. The size and geographic characteristics of the region contribute to this situation, of course.

Noy begins by summarizing the recent experience of the Pacific Rim with natural disasters. Many of the worst recent earthquakes, tsunamis, volcanic eruptions, floods, storms, and other natural disasters have occurred along the Pacific Rim. The chapter goes on to review the evidence on the possible impacts of climate change, and, while acknowledging the substantial uncertainties in prediction, echoes the concern that extreme events such as droughts and floods will become more common over time, as a result of global warming and associated changes in climate patterns. Indeed, later in the chapter there is a discussion of how events previously thought of as very rare (one in five hundred years, for example) have occurred several times in recent years.

Noy's chapter goes on to examine various economic aspects of natural disasters in the Pacific Rim, beginning with the economic costs. A conceptual distinction is made between direct and indirect economic impacts, and the piece provides econometric analysis as well as an extensive discussion of political economy factors, the role of inter-regional transfers, and the nature of fiscal impacts. Noy also surveys the relevance of the idea of "creative destruction," Schumpeter's concept of the cycle of obsolescence and innovation that drives capitalist economies. In this context, the term has a poignantly direct applicability, and Noy dispassionately examines the evidence for whether disasters afford reinvestment opportunities for the affected areas. As might be expected, given the complexity and diversity of the phenomena and responses, there is not a simple or uniform answer.

There are several other issues discussed in the chapter, which will ultimately have wider relevance to questions of economic development in the region. One major issue is the role of financial markets, ranging from insurance for disasters to financial instruments for rebuilding. Noy highlights some of the problems with achieving adequate insurance coverage, the incentive problems associated with insurance, and the possibilities for financial innovations such as "catastrophe bonds." Other important issues covered in the chapter include the role of out-migration after disasters in the recovery of affected regions and the spillover effects of natural disasters, ranging from the financial shock created for European economies (where the insurers were based) by the 1906 San Francisco earthquake to the disruption of global supply chains that followed the 2011 Japanese earthquake and tsunami. The chapter concludes with open policy questions, ranging from how to define and achieve more efficient insurance coverage, to the scope for, and impacts of, improved early-warning systems.

While the focus of Noy's chapter is not on climate change, clearly there is a close link between the issues addressed there, and the broader challenges of mitigation and adaptive responses to climate change, as surveyed in Roland-Holst's chapter. The latter concerns broader issues, in that climate change will not only affect the pattern and frequency of certain kinds of natural disasters, but will also lead to fundamental long run change in what is "normal," not just what is extreme. Both chapters should be read in conjunction with Jones's historical analysis of biological change in the Pacific Rim, which provides some insights into what the future might hold. Biological variation and change is an area that deserves further discussion by economists: the chapters by Roland-Holst and Noy focus most on geophysical and hydro-meteorological phenomena and impacts.

## People: Migration, Demographics, and Human Capital

Philip Martin provides a concise overview of international labor migration in the Pacific Rim in chapter 4. He begins by noting some of the heterogeneity in the region, with Japan and Singapore being at opposite extremes of rates of accepting foreign workers in their countries, and the Philippines being a major sender of labor abroad. Martin notes several dimensions that distinguish labor migration in the Asia Pacific region. International labor migration in the Asia-Pacific region is unique in three major ways. For example, Asian governments typically approach the challenge of managing low-skilled labor migration differently than governments in Europe and America. They are more cautious about immigration, and seek to avoid settlement and integration issues associated with low-skilled migrants. Furthermore, there is a large degree of within-region difference with respect to labor migration policies, unlike the similarities in other aspects of economic policy such as foreign-investment and export-orientation. Finally, Martin suggests that the policies of the major Asian migrant-sending governments are converging, sending more skilled workers to destinations inside and outside Asia to maximize remittances.

Martin's piece surveys the status of migration institutions and outcomes in the Asian Pacific region. He notes that there is significant migration from Asia to the developed nations of the Pacific Rim: Australia, Canada, New Zealand, and the United States, as well as among many of the countries of Southeast Asia. Because of the importance of the Middle East as a migration destination, he also considers the institutions of that region, specifically the countries of the Gulf Cooperation Council. The chapter explores the special cases of the Philippines and Vietnam in great detail, as both these countries are heavily influenced by their ties to the United States. In all of these cases, Martin notes the role of migration brokers, and the problems of migrants being tricked by recruiters and brokers in a market that is difficult to regulate or monitor effectively.

Turning to the economic impacts of migration, Martin's piece considers the effects of remittances as well as returns by migrants on the process of economic development. In the context of China, he also examines in detail the vast rural-urban migration that is taking place within that giant nation. The chapter concludes with an overall assessment of international labor migration, especially in the context of the Asian Pacific Rim. The author notes that international labor migration will be an increasingly important phenomenon, and will require more enlightened political and economic management in the future. He gives examples of how East Asian governments have been trying to design and implement policies to better manage international labor migration.

In chapter 5, Naohiro Ogawa examines the changes in demographics in selected Asian Pacific countries, and traces out the impacts of those changes for intergenerational transfers. East Asia has seen a demographic shift unprecedented in its rapidity. Declines in fertility as well as increases in longevity have been behind this phenomenon, with the former playing a more significant role till now, but with aging also becoming more important in the future. As Ogawa puts it, "the policy response to these age compositional changes will influence economic growth and poverty, intergenerational equity, and social welfare for decades to come." The implications of this shift for some aspect of fiscal policy in the countries of the region are touched on in the chapter by Kumar et al. in this volume.

A key analytical tool of Ogawa's piece is the system of "National Transfer Accounts" (NTA). The NTA provides a comprehensive framework for estimating consumption, production, and resource reallocations by age. The analysis draws heavily on the Japanese experience as the most advanced of the Asian Pacific countries in terms of its demographic transition, as well as its economic development, but it also applies the NTA approach to several other countries in the region. The NTA has two components. The first is a detailed accounting of income, production, and consumption. The second component measures economic resource flows from lifecycle surplus ages (working years) to lifecycle deficit ages (youth and old age). These flows are not quid pro quo transfers, but are either voluntary or determined by government policies. Ogawa highlights the advantages of the NTA approach over more basic dependency ratio-based analyses.

After surveying the demographic situation and projections for selected Asian countries, in East, Southeast, and South Asia, Ogawa's chapter provides detailed projections of demographic dividends for 10 of those countries, based on careful theoretical underpinnings. There are two aspects of demographic dividends. The first aspect is the rate of growth of the economic support ratio, which varies according to the age compositional transformation in the process of the demographic transition. The second aspect arises from the growth of productivity or output per effective worker, resulting from the accumulation of wealth as well as physical and human capital deepening.

The chapter concludes with an analysis of Japan's experience through the lens of the NTA approach. One interesting finding is that transfers from the "young elderly" in Japan flow to other age groups, providing an important societal cushion—the old are not uniformly recipients of transfers. The Japanese experience also is used to draw some brief lessons for the future of the rest of Asia, with respect to pension policies, financing methods, and the degree of permanence of the second aspect of the demographic dividend.

Anne Goujon, in chapter 6, documents the significant increases in human capital across the many countries of the Pacific Rim. Human capital is measured by educational attainment, and Goujon treats aspects of the changes that have occurred, such as relative improvements in the educational status of women, as well as likely future trajectories of educational upgrading. However, for developing countries, the process of catching up or convergence with advanced countries that have high levels of human capital will still take decades.

The discussion in the chapter begins with observations on the importance of human capital for economic development and the role played by demographics. Goujon brings out the effects of increases in educational attainment on the rapid decline in fertility in many of the region's countries, which has been the main driver of their demographic transition (as noted by Naohiro Ogawa in his piece for this volume). She also notes the importance of human capital accumulation in counteracting the effects of aging as the other part of the demographic transition.

Goujon's piece draws on a much larger study for 120 countries (K.C. et al., 2010), which provided a consistent data set for analysis of past experience and projections of the future of educational attainment. Here, she considers 27 out of 42 countries that she counts as being on the Pacific Rim, and which contain 99 percent of the population of the region. The period covered is from 1970 to 2010, and the advances in educational attainment for this period are no less than dramatic in their extent. There is also careful documentation and discussion of variation across countries and regions, with human capital increases being much less impressive in much of the Latin American portion of the Pacific Rim, and with developing countries on both sides of the ocean (e.g., Cambodia, Papua New Guinea, Guatemala, and Nicaragua) still suffering relatively high rates of illiteracy.

A large portion of the chapter documents the better relative achievement of women in the last four decades, and identifies cases where they have largely caught up with men in educational attainment. The analysis also considers the brain drain from many of the smaller and less-developed countries of the Pacific Rim, connecting to issues of international migration that are examined in Philip Martin's chapter in this volume. Future trends in human capital accumulation, based on past trajectories, current situations, and demographic trends, are also brought out in Goujon's chapter. Managing and improving these future trends will require policy attention, especially in the light of the effects of aging populations.

The chapters by Martin, Ogawa, and Goujon together highlight the challenges faced by much of the Pacific Rim with respect to the future trajectory of labor markets in the region. Some countries in the region are already facing rapid aging, while others are seeing bulges in their working-age populations. Human capital upgrading has been impressive in some countries in the region but not in others. Migration meets some of the challenges posed by demography and economic growth, but introduces other issues of social acceptance and integration. This complex of factors is likely to increase in importance in the Pacific Rim, just as it will around the rest of the world.

## Perspectives on Economic Growth and Development

In chapter 7, Barry Bosworth and Susan Collins explore key dimensions of economic growth in the Pacific Rim over the past half-century. They focus on 24 countries that encompass the region's large population centers, have an overwhelming proportion of the area's economic activity, and have reasonably complete national accounts. The last criterion is crucial for the authors' goal of comparing growth performances of different parts of the Pacific Rim since 1960. Given this far-reaching scope, for much of the analysis the authors find it useful to combine the countries along the Pacific Rim into three groupings: emerging Pacific Asia, Pacific Latin America (comprised of eight and eleven emerging market economies respectively), and the five high-income economies of the region (Australia, Canada, Japan, New Zealand, and the United States).

A basic fact of the regional growth experience highlighted by Bosworth and Collins is that, while the high-income economies have reasonably similar living standards, the differences within emerging Pacific Asia are very large and have not narrowed appreciably over time. On the other hand, the Pacific Latin American countries had similar standards of living in 1960, but have grown somewhat apart over time. Despite the rapid growth of East Asia, its average standard of living has gone up from 5 percent of the advanced economies to only 15 percent, and absolute differences have increased. Latin America started from higher levels, but has fallen dramatically back in relative terms.

Drawing on their own previous work, Bosworth and Collins conduct a detailed growth accounting analysis of the reasons for the differing performance of the sub-regions of the Pacific Rim. The growth accounting confirms that the Asia Pacific region's growth has been heavily dependent on capital accumulation, though less so after the Asian crisis of 1997-1998. Total factor productivity (TFP) growth has also been significant in contributing to growth. Pacific Latin America, on the other hand, has lagged behind the Asia Pacific in both these contributors to aggregate growth in output per worker. Bosworth and Collins also remark on the much lower female labor force participation rates in Latin America relative to East Asia.

The analysis of Bosworth and Collins reaffirms many economic truths through the comparison of emerging economies on the two sides of the Pacific Rim. The Asian group has had greater global economic engagement, higher rates of saving and investment, and better institutions of governance than Pacific Latin America (even though Asia still substantially lags behind the advanced economies on the last of these measures). Macroeconomic stability and educational attainment are yet two more dimensions where the Western side of the Pacific Rim has outstripped its Eastern counterpart.

There are bright spots on the Latin American side, with countries such as Costa Rica and Chile looking more like the Asian economies in the set of countries examined. This chapter perhaps suggests a set of questions that could be explored further. For example, what role is played by economic or societal inequality in differential performance? What are the interactions between different factors, such as savings and investment on the one hand, and macroeconomic stability on the other? Many of these issues have been tackled elsewhere in broader global contexts. Bosworth and Collins's empirical analysis of the two sides of the Pacific Rim provides a particularly sharp comparison that can be the basis for further analysis to increase our overall understanding of economic growth processes.

Chapter 8, by Justin Lin and Hinh Dinh, in several ways provides a complement to the Bosworth-Collins analysis. The focus is again on economic development in a subset of Pacific Rim economies, but the methodology and choice of the set of countries is quite different. Lin and Dinh examine the experience of 14 island nations of the Pacific. The total population of the group is less than 10 million, and even that figure is dominated by Papua New Guinea, with many of the others being minuscule in area and population. Precisely because of these characteristics, the analysis in this chapter is interesting and innovative, because it seeks to apply a paradigm developed by Lin and others as a general approach to understanding economic development.

The traditional neoclassical approach to economic policy for development is characterized by the authors as favoring complete liberalization of product and factor markets, with market forces determining what a country should produce and export. The alternative approach applied in the chapter is termed "new structural economics." It also begins with factor endowments, and acknowledges the importance of comparative advantage, the price system, and competitive market allocation, but simultaneously emphasizes the role of infrastructure, including educational, financial, and legal institutions, as well as physical infrastructure. Ultimately, the speed of economic development and associated industrial upgrading depends on the speed with which factor endowments and infrastructure can be upgraded, and the latter requires government action. As the authors put it, "Changes in infrastructure require collective action or at least coordination between providers of infrastructure services (which could be public, private or public-private partnerships) and industrial firms. For this reason it falls to government to introduce such changes or to coordinate them proactively." Note that the "new structural economics perspective" is conceived of in broader terms than the "big push," (Rosenstein-Rodan, 1943) though the conceptual similarities are apparent.

In applying the framework to the Pacific Island countries (PICs), Lin and Dinh bring out the similarities in their economic structures—though of course individual characteristics are not ignored. These include dependence on foreign aid, dominant public sectors, reliance on natural resources, undiversified exports, and large remittances from expatriates. There are associated observations about the lack of trade among these countries (reflecting their economic similarities, to some extent), the sensitivity to commodity price fluctuations, and the fragility of some macroeconomic indicators such as fiscal and current account balances.

Lin and Dinh proceed to outline a systematic approach to formulating strategies for sustained development of the PICs, beginning with a stock-taking of factor endowments and comparative advantage, and assessments of opportunities for economic development in various industries, including agriculture and fisheries, mining, light manufacturing, and tourism. The successful examples of Mauritius and the Maldives, island nations of the Indian Ocean, are used to illustrate potential avenues for development. One of the non-obvious parts of the analysis is the prominence given to light manufacturing as a contributor to development, even in these isolated island nations.

The authors are cognizant of the challenges of structural transformations and the role played by global economic conditions, especially for small nations. Given their focus, there is not much consideration of the possible effects of climate change, risks, and trade-offs between sectors such as light manufacturing and ecotourism, and the role of geopolitical considerations in creating external pressures on the PICs. The chapter does devote considerable attention to the difficulties of managing natural resources, including Dutch disease phenomena, price volatility and effective reinvestment of rents from extraction of mineral resources. Ultimately, one can take a broader perspective, and think of this chapter as providing important analytical underpinnings for thinking about preserving a unique part of the world's cultural and ecological resources, in a manner that provides meaningful livelihoods to the region's inhabitants, beyond just serving as stewards of these resources.

Chapter 9, which is by Manmohan Singh Kumar, Nirvikar Singh, and Jaejoon Woo, provides an overview of the fiscal situations of a set of Pacific Rim economies. Several South Asian economies are included for comparison in this exercise, for a total of 15 countries. The set of countries considered includes advanced, emerging, and low-income economies. The chapter begins by documenting the evolution of fiscal balances, public debt, and growth in the Pacific Rim economies. The piece also summarizes the revenue and expenditure ratios of the various economies in the sample. The data bring out the heterogeneity of the history and current fiscal situations of the sample of countries considered.

The authors next provide a brief summary of the role of policies and institutions that underlie these developments. They focus in particular on two sets of issues: budgetary policies, including tax and expenditure policies, and the impact of growth and low interest rates on the fiscal positions and debt sustainability (i.e., the impact of the interest-rate-growth differential, "RG"). The chapter documents the differing situations of most of the countries in the sample with respect to the level of RG. It then analyzes the role of budgetary institutions and fiscal frameworks that underlie the fiscal performance. The structures of governance and patterns of revenue and expenditure differ considerably across the different economies in the sample, in ways that are not merely determined by levels of income or resource endowments. For example, there are substantial differences in the relative reliance on direct versus indirect taxes. Patterns of spending also differ, but most of the economies share similar challenges of making government expenditure more effective, of broadening tax bases, and achieving greater efficiency in revenue collection.

The chapter makes clear that the need for greater efficiency and effectiveness of governments in the region is made more urgent by the fiscal challenges ahead, including those relating to demographics, the provision of social services, and the likely consequences for budgetary positions of financial sector reforms and opening up of capital accounts in some of the emerging economies. These developments, combined with possible slowing down of growth, could increase the challenges of managing fiscal balances. The chapter suggests that more forward-looking fiscal policies will be essential for the economies of the region.

The three pieces by Bosworth and Collins, Lin and Dinh, and Kumar et al. together provide different perspectives on the record of growth and development in the region. While each focuses on a different set of countries and different issues, together they highlight the factors that have contributed to the successful development of many of the economies of the region in the late twentieth century, as well as some looming policy challenges. In particular, demographic changes highlighted in Naohiro Ogawa's piece will have implications for national levels of savings and investment, and for government policies that impact these outcomes. While Kumar et al. do not document the Latin American experience, one is well aware of the fiscal fragilities that have been part of the macroeconomics of that continent, and the emerging economies of the Asian Pacific Rim will have to work hard to avoid that path.

## Regional Governance and Trade Linkages

Peter Petri and Wendy Dobson argue, in chapter 10, that Pacific Asia is gradually changing the landscape of regional and global economic cooperation. They note that, unsurprisingly, institutional reforms are underway to respond to the region's growing economic clout and pluralism. External expectations of Asian participation in collective goals are growing, with the Asian Development Bank (ADB), for example chastising the region's economies as "passive onlookers in the debate on global rule-making and reluctant followers of the rules."

A major thrust of Petri and Dobson's piece supports the ADB's characterization, so that, even though the economies of the Asia Pacific region have been major beneficiaries of the global economic system, they remain more comfortable with incremental change than with leading new initiatives or with enforcing global norms and rules. The chapter argues that this Asian reluctance to rock the boat, combined with natural reluctance on the part of the existing dominant players to revamp the governance structures in the global economic institutions, implies that the existing global order will change gradually, rather than in any dramatic fashion. The diversity of the region reinforces the desire for stability in slowing down change.

Petri and Dobson see global economic governance becoming more multi-polar, driven more by relationships than rules as compared to the past, with consensus building becoming more important as an approach to change, given the absence of a single dominant player, as was the case with the United States to varying degrees after World War II, and especially in the initial period after the collapse of the Soviet Union. The chapter does not take a simplistic view of regional attitudes as simply culturally determined (the "Asian values" school of thought) but carefully connects them to the complex history of Pacific Asia. The analysis is based on a cogent conceptual framework that examines the supply and demand for cooperation, ultimately resting on the theory of clubs. Trade-offs among different goals of universality, effectiveness, and democracy are discussed in a trilemma-like framework, drawing on the work of Kawai and Petri (2010). The analysis draws some implications of these trade-offs, arguing for a multi-layered global architecture of economic governance.

Petri and Dobson offer a rich discussion of existing governance institutions in the region, as well as the different levels and arenas of cooperation, including macroeconomic policies, development finance, and financial markets. There is a careful discussion of the different centers of political and economic power, and the interaction of regional and global groupings for collective action. Table 10.1 in Petri and Dobson, in particular, provides a snapshot of the many dimensions of international economic governance, and Asia's role in those various governance structures.

A new area of cooperation, climate change, is also highlighted as having specific challenges. The chapter argues that environmental cooperation could evolve more slowly than might be desirable, given that the countries of the Asia Pacific region face sharp trade-offs between their domestic priorities and the collective interest. However, the authors conclude by noting that, as Asia (particularly Pacific Asia) gains "votes and voice" in international governance institutions, greater investments in global public goods may be forthcoming. They suggest that time and patience will be needed.

Devesh Kapur and Manik Suri, examine, in chapter 11, the interaction of geopolitics and "geoeconomics" (the term and the idea of this interaction are attributed to Sanjaya Baru) in the Pacific Rim. Much of their story is centered on the rise of China. There are several major themes in the chapter, several of which find echoes in the pure economic analyses of authors Athukorala, Kaur, and Yang and Huang, also in this volume. First, they stress the importance of international supply chains, which they emphasize are regional in nature, rather than global. Their main point is that China dominates these supply chains in depth and breadth. They draw out implications for China's political presence in the region.

A second theme of the Kapur and Suri chapter is the role played by multinational firms (a topic explored in more detail by Yang and Huang). Again, the thrust of the analysis is that China's superior bargaining power gives it an advantage vis-à-vis even large multinationals, whereas there are many more firms, other than just the largest ones,that have invested in China. The authors view multinationals as being largely unfettered from ties to the nations in which they are nominally based, so that their loyalties are more to their return on capital than any domestic base.

Overall, this chapter suggests that there is a divergence between geopolitical objectives, which are pursued by countries such as the United States and Australia, seeking to contain China from a traditional security perspective, and the geoeconomic realities, which strengthen China's position. In fact, the authors see China's own alignment of geopolitical and geoeconomic goals as much tighter, with a strong state using national champions to pursue its strategic goals simultaneously on multiple fronts. In the longer run, however, the authors see some countervailing trends, which will balance the shift in economic power. These include innovations in manufacturing that displace low-cost labor, China's own demographic transition and increased labor costs, and natural resource constraints that will put a brake on growth.

Kapur and Suri argue that the Asian Pacific region's embrace of free markets, free trade, and private enterprise has enabled it to race ahead, epitomized by the case of China. The rise of China has counteracted what some earlier saw as looming economic dominance by the United States as a lone economic superpower. The authors conclude by noting several factors that will contribute to the pendulum swinging the other way: more favorable energy and natural resource positions in the West, both with respect to availability and efficiency; demographic trends that will favor the United States and India over China, Japan, and Europe; advances in manufacturing that will reduce economies of scale and favor skill intensive processes; and higher quality governance and other institutions in the West. These are broad-brush trends, but they highlight the idea that "past performance may not be an indicator of future returns," and open up possible new lines of research for the future of the different Pacific Rim economies.

In chapter 12, John Ravenhill provides an analysis of the political economy of trade agreements in the Asia-Pacific region. He begins by acknowledging that the conventional view of such trade agreements as "market-driven" is accurate, since the region lacks the over-arching institutions that guided European trade integration. However, the thrust of Ravenhill's piece is to challenge the perspective that economic considerations have been the driving force for what has transpired on this front: instead, he seeks to bring politics back in.

Ravenhill notes that Asian countries, with the exception of the case of ASEAN, eschewed preferential trade agreements (PTAs) prior to the Asian financial crisis of 1997–1998. Subsequently, as he documents, there has been a rush to create PTAs. Other regions had seen such PTAs prior to this period, and one of Ravenhill's goals is to examine whether the theoretical literature spawned by that experience is relevant for the recent developments in the Asia-Pacific region.

The evidence as presented in this chapter does not support rationales for PTAs based on increased economic interdependence or substantial economic benefits from such agreements. The structure of the initial PTAs was also quite weak. Ravenhill suggests that the process and outcomes can be understood in terms of the role of the state in the region's economies. To quote, "The relationship between the state and the private sector in many East Asian countries was an important factor contributing to a state-led process in decision-making on the selection of partners and timing and sequencing of the first generation of the region's PTAs." Ravenhill adduces signaling, symbolic, and prestige motives for the agreements, as well as complementarities with existing security and strategic relationships among the region's countries.

Ravenhill goes on to examine whether the Western Pacific region is seeing a new generation of PTAs that have different characteristics from the past. One new feature has been the reaching out beyond the region of countries like Japan and South Korea to seek PTAs. He also considers the US-driven Trans-Pacific Partnership (TPP), which seeks deeper agreements, exceeding the scope of the WTO in many respects. Investment, regulation, intellectual property rights regimes, and other difficult areas have become part of the agenda, well beyond the conventional focus on trade in goods. This reflects the concerns of advanced economies such as the United States, and the difference in interests between advanced and emerging or developing economies may increase tensions going forward, whether at a regional or global level.

The well-rounded discussion of this chapter also touches on the impacts of regional production networks (not so important in explaining the pattern of PTAs) and of floating exchange rates (which could swamp any effects of a trade agreement). Ravenhill is ultimately cautious, if not pessimistic, about the positive impacts of PTAs in the Asia Pacific region, and sees them as having the potential to undermine the deepening and consolidation of overall regional cooperation. An interesting recent development, subsequent to Ravenhill's analysis, is the May 2013 announcement of a Pacific Alliance by four Latin American countries (Chile, Colombia, Mexico, and Peru), which seeks to create a new (almost-)free trade area. How this plays out, and the balance between economic and political considerations, will be an interesting test of Ravenhill's analysis from the other side of the Pacific Rim.

Prema-chandra Athukorala, in chapter 13, offers a substantive new empirical analysis of trade patterns in East Asia, with special reference to the implications of the development of global production sharing. He points out that trade in parts and components and final assembly within production networks ("network trade") has generally grown faster than total world trade in manufacturing. Furthermore, "the degree of dependence of East Asia on this new form of international specialization is proportionately larger than elsewhere in the world." He emphasizes that complex transnational production networks have created difficulties for the interpretation of international trade data.

Athukorala carefully considers how to delineate network trade, using data from the United Nations (UN) trade data reporting system. This includes an analysis of how to distinguish parts and components from final goods. The chapter proceeds to document East Asia's role in world trade. Rapid export growth has been accompanied by a shift in exports from primary commodities toward manufacturing. Differences across countries are also noted in the discussion.

The heart of the chapter empirically examines the nature and extent of global production sharing, and more specifically, the role of East Asian countries within global production networks. A central feature of these developments has been the rise of China and its positioning within these production networks. Spatial patterns of international trade within the region have changed as a result, and there has been a magnification effect through multiple border-crossings of products in various stages of completion. Athukorala's analysis of the data tempers the view that China's export basket has become extraordinarily sophisticated. Instead, "what we observe is the rapid consolidation in China of final assembly stages of East Asia-centered global production networks of these products." He argues that China's export of manufacturing products is still based on its labor abundance and consequent comparative advantage, rather than any obvious leapfrogging. However, China's rise has created strong new trade complementarities with other economies in the region, as documented by the trade data.

The data also reveal that East Asia has not become more self-contained, nor decoupled from the global economy. The production networks established in the region are still connected to final goods demands outside the region. Indeed, as Athukorala shows, the regional trade response to the global economic crisis of 2008-2009 was consistent with such linkages. The chapter provides a detailed description of the pattern of trade contraction across countries and types of goods during the crisis.

A final aspect of the chapter is consideration of the challenges posed by global production networks for the conventional "flying geese" (i.e., changing comparative advantage) approach to the analysis of regional growth patterns. Athukorala lays out some of the issues, in particular suggesting that countries in the middle of the ladder of comparative advantage may be squeezed by the ability of the "lead geese" to hold on to segments of the value chain, while low-end labor intensive producers are still able to catch up from the rear.

Chapter 14, by Kar-Yiu Wong, examines the trade experience and performance of the Pacific Rim economies, looking at intra-regional trade as well as interactions with the rest of the world. The main focus is on the 21 members of the Asia-Pacific Economic Cooperation (APEC) group. The author begins by reviewing the basic economic characteristics of this still somewhat heterogeneous collection of economies. He points out that the average trade dependence of the group is less than the world average, but that this result is driven by the lower trade dependence of Japan and the United States, as large economies, the latter, in particular, having a continental cast to its economic activity. Investigating the link between GDP growth and foreign trade, Wong presents evidence suggesting that there is a strong positive link for the APEC economies, with the magnitude of the possible effect of trade on growth being stronger for this set of countries than for the set of all economies in the world.

The author goes on to provide a detailed empirical analysis of the trade patterns and trade interdependence of a selection of six major APEC economies, namely, the United States and Japan, as well as China, Mexico, Chile, and Australia. The chapter summarizes export and import patterns for these countries, considering changing patterns of comparative advantage, before going on to empirically characterize intra-industry trade for this set. Wong uses the Gruber-Lloyd index of intra-industry trade, and discusses some of the factors behind the observed patterns, including the role of NAFTA for the United States and Mexico. For the United States, China, and Japan, Wong provides a detailed analysis of their trade patterns in terms of types of exports and imports, and changes over time in the relative importance of different categories of exports and imports. He also contrasts the data for the two advanced economies, United States and Japan, with that of China as a developing country.

Wong also pays special attention to the trade nexus between China, Japan, and South Korea. These three countries are geographically close, have strong trade linkages, and are at different stages of economic development. The author documents these three nations' importance for each other in international trade, as well as their trade ties with the United States. He demonstrates the relative stability of rankings of trade ties, with China moving up somewhat, to overtake Japan and the United States, for example, in trade with South Korea. Finally, Wong calculates indices of relative comparative advantage, and shows that they match up quite well with levels of economic development among these three Pacific Rim economies.

The pieces in this volume on trade and regional governance of trade within the Pacific Rim suggest that the dynamics of the process are quite complex. Trade patterns have changed in ways that heighten interdependence within the region, especially on its Asian side, but also increase competition for trade with the rest of the world. While the data show that trade linkages in the region are already strong, and appear to have supported regional growth, efforts continue to deepen trade ties. Attempts to forge deeper economic integration through trade are complicated by the heterogeneity of the region's economies with respect to size and levels of development, as well as by security concerns. Security concerns and economic size both mark China out as a special and exceptionally significant player in the region, and how the politics of China's rise unfold and are managed could have a deep impact on the economic future of the Pacific Rim, indeed, of the global economy. How the increased economic importance of Pacific Asia is incorporated in global—and not just regional—governance institutions will be one aspect of this political process. The next set of chapters deals further with aspects of economic linkages in the region, while monetary and financial cooperation, yet another difficult aspect of regional interaction, is examined in some of the chapters in the last part of this volume.

## Industry, Innovation, and Domestic Policies

Chapter 15, by Inderjit Kaur, provides an analysis of a wide-ranging literature on catch-up industrialization, typically set out in the context of the experience of the Asian

Pacific economies. The author summarizes the flying geese or product cycle model of waves of industrialization, relating it also to the role of industrial policy in countries such as South Korea. There is a careful discussion of exactly what is the envisaged process of development. As Kaur points out, catch-up industrialization can take three forms—producing more capital-intensive goods, producing higher quality and more complex goods, and economy-wide transformation moving up the technological ladder. The common theme in these forms of industrialization is that of a hierarchy based on technological capability, with catch-up involving sequential shifts of comparative advantage. This approach clarifies some of the debates about structural change and comparative advantage that surface in earlier chapters, and the importance at different phases of industrialization of imitation and learning on the one hand and innovation on the other.

Kaur integrates a considerable amount of varied institutional and conceptual discussion of supply chains, service links across different components of these chains, and industry examples of the minutiae of the global division of labor, to draw out the essential economic changes taking place. This institutionally and conceptually rich discussion complements the trade data focus of Athukorala's chapter, and provides a deeper understanding of the economics of the flying geese model.

Kaur also touches on the connections between foreign direct investment (FDI) and trade, since FDI has been the basis of the creation of the Pacific Rim's production networks. The chapter by Yang and Huang deals with multinational firms and FDI in the context of the Pacific Rim, in a quantitative analysis.[2] Kaur's discussion also incorporates issues of innovation and the speed of product cycles, connecting to the treatments of innovation by Yusuf and Tschang, also in this volume, but providing clear analytical connections to the different phases of catch-up industrialization.

The discussion in Kaur offers somewhat different perspectives on a possible new version of the "flying geese" model, based on components and new kinds of agglomeration externalities, rather than mastery of entire production processes. The chapter brings out the increased importance of activity-level economies of scale as a result of the disaggregation of production into more specialized and dispersed stages. In a sense, China has illustrated this entry into the process of changing comparative advantage, and Kaur also discusses the complexities of China's role in the "rich matrix of global supply chains." Ultimately, this chapter suggests that sequential shifts in comparative advantage still matter, but at a different level, of components and intermediate products, than was the case before. The chapter also discusses the consequent challenges for late-entry countries, as they try to take advantage of previous economic development in the Asia Pacific to accelerate their own growth and development.

Yang and Huang examine, in chapter 16, the themes of changes in global organization that are central to the pieces by Athukorala and Kaur, but do so beginning with firms as the unit of analysis. By using data on the largest global multinational corporations (MNCs), the authors are able to provide different perspectives on the issues touched on in those earlier chapters. The chapter begins by documenting the importance of MNCs in the global economy, from their share of production, to their impacts on trade. The activities of MNCs affect the patterns of trade and have strong implications for trade policy. For example, China has argued that exports from China to the United States should be evaluated based on the country of ownership of the MNCs that drive these exports, through their FDI in China.

Yang and Huang characterize the top individual MNCs, and then rank countries by their MNC weights. The United States and Japan continue to top the list, while China has jumped to third place in recent years, paralleling its rapid ascent in other aspects of global economic activity. Hong Kong, South Korea, and Taiwan are also important MNC-generating economies. The authors show that patterns of FDI are positively correlated with the presence of large MNCs. This pattern may admit two possible explanations: large MNCs may drive the volume and location of FDI toward favored locations, seeking agglomeration benefits; and countries with large MNCs may themselves attract FDI through relationship or signaling effects.

The authors also use a clustering model (previously developed in the context of trade clustering) applied to bilateral FDI data to endogenously identify regional blocs. The empirical analysis reveals an East Asian FDI bloc that is quite distinct from a European-American bloc. Manufacturing FDI displays patterns similar to overall FDI.

A parallel clustering analysis for trade[3] shows that there are three trade blocs, NAFTA, EU, and East Asia, with the first two becoming closer after 2004. The trade data, unlike the FDI data, allow a multi-year analysis and therefore reveal changes in patterns over time. The chapter discusses in detail the evolution of sub-blocs within East Asia over the past decade. This also allows the authors to provide yet another perspective on the flying geese model as it pertains to Pacific Asia. Yang and Huang are bolder in their characterization of China as a "leapfrogger" in this context. The analysis of trade clusters before and after the financial crisis of 2008-2009 also provides a complement to the discussion by Athukorala. In particular, Yang and Huang argue that the global financial crisis of 2008-2009 had only minor impacts on the cluster structure within trade blocs, but increased the "distance" between the two major trade blocs.

Chapter 17, by Howard Pack provides a new perspective on analyzing industrial policy, using Taiwan as a case study. The previous extensive work on the role of government in shaping changes in industrial structure as part of the process of development has included country studies (e.g., Pack and Westphal, 1986, for South Korea, and Wade, 1990, for Taiwan), as well as conceptual discussions (e.g., Pack and Saggi, 2006, and Rodrik, 2008). As the author notes, "Industrial policy is a very elastic term." Differing views on the past and future role of industrial policy reflect differences in definition as well as different interpretations of the complexities of specific experiences. The Asian Pacific Rim has provided the key examples for the debates on these issues.

Pack suggests that "Taiwan may be the poster country for industrial policy if indeed this policy was the key source of growth," and this leads to his country choice and focus. The author begins with a brief qualitative review of Taiwan's experience, placed in the context of theoretical rationales for the use of industrial policy, such as overcoming externalities. The bulk of the chapter and its contribution lie in a quantitative examination of the impacts of industrial policy in Taiwan's growth experience.

The methodology of the chapter avoids the issues of endogeneity that have been criticized in previous quantitative studies of policy impacts across sectors: namely, the choice of sectors for promotion itself depends on their initial conditions. Here, the author does not try to explain differences in rates of TFP growth across sectors by instruments of intervention, but simply seeks to quantify the impacts of policy in terms of contributions to Taiwanese growth. The basic approach is to calculate the changes in sectoral composition of the economy, quantify their contributions to growth, and attribute these impacts to government policy. Hence, it is assumed that these changes would not have taken place in the absence of government intervention. To justify that assumption, one would presumably have to appeal to previous institutional studies such as that of Wade (1990). Pack acknowledges that his quantitative measures provide an upper bound on the impact of industrial policy.

The analysis proceeds through a growth accounting exercise. A key component of the analysis is the calculation of a counterfactual evolution of the Taiwanese economy's sectoral production structure, and this is done by averaging across countries with similar income levels in the different periods of comparison. Pack finds high TFP growth in promoted sectors as well as neglected sectors. There is some evidence that in the 1980s, versus the 1970s, promoted sectors did relatively better, which is suggestive of industrial policy indeed playing some role. Pack's discussion of his results seems to support the case for a broader view of industrial policy, including promotion of education and infrastructure, and not just narrow industry targeting.

The author also uses his methodology, combined with an input-output analysis, to consider spillovers from promoted to non-promoted sectors. While he finds strong interactions among promoted sectors, the empirical analysis suggests that broader spillovers were relatively unimportant. Ultimately, using his empirical methodology, Pack can attribute almost one percentage point of average growth, which was 9 percent a year, to industrial policy defined as sectoral targeting. As he discusses, the remainder of Taiwan's growth would be attributable to physical and human capital accumulation, good macroeconomic policies, and overall innovation. The author concludes with a nuanced discussion of the role of government in development, and a comparison of Taiwan and South Korea's experience. Certainly, the approach in this chapter is worthy of wider application, to understand processes of structural change in economic development.

In chapter 18, Ted Tschang breaks relatively new ground by considering creative industries in the Pacific Rim. The scope of what this term covers is quite broad, with UNCTAD enumerating the following areas: (1) design goods, including interior design, graphics, fashion accessories, jewelry, and toys; (2) audiovisuals, including film, television, and radio; (3) the visual arts, which includes everything from artwork to photography; (4) the performing arts; (5) traditional cultural expressions, which includes handicrafts; (6) publishing of printed media; and (7) new media, including video games. Tschang emphasizes that creative industries are increasingly driven by the use of digital technology, and he investigates the resulting role played by innovation in creative industries.

The chapter offers a rich set of observations. Tschang discusses the role of digital technology as a "general purpose technology" (potentially pervasive, with inherent potential for technical improvements, and innovational complementarities), as well as relating this framework to Schumpeter's ideas of creative destruction. The author provides a useful discussion of the process of diffusion and adaptation of technologies and of ideas, in the context of creative industries.

An interesting and significant discussion in this chapter concerns culture. Whereas "cultural" explanations for economic growth and progress have been used (and largely discredited) in the context of the Asian Pacific Rim, Tschang's point is different, since the output of creative industries is often culturally determined and there is a strong resultant home bias. At the same time, Tschang notes that there are adaptations and universal themes. He also examines these differences in the context of the creation of global value chains, which have been developed even in the case of creative industries. Therefore, Tschang examines both cultural roots and cross-cultural evolutions. In a similar complementary set of perspectives, he examines the role of individuals in innovation for creative industries (e.g., influential video game designers like Shigeru Miyamoto), as well as the importance of policy frameworks.

Tschang offers a tour of many of the key sites of creative industries in the Pacific Rim, especially California, Japan, South Korea, China, and Singapore, but also including some Latin American countries. In doing so, he provides specifics about individual country strengths in different niches, as well as idiosyncratic factors with respect to the demand for particular kinds of content.

Tschang's chapter also examines business models and industry structures, ultimately seeking to situate creative industries within broader ideas of national innovation systems. These national systems are also placed in the context of regional and global production networks, such as the offshoring of animation tasks. Tschang also makes the point that, for the Asian Pacific Rim, "catch-up" in the pure technological realm has been combined with frontier innovation in cultural production, leading to new patterns of economic development. Hence, this chapter provides a useful and broad overview of a topic that is likely to be of increasing importance globally, as well as in the Pacific Rim.

In chapter 19, innovation takes center stage in Shahid Yusuf's detailed and extensive contribution, and more broadly than in Tschang's treatment of creative industries. Yusuf begins with a survey of theories of growth and the role of learning and innovation in growth. He emphasizes the importance of innovation in sustaining economic growth, an idea now firmly ensconced in economics thanks to the work of Paul Romer and others on endogenous growth. The author discusses possible pathways for building innovation capacity at the national level. He then examines six different components of the "innovation economy," in the context of the Asian Pacific Rim: firms, the market and competitive environment, industrial composition, investment in technology, human skills, and cities as innovation clusters. The bulk of the chapter explores these components and their contributions to building innovative capacity.

First, Yusuf surveys the evidence on the role of entrepreneurship and new firm entry, as well as the aspects of firm culture that foster innovation. He particularly emphasizes the role of management and firm-level dynamism in fostering innovation, and surveys general empirical evidence for these impacts, as well as the Asian Pacific experience. Yusuf then reviews the East Asian experience with respect to market competition, and suggests that openness to trade helped support innovation, as did policy environments that made it easier for firms to do business. Next, the author discusses the different possibilities for innovation across different industries, and argues that the East Asian focus on manufacturing, and especially then-complex products such as automobiles, was conducive to innovation and industrial upgrading. He discusses how even late industrializers such as China are trying to spur the development of industries built around frontier technologies such as nanotechnology. He suggests that productivity improvements in services are also making their way into East Asia's economies. Yusuf's discussion is buttressed by reference to comparative data on intensities of research and development (R&D), across countries and industries.

With respect to investment in technology, Yusuf again surveys Asian Pacific experience, as well as that of the United States on the other side of the Pacific Rim. He details issues of R&D, commercialization, patent protection, financing, and other complexities of successful technology investment. The author then considers several different aspects of Asian Pacific educational systems, including education levels, fields of concentration, and industry linkages. Finally, he discusses the role of cities as innovation clusters, including economies of scale, agglomeration effects, and diversity. He notes that East Asian nations are seeking to make their cities centers of creativity to promote economic dynamism.

Yusuf concludes his chapter with a discussion of how East and Southeast Asia's policymakers are seeking to bring together the many components of policy required to accelerate innovation. He notes the different approach required once a country is on the global technology frontier, rather than just catching up. In terms of what is needed for innovation policy in the Asian Pacific region in the twenty-first century and the prospects for success, Yusuf ends on a somewhat agnostic note, especially with respect to the role of research and the possibility of making innovation more routine in these economies.

In sum, the chapters in this section provide a detailed and complex picture of the interaction of firms, national governments, and the societies in which they operate, deepening the understanding gleaned from the consideration of patterns of trade and institutions of economic governance considered in the previous set of chapters. Global production networks are shaped by national policies, multinational firms, and domestic innovation. While building broad national systems of innovation is a challenge, it seems that government policies can have targeted impacts, whether in rapidly changing industries such as those built on digital technologies, or industries where innovation is at the level of individual creativity with respect to design and content.

## Macroeconomics and Finance

In chapter 20, Anne Krueger analyzes and draws lessons from the Asian financial crisis of 1997-1998. She begins by reminding us that in the 1950s, most of the poorest countries in the world were in Asia. As with most developing countries, they suffered balance of payments problems. Krueger takes the position that import-substitution growth strategies, using high levels of trade protection to foster and protect new industries, were inefficient and failed to accelerate growth that was relatively slow. She traces the growth accelerations of the Asian Pacific countries, from Japan and Taiwan in the 1950s to China in the 1980s, to shifts in policy toward much greater outward orientation.

The "East Asian miracle" as described by Krueger is a backdrop for the extreme shock of the Asian crisis of 1997. In some respects, there was more than one crisis, since country experiences were different, and Krueger emphasizes this plurality, while providing a coherent picture of what happened. She does so by addressing four questions. First, what were the underlying factors that led to the crises, and how did these differ from those that had led to previous balance of payments crises? Second, what policies were adopted to control the crises and how effective were they? Third, what were the aftermaths of the crises in the affected countries? Fourth, what were the lessons learned from this entire experience?

To answer the first question, Krueger reviews the nature of crises (effectively, triggered by unsustainable policies), and the multiplicity of possible causes. In the Asian case, Japan's difficulties centered on its domestic financial system. Taiwan and Hong Kong successfully fended off international attacks on their currencies. Many Asian Pacific countries (including Indonesia, Malaysia, the Philippines, South Korea, and Thailand) had full-blown foreign exchange financial crises. In all these cases, Krueger explores the interplay of mobile global capital, exchange rate policies and controlled (distorted) domestic financial systems. The policy responses therefore included changes in exchange rate policies, financial sector reforms, and, in several cases, external support from multilateral agencies, particularly the International Monetary Fund. The aftermaths of the crises all involved drops and recoveries in growth rates, with Krueger arguing that the speed of recovery in the individual countries was directly related to the extent and quality of financial sector reforms.

The final and most important part of the analysis is Krueger's summary of lessons learned. She argues for the benefits of more flexible exchange rates, which she credits with helping the same Asian countries that suffered so much in 1997 in weathering the global crisis of 2008–2009 quite effectively. Krueger also notes the role of currency and maturity mismatches in 1997, and that these have been subsequently managed much better. Additional lessons adduced by Krueger are the benefits of adequate foreign exchange reserves and the dangers of overleveraging. The chapter therefore provides a coherent view of economic policymaking for countries facing a world of mobile financial capital, and a conditional optimism that countries that follow these policy guidelines can weather future storms.

In chapter 21, Joshua Aizenman and Hiro Ito build on their seminal and extensive analysis (jointly with Menzie Chinn) of empirical characterizations of intermediate policy stances toward the Mundell-Fleming "trilemma" or "impossible trinity." The trilemma hypothesis states that a country simultaneously may choose any two, but not all, of the three policy goals of monetary independence, exchange rate stability, and financial integration to the full extent. Note that these are intermediate goals, and Aizenman, Chinn, and Ito (2010) previously related the trilemma policy stance to more fundamental economic policy objectives such as controlling output volatility and inflation, all of which is explored as well in this chapter by Aizenman and Ito.

In practice, economies rarely choose two out of the three intermediate policy goals, instead seeking compromise positions, such as managed floats of the currency and partial restrictions on the capital account. A key foundation of the approach of this chapter is the development and calculation of trilemma indices for the three intermediate policy goals, permitting empirical characterizations of compromise policy stances. The authors find that emerging market economies have tended, on average, to gravitate toward some kind of "middle ground" in their trilemma policy stances. An important observation of the chapter is that the experience of East Asia has been different from other regions, with an earlier adoption of this middle ground policy stance. These economies have also seemed to give more weight to exchange rate stability, among the three objectives. The chapter also introduces and applies a new measure of policy divergence or convergence, essentially calculating the distance of the estimated policy stance from the edge of a unit simplex that represents the boundaries of the feasible trilemma policy stance. The chapter offers a rich empirical analysis of variations across regions and over time.

An important aspect of the analysis in the Aizenman-Ito chapter is the addition of the goal of managing risks of financial integration as a fourth policy objective. In this context, the authors (again building on previous work with Menzie Chinn) explore the choices and consequences of different countries with respect to international reserve holdings. The high levels of international reserves, a striking characteristic of East Asian economies in recent years, especially after the Asian financial crisis, can be justified as self-insurance driven by extreme precautionary motives. Empirical analysis in the chapter suggests that reserve holdings can soften the trade-offs involved with respect to the impacts of trilemma policy stances on more fundamental objectives such as reducing output volatility. The Aizenman-Ito analysis therefore can be said to emphasize the short-term pragmatism and rule-of-thumb approaches of Asian Pacific economies, as opposed to what might be desirable or optimal in the longer run.

Chapter 22, by Maria Socorro Gochoco-Bautista and Noli R. Sotocinal, focuses specifically on capital account liberalization, primarily in the context of the Asia Pacific experience, though Brazil and India are also considered to some extent. The chapter begins with a review of theoretical arguments for and against openness on the capital account. The case for openness rests on possibilities for more efficient use of capital as it moves to places where its marginal productivity, and hence returns, are higher. On the other hand, the existence of market imperfections associated with asymmetries of information, or the resulting incompleteness of asset markets, provide conceptual underpinnings for questioning that capital account openness has unambiguously positive impacts on economies that choose that policy orientation. The authors note that the IMF, after tending to be strong supporters of capital openness, has taken a more cautious view after the global crisis of 2008–2009.

The authors also review the empirical evidence for the impacts of capital account liberalization, and find that it is mixed. Financial integration can increase volatility of output, and its positive impacts on growth may depend heavily on the types of capital flows and the institutional capacity of the host country to productively absorb foreign capital. Other issues reviewed in the chapter include home bias, the reversal of capital flows, going from capital-poor to capital-rich countries, and the prevalence of herd behavior among international investors. The authors illustrate the association of increased cross-border capital flows with several financial crises in the last few decades, by charting the experience of several major Asian Pacific economies, as well as the United States and the Euro area. They assert that the growth rates of East Asian countries have become more synchronized after the Asian financial crisis of 1997–1998, and that the impact of crises has been more acute. They note the tightening of capital controls by Asian Pacific economies around the time of the most recent global crisis.

The chapter goes on to consider the imbalances in the global financial system (also the subject of the chapters by Chinn and Ito, and Ogawa and Nakamura in this volume) and the various kinds of capital control measures that have been tried in recent years. Capital account management is considered within the broader context of systemic risk and the increased recognition of the need for comprehensive approaches to macroprudential regulation. The role of exchange rate adjustment in the Asian Pacific economies is also discussed by the authors. Ultimately, the authors conclude that a return to financial autarky is not feasible, and that the new normal will be a world of greater regulation to manage a range of systemic risks, including those associated with cross-border capital flows. They stress the need for domestic financial development for developing economies, but clearly the specifics of policies that can and should be pursued are beyond the scope of this chapter, and remain to be worked out by economists.

In chapter 23, Eiji Ogawa and Chikafumi Nakamura examine the behavior of the Asia Pacific region's currencies through the lens of the global financial crisis of 2008-2009, and the global imbalances that have been a possible contributor to that crisis. In addition, the authors consider the challenges and prospects of regional monetary cooperation, tracing some of its history and institutional efforts toward various cooperative goals.

The analysis of the chapter begins with possible causes of global imbalances, particularly the "savings glut" hypothesis of Ben Bernanke, according to which East Asian export orientation and currency policies drove current account surpluses that mirrored the United States' large current account deficit. The authors also discuss other explanations, including the behavior of asset prices, as contributors to global imbalances, but much of the focus of the chapter is on the evidence for currency undervaluation. Indeed, the preponderance of studies quoted suggest some undervaluation, particularly of the

Chinese yuan (also known as the renminbi or RMB). The authors review three methods of judging currency valuations: purchasing-power parity (PPP) enhanced by the Balassa-Samuelson effect, the behavioral equilibrium exchange rate (BEER) approach, and the fundamental equilibrium exchange rate (FEER) approach.

The authors also consider the role of the United States' fiscal deficits and of the US dollar as the main international reserve currency in trying to understand the causality between global imbalances and the 2008–2009 financial and economic crisis. The international role of the dollar frames the authors' discussion of regional monetary cooperation, which forms the bulk of the chapter. They provide a careful review of the evolution and different aspects of the post-Asian crisis Chiang Mai Initiative (CMI) undertaken by the grouping known as ASEAN (Association of South East Asian Nations) +3 (Japan, China, and South Korea), as well as subsequent efforts such as the CMI Multilateralization Agreement of 2009. Institutional developments such as the creation of the ASEAN+3 Macroeconomic Research Office, for surveillance, and the development of swap facilities and other risk sharing arrangements are covered in the chapter.

The chapter continues with a detailed consideration of a possible Asian Currency Unit (ACU) or Asian Monetary Unit (AMU), and the possible behavior of this notional AMU after the recent crisis is discussed, in the context of the diverging behavior of its constituent national currencies. There is a discussion of issues of heterogeneity and possible convergence among the various Asian Pacific economies. The authors do not reach a strong conclusion, but the evidence that they survey, and the very recent experience of the Euro zone, together suggest that the goal of a common Asian currency might be viewed with considerable reservations or even skepticism. However, there is clearly value to exploring the possibility, since, as we have seen, the world can change dramatically in just a few decades, and the authors' contribution is important in summarizing our state of knowledge.

Menzie Chinn and Hiro Ito begin chapter 24 with the possible connection between global current account imbalances and the financial crisis of 2008-2009. This connection provides a motivation for analyzing how rebalancing can come about, though the mechanics of, and path to, rebalancing are of interest in their own right. Hence, the chapter focuses on the link between the rebalancing of the world economy and the contribution of the East Asian economies, especially China, to that rebalancing. The authors review several possible explanations for global imbalances, namely, trends in saving and investment balances, intertemporal trade-offs, mercantilist behavior, a global saving glut, and distortions in financial markets. They note that the explanations are not mutually exclusive, and go on to test the various hypotheses empirically.

The foundation of the empirical investigation is a panel data analysis of both industrialized and developing countries for the last four decades, which elucidates the cross-country determinants of current account balances. In turn, the empirical modeling is based on a careful consideration of alternative explanations of the emergence of current account deficits and surpluses. The empirical work in the chapter builds on previous work by Chinn and Prasad (2003), as well as Chinn and Ito (2007).

The empirical results are consistent with the twin deficits hypothesis: budget surpluses and current account surpluses move together, other things equal. Larger net foreign assets affect the current account balance positively, as one would expect based on the income such assets generate, while having a higher per capita income, being an oil exporting country, and having a lower dependency ratio all lead to stronger current account balances. The authors also find support for the hypothesis that more financial development leads to weaker current accounts, since strong financial institutions attract foreign capital.

A striking feature of the analysis is that Chinn and Ito proceed to go beyond the cross-country results to look at individual countries' experience. In fact, the estimated model does a poor job of prediction for China and the United States, the two biggest contributors to global imbalances. Previous work by these authors and other collaborators has also found this result, and has shown that country-specific fiscal and monetary policies do not capture too much of the country-specific variation. The authors here proceed to a detailed qualitative discussion of China's institutions and their impacts, including financial development and corporate finance, household savings behavior, and government savings mechanisms. Forecasting exercises based on the authors' econometric model suggest that US fiscal consolidation and similar measures will not by themselves achieve significant global rebalancing. Instead, China has to undertake significant changes in the way that its financial markets and institutions are organized, for rebalancing to make headway. The interplay between statistical and institutional analysis is a distinguishing feature of this contribution to the volume.

In chapter 25, Reuven Glick and Michael Hutchison examine financial linkages between China and the rest of East Asia, in the context of possible financial liberalization in China and internationalization of its currency. The latter term refers to the use of the currency for international trade and financial transactions, inside and outside the nation's borders, by foreigners as well as by Chinese. The authors begin by reviewing the literature on the extent of use of the Chinese yuan or renminbi, as well as differing assessments of likely future trajectories for its internationalization.

The authors extend earlier work of theirs, which examined the policy challenges faced by China in deciding how to sequence capital-account opening and currency internationalization with other policies, such as exchange-rate flexibility and financial market development, all of these being components of the country's long-run development strategy. In this chapter, they examine how these policy changes have been reflected in cross-border linkages of asset returns between China and the rest of East Asia. The analysis also tries to separate the role of direct financial market linkages from those induced by real economy factors such as international trade.

The chapter presents new empirical evidence on short-run and long-run linkages between China and East Asia for exchange rates, interest rates, and equity markets. The short-run analysis uses standard regression analysis, while the analysis of long-run linkages uses cointegration techniques. In the case of exchange rates, the authors confirm that other Asian Pacific economies have had more flexible exchange rates vis-à-vis the US dollar, and there is only a weak correspondence between China's limited exchange rate movements and those in the comparison countries. The authors go on to consider daily data for interbank interest rates, five-year government bond interest rates, and equity prices, each for Hong Kong, Korea, Taiwan, Malaysia, and Indonesia. The empirical analysis finds that China's short-term and long-term interest rate developments display broadly similar movements with the other economies over the long run, but also show substantial differences in the short run. On the other hand, equity prices show close linkages over the whole period. However, even such close movements are driven more by other factors, rather than by direct connections between China and the other Asian Pacific economies. In particular, the authors find that, once US equity price movements are controlled for, there is no long-run equilibrium (cointegration) relationship between Chinese and South Korean equity prices.

Glick and Hutchison's main conclusion is that domestic financial development in China (as of early 2012) has been modest, while internationalization of the currency and liberalization of capital controls has been limited. This is reflected in divergence of asset return behavior between China and several Asian Pacific economies. Equity market movements do not appear to reflect direct financial linkages, but, in the authors' view, are driven by trading relationships. How the future will unfold of course depends on a host of factors, including China's own policy direction.

The contribution by Yin-Wong Cheung and Hui Miao, chapter 26, also examines the internationalization of China's currency, but does so through a close analysis of the new offshore renminbi market in Hong Kong. This market represents one of China's recent initiatives to liberalize its financial markets and promote the international use of the renminbi, and the authors argue that its development is mainly driven and shaped by China's policies rather than market forces. While Hong Kong is part of Chinese territory, its special economic and political status mean that it is treated as an offshore market in terms of renminbi trading: this allows China to pursue a step-wise approach to internationalization, with Hong Kong as a convenient first step.

Cheung and Miao begin by tracing the different ways in which China has garnered international attention, as its role in the world economy has continued to grow and evolve. The focus has moved from China's ability to attract foreign direct investment, to its ballooning trade surplus, its staggering foreign exchange reserves, its exchange rate policy, its investments in other developing countries, and, more recently, to its promotion of the international use of the renminbi and its future role in the global financial architecture.

The authors provide detailed institutional and historical background on the establishment and growth of the Hong Kong renminbi market. From its 2004 inception, until the launch of the first renminbi-denominated bonds ("Dim Sum" bonds) issued in Hong Kong in 2007, the market's initial growth was quite slow. The Dim Sum bond market has really taken off in the last couple of years, however. The chapter provides a detailed analysis of both sides of this market, documenting its growth and the nature and motivations of participants in the market. Other financial markets analyzed in the chapter include settlement of cross-border trade, foreign exchange, commodities, and equities. The authors provide a detailed comparison of renminbi trading in Hong Kong and onshore, elucidating the role of differing market structures and of capital controls in creating divergences between the two markets.

The chapter discusses areas where the offshore renminbi market still lags. It still lacks some basic features, such as credit ratings of Dim Sum bonds and offshore renminbi benchmark interest rates. The quality of investor protection also remains an issue. The authors discuss the potential for competition as well as collaboration with other global financial centers, in developing a strong offshore market for renminbi-denominated assets. They conclude by putting the Chinese effort in this direction in the context of being less reliant on the dollar, both as a medium of exchange and as a store of value. Economic pragmatism is as important as possible symbolic and prestige considerations in promoting the internationalization of the renminbi. At the same time, as the authors bring out, political considerations also play a role for the countries of the Asia Pacific region in particular, in influencing the evolving role of the renminbi in international finance.

Together, the pieces in this section provide a significant summary of the interplay of macroeconomic policies and financial integration in the Pacific Rim, with a natural focus on its Asian side, and especially the role of China. The increased importance of global capital, driven partly by liberalization, but also as a sometimes unintended consequence of macroeconomic policy stances, has changed the way in which national governments think about managing capital flows, exchange rates, and, to some extent, monetary policy. The global economic crisis of 2008, with its roots in the financial sector, only heightened the policy challenges faced across the region. International reserves have assumed increasing importance in the Asia Pacific region, as have discussions on measures for cooperation in areas such as coordination of financial sector reforms and regulations. In all of these developments, the size and growth of China, and its future role in correcting global imbalances, through domestic reforms as well as steps toward internationalization of its financial sector, loom large, not just in the Pacific Rim, but globally.

## Conclusion

There is no doubt that China, as the largest, most dynamic economy in the Pacific Rim, will continue to exert an increasing influence on the world economy. The future of the region, even more than that of the world as a whole, will be bound up with that country's trajectory. Greenhouse gas emissions, natural resource use, innovation in manufacturing and services, and global financial development are among the economic areas where China's rise will matter more and more over time. At the same time, the United States will remain a major global power for the foreseeable future. Its interactions with China, and with the other countries in the region, will matter greatly for the global order.

All the countries of the region, in this context of economic dynamism and changing political balance, will be seeking to preserve their economic security, continue their own development, and find sustainable niches in an evolving economic ecosystem. Sometimes, the countries of the Pacific Rim have looked to the European model of cooperation, but recent events have exposed that model's own limitations, and the geography and history of the Pacific Rim is quite different from that of Europe. Hence, what emerges in the region in terms of individual and collective national responses will have a distinctive character and trajectory. What exactly will emerge? The contributions to this *Handbook* are not predictions about the future, but they collectively provide a set of insights that will be useful for anyone trying to understand the economics of the Pacific Rim, as a basis for drawing one's own conclusions about what the future might hold.

## Notes

1. This observation does not fully take account of the ecological harm created by European industrialization, and therefore the initial conditions inherited by late industrializers. Nevertheless, examples such as the slaughter of rhinos for horns because they are believed by some Asian consumers to be aphrodisiacs or cures for cancer are a matter of concern. It is also the case that market pressures are creating new demands—in some cases, claimed medicinal properties or animal body parts are recent inventions rather than reflections of long-standing traditions.
2. Other useful recent studies are: Thorbecke and Salike (2011), which considers factors determining FDI location, and Mora and Singh (2013), which suggests that FDI in East Asia has been positively correlated with the productivity levels (à la Rodrik, 2006) of exports and imports (those, in turn, having positive relationships with growth).
3. The fact that Yang and Huang, as well as Kaur, treat trade linkages in their analyses would have justified adding these two chapters to the previous group. On the other hand, their treatment of firms, industries, and (in the case of Kaur) domestic policies, provide connections to the subsequent chapters in this group, which look at industrial policy, creative industries, and innovation. Of course, readers are welcome to form their own judgments about the connections between various topics and chapters.

## References

Aizenman, Joshua, Menzie D. Chinn, and Hiro Ito (2010), The Emerging Global Financial Architecture: Tracing and Evaluating the New Patterns of the Trilemma's Configurations, *Journal of International Money and Finance*, Vol. 29, No. 4, pp. 615–641.

Chinn, Menzie D., and Hiro Ito (2007), Current Account Balances, Financial Development and Institutions: Assaying the World "Savings Glut," *Journal of International Money and Finance* 26(4), pp. 546–569.

Chinn, Menzie D., and Eswar Prasad (2003), Medium-Term Determinants of Current Accounts in Industrial and Developing Countries: An Empirical Exploration, *Journal of International Economics* 59(1), pp. 47–76.

Kawai, Masahiro, and Peter A. Petri (2010), Asia's Role in the Global Economic Architecture, Working Paper No. 235, Tokyo: Asian Development Bank Institute.

K. C., Samir, Bilal Barakat, Anne Goujon, Vegard Skirbekk, Warren C. Sanderson, and Wolfgang Lutz (2010). Projection of populations by level of educational attainment, age, and sex for 120 countries for 2005–2050, *Demographic Research* 22(15): 383–472.

Mora, Jesse, and Nirvikar Singh (2013), Trade Productivity Upgrading, Trade Fragmentation, and FDI in Manufacturing: The Asian Development Experience, *Indian Growth and Development Review* 6(1), pp. 61–87.

Pack, Howard, and Larry E. Westphal (1986), Industrial Strategy and Technological Change: Theory vs. Reality, *Journal of Development Economics* 22, pp. 87–128.

Pack, Howard, and Kamal Saggi (2006), he Case for Industrial Policy: A Critical Survey, *World Bank Research Observer* 21(2), pp. 267–297.

Rodrik, Dani (2006), What's So Special About China's Exports? *China & World Economy*, vol. 14(5), pp. 1–19.

Rodrik, Dani (2008), Normalizing Industrial Policy. Commission on Growth and Development, World Bank, Working Paper No. 3, Washington, DC.

Rosenstein-Rodan, P. N. (1943), Problems of Industrialisation of Eastern and South-Eastern Europe, *Economic Journal*, vol. 53 No. 210/211 (June-September), pp. 202–211.

Thorbecke, Willem, and Nimesh Salike (2011), Understanding Foreign Direct Investment in East Asia, Working Paper No. 290, Tokyo: Asian Development Bank Institute.

Wade, Robert (1990), *Governing the Market: Economic Theory and Taiwan's Industrial Policies*, Princeton: Princeton University Press.

# PART I

# THE NATURAL WORLD: HISTORY, CLIMATE, AND RISKS

CHAPTER 1

# THE HISTORY OF BIOLOGICAL EXPLOITATION ON THE PACIFIC RIM

ERIC JONES

Biological resources are natural capital, and the flow of ecosystem services from them may be conceived as notional interest on the stock. The interest includes the provision of food and raw materials, a range of indirect but indispensable services such as crop pollination and venues for eco-tourism, and even more indirect, insurance against pest explosions provided by the diversity within natural environments. In the literature, material on renewable resources is however often difficult to extricate from that on non-renewables. The extricability problem is severe. Resource economics is much concerned with mineral extraction and fossil fuels and tends to lump biological resources in with them.

Further difficulties exist with respect to isolating material on the Pacific: issues are considered globally for numerous academic purposes, each legitimate but overall masking the experience of the Pacific Rim. Treatments of the BRICs and similar groups of emerging economies, studies of East Asia, economic histories of North America and Latin America, and works on general economic development all amalgamate the experience of markedly diverse economies. Within countries surrounding the Pacific, coastal provinces seldom receive independent treatment.

Less attention is paid to the Pacific Basin than to the Atlantic, although more than to the Indian Ocean. After all, explorers entered the Pacific late in time and came from countries bordering the Atlantic. The interests of their home countries dominate discussions of colonization and trade. Studies of individual commodities tend to concentrate on supplies for the metropolitan market, centered on London. While the resources of much of the Pacific region were certainly under-developed before the European intrusion, economic history is distorted by disproportionate attention to Europe's role.[1]

The Pacific's size means the surrounding countries are widely separated and hard to conceive as a unity. They consist of very old and very new nation-states, descended from different civilizations, and varying in other respects such as physiography and population density. Accounts of the westward movement in the United States, though properly focusing on the acquisition of fresh land and resources, tend to peter out at the Rockies. Beyond the mountains, California—"where" in Joan Didion's phrase, "we run out of continent"—is sometimes described as an ecological island. University courses on the "Great Powers" typically include the rise of Meiji Japan but until recently often omitted China. The study of economic history was overtaken by the speed of the East Asian Miracle.

This relative neglect of the Pacific Rim occurs despite the fact that the Pacific Ocean occupies one-third of the earth's surface and is twice the area of the Atlantic. What is there to unify so large and diverse an area? Discussing the experience of individual states, commodities, or ecological regions quickly becomes seriatim description. Rather than inventories, historical processes would be a better means of integration, although sources are rarely arranged in a suitable form. Nevertheless there remains material from which to piece together examples illustrative of the opening of the region's resources, and to arrange them according to historical phases or processes of change.

## 1.1 Infinite Resources?

At the start of European exploration the biological resources of the area seemed boundless. The ocean presented itself as an open-access economy. New England whalers, for example, had so hunted their prey for its oil in the Atlantic that search costs were rising unbearably before they happened on the untapped stocks in the Pacific. This they found providential. Similar judgments were made with respect to a wide range of species. Despite the pressure soon placed on some commodities, optimism reigned. "The demand for gutta-percha is continually increasing," wrote Yeats in 1871, "and it is certain that a process too destructive to the trees is adopted... all the large trees having been felled... happily several other sources are known."[2]

Early exploitation of the Pacific Rim was often directed at offshore resources. Russian crossing of the Siberian land mass to the North Pacific and over to Alaska and California led to the unbridled harvesting of fur seals. Australia's settlement was at first pivoted, surprisingly, on island resources: the Tahitian pork trade, followed by sealing in Bass Strait and off southern New Zealand, and later Fijian sandalwood, New Zealand flax, and Kauri spars.[3] Until about 1835, Australia's main export was whale oil. Only when the Blue Mountains had been crossed and the inland plains occupied did wool become the country's prime export.

Meanwhile, in the fisheries abundance meant that the first fine careless rapture lasted a long time. Big salmon runs, things of the past in New York State long before the end of the nineteenth century, persisted in the Pacific Northwest until the late twentieth century. Yet by the 1980s only Alaska had enough fish left to sustain a fishery and what the biologist, Marston Bates, labeled humanity's "drunken spree" was staggering to its close. Thereafter the Alaskan Department of Fish & Game would not permit commercial fishing until subsistence openings for the Eskimo inhabitants were satisfied; not every year were salmon numerous enough for that.[4]

The salmon fishery of the Pacific Northwest has been documented by Anthony Netboy.[5] He charts the total weight of all salmonid species commercially landed in the Columbia River (Washington, Oregon, and Idaho) from 1866 to 1975. In several seasons between 1883 and 1925 over 40 million pounds were taken but between 1955 and 1974 eight million pounds was a peak take, rarely reached, though there was an additional sporting catch. The tale of declining stocks familiar with respect to Atlantic salmon was being repeated, merely taking place later in time. Habitat was destroyed by pollution or closed off by dams that prevented the fish from making their way upriver to spawn. Fishing became ever more intensive and fishing technology more effective. Catches that had been 13 million pounds in California in 1919 never attained as much as seven million in 18 consecutive years between 1926 and 1943. Although immediately after the Second World War the catch was higher, the fishery was soon obliged to move offshore and the Sacramento River was closed to commercial fishing in 1957.

## 1.2 The Columbian Exchange

Let us consider a longer history of human action. The presentist stance in economics implies that a global approach to resource exploitation is inappropriate before prices converged worldwide during the nineteenth century, but this is misleading. Granted, there was no large-scale intercontinental product or factor trade before modern times. Yet in the early modern period important crop species were transferred from the Americas in the form of the so-called Columbian Exchange. This raised food output in widely separated regions around the globe, which is reflected in figures for the human population.[6]

Standard histories claim that Imperial China absorbed little except tribute from the remainder of the world. Inevitably reference is made to the cessation of distant voyages after the expeditions of Zheng He in the early fifteenth century and the pronouncement of the emperor at the end of the eighteenth century that his domain needed nothing from elsewhere. This internalist story is reinforced when histories begin at the Opium Wars, portrayed as starting China's "opening." This misconceives the experience. A migration of population into the rich woodlands of southern China, ecologically as rich as those of Georgia in the United States, had already resulted in massive deforestation. Of the land surface 670 million acres or 28 percent succumbed to the logging frontier.[7] On this vast area, Chinese agriculture, by far the largest sector of the largest economy on the Pacific Rim, was transformed by crops from the Americas. In effect the Celestial Empire externalized the costs of exploration, upgrading its productive base with American crops brought in by Portuguese traders.

The Columbian Exchange was an extensive movement. In 1972 it was the subject of an important book by Crosby, though the topic had been raised by earlier scholars such as G. P. Marsh and Charles Elton. In 1968 the specific thesis had been advanced by Simkin in *The Traditional Trade of Asia*, when he observed that, "over the many centuries when peasants were four-fifths of the population the great economic benefit conferred by trade was the spread of useful plants and animals."[8] In short, global trade was less in products than in the means of production.

China's farming was remodeled. Dry-land crops from the New World that entered and spread during the sixteenth and seventeenth centuries included peanuts, sweet potatoes, and maize.[9] They were of signal importance in transforming the Empire's agricultural ecology. Peanuts were grown around Canton by 1516, sweet potatoes reached Yunnan in the 1560s, and white potatoes arrived in Fukien before 1700. All these crops could be grown on higher land than was feasible for irrigated rice. The adoption of maize was slower, but during the eighteenth century it spread like the other crops to the formerly forested uplands of southern China. Altogether the introductions are estimated to have supplied 20 percent of total food output. This underwrote population growth even though the rate of growth of rice production was slowing.

Whereas China's population had fallen by about 6 percent during the three-and-a-half centuries before 1400, it rose during the following three-and-a-half centuries by 115 percent. And while commodity flows were slight by later standards even they were growing in early modern times. For instance, Southeast Asian exports of pepper rose six-and-a-half times between 1500 and 1780.[10]

Hence the Columbian Exchange was a massive positive shock created by a redistribution of the world's biological potential. It may be viewed as a wave of technological innovation involving more intensive husbandry practices and the assimilation of unfamiliar crops into farming systems. Intercontinental trade in foodstuffs may have remained out of the question for centuries, and product prices did not converge around the world. Admittedly in that limited sense there was no "globalization" but the authors who make the point do not investigate price convergence within individual markets. Leaving international economic integration aside, China is so large that a convergence of its internal prices would have been of major significance.

## 1.3 European Intrusions

Before the stimulus imparted by European contacts, the chief economies around the Pacific Rim had been relatively immobile. As noted, China largely withdrew from deep sea voyaging after Zheng He, while the Tokugawa shoguns in Japan, eager to block foreign threats, forbade the use of sea-going vessels of any size. Exploration was left to the European powers, whose sometimes reckless use of the resources they found makes it easy to portray their entry into the Pacific world as impelled solely by profit, or as the sourer accounts express it, by greed. This was part of the motive, but the region's natural resources were often charted as a byproduct of exploration solely inspired by non-pecuniary interests.

Medical men and apothecaries in Europe, and later in the United States, had long engaged in natural history for hobbyist and scientific reasons. These became motives for exploration that it is facile to portray as wholly commercial in intent simply because it had stunning commercial results. Cook carried the naturalists Banks and Solander with him: they amassed large scientific collections that could scarcely have been justified by any economic return conceivable at the period. The enormous expenditure on Russian expeditions was also partly motivated by considerations of national *gloire*.[11]

Nor should the expeditions made in the 1820s and 1830s by the great shell collector, Hugh Cuming, be put down to the profit motive.[12] His collection of natural history specimens, eventually deposited in the British Museum, remains unequaled by any other individual. Cuming came from Devon and settled as a sailmaker at Valparaiso, Chile, but retired from business and devoted himself to science. His was the first vessel built solely for natural history collecting. Cuming's activities must stand here for all the scientists involved in reconnoitering the Pacific. Men whose primary aim was to exploit wildlife, land, and timber for gain tended to conceal from others what they had found, but the concern of the scientists was professional reputation. They published their results for all to read and enabled others to capitalize on the resources they found.

## 1.4 The Neo-Europes

European settlement modified the ecosystems of what are termed the neo-Europes. These lands lay within a climatic band suitable for Mediterranean styles of farming. Hitherto the regions had lived in ecological and epidemiological isolation from European organisms. Typically they had been occupied by hunter-gatherers who, like their habitats, were fairly easily overrun.[13] Scope for altering their biology was far greater than remained possible within long-settled Europe or in the old, densely occupied lands of East Asia. The most dramatic alteration was brought about by agriculture. The scale of the transition may be indicated by noting that whereas between 1870 and 1970 the arable area of Europe expanded by only 4.5 percent, it rose by 36 percent in China, 72 percent in Japan, and a staggering 475 percent in Australia.[14] Not surprisingly, the number of species and sub-species of mammals that became extinct in Europe after A.D. 1600 was a mere 7, compared with losses of 11 in Asia and 22 in Australia.[15]

Initially environmental differences were poorly understood and conceptual thought in the settler societies continued to mirror their European origins. Anatopisms resulting from the intellectual hegemony of the northern hemisphere raised the costs of development. For Australia, Seddon has shown how the European analogies coming automatically to their minds misled explorers, systematizers, and agriculturists; Stokes adds that Sturt projected two lines of bird flight in the mistaken belief that where they met would be a fertile region; while in recent years it has been demonstrated that northern hemisphere mammalian genetics does not cover the marsupial case and is not universally generalizable.[16]

The incomers gave to the new lands as well as taking away. A lengthy list of plants was deliberately or inadvertently brought to Australia, and firmly established there a mere 15 years after the First Fleet had landed in 1788; it included species picked up en route from Europe at Rio de Janeiro and the Cape. Besides the obvious European crops and livestock there were valuable lesser species—for instance bees, which are instrumental in pollinating crops, were introduced into Australia in 1822.[17] Some of the imported organisms exploded in population and burdened the settlers as pests. Lacking indigenous predators, their numbers ran away in the syncretic habitats created by agriculture; others escaped into the bush. The rabbit is the prime example of a truly costly introduction; in the 1880s Australian farmers were already investing in thousands of miles of supposedly rabbit-proof fencing.[18] Jump forward to 2010 and mobs of feral dogs and dingoes are wreaking havoc on sheep flocks in West Australia and big expenditures on new fences are planned.

Ecological change enabled some native species to breed to pest proportions. For instance, once dingoes had been (temporarily) suppressed, kangaroo numbers exploded on Australia's new sheep pastures. Dingoes, it should be noted, had themselves been introduced to Australia in the ancient past. In New Zealand the novel mixture of introduced and indigenous species has been testily described as a "witless menagerie." New Zealand's flora, too, was made more varied or became adulterated, according to whether one adopts a human-centered or environmentalist perspective. Whole professions arose to control the side effects of taming, or rather failing to tame, the new lands.

No doubt may be entertained that the European entry into the Pacific was thus accompanied by vast ecological changes, but two caveats should be noted. First, as indicated in the case of China, restricting discussion to the European intrusion truncates and therefore distorts history. Previous human activity had already modified many ecosystems within the Pacific Basin. The classic examples date from long before the arrival of the Europeans and relate to ancient occupations of Pacific islands that resulted in the loss of an astonishing 20 percent of the entire world's bird species.[19] In New Zealand, the Maori invaders had made major differences, among which exterminating the Moa is the best-known instance.[20] Aboriginal activity had altered the Australian environment to the extent that the Europeans are said to have poured through a half-open door—into "vacated niches" where the mega-fauna had been killed off in remote times.

The Pacific region was added to the already enormous overseas extension of Europe's resource base. A Eurocentric focus may seem odd, even objectionable, to nationalists in other continents, but there is no doubt it was European voyagers who opened up the Pacific and inspired most of its international trade. The major civilizations already on the Pacific Rim, China and Japan, did not much affect the remainder of the region. Although the completeness of China's withdrawal from the oceans can be exaggerated (Chinese regularly traveled to the north of Australia to gather trepang or *bêches de mer*), there were no longer official expeditions. In Japan, the Tokugawa shogunate pursued a policy of isolationism. Meanwhile, the ships of European nations entered the Pacific, competing with one another to acquire biological resources, such as spices, whales, furs, sandalwood, *mutatis mutandis*, according to the part of the region accessed.

There were generous harvests of first-generation staples such as whale oil, the securing of which for lighting and lubrication was part of a hunter-gatherer sector surviving within the early industrializing European and American economies. The high cost of transport restricted cargoes to commodities whose value was high relative to their bulk. But nineteenth-century improvements quickly reduced transport and storage costs and widened the range of exports. Australian wool became vital to English industrialization, supplementing or displacing sources in Saxony and Spain; raw wool is so bulky that the introduction of the hydraulic press was important in reducing its volume for shipment.

Since the value of wool per unit weight is 10 times that of wheat, the emergence of Antipodean pastoralism before much grain came to be exported is understandable. Later, refrigeration reinforced the importance of the livestock sector by making it possible to dispatch meat to faraway Britain. Railway and steam ship development lay at the heart of export expansion as it embraced ever bulkier commodities of lower unit value—for instance, timber. The timber trade is customarily associated with lumbering in the Pacific Northwest, yet in the nineteenth century more wood is believed to have been dispatched from Yarra Junction, in the Dandenong Hills east of Melbourne, than from any other town in the world except Seattle, Washington.

## 1.5 Ghost Acreage

The establishment of farming in the neo-Europes resulted in a huge increase of world agricultural supply. From the point of view of the metropolitan market and the populations it served, the effect of the opening of the Pacific Rim was to swell the "ghost acreage" of Britain and Europe. Ghost acreage is an area notionally added to the domestic resource base. It measures the tilled land that would be needed were domestic producers capable of supplying, with existing techniques, food and raiment of equal value to that now obtained from outside.

The acquisitions may be subdivided into, firstly, trade acreage, i.e., that notionally required to supply the equivalent of the net import of foodstuffs and fiber, and secondly, the marine acreage needed to procure from home waters a supply of animal protein equivalent to that derived from the distant fisheries, including whale fisheries. Ghost acreage should probably be extended to include the great source of fertility transferred from the Pacific Rim to the fields of nineteenth-century Britain in the forms of guano (bird dung) shipped from the Peruvian islands and nitrates mined in Chile to make nitrogenous fertilizer.[21]

In these respects the colonization, settlement, and trade of Pacific Rim countries was as if the economic area of the metropolis had magically expanded. The concept focuses on the importing countries. But trade—when it was not mere seizure—requires two partners: there had to be suppliers of the products and populations to service the export trades. This induced settlement and development around the Pacific Rim itself and in time usually led to political independence.

## 1.6 Negative Assessments of Resource Acquisition and Use

Views of heavy resource use are characteristically negative, starting with complaints about degraded ecological services and ending with prognostications that all productive capacity will be destroyed. Diminished water supplies and terminally eroded soils are commonly invoked. While it is reasonable to try to determine the social opportunity cost of diminished biodiversity and other resource depletion, there have been times when misplaced fears have provoked damagingly protectionist responses. The successful extension of free trade during the final quarter of the twentieth century made such fears seem passé but they were by no means abolished. In the early twenty-first century negative commentaries abound once more.

Already in 1945 Harold Williamson could entitle an article "Prophecies of Scarcity or Exhaustion of Natural Resources in the United States."[22] Williamson was writing at the end of a major episode in world history that saw an effort at securing resources militarily rather than by trade. This was the Pacific theatre of the Second World War, where Japan—feeling blocked by Allied imperialism and protectionism in mainland Asia—had attempted to seize farmland and sources of raw material such as rubber plantations. The Japanese apprehension of resource scarcity was partly a self-fulfilling prophecy, in that the military expansion needed to build the Greater East Asia Co-prosperity Sphere itself created much of the shortage.[23]

Forebodings of checks to economic activity recurred, with an early peak during the 1970s. They extended to claims that a majority of the world's population would starve before the end of the twentieth century. Other environmentalists took the view, implicitly or explicitly, that human welfare should not be privileged over what they termed "non-co-operating organisms." Such a judgment overrides the ordinary human-centered concerns of economists, which is the position adopted here. It is reasonable to temper the economist's position, nevertheless, by accepting that the gratuitous replacement of natural ecosystems is to be avoided on prudential, aesthetic, and scientific grounds. The key word is "gratuitous." We profess no sharp-edged means of making decisions about resource use but reject an extreme prudential stance that would sacrifice human living standards.

Negative predictions surfaced yet again in 1996 with Lester Brown's *Who Will Feed China*.[24] The suggestion was that Chinese demand for food would soon push the world into a new Malthusian age. This was perhaps ironic in that Hung Liang-Chi had already written two essays, *Reign of Peace* and *Livelihood*, in 1793, in which he presaged the essential point in Malthus, *An Essay on the Principles of Population* (1798), that population growth is inherently prone to outstrip the growth of agricultural output.

Brown's fears that China would so damage its soils that it would be unable to feed itself were shown by Lindert to be exaggerated.[25] The soil situation is complicated but the supply response quickly curbed the price spike of the mid-1990s and expanded the available stocks of grain. Yet alarmism perennially renews itself. At the end of the first decade of the twenty-first century concerns about global warming and continued population growth were being touted, notably with respect to Asia. Before the credit crunch, optimists asserted that financial crises were things of the past, saying, "it is different this time"; doomsayers say things will be different on the environmental front too, but they mean things will be worse, not better. The implication is that the opening of the Pacific was historically a flash in the pan, part of humanity's "drunken spree."

Around the Pacific Rim, as elsewhere in the world, agricultural intensification means diverting the energy flows of natural vegetation to plants that feed people, largely through monocultural crop production. The simplification creates super-habitats for often devastating eruptions of pests, meaning species that have energetically adapted to them. Human migrations, with their "living entourages" of other organisms, together with translocations of crops, inadvertently distribute species that compete vigorously with indigenous ones. Efforts to control these pests by chemical means sometimes produce costly side effects, while attempts at biological control have sometimes seen populations of the supposedly controlling species growing to pest proportions themselves. Among striking examples are the cane toad in Australia and insect pests on cotton in California, Mexico, and Peru.[26] Concomitant with these have been reductions, even extinctions, of native species that have become prey for introduced organisms or whose habitat has been restricted and fragmented by cultivation.

Economic growth has had additional unintended consequences. Pollution has increased. A New Zealand scientist early pointed out that the $CO_2$ emitted through the burning of vegetation during the late nineteenth-century expansion of agriculture, including in Australia and New Zealand, was the first environmental insult at a truly global level.[27] In recent years chimney-stack pollution from China—from factories partly supplying the American market—has become detectable in Hawaii and the West Coast of the United States. A University of California professor described an unintended consequence of globalization in 1999 by saying that, "the mountain (Mauna Loa, Hawaii) is effectively a suburb of Beijing in the spring."[28] The ocean itself has become afflicted by plastic debris. The North Pacific Gyre (a current circulating over an area twice that of Texas) contains millions of metric tons of circulating debris, mashing itself into smaller and smaller particles and entering the food chain of marine organisms.[29]

Alterations in human diet have also had significant effects. As per capita income rises a smaller proportion is spent on food, as stipulated by Engel's Law, but a larger fraction is laid out on animal protein. It is a couple of decades since a shift to "Western" meat-eating in Hong Kong began to be held responsible for a rise in heart disease to the level of a middle-income country. Japan's diet, too, for all that country's rice fetishism, now features more bread and meat.

To satisfy increasing demand for animal protein, East Asia has succeeded in externalizing some of its environmental costs. Japan's demand for blue-fin tuna supports intensive fishing as far away as the Mediterranean, and remains high for other marine organisms, including whales. Hence Japan resists protecting tuna and whales under CITES (Convention on Trade in Endangered Species of Wild Fauna and Flora). The scale of China's affluence also magnifies the world demand for fish; in 2010 France is expected to export to China 14.5 million metric tons of glass eels (immature eels), approximately half the total European catch.[30] This consumption has several consequences, ironically including some deleterious effects on human health (as indicated) and on the global environment (European eel populations have fallen drastically, due at least in part to intensive fishing).[31] The intensification of agricultural production needed to supply more and more meat is likewise troublesome, since livestock are inefficient converters of vegetable protein.

## 1.7 Ecological Shadow

The environmental impacts of modern economic activity are manifold. One relevant concept is that of "ecological shadow," which refers to the damaging extra-territorial reach of resource exploitation—the dark side of the expansion of ghost acreage. Exploitation at a distance may be viewed either way. Japan's ecological shadow has been criticized for causing immense deforestation outside its own borders. Timber imports from the Philippines, Sabah, and Indonesia have fallen away, but as the twenty-first century opened they remained high or rising from Sarawak, Papua New Guinea, the Solomons, and certain Southeast Asian countries.[32] By the 1990s the Philippines had turned into a net importer of timber. Indonesia has only one-quarter of its old-growth forest remaining, but this is of unparalleled significance since it is half of all that survives in Asia and holds more species of birds and plants than the entire continent of Africa.

In addition to an insatiable demand for timber, Japan continues to make an unrepentant call on fish and whale products. China has developed an even larger fishing industry, the largest in the world, accounting by 1999 for 30 percent of the world's total catch.[33] Its seafood consumption rose 7 percent between 2001 and 2007. East Asian demand inspired the Japanese asset manager, Amundi, to launch the world's first public mutual fund devoted to seafood in July 2010.

China's fish catch, together with its burgeoning demand for timber, means the country has overtaken Japan in casting the darker shadow over the regional environment. These two countries are not, of course, the only ones involved in the timber trade. By the mid-1990s firms from Indonesia, South Korea, and Malaysia were buying vast tracts of tropical forest in the extreme west of the Amazon basin (Brazil). There was some offset in a rapid expansion of plantation forestry around the Pacific. MITI (Japan's then Ministry for International Trade and Industry) was looking to shift the country's aging pulp mills closer to the resource, that is to plantations of eucalypts in Chile, Brazil, and South Africa.

## 1.8 Cultural Lag

There is irony in a further concept used to depict East Asia's environmental impact. This is "cultural lag." Affluence around the Pacific Rim, especially in East Asia, creates an unprecedented consumption of previously unfamiliar "Western" foods. Yet—almost paradoxically—higher incomes likewise permit people to consume more traditional dietary items. Cuisine begins to imitate high-income Western societies while simultaneously expanding the intake of what the modern West, forgetful of its own former intake of wild protein, regards as exotic, even vile, ingredients. These are the wildlife and marine organisms that fill East Asian markets and restaurants or are used in traditional medicine. In short, the East Asian Miracle produced what Reisner, concerned with the resultant poaching of endangered species in the United States, describes as "a strange muddle of hypermodernism and atavism."[34]

Demand in affluent East Asia expanded the market for what *The Economist* dryly calls the body parts of animals. These figure as food delicacies, medicines, or purported aphrodisiacs. The items are acquired or poached far from the centers of demand, for example from bears killed in the Pacific Northwest. Other commodities are sought for ornamentation: Japanese demand was primarily responsible for the decreasing numbers of large ivory-bearing mammals, notably African elephants, but also walrus in Alaska. Ivory carving is an old tradition throughout East Asia and parts of Southeast Asia, besides India. With the newfound wealth of East Asian countries, where they once were exporters, they are now consumers of other peoples' ivory, illegally acquired.

Luxury leather goods produced mainly in Japan often come from massive poaching of the hides of Louisiana alligators and Nile crocodiles. Poaching has similarly affected the entire range of tigers across South and Southeast Asia and the Russian Far East. There seems no part of the tiger that is not used in traditional medicine. Largely as a result, the global tiger population has been reduced to fewer than 3,000, compared with 100,000 a century ago.[35]

The supply of desired items from the wild is diminishing, especially as many target species occur in forests that are being cleared for farming. The impact on ecosystems that remain natural or at least in low-intensity use is considerable. For instance, the impact on the Mississippi was severe, where the old market for mussel shells to be made into ornaments was revived by Japanese demand about 1960. By 1966 the export of American mussel shells was worth almost nine million dollars annually at current prices.[36]

It is, however, conceivable that the surge in trade in endangered species is just that, a temporary surge before East Asian societies adjust away from consuming traditional items. Possibly, an autonomous shift in preferences will reduce the consumption of wild forms of protein, as it did in Europe, though whether this will be in time to prevent the extinction of certain species is debatable. Western conservationist groups have made a start at attempting to get certain wildlife items off the menus of restaurants in Vietnam.

## 1.9 Positive Assessments

Positive consequences and externalities of expanded resource use are often taken for granted or implicitly dismissed as weaker than the negative effects. Since they underwrite the economies of the region, this is unreasonable: gains in human well-being are scarcely calculable. Conservationist and animal liberationist critics attack the use of agricultural chemicals and intensive livestock production but, as Anderson points out, these methods raise yields. They reduce the area needed to produce grain and, via animal feed, meat. Through technological innovation the share of natural resource inputs per unit of output has been falling. Without the array of modern technologies even more of the earth's surface would have to be transformed from a wild state or be subjected to more intensive use.[37]

Expressed in this way, the trade-off becomes clearer. Restricting the applications of fertilizer, pesticides, herbicides, and fungicides would not necessarily have the benefits that command-and-control environmentalism expects. The negative externalities are in any case well-known, as is the cruelty involved in some forms of intensive livestock and poultry production, but the antidotes are well-understood too. Developed economies, where agricultural production is taxpayer-subsidized, have introduced legal curbs on farmers' misbehavior, and Pacific countries may eventually follow suit.

Anderson rejects the one-sidedness of resource appraisals by the environmental advocates who are numerous in the neo-Europes. The activists typically ignore second-order effects. Admittedly, when Anderson writes of the "huge technological strides that are changing fishing from a crude hunter and gatherer activity to high-tech deep-sea operations," he may be overstating his optimism, given the commonly accepted indications of over-fishing. Against this, not everyone accepts the conventional wisdom. Hannesson states that any "crisis" is hard to see in the statistics of the aggregate world fish catch; what is apparent is stagnation.[38] While some commercial stocks have been depleted, others have recovered, and institutional changes are increasing the incentives to conserve individual fisheries.

The optimistic alternative is a scenario in which environmental quality is improving and, apart from occasional price spikes like those for cereals in the mid-1990s and 2008, resource and product prices are continuing to fall in real terms. Optimists are able to point to reductions in resource inputs per unit of output and project indefinite technological advances and substitutions of materials. This opinion has almost as venerable a history as Malthusian negativism. When guano from islands off Peru first came onto the British market as fertilizer, a professor of chemistry remarked that it would "prove a great national service, if it shall teach us to imitate so valuable a natural production."[39] Nineteenth-century commentators tended to enthuse, not only about the prospects of discovering more or less infinite stocks of resources, but about the opportunities for substitution. Yeats, for example, approved of a contemporary saw that claimed that, "the addition of a new fact to a farmer's mind often increases the amount of his harvest more than the addition of acres to his estate."[40]

Scientific advance has made for fluent technological responses. Despite over-fishing in some zones (fisheries are where the problems of resource exhaustion first spring to mind) improvements in resource use as well as substitutions of materials have become commonplace. Thus despite, or rather because of, over-fishing, aquaculture increasingly substitutes for marine fisheries. World fishery production rose 13 percent from 2000 to 2008, but this came from farmed fish; the take of captured fish fell. Similarly, as part of a list of instances that could be extended, pearl-farming to produce cultured pearls in Indonesia and the Philippines is sufficient to keep depressing prices.[41] But to believe that renewable resources can invariably be refreshed or replicated is too Pollyana-ish. It ignores technological difficulties, as well as the competition among industries and nations that often frustrates institutional development.

We come, therefore, to the long-term consequences of biological exploitation. An important antidote is self-correction. Does the increasing scarcity of exploited organisms necessarily induce counter-measures? Conservation to ensure a permanent flow of resources is not new, not solely a product of European societies, and not only a product of modern affluence. It is environmental romanticism that is relatively new. Emperors in ancient China reserved huge areas, though their motive was the preservation of hunting. They issued strings of admittedly ineffective prohibitions on burning or clearing forest land. As long ago as the seventh century A.D., Japan's rulers also responded to shortages of timber by prohibitions on use which repetition shows were likewise seldom effective.

It was under the Tokugawa shogunate (1600–1868) that Japan took matters in hand.[42] The regional elite of the seventeenth and eighteenth centuries, and, in the nineteenth century, the central government as well, were driven to act because the growth of population and the area under tillage were rendering lumber and firewood scarce. This conservation campaign was instrumental rather than ideological. Shinto's "oneness" with nature cuts both ways: if wild creatures are accorded equal status with humanity, the corollary is that they should be able to look after themselves.[43] On the other hand, veneration for numinous places may favor habitat conservation.

Concern for safeguarding the harvest of fish was weak in Japan and new grounds were sought instead. Fishing stations were established in Sakhalin as early as the eighteenth century, despite the shogunate's disapproval of distant ventures.[44] Within Japan's own territory, big catches were made in the new fisheries of Hokkaido during the late nineteenth century. After the Second World War, Japanese and Russian fishermen contested the waters off the Russian Far East. In 1951, a report to the American Occupation authorities on the Japanese salmon industry claimed that Japan had never regulated any fishery for the sake of yields and simply shifted from one species to another as each was over-fished.[45] Between 1956 and 1960, the Japanese catch of salmon averaged 280,000 metric tons per annum but between 1967 and 1971 fell to an annual 188,000 tons.

Restricting catches of wild and edible species, providing nature reserves, and restoring impoverished habitats are the policies of affluent societies. In part they are functions of the scarcity of wildlife and undeveloped land consequent to economic growth. How widespread a "pure" or spiritual demand for conservation really is remains unclear. Questionnaires do not provide an answer since it is costless for respondents to applaud restrictions while continuing to "vote" the opposite way in the marketplace. People may settle for the so-called "Crete Scenario," accepting a pauperized environment for the sake of job creation and high incomes, provided they believe that wild land still exists and as long as zoos house exotic species that their children may enjoy. Television has made whole populations aware of conservation issues but by continually depicting rare species may have subliminally disguised their scarcity. That many people do not understand biodiversity is evident from answers to questionnaires, even when the phrasing of questions prompts pro-environment responses.[46]

Conservation organizations no longer remain economically marginal. They may nevertheless obtain credit for changes that would have occurred autonomously, through cleaner technologies and a shift in industrial composition away from smokestack industries. Comparative advantage shifts away from manufacturing as economies develop. Self-correction muffles or reverses impacts, one mechanism being the "natural resource Kuznets curve," whereby replanting begins to outstrip the level of the harvest. Net forest depletion has been calculated for forests in China: it rose fourteen- or fifteen-fold between 1975 and 1995 but had rapidly declined to half the peak area by 2000.[47] This is likely, however, to represent a shift to acquiring lumber beyond the country's borders.

With mobile species like fish and whales, catch effort rises but ceases once populations are reduced below the point at which effort is worthwhile. The residual stock is left unharvested and potentially able to recover on its own. Yet outcomes are indeterminate and the impact of usage must be assessed species by species. "Rat-farming" may dominate, which means that having been left with the best breeding grounds and food sources, survivors can recover from harvesting or pest control campaigns. Alternatively, the Allee effect may win out, meaning that survivors are so scattered they cannot find mates and the species goes into long-term decline.

## 1.10 Leisure and Ecotourism

Modern affluence in developed economies around the Pacific has sometimes gone beyond a straightforward consumption of more material goods; it has induced in the growing middle classes a taste for interacting with nature. This is now the basis of large leisure industries, though these are not novel in principle. To cite only the case of Japan, treatises on angling began to be published in the 1720s, only a couple of generations after the seminal publication of *The Compleat Angler* in England. The pastime received a boost when the artisan makers of military accoutrements, made redundant at the Meiji Restoration of 1868, switched to making equipment for anglers. Subsequent transport improvements generalized the hobby across Japan so that by the 1930s there were two million anglers.[48] In parallel with the translocation of plants and animals for husbandry and ornamental purposes, fish species were transplanted from one angling location to another.

Living standards rose in most countries around the Pacific toward the end of the twentieth century, though to different absolute levels. The reverse side of the coin is less-noticed: farming, lumbering, city growth, and other uses of the land rendered many wild species scarce. The notional value of wild species rises in inverse proportion to their numbers and this inspires hobbyist travel in search of them. Shooting and the collecting of specimens has slowly given way to observation and photography. Fishing has been a holdout in perpetuating the abuse of wild or feral organisms. Otherwise the consumption of nature has become kinder. Populations of European descent increasingly engage in bird-watching and the interest is spreading among societies with different cultural heritages. This generates expenditures on books, equipment, and eco-tourism. The political influence of natural history consumption has seen large areas dedicated as nature reserves, though once again this is not wholly new: reserves in Australia date from 1901.

## 1.11 Equilibria

Older sources thought of the European arrival in the neo-Europes as "destroying nature's equilibrium."[49] Is it true that previous equilibria were stable or, if one prefers, sustainable? An answer would mean specifying the time period, which will often be much longer than any normally contemplated by economists. Moreover, subtle changes may be hard to detect over a century or two, even when records exist. The contact period when Europeans arrived has generated most information on the topic. Understandably, the incomers seldom asked themselves whether what they found was or was not "permanent." They were more interested in the changes their own farming and species introductions caused.

Environmental history is a matter of trade-offs because any equilibrium will have involved numerical success for some species and loss for others; the net ecological costs and benefits involved may be vexatious to calculate. Optimal use requires a further decision, as to whether man-made and natural capital are substitutable in the long run. Optimists assume this will be so; pessimists insist that past successes are no guarantee for the future, though they are inconsistent in taking past losses as indicating inexorable trends.[50]

The future is in principle unknowable, and if the pessimistic view be taken the only decision rule about the proper level of resource use would be to adopt precautions so extreme they would sacrifice current living standards. These are often low enough as it is: fewer than 5 percent of the population may be undernourished in Australia, Canada, Chile, Mexico, and New Zealand, but the proportion rises to 9 percent in China, 15 percent in Ecuador, and 16 percent in the Philippines.[51] Under-nourishment may of course be the result of low entitlements (unequal income distribution) rather than inadequate production. Agricultural specialists are cautiously optimistic about prospects for increasing future physical supply.[52]

## 1.12 Extroversion

The possibility has been mooted that we are entering a super-cycle in which commodity prices must rise because of the entry into world markets of large new powers, China and India, which will have effects like those of the entry of the United Kingdom in the nineteenth century and the United States in the early twentieth century. This historical analogy seems to be over-influenced by the price spikes of 2007–2008 and ignores the extent to which American growth was based on the intensive use of its domestic resources.[53] The long-term trend has been for rising labor productivity in crop production to reduce the hours needed to supply a given unit of food. There is a lag before the elasticities of supply and substitution take effect but nothing to suggest that supply has ceased to respond to price incentives. The super-profits of 2007 induced an increase in world cereal output and brought prices down smartly.

This outcome did not prevent a number of East Asian countries from becoming anxious to seek land and resources far from their own borders. The World Bank has warned of this farmland "grab." For two centuries the Pacific Rim had seen resource exploitation bound up with Western colonization, notably in the neo-Europes and in plantation economies like those of the Indonesian archipelago. The East Asian countries, resource-poor relative to the size of their populations and target incomes, have now reversed the process. The Pacific Rim has turned outwards in a historically unprecedented process of extroversion.

Regular trade in foodstuffs has increasingly swept Latin America into the Chinese net. But this is normal trade. Beyond it, China and South Korea have purchased actual land holdings elsewhere in the world from which to source food for their own populations. These holdings chiefly lie in Africa and Central Asia, and may involve importing "virtual water" in grain carried from areas that are not water-rich. Similarly, Japan is acutely aware that it possesses fewer than 5 million hectares of arable land yet would need 17 million hectares for self-sufficiency at current nutritional standards. Unsurprisingly, it is the world's largest importer of grain, which is almost entirely maize from the United States. Japan has been slower to act than some of its East Asian neighbors but in 2010 established a body to coordinate public and private enterprises in world food markets.[54]

Rather than follow neighboring countries into markets for agricultural land where local populations may be short of food, Japan proposes to engage more vigorously in the international trade in foodstuffs. It aims to facilitate supply not only to the Japanese market but also to China, Southeast Asia, and the Middle East. The main exception to the self-denying ordinance over land acquisition is the fact that one Japanese company alone has leased 600,000 hectares in the Philippines in order to grow biofuel. Otherwise, Japanese investment will attempt to upgrade productive technologies, infrastructure, and distribution in Central and South America, Central Asia and Eastern Europe. The intended commodities are beans and maize.

All this activity, spurred above all by rising living standards in China, is likely to mean additional efforts at exploiting regions that are environmentally "difficult." *Ceteris paribus*, this will bring about a steep rise in the marginal price of commodities. Possible regions include the Russian Far East and Papua New Guinea. Already a Japanese company is considering entering West Papua. Parallel efforts will continue to aim at intensifying production on existing cultivated land, where China's norms, at any rate, still lag far behind the benchmarks of American practice. This will involve more research into plant production, where the prospects for raising yields are currently seen as promising.[55] As already remarked, higher yields work in the opposite direction from land acquisitions, because they reduce the land input needed per unit output. Given the demand created by world population growth and rising living standards, it remains unlikely, however, that scientific agriculture will be able to halt the incorporation of further wild or semi-wild tracts into farmland. Ecosystems around the Pacific and beyond will continue to be molded ever more intensively for human use.

## NOTES

1. E.g., W. Arthur Lewis (ed.), *Tropical Development 1880–1913: Studies in Economic Progress* (London: George Allen & Unwin, 1970), p. 283 on the Philippines.
2. John Yeats, *The Natural History of the Raw Materials of Commerce* (London: Cassell, Petter, and Galpin, 1871), p. 228.
3. J. M. R. Young, *Australia's Pacific Frontier* (Melbourne: Cassell Australia, 1967), p. 5.
4. Matt Weiland and Sam Wilsey (eds.), *State by State* (New York: Ecco, 2009), p. 19.
5. Anthony Netboy, *Salmon: The World's Most Harassed Fish* (London: Andre Deutsch, 1980), Part III and Appendix.
6. Eric Jones, *The Record of Global Economic Development* (Cheltenham: Edward Elgar, 2002), pp. 50–55.
7. Georg Borgstrom, *The Hungry Planet*, 2nd rev'd edn., (New York: Collier Books, 1972), p. 106.
8. Alfred Crosby, *The Columbian Exchange* (Westport, Conn.: Greenwood, 1972; C. G. F. Simkin, *The Traditional Trade of Asia* (London: Oxford University Press, 1968), p. 256.
9. Simkin, *Traditional Trade*, pp. 256–257.
10. *Ibid.*, p. 267.
11. Frank N. Egerton, "Naturalists Explore Russia and the North Pacific During the 1700s," *Bulletin of the Ecological Society of America* 89 (1), 2008, pp. 39–60.
12. Mary Saul, *Shells* (Garden City, New York: Doubleday, 1974), pp. 182–184.

13. Cf. map of indigenous and exotic flora in South Australia in A. Grenfell Price, *Island Continent: Aspects of the Historical Geography of Australia and its Territories* (Sydney: Angus and Robertson, 1972), p. 197.
14. Simmons *Changing the Face,* p. 245 table 5.20.
15. *Ibid.,* p. 288, table 5.33.
16. George Seddon, "Eurocentrism and Australian Science: Some Examples," *Search* 12/12 (1981–82), pp. 446–450; Edward Stokes, "The Outback Ocean," *The Geographical Magazine* LVIII (1986), pp. 402–408.
17. Australia's predominant native tree flora, the eucalypts, tend to be wind-pollinated.
18. Eric C. Rolls, *They All Ran Wild: The Story of Pests on the Land in Australia* (Sydney: Angus and Robertson, 1969).
19. D. W. Steadman, "Prehistoric Extinctions of Pacific Birds: Biodiversity Meets Zooarchaeology," *Science* 267 (1995), pp. 1123–1131.
20. The Maori were not averse to eliminating their human competitors, for instance killing off the Moriori in the Chatham Islands during the nineteenth century.
21. W. M. Mathew, "Peru and the British Guano market, 1840–1870," *Economic History Review* N.S. 23 (1), 1970, pp. 112–128; George Pendle, *A History of Latin America* (Harmondsworth, Middlesex: Penguin, 1967 edition), pp. 146–147.
22. Williamson, *American Economic Review,* 35 (1945), pp. 97–109.
23. Yasukichi Yasuba, "Did Japan Ever Suffer from a Shortage of Natural Resources Before World War II?" *Journal of Economic History* 56 (3), 1996, pp. 543–560.
24. Lester R. Brown, *Who Will Feed China?* (New York: W. W. Norton, 1994).
25. Peter H. Lindert, *Shifting Ground: The Changing Agricultural Soils of China and Indonesia* (Cambridge, MA: MIT Press, 2000).
26. E. L. Jones, "Ecological Accidents," *Biology and Human Affairs,* 40/1 (1974), pp. 37–47.
27. A. T. Wilson, "Pioneer Agriculture Explosion and CO2 Levels in the Atmosphere," *Nature* 273 (1978), pp. 40–41.
28. *Far Eastern Economic Review,* Mar. 25, 1999.
29. Charles J. Moore *et al.,* "A Comparison of Plastic and Plankton in the North Pacific Central Gyre," *Marine Pollution Bulletin* 42 (12), December 2001.
30. *Financial Times Magazine,* Mar. 27, 2010.
31. The benefits to human health should of course be taken into account.
32. Peter Dauvergne, *Loggers and Degradation in the Asia-Pacific* (Cambridge: Cambridge University Press, 2001), p. 151.
33. Loren Brandt and Thomas G. Rawski (eds.), *China's Great Economic Transformation* (Cambridge: Cambridge University Press, 2008), p. 269.
34. Marc Reisner, *Game Wars* (New York: Penguin, 1991), p. 82.
35. *The Observer/New York Times,* Mar. 21, 2010.
36. John Madson, *Up on the River: An Upper Mississippi Chronicle* (New York: Penguin, 1985), p. 90.
37. Kym Anderson, "Are Resource-Abundant Economies Disadvantaged?" Seminar Paper 97-03, Centre for International Economic Studies, Adelaide, 1997, p. 6.
38. Rognvaldur Hannesson, "Are the World Fisheries in Crisis?" Seminar, Institute for Advanced Study, La Trobe University, March 23, 2007.
39. Quoted in Mathew, "Peru and the British Guano Market."
40. Yeats, *The Natural History of the Raw Materials,* p. xiii.
41. *The Economist,* March 13, 2010.

42. Conrad Totman, *Japan before Perry: A Short History* (Berkeley: University of California Press, 1981), pp. 215–218.
43. J. Stewart-Smith, *In the Shadow of Fujisan: Japan and its Wildlife* (Harmondsworth, Middlesex: Viking, 1987, p. 44).
44. Netboy, *Salmon*, pp. 278ff.
45. *Ibid.*, p. 289.
46. Clive L. Spash and Nick Hanley, "Preferences, Information and Biodiversity Preservation," *Ecological Economics* 12 (1995), pp. 191–208.
47. Brandt and Rawski, *China's Transformation*, pp. 271–273.
48. Meizi Matuzaki, *Angling in Japan* (Japanese Government Railways, Board of Tourist Industry, 1940), pp. 14–15, 25.
49. Grenfell Price, *Island Continent*, pp. 205–206.
50. Eric Neumayer, "Scarce or Abundant? The Economics of Natural Resource Availability," *Journal of Economic Surveys* 14 (3), 2000, pp. 307–335.
51. Martin D. Smith, Sustainability and Global Seafood, *Science* 327 (Feb. 12, 2010), table 55. The outlying figure of 23 percent in North Korea has little to do with productive potential.
52. Peter Hazell and Stanley Wood, "Drivers of Change in Global Agriculture," *Philosophical Transactions of the Royal Society* Series B (2008), 363, pp. 495–515.
53. Gavin Wright, "The Origins of American Industrial Success, 1879–1940," *American Economic Review* 80 (1990), pp. 651–668.
54. I am grateful for details supplied by Professor Minoru Yasumoto, Komazawa University, Tokyo.
55. Wallace Huffman, Technology and Innovation in World Agriculture: Prospects for 2010–2019. Iowa State University, Department of Economics, Working Paper 09007 (2009). See also news reports (e.g., in *Financial Times*, March 26, 2010) of the fundamental discovery at the University of California, Davis, of plants with genetic material from only one parent, which have an increased propensity to pass on agronomically desirable traits.

CHAPTER 2

# CLIMATE RISK AND RESPONSE IN THE PACIFIC RIM

DAVID ROLAND-HOLST

## 2.1 Introduction

In modern times, exploiting prehistoric solar energy (carbon fuels) for industrialization has conferred living standards on humanity that are beyond the imagining of their forebears. Recently, however, we have awakened to the fact that this energy revolution is changing the natural world in fundamental and adverse ways. This unintended negative externality has given rise to what is often called the "mitigation agenda," a local, national, and global policy dialogue about how to limit greenhouse gas (GHG) emissions and other anthropogenic contributions to climate change.

Conversely, climate change has begun and will continue to present a broad array of challenges, as well as opportunities, to the Pacific Rim economies and their people. Response to long-term climate change is referred to as the "adaptation agenda." While both mitigation and adaptation are important environmental issues, unified in context of climate change, it is important to recognize their differences. Mitigation can improve environmental conditions and slow the progress of climate change. Mitigation activities are being discussed, negotiated, and promoted at all levels of society, and represent a complex agenda of environmental citizenship from the global to the individual level. Because mitigation is causative (i.e., behavior leads to an effect) and this externality is global, cooperation is essential to progress. Because of diversity in national environmental and economic circumstances, however, this kind appears to be very difficult under present conditions of uncertainty regarding climate risks.

The adaptation agenda is fundamentally different because it is responsive (i.e., effects induce behavior) and more localized. GHG emissions are the result of diverse local activities that affect the global environment; climate change is a global process with diverse effects on localities. Individuals, communities, and even states can debate their role in the mitigation agenda, but everyone has a responsibility to protect themselves from adverse effects of climate change. Regardless of what we do about emissions, climate change has begun and will continue for generations living and yet unborn. The extent of change will depend on mitigation decisions, but adaptation is necessary and inevitable.

More effective adaptation requires an understanding of complex challenges and opportunities to change behavior and innovate. In the next section, we review the basic economic theory of adaption. An economist's perspective only offers part of the insight society needs to advance the adaptation agenda, but the concepts presented here can elucidate how a changing climate will create economic risks and rewards. As they always have, these two incentives can be expected to animate human behavior and, if appropriately devised, move society along the path toward economic sustainability. Public agency is also discussed here because it will be essential to facilitate timely, cost-effective, and inclusive climate adaptation. Like private actors, policymakers need incentives to adapt their behavior, and the concepts below also recognize their essential role and the risks and rewards they face.

The remarkable diversity of the Pacific Rim countries will complicate the progress of both mitigation and adaptation. Historically, climate agreements (such as CFC reduction) have been most easily attained by small groups of countries with relatively similar economic structure and clearly shared interests. This region shares many interests, in, for example, trade, marine resources, etc., yet differences in stages of development arouse very different perspectives on mitigation priorities. Analogously, these countries share common biosphere resources (air, water, etc.), yet their geographic diversity will lead to very different kinds of climate change vulnerability. The Pacific Rim, for example, comprises many island nations, all of which should be rightly preoccupied with sea level and storm severity as overarching climate risks. Meanwhile, adaptation will have significant costs, and income diversity in the region implies very different levels of per capita adaptation capacity. In both the mitigation and adaptation context, some level of regional financial cooperation will be essential, but the architecture of such agreements will be complex.

## 2.2 Conceptual Perspective

This chapter addresses climate from an economist's viewpoint, assessing initial and future states of nature in terms of their impacts on livelihoods in Asia. Climate is such a pervasive phenomenon that it must touch on every dimension of economic life, but the challenges related to climate change and adaptation are of special relevance to six dimensions of microeconomic theory: Uncertainty, costs, timing, fairness, incentives, and institutions. We discuss each below.

### 2.2.1 Uncertainty

An essential consideration for all climate adaptation decisions is uncertainty and its economic avatar, risk. As we learn from the weatherman, uncertainty is endemic to our understanding of nature generally and climate processes in particular, and climate-economy linkages only compound this uncertainty. While we can never eliminate uncertainty, individual and social responses to climate change can be more constructive if better information is available about events and consequences. The importance of uncertainty for economics is that it complicates decision-making and can affect behavior in complex and often socially undesirable ways. Indeed, one of the main barriers to adaptation is inadequate information available to private and public actors. Generally speaking, today's available evidence is not relevant or authoritative enough to support timely and decisive policy.

Uncertainty in the context of adaptation takes six forms:

1. Climate processes
2. Baseline economic activity and resource availability
3. Impacts of climate change on economic resources and activities
4. Institutional constraints and capacity to respond to climate change
5. Technological change
6. Responses to adaptation measures

In this chapter we focus on evidence for the third and fourth areas, economic impacts and institutional responses, because we believe a stronger analytical foundation, candid discussion of risks and trade-offs, and greater consideration of the current and future effectiveness of institutions are most needed to advance proactive, sound decision-making. At the present time, the vast majority of information about climate change is in the first category, scientific evidence presented in terms of physical systems. However, financial markets, the insurance industry, and indeed most of the rest of the economy are not managed by scientists, and economic agents need to see climate costs and benefits in material terms if they are to change behavior and commit resources for adaptation. Government agencies need to understand the costs and benefits of different adaptation options if they are to make decisions that put public resources to their best use.

### 2.2.2 Costs

Two kinds of costs are relevant to the economic decisions about climate change: the costs of climate damage and the costs of adaptation. Evidence in this chapter is mainly about the former, but better information on what it costs to adapt will also be needed to move forward.

Because climate has such a complex relationship with the natural world, resources, and therefore the economy, there is a range of approaches to considering the economic impacts of climate change. In some cases, scientific information translates relatively directly into economic variables. For example, temperature-induced changes in crop yields can be converted to changes in expected harvest, and shortfalls can be assessed across a range of expected market prices. This can be contrasted with the complexity of more general climate risks, like fire risk to property. Unlike a farmer considering a specific crop, there is no model of fire incidence, severity, or timing to credibly inform individuals or communities about expected costs that are specific to their circumstances. In contexts like this, the best we can do is give estimates of total assets at risk and actuarial averages for fire frequency and severity. Given that the past may not be a reliable guide to the future, the insurance industry will need new approaches to risk assessment that provide the public with a better sense of the changing cost of risk.

A second complication relates to pricing risk and its attendant behavioral implications. To get fire safety incentives right, for instance, property owners should pay for protection in proportion to their individual (marginal) contribution to overall fire risk. Fire defense based on risk pooling and average cost calculations is generally inefficient because of heterogeneity in initial risk and ultimate damages. In a typical fire, some proportion of assets is catastrophically damaged while another portion is unscathed, and the former usually includes a disproportionate number of higher-risk properties. Risk pooling thus effects a financial transfer between these groups. Risk-based pricing, where insurance premiums better reflect individual risks, can provide more effective incentives for property owners, but is more costly and politically difficult to implement.

Pricing resources can be as complicated as pricing risk. In the electric power sector, for example, the fact that we pay time-averaged rates means that no one has an incentive to conserve during peak periods, which will become ever more problematic as per capita energy use in Asia rises with income. On the other hand, average cost pricing allows utilities to smooth price variability that might result from extremes. Like average versus marginal risk pricing, each approach as advantages and disadvantages.

Two final points are worthy of emphasis in the context of climate change costs. Firstly, more of the "disaster" assessments associated with extreme weather and other events remind us that, in the context of natural processes, the loss function is quite asymmetric. For example, a hurricane predicted to be a major storm might pass by with very limited long-term damage, or completely devastate communities. This asymmetry results from threshold processes (flooding, structural failure, evacuation orders, etc.), and it renders risk adjusted average costs of limited use because they overestimate the cost of most events and underestimate the cost of a catastrophic minority.

Secondly, despite much progress in environmental economics, the value of environmental services from baseline resources still plays only a minor role in climate assessment. Of course we are aware of our dependence on many amenities of today's world, but we have quite limited means of including these valuations in the baseline comparison for the cost of inaction, let alone the value of set priorities for restoring environmental services as part of the adaptation process. Much more progress is needed if we are to reliably factor these services into a more comprehensive cost-benefit analysis of climate policy.

### 2.2.3 Timing

In its most general form, climate policy can be seen as a form of insurance, incurring (mitigation and adaptation) costs at one time to avoid (climate damage) costs at another time. Thus, like other risk-based investments, timing plays a central role. Of course, with climate change, many mitigation, adaptation, and damage costs are uncertain, and so is the primary behavioral variable, the discount rate that mediates these values in determining the net present value of an adaptation choice. Further complicating this situation is the fact that adaptation can be proactive or reactive, occurring before or after the onset of damages.

As one might reasonably expect, this multidimensional uncertainty is a serious impediment to decision-making, individual or collective. Having said this, however, human institutions have remarkable capacity to manage complex risks and financial markets have already actively engaged the climate issue through insurance, venture capital, and other channels. All these developments can be considered tentative and even speculative, but available evidence continues to suggest that very large financial stakes will depend on the course of both climate change and adaptation. Better data on expected costs is certain to strengthen the capacity of markets for hedging climate risk, just as it will support better adaptation responses.

Uncertainty about timing makes adaptation decisions difficult and potentially more expensive, reinforcing any tendencies to defer them. For example, Neumann et al. estimate an uncertainty premium on California sea walls. If we borrow money at 3 percent to build walls 10 years before inundation, the project costs 35 percent more than it would if we could build the moment they were needed. Extending the margin of safety to 20 years increases the premium to 81 percent of the nominal project cost. At 5 percent, the same safety margins would add 63 percent or 165 percent to project costs.[1] Because sea level is in fact highly variable, subject to the dynamics of waves, tides, and storms, we must accept some degree of uncertainty and its attendant costs, but the question remains: How much?

The third source of uncertainty, the discount rate, has been seen by many observers as a major obstacle to progress of both the mitigation and adaptation agendas.[2] Not only do agents all have their own individual discount rates, but there can be significant disparities between them.[3] Financial markets offer some help here, and averaging investor discount rates gives general guidance about the opportunity cost of capital and inter-temporal asset comparison. Market interest rates are adequate proxies for discount rates in many other public and private investment decisions, and we do not believe climate adaption is any exception.

What is likely the greater barrier to financial commitment in this context is actual perception of risk-adjusted, discounted cost. Seismic risk offers a convenient metaphor. In the San Francisco Bay Area, a new bridge is being built to replace its seismically unsafe predecessor, even though the latter is still in full use. This proactive commitment was made because seismic risk is generally perceived as real, and the decision/cost is accepted because the public has internalized that risk. Why so with seismic and not climate risk? The reason is both credibility and timing. Every year, residents around the state get gentle reminders, usually while sleeping, that seismic risk is real and present. Thus we have a multibillion-dollar industry in earthquake engineering and retrofitting, but negligible investment to date in climate adaption.

Climate risks are not being internalized in part because of how risk is being communicated. Most climate change research addresses the middle or end of the present century, indeed much of the published research ignores events prior to 2030. This situation is changing now, however, with new evidence on accelerating change and the role of variability. We are awakening to the fact, for example, that not only averages (temperature, sea level, etc.) but variances of natural states are increasing. Sea level is not rising like water in a bathtub, but varies from week to week, hour to hour, and minute to minute because of the combined action of water temperature, tides, and wave action. These in turn are affected by random storm and other natural processes, and thus sea level risk will present itself decades before average sea level rises to inundate a given area all year around. Events arising from such variation will be the sentinels of climate risk that induce behavioral change.

### 2.2.4 Fairness

Economic fairness can be seen from many perspectives, but the most direct one is probably wealth distribution. From this angle, climate change has the potential to significantly impact global equity. This is to some extent inevitable because climate threatens such a diverse spectrum of economic assets, and does so in ways that are unequal. Different parts of the world will experience different temperature and sea level effects differently, for example. As with fire, heterogeneous risk can make risk pooling inefficient and inequitable, and may even increase damages by promoting risk-taking. Initial wealth inequalities may also be amplified because wealth represents adaptation capacity. Those with the means to invest in adaptation will suffer lower absolute, and perhaps net, costs, reinforcing prior inequality. Public (national and multilateral) investments in adaptation might correct some of this, but will likewise be differentiated in their incidence, benefiting some more than others.

How should mitigation and adaptation expenses be financed? When thinking about climate impacts, we might suppose that damage costs will fall on all three major players in the economy: households, enterprises, and government. In reality, however, the final bill will be passed through the markets and fiscal systems to households, who will face higher direct costs, combined with higher prices and taxes to cover costs incurred by the other two. The same logic of course applies to adaptation costs. The ultimate net costs may fall to the average global household, but to estimate them is a very complex cost allocation problem. Our estimates only make piecemeal contributions, but a few general conceptual rules are worth keeping in mind. In a more socially efficient and fair world, costs of climate risk should be borne by those whose behavior gives rise to those risks. Likewise, adaptation costs should be borne by those who benefit from the adaptations, be they publicly or privately financed.

Other metrics of fairness, such as economic vulnerability, occupational opportunity, mobility, can all be examined from a climate change perspective, but conceptual treatment of them is beyond the scope of present discussion. Lastly, it is important to recognize feedback between fairness issues and policymaking. Distributional effects are very important determinants of policy itself. Whom public spending, goods, and services affect, as well as how and when, are all intimately related to policy formation and implementation. Cost/risk averaging approaches that ignore this heterogeneity are unlikely to provide reliable guidance about the course of adaptation.

## 2.2.5 Incentives

Because mitigation and adaptation are forms of behavior, their economic characteristics can be better understood by examining incentives. For example, if the present value of climate damages exceeds the costs of adaptation that can avert these costs, there is a clear incentive to adapt. In this simple framework, we need only wait until climate change costs reach critical levels and we can expect to see waves of spontaneous private agency working to limit climate change and its adverse effects. To the extent that we do not see this, we could assume adaptation costs are too high, individuals rationally discount expected damages for credibility or time, institutional or other barriers stand in the way, or they have countervailing incentives of some kind.

The last case is of particular interest, since there are unfortunately many reasons why individual and social expected costs may be inconsistent. In the private sector, this kind of divergence usually arises from stakeholder diversity, uncertainty, and market failure. For example, a coal company might well calculate a different net benefit from mitigation policy than a kindergarten. These disparities in private interest are commonplace and form a solid basis for public interest initiatives by government, implementing policies that can redistribute net benefits to compensate adversely affected stakeholders and promote the greater good.

More difficult cases arise from policies that reinforce conflicting incentives or distort behavior. The most important of these is moral hazard, when incentives contradict the intention of a policy. Thus fire insurance, if it is priced below the marginal cost of the policyholder (i.e., the value of their individual fire risk), will promote risk-taking. This incentive flaw has been understood for at least a century, but the practice continues.[4] The same logic applies to a larger universe of climate risks. Some examples are obvious, like floodplain insurance, while others are more subtle, like public investments to protect high value private property. In broader financial markets, moral hazard is very difficult to eliminate because of public fiduciary responsibility. According to the World Bank, of the nearly 100 banking crises that have occurred internationally during the last 20 years, all were resolved by bailouts at taxpayer expense. Obviously, this kind of precedence seriously compounds moral hazard. In the case of catastrophic risk insurance, such as that which may accompany escalating climate risk, the same policy distortion is likely to emerge.

### 2.2.6 Institutions

If the world were organized by Adam Smith, individual agents would all make individual decisions based on individual information, acting on these autonomously and striving unconsciously for the collective good, achieving efficient resource allocation by each pursuing their self-interest. Here there would be no need for collective action or agencies like governments, producer groups, or labor unions to achieve efficiency. Obviously, we do not live in such a world, and institutions influence nearly every dimension of our lives. The significance of this for climate adaptation is that institutions may facilitate or retard our progress toward a more sustainable economy, reducing or even increasing the costs of climate change and/or adaptation.

Like the other conceptual topics discussed in this section, institutional economics occupies academic volumes of its own, so we can only touch on salient features related to climate risk. As has already been mentioned, adaptation is essentially a local issue, while climate change is global. This means that governmental institutions spanning these domains need some degree of consistency in responding to climate change. Unfortunately, the institutional landscape relevant to climate, mainly resource and regulatory agencies, is fragmented nationally, let alone globally. Examples from other global commons, like marine resources, are few in number and their experience offers only limited encouragement. Even at the national level, coherent decentralization of authority for emissions regulation, public investment, etc., remains a challenge even for OECD economies.

Another major institutional challenge is the political economy of interest groups. In Adam Smith's work all economic agents have equal, almost inaudible voices. The real world is of course very different, and concentrations of economic interests almost always coincide with concentrations of political influence. To the extent that such groups have short-term goals that diverge from effective long-term adaptation, the larger public interest may be undermined. For example, developers might push local governments for development rights in high flood risk areas, as neither is liable for flood damages. This problem need not be seen as some ethical failure, but simply a social distortion that applies different weight to different stakeholder interests. Our political system is sometimes interpreted as assigning equal per capita weights to things like welfare, opportunity, and entitlement, but the real economy often recasts this through political advocacy financed by stakeholder investment. In the context of climate damage, the most important implications of this problem are structural bias in favor of industry interests and short-term growth objectives. Both of these have historically contributed to higher expected climate risk and moral hazard with respect to the magnitude and ultimate incidence of climate damage costs.

A third important institutional issue relates to the behavior of office holders. These are the people to help make, implement, and enforce policies related to climate change and adaptation, and there are fundamental challenges to aligning their behavior with the longer-term, more inclusive perspective of present and future generations. Climate change may be happening faster than many people believe, and climate damage may come sooner than most expect, but there are very few predictions of significant adversity that fall within the next election cycle for any publicly elected. For this reason, even though action today might reduce adaptation costs for the majority of us, the result is unlikely to affect the next election. Officials are well aware of this and climate policy is therefore subordinated to decisions that have more immediate impacts, even though these impacts might be much smaller in the longer term.

More generally, we can see that, because their tenure is limited, office holders experience an inter-temporal version of moral hazard, focusing attention and resources on short-term public priorities at the expense of longer-term ones. Any uncertainty about the long-term consequences of their actions reinforces this by weakening their present accountability.

## 2.3 Climate Change Processes and Mitigation Challenges for the Region

Although the warming process associated with climate change is global, even a vast and diverse area like the Pacific Rim has special characteristics that regional public and private stakeholders need to consider. In this section, we review salient climate change and mitigation issues for the region.

### 2.3.1 Emissions Trajectories and Emerging Markets

The Pacific Rim includes the world's two largest national sources of GHG emissions, China and the United States. For this reason alone, the region will be decisive to the process of global warming. Per capita emissions are also nearly as unequally distributed across this region (Figure 2.1) as they are around the world (Figure 2.2). In this way the region encapsulates the negotiating challenges to any global agreement that could achieve lower long-term emissions. Wealthy countries have far higher per capita emissions, with about half of total current emissions from 20 percent of the regional

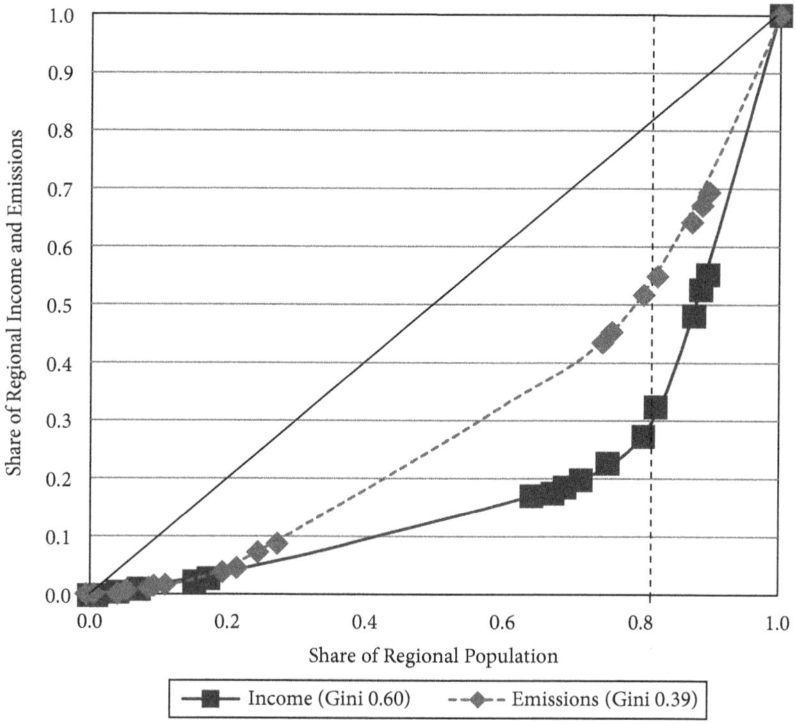


FIGURE 2.1 Distribution of National Global Greenhouse Gas Emissions, Pacific Rim

*Source:* Author estimates from World Bank, IEA, and UN data.

population. High income countries are also primarily responsible for 75 percent of the stock of GHG in the atmosphere that was emitted before 1950. Awareness of this legacy, combined with a desire to achieve comparable living standards, creates ambivalence toward significant emission reduction among developing and emerging economies, despite the essential need for their participation in any credible global mitigation agenda.

A deeper look at the origin of GHG emissions makes the mitigation challenge even more serious. Globally, over 80 percent of GHG emission currently comes from consumption of energy from carbon fuels and, as Figure 2.3 makes clear, energy and per capita income growth appear inextricably linked. Even emerging economies, which are producing energy-emission-intensive exports (raw materials and industrial goods) for OECD consumers, remain far below them in both income and energy use per capita. It is probably not realistic to imagine a significant decoupling of growth in per capita income and energy use. Although efficiency measures can help significantly (compare the US and Japan in Figure 2.3), lower net-carbon energy sources will have to play a major role to achieve incentive-compatible multilateral mitigation. Given the populations moving up this energy-income escalator, it is reasonable to imagine that conventional energy scarcity may drive part of this process.

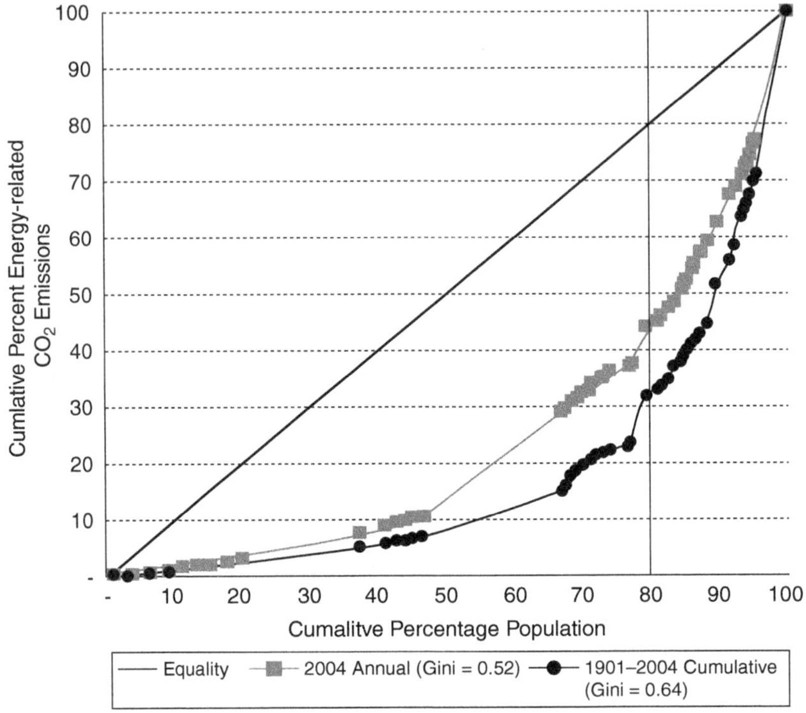


FIGURE 2.2 Distribution of National Global Greenhouse Gas Emissions, Global

*Source:* Kahrl and Roland-Holst: 2007.

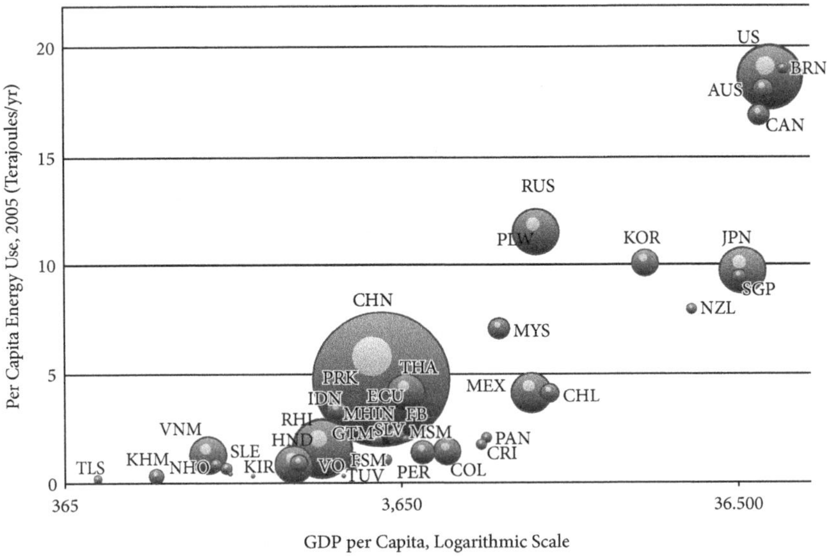


FIGURE 2.3 Emissions Intensity and Income, Pacific Rim Economies (Bubble diameter proportional to population)

*Source:* Author estimates from UN, IEA and World Bank data.

## 2.3.2 Residential Energy and Motorization

The primary driver of global energy use is middle-class demand for durable goods, most of which are energy-intensive in production and use. As Figure 2.4 suggests, this kind of demand can grow explosively in dynamic emerging economies. This depicts a schematic income distribution, with income milestones for difference types of personal transport technology. As average income grows moderately, perhaps at 4–8 percent per year, the eligible consumer population for each successive vehicle type grows with the area under the distribution (shaded), i.e., exponentially. Because each category is more energy intensive, energy consumption of course grows at a comparable or even greater rate. Similar reasoning holds for appliances and related durables.

During this kind of demand emergence, a sentinel commodity is one that represents an entire constellation of new behavior and consumption decisions. Automobiles are a classic example, and the diffusion of this technology in Pacific Rim countries will have a decisive influence on regional GHG emissions and resource use generally. As Figure 2.5 suggests, high-income countries in the region are becoming relatively saturated at 600–800 vehicles per thousand people, but China is still below 50 per thousand. The implications of this unmet demand potential are like a Holy Grail for the automotive industry, but are only beginning to be recognized in the climate policy dialogue.

Infrastructure requirements for this kind of motorization have also not been discussed explicitly in the climate policy context, yet they have far reaching implications for resource use. Figure 2.6 shows Asian Development Bank (ADB) estimates of road capacity needed to accommodate future global vehicle demand. The estimated paved-lane-km may be unattainable since it represents a quadrupling of total 2010 world paved road infrastructure by 2050, in China and India alone.

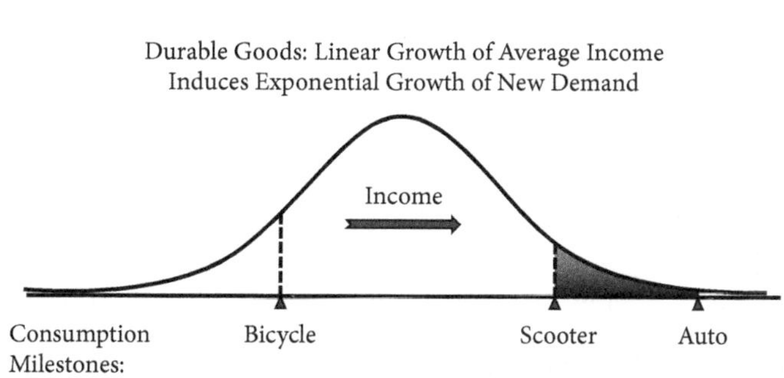


FIGURE 2.4 Affordability of Personal Transport

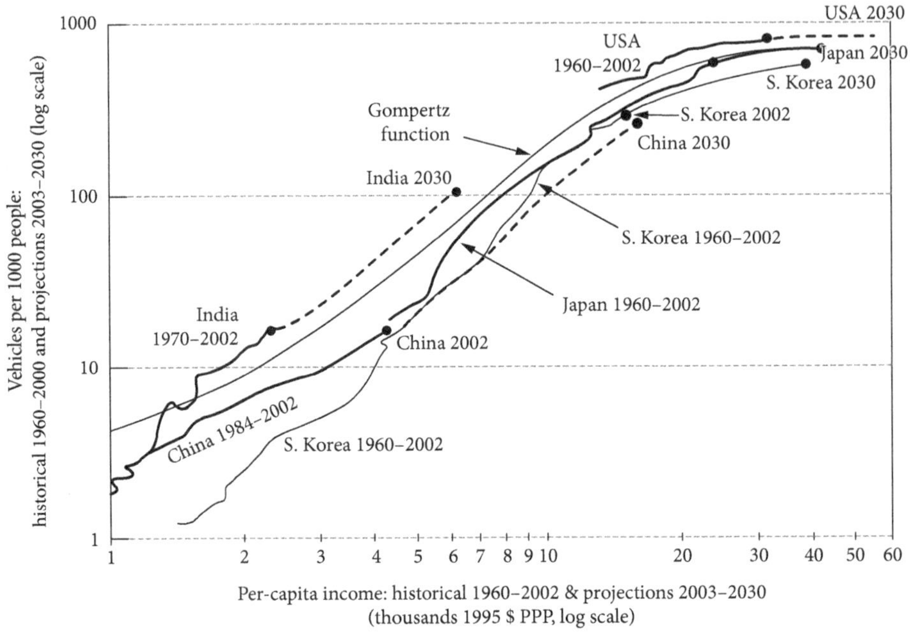


FIGURE 2.5 Passenger Vehicles, a Sentinel Commodity

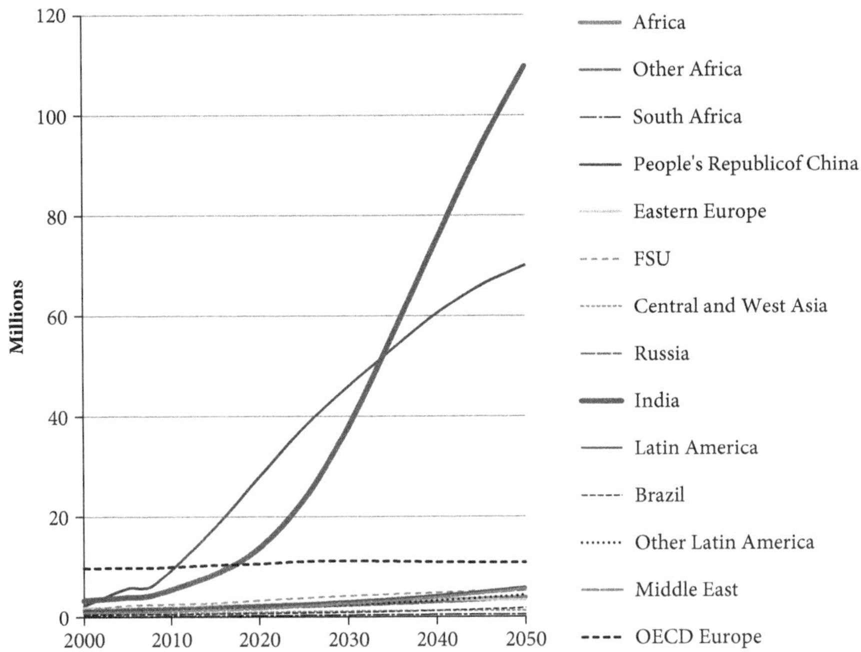


FIGURE 2.6 Paved-Road Requirements (km)

*Source:* ADB-IEA: 2011.

### 2.3.3 Development Rights and Global Climate Negotiations

One of the primary sticking points in global climate talks is the concept of "development rights," generally interpreted to mean that a principle of equal economic opportunity supersedes one of equal environmental commitment. Put another way, higher-income countries, because of legacy emissions and (perhaps) also because of ability to pay, should pay more per capita for global mitigation, even paying more as 1 percent of per capita emissions. Some see this as progressive environmental taxation on a global scale, while others call it green reparations. Obviously, this is a very complex ethical issue, and it should be no surprise that multilateral dialogue has had difficulty addressing it.

Figure 2.7 illustrates an essential aspect of this debate. Depicted here are estimated emissions to date and forward along a "450ppm" global emissions scenario, assuming we get GHG emissions down to levels that would limit global mean temperature increases below 2 degrees Centigrade. The green area represents developing and emerging economy emissions, while the solid and hatched blue areas combined represent the OECD. On a per capita equal emissions basis, the OECD would only be "entitled" to the solid blue area, suggesting a net "emissions debt" to the rest of the world equal to the intermediate (blue-green) area. Even assuming the higher-income countries can acknowledge the suggested ethical responsibility, the implied system of compensating transfers will be very challenging to design and implement. Experience with early prototypes, like the Clean Development Mechanism and Global Environmental Facility, have revealed serious incentive and agency issues that will further complicate progress.

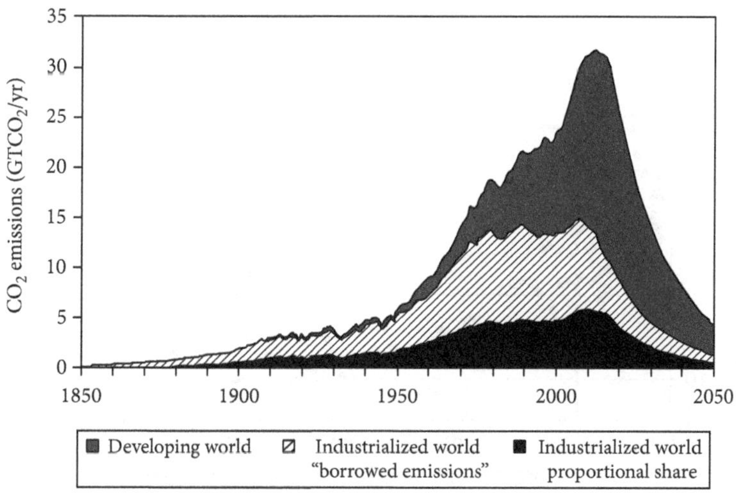


FIGURE 2.7 Global Emissions Balances to 2050

*Source:* Winkler et al.: 2006

Everything said above about global climate dialogue applies with at least equal force to the Pacific Rim, since this region is home to more than half of global emissions sources and represents much of the diversity that complicates our search of a lower-carbon future.

## 2.3.4 Agrifood Production and Food Security

Despite significant improvements in public health and life expectancy, global population growth has been relatively moderate over the last generation. Thus the Green Revolution was able to move us up to a trajectory of agrifood productivity, which along with subsidies to OECD producers has supported declining global food prices for several decades. Recently, however, global food markets have experienced serious price shocks. Looking at food expenditure shares for 118 countries (Figure 2.8), it is easy to see why these events are extremely sensitive. For the 80 percent of world population who live in countries to the left of the blue line, 35–75 percent of average disposable income is spent on food.

A detailed examination of recent food market turmoil is outside the scope of this chapter, but suffice to note for the moment two important components of the story: rising global food trade and Asian middle-class emergence (Jha et al.: 2011). The former has been with us for some time, as global agrifood trade rose 400 percent since 1970. Meanwhile, the very laudable economic successes of dynamic Asian economies have added hundreds of millions of people to the global middle class over the same period (Roland-Holst et al.: 2010). Indeed, the World Bank estimates that by 2030 over one-third of the world's middle class will come from China alone. Meeting the food demand of this emerging consumer population will be very different from the task of the Green Revolution. Rather than keeping up with the relatively modest dietary needs of the poor, agrifood systems will have to adjust to much more resource-intensive demand

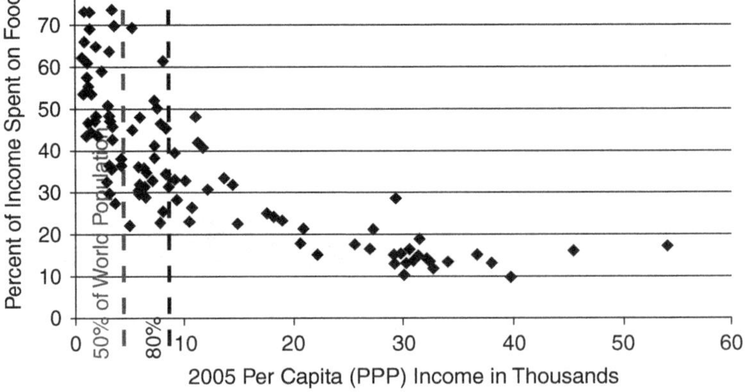


FIGURE 2.8 Food Expenditure and per Capita Income by Country

*Source:* Author estimates from official national and multilateral data.

patterns. As Figure 2.9 indicates, emerging market food needs will require much higher agrifood productivity growth than did the Green Revolution.

Merely shifting the diet toward meat, a signature feature of middle-class emergence in many countries, will make huge demands on global agricultural productivity. Because of this single food category, for example, China has gone in 15 years from self-sufficiency in soy products to the world's largest importer, buying 42 percent of the world's traded crop last year. As Figure 2.9, illustrates, the primary driver of this absorption is animal feed. Higher-income Asian economies that long ago shifted to meat as their main protein source all import more than 50 percent of their domestically

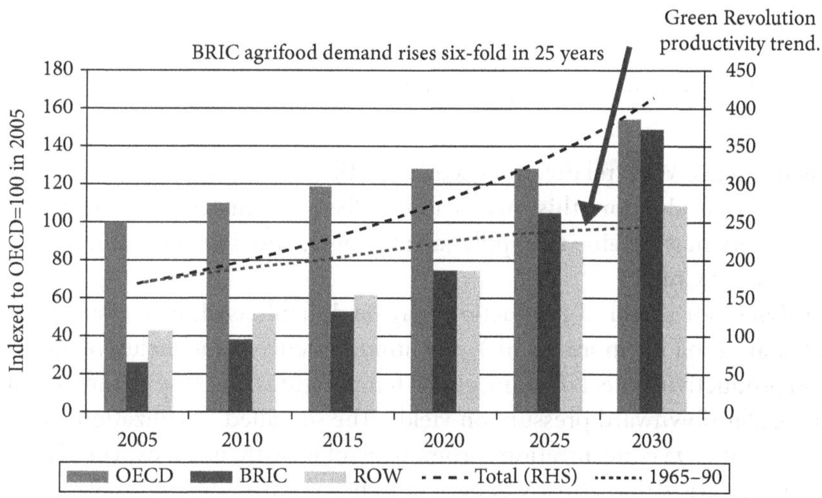


FIGURE 2.9A Global Agrifood Demand Trends

*Source:* Roland-Holst: 2012a.

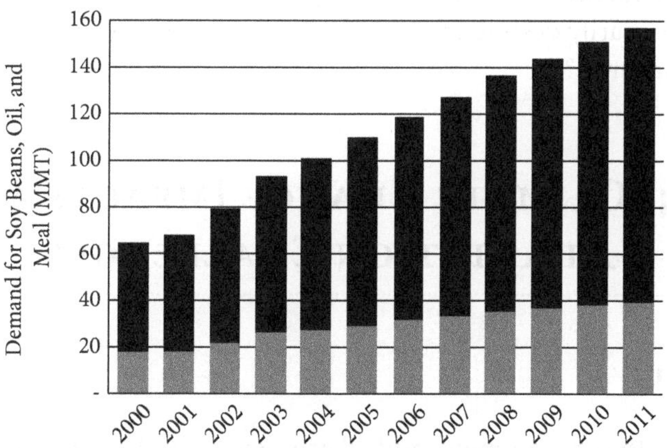


FIGURE 2.9B Soy Demand—China

*Source:* USDA/ERS.

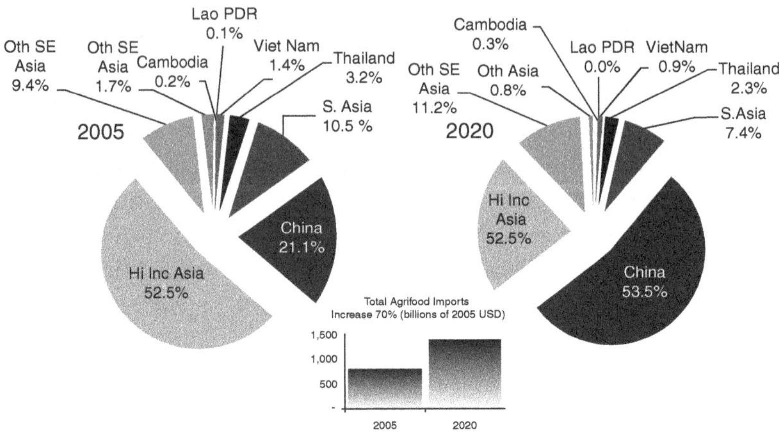


FIGURE 2.10 Asian Regional Food Imports, 2005 and 2020

*Source:* Jha et al.: 2011.

consumed cereals. With relatively closed comestible rice markets and limited land for extensive crop production, this means animal feed dominates their import bills. The world's farmers may be able to supply Japan, Korea, and Taiwan with more than half their cereals, but China?

Intensifying our agrifood production may be difficult as climate change progresses (see Liu et al.: 2004 for more details). Scientific evidence is inconclusive on the aggregate food productivity effect of rising global temperatures, but tropical areas will almost certainly suffer downward pressure on yields. The so-called "fertilization effect," when higher ambient CO2 concentrations promote plant growth, is not expected to compensate for this in areas that already experience chronic drought risk and water scarcity. Clearly, however, agrifood systems regionally and globally will be experiencing higher stresses and uncertainties as we are expecting more output from them. At the same time, middle-class emergence will be driving a 70 percent increase in Asian agrifood imports (Figure 2.10), primarily destined for Pacific Rim countries. Where will this food come from, and at what price?

## 2.4 Climate Change Impacts and Adaptation Challenges

### 2.4.1 Water

Essential to life, the environment, and all economic activities, renewable fresh water is very unequally distributed within and between countries around the Pacific Rim. Southeast Asia includes most of the countries in the top decile of annual rainfall and surface water per capita, yet China has 20 percent of global population and only

5 percent of the planet's renewable fresh water sources. Weather patterns distribute fresh water via storm systems, particularly in long monsoon and Pacific circulation cycles, while aquifers, snow, and ice reserve water for dry season use. The latter have been complemented by large investments in artificial storage and conveyance systems, distributing water across time and space to compensate for supply-demand mismatches. Climate change will profoundly affect all this, and necessitate significant regional adaptation. We review water challenges for the Pacific Rim from three perspectives, according to the source of water.

### 2.4.1.1 *Water from the Sky*

Most climate models agree that global warming will increase precipitation in temperate latitudes and reduce it in tropical ones. It is also expected that seasonality of rainfall will intensify, meaning shorter, more intense rain and longer dry periods. Subject to existing storage capacity, these trends would lead to a steady decline in total water availability, moderate increases in annual variability, and sharp increases in seasonal variability, meaning longer and deeper droughts. These trends will be aggravated by reductions

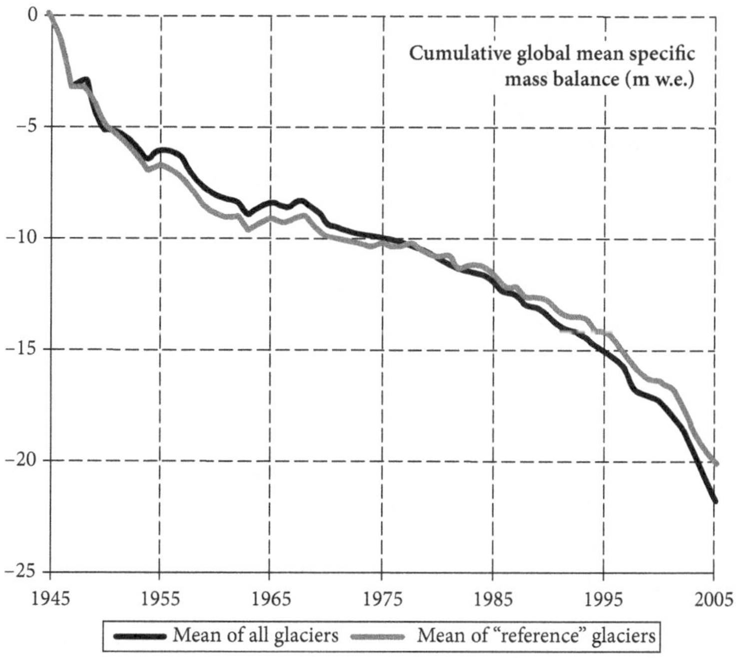


FIGURE 2.11 Global Average Glacier Mass Balances

Average of All Glaciers/Average of "Reference" Glaciers

*Ref:* GRIDA (2013), High Mountain Glaciers and Climate Change: An Interactive E-book, http://www.grida.no/publications/high-mountain-glaciers/e-book.aspx.

*Source:* UNEP/GRID-Arendal.

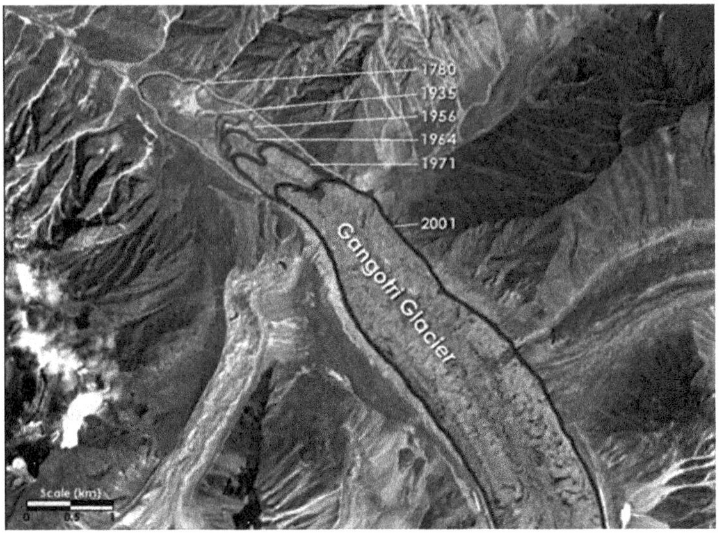


FIGURE 2.12 Historical Extent of the Gangotri Glacier

Source of 70 percent of Ganges River Summer Flow

*Source:* Earth Observatory, NASA.

in storage capacity, as aquifers are more aggressively exploited in dry spells, and snow packs shrink with global warming.

Demographic pressures will also affect the sustainable water supply. Clean and consistently available water has been one of the blessings of modernization, and most of the Pacific Rim's people have seen substantial improvements in water quality and availability over their lifetimes. This has happened primarily in cities and townships, however, where populations have been steadily migrating and per capita water use is much higher (2–3 times) than in rural areas. Thus we see water quality improving, but water availability is becoming less certain as urban use escalates. In many rural areas, the response to this has been increased groundwater exploitation, using more carbon fuel energy to extract an ever-receding resource. This combination is unsustainable and threatens both public health and food security. In populous Asian and smaller island economies in the region, determined initiatives for water efficiency, recycling, and scarcity pricing will be needed to avert more serious problems.

### 2.4.1.2 *Water from the Mountains*

Meanwhile, capacity of the world's second-largest fresh water storage facility, ice and snow, is expected to decline sharply as climate change progresses (Figure 2.11). So-called mid-latitude mountain ranges are very important to water supplies for Pacific Rim economies, including the Himalayas, Alps, Rocky Mountains, Cascade Range, and southern Andes. Glaciers in these ranges are showing the largest proportionate snow and ice losses as global temperatures have risen. The Himalayan plateau, for example,

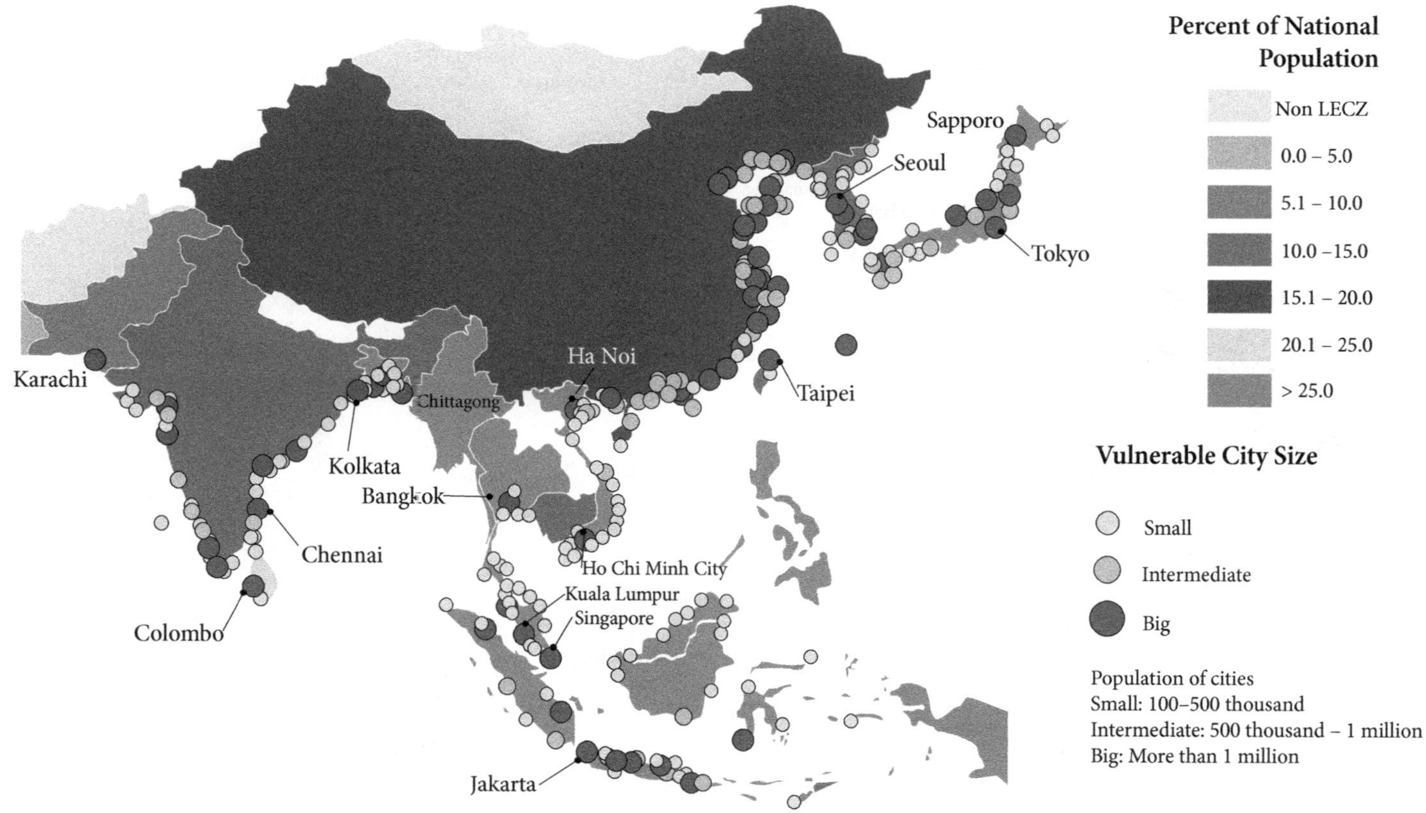


FIGURE 2.13 Population at Risk from Sea-Level Rise—Asia

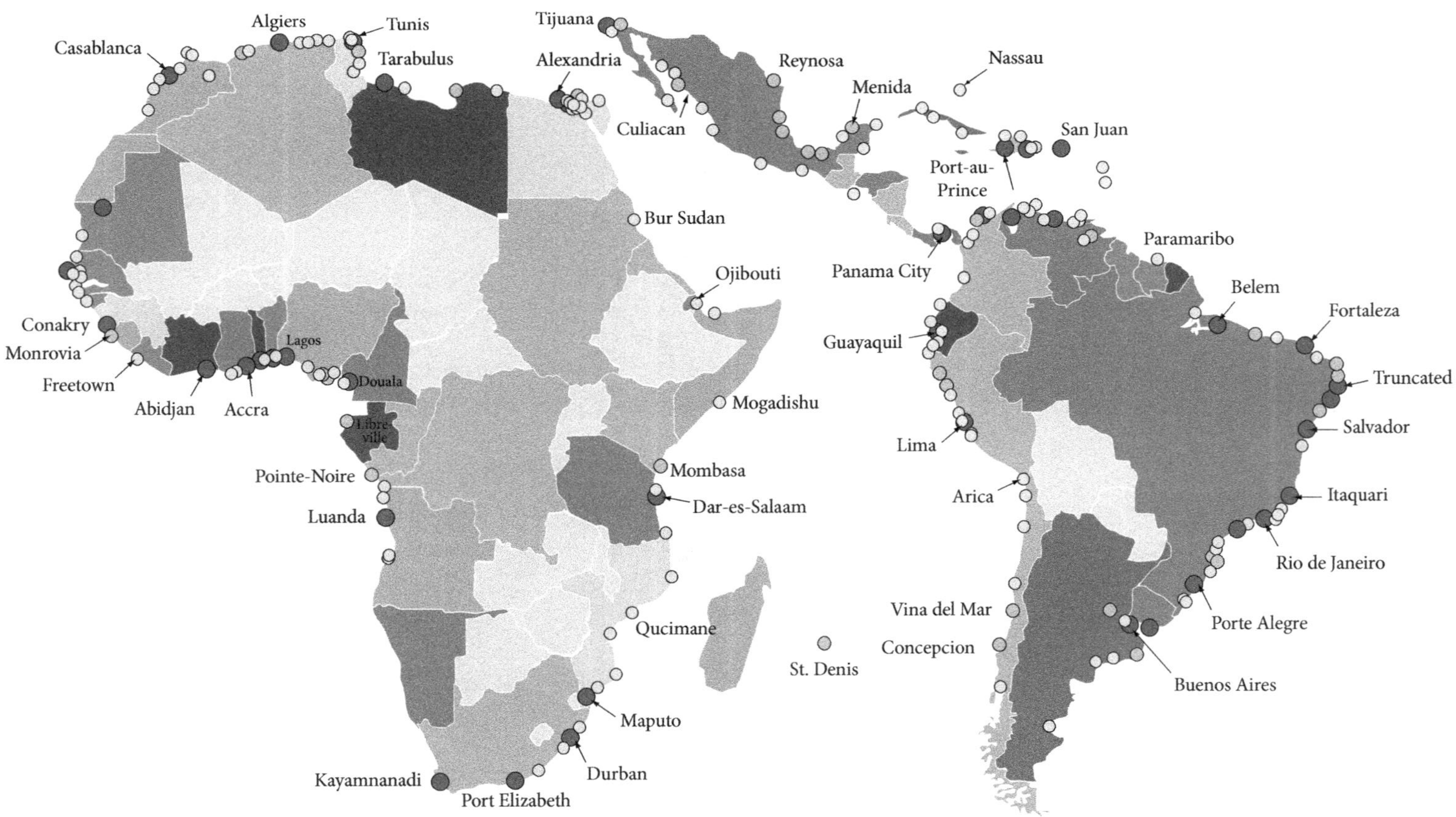


FIGURE 2.14 Africa and Latin America Will Be More Affected by Reduced Rainfall

with combined drainage basins serving some 3 billion people (almost half of the Earth's population) in 18 countries, is seeing about 90 percent of glaciers retreat (Figure 2.12). Even if total annual rainfall changes little, seasonal variation will escalate without montane water storage, and this could sharply curtail growing seasons and induce much more severe droughts in dry seasons.

### 2.4.1.3 *Water from the Sea*

Sea-level rise is one of the hallmark challenges of climate change, and for the Pacific Rim it will have special significance. The sea has been a catalyst for the region's collective prosperity, linking high-income markets to lower-income economies in globalization's continuing cycle of growth spillovers. In the case of sea-level rise, we shall again see shared destiny. Most of the defensive investments needed to protect people will be in export-oriented East and Southeast Asia.

Asia is home to 90 percent of the world's population at risk from rising sea level and, as Figure 2.13 suggests, this regional risk is concentrated in Pacific Rim Asian mega-cities (compare to, e.g. Africa and South America in Figure 2.14). By contrast, Canada and the United States, as well as countries in the Eastern Pacific and in western Central and South America, are significantly insulated by tectonic subduction, as the Pacific Plate has driven itself under both continents, raising extensive cliffs along most of their coastlines. In any case, these Pacific Rim countries have much lower coastal population densities than their Asian counterparts.

It must also be recognized that sea level is not a static object nor even a smooth trend. This kind of "bathtub" perspective greatly understates climate-induced sea level risk, both in terms of severity and timing. In fact, sea level is constantly subjected to variance from wave action, tides, and storm activity. Moreover, storm severity and frequency both appear to be escalating as a result of climate change. Taken together, these facts imply sea-level risk will become apparent sooner and more dramatically than simply average melting trends might suggest.

## 2.5 Demographic Challenges

Higher-income countries in the region generally have the financial capacity to protect their populations, particularly if they act early. The premia associated with resource-intensive consumption (higher energy and food costs) will largely be affordable for OECD members in the region, and for this group climate adaptation will generally be about protecting assets, including real estate and infrastructure. In lower-income countries, less financial capacity means people will be more directly threatened with food, energy, and habitat poverty, so the adaptation agenda in these countries will be focused on protecting people.

To the extent that this is unsuccessful, we can expect to see strong migratory pressures within and between countries in the Pacific Rim. Most well-known in this context are Bangladesh, 40 percent of whose population lives within 2 meters of sea level, and small island economies, some of which will lose the majority of their landmass in median sea-level scenarios (Figure 2.15). Domestic migration has been accommodated many times in these countries in the past, but transboundary spillovers may lead to more serious policy challenges.

## 2.5.1 Infrastructure

Emerging evidence of potential damages from climate change suggest there could be high private costs to adaptation, including large-scale relocation and investments to improve resilience of habitat, agrifood production, mobility and communication systems. To a significant extent, these costs can be offset by public commitments to infrastructure, particularly for defense against storm and flood damage, logistical disruption, and improved water storage/conveyance systems. The capacity for such investments will of course depend on government's ability to pay, and this will vary significantly across the Pacific Rim economies (Roland-Holst: 2009). As Figure 2.16 suggests, most of the assets at risk from sea level rise with their attendant defensive infrastructure costs, are concentrated in the Pacific Rim.

OECD regional economies can probably meet their needs over the long term, reprogramming large existing budgets for renewal and replacement. For lower-income economies, the situation will be quite different. Public funds already have a high opportunity cost in terms of advancing education, public health, and other basic needs and development initiatives, and climate defense may retard these advances. Many Asian regional economies could utilize external savings, from export surpluses, for such purposes, but this would necessitate fiscal changes that might undermine

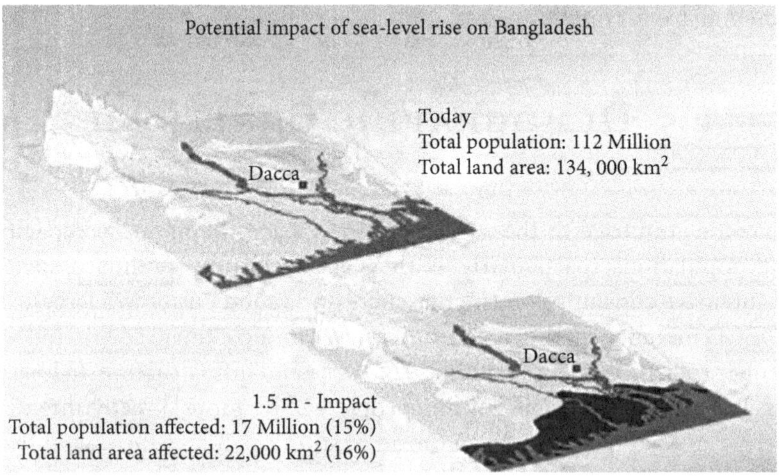


FIGURE 2.15 Climate Refugees—Everybody's Problem

*Source:* UNEP/GRID-Arendal.

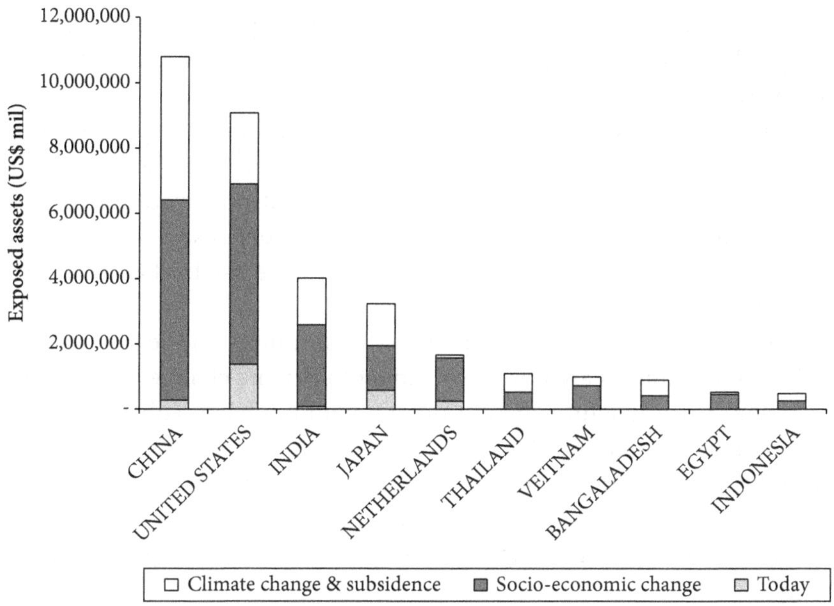


FIGURE 2.16 Top Ten Countries by Assets Exposed to Marine Climate Damage, Today and in 2070

*Source:* OECD: 2008.

competitiveness and in any case would undermine the growth dividend of export-led growth strategies.

## 2.6 Conclusion

This chapter reviewed an array of climate challenges facing the Pacific Rim. Each of these represents a different dimension of one overarching threat to our well-being, changes in the natural environment that will have profound and lasting adverse consequences unless we respond appropriately. Climate change is not only inevitable, it is already happening; but its ultimate consequences can be significantly mitigated by human and institutional adaptation.

If we do nothing, changes in the natural world will put our health, assets, and livelihoods at risk. The most expensive climate impacts for the Pacific Rim will be to human health and property. There are varying degrees of public and private sector risk: government would be contending with increased storm and flood severity; climate refugees would be displaced and made destitute; and the general public would mainly be affected through the price system (e.g., relatively more costly food, water, energy, and public goods and services). Who and where the affected people are will probably influence the timing of climate action, but it would be much less expensive to anticipate adaptation needs than to react to them. As we emphasize, huge potential wealth transfers can result from climate change—public-private, producer-consumer, producer-producer, and consumer-consumer. These will seriously complicate the politics of adaptation.

The good news is that the costs of adaptation are highly dependent on policy choices, and there are many choices open to the region. The bad news is that the most cost-effective and equitable solutions require strong institutions, only partially resembling their counterparts today. Moreover, expensive solutions are often capital-intensive extensions of the status quo and have established interest groups attached to them.

Because of this combination of ill-prepared institutions and legacy relationships, the Pacific Rim economies are unready to adapt to climate change. Over the last century the region's infrastructure, institutions, and politics have evolved in a small window of low climate variability. Like most disaster preparedness, we need to anticipate low probability events with very high cost and, like fire departments, this means overcommitting public resources most of the time. Public decision-makers need maturity to make such commitments against the cycles of economic growth and political seasonality.

For all its uncertainty and foreboding, we must recognize that climate adaptation also presents momentous opportunity, global need for innovation on a scale exceeding any period since (and perhaps including) the Industrial Revolution. Space programs were national and narrowly focused, the Green Revolution addressed only one supply chain (agrifood), and even World Wars concentrated most of their innovation in a few activities (ordnance, logistics, and transport). To address all the resource, livelihood, and habitat implications of climate change will require much more. Because of the technical nature of climate risks and impacts, effective adaption will require a knowledge-intensive revolution in our understanding of how to live in the natural world and use its resources sustainably. Within the climate challenge also resides a historic opportunity to sustain one of the most important lessons of the last century—peace and prosperity go hand in hand when we make credible commitments to multilateral cooperation.

## Notes

1. James E. Neumann, Daniel E. Hudgens, Jane Leber Herr, and Jennifer Kassakian, "Market Impacts of Sea Level Rise on California Coasts," Appendix XIII in Tom Wilson, Larry Williams, Joel Smith, and Robert Mendelsohn, "Global Climate Change and California: Potential Implications for Ecosystems, Health, and the Economy," PIER Report 500-03-058CF, 2003.
2. The underlying theory is summarized in Kenneth J. Arrow, William R. Cline, Karl-Göran Mäler, Moran Munasinghe, R. Squitieri, and Joseph E. Stiglitz, "Intertemporal Equity, Discounting, and Economic Efficiency," in J. Bruce, H. Lee, and E. Haites (eds.) *Climate Change 1995: Economic and Social Dimensions of Climate Change* (Cambridge: Cambridge

University Press, 1996). A detailed discussion of the discounting issue can be found in Yale Symposium, "Yale Symposium on the Stern Review," Yale Center for the Study of Globalization, Yale University, February 2007.

3. According to Ramsey, the standard discount rate $r = \delta + \eta g$, comprises $\delta$, a "pure" rate of time preference, a coefficient of relative risk aversion $\eta$, and the per capita growth rate of consumption g. A low value of the rate of pure time preference represents preference for intergenerational equity, while a high value of the coefficient of relative risk aversion implies equity over space and time.
4. Everett Crosby, "Fire Prevention," *Annals of the American Academy of Political and Social Science* 26 (1905): 224–238. More generally, Paul Krugman described moral hazard as, "...any situation in which one person makes the decision about how much risk to take, while someone else bears the cost if things go badly." See Paul Krugman, *The Return of Depression Economics and the Crisis of 2008* (New York: W.W. Norton Company Limited, 2009).

## References

Alllianz Group (Allianz) and World Wildlife Fund (WWF). 2006. *Climate Change and Insurance: An Agenda for Action in the United States*. New York: Allianz and WWF.

Baldocchi, Dennis, Simon Wong, and Andrew Gutierrez. 2005. "An Assessment of Impacts of Future CO2 and Climate on Agriculture." Public Interest Energy Research (PIER) White Paper.

Basu, Rupa, and Paul English. 2008. "Public Health Impacts from Climate Change." Draft CEC PIER-EA Discussion Paper.

Bureau of Transportation Statistics (BTS). 2005. *State Transportation Statistics 2005*. Washington, DC: BTS.

Carter, Lynne M. 2007. US National Assessment of the Potential Consequences of Climate Variability and Change Educational Resources Regional Paper: Pacific Northwest. Washington, DC: USGCRP.

Cayan, Dan, Peter Bromirski, Katharine Hayhoe, Mary Tyree, Mike Dettinger, and Reinhard Flick. 2006. "Projecting Future Sea Level." California Climate Change Center White Paper.

Changnon, Stanley A. 1999. "Impacts of 1997–98 El Niño-Generated Weather in the United States." *Bulletin of the American Meteorological Society* 80(9): 1819–1827.

Chestnut, L. G., W. S. Breffle, J. B. Smith, and L. S. Kalkstein. 1998. "Analysis of differences in hot-weather related mortality across 44 U.S. metropolitan areas." *Environmental Science and Policy* 1: 59–70.

CIC Research. 2008. "Overseas and Mexican Visitors to California, 2007." Report to the California Travel and Tourism Commission.

Cooley, Heather, Juliet Christian-Smith, and Peter H. Gleick. 2008. *More with Less: Agricultural Water Conservation and Efficiency in California: A Special Focus on the Delta*. Oakland: Pacific Institute for Studies in Development, Environment, and Security.

Croes, Bart. 2007. "California's Air Pollution and Climate Change Policies." Presentation at the 2007 Health Effects Institute Annual Conference, April 15–17, Chicago, Illinois.

Department of Energy (DoE). 2003. *"Grid 2030" A National Vision for Electricity's Second 100 Years*. Washington, DC: United States Department of Energy.

Deschênes, Olivier and Michael Greenstone. 2006. "The Economic Impacts of Climate Change: Evidence from Agricultural Profits and Random Fluctuations in Weather." MIT Joint Program on the Science and Policy of Global Change Report No. 131.

Deschênes, Olivier and Michael Greenstone. 2007. "Climate Change, Mortality, and Adaptation: Evidence from Annual Fluctuations in Weather in the US." Center for the Study of Energy Markets (CSEM) Working Paper 169.

Government Accountability Office (GAO). 2007. "Financial Risks to Federal and Private Insurers in Coming Decades are Potentially Significant." Highlights of GAO-07-760T, Testimony before the Committee on Homeland Security and Governmental Affairs.

Intergovernmental Panel on Climate Change (IPCC). 2007a. *Fourth Assessment Report*. Geneva: IPCC.

Intergovernmental Panel on Climate Change (IPCC). 2007b. *Fourth Assessment Report: Working Group II Report "Impacts, Adaptation and Vulnerability."* Geneva: IPCC.

Jha, Shikha, David Roland-Holst, Songsak Sriboonchitta, and Ryan Triolo (2011). "Food Security And Development In South And Southeast Asia," Working Paper, Erd, Asian Development Bank, Manila.

Johnson, David L. 2006. "Hurricane Katrina August 23-31, 2005." Service Assessment, U.S. Department of Commerce, National Oceanographic and Atmospheric Administration, and National Weather Service.

Julius, Susan Herrod, and Jordan M. West (eds.) 2008. *Adaptation Options for Climate-Sensitive Ecosystems and Resources*. U.S. Climate Change Science Program and the Subcommittee on Global Change Research Final Report, Synthesis and Assessment Product 4.4.

Kulesa, Gloria. 2002. "Weather and Aviation: How does weather affect the safety and operations of airports and aviation, and how does FAA work to manage weather-related effects?" in *The Potential Impacts of Climate Change on Transportation: Workshop Summary*. Proceedings from U.S. Dept. of Transportation Workshop, October 1–2, 2002.

Liu, X., D. Roland-Holst, D. Sunding, and D. Zilberman (2004). "The Economics of Climate Change in Agriculture," *Mitigation and Adaptation Strategies for Global Change* 9: 365–382.

Loomis, John B., and John Crespi. 1999. "Estimated Effects of Climate Change on Selected Outdoor Recreation Activities in the United States," in Robert Mendelsohn and James E. Neumann (eds.) *The Impact of Climate Change on the United States Economy*. Cambridge: Cambridge University Press.

Lott, J. Neal and Tom Ross. 2006. "Tracking and evaluating U.S. billion dollar weather disasters, 1980–2005." NOAA/NESDIS/NCDC.

Maynard, Trevor. 2008. "Climate Change: Impacts on Insurers and How They Can Help With Adaptation and Mitigation." *The Geneva Papers* 33: 140–146.

McConnell, Rob, Kiros Berhane, Frank Gilliland, Stephanie J. London, Talat Islam, W. James Gauderman, Edward Avol, Helene G. Margolis, and John M. Peters. 2002. "Asthma in Exercising Children Exposed to Ozone: A cohort study." *Lancet* 359: 386–391.

Mendelsohn, Robert, and Marla Markowski. 1999. "The Impact of Climate Change on Outdoor Recreation," in Robert Mendelsohn and James E. Neumann (eds.) *The Impact of Climate Change on the United States Economy*. Cambridge: Cambridge University Press.

Mills, Evan. 2005. "Insurance in a Climate of Change." *Science* 309: 1040–1044.

Nicholls, R. J., S. Hanson, C. Herweijer, N. Patmore, S. Hallegatte, J. Corfee-Morlot, J. Château, R. Muir-Wood (2008). "Ranking Port Cities with High Exposure and Vulnerability to Climate Extremes," OECD Environment Working Papers, No. 1, Paris.

Pielke Jr., Roger A., Mary W. Downton, J. Zoe Barnard Miller. 2002. Flood Damage in the United States, 1926–2000: A Reanalysis of National Weather Service Estimates. Boulder, CO: UCAR.

Pielke Jr., Roger A., Joel Gratz, Christopher W. Landsea, Douglas Collins, Mark A. Saunders, and Rade Musulin. 2008. "Normalized Hurricane Damages in the United States: 1900–2005." *Natural Hazards Review* 9(1): 29–42.

Roland-Holst, David, (2009). "Infrastructure as a Catalyst for Regional Integration, Growth, and Economic Convergence: Empirical Evidence from Asia," in Z. Fan (ed.), *From Growth to Convergence: Asia's Next Two Decades*, New York: Palgrave Macmillan.

Roland-Holst, David, Guntur Sugiyarto, and Yinshan Loh, "Asian Regional Income, Growth, and Distribution to 2030," *Asian Development Review*, Vol. 27, No. 2, pp. 57–81 (2010).

Savonis, Michael J., Virginia R. Burkett, and Joanne R. Potter. 2008. "Impacts of Climate Change and Variability on Transportation Systems and Infrastructure: Gulf Coast Study." Report by the U.S. Climate Change Science Program and the Subcommittee on Global Change Research.

Schugart, Herman, Roger Sedjo, and Brent Sohngen. 2003. *Forests and Global Climate Change: Potential Impacts on US Forest Resources*. Washington, DC: Pew Center on Global Climate Change.

Tanaka, Stacy, Tingju Zhu, Jay R. Lund, Richard E. Howitt, Marion W. Jenkins, Manuel A. Pulido, M'Elanie Tuaber, Randall S. Ritzema, and Ines C. Ferreira. 2006. "Climate Warming and Water Management Adaptation for California." *Climate Change* 76(34): 361–387.

Timmermann, Axel, Josef Oberhuber, Andreas Bacher, Monika Esch, Mojib Latif, and Erich Roeckner. 1999. "Increased El Niño frequency in a climate model forced by future greenhouse warming." *Nature* 398, 694–697.

United States Global Change Research Program (USGCRP). 2002. "Impacts and Adaptation," Chapter 6 in *Climate Action Report 2002*. Washington, DC: USGCRP.

Vafeidis, A. T., R. J. Nicholls, L. McFadden, R. S. J. Tol, J. Hinkel, T. Spencer, P. S. Grashoff, G. Boot, and R. J. T. Klein, 2008. "A New Global Coastal Database for Impact and Vulnerability Analysis to Sea-Level Rise." *Journal of Coastal Research*, 24(4), 917–924. West Palm Beach (Florida), ISSN 0749-0208.

WeatherBill Inc. 2007. "Impact of Climate Change on Golf Playable Days in the United States." WeatherBill Report.

Winkler, Harald, Bernd Brouns, Sivan Kartha (2006). "Future Mitigation Commitments: Differentiating Among Non-Annex I Countries," *Climate Policy*, 5, (5), 2006.

# CHAPTER 3

# NATURAL DISASTERS AND ECONOMIC POLICY FOR THE PACIFIC RIM

ILAN NOY

## 3.1 Disasters in the Pacific Rim

Many of the most destructive natural disasters of the past few decades occurred in Pacific Rim countries. During the past century for example, the most lethal earthquake (Tangshan, China, 1976), the most lethal tsunami (Aceh, Indonesia, 2004), and some of the most lethal storms and floods have all occurred in Asia bordering the Pacific.[1] Other catastrophic natural disasters, like the exceptionally strong earthquake in Chile in 1960 that generated a Pacific-wide tsunami; the Tohuku, Japan, 2011earthquake and tsunami that was the most destructive natural disaster in modern history in terms of destroyed property; the Mexico City earthquake of 1985; the Managua earthquake of 1972; and the periodic hurricanes that dramatically impact Honduras and El Salvador, are all examples of how natural disasters play a significant part in the economies of almost all the Pacific Rim countries.

Even without these catastrophic infrequent events, some Pacific Rim countries are buffeted by repeated and very frequent natural disasters (e.g., the Philippines experiences, on average, 5.8 destructive tropical storms annually). The countries of the Pacific Rim, as well as the volcanic islands and coral atolls of the Pacific Ocean itself, are also some of the most vulnerable to future disasters that may be associated with the changing climate and most are within the Ring of Fire—the globally most geologically active region.[2]

Robert Barro has argued that the infrequent occurrence of economic disasters has much larger welfare costs than continuous economic fluctuations of lesser amplitude (Barro 2006 and 2009). He estimated that for the typical advanced economy, the welfare cost associated with large economic disasters such as those experienced in the twentieth century amounted to about 20 percent of annual GDP, while normal business cycle volatility only amounted to a still substantial 1.5 percent of GDP. For developing countries, which usually suffer from more frequent natural disasters of all types, and of even greater magnitude than in advanced economies, these events have an even greater effect on the welfare of the average citizen.

Understanding the history of disasters in the Pacific Rim, their impact on development, on the spatial evolution of income, and the risks that the Pacific Rim region faces in terms of future events and their likely consequences all seem to be important components of an understanding of the region's economy. After all, the disruptions in many multinationals' supply chains that occurred after the 2011 Tohoku earthquake/tsunami demonstrated persuasively the potentially global impact of these types of disasters, an impact which is especially acutely felt in the Pacific region—whose countries' level of trade integration within the global economy is very high.

I employ a typology of disaster impacts that distinguishes between direct and indirect damages. Direct damages are the damage to fixed assets and capital (including inventories), damages to raw materials and extractable natural resources, and of course mortality and morbidity that are a direct consequence of the natural phenomenon. Indirect damages refer to the economic activity, in particular the production of goods and services, that will not take place following the disaster and because of it. These indirect damages may be caused by the direct damages to physical infrastructure or harm to labor, or because reconstruction pulls resources away from the usual production practices. These indirect damages also include the additional costs that are incurred because of the need to use alternative and potentially inferior means of production and/or distribution for the provision of normal goods and services (Pelling et al., 2002).

These costs can be accounted for in the aggregate by examining the overall performance of the economy, as measured through the most relevant macroeconomic variables, in particular GDP, the fiscal accounts, consumption, investment, and, especially important for the comparatively globalized countries of the Pacific Rim, the balance of trade and the balance of payments. These costs can also be further divided, following the standard distinction in macroeconomics, between the short run (up to several years) and the long run (typically considered to be at least five years, but sometimes also measured in decades). I use these distinctions in the discussion that follows.

## 3.2 Data on Disasters in the Pacific Rim

### 3.2.1 The Past

The Emergency Events Database (EM-DAT), maintained by CRED at the Catholic University of Louvain, is the most frequently used resource for disaster data.[3] EM-DAT defines a disaster as an event which overwhelms local capacity and/or necessitates a request for external assistance. For a disaster to be entered into the EM-DAT database, at least one of the following criteria must be met: (1) 10 or more people are reported killed; (2) 100 people are reported affected; (3) a state of emergency is declared; or (4) a call for international assistance is issued. Natural disasters can be hydro-meteorological, including floods, wave surges, storms, droughts, landslides and avalanches; geophysical, including earthquakes, tsunamis and volcanic eruptions; and biological, covering epidemics and insect infestations (these are much less frequent). The data report the number of people killed, the number of people affected, and the amount of direct damages in each disaster. Since biological events are much more anthropogenic, and the data collected on them are much less reliable, we will not discuss them in what follows.

We present disaster data for all the countries of the Pacific Rim, but exclude the small island-nations of the Pacific itself.[4] The disaster types we include are earthquakes, temperature extremes, floods, storms, volcanic events, and wildfires.

In the Pacific Rim, natural disasters, as defined in the EM-DAT database, are common events. Overall, we have some data on 3221 natural disaster events in the Pacific Rim for 1970–2008, but many of these do not include the full data on mortality, the number of people affected, and property damages; and many are quite small and would have no large economic consequences. The five worst disasters (in terms of the three measures of disaster magnitude) are given in Table 3.1. In the Pacific Rim region, the five disasters with the highest mortality are all earthquakes, with a total of almost 600,000 people killed. In terms of people affected, floods in China dominate the list, although aggregate mortality for these is fairly low (about 10,000 people in total). Hurricane Katrina in the U.S., and the Kobe earthquake in Japan were by far the costliest disasters (in terms of damage to infrastructure) until the March 2011 earthquake/tsunami in Tohoku, which dwarfs both disasters with damages estimated at 300 billion US$, more than twice as much as the amount estimated for Katrina.

A list of the three worst disasters for each Pacific Rim country and their aggregate toll (in terms of mortality), provided in Table 3.2, provides some limited insight into what are the vulnerabilities of each country both in terms of the kinds of disasters that are likely to wreak the most damages and how big these damages are likely to be. Not surprisingly, there are very few Pacific Rim countries for which earthquakes are not part of the most dangerous disaster list: Australia, Canada, Honduras, Korea, New Zealand, the U.S., and Vietnam. But, after the 2011 earthquake in Christchurch, New Zealand, that country can no longer be considered relatively earthquake safe, and most predictions are that a large West Coast quake in the U.S. will also dwarf any impact from other American disasters. Thus, past recent experiences is only of limited use in assessing future vulnerabilities in the face of catastrophic but rare events.

The last column in Table 3.2 measures vulnerability differently, by counting the number of large events in the past 40 years. In this case, we adopt a threshold that is 10 times higher than the one used by EM-DAT, since the dataset includes many relatively minor

**Table 3.1 Worst Disasters in the Pacific Rim 1970–2008**

| Country (year) | Type | # Killed | # Affected | Damages |
|---|---|---|---|---|
| *Worst Disasters (# of people killed)* | | | | |
| China PR (1976) | Earthquake | 242,000 | 164,000 | 5600 |
| Indonesia (2004) | Earthquake | 165,708 | 532,898 | 4451.6 |
| China PR (2008) | Earthquake | 87,476 | 45,976,596 | 30,000 |
| Peru (1970) | Earthquake | 66,794 | 3,216,240 | 530 |
| Guatemala (1976) | Earthquake | 23,000 | 4,993,000 | 1000 |
| *Worst Disasters (# of people affected)* | | | | |
| China PR (1998) | Flood | 3656 | 238,973,000 | 30,000 |
| China PR (1991) | Flood | 1729 | 210,232,227 | 7500 |
| China PR (1996) | Flood | 2775 | 154,634,000 | 12,600 |
| China PR (2003) | Flood | 430 | 150,146,000 | 7890 |
| China PR (1995) | Flood | 1437 | 114,470,249 | 6720 |
| *Worst Disasters (damages in US$ million)* | | | | |
| United States (2005) | Storm | 1833 | 500,000 | 125,000 |
| Japan (1995) | Earthquake | 5297 | 541,636 | 100,000 |
| China PR (1998) | Flood | 3656 | 238,973,000 | 30,000 |
| China PR (2008 | Earthquake | 87,476 | 45,976,596 | 30,000 |
| United States (1994) | Earthquake | 60 | 27,000 | 30,000 |

*Source*: Author's calculations from EMDAT.

events (from a macroeconomic perspective). Using this measure, Indonesia, China, and the Philippines stand out as highly vulnerable.

Figure 3.1, taken from Cavallo and Noy (2011), plots the average number of natural disaster events (hydro-meteorological and geophysical) per country 1970–2008. The figure shows that the incidence of disasters has been growing over time everywhere in the world. In the Asia-Pacific region for example, which is the region with the most events, the incidence has grown from an average of 11 events per country in the 1970s to over 28 events in the 2000s. In other regions, while the increase is less dramatic, the trend is similar. However, these patterns appear to be driven to some extent by improved recording of milder events, rather than by an increase in the frequency of disasters. Furthermore, truly large events—i.e., conceivably more catastrophic—are rarer. At this point, there is no credible evidence the frequency of catastrophic events is increasing, though that is most clearly a possible prediction given the projected evolution of climatic conditions in the next century.

**Table 3.2 Vulnerability—Worst Disasters per Country**

| Country | Worst Three Disasters (1970–2008)[1] | | | # killed[2] | # of large disasters[3] |
|---|---|---|---|---|---|
| Australia | Wildfire 1983 | Storm 1974 | Flood 1984 | 176 | 0 |
| Canada | Storm 1998 | Storm 1987 | Storm 1975 | 68 | 0 |
| Chile | Earthquake 1971 | Earthquake 1985 | Flood 1993 | 374 | 1 |
| China | Earthquake 1976 | Earthquake 1974 | Earthquake 2008 | 349,476 | 84 |
| Colombia | Volcano 1985 | Earthquake 1970 | Earthquake 1999 | 23,416 | 10 |
| Costa Rica | Storm 1988 | Storm 1996 | Earthquake 1991 | 126 | 0 |
| Ecuador | Earthquake 1987 | Flood 1983 | Flood 1998 | 5,525 | 3 |
| El Salvador | Earthquake 1986 | Earthquake 2001 | Flood 1982 | 2,444 | 5 |
| Guatemala | Earthquake 1976 | Storm 2005 | Flood 1982 | 25,133 | 4 |
| Honduras | Storm 1998 | Storm 1974 | Flood 1993 | 22,974 | 4 |
| Indonesia | Earthquake 2004 | Earthquake 2006 | Earthquake 1992 | 173,986 | 20 |
| Japan | Earthquake 1995 | Flood 1972 | Flood 1982 | 6100 | 10 |
| Korea | Flood 1972 | Flood 1998 | Storm 1987 | 1558 | 9 |
| Malaysia | Storm 1996 | Earthquake 2004 | Flood 1970 | 411 | 0 |
| Mexico | Earthquake 1985 | Flood 1999 | Storm 1976 | 1736 | 22 |
| N. Zealand | Storm 1988 | Flood 1985 | Storm 1997 | 13 | 0 |
| Nicaragua | Earthquake 1972 | Storm 1998 | Storm 2007 | 13,520 | 4 |
| Panama | Flood 1970 | Earthquake 1991 | Storm 1988 | 108 | 0 |
| Papua NG | Earthquake 1998 | Storm 2007 | Earthquake 1993 | 2407 | 2 |
| Peru | Earthquake 1970 | Earthquake 2007 | Storm 1998 | 67831 | 6 |
| Philippines | Earthquake 1976 | Storm 1991 | Earthquake 1990 | 14,368 | 17 |
| Russia | Earthquake 1995 | Ex temp 2001 | Ex temp 2001 | 2597 | 3 |
| Taiwan | Earthquake 1999 | Storm 2001 | Storm 2000 | 2453 | 2 |
| U.S. | Storm 2005 | Ex temp 1980 | Ex temp 1995 | 3763 | 19 |
| Vietnam | Storm 1997 | Storm 1985 | Storm 1989 | 5231 | 20 |

[1] The worst three disasters in terms of the number of fatalities.
[2] Measures the sum of fatalities in the three worst disasters experienced in each country.
[3] Measures the number of disaster events for which there were more than 100 fatalities, more than a thousand people affected, and damages of more than a million US$ (this is a significantly higher threshold than the one used by EMDAT—we further did not count disasters for which the number of fatalities was unavailable).
*Source*: author's calculations from EMDAT.

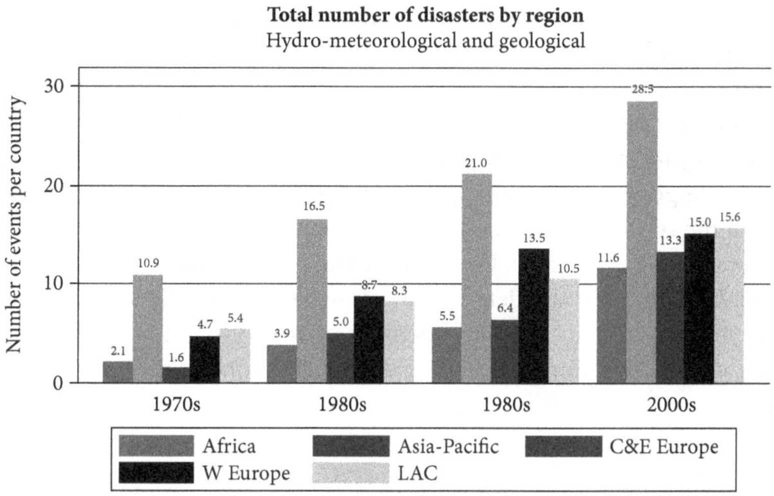


FIGURE 3.1 Frequency of Disasters by Geographic Region

*Source:* Cavallo and Noy (2011).

## 3.2.2 The Future

A recently announced Intergovernmental Panel on Climate Change (IPCC) summary of a *Special Report on Managing the Risks of Extreme Events and Disasters to Advance Climate Change Adaptation* concludes, after a review of the scientific literature, that there will be a "likely increase in heat wave frequency and very likely increase in warm days and nights across Europe.... likely increase in average maximum wind speed and associated heavy rainfall (although not in all regions).... very likely contribution of sea level rise to extreme coastal high water levels (such as storm surges).... [but] low confidence in drought projections for West Africa." (IPCC, 2011).[5] While the 2011 report is fairly skeptical about the robustness of much of the predictions available in the scientific literature about catastrophic high-risk low-probability natural disasters, it does argue that "For exposed and vulnerable communities, even non-extreme weather and climate events can have extreme impacts."

In its latest comprehensive report from 2007, the IPCC states that: "Warming of the climate system is unequivocal, as is now evident from observations of increases in global average air and ocean temperatures, widespread melting of snow and ice, and rising global average sea level" (IPCC, 2007). The IPCC report projects that by the year 2100, average global surface warming will increase by between 1.8° Celsius and 4° Celsius, depending on the success of emissions mitigation strategies.[6]

The projected increase in sea surface temperatures will potentially impact both the frequency and intensity of tropical storms, though there is limited understanding of these effects. One of the necessary conditions for hurricane formation is ocean water temperature greater than 26°C to a depth of about 50 meters. Several studies posit that, as global sea surface temperatures rise, hurricanes may become more numerous or intense, the range of hurricanes will increase to the north and south of the current "hurricane belt," or their location and typical paths will change (e.g., Webster et al., 2005 and Li et al., 2010).

While coupling climate models with storm-generation models is admittedly fraught with unknowns and maybe unknowables, Emanuel et al. (2008), for example, find that "Basin-wide power dissipation and storm intensity generally increase with global warming, but the results vary from model to model and from basin to basin. Storm frequency decreases in the Southern Hemisphere and north Indian Ocean, increases in the western North Pacific, and is indeterminate elsewhere" while Mendelsohn et al. (2009) also predict increased frequency and intensity of storms in the North Atlantic. Elsner et al. (2008) suggest that warming temperatures allow for already strong storms to get even stronger.

The 2007 IPCC report predicts that sea levels will rise between 0.18 and 0.59 meters by 2100. However, like predictions on temperature changes, more recent predictions of global sea-level rise are considerably more drastic as more information on glacial melting has become available. Rahmstorf (2007), for example, predicts a sea-level rise of 0.5 to 1.4 meters by 2100 while Vermeer and Rahmstorf (2009) predict rises of up to 1.9 meters. These sea-level rises, besides posing ongoing difficulties to low-lying areas, will certainly also increase the damages caused by storm wave surges and earthquake-induced tsunamis.

Other changes associated with climate change may also contribute to disaster occurrence and damage. For example, the absorption of carbon in the ocean has led to increased acidity and has resulted in widespread coral reef bleaching. This coral bleaching in turn leads to destruction of reef systems that protect coastal areas from storm surges.

Whatever climate models are used, however, there is wider agreement that the combination of sea-level rise and deteriorated coral reef ecosystems will make coastal areas considerably more vulnerable to storms, regardless of whether storms will indeed be more frequent or more intense (or both).

The impact of global climate change on the incidence of other types of natural disasters is even less well understood., but there is some preliminary evidence, mostly from model exercises, that droughts and floods will become more common and more severe (e.g., IPCC, 2007). For now, we have no evidence that the incidence of geophysical disasters is likely to change over time or be affected by any of the climatic changes that are predicted to occur. The frequency of large earthquakes appear to be fairly constant with, on average, 17 large earthquakes (magnitude 7.0–7.9) and about one mega earthquake (magnitude 8.0 and above) a year.[7] However, as we already observed about the future damages from earthquake-generated tsunami waves, one can easily conclude that even if the probability of geophysical events will not be impacted, the ways in which these natural events will interact with the local economy may clearly change over time. For example, if climate change will induce longer and more widespread droughts, then the soil erosion that will result will increase the damage incurred when earthquakes generate a mud-slides (as is frequent in Central America).

## 3.3 Determinants of Initial Disaster Costs

When evaluating the determinants of disasters' direct costs, most research papers estimated a model of the form: $DIS_{it} = \alpha + \beta \mathbf{X}_{it} + \varepsilon_{it}$; where $DIS_{it}$ is a measure of direct damages of all disasters in country *i* and time *t*; using measures of primary initial damage such as mortality, morbidity, or capital losses. $X_{it}$ is a vector of control variables of interest with each research effort distinguishing different independent variables. Typically $X_{it}$ will include a measure of the disaster magnitude (e.g., Richter scale for earthquakes or wind speed for hurricanes) and variables that capture the "vulnerability" of the country to disasters (i.e., the conditions which increase the susceptibility of a country to the impact of natural hazards). $\varepsilon_{it}$ is generally assumed to be an independently and identically distributed (iid) error term.

Kahn (2005) estimates a version of this model and concludes that while richer countries do not experience fewer or less severe natural disasters, their death toll is substantially lower. In 1990, a poor country (per capita GDP<2000 US$) typically experienced 9.4 deaths per million people per year, while a richer country (per capita GDP>14,000 US$) would have had only 1.8 deaths. This difference is most likely due to the greater amount of resources spent on prevention efforts and legal enforcement of mitigation rules (e.g., building codes). In particular, some of the policy interventions likely to ameliorate disaster impact, including land-use zoning, building codes, and engineering interventions are rarer in less-developed countries.

This finding, however, does not imply that higher damages in developing countries are inevitable. The contrast between storm preparedness in Cuba vs. Haiti, or in Burma vs. Bangladesh, clearly demonstrates that even poor countries can adopt successful mitigation policies and that successful mitigation does not only depend on financial resources and the ability to mobilize them. Even in wealthier countries, there are dramatic differences in the degree of preparedness; Japan, for example, constructed a nation-wide earthquake warning system that successfully managed to stop all high-speed rail a few seconds before the damaging earthquake shock waves arrived in the Sendai region on March 11, 2011—no other country has installed such a system.

A consistent finding of several studies (i.e., Kahn, 2005; Skidmore and Toya, 2007; Raschky, 2008; Strömberg, 2007) is that better institutions—understood, for instance, as more stable democratic regimes or greater security of property rights—reduce disaster impact. Typhoon Nargis, which hit Burma in May 2008, provides a tragic contrast to this insight. Apparently, the Burmese government was warned about the nearing storm two days before it arrived, but did little to warn coastal residents. In addition, the government interrupted post-disaster relief efforts and restricted access by international NGOs to the affected area; more than 138,000 people were killed. Nargis is an extreme case, but other countries that experience periodic storms and flooding, such as the Philippines, also appear comparatively unprepared.

Anbarci et al. (2005) elaborate on the political economy of disaster prevention. They conclude that inequality is important as a determinant of prevention efforts: more unequal societies tend to have fewer resources spent on prevention, as they are unable to resolve the collective action problem of implementing preventive and mitigating costly measures.

Besley and Burgess (2002), using data from floods in India, observe that disaster impacts are lower when newspaper circulation is higher, which leads to more accountable politicians and a government that is more active in preventing and mitigating impacts. Compounding this question of accountability is the apparent unwillingness of the electorate to punish politicians who had under-invested in preparedness, even though failure to provide generous post-disaster reconstruction funds does appear to be an important determinant of post-disaster electoral success (Healy and Malhotra, 2009). Thus, even in democracies, politicians rarely face the optimal incentives in terms of disaster prevention and/or mitigation.

To summarize, while the damage caused by disasters is naturally related to the physical intensity of the event, a series of economic, social, and political characteristics also affect vulnerability. A byproduct of this analysis, of course, is that these characteristics are therefore potentially amenable to policy action. In particular, the collective action problems that the literature identifies can potentially be overcome with the design of decision-making mechanisms that take these problems into account. There is growing awareness among the Pacific Rim countries' policymakers of the importance of not only mitigation but in reducing vulnerability to the economic pain that is likely in a disaster's aftermath. In the November 2011 ministerial meeting of Asia-Pacific Economic Cooperation (APEC), leaders issued a statement that details these concerns and describes the steps that APEC countries are encouraged to take in order to become more resilient (APEC, 2011).

## 3.4 Economic Impacts—Are Disasters a Poverty Trap?

A disaster's initial impact causes mortality, morbidity, and loss of physical infrastructure (residential housing, roads, telecommunication, and electricity networks, and other infrastructure). These initial impacts are followed by consequent impacts on the economy (in terms of income, employment, sectoral composition of production, inflation, etc.). These indirect impacts are not preordained, of course, and the policy choices made in a catastrophic disaster's aftermath can have significant economic consequences. For example, by using a non-equilibrium dynamic growth model, Hallegatte et al. (2007) show that a country experiencing disastrous events may find itself unable to adequately reconstruct and may remain stuck in a post-disaster poverty trap. Thus, while post-disaster policy choices clearly have a direct economic impact in the short run, these potentially also have long-run consequences.

### 3.4.1 Short-Run

The short-run impacts of disasters are usually evaluated in a regression framework of the form: $Y_{it} = \alpha + \beta X_{it} + \gamma DIS_{it} + \varepsilon_{it}$; where $Y_{it}$ is the measured variable of interest (e.g., per capita GDP), $DIS_{it}$ is a measure of the disaster's immediate impact on country *i* at time *t*, $X_{it}$ is a vector of control variables that potentially affect $Y_{it}$, and $\varepsilon_{it}$ is an error term. Noy (2009) estimates a version of this equation and, in addition to the adverse short-run effect already described in Raddatz (2007), he describes some of the structural and institutional details that make this negative effect worse. Noy (2009) concludes that countries with a higher literacy rate, better institutions, higher per capita income, higher degree of openness to trade, higher levels of government spending, more foreign exchange reserves, and higher levels of domestic credit but with less open capital accounts are better able to withstand the initial disaster shock and prevent further spillovers into the macro-economy. These findings suggest that access to reconstruction resources and the capacity to utilize them effectively are of paramount importance is determining the speed and success of recovery.

Raddatz (2009) uses vector autoregressions (VARs) to conclude that smaller and poorer states are more vulnerable to these spillovers, and that most of the output cost of climatic events occurs during the year of the disaster. His evidence, together with that of Becerra et al. (2013), also suggests that, historically, aid flows have done little to attenuate the output consequences of climatic disasters.[8]

Even if aid inflows are typically not substantial enough to assist in complete reconstruction, bigger countries may be capable of engineering the inter-sectoral and inter-regional transfers required to fully mitigate the economic impact of natural disasters (Coffman and Noy, 2010, and Auffret, 2003). The importance of inter-regional transfers was highlighted by the massive mobilization of reconstruction resources following the catastrophic Sichuan earthquake of 2008. The Chinese government spent lavishly on reconstruction, with about 90 percent coming from the central government and only 10 percent financed locally in Sichuan.[9] The rebuilt infrastructure in the destroyed counties (which were remote and under-developed pre-quake) appears to be significantly superior to its previous state. Therefore, while direct losses may be high in large countries because of the increased wealth exposure, the greater capacity to absorb shocks means that indirect losses may be lower, and/or that the size of the damage may be lower relative to the size of the country.

Noy and Vu (2010) further focus on the importance of inter-regional transfers in a developing country, Vietnam, and find that the post-disaster impact on economic activity across Vietnamese provinces appears to be determined by the provincial ability to attract reconstruction resources from the central government.

Very little research has attempted to examine household data and determine the effects of natural disasters on household expenditures. An important exception is Sawada and Shimizutani (2008), who examine household data after the 1995 Kobe earthquake in Japan. They find that, even in a rich country, credit-constrained households experienced significant reductions in consumption, while households with access to credit did not. Further evidence on the importance of credit is suggested by the Rodriguez-Oreggia et al. (2013) findings of a significant increase in poverty in disaster-affected municipalities in Mexico.

### 3.4.2 Long-Run

Theoretically, the likely impact of natural disasters on growth dynamics is not clear. Standard neo-classical frameworks that view technical progress as exogenous—e.g., the Solow-Swan model with exogenous saving rates and the Ramsey-Cass-Koopman model with consumer optimization—all predict that the destruction of physical capital will enhance growth since it will drive countries away from their balanced-growth steady states. In contrast, endogenous growth frameworks do not suggest such clear-cut predictions with respect to output dynamics, depending on the approach used to explain the endogeneity of technological change. For example, models based on Schumpeter's creative destruction process may also ascribe higher growth as a result of negative shocks (Hallegatte and Dumas, 2009), as these shocks can be catalysts for reinvestment and upgrading of capital goods. Yet, the AK-type endogenous growth models in which the technology exhibits constant returns to capital predict no change in the growth rate following a negative capital shock; though the economy that experiences a destruction of the capital stock will never go back to its previous growth trajectory. Endogenous growth models that have increasing returns to scale production generally predict that a destruction of part of the physical or human capital stock results in a lower growth path and consequently a permanent deviation from the previous growth trajectory.

To date, the empirical work on this question has also failed to reach a consensus. Skidmore and Toya (2002) use the frequency of natural disasters in a cross-sectional dataset to examine long-run growth impacts of disasters, while Noy and Nualsri (2007) use a panel of five-year country observations, as in the extensive literature that followed the work by Barro (1997). Intriguingly, they reach diametrically opposing conclusions, with the former identifying expansionary and the latter contractionary disaster effects. More recently, Jaramillo (2009) finds qualified support for the Noy and Nualsri (2007) conclusion.

Skidmore and Toya (2002) explain their somewhat counterintuitive finding by suggesting that disasters may be speeding up the Schumpeterian "creative destruction" process that is at the heart of the development of market economies. Cuaresma et al. (2008), however, find that for developing countries, disaster occurrence is associated with less knowledge spillover and a reduction in the amount of new technology being introduced rather than with an acceleration of these processes.

Cavallo et al. (2013) provide the most recent attempt to resolve this debate. They implement a new methodology based on constructing synthetic controls–i.e., a counterfactual that measures what would have happened to the path of the variable-of-interest in the affected country in the absence of the natural disaster. Using this methodology, they don't find any significant long-run effect of even very large disasters, except for very large events that were then followed by political upheavals. For these events, they find economically very substantial and statistically significant negative long-run effects on per capita GDP.

Another possibility is suggested in Coffman and Noy (2012), where the question is the impact of a specific event (a hurricane) on an isolated Hawaiian island. In this instance, the authors conclude that while there was no long-term impact on per-capita variables, this is largely because the disaster led to an out-migration from which the island has never completely recovered (the net population loss was a very significant 15 percent). Whether this pattern can be observed for other catastrophic events is not well-established, though casual observation suggests that these irreversible out-migrations also happened in the case of New Orleans after hurricane Katrina, while in the city of Kobe after the earthquake of 1995 the population did not move away in spite of persistent decreases in incomes (see Vigdor, 2008 and Dupont and Noy, 2012, respectively). There is much speculation that the same will be true for the Tohoku region of Japan that was hit by the March 2011 tsunami.

### 3.4.3 Fiscal Impacts

As we observed previously, disasters are likely to generate significant inter-regional transfers and/or international aid. Accurate estimates of the likely fiscal costs of disasters are useful in enabling better cost-benefit evaluation of various mitigation programs and to determine the appropriate level of insurance against disaster losses.[10]

On the expenditure side, publicly financed reconstruction costs may be very different from the original magnitude of destruction of capital; while on the revenue side of the fiscal ledger, the impact of disasters on tax and other public revenue sources has also seldom been quantitatively examined. Using panel VAR methodology, Noy and Nualsri (2011) and Melecky and Raddatz (2011) estimate the fiscal dynamics likely in an "average" disaster; however, they acknowledge that the impacts of disasters on revenue and spending depend on the country-specific macroeconomic dynamics occurring following the disaster shock, the unique structure of revenue sources (income taxes, consumption taxes, custom duties, etc.), insurance coverage and the size of the financial sector, and government indebtedness.

Borensztein et al. (2009) utilize data from Belize to estimate in a calibrated model the likely fiscal insurance needs of a government that is susceptible to large adverse shocks (hurricanes in the case of Belize), while Barnichon (2008) calculates the optimal amount of international reserves for a country facing external disaster shocks using a similar methodology.

The implications of these findings to the Pacific Rim region are quite obvious given the high degree of vulnerability of almost all countries in the region. Mexico's FONDEN provides an example of an ex-ante fiscal provisioning for disaster reconstruction, but this, while prudent, amounts to a form of self-insurance, which may be very costly in the case of a developing economy with substantial borrowing costs.[11] Chile, in contrast, has used some of the funds available in its Sovereign Wealth Fund (the Copper Fund) to pay for reconstruction following the destructive earthquake of February, 2010. Japan, which can easily pursue counter-cyclical fiscal policy,[12] resorted to additional borrowing to pay for the 2011 Tohoku earthquake reconstruction costs.

As we have already observed in section 3.3, political reluctance to engage in insurance purchase derives from the fact that there is little short-run benefit to be gained from entering into insurance contracts. Insurance involves costs today and a possible pay-off in the undetermined future, though by that time the government may have already changed hands. In addition to these time-incentive problems, disasters are widely considered as "acts of God" (or natural phenomena), and politicians are often not blamed for their occurrence and the damages they inflict. Politicians and policymakers therefore face very weak incentives for adopting relatively complex measures, such as purchasing market insurance, to offset hypothetical post-disaster costs.

One way to overcome this problem is for countries to mutually insure each other. While this is difficult to envision politically within any Pacific-Rim-wide grouping such as APEC, it may be more politically palatable and therefore practical in smaller and more geographically concentrated groups like ASEAN.

### 3.4.4 International Impacts: Trade, Financial Flows, and Emigration?

Odell and Weidenmeir (2004), in a historical investigation of the international impacts of the 1906 earthquake and fire in San Francisco, describe how the shock propagated to Europe, as about 40 percent of city's fire insurance policies were issued by European firms (the majority from the UK). Under the Gold Standard, these insurance payments required gold to flow across the Atlantic, and this eventually led to higher interest rates in Europe and restrictions on capital flows placed by European banks. This turmoil culminated with the 1907 U.S. financial panic. The earthquake and tsunami of March 2011 in Tohoku, Japan, was also propagated internationally. While a careful tabulation of that propagation is impossible at this time, preliminary reports frequently detail the difficulties in vertical production networks that were experienced after the tsunami destroyed manufacturers of key components.[13] Similar reports about interruption in vertical networks also surfaced after the Greater Bangkok floods of late 2011.

Several other papers examine various aspects of the international propagation of the economic shock that follow a natural disaster. For example, Gassebner et al. (2010) examine the impact of natural disasters on trade flows, while Yang (2008) and Bluedorn (2005) investigate the evolution of capital flows following disasters. Yet all these find fairly small impacts (if any). Even for foreign aid flows, Becerra et al. (2013) find that the increase in aid inflows following a disaster is on average substantially lower than the amount required to cover much of the cost of replacing destroyed property. All this suggests that international concern about disasters should focus not on the standard channels of trade and capital flows, but rather on production networks and contractual obligations through various financial instruments (e.g., large holders of CAT bonds), and is probably only relevant to the biggest economies in the global system.[14]

Whether disasters can potentially lead to migrations has not been studied thoroughly, and the likely impact may well be very different across time and circumstances (Hunter, 2005). The Irish Famine was, for example, a trigger for a dramatic out-migration from Ireland; and that migration turned out to be irreversible and initiated a long-term decline in the Irish population (Ó Gráda and O'Rourke, 1997). On the other hand, Halliday (2006) finds that the very large 2001 earthquake in El Salvador actually changed the household calculus of migration and led to a reduction in the number of people leaving El Salvador for the United States because the benefits to staying increased.

### 3.4.5 Disaster as an Opportunity?

Some argue that disasters provide an impetus for change, which can bring on positive economic changes that have long-term beneficial dynamic impact on the economy. Change can lead to "creative destruction" dynamics that entail replacing the old with new technologies and with upgrades of superior equipment, infrastructure, and production processes. The rapid growth of Germany and Japan after the destruction they experienced in World War II is widely used as an example of such beneficial dynamics. However, even for both these cases, empirical research failed to identify a long-term beneficial effect; but at best found a return to the pre-shock equilibrium (Davis and Weinstein, 2002, and Brakman et al., 2004).[15]

Besides the potential "creative" introduction of new technologies to replace the ones that had previously been destroyed, a large natural disaster changes political power dynamics in ways that may facilitate radical change. Rahm Emanuel, Barak Obama's former chief of staff, is often quoted as saying, "you never want a serious disaster to go to waste... it's an opportunity to do things you could not do before."[16] The evidence to date, however, does not suggest that after accounting for the loss of life and property, one can identify beneficial aspects to the destruction wrought by natural disasters.

## 3.5 Policies and Open Questions

Perrow (2007) argues that public policy should focus on the need to "shrink" the targets: lower population concentration in vulnerable (especially coastal) areas, and lower concentration of utilities and other infrastructure in disaster-prone locations. This advice also stems from the awareness that more *ex-post* assistance to damaged communities generates a "Samaritan's dilemma," i.e., an increase in risk-taking and a reluctance to purchase insurance when taking into account the help that is likely to be provided should a disaster strike.[17] However, apart from these *ex-ante* "shrink-the-target" policies, many other *ex-ante* and *ex-post* policies that can alleviate or worsen the economic impact of disasters will necessarily be weighed before and after any large event.

The need to construct efficient and timely warning systems is clearly a policy target that is less controversial and more easily implementable. The 2004 South-East Asian tsunami, for example, led to an extension of the Pacific Tsunami Warning System to regions of Indonesia and the Indian Ocean that were previously unprotected. Operating warning systems, however, remain a long-term goal that can still be improved in cost-effective ways in most countries of the Pacific Rim region.[18]

Scientific experts repeatedly describe the likelihood of future disasters in terms of one-in-X-year events. We have recently observed several one-in-500-year events, which suggest that this framing may not be very instructive given the shifting climatic conditions worldwide. This framing creates the lack of preparedness we have seen most recently in the Fukushima nuclear power plant. With hindsight, it is obvious that the operators of the seaside power plant should have had contingency plans in place for a failure in the electricity supply of both the grid and the emergency generators that were made inoperable by the tsunami. More generally, post-disaster energy supply difficulties and the collapse of communication networks seem to be two aspects of this and other recent disasters that were not planned for adequately. Vulnerability of industrial production, as exposed after this disaster, is a result of a dramatic increase in the vertical integration of production networks and the just-in-time supply chain management. These create vulnerabilities that can easily spread to unaffected regions, and are compounded by trends toward very specific specializations.

Beyond lack of preparedness and adequate mitigation of risks, Kunreuther and Pauly (2009) survey some of the problems associated with *ex-ante* insurance coverage for large natural events: uncertainty with regard to the magnitude of potential loses, highly correlated risk among the insured, moral hazard that leads to excessive risk taking by the insured, and an adverse selection of insured parties caused by imperfect information. As we already pointed out, many large disasters have very small probabilities associated with them and these make it difficult to develop relevant mitigation policies and likely also lead to under-insurance. In all recent disasters, even in ones that happened in heavily insured countries like the United States, only a relatively small portion of actual damages was insured. For example, Hurricane Katrina led to insurance claims totaling $46.3 billion; while the estimated damage of the storm was $158.2 billion.[19]

Implementing disaster insurance in many Pacific Rim countries, however, faces three types of obstacles: paucity of markets, political resistance, and inadequate institutional framework. For a number of reasons, markets have traditionally been insufficiently developed or simply nonexistent.

Private capital markets offer some complementary alternatives that may increase the availability of financing options as they continue to develop. The first capital market instrument linked to catastrophe risk ("CAT bonds") was introduced in 1994 as a means for reinsurers to transfer some of their own risks to capital markets, and these have since been used by various issuers, including governments. A typical structure of a CAT bond is one in which the investors purchase a highly rated bond for the desired amount of coverage and deposit it with a Special Purpose Vehicle (SPV) institution, which is legally distinct from the parties. The investors collect the interest on the bond plus the insurance premium that is paid by the insured party while the disaster does not occur. If the disaster strikes, however, their claim is extinguished and the SPV sells the bond and transfers the funds to the insured. While these are encouraging developments, the private and government CAT bond market is still in its infancy.[20]

Equally promising, but as yet even more undeveloped, are the possibilities for micro-insurance schemes that are indexed to measurable weather or other easily observable outcomes (rainfall, seismographic reading, river level rise, etc.). Instruments that, for example, tie insurance payments to measurable floods would have simplified immensely the difficult and prolonged sorting out of insurance claims that will likely follow the Greater Bangkok floods of October-November 2011—estimated at 13B US$.

Yet, even if the supply side of risk financing instruments becomes fully developed, many important questions remain unanswered. What is the optimal level of insurance for rare but catastrophic events? What is the optimal combination of alternative financing options? How are these answers tied to country-specific characteristics? What are the appropriate institutional arrangements that ensure the proper functioning of insurance schemes while minimizing moral hazard and adverse selection? What is the appropriate role of the government vis-à-vis the private sector in catastrophe insurance markets?

## Notes

1. The five most lethal events in the Pacific Rim (1970–2008) were all initiated by earthquakes: China 1976, Indonesia 2004, China 2008, Peru 1970, and Guatemala 1976. In these five events, 585,000 people died.
2. The Ring of Fire is an inverted U-shape region, whose Western tip is New Zealand. The region then encompasses the archipelagos of Indonesia, the Philippines, and Japan, the Russian Far East, the Aleutian Islands, Alaska, and then down the Western Coast of the Americas all the way to Tierra Del Fuego at the very southern tip of the continent. This region experiences by far most of the volcanic activity and earth movements recorded worldwide.
3. The data is publicly available at: [http://www.emdat.be/].
4. The following are included: Australia, Canada, Chile, China PR, Colombia, Costa Rica, Ecuador, El Salvador, Guatemala, Honduras, Indonesia, Japan, Korea (South), Malaysia, Mexico, New Zealand, Nicaragua, Panama, Papua New Guinea, Peru, Philippines, Russia, Taiwan, United States, and Vietnam.
5. By "very likely" the IPCC refers to 90–100 percent probability, while "likely" means 66-100 percent probability (IPCC, 2011).
6. Different climate models yield somewhat different results, but the consensus is well-represented by this range.
7. A one-point increase in earthquake magnitude entails a 10-time increase in earth movement and a 32-times increase in the amount of energy released, so a 9.0 earthquake

is dramatically different from an 8.0 one. For historical information about earthquake frequencies, see: [http://earthquake.usgs.gov/earthquakes/eqarchives/].

8. Loayza et al. (2009) note that while small disasters may, on average, have a positive impact (as a result of the reconstruction stimulus), large disasters always pose severe negative consequences for the economy in their immediate aftermath.
9. Data obtained from [http://www.china.org.cn/china/earthquake_reconstruction/2010-01/25/content_19302110.htm] (accessed on 11/11/11).
10. Insurance could be purchased directly (maybe through reinsurance companies), indirectly through the issuance of catastrophic bonds (CAT bonds), or through precautionary savings.
11. In addition to FONDEN, Mexico is also one of the biggest issuers of CAT bonds. Even so, the provisioning of FONDEN has recently been insufficient to cover the costs of disasters in 2010 (see [http://www.artemis.bm/blog/2010/09/16/fonden-mexicos-disaster-fund-exceeds-its-annual-budget/] accessed 11/12/11).
12. For some insights into why some countries can or cannot pursue counter-cyclical fiscal policy see, for example, Ilzetzki (2011).
13. The post-tsunami worldwide shortage of bismaleimide triazine resin—important in smartphones and other similar devices and produced almost exclusively by Mitsubishi Gas Chemical—is a relevant example (Noy, 2011).
14. The financial crisis that started in September, 2008, however, suggests that even smaller problems can percolate through the financial system and threaten the stability of larger markets.
15. In a related project, Miguel and Roland (2011) find that post-war Vietnam (a low-income country) also reverted to its pre-shock equilibrium with little evidence of a negative long-term effect (a poverty trap).
16. Emanuel, at a Wall Street Journal event (see *WSJ*, Nov. 21, 2008).
17. See, for example, the discussion in Raschky and Weck-Hannemann (2007).
18. That is one of the future policy goals in the region, as stated in the Hyogo Framework for Action adopted by the UN General Assembly in 2005. A recent review of progress in the Asia Pacific concluded that in preparing early warning systems: "achievement [in most countries is] neither comprehensive nor substantial." (UNISDR, 2011, p. 8).
19. Katrina insurance claim data are from Kunreuther and Pauly (2009), while the figure for total damages is taken from EM-DAT.
20. In January-November 2011, there were 21 different issues of CAT bonds, all but one issued by either insurance or reinsurance companies (the exception being the California Earthquake Authority). Information taken from: [http://www.artemis.bm/deal_directory/].

## References

Anbarci, N., M. Escaleras, and C. A. Register. 2005. "Earthquake Fatalities: The Interaction of Nature and Political Economy." *Journal of Public Economics* 89: 1907–1933.

APEC, 2011. APEC High Level Policy Dialogue on Disaster Resiliency. Available at: http://www.apec.org/Meeting-Papers/Ministerial-Statements/High-Level-Policy-Dialogue/2011_disaster.aspx

Barro R. 1997. *Determinants of Economic Growth: A Cross-Country Empirical Study*. Cambridge, MA: MIT Press.

______. 2006. "Rare Disasters and Asset Markets in the Twentieth Century." *Quarterly Journal of Economics* 121: 823–866.
______. 2009. "Rare Disasters, Asset Prices, and Welfare Costs." *American Economic Review* 99(1): 243–264.
Becerra, O., E. Cavallo, and I. Noy. 2013. "In the Aftermath of Large Natural Disasters, What Happens to Foreign Aid?" *Review of Development Economics*, forthcoming.
Borensztein, E., E. Cavallo, and P. Valenzuela. 2009. "Debt Sustainability under Catastrophic Risk: The Case for Government Budget Insurance." *Risk Management and Insurance Review* 12(2): 273–294.
Brakman, Steven, Harry Garretsen, and Marc Schramm. 2004. "The Strategic Bombing of Cities in Germany in World War II and Its Impact on City Growth." *Journal of Economic Geography* 4 (1), 1–18.
Cavallo, E., S. Galiani, I. Noy, and J. Pantano. 2013. "Catastrophic Natural Disasters and Economic Growth," *Review of Economics and Statistics*, forthcoming.
Cavallo, E., Noy, I. 2011. "The Economics of Natural Disasters—A Survey." *International Review of Environmental and Resource Economics* 5(1): 63–102.
Coffman, Makena and Ilan Noy. 2010. "A Hurricane Hits Hawaii: A Tale of Vulnerability to Natural Disasters." *CESifo Forum* 11(2): 67–72.
Coffman, M. and I. Noy. 2012. "Hurricane Iniki: Measuring the Long-Term Economic Impact of a Natural Disaster Using Synthetic Control." *Environment and Development Economics* 17(2): 187–205.
Cuaresma, J. C., J. Hlouskova, and M. Obersteiner. 2008. "Natural disasters as Creative Destruction? Evidence from Developing Countries." *Economic Inquiry* 46(2): 214–226.
Davis, Donald, and David Weinstein. 2002. "Bones, Bombs, and Break Points: The Geography of Economic Activity." *American Economic Review*, 92(5): 1269–1289.
Dupont, Will, and Ilan Noy. 2012. "Did Kobe Recover after Its 1995 Earthquake?" University of Hawaii Working Paper.
Elsner, J., J. Kossin, and T. Jagger. 2008. "The Increasing Intensity of the Strongest Tropical Cyclones." *Nature* 455: 92–95.
Emanuel, Kerry, Ragoth Sundararajan, and John Williams. 2008. "Hurricanes and Global Warming: Results from Downscaling IPCC AR4 Simulations." *Bulletin of the American Meteorological Society* 89(3): 347.
Gassebner, Martin, Alexander Keck, Robert Teh. 2010. Shaken, Not Stirred: The Impact of Disasters on International Trade. *Review of International Economics* 18(2), 351–368.
Hallegatte, S. and P. Dumas. 2009. "Can Natural Disasters Have Positive Consequences? Investigating the Role of Embodied Technical Change." *Ecological Economics* 68(3): 777–786.
Hallegatte, S., J.-C. Hourcade, and P. Dumas. 2007. "Why Economic Dynamics Matter in Assessing Climate Change Damages: Illustration on Extreme Events." *Ecological Economics* 62(2): 330–340.
Halliday T. 2006. "Migration, Risk and Liquidity Constraints in El Salvador." *Economic Development and Cultural Change* 54(4): 893–925.
Healy, A. and N. Malhotra. 2009. "Myopic Voters and Natural Disaster Policy." *American Political Science Review* 103: 387–406.
Hunter, Lori. 2005. Migration and Environmental Hazards. *Population and Environment* 26(4): 273–302.
Ilzetzki, Ethan. 2011. Rent-Seeking Distortions and Fiscal Procyclicality. *Journal of Development Economics* 96: 30–46.

IPCC. 2007. "Summary for Policymakers." In: *Climate Change 2007: Impacts, Adaptation and Vulnerability*. Contribution of Working Group II to the Fourth Assessment Report of the Intergovernmental Panel on Climate Change. M. L. Parry, O. F. Canziani, J. P. Palutikof, P. J. van der Linden and C. E. Hanson, Editors. Cambridge, UK: Cambridge University Press, 7–22.

IPCC. 2011. Summary for Policymakers. In: *Special Report on Managing the Risks of Extreme Events and Disasters to Advance Climate Change Adaptation*.

Landsea, C.W., B. A. Harper, K. Hoarau, and J. A. Knaff. 2006. "Can We Detect Trends in Extreme Tropical Cyclones?" *Science* 313(5785): 452–454.

Li, Tim, Min Ho Kwon, Ming Zhao, Jong-Seong Kug, Jing-Jia Luo, and Weidong Yu. 2010. "Global Warming Shifts Pacific Tropical Cyclone Location." *Geophysical Research Letters* 37(21).

Loayza, N., E. Olaberría, J. Rigolini, and L. Christiansen. 2009. "Natural Disasters and Growth-Going Beyond the Averages." World Bank Policy Research Working Paper 4980. Washington, DC: The World Bank.

Melecky, Martin and Claudio Raddatz. 2011. "How Do Governments Respond after Catastrophes? Natural-Disaster Shocks and the Fiscal Stance." World Bank Policy Research Working Paper 5564.

Miguel, Edward, and Gérard Roland 2011. "The Long-Run Impact of Bombing Vietnam." *Journal of Development Economics*, 96: 1–15.

Noy, I. 2009. "The Macroeconomic Consequences of Disasters." *Journal of Development Economics* 88(2): 221–231.

Noy, I. 2011. "The Economic Aftermath of the Recent Earthquake in Sendai, Japan." *European Business Review*, May-June, 2011.

Noy, I. and A. Nualsri. 2007. "What do Exogenous Shocks Tell Us about Growth Theories?" University of Hawaii Working Paper 07–28.

_____. 2011. "Fiscal Storms: Public Spending and Revenues in the Aftermath of Natural Disasters." *Environment and Development Economics* 16(1): 113–128.

Noy, I., and T. Vu. 2010. "The Economics of Natural Disasters in Vietnam." *Journal of Asian Economics* 21: 345–354.

Ó Gráda, Cormac, and Kevin H. O'Rourke. 1997. Migration as Disaster relief: Lessons from the Great Irish Famine. *European Review of Economic History* 1 (1997): 3–25.

Odell, Kerry A., and Marc D. Weidenmier. 2004. "Real Shock, Monetary Aftershock: The 1906 San Francisco Earthquake and the Panic of 1907." *Journal of Economic History* 64(4).

Raddatz, C. 2007. "Are External Shocks Responsible for the Instability of Output in Low-Income Countries?" *Journal of Development Economics* 84(1): 155–187.

_____. 2009. "The Wrath of God: Macroeconomic Costs of Natural Disasters." World Bank Policy Research Working Paper #5039.

Rodriguez-Oreggia, E., A. de la Fuente, and R. de la Torre et al. 2013. "The Impact of Natural Disasters on Human Development and Poverty at the Municipal Level in Mexico." *Journal of Development Studies* 49(3): 442–455. Sawada, Yasuyuki, and Satoshi Shimizutani. 2008. "How Do People Cope with Natural Disasters? Evidence from the Great Hanshin-Awaji (Kobe) Earthquake in 1995." *Journal of Money, Credit and Banking* 40(2–3): 463–488.

Skidmore, M. and H. Toya. 2002. Do Natural Disasters Promote Long-Run Growth? *Economic Inquiry* 40(4): 664–687.

UNISDR. 2011. *HFA Progress in Asia Pacific: Regional Synthesis Report 2009–2011*. United Nations International Strategy for Disaster Reduction.

Vermeer, Martin, and Stefan Rahmstorf. 2009. Global Sea Level Linked to Global Temperature. *Proceedings of the National Academy of Sciences*, Dec. 7, 2009.

Vigdor, J. 2008. "The Economic Aftermath of Hurricane Katrina." *Journal of Economic Perspectives* 22(4): 135–154.

Webster, P. J., G. J. Holland, J. A. Curry, and H. R. Chang. 2005. "Changes in Tropical Cyclone Number, Duration, and Intensity." *Science* 309 (5742): 1844–1846.

# PART II

# PEOPLE: MIGRATION, DEMOGRAPHICS, AND HUMAN CAPITAL

# CHAPTER 4

# INTERNATIONAL LABOR MIGRATION IN THE PACIFIC RIM

PHILIP MARTIN

INTERNATIONAL labor migration in the Asia-Pacific region is unique in three major ways. First, most Asian governments perceive the challenge of managing low-skilled labor migration differently than governments in Europe and the Americas. Just as some Asian countries achieved very rapid economic growth with foreign investment and exports (the Asian economic miracle), many Asian governments believe that they can rotate migrant workers in and out of their labor markets and avoid the settlement and integration issues associated with low-skilled migrants (World Bank, 1993).[1] Migrants with at least a university degree find it much easier to have their families with them and to stay for long periods while working in Asian countries.

Second, in contrast to similar foreign-investment-led and export-oriented economic policies, the migration policies of the major migrant-receiving countries create a triangle, with corners marked by Singapore, Japan, and Qatar. Korea and Taiwan lie closer to Singapore in rotating migrants in and out of jobs, while Malaysia and Thailand lie closer to the Gulf countries in their dependence on foreigners to fill low-skill jobs in some sectors but more like the United States in having high shares of unauthorized foreigners.

Third, the policies of the major Asian migrant-sending governments are converging, with all aiming to send more skilled workers to destinations inside and outside Asia to maximize remittances. Policies to achieve migrant promotion and protection goals include "marketing" workers abroad, improving the training of workers, and negotiating MOUs with migrant-receiving governments that set minimum wages and provide work-related benefits.

This paper reviews the major trends in Asian labor migration and migration's impacts on the major countries involved. After putting Asia-Pacific migration in a global context, we review the impacts of migrants in the major migrant-receiving countries and patterns of migration and their development impacts in major migrant-sending countries.

## 4.1 Asia-Pacific Migration in a Global Perspective

The Asia-Pacific region was home to almost 60 percent of the world's people and less than 30 percent of the world's migrants (Table 4.1). The 4.2 billion Asians in about 50 countries in 2010 included 1.3 billion Chinese and 1.2 billion Indians, that is, 60 percent of Asians are in the two population giants. Demographically, Asia includes some of the world's fastest-shrinking countries, including Japan, and some of the fastest-growing, including the Palestinian Territories, whose population is expanding by almost three percent a year.

In 2010, the UN estimated the migrant stock in Asia at 61 million, up from 48 million in 2005 (Table 4.2). There were two major reasons for this increase: the five million increase in the number of migrants in western Asia (Gulf oil exporters) and the inclusion of Central Asian countries such as Kazakhstan in UN data on Asian migrants—the "stans" had an estimated five million migrants in 2010.

Between 1980 and 2010, the stock of migrants in Asia almost doubled. There were distinct differences by region. The stock of migrants in Eastern Asia rose about 70 percent, while the stock of migrants in South-central Asia fell almost 15 percent, largely because of the shrinking number of persons resettled after wars for independence on the Indian

**Table 4.1 International Migrant Stock, Asia and World, 1960–2010 (mils)**

| | 1960 | 1965 | 1970 | 1975 | 1980 | 1985 | 1990 | 1995 | 2000 | 2005 | 2010 |
|---|---|---|---|---|---|---|---|---|---|---|---|
| Asia | **28.5** | **28.2** | **27.8** | **28** | **32.1** | **37.2** | **41.9** | **40.4** | **44.4** | **48.1** | **61.3** |
| Eastern Asia | 2.7 | 2.8 | 2.9 | 3.3 | 3.8 | 4 | 4.3 | 5 | 5.7 | 6.5 | 6.5 |
| South-central Asia | 18.4 | 17.7 | 16.9 | 16.1 | 16.6 | 18.6 | 19.7 | 15.6 | 15 | 13.2 | 14.3 |
| Southeast Asia | 3.6 | 3.3 | 3.5 | 2.9 | 3 | 2.9 | 3 | 3.5 | 4.8 | 5.7 | 6.7 |
| Western Asia | 3.8 | 4.4 | 4.5 | 5.8 | 8.8 | 11.7 | 14.9 | 16.3 | 19 | 22.7 | 28.5 |
| World | **75.5** | **78.4** | **81.3** | **86.8** | **99.3** | **111** | **154.9** | **165.1** | **176.7** | **190.6** | **213.9** |
| More Developed | 32.3 | 35.4 | 38.4 | 42.5 | 47.5 | 53.6 | 90.4 | 101.7 | 110.9 | 120.6 | 127.7 |

POP/DB/MIG/Rev. 2010
In 2010, international migration in Asia included five million immigrants in Central Asia (the "stans").
*Source*: UN Population Division, DESA.

**Table 4.2 Migrant Stock in East and Southeast Asia, 2000–2010 (000)**

| | 2000 | 2005 | 2010 | 2000-2010 Change |
|---|---|---|---|---|
| **East Asia** | **5,769** | **6,497** | **6,458** | **12%** |
| China | 513 | 596 | 686 | **34%** |
| Hong Kong | 2,701 | 2,999 | 2,742 | **2%** |
| Japan | 1,620 | 2,048 | 2,176 | **34%** |
| Malaysia | 1,392 | 1,639 | 2,358 | **69%** |
| Singapore | 1,352 | 1,843 | 1,967 | **45%** |
| South Korea | 597 | 551 | 535 | **-10%** |
| **Southeast Asia** | **4,126** | **5,664** | **6,715** | **63%** |
| **Total** | **9,895** | **12161** | **13,173** | **33%** |

Totals include migrants in countries with fewer than 500,000.
*Source*: United Nations, 2010.

subcontinent. The most rapid growth in migrants has been in Western Asia, where the migrant stock tripled between 1980 and 2010; almost half of the international migrants in Asia are in Western Asia, which includes the Gulf oil exporters. International migration is increasing alongside urbanization (Table 4.3).

The Pacific region or Oceania has the world's highest share of migrants among residents. Migrants were 17 percent of Oceania residents in 2010, the highest among world regions—North America was second at 14 percent. In Micronesia, 26 percent of

**Table 4.3 Urban Residents in Asia, 1950, 2000, 2030 (mils)**

| | 1950 | 2000 | 2030 |
|---|---|---|---|
| Asia | 230 | 1,254 | 2,441 |
| Eastern Asia | 121 | 617 | 1,065 |
| South-central Asia | 83 | 441 | 969 |
| Southeastern Asia | 26 | 196 | 407 |
| *Urban Share of Total Population (percent)* | | | |
| Asia | 17 | 35 | 52 |
| Eastern Asia | 18 | 42 | 63 |
| South-central Asia | 17 | 30 | 44 |
| Southeastern Asia | 15 | 38 | 56 |

*Source*: United Nations, 2002.

residents were migrants in 2010, followed by 22 percent in Australia and New Zealand. Migration issues in Oceania include the migrant selection systems of Australia and New Zealand and the threat of climate change induced migration in some Pacific islands (World Bank, 2006; McKenzie et al., 2008).

## 4.2 Major Migrant-Receiving Countries

Migration from Asia to traditional immigration countries was largely blocked until the mid-1960s, when policy reforms in Canada and the United States allowed Asian professionals who were offered jobs by Canadian and US employers to immigrate. These professionals usually arrived with their families, and most climbed the economic ladder quickly. Indeed, the earnings of foreign-born men caught up to those of US-born men of the same age and education within an average 13 years. Thereafter, Asian men earned more than similar US-born men, suggesting that the extra drive and ambition that prompts international migration could expand the US economy and raise average earnings (Chiswick, 1978).[2]

Today, Asian nations are a major source of immigrants to Australia, Canada, New Zealand, and the United States. After the Vietnam War ended in 1975, a million Southeast Asian refugees were resettled in Canada and the United States, forging new migration networks that continue to add immigrants via family unification. Many Asian students earn university degrees in traditional immigration destinations, and some settle and form or unite families.

Most international labor migration in Asia involves workers moving from one Asian nation to another for temporary employment. The first significant labor flows began after oil price hikes in 1973–74, when Gulf oil exporters turned to foreign contractors who hired foreign workers to build infrastructure projects such as roads and bridges (Abella, 1995). As the demand for labor shifted from construction to services, and from men to women, some predicted that Arabs would replace Asian migrants for language and cultural reasons (Birks and Sinclair, 1980). This did not happen and, despite efforts to "nationalize" Gulf work forces by prohibiting foreigners from filling some types of jobs, migrants from south and southeast Asia appear poised to continue to dominate private sector labor forces in most Gulf Cooperation Council countries.

There is also significant migration from one Asian country to a neighboring country, as exemplified by Indonesian workers in Malaysia and Burmese workers in Thailand (Hugo and Young). Migration policies in Malaysia and Thailand are in flux. The Malaysian government has several times announced plans to reduce the employment of migrants, but these have not been implemented. Meanwhile, the Thai government continues to register unauthorized migrants from Burma, Cambodia, and Laos periodically despite assertions that each registration is the last (Martin, 2003; Migration News).

UN data on migrant stocks by country over time include foreigners who have been in a country at least 12 months, and the data do not distinguish migrants by legal status or the purpose of migration. In East and Southeast Asia, the UN data show that South Korea had a decrease in its migrant stock between 2000 and 2010. However, the Korean Ministry of Public Administration and Security reported 1.2 million foreign residents in June 2010, more than double the 535,000 reported by the UN.[3]

## 4.2.1 Singapore, Hong Kong, and Taiwan

As mentioned above, migration policies of the major Asian countries receiving migrants can be framed by a triangle. At one corner is Singapore, welcoming foreign professionals and their families to settle but rotating less-skilled migrant workers in and out of the country. In 2010, 35 percent of Singapore's three million workers, over one million, were foreigners, and they dominated employment in construction, shipyards, and households (domestic helpers). The share of foreigners in Singapore's work force has increased more than ten-fold since 1970, when it was 3 percent.

The Singapore government welcomes "foreign talent." These professionals, mostly from China, India, and Malaysia, may move to Singapore with their families, achieve permanent residence status after two years, and become naturalized citizens after two more years. Less-skilled migrants, on the other hand, may not bring their families, are subject to removal if they become pregnant, and do not earn an automatic right to settle in Singapore, even by marrying a Singaporean citizen. Employers of low-skilled migrants are subject to dependency ceilings that regulate the mix of foreign and Singaporean workers in the workplace and must pay a significant levy or tax on the wages paid to the foreign workers they employ.[4]

The government believes that foreign talent is essential to Singapore's growth and prosperity and aims to induce more foreign professionals to immigrate and to raise fertility among more educated citizens. Former prime minister Lee Kuan Yew often reminds residents that their resource-poor country must compete on the basis of human capital. However, in response to fears of too many foreign workers, Finance Minister Tharman Shanmugaratnam in December 2009 said: "Growing dependence on foreign workers is not a sustainable strategy for the long term," and announced that the levy on foreign workers would increase July 1, 2010, from the current S$150 to S$470 a month, to slow the growth of the foreign work force (Migration News).

Hong Kong is another city-state with a welcome-the-skilled and rotate-the-unskilled migrant worker policy. As the financial and supply chain hub for southeastern China, Hong Kong's government has, since 1999, allowed employers to hire foreigners with professional skills not available locally who are paid market wages (for the first five years, half of such migrants had PhDs). Foreign professionals may arrive with their families and receive permanent residence status after seven years.

Hong Kong, with seven million residents, is less welcoming toward low-skilled foreign workers, most of whom are domestic helpers from the Philippines and Indonesia.

About 250,000 Hong Kong households employ a foreign woman to provide child and/or elder care.[5] Hong Kong requires that domestic helpers be paid a minimum wage, which was HK$3,580 dollars ($460) a month in 2010, and Hong Kong employers must also provide domestic helpers with room and board.[6] Filipino migrants in Hong Kong are well-organized, and they have protested against the migration policies of the Filipino and Hong Kong governments ([www.unifil.org.hk]).

In October 1989 Taiwan allowed the entry of foreign workers to help complete high-priority infrastructure projects, including highways and subways. This so-called open-door policy was small, giving Taiwan about 3,000 migrant workers in 1991. However, migrant workers soon spread to factories and later to private households, as foreigners became caregivers for children[7] and the elderly. By 2008, there were 375,000 migrant workers, and foreigners were 10 percent of all workers in low-skill jobs. The 2008-09 recession reduced the number of migrants employed in manufacturing, but the number of migrant caregivers remained stable.

Taiwan's migrants, most from Indonesia, the Philippines, Thailand, and Vietnam, often complain about the high fees they must pay to the brokers who arrange their employment. The maximum fee should be a month's wages for each year of a worker's contract, but many migrants report paying much more than 8 percent—reports of recruitment fees that are 20 to 30 percent of foreign earnings are common. Because of these high recruitment fees, which are deducted from the migrant's pay, some migrants can earn more as unauthorized workers, so they "run away" from the employer to whom they have been assigned. The Council of Labor Affairs (COLA), which regulates the employment of migrant workers in Taiwan, pays tips to residents who report violations of immigration laws.[8]

Migrants want to work in Taiwan because of relatively high wages, which were NT$17,280 ($510) a month in 2009 or about $3 an hour in all sectors except care giving, where the minimum wage is NT$15,840 a month. The COLA aims to reduce the growing dependence of some sectors on migrants, and in 2009 limited migrants to a maximum 20 percent of each manufacturer's work force.

### 4.2.2 Japan and Korea

Japan and South Korea are homogenous societies that have been largely closed to foreigners; less than 2 percent of residents are foreigners, versus 10 percent or more in industrial countries in Europe and North America. In both Japan and Korea, foreign professionals and the descendents of past emigrants are welcomed, although numbers are low. However, Japan and Korea have diverged on policies toward low-skilled migrant workers. Japan's low-skilled migrants are trainees, students, and unauthorized foreigners, while Korea in 2004 began to replace foreign trainees paid less than the minimum wage with migrant workers entitled to the minimum wage.

Japan had about 2.2 million foreign residents in 2009, including 943,000 permanent residents (410,000 were Koreans who settled in Japan before the end of WWII) and 1.2 million temporary foreign residents. Foreigners are about 1.7 percent of Japan's 128 million residents, and 40,000 foreigners a year obtain permanent resident status in Japan.

Almost a million foreigners were employed in Japan in 2009, including 230,000 Nikkeijin, the descendents of Japanese emigrants to Brazil and Peru a century ago. Japan also had 200,000 highly skilled foreigners, 170,000 unauthorized foreigners, and 122,000 foreign trainees and interns, but all these foreign workers were less than 2 percent of Japan's 62 million workers.

In 1989, the Japanese government in made it easier for employers to hire low-skilled foreign trainees, who are supposed to receive training in advanced production techniques that will be useful when they return to their countries of origin. However, the trainee program is controversial because trainees are not considered workers and thus not entitled to the minimum wage. Japan's minimum wage varies by prefecture, but averaged 713 yen ($8.60) an hour in 2010. First-year foreign trainees until 2011 received an allowance of 60,000 to 80,000 yen a month, or 375 to 500 yen an hour for those working 40 hours a week.

For most of the past two decades, foreign trainees were not considered workers, so they were not entitled to the Japanese minimum wage that varies by prefecture but averaged 713 yen ($8.60) an hour in 2010. Instead, first-year foreign trainees received an allowance of 60,000 to 80,000 yen a month, or 375 to 500 yen an hour for those working 40 hours a week.[9] However, concerns about overwork remain because several trainees in their 20s and 30s died, according to official reports, of karoshi (overwork).[10]

Japan has the world's fastest-aging society. Its median age of 44 and life expectancy of 83 in 2010 are among the world's highest, while fertility of 1.4 is among the world's lowest. The population of 127 million in 2010 is expected to shrink to less than 90 million by 2050, when 40 percent of Japanese are projected to be 65 or older. Many Japanese employers believe that Japan will have to open doors to migrants to maintain its economy, but a 2010 poll by the Asahi Shimbun newspaper found that two-thirds of Japanese opposed more immigration, fearing crime and cultural change. Ex-Prime Minister Junichiro Koizumi expressed the feelings of many Japanese: "Just because there is a labor shortage does not mean we should readily allow [migrants] to come in." (quoted in Kashiwazaki and Akaha, 2006).

Korea made one of the world's most rapid transitions from sending workers abroad to receiving migrant workers. The number of Koreans in Gulf Cooperation Council countries rose from 395 in 1974 to 162,000 in 1981 after the Korean government encouraged its construction firms to bid on contracts to provide jobs for Korean workers who were laid off as a result of the recession induced by higher oil prices. Korean workers earned $750 a month for 48-hour weeks in the Gulf, and remitted $1.4 billion in 1981 (Kapur and McHale, 2006, 175), and the experience gained by Korean firms and workers in the Middle East was applied to large-scale infrastructure projects in Korea in the 1980s.

Economic growth turned Korea into a net importer of labor by the early 1990s. The government allowed employers to bring foreigners to Korea as trainees who would work and learn skills in Korean-owned factories that could be applied at home in factories opened by Korean investors. However, the small and mid-sized manufacturing firms hiring trainees did not invest abroad, so the trainee program became a way for these firms to hire foreign workers to fill so-called three-D jobs, jobs that were dirty, difficult, and dangerous. Many trainees "ran away" from the Korean employers to whom they were assigned because they could earn more as illegal workers.

The Korean government recognized problems with the trainee system and began to replace foreign trainees with foreign workers under the Employment Permit System (EPS) ([www.eps.go.kr/wem/en/index.jsp]) in August 2004; the EPS has been the major avenue for low-skilled foreign workers to enter Korea since August 2008.[11] Korean employers with fewer than 300 employees in selected industries may apply for EPS migrants (90 percent are employed in small manufacturing) after a minimum 7-day failed effort to recruit Koreans (raised to 14 days in 2010). In a bid to protect migrants from abusive employers, EPS migrants may change employers three times during their typical three-year stay in Korea (raised to five years in December 2009).

Migrant workers are recruited in the 15 Asian countries that have signed bilateral agreements with the Korean government (Kim, 2008). Government agencies in migrant-sending countries recruit workers who have passed a test of the Korean language, and Korean employers select migrants from these recruitment lists. Each country is given a quota of workers that can be selected to work in Korea, and long lists in countries from Nepal to Vietnam ensure considerable frustration among potential migrants who assume that once they pass the Korean language test they will be on their way to a Korean factory and wages of $800 to $1,000 a month. About 200,000 migrants have been or are employed under the EPS, and the Korean government is working with partner sending countries to ensure that employment in Korea stimulates economic development in migrant-sending areas.

### 4.2.3 Gulf Cooperation Council

The Middle East, which stretches from Western Asia to North Africa, includes countries at the extremes of the labor migration spectrum, those that send most of their workers abroad and those that rely on migrant workers to fill most private-sector jobs. Some Middle East countries are uniquely dependent on remittances, including Palestine, and others both send workers abroad and receive migrants, including Jordan and Lebanon. After oil prices rose in the 1970s, migrant workers were employed in the Gulf oil-exporting states to fill the jobs created by the spending of higher oil revenues on infrastructure, and migrants are now over 90 percent of private-sector workers in most Gulf oil exporters.

The major migrant destinations are the Gulf Cooperation Council (GCC) countries of Bahrain, Kuwait, Oman, Qatar, Saudi Arabia, and the United Arab Emirates. The GCC countries had 15 million foreigners among 40 million residents in 2008; half of the foreigners were in Saudi Arabia. GCC countries have fast-growing populations and labor forces that seemingly belie the need for migrants. However, relatively few women work for wages in GCC countries, fertility is high, natives seek government- rather than private-sector jobs.[12] In 2010, the share of foreigners among residents ranged from a low of 28 percent in Oman to a high of over 86 percent in the UAE.

Migrant workers streamed into GCC countries after oil prices rose significantly in the mid-1970s. Most of the first migrants were from other Arab states; three-fourths in 1975. As the demand for migrants shifted from construction to services, the Arab share of migrant workers was expected to increase for language reasons. Instead, the Arab share of migrant workers fell to a third in the mid-1980s, where it has remained, which Kapiszewski (2006) believes reflects GCC government fears that too many Arabs could be a security threat.[13] Asian workers generally earn lower wages than Arab migrants, most arrive without families, and few settle.

The GCC countries have segmented economies and labor forces. Foreign- and native-born professionals operate the oil facilities that generate the region's wealth, native-born and foreign workers fill government jobs, and foreign workers fill most private-sector jobs. Some oil-rich governments guarantee government jobs to natives, a policy that is becoming unsustainable in the face of rapid labor force growth. In order to persuade private employers to hire local workers, some GCC governments have nationalization policies that make bar foreigners from filling certain jobs (Noland and Pack, 2007).

Foreigners in GCC countries must have local sponsors (kafala) to enter, work, and leave the country. Most households are allowed to employ five or more migrants to fill jobs ranging from domestic helper to gardener to driver. With sponsorships selling for $1,000 or more in migrant-sending countries, migrants often arrive in debt and must work for up to five months to repay sponsorship costs.[14] Migrant advocates have been critical of GCC governments as well as migrant-sending governments for not doing enough to protect migrants from the abuses of the sponsorship system (Human Rights Watch, 2004, 2008). In response, some GCC countries are making a government agency the sponsor of foreign workers in the country.

GCC countries often require employers to pay all recruitment-related fees, including the cost of mandatory health and criminal checks in migrant countries of origin. However, with more workers wanting to go abroad than there are jobs, many migrant workers nonetheless pay recruiters and their agents, believing it will help them to go abroad sooner. Governments have found it hard to eliminate or restrict recruitment fees in migrant-sending countries.

## 4.3 Migrant-Sending Countries

The two southeast Asian nations heavily influence by the United States are the Philippines and Vietnam. The Philippines is the major emigration country in Asia.

Almost 10 percent of Filipinos are abroad, about the same as the share of Mexicans abroad, but Filipinos are in many nations, while almost all Mexicans are in the United States. The Filipino government has developed what are often considered model agencies and regulations to promote the employment of Filipino workers abroad and to protect Filipino migrants while they are abroad.

Before 1989, Vietnam had labor cooperation agreements with several East European countries, including East Germany, under which workers were sent abroad to repay debts incurred by the government. Since 1991, Vietnam has allowed and increasingly promoted labor emigration, and had 400,000 migrant workers in 40 countries in 2006 (Anh Nguyen, 2007, 3–6); there were an estimated 500,000 Vietnamese workers abroad in 2010, including three-fourths in Malaysia, Taiwan, and Korea. Vietnam is aiming to increase the number of workers it sends to foreign labor markets to 100,000 a year (85,000 were sent abroad in 2010). Vietnamese workers have very good reputations with foreign employers, but persisting problems with high recruitment debts encourage some to run away from the employers to whom they have been assigned.

Sending workers abroad may accelerate development at home, so that the children of migrants to not have to follow their parents to jobs abroad. However, there is no automatic link between migration and development. Some emigration can promote more, as demonstrated by the Filipino experience.

### 4.3.1 Philippines

The Philippines had about 94 million residents in 2010, including at least five million employed temporarily abroad. Remittances from Filipinos abroad, $20 billion in 2009, are over 10 percent of Filipino GDP. In recognition of the importance of migrants and remittances, the Filipino president welcomes some returning migrants at Christmas in a "Pamaskong Handog sa OFWs" (welcome home overseas foreign workers) ceremony.[15]

A record 1.4 million Filipino migrants were deployed in 2009, including 1.1 million land-based workers and 330,000 sea-based workers. Most Filipinos complete multiple two- and three-year contracts abroad, sustaining what may be the world's major "migration economy"; opinion polls find that a majority of Filipino youth plan to work abroad for at least part of their lives.

International labor migration was seen as a temporary safety valve in 1974, when President Marcos issued Decree 442 to ensure "the careful selection of Filipino workers for the overseas labor market to protect the good name of the Philippines abroad." The Philippine Overseas Employment Administration (POEA) was created in 1982 to promote the migration of workers and to protect them during recruitment at home and employment abroad.

Over half of the migrants leaving the Philippines are women, and some are vulnerable to abuse in the private households in which many work abroad. In 1995, Flor Contemplacion, a Filipina domestic helper in Singapore, was hanged after killing another Filipina maid and a Singaporean child.[16] Philippine President Fidel Ramos was unable to win additional time to investigate the case, prompting the enactment of Republic Act 8042, the so-called Filipino migrant workers' Magna Carta, which obliges the government to actively seek to protect migrants abroad. One result is a minimum wage for Filipina women going abroad as domestic helpers, who must earn at least $400 a month since 2007 under the so-called "Supermaid" program.

Most Filipinos go abroad with the help of private recruiters who receive requests from foreign employers and recruit and screen Filipinos to fill foreign jobs. The POEA regulates private recruitment agencies and checks the contracts that recruiters provide to migrants ([www.poea.gov.ph]), seeking to enforce laws that generally limit recruitment fees to one month's foreign earnings, or about 4.8 percent of earnings on a typical two-year contract. In another bid to protect Filipino migrants, Filipino recruiters are jointly liable with foreign employers to fulfill the terms of the contracts that migrants sign before departure.

## 4.3.2 Vietnam

Vietnam was unified April 30, 1975, but the victorious North had no specific plans to integrate the South into a Vietnamese economy. Northern distrust of southerners who cooperated with Americans resulted in "re-education camps" and the departure of many ethnic Chinese who had been the glue of the South's economy. The result was a "lost decade" between 1975 and 1985, until the doi moi economic "renovations" of 1986 and 1989 led to a 1992 constitution that embraced a "multi-sector economy in accordance with the market, based on state management and socialist orientations."

In 2010, about two-thirds of Vietnamese lived in rural areas, primarily in the rice-growing Red and Mekong River basins. Farmers are poor: about 60 percent of Vietnamese workers are employed in agriculture, but they generate just 20 percent of GDP, explaining why young people flock to factories in the industrial estates surrounding cities and seek jobs abroad.

The government has two migrant-worker goals: to send 100,000 workers a year abroad, and to send more skilled workers abroad in order to generate more remittances and to enable migrants to better protect themselves. Almost 85,000 Vietnamese went abroad to work temporarily in 2010, including 28,500 to Taiwan, 11,700 to Malaysia, and 8,600 to Korea. Korea is a preferred destination because of high wages, typically $800 to $900 a month with overtime. Most Vietnamese employed in Taiwan are women caregivers earning $400 a month, while those in Malaysia are women employed in light manufacturing for $250 a month.

The Vietnamese Ministry of Labor, War Invalids, and Social Affairs ([www.molisa.gov.vn]) has a Bureau for Overseas Labor Management to regulate labor supply companies, and has since 1991 licensed recruiters to send migrants abroad. Decree 141/2005/ND-CP, issued November 11, 2005, establishes penalties of 20,000 to 20 million dong ($1,300) for collecting excessive recruitment fees, being illegally abroad, and "running away" or abandoning a foreign work contract. However, it is very hard to regulate the brokers who work on commission for licensed recruiters in rural villages, as they go from house to house, making oral promises about earnings and work abroad.

There are many stories of migrants being tricked by recruiters. A typical story recounts how a young person in a rural area paid $2,000 for a contract to work in Malaysia but received a tourist visa that did not permit work. When apprehended in Malaysia working illegally, migrants are fined and returned, where they find that their recruiters have disappeared. The fact that many migrants do not demand written contracts, and many believe oral promises, means that abuses are likely to continue until education of migrants and regulation of agents is improved ([http://ipsnews.net/migration/stories/exports.html]).

The contrast between the Philippines and Vietnam is clear. In both cases, most migrants leave with contracts to work for particular foreign employers. However, the Philippine government has agencies to check these contracts before the migrants depart, and holds the Filipino recruiter jointly liable with the foreign employer to abide by the terms of the agreement. The Vietnamese government, by contrast, puts more of the onus on migrant workers to abide by the terms of contracts that are not checked carefully by punishing those who run away from their assigned foreign employer.

### 4.3.3 Migration and Development

Many economists consider trade and migration to have similar effects on participating countries. Trade theory suggests that countries specializing in the production of the goods in which they have a comparative advantage, goods they can produce relatively cheaper than other countries, and trading for goods that other countries produce relatively cheaper, have larger economies than countries that are closed to trade. Dollar and Kraay (2002) found that the "aggregate annual per capita growth rate of the globalizing group [of developing countries] accelerated steadily from one percent in the 1960s to five percent in the 1990s. During that latter decade, in contrast, rich countries grew at two percent and nonglobalizer [developing countries] at only one percent."

Sending workers abroad should have effects similar to trade in goods on the economies and labor markets of migrant-sending and migrant-receiving countries. As migrants move over borders, wages rise in countries that workers leave and fall or rise more slowly in migrant-receiving countries.[17] Eventually, there should be convergence in wages and levels of economic development, reducing the incentive to migrate for economic opportunity.

However, there is no automatic link to ensure that more migration leads to faster development. Migration can accelerate development in countries poised to grow, such as was the case in the southern European countries in the 1960s and 1970s, or perpetuate underdevelopment, as in many island countries today.

The effects of migration on development are often grouped in the 3-R channels of recruitment, remittances, and returns. Recruitment refers to who goes abroad—international migration is generally most beneficial to developing countries if low-skilled workers who would have been un- or under-employed at home are recruited for jobs abroad. Remittances are that portion of the monies earned by migrants abroad that are sent home; with higher wages abroad, remittances usually exceed what migrants would have earned at home, so that migration can improve living standards for migrant families and provide additional capital to developing countries. Returns focus on what migrants do after a period of employment abroad, asking whether they acquired new skills that are useful for development or whether they return to rest and retire.

The impacts of recruitment on development can be captured by extreme examples summarized as virtuous or vicious circles (Martin, Abella, Kuptsch, 2005, Chapter 3). Sending Indian IT workers abroad provides an example of a virtuous migration and development circle, while the emigration of African doctors and nurses provides an example of a vicious circle. Virtuous circles are more likely if migrants are abroad for only a short time, they send home significant remittances, and they return with new skills and links to industrial countries that increase trade and investment. Vicious circles can be the outcome of migrants fleeing countries perceived to be sinking ships.

Most migrants remit some of their foreign earnings to family and friends at home. During the 1990s, when remittances to developing countries doubled, sending-country governments and development institutions became aware of rising remittances, which often provided the foreign exchange essential to cover balance of payments deficits and sustain economic development policies (Ratha, 2003). Leaders of major labor-sending countries began to acknowledge the importance of remittances by symbolically welcoming home some returning migrants at Christmas each year, as in the Philippines, or calling migrants "foreign exchange heroes," as with former Mexican President Vicente Fox.

Remittances should speed up development, creating jobs in areas receiving them and making migration less necessary in the future. Most remittances are spent on consumption, as would be expected since foreign earnings replace money that would have been earned locally. However, with earnings abroad typically higher than earnings at home, remittances often exceed what would have been earned at home. After the basic consumption needs of recipients are satisfied, most remaining remittances are used to build or improve housing, educate and provide health care to children, and expand or launch new businesses.

The major debate among Filipino economists is whether sending workers abroad will reduce out-migration over time, as would occur if remittances that are spent and invested in ways that spur stay-at-home development. World Bank studies conclude that remittances reduce poverty in households with migrants,[18] but migration and remittances may not prevent more migration in the future. Most Filipino remittances flow to already wealthier households, so that poor non-migrants may be worse off because of Dutch disease, as remittances increase the value of the peso and shrink the number of jobs in export-oriented manufacturing industries (Rodriguez, 1998).

Pernia concluded the "remittance windfall may have a moral hazard effect as the government softens in pursuing policy reform or improving governance while people are lulled into complacency, as appears to be happening in the Philippines," (2008, 8) so that "labor export cannot be relied upon as a policy for reducing poverty, redressing income inequality and, for that matter, fostering the country's long-run development." (2008, 21)

### 4.3.4 Rural-Urban Migration

Between 1950 and 2000, the number of Asians living in urban areas increased five-fold, from about 230 million to 1.2 billion, and the United Nations projects that over half of Asians will live in urban areas by 2030 (UN, 2002). In 1950, less than 20 percent of Asian residents lived in urban areas, and rates of urbanization were similar across regions. Urbanization is expected to proceed fastest in East Asia and slowest in South-central Asia, with significant differences between regions by 2030.

Perhaps the most studied internal migration underway is in China. China conducted its 2010 census in November 2010; projections suggest a total of 1.4 billion people, half in rural areas. The 2000 census reported almost 1.3 billion people, including 800 million people registered to live in rural areas.

The 2010 census is expected to report 160 million rural-urban migrants. Estimates of the number of rural-urban migrants vary with definitions and methodology—some include students studying away from home and traveling business people. Rural-urban migrants have a unique legal status because of the hukou household registration system, which generally limits access to public housing, education, medical and other benefits to the place where a person is registered. This means that rural-urban migrants must return to their place of registration to obtain marriage licenses or passports and to access most public services.

The Chinese government introduced the hukou household registration system in the 1950s, first to allocate grain and later to regulate internal migration (Chan, 1999). As a result, Chinese are generally registered in their place of birth, and it is often difficult to change registration from one place to another. Low-skilled migrants, especially, may find it difficult to access government services that range from housing to education to health care when they are away from the place where they are registered.

In 1978, before market reforms began, about 70 percent of Chinese were employed in agriculture, which generated 28 percent of GDP. By 2006, only 43 percent of the 760 million Chinese workers were employed in agriculture, which generated 12 percent of GDP. Most estimates find that up to half of the 327 million agricultural workers in China are redundant. However, many "surplus rural workers" are over 40 and less attractive to urban employers than younger rural-urban migrants. Young rural residents seeking higher wages are most of the rural-urban migrants.

Most of the 110 million workers employed in Chinese manufacturing are internal rural-urban migrants, as are most of China's construction workers. About 70 percent of China's internal migrants are between 15 and 35. Migrants in urban areas earn lower wages than urban residents, often less than half of the typical urban wage. However, the earnings of migrants in urban areas have been rising. Cai Fang of the Chinese Academy of Social Science's Institute of Population and Labor Economics estimated that migrant workers' wages rose from 700 yuan a month in 2003 to 1,200 yuan ($182) in 2010. Remittances from urban to rural China are estimated to exceed $80 billion a year.

The Chinese central government has been debating whether to loosen or abolish the hukou system. The National Development and Reform Commission (NDRC) in January 2008 recommended that the household registration system be ended within five years so that internal Chinese migrants have the same benefits in employment, education, healthcare, and housing as local residents. The NRDC, which said a "free flow" of migrants from rural to urban areas would maintain rapid economic growth, estimated that 43 percent of China's 1.3 billion residents lived in cities, including 200 million rural-urban migrants.

However, the most recent review by the Ministry of Public Security in 2005 concluded that local governments would have to extend to migrants the right to housing, education, and health care, which would cost money. The central government recently ordered urban schools to accept migrant children and not charge fees for K-9 education. However, some urban schools levy other fees, prompting some migrant parents not to enroll their children in regular public schools.[19] Cui Chuanyi, a rural development researcher at the State Council, China's Cabinet, said in 2007 that "Very few migrants sever their ties to the farm, not because they don't want to move but because their human rights in the cities are not protected."

Some local governments are making it easier for rural-urban migrants to access local services. Shenzhen, which had 2.1 million registered residents and eight million migrant workers, in July 2008 became the first Chinese city to offer "citizenship" to migrants. Residents ages 16 to 60 who have been living in the area at least 30 days but are registered elsewhere can obtain 10-year residence certificate smart cards that allow them to apply for driving licenses and business visas to visit Hong Kong or Macao. Children of persons holding residence certificate cards will be able to go to local public schools, and their families can apply to live in low-cost public housing.

Cities in Guangdong province, which encircles Hong Kong and has estimated 26 million rural-urban migrants, began to offer urban hukous to migrants in 2010 if they can achieve 60 points on a test that assesses level of education (20 points for high school graduates, 80 points for college graduates), skill level, and contributions to social security; there are also points for not violating China's family planning policies and for donating blood. Rural-urban migrants who acquire urban hukous must give up their right to farm land where they are registered.

Some employers reliant on rural-urban migrants complained of labor shortages. Factories in the Pearl River and Yangtze River deltas, which often assemble electronics and other goods for export, complain that they are squeezed between foreign buyers aiming to keep costs low and workers demanding higher wages as the cost of living rises. In 2010-11, some factories were aggressively recruiting workers from interior provinces for jobs in coastal-province factories.

## 4.4 Conclusions

The number of people outside their country of birth a year or more reached 214 million in 2010, meaning that 3 percent of the world's people were international migrants. International migration is likely to continue to increase because of demand-pull factors in receiving countries, supply-push factors in sending countries, and networks that create communications and transportation infrastructures and allow migrants to learn about opportunities abroad and move to take advantage of them. Managing migration by adjusting migrant rights, as when governments make it harder to apply for asylum or restrict migrant access to welfare benefits, can violate fundamental human rights and encourage smuggling and trafficking in people.

Every one of the world's roughly 200 countries participates in the international migration system as a destination for migrants, a country through which migrants transit, or an area of origin, and many participate in all three ways. Most migrants do not move far from home, and each of the world's continents has a migration system with unique characteristics, including the large number of unauthorized Mexican and Latin American migrants in the United States, the unexpected settlement of Southern European guest workers in Western Europe, and the very high share of contract foreign workers in private sector labor markets in the Gulf oil-exporting countries of western Asia.

The migration system in the Asia-Pacific region is unique in several respects. First, the share of migrants is far more variable in the major Asian migrant-receiving countries, far higher than the global average in the Gulf oil exporters and Singapore and far lower in Japan and Korea. Second, in contrast to similar economic policies aimed at attracting foreign investment to create factories that produced goods for export, Asian migration policies vary significantly. Japan is largely closed to low-skilled foreign workers, while Singapore relies on foreign workers to fill most low-skill jobs. Third, the policies of the major labor-sending countries are more similar, as all seek to send more skilled migrants to destinations inside and outside Asia in a bid to improve protections and increase remittances.

More Asian governments in migrant-receiving countries acknowledge that their economies are likely to employ more migrant workers in the medium term, prompting Korea and some other migrant-receiving countries to develop MOUs with migrant-sending countries that aim to improve the entire migration process, from recruitment to employment abroad to return and reintegration. In migrant-sending countries, governments that aim to protect their nationals during recruitment and while abroad from unscrupulous agents and employers, and cooperate to reduce the cost of remittances, can help to maximize the development impacts of the window of opportunity opened by migration.

Migration is usually a successful journey of hope. Most Asian migrants achieve the higher earnings they seek abroad, explaining why there are long lists of Filipinos, Indonesians, and Vietnamese waiting to go abroad. Women are the majority of migrants leaving many Asian nations, and their remittances often improve their family's housing and increase investment in the education and health of their children. However, returned migrants rarely form political organizations that advocate for the socio-economic changes that could make migration less necessary in the future. Instead, international labor migration more often acts as a safety valve in labor-sending countries that enables governments to postpone painful reforms that could speed growth.

Labor migration is a process to be managed, not a problem to be solved. Experience demonstrates that there is no universal best way to manage labor migration, but there are universal principles that can protect the human rights of migrants and local workers. Policies that adhere to fundamental principles, such as protecting local workers from "unfair" competition by treating migrants equally, and are flexible enough to change with circumstances, offer the most promise.

## Notes

1. The East Asian economic miracle stands in sharp contrast to the lack of similar African and Latin American investment- and export-led growth success stories.
2. Borjas (1994) reexamined Chiswick's findings and concluded they applied to the unique set of circumstances that accompanied the lifting of barriers to Asian immigration in the mid-1960s.
3. Over half of the foreign residents of Korea are Chinese, and two-thirds live in greater Seoul.
4. Singapore does not have a minimum wage, so the employer-paid levy of up to S$470 ($310) a month for unskilled migrant construction workers may lower the earnings of foreign workers. Employers of foreign workers must also post a bond for each non-Malaysian foreign worker they hire.
5. In Hong Kong, the fertility rate is one, meaning that the average woman has one child in her lifetime; a third of women in their mid-40s have no children.
6. Beginning August 1, 2008, the HK$400 a month levy that collects funds to retrain local workers was suspended as an inflation-fighting move. Wages and other rules for domestic helpers are on line at: [http://www.labour.gov.hk/eng/pub lic/wcp/FDHguide.pdf].
7. Taiwan has one of the lowest fertility rates in the world, 1.1 in 2008 ([www.prb.org]).
8. The COLA in 2010 offered NT$50,000 ($1,622) for each valid report of an unauthorized foreigner, and NT$20,000 for valid reports of employers who hire unauthorized foreigners.
9. Beginning in 2011, all foreign trainees have been reclassified as technical interns and covered by the Labor Standards Law and the Minimum Wage Act.
10. One Chinese trainee employed in a metal working plant died in June 2008 after working an average of 80 hours a week for the previous year; 34 foreign trainees, most in their 20s and 30s, died in 2008.
11. Since 2000, foreign professionals with IT, high-tech, and basic science qualifications can enter Korea for up to three years with their families, and foreigners investing at least $500,000 can obtain three-year green-card visas. Foreign students who graduate from Korean universities with science and engineering degrees can stay if a Korean employer hires them.
12. For example, in Saudi Arabia, the average woman has almost four children, 36 percent of the population is under 15, and the labor force is increasing rapidly.

13. Kapiszewski notes that some Arabs regard borders imposed by colonial powers as artificial and expect the emergence of a pan-Arab state to share oil wealth.
14. Most recruiting agents in GCC countries offer households 90-day guarantees, which means that if the first domestic helper is not satisfactory, she will be replaced at no additional cost to the employer. Many migrants report not being paid during their first three months abroad, a tactic used to encourage them to stay with the employer to whom they have been assigned, since breaking the contract could mean going home with no wages (those who break contracts within 90 days to return home are to have their return airfare paid by the recruiter).
15. An account of the December 20, 2007 welcome is at [www.devbankphil.com.ph/News/news_full.php?articleid=00350].
16. The events surrounding this case are covered in Asia Week. 1995. A Death in the Family. December 29. [www.asiaweek.com/asiaweek/95/1229/feat3.html].
17. Taylor and Williamson (1997, 27) conclude that mass migration from Europe to North America between 1870 and 1913 explains "very large shares of the convergence in labor productivity and real wages."
18. Adams and Page (2005) find that a 10 percent increase in the share of migrants in a country's population is associated with a 1.9 percent decrease in the share of residents living in poverty, defined as living on less than $1 a day, and that a 10 percent increase in the share of remittances in a country's GDP is associated with 1.6 percent reduction in poverty.
19. Fees for unofficial primary school in urban areas are often $25 or $50 a month. Current law requires high school students seeking to attend college to take entrance exams in the place they are registered to live. Most children who move to urban areas with their parents reportedly drop out of school.

## References


Abella, Manolo. 1995. Asian Migrant and Contract Workers in the Middle East in Cohen, Robin, Ed. Cambridge Survey of World Migrations. Cambridge University Press, pp. 418–423.

Adams, Richard, and John Page. 2005. Do International Migration and Remittances Reduce Poverty in Developing Countries? *World Development* Vol. 33. 1645–1669. October.

Anh Nguyen, Dang. 2007. Labor Export from Vietnam. *Mimeo*. May.

Birks, J., and C. Sinclair. 1980. *International Migration and Development in the Arab Region*. Geneva. International Labor Organization.

Chan, Kam Wing. 1999. The Hukou system and Rural-Urban Migration in China: Processes and Changes. *China Quarterly*. Vol. 160, December 818–855.

Chiswick, Barry. 1978. The Effect of Americanization on the Earnings of Foreign-Born Men. *Journal of Political Economy*, Vol. 86, October 897–921.

Dollar, David, and Aart Kraay. 2002. Spreading the Wealth. Foreign Affairs. January/February. www.foreignaffairs.org/20020101faessay6561/david-dollar-aart-kraay/spreading-the-wealth.html.

Hugo, Graeme, and Soogil Young. Eds. 2008. Labour Mobility in the Asia-Pacific Region: Dynamics, Issues and a New APEC Agenda. ISEAS. http://bookshop.iseas.edu.sg/ISEAS/Book.jsp?cSeriesCode=PIC183&cCategoryType=.

Human Rights Watch. 2004. Bad Dreams: Exploitation and Abuse of Migrant Workers in Saudi Arabia. http://hrw.org/reports/2004/saudi0704/.

Human Rights Watch. 2008. As If I Am Not Human. Abuses against Asian Domestic Workers in Saudi Arabia. http://hrw.org/reports/2008/saudiarabia0708/.

Kapiszewski, Andrzej. 2006. Arab Versus Asian Migrant Workers in the GCC Countries. UN Expert Group Meeting May 15-17. Beirut. www.un.org/esa/population/meetings/EGM_Ittmig_Arab/Ittmig_Arab.htm.

Kashiwazaki, Chikako, and Tsuneo Akaha. 2006. Japanese Immigration Policy: Responding to Conflicting Pressures. November. www.migrationinformation.org/Feature/display.cfm?id=487.

Kim, Nora Hui-Jung. 2008. Korean Immigration Policy Changes and the Political Liberals' Dilemma. *International Migration Review*, Vol. 42, No. 3. 576–596.

Martin, Philip L. 2003. *Thailand: improving the management of foreign workers.* Bangkok: ILO and IOM. www.ilo.org/asia/whatwedo/publications/lang--en/docName--WCMS_BK_PB_197_EN/index.htm.

Martin, Philip, Manolo Abella, and Christiane Kuptsch. 2005. *Managing Labor Migration in the Twenty-First Century*. New Haven, CT: Yale University Press.

McKenzie, David, Pilar Garcia Martinez, and L. Alan Winters. 2008. Who is coming from Vanuatu to New Zealand under the new Recognized Seasonal Employer program? *Pacific Economic Bulletin*, Vol. 23, No 3. 205–228.

Migration News. Since 1994. http://migration.ucdavis.edu.

Pernia, Ernesto. 2008. Is Labor Export Good Development Policy? UPSE DP 0813. October. www.econ.upd.edu.ph.

Ratha, Dilip. 2003. Workers' Remittances: An Important and Stable Source of External Development Finance. Chapter 7 in Global Development Finance 2003. World Bank. http://www.worldbank.org/prospects/gdf2003/.

Rodriguez, E. 1998. International Migration and Income Distribution in the Philippines. *Economic Development and Cultural Change* 48(2): 329–350.

United Nations. 2002. *World Urbanization Prospects: The 2001 Revision Data Tables and Highlights*, Department of Economic and Social Affairs, Population Division. New York.

World Bank. 1993. *East Asian Miracle*. Economic Growth and Public Policy. Oxford University Press. New York.

World Bank. 2006. Expanding Job Opportunities for Pacific Islanders Through Labor Mobility at Home and Away.

World Bank. 2005. Global Economic Prospects. The Economic Implications of Remittances and Migration. www.worldbank.org/prospects/gep2006.

CHAPTER 5

# AGE COMPOSITIONAL SHIFTS AND CHANGING INTERGENERATIONAL TRANSFERS IN SELECTED ASIAN COUNTRIES

NAOHIRO OGAWA

## 5.1 Introduction

In the second half of the twentieth century, Asia's demographic landscape sustained phenomenal changes. Until the early 1980s, many developing countries in Asia perceived population aging as an issue faced only by developed countries. However, as a consequence of their rapid fertility decline, coupled with remarkable improvements in longevity, Asian countries themselves have come to experience unprecedented changes in their age structures. While in some of these countries the child dependency ratio has been declining rapidly, the rise in old age dependency has been creating significant new policy challenges in a number of them. It should be stressed that the policy response to these age compositional changes will influence economic growth and poverty, intergenerational equity, and social welfare for decades to come.

Primarily because the fertility transition in many Asian countries, particularly in East and Southeast Asia, has been substantially shorter and more dramatic than in the developed countries of the West, the speed of population aging in Asia has been and will be much faster than that observed among the industrialized nations in the West (Ogawa and Retherford 1997; Ogawa 2005). In Asia, fertility decline first occurred in Japan. Its magnitude was the greatest among all the industrialized nations. By and large, the current demographic picture in Japan is similar to that of Europe.

It is axiomatic among demographers that declining fertility, not increased life expectancy, is the principal determinant of population aging. It should be stressed, however, that the mortality effect on population aging becomes increasingly strong as the process of demographic transition and economic development progresses (United Nations 1987). At present, the mortality effect on population aging seems relatively limited in most of the Asian countries, as compared with the fertility effect. However, if the recent trends in mortality improvement continue in these countries, mortality at advanced ages will fall substantially in the relatively near future, thus contributing to population aging as a major factor. It is generally considered that the role of mortality improvements in inducing the aging process becomes increasingly important over time, especially when life expectancy at birth exceeds 70 years (Myers 1988), which is what a number of developing Asian countries have already achieved.

At present, Japan's population aging level is by far the highest in Asia. Moreover, in 2005, the Japanese became the oldest national population in the world, surpassing the Italians (Ogawa, Chawla, and Matsukura 2010), and from that year, the total size of the Japanese population has been diminishing. Although Japan's demographic setting is considerably more advanced than that of any other country in Asia, Japan and a number of other Asian countries to a great extent share the same traditional cultural values. In view of these similarities, the present chapter will, to a significant extent, draw upon Japanese experiences of population aging and its socioeconomic impact, while discussing important policy issues related to population aging in developing Asia, particularly along the Pacific Rim.

To achieve this objective, we will utilize, as an analytical tool, the system of "National Transfer Accounts (NTA)," which, as will briefly be described in the next section, provides a comprehensive framework for estimating consumption, production, and resource reallocations by age. By taking advantage of a significant amount of analytical information generated by the NTA system for several Asian countries, this chapter sheds light mainly on the benefits of the youth bulge and on the economic costs and benefits of the growing number of the elderly. The chapter is structured as follows: (i) an introduction of basic features of NTA, (ii) a brief review of Asia's changing demographic landscape with emphasis on age structural shifts, (iii) the demographic transition and its relationship to the first and second demographic dividends, (iv) changing intergenerational transfers, and (v) a short summary with a few remarks on policy implications for Japan and other selected Asian countries.

## 5.2 A Brief Introduction to the NTA System

Approximately ten years ago, an international collaborative research project called "NTA" was initiated under the leadership of the East-West Center (Andrew Mason) and the Center on the Economics and Demography of Aging at the University of California, Berkeley (Ronald Lee). A number of collaborating institutions from various parts of the world are included in the project. As of the end of 2011, a total of 36 countries constitute the NTA membership, and 10 of them are situated in the Asia-Pacific region.

The purpose of NTA is to measure at the aggregate level how much persons at each age acquire and use economic resources (Lee, Lee, and Mason 2008; Lee and Mason 2011). NTA is constructed in a manner consistent with the National Income and Product Accounts (NIPA) and provides a comprehensive and coherent treatment of economic flows by age.

The following two principal components comprise the NTA system. The first of them is a detailed accounting of the economic life cycle, consisting of consumption, labor income, and their major constituent elements. As people move through their lives, there are periods when their material needs are not matched by their ability to produce goods and services. In childhood and old age, people consume far more than they produce, thereby generating life-cycle deficits, while during the prime working ages they produce considerably more than they consume, thereby generating life-cycle surpluses.

The second component of NTA measures the flows of economic resources from life-cycle surplus to life-cycle deficit ages. These economic flows are mediated by both the public and private sectors. Age reallocations come in two forms: transfers and asset-based reallocations. A defining feature of transfers is that they involve no explicit quid pro quo. Resources flow from one party to another either voluntarily in the case of most private transfers, or involuntarily in the case of public transfers. Asset-based reallocations rely on inter-temporal exchange. An asset acquired in one period can be used to support consumption, either from asset income or by disposing of the asset, in subsequent periods. When individuals accumulate pension funds or personal savings during their working years and rely on asset income and/or dis-saving of those assets during their retirement, they are relying on asset-based reallocations. Or when individuals borrow to finance their education or to buy a car or a home, they are relying on asset-based reallocations to consume more than their current labor income allows. A more detailed description of NTA is available at [www.ntaccounts.org].

## 5.3 Changing Age Structures in Selected Asian Countries: 1950–2050

To facilitate our analysis in the remainder of this chapter, let us examine, primarily drawing upon the 2010 United Nations population projection (United Nations 2011), the long-term demographic developments in Asia, both in the past and for the future. In 2010, Asia's total population exceeded 4.2 billion people, which is more than double the size observed in 1965. The annual growth rate of the population in Asia, however, has been declining continuously during the past four decades; as opposed to its peak value of 2.48 percent during 1965–1970, the current annual growth rate is estimated at 0.99 percent. With the emergence of slower population growth in the latter half of the twentieth century, Asia's demographic outlook of today is substantially different from that of only a few decades ago.

Such substantially slower population growth in Asia has been caused chiefly by a significant decline in fertility over the past few decades. In the 1960s, Japan was the only Asian country with below-replacement fertility (a total fertility rate, or TFR, of less than 2.1 children per woman). By 2005–2010, the number increased to 19 countries/areas, including China, Hong Kong, Taiwan Province of China (Taiwan hereafter), the Republic of Korea, Singapore, and Thailand. In terms of the population share, as shown in Figure 5.1, only 5.0 percent of Asia's population lived in countries with below-replacement fertility in 1965–1970, as compared to 43.4 percent in 1990–1995, when China's fertility rate fell below the replacement level. Moreover, since 2010 half of Asia's population has already been residing in societies with below-replacement fertility, and more than 80 percent of the Asian population will live in countries with a fertility rate below the replacement level in the early 2030s, when India is projected to attain the below-replacement level of fertility. In 2005–2010, Hong Kong, Macao, Taiwan, the Republic of Korea and Singapore were classified in the category of lowest-low fertility (i.e., those with a TFR below 1.3). In fact, East Asia's fertility is now the lowest in the

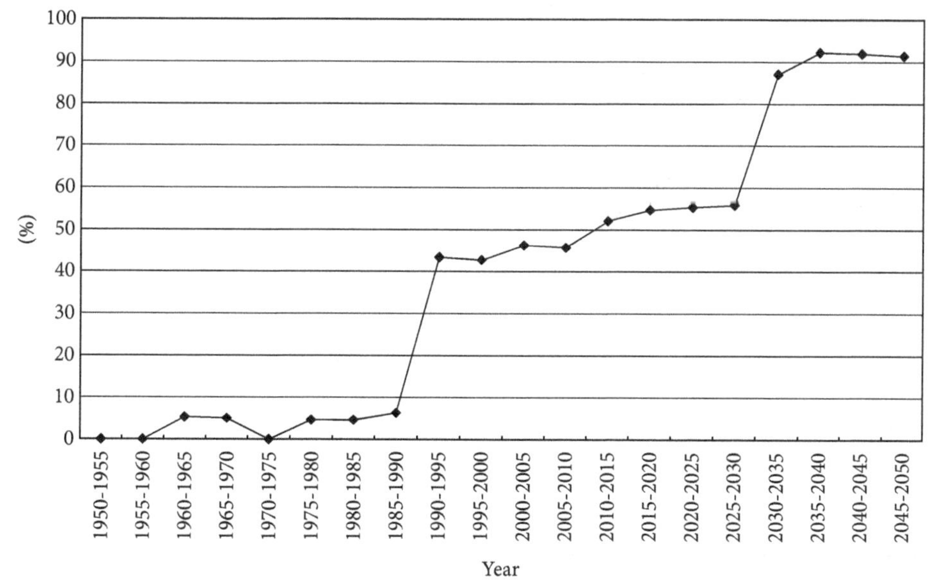


Note: Calculated by the author using data from the *World Population Prospects: The 2010 Revision* (United Nations 2011).

FIGURE 5.1 Proportion of the population of countries with below-replacement level fertility in Asia entire world (McDonald 2009; Jones and Gubhaju 2009), and among East Asia, Taiwan had the lowest TFR of 0.895 in 2010 (Ministry of the Interior, ROC (Taiwan), date unknown).

Parallel to the rapid decline in fertility, marked mortality improvements have been achieved in the Asian region. Particularly, the Japanese post-war experience is a case in point. When Japan joined the OECD in 1964, it had the lowest life expectancy at birth among the member countries, but by the early 1980s, it achieved the highest. At present, approximately 30 countries in Asia have life expectancies higher than 70 years. In the case of East Asia, four countries/areas (Hong Kong, Macao, Japan, and the Republic of Korea) have already surpassed the 80-year level.

As a result of these rapid fertility and mortality transformations in the second half of the twentieth century, we have witnessed phenomenal changes in Asia's demographic landscape in terms of population age distributions, with a relative increase in the number of the elderly and a relative decrease in the number of the young. As illustrated in Figure 5.2, Asia's total dependency ratio, which is defined as {[(aged 0–14) + (aged 65+)] / (aged 15–64)}, reached its peak value (0.803) in 1966, after which its projected long-term trend shows a U-shaped pattern, reaching the trough value (0.467) in 2016. This implies that in Asia as a whole, the share of the working age population has been increasing since 1966 to date, but is quickly approaching the end of growth. For Asia, this 50-year span, during which the share of the working age population continuously rises, corresponds to the period in which age structural transformations lead to a very direct and

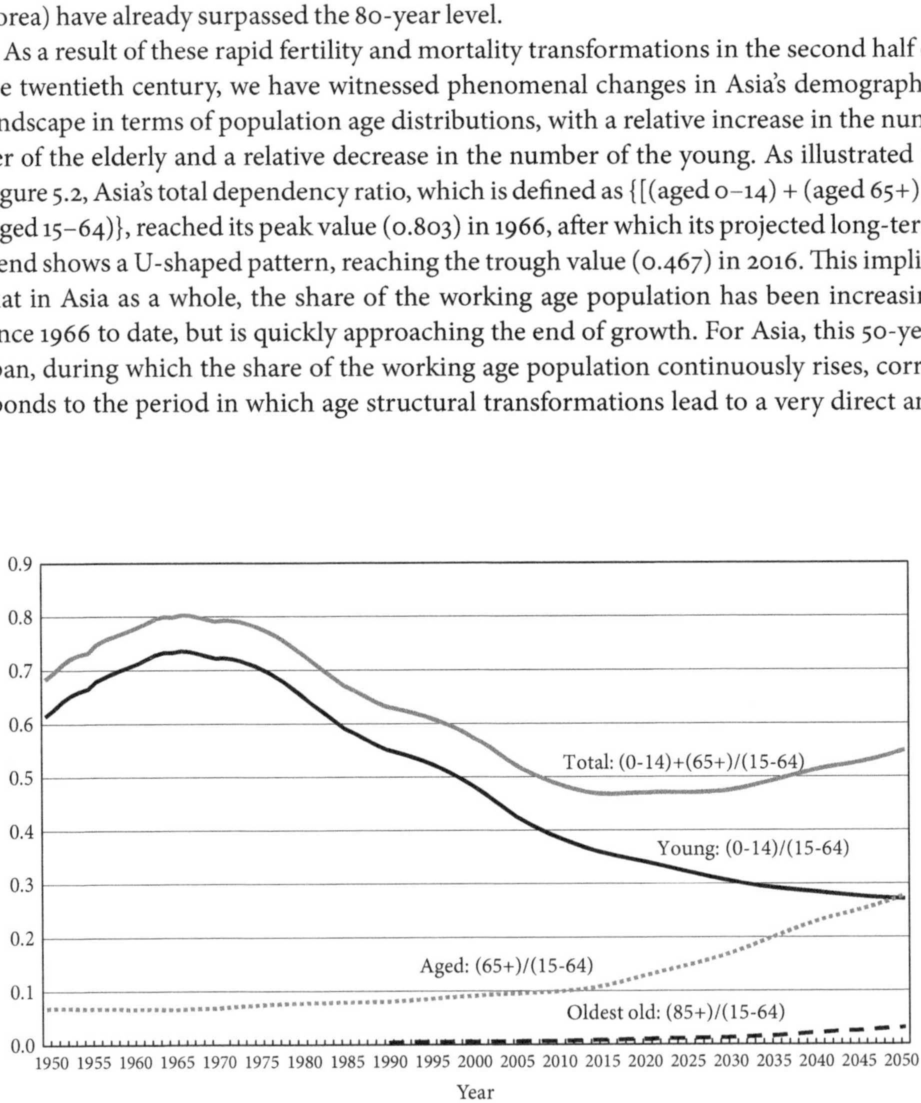


Note: Calculated by the author using data from the *World Population Prospects: The 2010 Revision* (United Nations 2011).

FIGURE 5.2 Changes in dependency ratios for Asia as a whole, 1950–2050 favorable impact on per capita income growth called "the first demographic dividend," as we shall see in more detail in the ensuing section.

In Asia, the broad outlines of the demographic transition are fairly similar in almost all of the countries in the region, although the speed and timing of the transition vary across countries. The age composition of each of the Asian countries has been changing rapidly since the mid-twentieth century (Ogawa 2003). As shown in Table 5.1, from 1975 to 2000, the total dependency ratio declined substantially in all of the three sub-regions and 10 countries listed. The extent to which the total dependency ratio decreased over the above-mentioned period in these countries is closely related to the magnitude of their fertility decline, as reflected in the inter-temporal change in the young dependency ratio, defined as [(aged 0–14) / (aged 15–64)]. Among the 10 countries in Table 5.1, Thailand had the largest reduction in total dependency ratio of 0.403, from 0.850 to 0.447, followed by Mongolia (0.372), the Republic of Korea (0.318), Indonesia (0.304), and China (0.290). The fact that all of these countries have shown substantial economic progress over the past decade or two may suggest that such steep declines in the total dependency ratio have facilitated the rapid economic growth in these countries.

The calculations based on the 2010 United Nations population projections shown in Table 5.1 indicate that the countries with high total dependency ratios will face a considerable reduction of the burden placed upon the working-age population in the first quarter of the twenty-first century and beyond. In these countries, the declining total dependency ratios are likely to facilitate their developmental process. In contrast, the countries with low total dependency ratios are expected to undergo a substantial increase in burden, mainly due to a rapid rise in the proportion of the elderly, as represented by the aged dependency ratio, expressed as [(aged 65+) / (aged 15–64)]. In the countries whose onset of fertility reduction was early, the changes in the aged dependency ratio are most pronounced. Clearly, Japan had the largest gain (+0.136), from 0.116 in 1975 to 0.252 in 2000. Among the countries listed in this table, the Republic of Korea showed the second largest gain (+0.042), followed by Singapore (+0.038).

A careful comparison of the index of aging, however, yields a picture substantially different from the one based upon the aged dependency ratios. Because the effect of fertility decline is immediately reflected in the index of aging, a marked increase in this index is observed among several developing countries under review, as presented in Table 5.1. Obviously, the countries that have shown a large increase in the aged dependency ratio, such as Japan, the Republic of Korea, and Singapore, have also seen a marked rise in their index of aging. Beside these countries, China and Thailand experienced a considerable increase in the index of aging during 1975–2000.

By 2000, Japan's index of aging had already exceeded the 100-level. Over the period 2000–2025 (to be exact, from 2005 to 2025), Japan is expected to remain the most aged society not only in Asia but in the entire world. By 2050, however, the value of the index of aging for the Republic of Korea is projected to be right behind that for Japan. These two East Asian countries will be closely followed by Singapore.

**Table 5.1 Age Structural Changes for Selected Asian Countries in 1975, 2000, 2025, and 2050**

| | 1975 | | | | 2000 | | | | 2025 | | | | 2050 | | | |
|---|---|---|---|---|---|---|---|---|---|---|---|---|---|---|---|---|
| | Dependency ratio | | | Index of aging | Dependency ratio | | | Index of aging | Dependency ratio | | | Index of aging | Dependency ratio | | | Index of aging |
| | Total | Young | Aged | | Total | Young | Aged | | Total | Young | Aged | | Total | Young | Aged | |
| Asia | 0.779 | 0.705 | 0.074 | 11 | 0.573 | 0.482 | 0.091 | 19 | 0.470 | 0.321 | 0.149 | 46 | 0.549 | 0.271 | 0.278 | 103 |
| *East Asia* | 0.730 | 0.647 | 0.083 | 13 | 0.476 | 0.360 | 0.117 | 32 | 0.445 | 0.223 | 0.222 | 100 | 0.667 | 0.225 | 0.442 | 196 |
| China | 0.771 | 0.690 | 0.081 | 12 | 0.481 | 0.377 | 0.104 | 27 | 0.422 | 0.223 | 0.199 | 89 | 0.640 | 0.221 | 0.419 | 190 |
| Japan | 0.475 | 0.359 | 0.116 | 32 | 0.466 | 0.214 | 0.252 | 117 | 0.721 | 0.216 | 0.505 | 233 | 0.958 | 0.262 | 0.696 | 266 |
| Mongolia | 1.011 | 0.909 | 0.102 | 11 | 0.639 | 0.578 | 0.062 | 11 | 0.493 | 0.404 | 0.088 | 22 | 0.574 | 0.352 | 0.222 | 63 |
| Republic of Korea | 0.713 | 0.654 | 0.060 | 9 | 0.395 | 0.292 | 0.102 | 35 | 0.512 | 0.216 | 0.296 | 137 | 0.851 | 0.244 | 0.607 | 249 |
| *South-East Asia* | 0.861 | 0.794 | 0.068 | 9 | 0.575 | 0.499 | 0.075 | 15 | 0.458 | 0.327 | 0.131 | 40 | 0.555 | 0.274 | 0.280 | 102 |
| Indonesia | 0.851 | 0.787 | 0.064 | 8 | 0.547 | 0.475 | 0.071 | 15 | 0.433 | 0.311 | 0.123 | 39 | 0.557 | 0.257 | 0.300 | 117 |
| Singapore | 0.586 | 0.521 | 0.065 | 13 | 0.405 | 0.301 | 0.103 | 34 | 0.509 | 0.214 | 0.295 | 138 | 0.812 | 0.236 | 0.576 | 245 |
| Thailand | 0.850 | 0.786 | 0.064 | 8 | 0.447 | 0.347 | 0.100 | 29 | 0.447 | 0.230 | 0.217 | 94 | 0.651 | 0.237 | 0.414 | 175 |
| *South-Central Asia* | 0.804 | 0.741 | 0.063 | 9 | 0.667 | 0.597 | 0.070 | 12 | 0.487 | 0.384 | 0.103 | 27 | 0.482 | 0.284 | 0.199 | 70 |
| Bangladesh | 0.972 | 0.903 | 0.069 | 8 | 0.704 | 0.636 | 0.069 | 11 | 0.417 | 0.332 | 0.085 | 26 | 0.464 | 0.231 | 0.233 | 101 |
| India | 0.774 | 0.714 | 0.061 | 9 | 0.638 | 0.568 | 0.069 | 12 | 0.486 | 0.378 | 0.108 | 29 | 0.480 | 0.281 | 0.199 | 71 |
| Pakistan | 0.885 | 0.815 | 0.070 | 9 | 0.828 | 0.756 | 0.072 | 9 | 0.536 | 0.454 | 0.081 | 18 | 0.451 | 0.299 | 0.152 | 51 |

*Note:* Calculated by the author using data from the *World Population Prospects: The 2010 Revision* (United Nations 2011).

# 5.4 Age Compositional Shifts and Two Demographic Dividends

## 5.4.1 Translating Demographic Changes into Economic Gains and Losses

In the second half of the 1990s, the term "demographic bonus" began to be widely used in economic and demographic research. It should be noted, however, that since then a number of new terms referring to the same or highly comparable demographic-economic nexus have appeared, ranging broadly from such an expression as "window of opportunity" to the term "demographic golden age."

Also, the definition of the total dependency ratio, which is used as a yardstick for assessing the timing and duration of the demographic bonus, often varies among researchers. Moreover, different criteria have been utilized to judge, on the basis of computed total dependency ratios, whether or not a country is at the stage of the demographic bonus. For instance, Komine and Kabe (2009) used the conventional total dependency ratio, namely, {[(aged 0–14) + (aged 65+)] / (aged 15–64)}, and chose to regard a country as experiencing a demographic bonus if the computed value for it falls continuously. In contrast, Cheung et al. (2004), although employing the same total dependency ratio, adopted a different criterion. That is, for them, the demographic bonus period corresponds to the stage where the computed value remains less than 0.5. Furthermore, Golini (2004) utilized a total dependency ratio defined in a slightly different manner, i.e., {[(aged 0–14) + (aged 60+)] / (aged 15–59)}. In his definition, the country is at the demographic bonus stage when the calculated value is below 0.66.

One of the most serious shortcomings in these studies lies in the fact that the conventional total dependency ratio and its variants are very crude measures for quantifying the impact of age structural transformations upon the overall economic productivity because the demographic and economic dependency ratios are inclined to be markedly different. The NTA-based approach rectifies this weakness.

## 5.4.2 Computational Steps for the First and Second Demographic Dividends

As extensively discussed elsewhere (Mason 2001, 2007; Mason and Lee 2006), one of the important linkages between demographic transformations and economic growth is the role of demographic dividends in the process of economic development. As a country advances along the stages of demographic transition, it undergoes considerable age structural shifts. When a country's fertility begins to fall, the first demographic dividend arises because changes in the population age structure have led to an increase in the working ages relative to non-working ages. In other words, the first demographic dividend arises because of an increase in the share of the population at ages during which production exceeds consumption. That is, the first demographic dividend is positive when the support ratio, which is defined as the ratio of effective workers to effective consumers, increases (Mason 2007).

Using relatively simple mathematical notations, we can provide a short description of how the first demographic dividend is measured. The calculus is as follows: income per effective consumer ($Y(t)/N(t)$), which is a measure of per capita income adjusted for age-variation in consumption, is the product of the support ratio ($L(t)/N(t)$) and income per worker ($Y(t)/L(t)$):

$$\frac{Y(t)}{N(t)} = \frac{L(t)}{N(t)} \times \frac{Y(t)}{L(t)} \tag{1}$$

Furthermore, $N(t)$, which represents the effective number of consumers, and $L(t)$, which represents the effective number of workers, can be expressed as:

$$N(t) = \sum_a \alpha(a) P(a,t)$$

$$L(t) = \sum_a \beta(a) P(a,t) \tag{2}$$

where $\alpha(a)$ and $\beta(a)$ are the age profiles of consumption and production, and $P(a,t)$ is the population. Hence, the estimates of the demographic dividends are heavily dependent upon the average age profiles of consumption (with both private and public sectors combined) and production (in both paid employment and self-employment) of the country under study. However, at the time of the writing, all the necessary data for each of the countries in question could not be obtained, which is why we chose to create the so-called "per capita age-specific profiles for developing Asia," by combining the following four Asian NTA member countries: India in 2004, Indonesia in 2002, the Philippines in 1999, and Thailand in 2004, as shown in Figure 5.3.

To identify the timing and duration of the first demographic dividend for each country, we need to discuss inter-temporal changes in the support ratio. Equation (1) can be expressed in growth terms as follows:

$$g\left(\frac{Y(t)}{N(t)}\right) = g\left(\frac{L(t)}{N(t)}\right) \times g\left(\frac{Y(t)}{L(t)}\right) \tag{3}$$

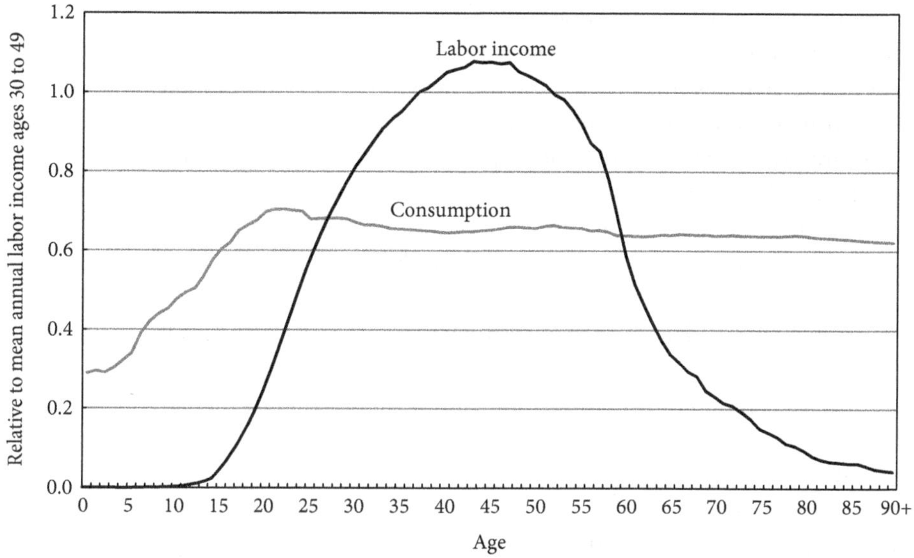


Note: This figure was prepared by the author.

*Indonesia (2002), Philippines (1999), Thailand (2004), and India (2004).

FIGURE 5.3 A typical Asian economic life cycle: NTA estimates on per capita consumption and labor income for four Asian countries* combined

The first demographic dividend is the rate of growth of the support ratio, which rises or falls, subject to the age compositional transformation in the process of the demographic transition. During the demographic transition when the support ratio is rising, income per effective consumer increases, given that there is no change in productivity. As the support ratio declines, however, income per effective consumer falls and the first demographic dividend disappears, which means that the increase in income per effective consumer is transitory. More importantly, the first demographic dividend can be realized only if employment keeps pace with the growth of the working age population.

Now, let us shift our attention to the second demographic dividend. This dividend corresponds to the growth rate of productivity or output per effective worker, which is induced by the accumulation of wealth as well as physical and human capital deepening. The second demographic dividend arises when individuals at all age groups increase demand for wealth in some form to support their old-age consumption. One possibility is that old-age economic security might heavily rely on transfers from public pension and welfare programs or from adult children and other family members. The other possibility is that individuals accumulate capital during their working years, which in turn serves as the source of support in retirement. Both of these forms of wealth can be utilized to support consumption in old age. However, attention should be drawn to the following key point: only capital accumulation will lead to an increase in productivity. Unlike the first demographic dividend, the second dividend is not transitory, and may lead to a permanent increase in capital deepening and income per effective consumer.

The second dividend, however, does not occur spontaneously, but can be brought about if consumers and policymakers are forward-looking and respond effectively to coming demographic changes by encouraging the development of an old-age support system that substitutes capital for transfer wealth.

There are two ways in which demographic factors cause an increase in the demand for life-cycle wealth and the second demographic dividend. First, there is a compositional effect, caused by an increase in the share of individuals who have nearly or fully completed their productive years. Second, there is a behavioral effect, caused by an increase in life expectancy and the accompanying increase in the duration of retirement, leading to an increase in demand for wealth. Demand for life-cycle wealth is mainly concentrated among older working adults who are approaching their peak earnings and have completed their childrearing responsibilities. Mason (2007) uses the wealth held by those aged 50 and older to measure the effect of demography on life-cycle wealth and the second demographic dividend.

Demand for life-cycle wealth is computed as the difference between the present value of lifetime consumption and the present value of lifetime production for adults. The present value of the future lifetime consumption of the cohort born in year *b* or earlier ($b=t\text{-}a$) is:

$$\bar{c}(t)PVN(<b,t)=\bar{c}(t)\sum_{x=0}^{\omega-a}e^{(g_c-r)x}N(\leq b,t+x) \tag{4}$$

where $N(\leq b,t+x)$ is the number of effective consumers born in year *b* or earlier who are alive in year $t+x$, $g_c$ is the rate of growth of the per capita age profile of consumption, *r* is the interest rate, and $\bar{c}(t)$ is consumption per effective consumer in year *t*.

Similarly, if the per capita age profile of production is shifted upward at $g_y$, the present value of the future lifetime production of the cohort born in year *b* or earlier ($b=t\text{-}a$) is:

$$\bar{y}^l(t)PVL(<b,t)=\bar{y}^l(t)\sum^{\omega-a}e^{(g_y-r)x}L(\leq b,t+x) \tag{5}$$

where $L(\leq b,t+x)$ is the number of effective producers born in year *b* or earlier who are alive in year $t+x$, and $\bar{y}^l(t)$ is production per effective producer in year *t*. Consequently, the ratio of wealth to labor income for those who were born in year *b* or earlier ($b=t\text{-}a$) is:

$$w(\leq b,t)=[\bar{c}(t)/\bar{y}^l(t)]=PVN(\leq b,t)/N(t)-PVL(\leq b,t)/L(t) \tag{6}$$

It should be noted that under the Golden Rule, the ratio is assumed to be 1, and the rate of productivity growth and the rate of growth of equivalent consumption, $g_y$ and $g_c$, are constant and equal to each other. Mason (2007) assumes that: (1) the growth of consumption and labor income are exogenously 1.5 percent per year and the interest rate is 3 percent; (2) age 50 is used as the cut-off age at which wealth accumulation begins;

(3) the transfer policy is constant so that the growth rates of the capital and life-cycle wealth are equal; (4) the elasticity of labor income with respect to capital is 0.5 (that is, the elasticity of output with respect to capital is 1/3). Thus, the second demographic dividend is calculated as half of the growth rate of the wealth to income ratio.

### 5.4.3 Computed Results on the First Demographic Dividend

Before examining country-specific computational results with regard to the first demographic dividend, let us discuss the calculated results for 10 Asian countries combined as a showcase. The selected countries here are the same as those listed in Table 5.1, i.e., China, Japan, Mongolia, the Republic of Korea, Indonesia, Singapore, Thailand, Bangladesh, India, and Pakistan.

With a view to identifying the timing and duration of the first demographic dividend for these 10 Asian countries combined, we have calculated the change in the support ratio over the period 1950–2050, by applying the computed age-specific results displayed in Figure 5.3 as statistical weights to adjust the entire population of the 10 countries combined. At this point, it is worth remarking that we have applied the same age-specific profiles of consumption and production as plotted in Figure 5.3 to the 10 populations combined for each year, assuming that these profiles remain unchanged throughout the entire period under review. This implies that the computational results solely reflect the effect of age structural change on the support ratio. We have used the 2010 United Nations population projection as the source of demographic data for the computation[1].

The computed results are shown in Figure 5.4. As can be observed in this graph, the first demographic dividend for the 10 Asian countries combined began in 1972, and is projected to come to an end in 2025, after which the combined countries are expected to enter into the phase of population aging. Thus, the duration of the first demographic dividend amounts to 53 years.

Based upon the same computational procedure and assumptions employed in the above case, we have, for comparative purposes, calculated an inter-temporal change in the support ratio for each of the 10 Asian countries. The results are listed in Table 5.2. There are marked differences in terms of both the timing and the duration of the first demographic dividend among the 10 selected countries. It should be noted that the year in which Japan entered its first demographic dividend stage is listed in the brackets. This is because Japan started experiencing the first demographic dividend in 1949, a year that falls outside the time frame of this table.

A few points of interest emerge from the results reported in this table. First, among the 10 countries, Japan was the earliest to enter the phase of the first demographic dividend, followed by the Republic of Korea and Singapore. It should be stressed that Japan's first demographic dividend ended in 1995, followed by Singapore in 2004, whereas the Republic of Korea is projected to shift from the stage of the first demographic dividend to that of population aging in 2012. Second, among the 10 countries, Singapore

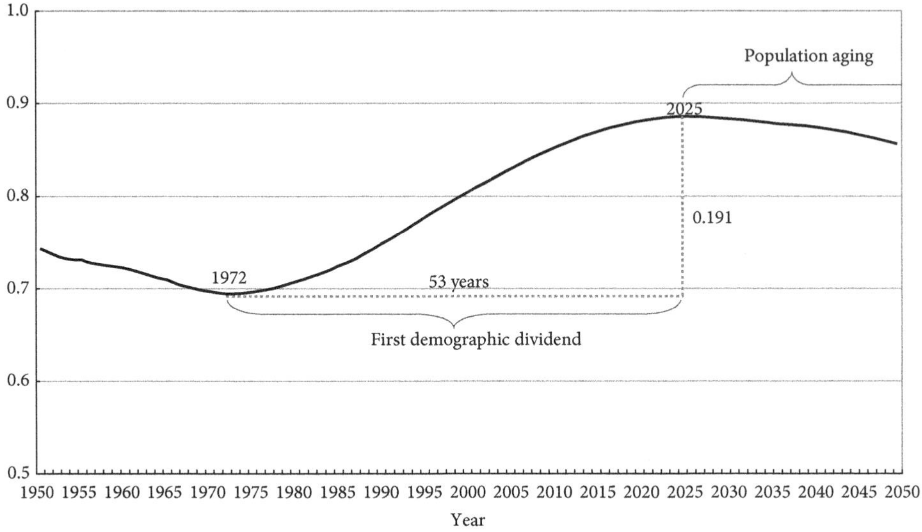


Note: This figure was prepared by the author.
*China, Japan, Mongolia, Republic of Korea, Indonesia, Singapore, Thailand, Bangladesh, India, and Pakistan.

FIGURE 5.4 Support ratio for selected Asian countries* combined

**Table 5.2. Timing and Duration of the First Demographic Dividend in the Selected Asian Countries**

| | First demographic dividend | | |
|---|---|---|---|
| | Beginning year | Ending year | Duration (years) |
| China | 1972 | 2020 | 48 |
| Japan | (1949)* | 1995 | 47 |
| Mongolia | 1981 | 2020 | 39 |
| Republic of Korea | 1965 | 2012 | 47 |
| Indonesia | 1977 | 2028 | 51 |
| Singapore | 1967 | 2004 | 37 |
| Thailand | 1972 | 2015 | 43 |
| Bangladesh | 1984 | 2039 | 55 |
| India | 1973 | 2045 | 72 |
| Pakistan | 1992 | 2050 | 58 |

*The reason why the beginning year of the first demographic dividend for Japan was bracketed is given in the text.
*Note:* Calculated by the author.

and Mongolia have the shortest duration of the first demographic dividend, i.e., 37 years from 1967 to 2004, and 39 years from 1981 to 2020. Thirdly, India is projected to have an extremely long period of the first demographic dividend, i.e., 72 years, from 1973 to 2045.

Next, we shall briefly examine the magnitude of the first demographic dividend in Asia by taking up the following four countries: the Republic of Korea (Figure 5.5), Mongolia (Figure 5.6), China (Figure 5.7), and India (Figure 5.8). The difference in the support ratio between the beginning year and the end year of the first demographic dividend varies considerably among these four countries. The largest magnitude was recorded by the Republic of Korea (0.278), followed by Mongolia (0.261) and China (0.252). India, however, is expected to have a rather low value of 0.200 in terms of magnitude, although its first demographic dividend is the longest among the 10 countries listed in Table 5.2.[2]

## 5.4.4 Computed results on the second demographic dividend

As mentioned earlier, the second demographic dividend corresponds to the growth rate of the wealth-income ratio, or capital stock. By closely following the procedure described by equations (4)–(6), we have computed the second demographic dividend in terms of capital stock growth rate for five out of the 10 countries listed in Table 5.2. The five selected countries are China, the Republic of Korea, Singapore, Thailand, and India, all of which have shown phenomenal economic growth performance in the past few decades. All the values reported in Table 5.3 represent the average annual growth rate

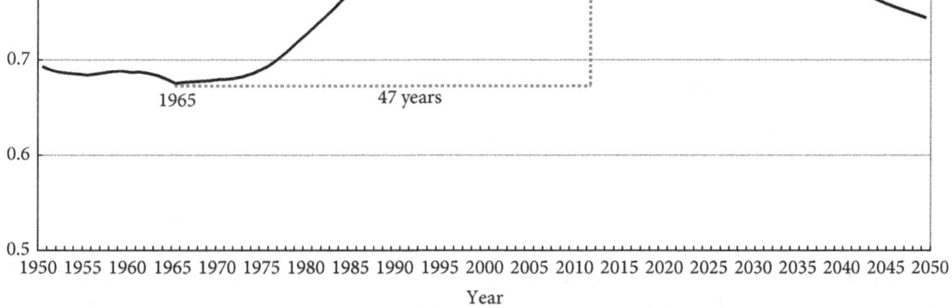


Note: This figure was prepared by the author.

FIGURE 5.5 Support ratio for the Republic of Korea, 1950–2050

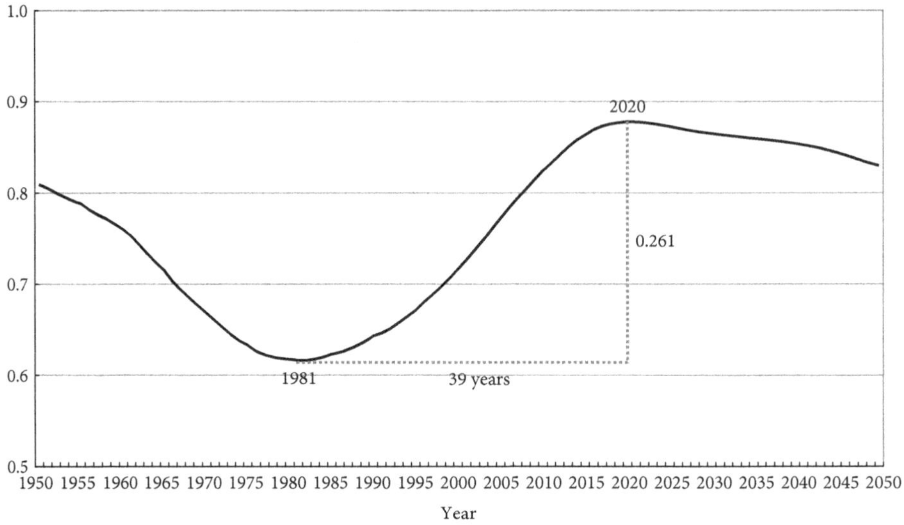


Note: This figure was prepared by the author.

FIGURE 5.6 Support ratio for Mongolia, 1950–2050

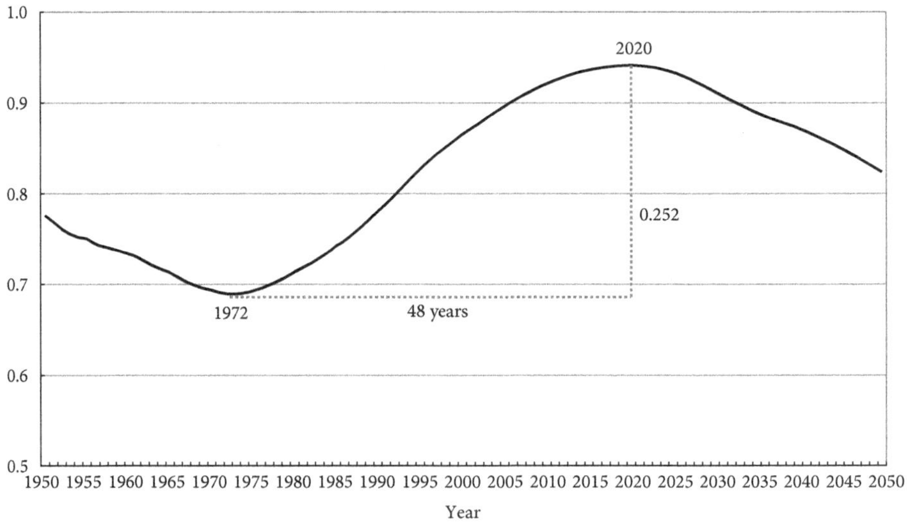


Note: This figure was prepared by the author.

FIGURE 5.7 Support ratio for China, 1950–2050

of capital stock for each decade over the period 2010–2030. In order to compare these results with those on the first demographic dividend, we have also prepared in Table 5.4 the average annual growth rate of the support ratio for the same countries in the same period.

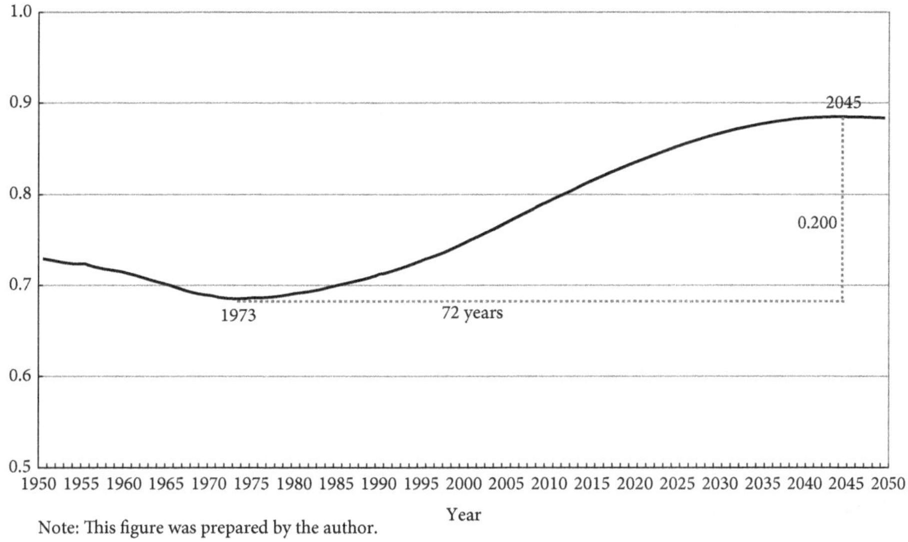


Note: This figure was prepared by the author.

FIGURE 5.8 Support ratio for India, 1950–2050

As can be seen from Table 5.3, all of the selected countries are likely to have a sizable second demographic dividend in the next 20 years. More importantly, a brief comparison of Tables 5.3 and 5.4 reveals that the magnitude of the second demographic dividend is far larger than that of the first dividend over the period under review. In the case of Singapore, however, although not shown in Table 5.3, the second demographic dividend is projected to become negative during 2030-2040, and then turn positive again in the subsequent decade.

It should be stressed that these projected results on the two demographic dividends reflect only the age compositional effect. The relationship between the demographic dividends and income growth is very policy-dependent. This point has been

**Table 5.3 Second Demographic Dividend in Five Asian Countries, 2010–2030, Expressed in Terms of the Average Annual Growth Rate (%)**

| | 2010–2020 | 2020–2030 |
|---|---|---|
| China | 1.86 | 1.14 |
| Republic of Korea | 1.84 | 1.03 |
| Singapore | 1.57 | 0.40 |
| Thailand | 2.02 | 1.31 |
| India | 2.28 | 1.74 |

*Note:* Calculated by the author.

**Table 5.4 First Demographic Dividend in Five Asian Countries, 2010–2030, Expressed in Terms of the Average Annual Growth Rate (%)**

| | 2010–2020 | 2020–2030 |
|---|---|---|
| China | 0.24 | −0.28 |
| Republic of Korea | −0.19 | −0.77 |
| Singapore | −0.31 | −0.77 |
| Thailand | 0.05 | −0.23 |
| India | 0.53 | 0.38 |

*Note:* Calculated by the author.

emphasized in the previous section but bears repeating. The first dividend arises in part because the working age population is growing rapidly. The economic gains can be realized only if employment opportunities expand as rapidly as the numbers of people seeking new jobs. The second dividend arises in part because prime-age adults save more to provide for their retirement. Their ability or willingness to save, however, may be undermined by the absence of developed financial markets or overly generous public pension programs. It is worth remarking that demographic transformations simply define possibilities, and that the outcome is heavily dependent on a large number of non-demographic factors.

## 5.5 Changing Intergenerational Transfers in Japan and Its Implications for Other Asian Countries

The calculated results for the selected Asian countries presented in the previous section clearly suggest that the magnitude, duration, and timing of the first and second demographic dividends are different from country to country. In addition, the computed results seem to substantiate the validity of the view that the magnitude of the first dividend is particularly large in countries where the fertility level has plummeted very rapidly. Obviously, these countries have already been in the midst of rapid age structural transformations, and the patterns of intergenerational transfers, both private and public, have been changing at an unprecedented rate. The NTA framework provides an extremely useful base for grasping these changes in intergenerational transfers. For the sake of convenience, we draw heavily upon NTA computational results for Japan, a forerunner of Asia's population aging process.

NTA, which measures intergenerational flows for a certain period of time (usually a calendar or fiscal year), is governed by the following relationship:

$$y^l + r(K+M) + \tau_g^+ + \tau_f^+ = C + I_K + I_M + \tau_g^- + \tau_f^- \tag{7}$$

where $y^l$ = labor income; $rK$ = returns to capital; $rM$ = returns to land and credit; $\tau_g^+$ = transfer inflows from the public sector; $\tau_f^+$ = transfer inflows from the private sector; $C$=consumption; $I_K$ = investment in capital; $I_M$ = investment in credit and land; $\tau_g^-$ = transfer outflows to the government; $\tau_f^-$ = transfer outflows to the private sector.

In addition, the life-cycle deficit (LCD), which is the difference between consumption and production, is matched by age reallocations consisting of reallocations through assets and net transfers as expressed below:

$$\underbrace{\underbrace{C - y^l}_{\text{Life-cycle deficit}} = \underbrace{y^A - S}_{\text{Asset-based reallocations}} + \underbrace{\underbrace{\tau_g^+ - \tau_g^-}_{\text{Net public transfers}} + \underbrace{\tau_f^+ - \tau_f^-}_{\text{Net private transfers}}}_{\text{Net transfers}}}_{\text{Age reallocations}} \tag{8}$$

Before proceeding to a discussion of the computational results, however, caution should be exercised with regard to the following two points. First, both "familial transfers" and "private transfers" are used interchangeably in this chapter; both of the terms refer to transfers coming from other family members of the same or different household. Second, although net private transfers are comprised of bequests and inter vivos transfers, the computation of the bequest component has not been completed at the time of writing. For this reason, the bequests are excluded from the computational results reported in this chapter. It is also important to note that the estimated values for the totals are adjusted on the basis of the National Income and Product Accounts (NIPA) values, which ensures consistency with NIPA.

Figure 5.9 compares the changing pattern of three components of reallocation of the life-cycle deficit for the entire Japanese population at 10-year intervals during 1984-2004 (Panels A, B, and C). The three components are net reallocations through assets, net public transfers, and net private transfers, measured in terms of 2000 constant prices on an annual basis.

A brief comparison of the three panels reveals the following two points of interest. First, the composition of net transfers to the elderly population changed dramatically over the 20-year period. The amount of net public transfers to the elderly population increased significantly, from 11.8 trillion yen in 1984 to 44.5 trillion yen in 2004. Similarly, the amount of net asset-based reallocations grew remarkably over time, from 6.1 trillion yen in 1984 to 46.1 trillion yen in 2004. In contrast, the relative importance of net familial transfers from the young to the elderly declined to an appreciable extent over the same time period. These results seem to indicate that the Japanese elderly have been increasingly dependent upon public transfers (predominantly old-age pensions and medical care services) and asset-based reallocations in supporting their retirement life.

Second and more importantly, as marked by two circles in Figure 5.9 (one in Panel B and the other in Panel C), the amount of net familial transfers to the relatively young

**Panel A. 1984**

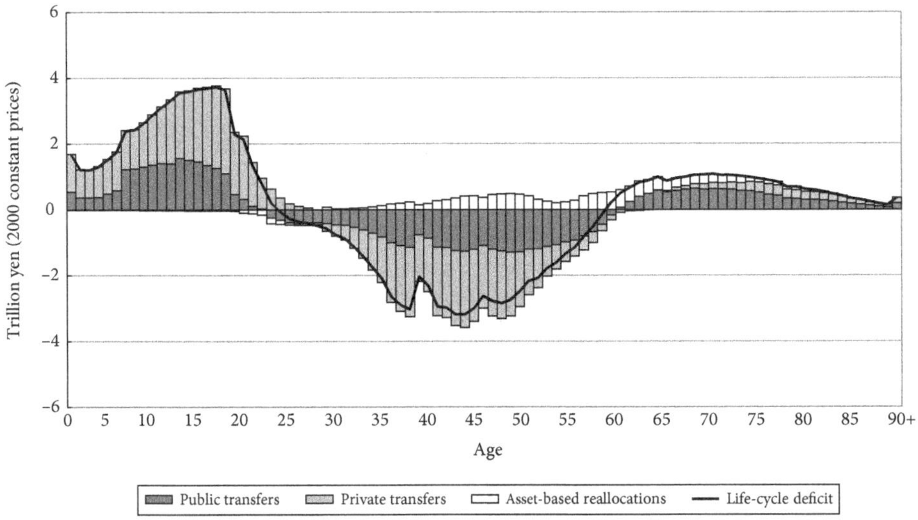


Note: This figure was prepared by the author.

**Panel B. 1994**

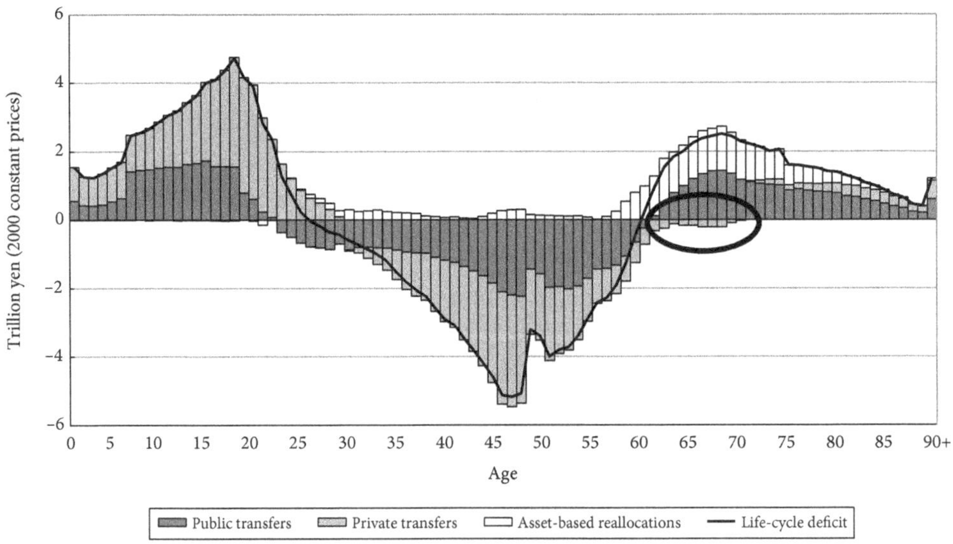


Note: This figure was prepared by the author.

FIGURE 5.9 Changing pattern of three components of reallocations: Japan, 1984–2004

Panel A. 1984, Panel B. 1994 and Panel C. 2004

Panel C. 2004

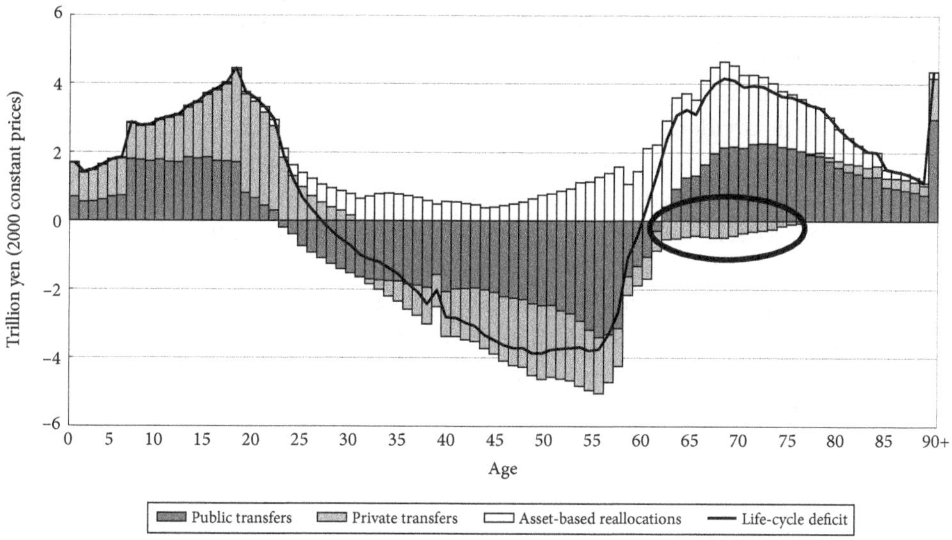


Note: This figure was prepared by the author.

FIGURE 5.9. *Continued*

elderly persons (roughly in their 60s and early 70s) was negative in both 1994 and 2004, implying that the amount of financial assistance the relatively young elderly persons provided to their adult children and/or grandchildren exceeded monetary assistance from the latter to the former. It is also worth noting that the amount of such negative net familial transfers from the relatively young elderly to other age groups rose during the period of "Japan's lost decade" (Yoshikawa 2002). These results suggest that despite the fact that multigenerational co-residence has been eroding over the past few decades, the Japanese elderly still play a vital role in providing financial support for their offspring when the latter encounter economic difficulties. Although older persons in Japan are often considered liabilities for the country, they are actually playing a key role as a safety net. For this reason, they should be considered latent assets in contemporary Japanese society.

## 5.6 Concluding Remarks

In this chapter, we have analyzed some of the important impacts of Asia's age structural changes on the first and second demographic dividends by heavily drawing upon the computed results generated under the global NTA project. The computed results for the developing countries in Asia indicate that the size of the two demographic dividends is quite substantial in most of these countries. In addition, it should be stressed that the first demographic dividend is basically transitory in nature, while the second demographic dividend could be permanent, depending upon policies to be implemented.

Although the awareness regarding the two demographic dividends is still fairly limited in developing Asia, their effective use, particularly that of the accumulated second demographic dividend that is likely to remain enormous for the next few decades, appears to be an attractive policy option for many Asian countries interested in placing their future economic growth on a steady path.

However, one crucial question arises: how should Asians make use of their accumulated assets and wealth in the years to come? The continent's future economic growth performance will differ considerably depending upon when and where they invest their future financial resources. Although the formulation and implementation of old-age pension programs are becoming increasingly vital policy issues in many Asian countries, attention should be drawn to their financing methods, since the amount of the second demographic dividend varies substantially in relation to the financing method, affecting the accumulation of capital to be utilized for boosting future economic growth. That is, if a country chooses the pay-as-you-go type of financing rather than the provident type of financing, the second demographic dividend may not emerge.

In the second half of this chapter, we have shown the impact of age structural shifts on the pattern of intergenerational transfers in Japan over the period 1984-2004. Although the discussion has been confined to Japan, its empirical findings should be applicable to other Asian countries for the following two reasons. First, many of the Asian countries have been following Japan in the pattern of demographic developments. Second, Japan and the other selected Asian countries share traditional cultural values to a considerable degree. In view of these similarities, the Japanese experiences of population aging and socioeconomic impacts brought about by aging will lend themselves useful to analyzing important policy issues related to population aging in developing Asia, particularly along the Pacific Rim.

## Acknowledgments

Research for this chapter was partially funded by two grants from the College of Economics, Nihon University: the Nihon University Multidisciplinary Research Grant for 2011 and the Collaborative Research Grant of the Research Institute of Economic Science.

## Notes

1. The only exception is Japan before 1950, for which we used population estimations for various years provided by the Statistics Bureau of Japan and data collected in population censuses, since no relevant UN projections were available.

2. We should point out that we have taken into account the sensitivity of the choice of the age-specific profiles of consumption and production in estimating the duration of the first demographic dividend. For each of the four Asian developing countries utilized to generate the Asian age-specific profiles, we have applied that country's own age-specific profiles to calculate the support ratio over the period of 1950–2050. In the case of Thailand, for example, the two computed support ratios are fairly comparable, thus substantiating the validity of our approach to calculating the timing and duration of the first demographic dividend for the various Asian countries listed in Table 5.2.

## References


Cheung, Siu Lan K., Paul Yip, Iris Chi, Antonio Golini, and Jean-Marie Robine. 2004. "Change in Demographic Window in Low Fertility Countries." Paper presented at the International Seminar on the Demographic Window and Healthy Aging: Socioeconomic Challenges and Opportunities, Beijing, May 10-11.

Golini, Antonio. 2004. "A Domestic and an International View from a Demographic Window." Paper presented at the International Seminar on the Demographic Window and Healthy Aging: Socioeconomic Challenges and Opportunities, Beijing, May 10–11.

Jones, Gavin W., and Bina Gubhaju. 2009. "Factors Influencing Changes in Mean Age at First Marriage and Proportions Never Marrying in the Low-Fertility Countries of East and Southeast Asia." *Asian Population Studies* 5(3): 237–265.

Komine, Takao, and Shigesaburo Kabe. 2009. "Long-term Forecast of the Demographic Transition in Japan and Asia." *Asian Economic Policy Review* 4(1): 19–38.

Lee, Ronald, and Andrew Mason, eds. 2011. *Population Aging and the Generational Economy: A Global Perspective.* Cheltenham and Northampton: Edward Elgar Publishing.

Lee, Ronald, Sang-Hyop Lee, and Andrew Mason. 2008. "Charting the Economic Life Cycle." In *Population Aging, Human Capital Accumulation, and Productivity Growth*, edited by Alexia Prskawetz, David E. Bloom, and Wolfgang Lutz, 208–237. A supplement to Vol. 34, 2008 of *Population and Development Review*. New York: Population Council.

Mason, Andrew, ed. 2001. *Population Change and Economic Development in East Asia: Challenges Met, Opportunities Seized.* Stanford: Stanford University Press.

Mason, Andrew. 2007. "Demographic Transition and Demographic Dividends in Developed and Developing Countries." In *United Nations Expert Group Meeting on Social and Economic Implications of Changing Population Age Structures, Mexico City, August 31-September 2, 2005*, edited by Department of Economic and Social Affairs, Population Division, United Nations, 81–101. New York: United Nations.

Mason, Andrew, and Ronald Lee. 2006. "Reform and Support Systems for the Elderly in Developing Countries: Capturing the Second Demographic Dividend." *GENUS* 62(2): 11–35.

McDonald, Peter. 2009. "Explanations of Low Fertility in East Asia: A Comparative Perspective." In *Ultra-low Fertility in Pacific Asia: Trends, Causes and Policy Issues*, edited by Gavin Jones, Paulin Tay Straughan, and Angelique Chan, 23–39. Abingdon: Routledge.

Ministry of the Interior, Republic of China (Taiwan). Date Unknown. "Statistical Yearbook of Interior." Accessed on August 5, 2011. http://sowf.moi.gov.tw/stat/year/elist.htm.

Myers, George C. 1988. "Demographic Aging and Family Support for Older Persons." Paper presented at the Expert Group Meeting on the Role of the Family in Care of the Elderly, Mexico City.

Ogawa, Naohiro. 2003. "Ageing Trends and Policy Responses in the ESCAP Region." *Population and Development: Selected Issues* (United Nations Economic and Social Commission for Asia and the Pacific Asian Population Studies Series 161): 89–127.

Ogawa, Naohiro. 2005. "Population Aging and Policy Options for a Sustainable Future: The Case of Japan." *GENUS* 61(3–4) (Proceedings of the International Conference: Trends and Problems of the World Population in the XXI Century: 50 Years Since Rome 1954, Rome, May 26-28, 2005, edited by Antonio Golini): 369–410.

Ogawa, Naohiro, Amonthep Chawla, and Rikiya Matsukura. 2010. "Changing Intergenerational Transfers in Aging Japan." In *Aging Asia: The Economic and Social Implications of Rapid Demographic Change in China, Japan, and South Korea*, edited by Karen Eggleston, and Shripad Tuljapurkar, 43–62. Baltimore: The Brookings Institution.

Ogawa, Naohiro, and Robert D. Retherford. 1997. "Shifting Costs of Caring for the Elderly back to Families in Japan." *Population and Development Review* 23(1): 59–94.

Statistics Bureau, Ministry of Internal Affairs and Communications, Japan. various years a. *Population Estimates*. Tokyo: Statistics Bureau, Ministry of Internal Affairs and Communications, Japan.

Statistics Bureau, Ministry of Internal Affairs and Communications, Japan. various years b. *Population Census of Japan*. Tokyo: Japan Statistical Association.

United Nations. 1987. "Global Trends and Prospects of the Age Structure of Population: Different Paths to Aging." In *Papers and Proceedings of the United Nations International Symposium on Population Structure and Development*. New York: United Nations.

United Nations. 2011. *World Population Prospects: The 2010 Revision*. New York: United Nations.

Yoshikawa, Hiroshi. 2002. *Japan's Lost Decade*. Tokyo: International House of Japan.

# CHAPTER 6

# HUMAN CAPITAL TRENDS IN THE PACIFIC RIM

ANNE GOUJON

## 6.1 Introduction

Overall human capital is of dramatic importance to economic and social development of a country (macro and societal level) as well as to the well-being of individuals (micro) as shown for instance in Lutz et al. (1998). The evolution of human capital is tightly entangled with demography. This statement is particularly true if we study human capital in the context of the demographic transition, a phenomenon that has been observed in all societies (with some exceptions to date in a few poor countries) by which a mortality decline is followed by a fertility decline, thus leading to rapid population growth during the transition period, as well as changes in the age structure (see, e.g., Goujon 2003). The fact that the population continues to grow for several years after childbearing rates have declined create a demographic bonus when both youth and old-age dependency ratios[1] are low and the adult, working-age population is very large and can enhance productivity. In fact, population change has been favorable to many countries in the Pacific Rim region and was one of the determining factors explaining the economic success of the miracle economies such as the four tigers—Hong Kong, Singapore, South Korea, and Taiwan (Mason 1997) and "second wave"[2] countries like Thailand, Malaysia, and Indonesia.

In the context of a demographic transition, human capital approximated here by the levels of educational attainment[3] of the population, especially of working age, plays a key role. It is at the same time an instrument and a consequence of the demographic transition. Education is instrumental in the sense that increases in the educational attainment of the population were proved to increase the pace of the demographic transition due to educational attainment's impact on components of demographic changes, especially death rates and birth rates (Lutz et al. 1998). The decline in fertility, whether caused or not by an increase in education, will induce further investments in education, as the decline is likely to stir a quality/quantity trade-off (Becker and Lewis 1973, Klemp and Weisdorf 2011), where parents invest substantially in the education of their children, an investment made possible by the decline in the number of births. In the miracle and second-wave countries, investments in human capital were particularly supported by governments whose commitment to education was steadfast and entailed the availability of a literate and educated workforce, notably of an adequate supply of qualified technicians and engineers for the development of the economy (Hobday 1995). The fact that education is the main ingredient in the formation of human capital provides important tracks for political action, since education is mostly driven by State investments. As a result of this, though not only for this reason, education and human resource development of the work force is believed by many to be the "central lever of economic growth" (Ashton and Green 1996, p. 1).

In the last phase of the demographic transition, as the bulged cohorts move in time, aging becomes the predominant demographic feature acutely pictured by two countries of the Pacific Rim: Japan and Russia. In that challenging stage, human capital is also key, with the potential of offsetting the potentially damaging consequences of increasing dependency ratios on economic growth and productivity, and increasing the competiveness of the country (Chawla et al. 2007). Mason et al. (2010, p. 50) note that "[investments in human capital and physical capital] . . . raise productivity and incomes far more significantly than declining support ratios diminish them."

As we will see in this chapter, a few decades ago, the Pacific Rim region used to be so polarized in terms of population and background characteristics such as levels of educational attainment that one would have had difficulties calling it a region. Just considering the three most populous countries in 2010, China, the United States, and Indonesia had little in common demographically 40 years ago besides their high density on the Pacific coast (Wong et al. 2006, Henriel and Plane 2006). In 1970, most countries along the Pacific Rim had the demographic and education characteristics of a developing country, with high fertility and low levels of educational attainment (other indicators of mortality, literacy, income, would lead to the same picture). As shown in Figure 6.1, in 1970, the level of fertility, measured here by the total fertility rate (TFR, a synthetic measure of average fertility) was very much correlated with the proportion of the population over 15 years of age with a high education (junior secondary and above), and Pacific Rim countries were spread across all possible stages of fertility and educational attainment. If we just consider the two extremes: Honduras with TFR above seven children per woman and only 10 percent of its population having at least achieved lower secondary education[4] (Vietnam's figures are very close) and at the other end of the spectrum Japan, already with below replacement fertility,[5] with a TFR of 2.07 children per woman and 90 percent of the population above 15 years of age having a junior secondary school education or more. In 2010, the fertility in most Pacific Rim countries is very low—half of the countries considered in the graph have a TFR below replacement level and two-thirds of those countries have a TFR below 2.5 children, meaning that those countries are reaching the end of the demographic transition with a large spectrum of education outcomes. For instance, Chile has a fertility rate of 1.8 children, with three-quarters

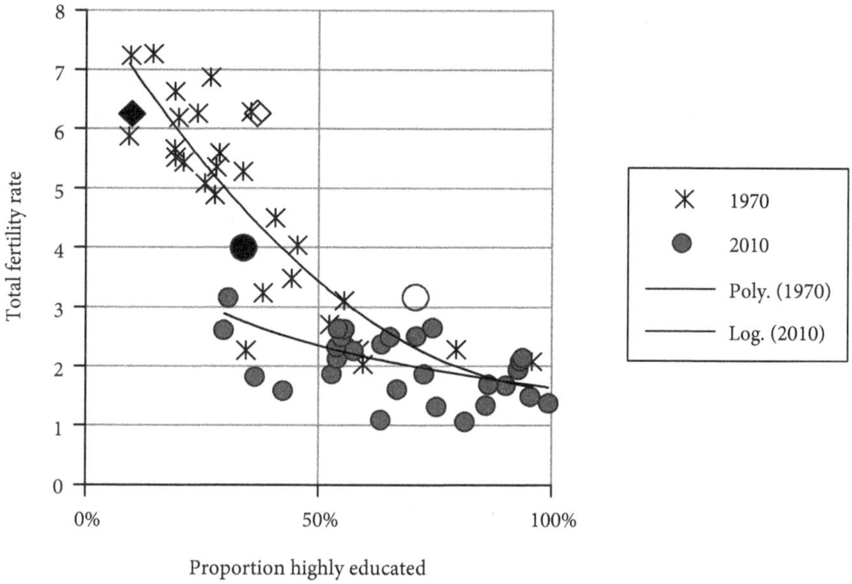


FIGURE 6.1 Proportion of the 15+ population with a high education and total fertility rate (TFR) in 1970 and 2010, Pacific Rim countries

*Source:* Lutz et al. 2007 and K.C. et al. 2010 for data on education and UN 2011 for data on TFR.

of its population with a a junior secondary school education or above, as opposed to Vietnam, with the same fertility rate but just one-third of the 15+ group being highly educated. Based on the Becker theory mentioned above, this would mean, among other things, that investments in education are likely to follow in the region.

This chapter will look in detail at progress made in terms of human capital from 1970 to 2010 in all countries where data is available on levels of educational attainment. Our approach will be gender-specific, since women have been catching up with men in this respect. We will also study human capital mobility and the particular issue of brain drain. In the last section, we will adopt a prospective point of view and see what the combination of demographic trends and increases of levels of educational attainment could mean for the Pacific Rim countries until the middle of the twenty-first century.

## 6.2 The Methodology

Most of the analysis developed in this chapter is based on an exercise of reconstruction and projection of levels of educational attainment by age and gender for 120 countries (Lutz et al. 2007, K.C. et al. 2010) that was conducted at the International Institute for Applied Systems Analysis, filling a gap in terms of consistent data within and across countries on levels of education and projections of human capital. This database is

**Table 6.1 Definition of Education Categories**

| No education | Primary education | Secondary education | Tertiary education |
|---|---|---|---|
| No formal education or less than one year of primary | Uncompleted primary, completed primary (ISCED 1), and uncompleted lower secondary | Completed lower/ junior secondary (ISCED 2), uncompleted and completed higher secondary (ISCED 3/4), and uncompleted tertiary education | Completed tertiary education (ISCED 5/6) |

*Source*: K.C. et al. 2010.

especially important since it contains the age structure of the population which, combined with education, gives substantial information on the characteristics of the labor force. The education categories that are used and their definition are shown in Table 6.1.

The analysis dealing with human capital in the countries of the Pacific Rim is based on 27 countries for which Lutz et al. (2007) found data for the analysis. Although this is relatively few compared to the 42 countries that have a border with the Pacific Ocean, actually these countries account for 99 percent of the 2010 population of the Pacific Rim region. Most of the countries for which data is missing are indeed small, little-populated islands and territories such as Nauru, Samoa, or Brunei. Two large countries are not in the sample of study because they do not have data on education, and these are North Korea and Papua New Guinea.

## 6.3 From the 1970s to 2010: Progress in Overall Levels of Educational Attainment

In 1970, more than one-fourth of the Pacific Rim population over 15 years of age had not received any education (see Figure 6.2). The situation was particularly acute—above 40 percent—in some countries in Latin America (El Salvador, Guatemala, and Honduras) but also in Asia, especially in Cambodia, China, Indonesia, Malaysia and Singapore. In a majority of countries, among the 15+ population, even if the individuals had been to school, they did not receive much beyond a primary education, as was the case in Cambodia, El Salvador, Guatemala, Honduras, Mexico, Thailand, and Vietnam, where more than 80 percent of the population over 15 years of age had not completed any lower secondary school graduation.

Figure 6.2 shows that by 2010, the region had been moving to higher levels of educational attainment so that only 5 percent have not received any education and 71 percent

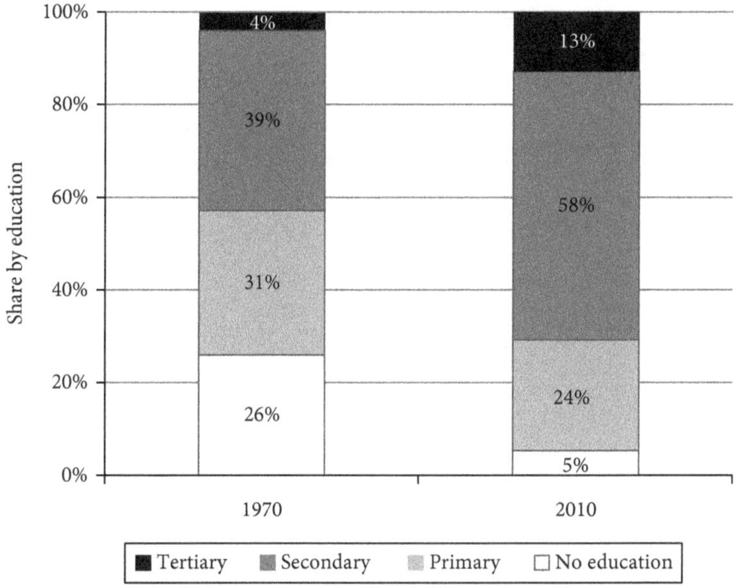


FIGURE 6.2 Share of population 15+ by levels of educational attainment, 1970 and 2010, Pacific Rim countries

*Source:* Adapted from Lutz et al. 2007 and K.C. et al. 2010.

have at least a secondary education, compared to 43 percent in 1970. Only a few countries have a high share of their population in the no-education group: Cambodia, El Salvador, Guatemala, Honduras, and Singapore. However, the mean age of that population with no education is quite high compared to the mean age of the population over 15 years of age who had received any education. For instance, in Singapore, those with no education have a mean age of 63 years, whereas the mean age of the population with a tertiary education was 38 years. Since education is acquired in younger ages, this means that the younger cohorts are benefiting from much higher levels of education compared to older cohorts that disappear slowly as the process of generation replacement proceeds. Figure 6.2 also shows that most improvements were achieved in bringing more children to secondary education and increasing the share of those with a tertiary education. Not surprisingly, the strongest increase toward higher levels of education occurred in the wealthier countries of Northern America and Asia (The United States, Canada, Japan, Australia, New Zealand, and the Russian Federation), where the population with a secondary education increased by more than 30 percent. This included a figure of almost 70 percent in Japan, and of more than 50 percent in the United States and the Russian Federation. As well, in those wealthy countries the population with a tertiary education increased by more than 15 percent (with large increases especially for the Russian federation and the United States). Obviously, these large populated countries are masking less impressive performances of other countries, especially those in Latin America (with the exception of Chile).

**Table 6.2 National Adult Literacy Rates (15+) and Youth Literacy Rates (15–24), 2000–2008 (Average Value)**

| Age | 15+ | | | 15-24 | | |
|---|---|---|---|---|---|---|
| Country | Total | Male | Female | Total | Male | Female |
| Brunei Darussalam | 93.4 | 95.6 | 91.2 | 99.2 | 99.3 | 99.3 |
| Cambodia | 74.9 | 84.8 | 66.3 | 84.7 | 88.7 | 82.2 |
| Chile | 96.7 | 96.7 | 96.7 | 99.0 | 99.0 | 99.2 |
| China | 92.3 | 95.9 | 88.5 | 99.1 | 99.3 | 98.9 |
| Colombia | 92.8 | 92.8 | 92.8 | 98.0 | 97.5 | 98.4 |
| Costa Rica | 95.4 | 95.2 | 95.6 | 97.9 | 97.4 | 98.3 |
| Ecuador | 87.6 | 89.8 | 87.0 | 95.9 | 95.8 | 96.1 |
| El Salvador | 83.2 | 86.2 | 80.7 | 94.8 | 94.3 | 95.3 |
| Guatemala | 70.7 | 76.8 | 66.0 | 83.5 | 87.4 | 81.0 |
| Honduras | 81.8 | 81.8 | 81.3 | 91.4 | 89.8 | 93.0 |
| Indonesia | 91.2 | 94.6 | 87.5 | 97.7 | 97.9 | 97.4 |
| Malaysia | 90.4 | 93.1 | 87.6 | 97.8 | 97.8 | 97.9 |
| Mexico | 91.6 | 93.3 | 90.0 | 97.7 | 97.8 | 97.6 |
| Nicaragua | 77.3 | 77.4 | 77.0 | 86.6 | 84.4 | 88.8 |
| Panama | 92.7 | 93.3 | 92.0 | 96.2 | 96.6 | 95.9 |
| Papua New Guinea | 58.5 | 63.5 | 53.3 | 66.6 | 66.9 | 66.3 |
| Peru | 88.5 | 94.1 | 82.9 | 97.2 | 98.1 | 96.4 |
| Philippines | 92.9 | 92.5 | 93.4 | 95.0 | 94.0 | 96.0 |
| Russian Federation | 99.5 | 99.7 | 99.3 | 99.7 | 99.6 | 99.8 |
| Samoa | 98.6 | 98.9 | 98.3 | 99.4 | 99.4 | 99.5 |
| Singapore | 93.5 | 97.0 | 90.1 | 99.7 | 99.6 | 99.7 |
| Solomon Islands | 76.6 | 83.7 | 69.0 | 85.0 | na | na |
| South Korea | 100.0 | 100.0 | 100.0 | 100.0 | 100.0 | 100.0 |
| Thailand | 93.2 | 95.4 | 91.0 | 98.0 | 98.2 | 97.9 |
| Tonga | 99.0 | 99.0 | 99.1 | 99.4 | 99.3 | 99.6 |
| Vanuatu | 79.2 | 81.1 | 77.9 | 92.6 | 92.9 | 92.8 |
| Viet Nam | 91.3 | 94.5 | 88.4 | 95.8 | 96.4 | 95.2 |

*Source*: UNESCO.

Most countries in the Pacific Rim have taken great strides toward eradicating illiteracy, and in the 2000s, this has almost been completed, as can be seen from Table 6.2. However, some pockets of illiteracy remain and are especially visible when looking at the illiteracy in the population 15–24, who, in ideal conditions, would have the possibility of enrolling in school and achieving literacy. In Cambodia, Guatemala, Nicaragua,

Papua New Guinea, and the Solomon Islands, the rates of illiteracy are still very high, above 15 percent of the 15–24 population. Interestingly, illiteracy in these particular countries affects men and women somewhat equally. The contrast is especially clear when looking at the gender differentials in illiteracy in the 15+ population where the gender bias was evident.

## 6.4 Women as the Major Achievers

Beside its sheer indicator of social imbalances within a population, gender inequality in education has been found to be a factor affecting economic growth and labor productivity (Klasen 2002, Knowles et al. 2002, Coulombe and Tremblay 2006) by lowering levels of human capital. The absence of a gender gap in the literacy levels of the developing countries in the Pacific Rim can be attributed to the huge improvements in the female level of educational attainment during the past 40 years. A lot of information can be gained from measuring the gap between men and women in terms of educational attainment, as shown in Figure 6.3. First of all there is a contrast between 1970, where women of working age were far behind men, to 2010, where one can measure the extent of the catching up that was achieved in terms of levels of intake and school life expectancy in primary education during that period. In 1970, if about one-fifth of the men in the region had not received any education, one-third of the women were deprived of any

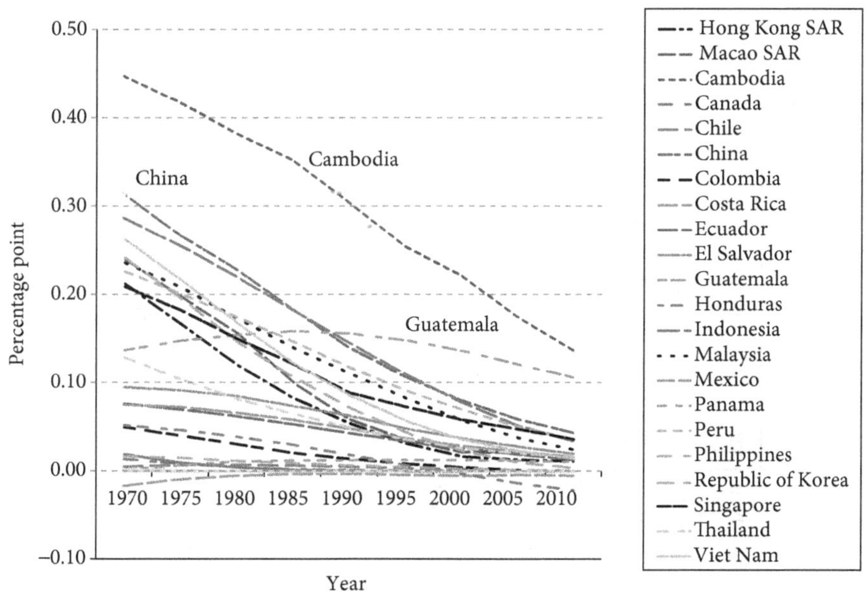


FIGURE 6.3 Gender gap in proportional terms with no education in population 20–64 (calculated as share of women minus share of men)

*Source:* Adapted from Lutz et al. 2007 and K.C. et al. 2010.

education. In 2010, even if women with no education were still twice more numerous than men with no education, nevertheless, the share of women with no education had fallen to 6 percent of the working-age population in 2010. This achievement concerns all countries of the Pacific Rim under study except for a few, especially Cambodia and Guatemala.

Progress was obvious at the level of lower secondary education: From 1995, there were more women with at least a lower secondary education than with a primary education or less—that particular threshold was already achieved in 1980 by men (in Figure 6.4). The increase was steep but went more or less in parallel for both sexes so that the gender gap was not removed. A closer look shows that in fact the gap was the largest in 1985 and has been declining, slowly, ever since. The difference in 2010 is about 7 percent points. There again, the situation varies quite strongly between countries as can be seen from Figure 6.5a. The share of women with a lower secondary education and above is almost universal (above 80 percent) for half of the women in the Pacific Rim, mostly living in OECD countries. Actually only 3 percent of all women in the region lives in a country where the majority of women have less than a secondary education, and that in a mix of Central American and Southeast Asian countries.

If progress was evident at the secondary level, it is less the case at the tertiary level, but surprisingly there, the women were able to close the gap with men, as the proportion in 2010 is 15 percent for both the male and female working-age population, increasing respectively from 7 percent and 4 percent in 1970. The absence of a gender gap at the

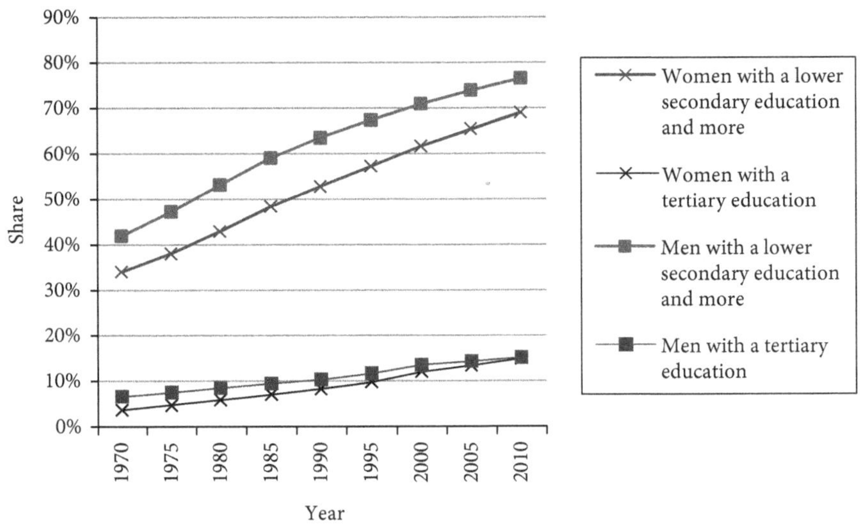


FIGURE 6.4 Proportion in the Pacific Rim of men and women aged 20–64 with a lower secondary education and more and with a tertiary education, 1970–2010

*Source:* Calculated from Lutz et al. 2007 and K.C. et al. 2010.

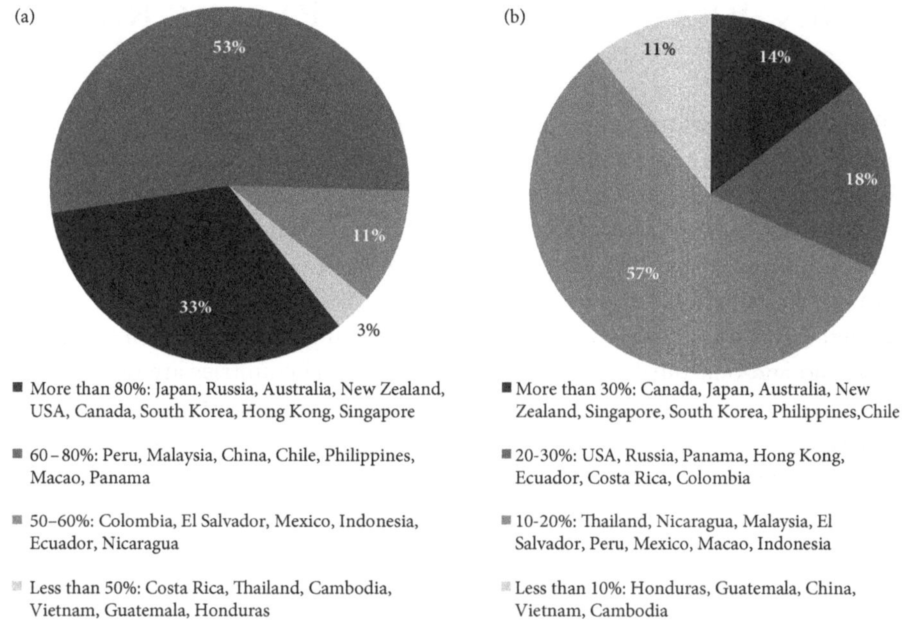


FIGURE 6.5 Pacific Rim country mapping of the proportion in 2010 of women in the 20–64 population with a lower secondary education and more (a), and with a tertiary education (b).

tertiary level is an indication that the bottleneck that handicaps girls rather than boys in their access to education is at the lower level and particularly at the primary level. The heterogeneity among countries is even more obvious at that level of attainment, as can be seen from Figure 6.5b, where women with a tertiary education were actually representing more than 30 percent of the working-age population in 2010. In six out of those eight countries, the percentage of women with a tertiary education is actually higher than that of men. For example, in Canada, 45 percent of women have a tertiary education compared to 38 percent of men. The United States and Russia are not in the high performer group and have a proportion of women with a tertiary education below 30 percent, although, as observed before, women there are more numerous. The reverse gender gap observed in many countries of the Pacific Rim is not a unique phenomenon, as it is occurring through much of the industrialized world. A study of the United States (Diprete and Buchmann 2006) shows that between 1964 and 2002, women experienced greater returns to higher education than men, not only in the labor market but also in the form of "a higher probability of marriage, a higher standard of living, and insurance against poverty" (p. 18). It does not seem to be the case in countries where tertiary education is not well spread but there again the gap is surprisingly not very large, less than 3 percent points.

## 6.5 Brain Drain in the Pacific Rim

The Pacific Rim has witnessed increased migration since the 1970s. Actually migration intensified the vitality of existing linkages between various Pacific countries, or was instrumental in creating new ones (Watters and McGee 1997). It is also one of the most affected regions by the brain drain, particularly small islands such as Samoa, Tonga, Nauru, and Tuvalu, as well as some Central American countries, such as El Salvador (Docquier and Marfouk 2006). The population originating from the Pacific Rim accounted for one-fourth (11 million) of the stock of migrants residing in OECD countries in 1990 and one-third (20 million) in 2000; OECD countries are receiving about 90 percent of the worldwide educated migration. Immigration to non-OECD countries is expected to be low, but there are a few exceptions of major receiver countries such as Hong Kong and Singapore, where about 17 percent of immigrants were tertiary educated. Most Pacific OECD countries are both major migration recipients and senders, since the eight Pacific Rim countries that are members of the OECD[6] made up for 18 percent of all immigrants to other OECD countries. As receiving countries, Australia, New Zealand, Canada, and the United States started implementing since the early 1990s "quality selective" immigration policies. This is clearly visible when looking at levels of educational attainment of the stocks of immigrants coming from Pacific Rim countries whose likelihood to be highly educated (with a post-secondary education) is three times higher than for other countries—38 percent compared to 11 percent for all world countries. It reflects as well the higher levels of education in the region compared to other sending countries.

Appendix Table A.1 shows that in 2000 migration represented a substantial share of the work force in a few small countries, for example, 46 percent in Samoa and Tonga, but also 21 percent in Fiji. The brain drain, considering the proportion of emigrants with a tertiary education, is substantial in those islands—Samoa, Tuvalu, Nauru, Tonga, Fiji, and Papua New Guinea—where more than two-thirds of the highly educated group was working abroad. The figures are less dramatic for the Pacific Americas, but one-fourth of the tertiary educated population, looking for better opportunites, is working outside of El Salvador, Honduras, Guatemala. Empirical studies of the brain drain have shown that the impacts on the country of origin are not necessarily negative, as it does not necessarily imply a loss of welfare (e.g., Government of Fiji 2002) and can also operate as an engine of development through remittances used for physical capital and human capital investments, that together with education help as a multiplier for human capital. Some researchers see the brain drain as a transitory stage, when the more educated do not find an outlet for their education until the country develops further (with the reinforcing effect of the remittances) and the economy can accommodate and utilize a larger share of the tertiary education. The theory unfortunately does not tell how long this transitory period can be. Some countries have, however, already witnessed a reversal of the brain drain, as shown by Simon (1995) in the case of Taiwan, South Korea, and Singapore.

## 6.6 The Future of Human Capital in the Region

Education has a large momentum, and whenever a country does not invest sufficiently in education, this lack of investment will show for a life time. Let us imagine a country where in 2011, the government fails to enroll in public schools 30 percent of all six-year-old children. If this cohort of six-year-olds does not manage to enroll in school in the following years, it will stay uneducated and 30 to 50 years later the labor force will still be plagued by this cohort of uneducated men and women. The difference between this example and the real world is that usually governments do not "forget" to ensure that all children enroll in primary education and the subsequent levels just for one year but for decades. This means that the size of cohorts suffering from a lack of education can be very large and dominate the labor force, with no hope of being curtailed except with costly adult educational programs such as adult literacy campaigns that can be successful but are cumbersome and cannot be exhaustive in terms of population covered. Multistate population projections by levels of educational attainment are very useful to see the momentum of education diffusion. In this section, we show results of the projections for most Pacific Rim countries conducted by K.C. et al. (2010) according to a Global Education Trend scenario, that "assumes that a country's educational expansion will converge on an expansion trajectory based on the historical global trend" (K.C. et al. 2010, p. 407).

Past neglects in education, showing large segments of the population with no education—above 10 percent—are especially visible in three Pacific Rim countries: Guatemala, Honduras, and Cambodia, where more than 10 percent of the working-age population have never been to school in 2010. Projected shares of the population with no education in those countries will remain above the 10 percent threshold until 2025-2035, even by implementing a scenario of strong convergence to high levels of education. The bottleneck is often at the level of intake to primary school, meaning that for those who have managed to enter school, the way to the upper levels of the education system are easier; this can be seen by the substantive percentage of the population with a secondary education or even a tertiary education (Table 6.3).

Patterns of education diffusion can be observed in the context of global demographic change. Figures 6.6 to 6.8 show three main patterns of demographic bonuses in the Pacific Rim region. In most central and Latin American countries (Figure 6.6), the fertility transition occurred somewhat late and rather slowly, so that the dependency ratios were still quite high in the last decades. In these countries, a group that also includes Malaysia, Philippines, and Cambodia, the dependency ratios that have steadily declined since the 1990s will reach their lowest level in the 2040s. The next group of countries shown in Figure 6.7 are countries where dependency ratios have already reached their lowest level (or will shortly like in Indonesia and Costa Rica) and will start increasing due to aging of the population, but the pace of the increase will be quite slow so that by 2070, the total

**Table 6.3 Share of the 2050 Population by Levels of Education, Global Education Trend scenario (GET)**

| Change in dependency ratios | Countries | No education | Primary education | Secondary education | Tertiary education |
|---|---|---|---|---|---|
| **Countries with rapid increase in dependency ratios** | **China** | 0.2 | 6.9 | 75.1 | 17.9 |
| | **Hong Kong** | 0 | 10.5 | 51.7 | 37.8 |
| | **Japan** | 0 | 0 | 34.9 | 65.1 |
| | **Macao** | 0 | 13.9 | 56.1 | 30 |
| | **Russia** | 0 | 0.5 | 55.6 | 43.9 |
| | **Singapore** | 0.1 | 6 | 35.4 | 58.5 |
| | **South Korea** | 0 | 0 | 38.9 | 61.1 |
| | **Australia** | 0 | 0 | 56.4 | 43.6 |
| **Countries with slow increase in dependency ratios** | **Canada** | 0 | 3.5 | 46.2 | 50.4 |
| | **Chile** | 0.1 | 6.2 | 41.2 | 52.5 |
| | **Costa Rica** | 0.4 | 19.9 | 43.2 | 36.5 |
| | **Indonesia** | 0.1 | 15.1 | 62.1 | 22.6 |
| | **New Zealand** | 0 | 0 | 56.9 | 43.1 |
| | **Thailand** | 0.5 | 17.8 | 42.6 | 39.1 |
| | **United States** | 0 | 5.2 | 52.9 | 41.9 |
| | **Viet Nam** | 1.4 | 33 | 50.7 | 14.9 |
| **Late transition countries** | **Cambodia** | 4.9 | 34 | 55.4 | 5.6 |
| | **Colombia** | 0.2 | 10.5 | 52.8 | 36.5 |
| | **Ecuador** | 0.5 | 17.3 | 41.8 | 40.4 |
| | **El Salvador** | 1.1 | 12.8 | 53.8 | 32.4 |
| | **Guatemala** | 5 | 27.8 | 48.7 | 18.5 |
| | **Honduras** | 3.6 | 36.6 | 42 | 17.8 |
| | **Malaysia** | 0.4 | 4.4 | 57.9 | 37.3 |
| | **Mexico** | 0.5 | 15.7 | 52.8 | 30.9 |
| | **Nicaragua** | 0 | 18.8 | 49.6 | 31.6 |
| | **Panama** | 0.6 | 11.5 | 47.3 | 40.6 |
| | **Peru** | 0.1 | 8.5 | 61.2 | 30.1 |
| | **Philippines** | 0.2 | 8.2 | 43.4 | 48.2 |

*Source*: Based on K.C. et al. 2010.

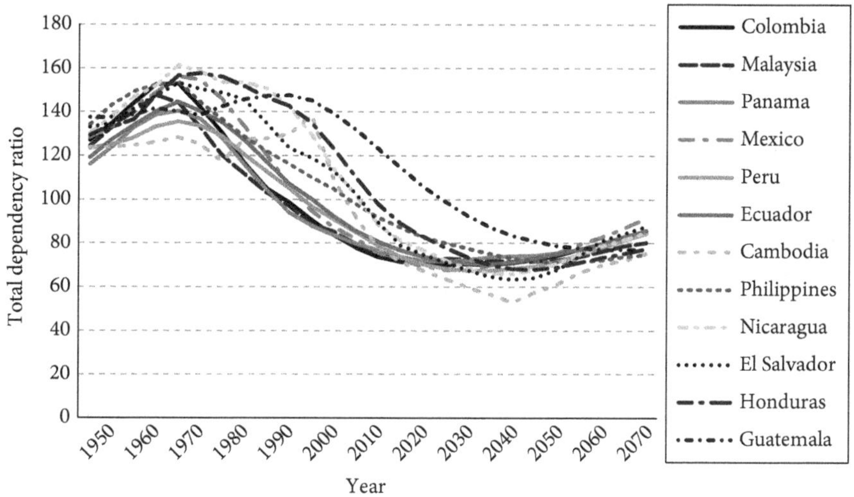


FIGURE 6.6 Total dependency ratios (ratio of population 0–19 and 65+ per 100 population), 1950–2070, *Late transition countries*

*Source*: United Nations (2011).

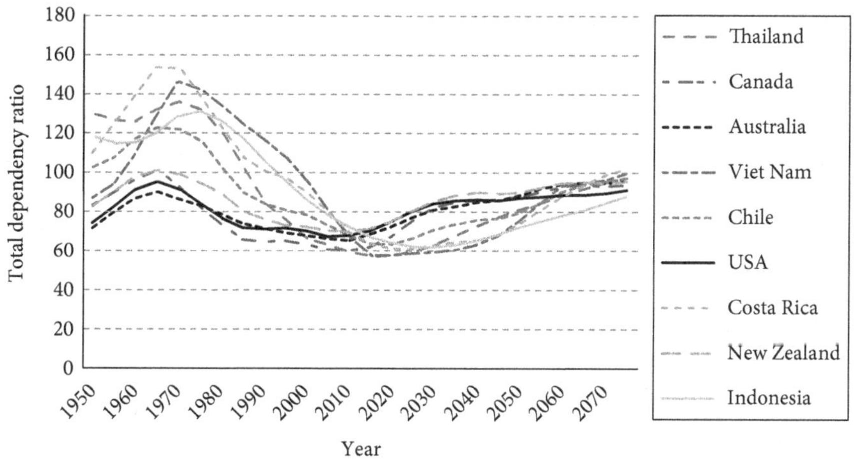


FIGURE 6.7 Total dependency ratios (ratio of population 0–19 and 65+ per 100 population), 1950–2070, *countries with slow increase in dependency ratios*

*Source:* United Nations (2011).

dependency ratio will still be below 100—meaning that for each active person, there is less than one (young and old) unproductive person. This group includes most of the Pacific OECD countries. In the last group shown on Figure 6.8, the countries including China and the Russian Federation also reach their lowest level of dependency ratio in 2010–2015, however those will increase rapidly thereafter so that by mid-century, those countries will have to deal with higher dependency ratios than the countries shown in Figure 6.7.

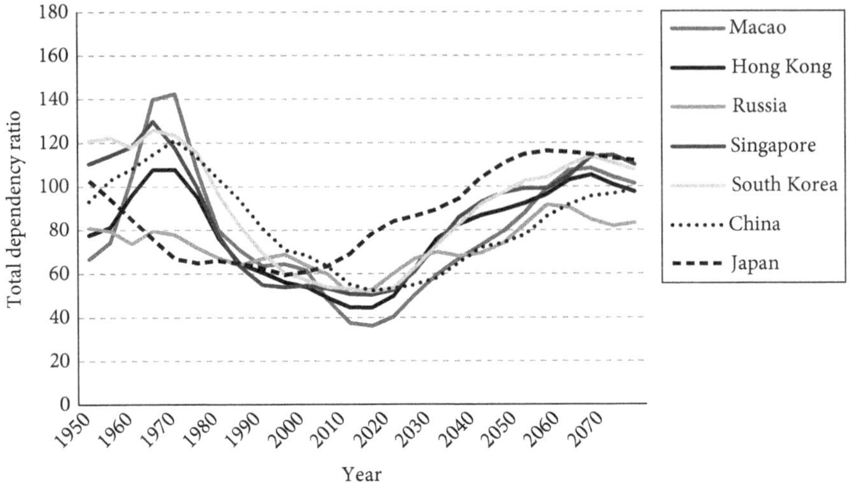


FIGURE 6.8 Total dependency ratios (ratio of population 0–19 and 65+ per 100 population), *countries with rapid increase in dependency ratios*

*Source:* United Nations (2011).

Countries experiencing an increase in the working-age population implied by the low dependency ratios will need one main demographic factor[7] to transform the bonus into a demographic and economic window of opportunity, that is an increase in the levels of educational attainment of the working-age population: this will also be a means to increase the female labor force participation by reducing gender gaps in education. Projections of educational attainment show that the gains in education of the working-age population will be quite substantial in those countries if they follow the global trend scenario. In 2050, the proportion of the population with no education would be reduced to zero in most countries. Only in Cambodia, Guatemala, and Honduras would the share of uneducated people somehow still be visible. In those three countries, this would still be linked to a large share, close to one-third of the working population with a primary education or less (this is also the case in Vietnam). However, even in those countries with pockets of low education, there will still be a large population with at least a lower secondary education.

Table 6.3 shows a quite uniformed distribution of the Pacific Rim countries' population according to lower secondary education or more. It is at the level of tertiary education that most differentials are found among the countries where the scenario has been implemented. The countries that will be experiencing rapid aging in the near future can rely on a very highly educated working-age population, e.g., around 60 percent in Singapore and South Korea, which would in principle have a positive impact on the country's level of innovation (see, for example, Dakhli and De Clercq 2004). The exception in this group is China, where the proportion with a university degree would still be below 20 percent in 2050. However the projection for China is based on the educational distribution in the 1990s, and the country has since then taken great strides in increasing participation in upper education levels of education. The next group of countries where the demographic bonus will last another few years is heterogeneous, with the Pacific OECD countries having a substantial share of the working-age population with a tertiary education, while the share will be much lower in Vietnam and Indonesia. The countries that will be experiencing long periods of declining dependency ratios in the last group, while pursuing an increase in the proportion of people acquiring a higher education, could benefit economically from a demographic bonus. These are especially located in Latin and Central America, in countries such as Colombia, Panama, Ecuador, and also the Philippines fall into this group. The progress in other countries as observed now would be too slow to reach sufficient levels of tertiary education to boost economic growth, like in Honduras, Guatemala, and Cambodia. It is worth noting that in all countries there will be more women with a tertiary education compared to men. This is particularly evident in Thailand, Panama, Philippines, Russia, and Australia, where the share of women in the labor force with a tertiary education would be at least 10 percentage points higher than that of men.

## 6.7 Conclusion

The study of past, present, and future human capital trends, presented in this chapter in terms of levels of educational attainment, shows several snapshots of Pacific Rim countries and of, with a few exceptions, the great efforts taken in increasing levels of educational attainment of the population. This has been key for the adoption of a strong human capital approach for development—including human development—and economic growth exemplified by the Asian miracle economies. It will become even more important in the context of aging. In Pacific Rim countries, men and women are converging in terms of qualifications, and women will increase their share of human capital, especially those who, in many countries, are on the verge of surpassing men in their level of higher education.

**Table A1 Migration Rates, in Percent of Total Population by Education and Sex, in Countries of Origin**

| | | Both sexes | | | Male | | | Female | | |
|---|---|---|---|---|---|---|---|---|---|---|
| Country of origin | Total | Primary | Secondary | Tertiary | Primary | Secondary | Tertiary | Primary | Secondary | Tertiary |
| Australia | 2 | 1 | 1 | 3 | 1 | 1 | 2 | 1 | 1 | 3 |
| Brunei | 3 | 1 | 8 | 15 | 1 | 6 | 14 | 1 | 10 | 16 |
| Cambodia | 4 | 3 | 5 | 21 | 3 | 5 | 27 | 3 | 6 | 17 |
| Canada | 4 | 7 | 2 | 5 | 6 | 2 | 5 | 8 | 3 | 5 |
| Chile | 2 | 1 | 2 | 6 | 1 | 2 | 6 | 1 | 2 | 6 |
| China | 0 | 0 | 0 | 4 | 0 | 0 | 3 | 0 | 0 | 7 |
| Colombia | 3 | 1 | 4 | 10 | 1 | 4 | 9 | 1 | 4 | 12 |
| Costa Rica | 3 | 1 | 6 | 7 | 1 | 6 | 6 | 1 | 6 | 9 |
| Ecuador | 7 | 4 | 12 | 10 | 4 | 13 | 8 | 4 | 12 | 11 |
| El Salvador | 20 | 16 | 33 | 32 | 16 | 38 | 31 | 15 | 30 | 32 |
| Fiji | 21 | 12 | 15 | 63 | 10 | 14 | 57 | 13 | 16 | 70 |
| Guatemala | 9 | 7 | 14 | 24 | 7 | 15 | 20 | 6 | 13 | 31 |
| Honduras | 8 | 5 | 15 | 25 | 5 | 16 | 19 | 5 | 15 | 32 |
| Indonesia | 0 | 0 | 1 | 3 | 0 | 0 | 2 | 0 | 1 | 4 |
| Japan | 0 | 0 | 0 | 1 | 0 | 0 | 1 | 0 | 0 | 2 |
| Malaysia | 2 | 1 | 1 | 11 | 1 | 1 | 9 | 1 | 1 | 13 |
| Marshall Iss. | 10 | 4 | 9 | 43 | 4 | 7 | 38 | 5 | 12 | 49 |
| Mexico | 12 | 14 | 7 | 15 | 16 | 8 | 14 | 12 | 6 | 17 |

| | | | | | | | | | | |
|---|---|---|---|---|---|---|---|---|---|---|
| Nauru | 7 | 2 | 26 | 72 | 1 | 20 | 62 | 2 | 36 | 84 |
| New Zealand | 13 | 9 | 9 | 22 | 9 | 10 | 22 | 8 | 9 | 22 |
| Nicaragua | 9 | 5 | 12 | 30 | 4 | 15 | 29 | 5 | 11 | 32 |
| Korea | 4 | 3 | 2 | 8 | 4 | 2 | 6 | 3 | 3 | 11 |
| Palau | 8 | 1 | 21 | 81 | 0 | 6 | 72 | 2 | 41 | 90 |
| Panama | 6 | 2 | 5 | 17 | 1 | 4 | 15 | 3 | 6 | 18 |
| Papua N. G. | 1 | 0 | 4 | 28 | 0 | 3 | 20 | 0 | 7 | 43 |
| Peru | 3 | 1 | 3 | 6 | 1 | 3 | 5 | 1 | 4 | 7 |
| Philippines | 5 | 2 | 3 | 14 | 1 | 2 | 12 | 2 | 4 | 15 |
| Russia | 1 | 1 | 0 | 1 | 1 | 0 | 1 | 0 | 0 | 2 |
| Samoa | 46 | 41 | 42 | 73 | 40 | 41 | 67 | 41 | 44 | 80 |
| Singapore | 3 | 1 | 2 | 14 | 1 | 2 | 12 | 1 | 2 | 17 |
| Solomon Iss. | 1 | 0 | 3 | 26 | 0 | 2 | 19 | 0 | 6 | 40 |
| Taiwan | 3 | 1 | 1 | 13 | 1 | 1 | 11 | 1 | 2 | 14 |
| Thailand | 1 | 0 | 1 | 2 | 0 | 1 | 1 | 0 | 2 | 3 |
| Tonga | 46 | 39 | 42 | 76 | 40 | 43 | 71 | 38 | 41 | 81 |
| Tuvalu | 13 | 10 | 28 | 65 | 8 | 23 | 59 | 12 | 36 | 74 |
| United States | 0 | 1 | 0 | 0 | 1 | 0 | 0 | 1 | 0 | 0 |
| Vanuatu | 1 | 1 | 1 | 8 | 1 | 1 | 6 | 1 | 1 | 12 |
| Vietnam | 3 | 2 | 5 | 27 | 2 | 4 | 31 | 2 | 6 | 24 |

*Source*: Extracted from the database and Docquier et al. (2009) [http://perso.uclouvain.be/frederic.docquier/filePDF/DataSetByGender_Aggregates.xls] [available on September 15, 2011].

## Notes

1. The dependency ratio represents the ratio of the population who is not in the labor force and who is dependent on the productive population in the labor force (the productive part). It is usually approximated by the population in age group 0-19 and 65+ on population aged 20-64.
2. This expression was used by McNicoll (2006).
3. As emphasized by Becker (1975), education and training, resulting in individual skills, are the most important investments in human capital, which also include expenditures in health (medical care). According to Becker, human capital is what cannot be separated from the people as opposed to "financial and physical assets," hence it also includes values such as honesty and punctuality.
4. Lower secondary education is equivalent to the completion of junior secondary education. Both terminologies are used in the chapter.
5. Replacement fertility is the fertility necessary for couples to replace themselves. In a world without mortality and equal birth ratios between boys and girls, replacement fertility level would be 2.0. Because of child and adult (especially maternal mortality), replacement fertility is approximately 2.1 children per women in developed countries, and is much higher in developing settings.
6. The eight OECD countries of the Pacific Rim are: Australia, Canada, Chile, Japan, Mexico, New Zealand, South Korea, and the United States.
7. Other factors are of course at play beyond demography such as "high and increasing rates of savings and investments" (Mason 1997, p. 4).

## References


Ashton, David and Francis Green (1996). *Education, training, and the global economy*, Cambridge University Press.

Becker, Gary S. (1975). *Human Capital: A Theoretical and Empirical Analysis, with Special Reference to Education, 2nd ed.* New York: Columbia University Press for NBER.

Becker, Gary S., and H. G. Lewis (1973). On the Interaction between the Quantity and Quality of Children, *Journal of Political Economy* 81: 279–S288.

Chawla, Mukesh, Gordon Betcherman, Arup Banerji (2007). *From Red to Gray: The "Third Transition" of Aging populations in Eastern Europe and the former Soviet Union*, Washington DC: The World Bank.

Coulombe, Serge, and Jean-François Tremblay (2006). Literacy and growth, *Topics in macroeconomics* 6(2), article 4: 1–32.

Dakhli, Mourad and Dirk De Clercq (2004) Human capital, social capital, and innovation: a multicountry study, *Entrepreneurship & Regional Development* 16: 107–128.

DiPrete, Thomas A. and Claudia Buchmann (2006) Gender-specific trends in the value of education and the emerging gender gap in college completion, *Demography* 43(1): 1–24.

Docquier, Frédéric, and Abdesalam Marfouk (2006). International migration by educational attainment (1990-2000)—Release 1.1. In C. Ozden and M. Schiff (eds), *International Migration, Remittances and Development* (pp. 151–199), New York: Palgrave Macmillan.

Docquier, Frédéric, B. Lindsay Lowell, and Abdeslam Marfouk (2009). A Gendered Assessment of Highly Skilled Emigration, *Population and Development Review* 35(2): 297–321.

Goujon, Anne (2003). Demographic Transition and Education in Developing Countries. In Sustainable Human Development, ed. Ismail Sirageldin, in *Encyclopedia of Life Support Systems (EOLSS)*, Developed under the Auspices of the UNESCO. Oxford, UK: Eolss Publishers. www.eolss.net.

Government of Fiji (2002) Impact of brain drain in Fiji. *RBF Quarterly Review (December 2002)*: 40–45.

Henrie1, Christopher J., and David A. Plane (2006). Decentralization of the Nation's Main Street: New Coastal-Proximity-Based Portrayals of Population Distribution in the United States, 1950–2000, *The Professional Geographer* 58(4): 448–459.

Hobday, Mike (1995). Innovation in East Asia: diversity and development, *Technovation* 15 (2): 55–63.

K. C., Samir, Bilal Barakat, Anne Goujon, Vegard Skirbekk, Warren C. Sanderson, and Wolfgang Lutz (2010). Projection of populations by level of educational attainment, age, and sex for 120 countries for 2005–2050, *Demographic Research* 22(15): 383–472.

Klasen, Stephan (2002) Low Schooling for Girls, Slower Growth for All? Cross-Country Evidence on the Effect of Gender Inequality in Education on Economic Development, *World Bank Economic Review* 16(3): 345–373.

Klemp, Marc, and Jacob Weisdorf (2011). The Child Quantity-Quality Trade-Off During the Industrial Revolution in England, *Discussion Papers 11-16*, University of Copenhagen. Department of Economics.

Knowles, Stephan, Paula K. Lorgelly, and P. Dorian Owen (2002). Are educational gender gaps a brake on economic development? Some cross-country empirical evidence, *Oxford Economic Papers* 54: 118–149.

Lutz, Wolfgang, Anne Goujon, and Gabriele Doblhammer-Reiter (1998). Demographic Dimensions in Forecasting: Adding Education to Age and Sex, *Population Development Review* 24: 42–58.

Lutz, Wolfgang, Anne Goujon, Samir K.C., and Warren Sanderson (2007). Reconstruction of population by age, sex and level of educational attainment of 120 countries for 1970-2000, *Vienna Yearbook of Population Research* vol. 2007: 193–235.

Mason, Andrew (1997) Will population change sustain the "Asian economic miracle"?, *Analysis from the East-West Center* 33 (October 1997). http://scholarspace.manoa.hawaii.edu/bitstream/handle/10125/3838/api033.pdf?sequence=1.

Mason, Andrew, Ronald Lee, and Sang-Hyop Lee (2010). The Demographic Transition and Economic Growth in the Pacific Rim. Ito, Takatoshi and Andrew Rose (Eds) *The Economic Consequences of Demographic Change in East Asia*, NBER-EASE Volume 19, 19–55. University of Chicago Press, Chicago.

McNicoll, Geoffrey (2006). Policy lessons of the East Asian Demographic Transition, *Policy research Division Working Papers No. 210*, Population Council, New York.

Simon, Denis Fred (1995). *The Emerging technological trajectory of the Pacific Rim*, Armonk, NY: M.E. Sharpe, Inc ("An East Gate Book").

United Nations, Department of Economic and Social Affairs, Population Division (2011) *World Population Prospects: The 2010 Revision*, CD-ROM Edition.

Watters, Ray F., and Terence G. McGee (eds.) (1997). *Asia-Pacific: new geographies of the Pacific Rim*, Wellington: Victoria University Press.

Wong, Poh Poh, Lee Boon-Thong, and Maggi W.H. Leung (2006) Hot Spots of Population Growth and Urbanisation in the Asia-Pacific Coastal Region, *Coastal Systems and Continental Margins* 10: 163–195.

# PART III

# PERSPECTIVES ON ECONOMIC GROWTH AND DEVELOPMENT

CHAPTER 7

# ECONOMIC GROWTH AND PERFORMANCE ON THE PACIFIC RIM

BARRY BOSWORTH AND SUSAN M. COLLINS

THE Pacific Rim encompasses a very diverse set of countries both economically and culturally.[1] In this paper, we explore key dimensions of its economic growth over the past half century. Our focus is on 24 countries that represent the large population centers, an overwhelming proportion of the area's economic activity, and have reasonably complete national accounts—enabling us to compare growth performances since 1960.[2] For much of the analysis, we combine the countries along the Pacific Rim into three groupings: Pacific Asia, Pacific Latin America (comprised of eight and eleven emerging market economies respectively), and the five high-income economies. For convenience, we often refer to these groupings as "regions."

Table 7.1 shows levels of GDP per capita at intervals from 1960 to 2008. While the high-income economies have reasonably similar living standards, the differences within emerging Pacific Asia are very large and have not narrowed appreciably over time. The Latin American countries all had similar standards of living in 1960, but have grown somewhat more diverse over time.

Regional differences are highlighted in Figure 7.1. In 1960, incomes in East Asia averaged less that 5 percent of incomes in the high-income countries. Even though Pacific Asia has sustained very high growth for nearly half a century, its average income is still only about 15 percent of that for the high-income group. In fact, because of the large differences in initial levels of income, the *absolute* differences in incomes between the high-income economies and emerging Asia have continued to grow.[3] These comparisons are of course greatly influenced by the inclusion of China because of its overwhelming size; but even if China is excluded, average income in Pacific Asia is still only about 20 percent of that in the high-income group.

The Latin American countries have had a very different experience. They began at much higher relative incomes in 1960, but have actually fallen further behind in both

**Table 7.1 GDP per Capita for Pacific Asia, Pacific Latin America, and Pacific High-Income Countries**

*'000 of PPP Constant 2005 International $*

| | Share of Regional GDP | 1960 | 1980 | 1990 | 2000 | 2008 |
|---|---|---|---|---|---|---|
| **Pacific High-Income** | **100** | **12.4** | **22.7** | **29.5** | **35.5** | **39.1** |
| Australia | 3 | 12.9 | 20.0 | 24.0 | 29.8 | 34.5 |
| Canada | 6 | 12.9 | 23.1 | 26.9 | 32.4 | 35.9 |
| Japan | 22 | 5.5 | 17.6 | 26.1 | 28.6 | 31.3 |
| New Zealand | 1 | 13.5 | 17.2 | 18.9 | 22.4 | 25.1 |
| United States | 68 | 15.9 | 25.5 | 31.9 | 39.6 | 43.3 |
| **Pacific Asia** | **100** | **0.5** | **1.1** | **1.9** | **3.7** | **6.4** |
| **Pacific Asia excluding China** | **46** | **1.1** | **2.8** | **4.4** | **6.5** | **8.4** |
| China | 54 | 0.3 | 0.5 | 1.1 | 2.7 | 5.7 |
| Indonesia | 9 | 0.7 | 1.4 | 2.1 | 2.7 | 3.7 |
| Korea | 14 | 1.6 | 5.5 | 11.4 | 18.7 | 25.5 |
| Malaysia | 4 | 2.1 | 4.9 | 6.6 | 10.3 | 13.2 |
| Philippines | 3 | 1.6 | 2.6 | 2.4 | 2.6 | 3.2 |
| Singapore | 2 | 3.6 | 14.5 | 23.4 | 36.8 | 48.0 |
| Taiwan | 8 | 1.8 | 7.0 | 13.2 | 22.8 | 28.6 |
| Thailand | 6 | 0.9 | 2.2 | 4.0 | 5.6 | 7.5 |
| **Pacific Latin America** | **100** | **4.2** | **7.5** | **7.3** | **8.7** | **10.3** |
| Chile | 8 | 4.0 | 5.4 | 6.6 | 10.5 | 13.4 |
| Colombia | 13 | 3.1 | 5.3 | 6.1 | 6.6 | 8.2 |
| Costa Rica | 2 | 3.6 | 6.4 | 6.2 | 8.1 | 10.4 |
| Ecuador | 3 | 3.5 | 5.8 | 5.5 | 5.5 | 7.6 |
| El Salvador | 2 | 3.4 | 4.4 | 3.7 | 5.2 | 6.3 |
| Guatemala | 2 | 2.2 | 3.9 | 3.3 | 4.0 | 4.4 |
| Honduras | 1 | 1.9 | 2.8 | 2.7 | 2.9 | 3.6 |
| Mexico | 60 | 5.2 | 10.4 | 10.1 | 12.1 | 13.4 |
| Nicaragua | 1 | 2.5 | 2.7 | 1.9 | 2.1 | 2.6 |
| Panama | 1 | 3.5 | 6.6 | 6.1 | 8.1 | 11.8 |
| Peru | 7 | 4.4 | 6.1 | 4.5 | 5.5 | 7.9 |

*Source*: World Development Indicators and authors' calculations. Regional GDP shares based on values for 2000.

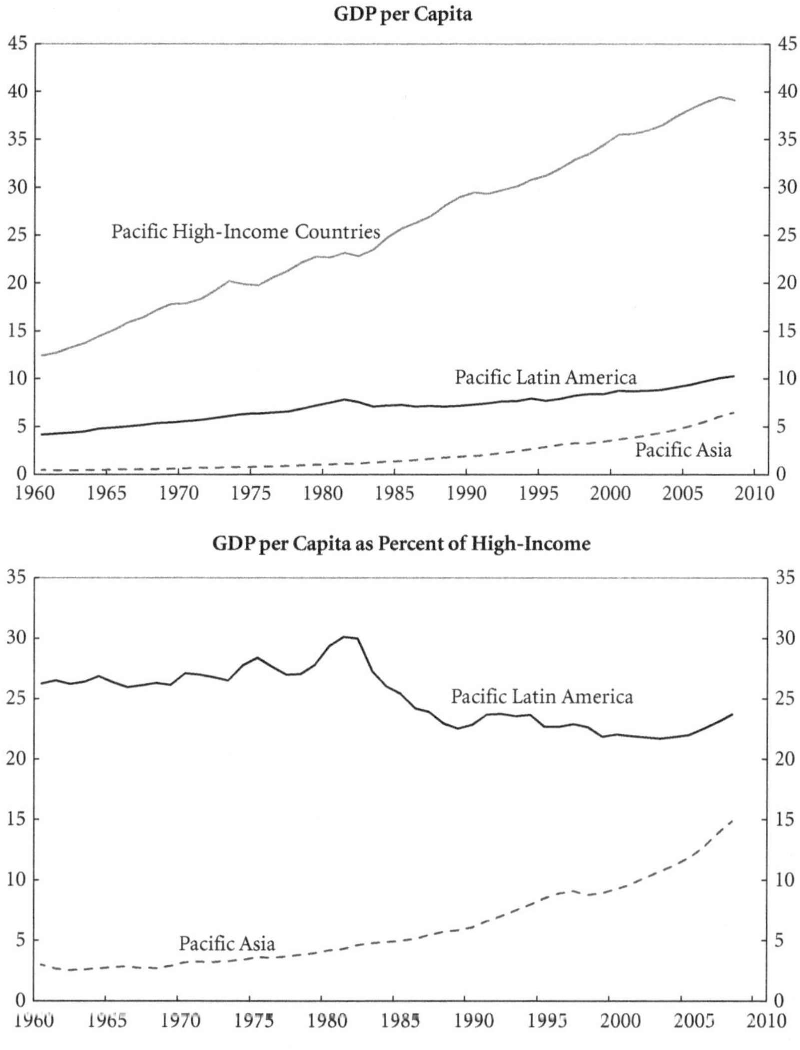


FIGURE 7.1 GDP per Capita, by Major Region, 1960–2008

Thousands of 2005 International $ (PPP)

*Source: World Development Indicators* and authors' calculations.

relative and absolute terms. As shown in the lower panel of Figure 7.1, they reached an average income of nearly one-third that of the high-income group in the 1970s, but then suffered huge losses in subsequent years, from which they still have not fully recovered. Most of that deterioration occurred during the 1980s, a period sometimes referred to as Latin America's "lost decade." Pacific Latin America has performed better in the 2000s, but the improvements in incomes remain much more modest than those of Pacific Asia.

Thus, there are striking and persistent differences in economic performance among the economies of the Pacific Rim. In the remainder of this paper, we first use growth accounting to document the sources of economic growth, thereby identifying some key dimensions of difference. We then explore a variety of possible explanations. Throughout our analysis, we find a significant portion of the differential performance to be associated with differences across regions. Our main findings are summarized in the final section.

## 7.1 Growth Accounts

GDP per capita, a measure of a country's standard of living, can be divided into two pieces:

GDP/population = GDP/worker * workers/population

Most of this section focuses on output per worker, the first of these components. However, the larger the proportion of workers in the total population (the second component), the greater impact a given change in output per worker will have on average living standards. In fact, the labor force has increased as a percentage of the total population in all three regions since 1960.

*Demographics and participation*. The top panel of Figure 7.2, with its focus on the proportion of the population of working age, highlights the demographic dimension. The emerging economies had relatively very high dependency rates 50 years ago, with children accounting for large shares of their population. As many countries in both emerging regions transitioned to lower birth rates, the share of their populations in the 15-64 age range began to rise, and has continued to increase steadily. The share for Pacific Asia has caught up with the high-income average, while the lower shares in Pacific Latin America reflect somewhat higher fertility rates. The sharp rise for China after 1980 associated with the one-child policy is very evident from the chart.[4]

The bottom panel of Figure 7.2 shows the economically-active (labor force), as a percentage of the working age population, in each region since 1960. The participation rate is rising in the high-income economies due to the increased participation of women, even though Japan stands out for its relative low rate (just 48 percent compared with 58 percent or more in the others). In Pacific Asia, labor force participation rates are somewhat higher for males but lower for females relative to the high-income group. China is once again an outlier with rates that are extremely high (though recently declining). Labor force participation in Pacific Latin America remains below that in the other regions. In fact, average rates for men actually *exceed* those in Pacific Asia, but the total is pulled down by very low rates for women, averaging just 46 percent.

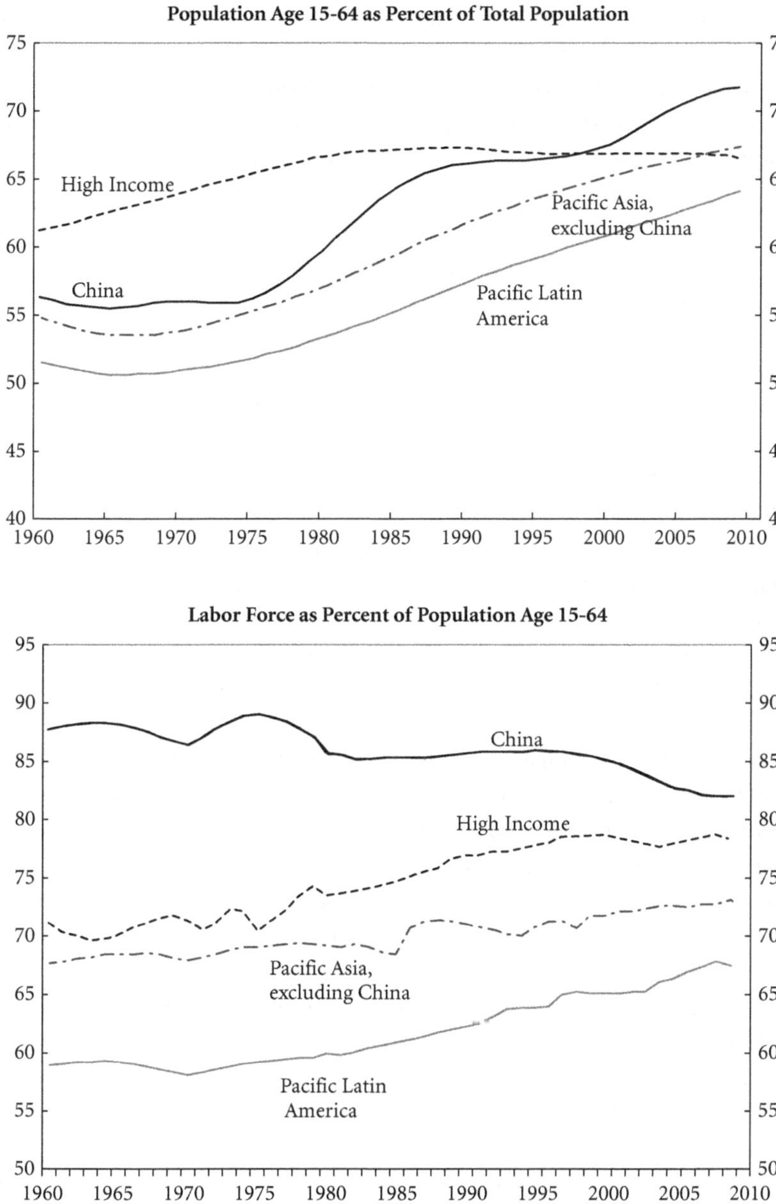


FIGURE 7.2 Demographic Structure by Region, 1960–2009

*Source: World Development Indicators* and authors' calculations.

*Growth in output per worker.* Understanding the characteristics and determinants of economic growth requires an empirical framework that can be applied to large groups of countries over a relatively long time frame. Growth accounts provide such a structure in a way that is particularly informative because it can be used to explore the channels (factor accumulation versus factor productivity) through which various determinants influence growth. While the information provided is, perhaps, best considered descriptive, it can be used in concert with other forms of analysis, such as in-depth case studies and econometric modeling, to generate a better understanding of the growth process.

Growth accounts provide a means of allocating observed output growth between the contributions of changes in factor inputs and a residual, total factor productivity (TFP), which measures a combination of changes in efficiency in the use of those inputs and changes in technology. In some high-income countries, researchers have developed large industry-level data sets that enable them to partition the growth accounts into a large number of inputs—including energy, purchased inputs, and different types of capital and labor—leading to a more refined measure of multi-factor productivity (MFP). At the level of individual industries, these accounts are used extensively to evaluate sources of change in productivity growth, contributions of information technology, and differences in individual country experiences. Growth comparisons across a highly diverse set of countries, such as those of the Pacific Rim, limits the analysis to a more aggregated and simplified framework.

The growth accounting methodology is explained in more detail in the appendix to this chapter, however the essential steps are as follows. First, indexes of growth in capital and labor inputs are combined into a single index using shares of capital and labor income weights. Then, the excess of output growth relative to growth of the inputs is attributed to TFP. The measure of output (value added) is GDP as reported in the national accounts of the individual countries. Estimates of labor input are compiled by the International Labor Organization. These are based on employment surveys in those countries where employment data are available. Otherwise, they are estimates of the economically active population (labor force) derived from periodic population surveys. Labor input measures are also adjusted for the improvement in quality that results from increased levels of education.[5] We have assumed that the flow of capital services is proportionate to the capital stock, which we construct as a cumulative sum of capital accumulation in the national accounts, with an assumed uniform depreciation rate of 5 percent per year. Finally, lacking specific data on the division of income between capital and labor, we use an estimate of 35 percent for the contribution of capital services. Thus, the accounts involve a substantial amount of approximation, but analyses in countries with more detailed data suggest that the conclusions are not particularly sensitive to any of these assumptions.

Results from the growth accounting exercise are shown in Table 7.2 and Figure 7.3 for the three regional groupings. China is shown separately because it is such an unusual case. Table 7.2 summarizes the accounts for the entire 1960-2008 period as well as for the years before and after 1980, and for each decade. The columns decompose growth in output per worker into the contributions from physical capital, education, and TFP.[6] Figure 7.3 shows how growth patterns have evolved over time. In each sub-chart, the dashed line marked "K/L contribution" shows the contribution of increased (physical and human) capital per worker to growth in output per worker. The thin line shows the contribution of changes in TFP. The multiplication of the two indexes equals output per worker, shown by the heavy line. Not surprisingly, capital's contribution changes

**Table 7.2 Sources of Growth, Major Regions, 1960-2008**

| Regions/Period | Output | Output per Worker | Contribution of: Education | Physical Capital | Factor Productivity |
|---|---|---|---|---|---|
| *Pacific Rim High-Income Countries (5)* | | | | | |
| 1960-2008 | 3.5 | 1.9 | 0.3 | 0.8 | 0.9 |
| 1960-1980 | 4.7 | 2.5 | 0.5 | 0.8 | 1.3 |
| 1980-2008 | 2.7 | 1.5 | 0.2 | 0.8 | 0.6 |
| 1980-1990 | 3.5 | 1.7 | 0.2 | 0.6 | 0.9 |
| 1990-2000 | 2.5 | 1.6 | 0.3 | 0.8 | 0.6 |
| 2000-2008 | 1.9 | 1.3 | 0.0 | 1.0 | 0.3 |
| *China (1)* | | | | | |
| 1960-2008 | 7.8 | 5.9 | 0.4 | 2.1 | 3.3 |
| 1960-1980 | 4.9 | 2.6 | 0.4 | 0.9 | 1.3 |
| 1980-2008 | 9.9 | 8.3 | 0.4 | 2.9 | 4.8 |
| 1980-1990 | 9.3 | 6.6 | 0.4 | 2.1 | 4.0 |
| 1990-2000 | 10.4 | 9.1 | 0.5 | 3.3 | 5.1 |
| 2000-2008 | 10.2 | 9.2 | 0.4 | 3.4 | 5.2 |
| *East Asia excluding China (7)* | | | | | |
| 1960-2008 | 6.6 | 3.8 | 0.5 | 2.1 | 1.1 |
| 1960-1980 | 7.6 | 4.3 | 0.6 | 2.5 | 1.2 |
| 1980-2008 | 6.0 | 3.4 | 0.5 | 1.8 | 1.0 |
| 1980-1990 | 7.4 | 3.9 | 0.6 | 2.1 | 1.1 |
| 1990-2000 | 5.8 | 3.5 | 0.5 | 2.3 | 0.7 |
| 2000-2008 | 4.4 | 2.6 | 0.5 | 0.7 | 1.4 |
| *Pacific Rim Latin America (11)* | | | | | |
| 1960-2008 | 4.2 | 1.1 | 0.4 | 0.5 | 0.1 |
| 1960-1980 | 6.0 | 2.6 | 0.4 | 0.7 | 1.5 |
| 1980-2008 | 2.9 | 0.0 | 0.5 | 0.4 | -0.8 |
| 1980-1990 | 1.9 | -1.5 | 0.6 | 0.1 | -2.2 |
| 1990-2000 | 3.6 | 0.8 | 0.4 | 0.4 | 0.0 |
| 2000-2008 | 3.2 | 1.0 | 0.4 | 0.6 | 0.1 |

a. Output growth data are averages of the countries in the region weighted by GDP measured in 2005 international dollars (PPP).

*Source*: Authors' calculations.

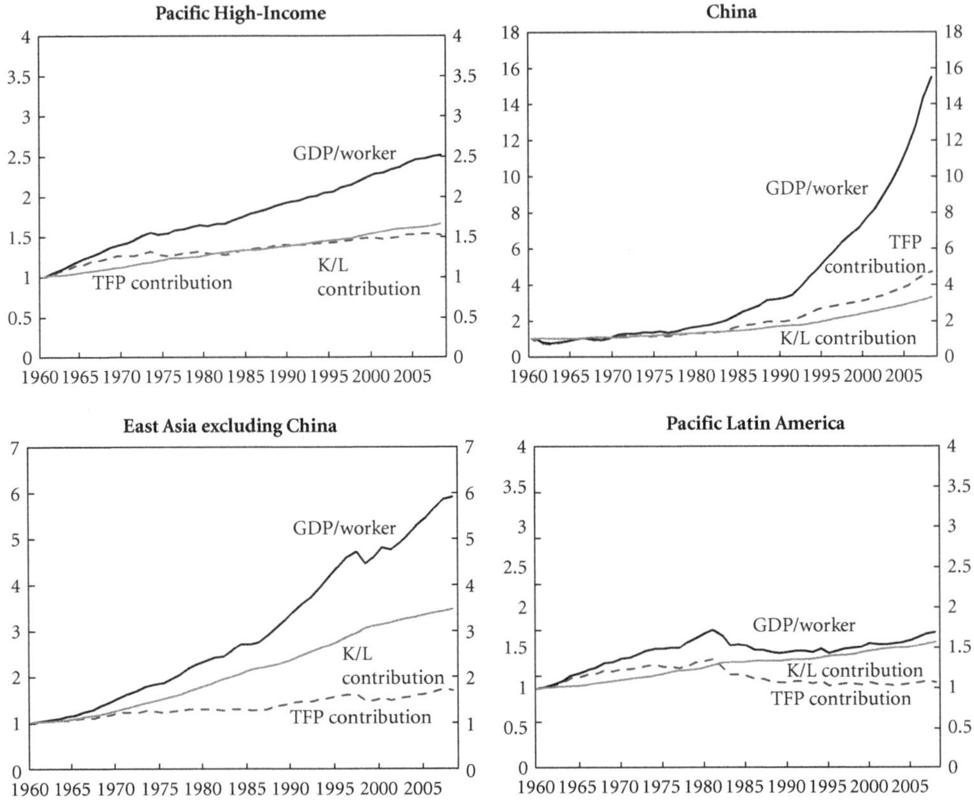


FIGURE 7.3 Output per Worker and Its Components, 1960–2008

*Source:* Table 7.2.

relatively smoothly over time, with most of the year-to-year fluctuations in GDP per worker reflected in TFP.

To begin with, the high-income countries show a relatively steady but modest rate of growth in output per worker. This pattern is consistent with their being on the technological frontier, where improvements in efficiency come slowly. The contributions to growth have been equally divided between increases in capital per worker and TFP, however there is some deceleration of growth after 1980 that is largely due to a slowing of TFP improvements.

China is separated out from the rest of Asia because it is so large and its growth has been so spectacular. It is probably true that the growth in China's GDP is overstated by 1½–2 percent per year (Maddison, 2007)—largely due to an underestimate of the rate of price increase—but because the precise amount remains in dispute, we opted to rely on the official measures. The acceleration in China's growth rate occurs in the post-1980 period with both the contribution of capital/worker and TFP growing at unprecedented rates that have been matched for only a few years in other high-growth economies, mostly within East Asia. The growth in TFP has averaged almost 5 percent per year for nearly a quarter century and is the component that most distinguishes China from other countries.[7] Much of this efficiency gain can be attributed to shifting workers from agriculture, where they were redundant, to industry and services.[8] China has also benefited from an extraordinary rate of capital accumulation, but high rates of saving and investment have been a feature of other economies during their years of rapid growth. China stands out for the long length of time over which it has sustained both the high rates of capital accumulation and TFP growth.

The other emerging economies of East Asia also achieved high rates of overall GDP growth, making substantial progress in converging toward levels of output per worker in the high-income countries. However, their growth has long been marked by a heavy reliance on increased capital per worker, with historically small contributions from gains in TFP. Interestingly, that pattern of growth seems to have changed for those countries impacted by the 1997–1998 Asian financial crisis. Their rates of capital accumulation fell dramatically in the 2000s and the share of GDP devoted to capital investment has remained below pre-crisis levels. This change is evident in the much smaller contribution of physical capital after 2000. (See Table 7.2.) Meanwhile the contribution from improvements in TFP has grown to represent almost half of the growth in output/worker recently, compared with only about one-third in the years before the crisis. There have also been strong improvements in educational attainment, but the regional average conceals substantial cross-national variations in the rate of progress.

Compared to Pacific Asia, the growth performance of Pacific Latin American has been disappointing for decades. However, much of the divergence from East Asia occurred during the disastrous reversal of growth in the 1980s. While the group's performance is dominated by Mexico, which accounts for more than half of the region's GDP, the 1980s economic crisis affected all of the countries, and was concentrated in sharp losses in TFP. Most countries in the region experienced a partial recovery during the 1990s and 2000s. However, overall growth has remained far below the rates of 1960-1980, and has been accompanied by particularly weak gains in TFP.[9] For the last three decades, living standards in these countries have fallen further behind those of the high-income countries, and they are on the verge of being surpassed by the countries of Pacific Asia. The regional differences are most evident in the area of physical capital, where the contributions to growth are far lower in Latin America. Contributions from education are roughly similar in the two regions. Finally, while Pacific Asia has achieved somewhat larger and more consistent efficiency gains, the modest TFP contributions are a surprise in both Latin America and the countries of East Asia other than China.

## 7.2 Explaining the Differences

The stark differences in the economic gains of East Asia and Latin America have generated numerous comparisons and efforts to identify the critical factors responsible for the disparate outcomes. It has been difficult, however, to develop a consensus. The list of potential explanations is long and it is very difficult to devise convincing tests to discriminate among them. In many cases, even the direction of causation is problematic since they may be products of the growth differences rather than causes. Some of the discussion centers around the distinction between proximate determinants of growth versus more fundamental causes. The latter involves debates over the role of geography, institutions, and cultures (Acemoglu, 2009). However, even the identification of proximate differences would help our understanding of why the outcomes in Latin America and East Asia have been so divergent.

Our own previous work consistently found empirical support for geographical indicators and measures of institutional quality as determinants of economic growth. These indicators do suggest some possible explanations for the differences in growth experiences between Pacific Asia and Latin America. In particular, our composite indicator of institutional quality in 1982 averages 0.61 for Pacific Asia compared with just 0.42 for Pacific Latin America. Arguably, this "beginning of period" indicator can be considered exogenous for growth experiences since 1980. Similarly, using our preferred geographical indicator—which clearly is exogenous—we find that the Pacific Asian countries enjoy a sizable "geographic advantage" relative to the Pacific Latin American countries (Bosworth and Collins 2003).[10] Geographical indicators have also been used to construct indices of a country's "predisposition to trade." Specifically, Frankel and Romer (1999) develop a measure using physical distance from trading partners as well as the other standard variables from a gravity equation to explain bilateral trade. This measure is also found to be a relatively robust determinant of economic growth. On average, the gravity-based trade indicator suggests that Pacific Latin America had a slightly *higher* pre-disposition toward trade than did Pacific Asia, however the indicators are very similar.[11]

One approach that focuses more on proximate causes comes from the 2008 Report issued by the Commission on Growth and Development. This group of government and business leaders as well as economists from around the world studied experiences of 13 countries that had accomplished high and sustained growth[12] They highlighted five key characteristics that distinguish the growth successes:

- Fully exploited the global economy
- Mustered high rates of saving and investment
- Had committed, credible and capable governments (Governance)
- Maintained macroeconomic stability, and
- Let markets allocate resources.

In the remainder of this section, we explore whether these characteristics also tend to distinguish economies in Pacific Asia from those in Pacific Latin America. Our discussion focuses on the first three characteristics, for which we find stronger evidence in the literature and based on our own data explorations.[13]

*Participation in the global trading system.* Trade is perhaps the most important mechanism through which countries can exploit the global economy. Export-led economic growth and trade openness have long been central to many explanations of why the East Asian economies grew so rapidly, and stand in sharp contrast to the import substitution strategies adopted by many countries in Latin America.[14] The contrast is reflected in Pacific Asia's much faster trade growth, and the fact that trade represents a much larger and rising share of the region's GDP.[15] Figure 7.4 compares trends in trade volume for the three country groupings. Since 1980, Pacific Asia's share of world trade has more than tripled, compared with a small rise for Pacific Latin America and a recent decline for the Pacific High-Income country grouping.

The dramatic differences in trade performance between Pacific Asia and Latin America are particularly striking given the earlier finding that the two have similar "predispositions" to trade. The strong suggestion is that differences in policy regime played a critical role. In fact, tariff rates are virtually identical in the two regions. The outcome difference appears to be attributable to the emphasis given to exports in East Asia. In Latin America, the high tariffs stimulated rent-seeking domestic behavior rather than promoting the birth of enterprises, as in Pacific Asia, that could compete on the global level. It remains puzzling why the inward-oriented, import-substitution policy persisted in Latin America well after its failures became evident (Taylor, 1998).

Beyond the contrasts in policy, others have stressed the importance of an integrated regional production network within East Asia, and the growth of intra-regional trade (Ng and Yeats, 2003; Athukorala, 2010). Mexico is also part of a production network, but its linkage is almost exclusively with the United States, unlike the multiple nodes in East Asia. As a result, there is less evidence of spillover effects in generating growth in inter-regional trade. Agosin (2007) emphasizes the importance of export diversification

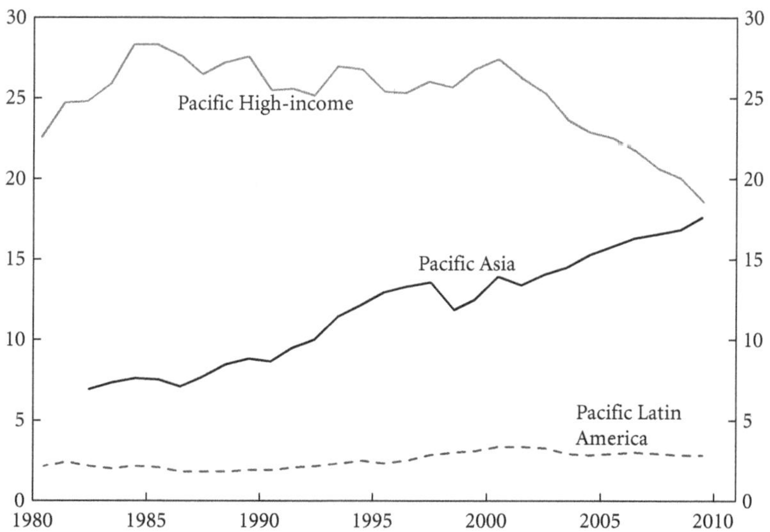


FIGURE 7.4 Regional Trade Flows, 1980–2009

*Source: World Development Indicators*, Balance of Payments. The sum of exports and imports of goods and services.

because it increases the range of a country's comparative advantage, and reduces the variance of overall export growth.

Foreign direct investment (FDI) is often perceived as another channel by which countries can benefit from interactions with a larger global economy. In particular, it could be a means of establishing cross-border linkages of production and distribution networks. Romer (1993), for example, argues that FDI can ease the transfer of technology and business practices to developing economies. However, the empirical evidence is decidedly mixed on whether FDI actually exerts a positive influence on growth versus a more endogenous role of signaling successful growth experiences (Carkovic and Levine, 2005). A recent study (Alfaro and others, 2010) suggest that the disparate evidence can be reconciled by linking the benefits of FDI to the development of the local financial system, but there is a growing consensus that FDI does not exert a positive influence on growth that is independent of other determinants.[16]

Aggregate FDI flow in and out of the Pacific Rim economies, as a proportion of the global total, is shown in Figure 7.5. The data are striking in several dimensions. First, the five high-income countries account for a large proportion of the global total, but their share has fallen substantially over the past quarter century. That is largely due to the growing role of FDI within Europe relative to the United States, and the fact that Japan has only a small amount of outward FDI and almost no inward flows. Second, while FDI flows of Pacific Asia were growing even more rapidly than trade in earlier decades, all that came to an end with the Asian financial crisis of 1997–1998, and it has never recovered. FDI of the region now accounts for a relatively stable 5–7 percent of the global total. And finally, whereas FDI flows in Pacific Latin America were negatively affected by the economic crises of the 1980s, they have always been a small share of the global total.

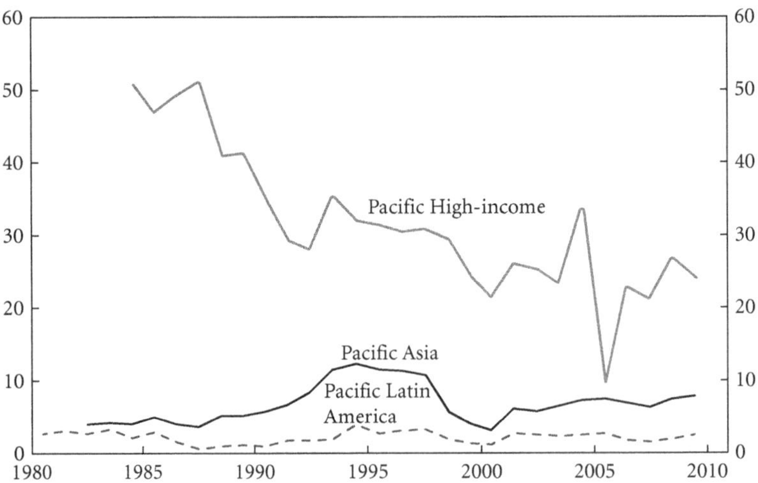


FIGURE 7.5 Foreign Direct Investment, Regional Totals, 1980–2009

*Source: World Development Indicators* and authors' estimates. Data for 2004-05 reflect a tax holiday for the repatriation of overseas profits by U.S. corporations, which is treated as a reduction in outward direct investment.

*Saving and Investment.* The growth accounts of the prior section have already drawn attention to the magnitude of difference in the contributions of physical capital accumulation between emerging East Asia and Latin America. Indeed, the contribution has been 4–5 times larger in East Asia than in Latin America. It is also useful to compare the annual flows of saving and investments, as shown in Figure 7.6. Even before the financial crisis, rates of saving and investment were low and trending down in the high-income countries, consistent with their moderate rates of economic growth. The shortfall of saving relative to domestic investment, shown in the figure, is largely traceable to developments within the United States.

In contrast, China has had extraordinarily high rates of both saving and investment throughout the past three decades. The saving rate rose further in the mid-2000s. Since this increase was not matched by investment, it resulted in the emergence of a large current account surplus after 2004. Historically, the other East Asian economies were also viewed as high-saving, high-investment economies. However, their investment rates fell precipitously during the Asian financial crisis and never recovered in subsequent years.[17] The average saving rate also fell, but by relatively modest amounts. As a result, these countries joined China in generating large current account surpluses during the 2000s.

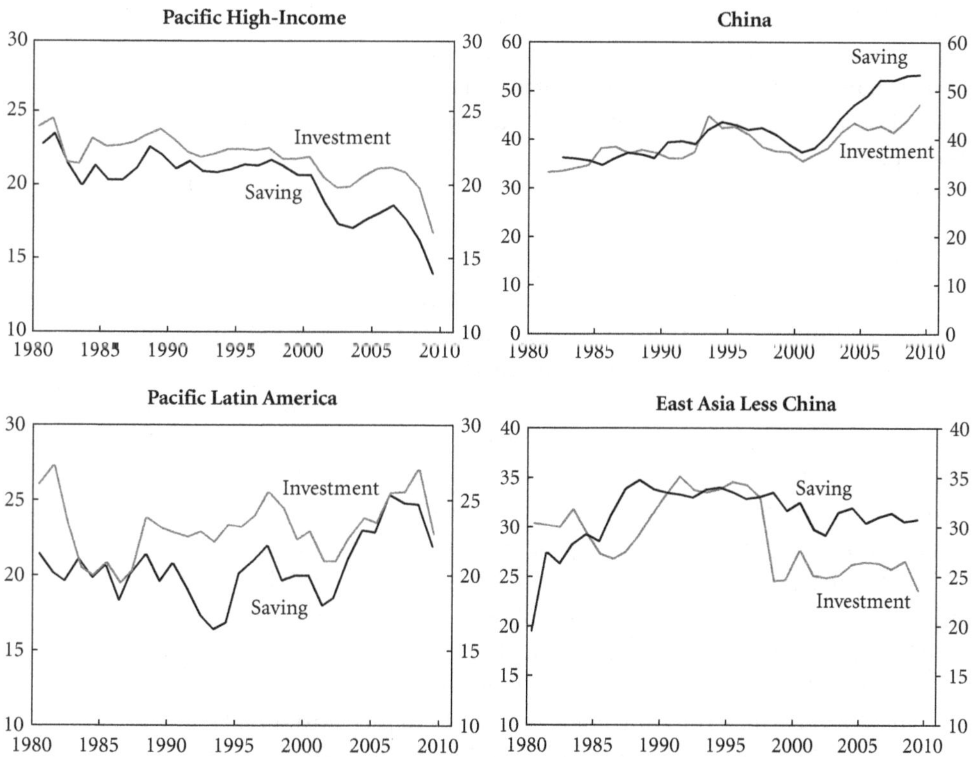


FIGURE 7.6 Saving and Investment by Major Country Groups on the Pacific Rim, 1980–2009

*Source:* World Development Indicators and authors' calculations.

Latin America has long been notable for low rates of national saving and a heavy reliance on foreign capital inflows to support domestic investment. That pattern is very evident among the Pacific Rim countries in the 1980s and 1990s. Rates of saving and investment in the region were consistently about 10 percent of GDP below those for East Asia. In an open global economy, low rates of domestic saving need not constrain the growth of individual countries because investment can be financed through capital inflows. But low saving does increase a country's vulnerability to a sudden disruption of the capital inflows—and such disruptions were common throughout Latin America. Most recently, the region has experienced a significant rise in saving with a corresponding decline in dependence on foreign capital inflows. While the gains in improved growth performance have been modest so far, the region was severely impacted by the financial crisis, and several years will be required to determine if the short-term trends can be sustained.

Finally, there has been a long-running debate about the direction of causation between saving and economic growth. Is it necessary to promote saving as prerequisite to growth, or does the growth itself translate into higher saving? It seems evident that the causation runs in both directions (Carroll and Weil, 1994); but if a country can access global capital markets, it can focus its initial efforts on creating conditions favorable to economic growth. The risks of excessive dependency on capital inflows, however, highlight the longer-term importance of increasing saving. In the absence of higher saving, a sustained rise in investment demand will drive up interest rates, appreciate the real exchange rate and choke-off exports. This process has impacted Latin America on several occasions, and appreciated real exchange rates have constrained the growth of the export sector.

*Governance and Institutions.* In the 1980s it was common to draw a distinction between East Asia and Latin America by characterizing the first as more authoritarian and the latter as more democratic, as part of an argument that authoritarian regimes are better for growth. Political problems were reflected in Latin America's extraordinary rate of inflation and chronic budget deficits that absorbed large portions of private saving. Several studies of Latin America's poor economic performance emphasized the instability of its political processes and the role of political populism (Dornbusch and Edwards, 1991, Edwards, 2010). Today, the situation seems more complex and it is difficult to draw clear conclusions. On the Pacific Rim, the leading Latin American economies have stable, well-functioning democracies, and for the last two decades have consistently pursued development programs that emphasize structural adjustment and trade liberalization; yet rates of economic growth remain well below those of East Asia. Many of the arguments that are made about aspects of populism in Latin America are also less applicable to this specific group of countries.

The World Bank has collected a wide range of indicators of the quality of governance and institutions since the mid-1990s, which do differ substantially across countries.[18] At the same time, many of the measures are highly correlated with the level of GDP per capita, while their influence on the rate of economic growth remains controversial. Still, the indexes indicate significant differences between the three regions. On a scale from

0 (worst) to 100 (best), the high-income countries have a simple average rank of 90 in 2009, compared with 56 for Pacific Asia and 45 for Pacific Latin American countries (see Table 7.3). But the rankings vary considerably within the Asian and Latin American groups. In particular, Chile and Costa Rica have ranks comparable to the highly rated countries of East Asia (South Korea, Singapore, and Taiwan), while Mexico—the largest country in Latin America—is rated much higher than either China or Indonesia.

Table 7.3 also contrasts the six individual governance indicators by region for 1996 and 2009. The indicators suggest most of the difference between Pacific Asia and Pacific Latin America is associated with relatively strong Asian scores in two of the governance categories: Government Effectiveness and Rule of Law. In 1996, there were also large gaps for Control of Corruption and Political Stability, but both gaps have shrunk over the past decade, as the average Asian indicators deteriorated, while those for Latin America improved somewhat. In contrast, the regional gap in Regulatory Quality has grown since 1996, with the Latin American indicator falling quite sharply. Finally, average indicators for Latin America remain above those for Asia in terms of Voice and Accountability. Again, these averages mask differences that are sometimes large within regional groupings.

In addition, closely related work by the World Bank (2011) has sought to develop other indicators that can compare countries in the extent to which their institutions maintain an efficient regulatory environment and encourage business creation and entrepreneurship. Thus, it publishes a set of indicators and rankings that seek to measure the ease of starting, operating and closing businesses. Again there are large differences among the three regions with an average rank of 8.6 for the high-income countries, 55 for East Asia,

**Table 7.3 Governance Indicators, Country Groups; 1996 and 2009**

| | Governance Indicators: Means | | | | | |
|---|---|---|---|---|---|---|
| | Pacific Asia | | Pacific Latin America | | Pacific High-Income | |
| Governance Measure | 1996 | 2009 | 1996 | 2009 | 1996 | 2009 |
| Voice & Accountability | -0.23 | -0.20 | 0.10 | 0.04 | 1.31 | 1.29 |
| Political Stability/No Violence | 0.02 | -0.20 | -0.60 | -0.42 | 0.96 | 0.84 |
| Government Effectiveness | 0.71 | 0.66 | -0.29 | -0.18 | 1.69 | 1.61 |
| Regulatory Quality | 0.65 | 0.51 | 0.41 | 0.14 | 1.05 | 1.52 |
| Rule of Law | 0.54 | 0.31 | -0.34 | -0.47 | 1.65 | 1.65 |
| Control of Corruption | 0.34 | 0.15 | -0.32 | -0.22 | 1.61 | 1.79 |
| Overall Ranking* | 60 | 56 | 44 | 45 | 89 | 90 |

Governance indicators are measured in units ranging from -2.5 to 2.5. Higher values correspond to better outcomes.

*Overall ranking averages the rankings for countries in each group, across all six indicators.

*Source*: The Worldwide Governance Indicators from the World Bank.

and 83 for the Pacific Rim countries of Latin America. However, there has been relatively limited research thus far in relating these measures to growth outcomes. Also, they are significantly correlated with the other governance indicators.

*Macroeconomic stability.* It has long been argued that macroeconomic stability is a crucial requirement for sustained growth (Fischer, 1993). The problems of Latin America in the 1980s and the relatively poor performance of African economies, for example, have commonly been blamed on the instability of the macroeconomic environment. However, numerous countries appeared to progress during the 1990s to much lower rates of inflation; and yet improvements in macroeconomic outcomes did not translate into more rapid rates of economic growth. As a result, many researchers became more questioning about the benefits of a stable macroeconomic environment. The skepticism also reflected a growing awareness of the problems of interpreting the causal role of policies that are themselves endogenous responses to economic circumstances. While the endogeneity of the policies certainly suggests some skepticism, the bulk of the empirical evidence still suggests that macroeconomic stability is an important ingredient in successful growth strategies.

As commonly construed, macroeconomic stability means avoiding large budget deficits, high rates of inflation, and distortions in the external exchange rate. Sirimaneetham and Temple (2009) developed an index of macroeconomic stability, based on averages of these three components over the period of 1970–1999, for 78 developing countries and ranked them. The six East Asian countries that were included had an average rank of 66 compared to an average of 30 for the seven countries in Pacific Latin America. They showed a significant difference in growth rates between countries in the bottom and top thirds of the ranking.[19] In his review of the sources of Chile's strong growth performance over the past several decades, De Gregorio (2004) places primary emphasis on its achievement of macroeconomic stability.[20]

## 7.3 Education

In this section, we look more closely at educational differences across regions in the Pacific Rim. In terms of simple increases in years of schooling, our growth accounting decomposition (Table 7.2) has already shown the contributions of education to growth to have been quite similar. During 1960–2008, education contributed 0.4 percentage points per year to growth for Pacific Latin America and a slightly higher 0.5 percentage points per year for Pacific Asia.

Table 7.4 provides additional information about education by region. The last column of the table shows the evolution of average years of schooling for those aged 15 or older. In 1960, Pacific Latin America had an average of three years of schooling—just one-third the average educational attainment among the high-income countries. Due to significant investments in human capital, that average has more than doubled to over eight years of schooling by 2010—two-thirds the new high-income schooling level. In

**Table 7.4 Educational Attainment by Region, 1960, 1980, 2010**

| Country Group | Year | No Schooling | Primary: Some | Primary: Completed | Secondary: Some | Secondary: Completed | Tertiary: Some | Tertiary: Completed | Average Years of Total Schooling |
|---|---|---|---|---|---|---|---|---|---|
| | | | (Percent of population aged 15 and over) | | | | | | |
| *Pacific High-Income* | | | | | | | | | |
| | 1960 | 1.68 | 16.78 | 22.80 | 19.90 | 27.44 | 5.40 | 6.04 | 9.00 |
| | 1980 | 0.92 | 6.38 | 12.38 | 23.98 | 33.82 | 11.10 | 11.46 | 10.87 |
| | 2010 | 0.52 | 2.76 | 8.12 | 18.68 | 33.58 | 16.00 | 20.32 | 11.99 |
| *Pacific Asia* | | | | | | | | | |
| | 1960 | 45.55 | 17.80 | 21.13 | 8.13 | 5.25 | 1.05 | 1.08 | 3.51 |
| | 1980 | 20.89 | 23.24 | 20.39 | 16.09 | 13.60 | 2.95 | 2.84 | 5.82 |
| | 2010 | 7.80 | 9.44 | 17.40 | 15.30 | 29.53 | 10.24 | 10.30 | 9.17 |
| *Pacific Latin America* | | | | | | | | | |
| | 1960 | 39.89 | 34.11 | 14.65 | 6.05 | 3.86 | 0.55 | 0.92 | 3.08 |
| | 1980 | 24.73 | 27.32 | 20.85 | 11.82 | 9.21 | 2.75 | 3.30 | 5.07 |
| | 2010 | 9.85 | 14.35 | 19.68 | 18.45 | 22.96 | 6.01 | 8.68 | 8.12 |

*Source*: Barro and Lee, 2010. Data are simple averages of national estimates.

1960, Pacific Asia's average education level was only slightly higher than that for Latin America. As shown, their somewhat larger investments in human capital have meant that their average schooling rose to over nine years by 2010, and the gap relative to Latin America rose to a full year. While average education levels are quite similar within the high-income group, the range is substantial larger among the emerging economies—especially within Latin America.

A growing literature explores the possible impact of education on economic growth. While there has long been clear evidence that education raises incomes from micro data, it has been much more difficult to establish a causal relationship in aggregated data. Much of the recent research emphasizes the possibility that the growth impact of a year of schooling depends on its characteristics.

Hanushek and Woessman (2007) argue that educational quality differs significantly across countries. Using performance on international standardized tests for 50 countries, they find school quality to be much more strongly correlated with growth than school quantity (years of schooling). Not all of our Pacific Rim countries are included in their sample. However, test scores for three of our Asian countries score above 500 while three score below 450. (These scores range from 350 to 550.) Only three of our Latin American economies are included, and all score well below 450.

Lutz, Cuaresma, and Sanderson (2008) argue that the distribution of a society's human capital is an important determinant of the effect of education on its growth. It is not simply that returns to schooling may differ by level of education. At early stages of growth a country may need to complement workers with a primary education with some who have attained at least some secondary education. For growth to continue at higher income levels, a country may also need some amount of workers who are educated at the tertiary level.

Table 7.4 also shows how the structure of each region's human capital has evolved. The average years of schooling discussed above masks considerable differences in educational distribution. In 1960, fully 45 percent of Pacific Asia's population had no schooling, compared with 40 percent for Latin America. However, Asia's educational distribution was somewhat bimodal, in the sense that 37 percent had completed primary schooling (or gone beyond) compared with just 26 percent for Latin America. By 1980, there had been large declines in the share with no schooling in both regions. The change is particularly dramatic for Pacific Asia, which now also has 35 percent of its population with at least some secondary schooling, compared with just 26 percent for Latin America. By 2010, half of Pacific Asia's population had completed secondary schooling or more, compared with just 37 percent for Pacific Latin America.

## 7.4 Concluding Remarks

In this paper, we have reviewed the growth experiences of the countries of the Pacific Rim. Our analysis focuses on three groupings: high-income countries and the emerging economies in Pacific Asia, and Pacific Latin America. While the Pacific Asia grouping is quite familiar as it coincides with East Asia, neither of the other two is a typical grouping to study. The primary finding will come as no surprise to most. Impressive economic growth in Pacific Asia has raised the region's living standards, creating a large middle class, and nearly catching up to those in Pacific Latin America. In contrast, Pacific Latin America's disappointing growth performance means that its living standards have deteriorated relative to those enjoyed in the high-income group. Even though Pacific Latin America has made progress in developing more stable economic policies and reducing its vulnerability to economic crises, those gains have not yet translated into significantly higher growth.

Much of the chapter is devoted to asking why the emerging regions have fared so differently. Recognizing the difficulties associated with apportioning causality among the many potential underlying causes, we set the less ambitious goal of exploring a number of the characteristics associated with growth success that have been identified in the literature. To what extent do these differ between Pacific Asia and Latin America? Perhaps significant differences in some key characteristics will point toward an explanation for the very different outcomes and a policy direction to help Latin America revive its growth.

Changes in output per capita can be divided into changes in output per worker and changes in workers as a share of the total population. In terms of the latter, countries in Pacific Asia and Latin America are at various stages in their demographic transitions, but sharp declines in fertility rates have reduced youth dependency ratios in most. The main reason that workers account for a larger share of the population in Asia is that labor force participation rates are so much higher for women there relative to Latin America. Workers have also risen as a share of the population in high-income countries—but there the dominant concerns focus on implications of population aging.

We use growth accounting to decompose changes in output per worker into the contributions from changes in factor inputs and the residual, TFP. We separate out China, because its growth is so high (from both capital accumulation and TFP) and reflecting concerns that it may be overstated. The rest of Asia's strong growth is dominated by capital accumulation until the financial crisis in the late 1990s, after which growth moderated and has become more balanced. Pacific Latin America's growth never recovered from the disastrous decade of the 1980s. TFP contributions have been modest at best, and contributions from capital accumulation consistently well below those in Asia.

In examining some of the characteristics associated with variations in economic performance, we note first that Pacific Asia has taken much greater advantage of opportunities for global engagement, as is evident in the large increase in its share of world trade. In contrast, Pacific Latin America has seen it share of global trade remained unchanged for a quarter century. Interestingly, FDI does not emerge as a key factor associated with North-South engagement. Instead, FDI is dominated by flows among high-income economies. Pacific Asia's global share has not grown since the 1997 financial crisis, and shares for Latin America have always been small.

Pacific Asia, and especially China, have been high saving and high investment economies. This has been associated with the large contributions to growth from physical capital accumulation. In contrast, Latin America has had relatively low saving, and relied on foreign capital to finance investment, making it much more vulnerable to external crises.

Evidence also points to differences in the quality of institutions. Pacific Asia ranks above Latin America though still well below the high-income group for governance measures overall. It does especially well in terms of Rule of Law and Government Effectiveness, although Latin America scores above Asia in terms of Voice and Accountability. Asia also scores relatively well on indicators associated with the ease of starting a business.

Pacific Asia has had a longer and more consistent record of macroeconomic stability (low inflation and budget deficits). However, Latin American economies have become considerably more stable in the past decade. While this has been identified by some as a key determinant of growth, our reading of the literature is that there is stronger evidence linking instability to poor growth performance than linking stable macroeconomic performance to growth success.

Educational attainment has increased significantly in both Pacific Asia and Latin America. However, the gains have been greater in Asia—both because of a sharp drop in the percentage of the population with no schooling and because of the growing share that has completed secondary school and beyond. Test score data also suggests large gaps in educational quality between the regions.

Thus, we find that, on average, Pacific Asia and Pacific Latin America differ along nearly every dimension we consider. It is important to note that regional averages mask considerable heterogeneity among countries, and that some countries in Latin America (such as Chile and Costa Rica) resemble Asian averages along some dimensions, and vice versa. We are left with the picture of a very diverse set of economies with widely varying living standards and very different economic concerns.

## Appendix

## Growth Accounting

Modern productivity analysis, following the framework provided by Solow (1957), begins with the concept of an aggregate production function relating output to the contribution of the factor inputs, capital and labor, and a Hicks-neutral shift in the production function:

$$Q_t = A_t F\left(K_t, L_t\right). \tag{1}$$

By combining the notion of a production function with the assumption of competitive markets where factors are paid their marginal products, it is possible to derive a simple index number formulation relating the growth in output to increases in factor inputs and a residual shift term that is identified with total factor productivity (TFP):

$$d\ln Q = v_k d\ln(K) + v_l d\ln(L) + \Delta \ln TFP, \tag{2}$$

where $v_k$ and $v_l$ are the shares of capital and labor income, respectively. Usage of income share weights is critical because this makes it possible to avoid imposing restrictions on the functional form of the production function. In empirical applications, the factor shares are replaced by average between period shares in a Tornqvist discrete time approximation. Thus $v_k$ is replaced by $(v_{kt} + v_{kt-1})/2$.[21]

As discussed more fully below, it is often difficult to obtain meaningful time series estimates of factor income shares. Thus, many studies adopt a more restricted Cobb-Douglas production function in which the contribution of each factor is assumed to be constant:

$$Q_t = A\left(K_t^{\alpha} L_t^{1-\alpha}\right)^{\gamma}. \tag{3}$$

Again, A represents TFP and $\gamma$ measures the extent of returns to scale. In this restricted formulation, the $s_k$ and $s_l$ of equation (2) are replaced with constants and many studies have simply assumed returns to scale of unity.[22]

*Quality Adjustment.* Factor inputs, particularly labor, are often adjusted to reflect changes in quality. Two approaches are common. One cross-classifies the workforce by a number of differentiating characteristics, such as education, age, occupation, and gender. Data on wage rates is used to compute each subgroup's share of total compensation. However, this is a very data-intensive process and some analysts object that the wage differentials may measure factors other than productivity differences, such as gender- or age-discrimination. The alternative is to use a simple index of educational attainment to adjust for skill differences. For example, our analysis uses an index of the form:

$$L^* = e^{as} L \tag{4}$$

that assumes each year of schooling, s, raises the average worker's productivity by a constant percentage, a. This formulation also parallels the vast empirical literature that uses "Mincer regressions" to measure the relationship between wage rates and years of schooling. Studies have been carried out around the world, typically finding a return to education in the range of 7 to 12 percent.[23] We used Barro and Lee (2010) as the source for data on years of schooling.

The capital input can also be adjusted for quality, although in most cases the adjustment really reflects changes in the composition of the capital services. The growing importance of short-lived, high-tech capital has increased the salience of compositional changes in the capital stock. Unfortunately, most countries do not have sufficiently detailed information—particularly at the level of individual industries—to make these compositional adjustments. Thus, we follow the common practice of using a simple estimate of the capital stock as the index of capital services.

*Income Shares.* There is an added complication for empirical applications. Although the use of income shares assumes that total value added has two components—labor and capital income—the national accounts classify income among three categories—wages, capital, and mixed income. The last category, which combines returns to labor and capital, refers to self-employed and family businesses. These are particularly important in developing countries, both because of the large agricultural sector and because family-run businesses with large numbers of unpaid relatives are common in many service-producing industries. However, data limitations make it difficult to plausibly partition mixed income into its labor and capital components. This often leads empirical researchers to assume fixed exogenous shares—although as noted above, the cost is a more restrictive formulation of the production function.

**Table A1. Sources of Growth, High-Income Countries, 1960–2008**

Annual percentage rate of change

| | | | | Contribution of: | |
|---|---|---|---|---|---|
| Regions/Period | Output | Output per Worker | Education | Physical Capital | Factor Productivity |
| *Australia* | | | | | |
| 1960–1980 | 4.1 | 1.9 | 0.5 | 0.7 | 0.8 |
| 1980–2008 | 3.3 | 1.3 | 0.1 | 0.8 | 0.4 |
| 2000–2008 | 3.3 | 1.0 | 0.1 | 0.9 | -0.1 |
| *Canada* | | | | | |
| 1960–1980 | 4.6 | 1.4 | 0.4 | 0.2 | 0.8 |
| 1980–2008 | 2.7 | 1.1 | 0.3 | 0.7 | 0.2 |
| 2000–2008 | 2.3 | 0.5 | 0.2 | 0.7 | -0.4 |
| *Japan* | | | | | |
| 1960–1980 | 7.4 | 6.2 | 0.3 | 3.5 | 2.4 |
| 1980–2008 | 2.2 | 1.7 | 0.3 | 1.1 | 0.3 |
| 2000–2008 | 1.3 | 1.4 | 0.3 | 0.6 | 0.6 |
| *New Zealand* | | | | | |
| 1960–1980 | 2.6 | 0.7 | 0.3 | 0.2 | 0.1 |
| 1980–2008 | 2.5 | 1.2 | 0.2 | 0.5 | 0.5 |
| 2000–2008 | 2.9 | 0.4 | 0.2 | 0.6 | -0.3 |
| *United States* | | | | | |
| 1960–1980 | 3.6 | 1.5 | 0.5 | 0.0 | 1.0 |
| 1980–2008 | 2.9 | 1.5 | 0.1 | 0.7 | 0.7 |
| 2000–2008 | 2.1 | 1.3 | -0.1 | 1.1 | 0.3 |

**Table A2 Sources of Growth, East Asia, 1960–2008**

Annual percentage rate of change

| Regions/Period | Output | Output per Worker | Education | Contribution of: Physical Capital | Factor Productivity |
|---|---|---|---|---|---|
| *China* | | | | | |
| 1960–1980 | 4.9 | 2.6 | 0.4 | 0.9 | 1.3 |
| 1980–2008 | 9.9 | 8.3 | 0.4 | 2.9 | 4.8 |
| 2000–2008 | 10.2 | 9.2 | 0.4 | 3.4 | 5.2 |
| *Indonesia* | | | | | |
| 1960–1970 | 4.1 | 2.1 | 0.6 | -0.1 | 1.6 |
| 1960–1980 | 6.0 | 3.4 | 0.5 | 1.1 | 1.8 |
| 1980–2008 | 5.3 | 2.6 | 0.5 | 1.8 | 0.3 |
| 2000–2008 | 5.2 | 3.2 | 0.6 | 0.8 | 1.8 |
| South Korea | | | | | |
| 1960–1980 | 7.7 | 4.0 | 0.8 | 2.5 | 0.7 |
| 1980–2008 | 6.5 | 4.5 | 0.5 | 2.4 | 1.4 |
| 2000–2008 | 4.4 | 3.0 | 0.4 | 1.3 | 1.2 |
| *Malaysia* | | | | | |
| 1960–1980 | 7.2 | 3.8 | 0.6 | 1.7 | 1.4 |
| 1980–2008 | 6.1 | 2.9 | 0.6 | 1.7 | 0.6 |
| 2000–2008 | 5.1 | 2.6 | 0.4 | 0.6 | 1.5 |
| Philippines | | | | | |
| 1960–1980 | 5.4 | 2.3 | 0.5 | 1.2 | 0.6 |
| 1980–2008 | 3.1 | 0.3 | 0.3 | 0.3 | -0.3 |
| 2000–2008 | 4.8 | 2.4 | 0.3 | 0.2 | 2.0 |
| *Singapore* | | | | | |
| 1960–1980 | 9.3 | 5.4 | 0.3 | 3.9 | 1.2 |
| 1980–2008 | 6.7 | 3.5 | 0.7 | 1.4 | 1.4 |
| 2000–2008 | 4.9 | 1.8 | 0.5 | 0.2 | 1.1 |
| *Taiwan* | | | | | |
| 1960–1980 | 9.8 | 6.5 | 0.8 | 3.6 | 2.0 |
| 1980–2008 | 6.1 | 4.3 | 0.6 | 2.1 | 1.5 |
| 2000–2008 | 3.3 | 2.0 | 0.7 | 1.1 | 0.1 |
| *Thailand* | | | | | |
| 1960–1980 | 7.5 | 4.3 | 0.2 | 2.8 | 1.3 |
| 1980-2008 | 5.7 | 3.9 | 0.5 | 1.6 | 1.6 |
| 2000-2008 | 4.8 | 3.3 | 0.5 | 0.3 | 2.5 |

**Table A3 Sources of Growth, Latin America, 1960–2008**

Annual percentage rate of change

| Regions/Period | Output | Output per Worker | Education | Contribution of: Physical Capital | Factor Productivity |
|---|---|---|---|---|---|
| *Chile* | | | | | |
| 1960–1980 | 3.5 | 1.4 | 0.4 | 0.1 | 0.9 |
| 1980–2008 | 4.8 | 2.2 | 0.4 | 0.9 | 0.9 |
| 2000–2008 | 4.2 | 1.2 | 0.4 | 1.0 | -0.3 |
| *Colombia* | | | | | |
| 1960–1980 | 5.4 | 2.5 | 0.4 | 0.2 | 1.9 |
| 1980–2008 | 3.5 | 0.3 | 0.4 | 0.5 | -0.5 |
| 2000–2008 | 4.6 | 1.9 | 0.3 | 0.4 | 1.2 |
| *Costa Rica* | | | | | |
| 1960–1980 | 5.8 | 1.7 | 0.4 | 1.0 | 0.3 |
| 1980–2008 | 4.2 | 0.7 | 0.4 | 0.4 | -0.1 |
| 2000–2008 | 4.9 | 1.4 | 0.3 | 0.5 | 0.5 |
| *Ecuador* | | | | | |
| 1960–1980 | 5.6 | 2.9 | 0.5 | 1.0 | 1.3 |
| 1980–2008 | 2.8 | -0.1 | 0.3 | -0.1 | -0.3 |
| 2000–2008 | 5.0 | 2.6 | 0.3 | 0.1 | 2.2 |
| *Guatemala* | | | | | |
| 1960–1980 | 5.6 | 2.7 | 0.3 | 1.0 | 1.4 |
| 1980–2008 | 2.9 | 0.1 | 0.3 | 0.1 | -0.3 |
| 2000–2008 | 3.8 | 0.1 | 0.3 | 0.1 | -0.3 |
| *Honduras* | | | | | |
| 1960–1980 | 5.1 | 2.0 | 0.4 | 1.0 | 0.5 |
| 1980–2008 | 3.5 | 0.4 | 0.4 | 0.4 | -0.4 |
| 2000–2008 | 5.0 | 2.7 | 0.4 | 0.8 | 1.6 |
| Mexico | | | | | |
| 1960–1980 | 6.7 | 3.1 | 0.4 | 0.9 | 1.6 |
| 1980–2008 | 2.6 | -0.3 | 0.5 | 0.4 | -1.2 |
| 2000–2008 | 2.4 | 0.2 | 0.5 | 0.7 | -0.9 |
| *Nicaragua* | | | | | |
| 1960–1980 | 3.5 | 0.0 | 0.3 | 1.8 | -2.1 |
| 1980–2008 | 1.7 | -1.3 | 0.4 | -0.3 | -1.4 |
| 2000–2008 | 3.4 | 0.7 | 0.4 | 0.0 | 0.3 |

**Table A3 Continued**

Annual percentage rate of change

| Regions/Period | Output | Output per Worker | Education | Contribution of: Physical Capital | Contribution of: Factor Productivity |
|---|---|---|---|---|---|
| *Panama* | | | | | |
| 1960–1980 | 6.0 | 2.9 | 0.5 | 1.3 | 1.1 |
| 1980–2008 | 4.1 | 0.7 | 0.4 | 0.3 | 0.1 |
| 2000–2008 | 6.3 | 3.4 | 0.3 | 0.5 | 2.6 |
| *Peru* | | | | | |
| 1960–1980 | 4.5 | 1.7 | 0.5 | 0.0 | 1.2 |
| 1980–2008 | 2.8 | -0.1 | 0.4 | 0.0 | -0.5 |
| 2000–2008 | 5.9 | 3.6 | 0.3 | 0.3 | 3.1 |
| *El Salvador* | | | | | |
| 1960–1980 | 3.9 | 0.5 | 0.3 | 1.0 | -0.8 |
| 1980–2008 | 2.3 | 0.7 | 0.5 | 0.4 | -0.3 |
| 2000–2008 | 2.8 | 1.6 | 0.4 | 0.9 | 0.3 |

**Table A4 Sources of Growth, Major Regions of the World, 1960–2008**

Annual percentage rate of change

| Regions/Period | Output | Output per Worker | Education | Contribution of: Physical Capital | Contribution of: Factor Productivity |
|---|---|---|---|---|---|
| *World (84)* | | | | | |
| 1960–1980 | 4.9 | 2.9 | 0.4 | 1.2 | 1.3 |
| 1980–2008 | 3.9 | 1.8 | 0.3 | 0.8 | 0.6 |
| 2000–2008 | 4.2 | 1.7 | 0.2 | 0.9 | 0.6 |
| *Industrial Countries (22)* | | | | | |
| 1960–1980 | 4.5 | 2.9 | 0.4 | 1.1 | 1.4 |
| 1980–2008 | 2.5 | 1.5 | 0.3 | 0.7 | 0.5 |
| 2000–2008 | 1.9 | 1.1 | 0.1 | 0.8 | 0.1 |

**Table A4 Continued**

Annual percentage rate of change

| Regions/Period | Output | Output per Worker | Education | Contribution of: Physical Capital | Contribution of: Factor Productivity |
|---|---|---|---|---|---|
| *China (1)* | | | | | |
| 1960–1970 | 3.6 | 1.7 | 0.4 | 0.2 | 1.1 |
| 1960–1980 | 4.9 | 2.6 | 0.4 | 0.9 | 1.3 |
| 1980–2008 | 9.9 | 8.3 | 0.4 | 2.9 | 4.8 |
| 2000–2008 | 10.2 | 9.2 | 0.4 | 3.4 | 5.2 |
| *East Asia, excluding China (7)* | | | | | |
| 1960–1980 | 7.6 | 4.3 | 0.6 | 2.5 | 1.2 |
| 1980–2008 | 6.0 | 3.4 | 0.5 | 1.8 | 1.0 |
| 2000–2008 | 4.4 | 2.6 | 0.5 | 0.7 | 1.4 |
| *Latin America (22)* | | | | | |
| 1960–1980 | 6.1 | 2.7 | 0.4 | 0.8 | 1.5 |
| 1980–2008 | 2.7 | -0.1 | 0.5 | 0.1 | -0.7 |
| 2000–2008 | 3.5 | 1.3 | 0.4 | 0.2 | 0.7 |
| *South Asia (4)* | | | | | |
| 1960–1980 | 3.8 | 1.6 | 0.3 | 1.0 | 0.3 |
| 1980–2008 | 5.8 | 3.5 | 0.4 | 1.3 | 1.7 |
| 2000–2008 | 6.9 | 4.6 | 0.4 | 1.7 | 2.4 |
| *Africa (19)* | | | | | |
| 1960–1980 | 4.5 | 2.1 | 0.2 | 0.8 | 1.1 |
| 1980–2008 | 2.8 | -0.5 | 0.5 | -0.3 | -0.7 |
| 2000–2008 | 4.9 | 2.2 | 0.4 | 0.2 | 1.5 |
| *Middle East (9)* | | | | | |
| 1960–1980 | 5.7 | 3.4 | 0.4 | 2.2 | 0.8 |
| 1980–2008 | 4.1 | 1.3 | 0.5 | 0.5 | 0.3 |
| 2000–2008 | 4.8 | 2.6 | 0.5 | 0.7 | 1.4 |

## Notes

1. We would like to thank Sveta Milusheva of the Brookings Institution and Joshua Montes of the University of Michigan for their assistance with the data in this chapter.
2. The lack of data accounts for the exclusion of Brunei, Cambodia, Papua New Guinea, Russia, and Vietnam.

3. Any comparison of relative incomes between such extremely different economies and over such a long time period should be viewed as having a considerable margin of error, but the differences would be even larger if we were to base them on commercial exchange rates instead of purchasing power parity.
4. There is a large and growing literature on the demographic transition and its implications. For example, see Mason, Lee, and Lee (2008) and Bloom, Canning, and Rosenberg (2011).
5. Again, details of the adjustment are provided in the appendix to this chapter but are based on the assumption that the earnings (productivity) of workers rise by an average of 7 percent for each year of schooling.
6. Results for the individual countries are reported in the appendix to this chapter.
7. As a residual calculation, the estimate of TFP reflects the potential overstatement of output growth in earlier years, but it would remain large even after any adjustment.
8. Bosworth and Collins (2008) provide estimates of the contribution to growth from reallocation of labor from agriculture to industry and services for the period 1978 to 2004.
9. Pagés (2010) highlights slow TFP growth as the main reason for Latin America's sluggish growth performance.
10. The most significant results were obtained when we used a composite average of the share of each country's land area located within the tropics and its number of frost days. This indicator averages –0.34 for the Pacific Asia group, compared with -0.77 for Pacific Latin America, and 1.12 for the high-income Pacific economics.
11. In addition to distance, this indicator is based on bilateral trade regressions that control for the extent of common borders, presence/absence of a common language, land area, trading partner population and whether either country is land-locked. Predicted trade values are constructed by aggregating across all trade partners. This indicator averages 2.86 for Pacific Latin America, 2.58 for Pacific Asia and 2.21 for the high-income Pacific countries.
12. Most striking, nine of the 13 success stories were located within the Pacific Asia region, but none from the Pacific Latin America group. Success was measured as achieving a growth rate that averaged in excess of 7 percent per year over the prior quarter century.
13. Elson (2006) also explores why economic growth was so much stronger in East Asia than in Latin America. His analysis highlights regional differences in global integration, macroeconomic stability and institutions.
14. A voluminous literature has developed on the empirical relationship between trade openness and growth and a recent critical survey is that of Rodriguez and Rodrik (2001).
15. The measures of trade openness need to be adjusted for the size of the country to reflect the fact that both the United States and China have relatively low trade shares.
16. Others have pointed to the existence of a well-developed trade sector as another precondition or conditioning influence.
17. In our growth accounts, the East Asian economies all have capital-output ratios in the range of about 2.5 times GDP. Balanced growth implies that the investment share of GDP should be equal to $k(g+d)$, where $g$ equals the growth of GDP, $d$ is the depreciation rate, and $k$ equals the capital-output ratio. Thus, the 10 percent annual growth rate of China's GDP would require an investment rate of about 45 percent of GDP. In contrast, the slowing of growth in the rest of the region is consistent with the observed drop in the investment rate to about 25 percent ($2.5\times(0.05+0.05)$).
18. A recent summary of the methodology and the results are provided in Kaufmann, Kraay, and Mastruzzi (2010).

19. In our 2003 paper, we found some influence of macroeconomic variables on economic growth, but the significance was limited.
20. Because they include the 1970s, Chile is only in the middle of the Sirimaneetham and Temple ranking.
21. The only restriction on the production function is the assumption of constant returns-to-scale. A summary of the literature is provided in Hulten (2001), and a detailed manual that elaborates on the major issues is available in OECD (2001).
22. This may not be a very important restriction, since income shares seldom show strong trend changes in those countries where they can be estimated with reasonable precision.
23. Summaries of many of these international studies are available in Psacharopoulos and Patrinos (2002).

## References


Acemoglu, Daron. 2009. *Introduction to Modern Economic Growth*, Princeton: Princeton University Press.

Agosin, M. R. (2007). "Trade and Growth: Why Asia Grows Faster Than Latin America," in *Growth with Equity in Latin America*, R. Ffrench-Davis and J. L. Machinea (eds.), Basingstoke: Palgrave-Macmillan, pp. 201–219.

Alfaro, L., A. Chanda, S. Kalemli-Ozcan, and S. Sayek. (2010). "Does foreign direct investment promote growth? Exploring the role of financial markets on linkages," *Journal of Development Economics* 91(2): 242–256.

Athukorala, Prema-chandra. 2010. "Production Networks and Trade Patterns in East Asia: Regionalization or Globalization?" ADB Working Paper Series on Regional Economic Integration, No. 56.

Barro, Robert, and Jong Wha Lee. 2010. "A New Data Set of Educational Attainment in the World, 1950–2010." NBER working paper No 15902. Data available at: http://www.barrolee.com/

Bloom, David, David Canning, and Larry Rosenberg. 2011. "Demographic Change and Economic Growth in South Asia." Harvard Program on the Global Demography of Aging, Working paper # 67.

Bosworth, Barry and Susan M. Collins. 2003. "The Empirics of Growth: An Update," *Brookings Papers on Economics Activity*, 2003, no. 2 pp. 113–206.

Bosworth, Barry, and Susan M. Collins. 2008. "Accounting for Growth: Comparing China and India," *Journal of Economic Perspectives*, Winter 2008, Vol. 22, no. 1, pp. 45–66.

Carkovic, Maria, and Ross Levine. 2005. "Does Foreign Direct Investment Accelerate Economic Growth?" in *Does Foreign Investment Promote Development?* ed. by Theodore H. Moran, Edward M. Graham, and Magnus Blomström, Washington: Institute for International Economics Center for Global Development, pp. 195–220.

Carroll, Christopher D., and David Weil. 1994. "Saving and Growth: a Reinterpretation," *Carnegie-Rochester Conference Series on Public Policy*, Elsevier, 40(1): 133–192.

Commission on Growth and Development. 2008. *The Growth Report: Strategies for Sustained Growth and Inclusive Development*. © Washington, DC: World Bank. https://openknowledge.worldbank.org/handle/10986/6507

De Gregorio, Jose. 2004. "Economic Growth in Chile: Evidence, Sources and Prospects." Working Paper No. 298, Central Bank of Chile, December.

Dornbusch, Rudiger, and Sebastian Edwards, editors. 1991. *The Macroeconomics of Populism in Latin America*, Cambridge: MIT Press.

Edwards, Sebastian. 2010. *Left Behind: Latin America and the False Promise of Populism*, Chicago: University of Chicago Press.

Elson, Anthony. 2006. "The Economic Growth of East Asia and Latin America in Comparative Perspective," *World Economics*, Vol. 7, No. 2:97–114.

Fischer, Stanley. 1993. "The Role of Macroeconomic Factors in Growth," *Journal of Monetary Economics*, 32(3): 485–512.

Frankel, Jeffrey A., and David Romer. 1999. "Does Trade Cause Growth?" *American Economic Review*, June 1999, Vol. 89, no. 3. pp. 379–399.

Hanushek, Eric, and Ludger Wößmann. 2007. The Role of *Education Quality in Economic Growth*, World Bank working paper WPS4122, Washington DC.

Hulten, Charles. 2001. "Total Factor Productivity: A Short Biography," in *New Developments in ProductivityAnalysis*, Charles R. Hulten, Edwin R. Dean, and Michael J. Harper, Eds., Studies in Income and Wealth, vol. 63, The University of Chicago Press for the National Bureau of Economic Research, Chicago, 1–47.

Kaufmann, Daniel, Aart Kraay, and Massimo Mastruzzi. 2010. "The Worldwide Governance Indicators: Methodology and Analytical Issues." World Bank Policy Research Paper No. 5430.

Lutz, Wolfgang, J. C. Cuaresma, and Warren Sanderson. 2008. "The Demography of Educational Attainment and Economic Growth," *Science* 319: 1047–1048.

Maddison, Angus. 2007. *Chinese Economic Performance in the Long Run, 960-2030 AD*, Development Centre Studies, OECD, Paris, second edition.

Mason, Andrew, Ronald Lee, and Sang-Hyop Lee. 2008. "The Demographic Transition and Economic Growth in the Pacific Rim." University of Hawaii—Manoa and East-West Center mimeo, August 2008.

Ng, Francis and Alexander Yeats. 2003. "Major Trade Trends In East Asia: What are Their Implications for Regional Cooperation and Growth?" Policy Research Working Paper Series No. 3084, World Bank.

OECD. 2001. *Measuring Productivity: Measurement of Aggregate and Industry-Level Productivity Growth*, OECD Manual (Paris).

Psacharopoulos, George, and Harry Anthony Patrinos. 2002. "Returns to Investment in Education: A Further Update," World Bank Policy Research Working Paper No. 2881.

Pagés, Carmen. 2010. (editor) *The Age of Productivity: Transforming Economies from the Bottom Up*, Washington, DC: Inter-American Development Bank.

Rodriguez, Francisco, and Dani Rodrik, 2001. "Trade Policy and Economic Growth: a Skeptic's Guide to the Cross-National Evidence," Bernanke, Benjamin and Kenneth Rogoff (Eds.), *NBER Macroeconomics Annual 2000*, Cambridge: MIT Press, 261–338.

Romer, Paul. 1993. "Idea Gaps and Object Gaps in Economic Development," *Journal of Monetary Economics*, Elsevier, 32(3): 543–573.

Sirimaneetham, Vatcharin, and Jonathan Temple. 2009. "Macroeconomic Stability and the Distribution of Growth Rates," *World Bank Economic Review* 23 (3): 443–479.

Taylor, Alan. 1998. "On the Costs of Inward-Looking Development: Price Distortions, Growth, and Divergence in Latin America," *Journal of Economic History* 58(1): 1–29.

World Bank. 2011. *Doing Business, 2011: Making a Difference for Entrepreneurs*, Washington DC: World Bank Group.

CHAPTER 8

# THE NEW STRUCTURAL ECONOMICS AND STRATEGIES FOR SUSTAINED ECONOMIC DEVELOPMENT IN THE PACIFIC ISLAND COUNTRIES

HINH T. DINH AND JUSTIN YIFU LIN[1]

ECONOMISTS have long been concerned about economic development—the transformation of countries from agrarian rural economies with low per capita incomes into industrial urban economies with much higher incomes. Countries that have stayed poor have failed to achieve structural transformations from their agrarian pasts (Lin, 2011b). The new structural economics, which takes into account lessons from the world's economic history and advances in economic theory, provides a pragmatic approach for facilitating structural change and sustained growth in developing countries.[2]

This chapter applies the new structural economics (NSE) framework to the developing Pacific Island countries (PICs)—the Cook Islands, Fiji, Kiribati, the Marshall Islands, the Federated States of Micronesia, Nauru, Niue, Palau, Papua New Guinea, Samoa, the Solomon Islands, Tonga, Tuvalu, and Vanuatu—to derive strategies for their sustainable growth and development.[3] These islands are home to about 8.5 million people, with Papua New Guinea accounting for 73 percent and Fiji for 10 percent, while Cook Islands and Niue each account for just 0.02 percent (Table 8.1). The total land area of these countries, dispersed across hundreds of small islands and atolls, is about 528,472 square kilometers.[4] But their sea area, controlled through exclusive economic zones, exceeds the land area of the United States.

The enormous diversity of the PICs in terms of population sizes and natural resources makes it impossible to develop a common sustainable development strategy for all of

**Table 8.1 Population, Land Area, and GDP Per Capita of the Pacific Island Countries**

| Country | Population (thousands) 2010 | Land area (sq. km) | GDP per capita (current US$) 2009 | GDP per capita (current US$) 1999 |
|---|---|---|---|---|
| Cook Islands | 1.3 | 236 | N/A | N/A |
| Fiji | 883.1 | 18,274 | 3,326 | 2,441 |
| Kiribati | 100.7 | 811 | 1,306 | 855 |
| Marshall Islands | 67.2 | 181 | 2,504 | 1,873 |
| Micronesia Fed. Sts. | 106.8 | 702 | 2,476 | 1,988 |
| Nauru | 9.3 | 21 | N/A | N/A |
| Niue | 1.3 | 260 | N/A | N/A |
| Palau | 21.0 | 458 | 8,074 | 6,010 |
| Papua New Guinea | 6,187.6 | 462,840 | 1,172 | 663 |
| Samoa | 193.2 | 2,831 | 2,776 | 1,316 |
| Solomon Islands | 516.0 | 28,896 | 1,030 | 1,192 |
| Tonga | 105.9 | 747 | 2,991 | 1,982 |
| Tuvalu | 11.1 | 26 | 2,447 | N/A |
| Vanuatu | 224.6 | 12,189 | 2,702 | 1,491 |
| **Total** | **8,484.4** | **528,472** | | |

*Source*: World Bank, World Development Indicators database and IMF.

them. Still, these countries share the geographic isolation and other features of many island economies. The new structural economics approach shows that the PICs could embark on strong, sustained growth paths by using their natural resources to develop tradable sectors—including some labor-intensive, light manufacturing goods, and services such as tourism—as well as remittances from workers overseas. Remittances play an important social protection role by providing steady income to vulnerable households. They can also help to ease some pressure on governments to create employment opportunities and safety nets. The new approach takes into account economic geography, which is part of factor endowment and comparative advantage of the PICs where small size, distance to major markets, and dispersal of populations (often across many islands) exert a serious impact on available opportunities.

Section 1 of this chapter discusses economic features of the PICs, including recent macroeconomic developments. Section 2 discusses the traditional approach to development policies and presents the new structural economics framework, with a focus on the central role of factor endowments and comparative advantages in guiding sustainable development policies. Section 3 reviews factor endowments of the PICs. Section 4 presents strategies for sustained development of the PICs based on the new structural economics. Section 5 concludes.

## 8.1 Economic Features of the Pacific Island Countries

The PICs' distances from world trade centers make them among the world's most isolated countries. For most, the closest major ports are Auckland (New Zealand), Sydney (Australia), or Tokyo (Japan)—which are, on average, more than 3000 kilometers away. Palau, the least remote island, is 1677 kilometers from Manila (the Philippines). By contrast, the small island countries of the Caribbean are less than 1000 kilometers from the huge U.S. market. Papua New Guinea is the largest PIC, with a total area of 462,840 square kilometers and a population of 6.2 million. Fiji is the second largest, with 18,274 square kilometers and a population of 883,100. Population densities in the PICs vary considerably, as larger countries like Papua New Guinea, Fiji, the Solomon Islands, and Vanuatu have very low levels while the Marshall Islands and Kiribati have very high levels.

The locations and small sizes of the PICs expose them to large oceanographic and weather vicissitudes, including annual cyclones, floods, and storms that affect all of the region's populations and economies. Natural resource endowments also vary enormously across the region, with some countries having extensive fertile land, others having mountainous terrain and unfertile land, and a few others having numerous atolls and reef islands, low rainfalls, and unfertile land. These endowments influence the compositions of their economic activities, even though their economies are virtually dominated by agriculture and tourism sectors.

Over the past decade per capita GDP growth in the PICs[5] averaged just 0.4 percent a year—less than a quarter of the rate in the slowest-growing developing region, Latin America and Caribbean, where growth averaged 1.9 percent a year. Even developing Sub-Saharan African countries grew more than five times faster than the PICs. But per capita GDP growth rates have fluctuated considerably both within and across the PICs. Fiji's per capita GDP growth averaged 2.2 percent in the 1990s, and then fell to 0.2 percent in the 2000s. Meanwhile, Samoa's per capita GDP growth averaged 0.5 percent in the 1990s but surged to 3.4 percent in the 2000s. Today, Papua New Guinea, Samoa, and the Solomon Islands have the region's highest per capita GDP growth rates. Though many PICs earned considerable revenues from the recent boom in commodity prices, most remain poor and suffer from dire socioeconomic performance.

Geographic constraints have shaped economic opportunities in the PICs. Nearly two-thirds of the region's people live in rural areas, which have a mix of cash and subsistence economies. Yet unlike most developing countries, agriculture accounts for only

21 percent of the region's GDP. Manufacturing is also limited in the PICs, accounting for less than 5 percent of GDP in countries such as Palau, the Solomon Islands, and Vanuatu. Services, on the other hand, account for about three times more of GDP than does agriculture, and about six times more than manufacturing.

### 8.1.1 Similarities

Despite the region's diversity, the PICs share some important similarities:

- *Dependence on aid.* Most PICs fall in the lower-middle-income category and, except Fiji, they are heavily dependent on foreign aid. Aid levels, both per capita and relative to GDP, are much higher than that of comparator countries with similar incomes. Most aid comes from bilateral donors; over the past five years the largest donors were (in order) Australia, the United States, New Zealand, Japan, and the European Union.[6] Australian aid focuses on Melanesia and Polynesia, U.S. aid on the north Pacific, and New Zealand aid on Polynesia.
- *Dominant public sectors.* Most PICs have large public sectors, a situation exacerbated by the inability of small populations to exploit returns to scale when providing public services, by community expectations for extensive state involvement in delivering services and performing other functions, and by the considerable foreign aid that finances government budgets. Government spending ranges from 20 percent of GDP in Vanuatu to 150 percent in Kiribati. Government employment accounts for nearly one-third of formal employment in Fiji and the Solomon Islands and about two-thirds in Kiribati. The region's large public sectors, combined with the considerable involvement of state enterprises in many economic activities, have crowded out private sector activity. High public sector wages tend to drive private sector wages, making many activities uneconomic for private firms—especially relative to the low-wage economies of Southeast Asia.
- *Undiversified exports.* Because of their limited resource endowments, small sizes, and geographic isolation, the PICs can export only a narrow range of goods and services—mainly primary commodities—and for most of these countries their imports are well in excess of their exports. In Tuvalu, for example, the value of imports is about 26 times that of exports. These features also raise the costs of commodity trade (Winters and Martin, 2004). The region's lack of export diversification makes its economies susceptible to terms of trade shocks—such as adverse weather conditions and sudden changes in global prices for exports and imports—particularly in economies that export almost exclusively primary commodities. The ratio of exports to GDP is quite high in larger countries, reaching almost one-third in Fiji and the Solomon Islands and about two-thirds in Papua New Guinea. But this ratio is much lower in smaller countries: for example,

6 percent in Tonga and 16 percent in Kiribati. In Micronesia and Palau food exports account for more than 90 percent of merchandise exports.

- *The importance of remittances.* Increasingly, many of the PICs are reliant on the mobility of the workforce—e.g., Pacific Islanders in the UN Peacekeeping Forces; seamen; workers in Australia, New Zealand, and Middle East—as a source of income.
- *Limited trade within the region.* Due to the similarities and lack of complementarities between PIC exports, inter-island trade accounts for a small share of the region's trade. Nearly all of these PICs, except Papua New Guinea, have large trade deficits.
- *Reliance on natural resources.* Residents of Pacific Island countries tend to depend on natural resources for their livelihoods, while governments depend on resource rents, making effective resource management a crucial issue for the region's economic development. But, due to their limited natural resource endowments, many Pacific Island countries face daunting challenges to develop more diversified economies beyond the small-scale agriculture, tourism sector, and fisheries. There are very few PICs that are endowed with rich natural resources. Among these few, Papua New Guinea has a large mineral sector, which accounts for about 22 percent of GDP in 2010 and is a key driver of economic development. Papua New Guinea and Fiji are the region's largest economies, accounting for 79 percent of its combined GDP of about US$14 billion in 2009 (Figure 8.1).
- *Effects of fluctuating commodity prices.* Between 2004 and mid-2008 global commodity prices soared, then plummeted between the second half of 2008 and end of 2009 (Figure 8.2). Given the diversity of the PICs, these rapid price changes

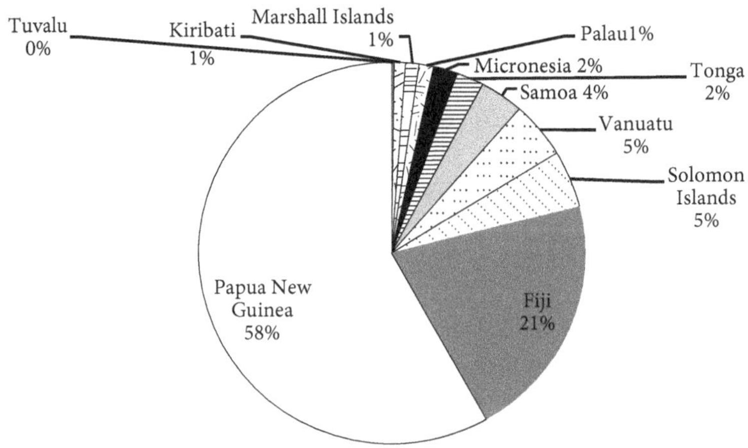


FIGURE 8.1 Distribution of GDP among selected Pacific Island countries, 2009

*Source*: World Bank, World Development Indicators database; authors' calculations.

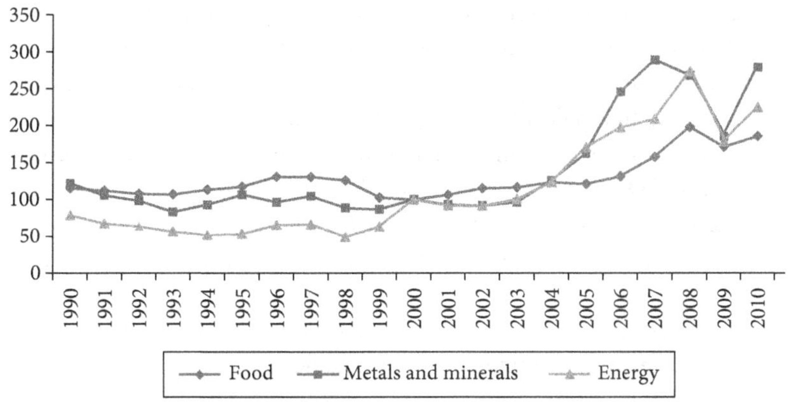


FIGURE 8.2 Global commodity price indexes, 1990–2010

(Index: 2000 = 100, constant 2000 US$)

*Source*: World Bank, World Development Indicators database; authors' calculations.

had mixed effects. In resource-rich countries like Fiji and Papua New Guinea, the boom in primary commodity prices provided windfall gains and boosted terms of trade. Prices for agricultural commodities—common exports from the PICs—also increased, particularly in 2008. But in most PICs these price hikes were more than offset by higher prices for imported foods and fuels.

Countries in the region are susceptible to price shocks in global markets partly due to their remoteness, which makes it costly to transport imports and exports and ultimately ensuing higher domestic prices. In addition, the countries' narrow export bases and dependence on food imports make them vulnerable to external shocks and hence macroeconomic instability. Since the late 1990s, current account deficits have grown in most PICs, reflecting high import bills and limited demand for Pacific island exports. Yet Papua New Guinea enjoyed a current account surplus between 2002 and 2008, mainly due to the commodity price boom—but sunk into a deep deficit in 2009.

## 8.1.2 Macroeconomic Performance

As noted, most PICs experienced weak economic growth over the past two decades. Recent growth in Papua New Guinea and the Solomon Islands has been driven by high global prices for minerals, timber, and oil. Policy reforms in Samoa, including support for new providers of telecommunications and aviation services, lowered the costs of doing business as well as prices for consumers, contributing to average per capita GDP growth of 3.4 percent in 2000-2008.

But other countries in the region have seen volatile, flat, or declining per capita GDP growth. In Fiji, Kiribati, Tonga, Tuvalu, and Vanuatu per capita GDP growth averaged less than 2 percent a year between 1990 and 2009, while the economies of the Marshall Islands and Palau contracted. In Fiji flooding and political uncertainty—triggered by a 2006 military coup—lowered business confidence and hurt tourism, and foreign remittances fell from 6.1 percent of GDP in 2005 to 5.0 percent in 2008. Other PICs also suffered declines in tourism. The number of tourists visiting Palau fell by 12 percent in 2008 and 11 percent in 2009,[7] leading per capita income to contract 5.4 percent in 2008 and 2.7 percent in 2009.

*Widespread current account and fiscal deficits.* Poor growth in most PICs has been accompanied by intermittent current account deficits—generally covered by aid and worker remittances (see below)—and large swings in fiscal balances. Fiscal deficits have been a persistent problem in these countries and have usually led to increased government borrowing, higher interest rates, and crowding out of private sector activity. In most of these countries—particularly Kiribati, Micronesia, the Marshall Islands, Palau, and Tuvalu—fiscal deficits (excluding grants) post a threat to fiscal sustainability and long-term growth prospects. These five countries saw fiscal deficits exceeding 30 percent of GDP in the 2000s.

*Inflation.* Aside from a sharp swing in 2008, perhaps due to higher global prices for food and fuels, most PICs managed to keep annual inflation in the single digits in recent years. Between 2000 and 2009 inflation was less than 5 percent in all the PICs except Fiji, Papua New Guinea, Samoa, the Solomon Islands, and Tonga. In Papua New Guinea annual inflation exceeded 10 percent in 1995-2003, when fiscal deficits and public borrowing were very high, affecting interest and exchange rates. But inflation dropped from nearly 15 percent in 2003 to about 1 percent in 2007, though it reverted to more than 10 percent in 2008 due to higher food and fuel prices, accumulation of foreign reserves, and expanding private sector credit. Tuvalu has one of the region's lowest inflation rates, averaging 2.5 percent in the 2000s.

In Micronesia inflation has stayed at 4–5 percent in recent years due to economic slack, extensive subsistence farming, and the country's use of the U.S. dollar as its official currency. In addition, the pass-through of higher prices for commodity imports was partly mitigated by a switch to lower-quality imports. Consumer prices have also been fairly stable in Palau, where inflation averaged 4 percent in 2000–2009. In Samoa inflation plummeted from 16 percent in 2004 to an average of 4 percent in 2005–2007 but became problematic in 2008–2009, when both domestic and external factors pushed it above 10 percent.

High inflation has been more persistent in the Solomon Islands, peaking at 24 percent in 2008. But the headline inflation rate fell to 3 percent in 2009, reflecting tighter monetary policy and lower global food and fuel prices. Tonga has also shown impressive performance in containing inflation in recent years, with the rate dropping from 12 percent in 2003 to just 1 percent in 2009. Tuvalu and Vanuatu have kept inflation below 10 percent since 1990, though both countries remain vulnerable to external shocks.

## 8.1.3 Poverty and Social Inequality

Most of the PICs have high per capita incomes by developing country standards and relatively productive subsistence sectors. Poverty in the Pacific may not be as visible or as extreme as in some of the countries in the South Asia and Sub-Sahara Africa, but countries such as Papua New Guinea (PNG) and Fiji rank on a par with Bangladesh, Tanzania, and Uganda. Poverty in the region is pervasive, largely due to poor economic performance accompanied with high rate of population growth and increasing inequalities. The human development indicators in Table 8.2 show a mixed picture for Pacific Island countries, with some countries, especially the smaller ones, doing much better than the larger ones, such as Fiji and PNG. It should be noted here that the size of these countries, both in terms of land size and population, as well as their

**Table 8.2 Poverty Indicators for Selected Pacific Island Countries**

| Country | 2009 GDP Per capita (2005 PPP$)* | GDP growth per annum (2000-09) | Population (thousands) 2010 | Population in basic needs poverty (percent) | Corresponding Gini coefficient | Pacific Human Development Index (2008) | Pacific Human Poverty Index (2008) |
|---|---|---|---|---|---|---|---|
| Fiji | 4,110 | 0.22 | 883 | 31.0 (2009) | 0.36 | 0.73 | 9.0 |
| Kiribati | 2,208 | -0.07 | 100 | 21.8 (2006) | 0.39 | 0.61 | 22.9 |
| Marshall Islands | N/A | 0.1 | 67 | 20.0 (1999) | 0.42 | 0.72 | 12.4 |
| Micronesia | 2,804 | -0.02 | 107 | 29.9 (2005) | 0.27 | 0.72 | 11.1 |
| Palau | N/A | -0.24 | 21 | 24.9 (2006) | 0.39 | 0.82 | 8.2 |
| Papua New Guinea | 2,072 | 0.14 | 6,187 | 37.0 (2009) | 0.48 | 0.44 | 41.8 |
| Samoa | 4,000 | 3.39 | 193 | 26.9 (2008) | 0.47 | 0.77 | 5.1 |
| Solomon Islands | 2,312 | -1.12 | 572 | 22.7 (2006) | 0.39 | 0.59 | 31.3 |
| Tonga | 4,055 | 0.82 | 106 | 22.5 (2009) | N/A | 0.75 | 4.5 |
| Tuvalu | N/A | N/A | 11 | 26.3 (2010) | 0.34 | 0.70 | 9.2 |
| Vanuatu | 4,030 | 0.96 | 225 | 15.9 (2006) | 0.58 | 0.65 | 19.8 |

*Source*: World Bank, World Development Indicators database; IMF, World Economic Outlook database; UNDP Human Development Report database; National Statistic Offices; Secretariat of the Pacific Community; Asian Development Bank data.
* PPP stands for purchasing power parity.

remoteness, create significant challenges in generating broad-based and sustained economic growth, making it difficult to meet the basic needs of the population—health, education, etc.

## 8.2 Economic Development in the Pacific Island Countries: The Traditional Approach and the New Structural Economics Approach

Given the diversity of the Pacific Island countries in terms of factor endowments, initial conditions, growth experiences, and potential, each country requires a different development strategy. The traditional neoclassical policy prescription calls for complete liberalization of factor and product markets, with market forces determining what countries should produce and export. For resource-rich, labor-abundant countries such as Papua New Guinea this means developing natural resources, despite global price volatility. Neoclassical policy recommends that wealth management funds be created to support prudent fiscal management and help achieve fiscal sustainability within the confines of resource availability. For small, resource-poor countries the traditional approach emphasizes adopting structural reforms, especially for public enterprises.

But beyond this general policy advice, no specific recommendations have been made to raise the productive capacity of these economies. This paper offers a specific, alternative development strategy for the PICs based on the new structural economics.

### 8.2.1 Identifying Factor Endowments

For the new structural economics, the starting point in analyzing a country's economic development is its factor endowments, which are fixed and determine a country's total budgets and relative factor prices at a specific point in time, but which change over time. Classical economists tend to think of a country's endowments as consisting only of land (or natural resources), labor, and capital (physical and human). These are indeed factor endowments that a country's firms can use in production.[8]

But other important endowments include beautiful scenery and moderate temperatures—as in the PICs—which are ideal for attracting tourism. As mentioned earlier, economic geography (small size, distance to major markets, and dispersal of populations) of the PICs is an integral factor endowment that has implications on their economic activities. Another endowment is infrastructure, whether hard (tangible) or soft (intangible). Hard infrastructure includes highways, ports, airports, telecommunications, electricity networks, and other public utilities. Soft infrastructure consists of institutions, regulations, social capital, value systems, and other social and economic features. Adam Smith discussed both factor endowments and infrastructure endowments in *The Wealth of Nations*. But the role of infrastructure was often neglected by subsequent economists. For example, there is no discussion of infrastructure in Alfred Marshall's *Principles of Economics*.

Countries at different stages of development have different economic structures due to distinct factor endowments. For countries at early stages of development, factor endowments typically reflect a scarcity of capital and an abundance of labor or natural resources. Accordingly, production activities tend to be labor- or resource-intensive—mostly involving subsistence agriculture, animal husbandry, fishing, and mining—and rely on conventional technologies to produce well-established products. Except for mining and plantations, such production has limited economies of scale. Firms are usually small and market transactions often informal, limited to local markets and familiar people. The hard and soft infrastructure required to facilitate such production and market transactions is limited and relatively simple. In developing countries with abundant unskilled labor and resources but scarce human and physical capital, only labor- and resource-intensive industries will have comparative advantages in open, competitive markets (Heckscher and Ohlin, 1991; Lin, 2003).

At the other extreme, high-income countries display a completely different endowment structure. Because they are industrialized, capital—not labor or resources—is typically their most abundant factor endowment. These countries tend to have comparative advantages in capital-intensive industries with economies of scale in production. Situated on the global technological and industrial frontier, these economies rely on creative destruction or the invention of new technology and products to achieve technological innovation and industrial upgrading (Schumpeter, 1942; Aghion and Howitt, 1992). Firms engaged in upgrading must undertake risky research and development activities that generate non-rival, public knowledge that benefits other firms in the economy (Jones and Romer, 2009; Rodrik, 2004; Harrison and Rodriguez-Clare, 2010).

For a developing country whose production is located on the global technological and industrial frontier, the structure of its factor endowments—that is, the relative abundance of factors—tends to determine its relative factor prices and optimal industrial structure, which in turn determine the distribution of firm size and the level and nature of risks for firms.[9] This is because the main force driving structural change in modern times is the change in endowment structure from a relatively low to relatively high ratio of capital to labor (Lin, 2003 and 2009b).[10] Such a change in endowment structure simultaneously increases an economy's total budget and changes its relative factor prices—the two most important parameters for firms' production choices.

These developments can be explained by a model in which an economy's aggregate output is composed of different goods, each of which is produced using technologies that differ in capital intensity. As capital becomes more abundant and hence relatively cheaper, optimal production shifts to more capital-intensive goods, gradually displacing more labor-intensive goods. This process generates endless V-shaped industrial dynamics—the "flying geese" pattern of economic development.[11] In addition, an economy's financial structure evolves endogenously as the demand for capital and the need for risk reallocation in production increase (Lin, Sun, and Jiang, 2009). Similarly, other economic and social structures will change accordingly.

Economic development is a process of sustained increases in per capita income, which require the continuous introduction of new and better technologies in existing industries and upgrading of labor- and resource-intensive industries to new, more capital-intensive industries.[12] Otherwise per capita income will stagnate, as predicted by Solow's neoclassical growth model. Because moving from the lower to the higher end of the spectrum is a gradual process, countries can move to many intermediate levels. Factor endowments, while changeable over time, must be taken as fixed at any specific time in the economy.[13] But developing countries have the advantage of being able to pursue a wide range of industries with different levels of capital intensity. To upgrade to highly capital-intensive industries, they must first upgrade their factor endowments, which requires that their stocks of capital grow faster than their labor forces (Ju, Lin, and Wang, 2009).

### 8.2.2 Exploiting Comparative Advantages

Economic diversification and acceleration of income growth are the main features of modern economic growth (Kuznets, 1966; Maddison, 2006) and hence employment creation. At any given point in time, all other things being equal, the relative abundance of a country's endowments determines its relative factor prices and thus its optimal industrial structure—the one that makes it most competitive (Ju, Lin, and Wang, 2009). A low-income country with abundant labor or natural resources and scarce capital will have a comparative advantage and be competitive in labor- or resource-intensive industries. Similarly, a high-income country with abundant capital and scarce labor will have a comparative advantage and be competitive in capital-intensive industries.

Thus a country's optimal industrial structure is endogenously determined by its endowment structure. For a developing country to reach the income levels of advanced countries, it must upgrade its industrial structure to the same relative capital intensity of advanced countries. But to do so, it must first close its endowment gap with advanced countries by exploiting its comparative advantages at each stage of development

Because a country's industrial structure at a given time is endogenous to its abundance of labor, capital, and natural resources, the speed of its development and industrial upgrading depends on the speed of its upgrading of factor endowments and infrastructure. Its production structure and legal, financial, and other infrastructure will also vary at each stage of development. In addition, factor endowments will change in line with an economy's capital accumulation or population growth, causing changes in its industrial structure.

Economies are most competitive when firms enter industries and adopt technologies consistent with their countries' comparative advantages, as determined by their factor endowments.[14] As competitive firms and industries grow, they claim larger market shares and create the greatest possible economic surplus in terms of profits and salaries.

Reinvested surpluses earn the largest possible return because the industrial structure is optimal for that endowment structure. Over time this strategy allows an economy to accumulate physical and human capital, upgrading its factor endowment structure as well as its industrial structure—and making domestic firms more competitive in capital- and skill-intensive products.[15]

For firms to spontaneously enter industries and choose technologies consistent with their economy's comparative advantages, the price system must reflect the relative scarcity of factors in the country's endowment. This only happens in an economy with competitive markets (Lin 2009a; Lin and Chang, 2009). Thus a competitive market should be an economy's fundamental mechanism for allocating resources at each stage of its development. That approach, based on following comparative advantages, may seem slow and frustrating in countries with major poverty challenges. But in reality, it is the fastest way to accumulate capital and upgrade the endowment structure—and the upgrading of industrial structure can be accelerated by the availability of technologies and industries already developed by more advanced countries. At each stage of their development, firms in developing countries can acquire the technologies and enter into industries appropriate for their endowment structures, rather than having to reinvent the wheel (Krugman, 1979; Gerschenkron, 1962). This possibility for using available technologies and entering existing industries is what has allowed some East Asian economies to sustain annual GDP growth rates of 8-10 percent.

As a country climbs the industrial and technological ladder, many other changes occur. The technology used by its firms becomes more sophisticated and capital requirements increase, as do the scale of production and the size of markets. Market transactions increasingly take place at arm's length. Thus a flexible, smooth industrial and technological upgrading requires simultaneous improvements in educational, financial, and legal institutions and in hard infrastructure so that firms in newly upgraded industries can produce sufficient amounts to achieve economies of scale and become the lowest-cost producers (Harrison and Rodríguez-Clare, 2010). Clearly, individual firms cannot internalize all these changes cost-effectively, and it is often impossible to achieve spontaneous coordination among many firms to meet these new challenges. Changes in infrastructure require collective action or at least coordination between providers of infrastructure services (which could be public, private, or public-private partnerships) and industrial firms. For this reason it falls to government to introduce such changes or to coordinate them proactively.[16]

## 8.2.3 The Growth Identification and Facilitation Framework

How can a country determine whether its tradable products reflect its comparative advantages? If a country's products are being successfully exported to global markets or are beating out imports in domestic markets with no government help, the country is sure to have a comparative advantage in those products. Similarly, if, without the recipient government's heavy subsidies, an industry producing exports is attracting a growing amount of foreign direct investment (FDI), the country has a comparative advantage in those goods too. Foreign direct investors have a keen sense of what countries can produce to compete internationally.

The approach proposed here to help the PICs create development strategies is based on two assumptions: that the government identifies industries in partnership with the private sector and that those are consistent with the country's comparative advantages. For existing products the concept of domestic resource cost can be used to identify industries in which the country has comparative advantages (Bruno, 1972). The domestic resource cost is useful because it directly measures a country's comparative advantages in an industry. Moreover, for import-dependent countries the domestic resource cost helps determine whether it makes economic sense for government to spend money to foster exports—which generate foreign exchange—or to support import replacement —which helps conserve foreign exchange. The domestic resource cost is a widely used index of economic efficiency in protectionist trade regimes.

For new tradable products the concept of *latent* comparative advantage, as introduced in Lin (2009b), can be used to identify new industries that are likely to be consistent with a country's comparative advantages. The most precise form of applying latent comparative advantage is found in Lin and Monga's (2011) Growth Identification and Facilitation (GIF) framework. The framework postulates that while a country's natural endowments—including its infrastructure—are fixed at a given time and determine its comparative advantages at that time, those endowments can change if a country grows quickly. That is, a successful country's comparative advantages are dynamic (Lin, 2009). Some of a successful country's dynamically growing industries will lose their comparative advantages as the economy's endowment structure upgrades. For instance, Hong Kong moved from a garment and electronic component assembly center in the 1980s to a high-tech and financial services-based economy by the late 1990s. The garments moved over the border to Shenzen and beyond, and even these are beginning to close as wages rise in Guangdong and there is a shift to more value-added industries and services. These sunset industries will become sunrise industries for latecomer countries with lower incomes and less capital-intensive endowments. That is, the latecomers will have latent comparative advantages in them. The criteria used for the Growth Identification and Facilitation framework are appropriate for low-income countries in Sub-Saharan Africa and for the PICs.

Drawing on the experiences of successful and failed industrial policies and applying the theories of comparative advantage and the benefit of backwardness, the Lin-Monga framework proposes a careful process for identifying industries in which developing countries may have latent comparative advantages and for creating conditions and removing constraints that impede the emergence of those industries (Lin and Monga 2011).

The industries identified through the above process should be consistent with a country's latent comparative advantage. Once pioneer firms enter successfully, other firms will enter these industries. Government's facilitating role is mainly limited to providing information, coordinating hard and soft infrastructure improvements, and compensating for externalities. Government facilitation through the above approach is likely to help developing countries tap into the potential advantages of backwardness and achieve dynamic, sustained growth.

### 8.2.4 Applying the New Structural Economics Framework to the Pacific Island Countries

How can a PIC tap its comparative advantages when it is rich in resources and has an abundant labor supply? A resource-rich country's comparative advantages first lie in developing resource-intensive industries. But resource-intensive industries such as extraction provide limited job opportunities (Lin, 2011a). In 2009 Papua New Guinea's Ok Tedi copper mine generated 40 percent of public revenues and accounted for 80 percent of exports. But the mine provided just 2000 jobs. Similarly, the country's Liquefied Natural Gas Project may double GDP over the next five years, but it will only create 8000 jobs in the construction phase, and less than a tenth of that when in full operation. Most of the country's population will continue to be poor, living off subsistence agriculture.

A resource-rich, labor-abundant economy like Papua New Guinea can also develop labor-intensive manufacturing industries. The country's wage rate is still low, and wages are the main cost of production for labor-intensive industries. Thus the country could be competitive in labor-intensive manufacturing industries—as in Cambodia, Indonesia, Thailand, the Philippines, and Vietnam. Labor-intensive manufacturing industries not only offer the potential to absorb surplus rural labor, but the development of such industries can also pave the way for continuous upgrading to higher value-added industries.

The exploitation and export of natural resources may be accompanied by the Dutch disease in resource-rich countries as export receipts from, say, oil, natural gas, or minerals push up the value of the currency, undermining the competitiveness of other exports. And if the wealth from natural resources is captured by powerful groups, the resources can become a curse. But Scandinavian countries have shown that it is possible to effectively manage the wealth generated by natural resources. By managing revenue transparently and investing in human capital and infrastructure, they have increased labor productivity, lowered production and transaction costs, and offset the adverse effects of the Dutch disease.

## 8.3 Factor Endowments of the Pacific Island Countries

The preceding discussion of the new structural economics shows that each PIC's development strategy must be determined by its comparative advantages, which in turn should be based on its factor endowments, including geography. This section analyzes these endowments and advantages.

## 8.3.1 Agriculture and Fisheries

Agriculture and fisheries, both subsistence and commercial, account for a large portion of private sector activity in the PICs, generating considerable employment, income, and livelihoods. In 2009 these two industries accounted for 20–39 percent of GDP in Kiribati, PNG, the Solomon Islands, Tonga, and Vanuatu (Figure 8.3). In the past two decades, PNG, Solomon Islands, and Vanuatu have maintained impressive agricultural growth (Figure 8.4), partly driven by the export-oriented activities. In the rest of Pacific economies, agriculture remained sluggish (Figure 8.4). Given the geographic location of the PICs, fishing has a great deal of potential to expand. Currently, the fishing industries have very low numbers of jobs and poor earnings. For instance, according to FAO (2010), PICs catch just \$200 million worth of tuna from its fisheries, while other nations in the vicinity and fishing in the same waters catch over \$1 billion.

## 8.3.2 Mining and Petroleum

In Papua New Guinea mining and petroleum account for two-thirds of exports and more than one-third of government revenue. Despite the sharp fall in global

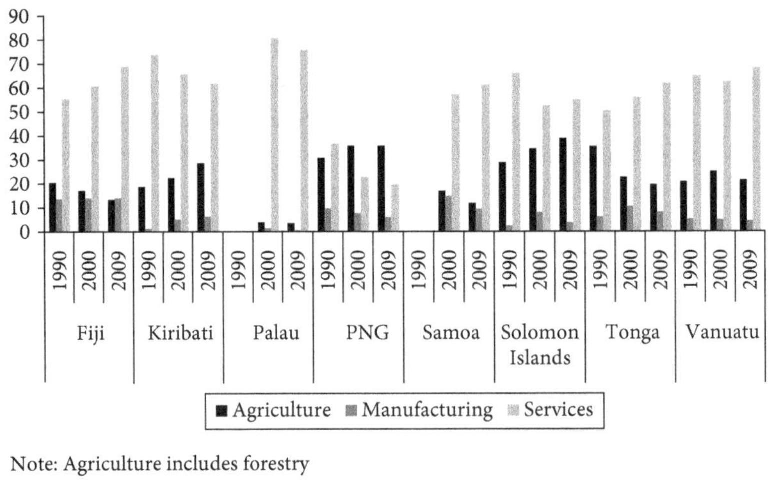


FIGURE 8.3 Sectoral contributions to GDP in selected Pacific Island countries, 1990–2009 (Percent)

*Note:* Agriculture includes fishery.

*Source*: World Bank, World Development Indicators database; authors' calculations.

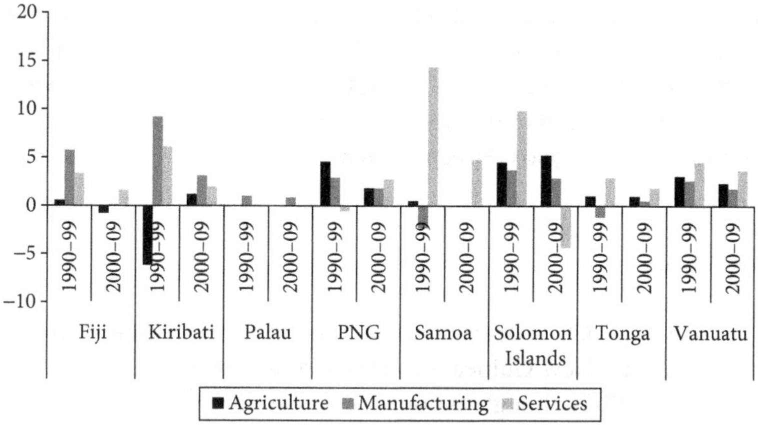


FIGURE 8.4 GDP growth by sector in selected Pacific countries, 1990–2009 (Percent)

*Note:* Agriculture includes fishery.

*Source*: World Bank, World Development Indicators database; authors' calculations.

commodity prices in 2008, mining remained the country's main source of growth. The industry is expanding significantly, with more exploration projects in the pipeline. But like many resource-rich countries, Papua New Guinea faces daunting challenges in managing mining projects and ensuring that revenue will be directed to broadly based employment generation and sustainable economic growth. The mining sector plays a negligible role in the economies of other PICs. In Fiji and the Solomon Islands mining is dominated by gold production but still accounts for less than 1 percent of GDP.

## 8.3.3 Manufacturing

The PICs have been less successful in diversifying their economic structures than have other developing countries. Manufacturing accounts for less than 5 percent of GDP for some countries in the region, and in many countries its share of GDP has stagnated or fallen in recent decades (see Figure 8.3). Fiji's manufacturing sector contributes much higher than most other PICs (14 percent of GDP), with two successful industries—sugar and garment. In the Fiji garment sector this success was facilitated in part by the introduction of a successful duty suspension scheme based on the Thai and Bangladesh models, which facilitate the duty-free imports of materials used for re-export. Some PICs may be too small to have viable manufacturing industries. But because Samoa, with a population size of 193,200, is able to attract FDIs to set up a factory employing 3000 people in its Foreign Trade Zone to make automobile electrical harnesses for an assembly plant in Australia, there is potential for larger PICs, such as Fiji, Marshall Islands, Papua New Guinea, Samoa, Solomon Islands, and Vanuatu to diversify into manufacturing sectors.

Because of the need for specialization and for clustering in the manufacturing sector to be competitive, it is important for small PICs to focus on a small number of subsectors within the manufacturing sector. In fact, Ireland's industrial policy, which began in the 1960s, was not successful until it focused on electronics, pharmaceuticals, software, and electronics in the late 1980s (Sweeney, 1998).

## 8.3.4 Services

The services sector, which is dominated by tourism, is an engine of growth in some PICs. Except in Papua New Guinea, services account for a larger share of GDP than agriculture in all the PICs, though its contribution to GDP varies across the region (see Figure 8.3). Between 1990 and 2009 tourism's share of GDP grew in Fiji, Samoa, Tonga, and Vanuatu. In 2009 tourism accounted for more than three-quarters of GDP in Palau.

## 8.3.5 Worker Remittances

Worker remittances are a major source of income and a safety net for poor people in some PICs. In 2008, officially recorded remittances accounted for 27 percent of GDP in Tonga and 19 percent in Samoa (Figure 8.5). Unlike official development assistance (ODA) and foreign direct investment (FDI), which are official transfers of capital, remittances are income that flows directly to households. In Tonga about 98 percent of households receive remittances, and in Fiji, 87 percent (UNESCO, 2008).

Remittances to the seven PICs, for which data are available, more than quadrupled between 1990 and 2009, jumping from US$107 million to US$445 million (Figure 8.6).

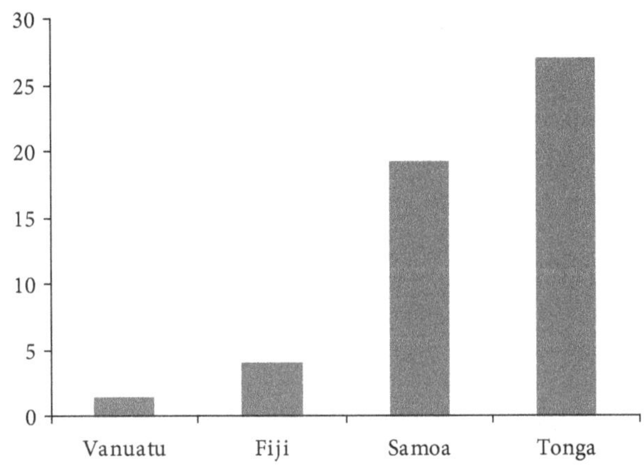


FIGURE 8.5 Remittances relative to GDP in selected Pacific Island countries, 2008

Percent

*Source:* World Bank, World Development Indicators database.

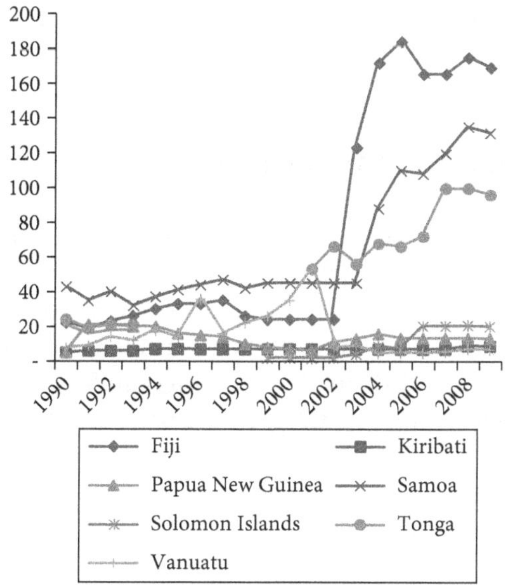


FIGURE 8.6 Remittances to selected Pacific Island countries, 1990–2008

US$ millions

But these flows are largely concentrated in Fiji, Samoa, and Tonga, which in 2009 accounted for 89 percent of the remittances received by these seven countries. Foreign aid plays a much larger role in the economies of these countries, though remittances are still higher in Fiji, Samoa, and Tonga.

## 8.3.6 Geography

As pointed out by the World Development Report 2009, when viewed along the three dimensions of economic geography: density, distance, and division, the PICs have to face the challenges of smallness and geographic isolation. They have low economic density, long distance from other centers of economic activity, and acute divisions from being sea-locked and remote. Export-oriented activities are constrained by countries' remoteness, high transport costs, and small export bases. The 2009 WDR noted that one of the most important factors to consider is that the PICs are unique in their remoteness. The islands rank 207 out of 218 countries on population and income weighted distance measures. The average Pacific Island is the 197th most remote country out of this group, while the average Caribbean island country is only the 100th most remote (Gibson, 2006). The geography implies that PICs' exports needs to focus on goods that have high value, such as many natural resource products, or are small in volume and light in weight such as spices, garments, and electronics, so that the costs of transportation will not be a burden on their competitiveness in the global market.

## 8.3.7 Aid and Foreign Direct Investment

Relative to their GDPs, the PICs are among the world's largest recipients of foreign aid—though in many countries these shares fell or hardly changed between 1990–1999 and 2000–2009 (Figure 8.7). Foreign direct investment (FDI) has played an increasingly significant role in PIC economies. FDI inflows vary considerably in terms of host counties. For the past two decades, Fiji, Kiribati, the Solomon Islands, and Vanuatu have attracted considerable FDI. Given declines in aid, it would be prudent for all the PICs to make greater efforts to attract FDI.

## 8.3.8 Labor

In most PICs formal employment accounts for a small portion of the total labor force, is concentrated in urban areas, and is dominated by the public sector and, to some extent, the tourism sector. Labor force participation rates vary considerably across the region (Table 8.3), though much of the variation may be due to differences in how economic activities are treated. For example, some countries consider all workers engaged in

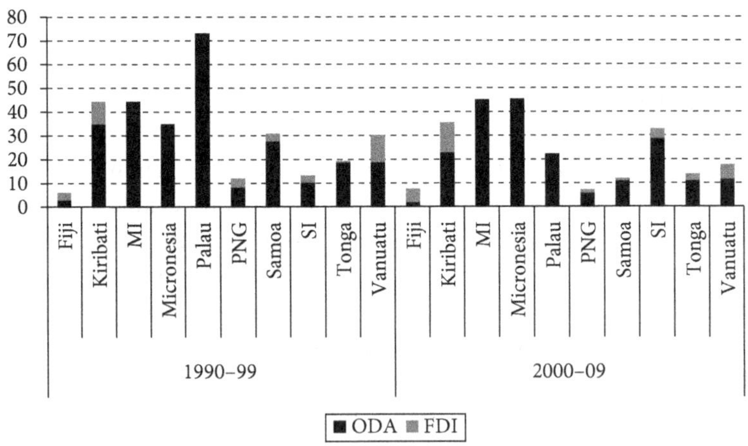


FIGURE 8.7 Foreign aid and investment in selected Pacific Island countries, 1990–2009

Percentage of GDP

*Source*: World Bank, World Development Indicators database.

*Note*: MI = Marshall Islands, PNG = Papua New Guinea, SI = Solomon Islands, ODA = official development assistance, and FDI = foreign direct investment.

**Table 8.3 Labor Force Participation Rates in Selected Pacific Island Countries**

| Country | Average (percent of total population ages 15 and over) | Percent of total labor force | | Percent of total population | |
|---|---|---|---|---|---|
| | | Female | Male | Rural | Urban |
| Fiji | 59 | 33 | 77 | 47 | 53 |
| Kiribati | 64 | 37 | 63 | 56 | 44 |
| Marshall Islands | 51 | 34 | 66 | 29 | 71 |
| Micronesia | 59 | N/A | N/A | 77 | 23 |
| Palau | 69 | | | 18 | 82 |
| Papua New Guinea | 73 | 49 | 51 | 87 | 13 |
| Samoa | 58 | 31 | 69 | 77 | 23 |
| Solomon Islands | 63 | 33 | 67 | 80 | 20 |
| Tonga | 65 | 42 | 58 | 75 | 25 |
| Tuvalu | N/A | 42 | 58 | 50 | 50 |
| Vanuatu | 84 | 47 | 53 | 75 | 25 |

*Source:* World Bank, World Development Indicators database, International Labor Organization and Asia Development Bank.

subsistence activities to be economically active, while others only include those who say that they work for cash. In most PICs many workers are unskilled, reflecting the dual nature of labor markets in these countries. Most rural employment is informal or based on subsistence production and cash cropping. In larger economies there is a healthy level of formal employment in the private sector, though urban areas also have many informal sector workers.

The nature of employment, formal and informal, in rural and urban areas of PICs reflects countries' economic structures and the relative sizes of their rural and urban populations. In Papua New Guinea, where most workers are engaged in subsistence or small-scale agricultural activities in the informal sector, about 90 percent of the country's 2.9 million workers are in rural areas. In contrast, more than half of the population in Fiji lives in urban areas, largely employed in the services sector. Lack of economic diversification and sluggish economic growth rates are the underlying reasons for these countries' vulnerability to external shocks and inadequate formal labor force participation. Employment opportunities in the PICs are limited by the region's narrow industrial bases, feeble private sectors, and small markets. In addition, most PICs lack adequately skilled workforces and have an excess supply of unskilled labor. In many countries a large number of professional positions—including skilled traders and technicians—are filled by foreign workers.

## 8.4 Strategies for Sustained Development of the Pacific Island Countries

As discussed above, in contrast to the traditional approach, the new structural economics emphasizes economic diversification, using resources currently available in the PICs to expand production in tradable goods, whether fishery, agriculture, manufacturing, or services, including tourism. In the case of large resource-based economies (Fiji, Papua New Guinea, the Solomon Islands, Vanuatu), as supplies of exhaustible resources dwindle, growth in non-mineral industries will become increasingly important. Thus efforts have to be devoted now to the supply of these tradable goods. Current resources extracted from mineral resources should be devoted to exploit growth opportunities in food production for the domestic market, high-value crops for export, plantation forestry and agro-industry, labor-intensive manufacturing, and tourism and other parts of the services sector. Harnessing the potential for economic growth in non-mineral industries will require increasing investment efficiency, improving the investment environment, and promoting entrepreneurship. For small, resource-poor PICs (the Cook Islands, Kiribati, the Marshall Islands, Micronesia, Niue, Palau, Samoa, Tonga, Tuvalu), in addition to the above sources of growth, prospects are also good for worker remittances (see below).

The new structural economics and the factor endowments of the PICs indicate that agriculture, fisheries, tourism, and worker remittances are four tradable goods and services on which all PICs could focus their strategies for sustainable development. With the exception of very small economies such as the Cook Islands, Kiribati, Marshall Islands, Micronesia Federal States, Nauru, Niue, Palau, Tuvalu, and Tonga, other PICs could also focus on developing light manufacturing as a viable source of growth, employment creation, and foreign exchange earnings.

Since these countries are geographically isolated from important world markets, their competitiveness in the world market may be hampered by low economic density, small markets, and other transaction costs, as pointed out by Winters and Martin (2004). Winters and Martin noted that there may be some "... very small economies that face such great absolute disadvantage that exporting at world prices is either impossible or generate factor incomes that are too low to subsist. In the limit free trade could mean no trade for these economies." For Cook Islands, Marshall Islands, Nauru, Niue, Palau, and Tuvalu, Winters and Martin's concern is valid because the population in each of these islands is only a few thousands or tens of thousands. For other PICs, their small size implies that their development policies need to focus on a very small number of products or service so that each product or service can have a large enough cluster to reduce transaction-related costs and become competitive in the global market. In fact, Mauritius's population was only approximately 820,000 when it started the garment and textile export process zone in 1970, and the populations of Seychelles and Maldives today are approximately 89,000 and 309,000, respectively. One of the important policy implications of the NSE is that even in cases where the countries will continue to require external aid or exceptional conditions to survive, the aid and conditions should be used to foster the environment for the growth of a few well-identified tradable goods and services, rather than going into general consumption.

In the following discussion, despite considerable variations among the PICs, we will treat the group as a whole, although the many special characteristics of Papua New Guinea may warrant a special treatment where applicable.

## 8.4.1 Agriculture and Fisheries

As noted, a large share of the PICs' workforce is engaged in agriculture, though the sector's contribution to GDP varies by country. Agriculture can play an important role in social and economic development. To do so, governments in the PICs need to identify certain crops that are suitable for local production but have global markets, such as sugar, coffee, coconut, copra, spices, vegetables, tropical fruits, and other cash crops. Governments should also actively attract foreign direct investments to promote modern farming techniques and should play a facilitating role in developing new varieties, research and extension efforts, marketing, and branding. In addition to their traditional crops, the government can also identify agricultural products that are produced in other countries with similar climate conditions and soil properties, countries such as Indonesia, the Philippines, Thailand, and Vietnam. Governments also need to play an enabling role for the smooth functioning of markets that facilitate private sector activities and market efficiency, so the produce can reach international markets efficiently.[17]

Fisheries are also one of the PICs' key economic resources. In recognition of the rising demand for fish in the region and around the world, governments in the PICs need to encourage domestic and foreign direct investments, to explore the fishery potentials and support national and regional efforts to increase the sustainable supply of fish and fish products. The government should ensure an enabling environment for sustainable fish production and for market efficiency and accessibility.

While the vast majority of the population in PNG earns its livelihood from agriculture, the sector's contribution in GDP is relatively low. To enhance agriculture productivity and hence the living standard of the rural population the government has an important facilitating role to play by providing better infrastructure services. It is also important to note here that the country should be able to diversify its economy away from the mineral sectors. The mineral sector needs to be used as an asset that would be used to stimulate or enhance the country's growth potential. Furthermore, if fully developed, the fishing industry in PNG can be the country's one of the most valuable export sectors. To achieve this, the government needs to create an enabling environment for the private sector (both domestic and foreign) to develop. The role of the government should also include ensuring sustainable development of the sector under responsible fisheries practices.

### 8.4.2 Tourism Development

Tourism in the PICs has enormous untapped potential to expand economic opportunities. This potential can only emerge if the business environment enables the local workforce to be integrated with value chains as employees, entrepreneurs, or beneficiaries. Governments in the region have important roles to play in tourism activities, from infrastructure to regulation. Their roles may involve attracting hotel investments and cruise operations, as well as building infrastructure like roads, water and power supplies, sea and airports—all essential for tourism development. Furthermore, there needs to be a mechanism for continuing advertisement of their countries in the international market.

In line with the New Structural Economics framework discussed above, the first step in promoting tourism in the region is to identify each country's comparative advantages (such as beaches, game reserves, national parks, accommodations, and other attractions and services) and, based on them, its potential tourism segments (such as source markets, socio-demographic groups, and the matching range of required services, from origin to destination). Maldives and Seychelles, both of which were quite poor a few decades ago, have achieved stunning advances in their per capita incomes, due largely to explosive growth in tourism.[18] As they are neighbors to the most dynamically growing regions in the world, i.e., East Asia and South Asia, PICs have enormous potential for increasing tourism.

### 8.4.3 Remittances and Aid

Demographic projections indicate that the PICs will continue to experience high population growth in the near future. Among other factors, high fertility rates, low formal sector employment, and limited migration options will create ever larger excess labor supplies. Industrial countries with scarce labor supplies could take advantage of this large pool of young workers, potentially providing for mutually beneficial movements of labor from the region.

Migration and worker remittances can help foster economic development and social stability. Remittances have deep, far-reaching benefits for close relatives and their communities—including reducing poverty. Lowering transaction costs for remittances could significantly increase the income received in the PICs.

The PICs could further enhance the benefits of labor mobility by allowing skilled workers to migrate from industrial countries. Though there is bound to be some symmetry in the number of workers flowing in and out, even a small increase in the number of skilled workers would likely have far more benefits than costs. Studies suggest that every skilled immigrant could create nearly 10 jobs for domestic workers in the PICs. Thus the PICs could benefit enormously from labor exchanges—especially under bilateral agreements—that allow the entry of skilled workers willing to provide capital, know-how, and employment. This move would transform labor mobility from a simple element of domestic immigration policy into a complex development issue (Winters and Martin, 2004; and Duncan and Lawson, 1997).

The Pacific is a region of dynamic migration. For years Pacific Islanders have migrated to work and, in many cases, settled in developed countries. As a result, remittances have become essential to residents of the PICs. This trend is expected to grow and become the main source of foreign exchange earnings—outstripping foreign aid—in a number of PICs. Thus remittances are a major source of current account financing, enabling higher levels of imports (including oil) while contributing to macroeconomic stability. Remittances also reduce pressure on governments to create jobs and provide safety nets. Accordingly, PICs need to work with various recipient countries to create an enabling environment for outmigration and provide better mechanisms for remittance inflows. This may include improving cash transfer mechanisms, reducing remittance taxes, and easing restrictions on recipients.

For many PICs, foreign aid is very likely to be an enduring feature of their economies for the foreseeable future. The challenge is to ensure that both the modalities of aid delivery and its usage become more effective. It would be more constructive for both donors and recipients to find a mechanism that takes their long-term development strategies into consideration. It would be more ideal if the support is used to buttress these countries' long-term growth prospects. Efficient and more customized scale-up strategies would help these countries to achieve a more sustainable economy and help the government provide services more efficiently.

A very effective way for the developed countries to help the PICs is to give preferential treatment to exports of goods and services of the latter, within the WTO framework, analogous to the African Growth and Opportunity Act (AGOA) in the US for Sub-Sahara Africa. This should be part of a comprehensive, long-term financial and technical assistance framework that PICs could negotiate with their traditional bilateral donors to support a sustainable development and growth strategy.

## 8.4.4 Light Manufacturing

The light manufacturing sector in the PICs is relatively small and focused on domestic consumption. The Pacific island countries face a number of distinct constraints to economic development—geographic dispersion and remoteness, small and scattered populations, limited natural resources, and exposure to natural disasters. PICs' inherent physical and geographic limitations pose serious challenges in developing the manufacturing sector. Furthermore, as pointed out by Winters and Martin (2004), there is likely to be a considerable challenge to find a balance between the cost of production in the Pacific and the world price in manufacturing, making it difficult for the PICs to compete in all but a few niche markets. The governments in the region can play a significant role by providing a facilitating environment for niche opportunities for the manufacturing sector.

The region's governments could create export processing zones and actively attract foreign direct investment, as countries like Mauritius and Costa Rica have done. Fiji, Papua New Guinea, and the Solomon Islands have the potential to jumpstart their industrialization through import replacement of simple, low-tech, bulky household appliances. Fiji, Papua New Guinea, Solomon Islands, and Vanuatu could, like Samoa, set up export processing zones to attract foreign export-oriented direct investments. Besides building reliable infrastructure such as roads, electricity, and water, their governments could play a key role in identifying and facilitating light manufacturing growth along the lines discussed in Section 8.2.

Among the PICs, Papua New Guinea, Fiji, and the Solomon Islands have the largest population size and are also resource-rich. These countries' needs for economic diversification and export expansion, as well as employment expansion, are the most urgent. Given the considerable macroeconomic instability related to the prices of the PICs' natural resource and primary exports, light manufacturing—and indeed, any manufacturing—should be encouraged.

The case for export-led growth has been well-established for developing countries (Chenery, 1980; World Bank 2009; Harrison and Rodríguez-Clare, 2010). Developing countries also need to export to earn the foreign exchange needed to import the skills and technology that would be required over time to move up the value chains. In addition, exposing resource-based industries to global competition offers important learning effects.

The structural characteristics of the PICs seem to justify why, in the past, researchers have been so pessimistic about the export prospects of countries rich in natural resources, particularly primary commodities (Prebisch, 1964). According to the natural resource hypothesis, countries that exported resource-based products were particularly growth-constrained because resource-based industries did not easily lend themselves to the technological progress that was essential for industrial upgrading and diversification into manufactured products. Sachs and Warner (1995) validated this view empirically. Yet similar exporters in rich countries such as Australia, Canada, and Finland did not share the same fate as their Latin American counterparts, motivating some researchers to delve deeper. Indeed, as discussed in Lederman and Maloney (2007) resource-based exports are not destined to fail. Their growth potential depends on what countries do with them.

The case for light manufactured exports from the PICs should also be examined based on the region's labor resources—that is, its comparative advantages in labor-intensive products given its abundant supply of unskilled labor. This is true for nearly all of the region's primary product and resource-based exporters. As shown in Figure 8.3, a large proportion of the region's workforce is employed in agriculture. Both activities reflect a significant surplus of unskilled workers who earn poverty-level or lower wages and offer a ready pool for light manufacturing.

Expanding light manufacturing in the PICs could also generate a large number of better-paying jobs outside agriculture and the informal sector. For most policymakers this reason alone usually generates considerable popular support. In addition, in the WIDER lecture, Lin (2011b) argues that light manufacturing may solve the problems facing natural resource exporters. Mineral industries are capital-intensive and create fewer jobs than light manufacturing industries. Although these countries have high and uncompetitive average wages (proxied by per capita incomes) and suffer from low labor productivity, Lin argues that shadow wages in agricultural and informal sectors are not much different than those of labor-intensive manufacturing exporters. Thus natural resource exporters should also have a potential comparative advantage in labor-intensive production. As noted above, by per capita incomes, most of the PICs fall in the lower middle-income category of countries. The prevalence of subsistence economic activities, coupled with relatively high living standards, may generate higher reservation wages in the PICs than other developing countries. In such circumstances, PICs need to enhance their labor force's human capital and target the development of sectors that will generate higher marginal labor productivity than otherwise.

The case of Mauritius is illustrative to PICs. Mauritius is a small, isolated island economy, remote to any major market. Before the 1970s, it was a monoculture economy, producing and exporting sugar. After the 1970s, it successfully diversified to garment and textile industries and became one of the most successful industrialization cases in Africa. Mauritius' success story is largely attributed to the government's encouraging measures that prompted foreign investors to move to the country and set up their businesses (Dinh and others 2013).

It could be argued that the experience of Mauritius may not be replicated elsewhere because of exogenous factors that helped Mauritius at various times: the Multi-Fiber Agreement in 1982, the appreciation of the Taiwanese Dollar in the early 1980s, the 1984 appreciation of the European currencies, political uncertainty in the 1990s over the future of Hong Kong's reintegration into China, preferential arrangements for sugar exports (90 percent above the market price to the European Union in 1977–2000). However, the favorable external conditions in the 1980s–1990s were common to all economies in the world. Yet only a few economies were able to take advantages of those conditions and succeeded in developing their textile/garment industry. Today, some of those favorable conditions in the 1980s–1990s disappeared but new favorable conditions, such as the wage increases in China, emerge. Therefore, if the governments in the PNG, Fiji, and Solomon Islands can identify the binding constraints in manufacturing and play an effective facilitating role, they may achieve similar success. In addition, major donor countries, such as Australia, may create some favorable conditions for Pacific Island countries.

Fiji (garment industry) and Samoa (electronics industry) have already made successful strides in processing and exporting light manufacturing products. With careful and pragmatic identification of industries and the government's effective facilitation in supporting domestic private entrepreneurs and attracting foreign direct investments, the success stories can be expected in PICs. It is also important to note here that the preferential access arrangements played an important role in Fiji's success in the garment industry, and the country may face a challenge as preferential access is removed. Similarly, Samoa's automobile industry is reliant entirely on preferential access to the Australian market. While the manufacturing sector in both Fiji and Samoa appear to be less stable, it also underscores the need for the role of the government in keeping the market alive and more competitive. What happened in Fiji, and the situation in Samoa, should be used as good examples for the role of the government in capturing possible opportunities and overcoming likely constraints to facilitate continuous industrial upgrading and diversification.

The manufacturing sector in Papua New Guinea is mainly focused on satisfying the domestic demand, and the sector has been undermined by the poor infrastructure. Given the country's immense potential, both in terms of natural resources and human capital, the government should be able to identify the potential tradable industries and play a greater role in facilitating conditions that will spur a more productive and efficient private sector. Besides infrastructure, the government may need to consider both financial and regulatory incentives.

## 8.5 Conclusion

The diversity of the PICs in terms of size, population, and stage of economic development calls for flexible development strategies based on their factor endowments and comparative advantages. The new structural economics offers these countries concrete elements for sustainable growth strategies focusing on diversification. The new structural economics emphasizes the need to expand tradable goods and services and to strengthen government's role as a catalyst in identifying and facilitating potential priority products and industries. For all PICs, there is enormous potential in agriculture, fishery, tourism, and worker remittances. With the exception of very small economies, light manufacturing offers potential for substantial employment creation, skill and technology transfers, and foreign exchange earnings. The NSE provides a consistent, unified theoretical framework for the PICs to formulate their development policies to achieve more diversified economies with progressive structural transformation and industrial upgrading.

## Notes

1. Hinh T. Dinh is Lead Economist, Office of the Senior Vice President and Chief Economist, the World Bank. Justin Yifu Lin is Honorary Dean and Professor, National

School of Development (NSD), Peking University, and former Senior Vice President and Chief Eonomist, the World Bank. We would like to thank Ephraim Kebede and Paul Holtz for excellent support in the preparation of this paper; Ferid Belhaj, Russell Muir, Vivek Suri, and Sona Varma for valuable comments; and Lucy Pan for data assistance. The analysis in this chapter was carried out in 2011 based on data available at that time.

2. The new structural economics applies a neoclassical approach to assess the determination and evolution of a country's economic structure. It is called new structural economics instead of structural economics to distinguish it from the structuralism that prevailed in the early years of development economics; see Lin (2010).
3. The Pacific Island Country Forum also includes Australia and New Zealand, which are developed countries. Note that data paucity is a major problem for the PICs.
4. All population and land data in this paper come from the World Bank's World Development Indicators database except those for the Cook Islands, Nauru, Niue, and Tuvalu, where other sources were used.
5. Due to data unavailability, the average figure does not include Cook Islands, Nauru, and Niue.
6. China is a growing donor to the region, though its contributions are difficult to measure because it does not separate aid from other forms of assistance. Still, by some accounts Chinese aid is equal to that from New Zealand, Japan, and the European Union.
7. Figures are based on data from the Palau Visitors Authority.
8. When analyzing a long-term dynamic development process, it is useful to start from a parameter that is fixed at a specific time, fundamental, and changeable. If the parameter is not fixed at a specific time, it cannot serve as a starting point for analysis. If it is not fundamental, the findings of the analysis will be trivial. And if the parameter is not changeable, the analysis will not provide useful knowledge that facilitates desirable changes in the economy. Factor endowments have all three properties. An economy's total factor endowments determine its total budget at a given time, while their structure determines the economy's relative factor prices at that time. The total budget and relative prices are two of the most important parameters in economic analysis. Over time, factor endowments and their structure can change through population growth and accumulation of capital in an economy.
9. The factor price equalization theorem does not hold in international trade due to transport costs, specialization, differences in technology across countries, and so on. Thus relative factor prices in both closed and open economies are largely determined by the structures of their factor endowments.
10. In pre-modern times an increase in the ratio of labor to land was the driving force for changes in structures and institutions (North 1981).
11. This pattern, documented by Akamatsu (1962) and Chenery (1960), is formalized in Ju, Lin, and Wang (2009).
12. The continuous introduction of new and better technology in existing industries is an important aspect of modern economic growth. Most people in low-income countries depend on agriculture for their livelihoods. Improvements in agricultural technology are essential to raising farmers' incomes and reducing poverty. But unless industries are diversified and upgraded to new, more capital-intensive industries, the scope for sustained increases in per capita income will be limited. Thus the discussion in the paper focuses more on industrial upgrading than technological innovation.

13. Cross-border labor mobility is still very limited in the world. Capital is more mobile than labor. But due to limited infrastructure endowments, returns to large capital inflows to the industrial sectors in developing countries are likely to be low. Such inflows are unlikely to be large enough to change the nature of relative capital scarcity in developing countries. Thus, despite the globalization of factor markets, factor endowments in any developing country can be taken as a given at any time.
14. The term *competitive advantage* was popularized by Porter (1990) who stated that nations will have competitive advantages in the global economy if their industries meet four conditions: they use their countries' abundant and relatively inexpensive factors of production, their products have large domestic markets, they form clusters, and there are competitive domestic markets for each industry. The first condition essentially means that industries' comparative advantages should be determined by countries' endowments. The third and fourth conditions will hold only if industries are consistent with countries' competitive advantages. Thus the four conditions can be reduced to two conditions: comparative advantage and domestic market size. Between these two conditions, comparative advantage is more important because if an industry corresponds to a country's comparative advantage, an industry's product will have a global market. That is why many of the world's richest countries are very small (Lin and Ren, 2007).
15. The proposition that countries need to specialize in industries consistent with their comparative advantages at each stage of their development is like the one that countries need to have free, competitive markets. It provides a theoretical framework for organizing an economy efficiently. In reality, just as no country has free, competitive markets in the perfect sense in the real world, no country perfectly follows its comparative advantages, especially given that those advantages change over time and industrial change is not instantaneous. For empirical testing on the impact of deviations from comparative advantages, see Lin (2009a).
16. This is a different argument from the coordination role that has often been proposed for developing country governments. That "big push" argument posited that if each potential firm's viability depended on inputs from another firm that did not yet exist, none of the potential firms might emerge. In that case, the government could theoretically move the economy to a higher-welfare equilibrium with a big push that led to the concurrent emergence of upstream and downstream firms (see Rosenstein-Rodan, 1961 and Murphy, Shleifer, and Vishny, 1989). But changing global conditions have made the big-push argument less applicable. In recent decades lower transport and information costs have resulted in global production networks in which many countries—developing and developed—produce only parts of a product based on their comparative advantages.
17. The success of Ecuador's cut flowers export in the 1980s is a good example (Dinh and others 2013). The fact that Ecuador had latent comparative advantages in producing and exporting cut flowers to the US market was known in the 1970s. However, the industry did not expand and exports did not take off until the government helped arrange regular flights and investment of cooling facilities near the airport in the 1980s (Harrison and Rodríguez-Clare, 2010). A similar story applied to Ethiopia's cut flowers' export to the European market. In the related issue of government support in the labor market, Germany's dual system of vocational education and training, involving both in-company training and education at vocational schools, has been a major factor in Germany's economic success over the past six decades.

18. Between 1971 and 2008 the number of tourists visiting the Seychelles shot from 3,000 to 159,000, while in the Maldives per capita income jumped from $268 in 1978 to $4760 today. To reduce dependence on tourism, the Seychelles has taken steps to diversify the economy by promoting the development of farming, fishing, small-scale manufacturing, and offshore financial services.

## References

Aghion, P. and P. Howitt. 1992. "A Model of Growth through Creative Destruction." *Econometrica* 60 (2), pp. 323–351.

Akamatsu, K. 1962. "A Historical Pattern of Economic Growth in Developing Countries" in *The Development Economies*. Tokyo. Preliminary Issue No. 1, pp. 3–25.

Bruno, M. 1972. "Domestic Resource Costs and Effective Protection: Clarification and Synthesis." *Journal of Political Economy* 80 (1), pp. 16–33.

Chenery, H. B. 1960. "Patterns of Industrial Growth." *American Economic Review* 50 (4), pp. 624–654.

Chenery, H. B. 1980. "Interactions between Industrialization and Exports." *American Economic Review* 70 (2), pp. 281–287.

Dinh, H. T., T. G. Rawski, A. Zafar, L. Wang, and E. Mavroeidi. 2013. *Tales from the Development Frontier: How China and Other Countries Harness Light Manufacturing to Create Jobs and Prosperity*. With contributions from X. Tong and P. Li. Washington, DC: World Bank.

Duflo, E. 2004. "Scaling Up and Evaluation," in Bourguignon, F. and B. Pleskovic (eds), *Accelerating Development*. Washington, DC and Oxford: World Bank and Oxford University Press, pp. 342–367.

Duncan, R. and T. Lawson. 1997. "Cost Structures in Papua New Guinea." Discussion Paper No. 69. Institute of National Affairs, Port Moresby.

FAO. 2010. "Marine Fishery Resources of the Pacific Islands." Fisheries and Aquaculture Technical Paper.

Flatters, F., & G. Jenkins. 1986. *"Trade Policy in Indonesia."* Harvard Institute for International Development. Cambridge, MA.

Gerschenkron, A. 1962. *"Economic Backwardness in Historical Perspective, A Book of Essays."* Cambridge, MA: Belknap Press of Harvard University Press.

Gibson, J. 2006. "Are the Pacific Island Economies Growth Failures?" Working Paper No. 3. Pasifika Interactions Project. University of Waikato. Hamilton, New Zealand.

Harrison, A. E., and A. Rodríguez-Clare. 2010. "Trade, Foreign Investment, and Industrial Policy for Developing Countries." In The Handbook of Development Economics, edited by D. Rodrik and M. R. Rosenzweig, 4039–4214. Handbooks in Economics, Vol. 5. Amsterdam: Elsevier North Holland.

Hausmann, R., D. Rodrik, and A. Velasco. 2005. "Growth Diagnostics." John F. Kennedy School of Government. Harvard University. Cambridge, MA. http://ksghome.harvard.edu/~drodrik/barcelonafinalmarch2005.pdf

Heckscher, E.F., and B. Ohlin. 1991. *Heckscher-Ohlin Trade Theory*. Cambridge, MA: MIT Press.

IMF. 2005. "Oil Market and Development Issues." Policy Development and Review Department. Washington, DC: International Monetary Fund.

Jones, C. I., and P. M. Romer. 2009. "The new Kaldor Facts: Ideas, Institutions, Population, and Human Capital." NBER Working Paper Series. No. 15094. Cambridge, MA.

Ju, J., J. Y. Lin, and Y. Wang. 2009. "Endowment Structures, Industrial Dynamics, and Economic Growth." Mimeo.

Krugman, P. 1979. "A Model of Innovation, Technology Transfer, and the World Distribution of Income." *Journal of Political Economy* 87(2): 253–266.

Kuznets, S. 1966. *Modern Economic Growth: Rate, Structure and Spread.* New Haven, CT: Yale University Press.

Lederman, D., and Maloney, W. F., (Eds). 2007. "Trade structures and growth" in Lederman, D., and Maloney, W. F, (eds), *Natural Resources: Neither Curse nor Destiny*. Washington, DC: The World Bank.

Lin, J. Y. 2003. "Development Strategy, Viability and Economic Convergence." *Economic Development and Cultural Change* 53 (2), pp. 277–308.

Lin, J. Y. 2009. "DPR Debate Should Industrial Policy in Developing Countries Conform to Comparative Advantage or Defy it? A Debate Between Justin Lin and Ha-Joon Chang." *Development Policy Review* 27 (5), pp. 483–502.

Lin, J. Y. 2009a. *Economic Development and Transition: Thought, Strategy, and Viability.* Cambridge: Cambridge University Press.

Lin, J. Y. 2009b. "Beyond Keynesianism." *Harvard International Review*, Summer 2009 31(2), pp. 14–17.

Lin, J. Y. 2011a. "Economic development in resource-rich, labor-abundant economies." http://blogs.worldbank.org/developmenttalk/economic-development-in-resource-rich-labor-abundant-economies.

Lin, J. Y. 2011b. "New Structural Economics." WIDER Lecture, 4 May, Maputo, Mozambique.

Lin, J. Y., and C. Monga. 2011. "Growth Identification and Facilitation: The Role of the State in the Dynamics of Structural Change." *Development Policy Review* 29 (3): 259–310.

Lin, J. Y., and Chang, H. 2009. "DPR Debate: Should Industrial Policy in Developing Countries Conform to Comparative Advantage or Defy It?" *Development Policy Review* 27(5): 483–502.

Lin, J. Y., and Ren, R. 2007. "East Asian Miracle Debate Revisited." (in Chinese) *Jingji Yanjiu* (Economic Research Journal) 42 (8), pp. 4–12.

Lin, J. Y., X. Sun, Y. Jiang. 2009. "Towards a Theory of Optimal Financial Structure." mimeo.

Maddison, A. 2006. *The World Economy*. Paris: Organization for Economic Cooperation and Development, 642.

Murphy, K., A. Shleifer, and R. Vishny. 1989. "Industrialization and the Big Push." *Journal of Political Economy* 97 (5), pp. 1003–1026.

North, D. 1981. *Structure and Change in Economic History*. New York: W.W. Norton.

Porter, M. E. 1990. *The Competitive Advantage of Nations.* New York: Free Press.

Prebisch, R. 1964. *Towards a New Trade Policy for Development*. New York: United Nations.

Rodrik, D. 2004. "*Industrial Policy for the Twenty-First Century.*" Harvard University, Cambridge, MA, http://www.hks.harvard.edu/fs/drodrik/Research%20papers/UNIDOSep.pdf

Rosenstein-Rodan, P. 1961. "Notes on the Theory of the 'Big Push'" in H. Ellis and H. Wallich (eds), *Economic Development for Latin America*. New York: St Martin's Press, pp. 57–67.

Sachs, J., and A. Warner. 1995. "Natural Resource Abundance and Economic Growth." NBER Working Papers No. 5398. Cambridge, MA.

Schumpeter, J. A. 1942. *Capitalism, Socialism and Democracy*. New York: Harper and Brothers.

Sweeney, P. 1998. *The Celtic Tiger: Ireland's Continuing Economic Miracle*. Dublin: Oak Tree Press, 1998.

UNESCO. 2008. *People on the Move: Handbook of Selected Terms and Concepts*. Paris: UNESCO.

Winters, L. A. and P. Martin. 2004. "When Comparative Advantage Is Not Enough: Business Costs in Small Remote Economies." *World Trade Review* 3 (3): 347–384.

World Bank, 2009. *World Development Report 2009: Reshaping Economic Geography*. Washington, D.C: World Bank.

CHAPTER 9

# THE EVOLUTION OF FISCAL DEVELOPMENTS AND POLICIES IN THE PACIFIC RIM

MANMOHAN SINGH KUMAR,

NIRVIKAR SINGH, AND JAEJOON WOO

## 9.1 Introduction

This chapter provides an overview and assessment of the evolution of the fiscal situation in 15 Asian economies that can be considered to be part of, or close to, the western side of the Pacific Rim. These economies include China, Hong Kong SAR, India, Indonesia, Japan, Laos, Malaysia, Mongolia, Myanmar, Nepal, Philippines, Singapore, South Korea, Thailand, and Vietnam. This includes three countries that could be classified as South Asian, but we include them to increase the balance of the sample across income levels, and for purposes of comparison. We do not provide any discussion here of what constitutes the boundary of the Pacific Rim. Note that we do not consider Latin American countries on the eastern side of the Pacific.

The goal of the chapter is to provide a compact assessment of the region's fiscal situation through mapping the experience of this set of economies, in the context of a global economy that is still recovering slowly from its worst shock in over 75 years. The financial crisis of 2008-2010 required individual and coordinated responses by governments to prevent economic activity from declining sharply, as financial markets seized up in a climate of fear and uncertainty. Governments around the globe used monetary and fiscal stimuli, as well as significant direct support to the banking sectors, to counteract and forestall the effects of a complete collapse of private sector confidence. The scope for such action, particularly on the fiscal front, and its efficacy varied considerably, however.

In many of the emerging Asian economies prudent policies and high economic growth rates in the preceding decade and a half provided substantial room for maneuver, while in others fiscal space was constrained.

Managing their fiscal situations remains an ongoing challenge for governments all over the world, including those in the Pacific Rim. An important factor in their ability to manage their post-crisis fiscal situations is the corresponding fiscal status before the crisis. Therefore, in this paper, we summarize 20 years of fiscal data, from 1990 to 2010.[1] An additional reason for looking at a longer period is that, beyond recovery from the crisis, the issue of managing demographic transitions and funding payments for increasing numbers of retired workers will loom larger for many of the Pacific Rim economies.

The description of developments is provided in Section 9.2, which discusses the evolution of fiscal balances, public debt, and growth in the Pacific Rim economies, and also looks at the revenue and expenditure ratios. Section 9.3 provides a brief summary of the role of policies and institutions that underlie these developments. It focuses in particular on two sets of issues: budgetary policies, including tax and expenditure policies, and alludes to the role of budgetary institutions, including fiscal rules, that underlie fiscal performance. Section 9.4 discusses the impact of growth and interest rates on the fiscal positions and debt sustainability (i.e., the impact of the interest rate-growth differential ("RG")), and the impact that public debt in turn can have on growth. This section also considers the fiscal challenges ahead, including those relating to demographics, the provision of social services, and the likely consequences for budgetary positions of financial sector reforms and opening up of capital accounts in some of the emerging economies. A last section concludes.

## 9.2 Summary of Fiscal Developments

The 15 economies are divided into three groups: Advanced (Hong Kong SAR, Japan, Singapore, and South Korea), Emerging (China, India, Indonesia, Malaysia, Philippines, and Thailand) and Low Income (Laos, Mongolia, Myanmar, Nepal, and Vietnam).

Figure 9.1 and Table 9.1 present the general government balance, as a percentage of GDP for the period 1990-2010.

- As is well-known, Japan has run large fiscal deficits over this period, as its economy slowed sharply following the bursting of the real estate and equity market bubble in the early 1990s, severe dislocation in the banking sector, and in recent years, population aging[2]. At the other end of this group, Singapore has run large fiscal surpluses, though these have become smaller over time. There is no discernible trend in Hong Kong or Korea's fiscal balance over the period. In all cases, the impact of the recent global crisis is evident, reflecting the discretionary fiscal

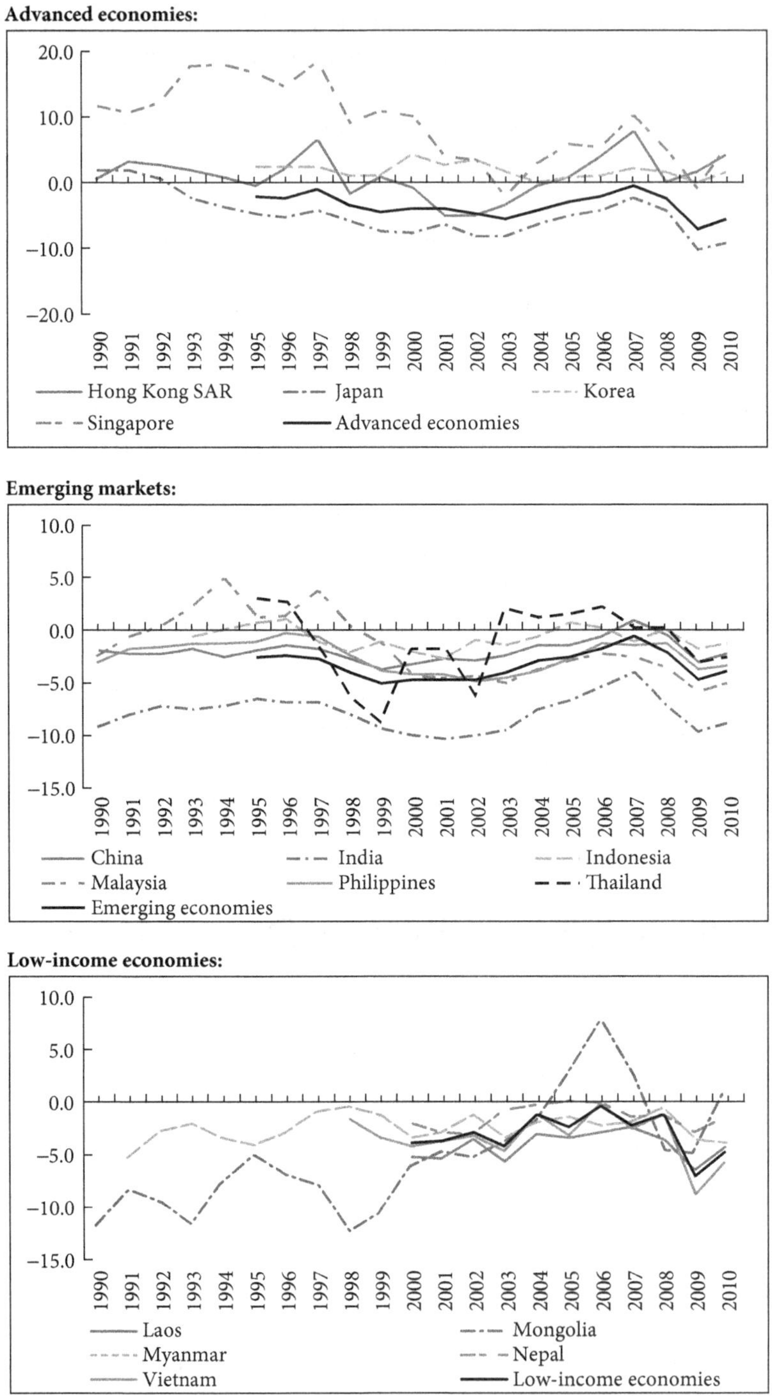


FIGURE 9.1 General Government Balance

**Table 9.1 General Government Balance (percent of GDP)**

| | 1990 | 1991 | 1992 | 1993 | 1994 | 1995 | 1996 | 1997 | 1998 | 1999 | 2000 | 2001 | 2002 | 2003 | 2004 | 2005 | 2006 | 2007 | 2008 | 2009 | 2010 |
|---|---|---|---|---|---|---|---|---|---|---|---|---|---|---|---|---|---|---|---|---|---|
| Hong Kong SAR | 0.7 | 3.3 | 2.7 | 2.1 | 1.0 | −0.3 | 2.1 | 6.4 | −1.8 | 0.8 | −0.6 | −4.9 | −4.8 | −3.2 | −0.3 | 1.0 | 4.1 | 7.7 | 0.1 | 1.6 | 4.3 |
| Japan | 1.9 | 1.9 | 0.8 | −2.4 | −3.7 | −4.6 | −5.1 | −4.0 | −5.6 | −7.4 | −7.6 | −6.3 | −8.0 | −8.0 | −6.2 | −4.8 | −4.0 | −2.4 | −4.2 | −10.3 | −9.2 |
| Korea | | | | | | 2.4 | 2.5 | 2.6 | 1.2 | 1.3 | 4.4 | 2.7 | 3.6 | 1.7 | 0.1 | 0.9 | 1.1 | 2.3 | 1.6 | 0.0 | 1.7 |
| Singapore | 11.9 | 10.6 | 12.3 | 17.8 | 18.1 | 16.9 | 14.7 | 18.3 | 9.2 | 10.9 | 10.1 | 4.0 | 3.4 | −2.3 | 3.0 | 5.8 | 5.3 | 10.2 | 5.2 | −0.8 | 5.4 |
| **Advanced Economies** | | | | | | **−1.9** | **−2.2** | **−1.1** | **−3.2** | **−4.3** | **−3.8** | **−3.8** | **−4.7** | **−5.3** | **−4.1** | **−2.8** | **−2.0** | **−0.3** | **−2.2** | **−7.0** | **−5.5** |
| China | −2.0 | −2.2 | −2.3 | −1.8 | −2.6 | −2.0 | −1.5 | −1.7 | −2.8 | −3.7 | −3.3 | −2.8 | −3.0 | −2.4 | −1.5 | −1.4 | −0.7 | 0.9 | −0.4 | −3.1 | −2.3 |
| India | −9.2 | −8.1 | −7.2 | −7.6 | −7.3 | −6.6 | −6.9 | −7.0 | −8.1 | −9.3 | −10.0 | −10.4 | −10.1 | −9.6 | −7.6 | −6.7 | −5.5 | −4.2 | −7.2 | −9.7 | −8.8 |
| Indonesia | | | | −0.6 | 0.0 | 0.7 | 1.1 | −1.1 | −2.1 | −1.0 | −2.0 | −2.7 | −0.9 | −1.4 | −0.6 | 0.6 | 0.2 | −1.0 | 0.0 | −1.8 | −1.2 |
| Malaysia | −2.4 | −0.6 | 0.4 | 2.2 | 4.9 | 1.2 | 1.4 | 3.7 | 0.3 | −1.2 | −4.4 | −4.5 | −4.5 | −5.1 | −3.7 | −3.0 | −2.3 | −2.6 | −3.6 | −5.9 | −5.1 |
| Philippines | −3.2 | −1.8 | −1.7 | −1.3 | −1.3 | −1.0 | −0.3 | −0.7 | −2.4 | −3.9 | −4.2 | −4.2 | −5.0 | −4.6 | −3.8 | −2.8 | −1.3 | −1.5 | −1.2 | −3.7 | −3.5 |
| Thailand | | | | | | 3.0 | 2.7 | −1.7 | −6.3 | −9.0 | −1.8 | −1.8 | −6.6 | 2.1 | 1.2 | 1.5 | 2.1 | 0.2 | 0.1 | −3.1 | −2.6 |
| **Emerging Economies** | | | | | | **−2.7** | **−2.4** | **−2.8** | **−4.1** | **−5.0** | **−4.8** | **−4.7** | **−4.8** | **−4.1** | **−2.9** | **−2.5** | **−1.7** | **−0.6** | **−2.1** | **−4.7** | **−3.9** |
| Laos | | | | | | | | | | | −5.2 | −5.5 | −3.6 | −5.7 | −3.1 | −3.4 | −2.9 | −2.5 | −3.6 | −6.5 | −4.2 |
| Mongolia | −11.8 | −8.4 | −9.5 | −11.7 | −7.8 | −5.1 | −6.8 | −7.9 | −12.4 | −10.6 | −6.1 | −4.7 | −5.2 | −3.7 | −1.8 | 2.6 | 7.6 | 2.6 | −4.5 | −5.0 | 1.2 |
| Myanmar | | −5.2 | −2.8 | −2.1 | −3.4 | −4.1 | −2.9 | −0.9 | −0.4 | −1.3 | −3.4 | −3.0 | −1.3 | −3.5 | −2.0 | −1.5 | −2.3 | −2.0 | −0.6 | −3.6 | −3.9 |
| Nepal | | | | | | | | | | | −2.0 | −3.0 | −3.1 | −0.7 | −0.3 | 0.0 | 0.0 | −1.5 | −1.3 | −3.0 | −1.4 |
| Vietnam | | | | | | | | | −1.6 | −3.3 | −4.3 | −3.8 | −3.3 | −4.8 | −1.2 | −3.3 | −0.2 | −2.5 | −1.2 | −9.0 | −5.7 |
| **Low-Income Economies** | | | | | | | | | | | **−4.0** | **−3.7** | **−2.9** | **−4.2** | **−1.4** | **−2.5** | **−0.5** | **−2.2** | **−1.3** | **−7.3** | **−4.8** |

response to the crisis and/or automatic stabilizers, with falls in the government balance in 2008 or 2009.

- Turning to the six emerging economies in our group, India is a clear outlier in its large negative general government balance. The sharp improvement in 2003-2007 appears to be somewhat of an aberration in the context of the entire 20-year period, and reflects both a marked pickup in economic activity leading to buoyant government revenues, as well as some positive effects following the adoption of the "Fiscal Responsibility and Budget Management Act" (FRBMA).[3] Only Thailand, of the other five emerging economies, has struggled with such a fiscal deficit, and its improvement was much sharper than India's, achieving a surplus several years in a row. All the six economies can be seen to have experienced rising fiscal deficits after the 1997 Asian crisis, as well as the recent global crisis. In the interim, however, they had improved their fiscal positions to the point where they were better placed (with India a partial exception) to deal with the latter shock.
- Data is somewhat more limited for the five low-income economies in the sample, but on the whole, they had relatively benign fiscal deficits before the latest crisis, and were able to increase those deficits sharply in the short run.

Turning next to the cumulative impacts of fiscal deficits, Figure 9.2 and Table 9.2 summarize the general government gross debt for the economies in the sample, as a percent of GDP.

- Among the advanced economies, Korea and Hong Kong SAR have very low debt positions, while Japan's is exceptionally high. Japan's debt ratio has been growing rapidly, reflecting both the large fiscal deficits and weak GDP growth. Despite the very low interest rates, the interest rate-growth differential has been unfavorable (see below) and it is difficult to foresee growth of the debt in this manner being sustainable. Although significantly less than that of Japan, Singapore's debt to GDP ratio is also somewhat high, and has been growing, albeit much more slowly.
- For the six emerging economies, India and China are at opposite extremes, with India's debt ratio high although easing somewhat due to earlier rapid economic growth. China's has been extremely low, though it has risen recently after the global crisis. Indonesia has managed to bring down its debt-GDP ratio substantially, while Thailand, after seeing a large increase following the Asian crisis, has managed to keep the level of debt steady as a percentage of GDP. On average, one can characterize government debt ratios as broadly sustainable for these emerging economies, at least at present.
- For the low-income economies, the data is quite limited, but what there is does not suggest strong concerns about the sustainability of government debt levels.

The next two sets of figures and tables, Figures 9.3 and 9.4 and Tables 9.3 and 9.4, provide two complementary ways of isolating non-cyclical components of the general government

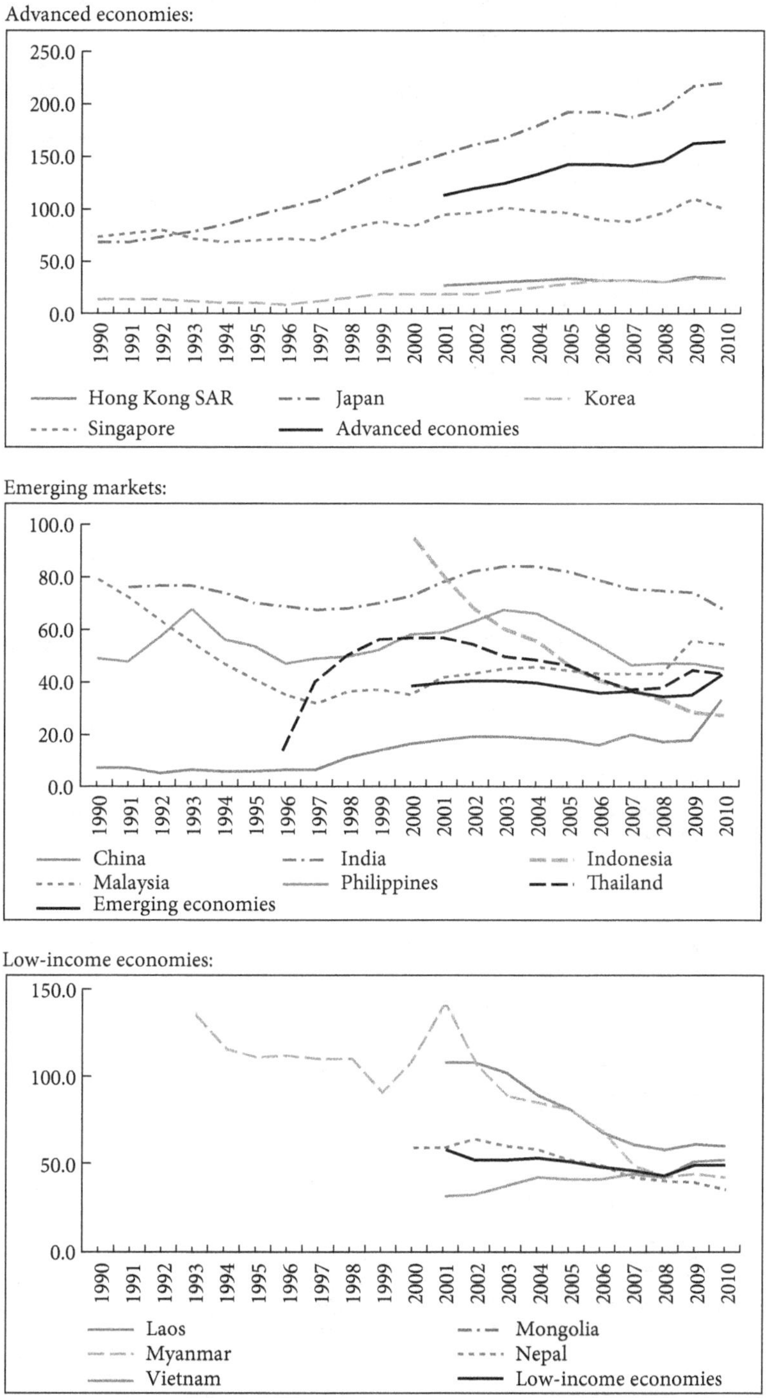


FIGURE 9.2 General Government Gross Debt

Table 9.2 General Government Gross Debt (percent of GDP)

| | 1990 | 1991 | 1992 | 1993 | 1994 | 1995 | 1996 | 1997 | 1998 | 1999 | 2000 | 2001 | 2002 | 2003 | 2004 | 2005 | 2006 | 2007 | 2008 | 2009 | 2010 |
|---|---|---|---|---|---|---|---|---|---|---|---|---|---|---|---|---|---|---|---|---|---|
| Hong Kong SAR | | | | | | | | | | | | 25.6 | 27.7 | 29.8 | 31.4 | 32.3 | 31.9 | 30.8 | 30.4 | 34.0 | 33.2 |
| Japan | 68.0 | 67.5 | 72.3 | 78.4 | 84.6 | 92.4 | 100.3 | 107.1 | 120.1 | 133.8 | 142.1 | 151.7 | 160.9 | 167.2 | 178.1 | 191.6 | 191.3 | 187.7 | 195.0 | 216.3 | 220.0 |
| Korea | 13.8 | 12.9 | 12.6 | 11.8 | 10.6 | 9.4 | 8.6 | 10.7 | 15.4 | 17.6 | 18.0 | 18.7 | 18.6 | 21.6 | 24.6 | 28.7 | 31.1 | 30.7 | 30.1 | 33.8 | 33.4 |
| Singapore | 73.1 | 75.6 | 79.4 | 71.5 | 67.4 | 70.1 | 70.7 | 69.4 | 81.0 | 87.4 | 82.6 | 94.8 | 96.6 | 101.3 | 98.0 | 95.8 | 89.4 | 87.6 | 95.3 | 109.3 | 99.1 |
| **Advanced Economies** | | | | | | | | | | | | **112.9** | **119.3** | **124.6** | **132.6** | **142.7** | **142.8** | **140.1** | **145.2** | **161.4** | **163.3** |
| China | 6.9 | 7.4 | 5.0 | 6.7 | 6.1 | 6.1 | 6.8 | 6.6 | 11.4 | 13.8 | 16.4 | 17.7 | 18.9 | 19.2 | 18.5 | 17.6 | 16.2 | 19.6 | 17.0 | 17.7 | 33.8 |
| India | | 76.4 | 76.8 | 76.9 | 74.1 | 70.4 | 68.7 | 67.6 | 67.8 | 70.1 | 72.7 | 77.8 | 82.2 | 84.3 | 84.1 | 81.8 | 78.5 | 75.4 | 74.7 | 74.2 | 67.3 |
| Indonesia | | | | | | | | | | | 95.1 | 80.2 | 67.8 | 60.5 | 55.8 | 46.3 | 40.4 | 36.9 | 33.2 | 28.6 | 27.4 |
| Malaysia | 79.5 | 72.2 | 63.4 | 54.9 | 46.9 | 40.9 | 35.2 | 31.8 | 36.1 | 36.9 | 35.3 | 41.3 | 43.1 | 45.1 | 45.7 | 44.4 | 43.2 | 42.7 | 42.8 | 55.4 | 54.2 |
| Philippines | 49.2 | 47.6 | 57.0 | 67.7 | 56.4 | 53.9 | 46.8 | 49.1 | 49.3 | 52.4 | 58.2 | 58.6 | 62.8 | 67.7 | 66.3 | 60.2 | 53.3 | 46.1 | 46.7 | 47.1 | 44.7 |
| Thailand | | | | | | | 14.9 | 40.2 | 50.3 | 56.2 | 57.0 | 57.2 | 54.0 | 49.5 | 48.2 | 46.2 | 41.2 | 37.3 | 37.5 | 44.3 | 43.3 |
| **Emerging Economies** | | | | | | | | | | | **38.1** | **39.4** | **40.4** | **40.6** | **39.8** | **37.8** | **35.4** | **36.2** | **34.2** | **34.8** | **42.7** |
| Laos | | | | | | | | | | | | 107.8 | 107.7 | 101.6 | 89.4 | 81.1 | 67.9 | 61.6 | 58.0 | 61.7 | 60.1 |
| Mongolia | | | | | | | | | | | | | | | | | | | | | |
| Myanmar | | | | 136.2 | 115.6 | 110.7 | 111.7 | 110.1 | 110.1 | 89.9 | 109.2 | 140.9 | 107.3 | 88.7 | 84.9 | 81.2 | 68.8 | 49.6 | 42.4 | 44.6 | 42.8 |
| Nepal | | | | | | | | | | | 59.7 | 59.1 | 64.3 | 60.7 | 58.3 | 51.9 | 49.3 | 42.8 | 40.4 | 39.5 | 35.9 |
| Vietnam | | | | | | | | | | | | 31.7 | 32.5 | 37.9 | 42.3 | 41.2 | 41.8 | 44.6 | 42.9 | 51.2 | 52.8 |
| **Low-Income Economies** | | | | | | | | | | | | **57.9** | **52.5** | **52.1** | **53.7** | **51.3** | **48.7** | **46.0** | **43.2** | **49.3** | **49.7** |

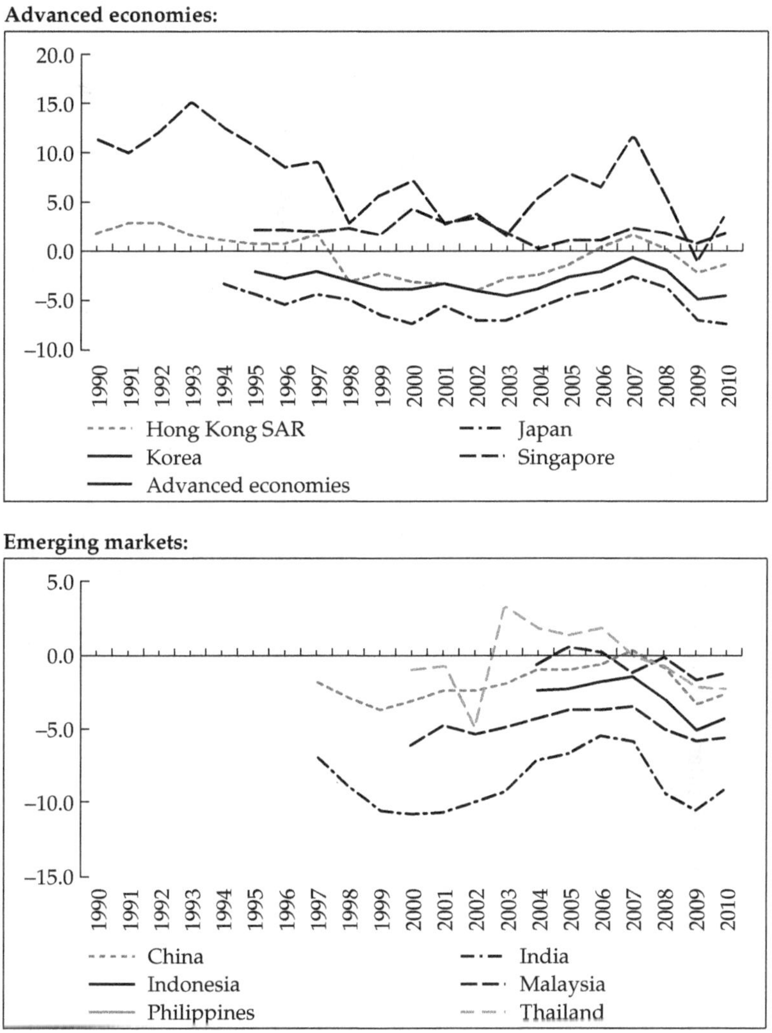


FIGURE 9.3 General Government Cyclically Adjusted Overall Balance

annual balances: the first set provides calculations of cyclically adjusted levels, while the second set estimates structural components of the balances.[4] These make it possible to obtain a perspective on whether the recent post-crisis fiscal response masks some underlying structural causes for concern. The data only permit us to perform this exercise for the advanced and emerging economies in the sample. The results for the two methods are similar: in all cases, comparing these figures with Figure 9.1, it appears that the structural component dominates the total general government balance. The cyclically adjusted balances appear to be less smooth, suggesting that on the whole, these economies do display some pro-cyclicality. For example, when the Indian fiscal balance improved during the high growth period of 2003-2007, the cyclical component partially counteracted a structural improvement.

**Table 9.3 General Government Cyclically Adjusted Overall Balance (percent of potential GDP)**

| | 1990 | 1991 | 1992 | 1993 | 1994 | 1995 | 1996 | 1997 | 1998 | 1999 | 2000 | 2001 | 2002 | 2003 | 2004 | 2005 | 2006 | 2007 | 2008 | 2009 | 2010 |
|---|---|---|---|---|---|---|---|---|---|---|---|---|---|---|---|---|---|---|---|---|---|
| Hong Kong SAR | | | | | | | | | | | | | | | | | | | | | |
| Japan | | | | | −3.4 | −4.4 | −5.5 | −4.5 | −5.0 | −6.5 | −7.4 | −5.7 | −7.0 | −7.1 | −5.8 | −4.6 | −3.9 | −2.6 | −3.7 | −7.1 | −7.4 |
| Korea | | | | | | 2.1 | 2.1 | 2.0 | 2.4 | 1.6 | 4.3 | 2.9 | 3.4 | 1.8 | 0.2 | 1.1 | 1.1 | 2.3 | 1.8 | 0.7 | 1.8 |
| Singapore | | | | | | 10.4 | 6.5 | 6.9 | 1.1 | 4.3 | 6.9 | 3.0 | 3.7 | 1.4 | 5.2 | 8.8 | 6.6 | 11.3 | 5.3 | −1.4 | 3.3 |
| **Advanced Economies** | | | | | | **−2.2** | **−3.2** | **−2.4** | **−3.0** | **−4.1** | **−3.9** | **−3.3** | **−4.1** | **−4.6** | **−3.9** | **−2.6** | **−2.3** | **−0.8** | **−2.0** | **−5.0** | **−4.7** |
| China | | | | | | | | −1.8 | −2.9 | −3.7 | −3.1 | −2.4 | −2.4 | −1.9 | −0.9 | −1.0 | −0.6 | 0.3 | −0.9 | −3.4 | −2.6 |
| India | | | | | | | | −6.9 | −8.9 | −10.5 | −10.8 | −10.7 | −9.9 | −9.3 | −7.1 | −6.6 | −5.5 | −5.8 | −9.4 | −10.6 | −9.2 |
| Indonesia | | | | | | | | | | | | | | | −0.7 | 0.6 | 0.2 | −1.2 | −0.2 | −1.7 | −1.2 |
| Malaysia | | | | | | | | | | | −6.0 | −4.8 | −5.0 | −4.8 | −4.2 | −3.7 | −3.6 | −3.9 | −5.4 | −6.3 | −5.1 |
| Philippines | | | | | | | | | | | −4.3 | −4.1 | −4.5 | −4.1 | −3.9 | −2.7 | −1.4 | −2.0 | −1.7 | −3.4 | −3.6 |
| Thailand | | | | | | | | | | | −1.0 | −0.7 | −5.2 | 3.2 | 1.9 | 1.4 | 1.8 | −0.1 | −0.8 | −2.1 | −2.3 |
| **Emerging Economies** | | | | | | | | | | | **−5.1** | **−4.6** | **−4.6** | **−3.8** | **−2.5** | **−2.3** | **−1.8** | **−1.5** | **−3.0** | **−5.1** | **−4.2** |

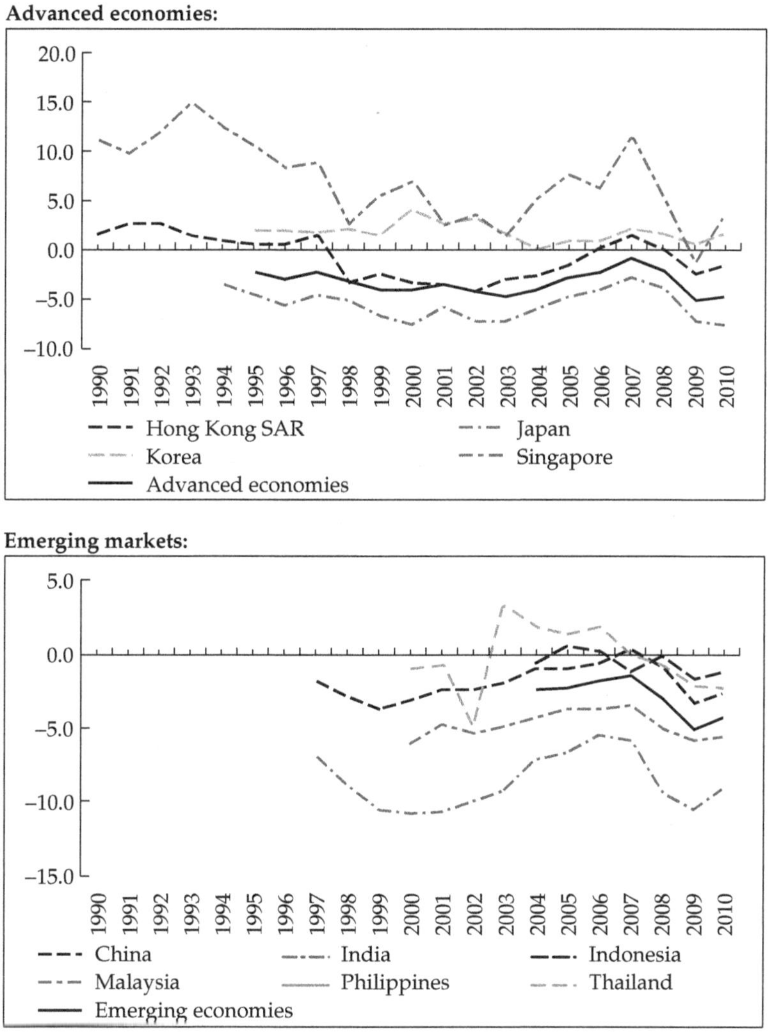


FIGURE 9.4 General Government Structural Overall Balance

Next, Figures 9.5 and 9.6 and Tables 9.5 and 9.6 report general government revenues and expenditures for the different economies in the sample. As is well-recognized, more advanced economies display larger government size, reflecting the role of the state and its ability and willingness to collect revenues and undertake expenditures[5]. However, it is notable that there is a wide degree of variation across countries in each grouping, suggesting that specific institutional factors also play an important role in determining this aspect of government capacity. In addition, there are structural differences at work, for example, an economy such as Indonesia's that has a substantial component of mineral extraction may find it relatively easier to raise tax revenue.

One other broad observation is possible for this group of countries: the rapid growth of most of these economies has not been accompanied by increases in the role of

**Table 9.4 General Government Structural Overall Balance (percent of potential GDP)**

| | 1990 | 1991 | 1992 | 1993 | 1994 | 1995 | 1996 | 1997 | 1998 | 1999 | 2000 | 2001 | 2002 | 2003 | 2004 | 2005 | 2006 | 2007 | 2008 | 2009 | 2010 |
|---|---|---|---|---|---|---|---|---|---|---|---|---|---|---|---|---|---|---|---|---|---|
| Hong Kong SAR | 1.8 | 2.9 | 2.9 | 1.6 | 1.0 | 0.7 | 0.8 | 1.6 | −3.1 | −2.2 | −3.1 | −3.3 | −4.1 | −2.8 | −2.5 | −1.4 | 0.5 | 1.7 | 0.2 | −2.2 | −1.4 |
| Japan | | | | | −3.4 | −4.4 | −5.5 | −4.5 | −5.0 | −6.5 | −7.4 | −5.7 | −7.0 | −7.1 | −5.8 | −4.6 | −3.9 | −2.6 | −3.7 | −7.1 | −7.4 |
| Korea | | | | | | 2.1 | 2.1 | 2.0 | 2.4 | 1.6 | 4.3 | 2.9 | 3.4 | 1.8 | 0.2 | 1.1 | 1.1 | 2.3 | 1.8 | 0.7 | 1.8 |
| Singapore | 11.4 | 9.9 | 12.1 | 15.2 | 12.7 | 10.6 | 8.6 | 9.0 | 2.7 | 5.8 | 7.2 | 2.7 | 3.7 | 1.4 | 5.3 | 7.9 | 6.5 | 11.5 | 5.4 | −1.4 | 3.5 |
| **Advanced Economies** | | | | | | **−2.0** | **−2.9** | **−2.1** | **−2.9** | **−3.9** | **−3.9** | **−3.3** | **−4.1** | **−4.5** | **−3.8** | **−2.6** | **−2.1** | **−0.7** | **−1.9** | **−4.9** | **−4.5** |
| China | | | | | | | | −1.8 | −2.9 | −3.7 | −3.1 | −2.4 | −2.4 | −1.9 | −0.9 | −1.0 | −0.6 | 0.3 | −0.9 | −3.4 | −2.6 |
| India | | | | | | | | −6.9 | −8.9 | −10.5 | −10.8 | −10.7 | −9.9 | −9.3 | −7.1 | −6.6 | −5.5 | −5.8 | −9.4 | −10.6 | −9.2 |
| Indonesia | | | | | | | | | | | | | | | −0.7 | 0.6 | 0.2 | −1.2 | −0.2 | −1.7 | −1.2 |
| Malaysia | | | | | | | | | | | −6.0 | −4.7 | −5.4 | −4.9 | −4.3 | −3.7 | −3.7 | −3.5 | −4.9 | −5.8 | −5.5 |
| Philippines | | | | | | | | | | | | | | | | | | | | | |
| Thailand | | | | | | | | | | | −1.0 | −0.7 | −5.2 | 3.2 | 1.9 | 1.4 | 1.8 | −0.1 | −0.8 | −2.1 | −2.3 |
| **Emerging Economies** | | | | | | | | | | | | | | | **−2.4** | **−2.3** | **−1.8** | **−1.4** | **−3.0** | **−5.1** | **−4.2** |

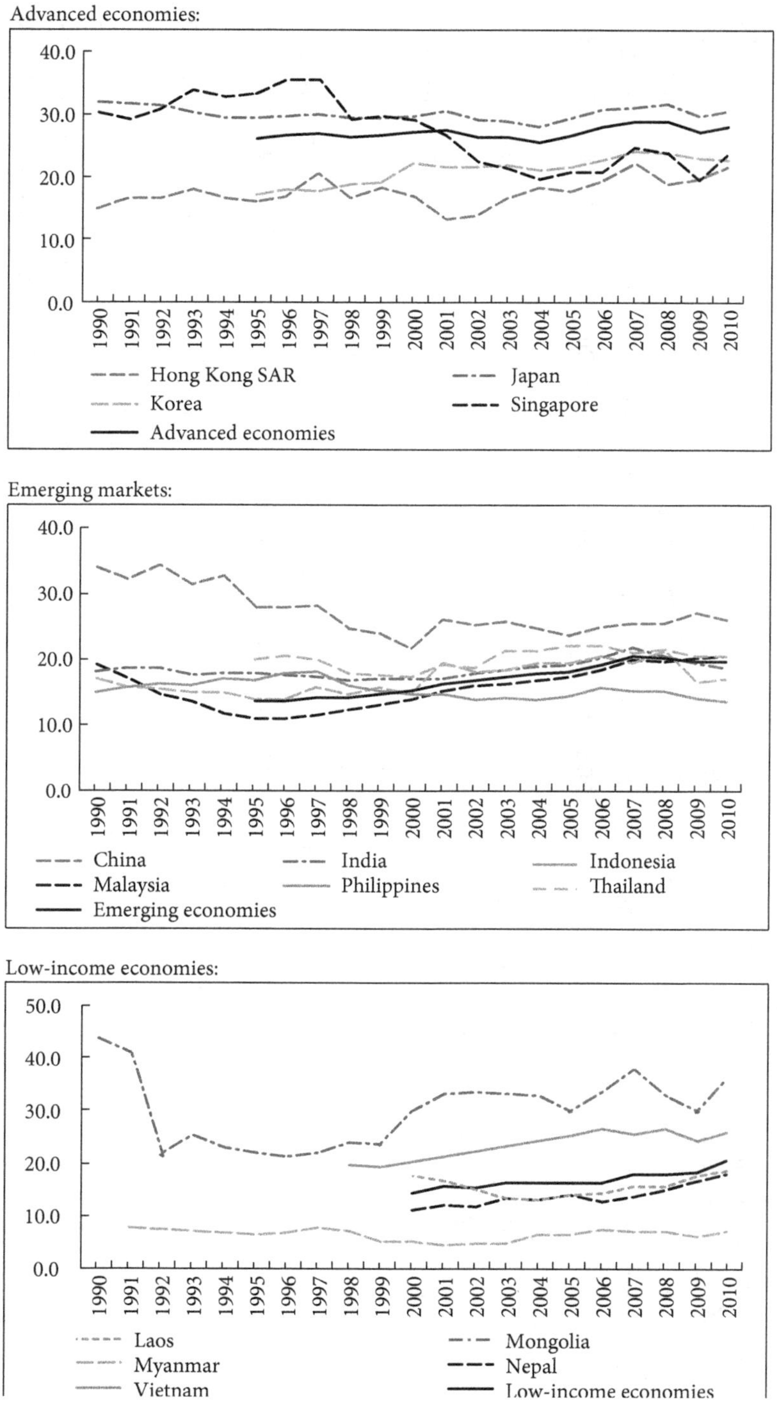


FIGURE 9.5 General Government Revenue

## Table 9.5 General Government Revenue (percent of GDP)

| | 1990 | 1991 | 1992 | 1993 | 1994 | 1995 | 1996 | 1997 | 1998 | 1999 | 2000 | 2001 | 2002 | 2003 | 2004 | 2005 | 2006 | 2007 | 2008 | 2009 | 2010 |
|---|---|---|---|---|---|---|---|---|---|---|---|---|---|---|---|---|---|---|---|---|---|
| Hong Kong SAR | 14.9 | 16.6 | 16.8 | 18.0 | 16.7 | 16.1 | 17.0 | 20.6 | 16.7 | 18.4 | 17.1 | 13.5 | 13.9 | 16.8 | 18.4 | 17.9 | 19.5 | 22.2 | 18.9 | 19.6 | 21.6 |
| Japan | 32.0 | 31.7 | 31.5 | 30.1 | 29.4 | 29.4 | 29.8 | 29.9 | 29.5 | 29.4 | 29.6 | 30.5 | 29.1 | 28.8 | 28.1 | 29.4 | 30.7 | 31.0 | 31.6 | 29.8 | 30.6 |
| Korea | | | | | | 17.3 | 18.0 | 17.9 | 19.0 | 19.3 | 22.3 | 21.8 | 21.6 | 21.9 | 21.2 | 21.8 | 22.7 | 24.2 | 24.0 | 23.0 | 22.9 |
| Singapore | 30.2 | 29.3 | 30.9 | 33.8 | 32.8 | 33.4 | 35.6 | 35.4 | 29.1 | 29.6 | 29.2 | 26.5 | 22.4 | 21.4 | 19.8 | 20.7 | 20.8 | 24.6 | 24.0 | 19.5 | 23.7 |
| **Advanced Economies** | | | | | | **26.2** | **26.7** | **27.0** | **26.5** | **26.6** | **27.3** | **27.5** | **26.3** | **26.3** | **25.7** | **26.7** | **27.9** | **28.8** | **28.9** | **27.3** | **28.1** |
| China | 19.0 | 16.9 | 14.6 | 13.6 | 11.6 | 10.7 | 10.8 | 11.4 | 12.1 | 13.1 | 13.8 | 15.1 | 15.9 | 16.2 | 16.6 | 17.2 | 18.2 | 19.8 | 19.7 | 20.0 | 20.4 |
| India | 18.0 | 18.4 | 18.4 | 17.5 | 17.8 | 17.7 | 17.4 | 17.3 | 16.7 | 16.8 | 17.0 | 17.0 | 17.6 | 18.2 | 18.9 | 19.1 | 20.2 | 21.8 | 20.3 | 19.3 | 18.5 |
| Indonesia | 16.8 | 15.6 | 15.3 | 14.8 | 14.8 | 13.7 | 13.6 | 15.5 | 14.4 | 15.5 | 14.6 | 19.3 | 17.9 | 18.3 | 19.3 | 19.4 | 20.3 | 19.3 | 21.3 | 16.5 | 17.1 |
| Malaysia | 33.8 | 31.9 | 34.0 | 31.3 | 32.6 | 27.8 | 27.8 | 28.1 | 24.6 | 23.9 | 21.3 | 26.0 | 25.3 | 25.6 | 24.5 | 23.7 | 24.8 | 25.4 | 25.3 | 27.0 | 26.0 |
| Philippines | 14.8 | 15.7 | 16.1 | 15.8 | 17.0 | 16.7 | 17.7 | 18.0 | 15.9 | 15.0 | 14.5 | 14.6 | 13.8 | 14.1 | 13.8 | 14.4 | 15.6 | 15.2 | 15.2 | 14.1 | 13.4 |
| Thailand | | | | | | 19.7 | 20.3 | 19.8 | 17.8 | 17.3 | 17.3 | 18.9 | 18.6 | 21.1 | 21.3 | 22.0 | 21.9 | 21.0 | 21.5 | 20.4 | 20.4 |
| **Emerging Economies** | | | | | | **13.5** | **13.5** | **14.0** | **14.0** | **14.6** | **15.0** | **16.3** | **16.8** | **17.2** | **17.7** | **18.1** | **19.1** | **20.3** | **20.0** | **19.7** | **19.7** |
| Laos | | | | | | | | | | | 17.8 | 17.0 | 15.3 | 13.5 | 13.1 | 14.4 | 14.6 | 15.8 | 16.0 | 17.9 | 18.7 |
| Mongolia | 44.0 | 41.2 | 21.7 | 25.4 | 23.0 | 22.3 | 21.6 | 22.2 | 24.0 | 23.7 | 30.0 | 33.5 | 33.8 | 33.4 | 33.1 | 30.1 | 33.8 | 37.9 | 33.1 | 30.2 | 36.5 |
| Myanmar | | 8.0 | 7.8 | 7.4 | 7.0 | 6.7 | 6.8 | 7.9 | 7.2 | 5.4 | 5.3 | 4.6 | 5.0 | 5.0 | 6.5 | 6.7 | 7.7 | 7.3 | 7.3 | 6.1 | 7.2 |
| Nepal | | | | | | | | | | | 11.4 | 12.1 | 12.0 | 13.4 | 13.4 | 14.1 | 12.9 | 14.0 | 15.3 | 16.8 | 18.2 |
| Vietnam | | | | | | | | | 20.0 | 19.4 | 20.4 | 21.4 | 22.5 | 23.4 | 24.6 | 25.4 | 26.9 | 25.9 | 26.8 | 24.4 | 26.0 |
| **Low-Income Economies** | | | | | | | | | | | **14.6** | **15.7** | **15.7** | **16.5** | **16.6** | **16.6** | **16.5** | **18.1** | **18.1** | **18.5** | **20.7** |

Advanced economies:

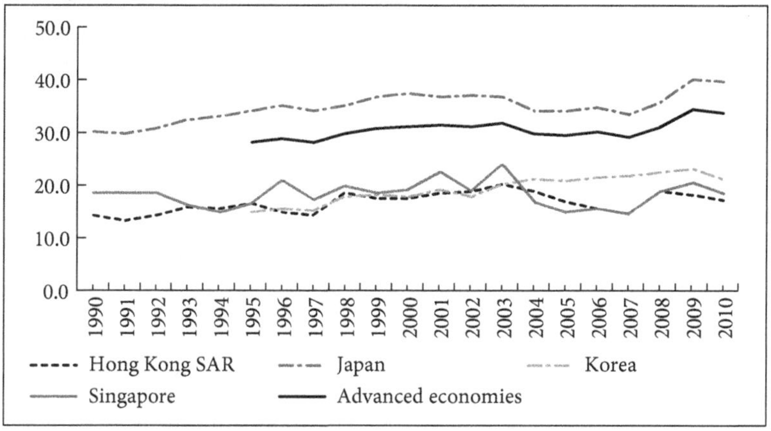


Emerging markets:

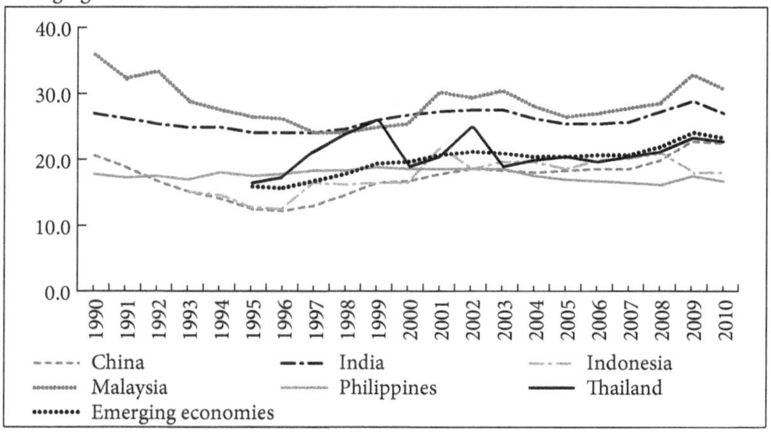


Low-income economies:

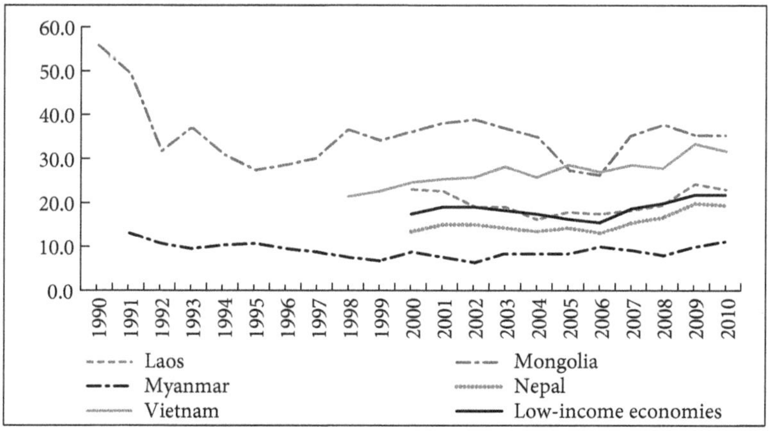


FIGURE 9.6 General Government Expenditure

**Table 9.6 General Government Expenditure (percent of GDP)**

| | 1990 | 1991 | 1992 | 1993 | 1994 | 1995 | 1996 | 1997 | 1998 | 1999 | 2000 | 2001 | 2002 | 2003 | 2004 | 2005 | 2006 | 2007 | 2008 | 2009 | 2010 |
|---|---|---|---|---|---|---|---|---|---|---|---|---|---|---|---|---|---|---|---|---|---|
| Hong Kong SAR | 14.3 | 13.4 | 14.1 | 15.9 | 15.7 | 16.4 | 14.9 | 14.2 | 18.5 | 17.6 | 17.7 | 18.4 | 18.7 | 20.0 | 18.7 | 16.9 | 15.4 | 14.5 | 18.8 | 18.0 | 17.3 |
| Japan | 30.1 | 29.9 | 30.8 | 32.5 | 33.1 | 34.0 | 34.9 | 34.0 | 35.1 | 36.8 | 37.3 | 36.8 | 37.1 | 36.8 | 34.2 | 34.2 | 34.7 | 33.4 | 35.8 | 40.1 | 39.8 |
| Korea | | | | | | 14.9 | 15.5 | 15.4 | 17.8 | 18.0 | 17.9 | 19.1 | 17.9 | 20.2 | 21.1 | 20.9 | 21.5 | 21.9 | 22.4 | 23.0 | 21.2 |
| Singapore | 18.4 | 18.6 | 18.6 | 16.1 | 14.7 | 16.5 | 20.9 | 17.1 | 19.8 | 18.7 | 19.0 | 22.5 | 19.0 | 23.7 | 16.8 | 14.9 | 15.5 | 14.4 | 18.8 | 20.4 | 18.4 |
| **Advanced Economies** | | | | | | **28.1** | **28.9** | **28.1** | **29.7** | **30.8** | **31.2** | **31.3** | **31.1** | **31.6** | **29.7** | **29.5** | **30.0** | **29.1** | **31.2** | **34.3** | **33.6** |
| China | 21.0 | 19.1 | 16.9 | 15.4 | 14.2 | 12.7 | 12.3 | 13.2 | 14.9 | 16.8 | 17.0 | 17.9 | 18.9 | 18.6 | 18.1 | 18.6 | 18.9 | 18.9 | 20.0 | 23.1 | 22.7 |
| India | 27.2 | 26.4 | 25.6 | 25.1 | 25.1 | 24.3 | 24.3 | 24.3 | 24.9 | 26.1 | 27.0 | 27.4 | 27.7 | 27.7 | 26.5 | 25.8 | 25.7 | 26.0 | 27.5 | 29.1 | 27.3 |
| Indonesia | | | | 15.4 | 14.8 | 13.0 | 12.6 | 16.7 | 16.5 | 16.6 | 16.6 | 22.0 | 18.7 | 19.7 | 19.9 | 18.8 | 20.1 | 20.3 | 21.3 | 18.3 | 18.3 |
| Malaysia | 36.2 | 32.5 | 33.6 | 29.1 | 27.7 | 26.6 | 26.5 | 24.4 | 24.3 | 25.1 | 25.8 | 30.5 | 29.7 | 30.7 | 28.3 | 26.6 | 27.1 | 28.0 | 28.9 | 32.9 | 31.1 |
| Philippines | 18.0 | 17.5 | 17.8 | 17.1 | 18.3 | 17.7 | 18.0 | 18.7 | 18.4 | 18.9 | 18.7 | 18.8 | 18.8 | 18.7 | 17.7 | 17.2 | 16.9 | 16.7 | 16.4 | 17.7 | 16.9 |
| Thailand | | | | | | 16.8 | 17.6 | 21.5 | 24.1 | 26.3 | 19.1 | 20.7 | 25.2 | 19.1 | 20.1 | 20.6 | 19.7 | 20.8 | 21.4 | 23.5 | 23.0 |
| **Emerging Economies** | | | | | | **16.2** | **15.9** | **16.8** | **18.1** | **19.7** | **19.8** | **20.9** | **21.5** | **21.2** | **20.6** | **20.6** | **20.8** | **21.0** | **22.1** | **24.4** | **23.6** |
| Laos | | | | | | | | | | | 23.0 | 22.5 | 19.0 | 19.2 | 16.2 | 17.8 | 17.5 | 18.3 | 19.6 | 24.4 | 22.9 |
| Mongolia | 55.8 | 49.7 | 31.2 | 37.0 | 30.8 | 27.4 | 28.4 | 30.1 | 36.4 | 34.3 | 36.0 | 38.2 | 39.0 | 37.1 | 35.0 | 27.5 | 26.2 | 35.3 | 37.6 | 35.2 | 35.3 |
| Myanmar | | 13.2 | 10.6 | 9.5 | 10.4 | 10.8 | 9.7 | 8.8 | 7.7 | 6.6 | 8.7 | 7.6 | 6.3 | 8.4 | 8.4 | 8.1 | 10.0 | 9.3 | 7.9 | 9.7 | 11.2 |
| Nepal | | | | | | | | | | | 13.4 | 15.1 | 15.1 | 14.2 | 13.7 | 14.1 | 13.0 | 15.5 | 16.6 | 19.8 | 19.5 |
| Vietnam | | | | | | | | | 21.6 | 22.8 | 24.6 | 25.2 | 25.8 | 28.2 | 25.8 | 28.7 | 27.1 | 28.5 | 28.0 | 33.4 | 31.8 |
| **Low-Income Economies** | | | | | | | | | | | **17.6** | **19.1** | **19.0** | **18.2** | **17.4** | **16.3** | **15.4** | **18.8** | **20.0** | **22.0** | **21.9** |

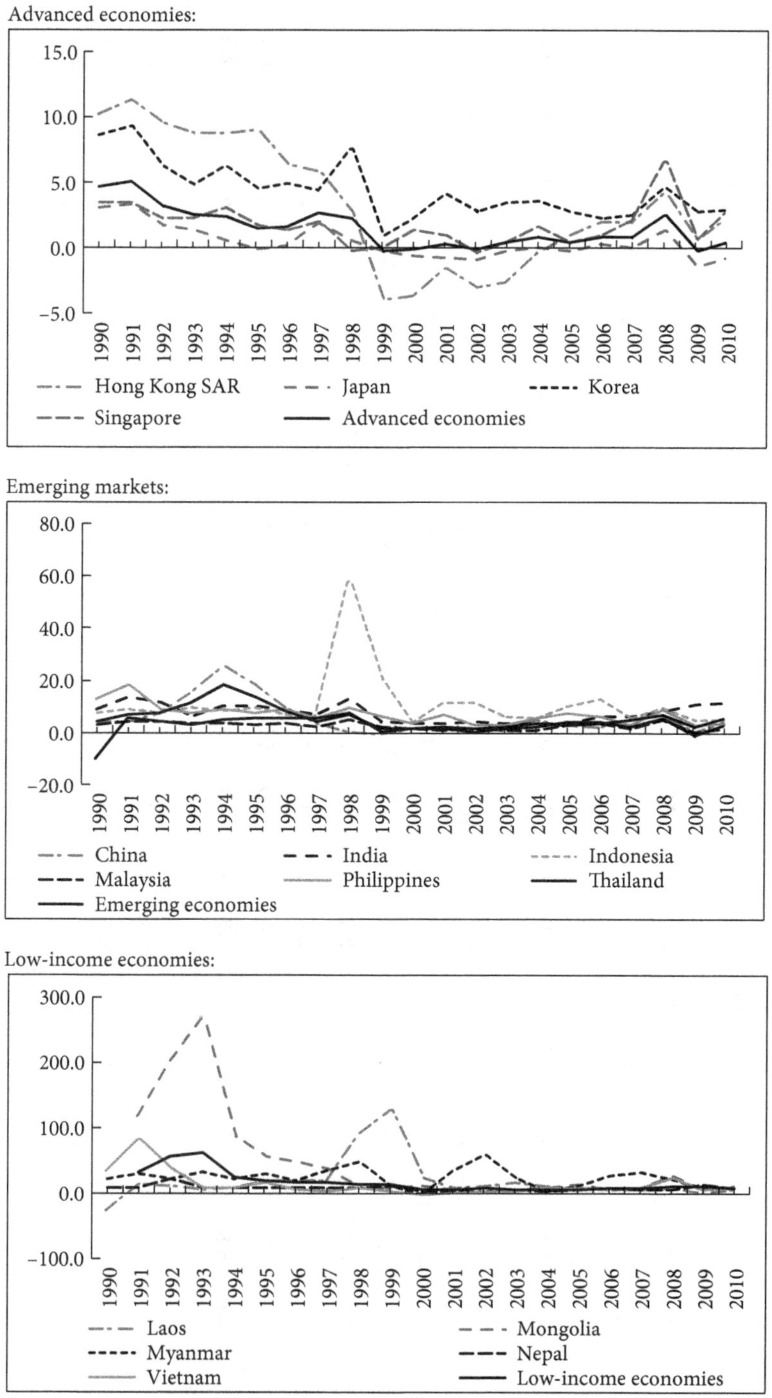


FIGURE 9.7 Inflation

**Table 9.7 Inflation (percent)**

| | 1990 | 1991 | 1992 | 1993 | 1994 | 1995 | 1996 | 1997 | 1998 | 1999 | 2000 | 2001 | 2002 | 2003 | 2004 | 2005 | 2006 | 2007 | 2008 | 2009 | 2010 |
|---|---|---|---|---|---|---|---|---|---|---|---|---|---|---|---|---|---|---|---|---|---|
| Hong Kong SAR | 10.3 | 11.3 | 9.5 | 8.8 | 8.8 | 9.0 | 6.3 | 5.8 | 2.8 | −3.9 | −3.7 | −1.6 | −3.1 | −2.6 | −0.4 | 0.9 | 2.0 | 2.0 | 4.3 | 0.6 | 2.3 |
| Japan | 3.1 | 3.3 | 1.7 | 1.3 | 0.6 | −0.1 | 0.1 | 1.9 | 0.6 | −0.3 | −0.7 | −0.8 | −0.9 | −0.3 | 0.0 | −0.3 | 0.3 | 0.0 | 1.4 | −1.4 | −0.7 |
| Korea | 8.6 | 9.3 | 6.2 | 4.8 | 6.3 | 4.5 | 4.9 | 4.4 | 7.5 | 0.8 | 2.3 | 4.1 | 2.8 | 3.5 | 3.6 | 2.8 | 2.2 | 2.5 | 4.7 | 2.8 | 3.0 |
| Singapore | 3.4 | 3.4 | 2.3 | 2.3 | 3.1 | 1.7 | 1.4 | 2.0 | −0.3 | 0.0 | 1.3 | 1.0 | −0.4 | 0.5 | 1.7 | 0.5 | 1.0 | 2.1 | 6.6 | 0.6 | 2.8 |
| **Advanced Economies** | **4.7** | **5.1** | **3.2** | **2.5** | **2.4** | **1.5** | **1.6** | **2.7** | **2.2** | **−0.2** | **−0.1** | **0.4** | **−0.1** | **0.5** | **0.9** | **0.5** | **0.9** | **0.8** | **2.5** | **−0.3** | **0.4** |
| China | 3.1 | 3.4 | 6.4 | 14.7 | 24.1 | 17.1 | 8.3 | 2.8 | −0.8 | −1.4 | 0.4 | 0.7 | −0.8 | 1.2 | 3.9 | 1.8 | 1.5 | 4.8 | 5.9 | −0.7 | 3.3 |
| India | 9.0 | 13.9 | 11.8 | 6.4 | 10.2 | 10.2 | 8.9 | 7.4 | 13.2 | 4.7 | 3.9 | 3.7 | 4.5 | 3.7 | 3.9 | 4.0 | 6.3 | 6.4 | 8.3 | 10.9 | 12.0 |
| Indonesia | 7.8 | 9.4 | 7.5 | 9.7 | 8.5 | 9.4 | 7.0 | 6.2 | 58.0 | 20.7 | 3.8 | 11.5 | 11.8 | 6.8 | 6.1 | 10.5 | 13.1 | 6.0 | 9.8 | 4.8 | 5.1 |
| Malaysia | 3.0 | 4.3 | 4.8 | 3.5 | 3.7 | 3.5 | 3.5 | 2.7 | 5.3 | 2.7 | 1.6 | 1.4 | 1.8 | 1.1 | 1.4 | 2.9 | 3.6 | 2.0 | 5.4 | 0.6 | 1.7 |
| Philippines | 13.2 | 18.5 | 8.9 | 7.6 | 9.0 | 8.1 | 9.1 | 5.8 | 9.7 | 6.4 | 4.0 | 6.8 | 3.0 | 3.5 | 6.0 | 7.6 | 6.2 | 2.8 | 9.3 | 3.2 | 3.8 |
| Thailand | −9.4 | 5.7 | 4.1 | 3.3 | 5.0 | 5.8 | 5.8 | 5.6 | 8.0 | 0.3 | 1.6 | 1.6 | 0.7 | 1.8 | 2.8 | 4.5 | 4.6 | 2.2 | 5.5 | −0.8 | 3.3 |
| **Emerging Economies** | **4.6** | **6.8** | **7.7** | **11.5** | **18.2** | **14.0** | **8.2** | **4.3** | **7.1** | **1.8** | **1.6** | **2.3** | **1.5** | **2.2** | **4.0** | **3.2** | **3.7** | **5.0** | **6.8** | **2.6** | **5.5** |
| Laos | −26.3 | 13.4 | 9.8 | 5.7 | 7.7 | 19.1 | 19.1 | 19.5 | 90.1 | 128.4 | 23.2 | 7.8 | 10.6 | 15.5 | 10.5 | 7.2 | 6.8 | 4.5 | 7.6 | 0.0 | 6.0 |
| Mongolia | | 120.2 | 202.5 | 268.4 | 87.6 | 56.8 | 46.8 | 36.6 | 9.4 | 7.6 | 11.6 | 6.2 | 0.9 | 5.1 | 7.9 | 12.5 | 4.5 | 8.2 | 26.8 | 6.3 | 10.2 |
| Myanmar | 21.9 | 29.1 | 22.3 | 33.6 | 22.4 | 28.9 | 20.0 | 33.9 | 49.1 | 10.9 | −1.7 | 34.5 | 58.1 | 24.9 | 3.8 | 10.7 | 26.3 | 32.9 | 22.5 | 8.2 | 8.2 |
| Nepal | 8.9 | 7.9 | 21.1 | 8.9 | 9.0 | 7.7 | 7.2 | 8.1 | 8.3 | 11.4 | 3.4 | 2.4 | 2.9 | 4.7 | 4.0 | 4.5 | 8.0 | 6.2 | 6.7 | 12.6 | 9.6 |
| Vietnam | 36.0 | 81.8 | 37.7 | 8.4 | 9.5 | 16.9 | 5.6 | 3.1 | 8.1 | 4.1 | −1.8 | −0.3 | 4.1 | 3.3 | 7.9 | 8.4 | 7.5 | 8.3 | 23.1 | 6.7 | 9.2 |
| **Low-Income Economies** | | **31.7** | **55.9** | **61.1** | **25.3** | **19.4** | **16.3** | **16.3** | **14.5** | **13.8** | **5.1** | **6.2** | **7.7** | **6.9** | **4.9** | **6.7** | **8.9** | **9.0** | **12.0** | **10.6** | **9.4** |

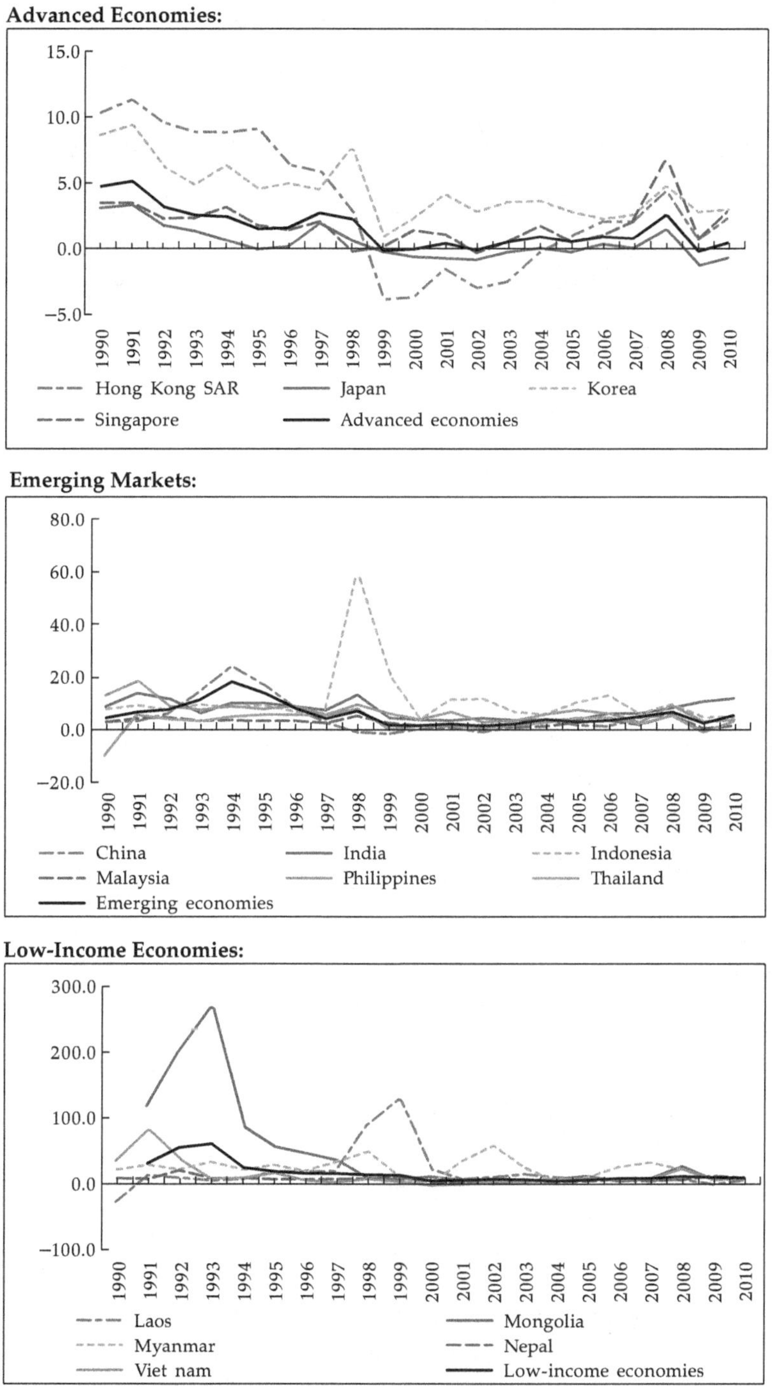


FIGURE 9.8 Growth Rates

**Table 9.8 Growth (percent)**

| | 1990 | 1991 | 1992 | 1993 | 1994 | 1995 | 1996 | 1997 | 1998 | 1999 | 2000 | 2001 | 2002 | 2003 | 2004 | 2005 | 2006 | 2007 | 2008 | 2009 | 2010 |
|---|---|---|---|---|---|---|---|---|---|---|---|---|---|---|---|---|---|---|---|---|---|
| Hong Kong SAR | 10.3 | 11.3 | 9.5 | 8.8 | 8.8 | 9.0 | 6.3 | 5.8 | 2.8 | −3.9 | −3.7 | −1.6 | −3.1 | −2.6 | −0.4 | 0.9 | 2.0 | 2.0 | 4.3 | 0.6 | 2.3 |
| Japan | 3.1 | 3.3 | 1.7 | 1.3 | 0.6 | −0.1 | 0.1 | 1.9 | 0.6 | −0.3 | −0.7 | −0.8 | −0.9 | −0.3 | 0.0 | −0.3 | 0.3 | 0.0 | 1.4 | −1.4 | −0.7 |
| Korea | 8.6 | 9.3 | 6.2 | 4.8 | 6.3 | 4.5 | 4.9 | 4.4 | 7.5 | 0.8 | 2.3 | 4.1 | 2.8 | 3.5 | 3.6 | 2.8 | 2.2 | 2.5 | 4.7 | 2.8 | 3.0 |
| Singapore | 3.4 | 3.4 | 2.3 | 2.3 | 3.1 | 1.7 | 1.4 | 2.0 | −0.3 | 0.0 | 1.3 | 1.0 | −0.4 | 0.5 | 1.7 | 0.5 | 1.0 | 2.1 | 6.6 | 0.6 | 2.8 |
| **Advanced Economies** | **4.7** | **5.1** | **3.2** | **2.5** | **2.4** | **1.5** | **1.6** | **2.7** | **2.2** | **−0.2** | **−0.1** | **0.4** | **−0.1** | **0.5** | **0.9** | **0.5** | **0.9** | **0.8** | **2.5** | **−0.3** | **0.4** |
| China | 3.1 | 3.4 | 6.4 | 14.7 | 24.1 | 17.1 | 8.3 | 2.8 | −0.8 | −1.4 | 0.4 | 0.7 | −0.8 | 1.2 | 3.9 | 1.8 | 1.5 | 4.8 | 5.9 | −0.7 | 3.3 |
| India | 9.0 | 13.9 | 11.8 | 6.4 | 10.2 | 10.2 | 8.9 | 7.4 | 13.2 | 4.7 | 3.9 | 3.7 | 4.5 | 3.7 | 3.9 | 4.0 | 6.3 | 6.4 | 8.3 | 10.9 | 12.0 |
| Indonesia | 7.8 | 9.4 | 7.5 | 9.7 | 8.5 | 9.4 | 7.0 | 6.2 | 58.0 | 20.7 | 3.8 | 11.5 | 11.8 | 6.8 | 6.1 | 10.5 | 13.1 | 6.0 | 9.8 | 4.8 | 5.1 |
| Malaysia | 3.0 | 4.3 | 4.8 | 3.5 | 3.7 | 3.5 | 3.5 | 2.7 | 5.3 | 2.7 | 1.6 | 1.4 | 1.8 | 1.1 | 1.4 | 2.9 | 3.6 | 2.0 | 5.4 | 0.6 | 1.7 |
| Philippines | 13.2 | 18.5 | 8.9 | 7.6 | 9.0 | 8.1 | 9.1 | 5.8 | 9.7 | 6.4 | 4.0 | 6.8 | 3.0 | 3.5 | 6.0 | 7.6 | 6.2 | 2.8 | 9.3 | 3.2 | 3.8 |
| Thailand | −9.4 | 5.7 | 4.1 | 3.3 | 5.0 | 5.8 | 5.8 | 5.6 | 8.0 | 0.3 | 1.6 | 1.6 | 0.7 | 1.8 | 2.8 | 4.5 | 4.6 | 2.2 | 5.5 | −0.8 | 3.3 |
| **Emerging Economies** | **4.6** | **6.8** | **7.7** | **11.5** | **18.2** | **14.0** | **8.2** | **4.3** | **7.1** | **1.8** | **1.6** | **2.3** | **1.5** | **2.2** | **4.0** | **3.2** | **3.7** | **5.0** | **6.8** | **2.6** | **5.5** |
| Laos | −26.3 | 13.4 | 9.8 | 5.7 | 7.7 | 19.1 | 19.1 | 19.5 | 90.1 | 128.4 | 23.2 | 7.8 | 10.6 | 15.5 | 10.5 | 7.2 | 6.8 | 4.5 | 7.6 | 0.0 | 6.0 |
| Mongolia | | 120.2 | 202.5 | 268.4 | 87.6 | 56.8 | 46.8 | 36.6 | 9.4 | 7.6 | 11.6 | 6.2 | 0.9 | 5.1 | 7.9 | 12.5 | 4.5 | 8.2 | 26.8 | 6.3 | 10.2 |
| Myanmar | 21.9 | 29.1 | 22.3 | 33.6 | 22.4 | 28.9 | 20.0 | 33.9 | 49.1 | 10.9 | −1.7 | 34.5 | 58.1 | 24.9 | 3.8 | 10.7 | 26.3 | 32.9 | 22.5 | 8.2 | 8.2 |
| Nepal | 8.9 | 7.9 | 21.1 | 8.9 | 9.0 | 7.7 | 7.2 | 8.1 | 8.3 | 11.4 | 3.4 | 2.4 | 2.9 | 4.7 | 4.0 | 4.5 | 8.0 | 6.2 | 6.7 | 12.6 | 9.6 |
| Vietnam | 36.0 | 81.8 | 37.7 | 8.4 | 9.5 | 16.9 | 5.6 | 3.1 | 8.1 | 4.1 | −1.8 | −0.3 | 4.1 | 3.3 | 7.9 | 8.4 | 7.5 | 8.3 | 23.1 | 6.7 | 9.2 |
| **Low-Income Economies** | | **31.7** | **55.9** | **61.1** | **25.3** | **19.4** | **16.3** | **16.3** | **14.5** | **13.8** | **5.1** | **6.2** | **7.7** | **6.9** | **4.9** | **6.7** | **8.9** | **9.0** | **12.0** | **10.6** | **9.4** |

**Table 9.9 Interest Rate-Growth Differentials (in percent) in Selected Countries, 1991–2010***

| | 1991–2000 | 2001–2010 |
|---|---|---|
| China | -7.29 | −9.84 |
| Hong Kong | | −1.20 |
| India | −3.79 | −3.96 |
| Indonesia | | −8.32 |
| Japan | 2.60 | 2.10 |
| Korea | −0.22 | 0.02 |
| Laos | −21.89 | −12.20 |
| Malaysia | −3.01 | −1.72 |
| Mongolia | −8.91 | −15.62 |
| Myanmar | −23.08 | −21.82 |
| Nepal | | −7.69 |
| Philippines | 0.95 | −0.27 |
| Singapore | −6.17 | −4.91 |
| Thailand | −1.54 | −4.26 |
| Vietnam | | −10.03 |
| Unweighted mean | −6.58 | −6.65 |
| Median | −3.79 | −4.91 |
| Advanced Economies | 1.31 | 0.20 |
| G-7 Economies | 3.08 | 1.69 |
| Emerging Economies | −0.55 | −3.70 |
| Low-Income Countries | −10.74 | −8.29 |

* The interest rate-growth differential, which is computed as $(r - g)/(1 + g)$, is the relevant factor for the debt dynamics.

government, such as has been observed in the advanced western economies. It may be that incomes have not reached the necessary levels to trigger such changes. However, since demographic transitions are occurring in a very different pattern than that of the historical past, Pacific Rim governments may need to pay more attention to increasing fiscal capacity to support the potential demand for increased government spending on social security, health care, and other forms of social insurance.

It is also useful to summarize the inflation and growth experience of this group of countries. Even if inflation ultimately reflects monetary factors, a country's fiscal balance affects the room for maneuver that monetary authorities possess. India's situation in 2011–2012 is a good example, where the central bank attempted to maintain a tightened monetary stance, in the face of stubbornly high inflation, meanwhile arguing that its room for loosening its policy in the face of a slowdown in economic growth was constrained by high fiscal deficits. Table 9.7 and Figure 9.7 summarize the inflation record over the last two decades. For the most part, the recent inflation picture is relatively benign, especially when compared to the 1990s. This is not to say that inflation has been low by advanced economy standards: indeed, several of the low-income countries are still dealing with inflation rates at or close to double-digit levels. Among the rest of the group (emerging and advanced) India is the clear outlier, with higher inflation than during its high-growth run of the early 2000s.

GDP growth of course has a very significant direct impact on government revenues, as well as, in most cases, on government expenditures. The impact of these "automatic stabilizers" varies considerably across countries, depending on the nature and progressivity of the tax system, the role the government plays in the provision of social safety nets, including unemployment benefits, and in the subsidy regime. In should also be noted that with regard to the impact on debt sustainability, the differential between the real interest rate and growth is key (see section below). As far as growth itself is concerned, as Table 9.8 and Figure 9.8 summarize, the record of the Asian economies has varied significantly across countries and over time. Despite the effect of the "Asian crisis" in the second half of the 1990s, growth has been generally high for the emerging economies over the last two decades, with China and India in particular registering an average of 10.5 percent and 6.5 percent per annum respectively, and with India showing a clear acceleration over the last decade. In the case of advanced economies, while Japan's performance has been weak, especially during the 1990s following the bursting of the asset price bubble, performance of the other smaller advanced economies has been strong. The growth performance of low-income economies has also been impressive, with high growth sustained in Vietnam.

## 9.3 Budgetary Policies and Institutions

Japan is a distinct member of the set of countries considered here, in terms of its income level and demographic composition. Having reached advanced country income levels as well as undergoing a demographic transition, its social security fund and spending are a significant fraction (about a third) of the total government size, considerably more than the OECD average. At the same time, overall government revenue and expenditure as percentages of GDP are smaller than the OECD average. Partially reflecting the age distribution, Japan's public spending is less on education and more on health, relative to the OECD average.

China and India also are distinct in terms of their sheer size. Each of them has a three-tier system of governance, and both have gone through periods of institutional reform in the 1990s, designed to manage provincial or state level fiscal imbalances. On the whole, following different specific paths to this reform, both countries succeeded in this, but India has been unable to maintain this fiscal rectitude at the central level. India also differs from China in having a much lower percentage of expenditure conducted at the local level—arguably, this has contributed to lower effectiveness of public spending in India relative to China, although other institutional factors no doubt play a role as well. Both countries have also instituted tax reforms to rationalize their indirect tax systems, again starting from very different initial points, but leading toward VAT-type systems with broad coverage. Overall, the revenue-to-GDP ratios of the two countries are quite similar.

Korea, while an advanced economy and member of the OECD, is a recent arrival to this status, and its government structure reflects this. Korea spends more on economic affairs than the OECD average, though the size of government is smaller than the average. Korea's history also plays a role, with a relatively large share of expenditure on defense. As the economy transitions to maturity, the size of government relative to GDP is increasing, and the government has been deliberately building up a social safety net as the population ages. Korea's tax-to-GDP ratio is also quite low in comparison to other OECD countries. There is a relatively heavy reliance (about 60 percent) on indirect taxes, chiefly a VAT system that was introduced in 1977. There are also individual and corporate income taxes, as well as local taxes.

Singapore and Hong Kong SAR are both city economies, but with very different political institutions. Their revenue and expenditure ratios are similar, but their official debt positions are quite different. The latter reflects the fact that Singapore has a sizable sovereign wealth fund, exceeding its gross debt stock. Singapore has invested heavily in public infrastructure and housing as well. Hong Kong SAR has a unique history, one that is still reflected in its tax system. Direct taxes are the main source of revenue, but rates are low, and the base is actually quite narrow. There is an ongoing debate about introducing a Goods and Services Tax (GST). Singapore, on the other hand, has a more traditional and comprehensive tax system, including GST, and mildly progressive direct taxes on individuals and corporations.

The remaining nine economies in the group are quite diverse, but all share to some extent the challenges faced by China and India, of making government expenditure more effective, of broadening tax base, and achieving greater efficiency in revenue collection. Of these economies, Malaysia is the richest, and has achieved the most in terms of public infrastructure development. Indonesia, Malaysia and the Philippines rely on universal food subsidies, rather than targeted income transfers. On the revenue side, Laos, Nepal and Thailand have relatively high reliance on indirect taxes, with Nepal and the Philippines also having high ratios of international trade taxes to government revenue. Malaysia relies the least on indirect taxes and has the highest ratio of direct taxes to government revenue.[6] For all these countries, as well as the two population giants, finding the right mix of transfers and investment, and revenues to finance them—essentially striving for what India's ruling coalition has dubbed "inclusive growth"—will be a continuing challenge (for some discussion of fiscal policy and political economy issues, see Woo 2009).

## 9.4 Debt and Growth

From the perspective of fiscal policy, the relationship between public debt and growth in the Asian economies deserves particular attention. There are two separate but interrelated aspects: first, the role of the differential between GDP growth and interest rates in the evolution of public debt; and second, the impact of high debt on GDP growth. We consider these in turn:

### 9.4.1 Interest-Growth Differential in Asian Economies

Public debt sustainability depends in an important way on the differential between interest rate on government debt and the GDP growth rate (RG).[7] A positive differential (interest rate exceeding growth rate) means that a government will require a primary surplus to stabilize any given debt ratio, with the required surplus being proportional to RG and the debt ratio. However, if RG is negative for an extended period, the debt ratio can decline toward zero even with a primary deficit—that is servicing existing debt with new borrowing. Sustained negative RG therefore implies a Ponzi scheme, that is, a government can roll over debt and interest without the debt ratio ballooning, and this is not tenable in the long run (see Blanchard and Weil 1992, and Bartolini and Cottarelli 1994).

Recent empirical analysis suggests a clear negative correlation between RG and GDP per capita (see Escolano, Shabunina, and Woo 2011). RG has been on average around 1 percentage point for large advanced economies over the past decade, but below -7 percentage points among non-advanced economies—exerting a powerful stabilizing influence on government debt ratios. While in general large negative RG differentials are due to real interest rates below market equilibrium—possibly stemming from financial repression and captive and distorted markets, in many of the Asian economies the convergence or income catch-up process has also played an important role.

What are the facts regarding the Asian economies? Table 9.9 provides the basic calculations for RG for each of the two decades of the sample period for these economies, and the averages for *all* emerging market and advanced economies.[8] As the calculations indicate, the experience of several of the Asian economies has been quite different from that of other emerging market economies.

- Consider first the industrial economies for which the average for all countries (unweighted) was 1.3 and 0.2 percent over the decades of the 1990s and 2000s, respectively. Japan's RG was substantially higher than the industrial country average, although relative to the G7 average, the outcome was not significantly different—it was somewhat lower in the first half of the sample period but higher in the second half of the period. As noted above, over the entire period, Japan saw over a three-fold increase in its debt ratio, reflecting both the RG and, in several years, large primary deficits. Korea's RG was substantially lower in the first half, but about the average for all industrial countries in the second half, while Singapore had significantly negative RG in both periods.

- In the case of Asian emerging market economies, the average RG was lower than that of the average of all emerging market economies. There is again significant variation across countries, with RG in the second half of the period ranging from −9.8 for China to −4 for India and −0.27 for the Philippines. Together with the situation on the primary balances, this has resulted in stable or declining debt ratios for many of these economies. A key point to note here is that in many instances, as in China and India, the negative RG is due relatively more to high sustained GDP growth than to low interest rates per se, which would reflect financial repression.
- In the case of low-income Asian economies, RG has been appreciably even more negative, ranging in the second half of the period from −23.1 percent for Myanmar to −15.6 percent for Mongolia, and -10 percent for Vietnam. In the case of several of these low-income economies, low interest rates are likely to have played a more significant role than high growth rates per se.

Looking ahead, changes in growth rates, shares of government revenue to GDP, and development of the financial system to reduce financial repression and facilitate investment (with higher, market-determined interest rates on government debt) will all factor into the prospects for RG and the sustainability of government debt. While the state of public finances in the Asian emerging market and the low-income countries is not alarming, to the extent that RG rises with financial integration and market development, and potential growth slows down as the catch-up process proceeds, there could be challenges for debt sustainability in some of these economies. These considerations could be reinforced by the adverse demographic developments in some of the economies (such as China; see for instance Baldacci et al. 2010), or the increasing emphasis on the provision of larger public social safety nets.

## 9.4.2 Impact of Public Debt on Growth

Given the above discussion, an interesting question arises regarding the extent to which Asian emerging market economies in particular have benefited from a virtuous cycle between low public sector debt and high growth: in other words, to what extent have they benefited from a positive feedback loop between low or significantly negative RG, leading to confidence in the sustainability of public finances which in turn had beneficial effects for GDP growth and which further strengthened public finances and reinforced fiscal sustainability. In this context, some quite recent literature on the effect of public indebtedness on investment, productivity, and growth is relevant and instructive in assessing the challenges that the Asian economies might face over the medium and long run.

There are several channels through which high public debt can impact medium- and long-run growth[9] : these include adverse effect on investment and growth via higher long-term interest rates (Gale and Orszag 2003; Baldacci and Kumar 2010), higher future distortionary taxation (Barro 1979; Dotsey 1994) and lower future public capital spending (Aizenman et al. 2007). In addition, higher inflation (Sargent and Wallace 1981; Cochrane 2010) and greater uncertainty about prospects and policies can adversely affect growth. In more extreme cases of a debt crisis, by triggering a banking or currency crisis, these effects can be magnified (Burnside et al. 2001). High debt is also likely to constrain the scope for countercyclical fiscal policies, which may result in higher volatility and further lower growth (see Woo 2009) on the effects of procyclicality and volatility of fiscal policy on growth).

In assessing the empirical magnitude of this effect, a variety of methodological issues, including reverse causality and simultaneity bias, need to be taken into account (see Kumar and Woo 2010 and 2013, and Rogoff and Reinhart 2010). When these methodological factors are taken into account, the broad conclusion of this analysis is that particularly beyond a certain threshold there is an inverse relationship between initial public debt and subsequent growth, controlling for other determinants of growth: on average, a 10 percentage point increase in the initial debt-to-GDP ratio is associated over the medium to long run with a slowdown in real per capita GDP growth of around 0.2 percentage points per year, with the impact being somewhat smaller in advanced economies than in emerging market economies[10]. There is some evidence of nonlinearity with higher levels of initial debt having a proportionately larger negative effect on subsequent growth. Further analysis through a growth decomposition exercise suggests that the adverse effect of public debt on growth largely reflects a slowdown in labor productivity growth, in turn mainly due to reduced investment and slower growth of capital stock.

In the light of the above findings, how can one interpret the experience of Asian economies? As far as the advanced economies are concerned, the position of Japan stands out, in that there has been a striking weakness in growth performance that has accompanied an equally striking increase in the public debt ratios. In other cases, particularly for the emerging market economies, public debt ratios have generally been on the relatively low side, with apparently no adverse effect on subsequent growth, and in the light of the above discussion contributing to the virtuous cycle of negative RG and high growth. In this context, India's growth performance may be seen to be somewhat of a puzzle in that its debt ratio has been high (although oscillating around a relatively stable path), and yet its growth rate has accelerated over the past decade. The answer to that puzzle may lie in part in the further empirical analysis that suggests that the nature and denomination of public debt may have a bearing on the extent to which high debt adversely affects growth (see Kumar and Woo 2013). This analysis suggests that when a country's economic and financial position vis-à-vis the rest of the world is weak or the share of its foreign-currency denominated debt is large, the adverse impact of initial public debt on subsequent growth tends to be more pronounced than when these factors are at more moderate levels. In India's case, both these elements may be of some import, in that the bulk of India's debt is held by domestic residents and is financed in local currency.

The above discussion further reinforces the challenges that the Asian emerging market and low-income economies could face if RG begins to turn less favorable. Whether that happens due to an increase in bond yields on government debt, or through a decline in potential growth, the resultant increase in the debt ratios, were it to be significant, could in turn begin to have an adverse effect on GDP growth. This could lead to adverse dynamics between high debt and low growth, exacerbating the fiscal challenges over the medium and long run.

## 9.5 Conclusion

The discussion in this chapter has highlighted the significant variation in fiscal developments and policies over the past two decades in the Pacific Rim countries. The heterogeneity in public finances, not only between the main groupings of countries but also within them, is not surprising given the enormous differences across countries in the level of development, per capita incomes, fiscal frameworks and institutions, growth performance, and other structural characteristics. This heterogeneity does mean, however, that fiscal challenges and the policies needed to deal with them vary substantially across countries.

Nonetheless, the discussion highlights the fact that in some countries, such as Japan, where debt ratios are already very high and where the benefit from negative interest rate growth differential is not available, sustained large primary surpluses would be needed to place public debt on a sustainable path. In some of the emerging market economies in the region, although negative interest-rate-growth differentials have had a significant beneficial impact, it is not clear how long such an effect can be counted on. This then increases the onus on sound fiscal policies to improve the primary balances and keep public finances sustainable.

In several countries in the region, public finances will likely be further under pressure due to the adverse demographics unfolding, with its impact both on potential growth following the decline in work force, and the increase in expenditures for government support of the social safety net. In other countries, the increased perceived need to strengthen these safety nets, or increase expenditures on public goods, including education and health, will put pressure on public finances. Lest these demands lead to increases in public debt ratios that begin to have adverse effect on growth itself, and set off a vicious cycle of high debt and low growth, it is essential for fiscal policies in many countries in the Pacific region to become even more forward-looking and prepare for the challenges ahead.

## Notes

1. For some countries, data are missing for several of the earlier years of the period under consideration.
2. See for instance, Saxonhouse, G., and R. Stern (eds) (2004).

3. FRBMA was enacted in 2003 to provide a framework for fiscal discipline, and reduce India's central fiscal deficit to 3 percent of GDP by March 2008. However, with the onset of the global crisis, the deadlines for achieving the targets were initially postponed and then suspended in 2009.
4. The *cyclically adjusted balance (CAB)* provides an estimate of the fiscal balance that would attain under current policies if the output gap were equal to zero. The *structural balance (SB)* is the difference between the CAB and two measures of other non-recurrent effects that go beyond the output cycle: one-time operations, that is, discretionary measures that are not expected to be repeated in the future (such as asset sales); and beyond-the-output-cycle effects, or cyclical fluctuations that do not coincide with the output cycle (e.g., changes in commodity prices, or asset prices). Such effects are often especially important for commodity exporters and financial centers.
5. The role of the provision of social security, health-care, education and other services, combined with demographics, is important in explaining the size of government in advanced economies generally.
6. This description is based on data from the World Bank World Development Indicators ([www.worldbank.org]). A breakdown of tax data is not available for Myanmar and Vietnam.
7. The discussion in this section draws on Escolano, Shabunina, and Woo (2011). The RG implications for debt sustainability are invariant to whether interest rate and growth rate are both measured in nominal or real terms.
8. RG is computed as the differential between the effective interest rate (actual interest payments divided by the debt stock at the end of the previous year) and the growth rate of nominal GDP, divided by the GDP growth rate plus one. The interest rate is adjusted for the change in the domestic currency value of foreign currency denominated debt due to exchange rate changes.
9. The discussion below draws on Kumar and Woo (2010, 2013).
10. See Kumar and Woo (2010). The analysis is based on a sample of 46 advanced and emerging market economies; a larger sample of 79 economies that includes in addition 33 developing countries yields similar results.

## References

Aizenman, J., K. Kletzer, and B. Pinto, 2007. "Economic Growth with Constraints on Tax Revenues and Public Debt: Implications for Fiscal Policy and Cross-Country Differences," NBER Working Paper No. 12750. (Cambridge, Massachusetts: National Bureau of Economic Research).

Baldacci, E., G. Callegari, D. Coady, D. Ding, M. Kumar, P. Tommasino, and J. Woo, 2010, "Public Expenditures on Social Programs and Household Consumption in China," IMF Working Paper WP/10/69.

Baldacci, E., and M. Kumar, 2010, "Fiscal Deficits, Public Debt and Sovereign Bond Yields," IMF Working Paper 10/184 (Washington: International Monetary Fund).

Barro, R., 1979, "On the Determinants of the Public Debt," *Journal of Political Economy*, Vol. 85 (5), pp. 940–71.

Bartolini, L., and C. Cottarelli, 1994, "Government Ponzi Games and the Sustainability of Public Deficits under Uncertainty," *Ricerche Economiche* 48, 1–22.

Blanchard, O. J., and P. Weil, 1992, "Dynamic Efficiency and Debt Ponzi Games under Uncertainty," NBER Working Paper No. 3992.

Burnside, C., Eichenbaum, M. and Rebelo, S. 2001. Prospective Deficits and the Asian Currency Crisis, *Journal of Political Economy* 109, 1155–1598.

Cochrane, J., 2010, "Understanding Policy in the Great Recession: Some Unpleasant Fiscal Arithmetic," Working Paper (Chicago: University of Chicago Press).

Dotsey, M., 1994, "Some Unpleasant Supply Side Arithmetic," *Journal of Monetary Economics*, pp. 507–524.

Escolano, J., A. Shabunina, and J. Woo, 2011, "The Puzzle of Persistently Negative Interest-Growth Differentials: Financial Repression or Income Catch-up?" IMF Working Paper, No. 11/260, November.

Gale, W., and P. Orszag, 2003, "The Economic Effects of Long-term Fiscal Discipline," Urban-Brookings Tax Policy Center Discussion Paper No. 8 (Washington: Brookings Institution).

Kumar, M.S., and J. Woo, 2010, "Public Debt and Growth," IMF Working Paper No. 10/174 (Washington: International Monetary Fund); Update, March 2012.

Kumar, M.S. and J. Woo, 2013, "Public Debt and Growth: An Update," Forthcoming, *Post-Crisis Fiscal Policy,Part 1*, IMF.

Reinhart, C., and K. Rogoff, 2009, "The Aftermath of Financial Crises," *American Economic Review*, Vol. 99 (2), pp. 466–472, May.

Reinhart, C., and K. Rogoff, 2010, "Growth in a Time of Debt," *American Economic Association Papers and Proceedings*, Vol. 100 (2), pp. 1–9, May.

Sargent, T., and N. Wallace, 1981, "Some Unpleasant Monetarist Arithmetic," *Quarterly Review*, (Fall) Federal Reserve Bank of Minneapolis.

Saxonhouse, G., and R. Stern (eds) (2004). *Japan's Lost Decade: Origins, Consequences and Prospects for Recovery.* Malden, MA: Blackwell.

Woo, J., 2003, "Economic, Political and Institutional Determinants of Public Deficits," *Journal of Public Economics*, Vol. 87(3), pp. 387–426, March.

Woo, J., 2009, "Why Do More Polarized Countries Run More Procyclical Fiscal Policy?" *Review of Economics and Statistics*, Vol. 91(4), pp. 850–870, November.

# PART IV

# REGIONAL GOVERNANCE AND TRADE LINKAGES

CHAPTER 10

# ASIA IN GLOBAL ECONOMIC GOVERNANCE

WENDY DOBSON[1] AND PETER A. PETRI

## 10.1 Asia's Involvement in Global Economic Governance

As its share of global output rises, Asia's role in global economic governance is rising as well. Even before the global financial crisis, the Bretton Woods institutions, created by the United States and its allies in 1944, were becoming less and less representative of the distribution of economic power. The global crisis highlighted gaps in cooperation and accelerated the relative rise of Asian and other emerging economies. As world leaders sought to respond to the crisis, they turned to the G20 as the new, more inclusive institution to formulate policy. Since then the G20 leaders forum has been designated the world's "premier forum" for economic cooperation. The transition to a new global architecture has begun.

What role will Asia play in this transition and what other new institutions are emerging? While Asia's interests and influence are more apparent, no other specific institutions or cooperative approaches have yet emerged. Much still depends on whether economic growth in Asia and the West slows or accelerates; whether political tensions within or among economies intensify; and whether global energy, resource, health, or other new issues radically change the priorities for international cooperation. Any of these areas could come to dominate trends in global governance. Even so, some central features of a transition are becoming clear:

- Economic governance will be multi-polar, mainly due to Asia's growing economic weight. The United States and the European Union will remain important centers of power for some time, but the global system will not be dominated by any one country or region as it was by the United States since the collapse of the Soviet Union.

- The modes of international cooperation will be conditioned by Asian preferences for consensus decision-making and a preference for relationships over rules and legal frameworks.
- The transition to new institutions will be gradual because of the inertia built into existing institutions and a natural resistance to change. Asian policymakers see economic and political stability as foundation stones for economic growth and influence and have varied interests in change. Significantly as well, Asia has been a major beneficiary of the existing world order and it will not be easy to find widely accepted alternatives.

These observations suggest that global governance will change as a result of Asia's rise, but not quickly or dramatically. We have called this environment one of "contested stability"—an era likely characterized by incremental additions to global rules, continuity of institutions, and ongoing tension about future directions. Given the important role of economic integration in the past half century, one might worry that such an ambiguous world order might lead to worse economic outcomes. This need not be so. It is important to distinguish between the level of integration and further liberalization. Economic integration is already high, and current rules, if sustained, provide ample room for efficient specialization. In the meantime, other development engines—especially technological innovation—can continue to drive growth, taking the place of incremental liberalization in the past.

Such expectations are not universally shared; some observers have urged Asia to pursue a more aggressive leadership role. For example, the Asian Development Bank has criticized Asian economies for being "passive onlookers in the debate on global rule-making and reluctant followers of the rules." Others have asked Asia to "deliver on its global responsibilities," given its strong relative economic position in the wake of the financial crisis, to promote a new global order based on open markets (Drysdale 2010).

We argue that Asian leadership is likely to emerge slowly, for both historical and utilitarian reasons. That may mean stalemates on issues that demand decisive global responses (for example, climate change), but will also give the world more time to adjust to the extraordinary transformation represented by Asia's rise. We begin by reviewing the distinguishing characteristics of international cooperation in an Asian context. We next consider the changing functions of the international system, examining both the demand for and supply of cooperation in the context of changing economic interactions. We then explore the implications for cooperation in key functional areas, focusing on the pressures facing existing institutions and their possible adaptations.

## 10.2 Cooperation with Asian Characteristics

The global financial crisis has diminished the prospects of the United States and Europe and boosted those of most Asian economies. Asia survived the crisis with less damage, stronger fundamentals, and typically less debt than Europe and the United States.[2] Figure 10.1 provides a projection of the shifts in global economic power by plotting the likely evolution of the shares of GDP (at market prices) for the United States, Asia and Europe. In 2010, the shares of all three are roughly equal in the 20 percent range. As the shares continue to shift over the next 20 years, Asia will reverse its relative position compared to the United States and Europe in 1990 (Petri 2010). Meanwhile, each bloc is also multi-polar; Asia itself consists of four major components with potentially diverging policy perspectives: China, Japan, India and ASEAN.

The dispersion of world economic activity has led to calls for revising the governance of the IMF, World Bank, and other global institutions, especially by providing a stronger role for Asia's emerging economies. The G20 leaders have tasked the global institutions to undertake particular roles in carrying forward their collective goals; they set up the Financial Stability Board, for example, and charged the IMF with carrying forward mutual assessment of economic policies. More accurate representation of current economic conditions will make global institutions more legitimate, but much depends on how the new votes will be exercised. More diffuse voting power and accountability could simply lead to more deadlock rather than better decisions. Asia's participation will be an important determinant of whether concerted global efforts are possible.

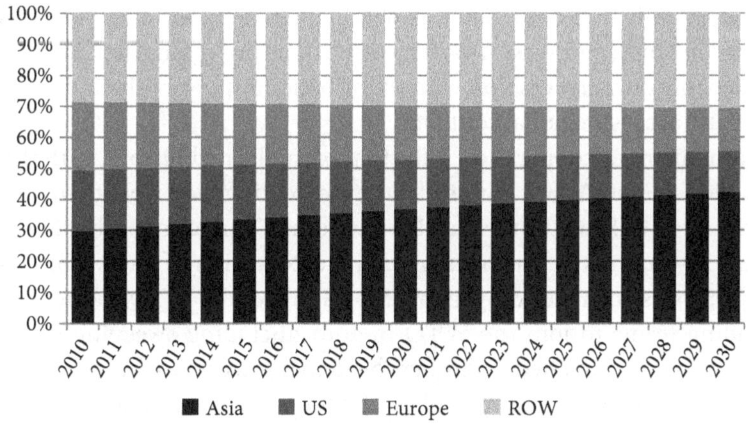


FIGURE 10.1 Changing Shares of World GPD (Purchasing Power Parity)

*Source:* ADB (2012). Asia includes ASEAN, China, India, and Japan. Europe includes the EU 25 plus Iceland and Norway.

Of course, there is no single Asian voice or perspective or set of economic interests. Asia is the largest region in the world, already in terms of population but eventually also in terms of output, and arguably the most diverse and complicated. Nevertheless, the approaches that dominate Asian cooperation have distinctive characteristics, in part developed to manage diversity. These characteristics and their contrasts with the prevailing global system provide a useful backdrop to analyzing the modalities of Asia's role in international governance.

History is a powerful factor in shaping contemporary Asian reactions to international cooperation. Skepticism and distrust of global systems and relationships is prevalent in Asia, despite the region's strong economic connections with the world. The roots are easy to understand; Asia's contacts with the West until well after World War II were based on sharply unequal power relations and are remembered as leading to humiliation and exploitation. Parts of all Asian countries, with the exception of Thailand, were occupied at one time or another by Western colonial powers, eventually joined by Japan. Even when not fully occupied, countries were required to accede to commercial treaties under the threat and occasional use of force. The opium trade marked a tragic low in the history of international trade. These deep-rooted memories may even help to explain Asia's bitter political reaction to the IMF during the Asian Financial Crisis; the political fallout from IMF interventions appears to have been greater in Asia than, say, in Latin America, where arguably harsher and longer-lasting conditionality was applied.

History pervades Asia's regional relations as well. Relative to Europe, Asia's historical tensions remain closer to the surface, flare up more frequently, and are less completely resolved. Thus they impede integration efforts. For example, while a complex network of bilateral free trade agreements now crisscrosses Asia, little progress has been made on a trade agreement to link the region's three largest economies: China, Japan, and Korea. Efforts to intensify such negotiations are periodically announced, but then fall prey to some new political event that ratchets tensions back to a level that no longer permits business as usual. Most recently, this was the effect of confrontations between China and Japan on islands that both claim as national territory. Political tensions are even more strained in South and West Asia. As a result of intra-regional tensions, many Asian countries depend on partnerships with extra-regional powers, including the United States, to ensure against regional conflicts.

Asia's mechanisms of cooperation reflect this complicated history, with three important implications. First, Asia is committed to the existing global economic framework. Trade played a central role in most Asian economic "miracles" and cooperation with international institutions was instrumental in the expansion of trade. China is a prominent example; it was not a founding member of GATT or the WTO and accepted unusually demanding terms to join the WTO in 2001, including sweeping revisions in its regulatory regimes.[3] China hedged its bets by denying access to foreign capital in some industries and by continuing to control capital flows, exchange rates, government procurement, and innovation. But it dramatically opened its economy by inviting foreign investment, signing new bilateral and multilateral agreements, and reaching out to the ASEAN-based regional framework. FDI inflows set new records among developing economies. Trade linkages intensified especially fast with the United States, a former enemy and new rival.

Second, Asia's ability to focus on economic development critically depends on peace and political stability. Wealth, not bullets, has been the route to power and influence in Asia. The United States, in turn, helped to underwrite this stability. Today China's economic power is rising and its political and military influence will inevitably grow. These trends have raised concerns among smaller countries in the region. To maintain stability and to build trust, China will need to extend its regional power cautiously, while assuring neighbors that Chinese markets and policies will continue to serve as a powerful regional locomotive (Zhang and Tang 2005).

Third, there is no Asian hegemon to impose an economic order in the region, nor is there enough trust among the largest economies to share leadership. To a large extent, China and Japan compete with each other by forming parallel regional integration initiatives. It falls on the smaller countries, such as the members of ASEAN and Australia, to conduct a delicate balancing act and convene regional cooperative forums and to launch initiatives such as the Regional Comprehensive Economic Partnership (RCEP).

Fourth, the principle of non-interference is enshrined in Asian institutions such as ASEAN and is frequently upheld as a pillar of Chinese foreign policy. It is also a source of contention between Western and Asian policy makers, for example with respect to economic relations with countries governed by oppressive regimes. The principle reflects Asian governments' intention to act in what they see as national interest, whether or not their actions conflict with "universal values" as seen from abroad. This issue has been highlighted by prominent Asian leaders such as Lee Kuan Yew, as they have attempted to formulate "Asian values" that could be distinguished from Western values.

These opposing threads—Asia's pride in its accomplishments and its internal divisions, juxtaposed with its recognition of the benefits of global connections and stability—will influence future trends. Asia has generally supported international institutions, but has yet to play a role commensurate with its power and (arguably) debt to the global system. For example, Japan has been blamed for preventing progress on global agricultural issues that would have facilitated a new Doha agreement between developing and developed countries. China and India, in turn, were central to the unresolved battle over safeguard policies that brought the Doha negotiations to a halt in July 2008. Except for pioneers like Singapore, smaller Asian economies have also failed to band together as champions of the world trading or monetary system, instead voicing narrower concerns about particular interests.

Asia's relative inexperience with international institutions also contributes to its global reticence. The region is focused on the still-urgent requirements of national development and is averse to complex legal systems and international rules. Although Asian economies have concluded many trade agreements in recent years, these have typically covered fewer products, areas of policy and issues than Western agreements. The agreements themselves are shorter and vaguer than the templates used, say, by Australia or the United States. Most intra-Asian agreements are limited primarily to tariff reductions and few have chapters on "behind the border" issues such as investment, services, competition and regulatory policy.

Viewed closer up, perspectives on the international system vary among Asian economies, ranging from the relatively global perspectives of Asia's most and least populous countries, China, India and Singapore, to the more regional focus of mid-sized East and Southeast Asian countries. The largest among these, Japan, Korea, and Indonesia, are attempting to balance regional and global engagement. But overall, the position articulated by Chinese President Hu Jintao in 2006, calling for peaceful development in an harmonious world (*hexie shijie*) is reasonably consistent with broader Asian views. The main elements of this vision include principles of independence, self-reliance, and peaceful coexistence, with differences resolved on the basis of mutual respect and cooperation. These principles do not envision conflict with the West, but nevertheless challenge Western views by omitting priorities such as human rights, democracy, transparency, and the rule of law. Critiques of the contemporary world order include (Wang and Rosenau 2009):

- The status quo order is "undemocratic"; the democratic deficit in international institutions, dominated by western nations and serving their own interests, (and tolerating US unilateralism) should be reduced;
- North-South economic disparities are growing and the wealthy advanced nations practice double standards in which they expect concessions from developing nations that are not reciprocated. These disparities should be reduced through "shared development and common prosperity."
- Countries have differing histories and cultures and therefore differing political systems and economic models. The international system should observe diversity and tolerance, and countries should not interfere in each other's affairs but seek "reconciliation amid differences."
- Cross-border conflicts should be resolved through cooperation rather than force.

These principles imply, among other things, that the United States should become a "normal" country and abide by international law; that western countries should open their markets more to developing countries; and there should be greater reliance on the UN system in multilateral diplomacy and world peace. These critiques also have substantial overlap with views often argued in the West, namely that the international order should be built on international regimes, democratic decision-making within international institutions, and should emphasize fairness, mutual respect, and development.

While Asian and Western prescriptions for the world order have substantial overlap, much uncertainty remains about how these principles will translate into action as Asia's power grows. Several contradictions will need to be resolved. President Xi Jinping's catchy but enigmatic new phrase, the China Dream, envisioned that, by "the mid-21st century, China will be turned into a modern socialist country that is prosperous, strong, democratic, culturally advanced and harmonious; and the Chinese dream, namely, the great rejuvenation of the Chinese nation, will be realized" (Xi 2013). For now, this vision is still at odds with China's still-low per capita income and evolving economic, legal, and political institutions. The phrase has been interpreted by some as a call for determined leadership of global and regional institutions, but the China Daily calls it "an inspirational vision of equilibrium between East and West, unity and diversity, progress and sustainability" (Gosset 2013). In the West, the concern is that China and other major Asian powers have so far kept a low profile, and have not played a large enough role in discouraging countries from violating international norms of conduct.

## 10.3 Functions and Constraints of Economic Governance

Tensions between Asia's rising power and slow ascent to leadership are playing out against the background of an increasingly complex international agenda. The market for international economic governance can be thought of as connecting demand and supply—the demand side reflecting the need for making cooperative decisions in the collective interest, and the supply side reflecting the ability of the international system to generate such cooperation. The good transacted in this market is a public good, namely the agreements and institutions needed to make international transactions predictable and cheap, with minimal negative side effects (such as environmental or financial risks). Thus, we can think of the rising demand for such public goods (due to the growing complexity of the international economy) to lead to rising supply, provided that the international system is capable of organizing the necessary cooperation.

The demand for international cooperation has grown sharply, in part because of burgeoning flows of goods and services. World trade has risen three times as fast as output and real international transactions were 14 times as great in 2008 as they were in 1960. In addition, economic exchanges have become more complex and multi-dimensional. Direct investment and intellectual property flows (as measured by patents or royalty payments) have grown faster than trade. The fragmentation of production has led to new requirements for logistics and flows of services, technology, and information. Financial flows—essential in their own right as well as for moving goods and capital—have added further complexity. Innovations in information technology have created vast opportunities for exchanging services that were previously untraded. All of these trends raise new questions about the coherence of a wide range of (historically) national policy decisions involving investment, intellectual property rights, the environment, and many other fields.

The supply of international cooperation, however, has arguably failed to keep pace with demand. One way to provide such public goods is to have a hegemonic leader impose rules and institutions through a combination of pressures and incentives. England in the nineteenth century and the United States in much of the twentieth century played this role; their large scale made it worth their while to offer significant benefits to other countries—principally through access to their own markets—to induce them to participate in an open world order. But in a multi-polar world the provision of global public goods encounters "free rider" problems; smaller economies prefer to benefit from access to others' markets without providing access to their own. As the relative power of the United States has declined, the prominence of free rider problems has grown, and the supply of global public goods has declined, notwithstanding the increased need for cooperation.

Some global public goods can be replaced by regional public goods that serve a smaller membership. In recent years, the world trading system has seen an explosion of regional agreements that benefit two or more partners. From a theoretical perspective, these agreements represent public goods provided by clubs—institutions that serve only their limited membership. This is possible for public goods that are non-rivalrous (more than one member of the club can use their services at the same time) but at least partially excludable (non-members can be denied access to them). While international trade agreements fall into this category, many other forms of collaboration do not. For example, since the benefits of reducing greenhouse gas emissions are universally available, whether or not countries signed the cooperative agreement to do so, regional policies cannot definitively mitigate climate change.

International organizations are a club that provides services that are essential, and under some conditions optimal, and yet cannot be produced privately. They are subject to the challenges generally faced by clubs. They are not easily scaled; expanding clubs become unwieldy because larger memberships make it harder for them to meet the preferences of all club members. They are also inflexible; charters and super-majority voting rules, designed to ensure the interests of a club's charter members, place strict limits on change. These problems are modest when clubs are formed: founding members have similar interests and create services to meet common needs, as did the participants at the Bretton Woods conference. But over time, as membership grows, interests diverge. This creates tensions among club members and, eventually, makes clubs unable to meet members' needs. These problems are compounded by charters that make it difficult to change governance.

The evolution of the IMF, the World Bank, and the WTO roughly follow the predictions of club theory. As Figure 10.2 shows, their memberships have multiplied since they were originally founded. Yet governance structures and voting shares have adjusted little. Quotas have been revised several times since they were first set in 1944, but have not kept pace with economic growth.[4] Emerging economies have much smaller voting shares than early members. As a result, international organizations find it increasingly difficult to carry out their responsibilities.

Ideally, international organizations should be universal (globally inclusive), democratic (responsive to individual members), and effective (able to adapt and deliver services quickly). As Kawai, Petri, and Sisli-Ciamarra (2009) argue, these three goals are very difficult to meet simultaneously, yielding a governance trilemma (Figure 10.3). Many organizations can satisfy two of the three goals but then fail on the third. For

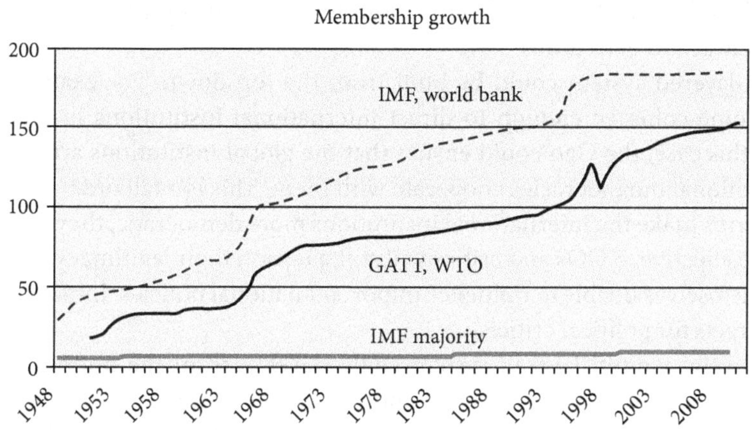


FIGURE 10.2 Growth of Membership of IMF, WB, and GATT/WTO

*Note*: IMF majority refers to the number of countries required to produce a majority vote.

*Source:* [www.wto.org], [www.imf.org]

example, the United Nations is universal and democratic, but has difficulty making and implementing decisions because of its large and diverse membership.

One solution to the trilemma is a layered architecture for making decisions. In such a structure, smaller "democratic and effective" institutions (say, regional trade groups) are the principal actors, ideally coordinated by a "universal" global framework (say, the G20 or a system of rules such as GATT article XXIV). This is akin to functional federalism within larger countries, and to the principle of subsidiarity in Europe (Casella and Frey 1992). This framework can generate a wider range of public goods than are possible under universal clubs. A layered institutional framework would permit global institutions to manage global interdependence while permitting deeper cooperation on

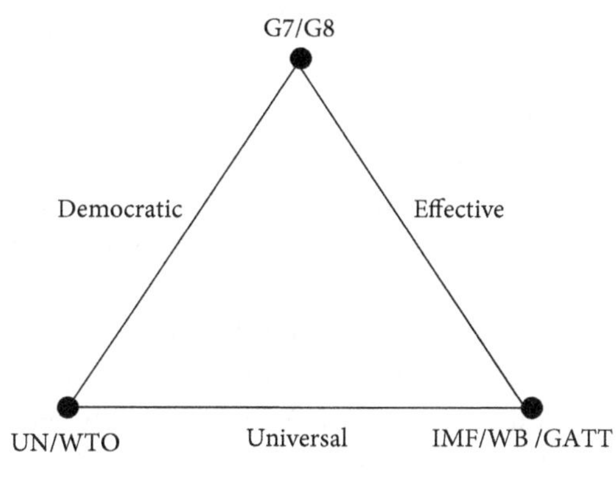


FIGURE 10.3 The governance trilemma

*Source:* Kawai et al. (2009).

sub-global tracks. The theoretical foundations for a layered approach rest on the theory of clubs (Kawai and Petri 2010).

A multi-layered system could be built from the top down. For example, the G20 might become cohesive enough to direct international institutions in administering policy. In this case, the G20 could ensure that the global institutions are strengthened and that national bureaucracies cooperate with them. This is a tall order: even if governance reforms make the international institutions more democratic, they may not make them more effective. NGOs and critics will still question their legitimacy, and they may still find themselves unable to influence important national policies. Inevitably, they will become targets for political criticism.

Alternatively, a multi-layered system could develop from the bottom up through increased cooperation among regional and functional institutions. In Asia, 14 "major economic cooperation groups" have been identified by the Asian Development Bank (ADB 2008). ASEAN, although struggling to implement the ASEAN Economic Community, an extensive economic integration agreement, is the most ambitious organization of its kind in the developing world. Many other groups, however, are little more than talk shops. To be effective, they would need more support from governments, including resources to monitor and enforce cooperative decisions. For example, a new model of emergency finance in the Chiang Mai Initiative Multilateralization (CMIM) would need to develop its own adequate monitoring and analytical capability as well as clear rules for coordination with the IMF. An even more difficult coordination problem confronts the myriad overlapping trade agreements that have been concluded in recent years.

A coherent, layered system would involve both global and sub-global (typically regional) institutions as well as strong connections among them. These connections may consist of explicit mechanisms (such as the monitoring role assigned to the IMF by G20 leaders) or rules that circumscribe the scope and jurisdiction of sub-global agreements and institutions. For example, a famous theoretical contribution by Kemp and Wan (1976) could be used to define a strategy that regional trade agreements should follow to be globally acceptable. In this case the strategy would require the members of the regional agreement to lower their trade barriers to non-members sufficiently to offset potential trade diversion effects.

Asia is active in initiatives that are both below and above the level of the global Bretton Woods institutions. Asian institutions *below* the global level include the ASEAN Economic Community, which is arguably the most ambitious integration effort in the developing world. Several high-level forums involving security, trade, and finance have also developed around ASEAN, including the Chiang Mai Initiative, an experiment in financial cooperation. As will be discussed later, free trade agreements have proliferated in the Asia, and a new set of regular, high-level bilateral and mini-lateral consultations have been established, ranging from the Strategic and Economic Dialogue between China and the United States to a similar meeting between the United States and India, and a new Triad meeting of the leaders of China, Korea, and Japan.

Asia is also prominent in the G20, the new layer of decision-making *above* the Bretton Woods institutions. The G20 includes five Asian countries (China, India, Indonesia, Korea, and Japan) and five more Pacific region countries that are members of APEC (Australia, Canada, Mexico, Russia, and the United States). The chair of ASEAN also attends G20 meetings. Yet despite these numbers and their considerable economic weight, Asian countries have not yet provided leadership in the G20 beyond South Korea as Chair in 2010.

## 10.4 Asia in the Emerging Structure of Economic Governance

Asian preferences and the logic of cooperation provide useful lenses for exploring recent trends in international cooperation. The 2008–2009 financial crisis highlighted the interconnectedness of the global economy and focused attention on global decision-making. The United States and Europe were at the epicenter of the crisis, but the effects of their recessions cascaded quickly through global supply chains to Asia and the world. Asia's financial institutions, having undergone reform following the 1997–1998 crises, escaped the worst of the crisis, but the region was nevertheless buffeted by sharp drops in demand. These shared problems opened a window for the overhaul of global summitry and rethinking the global governance system.

The principal elements of the international governance architecture are surveyed in Table 10.1. As this table shows, most major functional areas involve both global and Asian cooperative efforts. As it also shows, Asian interests vary significantly in each of the areas, both among countries and across modalities of cooperation. The next sections review the functional areas in further detail.

### 10.4.1 High-Level Cooperation

The most important public good required from the global system is high-level cooperation on problems that cut across major economies and fields of policy. The world had no institutions for providing this good at the outset of the global financial crisis. Leaders had to meet urgently and develop new mechanisms involving all economies essential to the task. A decade earlier, for similar reasons following the Asian financial crisis, finance ministers and central bank governors had begun to meet in a G20 framework, and elevating those meetings to the leaders' level was the practical choice. The G20 emerged in part as historical accident, with most (but not all) of its members representing the world's 20 largest economies.

The upgraded G20 initially focused on generating consistent national responses to the global financial crisis and monitoring the actions of international organizations in

**Table 10.1 Asia in International Governance**

| Function | Asian Objectives | Institutions |
|---|---|---|
| High-level cooperation | • Support global approach<br>• Accelerate transition to new international reserve system<br>• Resist formal targets | • G20 |
| Trade liberalization and dispute settlement | • Support global trade<br>• Reluctant to accept strict binding disciplines<br>• Varied detailed positions, but often oppose agricultural liberalization and strong intellectual property rights<br>• Interest in regional FTAs | • WTO<br>• Current focus on ASEAN+ regional agreements and (by some countries) on TPP<br>• Proposed regional agreements (EAFTA, CEPEA, TPP, FTAAP) |
| Monetary and macroeconomic cooperation | • Support global monetary oversight<br>• IMF as provider of global reserve currency<br>• RMB and yen as reserve currencies | • IMF<br>• Chiang Mai Initiative Multilateralization (CMIM) and Asian Macroeconomic Research Organization (AMRO) |
| Financial regulation | • Relaxed view of international rules due to strong current position of banks | • Financial Stability Board (FSB), Proposed Asian FSB |
| Development finance | • Support development finance<br>• Emphasis on infrastructure, resource development<br>• Emphasis on political relationships | • World Bank<br>• Asian Development Bank (ADB) |
| Climate change mitigation | • Green growth is a priority in several countries<br>• Concern about responsibility of developed countries for funding, mitigation<br>• Pledges plans to reduce carbon emissions based on development capacity | • UN Framework on Climate Change (UNFCC) |

carrying out their assigned tasks. The IMF was directed to provide appropriate emergency liquidity, strengthen its own monitoring functions, and reform its governance to reflect the changing shape of the global economy. They asked the WTO to monitor protectionist measures and to conclude the Doha round, and instructed the World Bank to mitigate the effects of the crisis on the poor in developing countries. They also decided to transform the Financial Stability Forum into a Financial Stability Board and to develop new international rules for financial oversight. In time, progress was made on all of these tasks.

Asia's G20 members have welcomed this new role on the world stage. Korea made extraordinary efforts to ensure the success of the 2010 Seoul summit, the first G20 leaders' meeting outside the G8 countries. It also used its role as a middle power, and not long ago one of the world's poor countries, to champion development. Some smaller Asian countries were less enthusiastic, but eventually Singapore and Vietnam were invited to the Seoul summit.

China, the world's most populous country and soon-to-be largest economy, is central to the G20. From early on, China was criticized in the G20 for its exchange rate and foreign exchange reserve policies. To some extent it deflected these criticisms and to some extent it responded to them. It increased the flexibility of its exchange rate prior to the June 2010 Toronto summit and accelerated yuan appreciation prior to the Seoul summit. China is still feeling its way on the G20 agenda. Expressing support for the G20, President Hu Jintao outlined priorities for shifting cooperation towards "...long-term governance and from passive response to proactive planning." He urged establishing "...a new international financial order that is fair, equitable, inclusive and well-managed" and policies that "...reject all forms of protectionism and unequivocally advocate and support free trade" (Xinhua 2010). But aside from listing these objectives and pressing for the inclusion of the yuan in the SDR, China has offered few concrete proposals.

So far, Asia's role in the G20 has been exercised through the individual (and typically muted) contributions of members. South Korea's efforts to prioritize development in 2010 were overshadowed by macroeconomic issues and attracted only modest support from other members. Japan has been preoccupied by internal economic problems, and ASEAN by the ASEAN Economic Community and "ASEAN-centric" approaches to regional cooperation. Thus, calls for concerted Asian positions and an Asian G20 caucus (Young 2009) have met with little support from governments. There was no collective Asian stimulus effort in the crisis or a common Asian strategy for the global monetary system. Instead, some countries experimented with other alliances. China and India joined dialogues in the "BRICS" grouping which, on the sidelines of the Cannes G20 summit in 2011, articulated the view that European bailouts should be managed by the IMF rather than through ad hoc arrangements.

The G20 plays a unique role in global governance, but much uncertainty remains about whether the G20 can evolve into a permanent, effective institution and whether an "Asian" voice could or should emerge within it. The emergency responses to the global crisis orchestrated by the G20 were broadly successful and, as our review of functional areas will show, progress has been also made on the G20's structural priorities. But as the urgency of the crisis receded and the details of implementation came to the fore, the momentum for action faded. Urgent regional issues, such as the European debt crisis, came to dominate the G20 discussions. In this context, consensus has been difficult to achieve and G20 meetings have become less conclusive.

In sum, so far the G20 has been more successful in responding to crises than in delivering sustained cooperation. The latter goal of course may not be attainable in the politics of the early twenty-first century. The G20 is playing a mid-field game: facilitating discussion while standing by for (rare) emergencies. This operational model more closely mirrors Asian than Western approaches to governance, and may be a harbinger of change in the global system. Meanwhile, practical cooperation, to the extent it is possible, is left to specialized institutions, both global and regional, in functional areas. We examine these in turn, focusing on the role of Asian economies in global and regional efforts.

### 10.4.2 Trade and Investment

Creating and sustaining a liberal, rules-based framework for trade is also a critical public good required from the international system. Extensive progress toward that framework was made in eight rounds of global trade agreements, the last being the Uruguay Round concluded in 1993, which established the WTO as a permanent institution for administering the global trading system. The Asian economic miracles are in part products of this remarkable achievement. The United States played a central role in building this system given its dominant role in the post-World War II global economy, but its relative position has diminished over time. In the increasingly multi-polar context, progress on global rules has stalled. At this writing the Doha Round is moribund and the momentum of trade liberalization has shifted to regional and bilateral trade agreements.

Despite the absence of new global agreements, most global trade continues to be conducted under the extensive rules and institutions of the WTO system. The WTO's dispute resolution mechanism is widely used and usually obeyed. Given the monitoring and safety valves it provides, protectionist responses to the global financial crisis appear to have been surprisingly muted.[5] Both developed and developing countries now use the WTO to resolve disputes and, with the addition of Russia in 2011, every large trading economy is now part of the WTO system.

Nearly all Asian economies recognize the value of the global system and support it. China and Vietnam worked intensively to join the WTO in 2001 and 2005, respectively. China used its 15-year accession negotiations as an instrument of domestic policy reform, transforming the institutions and managers of the planned economy into more market-oriented ones. Some terms were harsh—China accepted designation as a non-market economy in antidumping and safeguard cases and agreed to annual compliance reviews—but the concessions paid off. Value added in exports now accounts for around 20 percent of China's GDP, and China has become the leading emerging market destination for foreign direct investment (FDI). Similarly, Vietnam has greatly benefited from its accession; trade increased sharply in the five years following accession relative to the years before.

This support for the global system is confirmed by data on protection. Asia has relatively low trade barriers compared to the world and other regions such as Latin America, and has lowered barriers more rapidly over the last decade. Asia also participates reasonably actively in the WTO's dispute resolution system on both the complainant (and third parties supporting complainants) and respondent sides. To be sure, given the prominent role of governments in Asian development strategies, there have been many cases when governments promoted domestic sectors and technologies with measures seen as protectionist abroad. Nevertheless, Asia's interest in the global trading system is deeply rooted, even as countries jockey for perceived advantages from intervention.

The plurilateral Government Procurement Agreement under the WTO sets significant limits on government intervention through procurement and is a nuanced indicator of the role of Asian economies in the WTO system. Only the advanced economies—Korea, Japan, Singapore, and Chinese Taipei—are among the Agreement's 42 members. In 2010, nine years after it committed to join, China offered a negotiating proposal (Anderlini and Betts 2010), which, at the time of writing, in early 2013, remains under discussion. Southeast Asian economies, although targeting regional procurement provisions, have not entered the global negotiations.

The positions of Asia's advanced economies also differ from those of Asia's lower income countries in other ways. For example, Japanese and Korean positions on intellectual property rights and an investment framework are probably closer to those of Western countries than of other Asian exporters. Several countries have concluded FTAs with the United States or are involved in the TPP negotiations (discussed further below). Most welcome China's dynamism but are uneasy about the role of its large state-owned enterprises in the region's economy. Despite important common interests, Asian economies are far from comprising a monolithic block.

There are also other reasons why Asia has not assumed leadership in the WTO. Asia's principal markets in the developed countries are already reasonably open. At the same time, Asia's own barriers are reasonably entrenched. Japan's agricultural protection has prevented it from making obvious contributions and many countries generally resist liberalization in services, which they see as much more competitive in the United States and Europe. Many believe that so-called "new issues"—labor and environmental protection—are designed to undermine their own areas of comparative advantage. And now many are also concerned about Chinese competition in manufacturing. Most are in midst of rapid transformation and reluctant to take on additional policy challenges. As a result, rather than forcefully promoting the global system, Asian countries sometimes appear to be blocking it; for example, when several supported India's demands for special safeguard protection in July 2008, pouring cold water on the talks at a crucial stage.

Until recently, Asia has pursued trade initiatives on a less ambitious, regional scale. Regional negotiations are easier to manage because they allow for exceptions and typically focus mainly on tariff reductions. They provide light treatment of issues of interest to advanced economies, such as services, intellectual property rights, investment, and labor. In some cases, these include feature issues not found in other FTA projects, such as support for development through technical training to facilitate the extension of supply chains.

The China-ASEAN agreement, intended to upgrade China's political and economic relations with Southeast Asia, has been a catalyst for other large economies. Japan, South Korea, and India have followed suit. Competing proposals then appeared to expand these agreements into an ASEAN+3 agreement preferred by China (to include ASEAN,

China, Japan, and Korea) and an ASEAN+6 agreement proposed by Japan (adding Australia, India, and New Zealand). In 2011, a truce was negotiated by China and Japan, permitting both initiatives to move forward in parallel.

As pressure for a more ambitious agenda mounted, due partly to stalemate in the Doha negotiations and partly to the emergence of the TPP negotiations, in 2013 ASEAN launched a new negotiating framework—the Regional Comprehensive Economic Partnership (RCEP)—based on the ASEAN+6 group of countries. The negotiations are intended to harmonize ASEAN agreements and extend their reach across most of the Asian economy. In practice, however, RCEP's success will depend on consensus among China, Japan, and Korea, the region's three largest economies. Discussions among them have been underway for some time and also entered formal negotiations in 2013, but the uncertain and shifting political relationships of the three countries may make progress difficult.

Thus, despite extensive activity in Asian trade diplomacy, little progress has been made toward a comprehensive regional agreement. Economic studies show that such an agreement would produce results that are far superior to smaller ones (Park and Cheong 2008). Since benefits increase with the size of the area, ASEAN+6 generates somewhat greater gains than ASEAN+3 (Kawai and Wignaraja 2009), and an agreement that includes all 21 APEC economies (also the United States and countries on the Eastern edge of the Pacific) would be still better. Incorporating the United States is of interest to many economies, since it is a critical end market for Asian manufactures and a potential stabilizing force in the face of China's rising power. The 21 members of APEC agreed in 2008 to pursue a Free Trade Area of the Asia Pacific (FTAAP) as a long-term goal, eventually designating several pathways toward it.

Significantly, the United States has also entered the negotiating arena by promoting the Trans-Pacific Partnership (TPP), an agreement initiated by small Asian and Latin American economies that now encompasses 12 APEC economies with still others planning to join.[6] The TPP builds on a comprehensive, high-quality free trade agreement (encompassing New Zealand, Chile, Singapore, and Brunei) and intends to create a "twenty-first-century" standard for trade. But its ultimate benefits inevitably depend on all large Asian economies joining. While China has recently announced that it will study the TPP, it is likely to find it difficult to accept the terms of the agreement that now seems to be emerging in the near future. At the same time, the China-US dialogue appears to be intensifying in early 2013 and earlier Chinese concerns about the role of the TPP in containing China are easing. Nevertheless, no clear path has emerged so far for developing a truly a region-wide trading system.

Objective analysis suggests that the TPP is best seen as a move in a competitive liberalization game, and a potential stimulus for region-wide integration. Asian and Trans-Pacific FTA tracks that move in parallel and extensively overlap could well speed the integration of a region that has become splintered through many bilateral agreements (Petri et al. 2011). Progress on the tracks is likely to accelerate integration within each track and competition between them. In time, the tracks will increase the gains from consolidation to their dominant economies (China and the United States). This end result—a regional or global agreement—may not happen for some time. But in the meantime the tracks will generate forward momentum on trade liberalization, yielding real benefits at low cost to non-members.[7] The tracks are a "contest of templates" designed to shape the rules that govern eventual integration. In any case, the TPP strategy is ambitious, and there is still reason to worry whether it can clear the high political hurdles in its way.

A prominent feature of twenty-first-century trade agreements (and indeed of the TPP) is to offer better investor protection. With regional production networks a key feature of Asian economic and trade architecture, international investment is an increasingly important element of these linkages. Most high quality FTAs include investment provisions or are accompanied by investment agreements. An investment agreement was reached in 2012 by China, Japan, and Korea and, as of early 2013, is in the ninth round of negotiations between China and the United States. Investment concerns in Asia include sometimes-conflicting concerns such as attracting foreign investors while stimulating inward technology transfers, as well as promoting "infant industries" while protecting the right to invest in sensitive resource and technology sectors abroad. Despite some progress, these conflicting objectives make it difficult to design a comprehensive, consistent investment regime.

Some of the challenges faced by Asian firms in foreign markets are illustrated by some high-profile failures by Chinese firms to acquire foreign assets. Key resource acquisitions (CNOOC's of Unocal in the United States and Chinalco's bid for Rio Tinto assets in Australia) have failed for apparently political reasons. Chinese technology companies have also faced suspicions in India and the United States on national security grounds. These concerns have intensified with increased awareness of pervasive cyber espionage, conducted by both private and perhaps state actors. India temporarily blocked imports of Chinese equipment in its mobile telephone network. In the United States, politicians accused the electronics giant Huawei of having military ties and argued for blocking its access to the supply chains of the military and law enforcement sectors. Several Huawei efforts to acquire US assets failed (2Wire, a Motorola unit, and 3Com) and the US Committee on Foreign Investment (CFIUS) instructed the company to divest its interest in 3Leaf Systems, a small technology company it did manage to purchase. These cases raise difficult questions: does an acquisition reflect commercial goals or national strategic objectives? And in turn, do committees such as CFIUS reflect national security interests (as intended) or the interests of domestic firms?

Foreign investment regimes in some Asian economies have also raised concerns. In Korea and Japan, for example, foreign investment is far below levels predicted in international econometric studies, strongly suggesting explicit or implicit barriers. China has been open to many types of foreign investment, but has restricted access to others in an effort to foster technology transfers. The conviction and imprisonment of foreign executives (including an Australian and an American, on charges of bribery (in the first case) and violating laws on state secrets in both cases) has raised serious questions about inter-relationships among business, politics, and the Chinese legal system. These cases may have represented retaliation for discrimination against Chinese companies abroad.

The complexity and importance of such investment linkages represents a clear argument for strengthening rules-based approaches.

Overall, these trends in Asian trade and investment relations raise conflicting questions. Will the region continue to cede the leadership of the world trading system to the United States and Europe, as it has in much of the postwar period? Will it deepen regional cooperation, and if so, will it be through the Asian track promoted by China or the Trans-Pacific track championed by the United States? A more prominent role for Asia is inevitable, but will emerge gradually. The region's scale and connections with the world economy suggest that purely regional, even Asia-Pacific, initiatives will not accommodate its interests. Thus, Asian economies, as dominant Western economies before them, are likely to emerge as champions of a stable and open global system. The precise implications are unclear, but will need to bridge contemporary Western legal approaches with the flexible, relationship-based models of Asian integration.

### 10.4.3 Macroeconomic Cooperation

The global monetary system provides the frameworks for massive trade and investment flows that now connect the world economy. Yet increasingly it consists of a patchwork of compromise and ill-defined and often ignored rules. A safe and effective global monetary system will require substantial revisions in its central institution, the International Monetary Fund (IMF), and the gradual replacement of the dollar as the world's single dominant reserve currency.

The IMF was designed in 1944 to provide emergency lending in a dollar-based, fixed-exchange-rate world of limited international capital flows. As these initial conditions changed, the centrality of fixed exchange rates was replaced by flexible regimes and rising cross-border capital flows. Private capital flows now finance current account imbalances that would have been unimaginable a half century ago. The IMF, in turn, has specialized in providing short-term liquidity support in the face of balance of payment crises and macroeconomic oversight, mainly to developing countries in trouble. The role it played in the 1997–1998 Asian financial crisis brought it under attack when it was perceived, rightly or wrongly, to have deepened the crisis by treating Asian borrowers with liquidity problems as if they were insolvent with structural problems (Ito 2007). Resentful borrowers repaid their loans early and began self-insuring by accumulating foreign reserves larger than those needed to cover imports and short-term liabilities. By the time of the global financial crisis, the IMF's activities had sharply diminished and its resources, at around $250 billion, paled in comparison with those of Asia's central banks, whose foreign exchange reserves totaled nearly $5 trillion in 2010 (Truman 2007).

The G20 resuscitated the IMF by raising its resources to $1 trillion, proposing a major new SDR issue, and encouraging the Fund to revise its lending approach.[8] The IMF streamlined its lending by curtailing conditionality and providing adjustment support through short-term loans (including the flexible credit line facility, or FCL) that permit countries to qualify on an ex ante basis for funds up to five times their quota, without ex post conditions. In the long run, the operation of the international monetary system requires a credible, effective, lender of last resort, as well as effective surveillance of macroeconomic policies to prevent imbalances that lead to emergencies. It is now widely accepted that the IMF's effectiveness will depend on bringing its voting structure and management in line with the changing sizes of the world's major economies—that is, reducing Europe's influence and raising Asia's.

As emerging market economies, with China in the vanguard, move up the ranks of the world's largest economies, currencies such as the Chinese yuan are becoming more widely used in trade and other transactions, raising questions about the future of the US dollar as the world's principal reserve currency. How long this shift is likely to take is a matter of debate, as are the outlines of the new system: will it be based on the SDR, as the Bretton Woods architects envisaged in 1944? Or as multiple reserve currencies? The uncertainty surrounding the euro, the world's second-most popular reserve currency, has further clouded the outlook.

Among Asian currencies, the Chinese yuan is now the one most likely to become a significant global reserve currency. (Japan's earlier proposals for a multi-currency Asian basket have faded with the rapid progress and globalization of the Chinese economy.) China has begun the process of internationalizing the yuan, but major adjustments in its financial and monetary system will be required for the yuan to become a reserve currency. The Chinese central bank, which manages the exchange rate, also manages deposit and lender rates to provide the largely government-owned banks with generous riskless spreads (Dobson and Kashyap 2006; Dobson 2009; Prasad 2009). This system has created powerful interests vested in investment- and export-led industries. If the yuan is to be widely used internationally, opposition to more flexible exchange rates and interest rates will have to become overcome.

The Chinese measures to internationalize the yuan have included swap agreements with other central banks, increased foreign access to the interbank bond market, and agreements with foreign governments in Japan, the United States, and the United Kingdom to permit yuan-based international trade and investment transactions. The authorities have also created opportunities for holding yuan in offshore accounts in Hong Kong and elsewhere, and are expanding vehicles (such as the Qualified Foreign Institutional Investor funds) for investing some holdings in mainland securities. Many of these policy measures have been implemented on a limited, experimental basis so far, and much work remains before the capital account is opened and the yuan becomes fully convertible (Dobson and Masson 2009).

Looking ahead, as Asia's influence increases in the IMF and in the day-to-day conduct of finance, how might this influence be used? First, Asia is committed to maintaining as much independence as possible in managing national macroeconomic policy and the resulting global imbalances. China and other Asian countries have adopted important elements of the international system, but have been slow to change their domestic policies. One explanation for sluggish adjustment is that governments put an unusually high premium on the stability of manufacturing and export employment. To the extent that rapid adjustments might be forced by volatile short-term capital flows, Asian economies are willing to consider controls to dampen them. Since consensus is needed to adopt any formal approach in the G20, Asia's opposition to rapid changes in macroeconomic variables has effectively turned international macroeconomic coordination into a slow, informal negotiation—an approach consistent with the region's decision-making style.

Second, Asia's influence is reflected in growing calls for changes in the reserve currency system, in part to provide independence from policies pursued in the United States. During the Asian financial crisis, Japan advocated forming an Asian Monetary Fund, and perhaps also an Asian Currency Unit. Buffeted by capital flows, ASEAN countries have also supported greater cooperation. Most recently, the action has shifted to heavier use of the Chinese yuan. China's central bank governor Zhou Xiaochuan's (2009) argued that the current global arrangements are flawed because of conflicts between the domestic goals and international responsibilities of the United States, the provider of the world's principal reserve currency. As a result, the dollar-based system has become volatile, forcing both developing and emerging market economies to divert foreign exchange reserves to insurance from more productive uses. The United Nations Commission (2009) also proposed an expanded SDR, calibrated to the size of reserve accumulations. But these proposals have gained little traction because private investors have shown little enthusiasm for the SDR over the dollar and governments are reluctant to lead markets.

Third, Asia is hedging its bets by seeking its own emergency liquidity facility. In the aftermath of the Asian financial crisis in 2000, the ASEAN+3 governments adopted the Chiang Mai Initiative (CMI), a regional emergency financing mechanism based on bilateral currency swap agreements. The CMI did not make much progress in the next decade and did not prove useful in the global financial crisis. In 2010, the CMI was multilateralized (becoming the CMIM) and expanded to $120 billion with 80 percent contributed by China, Japan, and South Korea, and in 2012 it doubled the pool of funds to $240 billion (Adam and Sharp 2012).

Like the IMF, CMIM will provide short-term liquidity or balance of payments support within the region. But the difficult work of establishing procedures to activate the CMIM and provide associated surveillance has just begun; for now, substantial drafts on CMIM funds also require an IMF program. An Asian Macroeconomic Research Office has been established in Singapore to support the CMIM. Ideally, it will develop procedures consistent with IMF methodology so that support might combine IMF and CMIM funds, similar to the funding approach now used in Eastern Europe. Early indicators of the CMIM's success will be members' willingness to submit to multilateral peer review and surveillance of national policies and to reduce self-insurance.

Asia's rising influence and cautious policymaking style are now more evident in international monetary affairs. The region prizes stability and independence, and has blocked commitments to formal cooperation or rapid change. It is gradually pushing for a more multi-polar currency system and is hedging its bets by exploring regional arrangements. Most dramatically, Asian economies have built huge foreign exchange reserves, effectively buying insurance against a wide range of global shocks. But from this perspective of strength, Asian policymakers generally support the gradual reform—rather than dramatic reinvention—of the international system. There is wide agreement with Western observers on the diagnosis of problems and ultimate trends, although Asians would prefer some initiatives, such as the inclusion of the yuan in the SDR, to be implemented sooner rather than later. On the whole, Asia's rising influence does not appear to foreshadow major changes in the present, admittedly imperfect, mechanisms of monetary cooperation.

### 10.4.4 Financial Markets

The global crisis highlighted the paradox between the national scope of financial supervision and the global reach of capital markets and institutions. While strong and modern national financial systems are essential to stable markets, national regulators cannot prevent cross-border financial crises by acting on their own. They must coordinate and communicate among themselves. The Financial Stability Forum, set up by G7 governments after the Asian crisis, is based at the Bank for International Settlements and closely related to the Basel Committee, to facilitate such cooperation. But the institution lacked legitimacy and relied on voluntary implementation of its guidelines and recommendations. G20 leaders expanded its membership and changed its name to the Financial Services Board (FSB), charging it to work closely with the IMF in implementing its recommendations and guidelines through the Fund's surveillance and its Financial Sector Assessment Program (FSAP), which focuses on national financial systems and their prudential supervision. A group of East Asian economists has recommended intensified supervision of financial institutions engaging in cross-border business and an Asian Financial Stability Dialogue to deepen regional financial integration (Asian Development Bank Institute 2009), but the proposal has not gained much traction so far.

The new Basel III Accords agreed in 2010 provide a new framework for bank regulation in the wake of the global financial crisis. Although Asian economies were involved in the discussions leading up to the Accords, they did not play a central role in their design. For the most part, Asian banks have not been unduly strained by the new regulations; in many cases their asset structures were more conservative than those of Western banks and their equity positions were stronger, and so the implications of meeting the new standards are manageable. There is even a possibility that Asia's regional banks will make headway against global competitors, since a much smaller part of their income depends on fixed-income, currency, and commodities businesses, which will require more capital (Flatt 2012). Nevertheless, some objections were raised about the possibility that unnecessarily rigorous standards would be applied to banks with largely domestic operations, and that some of the requirements (for example, providing a favored treatment for government securities in judging liquidity) implicitly favored Western banks because of the greater availability of government securities in those markets. But on the whole the Accords have not increased calls for regional regulations, despite suggestions by the Asian Development Bank that a regional regulatory forum similar to the FSB be developed on a regional level.

## 10.4.5 Development Finance

The World Bank and the regional multilateral development banks provide development finance through loans and grants and technical assistance to developing countries to promote poverty reduction and economic development. The network of banks is more decentralized than the IMF system and the regional banks are largely run by countries in the regions. The World Bank is governed by its shareholders but developing countries criticize it for reflecting the development priorities imposed by the advanced countries rather than those of the developing countries themselves. Since 1980, China has had a harmonious relationship with the World Bank. China continues to borrow for projects ranging from energy efficiency and environmental projects to urban and rural development. In 2007 China became a net contributor to the World Bank's International Development Assistance mechanism and in 2010 its third-largest shareholder. A Chinese national was the World Bank's chief economist and a close collaboration between the World Bank and the Development Research Council generated a high-profile report on China's shifting development strategy (World Bank, 2013).

The Asian Development Bank (ADB) is active in promoting regional integration in Southeast Asia by providing substantial support for new transportation corridors and other infrastructure initiatives. The ADB has also scaled up its policy research efforts, aiming to match the analytical capacity provided by the international organizations with Asia-focused research capabilities. ADB capital was tripled in 2009 to $165 billion, permitting a significant increase in the loan portfolio. Its management has been dominated by Japan—its president has been always Japanese—but it operations are increasingly widespread and are likely, as in other development banks, to take on a more democratic configuration.

Perhaps because other development banks have established dominant country personalities, the rapid rise of China, with its massive foreign exchange reserves, is leading to some new directions in development lending, possibly resulting in a development bank, as discussed at the 2012 BRICS Summit in New Delhi (Fourth BRICS Summit). China has also offered loans to member states of the Shanghai Cooperation Organization, a grouping of six economies with Central Asian interests. And it has provided a variety of infrastructure investment support for African countries.

Finally, the China Investment Corporation (CIC), the sovereign wealth fund charged with investing part of China's foreign exchange reserves, has indicated substantial interest in undertaking "public-private partnerships" to develop infrastructure around the world, including in advanced countries such as the United Kingdom and the United States. These efforts represent an interesting new mix between initiatives designed to secure relatively safe and high returns, but due to their public dimensions inevitably play a role in China's international relations with the host governments.

These new initiatives suggest some "disintermediation" in the traditional lending functions, with funds shifting from general, global development banks to narrower asset portfolios and more direct political content. So far, and particularly in the wake of the global financial crisis, the trends have moved in parallel, with expansion in the lending programs of all lenders. Nevertheless, they suggest that Asia's new investments—led by China's resources—could be channeled in more direct ways to support national political and commercial objectives. These initiatives may, in turn, intensify competitive efforts among major economies to provide comparable support for its own political and commercial interests.

### 10.4.6 Environment

Owing to its rapid industrialization and large populations, Asia faces a wide range of environmental problems, ranging from water availability and quality to air pollution and carbon emissions. Three of the world's five largest producers of greenhouse gases (China, India, and Indonesia) are Asian economies, although Asia is still far down the list in per capita terms. With its many islands, long coast lines and great population concentrations in low-lying port cities, it is also the region most acutely threatened by climate change. Divisions on climate change policies are nevertheless substantial across Asia, reflecting the different levels of development.

Local pollution issues are likely to be addressed by Asian economies, as their resources permit. Air pollution and congestion have been brought under control in Tokyo and Seoul with policies ranging from gasoline standards and taxes to the development of rapid transit. Bangkok and many other large Asian cities in poorer countries are now following suit. China is also beginning to respond to widespread popular pressure to reduce particular pollution in its largest cities. These initiatives are at times costly—in China, for example, they will require the substitution of imported oil and gas, or even more expensive alternative fuels, for domestically produced coal.

The most vexing issues, however, involve carbon emissions and global climate change. Asian developing economies, particularly China and India, are reluctant participants in global climate negotiations. They are committed to rapid economic growth and are in the energy-intensive stages of their industrialization processes. They also rely heavily on fossil fuels and especially coal. They see pressures to generate binding commitments on emissions, especially given vague commitments by much wealthier nations, as efforts to constrain their economic catch-up with the West.

The central issue is a collective one: how to allocate responsibilities for mitigation among countries. There is much rhetoric and little agreement on how emissions targets should be determined. There are many questions: should responsibilities be allocated on the basis of emissions per capita, emissions per unit of GDP, or absolute emissions? Should emissions standards apply to what countries emit, or the global emissions induced by their consumption? Should past emissions be taken into account, since they have contributed to the buildup of greenhouse gases in the atmosphere? Should income be taken into account, since the wealthier countries have greater ability to pay for mitigation?

Asian economies have developed predictable positions on these issues, favoring principles and criteria that they will find easiest to meet. For example, China and other emerging countries prefer an emissions/GDP standard, because fast development reduces energy intensity by this measure, even as it increases other ratios. They also argue for taking past emissions into account, and for special treatment of developing countries, for example, through special funds that support adaptation in poor countries. The theory acts as an academic (and often not very seriously considered) backdrop to pragmatic politics; the positions of individual countries reflect the urgency of climate change issue in their domestic politics, and global cooperation as a whole in turn reflects the urgency of such political pressures around the world.

As a result of these divisions, global climate negotiations are making limited progress. Asian countries have played a prominent role in the UN Framework Convention on Climate Change. The Copenhagen Conference in December 2009 appeared to be headed for massive failure, but—in a last-minute agreement negotiated by Brazil—China, India, South Africa, and the United States agreed to a non-binding commitment to keep temperature increases under 2° Centigrade. Although many observers at the time saw this agreement as a face-saving gesture, it kept the negotiating process alive. The Durban Conference in November 2011, moved another step forward, committing to a negotiation—as outlined in the Durban Platform—to replace the Kyoto Protocol by a new treaty that would be negotiated by 2015 and implemented by 2020. This agreement was signed by both China and India (as well as the United States, which had not ratified the Kyoto Protocol), committing at least to the principle of accepting binding mitigation targets. Nevertheless, the pledges that countries had assembled so far did not add up to sufficient reductions in greenhouse gas emissions to meet global targets, and statements made by Chinese and Indian negotiators indicated that they were not prepared to make larger concessions than they had already offered. More recently, in their 2013 meeting in California, Presidents Xi and Obama pledged to intensify cooperation on climate change issues. Yet most Asian countries, including China and India, also recognize that the growth of global emissions could harm their development prospects, either directly through environmental risks, or indirectly through the threat of foreign pressure—for example, potential carbon tariffs by developed countries. They strongly oppose trade policy measures to implement environmental regulations. China's reaction to the European Union's plan to impose carbon taxes on airlines traveling to or from Europe is an early skirmish in this battle; China had apparently put on hold its Airbus orders in order to persuade the EU to drop the plan.[9]

At home, Asian economies are making significant commitments toward reducing energy intensity and developing alternative energy sources. These policies serve in part as insurance, should the pressure for a low-carbon growth strategy intensify. They also stimulate the development of technologies, such as wind power, that might generate important industries in the future. Some Asian countries, notably Japan and Korea, are leaders in green technologies and have become champions of global climate change mitigation. China is also entering the fray; its 12th Plan contains obligatory targets to increase renewable energy supplies to 15 percent of the primary energy mix and for 40–45 percent reduction by 2020 in carbon emissions as a ratio to GDP, and large investments are being made to develop globally competitive wind and solar power industries. Asia's growing emphasis on renewable energy—which, it is argued by competitors, is supported by subsidies and government procurement practices—could lead to major innovations and new industries. But it is also attracting complaints of unfair trade from the United States, and currently several anti-dumping investigations are underway on Chinese exports of alternative energy products to Europe and the United States.

Asia's attitude toward the environment is consistent with its broad stance toward global economic governance: participation in global processes and applying the brakes to initiatives that might constrain the region's future options and development prospects. Even so, in this area change might come relatively early, as the region increasingly faces serious environmental challenges that are being recognized in its internal politics. Meanwhile, innovations are helping to make alternative energy an important regional growth industry. Energy security concerns also argue for greater conservation. All these factors could turn the region toward more proactive policies, based as usual on pragmatic self-interest.

## 10.5 Conclusions

Asia's rise in the context of an increasingly multi-polar world economy is changing the landscape of global and regional cooperation. This trend has had arguably negative effects on established institutions of global cooperation so far. But it has also given rise to useful institutional experiments and deeper regional integration. The 2008-2009 crisis was handled mostly outside existing institutions, but it gave birth to the G20, a new high-level coordinating forum. The crisis also amplified dissatisfaction with global governance and led to increased hedging through alternative regional institutions in trade and finance.

It would be wrong to conclude that the changing configuration of global economic power is a harbinger of the wholesale replacement of the international system. Asia has benefited greatly from the liberal world economic order created in the aftermath of World War II and generally supports it. China and other Asian countries have made major adjustments in their domestic institutions to build relationships with the WTO and other international institutions. Despite their criticism of Western economic management, they share many Western views on how the world economy works and broad goals for macroeconomic and trade policy. So far, however, Asian powers have been reluctant to assume the costly responsibilities of global leadership or to invest more in international institutions than is justified by narrow, immediate interests.

The implication is that Asia's approach toward international governance—admittedly a difficult generalization to make, given the region's extraordinary complexity and diversity—will provide pragmatic but limited support for the international system. Asian countries will not want to undermine the current level of integration, but appear to have little appetite for deeper collaboration. This reflects historical suspicions of the international order and preoccupations with policy space for national development. Asian countries prize national independence and its corollary, non-intervention. And they prefer gradual, limited action to precedent-setting initiatives. Visionary pronouncements about long-term goals have become more common in Asian institutions such as ASEAN, perhaps to meet Western expectations, but actual decision-making—the "ASEAN way"—remains unintrusive and gradualist.

The shift toward Asian policy styles will undoubtedly shape international norms and institutions. Norms enforced by the IMF and the WTO might become more flexible, giving way to "tit for tat" self-enforcing norms in both trade and finance. It is unclear whether these changes will mean less satisfactory outcomes in trade or financial stability. Resistance to global legal agreements may lead to greater self-insurance, deeper regional initiatives, and more informal negotiations. Meanwhile, economic integration could continue to deepen, much as it has among Asian economies in the last two decades, with relatively little institutional support. What is less likely is new, formal, rules-based cooperation. This will disappoint economists invested in international rules, but it may not mean slower growth. The level of international interdependence is high, and self-enforcement may be enough to keep it in place while other drivers of growth—especially technological change—replace the role played by new liberalization initiatives in the past. On the positive side, Asia is likely to have the financial clout and commercial interest to make sure that international trade and financial systems survive serious threats.

Thus, Asia's rise is likely to mean stability for global institutions, both in the negative sense of making new initiatives more difficult, and in the positive sense of providing support and, if necessary, resources to keep pragmatic cooperation intact. The challenge will be to make this complex, informal global system more coherent and effective. As Asia gains votes and voice, perhaps it will become more comfortable in leading and coordinating. It may also see its way to making greater investments in global public goods than it has so far. Time and patience will be required to complete Asia's extraordinary transformation. This analysis suggests that the path forward appears to be different, but not intrinsically more, or less, hazardous than managing the global system has been in the past.

## Notes

1. Peter Petri is Carl J. Shapiro Professor of International Finance, Brandeis International Business School, and Senior Fellow, East-West Center, Honolulu Hawaii. E-mail: ppetri@brandeis.edu. Wendy Dobson is Professor and Co-director of the Institute for International Business, Rotman School of Management, University of Toronto. E-mail: Dobson@rotman.utoronto.ca.

2. This chapter is focused on the Asia Pacific, but growth poles have also emerged in Latin America, based on similar policy strategies. Latin American economic integration through MERCOSUR, a trade zone initially criticized for diverting more trade than it creates, has become more open by including the Andean Community countries and by gradually reducing extra-MERCOSUR barriers.
3. To join the WTO, 30 central ministries and departments were directed in 2002 to change 2300 laws and regulations (eliminating many of them) and 100,000 local laws and regulations at the provincial and autonomous region levels (Yu 2009:153).
4. The IMF's Board of Governors conducts general quota reviews every five years. Any proposed changes in quotas must be approved by an 85 percent majority.
5. In a comprehensive recent study, Christian Henn and Brad McDonald note that only 0.2 percent of world trade was subject to trade diversion due to new protectionist measures. See [http://www.imf.org/external/np/seminars/eng/2011/trade/pdf/session3-Henn-presentation.pdf].
6. The 12 current participants are Australia, Brunei, Canada, Chile, Japan, Malaysia, Mexico, New Zealand, Peru, Singapore, the United States, and Vietnam. Many observers expect Korea, Thailand, the Philippines and perhaps other countries to join eventually, although not necessarily in the first round of the agreement.
7. This is not a necessary result, but appears to be the empirical implication of the nature of existing economic relationships and the proposed agreements (Petri et al. 2011).
8. In April 2009 leaders authorized a one-time SDR allocation of $250 billion and $500 billion in new borrowing from Fund shareholders under the New Arrangements to Borrow (NAB). Japan and the EU each agreed to lend $100 billion and China indicated its willingness to provide $40 billion in other ways.
9. "EU to keep carbon tax," *China Daily*, March 10, 2012.

## References

Adam, Shamim and Andy Sharp, 2012. "Asia Doubles Reserve Pool to $240 Billion to Shield Region." Bloomberg News, May 3. Online: http://www.businessweek.com/news/2012-05-02/asia-set-to-double-reserve-pool-as-region-steps-up-cooperation.

Anderlini, Jamil, and Paul Betts, 2010. "China Forced to put a Value on Its 'Foreign' Friends," *Financial Times*, July 21.

Asian Development Bank, 2008. *Emerging Asian Regionalism: A Partnership for Shared Prosperity*. Manila: ADB.

Asian Development Bank Institute, 2009. *Recommendations of Policy Responses to the Global Financial and Economic Crisis for East Asian Leaders*. Available at http://www.adbi.org.

Asian Development Bank, 2012. *Highlights: The Great Transformation, ASEAN, China and India*. Manila: ADB.

Casella, Alessandra, and Bruno Frey, 1992. "Federalism and clubs: towards an economic theory of overlapping jurisdictions," *European Economic Review*, 36, 639–646.

Dobson, Wendy, 2009. *Gravity Shift: How Asia's New Economic Powerhouses Will Shape the 21st Century*, Toronto: University of Toronto Press.

Dobson, Wendy, and Anil Kashyap, 2006. "The Contradictions in China's Gradualist Banking Reforms," *Brookings Papers on Economic Activity*, Washington: Brookings Institution, No. 2.

Dobson, Wendy, and Paul Masson, 2009. "Will the Renminbi Become a World Currency?" *China Economic Review*, 20:1, 124–135.

Drysdale, Peter, 2010. "Asia's Global Responsibilities: Delivering through Global and Regional Arrangements," *East Asia Forum*, October 10.

Flatt, Daniel, 2012. "How Basel III Will Constrain Banks' Asia Ambitions," *Asiamoney*, February 14.

Fourth BRICS Summit, 2012. Delhi Declaration, New Delhi, March 29. Available at www.brics.toronto.ca/docs/120329-delhi-declaration.html.

Gosset, David, 2013. A shared world dream. *China Daily*, June 1, 2013.

Ito, Takatoshi, 2007. The Asian Currency Crisis and the International Monetary Fund, 10 Years Later: An Overview. *Asian Economic Policy Review*, 2:1, 16–49.

Kawai, Masahiro, and Ganeshan Wignaraja, 2009. Asian FTAs: Trends and Challenges. ADBI Working Paper No. 144. Tokyo: Asian Development Bank Institute.

Kawai, Masahiro, Peter A. Petri, and Elif Sisli-Ciamarra, 2009. "Asia in Global Governance: A Case for Decentralized Institutions." Processed.

Kawai, Masahiro, and Peter A. Petri, 2010. "Asia's Role in the Global Economic Architecture." Working Paper No. 235. Tokyo: Asian Development Bank Institute.

Kemp, Murray C., and H. Wan, 1976. "An Elementary Proposition Concerning the Formation of Customs Unions," *Journal of International Economics*, 6:1, 95–97.

Park, Y. C., and I. Cheong, 2008. "The Proliferation of FTAs and Prospects for Trade Liberalization in East Asia." In: Eichengreen, Barry, Yung Chu Park, and Charles Wyplosz, eds. China, Asia, and the new world economy. Oxford University Press, 2008. pp. 87–112.

Petri, Peter A. 2010. "Asia and the World Economy in 2030: Growth, Integration and Governance," in Ashley J. Tellis, Andrew Marble, and Travis Tanner, eds. *Asia's Rising Power and America's Continued Purpose*, Seattle: National Bureau of Asian Research. pp. 47–78.

Petri, Peter A., Michael G. Plummer, and Fan Zhai, 2012. *The Trans-Pacific Partnership and Asia-Pacific Integration: A Quantitative Assessment*. Policy Analyses in International Economics No. 98. Washington: Peterson Institute for International Economics.

Prasad, Eswar, 2009. "Is the Chinese Growth Miracle Built to Last?," *China Economic Review*, 20:1, 103–123.

Truman E. M., 2007. Sovereign Wealth Funds: The Need for Greater Transparency and Accountability. *Policy Briefs in International Economics*, PB07-06, Available at http://www.petersoninstitute.org.

United Nations, 2009. The Commission of Experts on Reforms of the International Monetary and Financial System: Recommendations. Available at http://www.un.org/ga/president/63/commission/financial_commission.html

Wang, Hongying and James N. Rosenau, 2009. "China and Global Governance," *Asian Perspective* 33:3, 5–39.

World Bank, 2013. *China 2030: Building a Modern, Harmonious and Creative Society.* Washington: World Bank.

Xi, Jinping, 2013. Working together toward a better future for Asia and the world. Speech delivered at the Boao Forum for Asia, 2013. In China Daily, April 9, 2013.

Xinhua, 2010. "Hu Calls for Balanced Global Economic Growth," China Daily website, http://www.chinadaily.com.cn/china/2010g20canada/2010-06/28/content_10028219.htm. July 6, 2010.

Young, Soogil, 2009. "The Case for an East-Asian Caucus on Global Governance: a Korean Perspective." Available at www.eastasiaforum.org/2009/04/12/the-case-for-an-east-asian-caucus-on-global-economic-governance-a-korean-perspective/html.

Yu Yongding (2009). "China's Policy Responses to the Global Financial Crisis", Snape Lecture, Melbourne, November 25.

Zhang, Yunling, and Tang Shiping (2005). "China's Regional Strategy," in David Shambaugh, ed., *Power Shift: China and Asia's New Dynamics*, Los Angeles: University of California Press, 48–68.

Zhou, X. (2009). Reform the International Monetary System. (http:www.pbc.gov.cn/english) accessed March 25, 2009.

CHAPTER 11

# GEOECONOMICS VERSUS GEOPOLITICS: IMPLICATIONS FOR ASIA

DEVESH KAPUR AND MANIK SURI

## 11.1 Growing Divergence between "Geoeconomics" and "Geopolitics" in Asia

### 11.1.1 Overview

This chapter examines causes and possible consequences of the growing divergence between the security imperatives of rapidly changing geopolitics in Asia and the economic interdependencies being woven by geoeconomics.

We first lay out these competing pressures as they bear on the relationship between a resurgent China and its major economic partners. We argue that geoeconomic trends are being driven by the individual rationality of investors and firms seeking to benefit from the world's biggest economic opportunity, but whose cumulative effects are generating major geopolitical consequences. The tension between the two is being partly mediated by cross-border production networks—and their attendant global supply chains—that are a hallmark of Asian economic integration in recent decades. Our primary focus on trade (rather than finance) arises from the fact that while 55.5 percent of total Asian trade was intra-regional in 2011, financial integration is still much more limited: only 23.7 percent of the region's cross-border assets were held in Asian equities and just 7.3 percent in debt securities.[1]

The chapter highlights two potential implications of these regional production networks. First, global supply chains may speed up industrialization but make it less resilient, particularly for smaller Asian countries that lack the bargaining power of a country like China. Second, these evolving production networks are potentially creating "Spiderman" ties that bind nations in Asia together more closely than ever before—but whether this regional dependency will amplify Beijing's *marge de manoeuvre* while constricting the strategic autonomy of smaller Asian economies is currently an open question. However, given China's economic trajectory, unmatched bargaining power with individuals firms, significant state capacity, and skillful leveraging of both inbound and outbound FDI, we believe that with time the former outcome is more likely.

The chapter then considers the implications arising from evolving financial networks in Asia. Financial integration lags behind real sector integration and regional financial integration is considerably less than global financial integration. The reasons are several: a greater role of the state (through state-owned enterprises) in domestic finance in the region; greater regulatory and trade barriers in professional services; capital account restrictions; and the more limited penalty of distance in international trade in financial services (compared to goods).[2] None of these factors are likely to fade away rapidly and hence financial sector integration will continue to be gradual in the foreseeable future.

The chapter concludes by stepping back and briefly reconsidering a first-order assumption that is largely taken for granted in discussions of "emerging Asia," namely, that economic and political power will continue shifting eastward amidst the "rise of the rest."[3] While this tremendous shift in global influence and power is a reality, we end by questioning the teleological assumption that this trend will continue into the foreseeable future and offer several reasons why the pendulum may not swing as much as generally assumed.

### 11.1.2 The Fundamental Tension between Geopolitics and Geoeconomics

Conventional geopolitical imperatives predict that states will engage in power balancing against rising powers.[4] In the Asian security context, this line of thought finds expression in recent discourse about "containing" or "hedging" against China's rise,[5] which some commentators have dubbed the "new Asian Great Game."[6] However, geoeconomic imperatives are at least as salient in Asia today, as profit-maximizing private actors pursue deeper trade and investment linkages, driven by factors such as wage differentials, rising productivity, the changing locus of consumer demand and technological advances underpinning complex cross-border supply-chains.[7] Again, the central actor in Asia's geoeconomic realm is China,[8] although there is a very substantial presence of other players, both regional (Japan, South Korea, Taiwan, ASEAN and India) and extra-regional (the United States, European Union, and Australia in particular).

Multinational firms seeking to secure gains from China's productive and (relatively) low-cost labor force (and a growing skilled-labor force), as well as access to market opportunities in the world's largest and fastest-growing economy, have been willing to do whatever it takes to get in—including provide significant transfers of knowledge, technology, and capital. However, the cumulative effect of rational decisions taken by individual firms is causing profound geopolitical consequences for relations between states in the region. The disjuncture between these two forces is creating fault lines evident in Asia today—and constitutes a defining feature of the relationship between China and some of its major economic partners.

These latter countries are increasingly caught in what Sanjaya Baru describes as a contest "between the pulls of geoeconomics and the pressures of geopolitics."[9] Specifically, firm-level decisions made under competitive dynamics and the prospect of gaining access to China's immense and fast-growing market are driving thousands of American, Japanese, Korean, and Taiwanese firms (amongst others) to help build their countries' foremost strategic competitor as they transfer knowledge and technological capabilities that could significantly impact their own long-term competitiveness. While the near-term economic opportunities may be unparalleled, the aggregate effect of these firm-level decisions threatens to potentially (though not necessarily) undermine their countries' long-term strategic interests.

Consider, for example, foreign direct investment (FDI) into China, which has largely come from the three countries most concerned about China's rise: Taiwan, Japan, and the United States.[10] Taiwan has been China's largest foreign investor over the past two decades, and China has accounted for about 80 percent of Taiwanese outward FDI (totaling between $130 billion and $150 billion). Alongside more than 70,000 Taiwanese firms operating in the mainland, in recent years, more than 20,000 Japanese firms have established operations in China as well. FDI from these potential competitors has undoubtedly helped propel China's emergence as an export powerhouse—and its resulting economic resurgence after three centuries into a great power once again.

In the case of Australia, the tension between geoeconomic "pull" factors drawing it closer to China and geopolitical "push" factors that compel strategic balancing has become increasingly evident. With bilateral trade crossing $105 billion annually, China is by far Australia's biggest trade partner—more than twice as large as the United States. Australia is also one of the leading destinations for outbound Chinese FDI, which was estimated at $34 billion between 2005 and 2010. Yet Canberra is simultaneously pursuing balancing against Beijing. In November 2011, for instance, Australia agreed to station several thousand US Marines in northern Australia and in early 2012 the two countries announced plans to develop a joint airbase on Australia's Cocos Islands in the Indian Ocean. Simultaneously, Australia has also taken steps to strengthen relations with Japan and India, laying the groundwork for potential geopolitical balancing in the region.[11]

### 11.1.3 Multinational Corporations: Driving the Wedge between Geoeconomics and Geopolitics

The principal actors driving the growing dichotomy between geoeconomics and geopolitics in Asia are Multinational Corporations (MNCs). Stagnant or slow-growing home country markets coupled with acute competition from firms across multiple political jurisdictions has meant that MNCs are willing to accept mandatory transfers of know-how, technology, and capital in order to secure near-term access to China's valuable market, even if doing so poses serious long-term strategic consequences.[12] The stark choice that MNCs seeking to enter China face is a result of astute "indigenous innovation" policies, such as local content and technology transfer requirements, instituted by Chinese planners to foster domestic industrial growth.[13] Beijing has skillfully employed such measures to channel FDI into creating "national champions" in strategically significant sectors, including high-speed rail, information technology, automobiles, advanced materials, and civil aviation.[14] Combined with weak enforcement of foreign firms' intellectual property rights, standard setting in favor of domestic players, and an opaque subsidy regime for state-owned enterprises, these policies are propelling China from a prolific low-cost manufacturer into a global technological leader in particular sectors.

By way of example, consider Beijing's monopoly in the strategic neodymium-boron magnet industry, which it secured by leveraging access to its auto market to acquire key technologies from General Motors (GM) in the 1990s.[15] Neodymium magnets are produced from a rare earth element that few countries other than China possess, and are necessary for everything from computer hard drives and hybrid cars to wind turbines and smart bombs. These specialized magnets had long been manufactured by a GM subsidiary, but in 1995, the American automaker decided to sell the division to an investment consortium backed by two companies that were partly owned by the Chinese government (the heads of each were son-in-laws of Deng Xiaoping). In a classic quid pro quo, GM gained inroads into China's burgeoning auto market, while Beijing secured a near-monopoly on neodymium magnets and their militarily significant technology.

A similar dynamic underlies the joint venture announced in 2011 between General Electric (GE) and state-owned Aviation Industry Corporation of China (AVIC).[16] While GE has sold engines to China for its large fleet of Boeing and Airbus jets for decades, it sought out this joint venture with AVIC to position itself for the future, namely to eventually sell avionics to the state-owned Commercial Aircraft Corporation of China—which intends to compete directly with Boeing. As part of its joint venture with AVIC, GE agreed to contribute advanced technology, including the "avionics brain" of Boeing's 787 Dreamliner, and promised to jointly develop new radars, controls, and guidance systems with its Chinese partner. By doing so, the American multinational secured itself access to China's burgeoning civil aviation market. Yet as the US-China Economic and Security Review Commission's annual report concluded in the wake of the deal: "Continued improvements in China's civil aviation capabilities enhance Chinese military aviation capabilities because of the close integration of China's commercial and military aviation sectors."[17]

## 11.1.4 "Rational" Tradeoffs: The Unfettering of MNC-State Ties

In earlier decades, MNCs leveraged their bargaining power to extract maximum concessions from host countries, whether in the form of tax breaks, exemptions on

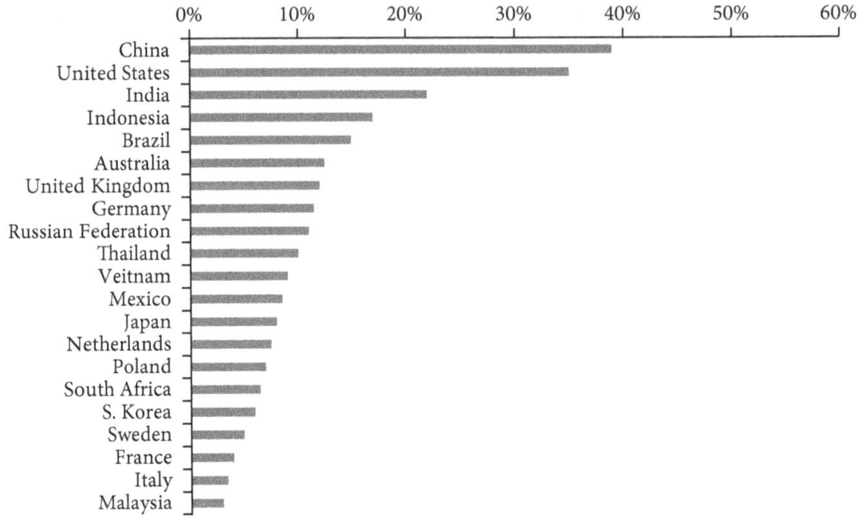


FIGURE 11.1 MNCs' Top Prospective Host Economies for 2012–2014*

*Percentage of respondents who selected economy as top destination (based on 174 validated company responses)

*Source:* UNCTAD World Investment Report 2012.

labor or environmental regulations, or state subsidies and investments that would boost their profit margins.[18] This is still the case in many poor countries, although these MNCs are now as likely to be from China, India, Mexico, or South Korea as from Western countries. In the case of China, however, the bargaining equilibrium favors the host country, and will continue to, as long as MNCs view China as the top destination for expansion (Figure 11.1). Thus, Beijing's indigenous innovation policies may be best understood as a premium charged in exchange for participation in its domestic market.

While it may be rational for individual firms to pay this premium and accept the embedded tradeoffs, MNCs' interests are distinct from—and increasingly misaligned with—those of the countries in which they are headquartered. For one, these countries account for a decreasing share of MNCs' revenues and profits. Recent data shows, for instance, that IT companies in the S&P 500 earn 54 percent of their revenues from outside the United States (up from 42 percent a decade ago). In the materials, consumer goods, and manufacturing sectors, those ratios have also risen by about 10 percent (to 45 percent, 35 percent, and 34 percent respectively). The proportion is far higher for some technology-intensive firms such as Texas Instruments (89 percent), Bristol Myers (82 percent) and Intel (79 percent).[19] Amongst the 100 largest non-financial MNCs in 2011, foreign assets, sales, and employment comprised 63 percent, 65 percent, and 59 percent respectively (Figure 11.2). These figures reveal a broader trend in the United States and globally: once-national firms are becoming less attached to domestic consumer and labor markets in their parent country.

| | 2011 | (%) |
|---|---|---|
| *Assets (USD billions)* | | |
| Foreign | 7776 | 63 |
| Domestic | 4584 | 37 |
| Total | 12360 | 100 |
| *Sales (USD billions)* | | |
| Foreign | 5696 | 65 |
| Domestic | 3077 | 35 |
| Total | 8774 | 100 |
| *Employment (millions)* | | |
| Foreign | 9.1 | 59 |
| Domestic | 6.3 | 41 |
| Total | 15.4 | 100 |

FIGURE 11.2 Internationalization Statistics for 100 Largest Non-Financial MNCs (2011)

*Source:* UNCTAD World Investment Report 2012

For the larger MNCs, China is becoming increasingly central to their commercial success (Figure 11.3)—and is expected to be even more so in the future.[20] Approximately one in seven leading MNCs, including companies like Mead Johnson, Cartier, BHP Billiton, and Advanced Micro Devices earned over 20 percent of their global revenue from China in 2011. And these numbers are expected to grow. Eight percent of MNCs already consider China to be their biggest market, 17 percent expect it to become their largest market within the next five years, and another 21 percent believe this will occur in five to ten years.[21]

Some observers take a sanguine view and contend that while such trade linkages and FDI flows have enhanced technological "catch-up" and spurred Chinese growth, they will not decisively propel Beijing to technology leadership. Instead, they claim that China's weak intellectual property protection, poorly regulated financial sector, restrictions on civil liberties, and an overbearing state and dominance of state-owned enterprises will continue to impede its long-term capacity for breakthrough innovation.[22]

Increasingly, however, this appears to be wishful thinking. According to the National Science Board, a policymaking arm of the US government's National Science Foundation, about 85 percent of the growth in R&D workers employed by US-based MNCs in the last decade has been abroad. This is partly a result of declining US educational performance, particularly in math, science, and reading, which as several reports have warned is undermining the country's ability to compete in a high-skill global economy.[23] Hence, despite high levels of domestic unemployment, more than 60 percent of US aerospace and life science firms claim to face shortages of qualified American workers. As the Chief Executive of 3M put it recently, his firm is expanding labs overseas

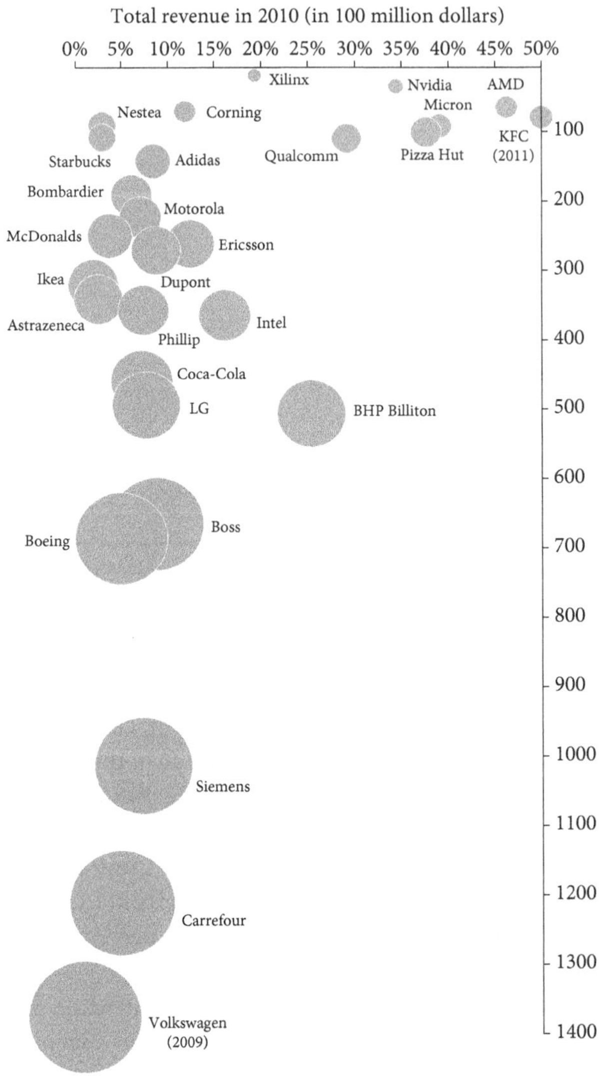


FIGURE 11.3 How Dependent are MNCs on China?

*Revenue in China as % of global revenue*

*Source:* Netease China Statistics (April 2012).

"in preparation for a world where the West is no longer the dominant manufacturing power... Given the moribund interest in science in the United States, this is strategically very important."[24]

At the same time, a wide variety of indicators based on inputs (R&D spending, students with advanced science and technology degrees, MNC R&D centers), as well as outputs (patents filings and citations, journal articles, share of "higher-technology goods"[25] within overall manufacturing exports), point to China's rapidly rising indigenous

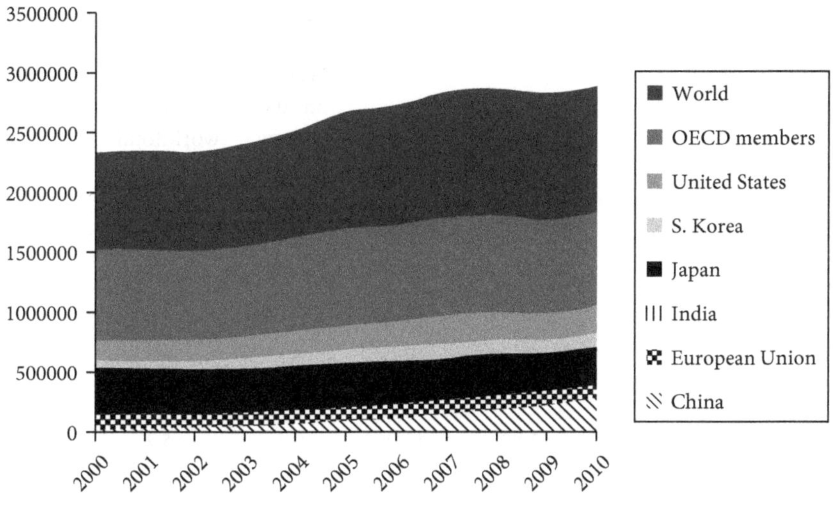


FIGURE 11.4 Patent Filings, 2000–2010*

*Worldwide patent applications filed through the Patent Cooperation Treaty procedure or with a national patent office for exclusive rights for an invention (a product or process that provides a new way of doing something or offers a new technical solution to a problem).

*Source:* World Bank Database

technological capacity and growing national knowledge stocks as drivers of future innovation (Figures 11.4 and 11.5). While factors ranging from foreign flows of knowledge and technology, training abroad, the burgeoning number of multinational R&D centers in China (400 of the Fortune 500 firms and more than a third of the world's top 1000 R&D-spending companies have captive R&D centers in China), and even simply unauthorized copying, have all played an important role, it is clear that this could not have occurred without the rapid development of domestic human capital capabilities within China.

## 11.1.5 The Role of Networks: Managing the Tension between Geoeconomics and Geopolitics

China's rising competitiveness—partly fueled by firm-level decisions in response to geoeconomic imperatives—has implications for its leading economic partners, some of whom are also its likeliest strategic competitors. Even as these countries' trade and investment flows with China continue to deepen, their leaders are cautiously pursuing balancing behavior, a trend that appears to have strengthened in the last few years. As has historically been the case with all rising global powers, China for its part has also begun to flex its muscles in pursuit of its perceived security interests, heightening this tension between geopolitics and geoeconomics. The countervailing "tension wires" in contemporary Asia are networks—particularly those involving production supply chains and to a lesser degree financial flows—as well as institutional frameworks such as ASEAN+3,

| Rank | Country | 1999 | 2009 | Average annual change (%) | 2009 worldtotal (%) | 2009 cumulative world total (%) |
|---|---|---|---|---|---|---|
| – | World | 610,203 | 788,347 | 2.6 | n/a | n/a |
| 1 | United States | 188,004 | 208,601 | 1.0 | 26.5 | 26.5 |
| 2 | China | 15,715 | 74,019 | 16.8 | 9.4 | 35.8 |
| 3 | Japan | 55,274 | 49,627 | −1.1 | 6.3 | 42.1 |
| 4 | United Kingdom | 46,788 | 45,649 | −0.2 | 5.8 | 47.9 |
| 5 | Germany | 42,963 | 45,003 | 0.5 | 5.7 | 53.6 |
| 6 | France | 31,345 | 31,748 | 0.1 | 4.0 | 57.7 |
| 7 | Canada | 22,125 | 29,017 | 2.7 | 3.7 | 61.4 |
| 8 | Italy | 20,327 | 26,755 | 2.8 | 3.4 | 64.7 |
| 9 | South Korea | 8,478 | 22,271 | 10.1 | 2.8 | 67.6 |
| 10 | Spain | 14,514 | 21,543 | 4.0 | 2.7 | 70.3 |
| 11 | India | 10,190 | 19,917 | 6.9 | 2.5 | 72.8 |
| 12 | Australia | 14,341 | 18,923 | 2.8 | 2.4 | 75.2 |
| 13 | Netherlands | 12,168 | 14,866 | 2.0 | 1.9 | 77.1 |
| 14 | Russia | 17,145 | 14,016 | −2.0 | 1.8 | 78.9 |
| 15 | Taiwan | 6,643 | 14,000 | 7.7 | 1.8 | 80.7 |
| 16 | Brazil | 5,859 | 12,306 | 7.7 | 1.6 | 82.2 |
| 17 | Sweden | 9,890 | 9,478 | −0.4 | 1.2 | 83.4 |
| 18 | Switzerland | 8,195 | 9,469 | 1.5 | 1.2 | 84.6 |
| 19 | Turkey | 3,223 | 8,301 | 9.9 | 1.1 | 85.7 |
| 20 | Poland | 5,100 | 7,355 | 3.7 | 0.9 | 86.6 |

FIGURE 11.5: Science & Engineering Journal Articles, 1999 and 2009*

*Countries shown produced >1000 articles in 2009. Article counts from set of journals covered by Science Citation Index (SCI) and Social Sciences Citation Index (SSCI). Articles classified by year of publication and assigned to country on basis of institutional address(es) listed on article. Articles on fractional-count basis, i.e., for articles with collaborating institutions from multiple countries, each country receives fractional credit on basis of proportion of its participating institutions.

*Source:* National Science Foundation, National Center for Science and Engineering Statistics, and The Patent Board; additional tabulations from Thomson Reuters (2011) the East Asia Summit, and similar bodies.[26] In this chapter we focus on the former (production and financial networks), in part because we are skeptical that Beijing will allow itself to be constrained by institutional frameworks in which it does not have a dominant role (unlike Washington in the US-created post-war institutional architecture).

If networks are the "glue" binding Asia together, what are the characteristics of these networks and how resilient are they? What role are they playing in the hedging strategies of countries in the region and how are these networks likely to evolve? A number of outcomes seem plausible. A "Spiderman" series of networks could become so intertwined that rupturing them would have such detrimental consequences as to effectively bind all parties. Alternatively, these evolving networks could become so asymmetrically balanced toward China that they begin to seriously and disproportionally limit other parties' strategic behavior. How would Japan respond, for instance, if China were to seize disputed territory in the region, given the sheer scale of investment and large number of Japanese nationals based in the mainland? If Tokyo's options appear uncertain, the uncertainty is substantial for China as well. To address these questions, the next section will analyze production and financial networks in Asia more closely.

## 11.2 Evolving Production and Financial Networks in Asia

### 11.2.1 Global Supply Chains and the Rise of "Factory Asia"

Deepening economic integration within Asia has been a predominant theme over the past several decades, as the share of intraregional (East Asia plus India) trade relative to total trade increased from a fifth in the early 1950s, to a third in the 1990s, and over a half in 2010 (Figure 11.6).[27] Asia's intraregional trade is growing faster than trade with traditional markets in the US and Europe (Figure 11.7).[28] Indeed the only major Asian country whose share of intra-regional trade has somewhat declined over the last decade has been China (Figure 11.6), indicating that while countries in the region have become more dependent on China, it has become less so as its vast economy expands into global markets. This expansion of intra-Asian trade has largely been driven by intermediate (rather than final) goods, as countries in the region import parts, add some value, and reexport the output (Figure 11.8). Whereas in 1985, developing nations in East Asia supplied most of their own intermediates, today countries in the region are much more dependent on cross-border flows of intermediate goods. A corollary trend has been the growth of cross-border production—involving specialization across vertically linked stages of the production process—which has given rise to so-called "Factory Asia."

In recent decades, as production stages have been sliced up and distributed across countries in Asia and beyond, a defining feature has been the emergence of global supply chains. Complex multi-component products such as engines, IT hardware, consumer

| | 2000 | 2011 |
|---|---|---|
| China | 51.4 | 47.4 |
| India | 36.6 | 53.7 |
| Japan | 36.0 | 59.5 |
| Korea | 47.0 | 62.7 |
| ASEAN | 23.0 | 68.5 |

FIGURE 11.6 Intraregional Trade Share, 2000 and 2011 (%)

*Source:* Authors' calculations based on UN COMTRADE database.

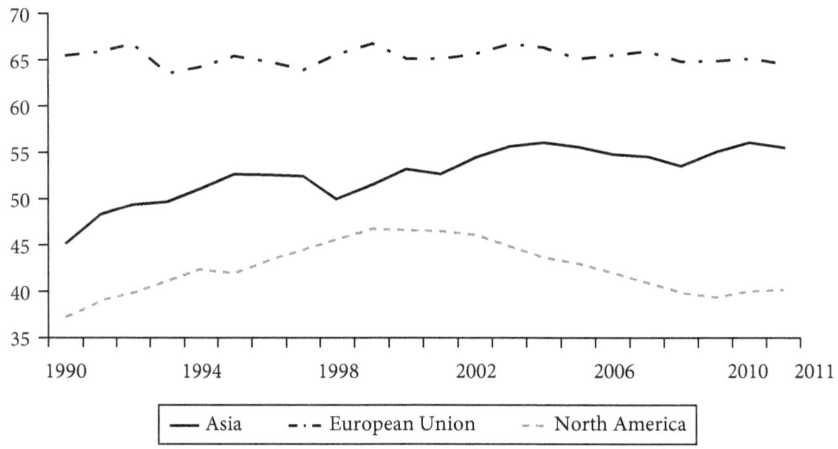


FIGURE 11.7 Intraregional Trade Share: World (%)*

*Intraregional trade share of region i is defined as $ITS_i = (X_{ii} + M_{ii})/(X_i + M_i)$; where $X_{ii}$ = exports of region i to region i, $M_{ii}$ = imports of region i to region i, $X_i$ = total exports of region I, and $M_i$ = total imports of region i.

*Source:* Asian Development Bank, Asian Economic Integration Monitor Report (July 2012).

durables etc... are now developed by multinational companies using horizontal segmentation, with various components being developed in parallel across multiple geographies and then assembled in China. Despite their prominence, analyzing these global supply chains in a systematic manner has proven difficult. A fundamental challenge is that the national accounts record data on gross shipments of goods across borders, rather than the locations at which value is added at different stages of the production process. As a result, trade statistics alone fail to provide a complete picture of underlying trends and linkages.

A leading explanation for the growing fragmentation of cross-border production and concurrent emergence of global supply chains in recent decades is a major shift in the nature of globalization around the 1980s—what some have termed a "second great unbundling"—in the form of falling transport costs and a revolution in information and

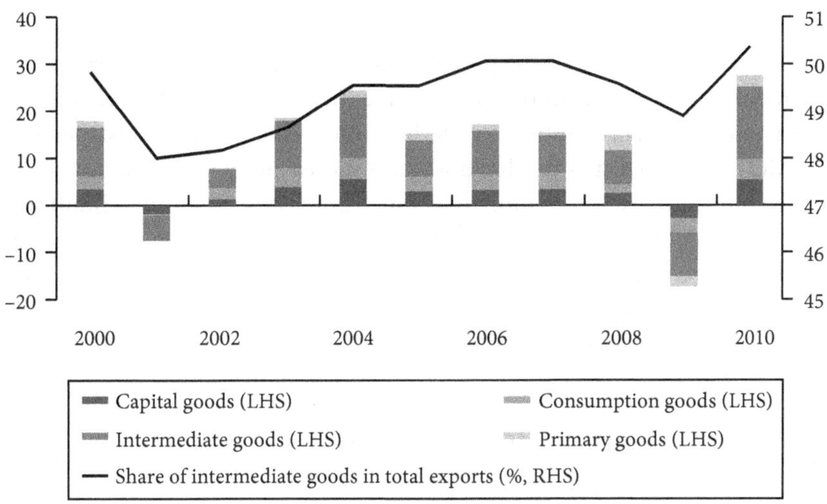


FIGURE 11.8 Contribution to Export Growth by Stages of Production—Asia (%)*

*Based on Broad Economic Categories, which classify traded goods by stages of production. Primary goods include food and beverages, and fuel, lubricants, and primary industrial supplies for industry. Intermediate goods include processed goods, mainly for industry, and parts and components for capital goods and transport equipment. Capital goods include machinery and equipment used by producers as inputs for production. Consumption goods are household goods and government final product purchases.

LHS = left-hand scale, RHS = right-hand scale

*Source:* Asian Development Bank, Asian Economic Integration Monitor Report (July 2012).

communication technology. Globalization's "first great unbundling" in the nineteenth and twentieth century was driven by steamships and railways that dramatically lowered transportation costs, enabling advanced economies like the United States and Great Britain (and later Japan and Korea) to industrialize by taking advantage of economies of scale. By contrast, in this more recent "second unbundling," an exponential decline in communication costs has enabled production to be broken up across ever-expanding multinational supply chains.

The emergence of global supply chains has given rise to a new form of trade, centered around what might be called a "trade-investment-services nexus" that encompasses: (1) trade in parts and components, (2) international movement of investment in production facilities, personnel training, technology, and long-term business relationships, and (3) services to coordinate dispersed production (particularly infrastructure services such as telecommunications, Internet, air cargo, trade-related finance, etc.).

By lowering the cost of coordinating complex activities at a distance, immense advances in information and communication technology have made the geographical dispersion of supply chains both feasible and profitable. As MNCs embraced such technologies, they were able to "offshore" segments of their value chains to developing nations. Yet to ensure that the output meshed seamlessly with continually evolving production processes in other nations, MNCs increasingly deployed firm-specific technology in their overseas manufacturing plants. As a result, global supply chains have had major implications for the process of economic development. Whereas industrialization once required a country to build an entire domestic supply chain, beginning in the mid-1980s and accelerating in the late 1990s, successful industrializing countries like Mexico, Malaysia, and Thailand have increasingly joined supply chains created by MNCs headquartered in more developed countries rather than build their own. While this has undoubtedly enabled them to grow rapidly, as off-shored production has brought technology, management know-how, and capital that countries like Taiwan and South Korea took decades to develop domestically, it has also (as we note later) made them more vulnerable to shifts in supply chains.

### 11.2.2 Strategic Implications of Evolving Production Networks

This growing fragmentation of cross-border production poses at least two strategic implications for Asian countries. One implication of evolving production networks is that industrialization may be faster, but potentially less resilient. Before the "second unbundling," a country had to develop a deep and wide industrial base in order to export advanced goods. Today, however, the ability to do so often merely signifies that a country is located along a particular segment of an international value chain. Whereas industrial power once rested upon robust technological capacity, many emerging markets now simply "borrow" technology from developed countries' firms. Could newly industrializing nations like Indonesia, Thailand, or Vietnam be vulnerable to the vicissitudes of MNC supply chains, which would come under severe stress if technologies change? We shall return to this question in the conclusion.

Importantly, however, the cross-border supply chain trend may have differential impacts on China versus other Asian countries. While MNCs attempt to limit technology transfers, they are less able do so vis-à-vis China both because of the sheer depth of a critical factor of production (labor) and its market size, but also due to the organizational capacity of the Chinese state at the local level and coherent vision of the country's leadership. Hence, Beijing leverages its size to extract concessions from MNCs that smaller Asian nations like Thailand or Vietnam cannot. A possible consequence is that limited spillovers from global supply chains may leave such countries mired in middle-income status, even as China continues to leverage its bargaining power to secure capital and technology that boosts its long-term competitiveness.

A second implication of evolving production networks in Asia is that they may be making economic integration less substitutable, and hence more "sticky," for all parties involved. In other words, geographic proximity matters—perhaps more than ever before. While today's fragmented production processes are commonly referred to as "global supply chains," they might be more accurately described as "regional supply chains," since they typically include geographically proximate countries. In fact, recent studies demonstrate that supply-chain fragmentation has been greatest among neighbors. This has given rise to regional industrial clusters, often described as the rise of "Factory Asia," "Factory North America," and "Factory Europe." Trade in auto parts, for instance, is concentrated within North America, while production and assembly of electronic components primarily occurs within East and South-East Asia.

A leading explanation is that proximity matters because the "trade-investment-services nexus" requires technicians and managers to travel between and coordinate across production facilities. Air travel may have grown cheaper, but time remains costly. One recent study estimates that a day in transit is equivalent to a tariff of between 0.6 percent and 2.3 percent, with the largest effects on parts and components trade. Rising fuel costs mean that transportation costs matter especially for low-margin goods. Although regional trade agreements have proliferated—as of January 2012, countries in the region had signed on to 126 agreements and were negotiating another 64—a majority were with countries outside Asia, and it does not appear that these institutional arrangements have had a marked positive impact.

In the Asian context, this regionalization of cross-border production networks appears to be binding nations closer to one another—particularly within East and Southeast Asia (Figure 11.9). China's massive "workbench" economy has played a central role as a low-cost manufacturing and assembly hub. With production increasingly divided across sequential blocks in various Asian countries, flows of intermediate and processed goods for assembly in China have grown rapidly. The share of Asia's primary and intermediate goods exports to China almost doubled—from 6 percent in 1998 to

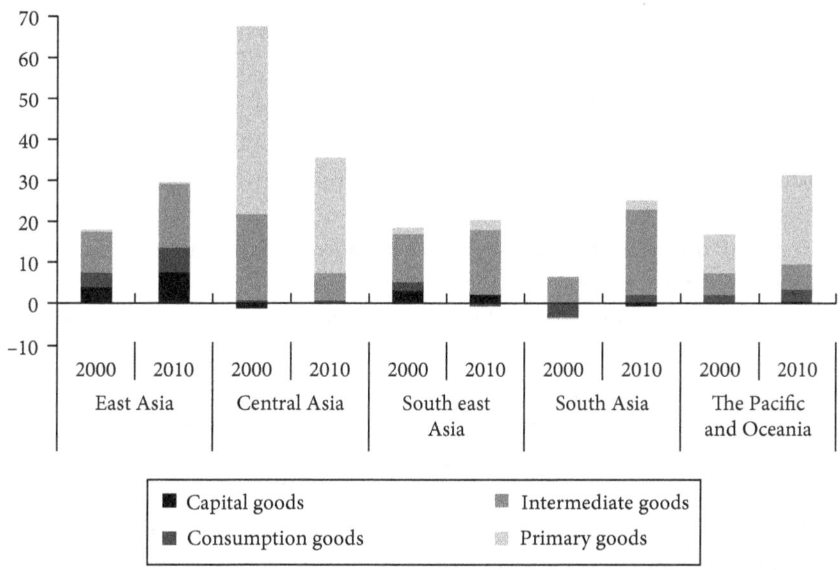


FIGURE 11.9 Contribution to Export Growth by Stages of Production—Asian Subregions (%)*

*Based on Broad Economic Categories, which classify traded goods by stages of production.

*Source:* Asian Development Bank, Asian Economic Integration Monitor Report (July 2012).

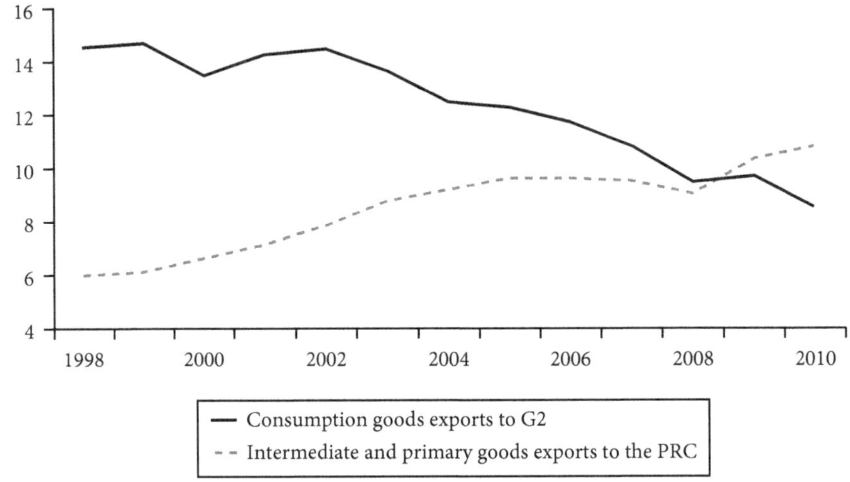


FIGURE 11.10 Exports to G2 and China (% of Total Exports)*

*Based on Broad Economic Categories, which classify traded goods by stages of production. See Figure 11.9 for definition of primary, intermediate, capital, and consumption goods.

*Source:* Asian Development Bank, Asian Economic Integration Monitor Report (July 2012).

about 11 percent in 2010, and is now larger (in value terms) than Asian exports of consumption goods to the United States and European Union combined (Figure 11.10).

Intraregional FDI has been the principal driver of cross-border production supply-chains: the share of intraregional FDI inflows to total inflows increased from 44.6 percent in 2007 to 60.0 percent in 2009. Unsurprisingly, some countries appear to be playing the FDI game better than others. China, in particular, has taken a strategic approach toward inbound FDI that has enabled it to leverage the creation of economic linkages through cross-border production networks that increase *intra-industry* trade across Asia, which is less substitutable than *inter-industry* trade and thereby generates more strategic interdependence.

If inward FDI into China has boosted the Chinese economy and helped make it the formidable strategic competitor today, what about the role of Chinese investment abroad? In 2010, China's outward FDI reached $68.8 billion (5.2 percent of total worldwide—Figure 11.11). By the end of that year, more than 13,000 domestic Chinese investing entities had established nearly 16,000 overseas enterprises across 178 countries; their accumulated outward FDI stock volume stood at $317.21 billion, and total assets of their foreign affiliates exceeded $1.5 trillion, with stakes in resource companies across the globe—from Sudan to Canada—particularly important.

However, Chinese FDI stands out in two respects. First, outbound Chinese FDI is largely driven by state-owned enterprises (Figure 11.12), hence the "geoeconomics" and "geopolitics" underpinning these outward capital flows are relatively more closely aligned. And second, much of China's FDI is in countries with which it runs trade deficits—particularly where it is seeking access to natural resources.

| | 2005 | 2010 |
|---|---|---|
| Australia | 587 | 7,867 |
| EU | 768 | 12,496 |
| India | 14 | 479 |
| Indonesia | 140 | 1150 |
| Japan | 150 | 1105 |
| S. Korea | 882 | 637 |
| Vietnam | 229 | 986 |
| USA | 822 | 4,873 |
| ASEAN | 1,256 | 14,350 |

FIGURE 11.11 Chinese Outbound FDI Stock, 2005–2010 (USD millions)

*Source:* Chinese Ministry of Commerce, 2010 Statistical Bulletin of China's Outward FDI.

| | Greenfield | % Share | M&A | % Share | All deals | % Share |
|---|---|---|---|---|---|---|
| *Number of deals* | | | | | | |
| Government-controlled | 40 | 29% | 30 | 23% | 70 | 26% |
| Private and public | 96 | 71% | 102 | 77% | 198 | 74% |
| | 136 | | 132 | | 268 | |
| *Total investment (USD millions)* | | | | | | |
| Government-controlled | 1,957 | 60% | 7,911 | 68% | 9,948 | 66% |
| Private and public | 1,307 | 40% | 3,754 | 32% | 5,062 | 34% |
| | 3,264 | | 11,746 | | 15,009 | |

FIGURE 11.12 Chinese Outbound FDI in the US by Ownership, 2003–2011

*Source:* The Rhodium Group; Stanford Center for International Development.

While this pattern of regional geographic dependency is not unique to Asia, a key difference is the simultaneity of increasing economic interdependence and rising strategic competition, to a degree that is simply not the case in any other part of the world. For the moment economic interdependencies do not appear to have muted the forces of nationalism in say, Hanoi, Manila, or Tokyo (or for that matter Beijing), although they may well have restrained these countries from acting on them. But their robustness is likely to ultimately affect how these countries manage conflicts, particularly with regard to contentious territorial claims. Given China's emergence as an economic colossus, at least some Asian countries, whose firms are embedded in increasingly "sticky" production and investment relationships with Beijing, might regard a loss of strategic autonomy as a price worth paying for doing business with it. Cambodia and Laos are examples in this regard.

### 11.2.3 Evolving Financial Networks in Asia

A significant gap still exists between trade and financial integration across Asia. In 2010, only 23.7 percent of the region's cross-border assets were held in Asian equities and just 7.3 percent in debt securities, whereas over 50 percent of total Asian trade was intraregional. Capital mobility within Asia has increased over the past two decades, as a result of both growing intraregional trade and individual countries' efforts to liberalize and deregulate markets. Yet the primary consequence has been deepening Asian linkages with global financial markets rather than an expansion of cross-border regional flows. As a recent ADB report notes, "Asian investors still prefer to invest either in their home markets or in mature markets such as the US and Europe,"[29] and to the extent that they invest within the region, their cross-border holdings are predominantly in equity rather than debt.

In the case of trade, Asian governments acted to create an enabling environment by reducing trade barriers and crafting policies conducive to attracting FDI. In the case of financial sector integration, the story is likely to be different. First, distance matters much less in finance than in trade. Second, the policy case for financial integration is weaker since gains from global diversification may be greater than those achievable solely through regional integration. Third, restrictions on the capital account—partly for macroeconomic stability and partly to manage an exchange rate conducive to exports—militate against strong intra-regional financial sector integration. And fourth, licensing and other regulatory practices protect powerful domestic incumbents, often state-owned enterprises.

Recently, however, there have been signs of growing financial integration across Asia, particularly in the wake of the global financial crisis, attributed to the region's robust growth prospects relative to weak and volatile markets globally as well as further liberalization of capital markets in key regional economies.[30] Regional cooperative efforts to safeguard the risks in capital account liberalization have been manifest in the Chiang Mai Initiative Multilateralization, which started as a complex network of bilateral swap agreements and has since become a single facility tasked with managing regional financial crises. However, other steps such as relaxing licensing standards for Asia-based foreign banks, setting common standards for domestic capital markets, and cross-border issues of financial products would be necessary for a region-wide capital market to emerge.

While overall financial integration still lags behind the rise of "Factory Asia," another key trend in the region's financial networks warrants serious attention: the emergence of a "Renminbi Bloc." In recent years, China's renminbi has begun to challenge the dollar's status as a global reference currency (one that other currencies track explicitly or implicitly) for the first time since World War II. Around the world, a growing number of emerging market currencies are tracking the renminbi since it resumed floating in mid-2010 (compared to its earlier period of flexibility between 2005 and 2008), while fewer are tracking the dollar and euro.[31] Moreover, a veritable "renminbi bloc" has emerged in East Asia—where seven out of ten countries (China, South Korea, Indonesia, Taiwan, Malaysia, Singapore, and Thailand) now track the renminbi more closely than the dollar. In fact, the average value of these seven currencies' co-movement relative to the renminbi may be as much as 40 percent greater than that for the dollar.

The renminbi's emergence as a key reference currency in East Asia is tied to regional trade and production networks, as "countries that sell to the growing Chinese market or are locked in supply chains centered on China see the advantages of maintaining a stable exchange rate against the renminbi."[32] Furthermore, China's international trade linkages are driving the renminbi's rise as a global reference currency, with countries from India and Israel to Turkey and South Africa now tracking the renminbi closely—in some cases more than the dollar.

China has been following its usual policy trajectory of gradualism to make the renminbi a reserve currency, beginning with using the renminbi in cross-border trade settlements, then allowing foreign firms investing in China to issue renminbi-denominated bonds, followed by allowing banks in Hong Kong to lend renminbi to companies in Shenzhen (and presumably to firms in other cities gradually), and most recently signing currency-swap agreements with an increasing number of countries. However, China's ability to make the renminbi rival the dollar as an international reserve currency faces three major challenges.[33] First its financial markets are still quite illiquid. This matters for central banks that value liquidity when deciding which currencies to hold as reserve. The liquidity of US Treasury bonds is critical for its acceptance as the world's leading reserve asset. Second, China would need to move to an open capital account for the renminbi to be accepted as a reserve currency, which entails considerable domestic risks for China. And third, and perhaps most critically, China's political system may perhaps be the biggest barrier to renminbi internationalization. Eichengreen (2012) has made the case that the principal reserve currencies of the nineteenth and twentieth centuries, the pound sterling and the dollar respectively, were issued by democracies which by design limit the arbitrary exercise of executive power—which is not the case with the Chinese political system. As Eichengreen argues, "democratically elected governments are best able to make the credible commitments needed to develop deep and liquid financial markets. They can commit not to expropriate creditors, since the latter will vote them out of office if they do. And the same respect for creditor rights that reassures domestic investors reassures foreign investors—both official and private—as well." Thus difficult political changes within China, limiting arbitrary executive power and strengthening creditor rights, may be needed before the renminbi emerges as an alternative reserve currency to the dollar.

This emerging "Renminbi Bloc" poses at least two strategic implications, one regional and the other global. Whereas cross-border production networks may be binding smaller Asian countries as well as China, this deepening currency linkage appears to be working more asymmetrically—generating regional dependency amongst Beijing's commercial partners while increasing its own strategic autonomy. Hence, Asian countries' growing dependence on the renminbi as a regional reserve currency seems to be *exacerbating* (rather than mitigating) the tension they face between geoeconomics and geopolitics, with China's neighbors being drawn closer toward the dynamic economic giant even as they seek to counterbalance its rising assertiveness on the security front. The emergence of a renminbi bloc in East Asia is also of global significance; it is yet another sign of the shifting locus of relative economic influence eastward, away from the United States and European Union.

## 11.3 Conclusion

The end of the Cold War coincided with the rise of the Washington Consensus—a set of beliefs organized around the superiority of free markets, free trade, and private enterprise. Legions of critics saw this as an attempt by the lone superpower to impose its economic ideology on weaker emerging economies and thereby strengthen its global hegemony. With "the end of history," MNCs—the embodiment of so-called Western (especially US) economic imperialism—were seen to be the instruments of this new economic order.

But as the saying goes, be careful what you ask for because you might actually get it—and then some. The "rise of the rest," led most spectacularly of course by China, was fueled by an ultra-rich diet of the "Washington Consensus." Within two decades, even in that poster-child of closed economies—India—trade to GDP ratios had tripled, exceeding those of Japan and the United States. Emerging market economies took up many elements of the Washington Consensus with a zeal unmatched in Washington itself. They welcomed MNCs, but many were from the region itself, particularly driven by the Chinese diaspora from Hong Kong, Taiwan, and ASEAN. Western MNCs arrived later, transferring technologies and exporting back to their countries with such rapidity as to quickly make China the largest creditor of the United States. US MNCs did indeed flourish in this era, but much of the profit they made overseas was parked outside the US—and its tax net. And as stated earlier, in doing what they were supposed to do (maximize profits) MNCs from advanced industrialized economies like Japan, the United States, and the European Union transferred knowledge and know-how that have gradually built up their most formidable strategic competitor: China.

While there is little doubt as to the magnitude of this eastward shift in global economic power, we believe that the pendulum is likely to swing back within the next decade or so, primarily as a result of five factors:

1. *Energy*: The shale gas revolution will make energy available in the United States in quantities and prices that will be unmatched in any other large economy, giving the United States renewed competitive advantage in energy intensive industries. The United States, which currently imports around 20 percent of its total energy needs, is expected to become self-sufficient by 2035, thanks to rising production and improved fuel efficiency, and North America is expected

to become a net oil exporter by around 2030.[34] As a result, the international oil trade will shift increasingly toward Asian markets, placing greater pressures on the security of strategic routes that link them to the Middle East.

2. *Manufacturing*: There is a silent revolution in manufacturing underway with sophisticated, relatively low-cost robots that can perform the task of workers from assembly lines to logistics. The advantages conferred by the availability of a low-cost, disciplined labor force will thus gradually diminish. This will have three major consequences: i) a shift in significant parts of manufacturing back to the West and especially the United States; ii) major disruptions in supply chain networks that are being established across Asia with countries possessing "shallow" industrial capabilities most adversely affected; iii) severe employment challenges in emerging markets with a younger demography.
3. *Natural Resources*: The most severe challenge facing rising powers in Asia in particular is the growing severity of natural resource constraints, especially land and water, which are not easily amenable to technological solutions and which (unlike energy) cannot be augmented by trade. This advantage in "natural capital" will favor the erstwhile Western powers well into this century.
4. *Demography*: The demographic transition in China is occurring much faster than previous projections. The fertility rate has dropped to just 1.4 and the labor force will shrink by nearly 30 million in this decade alone, putting a brake on a key driver of economic growth. Over the next few decades demographic trends are also unfavorable for the EU and Japan while relatively favorable for the United States and India.
5. *Institutional Quality*: In many emerging markets, the rapid emergence of the private sector has vastly outpaced the building of sound regulatory institutions. The resulting weakness of state capacity has led to the emergence of crony capitalism with pernicious effects in many countries such as Russia, India and even China. (In the United States the opposite has occurred—regulatory institutions that were in place have been weakened.)

Needless to say, these projections are all subject to a major caveat—namely, the vicissitudes of domestic politics. But that uncertainty is certain in all countries.

## NOTES

1. Asian Development Bank. *Asian Economic Integration Monitor Report.* July 2012.
2. Asian Development Bank, *Outlook 2012 Update*, Chapter 2, "Services and Asia's Future Growth,"Available at: [http://www.adb.org/sites/default/files/pub/2012/adou2012.pdf].
3. *See, e.g.*, ZAKARIA, Fareed. *The Post-American World.* New York: W.W. Norton & Company, 2008; WALT, Stephen. "The End of the American Era." *The National Interest.*October 25, 2011.
4. Here, "conventional" refers to contemporary realist theories of state behavior. Given their breadth and diversity, this chapter adopts an intentionally reductivist view of "realism" for the purpose of simplification. For an overview of various competing strains of realist

thought, *see* Michael W. Doyle, *Ways of War and Peace: Realism, Liberalism and Socialism* (1997), Part 1. *See also* Hans Morgenthau, *Politics among Nations: The Struggle for Power and Peace* (1948); Kenneth Waltz, *Theory of International Politics* (1979).

5. *See, e.g.*, Barrett L. McCormick, *Introduction*, in *What if China Doesn't Democratize? Implications for War and Peace* (Edward Friedman & Barrett L. McCormick, eds. 2000), 3–18; Eric A. Posner and John Yoo, "International Law and the Rise of China," 7 Chicago Journal of International Law 1, Spring 2006: 1–15; Margaret TALEV, "Obama's Asia Pivot Puts U.S. Approach to China on New Path," *Bloomberg*, November 19, 2011.
6. Kishore MAHBUBANI, "The New Asian Great Game." *The Financial Times*, November 23, 2011. [http://blogs.ft.com/the-a-list/2011/11/23/the-new-asian-great-game].
7. *See, e.g.*, Homi KHARAS and Indermit GIL, *An East Asian Renaissance: Ideas for Economic Growth*, The International Bank for Reconstruction and Development/The World Bank, 2007.
8. James MCGREGOR, *One Billion Customers: Lessons from the Front Lines of Doing Business in China*. New York: Simon & Schuster, 2005; C. FRED BERGSTEN, Charles FREEMAN, Nicholas R. LARDY, and Derek J. MITCHELL, *China's Rise: Challenges and Opportunities*, Petersen Institute for International Economics: Washington DC, 2008.
9. Sanjaya BARU, "Anchoring Australia," *The Business Standard*, November 28, 2011.
10. Devesh KAPUR, "The Geo-Strategic Implications of FDI," *The Business Standard*, January 9, 2012.
11. For the official Australian thinking on this issue see *Australia in the Asian Century White Paper* October 2012.
12. Theodore MORAN, "Foreign Direct Investment in China: Trading Competitiveness for Access?," *East Asia Forum*, April 11, 2011.
13. Numerous recent studies have examined Chinese indigenous innovation measures. *See, e.g.*, Nathaniel Ahrens, "Innovation and the Visible Hand: China, Indigenous Innovation, and the Role of Government Procurement." Carnegie Paper. Carnegie Endowment for International Peace. July 2010; James McGregor, "China's Drive for Indigenous Innovation: A Web of Industrial Policies," July 2010; Adam SEGAL, "China's Innovation Wall: Beijing's Push for Homegrown Technology." *Foreign Affairs*. September 28, 2010; United States International Trade Commission, "China: Intellectual Property Infringement, Indigenous Innovation Policies, and Frameworks for Measuring the Effects on the U.S. Economy," Publication 4199, November 2010.
14. Steve PEARLSTEIN, "Chinese Follow Same Old Script (and They Get the Punch Line)," *The Washington Post*, January 18, 2011.
15. Andrew LEONARD, "How G.M. Helped China to World Magnet Domination," *Salon.com*, August 30, 2010.
16. David BARBOZA, Christopher DREW, and Steve LOHR, "G.E. to Share Jet Technology With China in New Joint Venture," *The New York Times*, January 17, 2011.
17. U.S.-China Economic and Security Review Commission. "2011 Report to Congress." November 2011. [http://www.uscc.gov/annual_report/2011/annual_report_full_11.pdf].
18. *See, e.g.*, E. PENROSE (1959). "Profit Sharing Between Producing Countries and Oil Companies in the Middle East." *The Economic Journal*.69(274): 238–254; MORAN, T. (1974). *Multinational Corporations and the Politics of Dependence: Copper in Chile*. Princeton University Press. (Princeton, NJ); OTTO, J. et al. (2006.) *Mining Royalties: A Study of Their Impact on Investors, Government, and Civil Society*. The World Bank. (Washington, D.C.).

19. FactSet data cited in Gillian TETT, "Washington's Global Business Headache," *The Financial Times*, August 14, 2012.
20. The Economist Intelligence Unit, "Multinational companies and China: What Future?" November 2011. The report was based on surveys and in-depth interviews of non-Chinese executives, academics, and market analysts.
21. *Ibid.*
22. *See, e.g.*, "China's Indigenous Innovation Policy and U.S. Interests," Written Testimony of Dr. Philip I. Levy, Resident Scholar, American Enterprise Institute, Before the House Committee on Foreign Affairs Subcommittee on Terrorism, Nonproliferation, and Trade, March 9, 2011; Barun ROY, "'Mainland' for Innovation," *Business Standard*, February 9, 2012; Richard FLORIDA, "Why China Lags on Innovation and Creativity," *The Atlantic Cities*, April 2, 2012.
23. *See, e.g.*, Council on Foreign Relations, "U.S. Education Reform and National Security," Task Force Report. March 2012. [http://www.cfr.org/united-states/us-education-reform-national-security/p27618]; James Manyika, Susand Lund, Byron Auguste and Sreenivas Ramaswamy, "Help Wanted: The Future of Work in Advanced Economies," McKinsey Global Institute Report, March 2012.
24. James R. HAGERTY, "U.S. Firms Shift R&D to Asia," *The Wall Street Journal*, January 17, 2012.
25. This is defined by the U.S Census Bureau as roughly 600 manufactured-product categories with the greatest R&D content.
26. For an analysis on institutions of regional integration in Asia see Asian Development Bank *Institutions for Regional Integration: Toward an Asian Economic Community* December 2010.
27. Asian Development Bank 2012.
28. Asian Development Bank. *Asian Economic Integration Monitor Report.* July 2012.
29. *Ibid.*
30. *Ibid.*
31. Arvind SUBRAMANIAN and Martin KESSLER,"The Renminbi Bloc Is Here: Asia Down, Rest of the World to Go?" Petersen Institute for International Economics: Washington DC, 2008. Working Paper 12-19. October 2012.
32. Arvind SUBRAMANIAN and Martin KESSLER, "China's Currency Rises in the US Backyard," *Financial Times*, October 21, 2012.
33. Barry Eichengreen, "The renminbi challenge," Project Syndicate. Available at: [http://www.project-syndicate.org/commentary/can-china-have-an-international-reserve-currency-by-barry-eichengreen#6GHKTdroMIPQHGZj.99]
34. International Energy Agency *World Energy Outlook 2012.*

## References

Ahrens, Nathaniel. "Innovation and the Visible Hand: China, Indigenous Innovation, and the Role of Government Procurement." Carnegie Paper. Carnegie Endowment for International Peace. July 2010.

Asian Development Bank. *Asian Economic Integration Monitor Report.* July 2012.

Baldwin, Richard. "Trade and Industrialization after Globalization's 2nd Unbundling: How Building and Joining A Supply Chain Are Different and Why It Matters." NBER Working Paper No. 17716. December 2011.

"Bamboo Innovation: Beware of Judging China's Innovation Engine by the Standards of Silicon Valley." *The Economist*. May 5, 2011.

Barboza, David Christopher Drew, and Steve Lohr. "G.E. to Share Jet Technology With China in New Joint Venture." *The New York Times*. January 17, 2011.

Bergsten, C. Fred, Charles Freeman, Nicholas R. Lardy, and Derek J. Mitchell. *China's Rise: Challenges and Opportunities*. Washington, DC: Petersen Institute for International Economics, 2008.

Brahmbhatt, Milan, and Albert Hu. "Ideas and Innovation in East Asia." *The World Bank Research Observer* 25(2): 177–207. August 2010.

Bremmer, Ian. *The End of the Free Market: Who Wins the War Between States and Corporations?* New York: Penguin, 2010.

Chinese Ministry of Commerce. 2010 *Statistical Bulletin of China's Outward FDI*. http://english.mofcom.gov.cn/aarticle/statistic/foreigninvestment/201109/20110907742320.html.

Council on Foreign Relations. "U.S. Education Reform and National Security." Task Force Report. March 2012. http://www.cfr.org/united-states/us-education-reform-national-security/p27618.

Doyle, Michael W. *Ways of War and Peace: Realism, Liberalism, and Socialism*. New York: W.W. Norton & Co., 1997.

Eichengreen, Barry. "The Renminbi Challenge." *Social Europe Journal*, October 16, 2012.

Florida, Richard. "Why China Lags on Innovation and Creativity." *The Atlantic Cities*. April 2, 2012.

Fukasaku, K., B. Meng, and N. Yamano, "Recent Developments in Asian Economic Integration: Measuring Indicators of Trade Integration and Fragmentation," *OECD Science, Technology and Industry Working Papers*, 2011/03, OECD Publishing. 2011.

Hagerty, James R. "U.S. Firms Shift R&D to Asia." *The Wall Street Journal*. January 17, 2012.

Hont, Istvan. *Jealousy of Trade: International Competition and the Nation-State in Historical Perspective*. Cambridge: Harvard University Press, 2007.

Hummels, David, and Georg Schaur. "Time as a Trade Barrier." *NBER Working Paper No. 17758*. January 2012.

Johnston, David Cay. *Free Lunch: How the Wealthiest Americans Enrich Themselves at Government Expense (And Stick You With The Bill)*. New York: Penguin, 2008.

Johnson, Robert C., and Guillermo Noguera. "Fragmentation and Trade in Value Added over Four Decades." *NBER Working Paper No. 18186*. June 2012.

Johnson, Robert C., and Guillermo Noguera. "Proximity and Production Fragmentation." *American Economic Review: Papers & Proceedings 2012*, 102(3): 407–411.

Kharas, Homi, and Indermit Gil. *An East Asian Renaissance: Ideas for Economic Growth*. The International Bank for Reconstruction and Development / The World Bank. Washington, D.C., 2007.

Kim, S., and J-W. Lee. "Real and Financial Integration in East Asia." *Review of International Economics*. 20(2): 332–349. 2012.

Klein, Ezra. "The Upside of the Rise of the Rest." *The Washington Post*. May 17, 2011.

Lohr, Steve. "When Innovation, Too, Is Made in China." *The New York Times*. January 1, 2011.

Manyika, James, Susand Lund, Byron Auguste, and Sreenivas Ramaswamy. "Help Wanted: The Future of Work in Advanced Economies." McKinsey Global Institute Report. March 2012.

McCormick, Barrett L. "Introduction." In *What if China Doesn't Democratize?: Implications for War and Peace*, edited by Edward Friedman & Barrett L. McCormick, 3–18. Armonk: M.E. Sharpe, 2000.

McGregor, James. "China's Drive for Indigenous Innovation: A Web of Industrial Policies." July 2010. http://www.apcoworldwide.com/content/PDFs/Chinas_Drive_for_Indigenous_Innovation.pdf.

McGregor, James. *One Billion Customers: Lessons from the Front Lines of Doing Business in China*. New York: Simon & Schuster, 2005.

Moran, T. (1974). *Multinational Corporations and the Politics of Dependence: Copper in Chile*. Princeton: Princeton University Press.

Morgenthau, Hans. *Politics Among Nations: The Struggle for Power and Peace*. New York: Alfred A. Knopf, 1948.

"Multipolarity: The New Global Economy." *Global Development Horizons 2011*. The World Bank. 2011.

Otto, J., et al. *Mining Royalties: A Study of Their Impact on Investors, Government, and Civil Society*. Washington, DC: The World Bank. 2006.

Panagiotopoulos, Manuel. "East Asian Economic Integration." A Report for the Australian Trade Commission. March 2012.

Penrose, E. "Profit Sharing Between Producing Countries and Oil Companies in the Middle East." *The Economic Journal*, 69(274): 238–254. 1959.

Posner, Eric A., and John Yoo. "International Law and the Rise of China." 7 *Chicago Journal of International Law* 1, Spring 2006: 1–15.

Rosen, Daniel H., and Thilo Hanemann. "China's Changing Outbound Foreign Direct Investment Profile: Drivers and Policy Implications." *Peterson Institute for International Economics*. June 2009.

Segal, Adam. "China's Innovation Wall: Beijing's Push for Homegrown Technology." *Foreign Affairs*. September 28, 2010.

Sirkin, Harold L., Michael Zinser, and Douglas Hohner. "Made in America, Again: Why Manufacturing Will Return to the U.S." *The Boston Consulting Group*. August 2011.

Sturgeon, Timothy J. "Mapping Global Value Chains: Intermediate Goods Trade and Structural Change in the World Economy." United Nations Industrial Development Organization. Development Policy and Strategic Research Branch Working Paper 05/2010.

Tett, Gillian. "Washington's Global Business Headache." *Financial Times*. August 14, 2012.

The Economist Intelligence Unit. "Multinational Companies and China: What Future?" November 2011.

United Nations Conference on Trade and Development. Asian Foreign Direct Investment in Africa. UNCTAD/ITE/IIA/2007/1 United Nations Publication. 2007.

United Nations Conference on Trade and Development. *World Investment Report 2012*.

United States International Trade Commission. "China: Intellectual Property Infringement, Indigenous Innovation Policies, and Frameworks for Measuring the Effects on the U.S. Economy." Publication 4199, November 2010, 5–23. http://www.usitc.gov/publications/332/pub4199.pdf.

U.S.-China Economic & Security Review Commission. "Going Out: An Overview of China's Outward Foreign Direct Investment." March 30, 2011.

U.S.-China Economic and Security Review Commission. "2011 Report to Congress." November 2011. http://www.uscc.gov/annual_report/2011/annual_report_full_11.pdf.

Vaitheeswaran, Vijay V. "Need, Speed, and Greed." New York: Harper Business, 2012.

Walt, Stephen. "The End of the American Era." *The National Interest*.October 25, 2011.

Waltz, Kenneth. *Theory of International Politics*. Boston: McGraw-Hill, 1979.

Zakaria, Fareed. *The Post-American World*. New York: W.W. Norton & Company, 2008.

## CHAPTER 12

# THE POLITICAL ECONOMY OF ASIA-PACIFIC TRADE AGREEMENTS

JOHN RAVENHILL

Asia-Pacific regional economic integration is frequently characterized as "market-driven." In one sense such an assessment is accurate: the region lacks the deep and over-arching regional institutions that facilitated economic cooperation in Europe. On the other hand, it would be misleading to ignore the role that governments around the Pacific Rim have played in constructing an economic environment that facilitated the emergence of "Factory Asia." Tariff reductions, both through unilateral action and through participation in GATT/WTO rounds, the creation of export-processing zones and duty-drawback arrangements, and the negotiation of the WTO's Information Technology Agreement in 1996 (which substantially freed trade in the single most important category of Asian exports), were all important factors in removing impediments to the efficient management of regional supply chains.

What was distinctive about Asian approaches to liberalization until the financial crises of 1997-1998 was that it occurred predominantly on a non-discriminatory basis.[1] Governments on the Western Pacific Rim, long the victim of European practices that excluded their agricultural exports and that frequently attempted to limit their burgeoning exports of manufactures, were the most enthusiastic supporters of the global trading regime. The "open regionalism" principle that underlay the trans-regional Asia-Pacific Economic Cooperation (APEC) agreement, which had been established in 1989, emphasized the commitment to liberalization on a non-discriminatory basis and members' support for the global trade regime. At the time of the financial crisis, only one discriminatory trading agreement was in force in East Asia: the ASEAN Free Trade Area. And even this agreement was of little consequence: rather than being a genuinely regional arrangement, it was a series of bilateral pacts that, given the relatively low external (most favored nation—MFN) tariffs on the majority of goods traded within the region, created few preferential advantages (automobiles were the notable exception). Consequently, business made little use of the agreement (Ravenhill 1995, Baldwin 2007).

In the first decade of the new millennium, however, East Asia joined the global rush to preferential trade agreements (PTAs). By 2010, East Asian countries had concluded 124 agreements and were negotiating a further 55 (Table 12.1). In this chapter I consider whether the East Asian experience conforms to that of regional economic cooperation

**Table 12.1 Preferential Trade Agreements on the Western Pacific Rim (January 2010)**

| Country | Agreements Concluded | Agreements under Negotiation | Agreements Proposed | Total |
|---|---|---|---|---|
| *Northeast Asia* | | | | |
| People's Republic of China | 10 | 6 | 8 | 24 |
| Hong Kong, China | 1 | 1 | 0 | 2 |
| Japan | 11 | 5 | 4 | 20 |
| Republic of Korea | 7 | 9 | 8 | 24 |
| Taiwan | 4 | 2 | 1 | 7 |
| **Total NE Asia** | **33** | **23** | **21** | **77** |
| *SE Asia* | | | | |
| Brunei Darussalam | 8 | 1 | 4 | 13 |
| Cambodia | 6 | 1 | 2 | 9 |
| Indonesia | 8 | 2 | 6 | 16 |
| Lao PDR | 8 | 1 | 2 | 11 |
| Malaysia | 10 | 6 | 3 | 19 |
| Myanmar | 6 | 2 | 2 | 10 |
| Philippines | 7 | 1 | 4 | 12 |
| Singapore | 20 | 9 | 5 | 34 |
| Thailand | 11 | 7 | 6 | 24 |
| Viet Nam | 7 | 2 | 2 | 11 |
| **Total SE Asia** | **91** | **32** | **36** | **159** |
| *Oceania* | | | | |
| Australia | 8 | 6 | 6 | 20 |
| New Zealand | 8 | 3 | 4 | 15 |
| **Total Oceania** | **16** | **9** | **10** | **35** |
| **Western Pacific Rim Total** | **140** | **64** | **67** | **271** |

*Source*: Asian Development Bank (2011: Table 2.13 pp. 61–3).

elsewhere, and whether it can be adequately explained by the theoretical literature developed to account for regionalism in other parts of the world (the European experience, of course, remains the dominant referent for much of the literature). As part of this discussion, I consider the likely impact of these agreements, the dynamics they will set in train, and their possible consequences for the future of Asia-Pacific regionalism.

## 12.1 Explaining the Rush to Preferential Trade on the Western Pacific Rim

### 12.1.1 The Regional Literature

Several dimensions of the rush to preferential trade on the Western Pacific Rim defy commonplace explanations. Consider first the frequently stated argument that East Asian countries turned to PTAs in response to an increase in regional interdependence (see, for instance, Urata (2009: 33-40)). In support of this argument, authors frequently cite data from the Asian Development Bank that purportedly demonstrate that intra-regional trade as a share of East Asian economies' total trade had surpassed the equivalent figure for NAFTA and was approaching that of the EU. By the middle of the first decade of the new millennium, according to a study by Kawai (2007: Table 1 p. 12), the share of intra-regional trade in total East Asian trade had increased to over 55 percent. Certainly, with the rapid economic growth of China in these years, dramatic changes in trade patterns occurred in the region, with China emerging as the single largest export market for most countries of East Asian and Oceania. But the figure of 55 percent is arrived at only by counting trade between China and Hong Kong (which, because of the city port's entrepôt status, involves a substantial element of double-counting).[2] When, however, the analysis is confined to the ASEAN Plus Three (China, Japan, and Korea) grouping, the figure for the share of intra-regional trade in total trade for 2006 was only 38.3 percent, only slightly above that recorded a decade earlier (37.6 percent) and substantially below the figure for NAFTA (44.3 percent).

As work by Prema-chandra Athukorala (see chapter 13 in this volume) has demonstrated, while dense production networks generated a substantial increase in trade in components within East Asia, the region remains heavily dependent on extra-regional markets for the sale of final goods. Substantially more than half of the output of finished goods goes to markets outside the region. Moreover, the intra-regional trade intensity in East Asia (the ratio of intra-regional trade share to the share of world trade with the region) declined substantially in the quarter of a century after 1980 (Asian Development Bank 2011: Figure 2.3, p. 31).

Not only is there little support from the conventionally cited data for the argument that the rush to PTAs resulted from an increase in interdependence in the region, but such an interpretation is inconsistent with the initial choice of partners for PTAs.

A substantial share of the initial agreements was negotiated not with other countries in the region but with distant markets: Korea's first PTA was with Chile; Japan's second FTA was with Mexico; and Taiwan's initial PTAs (because China was then objecting to other countries negotiating with Taipei) were confined to the small Central American countries that recognized it as a sovereign entity. The choice of extra-regional partners could be consistent with arguments that the rush to regionalism was driven by concerns about managing interdependence (given the importance of extra-regional markets): however, many of the countries chosen for negotiations in the first generation of agreements were relatively minor trading partners. At the same time, countries that provided more important markets were shunned. If the logic of the "increasing costs of interdependence" argument applied, then Japan and Korea should have been seeking PTAs with China (where there were genuine concerns on issues such as respect for intellectual property rights) rather than with Chile or Singapore.

The choice of extra-regional partners also undermined arguments that the emergence of economic regionalism in Asia was "one of the most significant outcomes of the [Asian financial] crisis" (Kawai 2007: 10), that in the words of Kawai and Wignaraja (2010: 2) the "crisis made it clear that East Asia needed to address common challenges in the areas of trade and investment in order to sustain growth and stability." If Asian governments were indeed prompted to strengthen their cooperation with their neighbors by their dismay at extra-regional responses to their plight during the crises of 1997-1998 (see Krueger, chapter 20 in this volume), this concern was not reflected in their initial decision-making on which countries with which they would negotiate PTAs.

Finally, the content of the agreements provided little support for another popular argument (for instance, Kawai and Wignaraja (2010: 2)): that the rush to PTAs reflected governments' frustration with the slow rate of progress in the Doha Round of WTO negotiations. Such logic would have been persuasive if governments had committed themselves in the new PTAs to measures that went substantially beyond those to which they had signed up during the Uruguay Round. But this was seldom the case. Although the content of the agreements differed substantially, dependent on the parties involved (with agreements involving China, India, or ASEAN typically the least comprehensive and with the fewest legally binding commitments) (Dent 2006, Ravenhill 2008), few were WTO Plus in their content. The agreements between China and ASEAN, and India and ASEAN, for instance, contained no legally enforceable agreements that went beyond the current mandate of the WTO (World Trade Organization 2011: Appendix Table D.1 p. 157). Japan's first PTA, with Singapore, was similarly lacking in ambition: it contained only 3 legally enforceable provisions beyond the WTO's current mandate (World Trade Organization 2011: Appendix Table D.1 p. 157).

In short, although an intuitively plausible argument could be made that increasing levels of interdependence in East Asia, created by the deepening of regional production networks, would generate a new interest in PTAs among governments in the region, the actual experience provided little support for such expectations. The data offered in support of the argument that intra-regional trade had intensified at the expense of that with countries outside the region was unpersuasive; the agreements were often signed with relatively insignificant extra-regional partners. Moreover, authors failed to make a convincing case for a crucial component of the argument: they did not provide evidence that business was experiencing difficulties in managing regional supply chains under existing trade arrangements. That few of the agreements committed governments substantially beyond their obligations under the WTO indicated that they had little to do with supply chain management. The shallowness of the agreements had implications both for their impact on their parties and on non-members alike, a topic taken up later in this chapter.

### 12.1.2 The Political Economy Literature

The conventional understanding of the political economy of trade policymaking rests on the assumption that governments are utility-maximizing rational actors whose main preoccupation is with prolonging their stay in power. Policy outcomes will reflect the balance of pro-liberalization and protectionist forces to which rulers must respond. The great advantage of PTAs from the perspective of governments is that they are able to take advantage of the lax disciplines of the WTO on PTAs to exclude sensitive domestic sectors from agreements. Liberalization through PTAs therefore poses less of a political problem for governments than that undertaken multilaterally under the auspices of the WTO, where it is more likely that an economy-wide settlement will occur (Grossman and Helpman 1995).

The expectation in the literature on trade policymaking is that the trend toward tariff reduction—whether unilaterally or through negotiations at the regional or global levels—will strengthen domestic political economy forces that favor free trade while weakening anti-liberalization forces. A virtuous circle ensues from what Baldwin (2006) has termed a "juggernaut" effect. On the other hand, two other bodies of theoretical literature suggest reasons why protectionist forces may remain resilient. Collective action theories emphasize that it is easier to mobilize interests when the losses from a particular policy are concentrated—and difficult to counteract them when the gains from the policy are spread across a larger number of actors (Olson 1965). And prospect theory suggests that individuals are more likely to take risks when they perceive that action is required to avoid their suffering losses, and are more risk averse when action is being taken to generate gains (for an application to Japanese foreign economic policymaking see Katada and Solis (2010)).

A substantial literature also points out the importance of political institutions in trade policymaking. Some electoral systems—those with large constituencies and a "first past the post" electoral system—are associated with a greater incidence of protective barriers (Mansfield and Busch 1995). Electoral systems that lead to disproportionate representation of rural interests strengthen protectionist forces when the domestic agricultural sector is non-competitive internationally. In East Asia, rural over-representation has been problematic for trade policymaking in Korea and especially in Japan (Mulgan 2000, Mulgan 2002).

It is not just the electoral system that matters in translating the political preferences of domestic constituencies into policy—it is also the institutions of trade policymaking. Where these are fragmented and not subject to decisive central leadership, a single ministry (often captured by its "constituents") can wield disproportionate influence and act as an effective veto player. Despite efforts by the Koizumi administration to centralize trade policymaking in the office of Prime Minister, this remains an accurate characterization of the situation in Japan (Mulgan 2008). The consequence has been that Tokyo systematically favored countries with small agricultural exporting sectors in its choice of PTA partners. It has been unable to conclude PTA negotiations with major agricultural exporting countries such as Australia; meanwhile, ongoing agricultural protectionism prevented Japan from negotiating comprehensive PTAs with even minor agricultural exporters (Manger 2005).

Protectionist interests remain entrenched across the region: agreements that have the potential to bring larger welfare gains than those of the first generation of PTAs remain stalled because governments are unable to impose the associated adjustment costs on powerful domestic constituencies.

The discussion above has emphasized the domestic constraints on governments' freedom of action in trade policymaking. Political scientists, not just those writing in a neo-Marxian tradition, have long recognized that business enjoys a privileged position in policymaking because of its "structural" power (Lindblom 1977). Discerning the influence of business on policymaking is difficult in Asia's political systems—even in the region's democracies, policymaking is more opaque than that in the West. As Manger (2009: p. 21) notes, in contrast to the United States, "lobbying in Japan leaves no visible paper trail." Nonetheless, it is evident that business leaders can often pick up the phone and give voice to their policy preferences not just to senior administrators but to political leaders themselves.

On the other hand, a substantial literature on East Asia has asserted that the state has been both a relatively autonomous actor and the lead player in formulating economic policies—whether of a "developmental" type as in Northeast Asia (Johnson 1982, Deyo 1987, Amsden 1989, Wade 1990, Woo-Cumings 1999) or those that facilitate rent-seeking patrimonialism as in many Southeast Asian countries (Mackie 1988, MacIntyre 1991). The relative autonomy of the state is often facilitated either by the characteristics of the domestic business community and/or by the strategic context in which the state is situated. In Singapore, government-linked corporations dominate the local economy, providing an opportunity, Lee (2006) notes, for the state to impose its trade policy priorities with little domestic resistance. In Taiwan, Hsueh (2006: 170) asserts, a different logic of state action applies: because of the relative political weakness of sectoral interests and the government's preoccupation with the Cross-Straits relationship, "the Taiwanese government's trade policy is often made in response not to domestic economic interests, but rather to the international political economic environment of threat under which Taiwan is forced to operate" (see also Dent (2005)).

The relationship between the state and the private sector in many East Asian countries shaped the state-led process in decision-making on the selection of partners and timing and sequencing of the first generation of the region's PTAs. In Thailand, where the administration of former Prime Minister Thaksin Shinawatra embarked on an active policy of simultaneously negotiating multiple PTAs with partners as diverse as Croatia and Peru, Nagai (2003: 279) states bluntly that "the private sector does not play an important role in forming FTA policy." Pongsudhiriak (2010) suggests that civil society groups were more important in trade policymaking in Thailand than were business groups because their opposition to the Thaksin government's approach eventually served to cast doubt on its legitimacy. In Indonesia, Chandra and Hanim (2010) similarly find that business had little influence in trade policymaking. Even in Japan, the initial impetus for the signature of PTA was largely government-driven rather than the reflection of business lobbying, an attempt to (i) stimulate East Asian cooperation in the wake of the 1997/98 Asian financial crisis, and (ii) ensure Japan's centrality within the emerging regional architecture (Munakata 2006).

To gain a full understanding of the first generation of PTAs involving East Asian countries, we have to bring political considerations into the analysis.

### 12.1.3 Bringing Politics Back in

Missing from most of the literature on the new PTAs involving countries from the Pacific Rim is any discussion of the political/strategic context in which they were negotiated and of the impact of political considerations in government decision-making. While it would be naïve to suggest that economic factors played no role in states' move to preferential trade, it would be equally naïve to deny that trade agreements often serve multiple purposes, and that diplomatic/strategic considerations as well as domestic political factors enter into governments' calculations regarding the partners with which they choose to negotiate and/or the timing and sequencing of negotiations.

Political considerations can range from a cynical desire to have an "announceable" to enhance or secure a visit from another political leader—to exploit what Bhagwati (2008) terms the "CNN effect"—to the use of trade agreements to reinforce security relationships.[3] The idea that patterns of trade follow and reinforce alliance relationships is central to realist understandings of international relations, one that historically has found support in trade data (Gowa and Mansfield 1993, Mansfield and Bronson 1997)—although not a relationship that has been evident since the reintegration of China into the global economy (Ravenhill 2009). Security considerations have figured prominently in the US choice of partners to whom it has offered a PTA—and in the refusal to negotiate with countries whose foreign policies have irritated Washington (Higgott 2004, Kelton 2008, Aggarwal and Ahnid 2011). Australia, for instance, was offered talks on a PTA by the Bush Administration in recognition of the Howard government's support for US policies in the Middle East: in contrast, Washington repeatedly refused to negotiate with New Zealand because of its stance on visits by nuclear-powered and nuclear-armed warships and because of its criticism of US policies in the "war on terror."

For smaller countries, on the other hand, the negotiation of trade agreements with key strategic partners is often seen as a means of "anchoring" them in the region—one aim frequently stated by representatives of the Singapore government in explaining the island state's early activism in negotiating agreements with its major strategic partners. In Korea, Sohn and Koo (2011) suggest that the Rho Moo-hyun government's surprise decision to seek a PTA with the United States, and its willingness to make domestically unpopular concessions in the negotiations, represented an attempt to "re-securitize" bilateral economic relations. In contrast, Korea's PTA with the EU had very little to do with the country's security although it did serve domestic political purposes in tapping into nationalist sentiments about Korea's growing international status (Kelly 2012). Another dimension of security has also been important in shaping the PTA policies of Northeast Asian countries: a longstanding concern with "comprehensive security," manifested in particular in a desire to diversify reliable sources of supply for critical raw materials (for further discussion see Wilson (2012), and Jiang (2010) on China, and Aurelia George Mulgan (2011) on Japan).

Political considerations can enter calculations on the choice of partners in other ways. The rivalry between China and Japan for regional leadership has been reflected in their efforts to outdo one another in the number of agreements signed with other countries in the region (Mochizuki 2009). The offer by Chinese Premier Zhu Rongji of a free trade agreement to ASEAN leaders at the 2000 ASEAN-China summit took the proposed ASEAN partners and other countries in the region by surprise, and can itself be seen as a political as well as economic response to ASEAN fears that China's imminent entry into the WTO would cause problems for their economies. The proposal not only had the political advantage of reassuring ASEAN countries but also placed China's Northeast Asian rivals on the back foot: it was more difficult for them to offer a similar agreement because of domestic protectionist pressures (Ravenhill and Jiang 2009). Elsewhere, the Malaysian government decided to approach Pakistan for a PTA because it wanted to negotiate an "Islamic" trade agreement—even though its domestic business community preferred to give priority to an agreement with India, a more significant economic partner.

Once a trend toward the negotiation of PTAs developed, governments found themselves under pressure to follow suit—they feared a negative reaction from domestic constituencies if they appeared to be missing out on a new dimension of regional diplomacy—hence, for example, Taiwan's determination to pursue agreements with countries that consumed a trifling share of its exports. But it was not only diplomatic outcasts that were worried: Choi and Lee (2005: 15) note, for instance, that the Korean government expressed increasing alarm in the early years of the new millennium at being isolated as the only WTO member besides Mongolia that had not entered into a PTA. With the economy in disarray in the immediate post-financial crisis period, Korea had experienced difficulties in finding potential partners willing to negotiate with it (Park and Koo 2007). Governments also may find it difficult to resist invitations to negotiate from other countries for fear of causing offense: with the rush to PTAs, governments frequently found themselves under pressure to sign on to negotiations with relatively minor partners (or with partners in whose capacity or commitment to implement effective arrangements they had little confidence). In combination, these two factors generated a "political domino effect" (Ravenhill 2010): once momentum away from the region's traditional adherence to liberalization on a non-discriminatory basis was established, other countries rushed to join suit.

The argument here is not that economic factors played no role in the rush to regionalism on the Western Pacific Rim. Once a decision to negotiate was made, economic interests often reinforced the desire to reach an agreement (although sometimes the opposition of domestic protectionist interests complicated diplomatic initiatives). Some PTAs undoubtedly also had unintended consequences—positive spinoffs—in the economic sphere. In the first generation of PTAs involving Western Pacific Rim countries, however, political factors were often dominant considerations in the choice of partners and the timing/sequencing of negotiations.

A number of consequences follow from the prominent role of political motivations in the policymaking that drove the first generation of Asia-Pacific PTAs, and the often relatively small role that business interests played in the choice of PTA partners and the crafting of the content of the agreements. Agreements were:

- frequently concluded with relatively minor trading partners from outside the Western Pacific Rim: consequently, they covered a relatively small proportion of total trade, especially for the larger economies (the figure for Japan was only slightly over a quarter, for China slightly over a third—(Solis 2011: Table 2));
- were often shallow in their coverage, confined primarily to border barriers, and therefore rarely "WTO-Plus" in their content;
- included substantial carve-outs for sensitive import-competing domestic sectors;
- seldom included legally binding provisions or formal dispute settlement mechanisms: many of the PTAs were consistent with the longstanding East Asian preference for "soft law" arrangements (Kahler 2000)

Tariffs were already low across the region, and, as noted above, other government arrangements such as the creation of export processing zones further facilitated the free movement of components across national boundaries. The WTO calculates that 80 percent of the total value of Japan's imports in 2008 was subject to a zero MFN tariff rate; only 6 percent of imports benefited from preferential tariffs; 5.3 percent of total imports enjoyed a preferential margin of less than 5 percent. For Malaysia, the figures were similar: 78 percent of all imports entered the country at zero MFN rates; only 4.5 percent of imports benefited from a preferential tariff. Even for the traditionally relatively highly protected Chinese economy, close to half of all imports entered at zero MFN duties; only 5.8 percent of imports enjoyed a preferential tariff, the majority of these goods had margins of less than 5 percent (World Trade Organization 2011: Appendix Table 9 p. 224).

Products that attracted relatively high levels of tariffs because of their political sensitivity were typically excluded from the agreements.

The consequence was that business made relatively little use of the agreements. Even where the agreements created a preferential margin, the costs of completing the documentation required to demonstrate compliance with rules of origin were perceived to outweigh any benefits. All the evidence available to date suggests that not only is the utilization of PTA preferences in Asia low relative to that in other parts of the world but that it is very low in absolute terms (Baldwin 2006: 1491).

Consider the Asian PTA that has been in place for the longest period of time, the ASEAN Free Trade Agreement. In 2007, the share of exports from Malaysia to its ASEAN partners that took advantage of the preferences created by the ASEAN Free Trade Agreement was 19.1 percent. For the Philippines, a study of customs documentation suggested that in 2005 only 14 percent of exports to other ASEAN countries took advantage of AFTA preferences (Avila and Manzano 2007: 109). Anas (2007: 91) estimates that less than 4 percent of Indonesia's exports to other ASEAN economies makes use of AFTA's provisions; for Vietnam, the figure was under 8 percent (Van 2007). A study of the customs documentation by the Foreign Trade Department of the Ministry of Commerce in Laos indicates that only 0.1 percent of that country's trade with other ASEAN economies, by far the major trading partners of Laos, make use of AFTA preferences (Phetmany and Rio 2007: 105). Cambodia issued only 23 certificates of origin for AFTA in 2005, for trade with a total value of under one half of a million dollars (Kakada and Hach 2007: 70). Only Thailand, primarily because of its position as a regional hub for the (traditionally heavily protected) automobile industry, made more substantial use of AFTA preferences—but in 2007 this still amounted to only 30 percent of the country's exports to its ASEAN partners (Hiratsuka, et al. 2008: 415), a utilization rate far lower than that for agreements in Europe and the Americas.

Similarly low utilization rates have been reported for other preferential arrangements involving Asian countries. Thai customs data indicate that only 11 percent of Thai exports took advantage of the China–ASEAN FTA (CAFTA) in 2007 (Hiratsuka, et al. 2008: 415). Case studies based on the issue of the appropriate rules of origin documentation suggest even lower rates of utilization in other countries. Anas (2007: 91) estimated that only 2 percent of Indonesian exports were using the preferential provisions of this agreement. For Cambodia, only six certificates of origin were issued in 2005 for exports to China, for a total value of under $100,000 (Kakada and Hach 2007: 70). Chinese exporters similarly failed to make use of the agreement: in 2005, the value of trade covered by Form E, required for certification of rules of origin compliance under CAFTA, amounted to less than one third of one per cent of China's exports to ASEAN (Zeui 2007: 81).

Three caveats should be considered here. The first is to note that few countries in the region regularly publish customs information that enable a comprehensive examination of the use of trade preferences over time. Consequently, analysts frequently fall back on surveys of firms and their reported use of preferential arrangements—with all of the attendant problems of survey reliability (for one cross-regional analysis using firm surveys see Kawai and Wignaraja (2011): the data reported in the paragraphs above, however, are from customs documentation not surveys of firms). A second caveat can be quickly dismissed: the argument that the agreements have been in force for so brief a period that lack of familiarity has prevented business from taking full advantage of them. If it had been the case that business really had driven these agreements, then one would surely have seen greater uptake of them as soon as they were implemented—especially by larger firms whose export volumes would make an impression in trade data. A more substantial caveat is that, given the relatively small percentage of trade that benefits from preferential tariffs, a more relevant approach in estimating the use that business makes of the agreements would be to focus solely on imports that enjoyed a preferential margin—as seen in the utilization of ASEAN preferences by car exports from Thailand. Little evidence of this type is available for the Western Pacific Rim: one exception is a study of Australian PTAs by Pomfret, Kaufman, and Findlay (2010), who find that a very high percentage of imports took advantage of preferential margins when these were available The authors note, however, that the number of tariff lines benefiting from preferential margins was rapidly eroded over time. The strongest argument that can be made for the tariff preferences created by the PTAs, therefore, is that even in the relatively small number of cases where they are being used, they are becoming of less significance.

The converse of the PTAs conferring few benefits was that they created in aggregate few disadvantages for firms in countries that were not parties to an agreement. Again, care has to be taken in making such generalizations: specific companies and/or sectors were placed at a disadvantage by some agreements (for instance, New Zealand exporters of kiwi fruit suffered in the Korean market because of the tariff advantages their Chilean competitors enjoyed by virtue of the implementation of the Korea-Chile PTA). Overall, however, the first generation of PTAs on the Western Pacific Rim had a marginal impact on the operations of business. The consequence was that there was little enthusiasm for the agreements in the domestic business community. And the similarly minor disadvantages that the agreements created for non-beneficiaries in other countries were insufficient to generate a significant push from their business communities for equivalent arrangements to be negotiated. Little evidence existed of a business-driven "domino" effect that Richard Baldwin (1993) saw as an important factor in the proliferation of preferential agreements in Europe. In the absence of this dynamic, and in a context where agreements were often one reflection of geo-political rivalry, no foundations were laid for a consolidation/multilateralization of the increasingly complex "noodle bowl" of preferential arrangements.

## 12.2 A New Generation of Agreements?

Analysts are increasingly questioning whether the traditional analysis of PTAs, which focuses on their lowering or removal of border barriers, provides an adequate understanding of the effects of contemporary agreements and of actors' motivations in entering into them. Richard Baldwin (2011) has presented the most comprehensive case that "21st Century" trade agreements are a response to the internationalization of production networks and therefore about "disciplines that underpin the trade-investment-service nexus." Whereas twentieth-century regionalism was primarily about preferential market access, the new generation of agreements involves a bargain of "foreign factories for domestic reforms," that is, they are primarily about foreign direct investment and the management of supply chains. In a similar vein, Mark Manger (2009) argues that Japan's recent PTAs have been driven by concerns about enhancing or defending the interests of its transnational corporations' foreign investments rather than about securing market access.

To what extent are we seeing a new generation of PTAs involving Western Pacific Rim economies that differ substantially from the first generation? And, if so, what are the political economy forces driving them? An initial point would be to emphasize the capacity of economic actors to learn. In Malaysia, for instance, business groups, which had scarcely mobilized in response to the government's initial foray into PTAs, became much better informed about how PTAs might affect their interests and much more active in subsequent negotiations (Postigo-Angon 2011). The government heeded business concerns in adding a PTA with India to its earlier "Islamic PTA" with Pakistan. Governments similarly learned not just from their own experiences in negotiating PTAs but also from that of other countries: agreements typically became more comprehensive and detailed as the first decade of the twenty-first century progressed. In some instances (most notably Korea—whereas efforts in Japan were far less successful), the institutions for making trade policy were reorganized in an effort to circumvent entrenched protectionist interests in some ministries (Choi and Oh 2011)—although this reform was reversed by the President Park Geun-hye administration in 2013.

Arguably the most important development in the second half of the first decade of the new century was the signature of agreements with major trading partners for the first time (the superficial agreements that ASEAN countries individually and collectively had previously negotiated with China notwithstanding). Of particular importance in this context were the agreements that Korea negotiated first with the United States and then with the EU. These economies are respectively Korea's third and second largest export markets. Moreover, the agreements, following the templates that the larger partners had developed in other negotiations, were particularly comprehensive, containing a large number of legally enforceable provisions on issues not currently covered by WTO texts. Korea's (largely unexpected) success in these negotiations generated considerable concern among governments and business communities alike in other countries in Northeast and Southeast Asia. This alarm was particularly felt in Tokyo, where, as noted above, inability to overcome protectionist pressures from the agricultural lobby had limited the country's participation in PTAs—prompting the Japanese government not only to seek its own agreement with the EU but also to join the US-led Trans Pacific Partnership (TPP) negotiations.

US aspirations for the TPP are to create an agreement that is very much of the "21st Century" variety—one that goes beyond current WTO rules to establish new rules on investment, extension of intellectual property rights, etc. It also serves strategic purposes: as Ennis (2011) suggests, it represents an attempt by the United States to define "the terms of engagement to which China has to respond." The participants in the TPP negotiations in the middle of 2013, however, differed considerably in their negotiating priorities, and the US template could prove to be a significant obstacle to reaching an agreement. The proposed "deeper integration" provisions impose heavy demands on the TPP developing country participants that do not already have PTAs with the United States (Brunei, Malaysia, Vietnam), and may yet prove too difficult for them to digest even if they are granted longer time frames for implementation. Even those countries that have existing bilateral PTAs with the United States (Australia, Chile, Peru, and Singapore) have resisted US demands for change in their regulatory regimes; it is highly unlikely that governments will risk aggravating their domestic political constituencies especially when they will not receive much in return by way of improved access for their goods to the US market. Ironically, this proposed 21st Century agreement may founder largely because of "20th Century" protectionist forces in the United States that are resisting further liberalization of access to the US market for its TPP partners.

Ongoing US protectionism will affect the TPP in another manner. Whereas the original intention was that the TPP would be a single agreement (and thus contribute toward the multilateralization of existing agreements), once negotiations began, Washington indicated that it wanted to retain the market access arrangements in its existing bilateral PTAS with Australia, Chile, Peru, and Singapore, and to negotiate new market access arrangements with the other five countries. The resulting network of bilateral agreements would, as far as the United States was concerned, constitute the TPP. The United States adopted this approach largely for defensive reasons: US bilateral arrangements have a range of protectionist measures including carve-outs, long implementation periods, snap-back provisions, and product-specific rules of origin that are customized to protect domestic producers (Capling and Ravenhill 2012).

As Baldwin (2011: 16) notes, only technology-rich countries have the leverage to demand the substantial domestic reforms in their partners that are central to 21st Century regionalism. The approach inevitably is divisive—and in East Asia will pit the more advanced economies of the region against those, such as China, that are unwilling to subscribe to rules of the game that the more developed are attempting to dictate. Although the less-developed economies will indeed have an interest in continuing to attract foreign direct investment, their concern in PTAs is also with "20th Century" market access issues. Japan's experience in negotiating PTAs with Thailand and Mexico (Manger 2009) illustrates how its unwillingness to make concessions on domestic market access can frustrate efforts to negotiate agreements with "21st Century" content.

In short, it is too early to judge whether a push for "21st Century" PTAs will have a significant impact on economic cooperation among Western Pacific Rim countries. Rather than leading to a multilateralization of the noodle bowl, it may undermine the consolidation and deepening of cooperation within the region. Japan's decision to enter the TPP threatens to undercut the nascent steps toward deeper regional cooperation among the Northeast Asian "Big Three" (China, Japan, and Korea) seen in the institutionalization of the Trilateral Summit. Japanese Prime Minister Noda's enthusiasm for an Asia-Pacific approach to economic cooperation stood in direct contrast to that of his predecessor, Yukio Hatoyama, whose proposal for an East Asian Community envisaged deeper regional economic cooperation at a time when the global financial crisis had reinforced doubts about the continuing economic predominance of the United States (Emmers and Ravenhill 2011).

It remains unclear how many obstacles remain to the efficient management of supply chains across the region that a new generation of trade agreements might plausibly remove—and whether, in any event, PTAs would be the most effective means of addressing some of these issues. From a political economy perspective, a more efficient approach may be through bilateral investment treaties (BITs) (of which substantially more are in force than PTAs—in 2011, over 400 involving East Asian countries (United Nations Conference on Trade and Development 2011)). The logic here is that BITs are often easier to negotiate: the principal "negatives" of these agreements fall on governments in that they impose constraints on their actions rather than, as is the case with PTAs, adversely affecting private domestic actors (in import-competing sectors).

## 12.3 Conclusion

The paradox of the rush to preferential trade agreements on the Western Pacific Rim is that they have had minimal effect on aggregate welfare or even on patterns of trade. One reason could be that the proliferation of agreements has offset one another: any advantage for a privileged party is quickly offset when its rivals sign agreements with equivalent content. More plausible, however, is the probability that the effects of the agreements have simply been swamped by other factors that have influenced international trade, by the low-tariff context in which the agreements were implemented, by the content of the agreements themselves, and/or by the extent to which they have been utilized.

One of the most important confounding factors was the floating exchange rate environment, which could lead to any benefits from a PTA being offset or completely swamped by an appreciation of the domestic currency. This was the case, for instance, with the Australia-United States agreement: whereas the average benefit that Australian manufacturers received from the agreement was removal of US MFN tariffs that were less than 4 percent, Australian exporters were disadvantaged by the Australian dollar appreciating by more than 40 percent against the US currency in the first four years in which the agreement was in force. In a similar vein, trade with preferential partners (and its comparison with trade with non-beneficiaries of PTAs) can be swamped by changes in prices of key imports—particularly in the case of the large Northeast economies by fluctuations in the prices of natural resource imports. Other developments may have significant consequences on bilateral trade for reasons that have little or nothing to do with a preferential trade agreement. For instance, the substantial increase in Mexican exports of beef to Japan after the implementation of the Japan–Mexico agreement (the Mexican export that experienced the largest increase after the implementation of the PTA) was caused not by the preferences created by the agreement (which allowed for a duty-free quota of only 10 metric tons for the first two years) but by the BSE outbreak in the United States, which led to Japan's banning imports from this source (Ando 2007: 9).

Even with the assumption of a comprehensive liberalization of trade between parties, CGE models predict very low aggregate welfare gains from PTAs—typically less than 0.1 percent of GDP for an industrialized economy with low tariffs (Kimura 2006: 65). But the first generation of PTAs was seldom comprehensive in coverage, and their effects further limited by restrictive rules of origin. Moreover, the impact of the agreements was also constrained by the very low overall utilization rates discussed above.

An explanation of the paradox of why the region has enthusiastically embraced a proliferation of trade agreements that are often inconsequential requires an understanding of the politics of PTA negotiations, which have been driven as often by diplomatic/security considerations as by economic motivations. It is possible that a new generation of agreements, signed between countries that are important trading partners, will see a deeper integration that has a greater impact on welfare and on trade patterns. But for this development to materialize, the still substantial protectionist forces that continue to shape PTAs within the region will have to be overcome.

## Notes

1. This chapter mirrors the Handbook in that its principal focus is on the economies of the Western Pacific Rim, particularly those of East Asia (defined as the ten ASEAN countries, China, Japan, Korea and Taiwan). I follow the WTO in regarding all non-universal trade agreements as "regional" even though they may involve only two parties that are not necessarily geographically proximate.
2. Trade with Taiwan is also included in this figure.
3. Another political motivation observed in developing economies elsewhere is the use of PTAs to facilitate or lock in domestic economic liberalization (as is frequently asserted as a motivation for Mexico's enthusiasm for NAFTA)—but this has rarely applied in Western Pacific Rim countries, where protectionist forces have typically been able to shape agreements to safeguard their interests.

## References

Aggarwal, Vinod K., and Anders Ahnid. "Comparing EU and US Linkage Strategies in FTAs." Unpublished paper presented to *ANU MacArthur Foundation Asia Security Initiative Final Conference*. Beijing, Peking University 2011.

Amsden, Alice H. *Asia's Next Giant: South Korea and Late Industrialization*. New York: Oxford University Press, 1989.

Anas, Titik. "Indonesia." In *Preferential Rules of Origin: Policy Research Report*, edited by World Bank. Washington, D.C.: World Bank, 2007: 85–93.

Ando, Mitsuyo. "Impacts of Japanese FTAs/EPAs: Post Evaluation from the Initial Data." Tokyo: Research Institute of Economy, Trade and Industry, RIETI Discussion Paper Series 07-E-041, June 2007, http://www.rieti.go.jp/jp/publications/dp/07e041.pdf

Asian Development Bank. *Institutions for Regional Integration: Toward an Asian Economic Community*. Manaluyong City, Philippines: Asian Development Bank, 2011.

Avila, John Lawrence, and George Manzano. "Philippines." In *Preferential Rules of Origin: Policy Research Report*, edited by World Bank. Washington, D.C.: World Bank, 2007: 107–119.

Baldwin, Richard. "21st Century Regionalism: Filling the Gap between 21st Century Trade and 20th Century Trade Rules." No. 56. London: Centre for Economic Policy Research, May 2011.

——. "A Domino Theory of Regionalism." Working Paper No. 4465. Cambridge, Ma.: National Bureau of Economic Research, September 1993.

Baldwin, Richard E. "Managing the Noodle Bowl: The Fragility of East Asian Regionalism." Working Paper Series on Regional Economic Integration No. 7. Manila: Asian Development Bank, February 2007.

——. "Multilateralising Regionalism: Spaghetti Bowls as Building Blocs on the Path to Global Free Trade." *World Economy* 29, no. 11 (2006): 1451–1518.

Bhagwati, Jagdish N. *Termites in the Trading System: How Preferential Agreements Undermine Free Trade*. Oxford: Oxford University Press, 2008.

Capling, Ann, and John Ravenhill. "The TPP: Multilateralizing Regionalism or the Securitization of Trade Policy?" In *The Trans-Pacific Partnership: A Quest for a Twenty-First Century Trade Agreement*, edited by C.L. Lim, Deborah K. Elms, and Patrick Low. Cambridge: Cambridge University Press, 2012: 279–298.

Chandra, A.C., and L. Hanim. "Indonesia." In *Governments, Non-State Actors and Trade Policy-Making: Negotiating Preferentially or Multilaterally?*, edited by Ann Capling and Patrick Low. Cambridge: Cambridge University Press, 2010: 125–160.

Choi, Byung-il, and Kong-Jin Lee. "A Long and Winding Road: Ratification of Korea's First FTA." In *Korea and International Conflicts: Case Studies—Volume 1*, edited by Byung-il Choi. Seoul: Institute for International Trade and Cooperation, Ewha Womans University, 2005: 11–47.

Choi, Byung-il, and Jennifer Sejin Oh. "Asymmetry in Japan and Korea's Agricultural Liberalization in FTA: Domestic Trade Governance Perspective." *The Pacific Review* 24, no. 5 (December 2011): 505–527.

Dent, Christopher M. *New Free Trade Agreements in the Asia-Pacific*. Basingstoke: Palgrave Macmillan, 2006.

——. "Taiwan and the New Regional Political Economy of East Asia." *The China Quarterly* 182 (2005): 385–406.

Deyo, Frederic C., ed. *The Political Economy of the New Asian Industrialism*, Cornell Studies in Political Economy. Ithaca, NY: Cornell University Press, 1987.

Emmers, Ralf, and John Ravenhill. "The Asian and Global Financial Crises: Consequences for East Asian Regionalism." *Contemporary Politics* 17, no. 2 (2011): 133–149.

Ennis, Peter. "White House to Tap Obama Friend as Pentagon's Asia Chief." Dispatch Japan, http://www.dispatchjapan.com/blog/2011/03/white-house-to-tap-obama-friend-as-pentagons-asia-chief.html.

Gowa, Joanne, and Edward D. Mansfield. "Power Politics and International Trade." *American Political Science Review* 87, no. 2 (June 1993): 408–420.

Grossman, Gene M., and Elhanan Helpman. "The Politics of Free Trade Agreements." *American Economic Review* 85, no. 4 (September 1995): 667–690.

Higgott, Richard. "US Foreign Policy and the 'Securitization' of Economic Globalization." *International Politics* 41, no. 2 (2004): 147–175.

Hiratsuka, Daisuke, Kazunobu Hayakawa, Kohai Shiino, and Seiya Sukegawa. "Maximizing Benefits from FTAs in ASEAN." Chap. 11 In *Deepening East Asian Economic Integration*, edited by Jenny Corbett and So Umezaki. Eria Research Project Report 2008 No. 1. Jakarta: Economic Research Institute for ASEAN and East Asia, 2008.

Hsueh, Roselyn Y. "Who Rules the International Economy? Taiwan's Daunting Attempts at Bilateralism." In *Bilateral Trade Agreements in the Asia-Pacific: Origins, Evolution, and Implications*, edited by Vinod K. Aggarwal and Shujiro Urata. London: Routledge, 2006: 160–183.

Jiang, Yang. "China's Pursuit of Free Trade Agreements: Is China Exceptional?." *Review of International Political Economy* 17, no. 2 (2010): 238–261.

Johnson, Chalmers. *MITI and the Japanese Miracle*. Stanford, Ca.: Stanford University Press, 1982.

Kahler, Miles. "Legalization as Strategy: The Asia-Pacific Case." *International Organization* 54, no. 3 (Summer 2000): 549–571.

Kakada, Dourng, and Sok Hach. "Cambodia." In *Preferential Rules of Origin: Policy Research Report*, edited by World Bank. Washington, D.C.: World Bank, 2007: 65–73.

Katada, Saori N., and Mireya Solis. "Domestic Sources of Japanese Foreign Policy Activism: Loss Avoidance and Demand Coherence." *International Relations of Asia and the Pacific* 10, no. 1 (January 2010): 129–157.

Kawai, Masahiro. "Evolving Economic Architecture in East Asia." *The Kyoto Economic Review* 76, no. 1 (June 2007): 9–52.

Kawai, Masahiro, and Ganeshan Wignaraja, eds. *Asia's Free Trade Agreements: How Is Business Responding?* Cheltenham: Edward Elgar, 2011.

——. "Free Trade Agreements in East Asia: A Way toward Trade Liberalization?" ADB Briefs No. 1. Mandaluyong City, Philippines: Asian Development Bank, June 2010.

Kelly, Robert E. "Korea–European Union Relations: Beyond the FTA?." *International Relations of Asia and the Pacific* 12, no. 1 (January 2012): 101–132.

Kelton, Maryanne. "US Economic Statecraft in East Asia." *International Relations of Asia and the Pacific* 8, no. 2 (May 2008): 149–174.

Kimura, Fukunari. "Bilateralism in the Asia-Pacific: An Economic Overview." In *Bilateral Trade Agreements in the Asia-Pacific: Origins, Evolution, and Implications*, edited by Vinod K. Aggarwal and Shujiro Urata. London: Routledge, 2006: 50–71.

Lee, Seungjoo. "Singapore Trade Bilateralism: A Two Track Strategy." In *Bilateral Trade Agreements in the Asia-Pacific: Origins, Evolution, and Implications*, edited by Vinod K. Aggarwal and Shujiro Urata. London: Routledge, 2006: 184–205.

Lindblom, Charles Edward. *Politics and Markets: The World's Political Economic Systems*. New York: Basic Books, 1977.

MacIntyre, Andrew. *Business and Politics in Indonesia*. Sydney: Allen and Unwin, 1991.

Mackie, J.A.C. "Economic Growth in the ASEAN Region: The Political Underpinnings." In *Achieving Industrialization in East Asia*, edited by Helen Hughes. Cambridge: Cambridge University Press, 1988: 283–326.

Manger, Mark. "Competition and Bilateralism in Trade Policy: The Case of Japan's Free Trade Agreements." *Review of International Political Economy* 12, no. 5 (December 2005): 804–828.

Manger, Mark S. *Investing in Protection: The Politics of Preferential Trade Agreements between North and South*. Cambridge: Cambridge University Press, 2009.

Mansfield, Edward D., and Rachel Bronson. "Alliances, Preferential Trade Arrangements, and International Trade." *American Political Science Review* 91, no. 1 (March 1997): 94–107.

Mansfield, Edward D., and Marc L. Busch. "The Political Economy of Nontariff Barriers: A Cross-National Analysis." *International Organization* 49, no. 4 (Autumn 1995): 723–749.

Mochizuki, Mike M. "Political-Security Competition and the FTA Movement: Motivations and Consequences." In *Competitive Regionalism: FTA Diffusion in the Pacific Rim*, edited by Mireya Solís, Barbara Stallings, and Saori N. Katada. New York: Palgrave Macmillan, 2009: 54–73.

Mulgan, Aurelia George. *Japan's Failed Revolution: Koizumi and the Politics of Economic Reform*. Canberra: Asia Pacific Press, 2002.

——. "Japan's FTA Politics and the Problem of Agricultural Trade Liberalisation." *Australian Journal of International Affairs* 62, no. 2 (2008): 164–178.

——. "No Longer the 'Reactive State': Japan's New Trade Policy Activism." Asie. Visions No. 38. Paris: Institut français des relations internationals, May 2011.

——. *The Politics of Agriculture in Japan*. London: Routledge, 2000.

Munakata, Naoko. *Transforming East Asia: The Evolution of Regional Economic Integration*. Washington, D.C.: Brookings Institution Press, 2006.

Nagai, Fumio. "Thailand's FTA Policy: Continuity and Change between the Chuan and Thaksin Governments." In *Whither Free Trade Agreements? Proliferation, Evaluation and Multilateralization*, edited by Jiro Okamoto. Chiba, Japan: Institute of Developing Economies Japan External Trade Organization, 2003: 252–284.

Olson, Mancur. *The Logic of Collective Action*. Cambridge: Harvard University Press, 1965.

Park, Sung-Hoon, and Ming Gyo Koo. "Forming a Cross-Regional Partnership: The South Korea-Chile FTA and Its Implications." *Pacific Affairs* 80, no. 2 (2007): 259–278.

Phetmany, Thiphaphone, and Luz Julieta Rio. "Lao PDR." In *Preferential Rules of Origin: Policy Research Report*, edited by World Bank. Washington, D.C.: World Bank, 2007: 95–106.

Pomfret, Richard, Uwe Kaufmann, and Christopher Findlay. "Use of FTAs in Australia." Discussion Paper Series No. 10-E-042. Tokyo: Research Institute of Economy, Trade and Industry, August 2010.

Pongsudhiriak, T. "Thailand." In *Governments, Non-State Actors and Trade Policy-Making: Negotiating Preferentially or Multilaterally?*, edited by Ann Capling and Patrick Low. Cambridge: Cambridge University Press, 2010: 161–185.

Postigo-Angon, Antonio. "Policymaking of FTAs in Thailand and Malaysia." Unpublished manuscript, London School of Economics: January 2011.

Ravenhill, John. "Economic Cooperation in Southeast Asia: Changing Incentives." *Asian Survey* XXXV, no. 9 (September 1995): 850–866.

——. "The Economics-Security Nexus in the Asia-Pacific Region." In *Security Politics in the Asia-Pacific: A Regional-Global Nexus?*, edited by William Tow. Cambridge: Cambridge University Press, 2009: 188–208.

——. "The Move to Preferential Trade on the Western Pacific Rim: Some Initial Conclusions." *Australian Journal of International Affairs* 62, no. 2 (June 2008): 129–150.

——. "The 'New East Asian Regionalism': A Political Domino Effect." *Review of International Political Economy* 17, no. 2 (2010): 178–208.

Ravenhill, John, and Yang Jiang. "China's Move to Preferential Trading: A New Direction in China's Diplomacy." *Journal of Contemporary China* 18, no. 58 (2009): 27–46.

Sohn, Yul, and Min Gyo Koo. "Securitizing Trade: The Case of the Korea—US Free Trade Agreement." *International Relations of Asia and the Pacific* 11, no. 3 (September 2011): 433–460.

Solis, Mireya. "Global Economic Crisis: Boon or Bust for East Asian Trade Integration?." *The Pacific Review* 24, no. 3 (July 2011): 311–336.

United Nations Conference on Trade and Development. *World Investment Report 2011: Non-Equity Modes of International Production and Development*. New York and Geneva: United Nations, 2011.

Urata, Shujiro. "Exclusion Fears and Competitive Regionalism in East Asia." In *Competitive Regionalism: FTA Diffusion in the Pacific Rim*, edited by Mireya Solís, Barbara Stallings and Saori N. Katada. New York: Palgrave Macmillan, 2009: 27–53.

Van, Dang Nhu. "Vietnam." In *Preferential Rules of Origin: Policy Research Report*, edited by World Bank. Washington, D.C.: World Bank, 2007: 129–136.

Wade, Robert. *Governing the Market: Economic Theory and the Role of Government in East Asian Industrialization*. Princeton, N.J.: Princeton University Press, 1990.

Wilson, Jeffrey D. "Resource Security: A New Motivation for Free Trade Agreements in the Asia-Pacific." The Pacific Review 25, no. 4 (2012): 429–453.

Woo-Cumings, Meredith, ed. *The Developmental State*, Cornell Studies in Political Economy. Ithaca, N.Y.: Cornell University Press, 1999.

World Trade Organization. "World Trade Report 2011: Preferential Trade Agreements and the WTO: From Co-Existence to Coherence." Geneva: World Trade Organization 2011.

Zeui, Yang. "China." In *Preferential Rules of Origin: Policy Research Report*, edited by World Bank. Washington, D.C.: World Bank, 2007: 74–83.

CHAPTER 13

# GLOBAL PRODUCTION SHARING AND TRADE PATTERNS IN EAST ASIA

PREMA-CHANDRA ATHUKORALA

THE purpose of this chapter is to examine emerging trends and patterns of merchandise trade in East Asia with special emphasis on forces that mold world trade and the organization of production across national boundaries. A key theme running through the chapter is the implications of global production sharing[1]—that is, the breakup of the production processes into separated stages, with each country specializing in a particular stage of the production sequence—for rapid trade growth in these countries.

Over the past few decades global production sharing has opened up ever-increasing opportunities for countries to specialize in different slices (tasks) of the production process depending on their relative cost advantage and other relevant economic fundamentals. With rapid growth in cross-border dispersion of production, firms' decisions regarding how much to produce and for which target market are increasingly combined with decisions on where to produce and with what degree of intra-product specialization. While trade in parts and components and final assembly within production networks ("network trade") has generally grown faster than total world trade in manufacturing, the degree of dependence of East Asia on this new form of international specialization is proportionately larger than elsewhere in the world. Consequently, trade flow analysis based on data coming from a reporting system designed at a time when countries were trading predominantly only in final goods naturally distorted values of exports and imports and led to a falsification of the nature of emerging trade patterns in the region. The degree of falsification is likely to increase over time as more complex production networks are created with an ever-increasing number of participants.

The chapter begins with a discussion on the procedure followed in delineating network trade from data extracted from the United Nations (UN) trade data reporting system (Comtrade database). This is followed by an overview of East Asia's role in world trade. The next section examines the nature and extent of global production sharing and the role of East Asian countries within global production networks. This section also probes the implications of this new form of international exchange for intra-regional trade and for creating new supply-side complementariness among countries in the region, with emphasis on the emerging role of the PRC in regional production networks. The following two sections deal with two selected themes that are central to the contemporary policy debate on East Asia's rise in the global economy: challenges posed by global production sharing for the conventional changing comparative advantage ("flying geese") approach to the analysis of growth patterns in the region and the role of network trade in determining the impact of the global crisis on the export performance of East Asian economies. The final section summarizes the main findings and draws out some general inferences.

## 13.1 Data

Previous studies have used two alternative approaches to quantifying the magnitude and pattern of global production sharing.[2] The first approach relies on records kept by OECD countries (in particular the United States and the European Union [EU] in connection with special tariff provisions on overseas processing and the assembly of domestically produced components (outward processing trade [OPT] statistics) (Helleiner 1973; Sharpton 1975; USITC 1999; Gorg 2000). OPT records provide data on parts and components exported from source countries and assembled goods received in turn. However, the OPT schemes only cover a limited range of products, and the actual product coverage has varied significantly, both within and among countries over time. Perhaps more importantly, recent trends in unilateral trade and investment liberalization and the proliferation of bilateral and regional economic integration agreements have significantly reduced the importance of such tariff concessions in promoting global sourcing and, therefore, the actual utilization of these schemes. Moreover, by their very nature, these administrative records leave out cross-border transitions among third countries within global production networks.

The second approach, pioneered by Yeats (2001) and pursued in a number of subsequent studies (Ng and Yeats 2003, Athukorala 2005, Athukorala and Yamashita 2006, Ando and Kimura 2010) involves delineating trade in parts and components by using individual country trade statistics extracted from the UN trade data reporting system (Comtrade database). Compared to the OPT-based trade flow analysis, this approach provides comprehensive and consistent coverage of the parts and components trade, encompassing a large number of countries. But it suffers from two major limitations. First, the commodity coverage is limited to parts and components, which can be directly identifiable based on the commodity nomenclature of the U.S. Standard International Trade Classification (SITC) system. These items are confined to the product classes of machinery and transport equipment (SITC 7 and SITC 8). However, there is evidence that global production sharing has been spreading beyond SITCs 7 and 8 to other product categories, such as machine tools and various metal products (belonging to SITC 6). Second, and more importantly, even if we ignore the problem of under-coverage, parts and components are only one of the facets of network trade. As noted at the outset, there has been a remarkable expansion of network activities from pure component production and assembly to final assembly. Moreover, the relative importance of these two tasks varies among countries and over time in a given country, making it problematic to use data on the parts and components trade as a general indicator of the trends and evolving patterns of network trade over time and across countries.

The analysis in this paper makes use of data extracted from the U.S. trade data system following a procedure that aims to redress these two limitations to the extent permitted by the nature of data availability. We use a list of parts and components encompassing the entire spectrum of manufacturing trade. The list was compiled by mapping parts and components in the UN Broad Economic Classification (BEC) Registry[3] in the product list of the World Trade Organization (WTO) Information Technology Agreement with the Harmonize System (HS) of trade classification at the 6-digit level. Information gathered from firm-level surveys conducted in Thailand and Malaysia was used to fill gaps in the list.[4] Data compiled at the HS 6-digit level were converted to SITC for the final analysis using the UN HS-SITC concordance.

There is no hard and fast rule applicable to distinguishing between parts/components and assembled products in international trade data. The only practical way of doing this is to focus on the specific product categories in which network trade is heavily concentrated (Krugman 2008). Once these product categories have been identified, assembly trade can be approximately estimated as the difference between parts and components—directly identified based on our list—and recorded trade in these product categories. Guided by the available literature on production sharing, we identified seven product categories: office machines and automatic data processing machines (SITC 75), telecommunication and sound recording equipment (SITC 76), electrical machinery (SITC 77), road vehicles (SITC 78), professional and scientific equipment (SITC 87), and photographic apparatus (SITC 88). It is quite reasonable to assume that these product categories contain virtually no products produced from start to finish in a given country. However, admittedly the estimates based on this list do not provide full coverage of final assembly in world trade. For instance, outsourcing of final assembly does take place in various miscellaneous product categories such as clothing, furniture, sporting goods, and leather products. It is not possible to meaningfully delineate parts and components and assembled goods in reported trade in these product categories because they contain a significant (yet unknown) share of horizontal trade. Likewise, assembly activities in software trade have recorded impressive expansion in recent years, but these are lumped together in the UN data system with "special transactions" under SITC 9. However, the magnitude of the bias resulting from the failure to cover these items is unlikely to be substantial because network trade in final assembly is heavily concentrated in the product categories covered in our decomposition (Yeats 2001; Krugman 2008).

Regarding country coverage, East Asia (EA) is defined here to include Japan and developing East Asia (DEA), which covers the newly industrialized economies (NIEs) of North

Asia (South Korea, Taiwan, and Hong Kong), China, and members of the Association of Southeast Asian Nations (ASEAN). Among the ASEAN countries, Myanmar is not covered because of a lack of data, and Brunei, Cambodia and Laos are treated as a residual group because of data gaps. The East Asian experience is examined in the wider global context, focusing specifically on the comparative experiences of South Asia, North America, and the European Union (EU). Among the ASEAN countries, only the six largest economies—Indonesia, Malaysia, the Philippines, Thailand, Singapore, and Viet Nam—are covered in the statistical analysis. Brunei, Cambodia, Lao People's Democratic Republic (Lao PDR), and Myanmar are excluded because of data limitations. The East Asian experience is examined in the wider global context, focusing on the region's performance relative to the North American Free Trade Area (NAFTA) and the EU.

The data are tabulated using importer records, which are considered to be more appropriate for analyzing trade patterns than the corresponding exporter records. Compared to country records, importer records are also presumably less susceptible to double-counting and erroneous identification of the source/destination country in the presence of entrepôt trade (e.g., the PRC's trade through Hong Kong, and China and Indonesia's trade through Singapore) (Ng and Yeats 2003; Feenstra et al. 1999). Some countries also fail to properly report goods shipped from their own export-processing zones as these tend to be grouped into one highly aggregated category of "special transactions" under SITC 9. It is difficult to find a satisfactory solution for these problems. However, it is generally believed that data compiled from importer records are less susceptible to recording errors and reveal the origin and composition of trade more accurately than other records because there are normally important legal penalties for incorrectly specifying this information on customs declarations. Data for Taiwan, which is not covered in the UN data system, are obtained from the trade database (based on the same classification system) of the Council for Economic Planning and Development, Taipei. The analysis covers 1992 to 2008. The year 1992 was selected as the starting point because by this time countries accounting for over 95% of total world manufacturing trade had adopted the revised data reporting system. The year 2008 is used as the end point of time coverage given massive disruption in trade follows during the ensuing years due to the global financial crisis.

## 13.2 East Asia in World Trade: An Overview

Rapid export expansion has been the prime mover of East Asia's rise in the global economy. The combined share of East Asian countries in world non-oil exports recorded a three-fold increase, from 11% to 33%, between 1969-1970 and 2007-2008 (Table 13.1).[5] The region accounted for over 40% of the total increase in world exports over this period. In the 1970s and 1980s, Japan dominated the region's trade, accounting for nearly 60% of exports (and imports). The picture has changed dramatically over the

**Table 13.1 East Asia in World Trade (%)**

| | Total (non-oil) trade (%) | | | Manufacturing trade (%) | | | Manufacturing share in total exports (%) | | |
|---|---|---|---|---|---|---|---|---|---|
| | 1969–70 | 1989–90 | 2007–08 | 1969–70 | 1989–90 | 2007–08 | 1969–70 | 1989–90 | 2007–08 |
| *(a) Exports* | | | | | | | | | |
| East Asia | 11 | 23.8 | 30.7 | 12 | 26.7 | 34.8 | 72.5 | 90.3 | 86.6 |
| Japan | 6.3 | 10.4 | 4.6 | 8.9 | 12.7 | 7.4 | 93.4 | 98 | 93.2 |
| Developing East Asia | 4.7 | 13.4 | 24.4 | 3.1 | 14 | 27.4 | 44.3 | 84.3 | 84.9 |
| China | 0.8 | 2.9 | 12.7 | 0.5 | 3 | 14.9 | 45.1 | 83.6 | 93.4 |
| Hong Kong, China | 0.9 | 1.7 | 0.6 | 1.3 | 2 | 0.6 | 95.1 | 96.5 | 89.3 |
| South Korea | 0.3 | 2.2 | 3.0 | 0.3 | 2.6 | 3.5 | 75.4 | 93.6 | 87.6 |
| Taiwan | 0.6 | 2.7 | 2.0 | 0.6 | 3.1 | 2.4 | 71.5 | 91.9 | 91.8 |
| ASEAN | 2.1 | 3.7 | 6.0 | 0.3 | 3.3 | 5.8 | 21.1 | 72.0 | 73.2 |
| Indonesia | 0.3 | 0.5 | 0.9 | --- | 0.4 | 0.6 | 3.8 | 55.6 | 41.5 |
| Malaysia | 0.8 | 1.0 | 1.6 | 0.1 | 0.7 | 1.6 | 7.2 | 60.4 | 70.9 |
| Philippines | 0.5 | 0.3 | 0.6 | 0.1 | 0.3 | 0.6 | 10.3 | 62.8 | 83.8 |
| Singapore | 0.2 | 1.1 | 1.2 | 0.1 | 1.3 | 1.4 | 45.9 | 91.2 | 70.6 |
| Thailand | 0.3 | 0.8 | 1.3 | --- | 0.6 | 1.3 | 7.7 | 59.6 | 76.5 |
| Vietnam | ... | ... | 0.4 | ... | 0 | 0.3 | ... | 13.5 | 59.2 |
| *Memo items* | | | | | | | | | |
| South Asia | 1.1 | 0.8 | 1.2 | 0.9 | 0.7 | 1.2 | 72.1 | 71.6 | 69.2 |
| India | 0.9 | 0.6 | 1.1 | 0.7 | 0.5 | 1.1 | 71.8 | 71.5 | 67.7 |
| NAFTA | 25.5 | 17.5 | 13.8 | 24.1 | 16.2 | 13.6 | 62.8 | 74.5 | 71.1 |
| EU15 | 46.3 | 41.1 | 34.3 | 53.4 | 42.2 | 34.9 | 76.6 | 82.7 | 77.4 |
| Developing countries | 14.7 | 20.9 | 44.4 | 5.9 | 19.3 | 44.0 | 26.8 | 74.2 | 61.2 |
| Developed countries | 85.3 | 79.1 | 55.6 | 94.1 | 80.7 | 56.0 | 73.3 | 82.2 | 75.2 |
| World | 100 | 100 | 100.0 | 100 | 100 | 0.0 | 66.5 | 80.6 | 68.3 |
| US$ billion | 205 | 2386 | 12056 | 137 | 1922 | 9766 | | | |
| *(b) Imports* | | | | | | | | | |
| East Asia | 11.6 | 19.9 | 24.4 | 8.3 | 18.3 | 24.6 | 47.6 | 74.1 | 67.0 |
| Japan | 6.5 | 7 | 0.6 | 3 | 5 | 3.6 | 30.4 | 57.7 | 49.3 |
| Developing East Asia | 5.1 | 12.9 | 20.4 | 5.3 | 13.3 | 21.1 | 69.7 | 83 | 71.4 |
| China | 0 | 2.3 | 7.8 | 0 | 2.3 | 7.7 | | 81 | 70.0 |

**Table 13.1 Continued**

| | Total (non-oil) trade (%) | | | Manufacturing trade (%) | | | Manufacturing share in total exports (%) | | |
|---|---|---|---|---|---|---|---|---|---|
| | 1969–70 | 1989–90 | 2007–08 | 1969–70 | 1989–90 | 2007–08 | 1969–70 | 1989–90 | 2007–08 |
| Hong Kong, China | 1.3 | 3.1 | 3.4 | 1.3 | 3.4 | 3.9 | 69.5 | 87.5 | 90.2 |
| South Korea | 0.9 | 2.3 | 2.2 | 0.8 | 2.2 | 2.2 | 59.9 | 74.8 | 59.2 |
| Taiwan | 0.6 | 1.7 | 1.4 | 0.6 | 1.7 | 1.4 | 69.7 | 80.1 | 76.2 |
| ASEAN | 2.8 | 5.1 | 5.6 | 3.2 | 5.3 | 5.8 | 74.0 | 85.0 | 68.1 |
| Indonesia | 0.4 | 0.7 | 0.6 | 0.5 | 0.8 | 0.6 | 80.7 | 83 | 57.7 |
| Malaysia | 0.5 | 1 | 1.1 | 0.5 | 1 | 1.1 | 63.9 | 85.6 | 72.3 |
| Philippines | 0.5 | 0.4 | 0.4 | 0.6 | 0.3 | 0.4 | 77.3 | 76.4 | 65.3 |
| Singapore | 0.9 | 1.9 | 1.9 | 0.9 | 2.1 | 2.1 | 63.7 | 87.4 | 68.6 |
| Thailand | 0.5 | 1.1 | 1.1 | 0.7 | 1.1 | 1.1 | 85.9 | 84.1 | 68.5 |
| Vietnam | ... | ... | 0.5 | ... | ... | 0.5 | ... | 60.3 | 69.3 |
| *Memo items* | | | 0.0 | | | 0.0 | | | 0.0 |
| South Asia | 1.9 | 0.9 | 1.5 | 1.6 | 0.9 | 1.4 | 93.4 | 76.7 | 47.3 |
| India | 1.2 | 0.7 | 1.3 | 1.6 | 0.7 | 1.2 | 94.9 | 77.7 | 46.6 |
| NAFTA | 25 | 17.4 | 20.0 | 20.9 | 15.8 | 19.1 | 55.5 | 73.1 | 66.0 |
| EU15 | 45.5 | 40.8 | 35.4 | 46.2 | 41.1 | 34.5 | 67.7 | 81.1 | 67.9 |
| Developing countries[1, 2] | 16.5 | 21.6 | 40.1 | 18.6 | 21.4 | 40.2 | 74.9 | 80 | 68.3 |
| Developed countries[2] | 83.5 | 78.4 | 59.9 | 81.4 | 78.6 | 59.8 | 64.8 | 80.7 | 67.4 |
| World | 100 | 100 | 100.0 | 100 | 100 | 0.0 | 66.5 | 80.6 | 67.8 |
| US$ billion | 205 | 2386 | 12056 | 137 | 1922 | 9766 | | | |

*Notes:*
1 Including Asian developing countries.
2 Based on the UN country classification.
---negligible (less than 0.05 percent)... Data not available.
*Source:* Compiled from UN Comtrade database, and Trade Data CD-ROM, Council for Economic Planning and Development, Taipei (for data on Taiwan).

past two decades with the share of developing East Asian countries increasing rapidly in the face of a relative decline in Japan's position in world trade. By 2007-2008, these countries together accounted for almost 80% of total regional trade.[6]

The rise of China has been a dominant factor behind the share increase in DACs' world market shares from about the early 1990s, but the other countries in the region have also increased their world market shares (Table 13.1). In the global context, East Asia market share gains have come predominantly at the expense of developed countries.

**Table 13.2 Commodity Composition of Manufacturing Exports, 2007–08 (percent)**

| | | Resource based products (SITC 6–SITC 68) | | Machinery and transport equipment (SITC 7) | | | | Miscellaneous manufacturing (SITC 8) | |
|---|---|---|---|---|---|---|---|---|---|
| | Chemicals (SITC 5) | Total | Textiles | Total | ICT products[3] | Electrical goods[4] | Road vehicles (SITC 78) | Total | Apparel (SITC 84) |
| East Asia | 6.9 | 11 | 2.1 | 50.3 | 30.9 | 5.2 | 6.4 | 18.3 | 4.4 |
| Japan | 9.6 | 10.3 | 0.9 | 63.4 | 20.1 | 5 | 20.7 | 10 | 0.1 |
| Developing Asia | 6.3 | 11.2 | 2.4 | 47.1 | 33.6 | 5.3 | 2.9 | 20.4 | 5.5 |
| China | 4.4 | 13.7 | 3.1 | 46.6 | 32.5 | 6.9 | 1.6 | 28.8 | 8.4 |
| Hong Kong, China | 5.0 | 15.8 | 4.3 | 39.9 | 30.5 | 5.4 | 0.6 | 28.6 | 9.9 |
| Taiwan | 9.1 | 12.5 | 3.0 | 55.0 | 43.4 | 5.3 | 2.2 | 15.6 | 0.5 |
| South Korea | 10.4 | 11.2 | 2.2 | 57.2 | 33.3 | 3.9 | 10.2 | 8.9 | 0.5 |
| ASEAN | 7.2 | 6.3 | 1.1 | 42.8 | 33.7 | 3.0 | 2.2 | 11.0 | 3.2 |
| Indonesia | 4.7 | 9.7 | 2.3 | 15.0 | 9.0 | 2.8 | 1.4 | 12.2 | 5.2 |
| Malaysia | 4.8 | 5.2 | 0.6 | 53.0 | 47.5 | 2.7 | 0.6 | 7.8 | 1.7 |
| Philippines | 1.5 | 3.0 | 0.5 | 70.9 | 62.3 | 5.6 | 1.3 | 8.3 | 3.3 |
| Singapore | 15.8 | 2.9 | 0.2 | 45.6 | 36.3 | 1.9 | 0.5 | 6.4 | 0.1 |
| Thailand | 7.4 | 9.6 | 1.5 | 48.1 | 30.4 | 3.8 | 7.9 | 11.5 | 3.1 |
| Vietnam | 1.7 | 7.2 | 2.1 | 11.4 | 6.1 | 2.5 | 0.7 | 39.1 | 15.4 |
| *Memo items* | | | | | | | | | |
| South Asia | 11.6 | 29.6 | 9.5 | 11.3 | 2.4 | 1.6 | 2.3 | 16.5 | 9.6 |
| India | 12.5 | 27.8 | 6.2 | 12.3 | 2.6 | 1.0 | 2.5 | 15.1 | 8.1 |
| NAFTA | 12.2 | 8.3 | 0.8 | 41.5 | 11.4 | 3.3 | 10.4 | 9.1 | 0.5 |
| EU 15 | 17.2 | 13.6 | 1.4 | 37.1 | 7.2 | 2.9 | 11.9 | 9.6 | 1.4 |
| Developed countries[2] | 15.4 | 11.6 | 1.2 | 38.8 | 8.8 | 2.9 | 11.5 | 9.4 | 0.9 |
| Developing countries[1, 2] | 5.9 | 10.9 | 1.9 | 31.6 | 17.8 | 3.5 | 3.7 | 12.9 | 3.9 |
| World | 10.7 | 11.3 | 1.6 | 35.2 | 14.0 | 3.2 | 7.7 | 11.1 | 2.4 |

*Notes:*

1 Excluding Asian developing countries.

2. Based on the UN country classification.

3. ICT Information and communication technology products (SITC 75+76+772+776)

4. SITC 77 - 772–776

---Data not available

*Source:* Compiled from UN Comtrade database, and Trade Data CD-ROM, Council for Economic Planning and Development, Taipei (for Taiwanese data)

The combined share of other developing countries (that is, all developing countries less Asian developing countries) has increased throughout the period, although of course at a slower rate than DEA. Thus, on first inspection, there is no indication of China "crowding out" its neighbors—China's market share gains have been at the expense of that of the rest of the world, not from the rest of Asia. This observation is consistent with the inferences that can be derived from a number of recent studies that have systematically examined the impact of China's rise on exporter performance of the other countries in the region (Athukorala 2009, Greenaway at al. 2008; Eichengreen et al. 2007).

Rapid export growth in East Asia has been underpinned by a pronounced shift in export structure away from primary commodities and toward manufacturing. By 2007–2008, manufacturing accounted for 92% of total exports from Asia, up from 78% four decades earlier (Table 13.1). From about the early 1990s, manufactures accounted for over a four-fifths of total merchandise exports from these countries, up from 84% four decades ago. Given the nature of their resource endowments, the four Asian newly-industrialized economies (NIEs) (Hong Kong, Taiwan, Korea, and Singapore) relied very heavily on manufacturing for export expansion from the outset. However, beginning in the 1970s, a notable shift toward manufacturing is observable across all countries, at varying speeds and intensity. The combined shares of the ASEAN countries other than Singapore increased from a mere 11% to 71.0% between these two time points. Among individual countries Indonesia and Vietnam have a significantly lower share of manufactures in their exports, reflecting both their comparative advantage and their later adoption of export-oriented industrialization strategies.

Within manufacturing, machinery and transport equipment (SITC 7) have played a pivotal role in the structural shift in the export composition of DACs (Table 13.2). The share of machinery and transport equipment in the export structures of some of the more industrialized economies of East Asia is particularly high. By contrast, that for Indonesia, Vietnam. and all of South Asia is much smaller. Within the machinery and transport equipment category, ICT products have been the most dynamic component of Asian export expansion. By 2007–2008, over 58% of total world ICT exports originated from Asia, up from 30.8% in 1994/5; China accounted for 25.4% of total world ICT exports, up from 4.2% in 1994/5.[7] In electrical goods, China's world market share increased from 3.1% to 20.6% between these two years. As we explain in the next section, export dynamism in these product lines has been driven by the ongoing process of global production sharing and the increasingly deep integration of East Asian countries into global production networks.

## 13.3 Global production sharing and trade patterns

Linking East Asia to the global electronics production networks began in 1968 with the arrival in Singapore of two US companies, National Semiconductors and Texas

Instruments, to set up plants for assembling semiconductor devices (Athukorala 2008). From about the late 1970s, the MNEs with production facilities in Singapore began to relocate some low-end assembly activities in neighboring countries (particularly in Malaysia, Thailand and the Philippines) in response to the rapid increase in wages and land prices. Many newcomer MNEs to the region also set up production bases in these countries, bypassing Singapore. From about the early 1990s the emergence of China as the "global factory" of electrical and electrical goods assembly based on parts and component imported from other countries has contributed to rapid expansion of production networks in the region. More recently regional production networks have begun to expand to Vietnam. Over the past three decades, the process of global production sharing has created a new division of labor among countries in the region, based on skill differences involved in different stages of the production process and relative wages, and improved communication and transport infrastructure (Ando and Kimura 2010). As we will see below, the formation of production networks has dramatically transformed the spatial patterns of international trade in the region, with a notable "magnification" effect on recorded trade flows operating through multiple border-crossing of parts and components on the expansion of intra-regional trade.

Table 13.3 presents data on world trade based on global production sharing (network trade) and East Asia's relative position in this new international exchange. World network trade increased from US$ 1207 billion (about 23.8% of total manufacturing exports) in 1992-1993 to US$ 4850 billion (45.7%) in 2006-2008, accounting for nearly two-thirds of the total increment in world manufacturing exports during this period. This increase was underpinned by a palpable shift in global production sharing away from mature industrial economies toward developing countries and in particular toward East Asia. The share of developing countries in total network exports increased from 22.0% in 1992-93 to 46.1% in 2007-2008, driven primarily by the growing importance of East Asian countries in global production sharing. The share of East Asia (including Japan) increased from 32.2% in 1992-1993 to 40.3% in 2007-2008, despite a notable decline in Japan's share, from 18.4% to 9.5%. The major driving force has been China, whose share increased from 2.1% to 15.3%. Within East Asia, world market shares of ASEAN countries, with the exception of Singapore, have grown faster than the regional average. The mild decline in Singapore's share reflects a marked shift in its role in global production networks for high-tech industries away from the standard assembly and testing activities to oversight functions, product design, and capital and technology-intensive tasks in the production process. Some, if not most, of these new activities are in the form of services and are, therefore, not captured in merchandise trade data (Wong 2007; Athukorala 2008).

There has been a sharp increase in the share of parts and components (henceforth referred to as "components" for brevity) in network trade across all countries in the region. In all countries except the PRC and Thailand components accounted for well over half of total network export (and imports) by 2007-2008. Components' share is particularly high among ASEAN countries. There is a remarkable similarity in components' share figures on the export and import sides across countries, reflecting

**Table 13.3 Geographic Profile of World Manufacturing Trade: Total Trade and Network Trade (percent)**

| | Total Manufacturing | | Network Products: Parts and components | | Network Products: Final assembly | | Network Products: Total | | Share of parts and components in network products | |
|---|---|---|---|---|---|---|---|---|---|---|
| | 1992–3 | 2007–8 | 1992–3 | 2007–8 | 1992–3 | 2007–8 | 1992–3 | 2007–8 | 1992–3 | 2006–7 |
| *(a) Exports* | | | | | | | | | | |
| East Asia | 28.3 | 34.0 | 29.6 | 42.8 | 34.1 | 37.5 | 32.2 | 40.3 | 39.0 | 56.5 |
| Japan | 12.3 | 7.2 | 15.2 | 9.1 | 20.8 | 9.9 | 18.4 | 9.5 | 35.0 | 51.3 |
| Developing East Asia (DEA) | 16.0 | 26.8 | 14.4 | 33.7 | 13.3 | 27.6 | 13.8 | 30.9 | 44.3 | 58.1 |
| China | 4.5 | 14.3 | 1.7 | 13.5 | 2.4 | 15.7 | 2.1 | 14.5 | 35.0 | 49.4 |
| Hong Kong, China | 1.8 | 0.7 | 1.5 | 0.8 | 1.2 | 0.5 | 1.3 | 0.7 | 46.8 | 65.2 |
| Taiwan | 2.9 | 2.5 | 3.7 | 4.0 | 2.0 | 2.2 | 2.7 | 3.2 | 58.4 | 67.2 |
| South Korea | 2.3 | 3.4 | 2.2 | 5.6 | 2.0 | 3.7 | 2.1 | 4.7 | 45.0 | 63.5 |
| ASEAN | 4.5 | 6.0 | 5.2 | 9.8 | 5.8 | 5.5 | 5.6 | 7.8 | 39.9 | 66.9 |
| Indonesia | 0.6 | 0.6 | 0.1 | 0.5 | 0.1 | 0.5 | 0.1 | 0.5 | 40.3 | 56.1 |
| Malaysia | 1.2 | 1.7 | 1.7 | 3.4 | 1.9 | 1.8 | 1.8 | 2.6 | 40.5 | 68.1 |
| The Philippines | 0.3 | 0.7 | 0.5 | 1.8 | 0.2 | 0.4 | 0.4 | 1.2 | 61.6 | 82.1 |
| Singapore | 1.5 | 1.4 | 2.3 | 2.6 | 2.6 | 1.0 | 2.5 | 1.9 | 38.7 | 74.1 |
| Thailand | 0.8 | 1.3 | 0.6 | 1.4 | 0.9 | 1.8 | 0.8 | 1.6 | 32.7 | 47.5 |
| Viet Nam | 0.0 | 0.3 | 0.0 | 0.1 | 0.0 | 0.1 | 0.0 | 0.1 | 23.6 | 59.2 |
| South Asia | 0.9 | 1.3 | 0.1 | 0.4 | 0.1 | 0.2 | 0.1 | 0.3 | 44.1 | 72.7 |
| India | 0.6 | 1.0 | 0.1 | 0.4 | 0.1 | 0.2 | 0.1 | 0.3 | 47.2 | 73.5 |
| Oceania | 0.4 | 0.4 | 0.3 | 0.3 | 0.3 | 0.3 | 0.3 | 0.3 | 45.6 | 51.2 |
| NAFTA | 17.2 | 14.0 | 25.3 | 16.2 | 20.6 | 16.6 | 22.6 | 16.4 | 47.5 | 52.6 |
| EU 15 | 41.3 | 35.4 | 39.2 | 29.3 | 35.3 | 31.4 | 37.0 | 30.3 | 44.9 | 51.5 |
| Developed countries | 72.4 | 56.6 | 76.7 | 52.7 | 78.6 | 56.1 | 77.8 | 54.3 | 41.8 | 51.7 |
| Developing countries | 27.6 | 43.4 | 20.8 | 46.8 | 22.9 | 44.4 | 22.0 | 45.7 | 40.1 | 54.6 |
| World | 100 | 100 | 100 | 100 | 100 | 100 | 100 | 100 | 42.4 | 53.2 |

## Table 13.3 Continued

| | Total Manufacturing | | Network Products: Parts and components | | Network Products: Final assembly | | Network Products: Total | | Share of parts and components in network products | |
|---|---|---|---|---|---|---|---|---|---|---|
| | 1992-3 | 2007-8 | 1992-3 | 2007-8 | 1992-3 | 2007-8 | 1992-3 | 2007-8 | 1992-3 | 2006-7 |
| *(b) Imports* | | | | | | | | | | |
| East Asia | 21.7 | 23.7 | 30.1 | 36.6 | 14.3 | 18.1 | 21.0 | 28.1 | 61.2 | 70.3 |
| Japan | 4.1 | 3.5 | 4.0 | **3.8** | **3.0** | 3.3 | 3.4 | 3.5 | 49.9 | 57.7 |
| Developing East Asia (DEA) | 17.6 | 20.3 | 26.1 | 32.8 | 11.2 | 14.9 | 17.6 | 24.5 | 63.4 | 72.1 |
| China | 2.9 | 7.1 | 3.0 | 11.5 | 1.5 | 6.0 | 2.2 | 9.0 | 59.3 | 69.0 |
| Hong Kong, China | 4.4 | 3.6 | 5.4 | 6.3 | 2.8 | 2.1 | 3.9 | 4.4 | 59.4 | 78.2 |
| Taiwan | 2.1 | 1.6 | 3.1 | 2.3 | 1.4 | 1.2 | 2.1 | 1.8 | 62.1 | 69.9 |
| South Korea | 2.0 | 2.2 | 3.1 | 2.5 | 1.1 | 1.6 | 1.9 | 2.1 | 67.4 | 64.8 |
| ASEAN) | 6.2 | 5.8 | 11.5 | 10.2 | 4.4 | 4.0 | 7.4 | 7.3 | 66.1 | 74.9 |
| Indonesia | 0.8 | 0.4 | 1.1 | 0.3 | 0.3 | 0.3 | 0.6 | 0.3 | 74.7 | 58.0 |
| Malaysia | 1.4 | 1.3 | 3.0 | 2.4 | 1.1 | 1.2 | 1.9 | 1.9 | 66.7 | 69.4 |
| The Philippines | 0.4 | 0.5 | 0.6 | 1.2 | 0.2 | 0.4 | 0.4 | 0.8 | 68.6 | 77.9 |
| Singapore | 2.3 | 2.1 | 4.8 | 4.5 | 2.0 | 1.5 | 3.2 | 3.2 | 64.6 | 77.7 |
| Thailand | 1.3 | 1.1 | 2.0 | 1.4 | 0.8 | 0.6 | 1.3 | 1.0 | 66.2 | 74.4 |
| Viet Nam | 0.0 | 0.4 | 0.0 | 0.3 | 0.0 | 0.2 | 0.0 | 0.2 | | 66.2 |
| South Asia | 0.9 | 1.3 | 0.7 | 1.1 | 0.4 | 0.9 | 0.6 | 1.0 | 56.4 | 59.1 |
| India | 0.5 | 1.1 | 0.4 | 0.9 | 0.2 | 0.8 | 0.3 | 0.8 | 62.2 | 57.4 |
| Oceania | 16.6 | 18.6 | 31.8 | 19.6 | 8.5 | 17.9 | 18.5 | 18.8 | 73.7 | 56.3 |
| NAFTA | 1.8 | 2.4 | 2.7 | 3.2 | 1.0 | 2.0 | 1.7 | 2.6 | 67.4 | 65.5 |
| EU 15 | 42.0 | 35.2 | 45.5 | 29.9 | 7.5 | 15.9 | 23.8 | 23.5 | 81.9 | 68.8 |
| Developed countries | 71.4 | 61.1 | 82.7 | 52.3 | 68.8 | 66.8 | 74.7 | 59.0 | 47.3 | 47.8 |
| Developing countries | 28.6 | 38.9 | 17.3 | 47.7 | 31.2 | 33.2 | 25.3 | 41.0 | 29.3 | 62.8 |
| World | 100 | 100 | 100 | 100 | 100 | 100 | 100 | 100 | 42.8 | 54.0 |

*Source*: Data compiled from UN Comtrade database.

overlapping specialization patterns in component assembly and testing among countries in the region.

Table 13.4 presents comparative statistics on the share of network trade in total manufacturing exports and imports at the country and country group levels. It is evident that the share of network trade is much higher in East Asia than in all other regions of the world. In 2007-2008, exports within production networks accounted for over 60% of total manufacturing trade in East Asia, compared to the world average of 51%. Within

**Table 13.4 Share of Network Products in Manufacturing Trade, 1992-93 and 2006-08 (percent)**

| | Parts and components | | Final assembly | | Total network products | |
|---|---|---|---|---|---|---|
| | 1992-93 | 2007-08 | 1992-93 | 2007-08 | 1992-93 | 2007-08 |
| *(a) Exports* | | | | | | |
| East Asia | 20.2 | 34.3 | 31.6 | 26.4 | 51.8 | 60.7 |
| Japan | 23.9 | 34.3 | 44.5 | 32.3 | 68.4 | 66.6 |
| Developing East Asia (DEA) | 17.3 | 34.0 | 21.8 | 25.2 | 39.1 | 59.2 |
| People's Republic of China (PRC) | 7.4 | 25.5 | 13.7 | 26.6 | 21.1 | 52.1 |
| Hong Kong, China | 15.8 | 33.3 | 18.0 | 17.8 | 33.8 | 51.1 |
| Taiwan | 24.7 | 44.2 | 17.6 | 21.5 | 42.3 | 65.7 |
| Republic of Korea | 18.1 | 44.2 | 22.2 | 25.4 | 40.3 | 69.5 |
| ASEAN | 22.7 | 44.2 | 34.1 | 22.0 | 56.8 | 66.2 |
| Indonesia | 3.8 | 21.5 | 5.6 | 16.8 | 9.3 | 38.4 |
| Malaysia | 27.7 | 53.6 | 40.7 | 25.1 | 68.4 | 78.8 |
| The Philippines | 32.9 | 71.7 | 20.5 | 15.6 | 53.4 | 87.3 |
| Singapore | 29.0 | 49.3 | 45.9 | 17.2 | 74.9 | 66.5 |
| Thailand | 14.1 | 29.9 | 29.0 | 33.0 | 43.1 | 62.9 |
| Viet Nam | --- | 11.0 | --- | 7.6 | --- | 18.5 |
| South Asia | 2.3 | 8.2 | 2.9 | 3.1 | 5.1 | 11.3 |
| India | 3.0 | 10.4 | 3.4 | 3.8 | 6.4 | 14.2 |
| North American Free Trade Area (NAFTA) | 28.4 | 31.2 | 31.4 | 28.1 | 59.7 | 59.3 |
| Mexico | 42.1 | 34.6 | 30.8 | 42.1 | 72.9 | 76.6 |
| European Union (EU) 15 | 18.3 | 22.4 | 22.4 | 21.1 | 40.7 | 43.5 |
| Developed countries | 20.4 | 25.2 | 28.5 | 23.6 | 48.9 | 48.8 |
| Developing countries | 14.6 | 29.2 | 21.8 | 24.3 | 36.4 | 53.6 |
| World | 19.3 | 27.1 | 26.3 | 23.8 | 45.5 | 50.9 |

**Table 13.4 Continued**

| | Parts and components | | Final assembly | | Total Network products | |
|---|---|---|---|---|---|---|
| | 1992-93 | 2007-08 | 1992-93 | 2007-08 | 1992-93 | 2007-08 |
| *(b) Imports* | | | | | | |
| East Asia | 27.2 | 42.0 | 17.2 | 17.8 | 44.4 | 59.8 |
| Japan | 19.3 | 29.2 | 19.3 | 21.9 | 38.6 | 61.1 |
| Developing East Asia | 29.0 | 44.4 | 16.7 | 17.3 | 45.8 | 61.7 |
| PRC | 20.4 | 44.0 | 14.0 | 19.8 | 34.4 | 63.7 |
| Hong Kong, China | 24.1 | 48.5 | 16.5 | 13.5 | 40.6 | 62.1 |
| Taiwan | 29.5 | 38.9 | 18.0 | 16.8 | 47.5 | 55.7 |
| Republic of Korea | 30.1 | 31.9 | 14.6 | 17.4 | 44.7 | 49.3 |
| ASEAN | 36.0 | 47.8 | 18.4 | 16.2 | 54.4 | 64.0 |
| Indonesia | 27.0 | 21.8 | 9.2 | 15.8 | 36.1 | 37.7 |
| Malaysia | 40.5 | 50.0 | 20.2 | 22.0 | 60.7 | 72.0 |
| The Philippines | 32.6 | 61.3 | 15.0 | 17.4 | 47.6 | 78.6 |
| Singapore | 39.9 | 60.4 | 21.9 | 17.3 | 61.8 | 77.7 |
| Thailand | 30.6 | 36.1 | 15.6 | 12.4 | 46.2 | 48.5 |
| Viet Nam | --- | 19.1 | --- | 9.7 | --- | 28.8 |
| South Asia | 16.6 | 23.8 | 12.9 | 16.5 | 29.5 | 40.3 |
| India | 17.5 | 22.9 | 10.6 | 17.0 | 28.1 | 39.9 |
| NAFTA | 37.4 | 28.8 | 13.4 | 22.4 | 50.7 | 51.2 |
| Mexico | 29.4 | 36.1 | 14.2 | 19.0 | 43.7 | 55.1 |
| EU15 | 21.2 | 23.2 | 4.7 | 10.6 | 25.9 | 33.8 |
| Developed countries | 22.6 | 23.4 | 25.2 | 25.5 | 47.8 | 48.9 |
| Developing countries | 11.9 | 33.6 | 28.6 | 19.9 | 40.4 | 53.4 |
| World | 19.6 | 27.3 | 26.2 | 23.3 | 45.7 | 50.7 |

*Note*: ... = data not available

*Source*: Compiled from UN Comtrade database.

East Asia, ASEAN countries stand out for their heavy dependence on production fragmentation trade, which is a critical part of their export dynamism. In 2007–2008, network exports accounted for over two-thirds of total manufacturing exports in ASEAN, up from 57% in the early 1990s. The patterns observed on the export and import sides of the ASEAN are strikingly similar, reflecting growing cross-border trade within production networks.

### 13.3.1 China in Global Production Networks

China's phenomenal export expansion over the past two decades has been underpinned by a shift in the commodity composition of exports away from primary products and toward manufacturing. The share of manufactures in China's total merchandise exports increased from less than 45.1% in the late 1970s to nearly 83.6% in the early 1990s and to 93.4% in 2007–2008 (Table 13.1). Until about the early 1990s, traditional labor-intensive manufactures—in particular, apparel, footwear, toys and sport goods—were the prime movers of export expansion. Since then, there has been a notable shift in the export composition away from conventional labor-intensive product lines and toward more sophisticated product lines—in particular, those within the broader category of machinery and transport equipment (SITC 7) (henceforth referred to as "machinery"). China's phenomenal export expansion has been underpinned by a shift in the commodity composition of exports away from primary products and toward manufacturing. The share of manufactures in China's total merchandise exports increased from less than 40% in the late 1970s to nearly 80% in the early 1990s and to 92% in 2005–2006. Until about the early 1990s, traditional labor-intensive manufactures—in particular, apparel, footwear, toys, and sporting goods—were the prime movers of export expansion. Since then, there has been a notable shift in the export composition away from conventional labor-intensive product lines and toward more sophisticated product lines—in particular, those within the broader category of machinery and transport equipment (SITC 7) (henceforth referred to as "machinery") (Athukorala 2009).

The expansion of machinery exports from China has been brought about by its highly publicized export success in a wide range of "information and communication technology" (ICT) products (falling under SITC categories 75, 76 and 77). China's world market share of ICT products recorded a five-fold increase from 5% in 1992/3 to over 25% in 2005–06 (Athukorala 2009). Trade data showing this phenomenal structural shift have been used widely—not only in the popular press and policy reports of agencies involved in promoting R&D activities but also in some scholarly writings—to argue that China is rapidly becoming an advanced-technology superpower and the sophistication of its export basket is rapidly approaching the levels of those of most advanced industrial nations (e.g., Rodrik 2006, Yusuf et al. 2007). A closer examination of data, however, suggests that such an inference is fundamentally flawed. In reality, what we observe is the rapid consolidation in China of final assembly stages of East Asia-centered global production networks of these products. Ample supply of relatively cheap and trainable labor and the scale economies arising from China's vast domestic market (which enables firms to achieve low unit costs) are contributory factors to China's attractiveness as a global assembly center. China's so-called "high-tech" exports (such as notebook computers, display units, mobile phones, and DVD and CD players) are simply "mass-market commodities" produced in huge quantities and at relatively low unit cost using imported high-tech parts and components; they are not "leading edge-technology products."

The share of parts and components in total machinery imports of China increased from 32.5% in 1992–2003 to 64% in 2007–2008, with the import shared of the three ICT products (SITC 75, 76 and 77) recording a much faster growth. By contrast, final goods (total exports minus components) have continued to dominate the export composition. Over the past decade the share of final goods in total machinery exports has remained around 75%, with only minor year-to-year changes. Given the fact that the production of parts and component is generally more capital- and technology-intensive than final assembly, these figures clearly suggest that China's export success has so far been underpinned largely by its comparative advantage in international production arising from labor abundance. When components are netted out, more than 80% of total Chinese manufacturing exports from China can still be treated as labor-intensive products.

This inference is consistent with the findings of unit-value-based export quality analysis undertaken by Schott (2007) and Hallak and Schott (2010). Schott (2007) examines the relative "sophistication" of China's exports to the United States in 1972–2001. By comparing China's export bundle to that of the relatively skill- and capital-abundant members of the OECD as well as to that of similarly endowed US trading partners, he finds that China's export bundle increasingly overlaps with that of more developed countries, rendering it more sophisticated than that of the other countries with similar factor endowments. By contrast, his comparison of prices (unit values) within product categories reveals that China's exports "sell at a substantial discount relative to its level of GDP and the exports of the OECD countries" (Schott 2007: 15). Schott stops short of probing this rather puzzling contrast between the observed product sophistication and price trends, but it is certainly consistent with the nature of China's participation in fragmentation-based specialization in global manufacturing trade. China is engaged in the labor-intensive stages of production (mostly final assembly) in otherwise advanced industries. In an inter-temporal comparison by Hallak and Schott (2010) of change in quality of exports to the US from 43 countries between 1989 and 2003, China was found to be at the bottom 10% of the ranking with a modest move *down* the quality ladder between the two years (moved from rank 35 to 37).[8]

China's rise as a final assembler of a wide range of electrical and electronics goods has enhanced its trade complementarity with the other countries in East Asia that are involved in component assembly in the global value chain. The data on geographical profile of China's network trade (not reported here for brevity) point a persistent "component bias" in China's intra-East manufacturing trade. The intra-regional share in total component imports to China increased from 16% in 1992–1993 to 47% in 2007–2008. By contrast, the intra-regional share of China's final goods exports continued to remain less than 20% through this period.

## 13.3.2 Production Networks and Regional versus Global Economic Integration

There is a vast literature on what may be termed standard trade data analysis based on the traditional notion of horizontal specialization in which trade is an exchange of goods that are produced from start to finish in just one country. This literature unequivocally points to a persistent increase in intra-regional trade in East Asia, whether or not Japan is included, from about the early 1980s.[9] This evidence figures prominently in the current regional debate concerning the establishment of regional trading arrangements covering some or all countries in East Asia. Another implication of the highly publicized trade integration in the region was the so-called decoupling thesis, which was a popular theme in Asian policy circles in the first decade of the new millennium until the onset of the recent financial crisis.[10] This thesis held that East Asia had become a self-contained economic entity with the potential for maintaining its own growth dynamism independent of the economic outlook for the traditional developed market economies.

The above discussion on the emerging patterns of network trade casts doubts on the validity of these inferences. We have seen that component trade has played a much more important role in trade expansion in East Asia compared to the rest of the world. Conventional trade flow analysis can yield an unbiased picture of regional economic integration only if component trade and final trade follow the same geographic patterns. If component trade has a distinct intra-regional bias, as one would reasonably anticipate in the context of growing network trade in the region, then the conventional trade flow analysis is bound to yield a misleading picture in regard to the relative importance of intra-regional trade versus global trade for growth dynamism in the region. This is because growth based on assembly activities depends on the demand for final goods, which in turn depends on extra-regional growth.

Data on component intensity (percentage shares of parts and components) in bilateral flows of manufacturing trade are reported in Table 13.5. The data vividly show that components account for a much larger share of intra-regional trade in East Asia compared to these countries' world trade and trade with the EU and NAFTA. Moreover, the share of components in total intra-regional imports is much larger than in exports and has increased at a faster rate. This reflects the fact that the region relies more on the rest of the world as a market for final goods than as a market for components. Within East Asia, ASEAN countries stand out for the high share of components in their intra-regional trade flows. The share of components in total intra-regional exports in ASEAN countries increased from 34.6% in 1992-93 to 56.0% in 2007-08. On the import side, the increase was from 50.4% to 55.9% from 75.3% to 84.4%. According to country-level data (not reported here, for brevity), the share of components in manufacturing exports and imports amounted to more than four-fifths in Singapore, Malaysia, and the Philippines and over two-thirds in Thailand. Korea and Taiwan are also involved in sizable trade in components with other countries in the region.

Intra-regional trade shares estimated separately for total manufacturing trade, component trade, and final manufacturing trade (that is, total manufacturing trade less component trade) are reported in Table 13.6. The table covers trade in East Asia and three of its sub-regions, which relate to contemporary Asian policy debates on regional integration. Data for NAFTA and the EU are reported for comparative purposes. Estimates are given for total trade (imports + exports) as well as for exports and imports separately

**Table 13.5 Share of Parts and Components in Bilateral Trade Flows, 2007-08 (percent)**

| Reporting country | EA | Japan | DEA | PRC | ASEAN | NAFTA | EU15 | World |
|---|---|---|---|---|---|---|---|---|
| *(a) Exports* | | | | | | | | |
| East Asia (EA) | 47.6 | 32.9 | 50.1 | 51.6 | 54.5 | 25.1 | 24.1 | 34.1 |
| Japan | 42.0 | 0.0 | 42.0 | 41.5 | 47.9 | 31.5 | 30.4 | 34.4 |
| Developing East Asia (DEA) | 48.1 | 33.4 | 53.9 | 0.0 | 65.2 | 22.7 | 21.6 | 34.0 |
| China (PRC) | 36.2 | 25.2 | 40.6 | 0.0 | 49.1 | 17.1 | 16.3 | 25.6 |
| Korea | 61.9 | 51.5 | 63.5 | 57.3 | 63.7 | 36.6 | 26.8 | 44.2 |
| Taiwan | 51.5 | 59.0 | 50.5 | 39.5 | 61.2 | 35.0 | 37.6 | 44.2 |
| ASEAN10 | 58.2 | 39.9 | 61.4 | 64.0 | 56.0 | 32.1 | 33.9 | 44.2 |
| NAFTA | 46.7 | 36.5 | 49.8 | 34.8 | 67.9 | 28.8 | 30.6 | 31.2 |
| EU15 | 31.4 | 18.7 | 34.8 | 30.4 | 46.5 | 22.1 | 22.0 | 22.4 |
| *(b) Imports* | | | | | | | | |
| East Asia (EA) | 51.7 | 48.8 | 52.8 | 34.8 | 68.3 | 54.7 | 33.1 | 42.1 |
| Japan | 34.2 | 0.0 | 34.2 | 23.1 | 44.9 | 41.0 | 18.9 | 29.9 |
| Developing East Asia (DEA) | 55.5 | 47.7 | 59.5 | 0.0 | 74.3 | 40.3 | 31.7 | 44.2 |
| China (PRC) | 55.2 | 47.5 | 59.2 | 0.0 | 74.0 | 40.1 | 31.6 | 44.0 |
| Korea | 33.0 | 26.6 | 38.1 | 26.1 | 55.7 | 38.9 | 22.9 | 31.9 |
| Taiwan | 46.7 | 33.8 | 58.3 | 44.1 | 68.8 | 40.2 | 28.0 | 38.9 |
| ASEAN10 | 50.3 | 47.2 | 51.4 | 40.1 | 55.9 | 67.5 | 41.7 | 47.9 |
| NAFTA | 29.4 | 39.3 | 26.0 | 17.7 | 40.5 | 36.3 | 25.1 | 28.8 |
| EU15 | 25.0 | 33.6 | 22.8 | 14.9 | 37.9 | 34.1 | 22.1 | 23.4 |

*Note:*
1. EA: East Asia, DEA: Developing East Asia; ASEAN6: six main ASEAN countries; EU15: 15 member countries of the European Union; NAFTA: countries in the North American Free Trade Agreement (USA, Canada and Mexico).
*Source:* Compiled from UN Comtrade database.

to illustrate possible asymmetry in trade patterns resulting from East Asia's increased engagement in fragmentation-based international exchange. Trade patterns depicted by the unadjusted (standard) trade data affirm the received view that Asia, in particular East Asia, has become increasingly integrated through merchandise trade.

In 2007–2008, intra-regional trade accounted for 55.2% of total manufacturing trade in East Asia, up from 53.2% in 1992–1993. The level of intra-regional trade in East Asia was higher than that of NAFTA throughout this period and was rapidly approaching the level of the EU. For DEA and ASEAN, the ratios are lower than the aggregate regional

**Table 13.6 Intra-Regional Shares of Manufacturing Trade: Total, Parts and Components, and Final Trade, 1992–93 and 2006–08[1] (percent)**

| | East Asia | Developing East Asia | ASEAN | NAFTA | EU15 |
|---|---|---|---|---|---|
| *(a) Total trade* | | | | | |
| Exports | | | | | |
| 1992–93 | 47.2 | 38.2 | 20.7 | 44.4 | 61.2 |
| 2007-08 | 43.9 | 33.5 | 18.4 | 48.1 | 56.8 |
| Imports | | | | | |
| 1992–93 | 58.2 | 34.9 | 15.5 | 36.3 | 64.1 |
| 2007-08 | 64.4 | 46.6 | 20.8 | 32.0 | 57.8 |
| *Trade (exports + imports)* | | | | | |
| 1992–93 | 53.2 | 36.5 | 17.8 | 39.9 | 62.6 |
| 2007–08 | 55.2 | 40.4 | 20.1 | 38.4 | 57.5 |
| *(b) Parts and Components* | | | | | |
| Exports | | | | | |
| 1992–93 | 50.2 | 42.6 | 30.3 | 43.5 | 62.3 |
| 2007–08 | 61.1 | 53.9 | 25.4 | 46.9 | 55.9 |
| Imports | | | | | |
| 1992–93 | 65.9 | 35.3 | 20.2 | 39.5 | 58.0 |
| 2007–08 | 66.9 | 50.9 | 22.9 | 39.9 | 55.2 |
| Trade | | | | | |
| 1992–93 | 57.0 | 38.7 | 24.1 | 41.4 | 60.1 |
| 2007–08 | 63.0 | 52.2 | 23.3 | 43.2 | 55.5 |
| *(c) Final Goods*[3] | | | | | |
| Exports | | | | | |
| 1992–93 | 46.0 | 36.8 | 16.1 | 44.7 | 60.9 |
| 2007–08 | 36.9 | 28.3 | 15.9 | 48.7 | 57.0 |
| Imports | | | | | |
| 1992–93 | 55.4 | 34.7 | 12.9 | 35.3 | 65.6 |
| 2007–08 | 63.0 | 42.8 | 20.6 | 30.2 | 58.5 |
| Trade | | | | | |
| 1992–93 | 50.3 | 35.7 | 14.3 | 39.4 | 63.3 |
| 2007–08 | 44.2 | 34.1 | 18.1 | 37.4 | 57.3 |

*Note*: 1. Intra-regional trade shares have been calculated excluding bilateral flows between China and Hong Kong.
2. ASEAN+3=ASEAN+ Japan + Korea +China.
3. Total (reported) trade (a)—parts and components (b).
*Source*: Compiled from UN Comtrade database, and Trade Data CD-ROM, Council for Economic Planning and Development, Taipei (for data on Taiwan).

figure, but they have increased at a much faster rate. The intra-regional trade share of ASEAN has been much lower compared to the other two sub-regions. This asymmetry in intra-regional trade in East Asia reflects the unique nature of the involvement of Japan and the PRC in regional production networks. From about the late 1980s, Japan's manufacturing trade relations with the rest of East Asia have been predominantly in the form of using the region as an assembly base for meeting demand in the region and, more importantly, for exporting to the rest of the world (Athukorala and Yamashita 2008). The emergence of the PRC as a leading assembly center within regional production networks since the early 1990s further amplified this trade asymmetry. That is, the PRC is importing parts and components from the other East Asia countries to assemble final products, which are predominantly destined for markets in the rest of the world (Athukorala 2009).

However, the picture changes significantly when parts and components are netted out: the share of intra-East-Asian final trade (total trade—parts and components) in 2007–2008 was 44.2%, down from 50.3% in 1992–1993. The estimates based on unadjusted data and data on final trade are vastly different for East Asia, particularly for DEA and ASEAN. Both the level of trade in the given years and the change over time in intra-regional trade shares are significantly lower for estimates based on final trade. Interestingly, we do not observe such a difference in estimates for NAFTA and the EU.

The intra-regional shares calculated separately for imports and exports clearly illustrate the risk of making inferences about regional trade integration based on total (imports + exports) data. There is a notable asymmetry in the degree of regional trade integration in East Asia. Unlike in the EU and NAFTA, in East Asia the increase over time in the intra-regional trade ratio (both measured using unadjusted data and data for final trade) has emanated largely from a rapid increase in intra-regional imports as the expansion in intra-regional exports has been consistently slower. The dependence of East Asia (and East Asian country sub-groups) on extra-regional markets, in particular those in NAFTA and the EU, for export-led growth is far greater than is revealed by the standard intra-regional trade ratios commonly used in the debate on regional economic integration. For instance, in 2007–2008 only 43.9% of total East Asian manufacturing exports were absorbed within the region, compared to an intra-regional share of 64.4% in total manufacturing imports. For DEA, the comparable figures were 33.4% and 46.7%, respectively. This asymmetry is clearly seen across all sub-regions within East Asia. The asymmetry between intra-regional shares of imports and exports is therefore much sharper when components are netted out. This is understandable given the heavy component bias in Asian intra-regional trade and the multiple border-crossing of parts and components within regional production networks. On the export side, the intra-regional share of final goods declined continuously from 46% in 1995 to 37% in 2007, whereas the intra-regional import share increased from 56% to 63% between these two time points. The observed asymmetry in intra-regional trade in East Asia reflects the unique nature of the involvement of Japan and the PRC in regional production networks.

## 13.4 Production Sharing and Growth Patterns

The received view on growth patterns in countries in the Asia Pacific region stipulates a dynamic process of changing comparative advantage, a process in which each country rapidly shifts its output from raw materials to manufactures, and within manufactures shifts from labor-intensive to more capital- and technology-intensive sectors. The Japanese economists Akamatsu (1961) and Kojima (2000) dubbed this sequential growth pattern as the *flying geese* paradigm, which is consistent with the Heckscher–Ohlin explanations of how trade patterns are likely to change with the accumulation of human and physical capital (Balassa 1979). A large number of studies carried out in the 1980s and early 1990s have shown that the flying geese pattern of growth holds remarkably well in East Asia.[11]

This view of orderly, sequential economic transformation has profound implications for trade and industrial policy. The rapidly changing structure of exports implies that competitive pressure is experienced by countries at lower levels on the ladder, but it also means that there are new export opportunities for newcomers, as countries at higher rungs vacate export markets. For importing countries, according to this view, the source of competitive pressure in traditional labor-intensive products is expected to shift; however, to the extent that imports from one country merely displace imports from another, no new domestic resource adjustment costs arise. For instance, at the top levels of the ladder the United States and Japan find themselves in direct competition in technologically sophisticated products, but the competitive pressure is tolerable because most of these products create their own markets.

Has this sequential process of economic transformation been disturbed by the ongoing process of global production sharing? The flying geese growth paradigm is based on the conventional (product-based) division of labor among economies. It assumes a competitive relationship among countries in the growth process, rather than a complementary one that permits countries to climb the growth ladder on the basis of their own competitiveness achieved through policy reforms. By contrast global production sharing permits firms to relocate at each stage of the production process to places where production can be conducted at the lowest cost. This process could well disturb the sequential process of economic transformation, permitting firms in countries on the upper rungs of the growth ladder to remain internationally competitive in some segments of the production process (such as in product/component design, production of skill- and technology-intensive components, and various headquarter functions) even when rising incomes and related domestic cost pressures begin to erode their competitiveness in integrated production of the whole product at home. This, in turn, could constrain the growth process of countries on the middle rungs of the ladder, while countries on the lower rungs still benefit from their relative labor cost advantages. In other words, in the face of rapid expansion of fragmentation-based specialization in the world economy, countries at the middle levels are confronted with the increasingly challenging task of finding ways to "tech up" and enter the global knowledge economy, so as to escape from being trapped in standardized manufacturing segments in the manufacturing value chain (and, increasingly, in standardized services) (Garrett 2004).

In sum, the growing complementarity of production processes across countries resulting from global production sharing has implications for latecomers wishing to catch up in the growth process. This is an important subject for further research.

## 13.5 Production Networks and Trade Flows in Global Financial Crisis

A striking feature of the global economy following the onset of the global financial crisis (GFC) in late 2007 was the precipitous drop in global trade at a faster rate than during the Great Depression (Almunia et al. 2010, Krugman 2009). From April 2008 to June 2009 world trade contracted by about 20% which amounted to almost the total contraction in world trade during the first 30 months of the Great Depression (starting in April 1929).[12] Interestingly, the trade contraction experienced by the East Asian countries during this period has been even greater than the contraction in total world trade (Table 13.7).

Krugman (2009) points to the increased vertical integration of global production (the rise of globe production sharing) as a possible explanation for this surprisingly large trade contraction in the present crisis compared to the Great Depression. Vertical integration of production implies that a given degree of contraction in demand for a final (assembled) product has ramifications over trade flows between the many countries involved in the production chain. Also, demand for components is susceptible to rapid stock adjustment by producers compared to final goods. Given that global production sharing is much more important for trade expansion in East Asia, this explanation also seems relevant for East Asia's greater trade contraction compared to overall trade contraction at the global level. However, a number of other factors are also relevant for explaining the larger contraction in trade volume in the current crisis. These include the much larger contraction of trade credit, a greater share of consumer durables in contemporary world trade compared to the 1930s, and the effect of recent advances in communication technology on inventory cycle and just-in-time procurement practices. The current state of data availability does not permit us to systematically delineate the impact of production sharing on trade contraction while appropriately controlling for these other possible factors. Instead, this section puts together some readily available data that have some bearing on this issue in order to set the stage for further analysis.

All major East Asian countries (including China, which was expected by the decoupling enthusiast to cushion the rest of East Asia against a global economic collapse) experienced a precipitous trade contraction from about the last quarter of 2008

## Table 13.7 East Asia: Growth of Total Merchandise Exports and Imports, 2007Q1–2010Q2 (Year-on-year percent change)

| | 2007 q1 | 2007 q2 | 2007 q3 | 2007 q4 | 2008 q1 | 2008 q2 | 2008 q3 | 2008 q4 | 2009 q1 | 2009 q2 | 2009 q3 | 2009 q4 | 2010 q1 | 2010 q2 |
|---|---|---|---|---|---|---|---|---|---|---|---|---|---|---|
| *Exports* | | | | | | | | | | | | | | |
| East Asia (EA) | 14.3 | 13.3 | 11.6 | 17.4 | 19.0 | 20.8 | 18.1 | -7.7 | -24.1 | -25.3 | -20.0 | 6.0 | 32.9 | 35.6 |
| Japan | 9.7 | 6.9 | 9.1 | 14.0 | 20.2 | 18.0 | 13.0 | -9.6 | -41.5 | -35.5 | -25.5 | -6.2 | 53.2 | 44.0 |
| Developing EA | 14.7 | 13.9 | 11.9 | 17.7 | 18.9 | 21.1 | 18.6 | -7.5 | -22.4 | -24.2 | -19.4 | 7.2 | 30.9 | 34.7 |
| Hongk\ Kong | 8.4 | 11.1 | 7.8 | 8.6 | 11.0 | 8.2 | 6.0 | -1.4 | -20.9 | -12.1 | -13.5 | -1.9 | 24.9 | 24.6 |
| China | 27.3 | 27.6 | 26.4 | 25.8 | 24.6 | 22.4 | 19.1 | 17.6 | 3.5 | -22.2 | -18.0 | -16.1 | -2.3 | 35.5 |
| Korea | 16.4 | 14.8 | 11.4 | 19.4 | 19.2 | 22.4 | 20.7 | -14.2 | -32.3 | -27.6 | -22.3 | 8.9 | 37.2 | 35.7 |
| Taiwan | 8.6 | 6.8 | 9.7 | 15.2 | 16.9 | 18.2 | 7.5 | -25.1 | -37.5 | -31.9 | -20.5 | 16.9 | 54.8 | 45.3 |
| ASEAN | 14.5 | 13.1 | 10.6 | 18.1 | 19.5 | 23.3 | 22.1 | -8.6 | -22.8 | -24.7 | -20.0 | 10.7 | 32.4 | 34.3 |
| Indonesia | 22.2 | 19.9 | 8.8 | 13.1 | 21.8 | 18.9 | 22.4 | 1.4 | -22.3 | -14.8 | -11.1 | 17.5 | 38.9 | 27.6 |
| Malaysia | 7.3 | 7.4 | 6.9 | 16.2 | 19.5 | 29.2 | 21.2 | -12.5 | -28.9 | -33.3 | -26.3 | 9.8 | 40.5 | 33.1 |
| Philippines | 9.4 | 4.6 | 2.3 | 9.9 | 2.8 | 5.5 | 4.1 | -22.3 | -36.8 | -28.9 | -21.5 | 6.0 | 42.9 | 33.3 |
| Singapore | 9.9 | 7.4 | 8.6 | 14.7 | 21.4 | 26.0 | 21.4 | -13.4 | -32.7 | -30.6 | -22.5 | 11.5 | 38.1 | 36.5 |
| Thailand | 16.3 | 17.4 | 13.7 | 25.2 | 23.7 | 28.6 | 26.1 | -10.4 | -20.1 | -26.2 | -17.6 | 12.0 | 32.1 | 41.8 |
| Vietnam | 21.9 | 21.9 | 23.1 | 29.3 | 27.8 | 31.8 | 37.6 | 5.7 | 4.2 | -14.7 | -20.9 | 7.2 | 2.0 | 33.7 |
| *Imports* | | | | | | | | | | | | | | |
| East Asia (EA) | 11.1 | 12.5 | 12.8 | 19.8 | 29.7 | 28.2 | 25.3 | -0.6 | -26.9 | -26.4 | -18.6 | 4.2 | 38.6 | 37.7 |
| Japan | 4.0 | 3.5 | 3.4 | 15.6 | 25.6 | 29.1 | 35.2 | 7.4 | -29.1 | -37.3 | -31.6 | -19.2 | 25.9 | 40.4 |
| Developing EA | 11.8 | 13.4 | 13.7 | 20.2 | 30.1 | 28.1 | 24.3 | -1.4 | -26.7 | -25.3 | -17.3 | 6.5 | 39.9 | 37.5 |
| Hong Kong | 8.7 | 12.1 | 8.9 | 11.3 | 12.3 | 9.9 | 7.6 | -3.3 | -21.1 | -14.1 | -9.7 | 3.2 | 32.9 | 31.9 |
| China | 19.1 | 18.0 | 19.6 | 20.3 | 24.0 | 30.6 | 22.4 | 18.7 | 2.4 | -25.2 | -15.8 | -11.1 | 6.4 | 53.3 |
| Korea | 14.0 | 15.2 | 7.0 | 26.1 | 30.0 | 31.2 | 43.2 | -7.8 | -32.6 | -35.7 | -30.8 | 0.6 | 36.6 | 44.3 |
| Taiwan | 2.3 | 7.3 | 9.0 | 13.1 | 25.9 | 18.0 | 19.1 | -22.7 | -47.8 | -37.4 | -28.7 | 18.1 | 78.9 | 54.3 |
| ASEAN | 12.4 | 13.6 | 15.4 | 21.8 | 34.8 | 32.0 | 25.1 | 0.3 | -28.0 | -23.4 | -14.6 | 9.1 | 40.7 | 31.8 |
| Indonesia | 11.6 | 19.2 | 20.6 | 7.4 | 41.2 | 44.1 | 44.7 | 31.9 | -28.8 | -27.0 | -24.3 | -8.3 | 42.8 | 35.9 |
| Malaysia | 12.8 | 9.0 | 8.6 | 18.3 | 15.7 | 17.5 | 14.6 | -15.8 | -36.6 | -31.6 | -22.6 | 12.5 | 45.1 | 44.0 |
| Philippines | -1.1 | 12.0 | 22.4 | 25.2 | 13.8 | 2.9 | -5.3 | -3.0 | 5.0 | 9.3 | 14.4 | 13.9 | 16.4 | 11.3 |
| Singapore | 8.2 | 7.3 | 4.9 | 21.7 | 33.9 | 37.2 | 34.5 | -8.0 | -32.2 | -33.3 | -25.0 | 3.4 | 34.7 | 33.2 |
| Thailand | 5.4 | 6.9 | 7.7 | 16.1 | 35.0 | 30.0 | 39.4 | 5.3 | -38.3 | -33.1 | -28.4 | 1.5 | 63.6 | 44.8 |
| Vietnam | 37.6 | 27.5 | 28.5 | 42.4 | 69.0 | 60.1 | 22.7 | -8.9 | -37.2 | -24.8 | -1.5 | 31.9 | 41.5 | 21.8 |

*Note:* Growth rates calculated using current US$ values.
*Source:* Complied from CEIC Asia database.

(Table 13.4). The remarkably synchronized nature of the trade contraction across countries in the region, both in imports and exports, is generally consistent with the close trade ties among the East Asian countries forged within regional production networks and the unique role of the region within global production networks.[13]

Among the East Asian countries, Japan has been by far the worst hit. A large share of Japan's exports consists of capital goods and high-end durable consumer goods, such as cars and electrical machinery, machine tools and their components. Exports of capital goods and high-end consumer durables are heavily concentrated in the United States and other developed-country markets and are therefore directly exposed to the global economic decline. On the other hand, contrary to the predictions of the decoupling enthusiasts, Japan's growing exports to China have been indirectly affected by declining final (assembled) exports from China (Fukao and Yuan 2009). The degree of export contraction suffered by Taiwan and Korea has been smaller compared to Japan but, on average, notably higher compared to the other East Asian countries. As in the case of Japan, growing exports to China do not seem to have provided a cushion against collapse in world demand for these two countries. The relatively lower degree of export contractions experienced by Korea, Taiwan, and the second-tier exporting countries in the region compared to Japan could possibly reflect consumer preferences for price-competitive low-end products in the crisis context.

An inspection of growth rates of exports of individual East Asian countries by destination provides no support for the view that East Asian economies have become less susceptible to the worldwide trade contraction because of regional growth dynamism.[14] Intra-East Asia trade flows have in general contracted at a faster rate compared to these countries exports to the United States and EU.

A notable pattern in China's foreign trade following the onset of the crisis is the relatively sharper contraction in the category of machinery exports (in which network trade is heavily concentrated) compared to other product categories, in particular traditional labor-intensive products (textile and garments, footwear, and other miscellaneous manufactures). Exports belonging to the machinery category, in particular ICT products and consumer electronics are also predominantly consumer durables which, as already noted, are generally more susceptible to income contraction. In traditional labor-intensive products, developing country producers have the ability to perform better purely on the basis of cost competitiveness, even in a context of depressed demand.

Exports to China from most countries in the region have contracted at a much faster rate compared to their imports from China, perhaps an indication of destocking of components by Chinese firms, given the gloomy outlook for exports. China's imports from Japan, Korea, and Taiwan have shrunk more rapidly (at an average rate of 23.5%) than imports from other countries. This is not surprising, given the dominant role played by the former countries in the supply of components to ICT assembly activities in China, which are heavily exposed to contractions in import demand in the United States and other developed countries. Overall, China's imports from countries in the region intra-regional imports have contracted at a much faster rate compared to her imports from the United States and EU.

**Table 13.8 Growth Manufacturing Imports to the United States, 2008:Q1–2009:Q3 (year-on-year, percent)**

| | 2008 q1 | 2008 q2 | 2008 q3 | 2008 q4 | 2009 q1 | 2009 q2 | 2009 q3 |
|---|---|---|---|---|---|---|---|
| *East Asia (EA)* | | | | | | | |
| Total manufacturing | 2.0 | 4.1 | 4.9 | -6.8 | -22.3 | -24.2 | -22.0 |
| Parts and components | -2.5 | 3.9 | 2.6 | -14.3 | -29.1 | -29.3 | -23.9 |
| Assembly | 6.0 | 8.5 | 4.8 | -13.6 | -30.6 | -25.9 | -21.6 |
| Total network trade[1] | 2.6 | 6.7 | 4.0 | -13.8 | -30.0 | -27.2 | -22.4 |
| *Developing EA* | | | | | | | |
| Total manufacturing | 1.1 | 4.5 | 7.5 | -3.9 | -15.4 | -18.7 | -19.0 |
| Parts and components | -4.3 | 4.6 | 4.2 | -12.8 | -25.2 | -26.1 | -22.2 |
| Assembly | 5.3 | 9.8 | 10.0 | -9.5 | -17.6 | -15.5 | -16.1 |
| Total network trade[1] | 1.4 | 7.8 | 7.9 | -10.6 | -20.5 | -19.4 | -18.3 |
| *Association of Southeast Asian Nations (ASEAN)* | | | | | | | |
| Total manufacturing | 0.4 | 1.8 | -2.3 | -15.2 | -26.5 | -24.1 | -16.2 |
| Parts and components | -6.5 | 4.3 | -2.6 | -21.2 | -32.5 | -31.1 | -15.8 |
| Assembly | 3.0 | 4.8 | -6.3 | -25.1 | -39.6 | -36.5 | -26.5 |
| Total network trade[1] | -2.1 | 4.6 | -4.7 | -23.5 | -36.5 | -34.2 | -22.1 |
| *Japan* | | | | | | | |
| Total manufacturing | 4.6 | 2.9 | -4.1 | -16.6 | -42.3 | -42.5 | -33.5 |
| Parts and components | 1.6 | 2.1 | -1.0 | -17.7 | -37.1 | -37.4 | -28.5 |
| Assembly | 7.5 | 6.0 | -6.7 | -23.2 | -55.0 | -49.6 | -35.2 |
| Total network trade[1] | 5.3 | 4.5 | -4.7 | -21.4 | -49.0 | -45.3 | -33.0 |
| *Republic of Korea* | | | | | | | |
| Total manufacturing | 0.4 | 7.6 | 11.5 | -0.2 | -15.1 | -23.1 | -25.1 |
| Parts and components | -11.3 | 0.2 | 1.9 | -14.4 | -32.1 | -33.3 | -26.2 |
| Assembly | 4.3 | 13.9 | 14.4 | -2.1 | -9.4 | -12.6 | -17.7 |
| Total network trade[1] | -1.2 | 9.3 | 10.0 | -5.9 | -16.5 | -19.0 | -20.4 |
| *Taiwan* | | | | | | | |
| Total manufacturing | 5.8 | 2.8 | 4.1 | -10.3 | -28.5 | -32.3 | -22.9 |
| Parts and components | 11.8 | 12.1 | 3.9 | -16.4 | -30.8 | -33.1 | -21.2 |
| Assembly | 11.0 | 6.4 | 12.5 | -7.5 | -31.4 | -32.0 | -21.5 |
| Total network trade[1] | 11.0 | 9.3 | 7.8 | -12.4 | -31.1 | -32.6 | -21.3 |
| *People's Republic of China (PRC)* | | | | | | | |
| Total manufacturing | 1.3 | 5.3 | 10.1 | -0.6 | -11.2 | -16.0 | -18.4 |

**Table 13.8 Continued**

| | 2008 q1 | 2008 q2 | 2008 q3 | 2008 q4 | 2009 q1 | 2009 q2 | 2009 q3 |
|---|---|---|---|---|---|---|---|
| Parts and components | -1.6 | 5.9 | 7.7 | -8.7 | -20.2 | -22.3 | -23.6 |
| Assembly | 7.0 | 10.9 | 14.9 | -6.1 | -11.7 | -9.3 | -12.8 |
| Total network trade[1] | 3.7 | 9.0 | 12.4 | -7.0 | -14.8 | -14.0 | -16.5 |
| *Mexico* | | | | | | | |
| Total manufacturing | 2.8 | 3.9 | -4.2 | -11.8 | -25.2 | -27.6 | -17.0 |
| Parts and components | -3.6 | -4.3 | -7.6 | -15.1 | -31.0 | -32.7 | -17.7 |
| Assembly | 10.1 | 12.0 | -6.6 | -11.8 | -21.6 | -23.8 | -11.3 |
| Total network trade[1] | 3.3 | 4.1 | -7.1 | -13.2 | -26.0 | -27.8 | -14.1 |
| *World* | | | | | | | |
| Total manufacturing | 2.9 | 4.5 | 3.5 | -9.2 | -25.4 | -29.3 | -25.1 |
| Parts and components | -0.3 | 1.8 | 0.0 | -13.7 | -28.4 | -31.7 | -24.8 |
| Assembly | 4.5 | 7.2 | -0.1 | -16.5 | -31.9 | -30.1 | -22.6 |
| Total network trade[1] | 2.3 | 4.8 | 0.0 | -15.4 | -30.4 | -30.8 | -23.5 |

*Note:* 1. Parts and components plus final assembly.
*Source*: Compiled from US International Trade Commission online database.

Data on the growth of manufacturing imports to the United States are summarized in Table 13.8. A common pattern observable across the 10 source countries covered is that component imports have generally contracted at a faster rate compared with total imports and final goods imports. This pattern is consistent with the view that in the face of contraction in world demand, stock adjustment takes place at a faster rate in intermediate goods compared to final goods. The data also shows that the rate of contraction in final imports from the PRC has been much smaller compared to the dramatic contraction in imports from Japan. This perhaps reflects the fact that under depressed market conditions, consumers tends to substitute low-end products for high-end products.

## 13.6 Concluding Remarks

Global production sharing has become an integral part of the economic landscape of East Asia. Trade within global production networks has been expanding more rapidly than conventional final-goods trade. The degree of dependence on this new form of international specialization is proportionately larger in East Asia (particularly ASEAN) than in North America and Europe. The rapid integration of China into regional production networks is a critically important recent development in the international fragmentation of production. China's imports of components from ASEAN countries and other DEA countries have grown rapidly, in line with the equally rapid expansion of manufacturing exports from China to extra-regional markets, mostly in North America and Europe. The migration of some production processes within vertically integrated high-tech industries to China has opened up opportunities for producing original, equipment-manufactured goods and back-to-office service operations in other countries. In sum, China's emergence as a major trading power and an investment location has not been a zero-sum proposition from the perspective of the region. Rather, it seems to have added further dynamism to East Asia's role within global production networks.

Global production sharing has certainly played a pivotal role in the continued dynamism of East Asia and its increasing intra-regional economic interdependence. This does not, however, mean that the process has contributed to lessening the region's dependence on the global economy. A notable outcome of the rapid expansion of production networks has been the rapid growth of cross-border trade in parts and components within the regions; component share in intra-DAC trade is much higher compared to that of intra-regional trade in NATA and EU15. Driven largely by cross-border component trade, the share of intra-regional non-oil trade in total world trade of DACs increased significantly. However, there is no evidence of rapid intra-regional trade integration in final products. On the contrary, the region's growth based on vertical specialization depends inexorably on its extra-regional trade in final goods, and this dependence has increased over the years. This inference is basically consistent with the behavior of trade flows following the onset of the global financial crisis. The remarkably synchronized nature of trade contraction across countries in the region is generally consistent with close trade ties among East Asian countries forged within regional production networks. In addition, the PRC failed to provide a cushion against this export contraction as postulated by the decoupling thesis.

## NOTES

1. An array of alternative terms have been used to describe this phenomenon, including international production fragmentation, vertical specialization, slicing the value chain, and outsourcing. For a comprehensive survey of the related literature, see Helpman 2011, Chapter 6.
2. A number of recent studies have used imported input content of industrial production, estimated using input-output tables, to measure the growth of global production sharing in world trade at the industry/country level. According to this method, increase in the measured degree of imported-input content of exports between two time points is interpreted as an indicator of the growth of global production sharing (Campa and Goldberg 1997, Dean et al. 2008; Hummels et al. 2001). This approach is not relevant for the present study, which aims to examine the patterns and determinants of production-sharing-driven trade flows.

3. The BEC registry can be found at [http:/www. unstats.un.org/unsd/cr/registry].
4. The list of parts and components is given in the Appendix in Athukorala (2010). Total value of parts and components enumerated for the period 1992-2007 based on this list is on average 52% higher compared to the value based on the incomplete list used in Athukorala (2005).
5. Trade magnitudes throughout the chapter are measured in current U.S. dollars unless otherwise indicated. Inter-temporal comparison calculations are made for the two-year averages relating to the end points of the period under study, so as to reduce the impact of year-to-year fluctuations of trade flows. All data reported, unless otherwise stated, are compiled from the UN Comtrade database.
6. In this and other trade data tables, data are presented as two-year averages to smooth out the impact of yearly fluctuations in trade.
7. All data reported in this chapter, unless otherwise stated, have been compiled from the UN Comtrade database.
8. It is important to note that as an indicator of export quality unity values have a built-in measurement error whose extent is not known (Helpman 2011, p. 170).
9. See for example Drysdale and Garnaut 1997; Frankel and Wei 1997; and Park and Shin 2009.
10. See Yoshitomi (2007) and Park and Shin (2009) and the works cited therein.
11. See Petri (1993), Pearson (1994), and the works cited therein.
12. Numbers derived from Figure 5 in Almunia et al. (2010).
13. Discussion on export performance of individual countries in this section is based on monthly exports data extracted from the CEIC database (not reported here for want of space).
14. This inference is based on monthly exports data extracted from the CIEM database (not reported here for brevity).

## References


Akamatsu, K. (1961) "A Theory of Unbalanced Growth in the World Economy," *Weltwirtschaftliches Archiv*, 86: 196–217.

Almunia, Miguel, Austin Benetrix, Barry Eichengreen, Kevin H. O'Rourke, and Gisela Rua. 2010. "From Great Depression to Great Credit Crisis: Similarities, Differences and Lessons." *Economic Policy* April 2010: 219–265.

Ando, Mitsuyo, and Fukunari Kimura (2010), "The Special Patterns of Production and Distribution Networks in East Asia," in P. Athukorala (ed), *The Rise of Asia: Trade and Investment in Global Perspective*, London: Routledge, 61–88.

Athukorala, Prema-chandra. 2005. "Product Fragmentation and Trade Patterns in East Asia." *Asian Economic Papers* 4(3): 1–27.

Athukorala, Prema-chandra. 2008. "Singapore and ASEAN in the New Regional Division of Labour." *Singapore Economic Review* 53(3): 479–508.

Athukorala, Prema-chandra (2009), "The Rise of China and East Asian Export Performance: Is the Crowding-out Fear Warranted?." *World Economy*, 32 (2), 234–266.

Athukorala, Prema-chandra (2010), "Production Networks and Trade Patterns in East Asia: Regionalization or Globalization?" ADB Working Paper Series on Regional Economic Integration No. 56. Manila: Asian Development Bank.

Athukorala, Prema-chandra, and Nobuaki Yamashita (2006) "Production Fragmentation and Trade integration: East Asia in a Global Context," *North American Journal of Economics and Finance*, 17(4): 233–256.

Balassa, Bela (1979), "Changing Patterns of Comparative Advantage in Manufactured Goods," *Review of Economics and Statistics*, 61(2): 259–266.

Campa, Jose, and Linda S. Goldberg (1997), "The Evolution External Orientation of Manufacturing Industries: Evidence from Four Countries," *Federal Reserve Bank of New York Economic Policy Review*, 4: 79–99.

Dean, Judith, K.C. Fung, and Zhi Wang (2008), "Measuring the Vertical Specialization in Chinese Trade," *USITC Working Paper*. Washington, DC: U.S. International Trade Commission.

Drysdale, Peter and, Ross Garnaut (1997) "The Pacific: an application of a general theory of economic integration," pp. 183–224 in C.F. Bergsten and M. Noland (eds), *Pacific Dynamism and the International Economic System*, Washington DC: Institute for International Economics, 183–224.

Eichengreen, Barry., Rhee, Y., and Tong, H. (2007), "China and the Exports of Other Asian Countries," *Review of World Economics*, 143(2): 201–226.

Feenstra, Robert C., W. Hai, Wing Thye Woo, and S. Uao (1999), "Discrepancies in International Trade Data: An Application to China–Hong Kong Entrepôt Trade," *American Economic Review*, 89(2): 338–343.

Fukao, Kyoji and Tangjun Yuan (2009), "Why is Japan so heavily affected by the global economic crisis?," www.voxeu.org, 8 June.

Garrett, Geoffrey (2004) "Globalization's Missing Middle," *Foreign Affairs*, 83(6): 1–6.

Gorg, Holger (2000), "Fragmentation and Trade: U.S. Inward Processing Trade in the EU," *Weltwirtschaftliches Archive*, 136 (3):403–422.

Greenaway, D., A. Mahabir, and C. Milner C.(2008) "Has China Displaced other Asian Countries' Exports?," *China Economic Review*, 19(2): 152–169.

Hallak, Juan Carlos, and Peter K. Schott (2010), "Estimating Cross-Country Differences in Product Quality," *Quarterly Journal of Economics*, 94: 1108–1129.

Helleiner, Gerand K. 1973. Manufactured Exports from Less-Developed Countries and Multinational Firms. *Economic Journal*, 83(329): 21–47.

Helpman, Elhanan (2011), *Understanding Global Trade*, Cambridge, Mass: Belknap Press of Harvard University Press.

Hummels, David, Jun Ishii, and Kei-Mu Yi. 2001. The Nature and Growth of Vertical Specialization in World Trade. *Journal of International Economics*, 54(1): 75–96.

Kojima, Kiyoshi (2000) "The 'flying geese' Model of Asian Economic Development: Origin, Theoretical Extensions, and Regional Policy Implications," *Journal of Asian Economics*, 11(4): 375–401.

Krugman, Paul R. 2008. Trade and Wages, Reconsidered. *Brookings Papers on Economic Activity 1: Macroeconomics*, pp. 103–138.

Krugman, Paul. 2009. The Return of Depression Economics. Linoel Robbins Lectures (presentation and the summary by Geoff Riley and Paul Krugman at the London School of Economics) (http://cep.lse.ac.uk/_new/events/special_post.asp).

Ng, Francis, and Alexander Yeats. 2003. "Major Trade Trends in East Asia: What Are Their Implications for Regional Cooperation and Growth?" *Policy Research Working Paper 3084*. Washington DC: World Bank.

Park, Yung Chul, and Kwanho Shin. 2009. "Economic Integration and Changes in the Business Cycle in East Asia: Is the Region Decoupling from the Rest of the World?" *Asian Economic Papers*, 8(1). 107–140.

Pearson, Charles S. (1994) "The Asian export ladder," pp. 35–52 in Shu-Chin Yang (ed.), *Manufactured Exports of Asian Industrializing Economies: Possible Regional Cooperation*, New York: M.E. Sharpe.

Petri, Peter (1993). "The East Asian Trading Bloc: An Analytical History," pp. 21–48 in J.A. Frankel and M. Kahler (eds), *Regionalism and Rivalry: Japan and the United States in Pacific Asia*, Chicago: Chicago University Press.

Rodrik, Darny (2006) "What's So Special about China's Exports?," National Bureau of Economic Research (NBER) Working Paper 11947, Cambridge MA: NBER.

Schott, P. K. (2007), "The Relative Sophistication of Chinese Exports," *Economic Policy*, 23(53), 5–49.

Sharpton, Michael. 1975. "International Subcontracting." *Oxford Economic Papers* 27(1): 94–135.

USITC (United States International Trade Commission) (1999) *Production Sharing: Use of U.S. Components and Material in Foreign Assembly Operations, 1995–1998*, Washington DC: USITC Publication 3265.

Wong, Hpo Kam. 2007. "The Remaking of Singapore's High-Tech Enterprise System" in Henry S. Rowen, Marguerite G. Hancock, and Lilliam F. Miller (eds.) *Making IT: The Rise of Asian in High Tech.* Stanford: Stanford University Press. pp. 123–174.

Yeats, Alexander (2001), "Just How Big is Global Production Sharing?," in Seven Arndt and Henryk Kierzkowski (eds), *Fragmentation: New Production Patterns in the World Economy*, New York: Oxford University Press, pp. 108–143.

Yoshitomi, Masaru. 2007. "Global Imbalances and East Asian Monetary Cooperation," in Duck-Koo Chung and Barry Eichengreen (eds.), *Towards and East Asian Exchange Rate Regime*, Washington DC: Brookings Institutions Press, 22–48.

Yusuf, Shahid, Kaoru Nabeshima, and Dwight Perkins (2007), "China and India Reshape Global Industrial Geography," Chapter 3 in Alan L. Winters and Shahid Yusuf (2007), *Dancing with Giants: China, India, and Global Economy*, Washington DC: World Bank.

CHAPTER 14

# FOREIGN TRADE OF THE PACIFIC-RIM ECONOMIES

KAR-YIU WONG

## 14.1 Introduction

THIS chapter examines the trade experience and performance of Pacific-Rim (PR) economies and also the trade relations among themselves and with other economies. The analysis in this chapter will help us understand better how foreign trade is at work, how these economies are dependent on and affected by foreign trade, and how they are inter-dependent through trade activities.

There are many economies on both sides of the Pacific Ocean. It is not possible to have an in-depth examination of foreign trade of each of these economies. Moreover, many of them are small, and many of them have similar economic structures. There is therefore no need to look at every of these economies in detail. Instead, we will focus on a subset of them in order to get a good picture and understanding of foreign trade in these economies. In most parts of this chapter, we will focus on the members of Asia-Pacific Economic Cooperation (APEC). The list of these countries is given in the appendix. There are 21 members, all located on the rims of the Pacific Ocean.[1]

The 21 APEC members are far from being homogeneous. They differ very much in terms of culture, language, population, area, policy, national income, and the amounts of resources. However, the APEC economies are significant players in the world markets. They include the three biggest economies in the world: the United States, China, and Japan. Every year, they are responsible for more than half of the products and services the world produces. (See Table 14.1.) For example, in 1990, the sum of the real gross domestic products (at constant 2000 prices) of these economies was about US$14.5 trillion, which was around 58.8 percent of the world's GDP, the latter being US$24.6 trillion. The ratio of the APEC output to the world's output increased steadily though slowly in the past: In 2011, the real GDP of the APEC members rose to US$25.8 trillion, while the world's real GDP increased to US$43.1 trillion. The APEC GDP rose at a rate of 2.79 percent per year, which is slightly higher than that of the world, 2.70 percent. With a slightly

**Table 14.1 APEC Members Compared with the World, 1990–2011**

| | APEC | | | World | | |
|---|---|---|---|---|---|---|
| | GDP, US$tn | PC GDP, US$ | Trade-GDP, % | GDP, US$tn | PC GDP, US$ | Trade-GDP, % |
| 1990 | $14.5 | $6,329 | 24.9 | $24.6 | $4,628 | 33.7 |
| 1991 | $14.7 | $6,345 | 25.1 | $25.0 | $4,628 | 34.1 |
| 1992 | $15.1 | $6,440 | 26.0 | $25.6 | $4,659 | 34.9 |
| 1993 | $15.5 | $6,523 | 27.0 | $26.0 | $4,671 | 35.4 |
| 1994 | $16.0 | $6,681 | 29.1 | $26.9 | $4,756 | 37.5 |
| 1995 | $16.5 | $6,796 | 31.4 | $27.7 | $4,822 | 40.0 |
| 1996 | $17.1 | $6,978 | 32.7 | $28.6 | $4,914 | 41.3 |
| 1997 | $17.8 | $7,174 | 34.6 | $29.7 | $5,028 | 44.0 |
| 1998 | $18.1 | $7,220 | 34.5 | $30.3 | $5,068 | 45.0 |
| 1999 | $18.8 | $7,427 | 35.7 | $31.3 | $5,169 | 46.1 |
| 2000 | $19.6 | $7,683 | 39.1 | $32.7 | $5,318 | 50.0 |
| 2001 | $19.9 | $7,722 | 37.6 | $33.2 | $5,335 | 49.2 |
| 2002 | $20.3 | $7,837 | 38.7 | $33.8 | $5,375 | 50.1 |
| 2003 | $21.0 | $8,014 | 40.7 | $34.8 | $5,456 | 51.6 |
| 2004 | $21.8 | $8,279 | 44.7 | $36.2 | $5,609 | 55.3 |
| 2005 | $22.6 | $8,518 | 46.9 | $37.4 | $5,737 | 57.7 |
| 2006 | $23.4 | $8,774 | 49.5 | $38.9 | $5,897 | 60.8 |
| 2007 | $24.3 | $9,034 | 51.8 | $40.5 | $6,058 | 62.9 |
| 2008 | $24.6 | $9,076 | 52.9 | $41.0 | $6,069 | 63.9 |
| 2009 | $24.0 | $8,807 | 48.1 | $40.1 | $5,862 | 58.1 |
| 2010 | $25.2 | $9,176 | 53.8 | $41.9 | $6,054 | 63.5 |
| 2011 | $25.8 | $9,354 | na | $43.1 | $6,153 | na |

*Notes:* 1. PC GDP = per capita GDP; trade-GDP = (export+import)/GDP; na = not available.
2. GDP, PC GDP, and trade data are at 2000 constant US$.
3. The World and APEC figures include the corresponding data of Chinese Taipei.
*Source:* World Bank, World Development Indicators Databank
Accounting and Statistics, Executive Yuan, R.O.C.

higher rate, the ratio of the APEC's GDP to the world's GDP climbed to 60.0 percent in 2011.[2]

Many of the APEC members are rich, including developed countries such as the United States, Canada, Japan, and Australia. In 1990, the average real per capita GDP of the world was US$4628, but that of the APEC economies was US$6329, which was more than 36 percent higher. Over the following 21 years, the world's real per capita grew at an annual rate of 1.37 percent, reaching US$6153 in 2011. Over the same period of time, the real per capita GDP of the APEC members as a whole rose at an annual rate of 1.88 percent to US$9354 in 2011, which was more than 50 percent higher than that of the world.

This chapter will first examine the trade performance of the APEC member economies, including their trade volumes, their trade dependence, and the relation between trade and growth. It will then investigate how the APEC economies are interdependent. Intra-industrial trade of these economies will then be examined. In order to have a better understanding of the nature and features of trade in this region, we will look in more detail into the trade relations among China, Japan, and South Korea. These three economies are geographically very close to each other. The last section concludes.

## 14.2 Trade Performance

This section discusses the trade performance of the APEC economies. We will first examine their importance in the world markets, and then will see how they themselves depend on trade.

Table 14.2 shows the top 10 trading economies in the world. We use three criteria to rank the economies: their volumes of export, their volumes of import, and their total trade volumes (export plus import). The APEC economies are highlighted.

In 2010, on the top of the lists are the United States, China, and Germany. This ranking is the same in terms of either criterion: export volume, import volume, or total volume. The United States alone is responsible for more than 10 percent of the export, import, or total volume of the world. China is close, and with the rapid rise in the Chinese economy, it is quite possible that in the near future China will reach this 10 percent mark on both the export and the import sides. Germany also trades a lot with the rest of the world.

Japan and the United Kingdom were the distant fourth and fifth. Other economies that made it to the 2010 lists of top ten exporters and importers are France, Hong Kong, South Korea, and Singapore. Table 14.2 shows clearly how trade-oriented the APEC member economies are. In terms of the export volumes, seven of the top ten economies in 2010 were APEC members, or in terms of import or total volumes, six of the top ten economies were APEC members. The first two largest trading economies, the United States and China, are also the two largest economies in the world. The table also shows that all APEC economies contributed to slightly more than half of the export, import, and total volumes in the world.

To further investigate the trade performance of the APEC members, we determine the ratio of the trade volume of each of them to its GDP. This trade-GDP ratio of an economy is often used in the literature as an index to show the degree of openness of the economy. Strictly speaking, the trade volume of an economy depends on not only the size of the economy but also other factors such as technologies and preferences. A more reasonable interpretation of the trade-GDP ratio is how dependent on trade the economy is.

**Table 14.2 Top 10 Trading Economies, 2010**

| | Export | Import | Total |
|---|---|---|---|
| 1 | *United States (14.4%) | *United States (11.3%) | *United States (12.8%) |
| 2 | *China (8.3%) | *China (10.8%) | *China (9.6%) |
| 3 | Germany (7.2%) | Germany (7.7) | Germany (7.5%) |
| 4 | United Kingdom (4.4%) | *Japan (5.7%) | *Japan (4.9%) |
| 5 | *Japan (4.1%) | United Kingdom (3.9%) | United Kingdom (4.2%) |
| 6 | France (3.7) | *Korea, Rep. (3.7%) | *Hong Kong (3.4%) |
| 7 | *Hong Kong (3.4) | *Hong Kong (3.5%) | France (3.4%) |
| 8 | *Korea, Rep. (3.0%) | France (3.2%) | *Korea, Rep. (3.3%) |
| 9 | *Canada (2.9%) | *Singapore (3.0%) | *Singapore (2.8%) |
| 10 | *Singapore (2.7%) | Netherlands (2.8%) | Netherlands (2.7%) |
| | APEC (50.3%) | APEC (51.5%) | APEC (50.9%) |

*Notes:* 1. Economies with an asterisk are APEC member economies.
2. The number in parentheses after an economy's name represents the economy's world share.
3. The shares of all APEC economies are given at the bottom of the table.
*Source*: World Bank, World Development Indicators Databank.

Table 14.1 presents the ratio of trade volume to the GDP of the APEC members as a whole and that of the world. In 1990, the trade-GDP ratio of the APEC economies was 24.9 percent, while that for the world was 33.7 percent. Over the next 20 years, the trade dependence ratio of the APEC members rose steadily. In 2010, the trade dependence ratio of the APEC members was 53.8 percent, which can be compared with that of the world, or 63.5 percent. On the whole, the APEC economies have a trade-GDP ratio smaller than the world's average.

To interpret the numbers in Table 14.1, we can note that generally a large economy tends to have a smaller trade dependence ratio. The APEC group contains the three largest economies in the world. In general, large open economies will experience smaller price changes, and thus will not generate large trade volumes. This means that the trade-GDP ratio will tend to be smaller.

To see the last point more clearly, let us consider Table 14.3, which presents the trade dependence ratios of the APEC members. The ratios vary quite a lot. In 1990, Australia, China, Japan, Mexico, Peru, and the United States had trade dependence ratios less than 30 percent, while the corresponding ratios for Hong Kong, Malaysia, and Singapore were greater than 100 percent. Over time, all these economies got more and more trade dependent. However, in 2010, the overall ratio for these economies was still well below the average of the world.

A closer examination of Table 14.3 reveals more features of the trade dependence of the APEC economies. The United States and Japan are large economies, but they do not

**Table 14.3 Trade Dependence of APEC Members, 1990–2010 (in percent)**

| APEC members | 1990 | 1995 | 2000 | 2005 | 2010 |
|---|---|---|---|---|---|
| Australia | 28.1 | 34.6 | 40.7 | 44.6 | 49.9 |
| Brunei Darussalam | 95.2 | 116.8 | 103.2 | 102.4 | 94.9 |
| Canada | 54.8 | 70.2 | 85.4 | 82.1 | 77.1 |
| Chile | 44.3 | 53.4 | 61.3 | 75.4 | 83.4 |
| China | 25.3 | 31.5 | 44.2 | 74.6 | 78.6 |
| Hong Kong SAR, China | 172.9 | 256.8 | 282.1 | 344.6 | 365.4 |
| Indonesia | 60.7 | 74.5 | 71.4 | 81.9 | 82.2 |
| Japan | 15.1 | 16.6 | 20.3 | 24.2 | 25.8 |
| Korea, Rep. | 39.4 | 53.9 | 74.3 | 91.2 | 110.3 |
| Malaysia | 141.9 | 202.1 | 220.4 | 229.3 | 210.4 |
| Mexico | 25.6 | 38.7 | 63.9 | 70.0 | 81.2 |
| New Zealand | 53.7 | 62.3 | 68.4 | 74.3 | 76.5 |
| Papua New Guinea | 99.7 | 102.8 | 115.4 | na | na |
| Peru | 23.3 | 32.3 | 34.2 | 40.8 | 40.4 |
| Philippines | 66.8 | 95.2 | 104.7 | 102.8 | 101.2 |
| Russian Federation | 79.3 | 65.5 | 68.1 | 91.4 | 102.7 |
| Singapore | 260.5 | 340.1 | 371.8 | 453.6 | 456.2 |
| Chinese Taipei | 78.8 | 85.8 | 103.7 | 112.2 | 118.9 |
| Thailand | 86.1 | 109.9 | 124.9 | 133.6 | 132.6 |
| United States | 16.4 | 20.3 | 25.9 | 27.2 | 29.5 |
| Vietnam | 42.2 | 69.1 | 112.5 | 180.2 | 185.4 |

*Notes:* trade dependence = (export+import)/GDP; na = not available.
*Source:* World Bank, World Development Indicators Databank
Accounting and Statistics, Executive Yuan, R.O.C.

have very large trade volumes as compared with their GDPs. For example, the United States had a trade dependence ratio of 16.4 percent in 1990, and this ratio rose to a mere 29.5 percent in 2010. Japan had even smaller ratios within this period: 15.1 percent in 1990, rising to 25.8 percent in 2010. China, which has the second largest economy right now, depends more on trade as compared with the United States and Japan: Its trade dependence ratio increased sharply from 25.3 percent in 1990 to 78.6 percent in 2010. On the other hand, smaller economies tend to have larger trade-GDP ratios. Among the APEC economies, Singapore, Hong Kong, Malaysia, Viet Nam, Thailand, Chinese Taipei, South Korea, Russia, and the Philippines all had their ratios greater than 100 percent in 2010.

The APEC experience suggests a negative relation between the size of an economy and the economy's trade dependence. This relation, however, is not valid for all economies. China seems to be an obvious exception. Its economy grew rapidly in the past four decades, and is now the second-largest economy in the world. At the same time, China's trade-GDP ratio also grew substantially from 25.3 percent in 1990 to 78.6 percent in 2010. The China case shows that a large economy can be very much dependent on trade.

## 14.3 Trade and Growth

The previous section provides a discussion of the degrees of openness and trade dependence of the APEC economies. In this section, we will focus on the growth experience of these economies, especially the relation between growth and foreign trade of these economies.

Table 14.4 presents the growth rates of the GDPs (at constant 2000 prices) and foreign trade (export plus import, at constant 2000 prices) of various APEC economies in the period from 1991 to 2010.[3] The figures shown are their compounded annual growth rates. The rates for the APEC economies as a whole and those of the world are also shown for comparison.

These economies vary a lot in terms of the growth rates of their economies and the growth rates of their foreign trade. Some economies showed very impressive growth rates. For example, China, Viet Nam, Singapore, and Malaysia experienced growth rates of their economies higher than 5 percent. These economies also had their foreign trade volumes growing substantially in the same period. China was well ahead of other economies in terms of growth and trade, as it is the only economy among the APEC members that had double-digit growth rates of its economy and foreign trade.[4]

Among these economies, there were some of them that expanded fairly mildly in this period. Examples are Japan, Brunei Darussalam, and Russia: All had growth rates of their economies less than 2 percent, and these growth rates were well below the world's average, or the average for all the APEC economies. These three economies also experienced very slow growth rates of foreign trade.

Table 14.4 suggests a high correlation between the growth rates of economies and the growth rates of foreign trade. To examine this relation more rigorously, we ran a simple (OLS) regression of the following equation for the APEC economies:

$$g^{GDP} = \underset{(0.5655)}{0.2420} + \underset{(0.0685)}{0.5315}\, g^{FT}$$

**Table 14.4 Growth of GDP and Trade of APEC Economies, 1991–2010 (in percent)**

| Economy | Growth, GDP | Growth, trade |
|---|---|---|
| Australia | 3.41 | 6.45 |
| Brunei Darussalam | 1.73 | 1.33 |
| Canada | 2.64 | 4.27 |
| Chile | 4.98 | 8.43 |
| China | 10.52 | 17.13 |
| Hong Kong, China | 3.89 | 7.53 |
| Indonesia | 4.51 | 5.78 |
| Japan | 0.81 | 3.74 |
| Korea, Rep. | 4.89 | 10.42 |
| Malaysia | 5.66 | 7.35 |
| Mexico | 2.53 | 8.64 |
| New Zealand | 2.83 | 4.51 |
| Peru | 4.96 | 7.52 |
| Philippines | 4.04 | 6.17 |
| Russian Federation | 0.66 | 4.44 |
| Singapore | 6.37 | 9.48 |
| Chinese Taipei | 4.59 | 6.49 |
| Thailand | 4.18 | 6.30 |
| United States | 2.63 | 5.68 |
| Vietnam | 7.50 | 16.02 |
| APEC | 2.89 | 7.10 |
| World | 2.74 | 6.17 |

*Notes:* (a) Papua New Guinea, an APEC member, was not included in the table because of incomplete data.
(b) The growth rates are annual growth rates over the period from 1991 to 2010.
*Sources:* World Bank, World Development Indicators Databank
Accounting and Statistics, Executive Yuan, R.O.C.

$R^2 = 0.7698$, where $g^{GDP}$ is the growth rate of the real GDP and $g^{FT}$ is that of foreign trade.[5] This equation suggests a strong dependence of the growth rate of the GDP of an economy on its foreign trade. For example, for a typical APEC economy, a rise in one percent of the growth of its foreign trade leads to a growth of its GDP by 0.53 percent. This supports the usual argument that "Trade is the engine of growth."[6]

The same equation was also run for all the economies in the world. The result is

| | | | | | |
|---|---|---|---|---|---|
| $g^{GDP}$ | = | 1.6232 | + | 0.3147 | $g^{FT}$ |
| | | (0.2962) | | (0.0443) | |

$R^2 = 0.3289$. The implication of the growth of foreign trade on growth of an economy is less obvious for all the economies in the world as a whole, both in terms of the value of the coefficient of $g^{FT}$ and the value of $R^2$, although the estimated coefficient of $g^{FT}$ is still significant and positive.

## 14.4 Trade Interdependence

We now examine the directions of trade flows of these APEC economies. The analysis will give us good ideas of how these economies are interdependent and how they are dependent on the rest of the world. Because we want to get a closer and deeper investigation of the issue and because of the number of economies involved, we limit the study to the following major economies:

- the United States;
- China;
- Japan;
- Australia;
- Mexico;
- Chile.

The choice of these economies is based on the following criteria: the sizes and geographical locations of these economies. We first include the three biggest economies in the world: the United States, China, and Japan. We then consider one economy located in North America and two economies in Asia. We also take the biggest economy in South America, the biggest one in Central America, and Australia.

We first look at the major trading partners of these economies. Table 14.5 lists the five biggest destinations for the exports, and five biggest sources of imports of each of the Pacific-Rim economies in 2011. For the United States, Canada and Mexico are the top two markets for its goods, thanks to the North American Free Trade Agreement (NAFTA). These two markets accounted for more than 30 percent of the exports of the United States. China came in as a distant third, purchasing 7 percent of the United States' exports. Japan and the United Kingdom are the fourth and the fifth markets for the United States products. On the import side of the United States, in 2011, China was

**Table 14.5. Important Trading Partners of Selected PR Economies, 2011**

| Export | Import |
|---|---|
| (A) United States | |
| 1. Canada (19.0%) | 1. China (18.4%) |
| 2. Mexico (13.4%) | 2. Canada (14.1%) |
| 3. China (7.0%) | 3. Mexico (11.7%) |
| 4. Japan (4.5%) | 4. Japan (5.9%) |
| 5. United Kingdom (3.8%) | 5. Germany (4.4%) |
| (B) China | |
| 1. United States (17.1%) | 1. Japan (11.2%) |
| 2. Hong Kong (14.1%) | 2. Rep. of Korea (9.3%) |
| 3. Japan (7.8%) | 3. United States (7.1%) |
| 4. Rep. of Korea (4.4%) | 4. Germany (5.3%) |
| 5. Germany (4.0%) | 5. Australia (4.7%) |
| (C) Japan | |
| 1. China (19.7%) | 1. China (21.5%) |
| 2. United States (15.5%) | 2. United States (8.9%) |
| 3. Rep. of Korea (8.0%) | 3. Australia (6.6%) |
| 4. Hong Kong (5.2%) | 4. Saudi Arabia (5.9%) |
| 5. Thailand (4.6%) | 5. United Arab Emirates (5.0%) |
| (D) Australia | |
| 1. China (27.5%) | 1. China (18.5%) |
| 2. Japan (19.2%) | 2. United States (11.4%) |
| 3. Rep. of Korea (8.9%) | 3. Japan (7.9%) |
| 4. India (5.9%) | 4. Singapore (6.2%) |
| 5. United States (3.7%) | 5. Germany (4.7%) |
| (E) Mexico | |
| 1. United States (78.7%) | 1. United States (49.8%) |
| 2. Canada (3.1%) | 2. China (14.9%) |
| 3. China (1.7%) | 3. Japan (4.7%) |
| 4. Colombia (1.6%) | 4. Rep. of Korea (3.9%) |
| 5. Spain (1.4%) | 5. Germany (3.7%) |
| (F) Chile | |
| 1. China (22.8%) | 1. United States (20.2%) |
| 2. United States (11.2%) | 2. China (16.9%) |
| 3. Japan (11.1%) | 3. Brazil (8.3%) |
| 4. Brazil (5.5%) | 4. Argentina (6.3%) |
| 5. Rep. of Korea (5.5%) | 5. Germany (4.2%) |

*Source*: World Bank, World Development Indicators Databank.

without doubt the most important supplier of goods, while Canada and Mexico were the second and third sources of imported goods. These three suppliers were responsible for nearly half of what the United States imported in that year. Japan and Germany were the fourth and fifth suppliers.

China, with its rapid growth in the past decades, has now the second biggest economy in the world and is one of the major buyers and suppliers in the world markets. Table 14.5 shows that the United States has been consistently the most important market for the Chinese products. Hong Kong, a special administrative region of China, imported around 14 percent of China's exports, and a large fraction of these products was reexported to other places. Japan, South Korea, and Germany were also important destinations for the Chinese products. On the import side, Japan and South Korea were the two largest sources of China's imports. On the whole, we can see that China, Japan, and South Korea are close to each other not only in a geographical sense, but also in terms of foreign trade relations.[7] The United States, Germany, and Australia were also important suppliers in terms of China's imports.

Japan, the second largest economy in Asia, trades a lot with many countries in the world. In the past, the United States was its biggest trading partner, but the United States position has been taken over by China. Currently, Japan exports more goods to China than to the United States, and also imports more goods from China than from the United States. For example, in 2011, 21.5 percent of its imports came from China, while nearly 20 percent of its exports went to China.[8] The United States is now the number two trading partner of Japan. South Korea, Hong Kong, and Thailand are also major markets for the products from Japan. On the import side, Australia, Saudi Arabia, and United Arab Emirates are three major suppliers of what Japan imports. Saudi Arabia and United Arab Emirates are major suppliers of petroleum for Japan.

Australia is geographically far away from many other economies, but foreign trade is an important economic activity. China is clearly its most important trading partner right now, on both the export and the import sides. In 2011, more than 27 percent of Australia's products went to China, while 18.5 percent of Australia's imports came from China. Japan is also an important trading partner of Australia, being the second biggest market for Australia's products and the third biggest source of Australia's imports. The United States' role is less important in terms of the foreign trade of Australia. One interesting phenomenon is that New Zealand, despite its close proximity, is not a major trading partner of Australia, being only the sixth largest market and the eighth biggest supplier.

Mexico depends heavily on the United States, both on the export and import sides. In fact, its foreign trade is very highly concentrated on its relation with the United States. In 2011, nearly 80 percent of Mexico's exports went to the United States while about half of Mexico's imports came from the United States. There are many reasons for such heavy trade dependence. First, Mexico has a long border with the United States. So trade is relatively easy and inexpensive for both economies. Second, Mexico has many immigrants in the United States, and they like to consume Mexican goods imported directly from

Mexico. Third, the other countries bordering Mexico in the south, Guatemala and Belize, are much less developed in income and technology and are much smaller, as compared with the United States.[9] Mexico does not trade much with these economies. Fourth, the North American Free Trade Agreement (NAFTA) allows Mexican goods to enter the United States without duties and vice versa. This largely encourages trade between the two countries.[10] Fifth, the NAFTA allows not only free trade in goods, but also free movement of capital among the three countries. Because of the low labor costs in Mexico, many firms in the United States have been attracted to invest there. Many of these firms import intermediate products from the United States, and export finished products to the United States. This process leads to large trade volumes between the countries.

Perhaps one feature worth noting is that China has become a very important trading partner of Mexico, even though China is so far away.

Chile, an important APEC economy in South America, trades heavily with foreign economies. It is not surprising to see that it has large trade volumes with neighboring economies such as Brazil and Argentina. Historically, the United States was the major trading partner of Chile, but with the rise of China and the economic troubles in the US economy, China has recently become the biggest market for Chile's products. In fact, Chile's export to China in 2011 was more than double that to the United States.

To discuss the trade relations of these APEC economies further, we present in Table 14.6 the trade volumes among themselves and with economies in other regions in 2011. Panel (A) of the table shows the distribution of the export destinations of each of the six economies. For example, 0.19 percent of Australia's export went to Chile, or 51.06 percent were shipped to the other five economies, or 76.16 percent to other APEC economies, while the rest went to non-APEC economies.[11]

Table 14.6 shows that in 2011 the distributions of the export destinations of the six economies vary a lot. For China and the United States, only less than 30 percent of their exports went to the other five economies, or less than 60 percent to other APEC economies. Mexico, on the contrary, sent more than 80 percent of its exports to the other five economies, mainly because of its heavy reliance on the United States as a foreign market, as explained earlier. As a result, 86.38 percent of its exports were sold to other APEC members. It is true that on the whole, most of the APEC economies depended on other APEC members as a market.

Panel (B) of the same table shows the sources of the products these six economies purchased in 2011. For example, 0.41 percent of Australia's imports came from Chile, 39.1 percent from the other five economies, or 67.29 percent from other APEC economies. The interesting feature is that except for Mexico, the other five economies depended not so much on other APEC economies. For example, most of these economies have around 60 percent of their imports coming from other APEC members, except for Mexico, which had a figure of 81.59 percent, or Japan, with a figure of only 23.8 percent. The Mexico case can be explained in terms of its geographical proximity to the United States and the existence of the NAFTA. The case of Japan is also interesting, as it is due to the fact that Japan imported a lot of raw materials, including petroleum, from non-APEC countries.

**Table 14.6 Trade among Selected PR Economies, 2011**

| | Australia | Chile | China | Japan | Mexico | US |
|---|---|---|---|---|---|---|
| *(A) Export* | | | | | | |
| Australia | | 1.14 | 1.79 | 2.16 | 0.26 | 1.86 |
| Chile | 0.19 | | 0.57 | 0.28 | 0.59 | 1.07 |
| China | 27.52 | 22.85 | | 19.68 | 1.71 | 7.02 |
| Japan | 19.22 | 11.07 | 7.81 | | 0.65 | 4.47 |
| Mexico | 0.45 | 2.24 | 1.26 | 1.24 | | 13.35 |
| US | 3.68 | 11.16 | 17.12 | 15.51 | 78.67 | |
| region | 51.06 | 48.46 | 28.55 | 38.88 | 81.87 | 27.77 |
| APEC | 76.16 | 60.49 | 59.44 | 66.58 | 86.38 | 58.68 |
| ROW | 23.84 | 39.51 | 40.56 | 33.42 | 13.62 | 41.32 |
| world | 100.00 | 100.00 | 100.00 | 100.00 | 100.00 | 100.00 |
| *(B) Import* | | | | | | |
| Australia | | 0.70 | 4.74 | 6.61 | 0.28 | 0.46 |
| Chile | 0.41 | | 1.18 | 1.17 | 0.60 | 0.43 |
| China | 18.55 | 16.95 | | 21.51 | 14.89 | 18.44 |
| Japan | 7.91 | 3.95 | 11.16 | | 4.70 | 5.85 |
| Mexico | 0.78 | 3.37 | 0.54 | 0.47 | | 11.73 |
| US | 11.44 | 20.16 | 7.06 | 8.91 | 49.85 | |
| region | 39.10 | 45.13 | 31.72 | 38.66 | 70.32 | 36.91 |
| APEC | 67.29 | 54.63 | 57.23 | 23.80 | 81.59 | 61.10 |
| ROW | 32.71 | 45.37 | 42.77 | 76.20 | 18.41 | 38.90 |
| world | 100.00 | 100.00 | 100.00 | 100.00 | 100.00 | 100.00 |

*Note:* region = Australia, Chile, China, Japan, Mexico, and the United States.
Chinese Taipei was not included in the calculation.
*Source*: United Nations, Comtrade Databank.

## 14.5 Trade Patterns

In this section, we examine the patterns of trade of selected countries. Because of the space constraint, we focus on the three largest economies in this region and in the world: the United States, China, and Japan. We examine both the export volume and import volume of each of these three economies, using the Harmonized System (HS) two-digit codes, in 1996, 2001, 2006, and 2011. We group the two-digit commodities into four different types of goods: agricultural goods, raw materials and intermediate inputs, light manufacturing goods, and heavy manufacturing goods in the following way:[12]

- agricultural goods: HS codes 01–24;
- raw materials and intermediate inputs: HS codes 25–49, 68–83;
- light manufacturing goods: HS codes 50–67, 90–97;
- heavy manufacturing goods: HS codes 84–89.

The results for these three countries in selected years in the period from 1996 to 2011 are presented in Table 14.7, with panel (A) showing the exports of the economies to the world and panel (B) representing the imports of the economies from the world.

In the years considered, most of the exports of the United States were raw materials, intermediate inputs, and heavy manufacturing goods: The sum of the shares of these two categories remained around 80 percent over the years. There was a drop in the share of heavy manufacturing goods, but there was also an obvious rise in that of the raw materials and intermediate inputs. The export of agricultural goods and light manufacturing goods remained fairly constant in the same period, although there are signs that there was a small decline in the export volume of each group of goods.

China's exports were more diversified. In 2011, nearly half of its exports were heavy manufacturing products, and nearly half were light manufacturing products, raw materials, and intermediate inputs. Export of agricultural goods was only 3.1 percent. The importance of export of light manufacturing products could be explained in terms of the factor endowments of the country. China, despite its spectacular growth in the past decades, is still a developing country, with endowment abundance in labor. Its export performance can thus be explained in terms of the factor-endowment theory.[13] China is an important agriculture producing country, but its agriculture production productivity is low and it is also a big agriculture consuming country. So its export of agricultural goods was only 3.1 percent of the total export.

One interesting feature of China's export distribution over the years in this period is that the export of heavy manufacturing products is increasing significantly. For example, in 1996, 39.1 percent of its total export was due to light manufacturing products, and this export volume was about 1.6 times that of heavy manufacturing products. In 2011, the export of light manufacturing products was 24.4 percent of the total export, while the export of heavy manufacturing was about twice as much. This phenomenon is not surprising and can be explained using the factor-endowment theory: In the past decades, China has been accumulating physical and human capital at high rates, giving rise to a rapid increase in China's capital-labor ratio and enabling the country to produce and export more of the goods that are intensive in physical and/or human capital.

Japan's export distribution looks somewhat similar to that of the United States, but there are some important differences. On the one hand, Japan exported a lot of heavy manufacturing products, which were 61.1 percent of the total export in

**Table 14.7 Trade Patterns of the United States, China, and Japan**

| | | percent | | | |
|---|---|---|---|---|---|
| | | 1996 | 2001 | 2006 | 2011 |
| *(A) Export* | | | | | |
| United States | Agriculture | 10.8 | 7.9 | 7.1 | 9.6 |
| | Raw Mat. | 27.0 | 27.3 | 33.1 | 40.6 |
| | Light Manu. | 10.9 | 11.8 | 10.9 | 9.8 |
| | Heavy Manu. | 51.4 | 53.0 | 48.9 | 40.1 |
| China | Agriculture | 9.1 | 5.8 | 3.1 | 3.1 |
| | Raw Mat. | 28.5 | 25.2 | 42.7 | 24.6 |
| | Light Manu. | 39.1 | 33.5 | 23.3 | 24.4 |
| | Heavy Manu. | 23.4 | 35.5 | 30.9 | 47.9 |
| Japan | Agriculture | 0.5 | 0.8 | 0.5 | 0.6 |
| | Raw Mat. | 19.3 | 19.6 | 24.3 | 30.1 |
| | Light Manu. | 10.1 | 10.8 | 8.3 | 8.2 |
| | Heavy Manu. | 70.0 | 68.8 | 66.9 | 61.1 |
| *(B) Import* | | | | | |
| United States | Agriculture | 5.4 | 4.9 | 4.6 | 5.5 |
| | Raw Mat. | 32.1 | 33.3 | 42.2 | 44.4 |
| | Light Manu. | 16.1 | 16.9 | 14.3 | 13.4 |
| | Heavy Manu. | 46.3 | 44.9 | 38.9 | 36.7 |
| China | Agriculture | 6.1 | 4.0 | 3.0 | 4.5 |
| | Raw Mat. | 37.9 | 40.2 | 40.4 | 49.4 |
| | Light Manu. | 16.6 | 11.7 | 11.3 | 8.7 |
| | Heavy Manu. | 39.4 | 44.0 | 45.3 | 37.4 |
| Japan | Agriculture | 16.3 | 13.8 | 9.5 | 9.7 |
| | Raw Mat. | 43.7 | 43.5 | 52.9 | 58.3 |
| | Light Manu. | 15.2 | 15.1 | 12.7 | 10.8 |
| | Heavy Manu. | 24.8 | 27.7 | 24.9 | 21.2 |

*Source*: United Nations, Comtrade Databank.

2011 or 70.0 percent in 1996. Japan also exported a lot of raw materials and intermediate inputs. The export of light manufacturing products was less, at least in terms of the percentage of the total export volume. However, Japan's export of agricultural products was very small, suggesting the low productivity of its agriculture production.

On the import side, the three countries show quite different import patterns. In 2011, the United States imported relatively more raw materials and intermediate inputs, and also light manufacturing products. It also imported substantial amounts of agricultural products and heavy manufacturing products, a phenomenon suggesting intra-industry trade.[14] China also had a big import of raw material and intermediate inputs. As a matter of fact, the share of China's import of raw materials and intermediate inputs had been increasing, thanks to its rapid growth in recent years. The share of China's import of heavy manufacturing products had remained fairly constant in the period, but its shares of import of agricultural products and light manufacturing products were declining over time.

Japan, as a raw-material-scarce country, always has a great demand for raw materials, and this is shown clearly in Table 14.7. The share of Japan's import of raw materials and intermediate inputs increased steadily from 43.7 percent in 1996 to 58.3 percent in 2011. Japan also imported a lot of agricultural products, but the share had been declining.

The United States and Japan are commonly regarded as two of the most advanced countries in the region, in terms of technology and abundance in capital. Their trade patterns reflect, to a good extent, the trade performance of other advanced countries in the region. China, on the other hand, is a developing country, although it is more advanced than many other APEC economies.

## 14.6 Intra-Industry Trade

This section examines the existence and features of intra-industry trade of the APEC member economies. Our analysis again focuses on the six economies described above: the United States, China, Japan, Australia, Mexico, and Chile.

Intra-industry trade means a simultaneous import and export of identical or very similar products by an economy in the same period of time. Statistically, similar products refer to those products that are grouped in the same industry. Intra-industry trade can be compared with what we call inter-industry trade, the latter being a simultaneous import and export of very different products, or products that are grouped in different industries. For a long time, economists have been paying more attention to inter-industry trade than to intra-industry trade, and many theorems and results have been developed; for example, the Classical Theorems by Adam Smith and David Ricardo, the Heckscher-Ohlin Theorem, and the Law of Comparative Advantage. In the past two to three decades, many new theories were developed to explain the existence and effects of intra-industry trade; for example, the theories that focus on oligopolistic competition, and the theories that rely on the existence of internal increasing returns and differentiation of products. Intra-industry trade can exist horizontally or vertically. Horizontal intra-industry trade refers to trade in products at the same production stage; for example, trade in final products like cars or trade in intermediate products like engines. Vertical intra-industry trade is the import of an intermediate input or raw materials by an economy and the export of a processed product (could be another intermediate input) by the same economy.

Empirically, the measurement of intra-industry trade is not straightforward, and is often dependent on how industries or goods are defined. First, we rarely find goods produced by different firms in different countries identical. In other words, we are dealing with trade in differentiated or heterogeneous products. Then how heterogeneous products are grouped into different industries will affect the measurement of intra-industry trade. For example, consider an economy that experiences simultaneous import of foreign cars and export of domestic cars. This is an example of intra-industry trade when the car industry is considered. However, the imported foreign cars and the exported domestic cars are not exactly the same. If we consider the foreign car as one type of car belonging to one industry and the domestic car as another type of car belonging to another industry, then such trade could be regarded as import of one type of product and export of another type of product: This is inter-industry trade.

If we have already defined the industries of the products, then in the literature, intra-industry trade in each of the industries is usually measured in terms of the index suggested by Grubel and Lloyd (1995). For example, consider industry $i$ of an economy. The index of intra-industry trade is defined as

$$I_i = 1 - \frac{|E_i - M_i|}{E_i + M_i}, \tag{1}$$

where $E_i$ is the value of export of the good of industry $i$ in a particular period while $M_i$ is the value of import of the good of the same industry in the same period. This index allows a positive or negative net export of the good, and varies between zero and one: zero for no intra-industry trade when either $E_i$ or $M_i$ is zero while the other one is positive, and one for perfect intra-industry trade when $E_i = M_i > 0$. Also, a higher index means a higher degree of intra-industry trade.

Very often, it is needed to determine the degree of intra-industry trade for a group of industries or for the economy as a whole. This requires an aggregation of the relevant industries. The usual approach is to take the weighted average of the indices of the industries, using the total volumes of trade as weights. The aggregate index is then defined as:

$$I = \sum_{i=1}^{n} w_i I_i, \tag{2}$$

Where $n$ is the number of industries concerned, and $w_i = (E_i + M_i) / \sum_i (E_i + M_i)$. Substitute the definition of $I_i$ into (2) and rearrange the terms to give an alternative definition of the aggregate index:

$$I = 1 - \frac{\sum_{i=1}^{n} |E_i - M_i|}{\sum_{i=1}^{n} (E_i + M_i)}. \tag{3}$$

Grubel and Lloyd argue, however, that in the presence of positive or negative trade balance, the index defined in (3) underestimates the degree of intra-industry trade for the industries as a whole because the maximum possible value of the index is less than unity. They suggest another index defined as:

$$\bar{I} = \frac{\sum_{i=1}^{n} (E_i + M_i) - \sum_{i=1}^{n} |E_i - M_i|}{\sum_{i=1}^{n} (E_i + M_i) - \left| \left( \sum_{i=1}^{n} E_i - \sum_{i=1}^{n} M_i \right) \right|}. \tag{4}$$

This index lies between zero and one: zero when $E_i > 0$ and $M_i = 0$ or $E_i > 0$ and $M_i = 0$ for each of the industries, and one when $E_i = M_i$ for all industries, with $E_i = M_i > 0$ for some industries. Furthermore, a comparison of (3) and (4) shows that $\bar{I} < I$ when the trade balance is non-zero.

Using the formulas in (1) to (4), the degrees of intra-industry trade of different industries and for the whole economy for the each of the six economies are computed. We examine intra-industry trade in goods on the HS two-digit level. This means that the HS on the two-digit level is used to define industries. Then we compute the aggregate indices. The results are presented in Table 14.8. The first 97 rows show the degree of intra-industry trade for each of the industries on the two-digit level. The last two rows give the aggregate indices for the economy as a whole; index 1 ($\bar{I}$) represents the adjusted index defined in (4), while index 2 ($I$) shows the unadjusted index as defined in (2). As explained, as long as the trade balance is non-zero, index 2 < index 1.

In terms of either index, the United States has the highest degree of intra-industry trade. The country with the second highest degree is Mexico. This is interesting, and that shows the impacts of the NAFTA. China also has a high degree of intra-industry trade, with an adjusted index of 0.594. Chile, on the other hand, has a low degree of intra-industry trade.

For the United States in 2011, the first three industries with the highest degree of intra-industry trade are industries 48 (Paper and paperboard, articles of pulp, paper and

**Table 14.8 Intra-industry Trade of Selected Economies, 2011**

| HS code | US | China | Japan | Australia | Mexico | Chile |
|---|---|---|---|---|---|---|
| 01 | 0.613 | 0.795 | 0.187 | 0.204 | 0.302 | 0.862 |
| 02 | 0.510 | 0.479 | 0.011 | 0.137 | 0.437 | 0.956 |
| 03 | 0.550 | 0.674 | 0.164 | 0.890 | 0.676 | 0.025 |
| 04 | 0.662 | 0.316 | 0.025 | 0.495 | 0.233 | 0.674 |
| 05 | 0.985 | 0.378 | 0.144 | 0.908 | 0.293 | 0.949 |
| 06 | 0.382 | 0.720 | 0.236 | 0.431 | 0.674 | 0.583 |
| 07 | 0.673 | 0.346 | 0.023 | 0.482 | 0.143 | 0.498 |
| 08 | 0.963 | 0.975 | 0.069 | 0.853 | 0.457 | 0.046 |
| 09 | 0.231 | 0.206 | 0.060 | 0.129 | 0.458 | 0.234 |
| 10 | 0.151 | 0.464 | 0.004 | 0.046 | 0.118 | 0.458 |
| 11 | 0.815 | 0.959 | 0.254 | 0.228 | 0.508 | 0.765 |
| 12 | 0.183 | 0.137 | 0.058 | 0.198 | 0.067 | 0.598 |
| 13 | 0.503 | 0.278 | 0.219 | 0.155 | 0.828 | 0.402 |
| 14 | 0.890 | 0.518 | 0.039 | 0.076 | 0.427 | 0.033 |
| 15 | 0.841 | 0.090 | 0.166 | 0.948 | 0.210 | 0.359 |
| 16 | 0.576 | 0.045 | 0.180 | 0.313 | 0.499 | 0.598 |
| 17 | 0.606 | 0.754 | 0.096 | 0.886 | 0.768 | 0.145 |
| 18 | 0.498 | 0.685 | 0.114 | 0.464 | 0.929 | 0.474 |
| 19 | 0.811 | 0.960 | 0.414 | 0.878 | 0.599 | 0.996 |
| 20 | 0.776 | 0.157 | 0.030 | 0.323 | 0.721 | 0.373 |
| 21 | 0.759 | 0.602 | 0.632 | 0.389 | 0.883 | 0.779 |
| 22 | 0.589 | 0.633 | 0.204 | 0.906 | 0.428 | 0.260 |
| 23 | 0.393 | 0.797 | 0.054 | 0.946 | 0.213 | 0.743 |
| 24 | 0.961 | 0.999 | 0.101 | 0.585 | 0.725 | 0.542 |
| 25 | 0.837 | 0.742 | 0.556 | 0.994 | 0.994 | 0.845 |
| 26 | 0.705 | 0.008 | 0.008 | 0.023 | 0.454 | 0.141 |
| 27 | 0.436 | 0.210 | 0.112 | 0.732 | 0.772 | 0.087 |
| 28 | 0.903 | 0.772 | 0.606 | 0.429 | 0.706 | 0.824 |
| 29 | 0.888 | 0.767 | 0.875 | 0.096 | 0.407 | 0.480 |
| 30 | 0.740 | 0.688 | 0.320 | 0.504 | 0.562 | 0.266 |
| 31 | 0.786 | 0.607 | 0.325 | 0.390 | 0.232 | 0.873 |
| 32 | 0.577 | 0.904 | 0.509 | 0.939 | 0.470 | 0.158 |
| 33 | 0.976 | 0.781 | 0.783 | 0.495 | 0.961 | 0.253 |
| 34 | 0.596 | 0.897 | 0.660 | 0.412 | 0.987 | 0.092 |

**Table 14.8. Continued**

| HS code | US | China | Japan | Australia | Mexico | Chile |
|---|---|---|---|---|---|---|
| 35 | 0.888 | 0.868 | 0.901 | 0.916 | 0.337 | 0.314 |
| 36 | 0.918 | 0.210 | 0.435 | 0.451 | 0.567 | 0.936 |
| 37 | 0.801 | 0.703 | 0.147 | 0.197 | 0.621 | 0.150 |
| 38 | 0.636 | 0.873 | 0.715 | 0.410 | 0.411 | 0.300 |
| 39 | 0.828 | 0.786 | 0.670 | 0.290 | 0.527 | 0.445 |
| 40 | 0.673 | 0.951 | 0.673 | 0.102 | 0.560 | 0.380 |
| 41 | 0.322 | 0.124 | 0.988 | 0.160 | 0.636 | 0.777 |
| 42 | 0.208 | 0.118 | 0.023 | 0.098 | 0.517 | 0.284 |
| 43 | 0.935 | 0.481 | 0.015 | 0.169 | 0.294 | 0.028 |
| 44 | 0.794 | 0.835 | 0.019 | 0.889 | 0.383 | 0.184 |
| 45 | 0.254 | 0.542 | 0.191 | 0.186 | 0.069 | 0.319 |
| 46 | 0.077 | 0.013 | 0.008 | 0.038 | 0.928 | 0.059 |
| 47 | 0.586 | 0.024 | 0.865 | 0.878 | 0.128 | 0.033 |
| 48 | 0.996 | 0.563 | 0.861 | 0.476 | 0.483 | 0.891 |
| 49 | 0.865 | 0.625 | 0.791 | 0.406 | 0.747 | 0.619 |
| 50 | 0.226 | 0.121 | 0.758 | 0.125 | 0.020 | 0.007 |
| 51 | 0.439 | 0.870 | 0.679 | 0.077 | 0.546 | 0.548 |
| 52 | 0.210 | 0.975 | 0.812 | 0.083 | 0.367 | 0.295 |
| 53 | 0.157 | 0.804 | 0.454 | 0.112 | 0.075 | 0.750 |
| 54 | 0.835 | 0.455 | 0.560 | 0.215 | 0.507 | 0.259 |
| 55 | 0.852 | 0.487 | 0.520 | 0.251 | 0.415 | 0.263 |
| 56 | 0.879 | 0.512 | 0.934 | 0.294 | 0.507 | 0.132 |
| 57 | 0.693 | 0.111 | 0.116 | 0.220 | 0.332 | 0.076 |
| 58 | 0.809 | 0.276 | 0.693 | 0.190 | 0.398 | 0.134 |
| 59 | 0.928 | 0.431 | 0.550 | 0.256 | 0.323 | 0.160 |
| 60 | 0.920 | 0.372 | 0.280 | 0.266 | 0.080 | 0.515 |
| 61 | 0.102 | 0.029 | 0.027 | 0.067 | 0.866 | 0.296 |
| 62 | 0.105 | 0.073 | 0.030 | 0.064 | 0.594 | 0.318 |
| 63 | 0.263 | 0.036 | 0.125 | 0.154 | 0.739 | 0.333 |
| 64 | 0.103 | 0.072 | 0.026 | 0.068 | 0.758 | 0.257 |
| 65 | 0.197 | 0.020 | 0.383 | 0.142 | 0.916 | 0.143 |
| 66 | 0.107 | 0.007 | 0.004 | 0.088 | 0.124 | 0.023 |
| 67 | 0.101 | 0.138 | 0.046 | 0.033 | 0.398 | 0.127 |
| 68 | 0.729 | 0.309 | 0.746 | 0.149 | 0.958 | 0.217 |

**Table 14.8 Continued**

| HS code | US | China | Japan | Australia | Mexico | Chile |
|---|---|---|---|---|---|---|
| 69 | 0.469 | 0.100 | 0.947 | 0.171 | 0.876 | 0.122 |
| 70 | 0.932 | 0.664 | 0.571 | 0.275 | 0.858 | 0.512 |
| 71 | 0.959 | 0.703 | 0.894 | 0.789 | 0.175 | 0.051 |
| 72 | 0.921 | 0.832 | 0.425 | 0.880 | 0.678 | 0.647 |
| 73 | 0.705 | 0.333 | 0.653 | 0.241 | 0.751 | 0.507 |
| 74 | 0.908 | 0.221 | 0.575 | 0.438 | 0.938 | 0.007 |
| 75 | 0.708 | 0.250 | 0.406 | 0.391 | 0.235 | 0.034 |
| 76 | 0.889 | 0.688 | 0.469 | 0.435 | 0.384 | 0.466 |
| 78 | 0.376 | 0.923 | 0.877 | 0.039 | 0.263 | 0.492 |
| 79 | 0.281 | 0.369 | 0.972 | 0.039 | 0.385 | 0.015 |
| 80 | 0.382 | 0.341 | 0.269 | 0.623 | 0.385 | 0.069 |
| 81 | 0.975 | 0.578 | 0.863 | 0.747 | 0.390 | 0.556 |
| 82 | 0.802 | 0.451 | 0.541 | 0.413 | 0.755 | 0.225 |
| 83 | 0.623 | 0.265 | 0.988 | 0.203 | 0.942 | 0.409 |
| 84 | 0.822 | 0.721 | 0.543 | 0.276 | 0.946 | 0.159 |
| 85 | 0.719 | 0.881 | 0.833 | 0.191 | 0.964 | 0.149 |
| 86 | 0.761 | 0.243 | 0.489 | 0.207 | 0.811 | 0.140 |
| 87 | 0.735 | 0.862 | 0.215 | 0.168 | 0.625 | 0.183 |
| 88 | 0.397 | 0.215 | 0.959 | 0.462 | 0.852 | 0.025 |
| 89 | 0.639 | 0.089 | 0.028 | 0.213 | 0.978 | 0.725 |
| 90 | 0.918 | 0.759 | 0.708 | 0.508 | 0.987 | 0.080 |
| 91 | 0.373 | 0.939 | 0.650 | 0.306 | 0.512 | 0.277 |
| 92 | 0.770 | 0.287 | 0.793 | 0.086 | 0.919 | 0.023 |
| 93 | 0.823 | 0.127 | 0.734 | 0.245 | 0.535 | 0.258 |
| 94 | 0.362 | 0.090 | 0.348 | 0.097 | 0.617 | 0.203 |
| 95 | 0.396 | 0.080 | 0.574 | 0.186 | 0.762 | 0.378 |
| 96 | 0.488 | 0.182 | 0.770 | 0.160 | 0.957 | 0.192 |
| 97 | 0.991 | 0.202 | 0.895 | 0.740 | 0.604 | 0.055 |
| 99 | 0.818 | 0.090 | 0.477 | 0.946 | 0.483 | 1.000 |
| index 1 | 0.851 | 0.594 | 0.451 | 0.417 | 0.743 | 0.209 |
| index 2 | 0.673 | 0.569 | 0.442 | 0.407 | 0.742 | 0.200 |

*Source*: United Nations, Comtrade Databank and author's calculation.

board), 97 (Works of art, collectors' pieces, and antiques), and 05 (Products of animal origin, nes), while the three industries with the lowest degree of intra-industry trade are industries 46 (Manufactures of plaiting material, basketwork, etc.), 67 (Bird skin, feathers, artificial flowers, human hair), and 61 (Articles of apparel, accessories, knit or crochet).

China, as a developing economy, has an intra-industry trade pattern very different from that of the United States. In 2011, its first three industries with the highest level of intra-industrial trade are industries 24 (Tobacco and manufactured tobacco substitutes), 08 (Edible fruit, nuts, peel of citrus fruit, melons), and 52 (Cotton). The last three industries in terms of the degree of intra-industry trade are industries 66 (Umbrellas, walking-sticks, seat-sticks, whips, etc.), 26 (Ores, slag, and ash), and 46 (Manufactures of plaiting material, basketwork, etc.).

China trades a lot with other Asian economies. China has an economy quite different in structure from those of the United States, Japan, Australia and other developed economies, but the Chinese economy is closer in its development stage to Southeast Asian economies and the Korean economy. It is thus quite possible that the trade between China and other Asian economies has a high degree of intra-industry trade. In the next section we will see more details about the trade relations among China, Japan, and South Korea.

## 14.7 Trade among China, Japan, and South Korea

One of the best ways of investigating the growth and economic integration of the Pacific-Rim economies is to examine the performance of and trade relations among the three economies in the northeast part of Asia: China, Japan, and South Korea. There are two of the largest economies in the world, and all of the three economies trade heavily among themselves and with other economies. These three economies, which are so close to each other, are in different stages of economic development: The Japanese economy is believed to be the most advanced and most industrialized, while China is the least industrialized among the three. South Korea, one of the newly industrialized economies, is regarded as somewhere in between in terms of development. Thus, an examination of the performance of these three economies can reveal how economies at different development stages may cooperate and perform under foreign trade.

Figure 14.1 shows the growth of the three economies and the world economy in terms of their nominal GDPs. In order to compare the growth of these economies, we express the sizes of their economies using the values in 1980 as a base. China started to open up its economy at the end of the 1970s. Since then, China has made much of an effort to liberalize trade and integrate its economy with the rest of the world. Choosing 1980 as the

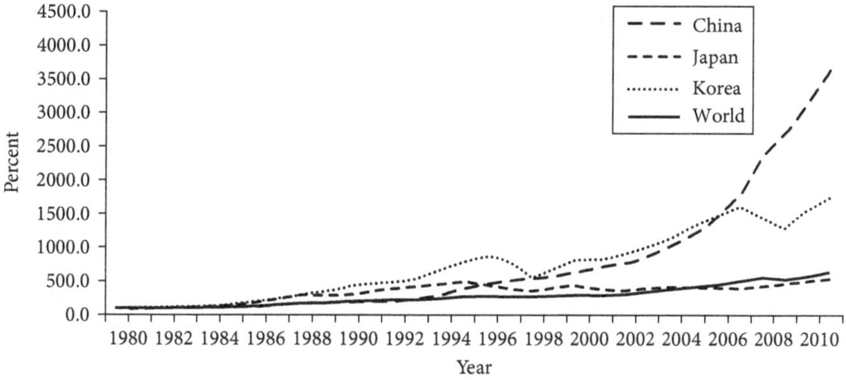


FIGURE 14.1 Nominal GDPs of Selected Countries, 1980–2011

*Source:* World Bank, World Development Indicators Databank.

base year allows us to see more clearly how the economy grew after the change in trade policy.

With 1980 = 100, the GDP of the world grew to 635.1 in 2011, with an annual growth rate of 6.1 percent. These numbers can be regarded as the average for all the economies in the world. Over these 31 years, the Japanese economy had a disappointing performance, while South Korea and China did much better than the average one. Japan experienced a recession in the early 1990s, and has not yet fully recovered. Its GDP reached a peak in 1995, but it dropped after that. It was not until 2010 that it rose back up to the 1995 level. The average growth rate of Japan in these 31 years was a mere 5.6 percent, which is worse than the world average.

South Korea and China performed much better than most other economies did in this period. South Korea grew to 1748.7 in 2011. This means that its GDP in 2011 was

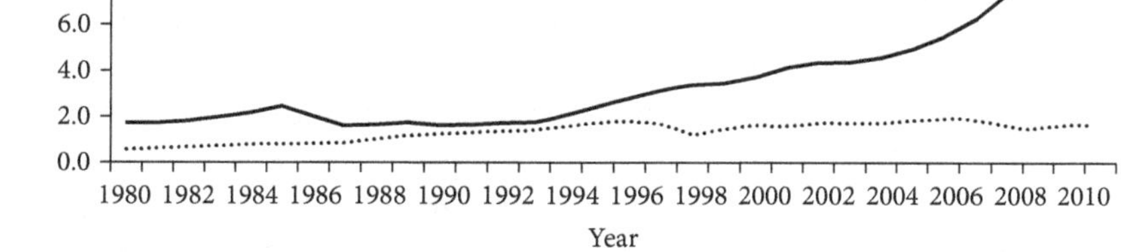


FIGURE 14.2 Shares of the GDP of Selected Countries in the World, 1980–2011

*Source:* World Bank, World Development Indicators Databank.

more than 17 times than that in 1980, with an annual growth rate of 9.7 percent. China's performance is even more spectacular: Its GDP in 2011 was more than 38 times that in 1980. The growth rate of China's GDP was 12.5 percent, which is higher than those of many other economies.

To highlight the growth of these three economies in Northeast Asia, we show in Figure 14.2 their shares in the world from 1980 to 2011. The curves reveal how the three economies grew as compared with the world. The share of the Japanese economy rose from 9.9 percent in 1980 and peaked at 18.1 percent in 1994. After that, the share fell gradually to 8.4 percent in 2011, a level even lower than what Japan had in 1980. On the contrary, China's economy was only 1.7 percent of the world, but it expanded to 10.5 percent in 2011. In 2010, China produced more goods and services than Japan did, surpassing the latter to become the world's second largest economy after the United States. The Korean economy did grow rapidly in this period as well. In 1980, its economy produced only 0.6 percent of the world's goods and services, but the share rose to 1.6 percent at the end of the period.

How did the growth, or different growth experiences, of these three economies affect the trade relations among these economies and those of the rest of the world? Table 14.3 shows how the APEC economies are dependent on trade from 1990 to 2011. We saw that among the three economies in northeast Asia, China and Korea are both very trade-dependent, and their trade dependence has been growing rapidly over time. For example, in 1990, China and Korea's trade dependence ratios (the trade-GDP ratios) were 25.3 and 39.4 percent, respectively, and these ratios rose substantially to 78.6 and 110.3 percent, respectively. The rise in the trade dependence of the economies was associated with their rapid growth. On the contrary, Japan did not show such dependence on trade as its trade-GDP ratio in 1990 was only 15.1 percent. Moreover, Japan's dependence ratio rose relatively slowly in this period: In 2011, its trade-GDP ratio rose to 25.8 percent. In other words, Japan became only slightly more trade dependent as its economy was recovering slowly from the economic recession in the nineties.

These three economies depend very much on each other. We already know from Table 14.5 the five biggest trading partners (on either the export side or the import side) of China, and those of Japan in 2011. We now try to go further to find out how China, Japan, and South Korea depend on each other. For China, even though its trade volumes have been rising substantially in the past decade, the lists of its major trading partners stay fairly constant, and the ranking of its trading partners has not changed much. For example, back in 2001, the five biggest overseas destinations for China's products are the United States, Hong Kong, Japan, South Korea, and Germany, while the five biggest suppliers of China's imports are Japan, the United States, South Korea, Germany, and Hong Kong. In 2011, these lists are about the same as those in 2001: The five major foreign destinations are the United States, Hong Kong, Japan, South Korea, and Germany (no change), while the five major import suppliers are Japan, South Korea, the United States, Germany, and Australia (small changes).[15] Note that Japan and South Korea are on both lists, showing that Japan and South Korea are important for China on the export side and the import side.

Table 14.5 also shows that in 2011, China was the most important destination for Japan's export and the most important supplier of international products to Japan. The dependence of Japan on the Chinese economy as a trading partner is spectacular. For a long time, at least up to 2001, the United States had been Japan's most important destination and foreign good supplier. This is especially more striking on the export side of Japan, because the United States' purchase of the Japanese goods was more than four times that of the second country, China. The importance of China as a trading partner has been rising steadily, and in 2011 China was the most important market for Japan's exports and the biggest supplier of goods Japan imported. The United States quietly became the second biggest (in value terms) trading partner. South Korea, despite having a smaller economy, remained one of the most connected trading partners of Japan. In 2001, South Korea ranked the third on both export and import sides of Japan. In 2011, South Korea stayed as the third market for Japan's exports, but fell to the sixth one on Japan's import side, because of the rise of Saudi Arabia and United Arab Emirates, as Japan became more dependent on foreign natural resources.

For South Korea, for a long time, the United States and Japan had been the two most important trading partners. For example, in 2001, the first three important markets for Korean products were the United States, China, and Japan, while the top three suppliers of Korean imports were Japan, the United States, and China. In 2011, these three countries remained to be the most important trading partners, but their rankings changed: The top three exporting destinations for Korea were China, the United States, and Japan, while the top three importing suppliers were China, Japan, and the United States. No doubt, China is now the number one trading partner of Korea, on both the export and the import sides.

After showing that the three countries in Northeast Asia have a very close trade relationship, the questions are, what goods do they trade and what comparative advantages do they have? To answer these questions, we determine the HS two-digit trade of these three economies among themselves and with the rest of the world. There are 97 industries on the two-digit level. We then group these industries into four main industries: (A) agriculture, (B) raw materials and intermediate inputs, (C) light manufacturing products, and (D) heavy manufacturing products. This is what we show in Table 14.7. However, there is some inconsistency between what different countries report to the United Nations; for example, the export of an industry by China to Japan, as reported by China, is not the same as the import of the product with the same HS code by Japan from China, as reported by Japan. We take the average of these two numbers so that the export of a good from China to Japan is equal to the import of the good by Japan from China. This will ensure that for each sector, the trade surplus of China versus Japan, say, is equal to the trade deficit of Japan versus China.

The comparative advantage of country $i$ versus another country $j$ in industry $k$ is represented by the index of relative comparative advantage, which is defined as

$$RCA_{ik}^{j} = \frac{E_{ik}^{j} - M_{ik}^{j}}{E_{ik}^{j} + M_{ik}^{j}}, \tag{5}$$

where $RCA_{ik}^{j}$ is the index of relative comparative advantage of country $i$ versus country $j$ in industry $k$, $E_{ik}^{j}$ is the export of good $k$ by country $i$ to country $j$, and $M_{ik}^{j}$ is the import of good $k$ by country $i$ from country $j$. The index lies between −1 and +1, and a negative number represents a relative comparative disadvantage, while a positive number shows relative comparative advantage. If $RCA_{ik}^{j} = 0$ while both $E_{ik}^{j}$ and $M_{ik}^{j}$ are positive, then it is a case of perfect intra-industrial trade. Furthermore, a bigger index stands for a stronger relative comparative advantage, while a more negative index points to an industry with a higher relative comparative disadvantage.

Table 14.9 shows the indices of relative comparative advantage of the three countries, China, Japan, and South Korea for trade among themselves and with the world in 1992, 2001, and 2011. The index of each country for trade with the world represents the overall relative comparative advantage, and it is used as a base for evaluating the indices of relative comparative advantage for trade with other Northeast Asian countries.

Historically, China has a comparative advantage in agricultural goods (industry A) and light manufacturing goods (industry C) for trade with other countries. For example, Table 14.9 shows that in 1992, China's indices of RCA for industry A and industry C were 0.436 and 0.444, respectively. This is consistent with the Heckscher-Ohlin Theorem, as China is abundant in land and labor, which are used intensively in agriculture and light manufacturing goods, respectively. For the same reason, China had relative comparative disadvantages in raw materials and heavy manufacturing goods. Another and probably more interesting phenomenon is the gradual change in China's comparative advantage over time as China grew continuously with astonishing rates. First, China was gradually losing its comparative advantage in agriculture but gaining comparative advantage in heavy manufacturing goods. As a matter of fact, China's index of RCA in agriculture changed from a positive number in 1992 to a negative number in 2011, while its index in heavy manufacturing goods switched from a negative number in 1992 to a positive number in 2011. These changes suggest two things: With the increase in China's income and wealth, there was a substantial rise in the consumption of agricultural products so that China changed from an exporter of these products to an importer, and with the rapid accumulation of physical and human capital and with sufficient progress in its technologies, China now has a comparative advantage in heavy manufacturing goods. On the other hand, China remained over these years a net importer of raw materials and intermediate inputs but a net exporter of light manufacturing goods.

China's trade with Japan and South Korea in these years showed a different picture. China had a very strong degree of relative comparative advantage in agricultural products with respect to Japan and South Korea. Even though China was a net importer of these products from the rest of the world, it had big export volumes to Japan and South Korea. China's position versus Japan was especially strong, as China's import of agricultural products was negligibly small. China relied heavily on Japan and South Korea in terms of raw materials, intermediate inputs, and heavy manufacturing products. In fact,

**Table 14.9 Patterns of Trade of China, Japan, and South Korea, 1992–2011**

| Industry | Year | vs World | vs Japan | vs Korea |
|---|---|---|---|---|
| *(1) China* | | | | |
| A | 1992 | 0.436 | 0.957 | 0.981 |
| | 2001 | 0.225 | 0.935 | 0.852 |
| | 2011 | -0.136 | 0.935 | 0.628 |
| B | 1992 | -0.146 | 0.074 | -0.144 |
| | 2001 | -0.185 | -0.026 | -0.432 |
| | 2011 | -0.285 | -0.171 | -0.269 |
| C | 1992 | 0.444 | 0.504 | 0.181 |
| | 2001 | 0.517 | 0.578 | -0.013 |
| | 2011 | 0.517 | 0.417 | -0.343 |
| D | 1992 | -0.384 | -0.794 | -0.507 |
| | 2001 | -0.061 | -0.189 | -0.260 |
| | 2011 | 0.179 | -0.191 | -0.288 |
| *(2) Japan* | | | | |
| A | 1992 | -0.901 | -0.957 | -0.840 |
| | 2001 | -0.873 | -0.935 | -0.669 |
| | 2011 | -0.885 | -0.935 | -0.645 |
| B | 1992 | -0.345 | -0.074 | 0.177 |
| | 2001 | -0.326 | 0.026 | 0.168 |
| | 2011 | -0.352 | 0.171 | 0.228 |
| C | 1992 | 0.078 | -0.504 | -0.236 |
| | 2001 | -0.107 | -0.578 | 0.262 |
| | 2011 | -0.173 | -0.417 | 0.450 |
| D | 1992 | 0.727 | 0.794 | 0.642 |
| | 2001 | 0.474 | 0.189 | 0.311 |
| | 2011 | 0.457 | 0.191 | 0.330 |
| *(3) South Korea* | | | | |
| A | 1992 | -0.358 | -0.981 | 0.840 |
| | 2001 | -0.500 | -0.852 | 0.669 |
| | 2011 | -0.584 | -0.628 | 0.645 |

**Table 14.9 Continued**

| Industry | Year | vs World | vs Japan | vs Korea |
|---|---|---|---|---|
| B | 1992 | -0.315 | 0.144 | -0.177 |
| | 2001 | -0.279 | 0.432 | -0.168 |
| | 2011 | -0.262 | 0.269 | -0.228 |
| C | 1992 | 0.432 | -0.181 | 0.236 |
| | 2001 | 0.224 | 0.013 | -0.262 |
| | 2011 | 0.209 | 0.343 | -0.450 |
| D | 1992 | 0.069 | 0.507 | -0.642 |
| | 2001 | 0.286 | 0.260 | -0.311 |
| | 2011 | 0.382 | 0.288 | -0.330 |

*Notes:* (i)industry A = agricultural goods; industry B = raw materials and intermediate inputs; industry C = light manufacturing goods; and D = heavy industry manufacturing goods
(ii) The HS two-digit level trade goods for China in 1911 were not available.
*Source:* United Nations, Comtrade databank and author's calculation.

Korea's light manufacturing products had become very competitive, and China became a net importer of the Korean products lately.

Japan had strong relative comparative disadvantages in agricultural products, raw materials, and intermediate inputs. It did have net exports of manufacturing products, but its comparative advantages in these products had been declining over time: the indices of RCA for light and heavy manufacturing products were dropping in these years, and as a matter of fact, the index for light manufacturing products switched from being positive in 1992 to being negative in 2001 and 2011.

Japan relied on China in terms of agricultural products and light manufacturing products, as its indices of RCA were consistently negative. Relative to China, Japan kept a comparative advantage in heavy manufacturing products, but the advantage was declining as its index of RCA was falling. Japan also imported substantially agricultural products from South Korea, but it could maintain strong competitiveness in raw materials, intermediate inputs, and manufacturing product over the years.

South Korea, like Japan, showed a relative comparative disadvantage in agricultural products, raw materials, and intermediate inputs with respect to the rest of the world, and again like Japan, had a relative comparative advantage in manufacturing goods. Trading with China, South Korea revealed a strong relative comparative disadvantage in agricultural goods, but very strong comparative advantage in nearly most other products. South Korea's comparative advantages for trade with China are the opposite of those for trade with Japan; for example, while South Korea has a relative comparative disadvantage in agricultural products versus China, but versus Japan, it has a relative comparative advantage in similar products. Interestingly, in terms of trade patterns, South Korea is revealed to be an economy somewhere in between China and Japan.

## 14.8 Concluding Remarks

This chapter examines the foreign trade of major economies on both sides of the Pacific Ocean. The objective of the present work is to find out how these economies are interdependent, how they are related to other economies in the world, and how foreign trade may contribute to economic growth. The chapter also studies in detail the trade relations among three of the important economies in Asia: China, Japan, and South Korea.

These economies are important players in the world markets, in terms of their sizes as well as their volumes of foreign trade. The economies under study include the three biggest economies in the world: the United States, China, and Japan, as their foreign trade and growth unavoidably have a strong impact on other economies in the world. Nearly all of these economies examined in the present project are highly trade-oriented, exporting goods and services to many other economies and buying goods and services from overseas. The two biggest economies, the United States and China, happen to be the two largest trading economies in the world, on both the export and the import sides. Other Pacific Rim economies perform very impressively in terms of foreign trade, as six to seven of the top 10 trading economies in the world are those located in the Pacific Rim region.[16]

The economies under the present study are not only trade-oriented, but also are some of the economies that grew rapidly in the previous decades. The more obvious ones are those in the northeast and southeast Asia. Among these economies, China is probably the one that has drawn most of the attention. Within three to four decades, the Chinese economy grew nearly without interruption and with impressive growth rate of around 10 percent per year. It now is the second largest economy in terms of GDP and the second largest trading economy in the world. The experience of China and many other Asian economies supports the argument that foreign trade contributes to the growth of an economy. Our study does show a strong relation between trade and growth.

Foreign trade is an important activity to integrate an economy with other economies. Nearly all Pacific Rim economies are heavily trade-oriented, and thus are interdependent and are linked to the rest of the world. Therefore, the growth of an economy can have strong spillover effects on its trading partners, and at the same time, each economy can also be affected by the growth of its trading partners.

This chapter examines various features of foreign trade of the Pacific-Rim economies, including their trade patterns and the degrees of intra-industrial trade. The trade patterns of economies are related to their factor endowments, technologies, and preferences. It is possible to explain some of these trade patterns in terms of trade theories such as the Heckscher-Ohlin Theorem. An interesting case is that of China. As it grew rapidly in previous decades, it got more and more developed and its exportables got more and more intensive in technology and human capital. This chapter also finds that these Pacific Rim economies have a high degree of intra-industrial trade. This is particularly true for economies in Asia, which have substantial import and export of intermediate inputs.

To examine in more detail the interdependency among some Pacific Rim economies, this chapter studies closely the trade relations among the three economies in northeast Asia: China, Japan, and South Korea. These three economies provide a very good case to study the roles of foreign trade and economic integration. Geographically, they are close to each other, and are very dependent on each other through trade. They are in different stages of economic development, with the Japanese economy the most advanced. China, and to a lesser extent, South Korea, are fast catching up and closing the development gaps. A study of these three economies allows us to see how growth may change their trade patterns. Furthermore, we can also see how the governments may want to use free trade agreements to bring their economies even closer together.

Although the present study focuses on the member economies of the APEC, some of the features of foreign trade of these economies can exist in other economies as well. For example, we examined the relation between foreign trade and economic growth of these economies, but the relation could be found in other economies as well.

## APPENDIX 1

### LIST OF ASIA-PACIFIC ECONOMIC COOPERATION MEMBERS

- Australia
- Brunei Darussalam
- Canada
- Chile
- China
- Hong Kong, China
- Indonesia
- Japan
- Korea
- Malaysia
- Mexico
- New Zealand
- Papua New Guinea
- Peru
- Philippines
- Russia
- Singapore
- Chinese Taipei

- Thailand
- United States
- Viet Nam

## APPENDIX 2

## AN ALTERNATIVE WAY OF GROUPING HS TWO-DIGIT INDUSTRIES

01–05 Animal & Animal Products
06–15 Vegetable Products
16–24 Foodstuffs
25–27 Mineral Products
28–38 Chemicals & Allied Industries
39–40 Plastics/Rubbers
41–43 Raw Hides, Skins, Leather, & Furs
44–49 Wood & Wood Products
50–63 Textiles
64–67 Footwear/Headgear
68–71 Stone/Glass
72–83 Metals
84–85 Machinery/Electrical
86–89 Transportation
90–97 Miscellaneous
98–99 Service

For more details, see, for example,

- [http://www.foreign-trade.com/reference/hscode.htm] or
- [http://www.vassl.com/hscode.htm]

## NOTES

1. There are, however, some economies not included in the APEC group, for example: Costa Rica; Guatemala; El Salvador; Panama; South Pacific economies like Fiji Islands, Tonga, and Tuvalu; and some other economies like North Korea and Macao, China. These economies are small, and thus are not considered explicitly here.
2. The GDPs reported here are real GDP at constant 2000 US dollars. Unless stated otherwise, the figures are from World Bank, World Development Indicators databank.
3. Papua New Guinea was excluded because of lack of data.

4. Viet Nam and South Korea were the other two APEC economies that had growth rates of their foreign trade higher than 10 percent in this period.
5. The numbers in parentheses are the corresponding standard deviation.
6. The equation suggests that the GDP growth of an economy depends on its foreign trade growth. However, it is possible that the foreign trade growth may also depend on the GDP growth of an economy. The estimation of the latter dependence is beyond the scope of this chapter.
7. These three countries have been negotiating for some time about forming free trade areas.
8. Slightly more than 5 percent of Japan's exports were sent to Hong Kong. It is believed that a big fraction of Japan's exports to Hong Kong would be later reexported to Mainland China. So we can conclude that more than 20 percent of Japan's export went to China.
9. Mexico is also close to other countries in Central America such as Honduras, El Salvador, Nicaragua, and Costa Rica, but all these countries are small developing countries with very low income levels.
10. Canada is the third member of the NAFTA, but Canada is far away from Mexico, as the two countries are separated by the United States.
11. Chinese Taipei was excluded in the numbers in Table 4.
12. There is no easy way of grouping published data into these four groups of products. First, a product can be used for many purposes; for example, a truck can be used as a consumption good or as an intermediate good. Second, many HS two-digit codes commodities may contain products that belong to more than one group of goods. A more accurate way is to use the HS six-digit codes, but that process would be much more time-consuming and costly.
13. The famous Heckscher-Ohlin Theorem states that a country exports the good that uses its abundant factor intensively. China is recognized as a labor-abundant country, and so according to the theorem it exports labor-intensive products such as textile, leather, and toy products. For more discussion about this theorem and its applications, see, for example, Wong (1995).
14. We will have more discussion about intra-industry trade later.
15. The list does not include China's import from China, which is believed to be the result of re-import/re-export.
16. The analysis earlier shows that the trade-GDP ratios of some of the APEC economies are not very high, and in a sense, they are not very trade-dependent.

## References

Grubel, Herbert G., and Peter J. Lloyd, (1975). *Intra-Industry Trade: The Theory and Measurement of International Trade in Differentiated Products*. New York: John Wiley & Sons.

Wong, Kar-yiu, (1995). *International Trade in Goods and Factor Mobility*. Cambridge, Mass.: MIT Press.

# PART V

# INDUSTRY, POLICY, AND INNOVATION

CHAPTER 15

# ARE THE GEESE STILL FLYING? CATCH-UP INDUSTRIALIZATION IN A CHANGING INTERNATIONAL ECONOMIC ENVIRONMENT

INDERJIT KAUR

*Komo na yo ga*—Will it come again
*Mata mo aro ka*—another night like this one?
*Tsuki ni kari.*—Wild Geese and the Moon.

—Hiroshige (1797–1858)

## 15.1 Introduction

Kaname Akamatsu, writing in Japanese in 1935, introduced the now famous metaphor of flying wild geese, depicting the catching-up process of post-war industrialization in Japan—a model successfully emulated by the East Asian "miracle" economies (World Bank, 1993), bringing hope to many other developing countries in Asia.[1] In that paradigm, sequential shifting of comparative advantage across economies, aided by factors such as foreign direct investment, structural change, infrastructure development, human capital formation, and industrial policy, unleashed trade-fueled economic development.

Throughout the 1990s a new international division of labor emerged based on the principles of the supply chain. The international economic landscape changed significantly, with international product fragmentation, agglomeration economies, intra-industry and intra-product trade, regionalization, and the emergence of two giant economies, China and India, as dominant forces; as well, many new players have been eyeing the field, including lower-tier Southeast Asian economies.

This chapter discusses some aspects of this changing international economic context and the relevance of the process of sequential shifting of comparative advantage as a basis for industrial upgrading, in the context of the economies of the Pacific Rim. Is catch-up industrialization still at work? In that sense, are the geese still flying? The discussion does not aim to consider all the theoretical and empirical issues surrounding the flying geese model of development. Rather than the details of the pattern, the focus here is on the process of sequential shifting of comparative advantage as a basis for progression on a scale of technological ability and catch-up industrialization.

## 15.2 Flying Geese

Akamatsu (1962) presented the flying geese pattern of industrial development as "a sort of formula for the industrial development of less-advanced countries after they have opened trade ports and entered into large-scale trade relations with the advanced Western European countries."[2] In that paradigm, trade liberalization ushers in the following process for manufactured goods. First imports increase, but as domestic production capabilities arise, imports diminish and eventually the imported goods become export goods. In other words, import-substitution is successfully followed by exports. The time series curves of imports, domestic production, and exports exhibit the inverse V shape similar to the formation of flying wild geese, as shown in Figure 15.1 for Japan for the period between 1870 and World War II.[3]

Akamatsu (1962) described three forms of the flying geese pattern: (1) with respect to manufactured consumer goods (which he termed the "fundamental wild-geese flying pattern"), (2) with respect to quality (the "wild-geese-flying development pattern from crude goods to elaborate goods"), and (3) with respect to economies (the "development of advanced and less-advanced countries in a flying-wild-geese pattern"). The first presents an inter-industry shift in products, from consumer to capital goods (e.g., textiles to machinery); whereas the second presents an intra-industry shift to more complex and refined goods (e.g., superior quality textiles). The flying geese in these two patterns are firms—a lead firm in an advanced economy, and followers in less developed economies, and the process is one of successful transition from import-substitution to export-promotion based on learning-by-doing in the lap of infant-industry protection. The third pattern refers to an economy-wide shift—transformation of entire economies up the industrialization ladder, from dominance of the primary sector, to labor-intensive, then to capital-intensive, and ultimately to the knowledge-intensive industrial sector. The flying geese here are economies; the less advanced trailing the advanced lead economy.

In other words, catch-up industrialization can take three forms—producing more capital-intensive goods (i.e., capital-intensity upgrading), producing higher quality and more complex goods (i.e., quality upgrading), and economy-wide transformation up

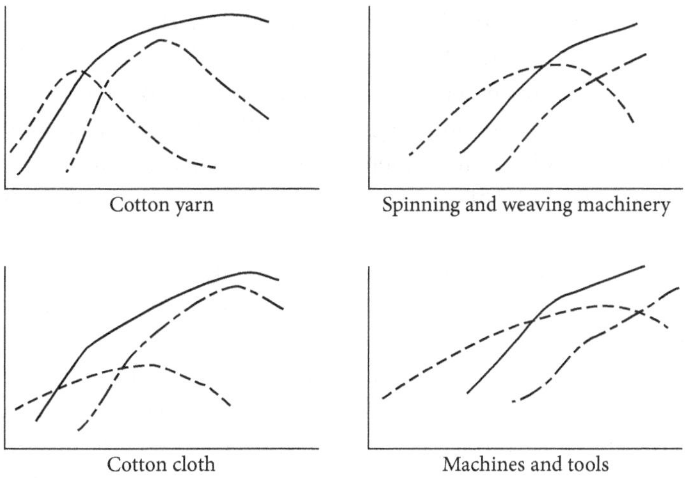


Notes : 1. These curves cover the period from about 1870 to World War II
2. ---- Import
—— Production
—-- Export
3. Vertical line denotes value

FIGURE 15.1 Wild-geese-flying pattern.

*Source:* Akamatsu (1962), p. 12

the technological ladder (i.e., economy-wide upgrading). The common theme is that there is a hierarchy that is based on technological capability, and catch-up involves sequential shifting of comparative advantage. In the earlier phases, imitation and learning suffice, but, ultimately, innovation is key.

While recognizing relatively lower costs of production as the basis of the process, Akamatsu also acknowledged the role of inputs (specifically energy), infrastructure (specifically transport), and industrial policy in enabling and shaping the details of the trends. Further, he recognized the role of the (naturally varying) relative pace of technological progress in determining the relative position of leading and trailing geese (countries), as well as possibilities of intersecting regional formations, and the ability of policy to alter the flying geese patterns.

A point that merits special emphasis is that this process requires continuous structural adjustment, namely phasing out industries with comparative disadvantage and nurturing those with comparative advantage in all economies. Such structural adjustments are, to say the least, challenging, and are often resisted by dying industries, and often create tensions within and across economies. Efforts on the part of an economy to resist this (due to employment and wage concerns) will inhibit the process of trade-led development along the comparative advantage ladder. Neither can the markets be left to navigate the process on their own. Structural adjustment policies need to keep abreast of structural changes.[4] Advanced countries need to succeed in shifting to new growth sectors.

Thus, flying geese catching-up development, even if market-driven, is not automatically achieved but requires active facilitating through public policy, on the part of both leading and following countries, keeping in view the dictates of comparative advantage.

The idea of countries progressing on a comparative advantage scale toward greater capital intensity is found in subsequent writings too, e.g., Balassa's (1977) "stages approach to comparative advantage." There too, as in the writings on catch-up industrialization, we find the example of Japan as the forerunner, followed by Korea and Taiwan.

Several factors contributed to Japan's early flying success, including: sufficient demand, both domestic and foreign, for the products; industrial policy, including infant-industry protection and export promotion; foreign direct investment and technology; technology adaptation and assimilation; trade-supporting infrastructure and networks; and high savings enabling capital accumulation. Kojima (1977), who rephrased the flying geese model as "catching-up product cycle of development" (a modification of Vernon's "product cycle" thesis[5] for developed economies), emphasizes the following for Japan:

> The key to a successful catching-up product cycle development was long run decreasing costs of the nature clearly revealed for steel, automobiles and so on. Foreign direct investment and technological knowhow were certainly important but the technological adaptability, active management and industrious skill of the Japanese were much more important. Foreign technology was often amended and assimilated in a way which made its application in Japan more efficient.
> (Kojima, 1977, p. 150)

Also noteworthy were the networks of linked firms. "Japan's unique trading firms played an important role in the expansion of trade. Their hundreds of subsidiaries and branches throughout the world were able to identify where Japan's comparative advantage lay, and to participate substantially in Japan's direct investments abroad" (Kojima, 1977, p. 151). With particular reference to Japan's position as head goose, a crucial factor was its ability to invent and innovate, or, in Kojima's terminology, its shift from engaging in catching-up product cycles to creating its own product cycles.

The four East Asian NIEs (the newly industrializing economies of South Korea, Taiwan, Hong Kong, and Singapore) followed Japan so well, and "flew" in such elegant formation, that their industrialization and growth was dubbed a "miracle" (World Bank, 1993). Many factors combined to facilitate East Asia's miraculous flight, including sound macroeconomic policy, infrastructure development, and human capital formation. In the context of catch-up industrialization, a key factor was the relatively efficient industrial policy. Promotional policies were conditional upon achievement of performance standards.

> For example, the government in South Korea disciplined its big business groups by means of price ceilings, controls on capital flight, and incentives that made diversification into new industries contingent on performing well in old ones. Board of Investment made subsidized credit and protection from competitive imports

> dependent on its clients' compliance with sequential performance standards, including exports and local content targets. Taiwan's state owned bankers have been held personally responsible for loans to business, and have carefully monitored them. (Amsden, 1991, p. 284)

This discipline was critical for creating the competitive edge that enabled participation in the catching-up process. The importance of quality over the extent of intervention cannot be overemphasized.

> The intervention schemes have worked closely with the market, and the state's alertness in using the signals emanating from world markets to judge dynamic efficiency has helped keep firms on their toes and prevent infant industries from turning into inefficient geriatric protection lobbies. . . . The other aspect of the quality of intervention that matters a great deal is the selectivity of intervention (in terms of strategic sectors, products and processes in the different stages of early industrialization). Such selectivity in targeting, as opposed to indiscriminate and blanket controls and regulations, saves on scarce administrative skills and makes it easier to pinpoint social costs of policies and adjust them in response to changing technical and market conditions. (Bardhan, 1990, p. 6)

"Advantages of backwardness"[6] played its role too, with advanced economies as trailblazers for the less developed.

> Deciding which industries to promote might seem a serious problem. However, it is not difficult for a developing country to pick an industry that is losing competitiveness in countries that are slightly further along in terms of economic development but have similar factor endowments and economic environments. Regional development, whether in nineteenth century Europe or in Asia in the 1980s, benefits from the market pressure and lessons learned from neighboring countries. (Ito, 1996, p. 53)

Trade-oriented foreign direct investment from Japan contributed, aiming at economic activities in which Japan was becoming comparatively disadvantaged (natural resource development, textiles, clothing, steel processing, and electronic components). Such complementarity strengthened comparative advantage in investing and receiving countries alike. It created export capacity in developing countries, while obtaining necessary imports for the more developed economy and accelerating internal structural adjustment.

The East Asian success further inspired catch-up development in Malaysia, Thailand, and Indonesia, and to some extent, in the Philippines. Growth was less miraculous, but take-offs in Southeast Asia were based on similar factors that enabled the Tigers. Thus, the geese flew, from Japan to Northeast Asia to Southeast Asia, riding ever-increasing waves of FDI in search of lower cost production. Furthermore, by opening its doors, China joined in as well, and has amazed the world with its "flying power."

## 15.3 A Panda among the Geese?—the Rise of China

"China is no goose," *The Economist* opined in 2001. "It does not conform to the... stereotype, because it makes simple goods and sophisticated ones at the same time, rag nappies and microchips."[7] Others have observed the steady rise of the level of sophistication of Chinese exports, noting China's export similarity to that of much higher income-level economies.[8] It appears that China has disrupted the orderly arrangement of East Asian catch-up industrialization. "With its economies of scale and other advantages, it has leapfrogged up the technological ladder. No other country in East Asia has the capacity to produce at all points between the lower and upper ends of the technology spectrum" (Gill et al, 2007a, p. 9). Thus, China has been seen as having the potential of dislodging all types of geese—the leading (Japan), the middle of the pack (Singapore, Hong Kong, South Korea, and Taiwan), and the trailing (Thailand, Malaysia, Indonesia, and the Philippines).

However, before accepting the "leapfrogging thesis" one must keep the extent of inward processing trade in mind, i.e., that a large proportion of industrial economic activity in China consists of assembly of imported components for re-export. Lardy and Branstetter (2006), e.g., argue that the exports of electronic and information technology products from China are mostly simply assembled high value-added parts and components with only 15 percent domestic value-added. "China, in short, does not in any real sense manufacture these goods"(Lardy, 2006, p. 38).[9] And "for many of these products it is doubtful that China is supplying anything but the labor required to produce these goods. China's provision of relatively low-wage 'assembly services' is completely consistent with its underlying comparative advantage" (Lardy, 2006, p. 38). Further, "most exports of electronic and information products are assembled not by Chinese owned firms but by foreign firms that are using China as an export platform" (Lardy, 2006, p. 39).

Similarly, Koopman et al. (2008) estimate that whereas the foreign content in Chinese exports overall is close to 50 percent, there is notable heterogeneity across sectors:

> Those sectors that are likely to be labeled as sophisticated or high-skilled, such as computers, electronic devices, and telecommunication equipment, tend to have especially low shares of domestic content. Conversely, many sectors that are relatively intensive in low-skilled labor, such as apparel, are likely to exhibit a high share of domestic content in China's exports. Finally,... foreign invested firms (including both wholly-owned foreign firms and Sino-foreign joint venture firms) tend to have a relatively low share of domestic content in their exports. (Koopman *et al.*, 2008, p. 18)

Several studies[10] have also noted that, within detailed products (e.g., shirts as opposed to apparel), China and other developing countries are found to export less expensive and lower-quality varieties relative to the more developed economies.

An important issue at hand is that conventional trade statistics can be misleading. For example, Linden et al. (2007) calculate, "For every $300 iPod sold in the U.S., the politically volatile U.S. trade deficit with China increased by about $150 (the factory cost). Yet, the value added to the product through assembly in China is probably a few dollars at most" (Linden et al., 2007, p. 10).

As Roland-Holst and Weiss (2004) have argued, "the *de facto* regional hierarchy of value-added in East Asia has not been substantially altered. Indeed, the most skill-intensive exporters, Japan and the NIEs (newly industrializing economies), have actually intensified their 'skill specialization' over the period 1996–2000" (Roland-Holst and Weiss, 2004, p. 1273). In fact, China has fitted into this overall economic landscape:

> Most countries have... found a niche in which they may retain competitiveness relative to China.... countries have the choice of (1) investing in China and selling to China or world markets; (2) exporting components to China and making it the assembly plant for exports to others; or (3) exporting raw materials to China. The United States and the European Union are focusing on the first channel. The four tigers and the more industrialized countries within ASEAN are focusing on the second. The less developed countries that possess natural resources are focusing on the third. (Gill et al., 2007a, p. 10)

Japan, for example, has a competitive advantage not only in frontier manufacturing technology but also in creativity in other sectors as well. "The strength of Japanese companies is not just technological sophistication. Goods and services such as pop culture, convenience stores, and fashion, which had been developed for and won the hearts and minds of selective and capricious Japanese consumers, started to attract the rapidly emerging middle class in China" (Munakata, 2003, p. 4).

Going back then to Akamatsu's three forms of catch-up industrialization, i.e., capital-intensity upgrading, quality upgrading, and economy-wide technological upgrading—China is very much still on the way up the ladder; albeit a very certain, steady, and rapid way up.

## 15.4 All the World's a Factory—"Flying" Direct Investment

In 2003 Yoshimatsu wrote, "Japan was the factory of the world in the 1970s and 1980s. China is succeeding this status in the new century" (Yoshimatsu, 2003, p. 95). However, by 2007 Gill et al. concluded, somewhat differently, "No single county within East Asia can dominate the production chain."[11] Indeed, one can argue that over the last two decades, a whole new mode of global production sharing has evolved.

Intensified technological advancement (particularly in information, communications and transportation technology) and trade liberalization have fundamentally altered the structure of foreign direct investment and foreign trade. Earlier, entire product lines shifted production. Now deverticalization by firms has created extensive international production networks of supply chaining. These networks include cross-border relationships between lead firms and their affiliates and subsidiaries, subcontractors, suppliers, and service providers.[12]

International product fragmentation is a vertical disintegration process wherein various components of a product are produced in different plants located globally, i.e., offshoring. A product is designed and engineered in one country, its components manufactured in many, and its assembly finished in yet another before it is sent off to distributions channels. Computers, e.g., are designed in the United States, but hard disks, monitors, and keyboards are produced in several different countries. Such intra-product specialization has resulted in a proliferation of complex webs of global supply chains, in many industries such as automobiles, aircrafts, and apparel (so that even a shirt label may often only claim, "*assembled* in Mexico").

Global production networks enable lead firms to source low-cost inputs and skills while specializing in core expertise. This enables a much finer division of labor and, therefore, many more participants in the supply chain. Figure 15.2 depicts a generic electronics supply chain.

In global production networks, the separated activities are coordinated by service links, as shown in Figure 15.3. The greater the product fragmentation, the more complex is the coordination.

These links encompass a whole host of functions, including demand forecasting, inventory management, marketing, distribution, telecommunication, and transportation. Thus, expanded sources of value added are available to private enterprise. In the apparel and shoe industries, for example, as production has relocated to China, Taiwan firms have moved on to supply chain management. Their expertise is to "locate suppliers in China, monitor the quality of their work, transmit orders and deal with buyers, organize shipments, and sometimes engage in rudimentary marketing."[13]

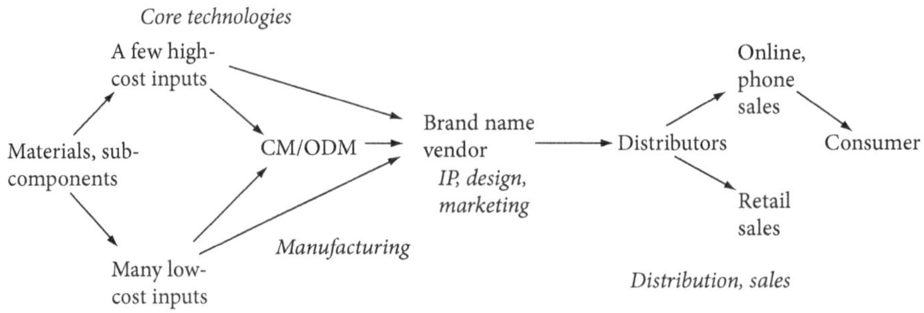


FIGURE 15.2 Generic electronics supply chain.

[CM is contract manufacturer; ODM is original design manufacturer.]

*Source:* Linden et al. 2007

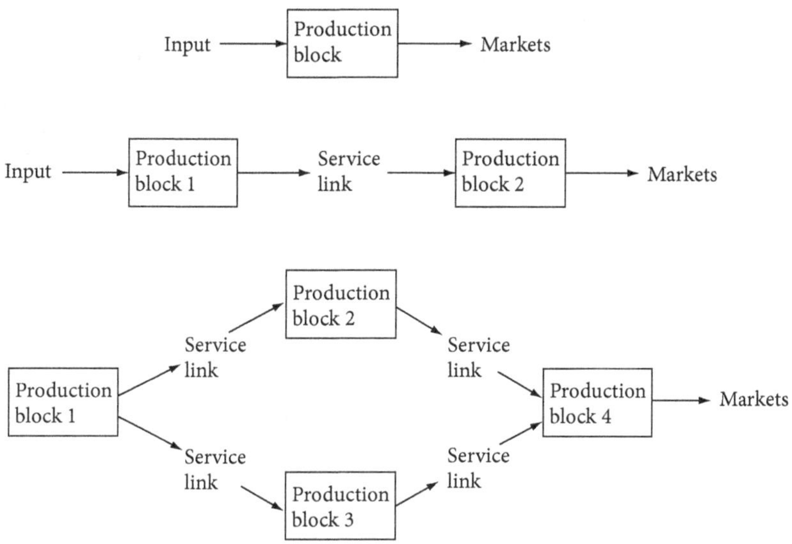


FIGURE 15.3 Fragmentation and service links.

*Source:* Arndt and Kierzkowski (2001) p. 3

The deeper vertical specialization in global production networks has increased the scope of activity-level economies of scale. From product development, to input (in particular, labor) sourcing, to marketing, producers can spread fixed costs over larger volumes of production, enabling per unit costs to fall steadily as the scale increases. With intra-product specialization, smaller firms can reap scale economies. Further, as a particular production activity gains ground in a particular location, it triggers complementary specialization in the vicinity, and agglomeration economies take effect, giving rise to industrial clusters (i.e., geographic concentrations of interrelated businesses and institutions in a particular field) and labor pools.

With expanded opportunities there are also new challenges. Competition is more intense. Efficiency-attributes such as on-time delivery, quality control, and flexibility take on added significance when activities are part of supply chains. Global product fragmentation has intensified, more than ever before, the "flying nature of foreign direct investment," i.e., its footloose characteristic of reallocating itself to the most advantageous international location. "CPNs (cross-border production networks) are assembled to access vocational advantages at each network node associated with the increasingly specialized technology, skills and know-how that are resident there."[14]

In Asia, the stage for the spread of global production networks was set by "flying geese" from Japan to the rest of East Asia and onward to Southeast Asia. Japanese *keiretsus* and Korean *chaebols* were tightly knit networks of production and distribution. Japanese outsourcing, first in the Tiger economies and then in the middle-income ASEAN countries and China, was joined by foreign direct investment from the United States. The Asian diaspora played its role, as members of the diaspora set up plants and distribution links back in their home countries. Managerial innovations such as the Toyota Way and distribution innovations such as the Li and Fung Global Distribution System led the way. Clusters of production and research and development emerged. Regional cascade effects ensued. Aided by factors such as rapid advances in telecommunications and logistics, congenial economic policies, and social networks, efficient East Asian firms became integral members of global production-sharing networks, making the region a substantial and vibrant part of the world factory.

## 15.5 Flying in a "Flat" World—Innovation, Education, and Infrastructure

A flat world, for our purpose here, is one where geography is irrelevant to the location of operation decisions. As mentioned above, with dramatic progress in information and communications technology, production activity has come to be allocated worldwide and guided more closely by comparative advantage, and more and more types of production activities have become footloose, ranging from routine, standardized manufacturing tasks to financial and legal services. The *New York Times* recently reported "knowledge process outsourcing," or "high-value outsourcing" of Wall Street jobs to India, citing, "Over all, United States banks will cut 200,000 employees by 2009, the banking consultancy Celent said in April."[15]

In a review of Thomas Friedman's *The World Is Flat*, Edward Leamer (2007) reminds us why geography remains relevant. He emphasizes that geography can be physical or cultural or informational. Hence we like local newspapers, music, and theater, and even websites from nearby countries.[16] And there are agglomeration externalities, which is why clusters succeed—movies in Hollywood, jazz and finance in New York City, and high-tech in Silicon Valley. In fact, "the most globalized firms depend heavily on capacities that benefit from local agglomeration economies."[17] Comparative advantage and specialization are localized phenomena, and often occur in economic clusters. "Of course, standardization, mechanization, and computerization all work to increase the number of footloose tasks, but innovation and education work in the opposite direction, creating relationship-based activities."[18] Sustaining high flying requires retaining "the immobile assets—the researchers (not the research), and infrastructure, including the parks and public spaces that these highly paid knowledge workers enjoy;"[19] indeed, high flying requires continuously developing created assets such as knowledge workers, intellectual property, and business infrastructure.

Innovation is an important determinant of the value-added ladder in a supply chain. At the apex are the lead firms, with design, management, and marketing skills, creating high value through intellectual property and brand reputation. And at the bottom are the suppliers of generic inputs, contributing little to innovation, competing with close substitutes and earning lean profit margins. As an example of the returns to innovation, consider the iPod:

> The iPod, like many other products, is made in several countries by dozens of companies, with each stage of production contributing a different amount to the final value.... The real value of the iPod doesn't lie in its parts or even in putting those parts together. The bulk of the iPod's value is in the conception and design of the iPod. That is why Apple gets $80 for each of these video iPods it sells, which is by far the largest piece of value added in the entire supply chain.... Those clever folks at Apple figured out how to combine 451 mostly generic parts into a valuable product. They may not make the iPod, but they created it. In the end, that's what really matters.[20]

How has the rapid spread of globalized supply chains affected the pace of globalization of innovation? After all, we can expect a complementarity between innovation and production—"ongoing cost-reducing process innovations can only be made by those who are actually producing the product."[21] Based on a collection of studies of 10 global industries (personal computing, software, semiconductors, flat panel display, lighting, pharmaceuticals, biotechnology, logistics, venture capital, and financial services), Macher and Mowery (2008) conclude that indeed, since the 1990s there has been a significant growth in innovative capabilities in countries like China, India, South Korea, and Taiwan, capabilities linked to the growth there of production, either manufacturing, or, in the case of India, software and services. And agglomeration economies have resulted in successful high-tech clusters—in Shanghai, Bangalore, and Hsinchu. While the United States still retains leading-edge capacity in most industries studied (with the exceptions of lighting and flat panel displays) there has developed a substantial international division of labor in innovation-related activities. Regarding personal computers, for example, "the global division of innovation-related activities within the industry is characterized as follows: component-level R&D (concept design and product planning) is performed in the United States and Japan; applied R&D and development of new platforms (particularly notebook computers) take place in Taiwan; and product development for mature products (mainly desktop computers) and a majority of production and sustaining engineering are performed in China."[22]

Figure 15.4 clearly shows sequential shifts in activities—catch-up industrialization is at work guided by shifts in competitive advantage.

> Industries and activities in which U.S. workers (defined in this case to include scientists and engineers) add less value are the most vulnerable to foreign competition and the most likely ones to move to foreign sites. The improved capabilities of scientists and engineers in many of these foreign locations, the identity of these locations themselves, and the changing outlook of demand and growth in the U.S. and foreign markets, however, may be causing more rapid shifts in competitive advantage and affecting a broader range of activities, including innovation-related activities, than in earlier decades.[23]

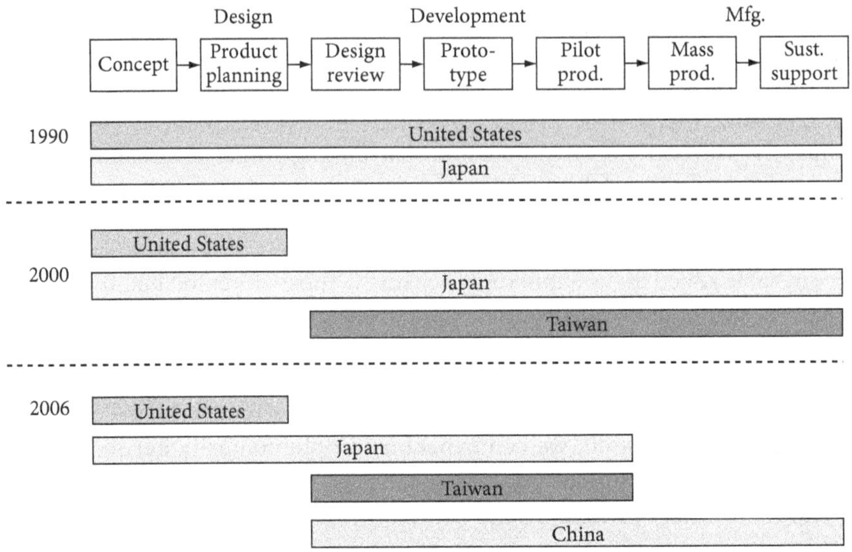


FIGURE 15.4 New global division of labor in the PC industry

*Source:* Macher and Mowery, ed. (2008) p.35

Within East Asia, high-income economies like Korea, Singapore, and Taiwan "now conduct formal R & D and patenting at the levels of the most advanced developed countries"[24] whereas low-income economies like Cambodia, conduct almost no R & D and patenting. "What is common to most East Asian economies though, is their success in absorbing knowledge from abroad."[25] Among lower-tier Southeast Asian economies, firms in low-income Cambodia "are among the most active in adopting and adapting activities."[26] For the higher-tier Northeast Asian economies, long-term contracts for original equipment manufacturing have been an important channel for building technological capabilities. Successful firms have achieved supplier-oriented industrial upgrading, i.e., sequential advancement from original equipment manufacturing to original design manufacturing to original brand manufacturing. Incremental innovation and user-driven innovation have been significant, especially in new personal computing products.

> Consumer markets for wireless and digital devices in countries such as South Korea, for example, are growing more rapidly than are similar markets in the United States. Equally important is the fact that many consumers in these markets (including firms producing advanced electronic-systems products) demand more advanced applications than is true of consumers elsewhere in the global economy. Users play a crucial role in demanding and in some cases developing or "co-inventing" new applications in the aforementioned industries, as well as in logistics.[27]

Such developments have hastened the speed of product cycling. Hence, "firms must combine product innovation and differentiation, and the learning and acquisition of specialized capabilities that implies, with high volumes, speed-to-market, competitive pricing, and the ability to penetrate new and uncharted markets."[28] Indeed, this has been at the core of the success of the small and medium Taiwanese firms. For instance:

> With flexible production and marketing networks, Taiwanese fashion shoe companies have managed to accommodate the rapidly changing fashion trends and small orders in the world market. As competition intensified in the mid-1980s, the number of product cycles grew from two to four and, eventually, eight per year. Taiwanese fashion shoe manufacturers received orders from international buyers who, in order to minimize risks in the increasingly unpredictable fashion markets, placed smaller orders more frequently, sometimes on a monthly basis. The lead-time between order placement and product delivery was compressed from 3–4 months to 1–2 months. Southeast Asian shoe manufacturers entered the competitive shoe export markets in the 1980s. Taiwanese shoe companies distinguished themselves by shifting from OEM (Original Equipment Manufacturing) to ODM (Original Development Manufacturing) arrangements with international buyers, and took greater initiatives in product design and development.[29]

Similarly, "China's competitiveness is derived not only from inexhaustible human resources but also from the diversity of foreign companies that interact and develop agile local players, a strength that has been hard to find in Japan."[30]

Investment and innovation also serve to lengthen quality ladders and deepen quality specialization. The greater the degree of product differentiation (e.g., the greater the variety of cotton shirts) the longer will be the quality ladder in that market and less likelihood that "wages in Los Angeles are set in Shanghai" [31].

An important aspect of the innovation at various nodes in the supply chain is the scope for cross-benefits. "The lead firms recognize how their products create potential value and they negotiate over its division with their partners. A successful firm understands that the creation of value through innovation is not a zero-sum game, and profits are needed all along the supply chain to sustain innovation by all participants."[32] Innovations may be spurred at the level of design, manufacturing or distribution. For example, "PC makers are pushed to incremental innovation by component makers (such as for semiconductors, storage, or power supply) who introduce frequent changes in their products (faster speed, greater capacity, smaller form factor, longer life) in efforts to gain greater market share within their industry sector. They also are pushed by consumers who want the latest technologies."[33] It can be easy to overlook the fact that "the ability to exploit offshore innovative talent has supported the entry and growth of numerous U.S. firms pursuing new business models and technology strategies."[34]

With innovation taking an expanded role at all levels of the supply chain, the value of education, at all levels and in new cross-disciplinary areas, is considerably magnified. From lead firms to component manufacturers, there is a need for a variety of skills, ranging from design to management, from software to hardware, and at interfaces, e.g.,"hardware engineers who can work with communications standards, and software engineers who can produce embedded software that enables customization of products for markets."[35]

All this requires infrastructure—appropriate educational and research institutions, funding, and collaboration between research institutions and private business. The quality of communications infrastructure (e.g., broadband access) is vital. The role of public policy as facilitator is far from trivial. From regulatory environments and tax structures that encourage innovation, to financial development and macroeconomic stability, all contribute significantly to the overall business environment for innovation. Intellectual property rights management includes far-sighted patenting and licensing policies:

> The international performance of firms, including multinationals, is affected by policy and other economic conditions in their home countries. And this link is especially strong for firms' innovation-related activities, which rely on a complex infrastructure of public and private institutions devoted to knowledge creation and transmission, personnel training, and other activities.[36]

For example, take the small story of the beginnings of a computer programming and pharmaceuticals hub in Hyderabad, India.

> Soon after N. Chandrababu Naidu became chief minister of the state of Andhra Pradesh in August 1995, he ordered that a partly built and abandoned government building here on the edge of the city be finished and turned into a college for computer software engineers. Today, the building houses one of 300 institutions of higher learning in a state that graduates 65,000 engineers a year, compared with 7,500 when Mr. Naidu took office.[37]

Alertness and quality of public policy are crucial.

## 15.6 The Gosling Challenge—Late-Entry Countries

For late entry Southeast Asian countries, like Cambodia, Laos, Myanmar, and Vietnam, catch-up industrialization in the contemporary global context of global production networks entails both new opportunities and challenges.

First, of course, there is the opportunity to join in as a small player in the extensive global value chain. Component manufacturing enables small firms to enter the global production network in specific and narrow activities of comparative-advantage. It eliminates the need for managing the complete production and marketing process of an end product. Further, intra-product specialization enables less-developed economies to focus on labor-intensive components of sophisticated products while benefiting from participation in a modern global supply network. The scope for knowledge transfer improves, and the goal of moving on to more skill, capital, and technology-intensive steps of production becomes more proximate. As we saw above, the complementarity between production and process innovation can usher a commensurate climb up the innovation ladder as well. Cambodian firms, for example, have done quite well in adopting and adapting products, processes, and methods from advanced countries.[38]

Also, once a particular node of a supply chain has been established in a country, the likelihood of local expansion of auxiliary activities improves substantially. These opportunities may be enhanced, for the Southeast Asian economies, by the simultaneous growth in China and India. As the more advanced ASEAN economies, with their comparative advantage in component production and resources, participate in the production networks created between these giant economies and others, growth externalities will be created for the lowest-income countries of the region. In short, there are real opportunities for "growth leverage."[39] In the realm of innovation too, "the emergence of East Asian national and regional knowledge stocks . . . are now providing an indigenous or regional foundation for new innovations and for cross-border knowledge flows."[40] It is worth emphasizing that "even in poor economies, some indigenous innovation effort increases the country's capacity to absorb knowledge from abroad."[41]

The prospects of the late-entry countries may also be well-served by stronger regional integration, in addition to the benefits of preferential treatment, standardization, and so on, this may also gather momentum for the development of strong reform constituencies within these countries. "Perhaps the best argument for economic integration is that it will make the fact more obvious that some countries are ahead and that some are behind. And the people of the lagging countries will start asking their governments the reason why."[42]

However, entry into a fiercely competitive international division of labor is not expected to be easy. Early entrants have preestablished relationships and markets. Further, in this scenario of trade in intermediates, product differentiation, and shortened product cycles, unlike in the earlier flying geese paradigm, there may be no immediate forerunner to copy and no period of import-substitution for learning-by-doing while serving a protected domestic market. In production for a global supply chain, timeliness and quality are imperative. It is not easy to acquire the nimbleness required to fit into an efficient and lean international production network. In addition, growth heterogeneity within China could make for the possibility that production networks may become focused within the large nation, delaying the emergence of outward waves of structural shifts.

For the growth leverage to work, these economies must make improvements in trade-facilitating infrastructure, including institutions of contract enforcement, regulation, and standards. In this complex and rapidly changing scenario, the role of the state as a major agent of catch-up industrialization will necessarily be more facilitating in nature. The importance of provision of infrastructure takes on significant proportions. A noteworthy aspect is the development of internal trading networks that can link the rural sector to the international, or at least regional, production network. Creation of a knowledge workforce is another prerequisite.

## 15.7 Conclusion

The international economic landscape has changed significantly since the flying geese paradigm unfolded, first in Japan, then in the Tiger Economies, and then in the ASEAN Four. That was a world where catch-up industrialization demanded mastery over entire product lines. In the contemporary scenario of complex webs of global supply chains, catch-up industrialization can begin with simple component manufacturing. There is more competition, but there are more opportunities too (in particular to master small phases of production), and significant spillover benefits.

However, the international division of labor, while finer, still rests on comparative advantage. This is true also of the international division of labor in innovation that has developed in conjunction with the spread of global production networks. There remains a hierarchy—akin to that of flying geese—of technology and innovation, and flowing from that, of value-added capture; and competitive advantage still drives the participation process. But instead of comparative advantage residing in complete end products, it is found typically in separate phases of production—design, engineering, and marketing are most often the realm of the more developed economies whereas the edge in the manufacturing and in the assembly of components belongs to the less developed.

For today's less developed economies the key to catch-up industrialization is to become a part of the rich matrix of global supply chains and to steadily climb the technology ladder. For the Asian developing economies in particular, the emergence of China and India offers opportunities for participation in rapidly expanding regional supply chains. In addition to this growth leverage, there are membership externalities—from the interaction with the more advanced members of the modern, global supply chain—of learning new and better ways of design, production, and management.

At the same time, these changes also mean a faster moving "air stream," if you will, and more crowded skies. With the global spread of technological ability, innovation-related activity and dynamic markets, shifts in comparative advantage have become more rapid, and affect a wider range of products. Product differentiation has multiplied and product cycles have shortened. "Flying" requires greater agility, on the part of all. Firm level efficiency, nimbleness, and creativity are crucial both to entering the supply chain and moving up the value chain.

Challenges notwithstanding, in the contemporary global context not only does the process of sequential shifting of competitive advantage remain the premise of catch-up industrialization, as when the flying geese roamed the newly industrializing Asian economies, but also the noteworthy factors contributing to participation and upgrading in the technological ladder are ever more significant. The value of innovation is widespread, spanning all nodes of the supply chain, from process to design, from manufacturing to distribution, to communications. Incremental innovation and user-driven innovation are contributing dynamism to industries. The scope for cross-benefits is extensive. The role of education is crucial—at all levels, in a variety of fields and in new cross-disciplinary directions. The significance of facilitating public policy cannot be overstated, in particular, infrastructure provision for education and innovation, and creating environments conducive to innovation. Quality and alertness of policy are the order of the day.

Looking at East Asia in particular, despite the transformed context of production activity, the regional hierarchy of value-added remains substantially unchanged, with Japan and the East Asian Tigers in the lead. Catch-up industrialization is ongoing, with its new opportunities and challenges. Sequential shifts in comparative advantage continue to drive the process, and in that sense, the geese continue to fly.

## Notes

1. This chapter is a revised version of University of San Francisco Center for the Pacific Rim Report No. 51, 2009. I am grateful for the Research Fellowship provided by The Kiriyama Chair for Pacific Rim Studies at the USF Center for the Pacific Rim. They are not responsible for the views expressed here, or for any errors or omissions.
2. Akamatsu (1962) p. 11.
3. Ibid., p. 12.
4. The "new structural economics," as discussed in chapter 8 of this volume, is pertinent to this aspect of the "flying geese" model. Further references to this general approach to fostering structural change are in chapter 8.
5. See Vernon (1966). The product cycle theory captures the process of invention of a product (in an advanced economy): its production and export, standardization of its production technology, and adoption and production by developing countries based on lower costs; all of this culminates in the original country importing the product. For a recent discussion of theoretical and empirical issues, see Kasahara (2004).
6. This term is Gerschenkron's (1962), from his classic work on economic development.
7. *The Economist* (2001) August 23.
8. See, for example, Rodrik (2006) and Wang and Wei (2008). Athukorala, in chapter 13 of this volume, provides somewhat of a corrective view to this characterization, in addition to the references in the text.
9. As noted, this view is reinforced by the work of Athukorala in chapter 13 of this volume.
10. See Khandelwal (2008), Xu (2007), and Schott (2008).
11. Gill (2007a) p. 11.
12. See, for example, Borrus (2000). Antras and Helpman (2004) provide a seminal theoretical analysis of global sourcing.
13. Yusuf and Evenett (2002) p. 150.
14. Borrus (2000) p. 2. See also Roland-Holst (2005) and Yusuf (2002).
15. *New York Times* (2008) August 11.
16. See Blum and Goldfarb (2006).
17. Borrus (2000) p. 11.
18. Leamer (2007) p. 83.
19. Ibid., p. 99.
20. Varian (2007).
21. Leamer (2007) p. 97.
22. Macher and Mowery, ed. (2008) p. 4.
23. Ibid., p.13

24. Brahmbhatt and Hu (2007) p. 4
25. Ibid.
26. Gill et al. (2007b) p. 128.
27. Macher and Mowery, ed. (2008) p. 11.
28. Borrus (2000) p 8.
29. Hsing (1999) p. 103.
30. Munakata (2003) p. 3.
31. Leamer (2007) p. 5.
32. Linden et al. (2007).
33. Macher and Mowery, ed. (2008) p. 22.
34. Ibid., p. 13.
35. Ibid., p. 49.
36. Ibid., p. 3.
37. See Bradsher(2002).
38. See Gill et al. (2007b) pp. 127–134
39. See Roland-Holst et al. (2005) p. 78. The lessons of late-comer industries in more advanced economies are also relevant: see, for example, Kimura (2007).
40. Brahmbhatt and Hu (2007) p. 4.
41. Ibid., p. 5.
42. Gill, ed. (2007a), p. 229.

## References

Akamatsu, Kaname, 1962, "A Historical Pattern of Economic Growth in Developing Economies," *The Developing Economies*, Preliminary Issue, No. 1, March-August, pp. 3–25.

Amsden, Alice H., 1991, "Diffusion of Development: The Late Industrializing Model and Greater East Asia," *The American Economic Review*, Vol. 81, No. 2, May, pp. 282–286.

Antras, Pol, and Elhanan Helpman, 2004, "Global Sourcing," Working Paper No.3-2004, The Foerder Institute for Economic Research and The Sackler Institute of Economic Studies.

Arndt, Sven W., and Henryk Kierzkowski (ed.) 2001, *Fragmentation—New Production Patterns in the World Economy*, New York: Oxford University Press.

Balassa, B., 1977, "A Stages Approach to Comparative Advantage," *World Bank Staff Working Papers*, No. 256.

Bardhan, P., 1990, "Symposium on the State and Economic Development, *Journal of Economic Perspectives*," Vol. 4, No. 3, pp. 3–7.

Blum, Bernardo S., and Avi Goldfarb, 2006. "Does the Internet Defy the Law of Gravity?" *Journal of International Economics*, Vol. 70, Issue 2, pp. 384–405.

Borrus, Michael (ed.), 2000, *International Production Networks in Asia: Rivalry or Riches*. Richmond, Surrey, GBR: Curzon Press Limited.

Bradsher, Keith, 2002, "A High-Tech Fix for One Corner of India," *The New York Times*, December 27.

Brahmbhatt, Milan, and Albert Hu, 2007, "Ideas and Innovation in East Asia," World Bank Policy Research Working Paper No. 4403.

*The Economist*, 2001, "A Panda Breaks the Formation," August 23.

Gerschenkron, A., 1962, *Economic Backwardness in Historical Perspective*, Cambridge, MA: Harvard University Press.

Gill, Indermit, Yukon Huang, and Homi Kharas, eds., 2007a, *East Asian Visions: Perspectives on Economic Development*, World Bank (Washington, DC) and Institute of Policy Studies (Singapore).

Gill, Indermit, and Homi Kharas, et al., 2007b, *An East Asian Renaissance: Ideas For Economic Growth*, World Bank, Washington, DC.

Hsing, You-tien, 1999, "Trading Companies in Taiwan's Fashion Shoe Networks," *Journal of International Economics*, Vol. 48, Issue 1, June, pp. 101–120.

Ito, Takatoshi, 1996, "Japan and the Asian Economies: A Miracle in Transition," *Brookings Paper on Economic Activity*, Vol. 1996, No. 2, pp. 205–272.

Kasahara, Shigeshisha, 2004, "The Flying Geese Paradigm: A Critical Study of its Application to East Asian Regional Development," *United Nations Conference on Trade and Development, Discussion Papers*, No. 169, April.

Khandelwal, Amit, 2008, "The Long and Short (of) Quality Ladders," Working Paper Series, Columbia Business School, New York.

Kimura, Seishi, 2007, *The Challenges of Late Industrialization: The Global Economy and the Japanese Commercial Aircraft Industry*, Basingstoke, UK: Palgrave Macmillan.

Kojima, Kiyoshi, 1977, *Japan and a New World Economic Order*, Boulder, CO: Westview Press, Inc.

Koopman, Robert, Zhi Wang, and Shang-Jin Wei, 2008, "How Much of Chinese Exports Is Really Made In China? Assessing Domestic Value-Added When Processing Trade Is Pervasive," National Bureau of Economic Research, Working Paper 14109, June.

Lardy, Nicholas, and Lee Branstetter, 2006, "China's Embrace of Globalization," NBER Working Paper Series, Working Paper 12373, July.

Leamer, Edward E., 2007, "A Flat World, a Level Playing Field, a Small World After All, or None of the Above? A Review of Thomas L. Friedman's *The World is Flat*," *Journal of Economic Literature*, Vol. XLV, March, pp. 83–126.

Linden, Greg, Kenneth L. Kraemer, and Jason Dedrick, 2007, "*Who Captures Value in a Global Innovation System? The Case of Apple's iPod*," Personal Computing Industry Center (PCIC), Irvine, California, June.

Macher, Jeffrey T., and David C. Mowery, ed., 2008, *Innovation in Global Industries: U.S. Firms Competing in a New World: Collected Studies*, The National Academies Press, Washington, D.C.

Munakata, Naoko, 2003, "*The Impact of the Rise of China and Regional Economic Integration in Asia—A Japanese Perspective*," Testimony, U.S.-China Economic and Security Commission Review, Washington DC.

*New York Times*, 2008, "Cost-Cutting in New York, but a Boom in India," August 11.

Rodrik, Dani, 2006, "What's So Special about China's Exports?" *China & World Economy*, Vol. 14, No. 5, 1–19, September/October.

Roland-Host, David, 2005, "Global Supply Networks and Multilateral Trade Linkages: A Structural Analysis of East Asia," in Charles Harvie, Fukunari Kimura, and Hyun-Hoon Lee ed., *New East Asian Regionalism: Causes, Progress and Country Perspectives*, Cheltenham, UK: Edward Elgar Publishing Limited, pp. 39-71.

Roland-Holst, David and John Weiss, 2004, "ASEAN and China: Export Rivals or Partners in Regional Growth?," *World Economy*, Aug., Vol. 27, Issue 8, pp. 1255–1274.

Roland-Holst, David, Jean-Pierre Verbiest, and Fan Zhai, 2005, "Growth and Trade Horizons for Asia: Long-term Forecasts for Regional Integration," *Asian Development Review*, Vol. 22, no. 2, pp. 76–107, Asian Development Bank.

Schott, Peter, 2008, "The Relative Sophistication of Chinese Exports," *Economic Policy* Vol. 53, 5–49, January.

Varian, Hal R., 2007, "An iPod Has Global Value. Ask the (Many) Countries That Make It," *New York Times*, June 28.

Vernon, Raymond, 1966, "International Investment and International Trade in Product Cycle," *Quarterly Journal of Economics*, LXXX, No. 2, May, pp. 190–207.

Wang, Zhi, and Shang-Jin Wei, 2008, "What Accounts For The Rising Sophistication of China's Exports?," National Bureau Of Economic Research Working Paper 13771, February.

World Bank, 1993, *The East Asian Miracle: Economic Growth and Public Policy*, Washington, DC: World Bank.

Xu, Bin, 2007, "Measuring China's Export Sophistication," China Europe International Business School, China, October.

Yoshimatsu, Hidetaka, 2003, *Japan and East Asia in Transition: Trade Policy, Crisis and Evolution, and Regionalism*, Palgrave MacMillan, New York.

Yusuf, Shahid, ed., 2004, *Global Production Networking and Technological Change in East Asia*, World Bank Publications, Washington, DC.

Yusuf, Shahid and Simon J. Evenett, 2002, *Can East Asia Compete? Innovation for Global Markets*, The World Bank, Washington DC.

CHAPTER 16

# MULTINATIONAL ENTERPRISES, FOREIGN DIRECT INVESTMENT, AND THE EAST ASIAN ECONOMIC INTEGRATION

TZU-HAN YANG AND DENG-SHING HUANG

## 16.1 Introduction

The increasing prominence of multinational enterprises (MNEs) in the current world economy has drawn considerable attention not only from international organizations and national government agencies, but also from local citizens. Through merging, procuring, and setting up new establishments, MNEs have operated businesses worldwide, by which they mobilize resources, develop vertical and horizontal production networks, and penetrate all market types across borders. These acts have changed state economy operations and the relationships among them. Willingly or not, state economies have been connected and become interdependent with one another. The result has created regional economic integration and intensified globalization.

Thanks to the openness of global trade and foreign investment advocated by the World Trade Organization (WTO) and responded to by national authorities, along with the use of advanced transportation and communication technologies, MNEs can rapidly expand with much fewer obstacles than previously. According to the survey of the Global 2000[1], the overall sales of these top 2000 firms in the world market grew 36.63 percent between 2004 and 2009, from $21.9 trillion to $30.0 trillion, with an annual growth rate of 6.44 percent, greater than the annual growth rate of 6.26 percent in world trade. The asset value grew 53.72 percent from $80.7 trillion to $124.0 trillion, with an annual growth rate of 8.98 percent[2], greater than that of 6.07 percent in world capital assets[3]. Gabel and Bruner (2003) also claimed that among the world's 100 largest economies, 53 of them are MNEs. They command greater resources and exert stronger influence than nearly three-fourths of all national states.

The effects of MNE investments on trade have also been recognized. Bonturi and Fusakaku (1993) found that the significant growth of intra-industry trade in the 1980s was mainly induced by FDI, and intra-firm trade accounts for approximately 35 to 40 percent of the total U.S. trade. UNCTAD (2002) indicated that foreign affiliates of MNEs accounted for 35 percent of world trade in 2001. Feenstra (1999) divided MNE trading into intra-MNE (parent-affiliate and affiliate-affiliate) trade and arm's length transactions (between MNEs and unaffiliated firms), and found that 34 percent of total U.S. exports and 43 percent of total U.S. imports were intra-MNE trade in 1992. In either case, these numbers of magnitude show that MNEs have been key players in global trade.

Because of the importance of MNEs in trade, the nature of MNE exports has been reconsidered. In the negotiations of U.S.-Japan trade disputes in the 1980s (and in the more recent U.S.-China negotiations), the representatives of Japan (and China) repeatedly indicated that a large portion of its exports to the United States was produced and traded by the MNEs of other countries and that portion should be treated as exports of these FDI source countries. Trade balances based on ownership (instead of geographical location) better show the trade relationship among countries. The United States later acknowledged this viewpoint. Since 1995, the U.S. Bureau of Economic Analysis has published an annual report on *An Ownership-Based Framework of the U.S. Current Account*, taking foreign MNE sales in the United States as extended exports of MNE source countries to the United States, and the sales of U.S. MNEs in foreign countries as extended U.S. exports. In this definition, MNE activities are considered an extension of the economic activities of source countries, largely reducing U.S. trade deficits.

Who, then, are the top MNEs in the global economic arena? Where do these MNEs come from and what types of businesses do they conduct? When MNEs invest overseas, where does the investment go? How might MNE activities affect the development of regional economies?

In this chapter, we attempt to answer these questions by first analyzing the structure of the top 2000 firms in the global market. Beginning from 2003, the *Forbes* Magazine has published an annual list of the top 2000 firms worldwide as "the Global 2000."[4] The ranking is determined based on a composite index considering profits, sales, assets, and market value.[5] The operation of these firms has gone beyond the boundary of their motherland and spreads across borders. The structural change of these firms may largely represent MNE development in the global economy.

We related the top MNE activities with national FDI to discover whether the countries with more large MNEs invest more outwardly, while simultaneously attracting more investment from abroad. By decomposing the regional distribution of national FDI and adopting the clustering analysis method, we are able to depict FDI networks and test the existence of regional concentration phenomena. Finally, we compare the structure of FDI networks with that of trade networks to trace the evolution of regional economic integration, particularly that in East Asia.

The rest of this chapter is organized as follows. The next section provides the descriptive statistics of the Global 2000 firms and analyzes the development trend. The third section describes the clustering analysis method and presents the empirical results to determine whether regional investment blocks exist and to trace the development of regional trade blocks. The fourth section summarizes our findings and offers a conclusion.

## 16.2 Multinational Enterprises and FDI

### 16.2.1 Who Are the Top MNEs and What Are They Doing?

For a quick glimpse of the top MNEs, in Appendix 1, we list the top 10 firms in the Global 2000 firms of 2011, and in Appendix 2, the top 10 manufacturing firms. Appendix 1 shows that the largest global firms are those doing business mainly in finance and energy exploration and drilling. (The only exception is the GE Company, which produces computer-storage devices, and is the only manufacturing firm in the list.) The top 10 manufacturing firms mainly produce computer products, automobiles, and medical products. In either case, U.S. firms have occupied at least half of the seats in each of these top-ten lists. Although the United States has remained the largest global investor, the ranking of the source countries where the Global 2000 firms are based has continued to change. As shown in Table 16.1, during 2004–2011, the United States and Japan retained their positions as the first and second largest source countries with the most Global 2000 firms, although the shares and numbers of their firms have significantly declined. Another country with a large decrease in firm number is the U.K., from 134 firms in 2004 to 90 in 2011. In contrast, the ones with the most rapid increase in the number of firms listed in the Global 2000 are China, India, and South Korea, each adding 115, 31, and 27 more firms, respectively, during 2004-2011. In 2004, China and India were ranked 17th and 14th, owning only 21 and 30 firms in the Global 2000. Yet in 2009, they became the third and eighth, owning 113 and 56 firms respectively. Maintaining the same ranking to 2011, the number of owned firms has increased to 136 and 61. In only five years, China surpassed technologically advanced and capital-abundant countries such as the U.K., France, Canada, and Germany, gaining a leading stand in the world investment race. In addition to China and India, the Asian newly industrialized economies (NIEs), including South Korea, Hong Kong,

**Table 16.1 The Source Countries Owning the Global 2000 Firms (ranked by firm number)***

| Source Country | 2011 | 2010 | 2009 | 2008 | 2007 | 2006 | 2005 | 2004 | 2011-2004 |
|---|---|---|---|---|---|---|---|---|---|
| United States | 1 (524) | 1 (536) | 1 (536) | 1 (551) | 1 (598) | 1 (659) | 1 (693) | 1 (711) | -186 |
| Japan | 2 (258) | 2 (260) | 2 (270) | 2 (288) | 2 (259) | 2 (291) | 2 (320) | 2 (326) | -68 |
| China | 3 (136) | 3 (121) | 3 (113) | 4 (91) | 4 (70) | 9 (44) | 15 (28) | 17 (21) | +115 |
| United Kingdom | 4 (90) | 4 (86) | 4 (90) | 3 (98) | 3 (120) | 3 (126) | 3 (125) | 3 (134) | -44 |
| South Korea | 5 (68) | 7 (61) | 9 (51) | 6 (61) | 8 (52) | 7 (52) | 7 (50) | 8 (41) | +27 |
| Canada | 6 (66) | 5 (67) | 6 (62) | 8 (55) | 6 (59) | 5 (61) | 5 (60) | 4 (67) | -1 |
| France | 7 (63) | 5 (67) | 5 (64) | 5 (72) | 5 (67) | 4 (66) | 4 (67) | 6 (62) | +1 |
| India | 8 (61) | 8 (57) | 8 (56) | 9 (47) | 10 (48) | 15 (34) | 13 (33) | 14 (30) | +31 |
| Germany | 9 (53) | 9 (54) | 7 (57) | 7 (57) | 6 (59) | 6 (57) | 6 (58) | 5 (63) | -10 |
| Hong Kong | 10 (48) | 11 (46) | 10 (49) | 13 (42) | 12 (39) | 8 (45) | 11 (36) | 12 (32) | +16 |
| Switzerland | 11 (45) | 10 (47) | 11 (48) | 10 (45) | 13 (37) | 13 (36) | 10 (39) | 9 (37) | +8 |
| Australia | 12 (44) | 12 (41) | 12 (45) | 10 (45) | 9 (50) | 10 (43) | 11 (36) | 9 (37) | +7 |
| Taiwan | 13 (42) | 13 (40) | 13 (39) | 10 (45) | 11 (42) | 11 (42) | 9 (41) | 11 (35) | +7 |
| Italy | 14 (34) | 15 (36) | 14 (38) | 14 (41) | 13 (37) | 11 (42) | 8 (46) | 7 (45) | -11 |
| Brazil | 15 (33) | 14 (37) | 15 (33) | 16 (31) | 15 (34) | 19 (22) | 18 (19) | 18 (19) | +14 |
| Russia | 16 (28) | 19 (26) | 17 (28) | 17 (28) | 16 (29) | 20 (20) | 23 (14) | 24 (13) | +15 |
| Spain | 16 (28) | 17 (27) | 16 (29) | 15 (33) | 16 (29) | 13 (36) | 14 (29) | 14 (30) | -2 |
| Sweden | 18 (25) | 16 (28) | 18 (27) | 18 (22) | 16 (29) | 17 (28) | 17 (26) | 16 (28) | -3 |
| Netherlands | 19 (24) | 17 (27) | 19 (23) | 18 (22) | 19 (25) | 16 (29) | 15 (28) | 12 (32) | -8 |
| South Africa | 20 (20) | 23 (17) | 19 (23) | 22 (17) | 22 (17) | 22 (16) | 19 (18) | 21 (17) | +3 |

*firm number in parenthesis.

*Note:* The year listed is one year before the publishing year. For example, the data published in 2012 is treated as the ranking of 2011.

*Source:* the Global 2000, the Forbes, various years.

and Taiwan, have remained steady in the list of the top 15 countries throughout the period.

If measured by sales, the ranking of emerging Asian countries is modestly falling behind. As shown in Table 16.2, except for China retaining its rank as third, South Korea, India, Taiwan, and Hong Kong show lower rankings than that counted by firm numbers. In 2011, India, Taiwan, and Hong Kong are listed as 16th, 17th, and 18th, whereas South Korea is ranked seventh. Although these emerging Asian countries have vigorously

**Table 16.2 The Rankings of the Source Countries of the Global 2000 Firms (by firm number and sales, 2011)**

| Country | The ranking by sales volume ($ billions) | The ranking by firm number (no. of firms) |
|---|---|---|
| United States | 1 (10846.9) | 1 (524) |
| Japan | 2 (4710.6) | 2 (258) |
| China | 3 (2418.0) | 3 (136) |
| France | 4 (2083.4) | 7 (63) |
| Germany | 5 (2019.3) | 9 (53) |
| United Kingdom | 6 (1999.5) | 4 (90) |
| South Korea | 7 (1269.8) | 5 (68) |
| Netherlands | 8 (1097.6) | 19 (24) |
| Switzerland | 9 (948.0) | 11 (45) |
| Canada | 10 (813.7) | 6 (66) |
| Italy | 11 (807.1) | 14 (34) |
| Brazil | 12 (701.2) | 15 (33) |
| Australia | 13 (630.6) | 12 (44) |
| Russia | 14 (617.7) | 16 (28) |
| Spain | 15 (587.8) | 16 (28) |
| India | 16 (583.3) | 8 (61) |
| Taiwan | 17 (505.3) | 13 (42) |
| Hong Kong | 18 (483.2) | 10 (48) |
| Sweden | 19 (289.7) | 18 (25) |
| Norway | 20 (194.4) | 42 (9) |

*Source*: the Global 2000, the *Forbes*, published in 2012.

invested overseas, the size of their business operation or their share of global sales is relatively smaller.

Although modest in size, the rapid growth of MNEs in emerging Asian countries has changed global-economy dominance. As shown in Fig. 16.1, the Herfindahl concentration index based on the shares of source countries owning Global 2000 firms, either measured by firm number or by sales, has declined over time. This may imply that the rise of emerging Asia has decentralized the distribution of global economic power and spread it more evenly among the three continents of Europe, America, and Asia.

FIGURE 16.1 The Herfindahl concentration index based on the shares of the source countries owning the Global 2000 firms

*The data of sales is not available for 2002.

*Source:* The Global 2000, the Forbes.

$$\text{The firm number index} = \sum_{\substack{i=\text{all Global 2000}\\ \text{source countries}}} \left[\begin{array}{l}\text{the number of the Global 2000}\\ \text{firms based on country i/2000}\end{array}\right]^2$$

$$\text{The sales index} = \sum_{\substack{i=\text{all Global 2000}\\ \text{source countries}}} \left[\begin{array}{l}\text{total sales of country } i\text{'s Global 2000}\\ \text{firms/total sales of all Global 2000 firms}\end{array}\right]^2$$

Table 16.3 shows the types of businesses conducted by these 2000 giant firms. Using the average data of 2004-2006, 2007-2009, and 2010-2011, we found that they have evenly covered all aspects of industries, and maintained a relatively stable structure over time. We classify different industries into five categories of finance, manufacturing, other services (services other than finance), resource type, and public facilities, and count the share of each category according to the number of firms. Taking the data of 2010-2011, we found that finance firms occupy the share of 29.35 percent and form the largest sector. This is reasonable because financial support is essential for investment, particularly foreign investment. Manufacturing firms take the second largest share of 23.08 percent, reflecting commodity production as one of the main purposes for overseas investment, as well as the fact that production fragmentation networks, either vertical or horizontal, have multiplied across countries. The other service firms hold the third stand or 17.83 percent, covering consumption services, production services, market access, and other miscellaneous services. Public facilities firms rank fourth and own the share of 15.90 percent, covering the businesses of communications, transportation, construction, and utilities. Resource-type firms own the smallest share, but it is the only sector showing a steady increasing trend from 10.90 percent of 2004-2006 to 12.97 percent of 2007-2009 and 13.85 percent of 2010-2011. The firm number of this type progressively increased from 200 of 2004 to 284 of 2012, which may reflect the fierce international

**Table 16.3 Industrial Distribution of the Global 2000 Firms***

| Industry | | 2010–2011 average (percent) | | 2007–2009 average (percent) | | 2004–2006 average (percent) | |
|---|---|---|---|---|---|---|---|
| Finance | Banking | 15.08 | 29.35 | 14.88 | 29.50 | 14.72 | 29.02 |
| | Diversified financial | 9.13 | | 9.55 | | 8.80 | |
| | Insurance | 5.15 | | 5.07 | | 5.50 | |
| Manufacturing | Capital goods | 8.78 | 23.08 | 8.35 | 21.78 | 7.92 | 22.05 |
| | Consumption goods | 8.43 | | 7.78 | | 8.08 | |
| | Intermediate goods | 5.88 | | 5.62 | | 6.05 | |
| Other services | Consumption services | 3.43 | 17.83 | 3.27 | 18.10 | 4.32 | 20.47 |
| | Production services | 5.70 | | 6.05 | | 6.32 | |
| | Market channels | 6.40 | | 6.25 | | 7.02 | |
| | Others | 2.30 | | 2.53 | | 2.82 | |
| Resources type | Material | 7.40 | 13.85 | 6.82 | 12.97 | 5.55 | 10.90 |
| | Oil and gas | 6.45 | | 6.15 | | 5.35 | |
| Public facilities | Communications | 3.13 | 15.90 | 3.60 | 17.68 | 3.50 | 17.57 |
| | Transportation | 3.40 | | 3.98 | | 3.93 | |
| | Construction | 3.55 | | 4.07 | | 4.13 | |
| | Utilities | 5.83 | | 6.03 | | 6.00 | |

*the percentage is counted by firm number.
*Source*: the Global 2000, the Forbes.

competition of procuring natural resources in recent years and the huge size of these investment projects.

This overall structure reflects that through FDI and MNE activities, a global business framework has largely formalized to constantly and evenly facilitate a freer flow of capital, goods, services, and resources.

In most industries, the United States and Japan have maintained their lead and ranked as first and second, whereas emerging Asian countries play different roles. For example, in the finance industry, as shown in Table 16.4, China and India have quickly promoted from 17th and 12th in 2004 to third and fourth in 2009, and have maintained these high rankings up to 2011. Because of high saving rates, rapid accumulation of capital, and government policy incentives encouraging outward investment[6], they have significantly advanced in financial business, through which they support their overseas investment. Their firm numbers even excelled in countries such as the U.K. and Switzerland, who are much more mature in financial development. Hong Kong, as the traditional East Asian financial center, held the sixth position in 2011, whereas Taiwan and South Korea were out of the top 10. Particularly, finance firms were traded and changed national identity most frequently, compared to firms in other industrial sectors.

**Table 16.4 The Source Countries Owning the *Finance* Firms in the Global 2000 (ranked by firm number)**

| Source Country | 2011 | 2010 | 2009 | 2008 | 2007 | 2006 | 2005 | 2004 |
|---|---|---|---|---|---|---|---|---|
| United States | 1 (108) | 1 (118) | 1 (119) | 1 (115) | 1 (140) | 1 (167) | 1 (162) | 1 (160) |
| Japan | 2 (81) | 2 (83) | 2 (81) | 2 (86) | 2 (86) | 2 (95) | 2 (104) | 2 (107) |
| China | 3 (39) | 3 (37) | 3 (28) | 3 (29) | 5 (22) | 13 (13) | 15 (8) | 17 (8) |
| India | 4 (23) | 4 (23) | 4 (21) | 6 (19) | 6 (19) | 9 (14) | 12 (13) | 12 (10) |
| UK | 5 (22) | 4 (23) | 4 (21) | 4 (24) | 3 (31) | 3 (33) | 3 (28) | 3 (27) |
| Australia | 6 (20) | 8 (16) | 6 (18) | 8 (18) | 4 (23) | 5 (18) | 8 (14) | 8 (14) |
| Hong Kong | 6 (20) | 6 (20) | 9 (16) | 6 (19) | 8 (16) | 5 (18) | 8 (14) | 11 (11) |
| Italy | 8 (18) | 7 (18) | 6 (18) | 5 (20) | 6 (19) | 4 (23) | 4 (26) | 4 (26) |
| Canada | 9 (17) | 11 (15) | 11 (15) | 14 (13) | 9 (15) | 7 (16) | 7 (15) | 8 (14) |
| Switzerland | 10 (15) | 8 (16) | 8 (17) | 11 (15) | 11 (14) | 8 (15) | 5 (17) | 6 (16) |
| Taiwan | 11 (14) | 12 (14) | 12 (14) | 11 (15) | 9 (15) | 9 (14) | 6 (16) | 7 (15) |
| South Korea | 11 (14) | 8 (16) | 16 (11) | 9 (16) | 11 (14) | 9 (14) | 13 (10) | 12 (10) |
| France | 13 (13) | 12 (14) | 12 (14) | 9 (16) | 13 (13) | 13 (13) | 8 (14) | 10 (12) |
| Germany | 14 (12) | 14 (12) | 14 (13) | 11 (15) | 15 (12) | 13 (13) | 8 (14) | 5 (17) |
| Spain | 15 (11) | 15 (11) | 15 (12) | 15 (11) | 17 (9) | 13 (13) | 14 (9) | 14 (9) |
| U. Arab Emirates | 16 (9) | 16 (9) | 17 (9) | 16 (10) | 16 (10) | --* | --* | --* |
| Israel | 17 (8) | 20 (7) | 20 (7) | 17 (9) | 30 (6) | 22 (6) | 21 (6) | 19 (6) |
| Brazil | 17 (8) | 18 (8) | 20 (7) | 21 (7) | 17 (9) | 27 (4) | 30 (3) | 30 (3) |
| Qatar | 17 (8) | 20 (7) | 30 (4) | 30 (4) | 39 (2) | --* | --* | --* |
| Sweden | 20 (7) | 18 (8) | 18 (8) | 27 (5) | 19 (8) | 17 (8) | 17 (7) | 14 (9) |
| No. of all finance firms in the Global 2000 | 583 | 591 | 578 | 585 | 607 | 601 | 576 | 564 |

*The country has no financial firm listed in the Global 2000 in the year.
*Source*: the Global 2000, the *Forbes*.

In the manufacturing sector, the United States owned 158 firms among all 470 manufacturing firms in the Global 2000 in 2011. This number is equivalent to the sum of the next four ranking countries (see Table 16.5). The sales of these 158 U.S.-based firms are 35.4 percent of all 470 manufacturing firms. The strong lead of the United States in manufacturing shows that even though the U.S. economy has transformed into a service-sector-dominated economy, it has remained the leading force in global manufacturing production.

On the other hand, the performance of East Asian countries in manufacturing is overall stronger. Japan, China, South Korea, and Taiwan are consecutively ranked as second, third, fourth, and fifth, followed by Singapore as 15th (see Table 16.5). The list can be illustrated as the leading goose (Japan) with the first follower geese (Asian NIEs) and the

**Table 16.5 The Source Countries Owning the Manufacturing Firms in the Global 2000 (ranked by firm number)**

| Source Country | 2011 | 2010 | 2009 | 2008 | 2007 | 2006 | 2005 | 2004 |
|---|---|---|---|---|---|---|---|---|
| United States | 1 (158) | 1 (150) | 1 (145) | 1 (156) | 1 (155) | 1 (162) | 1 (175) | 1 (179) |
| Japan | 2 (73) | 2 (74) | 2 (75) | 2 (86) | 2 (74) | 2 (84) | 2 (91) | 2 (96) |
| China | 3 (34) | 3 (31) | 3 (27) | 5 (18) | 10 (8) | 12 (7) | 20 (3) | 26 (1) |
| South Korea | 4 (22) | 6 (18) | 8 (12) | 6 (14) | 8 (12) | 8 (11) | 7 (13) | 8 (12) |
| Taiwan | 5 (21) | 4 (20) | 4 (19) | 3 (23) | 3 (22) | 3 (20) | 4 (18) | 6 (14) |
| France | 6 (19) | 4 (20) | 4 (19) | 4 (20) | 4 (21) | 3 (20) | 3 (21) | 3 (19) |
| United Kingdom | 7 (17) | 8 (13) | 8 (12) | 8 (13) | 5 (16) | 5 (17) | 4 (18) | 5 (18) |
| Germany | 8 (12) | 9 (12) | 7 (13) | 9 (12) | 5 (16) | 6 (15) | 6 (17) | 3 (19) |
| Switzerland | 8 (12) | 7 (15) | 6 (15) | 6 (14) | 7 (13) | 7 (12) | 7 (13) | 7 (13) |
| Sweden | 8 (12) | 10 (9) | 10 (9) | 10 (8) | 9 (10) | 9 (9) | 9 (8) | 10 (9) |
| Canada | 11 (8) | 10 (9) | 11 (7) | 11 (7) | 10 (8) | 10 (8) | 10 (7) | 9 (10) |
| India | 11 (8) | 13 (7) | 14 (6) | 12 (6) | 17 (4) | 15 (4) | 16 (4) | 14 (4) |
| Brazil | 13 (7) | 10 (9) | 11 (7) | 13 (5) | 12 (6) | 15 (4) | 16 (4) | 14 (4) |
| Ireland | 13 (7) | 16 (5) | 15 (5) | 30 (1) | 24 (2) | 23 (2) | 27 (1) | 26 (1) |
| Finland | 15 (6) | 16 (5) | 15 (5) | 13 (5) | 12 (6) | 13 (6) | 11 (5) | 12 (6) |
| Singapore | 15 (6) | 14 (6) | 15 (5) | 20 (4) | 17 (4) | 20 (3) | 23 (2) | 21 (2) |
| Netherlands | 17 (5) | 16 (5) | 15 (5) | 13 (5) | 12 (6) | 10 (8) | 11 (5) | 11 (7) |
| Italy | 17 (5) | 14 (6) | 15 (5) | 13 (5) | 15 (5) | 14 (5) | 11 (5) | 13 (5) |
| Denmark | 17 (5) | 21 (4) | 21 (4) | 13 (5) | 21 (3) | 15 (4) | 11 (5) | 14 (4) |
| Thailand | 17 (5) | 21 (4) | 27 (2) | 30 (1) | 30 (1) | --* | --* | --* |
| No. of all manufacturing firms in the Global 2000 | 470 | 453 | 436 | 442 | 427 | 427 | 445 | 451 |

*The country has no manufacturing firm listed in the Global 2000 in the year.
*Source*: the Global 2000, the Forbes.

newly joined goose (China), using the East Asian flying geese paradigm.[7] The production fragmentation networks among them are well-established and continue to intensify, notwithstanding the 1997 Asian financial crisis. The rise of China and the absence of the ASEAN4 countries[8] in large-scale foreign direct investment have triggered the discussion of China's catching-up and even outpacing ASEAN4 in the orderly sequence of industrial development.[9]

In contrast to their manufacturing advantage, the performance of emerging Asian economies is comparatively weaker in the services industry (other than finance). As shown in Table 16.6, in 2011, only Hong Kong was among the top five. China, South

**Table 16.6 The Source Countries Owning the Other Services Firms in the Global 2000 (ranked by firm number)**

| Source Country | 2011 | 2010 | 2009 | 2008 | 2007 | 2006 | 2005 | 2004 |
|---|---|---|---|---|---|---|---|---|
| United States | 1 (145) | 1 (152) | 1 (155) | 1 (143) | 1 (155) | 1 (173) | 1 (194) | 1 (211) |
| Japan | 2 (37) | 2 (40) | 2 (45) | 2 (46) | 3 (34) | 3 (43) | 2 (49) | 3 (48) |
| United Kingdom | 3 (22) | 3 (24) | 3 (30) | 3 (31) | 2 (42) | 2 (44) | 3 (45) | 2 (49) |
| France | 4 (17) | 4 (15) | 4 (14) | 4 (16) | 4 (13) | 4 (13) | 4 (13) | 4 (14) |
| Hong Kong | 5 (13) | 6 (11) | 5 (13) | 6 (10) | 8 (8) | 7 (9) | 8 (8) | 8 (7) |
| Germany | 6 (12) | 5 (12) | 6 (11) | 5 (12) | 5 (12) | 5 (11) | 5 (11) | 5 (12) |
| China | 7 (11) | 9 (9) | 10 (6) | 11 (4) | 12 (5) | 28 (1) | 25 (1) | 24 (1) |
| Canada | 8 (10) | 7 (10) | 6 (11) | 8 (9) | 6 (11) | 6 (10) | 6 (10) | 5 (12) |
| South Korea | 9 (7) | 7 (10) | 6 (11) | 6 (10) | 8 (8) | 7 (9) | 7 (9) | 10 (6) |
| India | 10 (6) | 13 (5) | 10 (6) | 11 (4) | 12 (5) | 13 (4) | 16 (3) | 16 (3) |
| Australia | 11 (5) | 11 (6) | 10 (6) | 9 (8) | 7 (9) | 9 (8) | 10 (7) | 8 (7) |
| Brazil | 11 (5) | 18 (4) | 13 (5) | 18 (3) | 21 (2) | 20 (2) | 22 (2) | 24 (1) |
| Ireland | 11 (5) | 11 (6) | 13 (5) | 18 (3) | 21 (2) | 20 (2) | --* | --* |
| Mexico | 11 (5) | 10 (7) | 9 (7) | 10 (7) | 10 (6) | 10 (7) | 10 (7) | 10 (6) |
| South Africa | 11 (5) | 13 (5) | 13 (5) | 11 (4) | 12 (5) | 12 (5) | 12 (5) | 12 (5) |
| Netherlands | 16 (4) | 13 (5) | 19 (3) | 11 (4) | 10 (6) | 11 (6) | 8 (8) | 7 (10) |
| Switzerland | 16 (4) | 13 (5) | 16 (4) | 11 (4) | 16 (3) | 13 (4) | 13 (4) | 13 (4) |
| Belgium | 18 (3) | 20 (3) | 19 (3) | 18 (3) | 16 (3) | 16 (3) | 16 (3) | 16 (3) |
| Chile | 18 (3) | 20 (3) | 23 (2) | 24 (2) | 21 (2) | 20 (2) | 22 (2) | 24 (1) |
| Spain | 18 (3) | 28 (1) | 23 (2) | 24 (2) | 21 (2) | 16 (3) | 25 (1) | 22 (2) |
| No. of all other service firms in the Global 2000 | 349 | 364 | 374 | 353 | 359 | 384 | 412 | 432 |

*The country has no services firms other than financial firms listed in the Global 2000 in the year.
*Source*: the Global 2000, the Forbes.

Korea, and India, by owning a handful of firms, listed as the seventh, ninth, and 10th, reflect their relative lagging-behind in service sector development.

Among the source countries where the Global 2000 firms are based[10], the top 10 countries hold a lion's share of all sales, showing high concentration of global businesses in a handful of countries, although the degree of concentration is slowly declining. As shown in Figure 16.2, the sales shares of the top 10 countries in all industries decreased from 86 percent in 2004 to 78 percent in 2011; and for each different

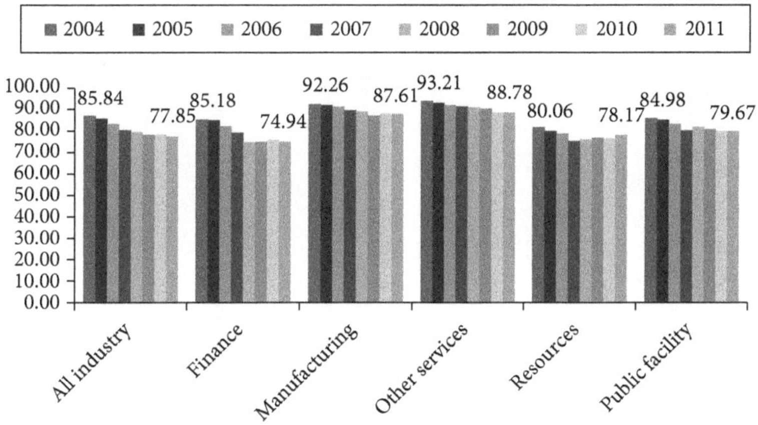


FIGURE 16.2 Sales concentration ratio of the top 10 Global 2000 source countries

*Source:* The Global 2000, the Forbes, calculated by authors.

industry, the concentration rate has remained over 75 percent. Among all, the other services and manufacturing industries hold the highest concentration, in that the rate of the former remained at 89 percent and the latter at 88 percent in 2011, despite the declining trend.

## 16.2.2 MNEs and FDI

How are MNE activities related to national FDI? Do more large MNEs activate constantly higher outward investment? Do more large MNEs attract inward investment? To answer these questions, we calculate the correlation coefficients between the number of Global 2000 firms and national FDI, including inward and outward FDI flows and stocks. As shown in Figure 16.3, high coefficient scores prove that large MNEs are highly connected to the volume of national FDI. For the stocks of both inward and outward FDI, the coefficients significantly remained above 0.8 in all sample years. The scenario may imply two tendencies. First, large MNEs have dominated the total volume of FDI. The overseas investment of small and medium enterprises either joins the investment of large MNEs to form industrial clusters or remains minor in national FDI. Second, the countries with more large MNEs tend to attract more foreign investment. They tend to invest in each other and shape an investment relationship similar to the gravity model of trade.[11] Would the gravity power of investment be affected by regional factors and form a structure of regional FDI blocks? If so, how are FDI blocks compared with trade blocks? In the next section, we develop the clustering analysis to discover the answers.

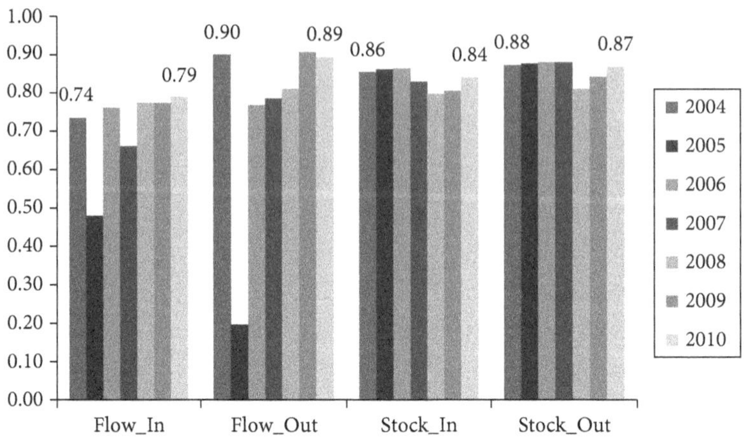


FIGURE 16.3 The correlation coefficients between the number of firms owned by a country in the Global 2000 and its national FDI

*Flow_In presents the correlation coefficients between the Global 2000 firm number and inward FDI flows; Flow_out the correlation coefficients between the Global 2000 firm number and outward FDI flows; Stock_in the correlation coefficients between the Global 2000 firm number and inward FDI stocks; and Stock_out the correlation coefficients between the Global 2000 firm number and outward FDI stocks.

*Source:* 1. the Global 2000, the Forbes. 2. World Investment Report, IMF, various years.

## 16.3 Examining FDI Regional Blocks Using Clustering Analysis

### 16.3.1 Methodology

The development of regional economic integration has caused academic studies on trading blocks and regionalism to flourish. For example, Eichengreen and Irwin (1995, 1996) applied the gravity model on 1928 data to investigate the effect of trading blocks and currency blocks on trade flows. Grant et al. (1993) indicated that regional block phenomena have grown faster since World War II. Frankel (1995) used the gravity model to show that Japan has formed a Yen-block in the East Asian and Pacific Basin in the 1980s through intensive intra-regional trade. Huang et al. (2006) derived from the (geographical) distance term of the gravity model to develop the concept of economic distance and measured the distance as the inverse of relative trade intensity. That is, the larger the share of bilateral trade to total world trade of a pair of countries, the higher the bilateral trade intensity and the shorter the economic distance between them. In this sense, the economic distance between country A and country B can be expressed as:

$$\text{Economic distance}_{AB} = 1/(\frac{BT_{A\to B} + BT_{B\to A}}{WT_A + WT_B})$$

$BT_{A\to B}$ is the bilateral exports from country A to country B, $BT_{B\to A}$ is the bilateral exports from country B to country A, and $WT_A$ and $WT_B$ are the world exports of country A and country B, respectively.

Using clustering analysis, the pair with the shortest distance among all countries is first identified as a potential inner core of a trade block. The inner core is then treated as a single joint economy and the bilateral trade intensities are recalculated for each pair of economies. By repeating the process, a sequence of economies with high trade intensity to the inner core are identified and added to it, and a trade block emerges with different layers, indicating the economic distance from the nearest to the farthest away.

The advantage of clustering analysis is that it does not presume the existence of regional blocks and their potential members but allows the blocks to emerge directly from the bilateral trade intensity. The multi-layer structure and the structural change over time also provide a good information source for discovering the evolution of trade blocks.

We applied the method also to the bilateral FDI to test whether regional investment block phenomena exist. We used the *Global Multi-sector Multi-region Foreign Direct Investment Database for GTAP*, published by the GTAP (Global Trade Analysis Project) Research Center of Purdue University,[12] which provides the bilateral FDI flows and stocks among 113 regions for each of the 57 industrial sectors in 2004.[13] The application steps are as follows. We first calculate the bilateral FDI intensity for each pair of the top 40 outward FDI countries.

$$\text{FDI Intensity}_{AB} = \frac{BI_{A\to B} + BI_{B\to A}}{WI_A + WI_B}$$

$BI_{A\to B}$ is the FDI from country A to country B, $BI_{B\to A}$ is the FDI from country B to country A, and $WI_A$ and $WI_B$ are the total outward FDI of country A and country B, respectively. The inverse of the FDI Intensity is also considered as the economic distance from the investment aspect.

The pair with the highest intensity is treated as a potential inner core of a FDI block. We again calculate the bilateral FDI intensity for each pair of 39 components (i.e., the 38 countries and the core). The pair with the highest FDI intensity is again taken as a core or an extended layer of the existing inner core. The calculation continues until all countries are included in a global cluster. The process is conducted for the total FDI stock and the manufacturing FDI stock to determine whether the FDI regional structure for commodity production differs from that of overall FDI.

## 16.3.2 FDI Clustering Analysis

Figures 16.4 and 16.5 show the empirical results of the total FDI clusters and manufacturing FDI clusters. In Fig. 16.4, we present a tree diagram of 25 countries that are

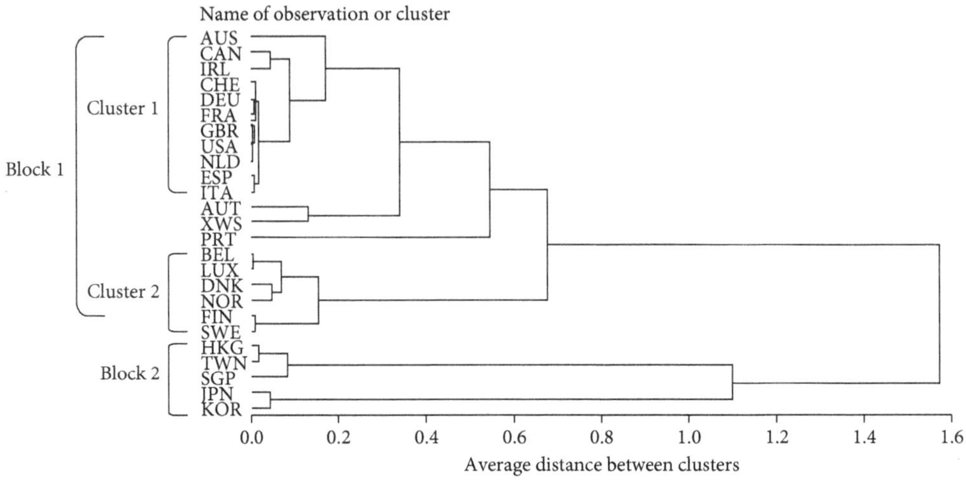


FIGURE 16.4 The tree diagram of the overall FDI blocks (2004)

adopted into the cluster structure after 25 calculation iterations and omit the remaining 15 countries, which are typically ranked lower in outward FDI stock and have invested in and received investment more equivalently from the other countries. Figure 16.4 shows two large blocks for the overall FDI with geographical proximity and historical origins. One block is composed of European and North American countries, and the other of East Asian countries. The European-American block consists of two main clusters. One evolves from the innermost core of the United States and the U.K. (GBR) and then extends sequentially to include France (FRA), Netherlands (NLD), Germany

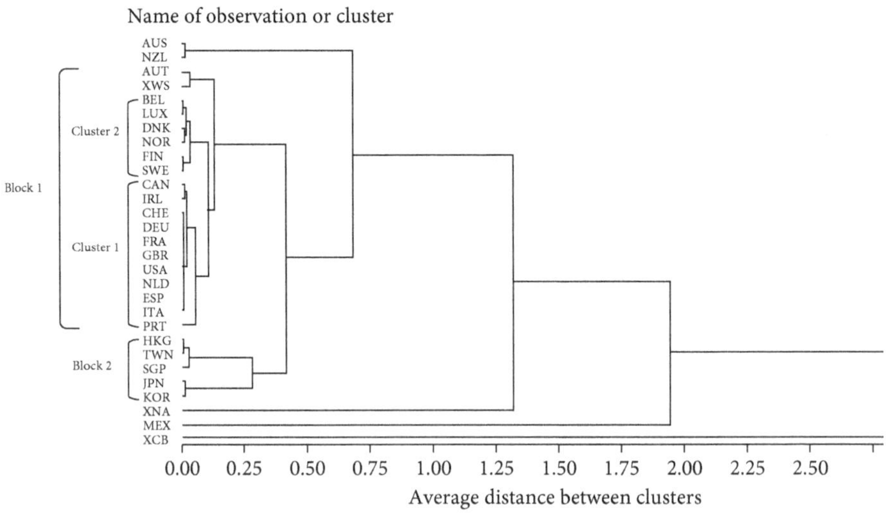


FIGURE 16.5 The tree diagram of the manufacturing FDI blocks (2004)

(DEU), Switzerland (CHE), the pair of Italy and Spain, the pair of Canada and Ireland, and Austria. The second cluster connects three pairs of countries, mainly in Central and Northern Europe, including the pairs of Belgium and Luxemburg, Denmark and Norway, and Finland and Sweden. The two clusters are ultimately connected with each other into one block.

The East Asian block is clearly separable from the European-American block, consisting of only five countries, with Japan and South Korea forming one inner core, and Taiwan and Hong Kong the other. The Taiwan-Hong Kong core is extended to include Singapore before they connect with Japan-South Korea core and become one block. The East Asian block and EU-American block do not link with each other until much later and form the outermost connection among all the clusters.

Because the East Asian NIEs started their outward FDI much later than those European and North American countries, the investment intensity among them is less imminent than that of the two European-American clusters. However, the diagram shows a structure that, through interwoven bilateral investment, the East Asian countries, particularly Japan and the four NIEs, have established close ties with one another and formed a regional block.

We then test the regional block phenomena for the manufacturing FDI stock. Figure 16.5 shows that the regional block structure of the manufacturing FDI is similar to that of the overall FDI. This structure remains the same as the two large blocks, one in the European-American region and the other in the East Asian region. The two main clusters within the European-American block also remain, except that Australia (AUS) was omitted and Portugal (PRT) was added to the Cluster 1 of the Europe-American block. These differences make the geographical proximity factor even more vivid.

The East Asian (manufacturing FDI) block incorporates the two inner cores as that in the overall FDI, one in North Asia (Japan and Korea) and the other in South Asia (Taiwan, Hong Kong, and Singapore). However, the block connects more closely to the EU-American block (or with shorter distance), compared with that of the overall FDI. The high consistency in Figures 16.4 and 16.5 may imply that FDI mainly serves the purpose of production division. Whereas the MNEs of European-American countries invested in the East Asian region with a greater manufacturing focus, they have established a production network that integrates economic resources and production capacities into one corporate system and have shortened the economic distance between the two regions.

Because the GTAP database provides a complete global bilateral FDI matrix for 2004 only, we are not able to follow up structural change of the FDI network for later years. Whereas FDI pushes forward production division within and among regions, it should cause more frequent intra- and inter-industrial trade. In the following section, we conduct clustering analysis for bilateral trade to determine whether block phenomena exist. If so, how does the block structure evolve?

## 16.3.3 Regional Clustering Analysis of Trade

The empirical results of clustering analysis on trade for the even years of the 2000-2008 period are presented in Figures 16.6 to 16.10 to demonstrate the evolution of regional block structure up to the eruption of the 2008-2009 global financial crisis.[14] These figures show three regional trade blocks of EU, NAFTA, and East Asia, with robust hierarchical layers throughout the period and only minor adjustments. We first analyze the broad relationship among the three blocks, and then focus on the structure of the East Asian block.

By observing the trade blocks during the first decade of the twenty-first century, we find a clear structural change before and after 2000 for either the broad relationship among the three blocks or the inner structure of the East Asian block. In 2000, the NAFTA block and the East Asian block showed a closer relationship with each other by joining together before they connected with the EU block (Figures 16.6). However, after 2000, the NAFTA block showed a closer relationship by joining with EU before they connected with the East Asian block. This is probably due to the dot-com bubble in 2000 and afterwards to the oil price surge and the high dependence of East Asian countries on the energy supply of Saudi Arabia and Indonesia. This is evidenced in that, starting in 2004, Saudi Arabia appeared to be one of the world's top 25 exporters, linking with the East Asian block before the broad East Asian block connected with the joint EU-NAFTA block.

The large expenditure of oil purchase formed a fat trade share between East Asia and the Middle East and shortened the economic distance between them. Whereas the NAFTA and EU countries had much less energy dependence on the two oil suppliers,

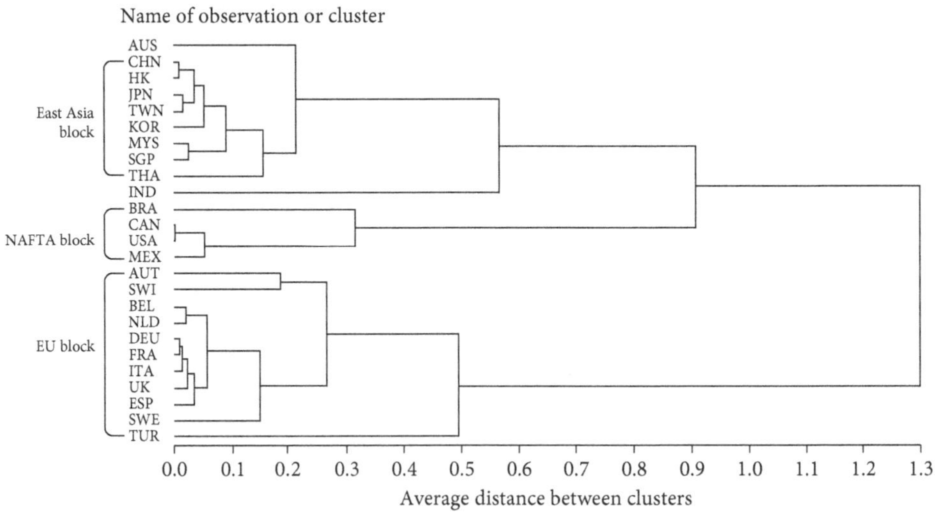


FIGURE 16.6 The tree diagram of the trade blocks in 2000

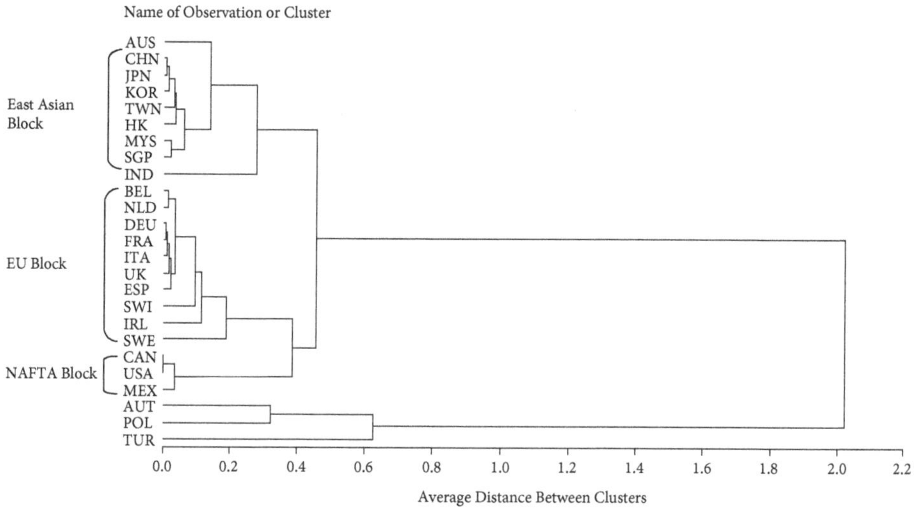


FIGURE 16.7 The tree diagram of the trade blocks in 2002

the economic distance between the East Asia (including Saudi Arabia and Indonesia) and NAFTA-EU blocks widened.

The structure of the East Asian trade block has also experienced subtle changes. In 2000, the East Asian block comprised two inner cores, namely the pair of China and Hong Kong and the pair of Japan and Taiwan. The two cores are connected to each other in the second layer and extended to include South Korea, followed by the Singapore-Malaysia core, and then Thailand (Fig. 16.6). This structure includes

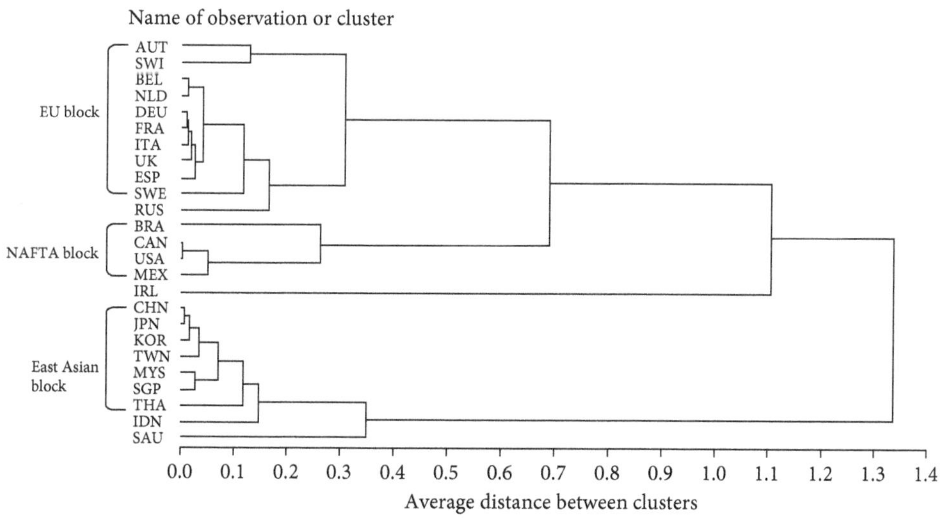


FIGURE 16.8 The tree diagram of the trade blocks in 2004

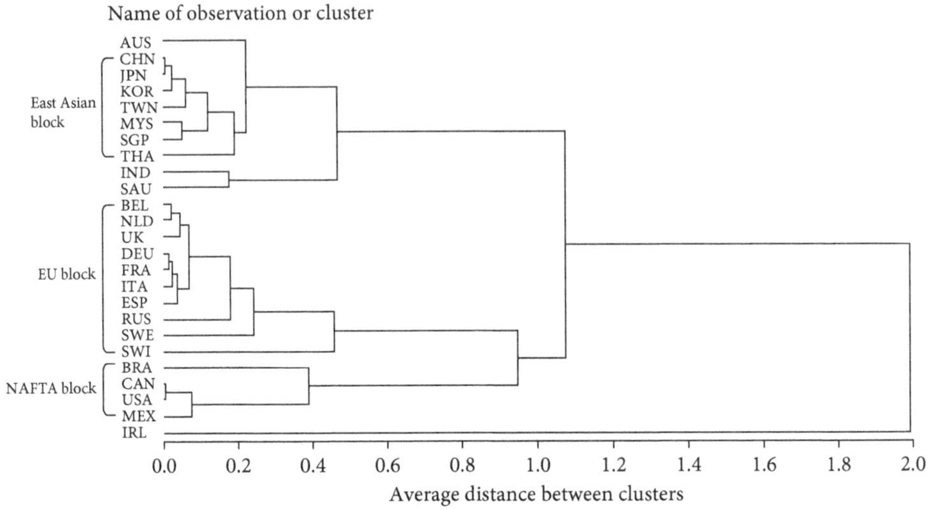


FIGURE 16.9 The tree diagram of the trade blocks in 2006

the key members of the East Asian flying geese paradigm, with Japan as the leading goose, followed by the four Asian NIEs of Hong Kong, Taiwan, South Korea, and Singapore, and the two of the ASEAN4: Malaysia and Thailand. The structure configuration provides further intuition of the East Asian economic integration. By comparing the trade blocks with the FDI and manufacturing FDI block, we find that, up to the early 2000s, the intensive bilateral investment between Taiwan and Hong Kong, which composed of the innermost core of the East Asian FDI block, played a key role in integrating the rising China into the East Asian economic cooperative system. They expanded

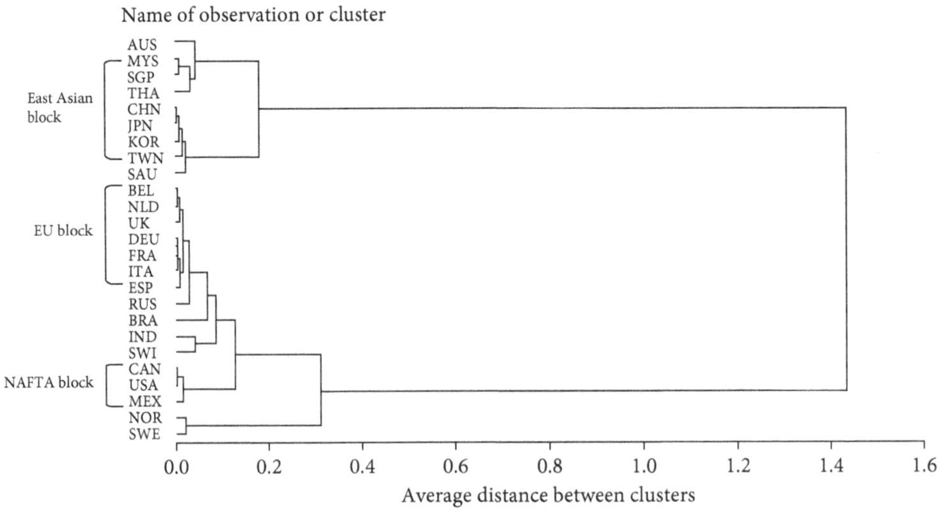


FIGURE 16.10 The tree diagram of the trade blocks in 2008

and deepened bilateral economic cooperation by first building a cross-border intra-firm labor division and then duplicating and extending the local industrial clusters of Taiwan to Hong Kong, which later moved into the east coast of Mainland China. Such development evolved into more frequent trading. The cooperative framework went upstream to link with Japan, which had been one of the important foreign investors and key provider of parts and components to Taiwan. This development fits well in the structure of the East Asian trade block of 2000, which consists of the inner core of China and Hong Kong and that of Japan and Taiwan, and the connection between the two.

However, in 2002 Taiwan and Hong Kong stepped back to the outer layers of the East Asian trade block, and in 2004, Hong Kong disappeared from the trade block and the two major inner cores reorganized and became one hierarchical cluster with Japan and China in the innermost core, followed by Korea, Taiwan, the core of Singapore and Malaysia, and Thailand. This new structure remained steady up to 2008.[15] The disappearance of Hong Kong and the marginalization of Taiwan from the inner core echo the findings of Ng and Tuan (1997) and Yang and Lin (2009), that the outward FDI has caused industrial restructuring and worsened the manufacturing productivity of Hong Kong and Taiwan, and hence their export performance. However, the aggressiveness of both inward and outward FDI of China may have strengthened its production capacity and trade competitiveness (Chen & Lin, 2008). The direct and intimate trade linkages between Japan and China and their joining the sole inner-core and driving force of the East Asian Trade block signify the change of the traditional East Asian flying geese pattern with Japan alone as the leading goose. The rise of China and its outpacing of the follower geese of the four NIEs and the ASEAN4 countries as the closest trade partner of Japan have shown its different development route from its predecessors. Chen and Huang (2009) depicted the traditional pattern of industrial catch-up and inheritance of East Asian countries as the sequence of Japan → Asian NIEs → ASEAN4 → China, in which Asian NIEs caught up with Japan and inherited its sunset industries of textiles, clothing, and household appliances in the 1980s, which transferred to the ASEAN4 and China in the 1990s. However, when the sample period is extended to 2002, China showed stronger comparative advantage than the ASEAN4 in three-fourths of total 742 4-digit SITC industries with numerous industries that China directly inherited from the United States, Japan, and the Asian NIEs (South Korea, Taiwan, Hong Kong, and Singapore) instead of from the ASEAN4. These results may imply that China may have broken the flying geese sequence and introduced a new era of regional development.

Similar to a leaping frog described by Brezis et al. (1993), China fulfills the conditions required for technological leaping and the shift from lagging to leading. Its considerably lower wages for skilled and unskilled workers have set an excellent stage for MNEs to experiment with new technology, whose application requires no experience with old technology, and which ultimately produces substantial productivity improvement over old technology. Furthermore, its abundant labor force and huge market provide the opportunity to support the development of both product supply and demand. In line with the structural change of the East Asian trade block in which China has entered from the outer layer to the innermost core and closely bonded with Japan, the leapfrogging theorem may provide an explanation.

The recent global financial crisis seemed to have only minor effects on the cluster structure within each trade block, but has significantly enlarged the distance between the two major trade blocks. By comparing the 2006 trade block diagram with that of 2008, the inner cores of the three regional trade blocks remain closely bonded. Only the outer layers are altered by either detaching from the original cluster or reorganizing into a different cluster. Whereas the major exporters in EU and NAFTA have become more closely united, the distance between the joint block of EU-NAFTA and the East Asian block has widened. This phenomenon may be explained by the differences between the intra-regional trade of the East Asian block and its inter-regional trade with the rest of the world. Athukorala (2008) found that while the contents of intra-regional trade in East Asia are mainly parts and components, those between East Asian countries and the rest of the world are mostly final goods. Whereas trade within East Asia is driven by cross-border production processing, most finished goods are shipped to advanced countries in Europe and North America to meet their final demand. Because the global financial crisis inflicted heavy losses on these advanced economies and decreased their purchasing power, their imports of East Asian goods drastically reduced, weakening their trade partnership. In contrast, the rising demand in East Asia, particularly household consumption demand in China, came to the rescue of East Asian countries in the global recession. The trade integration within the region became closer, and the interdependence more condensed. This phenomenon is expected to remain as Europe and North America will require time to reregulate and reestablish their financial system before they recover from the financial crunch.

## 16.4 Concluding Remarks

The phenomenon of fast-growing worldwide business activities of multinational enterprises has stimulated considerable interest in understanding its implications for world economy development and the relationship among national economies. By analyzing the world's top 2000 firms, published by the *Forbes* Magazine (the Global 2000), this chapter first investigates the contents and structural evolution of these giant multinational firms, and their relationship to national FDI. We then adopt clustering analysis to investigate the FDI and trade networks within and among regions showing the development of regional economic integration. The main findings are as follows.

First, the sales of Forbes Global 2000 firms have been progressing at a rate faster than international trade, and the growth of their asset value has outpaced that of world capital stock during the 2004-2009 sample period. Parallel with their expeditious growth, the industrial allocation of their investment has evolved into a balanced pattern, distributing relatively evenly among the sectors of finance, manufacturing, other services, resources, and public facilities. The degree of concentration of these MNEs, according to the countries they are based on, is declining due to the rapid increase of aggressive investment from Asian emerging countries, particularly China and India. Consequently, the rise of Asian emerging countries has altered the geographic distribution of the top MNEs and has spread them more evenly throughout the continents of Europe, North America, and Asia.

Second, the countries owning more large MNEs tend to invest more outwardly and attract more inward FDI. By applying the clustering analysis developed by Huang et al. (2006) to the world bilateral FDI stocks, we found that the large outward FDI countries are inclined to invest in each other more frequently in a regional manner. The empirical results show that both the overall FDI and manufacturing FDI share a similar structure of two multi-layer regional blocks. One block is composed of the countries of EU and North America, the other is of East Asian countries. Although they are similar in structure, the distance between the EU-North American block and the East Asian block, measured by the inverse of the bilateral FDI intensity, is much smaller for manufacturing FDI. This may imply a closer investment relationship for production purposes between the two regions.

By applying the same method to the global bilateral trade flows, the empirical results show three trade blocks of EU, NAFTA, and East Asia, which remained stable throughout the 2000-2008 period. However, the relationship among them varied. In 2000, the NAFTA block and East Asian block showed a closer relationship by joining with each other before they connected with the EU block. However, after 2004, the NAFTA block showed a closer relationship with EU by joining with EU before they connected with the East Asian block. This scenario is likely caused by the dot-com bubble and the oil price surge. The cluster structure of the East Asian block simultaneously had some modifications. In 2000, two inner cores existed for the East Asian block, whereas after 2000, the two inner cores were rearranged and became one, with Japan and China consisting of the sole inner core of the East Asian block. The more direct and intensive trade relationship between Japan and China, together with the quickly moving forward of China's ranking in the Forbes Global 2000, may signify the emergence of leapfrogging described by Brezis et al. (1993). By fulfilling the conditions of technology-leaping and position-switching from lagging to leading, China may have transformed from a follower goose to a joint leading goose with Japan in the new East Asian flying geese paradigm.

In its early stage, the 2008-2009 financial crisis did not seemingly have much effect on the cluster structure of each trade block, but obviously enlarged the distance between the EU-North American block and the East Asian block. This may be caused by the reduced purchasing power of EU and North American countries. The rising demand from Asian emerging countries, particularly the strong household consumption demand in China, has not only rescued East Asian countries in the world recession, but has more tightly integrated the regional economy.

## Appendix 1: The top 10 firms of the Forbes Global 2000 (2011)*

| Rank | Company | Country | Industry | Sales ($bil) | Profits ($bil) | Assets ($bil) | Market Value ($bil) |
|---|---|---|---|---|---|---|---|
| 1 | Exxon Mobil | US | Oil & Gas Operations | 433.5 | 41.1 | 331.1 | 407.4 |
| 2 | JPMorgan Chase | US | Major Banks | 110.8 | 19.0 | 2,265.8 | 170.1 |
| 3 | General Electric | US | Computer Storage Devices | 147.3 | 14.2 | 717.2 | 213.7 |
| 4 | Royal Dutch Shell | Netherlands | Oil & Gas Operations | 470.2 | 30.9 | 340.5 | 227.6 |
| 5 | ICBC | China | Major Banks | 82.6 | 25.1 | 2,039.1 | 237.4 |
| 6 | HSBC Holdings | UK | Major Banks | 102.0 | 16.2 | 2,550 | 164.3 |
| 7 | PetroChina | China | Oil & Gas Operations | 310.1 | 20.6 | 304.7 | 294.7 |
| 8 | Berkshire Hathaway | US | Investment Services | 143.7 | 10.3 | 392.6 | 202.2 |
| 9 | Wells Fargo | US | Major Banks | 87.6 | 15.9 | 1,313.9 | 178.7 |
| 10 | Petrobras-Petróleo Brasil | Brazil | Oil & Gas Operations | 145.9 | 20.1 | 319.4 | 180.0 |

*Source*: The Global 2000, the Forbes. April, 21, 2012. The data is available at: [http://www.forbes.com/global2000/list].

*: We treat the Global 2000 firm data as the performance of these firms in the year previous to the publishing year, so that the data published in 2012 is treated to reflect the performance of the firms in 2011.

## Appendix 2: The top 10 manufacturing firms of the Forbes Global 2000 (2011)

| Rank | Company | Country | Industry | Sales ($bil) | Profits ($bil) | Assets ($bil) | Market Value($bil) |
|---|---|---|---|---|---|---|---|
| 1 | General Electric | US | Computer Storage Devices | 147.3 | 14.2 | 717.2 | 213.7 |
| 2 | Volkswagen Group | Germany | Auto & Truck Manufacturers | 221.9 | 21.5 | 328.7 | 79.5 |
| 3 | Toyota Motor | Japan | Auto & Truck Manufacturers | 228.5 | 4.9 | 358.3 | 147.9 |
| 4 | Samsung Electronics | S. Korea | Semiconductors | 142.4 | 11.5 | 133.7 | 162.0 |
| 5 | IBM | US | Computer Hardware | 106.9 | 15.9 | 116.4 | 238.7 |
| 6 | Pfizer | US | Pharmaceuticals | 67.4 | 10.0 | 188.0 | 165.4 |
| 7 | Daimler | Germany | Auto & Truck Manufacturers | 138.0 | 7.3 | 188.7 | 66.3 |
| 8 | American Intl Group | US | Diversified Chemicals | 64.2 | 17.8 | 555.8 | 50.3 |
| 9 | Ford Motor | US | Auto & Truck Manufacturers | 136.3 | 20.2 | 178.3 | 47.5 |
| 10 | Johnson & Johnson | US | Medical Equipment & Supplies | 65.0 | 9.7 | 113.6 | 178.8 |

*Source:* the same as Appendix 1.

## NOTES

1. The ranking and relevant information of the Global 2000 firms published by the *Forbes* Magazine can be found in the website http://www.forbes.com/global2000/list/
2. The total sales of the Global 2000 firms decreased from US$31.5 trillion in 2008 to US$30.0 trillion in 2009 due to the global financial crisis. The growth rate between 2004 and 2008 was 43.7 percent, greater than the rate of 36.6 percent between 2004 and 2009. Sales consist of both domestic and foreign sales, which may reflect the scale of their operations in the global economy as a whole. On the other hand, asset value continued to grow in 2009 despite the effect of the financial crisis.
3. For world capital assets, we refer to the table of "domestic market capitalization, main and parallel market," published by the World Federation Exchange at: [http://www.world-exchanges.org/statistics/annual/2008/equity-markets-0]
4. The latest data is available at [http://www.forbes.com/2010/04/21/global-2000-leading-world-business-global-2000-10_land.html]
5. We treat the Global 2000 firm data to reflect firm performance at the year previous to the publishing year. The data published in 2005 represent firm performance in 2004. The first two editions published in 2003 and 2004 did not include industrial classification, which is added to later editions. Our article adopts only the data published in 2005-2012 to conduct industrial structure analysis.
6. For China's "going out" policy, see Chen and Lin (2008).
7. The flying geese paradigm was originally introduced by Akamatsu (1962) and has triggered profound discussion on the pattern of industrial development of East Asian countries. See Chen and Huang (2009), Fujita and Hill (1997), Kwan (2002), and Ozawa (1999, 2000, 2001a, 2001b, 2003) for more discussion of the East Asian flying geese formation and development, the effect of the 1997 Asian financial crisis, and the importance of foreign direct investment in forming the flying geese pattern.
8. The ASEAN4 (the 4 founding members of the Association of South-Eastern Asian Nations) are also called the four tigers. They are Malaysia, Indonesia, Thailand, and the Philippines.
9. See also the literature in note 7 and our article, Yang et al. (2011).
10. The Global 2000 firms were based on 47 different source countries in 2002. The number of source countries increased to 58 in 2004, 63 in 2006, 66 in 2007, and 68 in 2008 and 2009. This increasing trend is also an indicator of economic decentralization.
11. Numerous authors have used the gravity model to investigate FDI determinants. See Bevin and Estrin (2004); Egger and Pfaffermayr (2004); Dee and Gali (2005) for some examples.
12. For database details, see Lakatos and Walmsley (2010).
13. Unfortunately, this database provides the bilateral FDI data only for 2004. Therefore, we cannot follow the structure change in later years.
14. For the clustering analysis of trade in this section, we choose the top 25 exporters of each sample year and calculate the trade intensity for each pair of countries. The iterations continue until all countries are included in one global trade block.
15. In 2000 and 2002, Australia and India were added to the East Asian block and formed a large Asia Pacific block. However, in 2004, due to the oil price surge, Saudi Arabia and Indonesia were added to the East Asian Block. Australia reentered and stayed in the outer layer of the large Asian block in 2006 and 2008, whereas India joined the large Asian block again in 2006, but not 2008. However, Saudi Arabia has remained in the large Asian block since 2004. See Figures 16.6-16.10 for details.

## References

Akamatsu, K., 1962. A Historical Pattern of Economic Growth in Developing Countries. *The Developing Economies*, 1(1), 3–25.

Athukorala, P.-C., 2008. Multinational Production Networks and the New Geo-Economic Division of Labor in Pacific Rim countries. In Palacios, J. J. (Ed.), *Multinational Enterprises and the Emerging Network Economy in Asia and the Pacific* (pp. 139–162). London and New York: Routledge Press.

Bevin, A. A., & Estrin, S., 2004. The Determinants of Foreign Direct Investment into European Transition Economies. *Journal of Comparative Economics*, 32: 775–787.

Bonturi, M., & Fusakaku, K., 1993. Globalization and Intra-Firm Trade: An Empirical Note. *OECD Economic Studies*, 20: 145–159.

Brezis, E. S., Krugman, P. R., & Tsiddon, D., 1993. Leapfrogging in International Competition: A Theory of Cycles in National Technological Leadership. *The American Economic Review*, 83(5), 1211–1219.

Chen, E. K. Y., & Lin, P., 2008. Emerging Transnational Corporations from East Asia: the Case of Mainland China. In Palacios, J. J. (Ed.) *Multinational Enterprises and the Emerging Network Economy in Asia and the Pacific*, (pp. 183–207), London and New York: Routledge Press.

Chen, H.-Y., & Huang, D.-S., 2009. Shifting Comparative Advantage in East Asia: Re-examining the Flying Geese Paradigm. *Taiwan Economic Review*, 37(2), 185–211.

Dee, P. & Gali, J., 2005. The Trade and Investment Effects of Preferential Trading Arrangements. In Ito, T., & Rose, A., (Eds.) *International Trade in East Asia*, (pp. 133–175). Chicago and London: University of Chicago Press.

Egger, P., & Pfaffermayr, M., 2004. The Impact of Bilateral Investment Treaties on Foreign Direct Investment. *Journal of Comparative Economics*, 32: 788–804.

Eichengreen, B., & Irwin, D.A., 1995. Trade Blocks, Currency Blocks and the Reorientation of Trade in the 1930s. *Journal of International Economics*, 38: 1–24.

Eichengreen, B. & Irwin, D.A., 1996. The Role of History in Bilateral Trade Flows. *NBER Working Paper* No. 5565.

Feenstra, R. C., 1999. Facts and Fallacies about FDI. In Feldstein, M. (Ed.) *International Capital Flows*, (pp. 331–350), Chicago and London: University of Chicago Press and NBER.

Frankel, J. A., 1995. Is Japan Creating a Yen Block in East Asia and the Pacific? *NBER Working Paper, No. 4050.*

Fujita, K., & Hill, R. C., 1997. Auto Industrialization in Southeast Asia: National Strategies and Local Development. *ASEAN Economic Bulletin*, 13(3), 312–333.

Gabel, M. & Bruner, H., 2003. *Global Inc.: An Atlas of the Multinational Corporation*, New York: The New Press.

Grant, R. J., Papadakis, M. C., & Richardson, J. D., 1993. Global Trade Flows: Old Structures, New Issues, Empirical Evidence. In Bergsten, C.F., & Noland, M. (Eds.), *Pacific Dynamism and the International Economic System*, (pp. 17–63), Washington D.C.: Institute for International Economics.

Huang D.-S., Huang, Y.-Y., & Sun, Y.-C., 2006. Production Specialization and Trade Blocks. *Journal of Economic Integration*, 21(3), 474–495.

Kwan, C.H., 2002. The Rise of China and Asia's Flying-Geese Pattern of Economic Development: A Empirical Analysis Based on US Import Statistics. RIETI Discussion Paper Series 02-E-009. Available at http://www.rieti.go.jp/jp/Publications/dp/02e009.pdf.

Lakatos, C., & Walmsley, T. L., 2010. A Global Multi-sector Multi-region Foreign Direct Investment Database for GTAP. *GTAP Research Memorandum No. 18.*

Ng, L.F.Y., & Tuan, C., 1997. Evolving Outward Investment, Industrial Concentration, and Technology Change: Implications for Post-1997 Hong Kong. *Journal of Asian Economics,* 8(2), 315–332.

Ozawa, T., 1999. Pacific economic integration and the "flying geese" paradigm. In Rugman, A. M., & Boyd, G. (Eds.), *Deepening Integration in the Pacific Economies* (pp. 55–91), Cheltenham, UK and Northampton, MA, USA: Edward Elgar.

Ozawa, T., 2000. The "Flying-Geese" Paradigm: toward a Co-Evolutionary Theory of MNC-Assisted Growth. In Khosrow Fatemi, K., (Ed.), *The New World Order: Internationalism, Regionalism and the Multinational enterprises,* (pp. 209–223), New York: Pergamon Press.

Ozawa, T., 2001a. The "Hidden" Side of the "Flying Geese" Catch-Up Model: Japan's *Dirigiste* Institutional Setup and a Deepening Financial Morass. *Journal of Asian Economics,* 12(4), 471–491.

Ozawa, T., 2001b. The Internet Revolution, Networking, and the "Flying Geese" Paradigm of Structural Upgrading. *Global Economic Quarterly,* 2(1), 1–8.

Ozawa, T., 2003. Pax American-led Macro-Clustering and Flying-Geese-Style Catch-up in East Asia: Mechanisms of Regionalized Endogenous Growth. *Journal of Asian Economics,* 13(6), 699–713.

United Nations Conference on Trade and Development (2002). *World Investment Report: Transnational Corporations and Export Competitiveness.* New York and Geneva: United Nations Publications.

Yang, T.-H & Lin, Y.-C., 2009. How Does Outward FDI Affect Home Productivity?—Taiwan's Experiences in the 1990s. Mimeo.

Yang, T.-H., Huang, D.-S., Sun, Y.-C., & Chen, Y.-S., 2011. East Asian Flying Geese Framework and Industrial Competitive Advantages: The Cases of Textiles and Information Industries. The 2011 Annual Conference of Taiwan Economic Association, Dec. 17, 2011. (in Chinese)

CHAPTER 17

# THE IMPACT OF INDUSTRIAL POLICY ON ASIAN GROWTH: AN EXAMPLE FROM TAIWAN

HOWARD PACK[1]

## 17.1 INTRODUCTION

MANY nations have grown rapidly in the period after World War II that saw the decolonization of all nations. Yet the rapid economic growth that was widely anticipated has materialized in only a handful of nations, many of them in Asia. A great deal of attention has thus been focused on learning the secrets of the Asian "Miracle." Many explanations have been proffered including culture ("Confucian" with its emphasis on learning and civic virtue) and the alignment of nations such as Japan, Korea, and Taiwan (JKT) with the United States during the Cold War. Still others focus on government guidance of the industrial growth process, often under the rubric of industrial policy. Industrial policy (IP) is a very elastic term—it has been used to denote the building of infrastructure such as roads and railroads, improving education quantity and quality, and indeed any activity of the government that may accelerate development. Many of these government activities are familiar to public finance economists as having the characteristics of public goods: these characteristics include non-excludability (defense, environment), insufficiently developed capital markets to finance large scale projects such as roads, and civic externalities such as education. The desirable role of government is not limited to classic public goods from which users cannot be excluded—charges can be made for both electricity and ports, but these have generally been viewed as beyond the scope of private financing at the early stages of development, though this may be changing. Education is usually viewed as a joint good—providing the fundamentals of good citizenship plus economic skills valuable to potential employers.[2] There are many market failures that governments can potentially address in a quest to jump-start industrial development.[3] In the 1980s there were a spate of studies arguing that the Korean and Taiwanese governments had done precisely this in the 1960s and 1970s, closely following the earlier Japanese model. More recent analyses utilizing longer-term data are more skeptical of this success.[4]

There has been a particular concern with more narrowly defined industrial policy as an effort to initiate growth in manufacturing and change the structure of the sector from low to higher sophistication. For some, JKT provides a guideline of how to accelerate industrial development. These issues have generated an enormous literature on "how it was done" and the effects of such policies. Many reviews of this literature and analytic syntheses now exist (Noland and Pack, 2003; Pack and Saggi, 2006; and Harrison and Rodriquez-Clare, 2009). To examine the issues requires studies of individual countries, the policies they pursued, and the probable magnitude of the gains that accrued from the pursuit of such policies.

Until the financial crisis in Asia in 1997-1998, efforts to explain rapid growth in a number of countries focused on the efficacy of industrial policies. Since the crisis many analysts have in retrospect argued that the encouragement of selected sectors was one of the seeds of the ensuing problems. In particular, the targeting of low-interest loans to specific sectors and firms is viewed as having contributed to a weakening of the ability of the banking system to evaluate loans and channel saving to firms with the highest marginal product of capital. The experience of Taiwan, which did not experience the substantial downturn and financial crisis that occurred in Japan, Korea, and Thailand, has attracted considerable interest.

In retrospect, Taiwan may be the poster country for industrial policy if indeed this policy was the key source of growth. It transformed itself from a country that was dependent on the export of canned pineapples and sugar in 1960 to one that is a major supplier of the hardware of the global information technology sector. Much of this transformation to a major industrial power occurred from the mid-1960s through the 1980s, the period that is studied in this chapter. Several evaluations of the benefits Taiwan obtained from industrial policy have been skeptical about its beneficial impact (Smith, 1997, 2000, Thorbecke and Wan, 1999).[5] Moreover, some aspects of industrial policy were not pursued to foster the growth of new industries but to protect high cost sectors. For example, Smith (1997) showed that during the 1980s, public utilities were the largest beneficiary of loans to promote "strategic" industries. Taiwanese policies were typical of the efforts in Japan, Korea, and Taiwan to accelerate growth rates by transforming the manufacturing sector. By examining in detail the experience of one nation, many of the questions that have arisen of the role of IP more generally in Asia can be examined. Did productivity grow as a result of industrial policy; were there beneficial spillovers to non-promoted sectors; did the specific form in Taiwan lead to less vulnerability to external shock than the Heavy and Chemical industry effort in South Korea?

Section 1.2 analyzes the rationale for intervention. Section 1.3 proposes an empirical test to assess the likely magnitude of Taiwanese government policies on the rate of growth of the industrial sector. Section 1.4 presents empirical estimates. Section 1.5

considers the likely impact of intersectoral spillovers and provides measures of their likely magnitude. Section 1.6 contains conclusions.

## 17.2 The Case for Industrial Policy

Government guidance or industrial policy can be welfare improving in the presence of a number of market failures. These include:

a. Real external economies stemming from the growth of one sector that costlessly benefits others. One mechanism by which this occurs is the movement of individuals who have acquired non-firm specific human capital either from formal training or on-the-job experience. The knowledge spillovers may occur without such movement from informal exchanges in both professional and social contexts.[6] In the case of traded goods, real externalities improve welfare only if they allow goods to be produced at less than the imported c.i.f. price.[7]
b. Pecuniary external economies that arise when firms are established jointly at larger scales than would have prevailed in the absence of coordination argue for coordination of planned investment (Scitovsky, 1954). The market failure is that early in the development process current prices may not convey the information about the effects of prospective simultaneous expansion that is relevant to attaining a lower cost of production through larger plant size (Pack and Westphal, 1986).
c. Externalities conferred on other firms in an industry by the first entrant. These include the demonstration that the sector is physically and economically feasible and the diffusion of information on technology and marketing conditions by these initial entrants (Pack and Westphal, 1986).
d. The incomplete appropriability of the results of R & D and the possibility that its private riskiness exceeds social riskiness. In Taiwan, R & D was not of great importance early in its development but became larger in the mid-1980s.
e. Externalities that arise from the interaction of suppliers and buyers on the design or method of production of a product leading to a better or cheaper good than is available internationally. In this case, the source of the externality is the nontradablity of some types of inputs or knowledge—otherwise the improved method or product could be obtained from international suppliers.

In the cases just cited, public intervention may be effective if the government can redress the failures of the market. The view that industrial policy was *the* key rests on the assumption that the initiation of a sector is the critical intervention and once set in motion entrepreneurs inevitably play their assigned role as cost-reducing innovators. As the evidence from the many countries that engaged in import substituting industrialization demonstrates, tariffs or loans that enable the establishment of firms in a favored sector have generally not been successful (Pack, 2011). Protection or subsidies had to be continued as firms failed to improve productivity. Even in the presence of all of the market failures, there is a question of whether governments have the competence to address them as well as the danger of capture of the process by the intended beneficiaries. But undermining of the process may not arise solely from rent-seeking activities such as bribes offered to officials in return for obtaining the right to issues import licenses or obtain subsidized loans. It may simply derive from the reluctance of officials to acknowledge that some efforts may not be bearing fruit and should be ended; it may also result from the inability to overcome the opposition of either owners or workers who have benefited from the initial help.

Clark (1989), Gold (1986), Wade (1990), and Winckler and Greehalgh (1989) documented the extensive employment of tariffs, quantitative restrictions, and selective credit policies and argued that Taiwan's success in manufacturing was attributable to an intensive effort by the government to direct the sectoral evolution of the economy.[8] They correctly note that the earlier view that Taiwan approximated the laissez faire environment of Hong Kong is untenable in light of these carefully accumulated facts. A variety of industrial policies were pursued, including tariff protection, quantitative restrictions on imports, the provision of low-cost loans to selected sectors, and the establishment of public enterprises when private initiative was not forthcoming or the capital markets were reluctant or unable to fund very large projects. There was also the subsidization of the Industrial Technology Research Institute (ITRI), and of the Hsinchu Science Park, whose mission was to encourage new industries producing computer components and electronics, as well as to identify, transfer, diffuse, and efficiently absorb foreign industrial technologies and then undertake local innovation.[9] These latter institutions were largely introduced in the late 1970s and 1980s, though precursors existed in the 1960s.[10]

In Taiwan, government support may have played a role in the initial stages of a sector's growth, but the continuing entrepreneurship of firms was a critical component of success. And the government had a more limited role in these ongoing efforts to improve quality or lower cost. It seems likely that a key difference between the import substituting industrialing (ISI) countries such as India and Argentina, is that Taiwan had a relatively competitive internal market with considerable turnover of firms that weeded out inefficient ones that were replaced by more productive companies. (Nelson and Pack, 1999; Aw, Chen, and Roberts, 2001). In contrast to Korea, Taiwan had a more neutral stance with respect to the size of firms that were encouraged, and there was considerable turnover among firms. Although in Korea's early stages of development, policies were in place to monitor firms, especially large ones, by insisting on export performance, but gradually the discipline was lost as firms expanded into sectors in which international competitiveness was never achieved or into sectors that produced largely non-traded goods. This partly explains the differing experience in the late 1990s during the Asian financial crisis.

## 17.3 Quantifying the Impact of Taiwan's Industrial Policy

There have been numerous efforts to assess the impact of industrial policies on total factor productivity (TFP) growth of individual sectors in the export-promoting East Asian countries. The approaches have varied but most try to estimate the impact of specific policies such as tariffs and subsidies on individual sector TFP growth. TFP for each sector, calculated from an assumed production function, is regressed on a variety of measures of stimulation. Most of these studies have found no impact or a negative one.[11] These approaches have been criticized by Rodrik (2008) as difficult to interpret—roughly the more backward sectors may have received more protection—the amount of stimulus is endogenous and thus the empirical results are not convincing evidence of the failure of IP. In this chapter we do not attempt to explain differences in rates of TFP growth across sectors by instruments of intervention. Rather we *assume* that industrial policy was successful in altering both the sectoral structure of production and the rate of TFP growth and ask what its contribution to Taiwanese growth might have been.

Employing the standard growth decomposition, the intermediate term rate of manufacturing value added, $Q^*$, depends on the rate of growth of total factor productivity, $A^*$, the capital stock, $K^*$, and the rate of growth of the labor force, $L^*$ or

$$Q^* = A^* + \alpha K^* + (1\text{-}\alpha)L^* \qquad (1).$$

It is unlikely that industrial policies affect the size of $L^*$ although there is some evidence that birth rates in Taiwan decreased as a result of employment growth of young women that ultimately reduced $L^*$. If industrial policies targeted sectors with high labor intensity, it might have had such an effect but the sectors particularly encouraged were those in the higher capital intensity, higher technology industries whose labor intensity was not unusually high. Taiwan financed most of its capital accumulation from domestic saving and its high saving rate can largely be explained by the life cycle model (Deaton and Paxson, 1994). Thus the major channel through which industrial policy would have accelerated $Q^*$ is enhanced $A^*$.

Taiwan's policies were designed to alter the sectoral composition of manufacturing toward more capital and technology intensive industries and (implicitly) to raise the sector-wide $A^*$. The critical question is whether these goals were achieved and, if they were, how much of Taiwan's growth was attributable to the effort. Even if $A^*$ was increased by industrial policy, it does not follow that the policy was welfare-enhancing. This would require demonstrating that the present discounted value of additional producer surplus made possible was greater than the present discounted value of short-term welfare losses imposed, including the distortions generated by the imposition of taxes necessary to pay for subsidies—roughly the Mill-Bastable criterion. Industrial policy could also have improved welfare if there was an initial disequilibrium among sectors such that marginal value products of inputs, particularly labor, were not equal and industrial policy accelerated the movement of factors to higher marginal productivity sectors. There is a considerable body of evidence suggesting relatively competitive labor markets in Taiwan and the issue is of secondary quantitative importance (Fields, 1994).

A number of strategies are possible to assess the aggregate impact of industrial policy.[12] One is to relate the levels of effective rates of protection (ERP) to rates of TFP growth, as has been done for Korea (Lee, 1997), Japan (Beason and Weinstein, 1996), and Taiwan (Smith, 1997, 2000). Smith's analysis of Taiwan in the 1980s is exhaustive and she finds no relation between TFP growth and ERP or effective rates of subsidy, results similar to those of Lee for Korea. In Taiwan, however, other methods of promotion were also used, including the provision of centralized R & D that favored specific sectors and the establishment of industrial parks, particularly the Hsinchu Science Park that was designed to foster science-based sectors.[13] While Smith shows that protection levels were inversely related to TFP, proponents of industrial policy might argue that the non-trade and non-subsidy inducements were also very important and that ERP measures do not capture the full impact of industrial policies. Conversely, as noted above, Rodrik (2008) argues that tests that use TFP growth on the left hand side and measures of stimulation on the right are flawed insofar as the more backward sectors may have received greater stimulus and the absence of significance is thus not a demonstration of the ineffectiveness of industrial policy.

Thus, we propose an alternative test that acknowledges that many modes of stimulation were attempted and *assumes* they were efficacious in the sense of both increasing the relative importance of targeted sectors and their TFP growth and establishing the magnitude of the contribution of industrial policy. Such a measure implies that the research undertaken by ITRI and its diffusion would not have occurred under private auspices and indeed that entire sectors such as the computer chip sector would not have been established without such help. This approach helps to establish the upper bound estimates of the impact on TFP growth.

To assess the impact of selective intervention it is necessary to posit a counterfactual model. Ideally, a computable general equilibrium model is required. There have been no such studies at a level of sectoral disaggregation for the industrial sector that would permit analysis of the impact of industrial policies. Moreover, such models encounter difficulties of their own such as calibrating the large number of parameters. Instead, we utilize a sectoral decomposition to calculate the effects of industrial policy on the growth rate of total factor productivity. The rate of growth of TFP for the entire manufacturing sector, $A^*$ can be written as

$$A^* = \sum_i (VA_i/VA) A_i^* \qquad (2)$$

where *i* indicates individual branches within the manufacturing sector, $VA_i$ is value added originating in sector *i*, VA is value added for the entire manufacturing sector, and $A_i^*$ is the rate of TFP growth in sector *i* that reflects scale economies, learning, the effects of firm level and governmental research, and other productivity augmenting factors. Industrial policy affects sector-wide productivity by altering the structure of production $VA_i/VA$ as well as the rates of productivity growth, $A_i^*$. An increase in the weight of industries whose TFP growth is above average or an increase in $A_i$ that is induced by policy measures will accelerate the growth rate of overall productivity and this will also have further effects insofar as changes in $A_i^*$ will also induce a change in $(VA_i/VA)$ by altering relative product prices. *To obtain estimates of the maximum contribution of industrial policy to industrial growth, we will assume that all above average growth in either $(VA_i/VA)$ or $A_i^*$ was attributable to government policy rather than to decisions of firms that would have occurred in its absence.* Thus, our results provide an upper bound estimate of the impact of industrial policy.[14]

An induced flow of inputs into favored sectors will raise aggregate TFP growth rates for manufacturing if:

$$\sum_f (VA_f/VA)A_f^* > \sum_n (VA_n/VA)A_n^* \qquad (3)$$

where $f$ denotes favored sectors and n denotes sectors toward which the government is neutral and the value-added shares are those at the end of the period that reflect the altered sectoral composition. Even a successful industrial policy that increases both $A_f^*$ and $VA_f/VA$ will have smaller benefits, the larger is $A_n^*$. It is possible that $A_n^*$ is increased by spillover effects from policies designed to help the favored sectors and that our calculations could underestimate the effects of industrial policy. We will consider this in Section 17.6.

While these relations hold in a growth accounting sense, it is likely that branches with expanding productivity will also grow relative to others. However, the sectoral structure is not determined solely by competitive forces in economies in which a government intervenes in both product and factor markets. Deriving a measure of the impact of industrial policy thus requires the construction of a counterfactual for each of the components of (2). The following section describes the alternatives.

## 17.4 The Counterfactual Pattern

To calculate the change in sector-wide $A^*$ induced by policy, it is necessary to compare the measured value added shares $(VA_i/VA)_T$ for Taiwan with an alternative benchmark evolution, $(VA_i/VA)_B$ and that of $(A_i^*)_T$ and $(A_i^*)_B$ as well.

### 17.4.1 The Counterfactual Sectoral Structure of Production

We consider two periods, 1967-1978 and 1980-1991, the first corresponding to the labor-intensive growth phase and the latter reflecting the rapid expansion of technology and capital-intensive sectors. The government encouraged the chemical, basic metals, electrical, and machinery sectors during the late 1970s and early 1980s, and many of the effects should be manifest in this period. However, even in the earlier 1967-1978 period, efforts to encourage some of these sectors took place.

To obtain the values for the alternative or benchmark evolution of the sectoral structure, $(VA_i/VA)_B$ that can be compared to the observed growth of sectoral shares, it is necessary to construct a relevant counterfactual. Without government intervention, Heckscher-Ohlin (HO) theory predicts that the major determinant of international trade patterns and, in an economy as open as Taiwan, its production structure, is relative factor endowments.[15] Government macroeconomic and education policies may affect relative factor endowments by increasing saving, investment, and education levels, but these are not sectorally targeted and, by definition, are not part of industrial policy. Most of the research using the HO model as a framework for empirical research has generated relatively poor predictions of sectoral trade patterns (for example, Harrigan, 1995). Possible sources of the weak results include non-neutral differences in productivity, differences in consumer preferences across countries, and the effect of government interventions.

Given the lack of a rigorous econometric model for generating the counterfactual, we have derived the benchmark values for $(VA_i/VA)_B$ by averaging the observed individual values, $(VA_i/VA)_T$, for a number of countries that had similar income per capita in 1978 and 1991, the respective ends of the periods considered. The countries and their per capita incomes are shown in Table 17.1.[16]

Taiwan's value added in individual manufacturing sectors at the two-digit level relative to its per capita income peers is shown in Figures 17.1 and 17.2 for 17 sectors. By 1978 the eventual patterns had already emerged—Taiwan had relatively low income generated in food processing and relatively high activity in electrical and electrical products and precision instruments. These are sectors whose future development was encouraged by industrial policy. Paradoxically, the differences between Taiwan and its comparators decline over the next 13 years despite the intensive effort to foster the sector. By 1991 most Taiwanese sectors except for food, beverages, and tobacco were similar to those in the second set of benchmark countries, though Taiwan may have moved into more advanced subindustries.

The use of the sectoral structure derived from other countries to calculate numerical values for (3) implies that all of the observed differences between $(VA_i/VA)_B$ and $(VA_i/VA)_T$ are attributable to industrial policy rather than (unobserved) differences in factor endowments, tastes, or technology. Insofar as the favored sectors did indeed achieve greater shares of value added and higher values of $A_i^*$, calculations of (3) attribute the observed sectoral evolution entirely to industrial policy and may overstate its contribution. But the value thus calculated helps to establish upper bounds on the effect of industrial policy.

## 17.4.2 Productivity Growth in Individual Sectors

As the benchmark for productivity growth in Taiwan, we have calculated Tornqvist indices of TFP growth for the two periods, 1967-1978 and 1980-91 and converted them to annual growth rates. The Tornqvist index of inputs is

**Table 17.1 Benchmark Countries and Per Capita Income**

| Benchmark Countries | 1978 | Benchmark Countries | 1991 |
|---|---|---|---|
| *Jordan* | $1050 | *Greece* | $6340 |
| *Malaysia* | 1090 | *Taiwan* | 8,788 |
| *Korea* | 1160 | *Ireland* | 11,120 |
| *Turkey* | 1200 | *Israel* | 11,950 |
| *Mexico* | 1290 | *New Zealand* | 12,350 |
| *Panama* | 1290 | *Spain* | 12,450 |
| *Taiwan* | 1290 | *Hong Kong* | 13,430 |
| *Chile* | 1410 | *Singapore* | 14,210 |
| *Colombia* | 1540 | | |
| *Brazil* | 1570 | | |
| *Uruguay* | 1610 | | |

*Sources*: Taiwan, *Taiwan Statistical Data Book*, Council for Economic Planning and Development, Taipei, Taiwan, various issues; other countries, U.N. *Yearbook of Industrial Statistics*, various issues.

$$T_j = \sum_i [1/2(S_{i,j,t} + S_{i,j,t-1})(\ln x_{i,j,t} - \ln x_{i,j,t-1})] \qquad (4)$$

where $S_{i,j,t}$ is the share of value added of factor *i* in sector *j* in period *t* and $x_{i,j,t}$ is the quantity of the factor *i* used in period *t* in the sector. The value of the growth rate of TFP is then calculated as

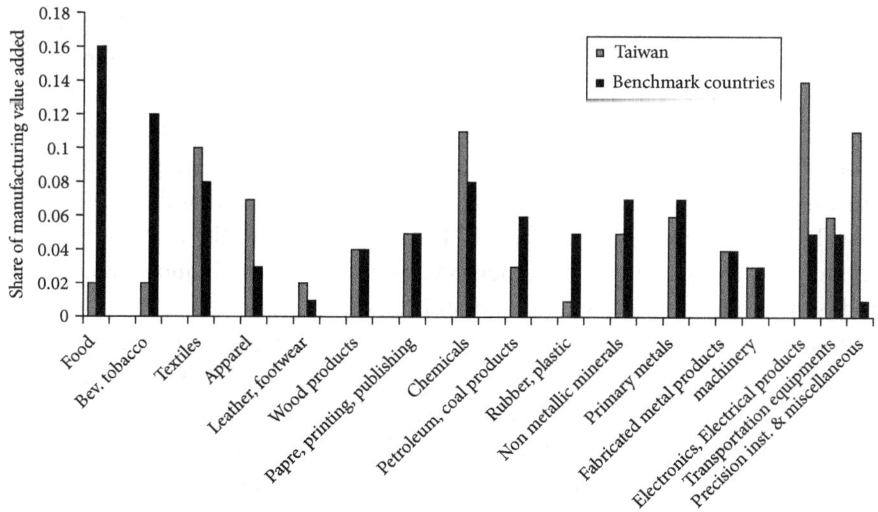


FIGURE 17.1 Sectoral Share of manufacturing Value Added Taiwan and Benchmark Countries—1978

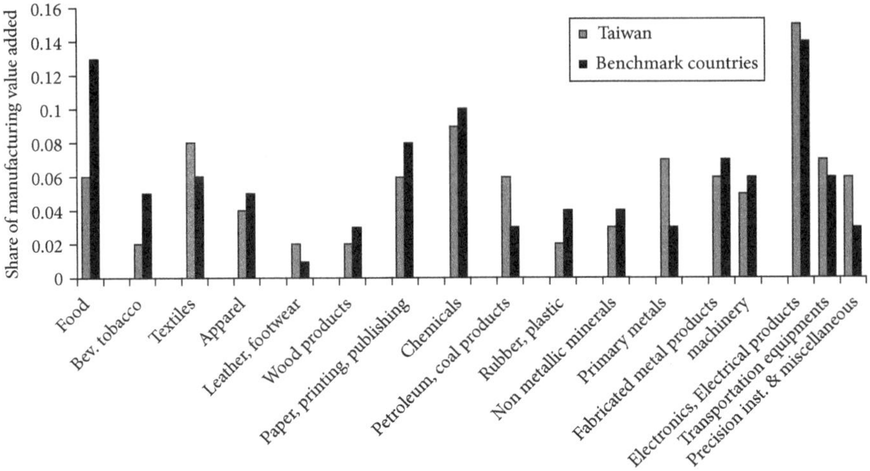


FIGURE 17.2 Sectoral Share of manufacturing Value Added Taiwan and Benchmark Countries—1991

$$A_{iT}^{*} = (\ln VA_{j,t} - \ln VA_{j,t-1}) - T_j \tag{5}$$

The results are shown in Table 17.4 for the periods 1967–1978 and 1980–1991. As education levels by two-digit manufacturing branch are not available, the calculated values of $A_i^*$ may reflect the differential growth of education by sector but data available for the end of the second period suggests not very dissimilar education levels across manufacturing sectors.

In both periods, in both the promoted and neglected sectors, TFP growth was quite high,[17] reflecting the rapid closing between initial TFP levels in Taiwan and world best practice. One source of these high rates was the rapid assimilation of international knowledge that contributed to a move toward international best practice in all sectors (Pack, 2001). For example, in 1967–1978 in sectors such as beverages, tobacco, apparel, leather, and footwear, $A_i^*$ was not very different from that in the promoted sectors such as chemicals, electrical machinery, and transport equipment. The weighted averages are 4.7 and 4.6 for the neglected and promoted sectors, suggesting that firm level efforts to increase TFP occurred in all branches. In the second period, the average for the promoted sectors was 5.96, that for the neglected ones, 4.21, which allows the possibility that industrial policies may have had a larger impact.

What is most striking about productivity in Taiwanese manufacturing is the high absolute values of $A_i^*$ in most sectors by international standards for the periods considered (Nishimizu and Page, 1987). These high sectoral values of $A_i^*$ imply that even if the impact of industrial policy achieved its goal of shifting factors among sectors, the cost of doing so was the foregone high productivity growth given up in the neglected sectors. Thus, unless the "neglected" sectors also benefited despite policies that implicitly discriminated against them, industrial policy could not have been a major factor in

Taiwanese industrial growth. We return to potential links between the promoted and neglected sectors in Section 1.6.

The most appealing TFP growth counterfactual would utilize the growth of $A_{iT}^*$ in each Taiwanese sector *i* relative to the average, in the benchmark countries, $A_{iB}^*$. Rates of productivity growth for individual industries in other countries, however, reflect many factors that are largely unrelated to industrial policy. For example, high and variable rates of inflation in some of the benchmark nations may have made it rational for firms to neglect productivity enhancements in order to concentrate on financial asset management and securing long-term contracts for intermediate inputs. In this case firms are likely to have neglected R & D, worker training, and improving plant layout. To attribute the higher rates of TFP growth in Taiwan in favored sectors compared to those in the benchmark countries to industrial policy alone would thus be inappropriate. In the periods considered, Brazil, Colombia, Israel, and Mexico all exhibited hyperinflation. Chile experienced a major change in political regime and then a large real appreciation of its currency, while Colombia and Jordan encountered internal conflict. We have thus utilized inter-industry productivity differences within Taiwan between favored and neglected sectors rather than international comparisons for identical branches. A number of sensitivity tests establish plausible bounds for estimating the impact of sectoral promotion.

## 17.5 Estimated Impact of Industrial Policy

To measure the potential effect of industrial policies we have calculated the value of equation (1) to establish Taiwan's industrial growth rate under various scenarios. First, we use the value-added shares in 1978 or 1991, shown in Figures 17.1 and 17.2, and the individual $A_i^*$ in Table 17.2. The actual growth calculated includes any beneficial impact of industrial policies, including induced deviations of the sectoral structure of production and any differences between $A_f^*$ and $A_n^*$. These values, 5.0 and 4.7, for the two periods, are shown in row 1 of Table 17.3.[18]

Three variations of the basic computation are utilized:

1.The first alternative shown in the second row of Table 17.3 employs value-added weights for the benchmark countries, $(VA_i/VA)_B$ from Figures 17.1 and 17.2 and the observed values of $A_i^*$ in Table 17.2:

$$A^* = \sum_i (VA_i/VA)_B \, A_i^* \qquad (6).$$

The values calculated, 3.7 and 4.9, imply that if it is assumed that the entire deviation in industrial structure from the benchmark group was due to industrial policy, Taiwan realized a 1.3 (5.0-3.7) percentage point gain in $A^*$ in 1967-78 but a.2 (4.7- 4.9) percentage

**Table 17.2 Total Factor Productivity Growth in Taiwanese Sectors**

| Sector | 1967–78 | 1980–91 |
|---|---|---|
| *Neglected Sectors* | | |
| Food | 1.9 | 4.0 |
| Beverages, Tobacco | 6.3 | 2.2 |
| Textiles | 6.0 | 7.1 |
| Apparel | 8.0 | 3.8 |
| Leather, footwear | 7.3 | 2.7 |
| Wood and wood products | .3 | 4.9 |
| Paper, printing, publishing | 4.5 | 2.4 |
| Rubber products | 4.1 | 7.4 |
| Non-metallic minerals | 4.2 | 3.4 |
| *Average* | 4.7 | 4.2 |
| *Promoted Sectors* | | |
| Primary metals | 2.8 | 6.1 |
| Chemicals | 3.8 | 7.1 |
| Fabricated metal. prod. | -2.7 | 4.3 |
| Machinery | 6.1 | 4.7 |
| Electrical machinery | 4.4 | 8.8 |
| Transportation equip. | 4.4 | 6.5 |
| Precision instruments | 13.7 | 4.2 |
| *Average* | 4.6 | 6.00 |

*Source*: Calculation of authors and Lin, 1995 from unpublished data, DGBAS.

point decrease in 1980-91. In the latter case, deviations in sectoral structure relative to benchmark countries was biased toward sectors with somewhat lower values of $A_i^*$.

2.In the third row, equation 5 is recalculated assuming that sectoral value added was the actual (Figures 17.1 and 17.2) and that productivity growth in the neglected sectors was not affected, but that the alternative values of $A_i^*$ in the favored sectors would have been two-thirds of their actual measured values, i.e., $A^*_f = .67A_f^*$. This reflects the assumption that the stimulation of these sectors increased their productivity growth rate by 50 percent, for example, by encouraging firms to undertake R & D and enabling them to benefit from the activities of ITRI. The recalculated growth rate is:

$$A^* = \sum_n (VA_n/VA)A_n^* + \sum_f (VA_f/VA)(.67A_f^*) \qquad (7)$$

and the computed values are shown in row 3 of Table 17.3. For both periods the assumption that productivity growth in the favored sectors was increased by 50 percent as a result of selective policy leads to a potential increase in $A^*$ of.3 =(5.0-4.7) percentage points in 1967-1978 and 1.5, (4.7-4.3) for 1980-1991.

3.$A^*$ is recalculated assuming that sectoral value added was the one in the benchmark countries and that the favored sectors experienced 50 percent greater growth rate of $A_i^*$.

$$A^* = \sum_n (VA_n/VA)_B A_n^* + \sum_f (VA_f/VA)_B (.5A_f^*) \qquad (8).$$

The calculated values are shown in row 4. This alternative is the one which provides the largest estimate of the effect of industrial policy, as it posits that growth in the promoted sectors would have been slower and that the promoted sectors would have experienced lower values of $A_i^*$. For 1967-1978, it implies that industrial policy accelerated TFP growth by.9 (5.0-4.1) percentage points and for 1980-1991 by.8, (4.7-3.9) points. The maximum improvement in TFP growth potentially ascribable to industrial policy is clearly a substantial one in both periods, increasing sector-wide A* by roughly 25 percent and 20 percent for the two eleven-year periods.

The results of Table 17.3 suggest that an upper bound for the gain from industrial policy was a bit less than 1 percentage point in both periods. A key element in the calculations is the assumption that values of $A_i^*$ were increased by 50 percent as a result of interventions such as the knowledge generated by the technology research institutes and science parks.[19] It is impossible with available data to establish the plausibility of this assumption. In both the traditional and newer sectors considerable technological effort was undertaken by local firms to identify and absorb internationally available technology. This activity does not appear to have been dependent on the promotional activities of the government (Gee, 1991). In some sectors such as electronics in the 1960s, foreign

**Table 17.3 The Effect of Industrial Policy on TFP Growth**

| | Values Used in Calculation | | | | |
|---|---|---|---|---|---|
| | $V_i$ | Values of $A_i^*$ | | Calculated Value of $A^*$ for All Manufacturing | |
| | Assumed Structure of Sectoral Value Added | Favored Sectors | Neglected Sectors | 1967–78 | 1980–91 |
| Eq. 2 | observed shares | measured | measured | 5.0 | 4.7 |
| Eq. 6 | benchmark countries | measured | measured | 3.7 | 4.9 |
| Eq. 7 | observed shares | .67 measured | measured | 4.7 | 4.3 |
| Eq. 8 | benchmark countries | .67 measured | measured | 4.1 | 3.9 |

*Source:* Calculations of author

direct investment was the critical source of transfer of technology (Gee and Kuo, 1998). The choice of Taiwan as a locale by multinational corporations had little to do with industrial targeting rather than the existence of a well-educated labor force, relatively low wages, and a stable macroeconomic environment. Finally, Taiwan's overall policy stance of neutrality with respect to firm size led to intense competition and considerable turnover among firms, a process that encouraged the exit of inefficient firms and the growth of more productive ones (Aw, Chen, and Roberts, 2001).

Say, however, that the maximum effect calculated in Table 17.3 did occur. Then one further beneficial impact of industrial policy needs to be calculated, namely, the inducement such productivity growth provided to additional capital accumulation. To analyze this it is necessary to consider the potential significance of the added TFP growth for the entire economy. Manufacturing accounted for about 30 percent of GDP and the added .9 percentage points of TFP growth would thus have increased aggregate TFP by roughly .27 per year. Hulten (1979) demonstrates that dividing the additional nationwide TFP growth by the labor share of output, roughly .4 in Taiwan, yields the true contribution of better productivity performance. In the case of Taiwan, .27/.4 = .68, suggesting that in the absence of industrial policy, Taiwan's 9 percent per annum aggregate growth rate would have been about 8.3. This is non-trivial and would be a welcome addition to growth in any country, remembering though that it depends critically on Taiwan having derived the maximum benefits from the *assumed* acceleration in productivity and shift in sectoral structure. Nevertheless, the 8.3 growth rate left after the effect of industrial policy is entirely attributable to more fundamental factors, namely, physical and human capital accumulation and productivity enhancement that accrues from a competitive environment.

This is far from trivial but it is not the entire explanation. The high rate of TFP growth in all sectors, even neglected ones, the high rate of saving and investment, even apart from the higher levels induced by industrial policy, and the acquisition of skills through education all played a significant role. Industrial policy was of significance but far from the entire story.

## 17.6 Spillover Effects

An argument often suggested for the pursuit of industrial policies is that it has externalities that improve the productivity of sectors vertically related to the promoted sector. If this is the case, calculating the aggregate impact of the promoted sectors is too narrow, as it assumes that rate of productivity growth in the neglected sectors was not affected by spillovers. If, however, $A_n^*$ was increased indirectly by the growth of the favored sectors, the calculations contained in Table 17.3 may underestimate the impact of industrial policy. Thus it is necessary to obtain some measure of the potential indirect impact of the promoted sectors. Real external economies could have arisen from three sources:

(1) local production of intermediates with special characteristics that improve productivity in the purchasing firm but are not available internationally
(2) movement by workers and managers from firms in promoted sectors to firms in other sectors, the movers bringing with them uncodified knowledge
(3) direct interactions with machinery design and manufacturing methods by local producers and buyers of machinery

All three are real externalities that are well-understood to be impossible to measure directly (Griliches, 1992). It is plausible, however, to assume that (1) and (2) depend on the magnitude of interaction between the promoted sectors and neglected sectors. For example, the knowledge generated in a promoted sector such as the metal working sector may accrue to machine producers if workers or engineers from the former are hired by the latter and carry with them knowledge of the metallurgical properties of specialty metals that were not previously understood by machine manufacturers. Even if machinery manufacturing was not specifically promoted, its productivity may be enhanced indirectly by the promotion of the metals sector. By contrast, if the domestic machinery sector purchases most of its metal from foreign suppliers, such indirect benefits are unlikely to accrue.

Such potential interactions can be measured by Leontief input-output coefficients. The n x n input-output coefficient table, A, consists of two sets of flows, the domestic intersectoral flows, $A_D$, and the import flow matrix, $A_M$, $A = A_D + A_M$. A typical coefficient of the domestic flow table is $a_{ij}$, while $m_{ij}$ denotes elements of the import matrix. The extent of interaction between favored and neglected sectors is given by the domestic input-output coefficient $a_{fn}$ which measures the purchases of an input from a favored sector per dollar of gross output of the neglected sector. The larger is $a_{fn}$, the more likely the neglected sector may derive some benefits from the existence of local producers.[20] The neglected sector may derive greater benefits if there are few imports that constitute an alternative source of specialized inputs. Thus, the lower is $m_{ij}$ relative to $a_{ij}$, the larger the potential impact of the availability of local production.

We first consider the magnitude of interaction between the promoted and neglected sectors. Several measures are derived from the Taiwanese input-output tables for 1976 and 1991, the available tables closest to our endpoint years, are shown in Tables 17.4 and 17.5. Column 1 in both tables shows the total purchases, $\sum_i a_{ij}$, of domestically produced intermediate goods by neglected and promoted industrial sectors. Column 2 shows the purchases of inputs from domestic metal, machinery, and electronics sectors, MME, denoted by $\sum a_{MME,j}$.[21] Column 3 shows the purchases from the chemical sectors that were promoted, $\sum_i a_{cj}$. The two groups of favored sectors are separated, as they sell to quite different domestic purchasers. Column 4 shows the value of all manufactured imports purchased by sector *j*, $M_j = \sum_i m_{ij}$.

Several features of Tables 17.4 and 17.5 stand out.

- In both years the direct input-output interaction between favored and neglected sectors is quite small. The promoted sectors account for a very small portion

**Table 17.4 Intersectoral Purchases—Taiwan, 1976**

| | Purchases from: | | | |
|---|---|---|---|---|
| Purchasing Sector | (1) all domestic sectors ($\sum_i a_{ij}$) | (2) primary metals, machinery, electronics ($\sum a_{MME,j}$) | (3) chemical Sectors ($\sum_i a_{cj}$) | (4) foreign suppliers ($M_j = \sum_i m_{ij}$) |
| Neglected Sectors: | .27 | .03 | .05 | .09 |
| Promoted Sectors: | | | | |
| Chemicals | .28 | .01 | .22 | .12 |
| Metal and Electronics | .30 | .21 | .02 | .20 |

*Source*: Calculations from DGBAS tapes.

**Table 17.5 Intersectoral Purchases—Taiwan, 1991**

| | Purchases from: | | | |
|---|---|---|---|---|
| Purchasing Sector | all domestic sectors ($\sum_i a_{ij}$) | primary metals, machinery, electronics ($\sum a_{MME,j}$) | chemical Sectors ($\sum_i a_{cj}$) | foreign suppliers ($M_j = \sum_i m_{ij}$) |
| Neglected Sectors: | .42 | .04 | .14 | .11 |
| Promoted Sectors: | | | | |
| Chem. material | .57 | .01 | .40 | .21 |
| Metal and Electronics | .58 | .41 | .05 | .21 |

*Source*: Calculations from DGBAS tapes.

of the domestically purchased inputs of most neglected sectors. For example, in 1976 chemicals accounted for an average of 5 percent of purchases by the neglected sectors and the machinery and electronics group accounted for an average of 3 percent of their total purchases.

- The promoted industries make extensive purchases among themselves, chemicals constituting 22 percent of total purchases by the chemicals sectors, and MME buying 21 percent of its total needs from itself in 1976 and 41 percent in 1991.
- The imports of the neglected sectors are substantial, the average in 1976,.09, being almost equal to the combined purchases from the favored domestic sectors, .08 (.03+.05).

These patterns suggest the following observations:

(a) Given the small domestic intermediate purchases by the neglected sectors from the promoted sectors and their substantial purchase of imported inputs, it is implausible that the promoted sectors were quantitatively critical in increasing the range of input availability. While domestic production of some unique, non-traded inputs may have been generated by industrial policies, these were almost surely small relative to the entire set of domestic and foreign purchases. Unless there is a very low elasticity of substitution between special local inputs and more generally available inputs, including imports, the quantitative effect of local supply of such inputs is likely to have been unimportant on the average, though some specific sectors may have benefited. Although interactions between local producers and users of intermediates may generate benefits, it would require strong assumptions about the quantitative importance of the purely local interaction to argue that a significant part of the observed values of $A_i^*$ in the neglected sectors stemmed from the promoted industries. If there were highly valuable missing intermediate inputs, many could have been obtained by imports. This was not necessarily true in the earliest stages of Taiwan's accelerated industrial development, say 1960-1970, when some inputs might not have been obtainable, but the period we are considering is largely after the initial spurt of industrialization.

(b) Insofar as movement of workers and managers transmitted important knowledge, the minor purchases by neglected sectors from the promoted sectors implies that such knowledge transmission would have had limited effects. Any tacit knowledge brought by workers and managers who had formerly been in the promoted sectors and then obtained employment in neglected sectors about the special properties of purchased inputs or how to use them more effectively, would affect only an insignificant component of total costs. While one can posit, as in the case of specialized inputs, that there is a critical piece of knowledge whose possession had exceptionally high marginal productivity for the recipient sector, the case seems implausible. Moreover, there would have been other channels by which to obtain such information, such as technology licensing agreements and foreign consultants, sources extensively used by Taiwan (Pack, 2001).

(c) Interactions across sectors are important in the case of the promoted sectors themselves, as they are substantial purchasers of each other's inputs, at least in the metal-based sectors. Any externalities from such interaction are already included in the calculations shown in Table 17.4 insofar as they utilize the observed values of $A_i^*$ that include any benefits from the posited spillovers within the sectors. The fact that there are significant purchases among the sectors leaves open the possibility that there were some gains from investment coordination.[22] Yet the presence of large imports into these sectors also suggests that the quantitative benefits conferred by coordination was probably small.

**Table 17.6 Imports of Machinery Relative to Domestic Production plus Imports**

| Sector | 1976 | 1989 |
|---|---|---|
| General Industrial Machinery and Machine Tools | .47 | .42 |
| Specialized Industrial Machinery | .47 | .43 |
| Other Machinery | .37 | .40 |
| Electrical Machinery | .23 | .43 |

*Source*: See Tables 17.4 and 17.5.

Some interactions are not be captured by input-output transactions shown in Tables 17.4 and 17.5. In particular, the interactions between machine producers and *final* purchasers of machines are not given by the input-output coefficients, investment being a final demand. One measure of the potential magnitude of such interactions is $I_D/(I_D + I_M)$, where $I_D$ denotes final sales of domestically produced machinery and $I_M$ denotes imports of machinery. These values are shown in Table 17.6.

In 1976, imports accounted for 47 percent of the total availability of general industrial machinery, machine tools, and specialized industrial machinery; 37 percent of other machinery; and 23 percent of electrical machinery. Except for the decline in electrical machinery, these had not changed much by 1989. Thus, even as late as 1989, Taiwan's local production was supplemented by extensive imports. It is difficult to argue that there were no imported substitutes or that special adaptations to local conditions are likely to have been quantitatively significant. Even if locally produced equipment conferred some cost reductions on its users that would not have been available from internationally available equipment, it would have affected about half of annual machinery investment as late as 1989 and none of the local construction costs. If a typical share of value added in gross output is 20 percent, of which 40 percent is the capital share, and if specialized machinery reduced capital costs by 25 percent, the typical reduction in overall cost (or increase in the level of TFP) would have been 2 percent. Thus, to come up with a significant impact from local production in the machinery sector would require that such equipment is also more productive in utilizing specialized intermediates and raw materials. But this is stretching a causal link much further than available evidence will permit.

## 17.7 Conclusions

Using a consistent set of estimates of TFP growth by sectors along with a variety of assumptions about the counterfactual development of both TFP and the sectoral structure of production, we have attempted to obtain a range for the probable impact of sectorally selective industrial policy in Taiwan. We found that Taiwan's manufacturing could have derived as much as a .9 percentage point increase in its growth rate as a result of industrial policy, inclusive of a measure of the likely importance of externalities. Even this, however, would still ascribe the major source of the extraordinary growth to factor accumulation and to TFP growth unrelated to industrial policy. And, at the aggregate level, even the extremely favorable assumptions employed in this paper yield an increase in growth rate of less than .3 points per year.

Many countries from Argentina to India have attempted to discriminate among sectors, most often with no success. One difference is that the Taiwanese promotion efforts were embedded in an economy in which almost all other policies were properly executed. These included fiscal and monetary discipline, remarkable constancy of the real exchange rate, and high resources devoted to education. Moreover, the household saving rate was exceptionally high.[23] Even if the government was sufficiently prescient to identify potentially successful sectors, without this favorable macroeconomic constellation, the development of a successful industrial sector could have been undermined by adverse movements in many variables that determine economic success.

The difficulty of demonstrating that the major source of either manufacturing or aggregate economic growth in Taiwan and other Asian nations was sectorally targeted industrial policies is not equivalent to denying the importance of a significant government role other than macroeconomic management in stimulating economic growth. This caveat holds for analyses of other nations that find that the industrial policy was not a major contributor to aggregate growth. Growth-enhancing measures that did not differentiate among sectors included large expenditures on primary and secondary education, the building of large and efficient social infrastructure, a favorable attitude toward international technology transfer, including both technology licensing and direct foreign investment and a substantial investment in public technology institutions (World Bank, 1993). The credible commitment of government to rapid development may itself have a positive effect on risk-taking in the private sector and have led firms to choose product or processes that promised greater return, though in other countries this phenomenon has not been observed. Policies that encouraged exports in all sectors may have generated a variety of learning benefits that would not have accrued from sales in the domestic market. There is also the possibility that close government monitoring of the private sector prevented major errors such as investment in sectors with worldwide excess capacity.[24]

Finally, we can ask whether the particular industrial development strategy pursued by Taiwan helped to forestall the crisis that dominated countries such as Korea and Thailand during the late 1990s. Without pursuing the sources of the Asian crisis in detail, one important difference between Taiwan's industrial policies and those of Korea was the less extensive emphasis on preferential lending to individual firms and, more generally, the size neutrality of Taiwan's policies. Its firms were not as leveraged as those in Korea and had also faced a more intense competitive environment. Though the industrial policies of the two countries had considerable similarities, Korea had pursued more intensively the promotion of individual products (semi-conductors and autos), whereas Taiwan's policy had encouraged a more diversified industrial base of small- and middle-sized firms that were neither as leveraged nor concentrated in one or two products. Thus when some declines in international markets such as semi-conductors occurred, Taiwan was less exposed. Similarly, Taiwanese firms were more dependent on domestic sources of finance and the rapid reversal of capital inflows to several Asian countries had only a minor impact on Taiwan.

## Notes

1. I thank without implicating David Lin, Justin Yinfu Lin, Marcus Noland, Janet Rothenberg Pack, and Kamal Saggi for very helpful discussions. I particularly thank David Yuh Yau Lin for permission to cite his 1995 dissertation at the University of Pennsylvania. Funding from the Wharton Global Initiatives Research Fund is gratefully acknowledged.
2. A good survey of the role of governments in the early history of OECD countries is provided by Lin and Monga, 2010.
3. Pack and Saggi (2006) provide an extensive discussion of the market failures that potentially could be addressed by industrial policy. Pack and Westphal (1986) suggested that the Korean government had addressed many of these successfully in its early efforts to industrialize.
4. On Korea see Jones and Sakong, 1980; Pack and Westphal, 1986; Pack, 2000. A recent article by Lee (2011) provides interesting perspectives on Korea's extensive interventions. On Taiwan see Wade, 1990. For a review and synthesis of still more recent studies see Noland and Pack, 2003; Pack and Saggi, 2006; and Harrison and Rodriquez-Clare, 2009.
5. Smith's analysis of the effects of Taiwanese policy is focused on the 1980s.
6. For a rich description of these informal mechanisms in the U.S. high technology sector see Saxenian, 1994.
7. This is not, however, sufficient to justify intervention. A socially successful intervention depends on whether the present discounted value (PDV) of future producer surplus exceeds the PDV of the social cost of subsidies.
8. For the views of a key Taiwanese policymaker see Li, 1988.
9. A thorough reevaluation of the extent of intervention is provided by Smith (2000). Dahlman and Sananikone (1997) provide a description of the modes of intervention.
10. The most thorough analysis of these institutions is contained in Dahlman and Sananikone, 1997.
11. Noland and Pack, 2003; Pack and Saggi, 2006; and Harrison and Rodriquez-Clare (2009) provide extensive surveys and evaluations of the analytic and empirical literature.
12. There have been some careful detailed studies of individual sectors (Wang 1998), such as information technology, that have discerned no measurable contribution.
13. Centralized research could be justified in terms of the argument noted above about incomplete inappropriability and the likelihood that social rates of return exceed private rates of return. The science park can be rationalized as encouraging agglomeration economies that stemmed from economies of scope for purchased inputs ranging from

accounting services to manufactured inputs produced by other firms in the park. The Hschinchu Park may also have been used to attract expatriate Taiwanese scientists back to Taiwan.

14. For example, we attribute sectoral shifts due to factor accumulation (that follows from the Rybczynski theorem) to industrial policy. As aggregate capital intensity increased due to the very high saving rate, the labor-intensive sectors declined in absolute size, while the more capital intensive sectors increased. Such sectoral shifts were not due to promotion.
15. For careful estimates of the factor endowment model for several Asian countries see Noland, 1997.
16. The countries and their per capita income relative to Taiwan do not change significantly when comparisons are made on the basis of purchasing power parity (PPP) using the Penn-World Tables, version 5.6. As we will be using the share of value added by manufacturing sector in GDP, which is not available in PPP terms given the nature of the construction of PPP, we have used GDP per capita conversions at official exchange rates.
17. The possibility that neglected sectors benefited indirectly from the stimulaton of favored sectors is considered systematically in Section 1.6.
18. As noted earlier, the values calculated for $A^*$ would be lower if growth in education in each sector were accounted for in the input measure. Data on education by sector are not available. Our conjecture is that if these were available, they would show a higher rate of growth of eductation in the promoted higher technology sectors, reducing the value of $A^*$ relative to that in the neglected sectors.
19. Sakakibara (1997) finds that participation in publicly supported R&D consortia in Japan was concentrated in slow growth sectors and that sharing fixed costs was not an important factor in determining participation.
20. It is possible to test whether indirect interactions mediated through other sectors have an effect by using the inverse coefficients of the Leontief matrix. But the potential sources of real external economies discussed in the text are not easily extended to indirect interactions.
21. More precisely iron and steel, non-electrical machinery, electrical machinery, household electronics, electronics, and transport equipment.
22. Pack and Westphal (1986) present a theoretical case for the potential importance of investment coordination.
23. Stiglitz, 1993, emphasizes the government's role in encouraging saving. Others have suggested that the emphasis on small-scale firms encouraged families to re-invest a high percentage of their income.
24. There were some notable but infrequent errors such as the encouragement of an automobile sector.

## References

Aw, Bee Yan, Hiaomin Chen, and Mark J. Roberts, 2001, "Firm-Level Evidence on Productivity Differentials and Turnover in Taiwanese Manufacturing," *Journal of Development Economics*, 66(1): 51–86.

Beason, Richard, and David E. Weinstein. 1996. "Growth, Economies of Scale, and Targeting in Japan (1955-1990)," *Review of Economics and Statistics*, 78(2): 286–295.

Caves, D. W., L. R. Christensen, and W. E. Diewert, 1982, "Multilateral Comparisons of Output, Input, and Productivity Using Superlative Index Numbers," *Economic Journal*, 92: 73–86.

Clark, Cal, 1989, *Taiwan's Development*, Greenwood, Westport, Conn.

Dahlman, Carl J., and Ousa Sananikone, 1997, "Taiwan, China: Policies and Institutions for Rapid Growth," in Danny Leipziger, ed., *Lessons from East Asia*, Ann Arbor, University of Michigan Press, 1997: 83–154.

Diewert, W. E., 1976, "Exact and Superlative Index Numbers," *Journal of Econometrics*, 4: 115–145.

Fields, Gary, 1994, "Changing Labor Market Conditions and Economic Development in Hong Kong, the Republic of Korea, Singapore, and Taiwan, China," *World Bank Economic Review*, 8 (3): 395–414.

Gee, San (ed.), 1991, "Technology, Investment, and Trade Under Economic Globalisation: the Case of Taiwan," in *Trade, Investment and Technology in the 1990s*, Paris, Organisation for Economic Cooperation and Development: 57–86.

Gold, Thomas, 1986, *State and Society in the Taiwan Miracle, M.E.* Sharpe, Armonk.

Griliches, Zvi, 1992, "The Search for R&D Spillovers," *Scandinavian Journal of Economics* 94: S29–S47.

Harrigan, James, 1995, "Factor Endowments and the International Location of Production: Econometric Evidence for the OECD, 1970-85," *Journal of International Economics* 39: 123–141.

Harrison, Ann, and Andrés Rodríguez-Clare, 2009, "Trade, Foreign Investment, and Industrial Policy," *Handbook of Development Economics*, Vol. 5, Dani Rodrik and Mark Rosenzweig (eds), North-Holland: 162–222.Please provide publisher name of Harrison and Rodríguez-Clare (2009).

Hulten, Charles R., 1979, "On the 'Importance' of Productivity Change," *American Economic Review*, 69 (1): 126–136.

Jones, Leroy, and Il Sakong, 1980, *Government, Business, and Entrepreneurship in Economic Development: the Korean Case*, Harvard University Press, Cambridge,.

Lee, Jong-wha. 1997. "Government Interventions and Productivity Growth in Korean Manufacturing Industries," *Journal of Economic Growth*. 1(3): 391–414.

Li, K. T., 1988, *The Evolution of Policy Behind Taiwan's Development Success*, Yale University Press, New Haven.

Lin, David (Yuh Yau), 1995, *Sources of Productivity Growth—Taiwan: 1966-1991* unpublished doctoral dissertation, The University of Pennsylvania.

Lin, Justin Yifu, and Celestin Monga, 2011, "Growth Identification and Facilitation—The Role of the State in the Dynamics of Structural Change," *Development Policy Review*. 26: 259–310.

Nelson, R. R., and Howard Pack, 1999, "The Asian Growth Miracle and Modern Growth Theory" *Economic Journal*, July, 1999.

Nishimizu, Mieko, and John M. Page, 1987, "Economic Policies and Productivity Change in Industry: An International Comparison." The World Bank. Washington D.C.

Noland, Marcus. 1997. "Has Asian Export Behavior Been Unique?," *Journal of International Economics*. 43: 79–101.

Noland, Marcus, and Howard Pack, 2003, *Industrial Policy in an Era of Globalization: Lessons from Asia*, Washington, D.C.: Institute for International Economics, 2003.

Pack, Howard, and Larry E. Westphal, 1986, "Industrial Strategy and Technological Change: theory vs. reality," *Journal of Development Economics*: 22: 87–128.

. . . , 2000, "Industrial Policy: Growth Elixir or Poison?" *World Bank Research Observer*, 15: 47–68.

Howard Pack 2001, "The Role of Foreign Technology Acquisition in Taiwanese Growth," *Industrial and Corporate Change*. 10(3): 713–733.

. . . , and Kamal Saggi, 2006, "The Case for Industrial Policy: A Critical Survey" *World Bank Research Observer*. 21: 267–297.

Howard Pack 2011, Industrial Policy in Historical Perspective, presented at American Economic Association Meetings, January, 2011.

Rodrik, Dani. 2008. "Normalizing Industrial Policy." Commission on Growth and Development, World Bank, Working Paper No. 3, Washington, DC.

Sakakibara, Mariko. 1997. "Evaluating Government Sponsored R&D Consortia in Japan: Who Benefits and How?," *CIPER Working Paper* 97–94. John E. Anderson Graduate School of Management, UCLA.

Saxenian, A., 1994, *Regional Advantage: Culture and Competition in Silicon Valley and Route 128*. Harvard University Press, Cambridge.

Scitovsky, Tibor, "Two Concepts of External Economies," *Journal of Political Economy*, April, 1954. 62: 30–48.

Smith, Heather. 1997. "Taiwan's Industrial Policy in the 1980s: An Appraisal," *Asian Economic Journal* 11(1): 1–34.

Smith, Heather. 2000. *Industry Policy in Taiwan and Korea in the 1980s*. Cheltenham: Edward Elgar.

Theil, Henri, 1968, "On the Geometry and the Numerical Approximation of Cost of Living and Real Income Indices," *De Economist*, 116: 677–689.

Thorbecke, Eric, and Henry Wan, 1999, *Taiwan's Development Experience: Lessons on Roles of Government and Market*. Kluwer Academic Publishers, Boston.

Wade, Robert, 1990, *Governing the Market: Economic Theory and Taiwan's Industrial Policies*, Princeton University Press, Princeton.

Winckler, Edwin A., and Susan Greenhalgh, eds., 1989, *Contending Approaches to the Political Economy of Taiwan*, M.E. Sharpe, Armonk, N.Y.

World Bank, *The East Asian Miracle: Economic Growth and Public Policy*, Washington, D.C.: World Bank, 1993.

CHAPTER 18

# CREATIVE INDUSTRIES: SOCIO-ECONOMIC TRANSFORMATION AS THE NEW FACE OF INNOVATION

F. TED TSCHANG

## 18.1 Introduction and Literature

The Pacific Rim has been and continues to be one of the most dynamic regions of the world.[1] One aspect of the Pacific Rim's ongoing socio-economic transformation, in particular, the one that is distinguishing its outputs on the world stage, is its development of creative industries.

I am foremost concerned with characterizing the emerging face of innovation, and the social milieu that may be shaping it. I will do this by focusing on selected creative industries (or sectors) as a window into creativity-based socio-economic transformations. Creativity is typically viewed as a front end to innovation, or to be the purview of the artistic sphere, and yet, it is increasingly considered to be critical to foster (as witnessed by China's and Singapore's policies to broadly foster creativity in education as well as focus on innovation in general) (Keane 2004). California is often acknowledged as the first mover in technological innovation, and aside from Japan, innovation in the Asian parts of the Pacific Rim are generally seen to be imitative. Increasingly however, innovation is seen to be based on creativity, to be having a local and regional characteristic, to be derived from culture, and to be based on content. While these aspects are seen to be happening in creative industries, information technologies are increasingly enabling content production, delivery and consumption, and even changing the nature of media. While we acknowledge the importance of traditional and popular culture, we will also discuss some of the trends by focusing on media that is newer, that is playing an increasing role, or that is technology-enabled, including games, animation, social media, and design.

Standard definitions of creative industries are too broad to be of use since they include everything from antiques to software (e.g., UNCTAD 2010). As the UN has pointed out, the term the creative industries (and set of sectors encompassed) has sometimes been distinguished from, and sometimes used interchangeably with, the older term known as the cultural industries (which include the parts of the economy dealing with "high culture," e.g., art, classical music, museums, and other traditional cultural forms), as well as popular (or pop) culture, such as contemporary music, film, and so on (UNCTAD 2010). A convenient analytical approach is to focus on specific sectors. I will pay some attention to popular culture (e.g., film and other traditional media), to the more industrialized parts of culture (e.g., fashion), and especially to newer media such as games and digital animation. Even the older of these sectors are roiling with change, as popular cultural influences shape and reshape the sectors. The UN suggests that in addition to the creative industries being creativity-based,[2] these sectors are also distinguished by their being "vehicles for symbolic messages to those who consume them, i.e., they are more than simply utilitarian insofar as they additionally serve some larger, communicative purpose"; and by their containing some intellectual property (IP) (UNCTAD 2010, p. 4).

Where possible, we will recognize the most dominant creative industry sectors within a given country, either by their renown in the international or regional sphere or their economic impact. The creative industries generally do not contribute more than a few percent to GDP, and it is hard to recognize the creative industries such as film, games, and social networking sites without recognizing that they operate in the shadow of the more dominant manufacturing and services. Yet, they have broader public (and global) recognition than most products, and account for ever greater amounts of use of individual time than traditional manufactures.

This chapter will attempt to illustrate the thesis that the character of creative industries' emergence, in particular in Asia, is largely due to cultural and societal history factors innate to the region and even a particular country. The combination of these factors in order to service uneven and unique markets are what have helped these sectors to emerge and sustain themselves in the countries that they have taken root in. (This is not to say that their time of emergence has occurred after certain stages of growth). I propose *four lenses* for viewing these trends as they occur across countries.

*Firstly, the nature of innovation typologies may change.* It is perhaps less useful to characterize innovations by conventional typologies, for example, as incremental or radical, or the model as market-led versus technology-push. *Innovations* may involve not only product or service innovations, but also innovations in the form of *experiences* (not all monetized), and *business models.*

*Secondly, innovations in the new creative industries are largely derived from culture.* For the most part, they involve some form of local cultural uniqueness or creativity. Standout cultures have products that become globally consumable by their uniqueness as well as their connections to global culture, making them relevant to regional and global markets. In regard to this, one common way of innovating is through *combinations*—of knowledge, of (creative) influences and means of doing business (i.e., the business model), and of local and global knowledge—all in order to situate or adapt an innovation (possibly imported) to the particular cultural context.

*Thirdly, as they are creativity-based,* innovations may occur through the acts of *particular individuals* (through individual creativity) set in a particular country's context, that is, individuals acting creatively and entrepreneurially. In this sense, it is a *general process,* but also *specific* with regards to the specific knowledge or influences acting on or through the individuals.

*Fourthly, the nature of policy frameworks* changes in culturally based regimes of innovation. Unlike industrial innovations, creative industry innovations are not induced by policy. Rather, policy tends to follow the emergence of a creative industry, and will tend to be *enabling* of these phenomena.

To a large degree, these processes and mechanisms are general beyond the Pacific Rim, but the specific knowledge of the past and present of these countries will shape the specific nature of creativity and trajectories of industrial and social development in the Pacific Rim countries.

### 18.1.1 Conceptual Lenses

This chapter examines creative industries as *industries*. In doing so, it largely adopts a rationalist stance, detailing actual business and industry cases as phenomena of economic growth, where standard understanding of entrepreneurship and risk-taking, capability, and participation in value chains actually matter for firms' fortunes. At the same time, there is a significant *literature* on the creative industries in the social sciences. This chapter taps into that literature where possible, recognizing the critical stance that this has on policies, and manner in which its approach is rooted in culture. In many cases, information technology is the *general purpose technology* (GPT) undergirding substantial structural change (and transformations in the products and services themselves) in sectors of interest.

Since many of the creative industries are media- or content-based, the Pacific Basin countries and creative industries cannot be understood without understanding the past and present cultural and socio-political history of the countries themselves.

In the technological industries, there have historically been strong connections between the production and consumption markets across the Pacific Rim region.[3] However, the question may arise as to why countries within the Pacific Rim would have particular affinities for each others' cultural products. In fact, many of the innovations in the creative industries arose and had their *first success* in their *country of origin*—that is, they were not innovations for a global or other market—but were later more broadly consumed within the region and even elsewhere in the world. This is the character of cultural innovation and diffusion. This repeats the technological innovations of the past, when general instances of innovation from elsewhere were heavily adapted for new localities.[4]

Nowadays, certain forms of a nation's culture may be broadly consumed worldwide. US popular culture has been as heavily consumed in Asia as it has been worldwide, but increasingly, Japanese popular culture and newer media are also likewise heavily consumed across Asia (Japanese animation and games have in fact made their way around the world). Chinese and Korean popular culture is following in this trend, starting within the region. In addition, films and music from different Asian countries are widely consumed in other Asian markets. In terms of export, animation has been offshored from the United States and other Western countries to the Philippines, Japan, and Korea (Yoon and Malecki 2009). All this cross-regional consumption of culture cannot help but influence the next generation of creative people (or creatives). It is perhaps safe to say that traditional culture (such as native dances) is not as exportable as popular culture products (e.g., pop music and television) and newer media (namely, games and animation), though traditional culture does influence or affect the other two cultures, however indirectly.

The next two sections examine first, specific countries and their key sectors, and second, the issues that are cross-cutting across sectors and countries, as highlighted above. The third section discusses how these issues can be reframed in economic terms, in particular, as they relate to the concepts of the GPT and Schumpeterian growth.

## 18.2 Regions

My first "take" is to look at particular countries' creative sectors that are either economically significant or that are popularly known in the press and literature. For reasons of space and the case-study nature of the evidence in this chapter, with a few briefly covered exceptions, I will limit my focus to selected countries of East and Southeast Asia, to California, and to Australia. As pointed out by UNCTAD's creative economy report, "In the Asia-Pacific region, the creative industries have been an important element in the development of mature economies such as Japan and the Republic of Korea, as well as of fast-growing economies such as Singapore and Malaysia. Many city authorities in China, Japan, the Republic of Korea and Singapore have formulated economic investment policies based on creativity and creative enterprise as a strategy for economic growth and competitive advantage" (UNCTAD 2010, p. 47). This suggests that a lens using this kind of industry may provide a window into the ongoing transformation of the Pacific Rim. This is reflected in UNCTAD trade statistics on the creative industries (UNCTAD 2010).

Six broad sectors are considered in UNCTAD's (2010) creative economies report: (1) design goods, which involves six main groups: interior design, graphics, fashion accessories, jewelry and toys; (2) audiovisuals, which includes film, television and radio; (3) the visual arts, which refers to everything from artwork to photography;

(4) the performing arts, consisting of music and stage art such as opera; (5) art craft, which includes handicrafts; and (6) new media, including video games.

The first thing that is noticeable from the pattern of exports in 18.1 is China's overwhelming influence on the world pattern of trade, especially in the exports of design goods, with a total export value of US$84.8 billion in creative goods in 2008 versus the US's $35 billion. In art craft, China leads the developing economies with US$10.7 billion, exceeding by a factor of five Belgium (not in the table), which leads the developed economies at US$2.09 billion. In the performing arts, Singapore leads the developing economies at US$1.08 billion and Germany the developed economies at US$5.65 billion. In the visual arts, China leads the developing countries with US$3.72 billion while the United States leads the developed countries with US$8.56 billion. In audiovisuals, the United States led the developed countries at US$27.2 billion, while China led the developing nations. The Pacific Rim countries of Korea, Mexico, and Thailand were also in the top 10 developing countries as far as the export of audiovisuals such as films and TV series. In publishing and printed media, China again leads the developing with US$2.42 billion, while Germany leads the developed with US$ 6.33 billion. In the new media sector, China leads the developing countries with US$8.38 billion and the United States leads the developed countries with US$3.79 billion.

One issue is that some of the statistics are incomplete, and hence, underreported. The new media data only cover videogames and digital records (whereas the UNCTAD classification also includes animation). We also have to consider that exports only indicate the popularity or "saleability" of a country's culture (or handiwork). In the absence of total output, another important, possibly leading indicator is imports (see Table 18.2), which suggests the countries' propensity to consume creative goods and services, and hence, is a partial measure of total consumption. Another rather aggregate indicator is that of the total (domestically hosted) production of the creative industries, seen in Table 18.2. It is also difficult to assess the meaning of the statistics on the creative industries' proportion of total GDP. There are likely to be variations in what sectors are counted, as it ranges up to 12 percent for some developing countries (unlike the few percent average for a typically "creative economy" such as the UK), and because doubling in sectoral output over a few years has been reported.

### 18.2.1 Descriptions of Countries and Significant Creative Sectors

Out of expediency, we will focus mainly on calling out and describing key sectors of the more prominent countries. Even within this, we will focus on the media- and technology-related sectors (or subsectors)—these being more subject to innovation and rapid change.

**Table 18.1 Creative Industry Exports by Sector—2008 Export (million US$) and Growth Rate**

| | 2008 exports (2003-2008 average growth rate) | | | | | | | | | | |
|---|---|---|---|---|---|---|---|---|---|---|---|
| | China | Taiwan | Hong Kong | USA | Chile | Mexico | Thailand | Japan | Australia | Korea | Singapore |
| **Creative goods**[5] (export) (value in millions of $) | 84,807 (16.9%) | 3,023 (NA) | 33,254 (6.33%) | 35,000 (13.3%) | 227 (5.92%) | 5,167 (9.1%) | 5,077 (10.31%) | 6,988 (14.7%) | 1022 (4.96%) | 4, 272 (1.05%) | 5, 047 (5.99%) |
| **Arts craft** (value in millions of $) | 10,722 (20.47%) | 780 (−0.54%) | 2,212 (−5.07%) | 1,531 (1.19%) | – | – | 399 (10.18%) | 442 (3.81%) | – | 1,447 (3.59%) | – |
| **Audio Visuals** (value in millions of $) | – | – | – | – | – | – | – | – | – | – | – |
| **Design** (value in millions of $) | 58,848 (15.45%) | – | 23,847 (5.01%) | 12,150 (14.25%) | – | 2,535 (1.40%) | 4,474 (10.80%) | 3,783 (17.21%) | – | – | 2,392 (16.21%) |
| **New Media** (value in millions of $) | 8,377 (25.64%) | 193 (22.13%) | 3,773 (29.70%) | 3,786 (5.43%) | – | 1,496 (99.09%) | – | 345 (2.40%) | – | 26 (−37.10%) | 368 (−31.59%) |
| **Performing arts** (value in millions of $) | 723 (36.65%) | 155 (14.04) | 634 (31.37%) | 3,642 (23.17%) | – | 361 (1.10%) | – | 940 (38.48 %) | – | 110 (17.90%) | 1084 (84.37%) |
| **Publishing and printed media** (value in millions of $) | 2,421 (8.70%) | – | 1,989 (3.91%) | 5,293 (6.18%) | 184 (13.19%) | 433 (−8.60%) | – | – | – | 605 (53.49%) | 713 (45.84%) |
| **Visual arts** (value in millions of $) | 3,715 (8.70%) | 204 (20.53%) | 769 (3.91%) | 8,558 (23.41%) | – | – | 95 (1.28%) | 677 (7.91%) | – | 890 (53.49%) | 399 (45.84%) |

**Table 18.2 Creative Industry Exports, Imports, and Contribution to GDP**

| | 2008 (2002-2008 average growth rate) | | | | | | | | | | | |
|---|---|---|---|---|---|---|---|---|---|---|---|---|
| | China | Taiwan | Hong Kong | Japan | USA | Chile | Mexico | Thailand | Canada | Australia | Korea | Singapore |
| **Creative goods contribution to GDP** (Year of study) | – | | | – | 11.09% (Year: 2004) | – | 4.77% (Year: 2003) | – | 2.4% (Year: 2004) | | | 5.67 (Year: 2001) |
| **Creative goods** (Export, 2008) | 84,807 (16.9%) | 3,023 (NA) | 33,254 (6.33%) | 6,988 (14.7%) | 35,000 (13.3%) | 227 (5.92%) | 5,167 (9.1%) | 5,047 (10.3%) | 9,215 (–0.94%) | 1022 (4.96%) | 4, 272 (1.05%) | 5, 047 (5.99%) |
| **Creative goods** (Import, 2008) | 2,914 (107%) | 2604 (NA) | 29,473 (10.16%) | 12,129 (53%) | 68,624 (31%) | 1,070 (21.81%) | 6,538 (11.23%) | 1974 (17.88%) | 8,214 (79%) | 7040 (12.32%) | 4,802 (16.21%) | 5,207 (15.30%) |
| **Creative services**[6] (Export, Year 2008) | 2620 | – | 265 | 155 | 13,598 | 111 | 87 | – | 10, 550 | 3,038 | 1,838 | 268 |
| **Creative services** (Import, Year 2008) | 2,195 | – | 140 | 1,215 | 1,878 | 47 | 227 | – | 6,440 | 3,144 | 6,257 | 278 |

#### 18.2.1.1 *United States (California)*

We start with our tour of the Pacific Rim by discussing the nature of innovation and creativity in the United States, and in particular, California, which has not only been a trendsetter, but has helped shape the global character of emergent industries, partly by creating knowledge in the "old" media epicenter of Hollywood, Burbank, and surroundings (Caves 2000, Scott 2005), and by developing and financing innovations in the high-tech and "new media" cluster of Silicon Valley (Kenney 2000).[7] The latter, advantaged by a copious ecosystem of venture capital, supporting institutions, and a skilled workforce, has helped promulgate different phases of the Information Technology (IT) revolution.[8] In recent years, California has contributed to the rise of social networking sites through Friendster, MySpace, Facebook (through its relocation from the East Coast), and Twitter, as well as virtual worlds like Second Life, Active Worlds, and There (these being more interactive types of social media). Many of these technologies have been replicated in and adapted to other regions' settings. For instance, China has seen the rise of a significant heavy Internet portal/search and social media industry, largely modeled after the Californian/American equivalents.[9]

#### 18.2.1.2 *Canada (Vancouver)*

Canada also has vibrant creative industries. One of the hotspots is Vancouver, which has a fairly strong film industry—largely because of the so-called "runaway" film productions from Hollywood, that is, productions that left the Greater Los Angeles area for cheaper filming locations (Coe 2001). Vancouver is also one of three hotspots in Canada (other than Montreal and Toronto) for videogame production, although this is primarily due to large foreign producers, i.e., publishers that have offices and studios there (Witheford and Sharman 2005). In this sense, the new media sectors in Vancouver are largely the direct offshoots of US and other Western economies.

#### 18.2.1.3 *Japan*

Japanese products based on its popular culture have been very popular (and the first in Asia to be so) across the world, in particular, videogames (both software and consoles) (Baba and Tschang 2001, Kohler 2004, Storz 2008) and animation (Aoyama and Izushi 2003, Lent 2001). While Japanese manga and anime has deep historical roots, it is also voraciously consumed by a subculture that includes youths in Asia and other regions, and its exports of popular culture-related products grew three-fold from 500 billion yen in 1992 to 1.5 trillion yen in 2002 (Iwabuchi 2008, p. 127). Japan also tends to spawn trendsetting if not also unusual trends, products, and experiences, and certain Japanese characters have become global brands, e.g., Sanrio's *Hello Kitty* was earning 1 billion USD annually as of 2003. Animation alone accounted for 3.5 percent of total Japanese exports to the United States in 2002 (Iwabuchi 2008, p. 127). Historically, this is suggested to be due to Japan's isolated nature and its manner of importing and then adapting foreign knowledge. Yet, this has served to bring about dramatic changes in products for users worldwide. All this has been said to occur, despite the limitations of a domestic industrial structure for facilitating the emergence of large dominant producers like those found in the United States (Dujarric and Hagiu 2009). Case-by-case evidence suggests that many of the standout productions in Japan appear to be the products of individual creators' minds (leaving aside the large teams also necessary for their production), such as video game creators like Maatsura, who largely fostered the "music playing game" genre; Hironobu Sakaguchi (who with his studio Square developed the Final Fantasy game series) (Baba and Tschang, 2001); Shigeru Miyamoto (the Nintendo designer of the *Donkey Kong* and *Mario* series); Hayao Miyazaki (and his production house, Studio Ghibli) for animation; and many other video game, film, animation, and manga creators (Aoyama and Izushi 2003, Lent 2001). On the international stage, Japanese achievements have also been made in architecture, fashion, and product design.

#### *18.2.1.4 Greater China*

By greater China, we refer in this case to the limited subset of countries (with ethnic Chinese majorities) of the People's Republic of China, Taiwan, and the Hong Kong Special Administrative Region. A comparison of the three is somewhat revealing of the sources of industrial strength by (selected) sector. The three countries have significant differences in size and economic composition.[10] All three countries are emphasizing the creative industries, in particular, China and Hong Kong. Hong Kong's creative industries' share of GDP was estimated to be about 2.6 percent in 2003, but competitive circumstances have led both legislature and government to utilize policy to emphasize these in recent years.

The size of the economy seems to matter for an industry's success, depending on the markets for a given product and the size of effort needed to create it. For instance, all three countries have vibrant film industries that are driven by both international and domestic markets. Hong Kong's film industry broke out and gained international acceptance much earlier (Cheung and Chu 2004), while Taiwan and China film industries are more recent arrivals to the international film arena. Taiwan's film industry is by now moderately successful, and recorded "breakout" films like the 2000 *Crouching Tiger, Hidden Dragon* by famed director Ang Lee. In fact, Hong Kong film also got its early start because of a series of famed directors, as well as the emergence of strong distributors.

Film is an interesting industry because of its strong ties to its past and present cultures, as well as domestic and global markets. Hong Kong's film industry is enviable, but not so its animation and games sectors. Strong distributors have helped Hong Kong's industry, but China's industry has come in with strong government support and influence, reportedly even to monitor the industry's content (Davis 2010).

Until a creative industry becomes international, its purview and success is totally dependent on the domestic market's size and strength. China, with its size of domestic market, also possesses both strong videogame and television (including animation) industries by that virtue (UKTI 2004). The earliest instances of the Chinese film industry cannot be comprehended without understanding recent Chinese history. Many films have revolved around societal themes, and due to the predominance of the government, societal themes will invariably reflect some aspect of the government—past or present (Davis 2010). Similarly, cinema and video games in greater China have rested one leg firmly on romanticized Chinese history, as depicted in historical novels such as the *Romance of the Three Kingdoms*. Film, radio, and music are said to be China's weakest creative industries (due to strict government oversight in the case of film), but multiplayer online games could have the greatest growth potential (UKTI 2004). Indeed, Chinese massively multiplayer online (MMO) game firms have overtaken the earlier Korean firms in being dominant in their own domestic market.

This suggests that the traditional media sectors are only one (balanced) model of developing creative industries, and that the newer media grows by very different innovative sources. While social media is prevalent throughout Asia, it is perhaps not taking off in as overwhelming fashion in the rest of Asia as it has in China. This has been suggested to be partly a result of China's one-child policy, but it has also been suggested that the demographics are broadening beyond the youth to their parents and grandparents.[11]

As part of this trend, online game revenue has shot up in recent years, suggesting that the strength of creative industries represents another model at work in China and parts of East Asia (UKTI 2004). This is in part due to China's technological strengths (as with Korea and Singapore), but also its strong policy emphasis (which it shares with Singapore).

Unlike in film (where Hong Kong's small market size was offset by the industry's early development and internationalization), the three countries' videogame industries are concomitant with their market sizes. Hong Kong's videogame industry is relatively weak, given the small scale of the market and largest scale of resources needed to fund games (Tschang 2010).[12] China's games industry is by far the biggest, with its MMO game industry (where it is harder for piracy to take hold) reaching revenues of well over several billion US dollars per year in 2009.[13] Hong Kong's industry shares some similar constraints to Taiwan in the size of its market, but Hong Kong is limited even more by its population's lower level of exposure to Chinese culture. A generally weak technological and technology (or technology related) entrepreneurship base also contributes to Hong Kong's weak games industry.

Interestingly, the sector with the smallest scale of effort—design—is where the differences in fortunes are reversed. Hong Kong has a reasonably strong design industry, suggesting that with its basis in individual designers and their ability to distinguish themselves, design can thrive even in a small economy, partly by adding value to products as toys, household items and clothes (traditionally exported).

Finally, a word about artistry and imitation. As in music, almost every creative industry has a fundamental difference between the ability to create and the technical virtuosity (or skill) to imitate. China's reputation for imitative production is well-known (Keane 2004). This carries over to newer creative industries, where a *Second Life* lookalike virtual world was launched, but is present in more traditional art (e.g., the single village of Dafen in Shenzhen is renowned for producing many thousands of copies of European masterworks each year) (Wong 2010). Chinese artists are also creating new traditions in their own right, though many times these are based (to varying degrees) on domestic cultural influences, or will at least harbor traces of historical culture (Kong and O'Connor 2009). As of 2006, it had been noted that the "reality (is) that China's creative content industries have yet to garner the international success claimed by Hong Kong, South Korea, Japan, and Taiwan." In part, the macro forces that are posited to constrain China's creativity may include the tendencies to be imitative on a large scale and the legacies of a "command" system (Keane 2006).

### *18.2.1.5 Korea*

Korea's creative industries are a reasonable second place to Japan's in terms of overall popularity in Asia as well as in breadth, even though it has perhaps not yet become well-known to the world. Korean popular culture has ridden a wave of popularity across Asia, led by the film and pop music industries and their stars (Shim 2006). Korea's export of TV programs went from \$12.7 million to in 1999 to \$37.5 million in 2003 (UNCTAD 2010, p. 20). Public policy has been instrumental in fostering this content development (UNCTAD 2010, p. 49).

In another setting, certain industries have ridden a tide of creative destruction fostered mainly by IT. Separately, the Korean online games industry has also become very strong and at one point dominated the Chinese market with as much as a 70 percent market share. Similarly, Chinese games are now commonly played around Southeast Asia.[12] It is largely due to the replication of cybercafés called "PC Bangs" that Korea's online industry got its fast start (Huhh 2008). This is perhaps a reflection of the IT sector in Korea—arguably one of the fastest moving in the world. Korea's economy is largely dominated by the chaebol, but the rise of significant levels of broadband connectivity and a vibrant IT financing and venture sector (also due in some part to the chaebols' entry as well as government policy) has led to an enviable IT industry with a broad basis in games, Internet business, and social media (Oh 2007, Chang 2003). In the latter case of games, however, government policy was not influential at the early stages of the game industry's beginning, but only augmented the industry after its initial success.

### *18.2.1.6 ASEAN (Singapore and Thailand as Examples)*

ASEAN as a whole covers countries at different states of economic development, ranging from the developed (e.g., Singapore) to the newly industrialized or emerging (for example, Thailand and Malaysia) to the developing (such as Indonesia and Indochina). Again, for the sake of selecting extreme cases, I focus on Thailand and Singapore.

*Thailand:* Within ASEAN, Thailand has the largest creative economy, one which contributes 12 percent to GDP (and plans to increase this to 20 percent by 2012 (UNCTAD 2010)). This is due to a strong design sector (like literally all countries in Table 18.1), as well as some traditional artcraft (mainly furniture and arts catered to tourism or exports). Thailand also has a domestic film industry, but unlike Bollywood or the Chinese film industry, the export market for this has, so far, been limited, and the domestic market is stronger. In fact, the larger Asian countries tend to have sizeable film industries. The Thai government has also invested in animation and the more advanced creative sectors.

*Singapore:* The Singapore case is worth a specific mention because in the high-tech creative sectors, Singapore continues to match its manufacturing era reputation of having the highest levels of policy-influenced industrialization. It is unique in Asia because "it is the only country in Asia to harness the shift to creative economy as a sustained national cultural policy imperative" (Yue 2006).[13] The cultural industries' share of Singapore's GDP was estimated to be 5.67 percent in 2001. As Singapore's cultural traditions are newer and smaller in scope than larger countries,' it has relied on technology to a large extent. At present, the programs and projects funded by the government appear to direct innovative output to be based on either a specific technology, purely creative work recombining existing games or genres, or an offshoring model where Singaporean facilities participate in a larger global value chain. Partly due to this trade as well as to the nature of training, the shape of new media emanating from Singapore has tended to resemble Western products more than Eastern ones (as has been the view of creativity education in China [Keane 2004]). In a recent five-year period, the Media Development Authority or MDA[14] provided half a billion Singapore dollars of funding to the interactive and digital entertainment sector for its development, to fund everything from R & D to proof of concept development.[15] In a similar manner, the government has embarked on a comprehensive design initiative—Design Singapore—expressly to "Increase design's direct contribution to GDP from S$2.15 billion to S$5 billion (or approximately 4 billion USD in 2011 terms)... (and to) Create 14,000 more jobs in the design cluster, from 32,000 to 46,000" (MICA 2008). The probability of success or a particular breakout success of a product funded by government policy initiatives is never predetermined, let alone such a product in the creative sectors, but as with many high-profile policy initiatives, it is possible that the outcome of the funding will be the seeding of a more competent, fertile environment for future growth of the industry by private sector forces.

### *18.2.1.7 Australia*

Even though Australia has made substantial state and private investments in creative industries, I will only briefly mention it, as it is disconnected from the cultural trends occurring in East Asia. Australia shares a similarity with Singapore in that the state has supported film, art, and new media industries. There is a tendency toward trade with the West, with the products being more Western-centric in culture than anything else in Asia. The creative economy generated $31 billion Australian dollars in 2007-2008, employing 5 percent of the workforce and generating 7 percent of national earnings (UNCTAD 2010, p. 30).[16]

### *18.2.1.8 Latin America (Mexico and Chile as examples)*

Latin America, including the Pacific Rim countries of Mexico and Chile (to name only two), has had a long cultural tradition. There are strong cultural traditions in literature (which includes Nobel- and other prize winning writers), as well as vibrant film, craft, and art traditions and industries. Chile has similar poetic and literary traditions. The new media has not yet taken root in these countries, although as with almost all countries, there are activities in these sectors and pockets of firms.

### 18.2.3 Summary

While across the Pacific Rim creative industries are emerging in the stronger and more developed economies, there are still leaders and emergent industries. Aside from the dominance of the United States in film, music, and new media, the Japanese cultural products of animation and games are still second to none in Asia with regards to their strength and appeal, and in many respects, are world co-leaders at least. Most Asian countries aspire to follow the Japanese, but realistically speaking, while popular culture like music and TV are broadly consumable across many borders, it has and will not been easy to "turn" domestic culture into a readily consumable export. Some sectors have become offshoring locations for the West, such as animation industries in Korea, Philippines, and China, so only time can tell if domestic content becomes globally consumable, if at all. Still, popular culture and new media such as online games (in Korea and China) show intra-regional patterns of media consumption to be an alternative.

## 18.3 Cross-cutting Issues and Mechanisms Shaping Creative Industries

To move our understanding of creativity-based innovations and creative industries (as instances of innovations) forward, it may be useful to start a process of theorizing by laying out some observations that can support beginning propositions, no matter how superficial they may be. I construct this on the basis of selected case studies. While these cases only highlight certain conceptions of production and consumption and are often outliers (i.e., extreme successes or only successes), they were collected with sufficient nuance to allow us to ascertain some of the limits to their findings.

### 18.3.1 Nature of Production and Industry Structure

Creative industries have a production process that typically stretches from the conceptualization phase to preproduction (e.g., involving prototyping) to full production and testing (there is also postproduction for film and animation). The industries may consist of individuals (e.g., lone artists) or teams (acting as studios), but usually, all are supported by intermediaries. That is, creative industries have a dual layer involving intermediaries that finance and carry products to market. While it is true of conventional industries like film, publishing, and art (Caves 2000), it is as true of newer ones like games and digital animation (Tschang 2007, Tschang and Goldstein 2010). This is in part because the industries are characterized by a "hits" nature—for the many failures and ignominious products, there are a few major hits (Caves 2000). As such, deep pockets are needed to sustain firms or creators.

The question is whether such industries can exist in a given country without the needed intermediaries. It appears that in many Asian countries, strong intermediaries are present (Shim 2006); at the same time, in other countries, the lack of intermediaries may or may not affect the ability to foster creative work, so long as global intermediaries are willing to play the role. Some Asian countries have developed strong distributors for film, animation, and games, partly by developing and controlling intellectual properties, such as Sanrio's *Hello Kitty*, which earns some 1 billion USD in sales per year (Keane 2004). Some of the largest online gaming firms in Korea and China are vertically integrated and produce their own content as well as "operate" it (i.e., they run the servers that service the millions of users of the software), for example, The 9, which until recently held the license for and profited from Blizzard's *World of Warcraft*. (Tschang and Tsang 2008).

It is worth noting that the structure of processes and production can facilitate the offshoring of the more routine parts of the production (see for example Tschang and Goldstein [2010] for the case of animation), but also shapes local economies. The more large-scale and project-intensive industries like film may reap benefits from strong "local" clusters of suppliers or labor pools (e.g., Caves 2000, Scott 2005). At the same time, the offshoring of whole stages of production is increasingly feasible in sectors like film and animation (Coe 2001, Goldstein and Tschang 2010). While it can be said that technology can intercede in creative industries, it is useful to think of technology as being the basis for the product itself (such as in 3D animation), or in its reshaping structure (e.g., by reducing and displacing workforces (as occurred in animation), or by reshaping production, as with user participation in content creation (Jenkins 2006).[19]

## 18.3.2 The Combinative, Contextualized, and Cross-Cultural Nature of Innovation

Much has been made in Western media studies of how media is recombined (also variously known as remix, combination, remediation, and media convergence) as it makes its way across time, media, and even borders in an ensuing process of globalization, often facilitated by new technologies like the Internet (Jenkins 2006). Culture is also "localized" or can have elements transplanted into more local media (Shim 2006). For example, the Taiwanese drama *Meteor Garden*, which, while based on a Japanese manga, ". . . . blend(s) a variety of local elements, and are far more than mere imitations of Japanese shows." Similarly, while one of the earliest South Korean series seemed similar to a Japanese show, the Koreans have "produced drama series portraying Asia's here and now with their own appeal," and which have now beat out Japanese serials in terms of current popularity across parts of Asia (Iwabuchi 2008, p. 132.) Davis (2010) gives examples of Chinese blockbuster films modeled on Hollywood equivalents. In games, the Hong Kong studio Firefox interprets anime through Chinese anime fans' eyes for both the Hong Kong and wider, including Japanese, markets (Tschang 2010); this even as the Japanese "Go West." Some Japanese game designs have been heavily adapted for the US market by stripping out the cultural content and replacing it with familiar ones, even while keeping the game play the same (Kohler 2004).

Thus, innovations like media are "consumed" in regions not of their origination through a process of adaptation that is less about "localization" as it is about "glocalism" (Iwabuchi 2008, p. 128). The transference of culture (and its acceptance) from one country to another is arguably one of the more important lenses with which to understand how well culture exports. Japanese and Korean popular culture has swept across East and Southeast Asia (Shim 2006, Dujarric and Hagiu 2009).

Interestingly, despite the significant cultural differences, in part due to rationalization and codification of production processes, a given country can also develop competencies for developing content for a different culture, as the location of Toei's overseas animation studio in the Philippines and Fox's production of *The Simpsons* in Korea illustrate (Tschang and Goldstein 2010). In fact, the Philippines' history as a Western colony may have partially helped it to become an offshoring location, since Philippine animation studios (and business process outsourcing [BPO] broadly speaking) are partly advantaged by the fluency in English and the "Western" attitudes such as humor. The flip side of this work is that these instances are of studios doing production-stage work, after the initial conceptualization (story lines, characters, etc.) is determined. That is, the most creative parts of the work are still usually done in the home market.

Localization has historically been used to refer to simpler processes of adaptation, such as substituting local languages for foreign languages, or simplifying products for lower cost and other forms of dealing with a "lower value-added" product. But as shown by the cases of creative industry products, local cultural taste shapes receptivity to a product, so products need to be reformulated to make them consumable. Thus, rather than treat innovation as a pattern involving localization of a global product, I think it is important to view it as a possible phenomenon of contextualizing innovations to a local environment that includes aspects of combination.[20] Business model innovations also have some characteristic of a "localized" nature. For instance, game revenue models (and the way in which the games have played) have been adapted to local circumstances, such as in being adapted from Korea to China.

## 18.3.3 Toward a View Encompassing Individuals, Cultures and Industries in National Systems of Artistic Innovation

Studies of individual creativity in the West note that the creativity of individuals is shaped by exposure to a wide variety of societal influences at different scales (Csikszentmihalyi 1999). Such individuals have shaped many if not all of the industries mentioned, including those of film and games. Hong Kong's talented corps of film directors has been absolutely critical to the industry's past success as well as its recent renewal.

The more commercial creative industries are also IP-driven, and hence can also benefit from cross-industry linkages. Hong Kong's strength in computer generated imagery (CGI) has been due largely to early linkages with the local film industry, but in recent developments, one firm acquired intellectual properties such as the *Teenage Mutant Ninja Turtles* and *Astroboy* (originally from Japan) through its business acumen, and this has helped it, and the sector, to grow both regionally and internationally (Tschang 2010).

The same concept applies to the reuse and "influence" of human capital. An earlier study showed how the Japanese games sector sourced human capital from preexisting adjacent creative industries (Aoyama and Izushi 2003). Taken together, these suggest the idea that creative industries could be viewed as national innovation systems possessing the ability to reshape the linkages and hence the interactions between actors (Storz 2008, Keane 2006). This ties together the entirely culturally situated view held by media studies with the view of individuals in creativity studies and the view of industries. Understanding competitive advantages of creative industries requires us to understand resources as human, creative, and culturally influenced in all their uniqueness.

### 18.3.4 Business Models as Innovations Helping to Contextualize Technological Innovations

Business models first saw light during the dot-com boom of the late 1990s/early 2000s, but have recently resurfaced (and are being more broadly applied) in broader management contexts. While there is some debate that business model frameworks are talking about nothing more than the reconfiguration of the value chain, and that business strategy still has to revolve around staid strategy concepts such as competitive advantage, the plethora of frameworks suggest that others are.

The idea of a business model is naturally suited to describing how firms involved in digital content, especially online content, can gain competitive advantage. One by now well-known example is that of online games, which started out with revenue models based on monthly fees. In recognition of consumers' ability to pay and the prevalence of retail stores' offering of services, games in Korea and China moved toward prepaid cards as a means of payment, and in the last few years, have moved toward the "free to play" type of model (which generates revenue by sales of "virtual goods").[21] While this appears to be a change in the revenue model on the surface, it has implications for the game and how it is experienced as well, since the company makes money from players' purchasing of virtual goods (often from the company itself), especially if they want to advance faster. This changes the dynamics of gameplay, since some players are paying to play, while others are playing for free, and the overall game itself has to be "balanced" in order to accommodate these different kinds of consumers. Thus, in a business model, the good or service changes from its traditional structure or form (i.e., how the customer accesses it), as well as how the customer experiences it and even pays and gains access to it).[22]

The potentially important conceptual leap that this suggests is that of the business model as a mechanism for further contextualizing an innovation (whether made locally or elsewhere) and to make it "consumable." Business models are already seen to be responsible for opening up new customer segments (e.g., Gillette's razor and blades business model, which sells to those wanting a better razor with disposable blades), or to new means of consuming music (e.g., Apple's iPod).[23] This is consonant with the new interpretation of Schumpeterian combination advanced by Knudsen and Swedberg (2009), whose rereading of Schumpeter highlights how combinations could take place between not only technologies, but elements in the wider economic sphere of production, including elements of the business and value chain (Schumpeter 1934).

> Every method of production signifies some such combination. This concept may be extended even to transportation and so forth, in short to everything that is production in the widest sense. An enterprise as such and even the productive conditions of the whole economic system we shall regard as "combinations" (Schumpeter 1934, p. 66).

The notion of the business model can thus be seen to be one manifestation of the combination of a business type with a technology or other artifact. This itself relates to a more traditional view of firms that have become embedded in production networks. The tendency is for the production advantages of incumbents to shift over time as their competitiveness declines in relation to the business environment. Businesses have to be fast adapters to changes that are often socially or technologically induced. On top of this, social media and a culture of amateur production are also further reshaping the relationship between producers and users in the newer, social media, with user-generated content accounting for more of the content.

In older creative industries such as US animation, the shift to a flexible model involving a largely temporary workforce has meant that a larger proportion of employment is now undertaken by freelancers. This has become one feature in the industrialization model in the Philippines as well, even as the Philippines and other countries become the site for globally outsourced production (Tschang and Goldstein 2010). There are also different ways in which production and value chains are shaped across continents, e.g., some studios who are outsourcing providers engage in co-production deals, where they invest more of their own time and resources upfront for a percentage of the profits later (Keane 2004, Lent 2001, Tschang and Goldstein 2010), between countries such as Japan and the Philippines, and between Western countries such as Canada and France.

There are significant overlaps between the services economy and the creative economy.[24] While this chapter does not try to concentrate on conventional technological innovations, it is worth acknowledging that the business model innovation is perhaps symptomatic of a broader class of innovations involving innovation in the services, and in how products are consumed and delivered. It is worth making a brief comparison with some of the purer services as they exist in, and enable, the emerging economies of the Pacific Rim. No discussion of this in Asia would be complete without mentioning Li and Fung, arguably the most influential "logistics" firm. Consisting largely of a supply chain, Li and Fung weaves together manufacturing firms large and small in China with logistics to create global supply chains for giant retailers like Walmart. Li and Fung is now turning its view inwards toward "supplying" China. By the same measure, dramatic potential for innovation also exists in Indonesia, a highly fragmented archipelago that amounts to the sixteenth largest land mass in the world.

If 92 percent of Hong Kong's GDP was comprised of the service (and creative) economy in 2009 (Hong Kong SAR 2009), it is largely due to the transition of economic power to firms like Li and Fung. A similar story at a different end of the retail scale is represented by 7-11 Japan. The one time subsidiary of the US convenience store chain acquired the home country's (US) headquarters after demonstrating a keen ability to use IT networks with Japanese just-in-time systems at the point of sale.

Many countries are taking to e-commerce not merely in a business-to-business or business-to-consumer way, but in ways that empower consumers acting as intermediaries. China's creative economy is heavily underpinned by social networking sites like RenRen (formerly Xiaonei), while use of the Internet to facilitate individual-to-individual commerce is afforded by the proliferation of portals such as Taobao, which provide active trading, reshaping the commerce landscape. In Singapore, a similar, differently organized phenomenon of "blog shops" has students and other young entrepreneurs self-organizing over the Internet, by sourcing unique fashions and other items for sale to their communities.

## 18.3.5 Rethinking the Role of Policy

Asian governments have always had a strong hand in guiding industrial policy, but with the "bubble up" nature of the culture-based creative industries, policy frameworks are having to change. It is no surprise that governments have been influential in some countries, for example, Singapore, with its thrusts on integrated digital media and design and China with its 11th five-year plan, and to some extent Korea (on games) and Japan (on cultural industries broadly speaking). More recently, the most laissez-faire of economies, Hong Kong, formulated a creative industries framework policy and investments toward promoting these as the city's competitive advantages in adding value to other industries. Most of these have to address that policies cannot be used to instigate industrial change or private-sector development, let alone to shape the cultural milieu, but instead to address fundamental factors such as human resources.

The question is whether public policy beyond that of supporting the basic factors of production actually improves the chances of industrial development. Certainly, using policies to support human capital and other basic factors after a creative industry has emerged can help. There is some evidence that a lack of such policies can constrain such industry development (Tschang and Goldstein 2010). There is also ample evidence that state influence over TV media does not lead to strong enterprises, since this creatively constrains the content, making it less saleable overseas (Keane 2006). While states cannot substitute for private sector forces, a state can still play a role in bringing about change (however circuitously), as the case of Korea suggests (Shim 2006).

Another issue that is different regarding creative industries is that national policies will also tend to balance political views of social considerations, such as the national considerations to tap into older cultural roots as a form of preserving them and to energize the new sectors, to present nationalist pride, and to use this as a form of national education (Keane 2004).

### 18.3.6 Relating the Creative Industries, General Purpose Technologies, and Creative Destruction to Growth and Development

The country and industry cases we have examined open a window into how creative industries relate to growth and development. To understand the role of the driving technological forces, we need to develop stylized views of how technological progress is interwoven with industrial progress by drawing on additional observations.

The first point I want to make is that the products undergirding many of the newer creative industries have tapped into core general purpose technologies (GPTs) even as they have combined these with other elements in new applications. A GPT has been defined to be a technology possessing the three characteristics of: (1) *pervasiveness*, or its ability to spread to most sectors, (2) *improvement*, or its ability to improve over time, and thus to lower the costs of its use, and (3) *innovation spawning*, or the notion that it helps in the invention of other new products and processes (Jovanovic and Rousseau 2005). Many industries and firms involved in making old and new products coexist with one another. For instance, online games coexist with traditional and even the more modern forms of media. In this way then, industrial change is not only about Schumpeterian creative destruction completely wiping away the old, but it is also a story about new products industries overlapping with the old, even as the old products also find ways to recharge themselves with the new technologies.

A second point that reinforces the model of Schumpeterian combination highlighted earlier is that, as GPTs propagate throughout economies, the Schumpeterian (industrial) change that occurs in different countries or contexts comes about through the combination of these new technologies into new products, and with other cultural elements embedded in those products, and economic elements involved in their making (in the case of online games, new cultural content and business models) (Knudsen and Swedberg 2009). This corresponds to the traditional view of how technologies were adapted over time, since this adaptation involves making corresponding organizational changes, in this case, the business models that help contextualize the product or content to a new setting. All of this is possible because we are talking about products delivered as IT services whose value can be demonstrated and consumed in different ways than with conventional products and human services, and which can be reconfigured to do so. This adaptation is also seen when new entrants overcome existing competitive forces in the same industry by configuring the products with new constituents, for instance, the fortunes of Korean MMO firms and other early foreign entrants in online games to China have ebbed and swayed as domestic firms have learned the technology and improved its application by integrating it with Chinese cultural content.[25] So the real issue is that of how a kind of combinative creativity—involving not just technology or products, but also content and business models and the adaptation of content to new local contexts—can help us to understand the process of industrial change across countries.

A third point is about the circuitous or nonlinear manner by which economic impacts were felt from this technological progress. The general concept of a GPT is meant to describe how technologies and industries benefit from the general process by which technological innovations radiate outwards from the central (core) GPT.[26] In order to understand how IT had an impact as a GPT, we have to look at what impacts key information technologies have had on the various industrial sectors and their products. The key technologies in videogames are those of the hardware and of the software that implements the games. The latter includes, amongst other things, the graphics engine (that generates the graphics via computer graphic algorithms), and artificial intelligence (AI) (aside from all the content and designs that are needed to differentiate the games from one another). Some of these technologies, especially the AI and computer graphics techniques, made their way into games from other industrial sectors, including computer animation (used in animation films) and computer imagery (i.e., three-dimensional (3D) special effects used in films). Thus it is the use and extension of these techniques by other sectors that have led to the techniques becoming important constituents, both in the evolution of a product (e.g., games), as well as within that type of product (e.g., the evolution of different genres of games). This is the aforementioned "radiative" effect of GPTs. More subtly, I want to emphasize that this use of IT also demonstrates a "pass-through" effect, as its improvement of the entertainment sectors is only a pit stop on its way from improving business applications, to other uses that incorporate game-related technologies into other sectors (e.g., new algorithms, business models, and even games themselves (the latter being embedded in other services in a process termed "gamification"). An example of this is how what was originally videogame technology (real-time rendering) became useful for virtual worlds like Linden Lab's *Second Life*, a type of product that many companies have been seeking to develop commercial value out of, for example, by making the Internet into a 3D-immersive environment that provides for collaborative, communicative, and training uses.

The fourth point is that, unlike what is seen in the traditional industrial progress, where advances involve productivity increases and overall economic progress, the application of GPTs in the entertainment sectors and to leisure goods is fundamentally about creating aesthetic experiences and meanings. In this sense, new meanings and purposes could be made by combining existing technologies and cultural knowledge. On the consumption side, consumption is facilitated by the society's and the individual's appreciation of aesthetics. On the production side, this process is fed by the expansion of a society's cultural base of knowledge, since the expanding set of cultural motifs is always available for future production, and possibly, productivity gains. In this sense then, cultural knowledge is also a factor in growth (of these sectors). In the end, while leisure goods do not promote productivity in themselves, they at least add positively to a nation's output.

## 18.4 Conclusion

We have provided a brief scan of the Pacific Rim. Within that, the region emerging as a new economic power is that of the Asian side. While Asia as a whole has popularly and academically been seen to be a set of "catch-up" economies, we also see and hear of a whole other side of Asian innovation—one that involves cultural and technological engagement with the Pacific Rim and the world at large, and one largely of its own making. Why do these two models of development coexist? It may be because the creative, design-oriented one is located within the local, cultural sphere of production, where meanings are made (rather than functions); where in design, meaning is far more subject to varying and local interpretation. Conflicting views are also presented by traditional culture, which is what tourism caters to, and the newer economy, which is often locally and regionally consumed, and increasingly (for selected genres and industries), globally appreciated and consumed. In these parts of the economy, media is interpreted through a cultural lens, to become a "whole other something." Aside from the cultural basis of production (especially in content), and apart from the fact that only some countries' creative industries have enjoyed export success, this pattern of success also partly involves strong creatives and entrepreneurs; eventually, stronger firms; and to some extent, enabling policies.

## Notes

1. It encompasses the second largest economy in the world (China); the third-largest (and former second-largest) economy (Japan); the US state with the eighth-largest economy in the world (California), which houses the three most dynamic IT firms in the world (Google and Apple in Silicon Valley, and Microsoft in Washington); the "Four Tigers" or "Dragons" of the East Asian Industrial Revolution (Hong Kong, Singapore, Taiwan, and Korea); and two of the largest and most dynamic economies of Latin America—Mexico and Chile. New technology and media trends continue to erupt.
2. While one standard definition of creative industries is that they are the products of individual creativity, teamwork is increasingly involved in the creation of such products, particularly as they involve media IP or technology.
3. Technological collaboration and production networks have emerged between Asia and the United States, or within Asia. For instance, Silicon Valley has focused on being a design center, and has used other Asian countries as manufacturing offshoring locations.

Singapore used to be the manufacturing center for the US hard disk drive industry, while firms in Taiwan and China have been used for Apple Computer's parts and manufacturing.

4. This is in fact the story of Japanese innovation since the earliest days, e.g., Toshiba, which created the first small footprint washing machine (similar to modern washers), and Sony's transistor radio.
5. *Creative Goods* are goods that fall under the criteria of the UNCTAD classification of "the cycle of creation, production and distribution of a tangible product with creative content, economic and cultural value and a market objective."

   They include all 211 codes selected from the list of HS 2002 based on the UNCTAD classification and methodology for a trade model for creative industries; these are grouped into 7 broad categories—art craft, audiovisuals, design, new media, performing arts, publishing and printed media, and visual arts.
6. *Creative Services* comprises, though not exclusively, the following categories of services—advertising, market research, and public opinion services (EBOPS 278, level 3); architectural, engineering, and other technical services (EBOPS 280, level 3); research and development services (EBOPS 279, level 3); personal, cultural, and recreational services (EBOPS 287, level 1); audiovisual and related services (EBOPS 288, level 2); and other personal, cultural, and recreational services (EBOPS 897, level 3). The fifth edition of the IMF Balance of Payments Manual defines each category as such:
   - Advertising and market research and public opinion polling services (Advertising): Advertising and market research services transacted between residents and non-residents cover the design, creation and marketing of advertisements by advertising agencies; media placement, including the purchase and sale of advertising space; exhibition services provided by trade fairs; the promotion of products abroad; market research; and public opinion polling abroad on various issues.
   - Architectural, engineering and other technical services (Architectural): Architectural, engineering and other technical services cover resident and non-resident transactions related to architectural design of urban and other development projects; planning and project design and supervision of dams, bridges, airports, turnkey projects, etc.; surveying, cartography, product testing and certification, and technical inspection services.
   - Research and development services (R & D): "Research and development services cover those services that are transacted between residents and non-residents and associated with basic research, applied research, and experimental development of new products and processes. In principle, such activities in the sciences, social sciences and humanities are covered; included is the development of operating systems that represent technological advances."

     Personal, cultural, and recreational services (Personal recreation): "Personal, cultural, and recreational services involving transactions between residents and non-residents are subdivided into two categories."
7. "In Silicon Valley, the Night is Still Young," Claire Cain Miller, *New York Times*, August 20, 2011. [http://www.nytimes.com/2011/08/21/technology/silicon-valley-booms-but-worries-about-a-new-bust.html?_r=1&hpw]. (Accessed August 21, 2011.)
8. This ranges from being the location of early key nodes in the Arpanet (precursor to the Internet), to being the seat of the personal computer industry, to a significant participant in the dot-com boom, and finally, one of the earliest locations of the computer gaming (or videogame) industry.

9. At the heart of Silicon Valley is a can-do attitude that promotes risk-taking (Chong-Moon et al. 2000), and perhaps an openness to change that accepts not only new migrants, but ideas (Florida 2002).
10. Hong Kong has the smallest economy, as Taiwan has a rich manufacturing past, China is an emerging market and now an emerged major economic power, and Hong Kong has the strongest service sector. They all have selected strengths in the creative industries.
11. The Game of Being Social: A Case Study of Intersections between Social, Geosocial and Mobile Media in China, L. Hjorth and M. Arnold, paper presented at Games and Innovation Seminar, Tampere University, Tampere, May 2011.
12. Taiwan's game industry is somewhat better off, but not by much. PC games that were marketed with a strong Chinese historical content would have done well in China and Taiwan alike, but severe piracy in Taiwan and China have taken their toll on videogames for PCs.
13. "Chinese Online Game Market Reaches 25.8 billion Yuan" *People's Daily Online*. [http://english.peopledaily.com.cn/90001/90778/90860/6874963.html]. Accessed August 21, 2011.
14. S. Tsang and F.T. Tschang, mimeo.
15. Like Thailand and other countries, it has the ambitious goal to diversify its sources of economic growth beyond manufacturing, and to include a strong component from the creative sectors. Singapore invested heavily in creative industries, ranging from R & D funding to large-scale training in polytechnics, creativity programs in schools, and new film and television funding and programming; it also attracted foreign investments by international game and animation studios.
16. Much of the national R & D funding, including that which the Media Development Authority (or MDA—the lead authority for the videogame and digital entertainment sector) has awarded, has gone to technology-related projects.
17. Introduction, Interactive and Digital Media (program), National Research Foundation. [https://rita.nrf.gov.sg/IDM/default.aspx]. Accessed August 21, 2011.
18. Like many other sectors, New Zealand's is notable for the influence that director Peter Jackson had on shaping the local economy, when he brought the "runaway" Lord of the Ring's production to the country. In addition to stimulating local supporting enterprises and strong special effects firms, it has also impacted the country's tourism.
19. Also known as user-led innovation or peer production, depending on the discipline.
20. In logical terms relating to creativity and product development, this convergence (or contextualization of innovations) can be viewed as part of a general process or mechanism of knowledge creation that is more akin to the technological form of combination (Arthur 2009) historically embedded in Schumpeterian models of technological change and industrial growth. In fact, most if not all innovations could be said to have this nature of contextualizing global (or other local) knowledge—where local is not necessarily spatial, but could be in terms of field of specialization or economic sector (or human sphere) of application.
21. S. Tsang and F. T. Tschang, mimeo.
22. Ibid.
23. A simple analogy with a conventional formulation of firms provides an illustration. If publishers of games possess scale and scope economies and are focused on intellectual property generation, they are less likely to be able to see the opportunities in or to take advantage of the advent of user-generated content enabled by small (e.g., single-person)

operations or studios. This was the case with *Mindcraft*—a Web-based game that allows users to generate their own creations.

24. Starbucks (also from the Pacific Rim, having emanated from Seattle) could have been said to have been a service innovation, but it embedded products, experiences, logistical services and so on, to get those products into the hands of consumers. In media itself, all online games, and many games, are delivered as services, and the manner in which the game is played and technologically constructed (e.g., the software architecture and its ability to deliver content) embed services to the player (e.g., payment models, means of handling content, etc.). Many services such as airlines' in-flight service are essentially also considered as "experiences."
25. S. Tsang and F. T. Tschang, mimeo.
26. The definition of a GPT is that it should have: (1) pervasiveness, or the spread to most sectors, (2) technological dynamism, or the ability to improve over time, and (3) innovational complementarities, or the ability to improve the productivity of downstream sectors.

## References


Aoyama, Y, and H. Izushi (2003). Hardware Gimmick or Cultural Innovation? Technological, Cultural, and Social Foundations of the Japanese Video Game Industry, *Research Policy*, 32(3): 423–444.

Arthur, W. B. (2009). *The Nature of Technology: What It Is and How It Evolves*, New York: Free Press.

Baba, Y., and F. T. Tschang (2001). "Product Development in Japanese TV Game Software: The Case of an Innovative Game," *International Journal of Innovation Management*, 5(4): 487–515.

Jovanovic, B., and P. L. Rousseau (2005). General Purpose Technologies, chapter 18, in *Handbook of Economic Growth*, P. Aghion and S. N. Durlauf, eds., 1181–1223, Amsterdam: Elsevier B.V.

Caves, R. E. (2000). *Creative Industries: Contracts Between Art and Commerce*, Cambridge: Harvard University Press.

Chong-Moon, L., W. F. Miller, M. Gong Hancock, and H. Rowen (2000). *The Silicon Valley Edge: A Habitat for Innovation and Entrepreneurship*, Palo Alto: Stanford Business Books, Stanford University Press

Chang, S. J. (2003). Korea's Internet Economy, chapter 8, in *The Global Internet Economy*, B. Kogut ed., 263–290, Cambridge: MIT Press.

Cheung, E. M. K., and Y. W. Chu (2004) Between Home and World: A Reader in Hong Kong Cinema, http://hub.hku.hk/handle/10722/123343. Accessed August 19, 2011.

Coe, N. M. (2001). "A Hybrid Agglomeration? The Development of a Satellite-Marshallian Industrial District in Vancouver's Film Industry," *Urban Studies*, 38(10): 1753–1775.

Csikszentmihalyi, M. (1999). Implications of a Systems Perspective for the Study of Creativity, chapter 16, in *Handbook of Creativity*. R. J. Sternberg ed., 313–338, Cambridge: Cambridge University Press.

Davis, D. W. (2010). "Market and Marketization in the China Film Business," *Cinema Journal*, 49(3): 121–125. Spring 2010

Dyer-Witheford, N., and Z. Sharman (2005). "The Political Economy of Canada's Video and Computer Game Industry," *Canadian Journal of Communication*, 30(2): 187–210.

Dujarric, R., and A. Hagiu (2009). Capitalizing on Innovation: The Case of Japan, Harvard Business School Working Paper 09-114.

Florida, R. L. (2002). *The Rise of the Creative Class: and How It's Transforming Work, Leisure, Community and Everyday Life*, New York: Basic Books.

Hong Kong as a Service Economy, Hong Kong SAR government, http://www.gov.hk/en/about/abouthk/factsheets/. Accessed August 19, 2011.

Huhh, J. S. (2008) "Culture and business of PC bangs in Korea," *Games and Culture*, 3(1): 26–37.

Iwabuchi, K. (2008). "Symptomatic Transformations: Japan in the Media and Cultural globalization," chapter 7, in *A New Japan for the Twenty-First Century: An Inside Overview of Current Fundamental Changes and Problems*, R. T. Segers ed., 125–140, New York: Routledge

Keane, M. A. (2004). "Brave New World: Understanding China's Creative Vision," *International Journal of Cultural Policy*, 10(3): 265–279.

Keane, M. A. (2006). "From Made in China to Created in China," *International Journal of Cultural Studies*, 9(3): 285–296.

Kenney, M. (2000). *Understanding Silicon Valley: The Anatomy of an Entrepreneurial Region*, Palo Alto: Stanford University Press.

Knudsen, T., and R. Swedberg (2009). Capitalist entrepreneurship: making profit through the unmaking of economic orders. Capitalism and Society, 4(2).

Kohler, C. (2004). *Power-up: How Japanese Video Games Gave the World an Extra Life*, Indianapolis: Bradygames.

Kong, L., and J. O'Connor (2009). *Creative Economies, Creative Cities: Asian-European Perspectives*, New York: Springer.

Lent, J. A. (2001). *Animation in Asia and the Pacific*, Bloomington: Indiana University Press.

Lent, J. A. (2006). Keynote speech, "Asian Animation: The Digital Age and Before." International Conference, "Digital Communication: The Challenge of the New Era." Chulalongkorn University, Bangkok, Thailand, November 29, 2006.

Jenkins, H. (2006). *Convergence Culture: Where Old and New Media Collide*, New York: New York University Press.

MICA (2008). Dsg-II: Strategic Blueprint of the Designsingapore Initiative, Ministry of Communication, Information and the Arts (MICA), 2008.

Oh, E. (2007). Project Organization, Diverse Knowledge, and Innovation Systems in the Korean Game Software Industry, PhD Dissertation, School of Public Policy, Georgia Institute of Technology.

Schumpeter, J. A. (1934). *The Theory of Economic Development*, Cambridge: Harvard University Press.

Scott, A.J. (2005). *On Hollywood: The Place, The Industry*,Princeton: Princeton University Press.

Segers, R. T. (2008). *A New Japan for the Twenty-First Century*, R. T. Segers, ed. New York: Routledge.

Shim, D. (2006). "Hybridity and the Rise of Korean Popular Culture in Asia," *Media, Culture and Society*, 28(1): 25–44, London: Sage.

Storz, C. (2008). "Dynamics in Innovation Systems: Evidence from Japan's Game Software Industry," *Research Policy*, 37(2008): 1480–1491.

Tschang,F. T. (2010). Kong's New Creative Industries: The Example of the Video Games Sector, chapter 11, in *Innovation Policy and the Limits of Laissez-Faire: Hong Kong's Policy in Comparative Perspective*, D. B. Fuller ed., 267–294, Basingstoke, UK: Palgrave.

Tschang, F. T. (2007). "Balancing the Tensions Between Rationalization and Creativity in the Video Games Industry," *Organization Science*, 18(6): 989–1005

Tschang, F. T. and Goldstein, A. (2010). "The Outsourcing of 'Creative' Work and the Limits of Capability: The Case of the Philippines' Animation Industry," *IEEE Transactions on Engineering Management*, 57(1): 132–143

Tschang, F. T. and S. Tsang (2008). China's New Media Sectors: Domestic Culture as Competitive Advantage, chapter in *Innovation in Greater China*, H. S. Rowen, M. G. Hancock and W. F. Miller, eds., Shorenstein APARC (center), 371–392, Palo Alto: Stanford University Press.

UKTI (2004). Changing China—The Creative Industry Perspective: A Market Analysis of China's Digital and Design Industries, Executive Summary to report, UK Trade and Investment.

UNCTAD (2010). *Creative Economy Report 2010*, Geneva: United Nations Conference on Trade and Development.

Wong, W. W. Y. (2010). After the Copy: Creativity, Originality and the Labor of Appropriation: Dafen Village, Shenzhen, China (1989-2010). PhD Thesis, Department of Architecture, MIT.

Yoon, H., and E. J. Malecki (2009). "Cartoon Planet: Worlds of Production and Global Production Networks in the Animation Industry," *Industrial and Corporate Change*, 19(1): 239–271.

Yue, A. (2006). "The Regional Culture of New Asia: Cultural Governance and Creative Industries in Singapore," *International Journal of Cultural Policy*, 12(1): 17–33.

CHAPTER 19

# THE ROAD TO INNOVATION IN EAST ASIA

SHAHID YUSUF

## 19.1 Introduction: From Learning to Innovation

For policymakers the world over, innovation is the passport to faster GDP growth and is increasingly viewed as the source of solutions to myriad problems. For business people, it holds out the promise of greater competiveness and profitability. But as it has gained currency, the meaning of innovation has tended to blur. Innovation should refer to a product, a process, a design, an organizational form, or a way of conducting business that is a tangible improvement over current products and practices. Even incremental innovation—and most innovation falls in this category—entails a nontrivial change in a process or an attribute of a product. Innovation that is commercially viable and proves to be scalable swells the ranks of successful (that is, profitable) firms and can lead to higher GDP growth by enhancing productivity,[1] widening domestic as well as foreign markets for products and services, raising the quality of what is produced, and creating new wants where none existed. The degree to which innovation can contribute to a sustained increase in GDP is the true acid test: from the policymakers' perspective, the value of innovation and the reason for pursuing it lies in its contribution to the economic bottom line.

An emerging consensus among researchers is that growth in high- and middle-income countries will increasingly hinge on continuous gains in productivity through innovation. Moreover, low-income countries can add a few valuable percentage points to their growth rates by narrowing cross-sectoral technology gaps so as to raise factor productivity (Jones and Romer 2009). This is no way minimizes the role of investment, which is likely to remain dominant, especially in countries where the ratio of capital to labor is low[2] and where industrialization is in its early stages. It is well-established that much technological catching-up is through embodied technology and such technical change can require new rounds of investment in capital and technical skills (Nelson and Winter 1975).

For the majority of lower- and middle-income countries, the first order of business (which can take two or three decades) is to acquire production capabilities and to narrow technological and intra-industry efficiency gaps in key subsectors (Acemoglu, Aghion, and Zilibotti 2006). Once these objectives are close to being achieved, further gains in productivity are likely to be paced by innovation in a variety of areas. Innovation as a productivity multiplier is a valuable asset at any stage of development and in any sphere of activity; however, its importance increases as technological catch-up shrinks the pool of unexploited possibilities. Then new combinations of existing ideas and pushing of the knowledge frontier acquire greater salience. At this stage, the contribution of skilled labor increases because innovation is skill-intensive and the returns to R & D rise the closer a country is to the technology frontier (Vandenbussche, Aghion, and Meghir 2005).

Building innovation capabilities requires a lengthy apprenticeship. The less industrial a country is and the weaker its knowledge base, the longer its apprenticeship. But many low- and middle-income economies, seduced by the possibility of "stage skipping" and of "leapfrogging," are impatient.[3] They are looking for a short route to an innovative economy that will deliver the growth they are unable to generate from other sources, especially capital investment. Because innovation has come to be viewed as a panacea for firms and economies in a hurry, its meaning is being confused with learning and technology absorption in the preparatory stage of development. Mastering an existing body of technology and associated scientific knowledge and translating this mastery into production capabilities, whether in manufacturing or in services, is a necessary prelude to the kind of activity that seeks to push the technology frontier through ideas, research, and innovations.[4] Accumulating a substantial fund of knowledge, expertise, tacit understanding, and research and production skills is a necessary prelude to sustaining innovation.[5] (See Figure 19.1, which underscores the concentration of innovation in high-income countries.) A large percentage of the gains in productivity attained by developing economies is from an internalization of what is already commonplace in more advanced countries.

How quickly an economy—or more precisely, firms and other entities in an economy—can catch up is the true test of good policy, effective institutions,[6] entrepreneurship, and an enabling culture of industrial learning that includes the capacity to reverse-engineer.[7] In this catching-up process, a small subset of firms invariably takes the lead in borrowing and mastering technologies from abroad, and within subsectors, a wide gap can separate the pacesetters in an economy from the rest (Bloom, Eifert, and others 2010). This gap is the source of opportunities for productivity growth through intra-sectoral reallocation of resources (Syverson 2010). Thus, for low- and middle-income countries, there is vast scope for ratcheting up productivity in all segments of the economy through efficiency gains and by moving to higher-value products.[8] The learning, mastering, and applying of technological knowledge as it evolves underpins innovation by leading firms once they pull abreast of the global leaders.

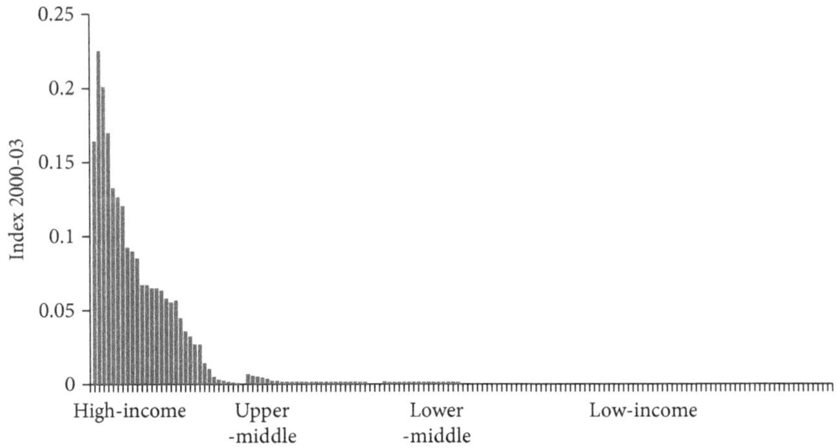


FIGURE 19.1 Scientific Innovation: Penetration of New Technologies, 2000–2003

*Source:* Chandra and others 2009.

Innovation capacity indexes constructed by various groups of researchers (see Tables 19.1 and 19.2) provide a window onto the relative standing of countries by using a variety of quantitative indicators[9] combined with subjective assessments. In East Asia, the front-runners, not surprisingly, are Japan, the Republic of Korea, Singapore, and Taiwan. According to these indexes, firms in China, and Malaysia, for example, are now demonstrating the ability to innovate. But the signs of nascent and fitful innovative activity in these middle-income countries draw attention to the broad-ranging effort required to fully assimilate the technology that is already in circulation before trying to extend it in fresh directions.

The balance of this chapter is divided into seven parts, each addressing a key element of an evolving innovative economy:

- The role of firms
- Market competition
- Industrial composition and innovation
- Investment in technology
- Human skills and innovation
- Smart cities that are part and parcel of an innovative modern economy

A brief, final section highlights the policy issues.

## 19.2 Firms: The Prime Movers

The epicenter of technology learning and application is the business sector, and firms are the prime movers. For industrializing countries, the cycle of learning technologies

**Table 19.1 Innovation Capacity Index**

| 2009–2010 | | | 2001–2002 | | |
|---|---|---|---|---|---|
| Country | Rank | Score | Country | Rank | Index |
| Singapore | 6 | 76.5 | Japan | 12 | 26.4 |
| Taiwan, China | 13 | 72.9 | Singapore | 13 | 26.0 |
| Japan | 15 | 72.1 | Taiwan, China | 14 | 26.0 |
| Korea, Rep. of | 19 | 70.0 | Korea, Rep. of | 23 | 22.9 |
| Malaysia | 34 | 57.3 | China | 43 | 18.1 |
| Thailand | 43 | 54.6 | Thailand | 46 | 17.4 |
| China | 65 | 49.5 | Malaysia | 52 | 16.8 |
| Philippines | 75 | 47.0 | Indonesia | 54 | 16.4 |
| Vietnam | 78 | 46.4 | Philippines | 56 | 15.8 |
| Indonesia | 88 | 44.9 | Vietnam | 61 | 13.8 |
| Cambodia | 112 | 37.5 | Cambodia | n.a. | n.a. |

*Note:* n.a. = not applicable.
*Sources:* López-Claros and Mata 2010; Porter and Stern 2001.

starts at the level of the firm and, depending on policies and circumstances, is complemented and reinforced by a strengthening of market and intellectual property institutions, the accumulation of human capital, improvements in infrastructure, lowered

**Table 19.2 Boston Consulting Group/National Association of Manufacturers Global Innovation Index, 2009**

| Country | Rank | Overall score | Innovation input score | Innovation performance score |
|---|---|---|---|---|
| Singapore | 1 | 2.45 | 2.74 | 1.92 |
| Korea, Rep. of | 2 | 2.26 | 1.75 | 2.55 |
| Japan | 9 | 1.79 | 1.16 | 2.25 |
| Malaysia | 21 | 1.12 | 1.01 | 1.12 |
| China | 27 | 0.73 | 0.07 | 1.32 |
| Thailand | 44 | 0.12 | −0.12 | 0.35 |
| Philippines | 54 | −0.15 | −0.76 | 0.48 |
| Indonesia | 71 | −0.57 | −0.63 | −0.46 |
| Vietnam | 73 | −0.65 | −1.09 | −0.16 |

*Source:* Andrew, DeRocco, and Taylor 2009.

transaction costs, and so on. In all countries, firms' entry, survival, competitiveness, profitability, and growth depend in large part on how effectively they organize themselves and deploy their resources to learn and apply available technologies. This is the first order of business for the majority of firms. Innovation comes much later, if it figures at all in their decision-making calculus. Where firms are slow to take the initiative, efforts to educate workers and to build knowledge and physical infrastructure will make limited headway in inducing the assimilation of technology and preparing the ground for an innovative economy. Such lethargy is surprisingly widespread. Investment climate surveys conducted by the World Bank in Malaysia, Thailand, Philippines, Vietnam, and South Africa, for example, uncover persistent dissatisfaction with the level and quality of skills; but most small firms and many large firms as well are reluctant to ramp up their internal training, to work with private and public providers to enhance the supply of skills, and to take advantage of the incentives offered by the state. Small firms are more passive in this respect and often express ignorance of training and incentive schemes.

If firms are the primary movers, then it stands to reason that entrepreneurship and management skills have a vital role to play in the technology cycle. Entrepreneurs not only bring firms into existence; they also, together with professional managers, are important conduits for technology and drivers of technological change in their companies (Audretsch 2008; Glaeser 2007). Innovative firms are frequently the brainchild(ren) of entrepreneurs who are ready to test the commercial potential of fresh ideas and technologies.[10] In Korea during the 1960s and 1970s; in Taiwan, China, from the 1950s onward; and in China after the mid-1980s, the nurturing of entrepreneurship[11] and of policies to promote new starts—as well as the rapid expansion of existing firms and the ambition to enter foreign markets—were responsible for a virtuous spiral of industrial development, fueled by investment and technology acquisition.

Entrepreneurship[12] transfers ideas into the commercial domain. It is vital not only to the absorption of existing technologies by industrializing countries but also to the process of innovation. Talented risk takers, many with some business experience drawn from firms, universities, and research centers, are the ones who promote technological advances. Increasingly, as technologies become more sophisticated, such risk-takers tend to have tertiary-level training, and entrepreneurs in bio- and nanotechnology industries are frequently university researchers and faculty members. Many of the people who launched electronics firms started out working for companies in the same or related industries.[13] Then there are the stories of inspired and lucky mavericks who started out tinkering in their garages, but one hears of fewer such inventors now. Most innovative new starts are by two or three individuals; venture capitalists prefer dealing with more than one person and attach value to business experience as well.[14] The point is that (a) entrepreneurship matters; (b) it can be assisted by a cultural environment that is more tolerant of failure; (c) the essentials of good entrepreneurship can be taught, although little evidence shows that schools offering courses on entrepreneurship induce more students to take the plunge; and (d) entrepreneurs can benefit from the assistance of managers, angel investors, and other service providers.

There are wide differences in productivity among firms in the same industry, especially in industrializing countries. Several factors account for this divergence. In particular, the quality of management, when reinforced by product competition in domestic and foreign markets, affects the productivity of firms through several channels, including the emphasis on innovation, the utilization of information technology (IT),[15] and personnel management. Several researchers ascribe the large intra-industry differences in the productivity of firms to managerial shortcomings in industrializing countries that result in a long tail of firms performing far below par (Bloom, Eifert, and others 2010; Bloom, Mahajan, and others 2010; Bloom, Sadun, and Van Reenen 2009; Bloom and Van Reenen 2010). The shortcomings can be remedied in time, though management know-how accumulates slowly.

From the standpoint of innovation, the entry of many new firms and the churning of firms are advantageous because they accelerate the technology refresh-rate and raise growth rates (Rosenthal and Strange 2008). One reason the United States is the innovation front-runner is that it provides a hospitable environment for large numbers of young, innovative firms that contribute to both R & D and sales.[16]

Recent research has revealed how the activities of a minority of firms, prompted by opportunities inherent in exporting, can initiate a cycle of technology enhancement and rising productivity (see, for example, Bernard and Jensen 2001; Bernard, Redding, and Schott 2006; Melitz 2003). Firms active in international markets are quicker to extract the maximum productivity advantage from technological learning, imitating, and upgrading, and at raising productivity.[17] The actions and the example of this minority of pioneering exporters generate spillovers and set the pace for other domestic firms that have not ventured abroad. These pioneering firms can trigger the exit of less productive firms and the entry of competitors and, in so doing, infuse dynamism into the industry, a process that contributed to the unusual performance of the leading East Asian countries.

Firms such as Samsung, LG, SK, and Hyundai in Korea; their counterparts in China such as Lenovo, Huawei, ZTE, Wanxiang, BYD, CIMC, SAIC, TSMC, and Mediatek in Taiwan; and similar firms in other Southeast Asian economies were—and are—the standard-bearers of Asia's signature export-led growth model.[18] These firms are now helping to build the innovation capabilities of their respective economies, having first drawn abreast of the global technological frontier.

Large companies do the lion's share of applied research and innovation.[19] Such companies are responsible for most of the incremental process and product innovation, and through their own efforts and the perfecting, customizing, and marketing of more radical innovations by smaller companies that they acquire.[20] Large firms are generally less receptive and often do not give rise to breakthrough innovations (especially low cost), for *lock-in* reasons delineated by Christensen and Raynor (2003); nevertheless, their development and marketing inputs frequently determine the success of disruptive innovations.[21] Some research by Zucker and Darby (2007) also shows that, notwithstanding the drawbacks of industrial concentration and oligopolistic producers, consumers derive more generous welfare gains from the innovativeness of oligopolistic firms. In fact, no substitute exists for the initiative and leadership that large firms with transnational strategies can provide. Government incentives and purchasing policies can encourage innovation, universities and research institutions can assist, business incubators can nurture new ideas, and science parks can offer space and enabling infrastructure, but large firms that seek to compete and earn profits on the basis of innovation must provide a good part of the impetus—the demand for innovation—and some of them must evolve into the innovation hothouses.

One striking finding from the research on leading international firms is that only a weak relationship seems to exist between the level of research and development (R & D) spending and the metrics used to measure the financial and market related performance of firms. Increasing R & D can raise the number of patents, but patents do not readily translate into desired business outcomes such as profitability and market share. In fact, excessive spending can be dysfunctional if it throws up barriers to innovation by making scientists into constituents who become wedded to the status quo (Jaruzelski, Dehoff, and Bordia 2005). The most successful innovative companies are ones that can extract the maximum innovation from a moderate R & D budget. These companies share a number of characteristics:

- They have an innovation culture deliberately cultivated and constantly reinforced by top management and an innovation strategy fully aligned with corporate strategy.
- The innovation strategy is comprehensive and keyed to long-run competitiveness and the avoidance of frequent restructuring and changes of direction.[22] It embraces not only products but also process innovation, innovations in marketing, associated services, and the business model of the firm itself. A study of innovative firms by Hargadon and Sutton (2000: 158) found that serial innovators had perfected a "knowledge brokering cycle made up of four intertwined work practices: capturing good ideas, keeping ideas alive, imagining new uses for old ideas, and putting promising concepts to the test." Some research suggests that the firms with the most innovative business models—and not the ones with the innovative products—achieved the highest stock market returns and growth of revenues (Hagel, Brown, and Davison 2008).
- Successful innovators adopt an open and collaborative approach to innovation, recognizing that they cannot excel in more than a few areas of research and need to canvass ideas from a variety of sources.[23]
- The focus of the research efforts and the quality of leadership is critical to success, as is the closeness of interaction between the research wing of the firm and the production and marketing departments.[24]
- Successful innovators tend to have a flatter and nimbler managerial structure and effective procedures for vetting research proposals, tracking progress, and screening out failures (Lynch 2007). These companies also have well-articulated procedures for developing and commercializing products.

- In industrializing East Asian countries, the successful innovators have leveraged their knowledge of the local market to innovate by customizing products and tuning distribution networks. This explains the success of Lenovo in China (Zeng and Williamson 2007). They also innovate in the distribution of products.

Bolstered by policy support, entrepreneurship allied with management skills and technological expertise can, through the medium of firms, generate productivity gains during the catch-up stage of development and enable an economy to transition to a stage where productivity accrues more from innovation than from learning. But the formation and growth of firms, their responsiveness to incentives, and their capacity to push technological change are not independent of other factors. Firms may be the prime movers, but how fast they move, how effectively they mobilize technology, how much innovation they are capable of, and the quality of this innovation are functions of other factors.

## 19.3 The Market Environment

The smaller East Asian economies, by embracing export-oriented industrialization, moved in measured steps to a relatively open market environment that gradually subjected firms to market discipline by dismantling the trade barriers and incentivizing exports. To survive through trade, companies were forced to be competitive; this approach to trade liberalization encouraged the more dynamic firms with government help to move up the learning curve, deepen manufacturing capabilities, and bring levels of productivity and quality closer to international norms.

All the East Asian economies retained degrees of protectionism in a variety of guises (many of the non-tariff variety)[25] and supported their growing industries with incentives that were compatible with international treaties—with tax incentives for investment and R & D, depreciation allowances, duty free access to imported inputs for exports, government procurement, and credit at attractive terms among the more common. None of the economies introduced competition policies until quite late in the day, and even those economies that do have such policies on the books have enforced them sparingly, flexibly, and with modest conviction.

Notwithstanding those market protections, the East Asian economies embraced systems that were progressively more open and increasingly better equipped with market and legal institutions and adequate mechanisms of governance. Under conditions of macroeconomic and political stability, relatively open market economies provided the environment for the development of competitive firms. As Tables 19.3 to 19.6 show, the innovation capacity indexes partially match the rankings of competitiveness and of openness. Singapore and Taiwan are usually top-ranked. Taiwan's "Doing Business" ranking was low through 2009, however, it has since improved rising to 16th place in 2013. Malaysia and Thailand are consistently ranked near the middle (although Malaysia

**Table 19.3 IMD Global Competitiveness Ranking, 2004–2008**

| Economy | 2004 | 2005 | 2006 | 2007 | 2008 |
|---|---|---|---|---|---|
| Singapore | 2 | 3 | 3 | 2 | 2 |
| Taiwan, China | 12 | 11 | 17 | 18 | 13 |
| China | 22 | 29 | 18 | 15 | 17 |
| Malaysia | 16 | 26 | 22 | 23 | 19 |
| Japan | 21 | 19 | 16 | 24 | 22 |
| Thailand | 26 | 25 | 29 | 33 | 27 |
| Korea, Rep. of | 31 | 27 | 32 | 29 | 31 |
| Philippines | 43 | 40 | 42 | 45 | 40 |
| Indonesia | 49 | 50 | 52 | 54 | 51 |

*Note:* Economies are ordered by their rank in 2008.
*Source:* IMD 2009.

is second only to Singapore with respect to openness because of its large processing industry), and Indonesia and the Philippines are consistently near the bottom. Thus, a competitive business environment helps set the stage for technological advance and, eventually, innovativeness.

## 19.4 Industrial Mix, Research Intensity, and Innovation by Firms

A competitive environment stimulates, but technological change and innovation are strongly influenced by the composition of industry. Historically, the pattern of scientific inventions has tended to be concentrated in certain fields, and this concentration is reflected in the intensity of innovation. Certain industries are far more innovative than others, and countries specializing in these industries have greater opportunities for catching up and for developing new products and processes. Countries whose market forces are abetted by the nudging from industrial policy[26] can develop a suite of technologically dynamic industries that increase their chances of becoming innovative economies, if they can establish a viable system for generating ideas and translating those ideas into commercial practice. How effectively the system performs depends on the fruitful interplay and coordination between the factors listed above in the two preceding sections.

Producers of garments, food products, footwear, furniture, light consumer electrical devices, and a variety of services have been innovation laggards in most countries. Where these industries have registered gains in productivity, those gains have occurred because the industries have moved closer to an international production frontier and

**Table 19.4 World Economic Forum Global Competitiveness Index, 2006–2007 and 2007–2008**

| Economy | 2006-2007 | 2007-2008 |
|---|---|---|
| Singapore | 8 | 7 |
| Japan | 5 | 8 |
| Korea, Rep. of | 23 | 11 |
| Taiwan, China | 13 | 14 |
| Malaysia | 19 | 21 |
| Thailand | 28 | 28 |
| China | 35 | 34 |
| Indonesia | 54 | 51 |
| Philippines | 75 | 67 |

*Note:* Economies are ordered by their rank in 2007-2008.
*Sources:* López-Claros and others 2006; Porter, Schwab, and Sala-i-Martin 2007.

**Table 19.5 "Doing Business" Indicators, 2006–2009**

| Economy | 2006 | 2007 | 2008 | 2009 |
|---|---|---|---|---|
| Singapore | 2 | 1 | 1 | 1 |
| Japan | 10 | 11 | 12 | 12 |
| Thailand | 20 | 18 | 15 | 13 |
| Malaysia | 21 | 25 | 24 | 20 |
| Korea, Rep. of | 27 | 23 | 30 | 23 |
| Taiwan, China | 35 | 47 | 50 | 61 |
| China | 91 | 93 | 83 | 83 |
| Indonesia | 115 | 135 | 123 | 129 |
| Philippines | 113 | 126 | 133 | 140 |

*Note:* Economies are ordered by rank in 2009.
*Sources:* World Bank 2005, 2006, 2007, 2008.

more rarely because innovations have shifted the frontier outward. Industries producing electronics, telecommunications and office equipment, machinery, and engineering products have been in the vanguard of productivity advances in the manufacturing sector, and in the United States, finance, retailing, and wholesaling also registered significant gains in the past two decades. The findings for manufacturing industries in the United States approximately resemble the Japanese experience.[27]

**Table 19.6 Exports and Imports of Goods and Services, 2007**

| Economy | Percentage of GDP |
|---|---|
| Singapore | 463.0 |
| Malaysia | 210.0 |
| Taiwan, China | 140.0 |
| Thailand | 132.5 |
| Philippines | 83.3 |
| Korea, Rep. of | 90.4 |
| China[a] | 72.0 |
| Indonesia | 54.7 |
| Japan[b] | 27.3 |

a. Data are for 2006.
b. Data are for 2005.
*Source:* World Bank World Development Indicators database.

Figures 19.2 and 19.3 show how industries compare with respect to productivity outcomes since 1960 in the United States and Japan. Of the U.S. manufacturing industries, firms producing machinery, instruments, telecommunications equipment, and rubber and plastic products were among the industries that registered the greatest gains in total factor productivity between 1960 and 2004 (Jorgenson, Goettle, and others 2008). A number of factors contributed to these gains, and it is not surprising that innovation is prominent among them. The most productive manufacturing industries are also the most research-intensive, and this research has produced numerous patents that tangibly delimit the extent of technological advance and the expanding scope for innovation. This is also apparent from Figure 19.7 correlating the innovation capacity index with R & D spending in East Asia.

Figure 19.4 shows the R & D intensities (measured by R & D spending as a share of sales) among different subsectors based on the top 1000 R & D corporate spenders globally. Figure 19.5, which uses data from 10 leading Organization for Economic Co-operation and Development (OECD) countries, presents the variation in research intensity across different subsectors. Clearly, the manufacturing industries, led by office and computing machinery, are in the forefront, followed by pharmaceuticals and by machinery, professional goods, and transport equipment. The contributions to productivity via innovations of the science-based industries such as electronics and pharmaceuticals and the specialized suppliers producing complex capital goods in the OECD countries, are reinforced by Castaldi (2009: 721), who states that these industries "remain fundamental contributors to technologies, knowledge and aggregate productivity growth."

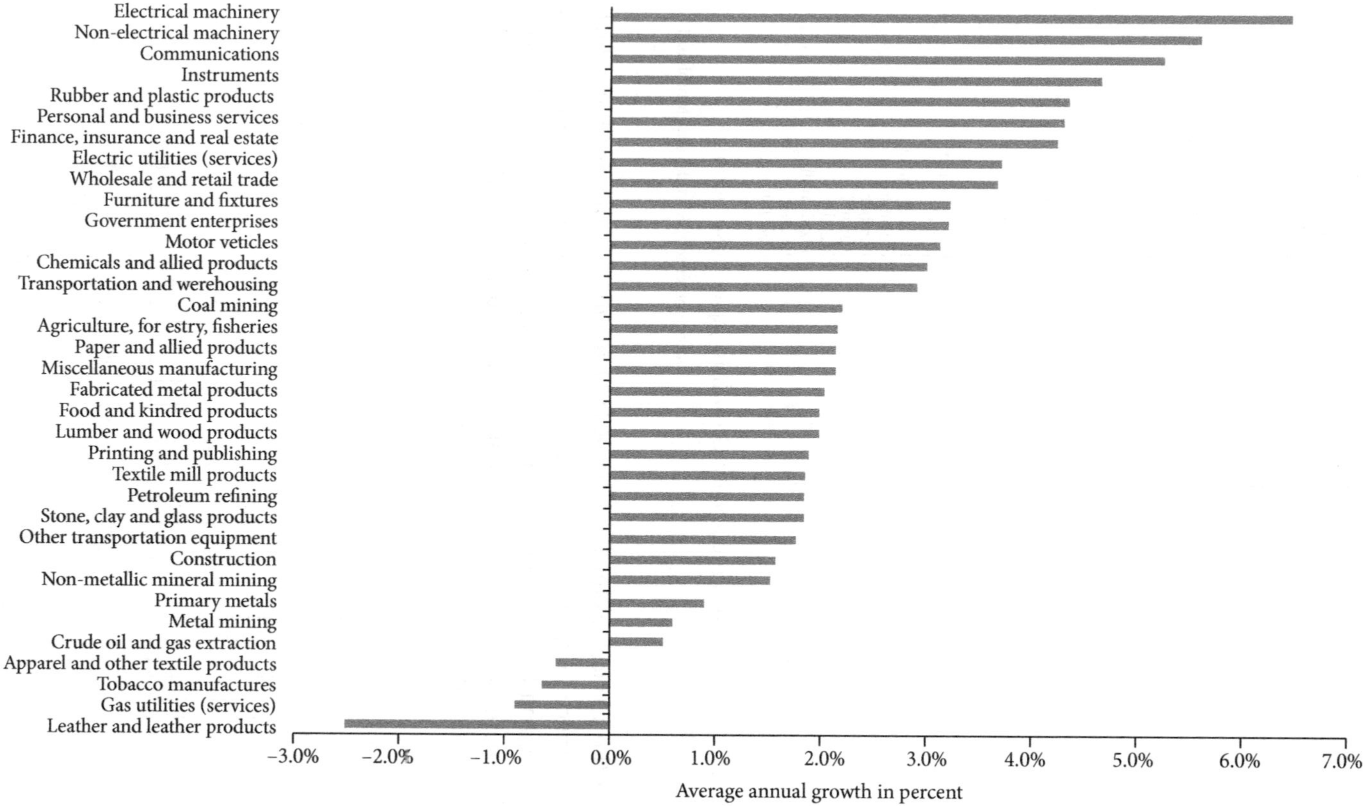


**FIGURE 19.2** Growth of U.S. Total Factor Productivity 1960–2004

*Source:* Jorgenson, Goettle, and others 2008.

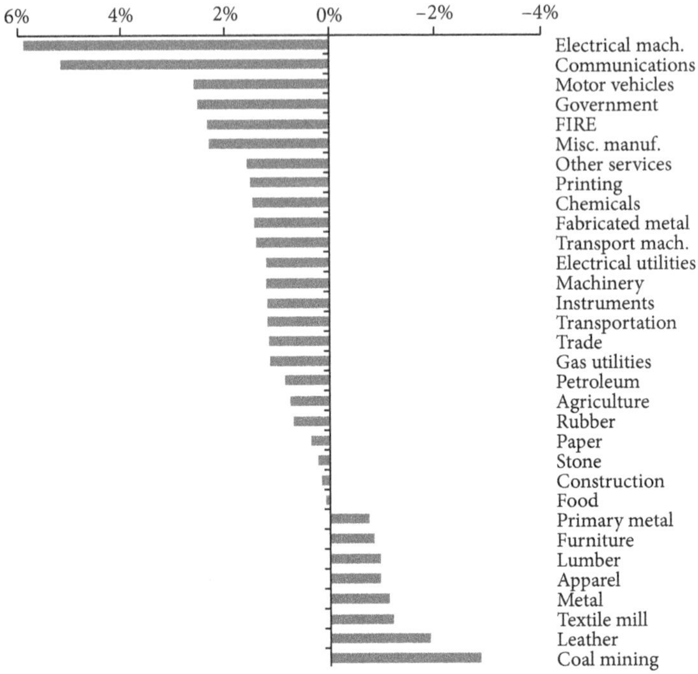


FIGURE 19.3 Average Total Factor Productivity Growth in Japan, 1980–2000

*Source:* Jorgenson, Kuroda, and Motohashi 2007.

The share of the services sector in global R & D spending is the smallest, which is not to say that service industries do not innovate. In fact, they do, but formal R & D plays a small role, and fiscal incentives that seek to promote spending on R & D will have little effect on innovation in services. For services, business model, IT-related and service-delivery innovations are more important.

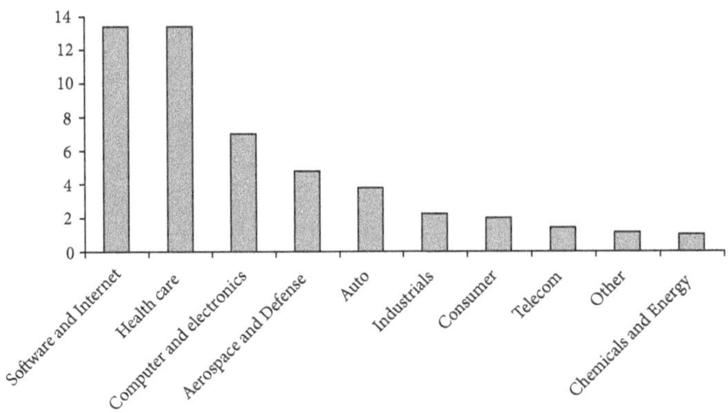


FIGURE 19.4 Global R & D Intensity as a Share of Sales in 2006

*Source:* Jaruzelski and Dehoff 2007.

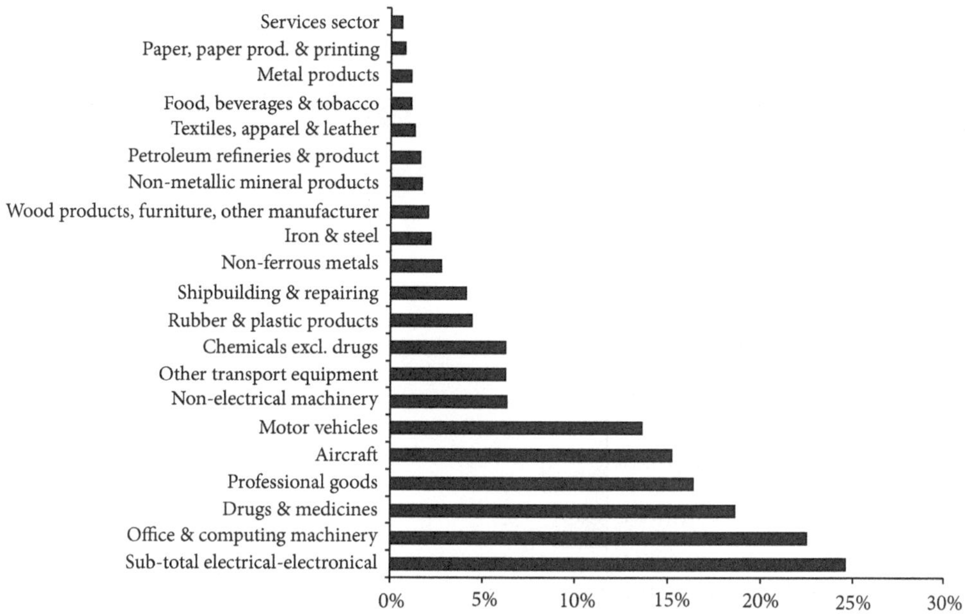


**FIGURE 19.5** R & D Intensity by Industry in 10 OECD Countries for 1991–2002

*Source:* Mathieu and van Pottelsberghe de la Potterie 2008.

Patent data from the U.S. Patent and Trademark Office (USPTO) reaffirm the relative importance of innovation in manufacturing. Invention patents are more numerous in manufacturing industries, notwithstanding a considerable jump in patents for services (inventions) over the past decade. Within manufacturing industries, only a dozen or so industrial subsectors account for 60 to 70 percent of the invention patents (Figure 19.6).

Innovative manufacturing industries can be grouped into three categories. The first category comprises producers of customized, complex capital goods (for example, plant equipment, power-generating equipment, and transport equipment). These industries depend on a slow accumulation of learning, tacit knowledge, and specialized skills. They have significant backward links and involve a host of specialized suppliers that frequently cluster near the main assemblers. Suppliers collaborate in conducting R & D programs to meet specific needs of end-users and in producing new generations of equipment.[28] With respect to innovations in the capital goods and components industries, Cooke and others (2007: 57) note that these innovations:

> are characterized by a *synthetic knowledge base*. In such settings, the application of existing knowledge or the new combination of available knowledge may lead to innovations. This often occurs in the need to solve actual problems on the shop floor or in interaction with key customers or users and suppliers. Research and development are generally less important... University-industry links are less

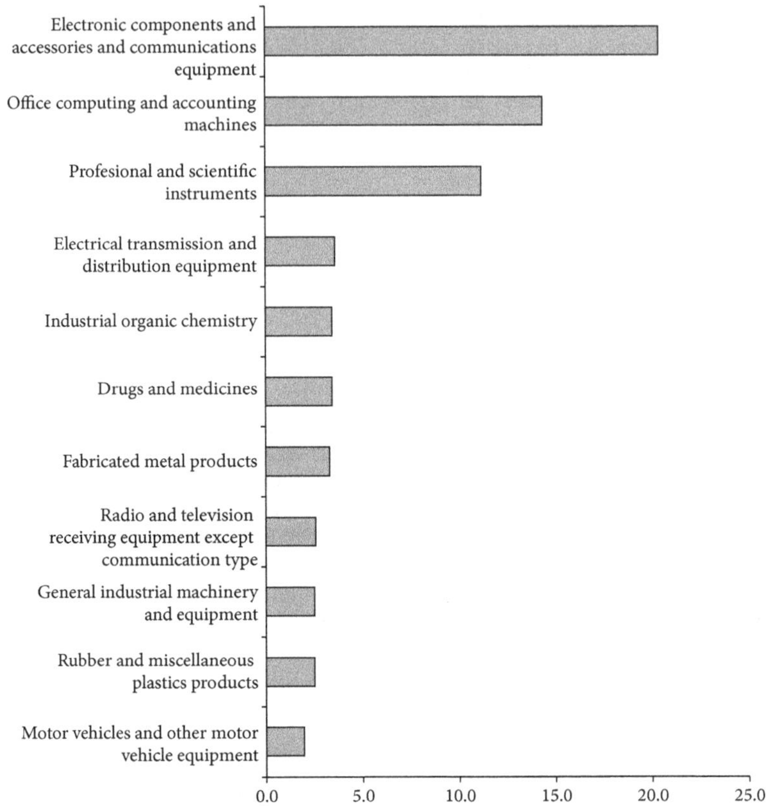


FIGURE 19.6 Share of U.S. Patents by Industry, 2006

*Source:* Authors' calculation based on U.S. Patent and Trademark Office data.

> frequent... Accordingly, knowledge is created... through... an inductive process of testing, experimentation, or through practical work.

Such industries also derive substantial revenues from after-sales services by maintaining, upgrading, refurbishing, or rebuilding existing equipment (for example, aircraft, earthmoving and power generating equipment, engines, and locomotives) and by supplying spare parts for long-lived capital goods (in fact, services of all kinds including finance, insurance and logistics account for almost a third of value added by manufacturing). Global suppliers of complex goods can sustain a flotilla of affiliated firms that provide well-paid jobs in an urban environment. (Complex capital goods, components, and electrical equipment are among the industrial products most suited for capital-abundant economies with a skilled and high-wage workforce.)[29]

A second category of manufacturing activities with growing appeal is profitable because these activities innovate incrementally and, every so often, introduce a revolutionary (disruptive) new product that redraws market boundaries and brings new firms to the forefront.[30] This category of manufacturing industries ranges from cosmetics to white goods to medical imaging, and from nanotechnology to new materials. But all of these industries share several distinctive characteristics. They all are R & D-intensive, often rely on research covering several fields, and frequently draw on the basic or applied research conducted in universities or specialized institutes (Boozer and others 2003; Jaruzelski and Dehoff 2007; Jaruzelski, Dehoff, and Bordia 2005, 2006). Small and medium-size firms are the lifeblood of these industries because they are responsible for a significant share of innovation. Firms in industries associated with the life sciences and with advanced materials not infrequently are started by university faculty from nearby schools; draw on the research conducted in universities; and are heavy users of legal,[31] consulting, managerial, and financial services. Consequently, they integrate closely with the service providers in urban centers (see Bresnahan and others 2001). Both types of industries depend for their growth, profitability, and longer-term survival on knowledge deepening and on product differentiation through customization, innovation of all kinds (including business models), and packaging of products with services ("The World's Most Innovative Companies" 2006).[32] Industrializing East Asia's focus on manufacturing has positioned it to benefit from advances in the most technologically dynamic subsectors. And led by Korea, Taiwan, and China these economies are now attempting to develop indigenous capabilities in electronics, telecoms, and nanotechnology.

The automobile industry, a leading sector in Japan, Korea, and now China falls into the third category with a widening scope for innovation for a number of reasons. First, the development of commercially viable "clean" automobiles and the supporting infrastructure will absorb a large volume of R & D in hybrid, electric, and fuel cell technologies, plus other alternatives, and in the physical facilities for delivering fuel or power.[33] In just a decade, Chinese producers of hybrid and electric vehicles have entered the field that latterly was dominated by Japan and Western producers. Second, the increasing use of electronics in improving the performance of automobile engines, entertainment systems, sophisticated IT-enriched dashboard displays, and safety and handling features opens fruitful opportunities for innovation, including in embedded software and sensors (leading eventually to driverless cars supported by the 'Internet of things'), which is a strength of IT firms in China and Taiwan. Third, the auto industry is also investing in advanced materials that can reduce weight without compromising safety and can facilitate the repair and recycling of the vehicle (Charette 2009; Zhao 2006).[34]

Innovation is also responsible for rising productivity in several service industries, such as wholesale and retail trade, real estate, and banks. Much of this increase occurred after the mid-1990s in the United States and Europe as a result of major advances in IT, the parallel reorganization of work practices and logistics, coupled with innovations in business models (Brynjolfsson and Hitt 2003; Brynjolfsson and Saunders 2009; Gordon 2003; Oliner and Sichel 2000). The introduction of new equipment (computers, other office equipment, and telecommunication equipment and software)[35] has enabled providers of services to increase the quality and variety of their services (for example, in finance); to raise the efficiency of their supply chains and warehousing; to consolidate

Table 19.7 R & D Spending, by Country, 1996–2006

| Economy | 1996 | 2000 | 2002 | 2004 | 2005 | 2006 |
|---|---|---|---|---|---|---|
| China | 0.6 | 0.9 | 1.1 | 1.2 | 1.3 | 1.4 |
| Indonesia | – | 0.1 | – | – | – | – |
| Japan | 2.8 | 3.0 | 3.2 | 3.2 | 3.3 | 3.4 |
| Korea, Rep. of | 2.4 | 2.4 | 2.5 | 2.9 | 3.0 | 3.2 |
| Malaysia | 0.2 | 0.5 | 0.7 | 0.6 | – | – |
| Philippines | – | – | 0.2 | – | – | – |
| Singapore | 1.4 | 1.9 | 2.2 | 2.2 | 2.4 | 2.4 |
| Thailand | 0.1 | 0.3 | 0.2 | 0.3 | – | – |
| Vietnam | – | – | 0.2 | – | – | – |

*Note:* – = not available.
*Source:* World Bank World Development Indicators database.

their activities; and to outsource and massively reduce the labor intensity of their operations.

This surge of productivity in services, which is filtering into the East Asian industrializing countries, foreshadows vast opportunities for catch-up and gains in productivity.

## 19.5 Investment in Technological Capacity, Technology Absorption, and Innovation Potential

Clearly, industrial composition is a major determinant of innovation and productivity. However, the level of research activity can reinforce the technological capacity inherent in the industrial structure. Expenditure on R & D is the most frequently used input metric of technological capacity and as can be seen from Figure 19.7, R & D spending does on balance enhance innovativeness.[36] Japan is by far the largest spender of R & D as a share of GDP, with 3.4 percent of GDP devoted to R & D in 2006 (see Table 19.7). Korea spends 3.2 percent of GDP on R & D, rivaling Japan. Singapore also has been increasing its spending on R & D, which in 2006 accounted for 2.4 percent of GDP. All three economies rely on manufacturing as the drivers of growth and exports. By far the fastest increase has occurred in China, a manufacturing economy par excellence, with outlay on R & D rising from 0.6 percent of GDP in 1996 to 1.7 in 2009 and 2 percent in 2012. Given the rapid economic growth during this period, the increase in the volume of resources committed to R & D was phenomenal. By comparison, the spending on R & D by Southeast Asian economies is quite low, with less than 1 percent of GDP devoted to R & D, because manufacturing activity is mostly oriented toward processing and assembly.

**Table 19.8 Composition of R & D Spending**

| Economy | Business enterprise (%) | Government (%) | Higher education (%) | Private nonprofit (%) |
|---|---|---|---|---|
| China | 71.1 | 19.7 | 9.2 | – |
| Hong Kong, China | 48.3 | 2.2 | 49.5 | – |
| Indonesia | 14.3 | 81.1 | 4.6 | – |
| Japan | 77.2 | 8.3 | 12.7 | 1.9 |
| Korea, Rep. of | 77.3 | 11.6 | 10.0 | 1.2 |
| Malaysia | 71.5 | 10.4 | 18.1 | – |
| Philippines | 68.0 | 19.1 | 11.1 | 1.8 |
| Singapore | 65.7 | 10.4 | 23.9 | – |
| Thailand | 43.9 | 22.5 | 31.0 | 2.6 |
| Vietnam | 14.5 | 66.4 | 17.9 | 1.1 |

*Note:* – = not available. Data for Hong Kong, China; India; Malaysia; and Sri Lanka are for 2004. Data for the Philippines and Thailand are for 2003. Data for Vietnam are for 2002. Data for Indonesia are for 2001.
*Source:* UNESCO Institute for Statistics Data Centre.

Mirroring the overall pattern in the OECD, firms account for two-thirds or more of R & D spending in East Asia, except in Hong Kong, Indonesia; Thailand; and Vietnam (see Table 19.8). In China, the business sector is responsible for more than 70 percent of R & D outlay compared with 40 percent in the mid-1990s.[37] Both in Indonesia and Vietnam, the government is the major source of R & D spending. In Hong Kong, China, universities are the largest spenders on R & D. In Thailand, half of the spending on R & D is by the public sector and by universities. Although the public sector usually finances the bulk of basic and early-stage applied research, the task of technology development and the commercializing of innovation falls on firms. R & D spending during the early stage of development can be thought as a part of the effort by manufacturing industries to assimilate and internalize foreign technology as well as building the foundations of a national innovation system. During the rapid growth phase of Japan, more than 30 percent of R & D was devoted to learning. Firms are in a much better position to identify the technologies with the greatest commercial payoff, and they need to expend some effort in understanding these technologies.

Larger firms generally engage in some form of R & D and take the lead in establishing the infrastructure and assembling teams of researchers. Increasing attention to process innovation by firms prepares the ground for competition strategies alive to the need for continuous innovation, because improved processes can be integrated more readily into the operations of a firm and because the returns accrue quickly. Once process innovation, which is generally incremental, gathers momentum and its utility is widely perceived, R & D gains stronger adherence both within and beyond the firm and

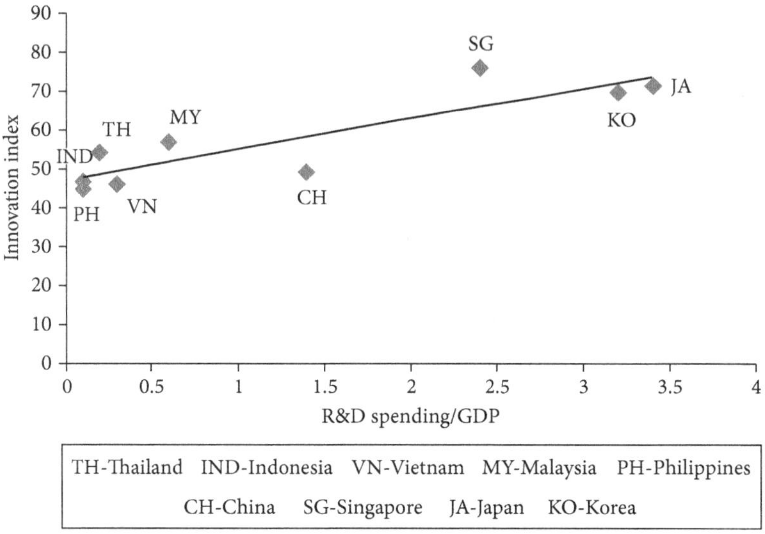


FIGURE 19.7 Correlation between Innovation Capacity Index and R & D Spending

*Source*: World Development Indicators and Table 19.1 in this chapter.

becomes better integrated into the operations of an entire industry. Policies that seek to augment the volume of basic research in universities and public research institutions with the help of public financing may raise the supply of scientific findings, but tangible economic results are linked to the slow process of innovating via applied research and commercialization that can take from five to fifteen years depending upon the type of product involved, industrial composition and the profitability of innovating.

## 19.5.1 Technology Generation and Absorption

Royalty and license fee payments are a proxy for technology absorption. In this regard, China and Singapore stand out in part because of the presence of multinational corporations (MNCs) in these countries. Korea also actively purchases technologies from abroad, although the pace of increase has slowed in the past five years. Other economies in East Asia are not active in the market for technology, despite the scale of manufacturing activities and role of MNCs, probably because the focus is mainly in assembly and processing and the innovation systems are weak (Figure 19.7).

Japan is the major "technology provider" in a sense that it maintains a surplus in this area, even though Japan became a net provider of technology only in the past few years. Since 1998, royalty and license fee receipts of Korea have increased dramatically, although there was a slowdown between 2001 and 2002 (see Figure 19.8). Singapore is actively engaged in the trade of technologies in both directions through foreign affiliates. It has increased its license fee receipts since 2003. These data suggest an emergence of technological capabilities in Korea and Singapore in the past 10 years. The sale of technology by other countries is insignificant, reflecting their modest technological capacities (Figure 19.8).

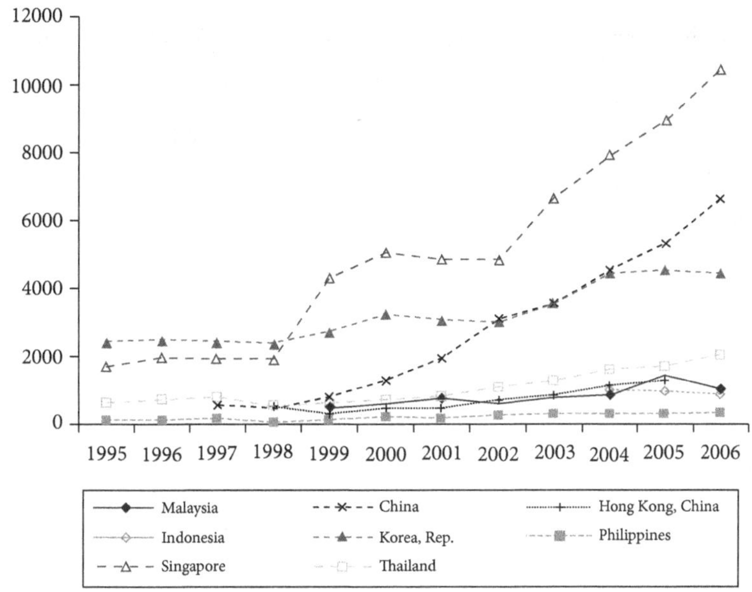


FIGURE 19.8 Royalty and License Fee Payments, 1995–2006 (in 000s of U.S. dollars)

*Source:* World Bank World Development Indicators database.

China is currently the leading importer of technologies and Chinese firms are supplementing licensing with the takeover of foreign firms with promising technologies or other intangibles.[38] Other economies in East Asia are not actively importing technologies from abroad or generating many technologies themselves.

## 19.5.2 Patenting and Innovation Potential

R & D spending is an input measure that is usefully complemented by a measure of innovation output. The number of patents, although far from ideal as an indicator of the productivity of R & D,[39] is generally the metric of choice (Scotchmer 2004), and patents granted by the USPTO are preferred as the yardstick for several reasons.[40] First, because the criteria for submission, the examination of patents, and the decision to award patents differ across countries, the number of patents granted by any one country is not directly comparable with that of another and the quality of patents differs. Using data from a specific patent office eliminates this incompatibility. Because the United States has been the major market for East Asian economies, using data from the USPTO is appropriate. Second, applying to a foreign patenting office is more expensive. Therefore, only high-quality patents are submitted for approval, reducing the "noise" in the data.

Table 19.9 lists the number of patents granted to East Asian economies in 1992, 2000, and 2008. Japan is the leader by a wide margin, with more than 36,000 patents awarded in 2008.[41] Korea is a distant second, followed by Taiwan. The number of patents granted to these economies grew quite rapidly between 1992 and 2008. China ranked fourth among East Asian economies in 2008 and also in 2012. In 2000, China received 119

**Table 19.9 Number of Patents Granted by the USPTO, 1992, 2000, and 2008**

| Economy | 1992 | 2000 | 2008 |
|---|---|---|---|
| Japan | 23,151 | 32,922 | 36,679 |
| Korea, Rep. of | 586 | 3,472 | 8,731 |
| Taiwan, China | 1,252 | 5,806 | 7,779 |
| China | 41 | 163 | 1,874 |
| Singapore | 35 | 242 | 450 |
| Malaysia | 11 | 47 | 168 |
| Thailand | 2 | 30 | 40 |
| Philippines | 7 | 12 | 22 |
| Indonesia | 9 | 14 | 19 |
| Vietnam | 0 | 0 | 0 |

*Source*: U.S. Patent and Trademark Office.

patents, less than Singapore, which had 218 patents. However, by 2012, Chinese residents received nearly six times the number of patents granted to residents of Singapore (4637 as against 810) http://www.uspto.gov/web/offices/ac/ido/oeip/taf/cst_utl.htm. Malaysia also saw the number of patents granted to its residents increase steeply during this period, albeit starting from a base of just 11. Thailand, the Philippines, and Indonesia have not received many patents from the USPTO during this period, and the numbers of patents granted to their residents is growing at a slow pace. Vietnam, a latecomer, did not receive any patents during this period.

Spending on R & D and the volume of patenting help to move economies closer to the technological frontier and prepare the ground for innovation. But the productivity of R & D spending—the assimilation of technology and the effective commercialization of innovative ideas—requires the mobilization of specific skills.

As countries approach the technology frontier, the sophistication of technologies and, in certain types of industry, the start-up of innovative activities and the growth of firms lend greater importance to the roles played by financial institutions, angel investors, and venture capitalists.[42] These investors are a source of patient capital, mentoring, contacts, technical advice, network connections, and other forms of assistance. However, their role needs to be kept in perspective.

In the vast majority of cases, whether in East Asia or the United States, banks—public or private—have provided the financing for firms that are entering the mezzanine or more advanced stages and the supplementary financing for start-up firms, whose primary source of funding is invariably the founders' own resources and those of family and friends. Venture capitalists (or more rarely in industrializing countries, angel investors), especially if they are highly experienced, well-established providers with deep pockets (this is rarely the case with VCs in East Asia), can make a difference to the prospects of start-up firms with innovative ideas, but they do not change the pace of innovation itself (Hirukawa and Ueda 2008a, 2008b). Nevertheless, venture capitalists can make this difference only under certain conditions. First, they have to be highly selective and skilled in picking potential winners with the right venture capital-friendly technologies. Second, they need to be in a position to put up a significant amount of financing over a number of years with reference to performance and to assist firms actively in management, product development, and marketing. Third, venture capitalists' own profitability rests on investing in companies that can establish their worth in not much more than five years (Puri and Zarutskie 2008).[43] The refinement, testing, development, and marketing of most biopharmaceuticals and advanced materials can easily take 10 to 15 years, which is longer than venture capitalists are willing to wait. Hence, they either select firms promising an early payoff or provide mezzanine financing to companies with a proven product. East Asian publicly owned providers of patient capital, which can be development banks or venture capitalists, can wait longer, but their success rate is also low.[44] International experience suggests that combining private with public financing gives better results, and complementing financing with business services of the kind that technology-intensive small and medium-size enterprises find valuable also improves outcomes. Governments can also raise the odds against failure by building a monitoring and auditing process into public venture funding schemes, as Israel and Taiwan have done (Kenney, Han, and Tanaka 2004).

Perhaps the most successful investment model is the following:

- It includes several large firms that depend on growth through innovation and that are on the lookout for firms with good products.[45]
- It finances start-ups using public funds channeled through banks and other public agencies and complemented by private venture capitalists.
- It comprises emerging clusters of networked firms that provide a base of specialized suppliers and mutually reinforcing R & D activities that are a source of valuable technological spillovers.
- It includes seasoned foreign VCs many of whom are becoming active in China and Southeast Asia. This is still something of a rarity in the Southeast Asian middle income economies.

## 19.6 Innovation and the Human Capital Dimension

Creating a manufacturing base that can lead to technological development and innovation and that can flexibly accommodate new research-intensive industries as existing ones migrate must go hand in hand with the building of the human sources of knowledge and technical expertise.[46] The relationship between the innovation capacity index and higher education enrollment in East Asia is apparent from Figure 19.10. The starting point is the quality of the education imparted by schools, how effectively it instills science

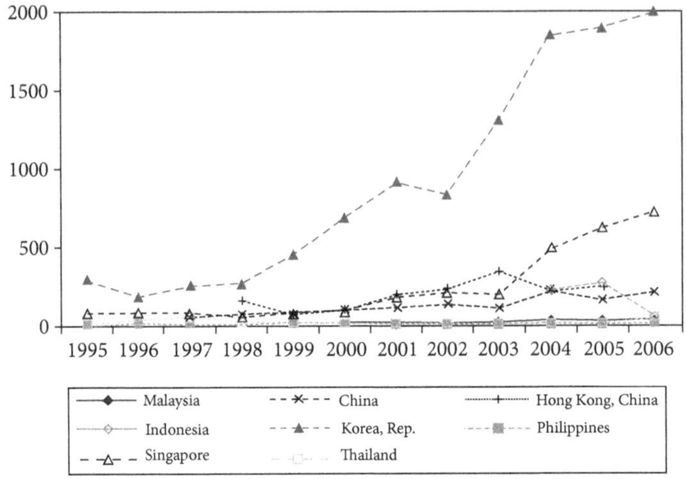


FIGURE 19.9 Royalty and License Fee Receipts, 1995–2006 (in 000s of U.S. dollars)

*Source:* World Bank World Development Indicators database.

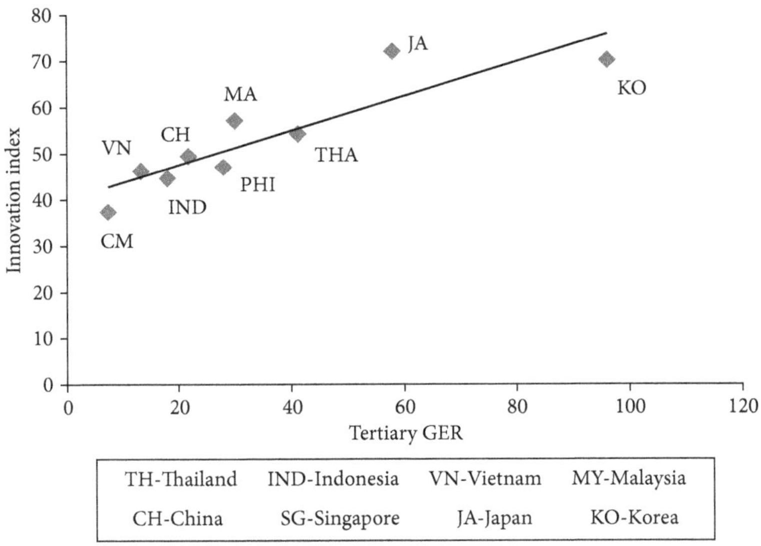


FIGURE 19.10 Correlation between Innovation Capacity Index and Higher Education GER

*Source*: World Development Indicators and Table 19.1 in this chapter.

and math skills, and whether it nurtures a spirit of inquiry and an aptitude for solving problems (Yusuf 2009). A solid base of primary, secondary, and technical or vocational schooling serves as a foundation. A sound university system with several world-class universities builds on this foundation and produces the advanced STEM (science, technology, engineering, and mathematics) skills and the talent for management, design, and marketing required by dynamic industries, whether manufacturing or services.[47]

As can be seen from Figure 19.11 the share of science and engineering enrollment at the tertiary level is even more tightly linked to the innovation capacity index.

The research establishment augments and extends the basic tertiary-level education to services. It usually centers on a few key universities and major firms but also embraces private and public research institutions, which collaborate with leading local or multinational companies. Openness and networking among local researchers and their interaction with peers around the world constitute a knowledge multiplier whose value is increasingly recognized.

The competitiveness of industry and services, the pace of diversification into new activities, and the capacity to innovate are closely linked to the quality of education. Those individuals with more education of better quality have a higher probability of starting a technology-intensive business, hiring skilled workers, and engaging in innovation.[48] Workers who have a solid grounding in the sciences and in engineering and who have good analytic problem-solving and team-working capabilities require less remedial training once they join a firm and can more fruitfully contribute to incremental process innovations.[49]

East Asian economies have relatively high levels of primary and secondary gross enrollment (see Figure 19.12, but quality is a different matter, and in fact there is wide dispersion. Higher-income economies such as Hong Kong, China; Japan; Korea; Singapore; and Taiwan, China, are among the top-ranked in terms of international test scores in math and science (see Tables 19.10 and 19.11). This was reaffirmed by the results of the OECD administered Program for International Student Assessment. This compares the performance of 15-year-olds from 60 nations. Students from Shanghai, Hong Kong, Singapore, Japan, and Korea were in the top six for science and in the top nine for mathematics in the test administered in 2009 (OECD 2010). The Northeast Asian countries and Singapore are followed mainly by Southeast Asian economies, all of which fall

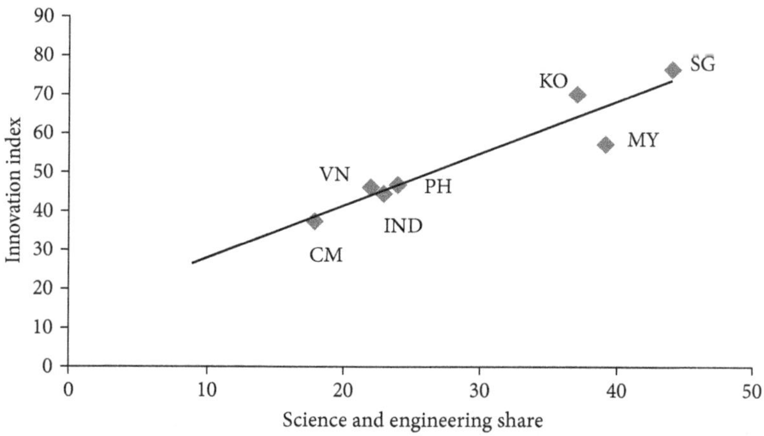


FIGURE 19.11 Correlation between Innovation Capacity Index and Higher Education Science and Engineering Share

*Source*: Table 19.1 in this chapter and EdStats.

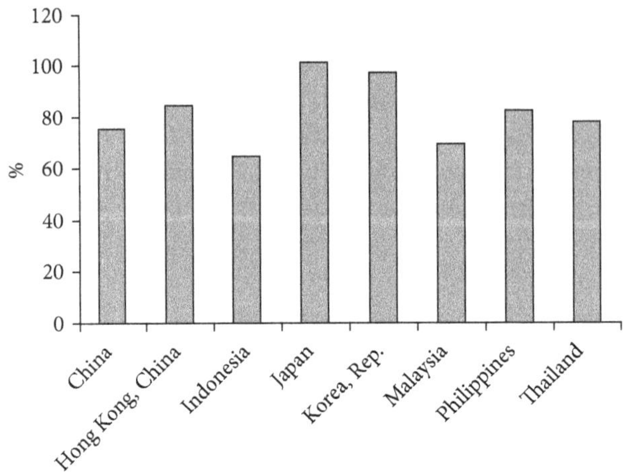


FIGURE 19.12 Secondary School Gross Enrollment Ratio, 2006

*Note:* Data for the Republic of Korea are from 2007; data for Malaysia are from 2005.

*Source:* World Bank World Development Indicators database.

**Table 19.10 Eighth-Grade TIMSS Scores for Mathematics for Selected East Asian Economies, 1999, 2003, and 2007**

| Economy | 1999 | 2003 | 2007 |
|---|---|---|---|
| Taiwan, China | 585 | 585 | 598 |
| Korea, Rep. of | 587 | 589 | 597 |
| Singapore | 604 | 605 | 593 |
| Hong Kong, China | 582 | 586 | 572 |
| Japan | 579 | 570 | 570 |
| United States | 502 | 504 | 508 |
| International average | 487 | 466 | 500 |
| Malaysia | 519 | 508 | 474 |
| Thailand | 467 | n.a. | 441 |
| Indonesia | 403 | 411 | 397 |
| Philippines | 345 | 378 | n.a. |

*Note:* n.a. = not applicable; TIMSS = Trends in International Mathematics and Science Study. Economies are ranked by their score in 2007.

*Sources:* Gonzales, Guzman, and others 2004; Gonzales, Williams, and others 2008; Mullis and others 2000.

**Table 19.11 Eighth-Grade TIMSS Scores for Science for Selected East Asian Economies, 1999, 2003, and 2007**

| Economy | 1999 | 2003 | 2007 |
|---|---|---|---|
| Singapore | 568 | 578 | 567 |
| Taiwan, China | 569 | 571 | 561 |
| Japan | 550 | 552 | 554 |
| Korea, Rep. of | 549 | 558 | 553 |
| Hong Kong, China | 530 | 556 | 530 |
| United States | 515 | 527 | 520 |
| International average | 488 | 473 | 500 |
| Malaysia | 492 | 510 | 471 |
| Thailand | 482 | n.a. | 471 |
| Indonesia | 435 | 420 | 427 |
| Philippines | 345 | 377 | n.a. |

*Note:* n.a. = not applicable; TIMSS = Trends in International Mathematics and Science Study. Economies are ranked by their score in 2007.
*Sources:* Gonzales, Guzman, and others 2004; Gonzales, Williams, and others 2008; Mullis and others 2000.

below the international average. Among the Southeast Asian economies, Malaysia is closest to the international average and leads other economies. The quality of secondary education in Indonesia and the Philippines is low, especially in mathematics.

Except for Korea, Japan, and Thailand, East Asian countries are lagging with respect to tertiary education enrollment (see Table 19.12). Although the gross enrollment rate in Korea is 93 percent (much higher than that of the United States), the enrollment rates in Japan and Thailand are 57 percent and 46 percent, respectively. Gross enrollment rates in other East Asian economies range from 17 percent in Indonesia to 30 percent in Malaysia (see Figure 19.13). Most East Asian economies rely on private universities to accommodate an increase in demand for tertiary education. Though this system has lessened the fiscal burden (in fact, East Asian economies do not spend much on higher education relative to other countries, especially European ones), equity of access is imperiled.

University graduates enter the job market with grounding in theory (often outdated, as in Vietnam) but with little practical knowledge and few analytical skills. This problem is experienced in many countries[50] and is addressed perhaps most comprehensively by Singapore through action at the level of general education and also through vocational training.[51] Employers ascribe this lack to continuing reliance on rote learning and on training to take tests, which remains the rule across the East Asian region; to the knowledge and pedagogical techniques of many of the teaching staff, which could be seriously

**Table 19.12 Gross Enrollment in Tertiary Education**

| Country | 1998 | 2000 | 2002 | 2006 |
|---|---|---|---|---|
| Korea, Rep. of | 66.0 | 78.4 | 86.8 | 92.6 |
| Japan | 43.7 | 47.4 | 50.5 | 57.3 |
| Thailand | – | 35.2 | 41.0 | 45.9 |
| Malaysia | 22.1 | 25.9 | 28.0 | 30.2 |
| Philippines | 27.3 | – | 30.4 | 28.5 |
| China | – | 7.7 | 12.7 | 21.6 |
| Indonesia | – | – | 15.0 | 17.0 |
| Vietnam | – | 9.5 | – | – |

*Note:* – = not available.
*Source:* World Bank World Development Indicators.

outdated; to the low quality of textbooks; to the limited attention given to practical training and interaction with potential employers; and to the obsolescence of the laboratory and testing equipment that is available to the students. This is especially serious in Vietnam, the Philippines, and Indonesia. A massive expansion in tertiary enrollment can exacerbate all these factors.

Because the potential capacity to absorb and develop technology depends on STEM skills and the importance of these skills increases as a country approaches the technology frontier, enrollment in science and engineering fields is a better indicator than the

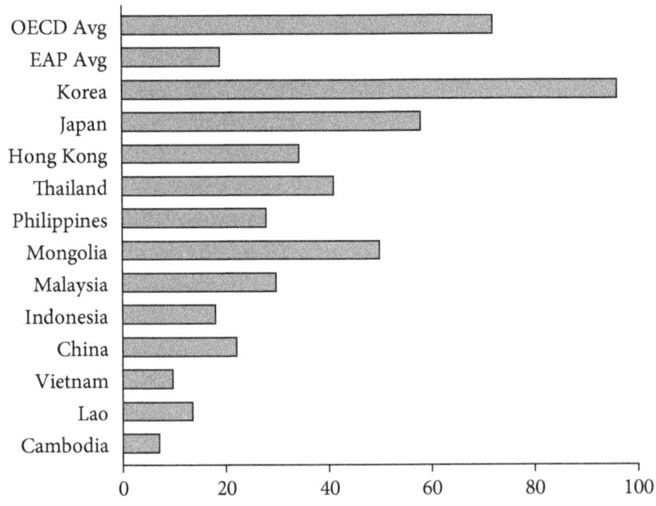


FIGURE 19.13 Tertiary Gross Enrollment Rates in East Asia and the OECD Average

*Note*: EAP Average includes Timor L'Este, Papua New Guinea, and North Korea

**Table 19.13 Percentage of First University Degrees in Science and Engineering**

| *Country* | *Year* | *Percentage* |
|---|---|---|
| China | 2004 | 56.2 |
| Hong Kong, China | 2004 | 37.7 |
| Japan | 2005 | 63.3 |
| Korea, Rep. of | 2004 | 45.6 |
| Philippines | 2006 | 27.4 |
| Singapore | 2004 | 58.5 |
| Taiwan, China | 2005 | 40.8 |
| Thailand | 2001 | 68.9 |

*Sources:* National Science Board 2008. Data for the Philippines are from the World Bank Knowledge Assessment Methodology data set ([http://www.worldbank.org/kam]).

overall enrollment rates in tertiary education. The experience of leading East Asian economies suggests that indigenous technological capabilities require an abundance of scientists and engineers, necessitating the enrollment or graduation percentage in these fields of between one-third and one-half of the totals in the earlier stages of industrialization (see Figure 19.11). More than one half of students earn science and engineering degrees in China, Japan, Singapore, and Thailand (see Table 19.13). A significant percentage of students in Hong Kong, China; Korea; and Taiwan, China, also earn their degrees in science and engineering fields, while relatively few students are graduating with science and engineering degrees in the Philippines. The situation in the Philippines is much worse if one looks at the number of students receiving advanced degrees in STEM fields. Only 315 received master's degrees in engineering, 153 received master's degrees in the natural sciences, and 203 received them in math and computer science; only a handful received doctoral degrees (6 in engineering, 13 in the natural sciences, and 6 in math and computer science).

## 19.6.1 Quality of Tertiary Education

The quality of tertiary education in the low- and middle-income East Asian economies is a matter of rising concern. It is reflected in the ranking of universities compiled by Times Higher Education Supplement, which lists 9 East Asian universities in the top 50 (see Table 19.14).

East Asian countries lag significantly compared with other OECD countries. Even the leading East Asian countries—Japan, Korea, and Singapore—produced far fewer scientific and technical articles than did the top performers, such as Finland, the United Kingdom, and the United States. Finland produces nearly 1000 scientific and technical articles per million inhabitants, while the United Kingdom and the United States

**Table 19.14 Ranking of Selected Universities in East Asia, 2007 and 2008**

| *International rank* | | *Regional rank* | | |
|---|---|---|---|---|
| *2008* | *2007* | *2008* | *School* | *Economy* |
| 19 | 17 | 1 | University of Tokyo | Japan |
| 25 | 25 | 2 | Kyoto University | Japan |
| 26 | 18 | 3 | University of Hong Kong | Hong Kong, China |
| 30 | 33 | 4 | National University of Singapore | Singapore |
| 39 | 53 | 5 | Hong Kong University of Science and Technology | Hong Kong, China |
| 42 | 38 | 6 | Chinese University of Hong Kong | Hong Kong, China |
| 44 | 46 | 7 | Osaka University | Japan |
| 50 | 36 | 8 | Peking University | China |
| 50 | 51 | 9 | Seoul National University | Korea, Rep. of |
| 56 | 40 | 10 | Tsinghua University | China |
| 166 | 223 | 23 | Chulalongkorn University | Thailand |
| 230 | 246 | 33 | Universiti Malaya | Malaysia |
| 250 | 309 | 35 | Universiti Kebangsaan Malaysia | Malaysia |
| 251 | 284 | 36 | Mahidol University | Thailand |
| 276 | 398 | 39 | University of the Philippines | Philippines |
| 287 | 395 | 41 | University of Indonesia | Indonesia |
| 313 | 307 | 43 | Universiti Sains Malaysia | Malaysia |
| 315 | 369 | 44 | Bandung Institute of Technology | Indonesia |
| 316 | 360 | 45 | Universitas Gadjah Mada | Indonesia |
| 320 | 364 | 46 | Universiti Putra Malaysia | Malaysia |
| 356 | 401–500 | 51 | Universiti Teknologi Malaysia | Malaysia |

*Source:* Times Higher Education Supplement ([http://www.topuniversities.com/university_rankings/results/2008/overall_rankings/fullrankings/]).
Source: EdStats (2009) and UIS (2009).

generate more than 700 scientific and technical articles per million people. Mid- or low-ranked universities in East Asia with modestly scaled doctoral, postdoctoral, and research programs generate a limited number of scientific publications, another measure of quality.

Since the mid-1990s, China has given the highest priority to the development of technology capabilities, and it is now attempting to accelerate the pace to catch up with the leading economies in East Asia, through investment in tertiary education and R & D.

The vast and increasing numbers of Chinese students studying overseas and conducting research is a source of vital experience and exposure to new ideas and different ways of thinking. That an increasing number of Chinese graduates and PhDs return to China after a stint abroad is a testimony of the opportunities they see in their home country and in the East Asian region. Since 2002, China has made great strides toward closing the technology gap (for example, as measured by manufacturing capacity in power generating and transport equipment, telecommunications equipment, solar cells, wind turbines, and iron and steel; and by patents granted to Chinese entities). The other East Asian economies, though they acknowledge the importance of innovation in their policy statements, lag far behind. Innovative countries such as Korea and Japan are in danger of losing their edge because of brain drain (from Korea) since the late 1990s and declining contact with foreign researchers and exposure to other research environments (for Japanese researchers).[52]

## 19.6.2 Beyond Education: Links with Firms

Universities and other tertiary entities can assist firms in assimilating and upgrading technology, provided that the overall quality of the faculty, and of researchers in science and engineering departments in particular, is adequate to follow the latest technologies and that they have the time and incentives to engage with business entities.[53] These institutions are in a position to advise firms on the availability of such technologies and to help firms harness and adapt them to local use, potentially introducing improvements. Except in China, universities have been slow to cultivate links and this is inducing governments throughout the region to introduce reforms, often packaged together with governance reforms and a tapering of state financing (such as university autonomy) to increase university-industry links.[54]

Firms in East Asia have been equally tardy in tapping the research capacity of universities. The problem is universal and stems from the difference in capabilities between universities and firms. The advantage of universities lies in their knowledge of a given subject area and multidisciplinary reach. At the same time, their knowledge tends to be more theoretical. Although theoretical knowledge is an asset for industries that are more science-oriented, such as chemical, metallurgical, electronics, and telecommunications, for the other industrial subsectors, practical knowledge is more relevant. In addition, firms may lack the capability to identify and use the knowledge that is available at universities (Kodama and Suzuki 2007). Hence, the demand from firms to collaborate with universities is relatively weak throughout East Asia, although members of certain faculties may engage in consulting assignments.[55] Even where there is a demand from firms, domestic universities and research institutes may not be capable of or interested in collaborating with firms.

This is not to deny episodic examples throughout the region of advantageous collaboration,[56] but these episodes are not numerous, and there is as yet no trend pointing to an intensification of university-industry links (World Bank and NESDB 2008; Yusuf and Nabeshima 2007).

## 19.7 Innovative Cities

Technological change and innovation are concentrated geographically in a few cities, with a mix of technologically dynamic activities, a strong research infrastructure, and an urban environment that is attractive to knowledge workers or, as Florida (2002; 2004) describes them, members of the creative class.[57] Research by Gerald Carlino and his coauthors shows that in the United States, the rate of invention is correlated with city size; however, the availability of human capital appears to be the principal driver (Glaeser 2011). On balance, there is some evidence of increasing returns to the overall scale of industrial activities[58] but not to the increasing concentration of industry, which suggests that inter-industrial knowledge spillovers are rather more important than intra-industrial ones (see Buzard and Carlino 2009; Carlino, Chatterjee, and Hunt 2007; Carlino and Hunt 2007, 2009).

The importance of city size for inventive activity, innovation, and urban productivity has been much debated, and no clear answer has emerged. Though patenting is concentrated in a few metropolitan regions in the United States (Chapple and others 2004), some of the most innovative hotspots in the United States and in Europe are medium-size cities. Silicon Valley in California has a population of 2.6 million, and innovative cities in Europe have populations of well under 2 million. Cambridge, United Kingdom, has a population of 600,000. East Asia is home to many large cities, some of which, such as Tokyo, Kyoto, and Seoul, are already viewed as creative places. Others, such as Shanghai, Beijing, Shenzhen, Guangzhou, Tianjin, and Singapore are approaching the threshold of innovativeness. In addition to these mega-cities, international experience suggests that a number of smaller cities in East Asia could, in time, join their ranks.

One attribute shared by all "smart cities" is that they have high ratios of college-educated workers. The presence of workers with tertiary education promotes innovation, which in turn raises productivity and industrial competitiveness and contributes to job growth (Shapiro 2005).

Moreover, cities that attract many visitors, migrants and students from within the country and abroad benefit from the influx and circulation of diverse ideas and talent. As E. L Glaeser (2009: 50) notes, "Attracting and retaining skilled people is a critical task for local governments." The experience of the United States and of European countries suggests that, in conjunction with major universities, consumer amenities—theaters, galleries, museums, bars and restaurants, public spaces, and green spaces[59]—underpinned by efficient public services are the most effective means of building and retaining the skilled workforce that is invaluable under any set of circumstances, but they are especially important when as in East Asia, accelerating technological change is the objective. Phillips (2008: 731) presciently observes, "Most cities are the longest running examples of large open source projects. Cities can also instill the culture of inquiry and interest in sciences by actively promoting science-oriented conferences, fairs, and exhibitions. Cities were open source long before Linux." Cities that invest in the quality of the socio-cultural environment, cultural diversity, amenities, and physical aesthetics benefit from faster growth of populations and also of employment (Carlino and Saiz 2008).

Leading East Asian cities in industrializing countries have only some of these attributes. In their haste to modernize, Asian cities in industrializing countries run the risk of losing sight of the mistakes made by others. "Urban deserts" do not breed innovation.[60] And cities that do not benefit from in-migration (or worse are faced with declining and aging populations, as is the case with many of the secondary cities in Japan) and are resistant to diversity quickly lose dynamism and entrepreneurial vigor, which in time can result in declining growth.

A few cities are now waking up to the need to make density more appealing and to redesign and reengineer to usher in a greener lifestyle. These attributes, among others, will determine whether they can move beyond the current industrial mix and technology levels and initiate a cycle generating a succession of knowledge-intensive industries.

Many cities in East Asia are aspiring to be "creative"; few will succeed. Landry (2008: 244) lists several attributes of a creatively viable and vital city. They include "critical mass [of talent]; diversity; accessibility; linkage and synergy; competiveness; and organizational capacity."[61]

Initiatives taken by urban centers in a number of OECD countries are instructive. Cities, both with and without central government participation, have embarked on regional innovation strategies, defined visions, passed innovation laws, established innovation funds, tested and mainstreamed ideas, and created institutions. Often, pressures resulting from the decline of existing industries catalyzed these strategies (OECD 2008). Local efforts attempt bottom-up approaches aimed at making city regions innovative through spatial planning for facilities (such as science parks and incubators), cluster networking support, and special programs with higher education institutions.

For cities in East Asia to emerge as trendsetters in the world, a committed local leadership with a strategic vision must compete for a cosmopolitan creative class and for innovative companies by creating an attractive and affordable urban environment, by focusing on the excellence of universities, and by offering firms the space and services they need to leverage local human capital and build a dynamic knowledge economy.

## 19.8 A Brief Summing Up

Technological change seems to be influenced by five sets of policies and institutions:

- Policies that affect the composition of industry, the competitiveness of firms, and the building of technological capability.
- Education and research policies that determine the foundation-building strengths of primary and secondary schooling; the quality of tertiary education; and the volume and productivity of R & D in universities, firms, and specialized institutes.[62]

- Sociopolitical institutions that assign status and recognition to learning and encourage intellectual achievement, safeguard intellectual property, and promote openness to ideas and to the circulation of knowledge workers.
- Policies that affect the productivity and innovativeness of urban centers.

Policymakers are working on all these registers; there is plenty of evidence indicating that technological catch-up has been rapid in several East Asian economies, less convincing as yet (except arguably in Japan), is evidence of sustained and cross-sectoral innovativeness, especially in services where the scope for innovation might be larger, especially for the more industrialized countries (Chesbrough 2011). This may soon change now that many MNCs are shifting more of their operations to East Asia; as experienced researchers, intermediaries, and venture capitalists are aggregating into critical masses, and an innovation culture is beginning to gel in cities such as Singapore, Seoul, Shanghai, and Shenzhen. Typically, a strong desire exists to hurry the process along. But acquiring broad-based innovation capabilities—as distinct from the capacity for incremental innovation in a few manufacturing industries, which is apparent in Japan, Korea, Taiwan, and Singapore—involves the time-consuming accumulation of not just skills but also tacit knowledge, institutions, and a culture that values openness and enquiry. The potential supply of innovations must be matched by discerning market demand. Innovation in the United States and in Japan has been pulled by the willingness of consumers to experiment with new products and to embrace new processes and services. The rapid spread and efficient assimilation of IT products and processes in the United States more than any other country testifies to the existence of a market environment enormously hospitable to innovation. Most Asian countries still lack such a welcoming and discriminating mass market that encourages innovation and facilitates scalability.[63]

After countries have acquired substantial technological depth and are near the frontiers of knowledge, what further action might push the system they have created to deliver high and persisting levels of innovation, or any significant innovation, is difficult to determine. Spending on R & D can help. Also, the innovation strategies of major firms can make a contribution, especially if they spin off innovative firms. New entrants can serve as bearers of technology, and the excellence of the research universities can feed the pool of skills, ideas, and entrepreneurship. Beyond these observations, whether research can fulfill the demands of national policymakers and chief executive officers who would like to make innovation routine remains an open question.[64]

## Notes

1. Hulten and Isaksson (2007) estimate that the major differences in levels of income between countries are explained by total factor productivity, although more than half the growth rate in incomes is traceable to differences in capital investment. Similar findings are reported by Comin, Hobijn, and Rovito (2008) who ascribe GDP per capita gaps to gaps in technology usage and find that usage lags are correlated across technologies.

2. Jorgenson and Vu's (2009) estimation of the global sources of growth during 1989 and 2006 shows that, over the entire period, capital dominated; however, its share declined from 54 percent during 1989–1995 to 46 percent during 1995–2000 and then to 41 percent during 2000–2006. The contribution of total factor productivity climbed from 16 percent to 36 percent between 1989–1995 and 2000–2006. Estimates by Jorgenson, Ho, and Samuels (2010) for the United States during 1960–2007 reaffirm the primacy of capital. It contributed 60 percent of the growth, productivity about 12 percent, but in their view, innovation undergirding productivity will be vital for maintaining future living standards in the United States. Jorgenson and his collaborators draw special attention to the contribution in recent years of ICT capital.
3. Gottinger (2006) examines how firms engage in technological races and what leads to leapfrogging, the size of a jump, frontier sticking, and other criteria of performance in races. On the Korean experience with catching-up and leapfrogging in the electronics, telecommunications, computer and machinery industries, see Lee and Lim (2001).
4. Viotti (2002) sees the national learning system as the foundation of what can in time become an innovation economy. Indigenous R & D enables firms to search for technologies more effectively and absorb them faster. Research intensive local firms are also better at exploiting technology spillovers from MNCs and other sources. (see Cohen and Levinthal 1989; and Cohen and Levinthal 1990).
5. One cannot exclude the possibility of chance innovations, which are like manna from heaven.
6. Jones and Romer (2009) assign special significance to institutions.
7. Koreans and more recently the Chinese have demonstrated a remarkable capacity to reverse-engineer complex products and master the associated production capabilities in an amazingly short period of time.
8. Petrin, White, and Reiter (2011) use data from a sample of U.S. firms from the period 1976–1996 to compute the relative shares of technical efficiency and of resource reallocation and find that the contribution of reallocation overshadows technical efficiency.
9. Lopez- Claros and Mata (2010) describe the construction of the Innovation Capacity Index.
10. Graham (2008, 2010) provides valuable insights into the attributes responsible for the success of entrepreneurs from his rich experience as a venture capitalist.
11. The rise of an entrepreneurial tradition in these countries dates back to the (proto) industrialization stage in the 1920s and 1930s, which survived a long spell of dormancy in the 1940s and 1950s in Korea and Taiwan, China, and an even longer dormancy in China.
12. Antoinette Schoar (2009) draws an interesting distinction between *subsistence entrepreneurs* and *transformational entrepreneurs*. Subsistence entrepreneurs set up small businesses with their own capital or the small amounts available from relatives, friends, and microfinance providers. These firms rarely grow. Transformational entrepreneurs have access to larger amounts of capital and are able to initiate ventures with the potential for growth. Such financing cannot be supplied by microfinance providers or venture capitalists; it must come from banks. Transformational entrepreneurship is also influenced by the regulatory environment, and innovation by smaller firms is promoted by competition with foreign firms (Hall, Lotti, and Mairesse 2008).
13. Companies that are fecund in ideas because of the volume of research they conduct, give birth to many start-ups. In its heyday, Silicon Valley firms such as Fairchild Semiconductor and HP were notable in this respect.

14. See the interviews with Vinod Khosla, (2000, http://hbr.org/2000/07/starting-up-in-high-gear/ar/1; http://techcrunch.com/2009/09/12/interview-vinod-khosla-is-on-the-hunt-for-great-technologies/) one of the leading VCs in Silicon Valley, and with Paul Graham, the driving force behind the Combinator [http://www.paulgraham.com/founders.html].
15. Haacker (2010) finds that capital investment in IT and telecommunications equipment both contribute although IT equipment yields more technological progress.
16. Veugelers (2009) lists the following innovations by small U.S. firms in the twentieth century: air conditioning, biomagnetic imaging, electronic spreadsheets, heat sensors, high-resolution computed axial tomography (CAT) scanners, hydraulic brakes, kidney stone lasers, microprocessors, magnetic resonance scanners, optical scanners, pacemakers, Polaroid cameras, quick-frozen food, soft contact lenses, and two-armed mobile robots.
17. Chinese firms such as China International Marine Containers (CIMC), Huawei, ZTE, SMIC, have all succeeded by aggressively learning from and imitating their international competitors and then improving on their products (see Zeng and Williamson 2007; RedTech Advisers 2011). Imports can also promote upgrading and competitiveness (Fernandes and Paunov 2009).
18. See the reviews by the Boston Consulting group of the "New Challengers" from industrializing nations; [http://www.bcg.com/documents/file70055.pdf]; [http://www.bcg.com/documents/file20519.pdf].
19. In China, Huawei Technologies, Datang Telecom Technology, and Zhongxing Telecom lead the way, each devoting about 10 percent of sales revenue to R & D (Cao 2008).
20. Baumol (2004: 4) notes that "technical progress requires both breakthrough ideas and a protracted follow-up process of cumulative incremental improvement of those breakthroughs with the combined incremental contribution of this second phase often exceeding that of the first." Baumol (2004d: 10) continues, "In today's economy, many rival firms use innovation as their main battle weapon with which they protect themselves from competitors... The result is precisely analogous to an arms race."
21. The spread of electricity and the internal combustion engine was expedited by takeovers that consolidated production in a few large firms that could reap scale advantages and sustain technological advances.
22. The Hay Group finds that companies that have consistent and stable strategies and can avoid paroxysms of restructurings have a better chance of forging and sustaining a reputation for performance ("World's Most Admired Companies" 2009). The experience of General Motors highlights the limited utility of frequent restructurings that leave the firm culture and the fundamental strategic orientation untouched.
23. The "open" approach to innovation emphasizes tools such as alliances, licensing, consortia and innovation exchanges, and joint ventures. It assumes that few if any firms can develop all the capabilities required in-house and find it advantageous to specialize and to work with others so as to maximize their innovation potential. Innovation is viewed as a cumulative process that requires melding a number of different and intersecting technologies (see Chesbrough 2006). Tetra Pak, for example, concluded that it had to draw on the expertise of a number of other companies before it could develop a paperboard container that could be sterilized and was lightweight, rectangular, and easy to hold and pour. Similarly, Cargill managed to perfect a new family of corn-based plastics only when it teamed up with Dow Chemical (Rigby and Zook 2002). During World War II, the large-scale production of

penicillin became a reality after U.S. agricultural scientists and technicians who knew a lot about culturing molds became involved. However, even though open innovation enables a company to tap a large pool of ideas, building the capability to harness a variety of sources is costly, and lack of trust and the inability to resolve intellectual issues can impede progress. (see Birkinshaw, Bouquet, and Barsoux 2011).

24. Toyota has sought to achieve close integration by rotating staff among departments and in particular exposing researchers to the production and marketing departments of the company.
25. Protection of services was more stringent and this accounts for the low productivity of services in East Asia as well as the limited share of services in the region's trade. See Miroudot, Sauvage, and Shepherd (2011).
26. The "hard" industrial policies of yesteryear (1960s through the 1980s) emphasizing industrial targeting supported by low-interest directed credit and fiscal subsidies, have in the post WTO era been superseded by "soft" policies seeking to sharpen competitiveness by measures to improve skills, innovation and the investment climate. (See Harrison and Rodriguez-Clare 2009, [http://www.nber.org/papers/w15261])
27. See Jorgenson, Ho, and Samuels (2010).
28. This collaborative activity between assemblers and their suppliers, most notably in the transport sector, is well-known and associated with the embracing of just-in-time delivery practices. Subcontractors have taken on the responsibility for major modules (see Smitka 1991). Collaboration and proximity might be taken a step further if Toyota, for example, realizes its ambition to further minimize the movement of parts (Stewart and Raman 2007).
29. The most dynamic firms in Japan's and Germany's shrinking manufacturing sector are ones that specialize in components; in engineering, transport, and plant equipment; and in materials technologies. These companies contribute to the success of some of the latest Apple products and the newest generation of jet airliners, most notably the Boeing 787 Dreamliner (Schaede 2008).
30. Leading firms are reorganizing the way in which they conduct their R & D by embracing an open approach to innovation to enrich and extend their own efforts in fruitful ways to promote radical innovation. Their strategy includes the establishing of R & D labs and sentinel offices in innovation hotspots worldwide and selective acquisition of foreign firms with valuable IP ("The World's Most Innovative Companies" 2006). Two Indian firms, the Tata Group and Reliance Industries, were included in the 2008 edition of *Business Week*'s "The World's 50 Most Innovative Companies." See also Christensen and Raynor (2003).
31. Intellectual property protection is frequently a concern for high-tech firms in areas such as pharmaceutical, biotechnology, and electronics.
32. The success of innovations in advanced materials has been closely associated with complementary innovations that can delay adoption or widespread use for many years. Realizing the full potential of glass fiber was paced by the evolution of laser technology, which brought the fiber-optic infrastructure into existence. Kevlar came into widespread use following advances in the design of body armor. Currently, proton exchange membrane fuel cells for automobiles are in a holding pattern waiting for other innovations that will reduce production costs and lead to superior catalysts and fuel cell stacks that together will result in an economically viable substitute for the internal combustion engine (Maine and Garnsey 2005).

33. To stimulate the demand for hybrid and electric cars, the Chinese government is requiring the power companies to install charging stations for electric cars in Beijing, Shanghai, and Tianjin (Bradsher 2009).
34. Automobiles have evolved into highly complex systems, and the trend with hybrids, electric, and fuel cell-based automobiles is toward greater technical complexity, entailing a vast amount of groundbreaking research, in particular research that results in better integration of IT, and in storage batteries (a slow and difficult process) currently accounting for a large part of the price and weight of electric cars (see "A Road Trip into the Future" 2011; and "Building a Better Battery" 2010). A premium car now has 70 to 100 microprocessor-based electronic control units, which can execute up to 100 million lines of code. This quantity is comparable to the number of electronic control units in the Airbus 380 (not including the aircraft's entertainment system). A car's electronics and software amount to between 15 and 40 percent of the vehicle's total cost and as cars become smarter, this share could soon approach 50 percent (Charette 2009).
35. Digital technology has been reinforced by organizational changes, changes in work practices, and training.
36. R & D expenditures represent only a fraction of the resources firms devote to innovation—by one estimate, they may represent only a quarter. Other expenditures include investment in equipment, in prototyping, and in gathering market intelligence. See Danguy and others (2010).
37. With more than 1.3 million researchers, China is placed second in the world after the United States. In terms of (PPP adjusted) absolute amount spent on R & D, China also ranks second after the United States.
38. The investment by MNCs in R & D facilities in China is another important conduit for technology transfer and a source of spillovers.
39. Duguy and others (2010: 4) in echoing a consensus among researchers, observe that "patent counts reflect more the propensity to patent than innovative performance or research productivity." Firms' propensity to patent is driven by the availability of "alternative protection mechanisms and strategic behavior."
40. Triadic listings with the USPTO, the EPO, and the JPO are viewed as an indicator of quality because of the cost entailed and the more rigorous evaluation standards of the EPO. Cross-listing is also becoming more common with globalization.
41. In fact, among the foreign countries, Japan receives the most patents (60 percent), followed by Germany. In any given year, about half of patents granted by the USPTO are to foreign residents.
42. Research by Dabla-Norris, Kersting, and Verdier (2010) points to the contribution of efficient financial systems to the diffusion of productivity enhancing innovation.
43. Interestingly, the likelihood of a new company succeeding with venture capital or other traditional sources of financing is about even, although at the end of five years, firms that received financing from venture capitalists are likely to be larger.
44. East Asian experience resonates with that of public VCs in advanced countries (on venture capital in East Asia, see Yusuf and Nabeshima 2009; Zhang and Zeng 2009; and Kenney, Han, and Tanaka 2006). In 2009, an evaluation of 782 firms that were provided venture capital by the U.K. government indicated that the results were disappointing; on average, the financing created only 1.8 jobs per company invested on average (Arnold 2009). See also Lerner (2009) for similar findings drawn from other countries.

45. Lewis Branscomb (2008: 916) notes that "Cisco is passionate about innovation [and] its most important innovation is its partnership with both customers and competitors making a true networked enterprise."
46. See for instance Roper, Du, and Love (2006) and the references cited therein.
47. In the United States, math-related occupations are the most well-paid (Needleman 2009).
48. Entrepreneurial performance is associated with the quality of formal schooling (Berry and Glaeser 2005, Glaeser 2007; van der Sluis, van Praag, and Vijverberg 2008).
49. Leading firms that attach importance to innovation look for a number of attributes in their new hires. For example, they value industry experience, a "big picture mindset," creativity, and the ability to "think outside the box." Firms did not cite education and training as the distinguishing feature of graduates from the best schools. Nor did they comment on readiness to work long hours (Wadhwa and others 2007; authors' interviews with firm representatives).
50. It is worsened by the inadequate qualifications of many of the teachers (as in Thailand, the Philippines, and Vietnam), and the looming problem posed by retirement of experienced faculty and the inability to attract suitable replacements.
51. Singapore established its first vocational institution in 1964. By 1972, displaying considerable foresight, the government had set up nine institutions, training more than 4000 students a year. As the economic structure became more skill-intensive, the curriculum of general and vocational education and the skills emphasized were adjusted n parallel. The Institute of Technical Education, which orchestrates vocational training, caters mainly to those who are not academically inclined and equips them with necessary technical skills in close collaboration with industries and with the help of the latest equipment, some of it donated by industry. Singaporean experience shows that good vocational education costs 50 percent more per year than general schooling (Seng 2009). However, the Singaporean experience with vocational education has proved hard to replicate in Korea and Indonesia, for example, partly because parents continue to prefer general to vocational education and partly because—as in Indonesia—returns to vocational education are lower, even though the cost per public school student is 28 percent higher (Newhouse and Suryadarma 2009).
52. "Will Homebody Researchers" (2010).
53. The absence of career and salary-related incentives can discourage university faculty from pursuing research with the intent to commercialize. Publications are more rewarding career-wise in most East Asian universities than applied research. Heavy teaching loads also inhibit university researchers from pursuing commercial leads.
54. Firms conducting R & D are more likely to establish research links with universities. Their support can be invaluable for government initiatives to improve the quality of tertiary education, to strengthen the research capabilities of universities, and to develop a local research culture.
55. Faculty members in some departments are sometimes compelled to do this so as to augment meager salaries.
56. Leading Japanese research universities have maintained informal and formal research ties with companies for some time. There are examples of fruitful collaboration in Thailand and China but overall, the extent of university industry linkages is sparse, although government and budgetary pressures could result in a widening of collaboration. Whether it will substantially increase innovation by the business sector remains to be seen.
57. Cities can confer numerous economic and social benefits as described by Glaeser (2011).

58. This evidence appears to buttress the findings on the productivity gains accruing from urbanization to large cities, which can be as high as 10 to 12 percent. However, a meta-study of the research on agglomeration economies arrives at a more conservative figure of about 3 percent as the likely productivity bonus gained by large cities (Melo, Graham, and Noland 2009).
59. These facilitate the face-to-face interaction so crucial to the germinating of ideas and the exchange of tacit knowledge (see Leamer 2007; Storper and Venables 2003; Leamer and Storper 2001).
60. Planning, designing, and cross-linking of public spaces are frequently ignored to the detriment of the urban environment. Cities such as Barcelona and Munich have enriched the urban milieu by making public spaces an integral part of their planning efforts (Landry 2008).
61. Jean-Claude Biver, chief executive officer of Hublot, speaks for most businesspeople when he maintains that a city must address the "quality of environment, quality of the air, quality of the traffic, good communication, a strong and effective university, good recruitment possibilities, important artistic activities, and good connections" ("Ask the Boss" 2009: 86).
62. Patenting by Korean residents has been influenced by both the spread of higher education and the increasing expenditure on R & D (Lee and Kim 2009).
63. See Bhide (2006).
64. Not that there is a shortage of suggestions on how to improve innovation capabilities. See, for example, World Bank Institute (2007).

## References


Acemoglu, Daron, Phillipe Aghion, and Fabrizio Zilibotti. 2006. "Distance to the Frontier, Selection and Economic Growth." *Journal of the European Economic Association* 4(1): 37–74.

Andrew, James P., Emily Stover DeRocco, and Andrew Taylor. 2009. "*The Innovation Imperative in Manufacturing: How the United States Can Restore Its Edge.*" Boston Consulting Group, Boston.

Arnold, Martin. 2009. "U.K. Government under Fire on Venture Capital." *Financial Times*, September 2.

"Ask the Boss." 2009. *Monocle* 3 (25): 86.

Audretsch, David B. 2008. *The Entrepreneurial Society*. New York: Oxford University Press.

Baumol. 2004. "Education for Innovation: Entrepreneurial Breakthroughs vs. Corporate Incremental Improvements." NBER Working Paper 10578, National Bureau of Economic Research, Cambridge, MA.

Bernard, Andrew B., and J. Bradford Jensen. 2001. "Who Dies? International Trade, Market Structure, and Industrial Restructuring." Working Paper 01-04, Center for Economic Studies, U.S. Census Bureau, Washington, DC.

Bernard, Andrew B., Stephen J. Redding, and Peter K. Schott. 2006. "Multi-product Firms and Trade Liberalization." NBER Working Paper 12782, National Bureau of Economic Research, Cambridge, MA.

Berry, Christopher, and Edward L. Glaeser. 2005. "The Divergence of Human Capital Levels across Cities." NBER Working Paper 11617, National Bureau of Economic Research, Cambridge, MA.

Bhide, Amar. 2006. Venturesome Consumption, Innovation and Globalization. Venice Summer Institute 2006. IFO Institute for Economic Research. Venice. July 21/22.

Birkinshaw, Julian, Cyril Bouquet, and J-L Barsoux. 2011. "The 5 Myths of Innovation." *MIT Sloan Management Review*. 43–50. Winter.

Bloom, Nicholas, Benn Eifert, Aprajit Mahajan, David McKenzie, and John Roberts. 2010. "Does Management Matter? Evidence from India." Department of Economics, University College London, London.

Bloom, Nicholas, Aprajit Mahajan, David McKenzie, and Donald John Roberts. 2010. "Why Do Firms in Developing Countries Have Low Productivity?" Working Paper, Department of Economics, Stanford University, Stanford, CA.

Bloom, Nicholas, Raffaella Sadun, and John Van Reenen. 2009. "Americans Do I.T. Better: U.S. Multinationals and the Productivity Miracle." NBER Working Paper 13085, National Bureau of Economic Research, Cambridge, MA.

Bloom, Nicholas, and John Van Reenen. 2010. "Why Do Management Practices Differ across Firms and Countries." *Journal of Economic Perspectives* 24 (1): 203–224.

Boozer, Michael, Gustav Ranis, Frances Stewart, and Tavneet Suri. 2003. "Paths to Success: The Relationship between Human Development and Economic Growth." Discussion Paper 874, Economic Growth Center, Yale University, New Haven, CT.

Bradsher, Keith. 2009. "China Vies to Be World's Leader in Electric Cars." *New York Times*, April 21.

Branscomb, Lewis. 2008. "Research Alone Is Not Enough." *Science* 321: 915–916.

Bresnahan, Timothy, Alfonso Gambardella, AnnaLee Saxenian, and Scott Wallsten. 2001. " 'Old Economy' Inputs for 'New Economy' Outcomes: Cluster Formation in the New Silicon Valley." SIEPR Discussion Paper 00-43, Stanford Institute for Economic Policy Research, Stanford, CA.

Brynjolfsson, Erik, and Lorin M. Hitt. 2003. "Computing Productivity: Firm-Level Evidence." *Review of Economics and Statistics* 85 (4): 793–808.

Brynjolfsson, Erik, and Adam Saunders. 2009. *Wired for Innovation: How Information Technology Is Reshaping the Economy*. Cambridge, MA: MIT Press.

"Building a Better Battery" 2010. *Science* 30: 1485.

Buzard, Kristy, and Gerald A. Carlino. 2009. "The Geography of Research and Development Activity in the U.S." Working Paper 09-16, Federal Reserve Bank of Philadelphia, Philadelphia, PA.

Cao, Cong. 2008. "Technological Development Challenges in Chinese Industry." In *China's Science and Technology Sector and the Forces of Globalization*, ed. Elspeth Thomson and Jon Sigurdson, 1–30. Singapore: World Scientific Publishing.

Carlino, Gerald A., Satyajit Chatterjee, and Robert M. Hunt. 2007. "Urban Density and the Rate of Invention." *Journal of Urban Economics* 61 (3): 389–419.

Carlino, Gerald A., and Robert M. Hunt. 2007. "Innovation across U.S. Industries: The Effects of Local Economic Characteristics." Working Paper 07-28, Federal Reserve Bank of Philadelphia, Philadelphia, PA.

———. 2009. "What Explains the Quantity and Quality of Local Inventive Activity?" Working Paper 09-12, Federal Reserve Bank of Philadelphia, Philadelphia, PA.

Carlino, Gerald A., and Albert Saiz. 2008. "City Beautiful." Working Paper 08-22, Federal Reserve Bank of Philadelphia, Philadelphia, PA.

Castaldi, Carolina. 2009. "The Relative Weight of Manufacturing and Services in Europe: An Innovation Perspective." *Technological Forecasting and Social Change* 76 (2): 709–722.

Chandra, Vandana, Deniz Erocal, Pier Carlo Padoan, and Carlos A. Primo Braga. 2009. *Innovation and Growth: Chasing a Moving Frontier*. Paris: OECD Publishing.

Chapple, Karen, Ann Markusen, Daisaku Yamamoto, Gregory Schorock, and Pingkang Yu. 2004. "Gauging Metropolitan 'High-Tech' and 'I-Tech' Activity." *Economic Development Quarterly* 18 (1): 10–24.

Charette, Robert N. 2009. "This Car Runs on Code." *IEEE Spectrum*, February. http://www.spectrum.ieee.org/feb09/7649.

Chesbrough, Henry. 2006. *Open Business Models*. Boston: Harvard Business School Press.

———. 2011. *Open Services Innovation*. New York: Jossey Bass—John Wiley.

Christensen, Clayton M., and Michael E. Raynor. 2003. *The Innovators' Solution*. Boston: Harvard Business School Press.

Cohen, Wesley, M., and Daniel A. Levinthal. 1989. "Innovation and Learning: The Two Faces of R&D." *Economic Journal* 55 (September): 569–596.

———. 1990. "Absorptive Capacity: A New Perspective on Learning and Innovation." *Administrative Science Quarterly* 35: 128–152.

Comin, Diego, Bart Hobijn, and Emilie Rovito. 2008. "Technology Usage Lags." *Journal of Economic Growth* 13: 237–256.

Cooke, Philip, Carla Laurentis, Franz Tödtling, and Michaela Trippl. 2007. *Regional Knowledge Economies: Markets, Clusters and Innovation*. Northampton, MA: Edward Elgar.

Dabla-Norris, Era, Erasmus Kersting, and Genevieve Verdier. 2010. "Firm Productivity, Innovation and Financial Development." IMF Working Paper. 10/49. IMF. Washington DC.

Danguy, Jerome, Gaetan de Rassenfosse, and Bruno van Pottelsberghe de la Potterie. 2010. "The R&D Patent Relationship: An Industry perspective." CEPR Working Paper No. 8145. Centre for Economic Policy Research. London.

Fernandes, Ana, M., and Caroline Paunov. 2009. Does Trade Stimulate Innovation? Evidence from Firm—Product Data. World Bank. Washington DC. Processed. November 23rd.

Florida, Richard. 2002. *The Rise of the Creative Class and How It's Transforming Work, Leisure and Everyday Life*. New York: Basic Books.

Florida, Richard. 2004. *Cities and the Creative Class*. New York: Routledge.

Glaeser, Edward L. 2007. "Entrepreneurship and the City." NBER Working Paper 13551, National Bureau of Economic Research, Cambridge, MA.

———. 2009. "Growth: The Death and Life of Cities." In *Making Cities Work: Prospects and Policies for Urban America*, ed. Robert P. Inman, 22–62. Princeton, NJ: Princeton University Press.

Glaeser, Edward, L. 2011. *Triumph of the City*. New York: Penguin Press.

Gonzales, Patrick, Juan Carlos Guzman, Lisette Partelow, Erin Pahlke, Leslie Jocelyn, David Kastberg, and Trevor Williams. 2004. *Highlights from the Trends in International Mathematics and Science Study (TIMSS) 2003*. Washington, DC: National Center for Education Statistics.

Gonzales, Patrick, Trevor Williams, Leslie Jocelyn, Stephen Roey, David Kastberg, and Summer Brenwald. 2008. *Highlights from TIMSS 2007: Mathematics and Science Achievement of U.S. Fourth- and Eighth-Grade Students in an International Context*. Washington, DC: National Center for Education Statistics.

Gordon, Robert J. 2003. "Hi-Tech Innovation and Productivity Growth: Does Supply Create Its Own Demand?" NBER Working Paper 9437, National Bureau of Economic Research, Cambridge, MA.

Gottinger, Hans Werner. 2006. "Global Technological Races." *Japan and the World Economy* 18 (2): 181–193.

Graham, Paul. 2010. The Disruptor. *Forbes*. November 8, 72–80.

Haacker, Markus. 2010. "Quantifying the Impact of ICTs on Growth in Developing Economies." In *The Innovation for Development Report 2009–2010*, ed. Augusto López-Claros, New York: Palgrave Macmillan.

Hagel, John III, John Seely Brown, and Lang Davison. 2008. "Shaping Strategy in a World of Constant Disruption." *Harvard Business Review* (October): 81–89.

Hall, Bronwyn, Francesca Lotti, and Jacques Mairesse. 2008. "Innovation and Productivity in SMEs: Empirical Evidence for Italy." NBER Working Paper 14594, National Bureau of Economic Research, Cambridge, MA.

Hargadon, Andrew, and Robert I. Sutton. 2000. "Building an Innovation Factory." *Harvard Business Review* 78 (3): 157–166.

Hirukawa, Masayuki, and Masako Ueda. 2008a. "Venture Capital and Industrial 'Innovation.'" CEPR Discussion Paper 7089, Centre for Economic Policy Research, London.

———. 2008b. "Venture Capital and Innovation: Which Is First?" CEPR Discussion Paper 7090, Centre for Economic Policy Research, London.

Hulten, Charles R., and Anders Isaksson. 2007. "Why Development Levels Differ: The Sources of Differential Economic Growth in a Panel of High and Low Income Countries." NBER Working Paper 13469, National Bureau of Economic Research, Cambridge, MA.

IMD (International Institute for Management Development). 2009. *World Competitiveness Yearbook*. Laussane, Switzerland: IMD.

Jaruzelski, Barry, and Kevin Dehoff. 2007. "The Booz Allen Hamilton Global Innovation 1000: The Customer Connection." *Strategy+Business* 49: 1–16.

Jaruzelski, Barry, Kevin Dehoff, and Rakesh Bordia. 2005. "The Booz Allen Hamilton Global Innovation 1000: Money Isn't Everything." *Strategy+Business* 41: 1–14.

———. 2006. "The Booz Allen Hamilton Global Innovation 1000: Smart Spenders." *Strategy+Business* 45: 46–61.

Jones, Charles I., and Paul Romer. 2009. "The New Kaldor Facts: Ideas, Institutions, Population, and Human Capital." NBER Working Paper 15094, National Bureau of Economic Research, Cambridge, MA.

Jorgenson, Dale W., Richard J. Goettle, Mun S. Ho, Daniel T. Slesnick, and Peter J. Wilcoxen. 2008. "U.S. Labor Supply and Demand in the Long Run." *Journal of Policy Modeling* 30 (4): 603–618.

Jorgenson, Dale W., Mun S. Ho, Jon D. Samuels, and Kevin J. Stiroh. 2007. "Industry Origins of the American Productivity Resurgence." *Economic Systems Research* 19 (3): 229–252.

Jorgenson, Dale W., Masahiro Kuroda, and Kazuyuki Motohashi. 2007. *Productivity in Asia: Economic Growth and Competitiveness*. Northampton, MA: Edward Elgar.

Jorgenson, Dale W., and Khuong M. Vu. 2009. "Growth Accounting within the International Comparison Program." *ICP Bulletin* 6 (1): 3–28.

Kenney, Martin, Kyonghee Han, and Shoko Tanaka. 2004. "Venture Capital Industries." In *Global Change and East Asian Policy Initiatives*, ed. Shahid Yusuf, M. Anjum Altaf, and Kaoru Nabeshima, 391–427. New York: Oxford University Press.

Kodama, Fumio, and Jun Suzuki. 2007. "How Japanese Companies Have Used Scientific Advances to Restructure Their Business: The Receiver-Active National System of Innovation." *World Development* 35 (6): 976–990.

Landry, Charles. 2008. *The Creative City: A Toolkit for Urban Innovators*. London: Earthscan Publications.

Lee, Keun, and Byung-Yeon Kim. 2009. "Both Institutions and Policies Matter but Differently for Different Income Groups of Countries: Determinants of Long-Run Economic Growth Revisited." *World Development* 37 (3): 533–549.

Lee, Keun and Chaisung Lim. 2001. "Technological Regimes, Catching-Up and Leapfrogging: Findings from the Korean Industries." *Research Policy* 30: 459–483.

Lerner, Josh. 2009. *Boulevard of Broken Dreams: Why Public Efforts to Boost Entrepreneurship and Venture Capital Have Failed—and What to Do about It.* Princeton, NJ: Princeton University Press.

López-Claros, Augusto, and Yasmina N. Mata. 2010. "The Innovation Capacity Index: Factors, Policies, and Institutions Driving Country Innovation." In *The Innovation for Development Report 2009–2010*, ed. Augusto López-Claros, 50–66. New York: Palgrave Macmillan.

López-Claros, Augusto, Michael E. Porter, Klaus Shwab, and Xavier Sala-i-Martin. 2006. *The Global Competitiveness Report 2006–2007.* New York: Palgrave Macmillan.

Lynch, Lisa M. 2007. "Organizational Innovation and U.S. Productivity." VoxEU.org, December 6. http://www.voxeu.org/index.php?q=node/775.

Maine, Elicia, and Elizabeth Garnsey. 2005. "Commercializing Generic Technology: The Case of Advanced Materials Ventures." Working Paper 2004/04, Centre for Technology Management, University of Cambridge, Cambridge, U.K.

Mathieu, Azele, and Bruno van Pottelsberghe de la Potterie. 2008. "A Note on the Drivers of R&D Intensity." CEPR Discussion Paper 6684, Centre for Economic Policy Research, London.

Melitz, Marc J. 2003. "The Impact of Trade on Intra-industry Reallocations and Aggregate Industry Productivity." *Econometrica* 71 (6): 1695–1725.

Melo, Patricia C., Daniel J. Graham, and Robert B. Noland. 2009. "A Meta-analysis of Estimates of Urban Agglomeration Economies." *Regional Science and Urban Economics* 39 (3): 332–342.

Miroudot, Sebastien, Jehan Sauvage, and Ben Shepherd. 2011. Lowering Trade Costs in Services markets: The Final Frontier? VOXEU.org January 17th

Mullis, Ina V. S., Michael O. Martin, Eugenio J. Gonzalez, Kelvin D. Gregory, Robert A. Garden, Kathleen M. O'Connor, Steven J. Chrostowski, and Teresa A. Smith. 2000. *TIMSS 1999 International Mathematics Report: Findings from IEA's Repeat of the Third International Mathematics and Science Study at the Eighth Grade.* Boston, MA: International Study Center, Boston College.

National Science Board. 2008. *Science and Engineering Indicators 2008.* Vols. 1 and 2. Arlington, VA: National Science Foundation. http://www.nsf.gov/statistics/seind08/.

Needleman, Sarah E. 2009. "Doing the Math to Find the Good Jobs." *Wall Street Journal*, January 6.

Nelson, Richard, R, and Sidney G. Winter. 1975. Growth Theory from an Evolutionary Perspective: The Differential Productivity Puzzle. *American Economic Review.* May, 65(2): 338–344.

Newhouse, David, and Daniel Suryadarma. 2009. "The Value of Vocational Education: High School Type and Labor Market Outcomes in Indonesia." Policy Research Working Paper 5035, World Bank, Washington, DC.

OECD (Organisation for Economic Co-operation and Development). 2008. *OECD Reviews of Regional Innovation: North of England, U.K.* Paris: OECD.

OECD, 2010. *PISA 2009 at a Glance.* Paris. OECD.

Oliner, Stephen D., and Daniel E. Sichel. 2000. "The Resurgence of Growth in the Late 1990s: Is Information Technology the Story?" *Journal of Economic Perspectives* 14 (4): 3–22.

Petrin, Amil, T. Kirk White, Jerome P. Reiter. 2011. "The Impact of Plant Level Resource Reallocations on U.S. Macroeconomic Growth." NBER Working Paper. No 16700. National Bureau of Economic Research, Cambridge, MA.

Phillips, Fred. 2008. "Change in Socio-technical Systems: Researching the Multis, the Biggers, and the More Connecteds." *Technological Forecasting and Social Change* 75 (5): 721–734.

Porter, Michael, Klaus Schwab, and Xavier Sala-i-Martin. 2007. *The Global Competitiveness Report 2007–2008*. New York: Palgrave McMillan.

Porter, Michael, and Scott Stern. 2001. "National Innovative Capacity." In *The Global Competitiveness Report 2001–2002*, ed. Klaus Schwab, Michael Porter, and Jeffrey D. Sachs, 102–119. New York: Oxford University Press.

Puri, Manju, and Rebecca Zarutskie. 2008. "On the Lifecycle Dynamics of Venture-Capital- and Non-Venture-Capital-Financed Firms." NBER Working Paper 14250, National Bureau of Economic Research, Cambridge, MA.

RedTech Advisors. 2011. *"Incremental Innovation."* GaveKal Dragonomics. Beijing China.

Rigby, Darrell, and Chris Zook. 2002. "Open-Market Innovation." *Harvard Business Review* 80 (10): 80–89.

"A Road Trip into the Future." 2011. *Financial Times*. January 14, p. 10.

Roper, Stephen, Jun Du, and James H. Love. 2006. *The Innovation Value Chain*. Aston Business School. Birmingham U.K. December 18.

Rosenthal, Stuart S., and William C. Strange. 2008. "Small Establishments/Big Effects: Agglomeration, Industrial Organization, and Entrepreneurship." In *Agglomeration Economics*, ed. Edward L. Glaeser, 277–302. Chicago: University of Chicago Press.

Schaede, Ulrike. 2008. *Choose and Focus: Japanese Business Strategies for the 21st Century*. Ithaca, NY: Cornell University Press.

Schoar, Antoinette. 2009. "The Divide between Subsistence and Transformational Entrepreneurship." NBER Working Paper 14861, National Bureau of Economic Research, Cambridge, MA.

Scotchmer, Suzanne. 2004. *Innovation and Incentives*. Cambridge, MA: MIT Press.

Seng, Law Song. 2009. *"Vocational Technical Education and Economic Development: The Singapore Experience."* ITE Education Services, Singapore.

Smitka, Michael J. 1991. *Subcontracting in the Japanese Automobile Industry*. New York: Columbia University Press.

Stewart, Thomas A., and Anand P. Raman. 2007. "Lessons from Toyota's Long Drive." *Harvard Business Review* 85 (7–8): 74–83.

Syverson, Chad. 2010. "What Determines Productivity?" NBER Working Paper 15712, National Bureau of Economic Research, Cambridge, MA.

Vandenbussche, Jerome, Phillipe Aghion, and Costas Meghir. 2005. Growth, Distance from the Frontier and Composition of Human Capital. CEPR Discussion Paper No 4860. Center for Economic and Policy Research. London UK.

van der Sluis, Justin, Mirjam van Praag, and Wim Vijverberg. 2008. "Education and Entrepreneurship Selection and Performance: A Review of the Empirical Literature." *Journal of Economic Surveys*. 22 (5): 795–841.

Veugelers, Reinhilde. 2009. "A Lifeline for Europe's Young Radical Innovators." Breugel *Policy Brief*. Issue 2009/01. March http://ideas.repec.org/p/bre/polbrf/289.html.

Viotti, Eduardo B. 2002. "National Learning Systems: A New Approach on Technological Change in Late Industrializing Economies and Evidences from the Cases of Brazil and South Korea." *Technological Forecasting and Social Change* 69 (7): 653–680.

Wadhwa, Vivek, Gary Gereffi, Ben Rising, and Ryan Ong. 2007. "Where the Engineers Are." *Issues in Science and Technology* (Spring).

World Bank. 2005. *Doing Business in 2006*. Washington, DC: World Bank.

———. 2006. *Doing Business in 2007*. Washington, DC: World Bank.
———. 2007. *Doing Business in 2008*. Washington, DC: World Bank.
———. 2008. *Doing Business in 2009*. Washington, DC: World Bank.
World Bank Institute. 2007. *Building Knowledge Economies: Advanced Strategies for Development*. Washington, DC: World Bank.
World Bank and NESDB (National Economic and Social Development Board). 2008. *Towards a Knowledge Economy in Thailand*. Bangkok: World Bank.
"The World's Most Innovative Companies." 2006. *BusinessWeek*, April 24.
"The World's 50 Most Innovative Companies." 2008. *BusinessWeek*, http://bwnt.businessweek.com/interactive_reports/innovative_companies
"World's Most Admired Companies." 2009. *Fortune*, March 16.
"Will Homebody Researchers Turn Japan into a Scientific Backwater?." 2010. *Science* 330: 1475. http://www.sciencemag.org/content/330/6010/1475.summary
Yusuf, Shahid. 2009. "From Creativity to Innovation." *Technology in Society* 31 (1): 1–8.
Yusuf, Shahid, and Kaoru Nabeshima. 2007. *How Universities Promote Economic Growth*. Washington DC: World Bank.
Yusuf, Shahid, and Kaoru Nabeshima. 2009. *Tiger Economies Under Threat*. Washington DC. World Bank.
Zeng, Ming. and Peter W. Williamson. 2007. *Dragons at Your Door: How Chinese Cost Innovation is Disrupting Global Competition*. Boston: Harvard Business School Press.
Zhang, Chunlin, and Douglas Zhihua Zeng. 2009. *Promoting Enterprise Led Innovation in China*. Washington DC: World Bank.
Zhao, Jimin. 2006. "Whither the Car? China's Automobile Industry and Cleaner Vehicle Technologies." *Development and Change* 37 (1): 121–144.
Zucker, Lynne G., and Michael R. Darby. 2007. "Star Scientists, Innovation, and Regional and National Immigration." NBER Working Paper 13547, National Bureau of Economic Research, Cambridge, MA.

# PART VI

# MACROECONOMICS AND FINANCE

# CHAPTER 20

# ASIAN FINANCIAL CRISES

ANNE O. KRUEGER

In the 1950s, most of the poorest countries in the world were in Asia. The majority had difficulty managing their balance of payments (as did most other developing countries), and growth was relatively slow. They adopted "import-substitution" growth strategies, under which high walls of protection (both tariff barriers and quantitative restrictions) were intended to foster and protect new industries. However, import substitution proved to be import-intensive and inefficient.

Many Asian countries, including India, Myanmar, Pakistan, the Philippines, and Sri Lanka, had severe economic crises during the course of the next 20 years and needed IMF support to resolve the major policy issues that had arisen. Japan was, of course, a more developed country, but the economy had been devastated by the war. Japanese per capita income was precariously low, and the country had fairly severe exchange controls and import licensing during the decade of the 1950s and needed an IMF program. Japan, however, abandoned those policies by the late 1950s and began growing rapidly. As an industrial country, Japan was and is regarded differently from the emerging markets in Asia. Here, focus is on crises in Asian emerging markets, with only a little attention to Japan's financial crises.

Starting with Taiwan in the mid-1950s, one by one Asian countries' economic growth began accelerating rapidly. The Japanese government put forth its income-doubling plan in 1959, and achieved that goal ahead of schedule by 1967, and continued growing rapidly. By 1960, South Korea's economic policies were being drastically reformed, and South Korea switched from import-substitution to an outer-oriented trade strategy, with many other economic policy reforms accompanying and following the shift in trade policy. Singapore and Hong Kong also oriented their policies toward an open economy and export growth, and began growing rapidly. By the 1980s, many Southeast Asian countries, witnessing the successes in East Asia, were in the midst of the reform process. Even more significant, the People's Republic of China began its long process of reform in the early 1980s, having been an almost entirely closed economy prior to that date, and switched to an export-led strategy as the lynchpin for its rapid growth strategy.

The success of the East and Southeast Asian countries contrasted sharply with the relatively sluggish performance not only of the rest of Asia but also of most other developing countries at that time. By the 1990s, Asia's share of world trade and world GDP was rising rapidly, and Asia's successful rapid economic growth, with rising living standards, stable macroeconomic policies, and rapidly growing trade was the envy of the world.

It seemed that Asian policymakers, especially the East Asian "tigers" (Hong Kong, Singapore, South Korea, and Taiwan), could do no wrong. For more than three decades, the reformed economics had performed well even as oil price increases and the debt crisis of the 1980s led to severe shocks and slow growth in other developing countries. As they sustained growth while other economies faltered, the Asian economies came to be viewed as immune from the difficulties confronting others; their rapid growth continued and policymakers seemed to meet all the challenges arising from growth and changes in world economic conditions.

Then, in 1997, there came an abrupt shock. After more than 30 years of unbroken successful performance, sharp difficulties arose in Indonesia, Malaysia, the Philippines, South Korea, and Thailand.[1] Contagion effects even rocked Hong Kong, Taiwan, and, to a degree, Singapore. The Asian financial crisis erupted. In many regards, these crises were different from the older balance of payments crises that had afflicted developing countries in the earlier years and continued to occur in countries still wedded to the old, inward-looking policies. India, for example, still following import-substitution policies, had a major balance-of-payments crisis in 1991, in which a shortage of foreign exchange was the precipitating factor.[2]

It is the purpose of this chapter to assess the Asian financial crises of the 1990s. Four questions are addressed in turn. The first focuses on the underlying factors that led to the crises, and the ways in which these factors differed from those that had precipitated the balance of payments crises of earlier years. A second question concerns the policies that were adopted to stem the crises and their effectiveness. The third centers on the aftermaths of crises in the afflicted countries. Finally, the lessons that were learned from these crises are reviewed.

Before starting, it should be noted that the financial crises of the great recession of 2007–2009 did not result in crises in the Asian countries (including India), but centered in the industrial countries. There were spillover effects that impacted the Asian economies largely through the reduction in demand for exports from the Asian countries. However, the Asian economies were by that time strong enough so that no crises resulted.[3] While the crises of the industrial countries were as severe as they were because of difficulties in their financial sectors,[4] the Asian economies' financial sectors were generally strong enough (and their financial institutions held few "toxic assets") to emerge relatively unscathed. Growth rates fell, and real GDPs even dropped, largely because of spillovers from the industrial countries as exports shrank sharply in the early part of the recession.[5] However, most of the East Asian countries resumed growth sooner, and with sharper rebounds, than did the industrial countries. A major reason was the enhanced strength of their financial systems after the crises of 1997–1998.

As will be discussed briefly in Section 4, the fact that the Asian countries did not experience a crisis does not prove that they will be immune from any future crises. However, focus until Section 4 is on the crises of the late 1990s and their lessons.

## 20.1 What Led to the Financial Crises

Each crisis arises and evolves in a unique way, depending on the particular characteristics of the afflicted economy, the policies in place leading up to the crisis, the ways in which the authorities address difficulties in the months leading up to the crisis, and external factors such as the state of the world economy. How rich the country is, the size and composition of its tradable goods sector, its history of fiscal probity or laxity, its overall financial position (in both the public and the private sectors), its state of financial development, and many other attributes play a role. But while that is true, there are also certain commonalities.[6]

A crisis comes about when the authorities are unwilling or unable to accept the rising costs of continuing with the economic policies currently in place. This might happen either because available foreign exchange is insufficient to finance even imports deemed essential for maintenance of economic activity (a balance of payments crisis) and/or because it is not possible to service foreign debt (a capital account crisis) and the country can no longer access international capital markets. In some countries, the authorities have not acted until real GDP has been seen to start dropping because of restricted imports. In other countries, the prospective lack of foreign exchange to service debt has triggered action. In that circumstance, the choice is to default on outstanding obligations and in so doing accept the strong likelihood that real GDP will fall, or to undertake sufficient changes (which may not be possible without outside financial support) to enable at least some financing of imports and meeting financial obligations. Alternatively, the crisis might arise when the domestic banking or financial system is faced with the threat of collapse, which would be calamitous for the functioning of any modern economy, whether industrial, emerging market, or low-income.[7]

Often, it is difficult to disentangle the roles of the financial sector, the public finances, debt and debt-servicing obligations, and the exchange rate regime. For example, while having a fixed exchange rate, a country's government might incur large fiscal deficits, initially financing them by borrowing from abroad (with obligations denominated in foreign currency). As that set of policies continued, foreign debt and debt-servicing would mount, and at the same time there would likely be inflationary pressures in the domestic economy. At some point, foreign lenders would be willing to roll over existing debt and finance additional debt, if at all, only with the inducement of higher interest rates and shorter maturities. This in itself would increase debt-servicing obligations and the fiscal deficit, while export earnings (at the fixed exchange rate) would likely fall, making the country's future ability to service its debt even more dubious. At some point, in the absence of policy changes, default on the debt would be inevitable. This would immediately force policy changes.[8]

Of course, creditors and observers (domestic and foreign) can anticipate the likely outcome in the absence of policy change, and usually do not wait until a country's reserves and borrowing capacity are entirely exhausted. Rather, as indicators of laxity persist and mount, if the authorities do not show signs of acting to address the situation, creditors refuse to roll over existing debt or buy new debt except at higher interest rates and shortened maturities. If a country has a good macroeconomic track record of economic and financial stability, would-be creditors initially believe that a turnaround in policies will occur. But the longer these policies persist or become more lax, the more doubt about a turnaround arises.

For analytical clarity, economists conceptualize a "macroeconomic soundness" indicator, ranging from countries whose policies have been, are, and are likely to continue to be sound to countries where indebtedness and indicators of macroeconomic policy (including the authorities' failure to address their issues) are so poor that action must be taken. Many countries are in between, some with improving indicators as policy changes are undertaken, some are deteriorating as policies persist and debt mounts.

To be sure, no country is totally immune, although high levels of reserves, current account surpluses, low levels of gross and net debt, rapid economic growth, countercyclical fiscal policies (with a zero or slightly positive balance over the cycle), and a history of good economic management are found in a number of countries. These countries are deemed creditworthy and can, when entering the market, do so with little or no spread over LIBOR.

Germany, prior to the introduction of the euro, was such a country where conservative fiscal and monetary policies, a very low rate of inflation, and current account surpluses resulted in excellent credit ratings. Germany was able to borrow at a very low interest rate, even when there was a large fiscal expansion after the fall of the Berlin Wall.

At the opposite end of the spectrum, Argentina was, in 2001, an example of a country in which imbalances had been building for at least five years and finally became unmanageable. By early 2001, Argentina had very large debt-servicing obligations, a sizeable (and growing) fiscal deficit, and rising current account deficits. Even with spreads of over 2600 basis points, Argentina was unable to access international capital markets and could not service her debt obligations.[9]

Asian crises differed. There was Japan, whose difficulties were domestic, centering on the financial system.[10] Then there were those that successfully fended off international attacks on their currencies. These included Taiwan and Hong Kong. Finally, there were countries that had full-blown foreign exchange financial crises. These included Indonesia, Malaysia, the Philippines, South Korea, and Thailand.

Japan had experienced rapid growth, as already mentioned, through the 1980s. During that decade there had been a rapid run-up in prices of residential and commercial real estate, not dissimilar to the real estate bubble in the United States prior to 2007. When the bubble burst in the early 1990s, the Japanese banking system was very weak, as NPLs (nonperforming loans) mounted with falling property prices. However,

Japan's external position was good: virtually all debt was domestic and Japan was running current account surpluses so that there was a sizeable positive net foreign asset position. The crisis was, therefore, entirely a domestic one centered on the financial sector.[11]

The crises in the Asian Newly Industrialized Countries (NICs) and developing countries in 1997-1998 differed from the situations in most earlier crises in that the afflicted countries had pursued conservative fiscal policies and did not have sizeable fiscal deficits or public debt.[12] However, in each of the countries, governments had controlled their banking systems, directing credits and placing ceilings on interest rates in order to stimulate investments and economic growth. When growth had tended to decelerate, credit expansion was used in an effort to offset the slowdown. Inevitably, over time an increasing volume of directed credits became NPLs,[13] and the solvency of the banking system was undermined. As that happened, domestic residents and foreigners withdrew their funds from the banking system to place them overseas, while at the same time domestic banks were lending abroad to countries where interest rates were high, in an effort to offset the low interest rates they were receiving on their performing loans, and the lack of income from their NPLs.[14]

In the cases of Thailand, Indonesia, and Malaysia, the exchange rate had been held constant, or permitted to fluctuate only with a narrow range, for several decades before the crises. Although inflation rates had been moderate by standards of developing countries, they were nonetheless higher than those in industrial countries. Hence, the real exchange rates appreciated over time and consequently export earnings had not grown very rapidly. The result was that competitiveness, as well as the health of the banking system, was an issue.

As funds began to flow out of these countries, other foreign and domestic creditors naturally became increasingly alarmed. Despite the authorities' efforts (raising domestic interest rates, attempting to prevent capital outflows, etc.), the outflow grew until it was clear that the country's defenses would be exhausted. In Thailand, which had begun experiencing severe difficulties in January 1997, the authorities finally recognized the futility of further efforts to stem the flows, and undertook a major reform program, supported by the IMF, in July 1997. Malaysia had a similar situation, in that the exchange rate had for long been fixed, although the banking system was not as weakened as was the Thai system. Nonetheless, Malaysia adjusted the exchange rate and undertook a number of other measures later in the summer of 1997.[15] Indonesia, South Korea, and Thailand all had short-term debts to banks that exceeded their reserves—by a factor of 2.1 in South Korea, 1.6 in Indonesia, and 1.4 in Thailand.

By late summer 1997, a number of other East and Southeast Asian economies were experiencing difficulties. There were strong capital outflows from both Taiwan and Hong Kong, although in both cases the underlying policy framework, the initial levels of reserves, the low levels of indebtedness, and current account surpluses enabled the authorities successfully to stave off the attacks on their currencies and meet demands for foreign exchange. The Philippine economy also experienced major difficulties and quickly resorted to a stabilization program.

In Korea and Indonesia, however, the situation was more complex, although in very different ways. South Korean growth had been spectacular over the preceding three and a half decades and the country had been transformed from a very poor, slowly growing, aid-dependent economy into an industrial one, even joining the OECD in 1996. As mentioned earlier, because of its dramatic success and transformation, South Korean economic policy was viewed almost with awe by foreign observers. However, difficulties had been building up largely unnoticed since the late 1980s. While economic policy reforms had earlier transformed the economy, with a successful export-oriented growth strategy, the abandonment of exchange controls, major reductions in non-tariff barriers to trade and stable macroeconomic policy, the financial system had remained tightly controlled.[16] The growth rate had been slowing, and the authorities attempted to revive growth by instructing the banks to increase their lending at reduced interest rates.[17]

Although growth temporarily revived in 1993-94 (partially in response to the increased low-interest credits that were extended), the indebtedness of the Korean chaebol (the large industrial houses) shot up, and with it their ability to service their debts diminished.[18] The first chaebol bankruptcy, something previously regarded as unthinkable, was in late 1996. As it became evident that other chaebol were in difficulty, capital inflows diminished and outflows increased. When Thailand devalued the baht, Korean banks, which had lent in baht and rupiah (among others) to secure higher interest rates, took additional losses.[19] As growth further slowed, chaebol debt-servicing capacity was further reduced and, having lost income and principal from their overseas exposures as well as the NPLs of the chaebol, the Korean banking system was threatened. Creditors were increasingly reluctant to roll over their outstanding loans, capital outflows were increasing, and Korean reserves were diminishing rapidly.

To make matters worse, the South Korean Presidential elections were scheduled for December 1997, and there were three major candidates, each of whom vowed that they would under no circumstances approach the International Monetary Fund for assistance.[20] That, of course, increased uncertainty and seemed to make it less likely that South Korea would be able voluntarily to service all of her debt. By early December (prior to the vote), South Korea was running out of reserves, and action had to be taken or default on debt would have been imminent (which would have been disastrous for a country with as much involvement in international trade as Korea had).

By early December, the authorities faced the inevitable. An IMF team flew to Korea and a policy package was drawn up, with all three presidential candidates publicly indicating their support for it.[21] In fact, the first IMF program package did not calm the markets, and a second package was agreed late in December before the panic subsided.

Indonesia's situation was different yet again. There had been a long period of sustained growth, with rising living standards, starting in the late 1960s. However, the exchange rate was permitted to fluctuate only within a narrow range (with inflation above that of the country's major trading partners). Moreover, the country's President

Suharto had been in office since the mid-1960s, and there was increasing uncertainty as to the political future. As investors witnessed the downfalls of other East Asian countries, they reevaluated the Indonesian situation, and capital outflows began. These intensified as the Indonesians announced the closure of some 16 banks, as NPLs had mounted during the latter phase of Indonesia's growth prior to 1997.[22] Depositors naturally then became concerned about the remaining banks, with attendant increases in outflows.

Thus, despite somewhat different circumstances, most of the Asian countries had held relatively fixed, or fixed, exchange rates, had sizeable outstanding debts to the rest of the world that were denominated in foreign exchange, and had banking systems that had gradually weakened.[23]

## 20.2 Policies Adopted to Stem the Crises

After the early 1990s, the Japanese government was confronted with crises in the financial system on several occasions. Each crisis was met with policies that proved to be inadequate to restore the banks to health. Despite tentative signs of recovery on several occasions, the economy again lapsed into stagnation and deflation. But until 2003, efforts to restore the banking system to health were insufficient: a Financial Services Agency was established in 1998 and was able to resolve two bad banks, but until 2003 regulatory forbearance for the banks' capitalization was the norm. Only in 2005-2006 did the economy and the banking system show signs of sustained recovery; but with the great recession starting in late 2007, the Japanese economy again floundered.[24] Policy changes were largely confined to repeated measures intended to restore the banking system to health. Fiscal policy was loosened, and fiscal deficits were between 5 and 8 percent. One result was a buildup of Japanese government debt to over 200 percent of GDP by 2010. The interest rate, however, was close to zero, Japan was incurring current account surpluses, and the debt was and is held mostly by Japanese nationals. Hence, there were few international spillovers from the Japanese plight, except insofar as the sluggish economy resulted in less Japanese demand for goods and services from abroad.

In the cases of Taiwan and Hong Kong, the authorities were able to meet the capital outflows and avoided a full-blown crisis.[25] Malaysia's banking system was somewhat stronger than that in the other crisis countries, and the mounting capital outflow started somewhat later. The Malaysian authorities devalued the currency and, in the winter of 1998, imposed capital controls. As stated above, whether these controls were effective or whether the other measures taken by the Malaysians were sufficient and the crisis would have subsided anyway is still a matter of dispute.

Thailand, South Korea, and Indonesia had full-blown crises which could not be addressed satisfactorily without external support.[26] In these three instances, the

International Monetary Fund extended sizeable financial support to the countries; there were IMF programs in each instance.[27] It was these three countries whose crises were the major headlines during 1997–1998.

All three countries permitted their exchange rates to float. In Indonesia and Thailand, there had earlier been a fixed exchange rate, while in South Korea the authorities had intervened extensively to prevent any sizeable depreciation. By the end of 1998, the rupiah had depreciated to 8025 rupiah per U.S. dollar from Rp 2383 at the end of 1996 and Rp 4650 at the end of 1997. The Thai baht depreciated from 25.6 per U.S. dollar at the end of 1996 (still the fixed exchange rate that had been in force for more than a decade) to 47.2 at the end of 1997. South Korea's exchange rate depreciated from 844 won per U.S. dollar at the end of 1996 to 1695 won per U.S. dollar at the end of 1997.[28] In all three countries, future intervention in the foreign exchange market was to be very limited.

These real depreciations intensified financial difficulties whenever there were mismatches between the currencies in which assets and liabilities were denominated. However, they also encouraged rapid increases in exports, which offset part of the reduction in domestic demand brought about by the reductions in monetary and fiscal stimuli and the real depreciation of the exchange rates.

All three countries received financial support during the time they were undertaking domestic economic policy changes to restore their economies to health. But each reform program, as outlined in the LOI, was different, depending on the country's situation. In Korea's case, there was fiscal and monetary tightening (which could be expected to make it more attractive to hold Korean won and thus reduce the incentives for capital outflow), banking reform including both the establishment of a "bad bank" to remove the bad loans from the banks' books and recapitalization of the banks, and changes in corporate governance and a move to arm's-length lending.

All three programs addressed problems in the financial sector. In each, there were policy changes specific to the individual country's situation. In Korea, for example, there was emphasis on corporate governance and moving toward arm's-length lending between banks and the chaebol.[29]

### 20.2.1 Aftermath of Crises

The South Korean authorities moved rapidly to adopt reforms. Even so, the first program (early December 2007) was insufficient to stem the capital outflow, and a revised program was adopted within a short period of time. However, in South Korea, as in Thailand and Indonesia, the initial drop in real GDP was greater than had been anticipated, and the fiscal components of all three programs were relaxed.[30]

Thailand's reforms were implemented, but somewhat more slowly than was the case in South Korea. However, the Indonesian authorities did not fully carry out the reforms to which they had committed. As already seen, 16 banks had been closed in November 1997.[31] However, the president's son reacquired his banks by acquiring the name of another bank, raising questions in many minds as to whether anything had happened. Withdrawals from other banks accelerated; and the monetary tightening and high interest rates, that had been a part of the program, were not maintained. Indonesia's policy reforms fell far short of those envisaged in the program.[32]

All three countries initially experienced large drops in real GDP. South Korea's fell by 6.9 percent between 1997 and 1998. Thailand's fell by 10 percent and Indonesia's by 13.4 percent over that same period.[33]

The speed and extent of recovery appear to have been directly related to the alacrity with which reforms were undertaken. South Korea's economy turned around by mid-1998, and in 1999 was 2 percent above its 2007 level, while Thailand's real GDP attained its pre-crisis level only in 2001. Indonesia's recovery began later, and was much less buoyant. In 2000, Indonesia's GDP was still only at 90 percent of the 1997 level and did not surpass it until 2004.

But growth resumed in each country. Except for Indonesia, where political change played a major role (both in the slow adoption of the necessary reforms and in the uncertainty as to future policies), growth resumed far more quickly than had been forecast at the time of the crises.

Growth of all three countries accelerated early in the next decade, and continued until the Great Recession of 2007–2008. Even then, the financial sectors of the East Asian countries were sufficiently robust as a result of reforms to avoid any of the difficulties experienced in some of the industrial countries. While real GDP fell in each country early in the recession, the downturns were shorter-lived than in most countries, and the ensuing upturns were fairly sharp and resulted in fairly high growth rates. Indeed, many analysts pointed to the role of significant demand from China and India played in cushioning the downturn and supporting the upturn.

## 20.3 Lessons Learned from the 1997–1998 Experience

Some have termed the Asian crises of 1997–1998 "the first crises of the twenty-first century." While the earlier (1994) Mexican crisis also was driven by the capital account, many analysts had seen special features, such as entry into NAFTA, the depreciation of the nominal exchange rate at a rate slower than the rate of inflation, and political change, as important. While the Mexican banks were in great difficulty, that was seen largely as a function of a currency mismatch between Mexican assets and liabilities, and of the increased cost of servicing foreign-exchange denominated debt after the peso depreciated.

These factors were clearly at work as well in the Asian crisis countries. But the extent to which the open capital account, and especially the banks' borrowing from abroad, deepened the crisis was much more evident in Asia.

Connected to that, the feasibility of maintaining a fixed nominal exchange rate was called into serious question. As seen, the crisis countries all moved to a flexible exchange rate with little intervention. Exchange rate flexibility served them well during the Great Recession, as impact of the drop in foreign demand for domestic firms' exports was partially offset by higher domestic prices received for their goods.

A first and major lesson of the 1997–1998 episodes was an increased appreciation of the merits and desirability of a flexible exchange rate regime with little or no intervention. Questions arose as to whether it was even possible to choose a "middle path," with fixed but adjustable exchange rates that had characterized earlier years. While it was recognized that a fixed nominal exchange rate regime could be maintained, as Hong Kong had done, doing so would require disciplined monetary and fiscal policies that focused on insuring that macroeconomic variables were consistent with that rate.[34]

A second major lesson was the importance of avoiding currency mismatches to the extent possible. When a government borrowed in foreign currency[35] and then the currency was devalued or depreciated, the domestic burden on fiscal resources always rose.[36] With open capital accounts, however, currency mismatches could and did arise in the financial systems, with serious threats to financial stability.[37]

A third lesson followed from the second. That is the importance and desirability of maintaining foreign exchange reserves at least equal to one year's short-term foreign liabilities. When reserves are adequate to meet financing needs over a long period, doubts about the sustainability of the exchange rate and the currency regime and of debt-servicing capacity are far less likely to arise.

A fourth lesson focused on the economic fragility that arises when firms or countries are overleveraged and when financial regulation is too weak. Strengthening the banks, removing NPLs from their balance sheets (as was done well in Korea), and increasing their equity were all essential parts of the crisis resolution packages. While there is still much to be learned about "best practice" regulation, it was evident in the Asian crisis countries that connected lending, poor loan evaluation, and other practices had negatively affected growth before the crises, and that these issues had to be dealt with as part of crisis resolution.

## 20.4 Conclusion

With economic growth, economic structures necessarily change. As they do so, the factors that may bring about fragility of the economy or the financial system change. As Reinhart and Rogoff (2009) point out, crises have always been with us, and probably always will be. The most that can be done is to identify the fragilities that led to past crises, find ways to strengthen the weak links in the economy and financial system, and remain alert to signs of danger. This can reduce the magnitude of any potential future crises and even avoid some. To avoid all would be expecting too much.

The Asian countries' economies, however, are much stronger than they were in the mid-1990s, and have, of course, grown larger as well. They all have issues—such as the very low level of Chinese consumption—that must be addressed, but weaknesses in the financial systems that led to the crises of the 1990s have been largely eradicated. If the lessons from the 1990s were learned, it is likely that growth can proceed for a substantial period of time before yet another source of instability threatens these economies.

## Notes

1. Japan experienced financial crisis and a period of economic stagnation starting in the early 1990s. This never spilled over into a balance of payments crisis and was largely a domestic financial crisis, accompanied by stagnation in economic growth. This is discussed further below.
2. Pakistan has continued in IMF programs to the time of writing (spring 2011), although armed conflict and political difficulties have been major factors. The Indian government undertook significant policy reforms after the 1991 crisis, including removal of high levels of protection to domestic industry. Indian economic growth accelerated subsequently. To date, there has been no financial crisis since 1991 so that country is not discussed further in this chapter.
3. In part, this was because of the buildup of foreign exchange reserves in those countries. After the 1997–98 crises, policy makers resolved that they would never again be caught out as they had been. Part of their response was the huge increase in reserves over the following decade.
4. This is not to say that the financial sector, as such, "caused" the Great Recession, as it came to be called. Analysis of the factors leading to the Great Recession will continue for years. While the financial meltdown following the collapse of Lehman Brothers clearly intensified the Recession, it can be argued that other, "real," factors, such as global imbalances and/or the housing bubbles in a number of industrial countries, were the underlying issues.
5. 2. For analyses of the factors leading to the sharp shrinkage in trade, see the symposium in *IMF Economic Review*, Vol. 58, Number 2.
6. See Reinhart and Rogoff (2009) and Edwards and Frankel (2002), who trace the history of crises since the tenth century. They term the crises of 2007–09 as "the first crises of the twenty-first century," reflecting their view that there have always been financial crises and always will be.
7. In many cases, measures taken to ameliorate foreign exchange difficulties (including especially devaluations or sizeable depreciations) can precipitate a financial crisis.
8. Assuming that the fiscal deficit was greater than interest previously paid on outstanding obligations, the government would be forced to print money (highly inflationary), or cut back on its expenditures and raise taxes immediately even with default, as foreigners would no longer be willing to buy government-issued securities.
9. Argentina had been viewed as highly creditworthy in the mid-1990s after a set of policy reforms in 1991–3 that resulted in a sharp reduction in the rate of inflation and an apparent contraction in fiscal deficits. But a fixed exchange rate made Argentine exports increasingly uncompetitive (resulting in rising current account deficits), and the debt ratio rose as off-budget expenditures were financed by borrowing. As these imbalances grew, creditors

became increasingly concerned about Argentina's creditworthiness and ability to sustain the convertibility plan. By the end of 2001, Argentina suspended servicing of the debt, abandoned the quasi-currency board (fixed exchanger rate) system and had to undergo a series of policy reforms. Abandonment of the currency board and the manner in which banks were treated (with liabilities converted at a 3:1 ratio while bank assets were converted at 1:1, wiping out the equity of the banking system) led to a large drop in real GDP.

10. Most references to the "Asian financial crises" refer to those in the emerging markets, and do not focus on Japan. But in fact, the Japanese economy has undergone two decades of stagnation, with a real estate bubble that burst in the early 1990s, and several severe threats to the financial system. See Krueger (2009) for a discussion.
11. See Hoshi and Kashyap (2009) and Krueger (2009) for a full analysis.
12. Japanese fiscal policy had also been quite conservative.
13. For a considerable period of time, the authorities overlooked the "evergreening" of loans, as firms unable to service their debts borrowed more to pay interest obligations. When these NPLs came to light, it was evident that the equity of many banks had been severely depleted or wiped out.
14. See Dornbusch (2002) for an analysis of the "old-style" balance of payments crises and the financial crises. As he points out, financial crises are often closely associated with balance of payments difficulties as domestic residents and foreigners are trying to move their funds out of a country.
15. The Malaysian authorities did not enter into an IMF program and instead imposed capital controls in the early winter of 1998. There is much controversy over the effectiveness of these controls: some argue that they were imposed when the worst was already over; the Malaysian authorities believed that the imposition of capital controls had successfully reduced or removed the pressures of the crisis (Kaplan and Rodrik, 2002).
16. Capital controls had been liberalized for short-term flows, which also contributed to the difficulties. Most analysts believe that long-term capital flows should have been liberalized first.
17. See Mason et al. (1980), for an economic history of the first 25 years after Korean independence and Cha et al. (1997) for an account of the first 50 years. South Korea's real GNP grew at an average annual rate of less than 5 percent from the end of the Korean War in 1953 to 1960, despite the opportunities for more rapid growth that accompany the end of hostilities. Exports constituted only 3 percent of GDP in 1960, and foreign aid equaled 10 percent of GDP. The inflation rate in the 1950s was among the highest in the world, and more than 70 percent of the population resided in rural areas and was dependent on primary commodities (mostly agricultural) for their livelihood.
18. By the time of the financial crisis in South Korea, it is estimated that the average leverage ratio among the large chaebol was well over 400 percent. Prior to the crisis, banks had been encouraged to roll over the existing debt of the chaebol when they were unable to service it, and to extend new credit to them. This "evergreening" of outstanding credits to the chaebol hid the extent of the NPLs until the crisis broke. See Coe and Kim (2002).
19. There was considerable "evergreening" (lending to firms so they could pay the bank the debt service owed) of lending, which makes it difficult to ascertain the true extent of the banks' difficulties.
20. This meant that there were few preliminary discussions between Korean and IMF officials, and that, when IMF support was sought, the IMF staff needed to draw up plans in haste.
21. See Coe and Kim (2002), for analyses of the crisis and recovery.

22. It was almost certainly unwise to close 16 banks without examining the others and providing assurances that they were sound. The abrupt closure of the 16 has been widely criticized, and blamed for the intensification of the crisis. See Fischer (2002) p. 347 for a statement of this view.
23. See Hoshi and Kashyap (2004) and (2009) and references therein for a fuller account.
24. Japan's labor force began falling in the 1990s, and population has actually been falling since 2010. This demographic has complicated efforts to move the economy toward a sustainable growth path.
25. Singapore was not attacked as much as Hong Kong and Taiwan, and was not even threatened with a serious crisis.
26. For an overview of the three crises, see Ito (2007) and Wijnholds (2011).
27. The International Monetary Fund's Articles charge it with maintenance of financial stability. It can lend significant sums to member countries only when it is satisfied that the loan, and the policies that the country intends to adopt to meet the crisis, will enable the country to overcome its initial difficulties and to repay the loan. Hence, the policies proposed to be followed are set forth in "Letters of Intent" (LOIs) from the countries' authorities to the IMF Managing Director. These LOIs set forth the intended fiscal, monetary, and exchange rate policies that will be followed, along with other changes deemed necessary to restore sustainability and growth.
28. The South Korean won and Thai baht both appreciated once the upturn had begun and the economy had stabilized, although neither currency appreciated sufficiently to reach its earlier level. Data are from IMF, *International Financial Statistics*, various Yearbooks.
29. There were well over 100 policy reforms set forth in the Indonesian LOIs. Many observers criticized this as excess conditionality. While some of the reforms were clearly essential to the stabilization of the economy, some were aimed at enabling healthier future growth. It was these latter reforms that spurred criticism. See Fischer (2002, p. 352) for a discussion of the structural reforms in the Indonesian program.
30. It has been argued that the relaxation proves that the initial programs were too austere. There is no satisfactory way of testing this hypothesis. That they were relaxed certainly shows that the initial programs were not too loose. However, in the midst of a crisis, it must be remembered that "too weak" a program will intensify panic and outflows (and did so in South Korea); it is almost certainly preferable to tighten policies and loosen them if need be, rather than to start without sufficient tightening and witness further outflows.
31. Some have argued that this was a mistake because the closure of those banks (with cuts in the value of deposits for large shareholders), without assurance that the other banks were sound, may have triggered further withdrawals of deposits.
32. See Wijnholds (2011) for a fuller discussion.
33. Data are from IMF, *International Financial Statistics Yearbook*, 2006, country pages.
34. Economists accept the validity of the proposition of the "impossible trinity," by which is meant that over the longer term it is not possible for a country to maintain an open capital account, independent monetary and fiscal policy, and a fixed nominal exchange rate.
35. Until recently, most lenders to developing countries were not willing to denominate their loans in the currency of the borrower, presumably because of their concern about the risks of currency depreciation or devaluation. In the past decade, some of the more successful emerging markets have begun to be able to sell bonds abroad denominated in local currency.

36. In older "balance of payments crises," foreign exchange earnings could be insufficient for debt-servicing obligations as the government might not be able to acquire sufficient foreign exchange. While a crisis might arise, it involved the domestic banking system to a much more limited extent.
37. "Indirect" mismatches can also arise when local (importing) firms borrow from domestic banks and the currency depreciates. If the costs of the indebted firms rise with devaluation, some of those firms may be unable to service their obligations to the domestic banking system.

## References

Cha, Dong-Se, Kim, Kwang Suk, and Dwight H. Perkins, editors, 1997, *The Korean Economy 1945-1995: Performance and Vision for the 21st Century*, Korea Development Institute, Seoul.
Coe, David T., and Se-Jik Kim, 2002. *Korean Crisis and Recovery*, International Monetary Fund and Korea Institute for International Economic Policy, Washington D.C.
Dornbusch, Rudi, 2002. "A Primer on Emerging Market Crises," pp. 743–754 in Edwards and Frankel.
Edwards, Sebastian, and Jeffrey Frankel, editors, 2002. *Preventing Currency Crises in Emerging Markets*, University of Chicago Press, Chicago.
Fischer, Stanley, 2002. "IMF Stabilization Programs," pp. 347–352 in Edwards and Frankel.
Hoshi, Takeo, and Anil Kashyap, 2004, "Japan's Financial Crisis and Economic Stagnation," *Journal of Economic Perspectives*, Winter 2004, pp. 3–26, Vol. 18, No. 1.
Hoshi, Takeo, and Anil Kashyap, 2009. "Will the U.S. Bank Recapitalization Succeed? Eight Lessons from Japan," NBER Working Paper 14401, August.
Ito, Takatoshi. 2007. "Asian Currency Crisis and the International Monetary Fund, 10 Years Later: Overview," *Asian Economic Policy Review*, No. 2, pp. 16–49.
Kaplan, Ethan and Dani Rodrik, 2002. "Did the Malaysian Capital Controls Work?," pp. 393–431 in Edwards and Frankel.
Krueger, Anne O., 2009, "Lessons from Asian Financial Experience" pp. 93–114 in Reuven Glick and Mark M. Siegel, *Asia and the Global Financial Crisis*, San Francisco, CA: Federal Reserve Bank of San Francisco, 2009.
Mason, Edward S., Mahn Je Kim, Dwight H. Perkins, Kwang Suk Kim, and David C. Cole, 1980. *The Economic and Social Modernization of the Republic of Korea*, Harvard University Press, Cambridge, MA
Reinhart, Carmen M., and Kenneth S. Rogoff, 2009. *This Time is Different: Eight Centuries of Financial Folly*, Princeton University Press, Princeton NJ.
Wijnholds, Onno de Beaufort, 2011. *Fighting Financial Fires*. Palgrave Macmillan, New York.

CHAPTER 21

# THE "IMPOSSIBLE TRINITY," THE INTERNATIONAL MONETARY FRAMEWORK, AND THE PACIFIC RIM

JOSHUA AIZENMAN AND HIRO ITO

## 21.1 Introduction

EVER since the breakout of the global financial crisis of 2008-2009, policymakers have gathered and discussed the future of the international monetary system. Policymakers from many countries have questioned the current international monetary system that has been essentially a uni-currency system heavily dependent on the U.S. dollar, the currency at the epicenter of the crisis, as the international reserve currency. China, with its mighty economy that has been growing at an impressive rate in the last two decades, has been one of the biggest challengers to the current international financial framework. However, while it challenges the dollar-dominant system and criticizes the U.S. profligacy for being responsible for the crisis, China itself is the largest holder of dollar reserves. It holds more than $3 trillion of foreign reserves, more than 30 percent of the world's foreign reserves, with more than two-thirds denominated in the U.S. dollar.

The global financial crisis of 2008-2009 has been followed by the European debt crisis, damaging the credibility of the euro as the second largest international reserve currency and, consequently, leaving the U.S. dollar as the sole safe haven currency. Despite the feeble recovery of the U.S. economy, and given no other alternative international currency that can replace the role of the dollar or the euro, international investors choose the U.S. dollar as the sole safe haven currency only after the process of elimination. That means, the U.S. still maintains the "exorbitant privilege" even though it is its profligacy, partially financed by capital inflow, that started the chain of crises. In such an international monetary system, frustration has mounted among high-growth developing countries, such as the BRIC countries—Brazil, Russia, India, and China—that are increasing their presence in the world economy. While the global financial crisis of 2008-2009 barely left a dent on these economies' economic growth, the U.S. attempts to provide ample liquidity through extremely loose monetary policy have caused an influx of capital to these high-growth economies, sowing seeds for asset inflation, especially in emerging market economies with de facto exchange rate fixity to the dollar.

With the low yield and expected depreciation trend of dollar-denominated assets, the opportunity cost of holding dollar assets has been increasing rapidly among the countries that hold massive international reserves (Jeanne 2011), although they cannot find alternative international reserve currencies that can provide the same level of safe haven and liquidity to the extent of the U.S. dollar. Some developing economies, most notably China, hold so large an amount of dollar assets that any attempt of selling off dollar assets could exacerbate the US dollar depreciation trend, increasing capital losses.

In sum, the international monetary system is facing the Triffin dilemma again. Countries created the Special Drawing Rights (SDRs) as a solution to the dilemma in the 1960s, and powerful developing countries are now seeking for a drastic reform in the SDR as well as the international monetary system. However, a rise in the relative economic power has not been matched by a proportional rise in the status of these economies' currencies. One main reason for this is that it is only in the last two decades that middle-income developing countries have been actively opening their financial markets. Slow and cautious process for financial liberalization is due to its double-edged sword nature; while it can supplement domestic financial intermediation, financial opening can make countries exposed to economic and financial turmoil.

However, moving toward further financial globalization seems to be an irreversible trend for developing countries. At least, that is how policymakers in those economies perceive financial liberalization, even including those in financially closed economies such as China. Now the question is, how to proceed with financial liberalization, especially in a way that would not put the country in a turbulence. Such a task can be complex in such a globalized environment.

Despite the complexity of policy management, policymakers face a simple, old theoretical constraint, called the "impossible trinity," or "trilemma." This is a hypothesis that was first made popular by Mundell (1963). The hypothesis states that a country simultaneously may choose any two, but not all, of the three policy goals: monetary independence, exchange rate stability, and financial integration. This hypothesis has been widely taught and recognized, as it is quite intuitive and helpful to understand the constraints policymakers must face in an open economy setting.

Despite its pervasive recognition, the hypothesis has not faced much empirical scrutiny until recently. The main reason for that is because it is quite difficult to create systematic metrics that measure the extent of achievement in the three policy goals of the trilemma. If one does not know to what extent each of the policy choices has been achieved, it is difficult to estimate what kind of other policy choices are still available and to what extent.

Aizenman, Chinn, and Ito (2010) developed a set of "trilemma indexes" that measure the degree of achievement in each of the three policy choices for a wide coverage of countries and years. Using the indexes, they empirically proved that the hypothesis is valid by showing that the three measures of the trilemma are linearly related to each other.

In this chapter we will characterize the policy choices developing economies have adopted over years from the perspective of the powerful hypothesis of the trilemma. For this attempt, we will use the "trilemma indexes" of Aizenman et al. (2010), empirically proving that the hypothesis is "binding"—the three policies are linearly related to each other so that policymakers must face a trade-off in choosing a combination of two out of the three open macro policies. Lastly, we will focus on a characteristic of emerging market economies that have been evident in recent decades. That is the tendency for the "middle-ground convergence"—emerging market economies tend to choose a policy combination composed of intermediate levels of all three policies. We provide some evidence that a country equipped with intermediate levels of the three trilemma policies tend to experience a lower level of output volatility. That may explain the recent tendency of middle-ground convergence among emerging market economies.

## 21.2 The Trilemma Theory and Evidence

### 21.2.1 The Trilemma Hypothesis

The trilemma is illustrated in Figure 21.1. Each of the three sides of the triangle—representing monetary independence, exchange rate stability, and financial openness—depicts a potentially desirable goal, yet it is not possible to be simultaneously on all three sides of the triangle. For example, the top vertex, labeled "floating exchange rate," is associated with the full extent of monetary policy autonomy and financial openness, but not exchange rate stability.

History has shown that different international financial systems have attempted to achieve combinations of two out of the three policy goals, such as the Gold Standard—guaranteeing capital mobility and exchange rate stability—and the Bretton Woods system—providing monetary autonomy and exchange rate stability. The fact that economies have altered the combinations as a reaction to crises or major economic events may be taken to imply that each of the three policy options is a mixed bag of both merits and demerits for managing macroeconomic conditions.

Greater monetary independence could allow policymakers to stabilize the economy through monetary policy without being subject to other economies' macroeconomic management, thus potentially leading to stable and sustainable economic growth. However, in a world with price and wage rigidities, policymakers could also manipulate output movement (at least in the short run), thus leading to increasing output and

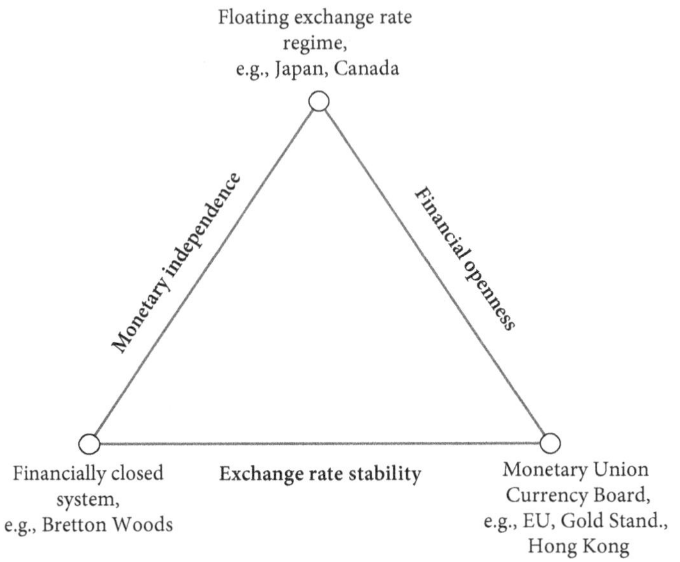


FIGURE 21.1 The Trilemma

inflation volatility. Furthermore, monetary authorities could also abuse their autonomy to monetize fiscal debt, and therefore end up destabilizing the economy through high and volatile inflation.

Exchange rate stability could bring out price stability by providing an anchor, and lower risk premium by mitigating uncertainty, thereby fostering investment and international trade. Also, at the time of an economic crisis, maintaining a pegged exchange rate could increase the credibility of policymakers and thereby contribute to stabilizing output movement (Aizenman et al., 2012). However, greater levels of exchange rate stability could also rid policymakers of a policy choice of using exchange rate as a tool to absorb external shocks.[1] Hence, the rigidity caused by exchange rate stability could not only enhance output volatility, but also cause misallocation of resources and unbalanced, unsustainable growth.

Financial liberalization is perhaps the most contentious and hotly debated policy among the three policy choices of the trilemma. On the one hand, more open financial markets could lead to economic growth by paving the way for more efficient resource allocation, mitigating information asymmetry, enhancing and/or supplementing domestic savings, and helping transfer of technological or managerial know-how (i.e., growth in total factor productivity).[2] Also, economies with greater access to international capital markets should be better able to stabilize themselves through risk-sharing and portfolio diversification. On the other hand, it is also true that financial liberalization has often been blamed for economic instability, especially over the last two decades, including the current crisis. Based on this view, financial openness could expose economies to volatile cross-border capital flows resulting in sudden stops or reversal of capital flows, thereby making economies vulnerable to boom-bust cycles (Kaminsky and Schmukler 2002).

Thus, theory tells us that each one of the three trilemma policy choices can be a double-edged sword, which should explain the wide and mixed variety of empirical findings on each of the three policy choices.[3] Furthermore, to make the matter more complicated, while there are three ways of pairing two out of the three policies (i.e., three vertices in the triangle in Figure 21.1), the effect of each policy choice can differ depending on what the other policy choice it is paired with. For example, exchange rate stability can be more destabilizing when it is paired with financial openness, whereas it can be stabilizing if paired with greater monetary autonomy. Hence, it may be worthwhile to empirically analyze the three types of policy combinations in a comprehensive and systematic manner.

## 21.2.2 Development of Policy Combinations in the Trilemma Context

Despite its pervasive recognition, there has been almost no empirical work that we are aware of that tests the concept of the trilemma systematically. Many of the studies in this literature often focus on one or two variables of the trilemma but fail to provide a comprehensive analysis of all of the three policy aspects of the trilemma.[4] This is partly because of the lack of appropriate metrics that measure the extent of achievement in the three policy goals.

Aizenman et al. (2008) overcame this deficiency by developing a set of "trilemma indexes" that measure the degree to which each of the three policy choices is implemented by economies for more than 170 economies for 1970 through 2010.[5] The monetary independence index (MI) is based on the correlation of a country's interest rates with the base country's interest rate. The index for exchange rate stability (ERS) is an invert of exchange rate volatility, i.e., standard deviations of the monthly rate of depreciation, using the exchange rate between the home and base economies. The degree of financial integration is measured with the Chinn-Ito (2006, 2008) capital controls index (KAOPEN). More details on the construction of the indexes can be found in the appendix to this chapter, as well as in Aizenman et al. (2008).

Figure 21.2 shows the trajectories of the trilemma indexes for different income–country groups. For the industrialized economies, financial openness accelerated after the beginning of the 1990s, while the extent of monetary independence started a declining trend. After the end of the 1990s, exchange rate stability rose significantly. All these trends seem to reflect the introduction of the euro in 1999.[6]

Developing economies, on the other hand, do not present such a distinct divergence of the indexes, and their experiences differ depending on whether they are emerging or non-emerging market economies.[7] For emerging market economies, exchange rate stability declined rapidly from the 1970s through the mid-1980s. After some retrenchment around early 1980s (in the wake of the debt crisis), financial openness started rising from 1990 onwards. For the other developing economies, exchange rate stability declined less rapidly, and financial openness trended upward more slowly. In both cases though, monetary independence remained more or less trendless.

Interestingly, for the emerging market economies, the indexes suggest a convergence toward the middle ground, even as talk of the disappearing middle has been

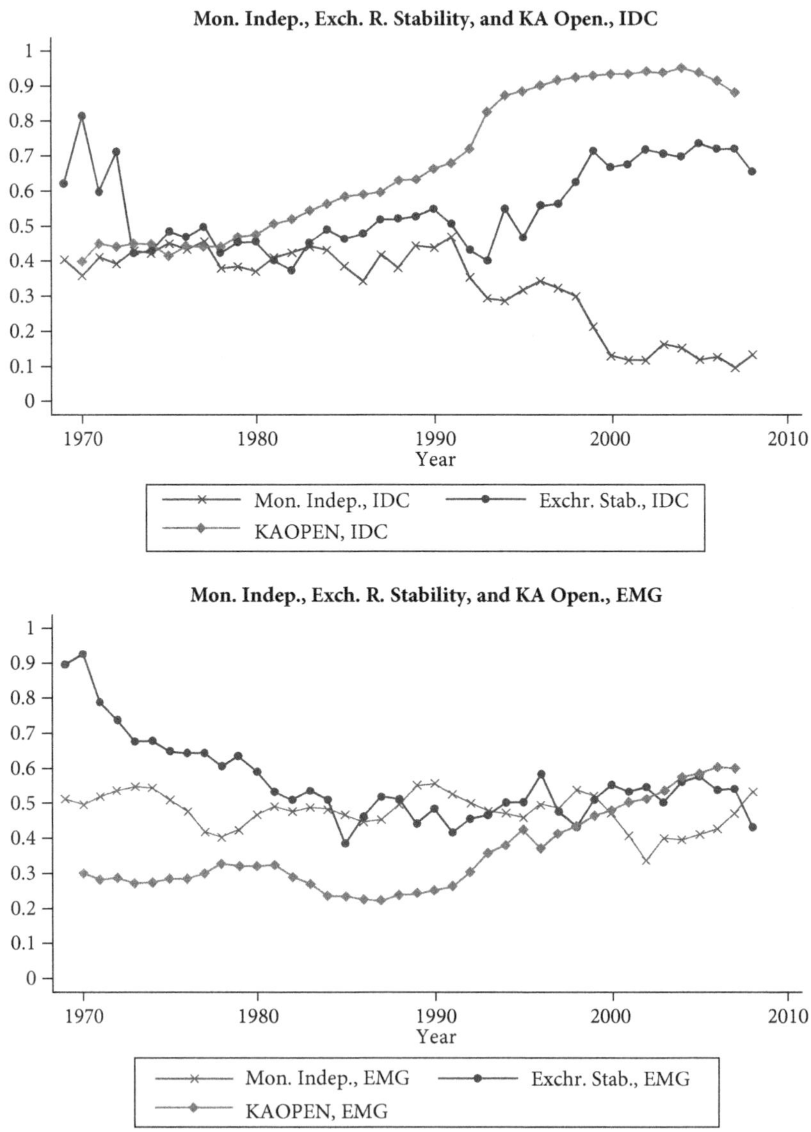


FIGURE 21.2 Development of the Trilemma Configurations Over Time (a) Industrialized Countries (b) Emerging market economies (c) Non-Emerging Market Developing Countries

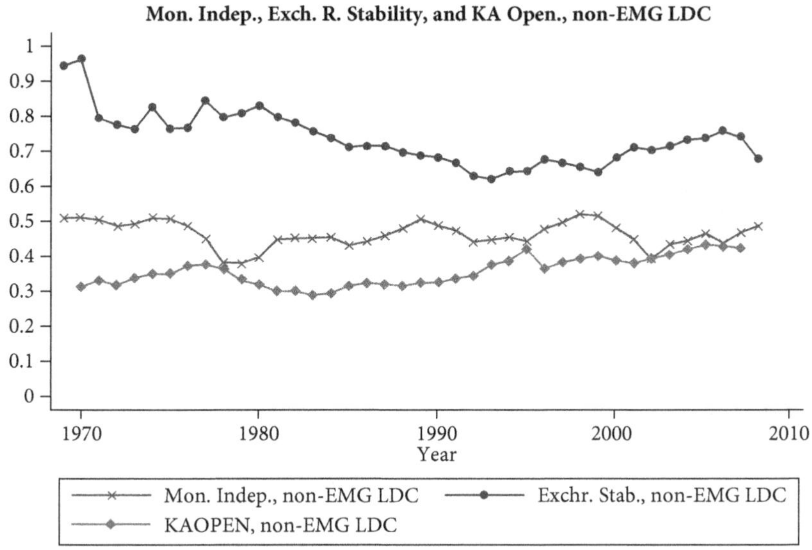


FIGURE 21.2 Continued

doing the rounds. This pattern of results suggests that developing economies may have been trying to cling to moderate levels of both monetary independence and financial openness, while maintaining higher levels of exchange rate stability. In other words, they have been leaning somewhat against the trilemma over a period that interestingly coincides with the time when some of these economies began accumulating sizable international reserves (IR), potentially to buffer the trade-off arising from the trilemma.

None of these observations is applicable to non-emerging developing market economies (Figure 21.2[c]). For this group of economies, exchange rate stability has been the most aggressively pursued policy throughout the period. In contrast to the experience of the emerging market economies, financial liberalization has not been proceeding rapidly for the non-emerging market developing economies.

Furthermore Asia, especially those economies with emerging markets, stands out from other geographical groups of economies.[8] Panel (a) in Figure 21.3 shows that for Asian emerging market economies, this sort of convergence is not a recent phenomenon. Since as early as the early 1980s, the three indexes have been clustered around the middle range. However, for most of the time, except for the Asian crisis years of 1997-1998, exchange rate stability seems to have been the most pervasive policy choice. In the post-crisis years in the 2000s, the indexes diverged, but seem to be converging again in the recent years. This characterization does not appear to be applicable to non-emerging market economies (non-EMG) in Asia, as shown in Figure 21.3 panel (b), or in Latin America, (Figure 21.3, [c]). For non-EMG economies in Asia or non-Asian developing economies, convergence in the trilemma configurations seems to be the case in the last decade.

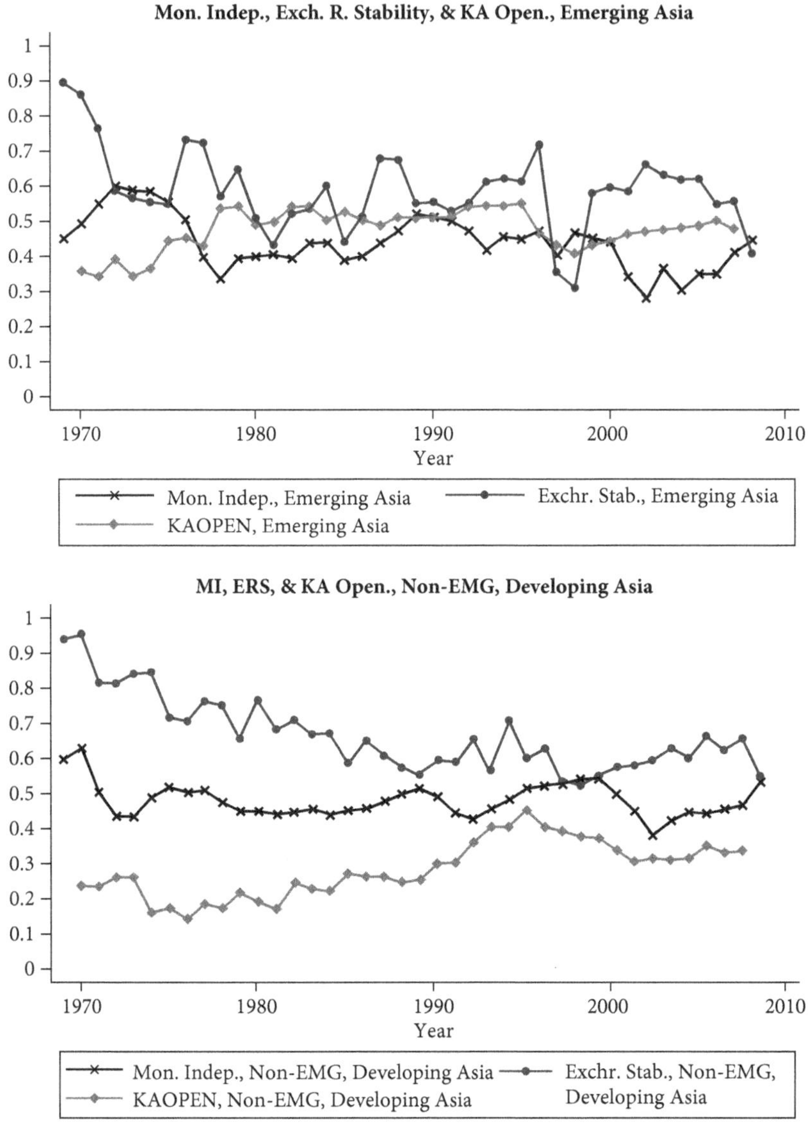


FIGURE 21.3 Regional Comparison of the Development of the Trilemma Configurations (a) Emerging Market Economies (EMG) in Asia (b) Non-EMG, Developing Asia (c) Latin American Countries (d) Less-Developed Countries (LDC) excluding Asia

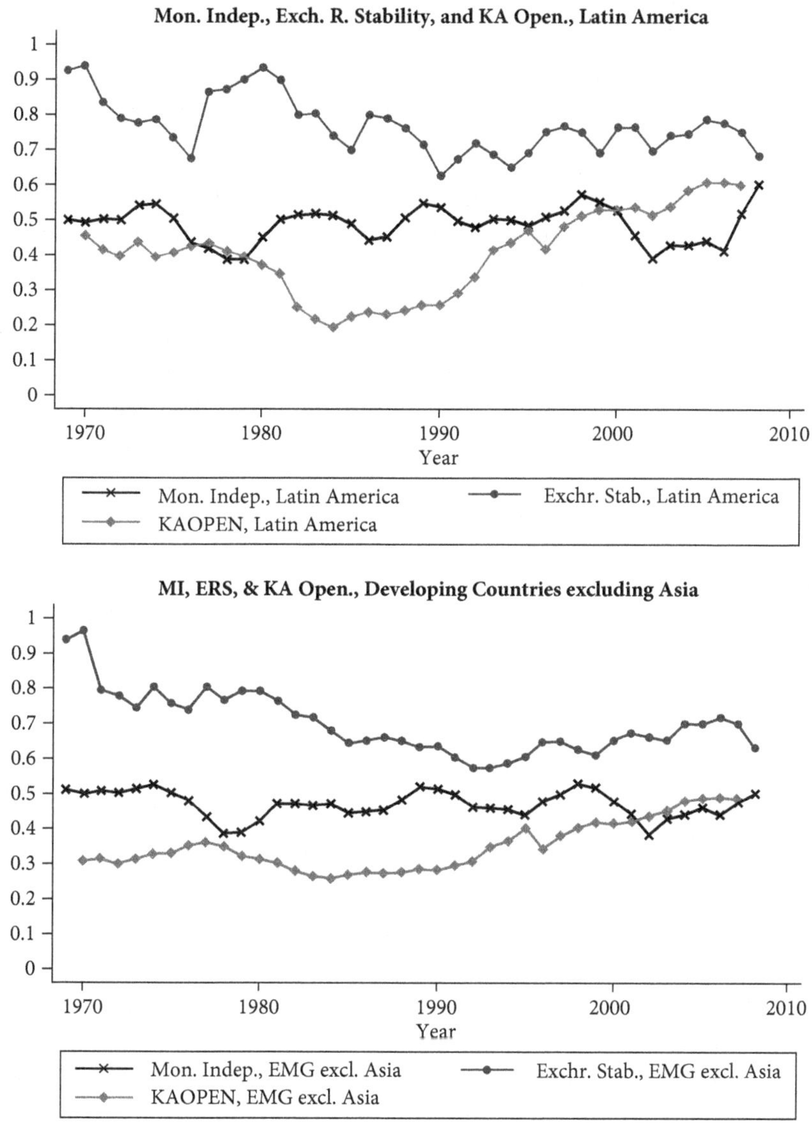


FIGURE 21.3 Continued

## 21.3 Linear Relationships of the Trilemma Indexes

While the preceding analyses are quite useful for tracing out the evolution of international macroeconomic policy orientation, we have not demonstrated whether these three macroeconomic policy goals are "binding" in the sense of the impossible trinity. That is, it is important for us to provide evidence that countries have faced the trade-offs based on the trilemma. A challenge facing a full test of the trilemma tradeoff is that the trilemma framework does not impose any obvious functional form on the nature of the tradeoffs between the three trilemma variables. To illustrate this concern, we must note that the instrument scarcity association with the trilemma implies that increasing one trilemma variable, say higher financial integration, should induce lower exchange rate stability, or lower monetary independence, or a combination of these two policy adjustments.[9] Hence, we test the validity of the simplest possible trilemma specification—a linear tradeoff. Specifically, we test whether the weighted sum of the three trilemma policy variables equals a constant. This reduces to examining the goodness of fit of this linear regression:

$$1 = a_j MI_{i,t} + b_j ERS_{i,t} + c_j KAOPEN_{i,t} + \varepsilon_{i,t} \quad (1)$$

where $j$ can be either IDC, ERM, or LDC.

Because we have shown that different subsample groups of countries have experienced different development paths, we allow the coefficients on all the variables to vary across different groups of countries—industrialized countries, the countries that have been in the European Exchange Rate Mechanism (ERM), and developing countries—by allowing for interactions between the explanatory variables and the dummies for these subsamples.[10] The regression is run for the full sample period as well as the subsample periods that are divided by major economic event and crises, i.e., the collapse of the Bretton Woods system in 1973, the Mexican debt crisis of 1982, and the Asian crisis of 1997-1998. The results are reported in Table 21.1.

The rationale behind this exercise is that policymakers of an economy must choose a weighted average of the three policies in order to achieve a best combination of the two. Hence, if we can find the goodness of fit for the above regression model is high, it would suggest a linear specification is rich enough to explain the trade-off among the three policy dimensions. In other words, the lower the goodness of fit, the weaker the support for the existence of the trade-off, suggesting either that the theory of the trilemma is wrong, or that the relationship is non-linear.

Secondly, the estimated coefficients in the above regression model should give us some approximate estimates of the weights countries put on the three policy goals.

However, the estimated coefficients alone will not provide sufficient information about "how much of" the policy choice countries have actually implemented. Hence, looking into the predictions using the estimated coefficients and the actual values for the variables (such as $\hat{a}MI$, $\hat{b}ERS$, and $\hat{c}KAOPEN$) will be more informative.

Thirdly, by comparing the predicted values based on the above regression, i.e., $\hat{a}MI + \hat{b}ERS + \hat{c}KAOPEN$, over a time horizon, we can get some inferences about how "binding" the trilemma is. If the trilemma is found to be linear constraint, the predicted values should hover around the value of 1, and the prediction errors should indicate how much of the three policy choices have been "not fully used" or to what extent the trilemma is "not binding."

Table 1 presents the regression results. The results from the regression with the full sample data are reported in the first column, and the others for different subsample periods are in the following columns. First of all, the adjusted R-squared for the full sample model as well as for the subsample periods is found to be above 95 percent, which indicates that the three policy goals are linearly related to each other, that is, countries face the trade-off among the three policy options. Across different time periods, the estimated coefficients vary, suggesting that the nature of the tradeoffs varies, either because of changes in the governments' objective functions, or the changing nature of the economies.

Figure 21.4 illustrates the goodness of fit from a different angle. In panel (a) as well as in panel (b), the solid lines show the means of the predicted values (i.e., $\hat{a}MI + \hat{b}ERS + \hat{c}KAOPEN$) based on the full sample model in the first column of Table 21.1 for the groups of industrial countries (top) and developing countries (bottom).[11] To incorporate the time variation of the predictions, the subsample mean of the prediction values as well as their 95 percent confidence intervals (that are shown as the shaded areas) are calculated using five-year rolling windows. [12] The panels also display the rolling means of the predictions using the coefficients and actual values of only two of the three trilemma terms— $\hat{a}MI + \hat{b}ERS$, $\hat{a}MI + \hat{c}KAOPEN$, $\hat{b}ERS + \hat{c}KAOPEN$. The regression results allow a simple description of the changing ranking of policy combinations (of the two out of the three trilemma policy goals) over time.

From these panels of figures, we can first see that the predicted values based on the model hover around the value of one closely for both subsamples. For the group of industrial countries, the prediction average is statistically below the value of one in the late 1970s through the beginning of the 1990s. However, since then, one cannot reject the null hypothesis that the mean of the prediction values is one, indicating that the trilemma is "binding" for industrialized countries. For developing countries, the model is under-predicting from the end of the 1970s through the late 1990s. However, unlike the IDC group, the mean of the predictions becomes statistically smaller than one in the early 2000s and goes back to around the value of one in the last few years of the sample period. More importantly, for both subsamples, the mean of the predictions never rises above the value of one in statistical sense, implying not only that the three macroeconomic policies are linearly related with each other, but also that countries have never implemented an infeasible combination of policies. [13]

**Table 21.1 Regression for the Linear Relationship between the Trilemma Indexes:** $1 = a_j MI_{i,t} + b_j ERS_{i,t} + c_j KAOPEN_{i,t} + \varepsilon_{i,t}$

| | (1) FULL | (2) 1970–72 | (3) 1974–81 | (4) 1983–96 | (5) 1999–2010 |
|---|---|---|---|---|---|
| Monetary Independence | 1.084 | 0.932 | 1.354 | 0.970 | 0.708 |
| | (0.040)*** | (0.132)*** | (0.068)*** | (0.065)*** | (0.128)*** |
| Exch. Rate Stability | 0.568 | 0.640 | 0.582 | 0.665 | 0.077 |
| | (0.030)*** | (0.075)*** | (0.084)*** | (0.050)*** | (0.081) |
| KA Openness | 0.457 | 0.398 | 0.295 | 0.415 | 0.817 |
| | (0.020)*** | (0.047)*** | (0.062)*** | (0.033)*** | (0.056)*** |
| ERM x MI | -0.175 | - | 0.356 | -0.232 | -0.379 |
| | (0.073)** | - | (0.343) | (0.119)* | (0.150)** |
| ERM x ERS | -0.024 | - | 0.299 | 0.024 | 0.017 |
| | (0.053) | - | (0.189) | (0.075) | (0.080) |
| ERM x KAOPEN | 0.013 | - | -0.282 | 0.041 | 0.094 |
| | (0.049) | - | (0.131)** | (0.057) | (0.058) |
| LDC x MI | 0.149 | 0.532 | -0.102 | 0.364 | 0.333 |
| | (0.045)*** | (0.163)*** | (0.095) | (0.070)*** | (0.132)** |
| LDC x ERS | -0.151 | -0.398 | -0.142 | -0.254 | 0.399 |
| | (0.033)*** | (0.091)*** | (0.091) | (0.053)*** | (0.079)*** |
| LDC x KAOPEN | -0.185 | -0.222 | -0.082 | -0.144 | -0.485 |
| | (0.027)*** | (0.075)*** | (0.080) | (0.048)*** | (0.064)*** |
| Adjusted R-squared | 0.95 | 0.98 | 0.95 | 0.96 | 0.96 |
| Observations | 2,450 | 180 | 480 | 840 | 710 |

*Notes:* Robust standard errors in brackets * significant at 10 percent; ** significant at 5 percent; *** significant at 1 percent. The dummy for ERM countries is assigned for the countries and years that corresponds to participation in the ERM (i.e., Belgium, Germany, France, Ireland, Italy, and Luxembourg from 1979 on; Spain from 1989; U.K. only for 1990–91; Portugal from 1992; Austria from 1995; Finland from 1996; and Denmark and Greece from 1999) or ERM II (Estonia, Lithuania, and Slovenia from 2004; and Cyprus, Latvia, Malta, and Slovak Rep. from 2005).

The top panels also show that, among industrialized countries, the policy combination of increasing exchange rate stability and more financial openness became increasingly prevalent after the beginning of the 1990s, whereas that of monetary independence and exchange rate stability has been consistently declining over the years. Among developing countries, the policy combination of exchange rate stability and financial openness has been the least prevalent over the sample period, most probably reflecting the bitter experiences of currency crises. The policy combinations of monetary independence and

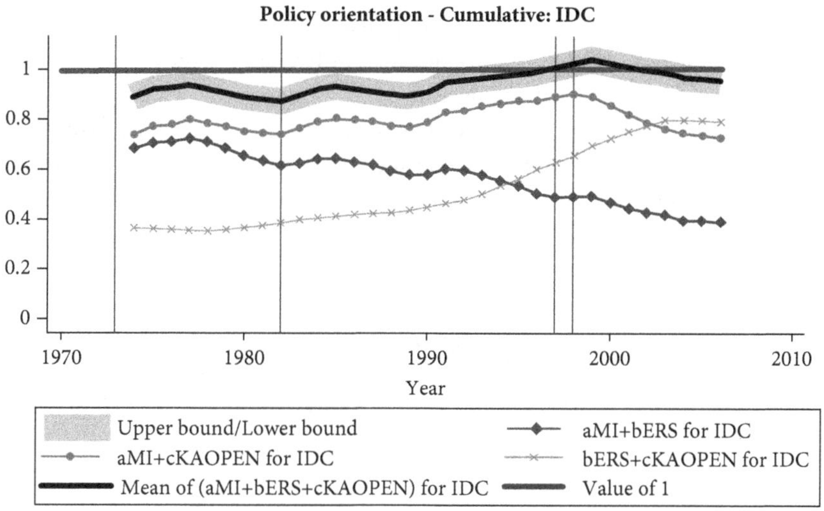


Note: The vertical lines correspond to the candidate break years.
The shaded areas indicate the 95% confidence interval for aMI+bERS+cKAOPEN.

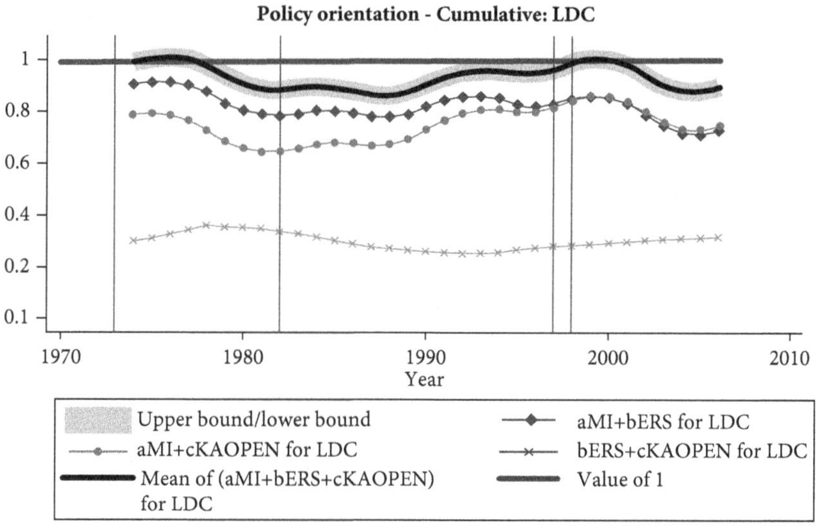


Note: The vertical lines correspond to the candidate break years.
The shaded areas indicate the 95% confidence interval for aMI+bERS+cKAOPEN.

FIGURE 21.4 Policy Orientation of IDCs and LDCs.
Cumulative Effects:

$(\hat{a}MI + \hat{b}ERS), (\hat{a}MI + \hat{c}KAOPEN), (\hat{b}ERS + \hat{c}KAOPEN)$, and $(\hat{a}MI + \hat{b}ERS + \hat{c}KAOPEN)$

(a) Industrial Countries (b) Developing Countries

financial openness or that of monetary independence and exchange rate stability has been quite dominant, but that is mainly because of the dominant preference for monetary independence through the time period.

We also repeat the exercise using the regression models for each of the subsample period (excluding the break years corresponding to the end of the Bretton Woods system and the two crises). The results (not reported) are qualitatively the same as in Figure 21.4.

# 21.4 Further Look into the "Middle-Ground" Convergence

Now that we have empirical evidence for the theoretical validity of the indexes, let us take a closer look at the distribution of the indexes. We pay particular attention to the tendency of the "middle-ground convergence"—a tendency that the indexes cluster around the intermediate levels for all three policy choices—especially among emerging market economies.

## 21.4.1 The Index of Policy Convergence

To see how much convergence is taking place, we calculate a new variable that measures the extent of divergence in all three trilemma indexes. The measure of triad policy divergence $d_{it}$ is calculated as follows:

$$d_{it} = \sqrt{(mi\_r_{it} - 1)^2 + (ers\_r_{it} - 1)^2 + (ka\_r_{it} - 1)^2}$$

where $X\_r_{it} = X_{it} / \overline{X}_t$ for $X = MI, ERS,$ and $KAOPEN$, and $\overline{X}_t$ is cross-country average of $X$ in year $t$. Here, we can consider $d_{it}$ as the measure of dispersion in all three policies in a particular year. The higher the $d_{it}$ is, the more dispersion among the three indexes in a particular year we can expect for country $i$, meaning that country $i$ tends to have a combination of distinctively different triad policies. In terms of the triangle shown in Figure 21.1, a country with a higher $d_{it}$ is considered to be closer to one of the corners or the sides of the triangle whereas a lower $d_{it}$ represents a policy combination closer to the middle of the triangle (see Aizenman and Ito 2012).

Figure 21.5 illustrates the average of $d_{it}$ for different subgroups of countries based on income levels. Essentially, this figure allows us to observe Figure 21.2 from a different perspective.

We can make several interesting observations based on this figure. For the last two decades, advanced economies tend to have combinations of distinctive policies. Not surprisingly, the Euro country group has the highest degree of policy divergence among the country groups, followed by the group of non-Euro advanced economies. As we have observed in Figure 21.2, the group of emerging market economies has had the lowest degree of policy convergence in the last two decades. Since the beginning of the 1980s, developing economies, whether or not with emerging markets, have had relatively stable movement in the degree of policy convergence except for the mid-1990s when both subgroups of developing economies experienced a drop in the degree of policy divergence. In the crisis years of 1982, 1997–1998, and 2008–2009—the Mexican debt crisis, the Asian financial crisis, and the global financial crisis, respectively—interestingly, the policy convergence measure tends to fall in the years prior to the crisis years.

To see what is driving the trajectories in Figure 21.5, we look at the group mean of the ratios of each of the three indexes to its cross-country mean. We focus on developing economies and report the average ratios for emerging market economies and non-emerging market developing economies in Figures 21.6 and 21.7, respectively.

These figures show clear differences between emerging market economies and non-emerging market developing economies. First, from the beginning of the sample period through the end of the 1990s, it is exchange rate stability that non-emerging market developing economies have prioritized. In the same period, emerging market economies, on the other hand, have pursued monetary independence. Second, despite the prevalent anecdotal view that emerging market economies have pursued greater exchange rate stability, exchange rate stability has not been given the first priority over

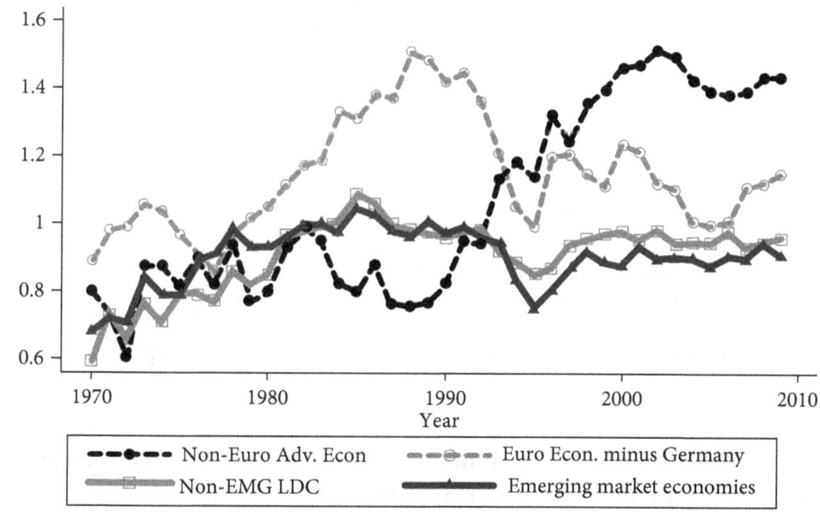


Note: "Euro economies" include Austria, Beligium, France, Italy, Netherlands, Finland, Greece, Ireland, Portugal, and Spain

FIGURE 21.5 Degree of Policy Dispersions among Different Income Groups of Countries

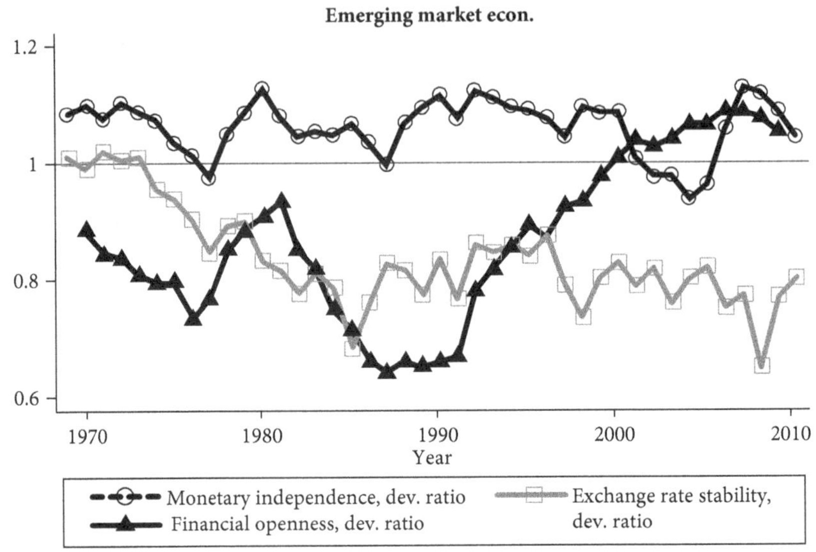


FIGURE 21.6 Deviations from the Means—Emerging Market Economies

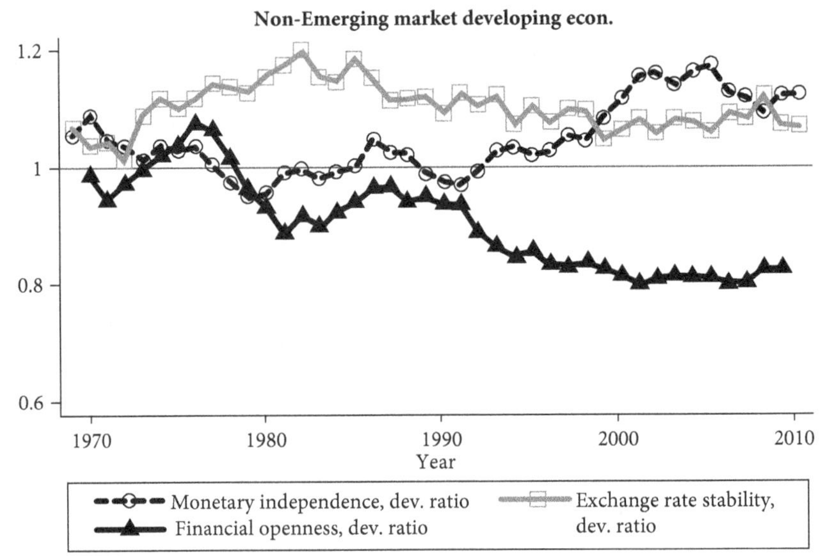


FIGURE 21.7 Deviations from the Means—Non-Emerging Market Developing Economies

the sample period. Third, most distinctively from the non-emerging market group, emerging market economies have increased the extent of financial openness very rapidly in the last two decades. Fourth, while the role of retaining monetary independence has been increasing for non-emerging market developing economies in the first half of the 2000s, the opposite is true for emerging market economies. However, facing the global financial crisis of 2008–2009, emerging market economies rapidly regained monetary independence.

We are also curious to see if there are any regional characteristics in the formation of triad open macro policies. Externality can play a role in concerting policy decision makings among neighboring countries in a region. Plus, there can be a regional economic integration such as the case of East Asian supply chain network. Figure 21.8 illustrates the averages of the policy dispersion measure ($d_{it}$) for different regional country groups.

One interesting observation we can make is that both Asian emerging market economies and countries in the middle east and northern Africa experienced high levels of policy divergence from the beginning of the 1980s through the early 1990s. This is mainly because the countries in both regional groups achieved higher levels of financial opening compared to the average of developing economies.[14] More interestingly, since the last few years of the 1990s, which coincides with the Asian Crisis period, the degrees of policy divergence have been persistently small among all regional groups. This policy convergence among developing economies may reflect the great moderation, but the convergence seems to be still in place in the last few years of the sample despite the global financial crisis. Lastly, despite its high levels of policy divergence in the 1980s, emerging market economies in Asia have been experiencing lowest levels of policy divergence. Aizenman, Chinn, and Ito (2011) examined econometrically how the triad open macro policy combinations can affect macroeconomic performances such as output growth and volatility, inflation, and inflation volatility. They concluded that the policy combinations implemented by emerging market economies in Asia have allowed these economies to experience low levels of output volatility. The figures here suggest

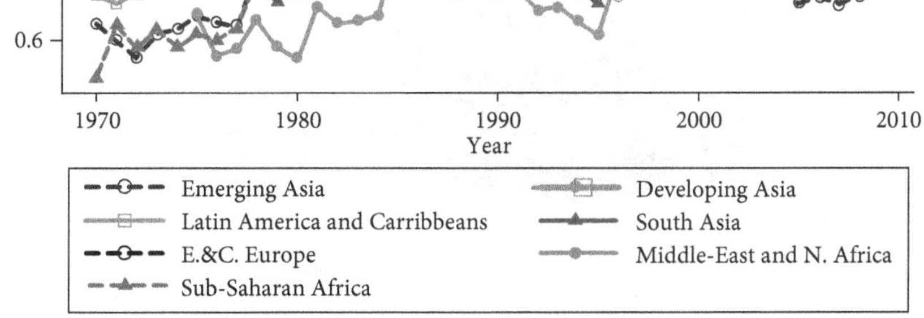


Note: "Emerging Asia" include China, Hong Kong, Korea, Indonesia, Thailand, Malaysia, Philippines, and Singapore

FIGURE 21.8 Degree of Policy Dispersions among Different Regional Country Groups that the "middle-ground convergence" of the triad open macro policies may also have contributed to the stability of these economies' output performances.[15]

## 21.4.2 Effect of Policy Convergence

Given that Asian emerging market economies, as well as developing economies in general, were barely affected by the global financial crisis of 2008-2009, the high degree of policy convergence we observe for developing economies, especially emerging market economies, may have also contributed to more stable output performances of developing economies. We focus on this issue in this subsection.

An economy with its triad open macro policies clustered around the intermediate levels, as is the case with many emerging market economies, may be able to retain stability in its output performance. By avoiding a policy combination of distinctive choices among the three open macro policies, the economy may be able to dampen the negative aspects of each of the three policy choices we discussed in a previous section. If that is true, we can expect smaller the $d_{it}$'s to be correlated with smaller output volatilities.

Figure 21.9 displays a scatter diagram for the correlation between five-year standard deviations of per capita output growth (in local currency) and the five-year average of the policy divergence measure $d$ for non-overlapping five-year panels from 1970 through 2009. The gray triangles are for the group of non-emerging market developing economies whereas the black diamonds are for emerging market economies. Both subsamples have slightly positive correlation coefficients as our prior suggested, but the coefficients are insignificant.

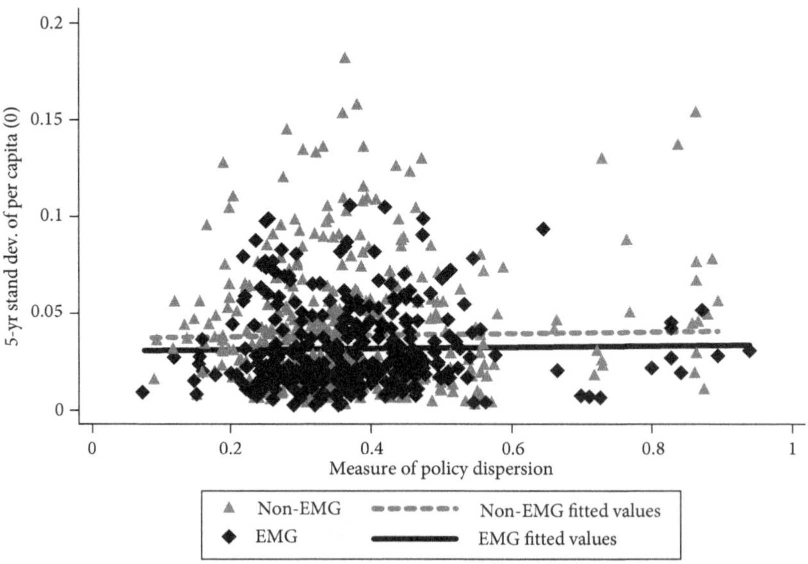


FIGURE 21.9 Correlations between Policy Dispersion and Output Volatility: EMG vs. Non-EMG

For the last two decades, some of the developing economies have been actively opening up their financial markets. One other conjecture we can make is that countries may try to have a smaller degree of policy divergence to be prepared for potential negative consequences of financial liberalization. If that is true, more financially open economies may experience smaller output volatility when they adopt a policy combination with smaller policy divergence. Let us see if the data are consistent with this conjecture.

Figure 21.10 again illustrates the correlation between output volatility and the measure of policy divergence, but now the sample is divided into two groups: financial open economies and financial closed economies. A country is categorized as a financial open economy if its measure of financial openness is greater than the median of the measure among developing economies in a particular year. Financially open economies are shown in black diamonds and financially closed economies are in gray triangles. As we suspected, financially open economies have a positive, but insignificant, correlation between output volatility and policy dispersion whereas financially closed economies have a slightly negative, insignificant correlation. The statistical significance of the positive correlation is lower than that of the negative correlation.

What if we focus on the time period when developing economies, especially those with emerging markets, have been actively liberalizing financial markets? Figure 21.11 is a recreation of Figure 21.9, but we now restrict the sample to the 1990-2009 period. We see a clear difference between emerging market economies and non-emerging market economies. Emerging market economies with lower levels of policy dispersion measure tend to experience lower levels of output volatility—the correlation coefficient is significant with a conventional significance level. Non-emerging market economies,

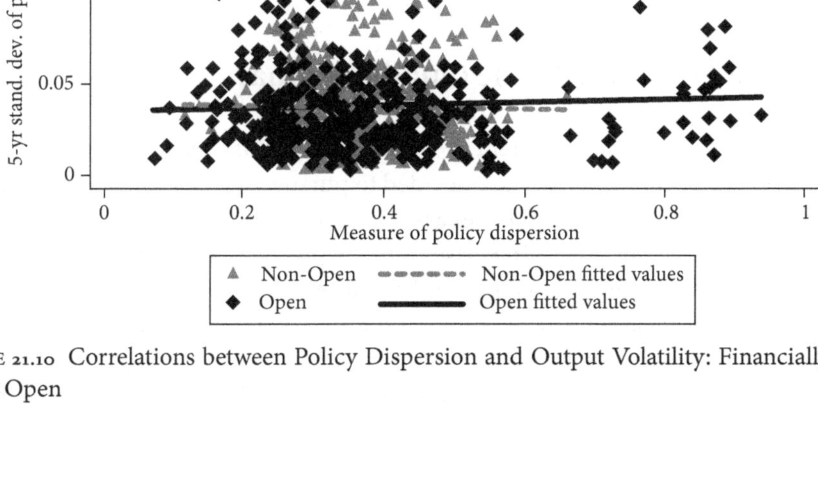


FIGURE 21.10 Correlations between Policy Dispersion and Output Volatility: Financially Open vs. Not Open

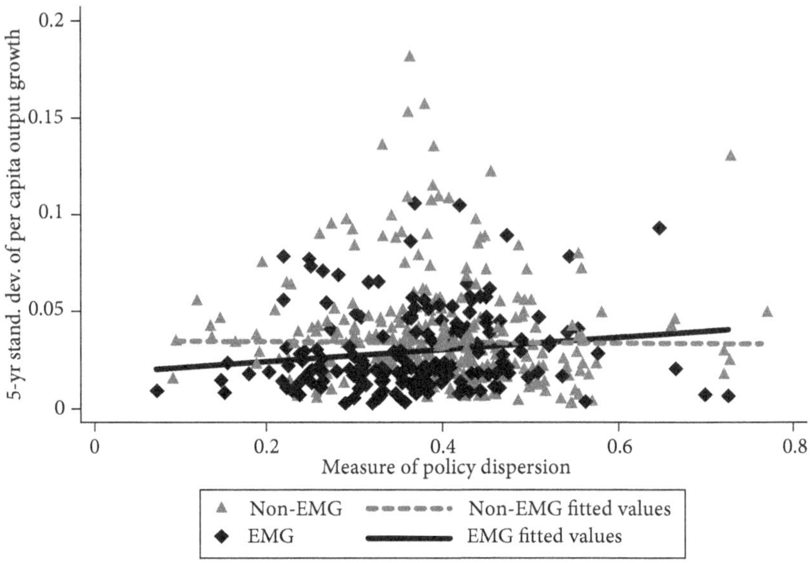


FIGURE 21.11 Correlations between Policy Dispersion and Output Volatility: EMG vs. Non-EMG since 1990

on the other hand, tend to experience *higher* levels of output volatility if they pursue lower levels of policy dispersion though the correlation coefficient is insignificant. It appears that emerging market economies have dealt with financial globalization better than non-emerging market developing economies by having more converged policy combinations.

Figure 21.12 is a re-creation of Figure 21.10, but focuses on emerging market economies in the 1990-2009 period. Emerging market countries without open financial markets have a significantly positive and high correlation between policy convergence and output volatility, while those with open financial markets have an insignificantly positive correlation (with a smaller magnitude). This result can be counter-intuitive for those who believe that an economy can experience a turbulence if it pursues greater financial openness and a more distinctively divergent policy combination.

## 21.4.3 The Trilemma to the Quadrilemma?

Open macroeconomic management is never an easy task especially for developing countries. Those economies that have decided to pursue greater financial openness have to be prepared for financial turbulences associated with sudden stops of inflows of capital, capital flights, and deleveraging crises. One byproduct of pursuit for greater financial openness while retaining financial and economic stability is rapid accumulation of international reserves among developing economies. As many researchers have pointed out, developing countries, especially emerging market economies, have increased the amount of international reserves holding significantly in recent years. While the

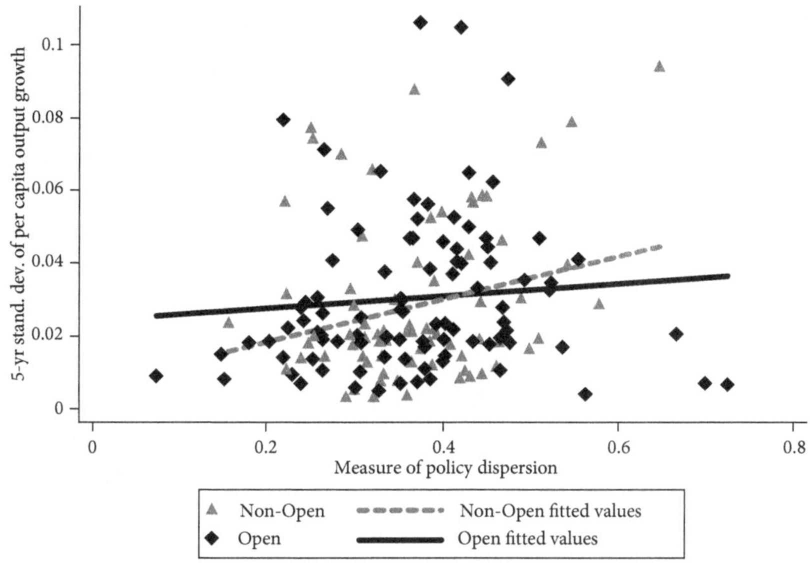


FIGURE 21.12 Financially Open vs. Not Open Since 1990

international reserves/GDP ratio of industrial countries was overall stable, hovering below 10 percent, the reserves/GDP ratio of developing countries increased dramatically, close to tripling in 25 years. By 2007, about two-thirds of the global international reserves were held by developing countries. Most of this increase has been in Asia. The most dramatic changes occurred in the China, increasing its reserve/GDP from below 5 percent in 1980, to about 50 percent in 2009. As has been widely discussed, a rapid increase in international reserves holding, especially in Asia, started in the post-Asian crisis period, suggesting that insurance motives are one of the motivations for developing economies to hold massive international reserves (Aizenman and Marion 2004).[16]

Before financial liberalization became more of a general trend for developing countries in the 1990s, the demand for reserves provided self-insurance almost merely against volatile trade flows. However, as financial liberalization efforts created externality among developing countries, leading to abundant but volatile capital flows across countries, countries started finding a strong need to self-insure against volatile financial flows. By the nature of financial markets, the exposure to rapidly increasing demands for foreign currency triggered by financial volatility exceeds by a wide margin the one triggered by trade volatility. The East Asian crisis was a watershed event, as it impacted high-saving countries with overall balanced fiscal accounts. These countries were viewed as being less exposed to sudden stop events as compared with other developing countries prior to the crisis. With a lag, the affected countries reacted by massive increases in their stock of reserves.

Recent studies validate the importance of "financial factors" as key determinants, in addition to the traditional trade factors, in accounting for increased international reserves/GDP ratios. Indeed, recent research has revealed that the role of financial factors has increased in tandem with growing financial integration. More financially open, financially deep countries, with greater exchange rate stability, tend to hold more reserves. Within the emerging market sample, the fixed exchange rate effect is weaker, but financial depth (measured by M2/GDP) is highly significant and growing in importance over time (Cheung and Ito 2009, Obstfeld et al. 2010). Trade openness is the other robust determinant of reserve demand, though its importance seems to have diminished over time (Cheung and Ito 2009). The growing importance of financial factors helps in accounting for a greater share of the international reserves/GDP ratios (Aizenman and Lee 2007). These results are in line with a broader self-insurance view, where reserves provide a buffer, both against deleveraging initiated by foreign parties, and against the sudden wish of domestic residents to acquire new external assets. That is, developing countries often face "sudden capital flight" (Calvo 1998, 2006; Aizenman and Lee 2007) in the form of "double drains" or "external and internal drains" (Obstfeld et al. 2009).[17]

All these issues suggest that developing countries may need to manage their open macro policies on the basis of the "quadrilemma" rather than the trilemma.

The "diamond charts" in Figure 21.13 are useful to trace the changing patterns of the "quadrilemma" configurations. Each country's configuration at a given instant is summarized by a "generalized diamond," whose four vertices measure monetary independence, exchange rate stability, International Reserves/GDP ratio, and financial integration. The origin has been normalized so as to represent zero monetary independence, pure float, zero international reserves, and financial autarky. The panels of figures summarize the trends for industrialized economies, emerging Asian economies, non-emerging market developing Asian economies, non-Asian developing economies, and Latin American emerging market economies.

In Figure 21.13, we can observe again the divergence of the trilemma configurations for the industrial economies over the years—a move toward deeper financial integration, greater exchange rate stability, and weaker monetary independence—while reducing the level of IR holding over years. Asia, especially those economies with emerging markets, appears distinct from other groups of economies; the middle-ground convergence observed for the emerging market group is quite evident for this particular group of economies. Again, however, this is not a recent phenomenon for the Asian emerging market economies. Since as early as the 1980s, the three indexes have been clustered around the middle range, though exchange rate stability has been the most pervasive policy choice and the degree of monetary independence has been gradually declining. This characterization is not applicable to the other groups of developing economies such as Latin American emerging market economies. Most importantly, the group of Asian emerging market economies stands out from the others with their sizable and rapidly increasing amount of IR holding, making one suspect potential implications of such IR holdings on trilemma policy choices and macroeconomic performances.

Aizenman et al. (2010) empirically show that pursuing greater exchange stability can be increasing output volatility for developing economies, but that that can be mitigated

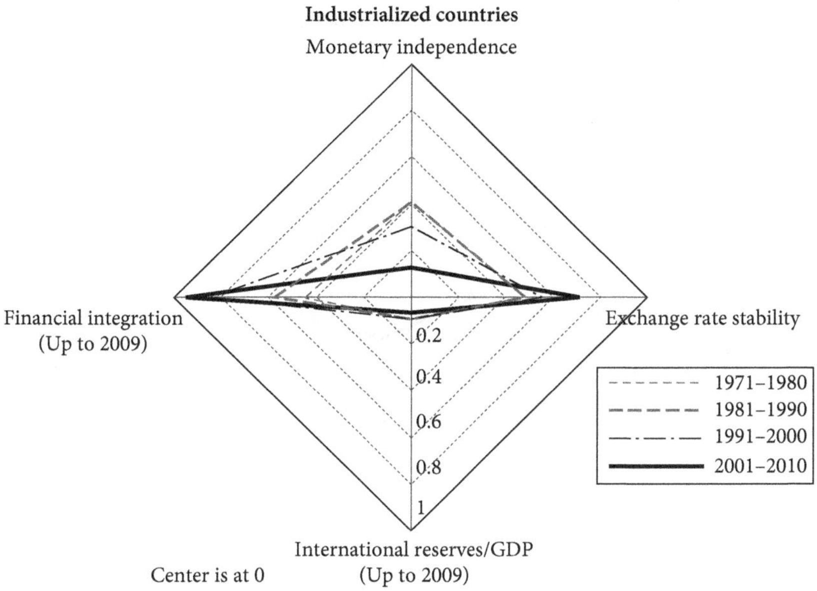


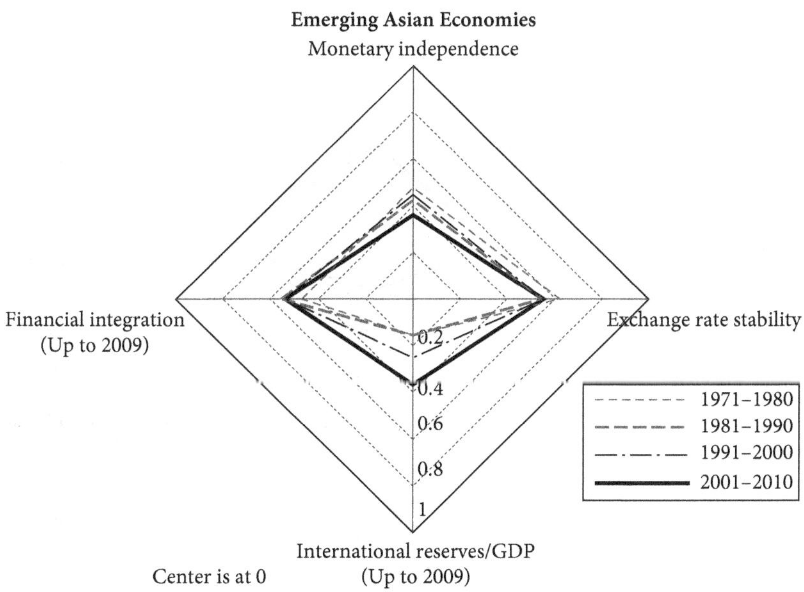


FIGURE 21.13 The "Diamond Charts": Variation of the "Quadrilemma" across Different Country Groups

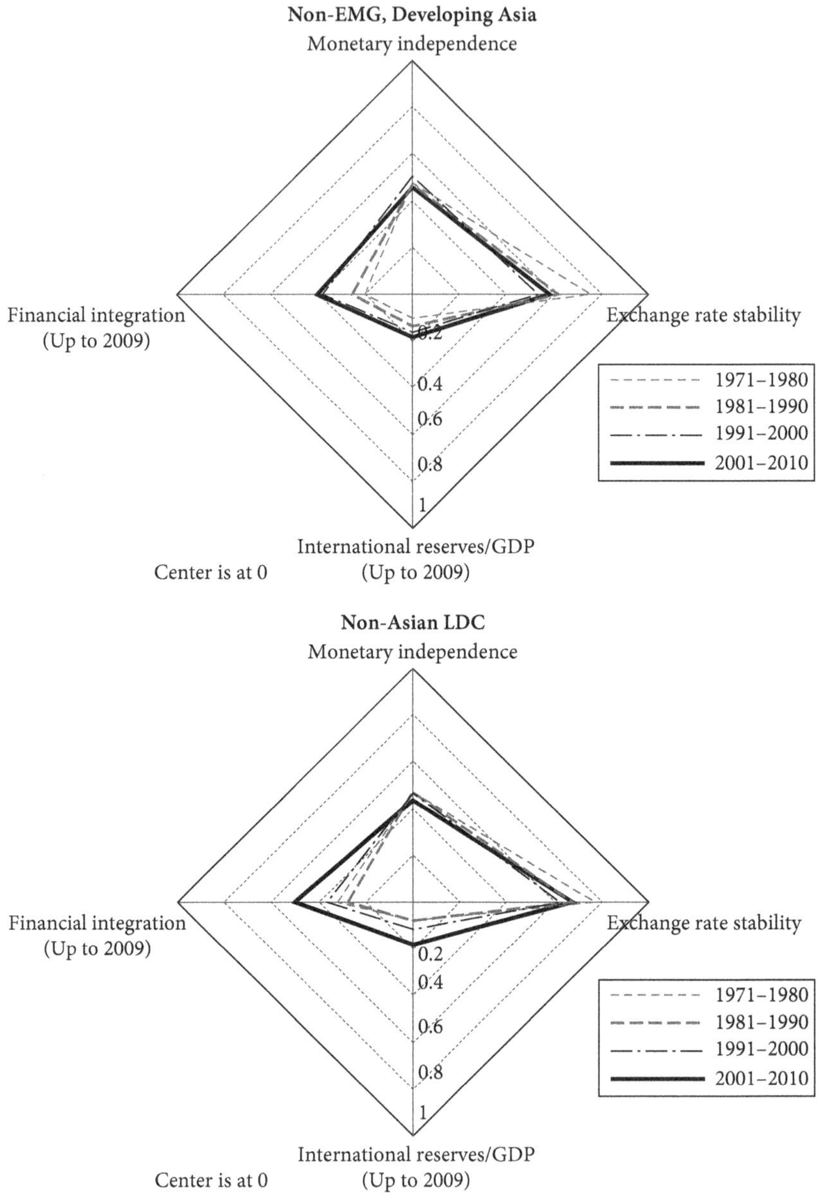


FIGURE 21.13 Continued

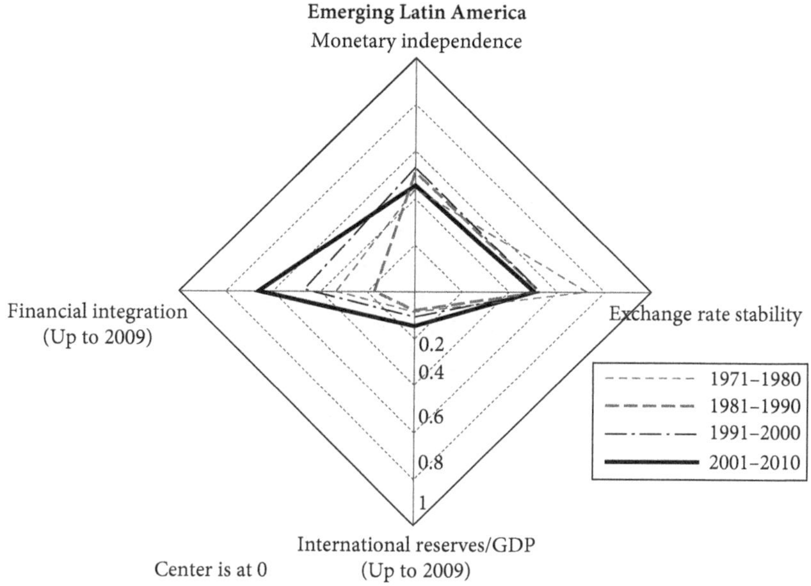


FIGURE 21.13 Continued

by holding a greater amount of international reserves than the threshold of about 20 percent of GDP. Aizenman et al. (2011) find that emerging market economies seem to have adopted a policy combination of the three trilemma policies and international reserves that allow these economies to lessen output volatility through reduced real exchange volatility. Thus, it is not surprising for developing economies to have become active in accumulating international reserves in recent years.

Lastly, let us examine the impact of holding international reserves in the context of policy convergence. Figure 21.14 again displays a scatter diagram for the correlation between output volatility and the measure of policy divergence for emerging market economies in the 1990–2009 period. The sample is divided into two subgroups: one composed of emerging market economies that hold international reserves more than the annual median level among developing countries and the other of those economies with reserves lower than the median. Those emerging market economies with lower levels of international reserves have a significantly positive correlation, while those with higher levels of reserves have an insignificantly negative association. One interpretation of this result is that holding high levels of international reserves may give countries a wider choice for the degree of policy divergence. For countries with low international reserves, it is better to have more convergence, but high-reserve holders do not face the same kind of trade-off.

What if we restrict the sample to those emerging market economies that have more open financial markets? Figure 21.15 is the same as Figure 21.14, except that the sample is now restricted to only emerging market economies with more open financial markets ("open" as defined in Figure 21.10). Figure 21.15 illustrates that emerging market

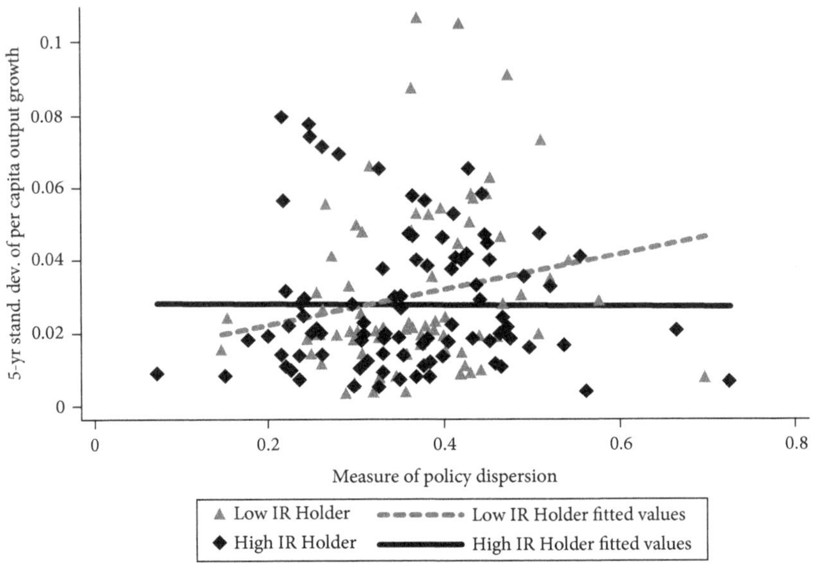


FIGURE 21.14 EMGs with and without High IR Holding since 1990

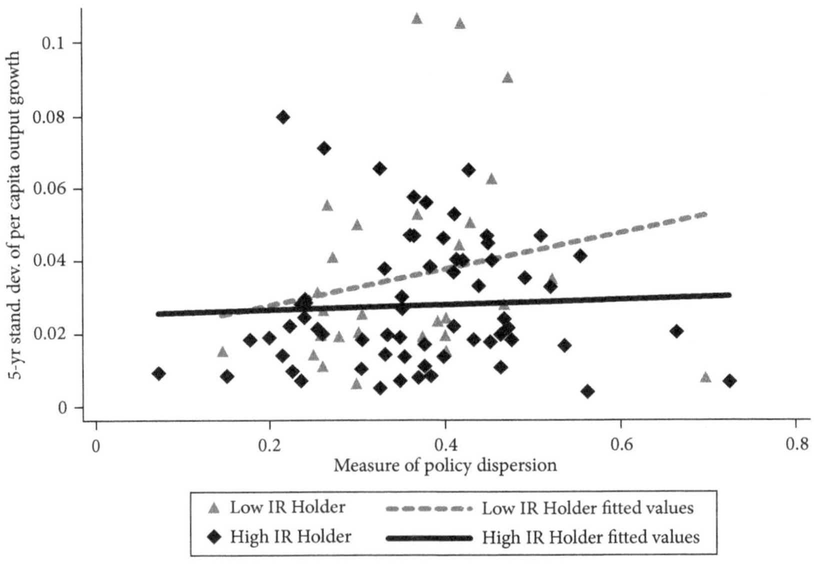


FIGURE 21.15 EMGs w/ Open Financial Markets and High IR Holding vs. Those w/ Open Financial Market, but w/ Low IR Holdings

economies with more open financial markets may face higher levels of output volatility if they pursue higher degrees of policy divergence but do not hold high levels of international reserves, though the positive association is not statistically significant. For emerging market economies with more open financial markets and high levels of international reserves, the level of policy divergence does not seem to have an effect on output volatility levels.

Having seen these results, we can conclude not only that the tendency for emerging market economies to have more converged policy combinations help them to experience lower levels of output volatility, but also that holding a higher level of international reserves may help them to get prepared for a future choice of policies that are more distinctively different from each other.

Now that we know holding high levels of IR may allow countries to have a wider range of policy divergence than those without and may help those with wider policy divergence to avoid experiencing higher output volatility, we wonder how emerging market economies performed during the global financial crisis of 2008-2009. Although the epicenter of the crisis was not in any emerging market economies but in the advanced economies (mostly the United States), emerging market economies could have been exposed to contagion from the crisis. However, except for a few emerging market economies in Eastern Europe, most of emerging market economies were barely affected by the crisis. In such circumstances, we wonder what was the role of international reserves holding for emerging market economies.

Figures 21.16 and 21.17 are helpful to answer this question. Figure 21.16 shows the correlation between output volatility and the degree of policy divergence for the group of

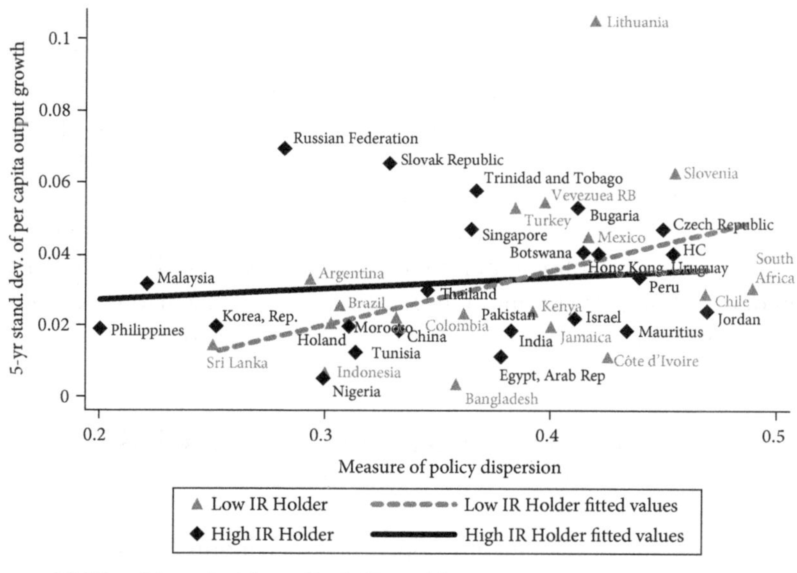


FIGURE 21.16 EMGs with and without High IR Holding in 2005–09

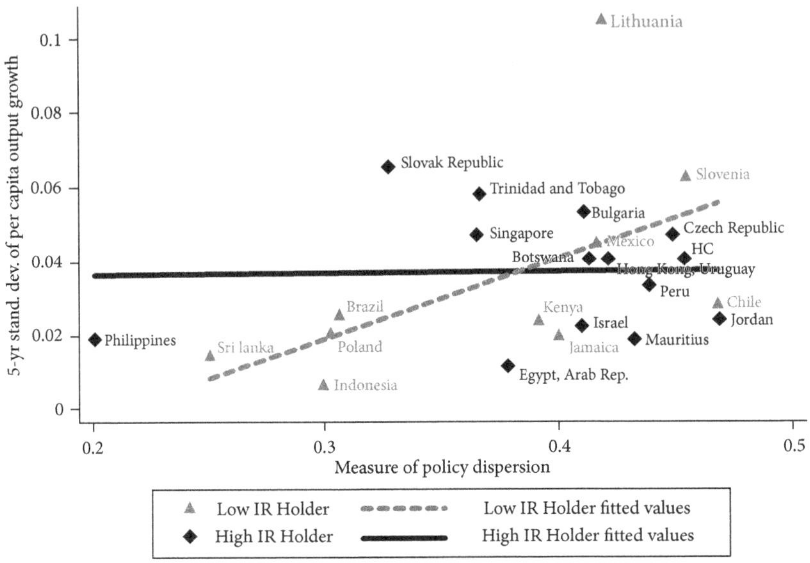


FIGURE 21.17 EMGs with Open Financial Markets and with and without High IR Holding in 2005–09

emerging market economies but only for the five-year period of 2005 through 2009, which corresponds to the years prior to and during the global financial crisis. In the figure, we see again that the correlation is weaker for the countries that hold higher levels of international reserves—while the correlation is significantly positive for the low IR holders with a conventional significance level, that for the high IR holders is small and insignificant.[18]

The effect of holding IR should be greater for those economies with more open financial markets. Hence, we restrict our sample to only those economies with more open financial markets (as defined previously) and show the result in Figure 21.17. The result is clear; those economies which do not hold high levels of IR experienced higher levels of output volatility if they have trilemma policy combinations with a greater degree of divergence.[19] The high IR holders on average do not face such a positive correlation. Compared to Figure 21.16, the magnitude of the correlation is higher, suggesting that countries with more open financial markets and higher degrees of policy divergence would have to face higher levels of output volatility if they do not hold high levels of IR. With these results, high levels of IR holding may be one of the reasons for emerging market economies to be able to avoid contagion from the outbreak of the global financial crisis.

## 21.5 Concluding Remarks

We have examined the development of open macroeconomic policy choices among developing economies from the perspective of the powerful hypothesis of the "trilemma"—a country may not simultaneously pursue the full extent of achievement in all of the three policy goals of monetary independence, exchange rate stability, and financial openness. Using the metrics introduced by Aizenman, Chinn, and Ito (2010), or the "trilemma indexes," that measure the extent of achievement in each of the three policy choices, we have observed several interesting characteristics of the international monetary system.

There are striking differences in the choices that industrialized and developing countries have made over the 1970–2009 period. More importantly, recent trends suggest that among developing countries, the three dimensions of the trilemma configurations are converging toward a "middle ground" with managed exchange rate flexibility, underpinned by sizable holdings of international reserves and intermediate levels of monetary independence and financial integration. Industrialized countries, on the other hand, have been experiencing divergence of the three dimensions of the trilemma and have moved toward the combination of high exchange rate stability, financial openness, and low monetary independence (most clearly exemplified by the advent of the euro).

To ensure the validity of the results based on the trilemma indexes, we also tested whether the three macroeconomic policy goals are "binding" in the context of the impossible trinity, by estimating the nature of the trade-offs faced by countries. Because there is no specific functional form of the trade-offs or the linkage of these three policy goals, we estimated the simplest linear specification for the three trilemma indexes and examined whether the weighted sum of the three trilemma policy variables equals a constant. Our results confirmed that countries do face a binding trilemma. That is, a change in one of the trilemma variables induces a change with the opposite sign in the weighted average of the other two variables. In that sense, we have provided substantial content to the hypothesis of the "impossible trinity."

We also focused on the characteristics of the "middle-ground convergence" among emerging market economies. When we examined the correlation between the measure of policy divergence and the level of output volatility, we found that emerging market economies with more converged policy choices tend to experience smaller output volatility in the last two decades. In a world with rapidly proceeding financial globalization, financial liberalization can be a risky policy for developing economies, raising the importance of holding a large amount of international reserves as it has happened in the last decade. On that issue, we found some evidence that emerging markets with low levels of international reserves holding could experience higher levels of output volatility when they choose a policy combination with a greater degree of policy divergence. The greater output volatility associated with greater degree of policy divergence does not apply to economies with high levels of international reserves holding. This may indicate that holding a high volume of international reserves may give room to emerging market economies to choose a policy combination from a wider spectrum of policy combinations.

We also found that this generalization is true for emerging market economies during the period around the global financial crisis of 2008–2009. In the 2005–2009 period, economies with high levels of IR holding do not seem to have faced the positive correlation between policy divergence and output volatility, though the correlation is quite evident for those economies which did not hold high levels of IR. These results may indicate that high levels of IR holding may be one of the reasons for emerging market economies to be able to avoid contagion from the outbreak of the global financial crisis.

## Appendix

## CONSTRUCTION OF THE TRILEMMA MEASURES

### Monetary Independence (MI)

The extent of monetary independence is measured as the reciprocal of the annual correlation between the monthly interest rates of the home country and the base country. Money market rates are used for the calculation.[20]

The index for the extent of monetary independence is defined as:

$$MI = 1 - \frac{corr(i_i, i_j) - (-1)}{1 - (-1)}$$

where $i$ refers to home countries and $j$ to the base country. [21] By construction, the maximum value is 1, and the minimum value is 0. Higher values of the index mean more monetary policy independence.[22]

Here, the base country is defined as the country that a home country's monetary policy is most closely linked with, as in Shambaugh (2004). The base countries are Australia, Belgium, France, Germany, India, Malaysia, South Africa, the United Kingdom, and the United States. For the countries and years for which Shambaugh's data are available, the base countries from his work are used, and for the others, the base countries are assigned based on the International Monetary Fund's *Annual Report on Exchange Arrangements and Exchange Restrictions (AREAER)* and *Central Intelligence Agency Factbook*.

### Exchange Rate Stability (ERS)

To measure exchange rate stability, annual standard deviations of the monthly exchange rate between the home country and the base country are calculated and included in the following formula to normalize the index between 0 and 1:

$$ERS = \frac{0.01}{0.01 + stdev(\Delta(\log(exch\_rate))}$$

Merely applying this formula can easily create a downward bias in the index, that is, it would exaggerate the "flexibility" of the exchange rate, especially when the rate usually follows a narrow band, but is de- or revalued infrequently.[23] To avoid such downward bias, we also apply a threshold to the exchange rate movement, as has been done in the literature. That is, if the rate of monthly change in the exchange rate stayed within +/-0.33 percent bands, we consider the exchange rate is "fixed" and assign the value of one for the ERS index. Furthermore, single-year pegs are dropped because they are quite possibly not intentional ones.[24] Higher values of this index indicate more stable movement of the exchange rate against the currency of the base country.

### Financial Openness/Integration (KAOPEN)

Without question, it is extremely difficult to measure the extent of capital account controls.[25] Although many measures exist to describe the extent and intensity of capital account controls, it is generally agreed that such measures fail to capture fully the complexity of real-world capital controls. Nonetheless, for the measure of financial openness, we use the index of capital account openness, or *KAOPEN*, by Chinn and Ito (2006, 2008). *KAOPEN* is based on information regarding restrictions in the International Monetary Fund's *Annual Report on Exchange Arrangements and Exchange Restrictions* (*AREAER*). Specifically, *KAOPEN* is the first standardized principal component of the variables that indicate the presence of multiple exchange rates, restrictions on current account transactions and on capital account transactions, and the requirement of the surrender of export proceeds.[26] Since *KAOPEN* is based on reported restrictions, it is necessarily a de jure index of capital account openness (in contrast to de facto measures such as those in Lane and Milesi-Ferretti [2006]). The choice of a de jure measure of capital account openness is driven by the motivation to look into policy intentions of the countries; de facto measures are more susceptible to other macroeconomic effects than solely policy decisions with respect to capital controls.[27]

The Chinn-Ito index is normalized between zero and one. Higher values of this index indicate that a country is more open to cross-border capital transactions. The index is originally available for 181 countries for 1970 through 2006. The data set we examine does not include the United States.

## Notes

1. Prasad (2008) argues that exchange rate rigidities would prevent policymakers from implementing appropriate policies consistent with macroeconomic reality, implying that they would be prone to cause asset boom and bust by overheating the economy.
2. Henry (2006) argues that only when it fundamentally changes productivity growth through financial market development, could equity market liberalization policies have a long-term effect on investment and output growth. Otherwise, the effect of financial liberalization should be short-lived, which may explain the weak evidence on the link between financial liberalization and growth.

3. As for monetary independence, refer to Obstfeld et al. (2005) and Frankel et al. (2004). On the impact of the exchange rate regime, refer to Ghosh et al. (1997), Levy-Yeyati and Sturzenegger (2003), and Eichengreen and Leblang (2003). The empirical literature on the effect of financial liberalization is surveyed by Edison et al. (2002), Henry (2006), Kose et al. (2006), Prasad et al. (2003), and Prasad and Rajan (2008).
4. Notable exceptions include works by Obstfeld, Shambaugh, and Taylor (2005, 2009, and 2010) and Shambaugh (2004).
5. The data are available at http://web.pdx.edu/~ito/trilemma_indexes.htm.
6. If the euro economies are removed from the sample (not reported), financial openness evolves similarly to the IDC group that includes the euro economies, but exchange rate stability hovers around the line for monetary independence, though at marginally higher levels, after the early 1990s. The difference between exchange rate stability and monetary independence has been slightly diverging after the end of the 1990s.
7. The emerging market economies are defined as the economies classified as either emerging or frontier during 1980–1997 by the International Financial Corporation.
8. The sample of "Asian Emerging Market Economies" include Cambodia, China, Hong Kong, India, Indonesia, Rep. of Korea, Malaysia, Philippines, Singapore, Thailand, and Vietnam.
9. More generally, increasing of one Trilemma variable should induce a drop of the second Trilemma variable, or a drop in the third Trilemma variable, or a combination of the two.
10. The dummy for ERM countries is assigned for the countries and years that correspond to participation in the ERM (i.e., Belgium, Germany, France, Ireland, Italy, and Luxembourg from 1979 on; Spain from 1989; U.K. only for 1990-1991; Portugal from 1992; Austria from 1995; Finland from 1996; and Denmark and Greece from 1999) or ERM II (Estonia, Lithuania, and Slovenia from 2004; and Cyprus, Latvia, Malta, and Slovak Rep. from 2005).
11. For this exercise, predictions also incorporate the interactions with the dummy variables shown in Table 1.

12. Both the mean and the standard errors of the predicted values are calculated using the rolling five-year windows. The formula for the mean and the standard errors can be shown as and $\overline{x}_{t/t-4} = \sum_{t}^{t-4} \sum_{i=1}^{n} \hat{x}_t / n \times 5 \; SE(\hat{x}) \sqrt{\sum_{t}^{t-4} \sum_{i=1}^{n} (\hat{x} - \overline{x}_{t|t-4})(n \times 5 - 1) / \sqrt{n \times 5}}$, respectively, where $n$ refers to the number of countries in a subsample (i.e., IDC and LDC), $\hat{x}_{it}$ to the prediction values, and $\overline{x}_{t|t-4}$ to the mean of $\hat{x}_{it}$ in the rolling five-year window. Because of the use of rolling five-year windows, the lines in the figures only start in 1974.
13. One may question the uniqueness of this regression exercise by pointing at the left-hand side variable being an identity scalar. As a robustness check, we ran a regression of $MI_{i,t}$ on $ERS_{i,t}$ and $KAOPEN_{i,t}$, recovered the estimated coefficients for $a_j$, $b_j$, and $c_j$.in equation (1), and recreated panels of figures comparable to those in Figure 21.4. These alternative figures appeared to be very much comparable to Figure 21.4 and therefore confirmed our conclusions about the linearity of the trilemma indexes as well as the development of the subsample mean of prediction values based on equation (1).
14. Plus, Latin American countries, many of which went through debt crises, retrenched financial openness around the same period, dragging down the average.
15. The methodology outlined in the section has been applied for several studies, including Hutchison, Sengupta, and Singh (2012), Cortuk and Singh (2011), and Popper, Mandilaras, and Bird (2011).

16. These economies also cannot expect stable access to the international financial market to the same extent of advanced economies (Obstfeld, et al. 2009). Further, distaste among developing countries for rescue programs offered by the International Monetary Fund (IMF) since the Asian crisis period could have also motivated these economies to be prepared on their own for a rainy day.
17. The high positive co-movement of international reserves and M2 is consistent with the view that the greatest capital flight risks are posed by the most liquid assets, i.e., by the liquid liabilities of the banking system as measured by M2.
18. The result is independent of whether or not Lithuania, a clear outlier with its high output volatility, is included.
19. Again, the positive correlation is significant irrespective of Lithuania.
20. The data are extracted from the IMF's *International Financial Statistics* (60B...ZF...). For the countries whose money market rates are unavailable or extremely limited, the money market data are supplemented by those from the Bloomberg terminal and also by the discount rates (60...ZF...) and the deposit rates (60L...ZF...) series from *IFS*.
21. The index is smoothed out by applying the three-year moving averages encompassing the preceding, concurrent, and following years ($t-1$, $t$, $t+1$) of observations.
22. We note one important caveat about this index. Among some countries and in some years, especially early ones, the interest rate used for the calculation of the MI index is often constant throughout a year, making the annual correlation of the interest rates between the home and base countries ($corr(i_i, i_j)$ in the formula) undefined. Since we treat the undefined *corr* the same as zero, it makes the MI index value 0.5. One may think that the policy interest rate being constant (regardless of the base country's interest rate) is a sign of monetary independence. However, it can reflect the possibilities not only that (i) the home country's monetary policy is independent from the base country's; but also (ii) the home country uses other tools to implement monetary policy than manipulating the interest rates, such as changing the required reserve ratios and providing some window guidance (while leaving the policy interest rate unchanged); and/or that (iii) the home country implements a strong control on financial intermediary, including credit rationing, that makes the policy interest rate appear constant. To make the matter more complicated, some countries have used (ii) and (iii) to exercise monetary independence while others have used them while strictly following the base country's monetary policy. The bottom line is that it is impossible to incorporate these issues in the calculation of MI without over- or under-estimating the degree of monetary independence. Therefore, assigning an MI value of 0.5 for such a case should be a reasonable compromise. However, it does not preclude the necessity of robustness checks on the index, which we plan to undertake.
23. In such a case, the average of the monthly change in the exchange rate would be so small that even small changes could make the standard deviation big and thereby the ERS value small.
24. The choice of the +/−0.33 percent bands is based on the +/−2 percent band based on the annual rate that is often used in the literature. Also, to prevent breaks in the peg status due to one-time realignments, any exchange rate that had a percentage change of 0 in 11 out of 12 months is considered fixed. When there are two re/devaluations in 3 months, then they are considered to be one re/devaluation event, and if the remaining 10 months experience no exchange rate movement, then that year is considered to be the year of fixed exchange

rate. This way of defining the threshold for the exchange rate is in line with the one adopted by Shambaugh (2004).

25. See Chinn and Ito (2008), Edison and Warnock (2001), Edwards (2001), Edison et al. (2002), and Kose et al. (2006) for discussions and comparisons of various measures on capital restrictions.
26. This index is described in greater detail in Chinn and Ito (2008).
27. De jure measures of financial openness also face their own limitations. As Edwards (1999) discusses, it is often the case that the private sector circumvents capital account restrictions, nullifying the expected effect of regulatory capital controls. Also, IMF-based variables are too aggregated to capture the subtleties of actual capital controls, that is, the direction of capital flows (i.e., inflows or outflows) as well as the type of financial transactions targeted.

## References


Aizenman, J. and Ito, H. 2012. "Trilemma Policy Convergence Patterns and Output Volatility." *The North American Journal of Economics and Finance*. 23(3): 269–285.

Aizenman, J., M. D. Chinn and H. Ito. 2012. "The Financial Crisis, Rethinking of the Global Financial Architecture, and the Trilemma." In P. Morgan and M. Kawai, eds., *Monetary and Currency Policy Issues for Asia: Implications of the Global Financial Crisis*, Edward Elgar: 143–192.

Aizenman, J., M. D. Chinn and H. Ito. 2011. Surfing the Waves of Globalization: Asia and Financial Globalization in the Context of the Trilemma. *Journal of the Japanese and International Economies*, 25(3): 290–320.

Aizenman, J., M. D. Chinn and H. Ito. 2010. The Emerging Global Financial Architecture: Tracing and Evaluating the New Patterns of the Trilemma's Configurations. *Journal of International Money and Finance* 29 (4): 615–641.

Aizenman, J., M. D. Chinn and H. Ito. 2008. Assessing the Emerging Global Financial Architecture: Measuring the Trilemma's Configurations over Time, NBER WP no. 14533, forthcoming. *Review of International Economics*.

Aizenman, J. and Lee, J. 2007. International Reserves: Precautionary versus Mercantilist Views, Theory and Evidence, *Open Economies Review*. 2007, 18 (2): 191–214.

Aizenman, J. and Marion, N. 2004. International Reserves Holdings with Sovereign Risk and Costly Tax Collection. *Economic Journal* 114: 569–591.

Calvo, G. 1998. Capital Flows and Capital-Market Crises: The Simple Economics of Sudden Stops. *Journal of Applied Economics* 1: 35–54.

Calvo, G. 2006. Monetary Policy Challenges in Emerging Markets: Sudden Stop, Liability Dollarization, and Lender of Last Resort. Working Paper 12788, National Bureau of Economic Research.

Cheung, Y. W, and H. Ito. 2009. Cross-Sectional Analysis on the Determinants of International Reserves Accumulation. *International Economic Journal* 23 (4): 447–481.

Chinn, M. D. and H. Ito. 2008. A New Measure of Financial Openness. *Journal of Comparative Policy Analysis* 10 (3): 309–322.

Chinn, M. D. and H. Ito, 2006. What Matters for Financial Development? Capital Controls, Institutions, and Interactions. *Journal of Development Economics* 81(1): 163–192.

Cortuk, O. and N. Singh. 2011. Turkey's Trilemma Trade-Offs: is There a Role for Reserves? Manuscript.

Edison, H. J. and Warnock, F. E. 2001, September. A simple measure of the intensity of capital controls. International Finance Discussion Paper #708.Washington, DC: Board of Governors of the Federal Reserve System.

Edison, Hali J., M. W. Klein, L. Ricci, and T. Sløk. 2002. Capital Account Liberalization and Economic Performance: A Review of the Literature. IMF Working Paper. Washington, D.C.: International Monetary Fund (May).

Edwards, S. 2001. Capital mobility and economic performance: Are emerging economies different? NBER Working Paper No. 8076.

Eichengreen, B., and D. Leblang. 2003. Exchange Rates and Cohesion: Historical Perspectives and Political-Economy Considerations. *Journal of Common Market Studies* 41 (5): 797–822.

Frankel, J.A., S.L. Schmukler, and L. Serven. 2004. Global Transmission of Interest Rates: Monetary Independence and Currency Regime. *Journal of International Money and Finance* 23 (5,Sep): 701–733.

Ghosh, A., A. Gulde and J. Ostry. 1997. Does the Nominal Exchange Rate Regime Matter? NBER Working Paper No 5874.

Henry, P. B. 2006. Capital Account Liberalization: Theory, Evidence, and Speculation. NBER Working Paper No. 12698.

Hutchison, M., Sengupta, R., and Singh, N. 2012. India's Trilemma: Financial Liberalization, Exchange Rates and Monetary Policy, *The World Economy*, 35 (1): 3–18.

Jeanne, O. 2011. The Triffin Dilemma and the Saver's Curse, prepared for the 4th Santa Cruz Institute for International Economics (SCIIE)—Journal of International Money and Finance Conference, September 23-24, 2011.

Kaminsky, G. and S. L. Schmukler. 2002. Short-Run Pain, Long-Run Gain: The Effects of Financial Liberalization. World Bank Working Paper No. 2912; IMF Working Paper No. 0334. Washington, D.C.: International Monetary Fund (October).

Kose, M. A., E. Prasad, K. Rogoff, and S. J. Wei, 2006, Financial Globalization: A Reappraisal. IMF Working Paper, WP/06/189. Washington, D.C.: International Monetary Fund.

Lane, Philip R. and Milesi-Ferretti, Gian-Maria. 2006. The External Wealth of Nations Mark II: Revised and Extended Estimates of Foreign Assets and Liabilities, 1970-2004, IMF Working Papers 06/69, International Monetary Fund.

Levy-Yeyati, E. and F. Sturzenegger. 2003. To Float or to Fix: Evidence on the Impact of Exchange Rate Regimes on Growth. *The American Economic Review* 93 (4): 1173–1193.

Mundell, R. A. 1963. Capital Mobility and Stabilization Policy under Fixed and Flexible Exchange Rates. *Canadian Journal of Economic and Political Science* 29 (4): 475–485.

Obstfeld, M., Shambaugh, J. C. and Taylor, A. M. 2010. Financial Stability, the Trilemma, and International Reserves. *American Economic Journal: Macroeconomics* 2: 57–94.

Obstfeld, M., J. C. Shambaugh, and A.M. Taylor. 2009. Financial Instability, Reserves, and Central Bank Swap Lines in the Panic of 2008. NBER Working Papers 14826. Cambridge, MA: National Bureau of Economic Research (March).

Obstfeld, M., J. C. Shambaugh, and A. M. Taylor, 2005. The Trilemma in History: Tradeoffs among Exchange Rates, Monetary Policies, and Capital Mobility. *Review of Economics and Statistics* 87 (August): 423–438.

Popper H., A. Mandilaras, and G. Bird, 2011, Trilemma Stability and International Macroeconomic Archetypes, manuscript, Santa Clara University, California.

Prasad, E. S., 2008. "Monetary Policy Independence, the Currency Regime, and the Capital Account in China." In Goldstein, M. and N. R. Lardy (Eds.), *Debating China's Exchange Rate Policy*, Washington, D.C.: Peterson Institute for International Economics: 77–92.

Prasad, E. S., and R. Rajan. 2008. A Pragmatic Approach to Capital Account Liberalization. NBER Working Paper #14051. (June).

Prasad, E.S., K. Rogoff, S. J. Wei, and M. A. Kose. 2003. Effects of Financial Globalization on Developing Countries: Some Empirical Evidence. Occasional Paper 220. Washington, D.C.: International Monetary Fund.

Shambaugh, C. Jay. 2004. The Effect of Fixed Exchange Rates on Monetary Policy, *Quarterly Journal of Economics* 119 (1): 301–352.

# CHAPTER 22

# RETHINKING CAPITAL ACCOUNT LIBERALIZATION

MARIA SOCORRO GOCHOCO-BAUTISTA
AND NOLI R. SOTOCINAL

## 22.1 INTRODUCTION

CAPITAL account liberalization reduces or eliminates the barriers to flows of capital across sovereign borders. By allowing the flow of capital from resource-rich to resource-poor countries, allocative efficiency is promoted, enabling consumption smoothing and risk diversification. Capital-rich countries would benefit from a higher rate of return on capital, while recipient countries would be able to borrow at lower interest rates relative to autarky levels. Lower interest rates in capital-scarce countries would raise investments and spur consumption and economic growth. In theory, therefore, capital account liberalization is unambiguously welfare-enhancing for both countries.

Critics, however, question the validity of welfare-improving outcomes from unfettered cross-border capital flows. Bhagwati (1998) points out that the international trade in financial assets is not the same as trade in goods. International trade in financial assets involves inter-temporal decisions to save and invest made under conditions of information asymmetry between borrower and lender. Borrowing countries, for example, may invest in poor projects or use foreign capital only to consume today so that no future increase in output with which to pay lending countries is forthcoming. Note that the promised payment of a borrower and returns to investors are contingent on some future state. Information asymmetries on either side of transacting parties introduce moral hazard and adverse selection. The outcome is thus not unambiguously welfare-improving for the borrowing or lending country. Rodrik (1998) points out that information asymmetries, incomplete markets, and bounded rationality that are endemic to financial markets result in boom-bust cycles. Stiglitz (2010) attributes sub-optimal results to the absence of a complete set of Arrow-Debreu securities,[1] as the actions of each agent generates externalities on others, causing herding behavior and adverse results.

Critics thus see capital account liberalization as having questionable or non-existent benefits. Furthermore, whatever potential benefits there are come with large downside risks. The main reason unfettered flows of international capital are not unambiguously welfare-improving is that markets are never complete nor free from distortions as Eichengreen (1998) and Cooper (1999) emphasize. Liberalizing capital flows to and from countries with underdeveloped domestic financial systems, where there are substantial information asymmetries, distorted incentives, and structural problems could fail to deliver the purported gains in growth and welfare and simultaneously expose an economy to a substantial amount of risk.

Indeed, three decades after the adoption of the financial and capital account liberalization policy, the frequency and scale of financial crises have increased. Emerging economies, in particular, which willingly embraced financial and capital account liberalization in the 1980s, have resorted to using various forms of restrictions on capital account openness in the 1990s and more recently, especially in the aftermath of the Global Financial Crisis (GFC) of 2008–2009. These economies are wary of capital inflows that may lead to real currency appreciation and loss of export competitiveness and "Dutch disease" effects, financial instability or crises due to inflows that are large, suddenly stop or reverse course, and the loss of monetary independence due to the lack of instruments to anchor inflationary expectations, maintain a competitive level of the exchange rate, and protect the financial sector from the risk of large capital inflows that cannot be efficiently intermediated and deleveraging.

Three decades after espousing financial liberalization, the IMF itself has began to reconsider the wisdom of capital account liberalization and now includes the use of "capital management measures" as part of a country's macroeconomic management tool kit. Ostry et al. (2011) find evidence that such measures and other macro prudential policies can mitigate risks and asset price booms arising from cross-border capital flows. Nevertheless, the adoption of such measures by any one country has externalities on others. Unfortunately, there is currently no multilateral approach to the adoption of capital restrictions by countries, and rules that factor in such externalities on others still await formulation. The recent surge in capital flows is viewed by some quarters in a more sinister light—"currency wars" became the "hot button" issue in October 2010. The presence of large and persistent global imbalances, especially in systemically important countries, was perceived as being largely the result of currency manipulation and insufficient domestic absorption by some, as well as unsustainable and profligate spending by others. Many emerging markets regarded the use of capital controls as a legitimate response to large capital inflows from such perceived currency manipulation that resulted in unwarranted currency appreciation of their currencies.

The rest of the chapter is organized as follows: section 22.2 presents a review of empirical studies and findings, section 22.3 discusses the risks associated with unfettered capital flows, section 22.4 presents recent trends in the use of de jure capital controls, and section 22.5 presents a synthesis of issues.

## 22.2 Gains and Downside Risks from Capital Account Liberation

The gains from capital account liberalization and financial globalization are well-known. Financial globalization is broadly defined as the increasing amount of global linkages created through cross- border capital flows.[2] The degree of capital account openness and volatility is driven by a number of factors, that include the nature and persistence of shocks to the system. Mendoza (1994), for example, finds that output volatility increases with financial integration when shocks are large and persistent. Buch, Dopke, and Pierzoch (2002) find that monetary policy shocks increase the volatility of output but lower that of consumption. They also find that fiscal policy shocks have the opposite effect on output and consumption.

Prasad et al. (2003) note that financial globalization could foster growth though direct and indirect channels. Direct channels include the augmentation of domestic savings, reduction in the cost of capital, technology transfer from more advanced economies, and the development of the domestic finance sector. Indirect channels include increased production specialization due to better risk management and induced improvements in macroeconomic policies and institutions driven by the competitive pressures of globalization.

There is evidence that the level of domestic finance sector development has an important positive role in making capital flows productive. More developed financial sectors are also able to absorb large capital inflows. This suggests that domestic finance sector development is a key component in a country's development and globalization agenda.

Nevertheless, the existence of a number of puzzles showing a disconnect between theory and reality casts doubt on the supposed welfare-enhancing effects of capital account liberalization.[3] One example is the Feldstein-Horioka puzzle,[4] which essentially highlights the persistently high correlations between savings and investments in OECD member countries. Under the prediction of the Intertemporal Theory of the Current Account of full capital mobility, domestic saving and domestic investment should have a low correlation since with capital moving from capital-rich economies to capital-poor economies, the amount of domestic saving should not be a binding constraint on a country's domestic consumption and investment. Consumption smoothing should be enhanced. Yet many studies have shown that domestic saving and domestic investment remain highly correlated in Asian economies[5] and that the increase in consumption volatility occurred when countries liberalized their capital accounts. Kose, Prasad, and Terrones (2003), for example, find that the volatility of consumption growth relative to income growth actually increased for some mid-range financially integrated economies that experienced large inflows in the 1990s. This is consistent with the observed procyclicality of capital flows and threshold effects, where reversals tend to occur after inflows reach a particular level. In contrast, less financially integrated developing countries experienced a reduction in their volatility of consumption growth relative to income growth in similar periods. Obstfeld (2008) argues that domestic finance sector development matters to the realization of gains and mitigation of risk from the liberalization of the capital account. Underdevelopment in other sectors also matters, as he notes that, "an extensive domestic financial development makes it harder to police and enforce binding financial-account restriction."

Another puzzle is the Home Bias Puzzle. French and Poterba (1991) document the disproportionately high share of domestic assets in equity portfolios of investors in the United States, UK, Japan, France and Germany and the lack of cross-border diversification. This tendency to invest in equities markets locally evidently persists even if capital is relatively mobile internationally and there are relatively higher return investments elsewhere. A recent study by Coeurdacier and Rey (2011) shows that home bias is also a feature in bond markets today: Asia, followed by Central and South America, exhibits the highest levels of home bias in bonds among emerging economies. There thus appear to be no gains from risk diversification despite the international mobility of capital. Instead, Prasad et al. (2003) note that there is evidence that international investors in developing and emerging economies tend to conduct momentum trading and exhibit herding behavior.

Finally, the Lucas paradox[6] concerns the failure of capital to flow from capital-rich countries to capital-scarce ones. In the case of many emerging economies in Asia and Latin America today, not only does capital not flow from the advanced capital-rich economies such as the United States, capital flows perversely from emerging economies to the United States and other advanced, capital-rich economies.

Apart from the theory-reality disconnect, most of the empirical studies on gains from financial and capital account liberalization or greater financial integration show mixed results. Prasad et al. (2003), for example, cite studies in which only 3 of 14 show a positive effect of financial integration on growth. Prasad, Rajan, and Subramaniam (2007) find that reduced reliance on foreign capital is associated with higher growth. Given the puzzles mentioned earlier, it is not surprising that the literature on the effects of greater financial integration on economic growth cannot easily establish a positive relationship between them. The efficiency gains from capital account liberalization are welfare-maximizing through risk reduction and consumption-smoothing only provided financial markets are sufficiently deep to be characterized as complete.[7] The underlying assumptions of market completeness, information efficiency, and the absence of distortions are, however, sometimes overlooked by policy makers.

Micro-level distortions, if widespread, could lead to asset price bubbles and manic trading in financial assets. These, in turn, could result in market panic and financial crisis when the bubble bursts after some information event, and the market suddenly realizes that such assets are fundamentally overvalued and simultaneously liquidate financial assets. The increasing complex trading relations in the financial sector and the nature of the financial assets themselves as these are converted into derivative assets, de-links the transactions between the borrower and the lender through layered intermediation and exacerbates information asymmetries. One example is the irrational lending behavior of mortgage originators and the increasingly evident moral hazard of investment banks as regards the creation of mortgage and asset-backed securities, which eventually led to the US Mortgage Crisis of 2007 (Stiglitz, 2010).

Theory and empirical evidence also point to the effect of distortions in the real side of the economy. Under capital account liberalization, domestic industries with little or no comparative advantage have access to cross-border capital flows, resulting in resource misallocation and efficiency losses. Distortionary effects of differences in marginal tax rates across countries with liberalized capital accounts could also matter, as capital may flow to a country with low tax rates regardless of the productivity of capital in a particular country.

Another reason may be that financial integration requires several prerequisites to be in place ex-ante, including a fairly high degree of financial development and absorptive capacity, sound macroeconomic policies, good governance and strong institutions, macroeconomic policies, prudent debt management, a flexible exchange rate regime, and transparency in the conduct of policy. Kawai and Takagi (2008), however, argue that there are no simple rules on the pace and sequencing of capital account liberalization and certain preconditions must exist so as to mitigate financial risks arising from unhindered cross-border capital flows.

## 22.2.1 Problems with Econometric Methods

There are problems with econometric methods to test the effects of capital account openness and financial liberalization on the economy. One is the problem of making the correct distinction between employing incorrect or problematic empirical tests that negate finding positive results from greater financial and capital account liberalization versus these positive effects being non-existent in reality. It is difficult to find explanatory variables that correctly represent a variable of interest or correctly quantify certain variables. Findings regarding consumption smoothing could be spurious, especially in cases where there is a large amount of real exchange rate fluctuations such as during crises. Indirect benefits from financial globalization, such as better institutional governance, are difficult to assess and quantify (Kose et al., 2009). Moreover, these benefits may be dependent on certain threshold levels of financial and institutional development unknown to the econometrician, and may differ depending on the type of capital flow—whether foreign direct investments (FDI), portfolio equities or debt liabilities.[8] Reisen and Soto (2001), for example, find a positive impact of capital account openness on growth from FDI and equity flows but not from other types of capital flows.

Another problem involves the failure to distinguish between permanent and temporary effects. Studies could be trying to empirically capture permanent effects of capital account liberalization on growth—such as a one-time permanent increase in the level of GDP—even though the impact on growth is only temporary (Henry, 2007). There are also various causality and endogeneity issues that are difficult to overcome. Whether opening the capital account leads to benefits such as the development of domestic financial markets or whether the development of domestic financial markets allow capital account to be beneficial is not known.[9]

Even as the empirical evidence on the benefits from capital account liberalization remains unclear, the estimated gains to be had from capital account liberalization may not be substantial. Gourinchas and Jeanne (2006), for example, conduct a policy experiment on two calibrated models of economic development, and find that the potential gains from capital liberalization are likely to be small, not exceeding a 1.7 percent increase in real consumption given estimated parameter values in production and inter-temporal substitution. Having employed a neoclassical growth model à la Ramsey-Cass-Koopmans and a Macro Mincer model that incorporates human capital and distortions, their findings imply that improvements in factor productivity need to occur for the benefits from capital account liberalization to be substantial.

While gains from opening up the capital account may be empirically established, tail risks, exemplified by increased output volatility and/or the occurrence of financial crisis, are substantial. This is seen in Figure 22.1, where crises incidence and output volatility from the 1990s onwards, the period in which capital account liberalization was embraced by most countries, where the magnitude of recessions is greater. The global economy suffered three financial crises over a span of twelve years, all of which coincided with large and volatile cross-border flows of capital and the creation of asset price bubbles.

The 1973–1974 Oil Price shocks and the Latin American Debt Crisis in the early 1980s led to a deceleration of economic growth in Asia, but not by as much as the financial crises after the progressive liberalization of capital accounts in the late 1980s and 1990s.[10] The growth rates of East Asian countries have become more synchronized after the Asian Financial Crisis, and the impact of the various financial crises more acute. This

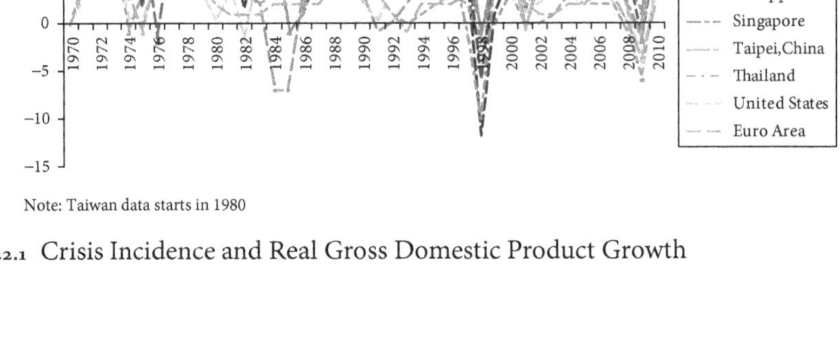


FIGURE 22.1 Crisis Incidence and Real Gross Domestic Product Growth

is consistent with the notion that closer economic integration and increased capital account openness introduces systemic risks.

### *22.2.1.1 Capital Account Liberalization and Recent Financial Crises*

Capital accounts in different countries were progressively liberalized in the 1980s and 1990s. Figure 22.2 shows the relative openness of capital markets as countries embraced capital account liberalization policies:

The capital control indices for 1995 to 2004 are from Schindler (2009), subsequently updated using the same methodology. The index is a measure of de jure capital controls, with zero indicating the absence of controls and unity implying complete restriction. The difference in the degree of openness as regards cross-border capital flows is easily seen in Figure 22.2, with OECD countries generally having more open capital accounts relative to Asian Emerging Market Economies (EMEs). Note that almost all Asian EMEs tightened controls on cross border-flows during 2005–2009.

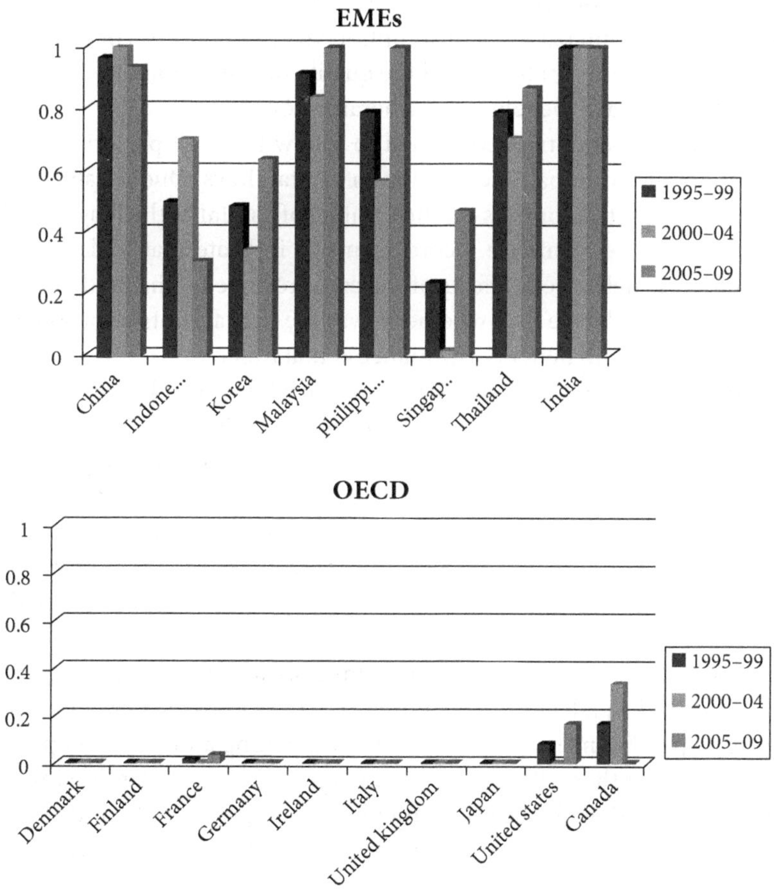


FIGURE 22.2 Capital Control Indices in OECD Member Countries and in Emerging Asian Markets

The flow of capital and economic performance in the emerging market economies in the run-up to and during the 1997 Asian Financial Crisis is reflective of increased capital account openness. The relatively unregulated cross-border flows of capital, however, gave birth to a double mismatch problem; the domestic finance market sectors' balance sheets long-term assets were largely backed by short-term liabilities, and in terms of foreign currency. The sudden stop of inflows after the Thai Baht's depreciation in 1997 eventually led to a reversal of flows and a full-blown crisis in several Asian economies. Felman et al. (2011) note that the bank-centric nature of ASEAN financial markets, as well as excessive dependence on foreign capital flows, contributed to the 1997 crisis. The relatively undeveloped finance sector was largely dominated by banks, which were in turn heavily exposed to foreign currency-denominated short-term liabilities.

The Asian Financial Crisis sparked an ensuing review and debate about the merits of full capital account liberalization. Prasad et al. (2003) summarizes the tone of the debate and provides an overview of factors that could affect the realization of benefits from financial globalization. They point to the procyclical nature of cross-border capital flows as a factor for the increase in consumption volatility in times of crisis. They note that sound macroeconomic policies, and the quality of institutions and governance are important for the accrual of benefits from liberalization.

Most of the ASEAN countries continued to follow the IMF prescriptions of financial liberalization and minimal intervention in capital flows. One notable exception is Malaysia, which instituted controls on the outflow of capital at the height of the Asian Financial Crisis. The performance record seems to indicate that Malaysia was better able to minimize the deleterious effects of the crisis relative to Thailand and Indonesia, although there is still a debate as to whether it was the capital controls or something else that helped Malaysia attain better performance at that time.[11]

After recovering from the 1997 Asian Financial Crisis, the region's emerging economies managed the risk of sudden stops or reversals of capital inflows through the accumulation of excessively large amounts of foreign currency reserves. This over-insurance behavior is costly and inefficient, as massive sterilization was used to prevent inflationary pressures, but more often than not, to prevent currency appreciation. Persistently large current account imbalances, with the majority of emerging market economies posting large surpluses and having to sterilize these, fueled the large reserve accumulations.

Much of the current account surpluses from Asia and other emerging economies is also intermediated in advanced economies like the United States, and is argued by some to have helped finance unsustainable fiscal spending and fuel asset price bubbles in the housing market there. Bernanke (2005) argues that the Asian "savings glut" was one of the key factors that allowed the United States to persistently, and as it turns out unsustainably, incur large deficits. The key argument is that Asia was earning too much, and spending too little. Others argue however, that the same thing could be said about the United States: it was spending too much and earning too little. From this perspective, exchange rate over- and undervaluation may have also contributed to the large imbalances, and it was partially made possible by the relatively open cross-border flow of capital. Gochoco-Bautista and Remolona (2012) have also argued that the lack of financial market development and depth in Asian countries have resulted in inefficient intermediation of the region's savings in distant financial centers. These savings then return to Asia in various forms of capital flows.

The status of the US dollar as the principal reserve currency also necessitates that it run current account deficits, which according to the Triffin Dilemma,[12] results in undermining the value of the US dollar. As the monopoly issuer of the dominant global reserve currency, the United States enjoys an "exorbitant privilege" and faces few incentives to undertake necessary adjustments to increase net savings and trim its large deficits. The United States earns seignorage on global US dollar holdings. Indeed, the bulk of such seignorage is now earned from US dollar holdings abroad. The heightened aversion of Asian countries to financial crisis after 1997, which led to the buildup of large reserves, further diminished the incentive for US authorities to reduce its large current account deficit, as the incremental increase in the demand for global US dollar reserves partially financed its deficit.

The 2008 Global Financial Crisis, the status of the US dollar as the global reserve currency, and the relatively open flow of capital internationalized the 2007 U.S. Mortgage crisis. Stiglitz (2010) presents an accounting of the 1987 mortgage crisis, and the complicity of various economic agents within the United States' relatively unregulated finance sector who, while acting rationally, led to systemic problems caused by moral hazard and adverse selection. The openness of capital markets and the status of the US dollar as the global reserve currency practically ensured the transmittal of the US financial crisis to other countries with substantial holdings of US financial assets. The resulting economic contraction in US output and employment also led to a decline in real demand for goods and services from the rest of the world.

Weak and protracted US recovery in 2009 and 2010, exacerbated by the ensuing Eurozone debt crisis that began in 2009, forced US monetary authorities to conduct several rounds of monetary quantitative easing. This led to the depreciation of the US dollar, which effectively forced an appreciation of the currencies of other countries and severely affected the exports of its trading partners, as well as reduced the value of US dollar-denominated assets. Given low prevailing interest rates in the United States and buoyant economies in the Asian and other EMEs, capital flows to the latter further increased currency appreciation pressures that eventually spawned allegations of currency wars.

The recent global crisis reinforced the argument for a rethinking of unbounded capital account liberalization. The IMF heightened efforts to formulate a framework for the use of "capital management measures" as part of a country's macroprudential toolkit, in order to address systemic risks arising from volatile cross border capital flows. The following section presents a brief overview of these efforts.

### 22.2.1.2 *Capital Controls and the Macroprudential Toolkit*

In the aftermath of the 1997 Asian Financial Crisis, there was a resurgence and acceleration of volatile capital flows into emerging economies.[13] Ostry et al. (2010) note that at its inception, even the IMF's Articles of Agreement recognize that members may generally exercise controls as are necessary to regulate capital movements subject to their Article IV obligations on IMF surveillance. However, just like the empirical record on the merits of capital account liberalization, results arising from research on the effectiveness of capital controls are mixed.

In a review of empirical studies on the effectiveness of capital controls, Hutchison (2012) finds that effects on the volume of outflows and inflows show mixed results, albeit it seems that there is a consensus on the significant effect on the composition of capital flows. Gochoco-Bautista, Jongwanich, and Lee (2012); Jongwanich and Kohpaiboon (2012); and Kim and Yang (2012) find that capital controls have temporary effects on the volume of inflows. Gochoco-Bautista and Francisco (2011) find that the effectiveness of controls in Asian emerging markets depends on regional factors and income levels, and that capital controls have significant effects to varying degrees on foreign direct investment inflows and on debt inflows and outflows.

In general, there is sufficient evidence that capital controls are, at the very least, temporarily effective. The importance of their persistent effect on the composition of capital flows should not be understated, as they tend to bias toward longer-maturity instruments. The emerging consensus in the literature is that specific types of capital controls have different effects on the components of capital flows. Unremunerated reserve requirements, for example, were found by Edwards, Valdez, and De Gregorio (2000) to have pushed capital inflows into Chile as assets with longer term maturities. Ostry et al. (2010) note that inflow taxes on short-term debt will also tend to create a wedge between short- and long-term debt, and induce substitution for the latter. A tax on financial transactions will have a similar effect. The effect of various capital controls on the composition of flows is important, since short-term debt and portfolio investment flows are typically more volatile than others.

It should be noted though, that capital controls are not the only tools that should be used, and not necessarily the first to be considered even for macroprudential reasons. Ostry et al. (2010) propose a framework in which capital controls may be used in conjunction with macroeconomic and prudential policies in order to address potential problems associated with surges in capital flows. The IMF's Monetary and Capital Markets Department also released a report on Organizing Framework for Macroprudential Policy[14] that subsumes and generalizes much of the effort in the development of an acceptable macroprudential framework. The document outlines not only the tools for mitigating systemic risk, but also the required governance and monitoring structures that are necessary to ensure that these are used correctly and effectively. It suffices to note that capital measures are only part of a toolbox that could be employed for macro-financial risk mitigation. Just like any tool, however, capital restrictions could be used for an entirely different purpose that is not prudential and that could impose negative externalities on other countries.

### 22.2.1.3 *Capital Flows and Controls after the GFC: Currency Wars?*

The low interest rates in the United States as the monetary authorities embarked on and continue with accommodative policies, the relatively buoyant economic recoveries in emerging economies coupled with the availability of high yielding-investment instruments ensured that mobile capital would flow to emerging markets. To contain volatility, a number of EMEs imposed or heightened the use of capital controls, as well as continued to accumulate large foreign currency reserves.

The use of capital controls appears to be the "new normal."[15] The IMF itself has evidently reconsidered its position on the use of "capital management measures" as part of its toolkit within a framework of macroprudential regulation (Ostry et al., 2010). South Korea, for example, announced in June 2010 that it would impose currency controls that were wider in scope than the foreign exchange liquidity controls it had imposed a year earlier in order to hold down the amount of short-term foreign debt inflows and prevent sudden reversals of capital. Brazil doubled the tax levied on foreign investments in fixed-income bonds to 4 percent in October 2010, but kept its foreign equity investment taxes at 2 percent. Thailand introduced an unremunerated reserve requirement of 15 percent of cross border inflows in October 2010. These only illustrate the increasing popularity of the use of capital controls by EMEs and by no means present an exhaustive list.

Even with the increasing use of capital controls for supposedly macroprudential purposes, there is also a seemingly general consensus that capital controls could also be used to create commercial advantage in exports and further fuel the problem of current account imbalances. This possibility was the gist of Brazil's Finance Minister Guido Mantega's comments, which called the perceived forced appreciation of other currencies relative to the dollar from QE2, the so-called "currency wars." Mantega's comments were in response to the Brazilian real's persistent appreciation against the U.S. dollar,[16] despite its current account deficits from 2008-2010.

Figure 22.3 illustrates the extent of capital inflows to Brazil and selected emerging market economies in Asia.

China and Brazil are systemically important countries given that they account for a relatively large volume of cross-border capital movements into the EMEs. As seen

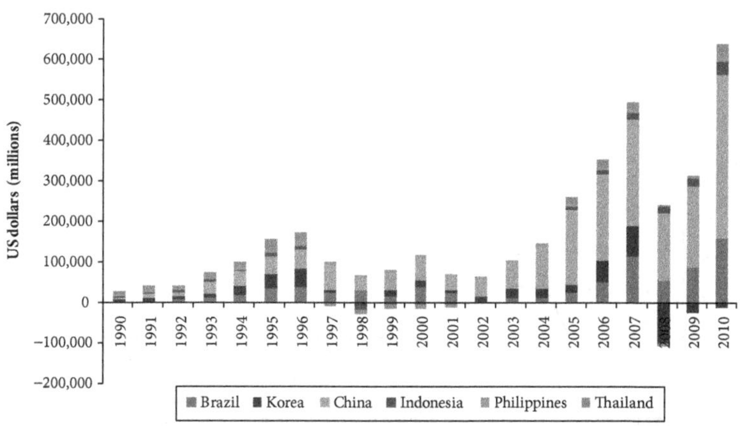


Note: Capital inflows include direct investment, portfolio, financial derivatives, and other investment inflows

FIGURE 22.3 Capital Inflows to Selected Emerging Market Economies in Figure 22.4, the rapid growth of inflows into these key economies would tend to strengthen local currencies against the US dollar.

Except for Indonesia and China, the various local currencies in the given sample tend to strengthen as with the acceleration of the influx of capital. However, the persistence of current account imbalances implies that exchange rates need to adjust further. To a certain extent, the current account deficits of some countries are more than offset by a strong influx of volatile capital flows, and disrupting external balance adjustments through the exchange rate channel. Figure 22.5 shows the extent of capital flows into some emerging economies during and after the 2008 Global Financial Crisis.

Among the components of cross-border capital flows, note that portfolio investments closely followed by other investments (i.e., includes debt securities). These volatile capital flows, exceeding 5 percent of GDP for Thailand, China, and Brazil, led to a strengthening of emerging economies' currencies, as seen in Figure 22.6.

Except for Brazil and Korea, other currencies generally weakened against the dollar at the height of the 2008-2009 crisis, but generally strengthened in nominal and real terms with the resurgence of capital inflows.

Cline and Williamson (2010) provide estimates for the fundamental equilibrium exchange rates (FEER)[17] of various countries, and note that China, Hong Kong, Taipei,China, Malaysia, Singapore, and Switzerland have undervalued currencies relative to their FEER in the period after the GFC but continue to employ, if not heightened, capital controls. They note that Korea, Indonesia, the Philippines, Argentina, and Israel use capital controls but have FEERs that are approximately in equilibrium. India, Thailand, Japan, South Africa, and Brazil have overvalued currencies, and employed capital controls in order to prevent further currency appreciation.

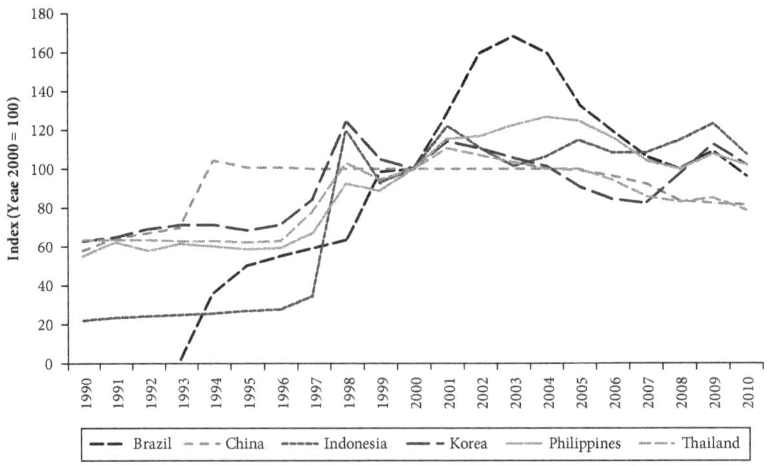


Note: Declining index values indicate that the U.S. dollar is depreciating

FIGURE 22.4 Index of Nominal Exchange Rates to the US Dollar

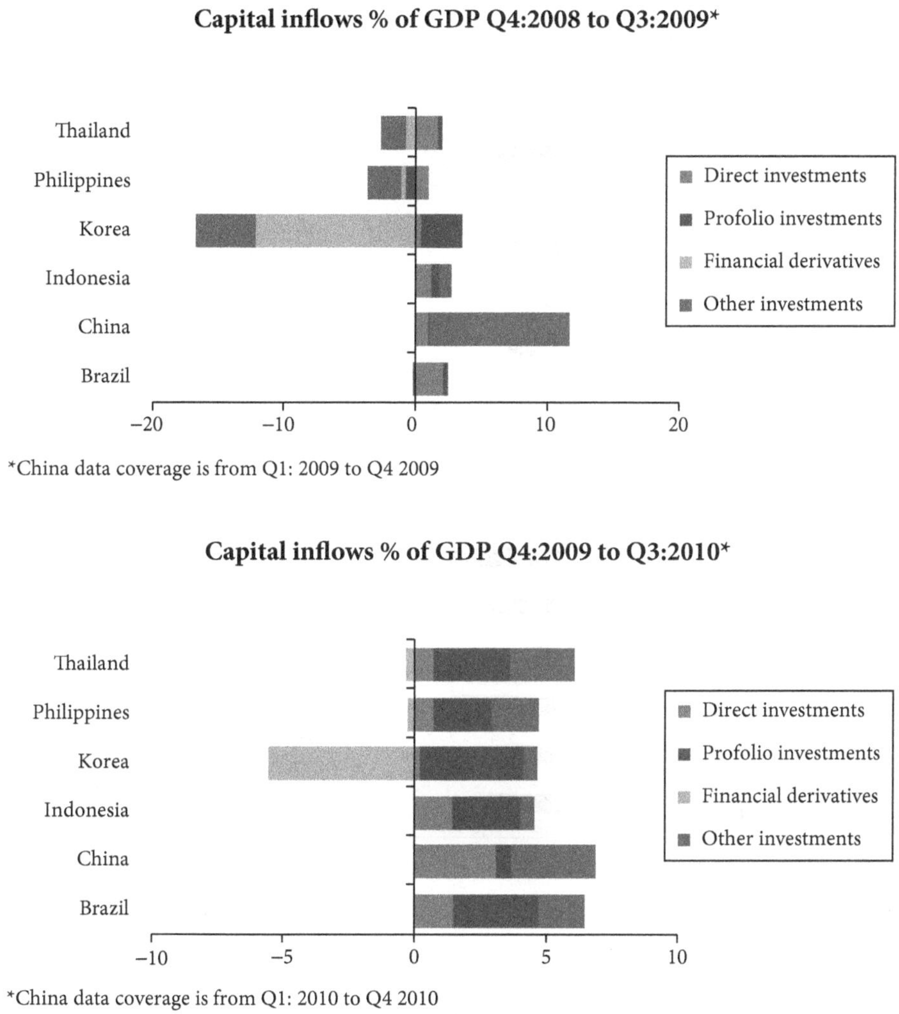


FIGURE 22.5 Capital Inflows into Selected Emerging Economies

The prudential use of capital controls is becoming acceptable as a legitimate way of minimizing the risks associated with intertemporally-mobile capital. On the other hand, it could also be strategically used to create commercial advantage in trade, and ultimately fuel the persistent problem of current account imbalances. While each country has the sovereign right to implement policies that would maximize its societal welfare, its own use of capital controls could have negative spillover effects to its trading partners. Should all, or at the very least, most countries employ this strategy, a sub-optimal welfare equilibrium will prevail, where each and every country is implementing its own nationalist, beggar-thy-neighbor agenda. There is therefore a need for a universally accepted framework on the prudential use of capital controls; the implementation of which supervised and controlled by a multilateral body like the IMF.

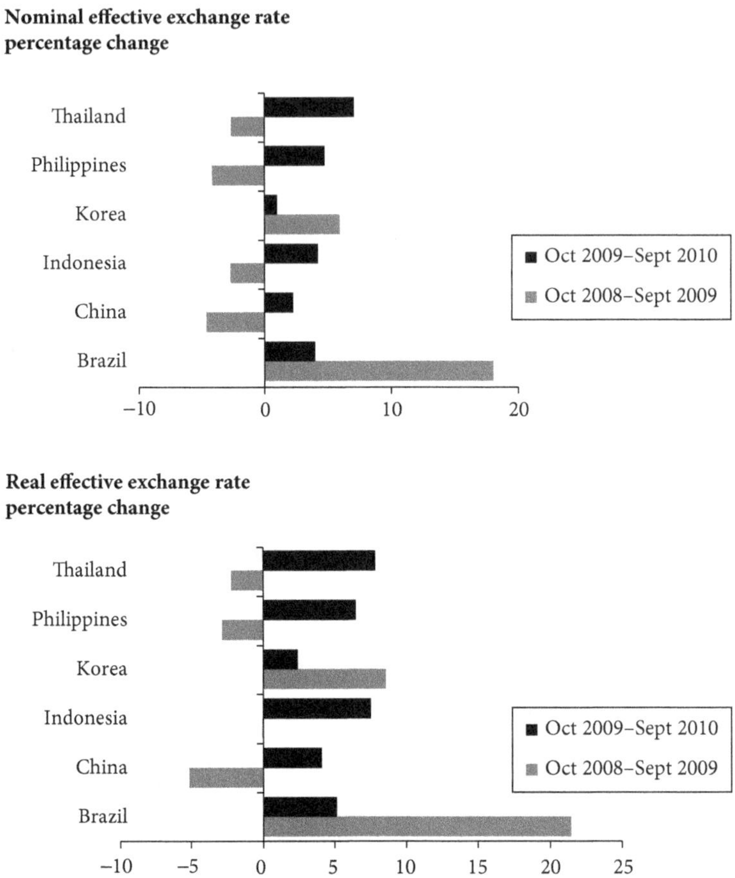


FIGURE 22.6 Effective Exchange Rate Appreciation against the US Dollar

# 22.3 Rethinking Capital Account Liberalization

Capital account liberalization has not unambiguously delivered on its promise of significant improvements in welfare. It has also exposed a large number of countries to risks of heightened output and consumption growth volatility, and financial crisis. At a theoretical level, a number of unexplained puzzles tend to undermine the basis for capital account liberalization. More importantly, pragmatic issues like the underdevelopment of the necessary market infrastructure and institutions to approximate the conditions of negligible transaction costs and distortions introduce significant friction that not only prevents welfare gains, but also fuels the adverse effect of welfare destruction.

While the promises of capital account liberalization have not all been met, it is still widely viewed that the polar opposite of returning to financial autarky is not a desirable option. There is recognition of the fact that a generally overall open environment for cross-border flows of capital must remain, as it is a necessary tool for the facilitation of trade and investment to foster growth. The use of temporary capital control measures, ideally implemented with multilateral consequences factored in, provides authorities with an additional instrument to mitigate the risks arising from the trade in financial assets. The conduct of sound macroeconomic and macroprudential policies are needed to ensure that financial fragility is minimized.

From the perspective of economic development, it is imperative that domestic financial markets be developed *pari passu* with the necessary infrastructure and institutions that markets need to operate efficiently. Although there is no simple rule on the sequence by which the foundations for economic growth must be developed, each developing or emerging country needs to continue to do so.

There is a need to further develop and fine-tune existing policies aimed at mitigating the increased risk associated with heightened global financialization. So as to prevent adverse systemic effects arising out of individual level incentives, a framework for multilateral cooperation must be crafted and a consensus arrived at soonest.

## Notes

1. Arrow-Debreu securities are contingent claims against the occurrence of a particular state or outcome.
2. Prasad et al. (2003).
3. Gochoco-Bautista and Remolona (2012).
4. Feldstein and Horioka (1980).
5. Kim et al. (2011) find evidence of home bias in Asian investments, as reflected by the liquidity risk premia levied over dollar and local currency denominated assets.
6. Lucas (1990).
7. Cochrane (2001) Please note the year discrepancy "Cochrane (2001)" in footnote and "Cochrane (2005)" in references.
8. Kose, Prasad, and Taylor, 2009 Please note the year discrepancy "Kose et al. (2009)" in cross-reference and "Kose et al. (2006)" in reference; Eichengreen and Leblang, 2002; Arteta et al., 2001; Stiglitz, 2000.
9. Mohan, 2008, p.2.
10. The exception to this is the Philippines, which suffered a political and economic crisis in 1984-1985 following the assassination of opposition leader Benigno Aquino Jr. in November 1983.
11. An argument against the effectiveness of Malaysia's control on capital outflows is underpinned by the "barn door" fallacy, which argues that controls were instituted after much of the mobile capital already fled the country. Others note that Malaysia's current anemic FDI flows relative to GDP are a lingering byproduct of its use of capital controls during the Asian Financial Crisis.
12. The Triffin Dilemma states that it is not possible for a reserve-issuing country to maintain both a balance in its current account and the value of its currency.
13. Ariyoshi et al. (2000) discusses the experiences of Latin American and Asian countries with capital controls in the early 1990s.

14. Macroprudential Policy: An Organizing Framework, IMF Monetary and Capital Markets Department
15. Grabel, 2010.
16. The Brazilian real appreciated against the U dollar by 30 percent between January 2009 and December 2010.
17. Cline and Williamson define the FEER as the exchange rate that results in internal and external balance.

## References


Arteta, C., B. Eichengreen, and C. Wyplosz (2001). "When Does Capital Account Help More Than It Hurts?" NBER Working Paper No. 8414.

Ariyoshi, A., K. Habermeier, B. Laurens, I. Otker-Robi, J. Canales-Kriligenko, and A. Kriligenko (2000). "Capital Controls: Country Experiences with Their Use and Liberalization." International Monetary Fund, Washington D.C.

Bernanke, B. (2005). "The Global Savings Glut and the U.S. Current Account Deficit," Speech delivered at the Sandridge Lecture, Virginia Association of Economics, Richmond, Virginia, March 10.

Bhagwati, J (1998). "The Capital Myth: The Difference between Trade in Widgets and Dollars." *Foreign Affairs* 7 (May/June), pp. 7–12.

Buch, C., J. Dopke, and C. Pierdzioch (2002). "Business Cycle Volatility in Germany," Kiel Institute for World Economics Working Paper.

Cline, W., and J. Williamson (2010). "Currency Wars?" Policy Brief No. 10-26, Peterson Institute for International Economics.

Cochrane, J. (2005). "*Asset Pricing.*" Princeton University Press, Princeton, New Jersey.

Coeurdacier, N., and H. Rey (2011). "Home Bias in Open Economy Financial Macroeconomics," NBER Working Paper No. 17691, December.

Cooper, R. (1999). "Should Capital Controls be Banished?," Brookings Papers on Economic Activity, No. 1, pp. 89–125.

Edwards, S., R. Valdez, and J. De Gregorio (2000). "Controls on Capital Inflows: Do The Work?," NBER Working Paper No. 7645, April.

Eichengreen, B. (1998). "International Economic Policy in the Wake of the Asian Crisis". Center for International and Development Economics Research. University of California, Berkeley. Available on-line at http://escholarship.org/uc/item/78c3z577.

Eichengreen, B., and P. Leblang (2002). "Capital Account Liberalization and Growth: Was Mr. Mahathir Right?" NBER Working Paper No. 9427.

Feldstein, M., and C. Horioka (1980). "Domestic Savings and International Capital Flows," *Economic Journal* Vol. 90 No. 358, pp. 314–329.

Felman, J., S. Gray, M. Goswami, A. Jobst, M. Pradhan, S. Peiris, and D. Seneviratne (2011). "ASEAN5 Bond Market Development: Where Does It Stand? Where is it Going?" IMF Working Paper 11-137

French, K. R., and J. M. Poterba (1991). "Investor Diversification and International Equity Markets," *American Economic Review* Vol. 81, 222–226.

Gochoco-Bautista, M. S. (2009). "To What Extent Should Capital Flows be Regulated?" Unpublished Monograph, University of the Philippines and Asian Development Bank.

Gochoco-Bautista, M. S., and E. M. Remolona (2012). "Going Regional: Deepening ASEAN's Financial Markets," Asian Development Bank Working Paper no. 300, January.

Gochoco-Bautista, M. S., J. Jongwanich, and J. W. Lee (2012). "How Effective Are Capital Controls in Asia?" *Asian Economics Papers*, MIT Press, Vol. 11(2), pp. 122–143, June.
Gochoco-Bautista, M. S., and R. Francisco (2011). "Effectiveness of Capital Restrictions: Do Regional and Income Differences Matter?," ADB Economics Working Paper Series No. 261, June.
Gourinchas, P. O. and O. Jeanne (2006). "The Elusive Gains from International Financial Integration," *Review of Economic Studies*, Vol. 73(3), pp. 715–741
Grabel, I. (2010). "Capital Controls, 'Currency Wars', and the New Global Financial Architecture," in Global Perspectives on Finance, Development and Environment, www.triplecrisis.com.
Henry, P. B. (2007). "Capital Account Liberalization: Theory, Evidence and Speculation." *Journal of Economic Literature*, Vol. 45, pp. 887–935.
Hutchison, M. (2012). "A Brief Review of Literature on the Effectiveness of International Capital Controls". Asian Development Review Vol. 29 (1). Asian Development Bank, pages 102–103, December.
Jongwanich, J., and A. Kohpaiboon (2012). "Effectiveness of Capital Controls: Evidence from Thailand," *Asian Development Review*, Vol. 29(2), pp. 50–93, December.
Kawai, M. and S. Takagi (2008). "A Survey of the Literature on Managing Capital Flows," ADBI Working Paper No. 100.
Kim, S., S. Kim, and C-Y Park (2011). "International Capital Mobility of East Asian Economies: Is Domestic Investment Financed by Regional or Global Saving?" in *The Dynamics of Asian Financial Integration*, ed. by M. B. Devereux, P. R. Lane, C-Y Par and S-J Wei. ADB and Routledge.: New York, U.S.A. pp. 52–75.
Kim, S, and D-Y Yang (2012), "Are Capital Controls Effective? The Case of Korea," *Asian Development Review*, Vol. 29(2), pp. 96–133, December.
Kose, M., E. Prasad, and M. Terrones (2003). "Financial Integration and Macroeconomic Volatility." IMF Working Paper WP/03/50. IMF Staff Papers Vol. 50, pp. 119–142.
Kose, M., E. Prasad, and A. Taylor (2009). "Thresholds in the Process of International Financial Integration." NBER Working Paper No. 14916.
Lucas, R. (1990). "Why Doesn't Capital Flow from Rich to Poor Countries?" *American Economic Review* Vol. 80 (2), pp. 92–96.
McKinnon, R. (2002). "Limiting Moral Hazard and Reducing Risk in International Capital Flows: The Choice of an Exchange Rate Regime." *Annals of the American Academy of Political and Social Science*, Vol. 579.: pp. 200–218.
Mendoza, E. (1994). "The Robustness of Macroeconomic Indicators of Capital Mobility," in L. Leiderman and A. Razin (eds.), *Capital Mobility: The Impact on Consumption, Investment and Growth*, Cambridge University Press, Cambridge, U.K., pp. 83–111.
Mohan, R. (2008). "Liberalization and Regulation of Capital Flows: Lessons for Emerging Market Economies." Asian Development Bank Institute Working Paper.
Obstfeld, M. (2008). "International Finance and Growth in Developing Countries: What Have We Learned?" World Bank Commission on Finance and Growth, Working Paper No. 34. Published in IMF Staff Papers (2009), Vol. 56 No. 1.
Ostry, J., A. Ghosh, K. Habermeier, M. Chamon, M. Qureshi, and D. Reinhardt (2010). "Capital Inflows: The Role of Capital Controls." IMF Staff Position Note 10-04.
Ostry, J., M. Qureshi, A. Ghosh, and M. Chamon (2011). "Managing Capital Flows: The Role of Capital Controls and Prudential Policies," NBER Working Paper No. 17363.
Prasad, E., K. Rogoff, S. Wei, and M. Kose (2003). "Effects of Financial Globalization on Developing Countries: Some Empirical Evidence." IMF Occasional Paper 220.

Prasad, E., R. Rajan, and A. Subramaniam (2007). "Foreign Capital and Economic Growth." NBER Working Paper No. 13619, November.

Reisen., H. and M. Soto (2001). "Which Types of Capital Inflows Foster Developing Country Growth?" *International Finance* Vol. 40, pp. 1–14.

Rodrik, D. (1998). "Who Needs Capital Account Convertibility," in Should the IMF Pursue Capital Account Convertibility? Princeton Essays in International Finance No. 207, pp. 55–64.

Schindler, M. (2009). "Measuring Financial Integration: A New Data Set." IMF Staff Papers

Stiglitz, J. (2000). "Capital Market Liberalization, Economic Growth and Instability." *World Development*, Vol. 28, pp. 1075–1086.

Stiglitz, J. (2010). *Freefall: America, Free Markets and the Sinking of the World Economy.* W.W. Norton.: New York.

CHAPTER 23

# ASIAN CURRENCIES IN THE GLOBAL IMBALANCE AND GLOBAL FINANCIAL CRISIS

EIJI OGAWA AND CHIKAFUMI NAKAMURA

## 23.1 INTRODUCTION

GLOBAL imbalances, which showed signs of expansion from the latter half of 1990s, expanded rapidly from early 2000s. Current account deficits expanded in the United States, while current account surpluses expanded in China, other Asian emerging countries, and oil-exporting countries in the Middle East. In the global imbalances, housing bubbles occurred in the United States, which fell into the excessive current account deficit due to insufficient savings. It is helpful to consider persistent global imbalances as the continuous financing of US consumption with the net savings of the surplus countries. Because the financial institutions, not only in the United States, but also in Europe, invested in subprime mortgage-backed securities, they worsened their own balance sheets following the burst of housing bubbles. Thus, in the background of the global imbalances, the financial crisis that started from the United States has developed into a global financial crisis. At the same time, both the negative wealth effects due to the fall of asset prices and credit crunch by the financial institutions have brought the United State and European economies to recession under the global financial crisis. As a result, the world economy came to face a simultaneous economic slowdown further through sharp declines in their exports to these economies.

Under the influences of the global economic slowdown, fiscal deficits have expanded rapidly in many countries because each government increased its government expenditures to inject capital into financial institutions and to give fiscal stimulus to its domestic economy. In the United States, the government planned to increase its fiscal deficits from 450 billion dollars in FY2008 to 1.75 trillion dollars in FY2009, which means nearly four times on a year-on-year basis. Moreover, the expansion of fiscal deficits was observed in many other countries. The Greece fiscal crisis occurred as its typical result in 2010. The euro zone countries have given a financial rescue to the Greek government with the International Monetary Fund (IMF) under the IMF's strict conditionality.

Both the global imbalance and the global financial crisis have had effects on East Asian currencies because of active capital flows, although the global financial crisis has had minimal direct effects on the financial sector in East Asia. The Japanese yen has appreciated after the global financial crisis while the Korean won has depreciated at the same time. This chapter focuses on the relationship between Asian economies, the global imbalances, and the global financial crisis, and it also provides an overview on regional monetary cooperation in East Asia. It refers also to recent studies that consider possibilities of creating a regional common currency unit.

## 23.2 Global Imbalances

### 23.2.1 Causes of Global Imbalances

Since the 1990s, causes of global imbalances have been one of the most important issues in international macroeconomics. Many different factors are intertwined behind the global imbalances and have been widely discussed.

One of the most famous hypotheses is "the global savings glut" in Bernanke (2005) as the cause of the world's large trade imbalances in general, and in particular, the large current account deficits of the United States. This hypothesis suggests that the global imbalances were caused by an increase in the global supply of savings, since 1995, with China as one of the most important suppliers of savings. Bernanke (2005) argued that the US current account deficits do not reflect the trade structure of the United States. Rather he pointed out the excess savings in emerging countries, in other words the "saving glut" as a main cause of the global imbalances. According to Bernanke (2005), the present global imbalances are due to excess savings in Asian countries and resource-producing countries. The insufficient savings in the United States are the outcome of a corresponding global downward trend in interest rates that was caused by the excess saving in a number of emerging countries, as shown in Dunaway (2009), Portes (2009), and Bernanke et al (2011). Therefore, the US current account deficit results from having achieved surpluses in the current account in Asian countries since Asian currency crisis in 1997–1998.

There are two reasons behind the current account surpluses in Asia. One reason is that the monetary authorities should prepare for an unforeseen economic crisis. Another is that governments should conduct their export-oriented economic strategies for their economic growth. They hold down appreciations of their home currencies in order to stimulate their exports and their trade surpluses, which lead to accumulate enormous foreign reserves in the region. In fact, in Indonesia, Thailand, South Korea, and Malaysia all of which experienced the Asian currency crisis, they have moved from deficit to surplus in their current account. In addition, Singapore and China have expanded their current account surpluses. In so doing, most Asian countries has been running large current account surpluses, and there has been an accelerated accumulation of their foreign reserves.

Therefore, Bernanke (2005) argued that the saving glut was the main factor for driving large capital inflows into the United States, which triggered consumption and a housing investment boom and, expanded large current account deficits. Fogli and Perri (2006) showed that excess savings in emerging countries after the financial crisis in 1990s, or a fall of precautionary savings in the United States with less business cycle volatility since the 1980s explained the dynamic of persistent negative external position of the United States. Caballero, Fahri and Gourinchas (2008) focused on the global asset shortage. Excess saving countries such as Asian and oil-exporting countries have boosted huge demand for safe assets that are highly liquid and expected to store value, but their domestic supply can never meet it because of their limited ability to produce these assets. They pointed out that this global asset shortage is one of the main forces behind the global imbalances.

Regarding the background on the global imbalances, some studies pointed out that changes of asset prices caused the global imbalances. Laibson and Mollerstrom (2010), Obstfeld and Rogoff (2009), and Basco (2009) pointed out a relationship between asset price and global imbalances. Especially, Laibson and Mollerstrom (2010) revealed that the increase in housing prices was a major driving force of consumption booms and the subsequent US current account deficit. Moreover, they showed that movements of housing prices significantly account for the variation of trade deficits in 18 countries. This relation between housing prices and current account deficits seems to hold empirically and has also been studied by Aizenman and Jinjarak (2008). In addition, Greenspan and Kennedy (2008) showed that the increases in housing prices contributed substantially to expanding personal consumption expenditures through home equity loans and mortgage refinancing cash-outs.

## 23.2.2 Global Imbalances and Asian Emerging Market Countries

As described above, current account surpluses of Asian emerging market countries might have played a significant role as one of major causes of global imbalances after the Asian currency crisis. It has risen sharply especially since 2003. Many studies gave explanations for Asian countries' surpluses, focused on their high saving rates. For instance, IMF (2006) focused on precautionary savings in Asian countries as one of the sources underlying the global imbalances. China has been a particular focus of attention due to the markedly high savings rate, as shown in Weimer (2008) and Kujis (2005).

At the same time, many previous studies pointed out undervaluation of Asian currencies as a cause of global imbalances. It is evident that there have been rapid increases in foreign reserves in Asian emerging market countries, especially China. This point means that relatively rigid exchange rate management in Asian countries has been used to maintain competitive exchange rates in order to boost their exports, and it has caused the large current account surplus in the region. The systematic intervention in foreign exchange markets to maintain such competitiveness of their exchange rate leads to accumulate enormous foreign reserves in the region.

Many papers investigate the undervaluation problem of Asian currencies. Undervaluation of the Chinese yuan or the RMB has been one of the most serious issues. In light of sharp increases in exports and foreign direct investments into China since 1994, the RMB would have appreciated against the major currencies if only market forces had determined its exchange rate in the foreign exchange market. In fact, China has accumulated US$ 3.2 trillion of foreign reserves in December 2011 because the monetary authority of China has kept preventing appreciation of the RMB.

As shown in Cline and Williamson (2008), we can classify a number of recent studies estimating the equilibrium exchange rate of the RMB into the following three approaches: purchasing-power parity (PPP) enhanced by the Balassa-Samuelson effect,[1] behavioral equilibrium exchange rate (BEER), and fundamental equilibrium exchange rate (FEER) approaches.

The PPP approach is the most famous and popular approach to measure an equilibrium exchange rate in long term. Although the PPP approach is a very simple idea that is based on the law of one price, it has been proven to be inappropriate in analyzing an equilibrium level of the exchange rate. The Balassa-Samuelson effect is one of the factors that causes persistent deviations of market exchange rate from its PPP level. For the reason, the enhanced-PPP incorporates the Balassa-Samuelson effect by using levels of productivity or per capita income. Coudert and Couharde (2005) used the enhanced PPP approach to find that undervaluation of the RMB is estimated in the range between 43 and 50 percent in terms of its bilateral exchange rates. Recently, Subramanian (2010) also found that the RMB is undervalued by almost 31 percent. In contrast, Cheung, Chinn, and Fujii (2007) conducted panel estimation on the relationship between the relative price and the relative per capita GDP with a large data set including 160 countries over a 30-year period from 1975-2004. They showed that the deviation from the predicted RMB equilibrium value is not significantly different, although the point estimates indicate that the RMB is undervalued in almost all samples.

The BEER approach, proposed by Clark and MacDonald (1998), directly estimates the equilibrium relationship between macroeconomic fundamentals and the real exchange rate, while taking into account the Balassa-Samuelson effect. Thus, this approach is based on the concept that the real exchange rate must change with a change in macroeconomic fundamentals in the medium term. It is important to note that the estimated BEER does not necessarily mean to be consistent with macroeconomic balance. The estimated BEER just means an equilibrium exchange rate to be consistent with current fundamentals. It is because it is not necessary that the level of fundamentals at some point in time is consistent with the macroeconomic balance, especially the external balance. Coudert and Couharde (2005) conducted the BEER approach to show that a real exchange rate of the RMB in terms of the US dollar is undervalued by almost 18 percent.

Bénassy-Quéré, Lahrèche-Révil and Mignon (2006) also found a large undervaluation of the RMB, which ranges from 30 to 59 percent. However, Wang, Hui, and Soofi (2007) argued that a degree of deviation of the RMB from the BEER is quite small (at most 5 percent) during a period of 1980-2004.[2]

The FEER approach, which was proposed by Williamson (1985), is the most popular approach in the literature on equilibrium exchange rates. The FEER approach estimates equilibrium exchange rates in the medium term by adjusting the country's internal and external macroeconomic balance to equilibrium simultaneously. The internal balance corresponds to a zero output gap consistent with the Non-Accelerating Inflation Rate of Unemployment (NAIRU). The external balance is interpreted as a sustainable current account position.[3] However, this approach has a variety of discussions on how to determine a normative level of external balance and there is no consensus on it.[4] As empirical studies based on the FEER approach, Coudert and Couharde (2005) estimated that an exchange rate of the RMB in terms of the US dollar is undervalued, ranging from 44 to 54 percent. Recently, Cline and Williamson (2010) show the RMB is undervalued in terms of the US dollar by almost 40 percent.

Table 23.1 summarizes recent major findings that show that the real effective exchange rates of the RMB are undervalued in the range between 21 percent and 45 percent. In the case of bilateral exchange rates, the results vary widely from 24 percent to 59 percent. The IMF also estimated the RMB to be substantially undervalued from a medium-term perspective. In IMF (2011), undervaluation of the RMB against a basket of currencies is estimated in the range between 3 percent and 23 percent.[5] Although we need to note that the estimation results depend on which methodology is used,[6] in light of these empirical results and recent sharp increases in foreign currency reserves in Asian countries, including China, it is a fact that their exchange rate policies contribute to the expansion of the global imbalances. The foreign exchange interventions have propped up the US current account deficit.[7]

## 23.3 Causality and Relationship between Global Imbalances and Global Financial Crisis

The global financial crisis started from the subprime mortgage problem in the United States and extended to financial institutions in Europe. The origins of the crisis are deeply related to the US current account deficits.

First of all, we need to understand that the causes of the US current account deficits varied over time from the latter half of 1990s to 2000s. During the latter half of 1990s, the current account deficits were caused mainly by growing investments because of the information and communication technology (ICT) boom in the United States. In the end of the 1990s, the ICT boom took on the features of a bubble, as expansion of

**Table 23.1 Summary of the Studies on the RMB Undervaluation**

| Paper | Approach | Period | REER range | Against US$ |
|---|---|---|---|---|
| Coudert and Couharde (2005) | PPP-E | 2003 | – | 43–50% |
| | BEER | 2002 | – | 17.8% |
| | FEER | 2003 | 23–30% | 44–54% |
| Bénassy-Quéré, Lahrèche-Révil and Mignon (2006) | BEER | 2004 | 31-45% | 30–59% |
| Wang, Hui and Soofi (2007) | BEER | 1980–2004 | The degree of deviation from the long-run equilibrium is quite small. | |
| Cheung, Chinn, and Fujii (2007) | PPP-E | 1975–2004 | There's little statistical evidence. | |
| Subramanian (2010) | PPP-E | | – | 31.3% |
| Cline and Williamson (2010a) | FEER | | 21.4% | 40.2% |
| Cline and Williamson (2010b) | FEER | | | 24.2% |

*Notes:* REER: real effective exchange rate. PPP-E: PPP-enhanced. BEER: behavioral equilibrium exchange rate. FEER: fundamental equilibrium exchange rate.

ICT-related investments and its related current account deficits continued accelerating in the United States. The investments and the current account deficits in the United States were financed by huge capital inflows from Europe.

Early in the 2000s, the fiscal deficits of the United States increased to avoid the after-effects of its ICT bubble burst. Moreover, the surging military spending relating to anti-terrorism in Afghanistan accelerated worsening the US fiscal deficits. At the same time, rapid cuts in interest rates and the low-interest rate policy that the Federal Reserve Bank instituted for measures to recover the economy caused a housing bubble. The housing bubble was deeply related to subprime mortgages and subprime mortgage-backed securities. The subprime mortgages, which were in a higher-risk category of housing loans based on expectation of rising housing prices, encouraged housing investments in the United States from 2003 to 2006. This reinforced the US current account deficits.

Thus, causes of the US current account deficits expansion from the latter half of the 1990s to the 2000s have changed. However, insufficient savings in the private sector in the United States have been pointed out to be a fundamental source of the current account deficits over time. Owing to the insufficient savings in the domestic private sector, capital inflows from the foreign countries have continued to meet large capital demands in the United States such as the ICT boom, the housing bubble, and the runaway fiscal deficits. As a result, the current account deficits have expanded with the growing capital demands.

As shown in Figure 23.1, the US current account deficits are financed by current account surpluses in East Asian countries, especially China. Bernanke (2005) pointed

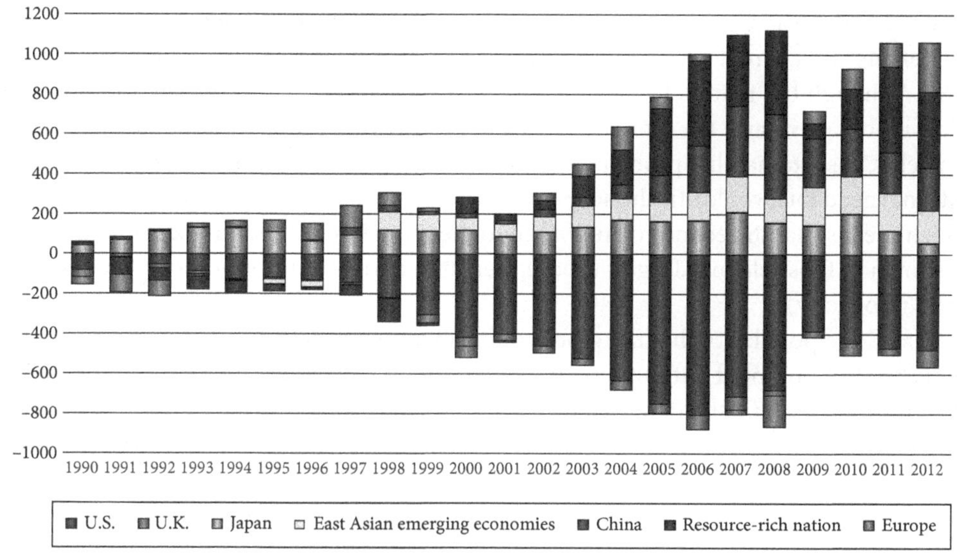


FIGURE 23.1 Global Current Account Imbalances (US$ billion)

*Note:* East Asian emerging economies are composed of Hong Kong, South Korea, Singapore, Taiwan, and ASEAN-5. Europe is composed of the Euro area and Switzerland. The resource-rich nation category is composed of Russia, the Middle East and North Africa, and Latin America and the Caribbean.

*Source:* IMF, World Economic Outlook Database April 2013.

out that the global imbalances are attributed to the global saving glut, although the hypothesis is debatable, as shown already in this chapter. It is also true, however, that savings in Asian countries go toward Treasury Bills and Government Bonds of the United States and, in other words, the savings are used for the United States to finance the large current account deficits.

Moreover, financial institutions in Europe have played a role as an international financial intermediary from countries with excess savings to the United States with insufficient savings. In particular, the oil-exporting countries grew current account surpluses, which were caused by increases in the oil price in the 2000s. On one hand, the European Union (EU) as a whole did not have large current account imbalances,[8] but on the other, European financial institutions had heavily invested in US mortgage-backed securities. This implies that they acted as go-between for the surplus countries such as the oil-exporting countries and the United States.

Thus, it is savings in Asia and oil money of oil-exporting countries that financially support insufficient savings and current account deficits in the United States. Also, it is European financial institutions that allow for international financial intermediation. It is possible for the United States to finance internationally, even though it is a large external net debtor. However, if it were the other country, it could not have been burdened by such huge cumulative external debts under the same circumstances. As described later, it is the US dollar's special status in the world economy that makes it possible.

In the 1980s, the US economy was faced with "twin deficits," which include both fiscal deficits and current account deficits, and fell into an external net debtor country in 1985. Although the twin deficits were temporarily-improved from the late 1980s to the early 1990s, afterward, the United States has steadily increased the amount of external net debts. A sustainability problem was supposed to occur because the huge cumulative external net debts would stir the suspicion about a capability of repayment in the future, which means that the economy might fail to meet the intertemporal budget constraint, as shown in Obstfeld and Rogoff (2003), Bergsten and Williamson (2004), and Ogawa and Kudo (2007).

In fact, the possibility that the global imbalances potentially cause a global financial crisis has been pointed out in many previous studies. Edwards (2002) found that large current account deficits might enhance the probability of a financial crisis.[9] Moreover, Edwards (2005a, 2005b) showed that the US current account would have to go through a significant adjustment in the near future with a portfolio model of the current account, even under an optimistic assumption that the foreigners' net demand for the US assets would double from its current level during the last five years.

However, it might be possible for the United States to finance its current account deficits without any problems, even though it is the largest net debtor country in the world. Behind it, there is a current international monetary system where the US dollar has been a dominant key-currency in the world economy, even after the Bretton Woods System collapsed in 1971. It is a fact that the US dollar is widely used as a major currency for international settlement. Under the international monetary system, there would be continuous demands for the US dollar as a settlement currency even if the huge external net debts made the current account unsustainable in terms of intertemporal budget constraints. The international monetary system makes the United States easily supply the US dollar into the world economy without making the United States reluctant to expand its current account deficits and accumulate external net debts. Therefore, it is no exaggeration to say that the global imbalances occurred in the context of the current international monetary system with the US dollar as a key currency.

## 23.4 Regional Monetary Cooperation in Asia

The monetary authorities of East Asian countries, especially ASEAN (Association of South East Asian Nations) +3 (Japan, China, and South Korea), have been strengthening their regional monetary cooperation ever since they experienced the Asian currency crisis in 1997-1998. They established the Chiang Mai Initiative (CMI) for prevention and resolution of the financial and currency crisis in 2000. Under the CMI, the monetary authorities of ASEAN+3 countries established a network of bilateral swap arrangements for managing a currency crisis in the member countries as well as a surveillance process over macroeconomic variables that include GDP growth rates, inflation rates, and soundness of the banking sector.

In May 2009 in Bali, Indonesia, the Finance Ministers and Central Bank Governors of the ASEAN+3 and the monetary authority of Hong Kong announced the signing of the Chiang Mai Initiative Multilateralization (CMIM) Agreement, which went into effect on March 24, 2010. The CMIM strengthens the region's capacity to safeguard against increased risks and challenges in the global economy. The CMIM provides financial support through the currency swap arrangements for the CMIM participants facing balance-of-payments and short-term liquidity difficulties. The total of the currency swap arrangements under the CMIM amounts US$120 billion.

There are two major objectives of the CMIM: (i) to address balance-of-payments and short-term liquidity difficulties in the region and (ii) to supplement the existing international financial arrangements. Each CMIM member is entitled, in accordance with procedures and conditions set out in the CMIM Agreement, to swap its local currency with US dollars for an amount up to its contribution multiplied by its purchasing multiplier. The CMIM Agreement, a multilateral currency swap arrangement that covers all ASEAN+3 members, was developed from the CMI bilateral swap network to facilitate prompt and simultaneous currency swap arrangements through establishing a common decision-making mechanism under a single contract.

Moreover, ASEAN+3 members also reached an agreement on establishing a surveillance office in Singapore in early 2011, which was named the ASEAN+3 Macroeconomic Research Office (AMRO). The AMRO performs a key regional surveillance function as part of the US$120 billion CMIM currency swap facility. Finance Ministers of the ASEAN+3 now have to ensure that technical details are ironed out. To support the CMIM, the AMRO is tasked with monitoring and analyzing the macroeconomic situation and financial soundness of the ASEAN+3 Countries, a process that ideally will contribute to early detection of possible currency crises, swift implementation of remedial actions, and effective decision-making in the region.

Under the framework, the monetary authorities should engage in a surveillance process for preventing a currency crisis in the future. However, the monetary authorities have had no standing institution for carrying out any surveillance process in East Asia. Instead, the ASEAN+3 Finance Deputy Ministers' Meeting regularly holds a so-called Economic Review and Policy Dialogue for surveillance over their macroeconomic performance.

The monetary authorities of East Asian countries should prevent biased changes in the relative prices caused by the US dollar depreciation under the different exchange rate systems in East Asian countries. For this purpose, they need to coordinate their choice of their exchange rate systems and exchange rate policies.

Kawai, Ogawa, and Ito (2004) suggested the following advice concerning exchange rate policy in East Asia. First of all, the monetary authorities of the ASEAN+3 should discuss the exchange rate issue as a part of the surveillance process. They should focus on the exchange rate issue as well as on domestic macroeconomic policies and on the soundness of their financial sectors: the exchange rates of a home currency against neighbouring countries' are indeed related with terms of trade of the home country against the neighbouring countries and its international price competitiveness.

Each of the East Asian countries has strong economic relationships with the other regional countries as well as with the European countries and the United States. Movements in intra-regional exchange rates among the regional currencies affect economic activities in each country of East Asia through intra-regional trade, investment, and finance. The monetary authorities should not only monitor account movements of the exchange rates but also their deviations from the regional averages and, in turn, their exchange rate policies per se.

The surveillance process, in itself, might not be sufficiently solid to preserve regional policy coordination in the long run because the monetary authorities from each country are not committed to policy coordination. They might make a limited contribution to policy coordination. Thus, it's necessary to have a mechanism that will be able to preserve regional coordination in the long run by compelling the monetary authorities to be committed to such coordination.

## 23.5 Common Currency Unit in Asia

The concept of a regional common currency unit have been addressed and discussed in East Asia after the 1997 Asian Currency Crisis. Several concepts and names regarding a regional common currency unit have been addressed: Regional Monetary Unit (RMU) by IIMA (2007, 2008) and ASEAN+3 Finance Ministers' Meeting; Asian Currency Unit (ACU) by Kuroda and Kawai (2002) and Kawai (2009a, 2009b); Asian Monetary Unit (AMU) by Ogawa and Shimizu (2005); and Regional Currency Unit (RCU) by Moon, Rhee, and Yoon (2006). It seems there is not so much difference among them, as IIMA (2008) pointed out.

A roadmap to introduce an ACU has already been proposed to ASEAN+3 Finance Ministers' Meeting in 2007 and 2008, as shown in IIMA (2007, 2008). The roadmap has two paths, as Ogawa (2011) pointed out. One path is for surveillance, and the other is for transactions. An ACU for surveillance would be used for macro-economic surveillance. All the currencies of the member countries in that surveillance should be included. On the other hand, an ACU for transactions would become a composite currency for financial products, especially Asian bonds, when we take into account the Asian Bond Market Initiative (ABMI) and Asian Bond Fund (ABF) initiative. Only currencies that meet several criteria, including convertibility, should be included.

The two paths could converge into one, with sufficient regional economic and financial integration achieved in the longer-term. The difference between high-income developed countries, which include Japan, Korea, and Singapore, and middle-income developing countries, which include China, Thailand, Malaysia, Indonesia, and the Philippines, will be reduced in terms of the economies, in particular the development stages of financial systems and financial and capital markets.

Developments in the two paths would facilitate regional economic and financial integration as well. An ACU for surveillance would contribute to avoiding misalignments and excess volatility in intra-regional exchange rates among East Asian currencies, and would strengthen mechanisms for regional surveillance. The reduced misalignments and volatility would lead to facilitating regional economic integration. An ACU for transactions would offer financial products for diversification of foreign exchange risk because the weighted average interest rates of their component currencies should have portfolio effect to reduce foreign exchange risk. It would promote intra-regional financial intermediation (a bridge between savings and investment) within the region while it, at the same time, would facilitate regional financial integration in East Asia. Thus, the two paths for an ACU and for regional economic and financial integration are mutually complementary.

Ogawa and Shimizu (2005a) calculate an AMU (Asian Monetary Unit) according to the method used to calculate the ECU under the EMS prior to the introduction of the euro in 1999. In the same way that the ECU was defined as a basket of currencies of EU member countries, the AMU is defined as a basket currency of the ASEAN10+3 countries. The weight of each currency in the basket is based on both the countries' respective shares of GDP measured at Purchasing Power Parity (PPP), and trade volumes (the sum of exports and imports) in the total of sampled countries for the relevant country; Kawai (2009a, b) takes into account relative size of domestic capital markets and Ogawa and Shimizu (2005b) take into account liberalization of capital markets and international capital control.

IIMA (2008) found little difference among the candidates for ACU in basic statistics of movements in ACU and ACU Deviation Indicators of East Asian currencies. Given that the candidates for ACU are not very different from one another, we should consider the easiest method of selecting among them. The ASEAN+3 Finance Ministers Meeting on May 3, 2009 in Bali, Indonesia has already come to agreement on the contribution share of each of ASEAN+3 countries to their pooled foreign reserves under the Chiang Mai Initiative Multilateralization (CMIM). It is the easiest for us to follow the CMIM contribution share to have a consensus that an ACU should be based on CMIM contribution share because they have already made the consensus in terms of contribution share to pooled foreign reserves.

The CMIM-based ACU has the following characteristics: the basket share of CMIM-based ACU is based on the individual country's contribution proportion of CMIM (the total size of the CMIM is USD 120 billion). The Hong Kong dollar, as well as ASEAN+3 currencies, participate in the composition currencies of CMIM-based ACU. The basket weights of CMIM-based ACU are shown in Table 23.2.

The calculations of the CMIM-based ACU and CMIM-based ACU Deviation Indicators are almost the same as those of the ACU that have been discussed based on shares of GDP, international trade, and capital markets. However, the basket weights of the CMIM-based ACU are not revised as long as contribution shares of East Asian countries are kept. The benchmark period, which fixes the benchmark exchange rates,

**Table 23.2 Weights of East Asian Currencies for CMIM-based AMU (benchmark year = 2000/2001)**

| | CMI contribution* (USD billion) | CMI share % (a) | Benchmark exchange rate** (b) | AMU weights (a)/(b) |
|---|---|---|---|---|
| Brunei | 0.03 | 0.025 | 0.589114 | 0.0004 |
| Cambodia | 0.12 | 0.100 | 0.000270 | 3.6969 |
| China | 34.20 | 28.500 | 0.125109 | 2.2780 |
| Hong Kong | 4.20 | 3.500 | 0.132842 | 0.2635 |
| Indonesia | 4.77 | 3.975 | 0.000113 | 352.8940 |
| Japan | 38.40 | 32.000 | 0.009065 | 35.3024 |
| South Korea | 19.20 | 16.000 | 0.000859 | 186.1856 |
| Laos | 0.03 | 0.025 | 0.000136 | 1.8342 |
| Malaysia | 4.77 | 3.975 | 0.272534 | 0.1459 |
| Myanmar | 0.06 | 0.050 | 0.159215 | 0.0031 |
| Philippines | 3.68 | 3.067 | 0.021903 | 1.4001 |
| Singapore | 4.77 | 3.975 | 0.589160 | 0.0675 |
| Thailand | 4.77 | 3.975 | 0.024543 | 1.6196 |
| Vietnam | 1.00 | 0.833 | 0.000072 | 116.4928 |

*CMI contribution was decided by the 12th ASE AN+3 Finance Ministers' Meeting on May 3, 2009. Total amount is USD 120 billion.
**The Benchmark exchange rate ($-euro/Currency) is the average of the daily exchange rate in terms of US$-euro in 2000 and 2001.
*Source:* RIETI's website ([http://www.rieti.go.jp/users/amu/en/cmi.html])

might be decided by the average of daily exchange rates between 2000 and 2001 in the same way as the AMU in Ogawa and Shimizu (2005a).

Figure 23.2 shows movements in values of CMIM-based ACU in terms of a currency basket of the US dollar and the euro[10], the US dollar, and the euro. The CMIM-based ACU is relatively stable against a currency basket of the US dollar and the euro although it has been appreciating by about 15 percent since spring in 2009. Values of the CMIM-based ACU in terms of the euro as well as those in terms of the US dollar are much more fluctuating, which reflects large fluctuations in exchange rate of the euro in terms of the US dollar.

An Asian Monetary Unit (AMU) is a weighted average of East Asian currencies where weights on currencies are based on shares of intra-regional trade and GDP is measured at Purchasing Power Parity (PPP). Daily and monthly data are available at a website of RIETI ([http://www.rieti.go.jp/users/amu/en/index.html#data]). Figure 23.3 shows movements in values of AMU in terms of a currency basket of the US dollar and

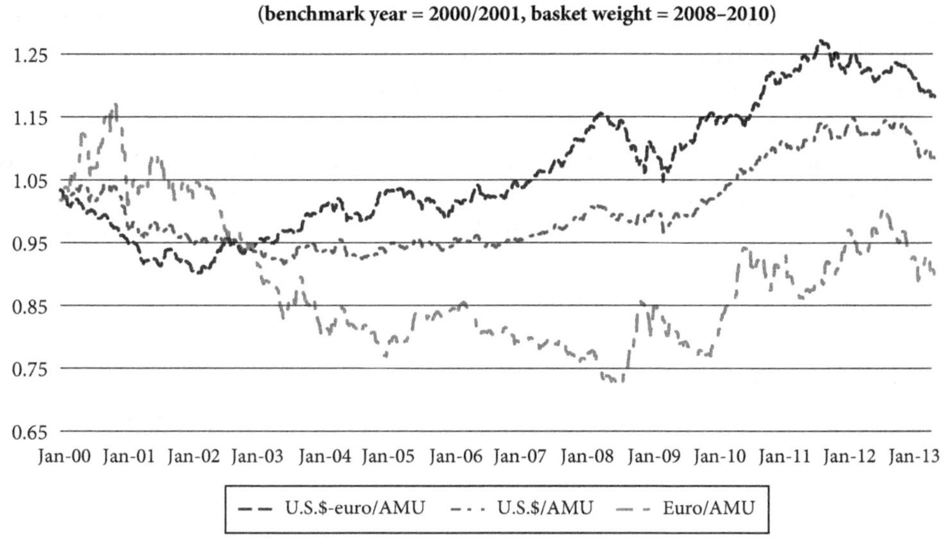


FIGURE 23.2 CMIM-based AMU in terms of the US$-euro

Data: RIETI's website ([http://www.rieti.go.jp/users/amu/en/cmi.html])

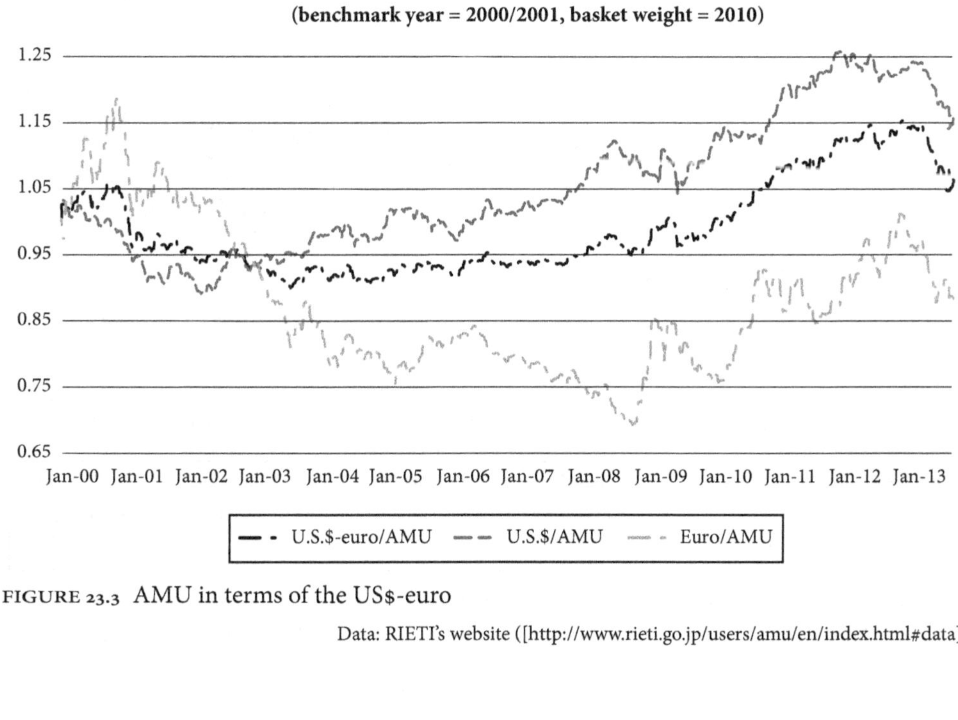


FIGURE 23.3 AMU in terms of the US$-euro

Data: RIETI's website ([http://www.rieti.go.jp/users/amu/en/index.html#data])

the euro, the US dollar, and the euro. Comparison between Figures 23.2 and 23.3 tell us that the CMIM-based ACU has almost the same movements with the AMU, where weights on currencies are based on shares of intra-regional trade and GDP measured at PPP.

The nominal exchange rate of each East Asian currency in terms of the CMIM-based ACU is used to calculate a nominal CMIM-based ACU Deviation Indicator for each East Asian currency from the Benchmark Exchange Rate from the viewpoint of deviation from the CMIM-based ACU, which is a weighted average of East Asian currencies determined according to the following formula:

$$\text{Nominal Deviation Indicator (\%)} = \frac{\text{actual exchange rate of ACU / a currency} - \text{benchmark exchange rate of ACU / a currency}}{\text{benchmark exchange rate of ACU / a currency}} \quad (1)$$

Figure 23.4 shows movements in nominal CMIM-based ACU Deviation Indicators. Figure 23.4 tells us that some Asian currencies were overvalued before the global financial crisis, while other currencies were undervalued. The global financial crisis has depreciated the overvalued Asian currencies, whereas it has appreciated the undervalued currencies.

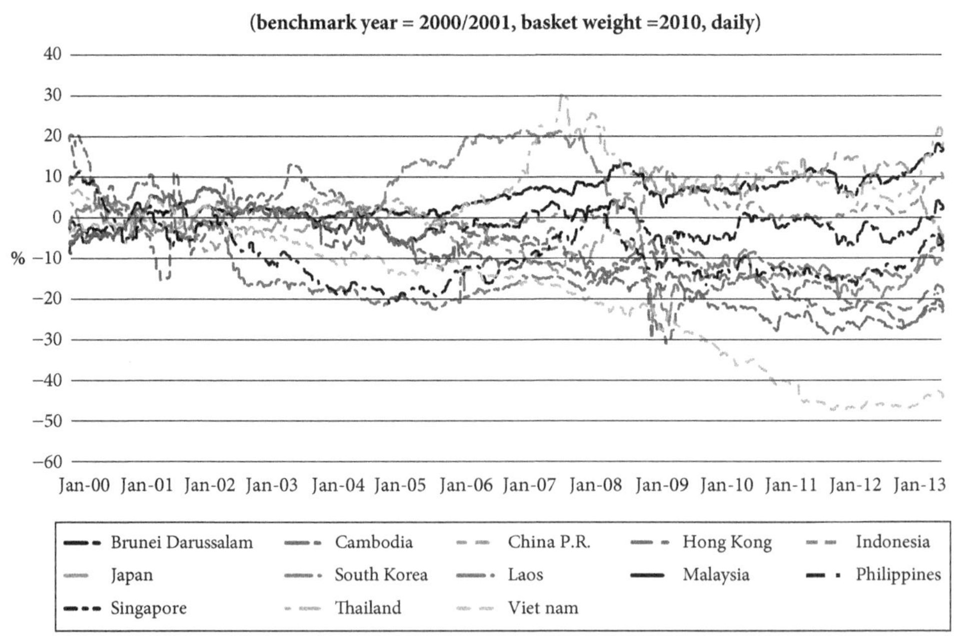


FIGURE 23.4 Nominal CMIM-based AMU Deviation Indicators
Data: RIETI's website ([http://www.rieti.go.jp/users/amu/en/index.html#data])

Next, CMIM-based ACU Deviation Indicators in real terms are calculated by taking into account inflation rate differentials. Given that the Nominal CMIM-based ACU Deviation Indicator is defined as equation (1), a Real CMIM-based ACU Deviation Indicator is used according to the following equation:

$$\begin{aligned}&\text{Rate of change in Real Deviation Indicator (\%)}\\&\quad=\text{Rate of change in Nominal Deviation Indicators}\\&\qquad-(\text{inflation rate in East Asia - inflation rate in home country})\end{aligned} \tag{2}$$

Consumer Price Index (CPI) data are used as a general price index in calculating the Real CMIM-based ACU Deviation Indicator. Since CPI data are available only on a monthly basis, we calculate the Real CMIM-based ACU Deviation Indicator monthly. As for the inflation rates in East Asia, we calculate a weighted average of the CPI for East Asia using the shares that are used in calculating the CMIM-based ACU. Figure 23.5 shows movements in the Real CMIM-based ACU Deviation Indicators on a monthly basis for each of the East Asian currencies.

## 23.6 Asymmetric Responses of Asian Currencies to the Global Financial Crisis

Both Figures 23.2 and 23.3 show that the AMU has been gradually depreciating against the currency basket of the US dollar and the euro before May 2003 when the AMU depreciated about 10 percent compared with the benchmark years of 2000 and 2001. However, it reversed its trend to upward direction and returned to almost the same level as in the benchmark years before the end of 2008. It has kept appreciating against the currency basket of the US dollar and the euro over time after then. In other words, the AMU has become relatively more stable with an appreciating trend after the global financial crisis. On one hand, the AMU has an appreciating trend against US dollar as well as the euro during and after the global financial crisis. However, it has been fluctuating against each of them because of euro turmoil related to the global financial crisis and the European fiscal crisis.

Figure 23.4 shows movements in AMU deviation indicator of each of East Asian currencies or movements in each of East Asian currencies against the AMU in terms of nominal exchange rates from the benchmark years. It is clear that the East Asian currencies have had a deviating tendency since 2005. Moreover, some East Asian currencies, including the Japanese yen, have kept overvalued over time since the Lehman shock, while other East Asian currencies including the Korean won, have kept undervalued over time. In particular, the Korean won and the Japanese yen had characteristic and asymmetric movements before and after the global financial crisis. The Korean won was overvalued against the AMU or a weighted average of East Asian currencies from the end of 2004 to early 2008. It was overvalued by more than 20 percent compared with the benchmark years, especially from March 2006 to July 2007. However, the Korean won has been depreciating quickly since the end of 2007. It has been undervalued by 20 percent to 30 percent compared with the benchmark years during and after the global financial crisis. On the other hand, the Japanese yen has asymmetric movements against the Korean won.

Figure 23.5 shows movements in deviations of East Asian currencies against the AMU in terms of real exchange rates from the benchmark years. The Real AMU Deviation Indicators of East Asian currencies were limited within plus 20 percent and minus 10 percent during a period from 2000 to 2001. The Indonesia rupiah and the Lao kip have appreciated against the AMU in terms of real exchange rates because of higher inflation since 2003. Also, the Vietnamese dong has abruptly appreciated since 2010 because of higher inflation that exceeds its devaluation. The Korean won was overvalued against the AMU, also in terms of real exchange rates, due to the appreciation of the nominal exchange rate from the end of 2004 to October 2007, although it has been depreciating quickly due to the depreciation of the nominal exchange rate. On the other hand, the Japanese yen was depreciating because of a combination of yen depreciation in terms of nominal exchange rate and the deflation in prices from January 2005 to July 2007. It recorded that it was undervalued by 30 percent compared with the benchmark years in July 2007. However, the Japanese yen has been appreciating in terms of real exchange rate since August 2007.

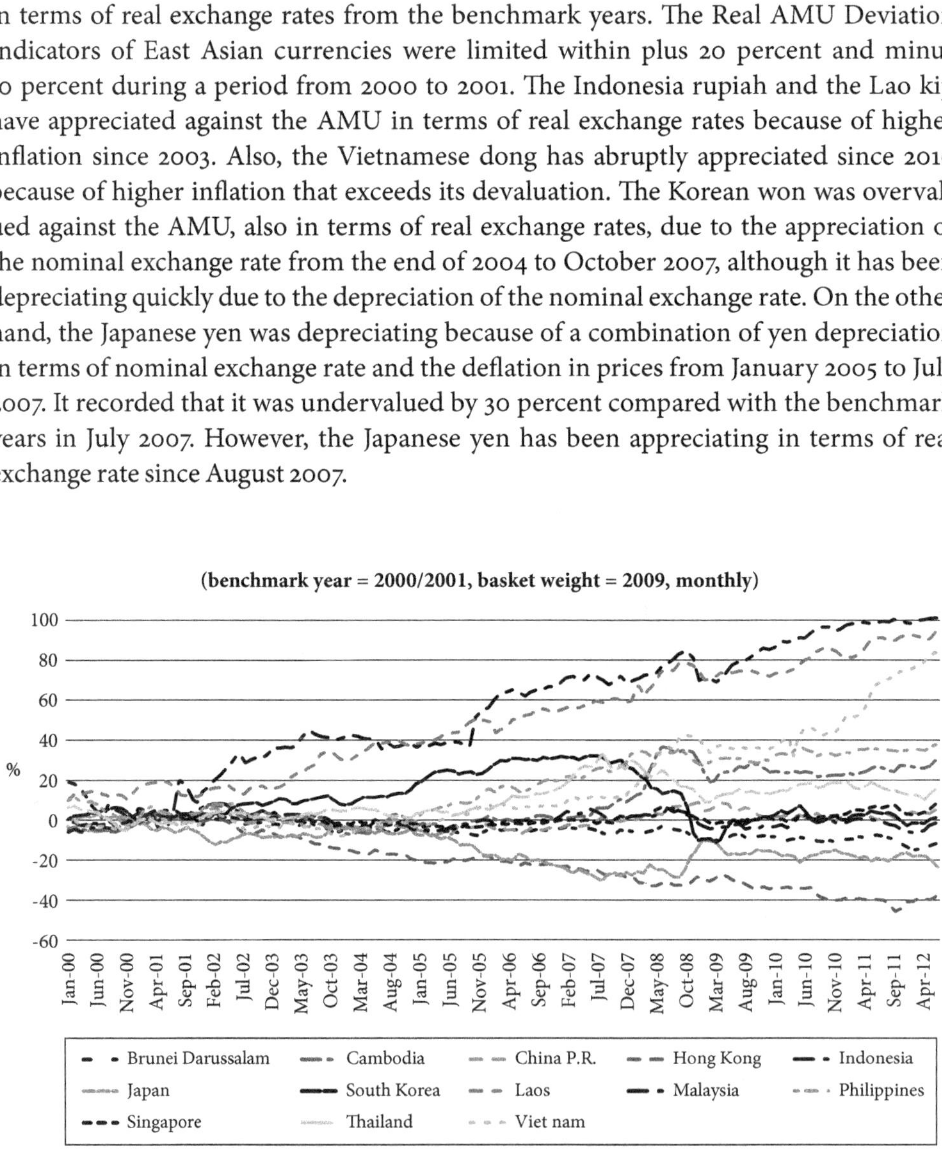


FIGURE 23.5 Real CMIM-based AMU Deviation Indicators

Data: RIETI's website ([http://www.rieti.go.jp/users/amu/en/index.html#data])

Ogawa and Yoshimi (2010) focused on recent events, which include the RMB reform in China and the global financial crisis, to investigate statistically recent diverging trends among East Asian currencies. Data on AMU Deviation Indicators were used to analyze both $\beta$ and $\sigma$ convergences of East Asian currencies. The analytical results show that the monetary authority of China has still kept stabilizing the exchange rate of the Chinese yuan against only the US dollar even though it announced its adoption of a managed floating exchange rate system with reference to a currency. Analytical results on $\beta$ and $\sigma$ convergences show that deviations among the East Asian currencies have been diverging in recent years, especially after 2005. The widening deviations reflect not the RMB reform but recent international capital flows and the global financial crisis. In addition, it is important that the monetary authorities of the countries are adopting a variety of exchange rate systems. In other words, a coordination failure in adopting exchange rate systems among these monetary authorities increases volatility and misalignment of intra-regional exchange rates in East Asia.

## 23.7 Conclusion

The global imbalance grew especially between the United States and East Asia, including China. The global imbalance changed exchange rates not only among the US dollar, the euro and other industrial country currencies but also among East Asian currencies which include the Japanese yen. This chapter considered movements in East Asian currencies in the global imbalance. To this end, it looked at causes of the current account imbalances. It focused on issues of whether undervalued currencies or saving glut caused the current account surplus. However, some East Asian currencies have depreciated during the global financial crisis. No currency swap arrangements under the Chiang Mai Initiative were implemented to stop the depreciation while the Chiang Mai Initiative has been multilateralized at the same time. Issues regarding the regional monetary cooperation in East Asia were considered in this chapter.

### Notes

1. The Balassa–Samuelson effect relies on differences in the relative productivity of the tradable and non-tradable sectors among countries.
2. This result may depend on their sample size. They conducted the estimation on a panel of countries like other studies, but on a single country. Coudert and Couharde (2005) pointed out that the small size of the sample compared to the number of regressors makes the fitted value of the regression very close to the observed value.
3. Thus, the macroeconomic balance is identified as the rate that equates the current account at full employment with sustainable net capital flows.
4. Most previous studies employ the fundamental current account balance obtained by panel estimation, using a set of macroeconomic fundamentals.

5. These results depend on the methodologies used to calculate the theoretical value: equilibrium real exchange rate (ERER) approach is 3 percent, external sustainability (ES) approach is 17 percent, and macroeconomic balance (MB) approach is 23 percent. We can categorize ES approach and MB approach as FEER, and ERER approach as BEER, respectively.
6. There is no strong consensus over the methodology used to estimate how undervalued the RMB is.
7. Dooley, Folkerts-Landau and Garber (2004) labeled the international monetary system "Bretton Woods II."
8. Each country in the EU has current account imbalances against other EU countries. In short, the EU faces a problem of internal imbalances.
9. The result depends on empirical analyses using a large data set that covers 128 emerging countries during 1970-1997.
10. A currency basket of the US dollar and the euro is 65 percent: 35 percent according to trade shares of the East Asia with the United States and the euro zone.

## References


Aizenman, J., and Jinjarak, Y. (2008), "Current account patterns and national real estate markets." NBER Working Paper No. 13921.

Bénassy-Quéré, A., Lahrèche-Révil, A., and Mignon, M. (2006), "World Consistent Equilibrium Exchange Rates," CEPII working paper no. 2006–20.

Bergsten, F., and Williamson, J. (2004), "Dollar Adjustment: How Far? Against What?," Institute for International Economics, Washington, DC.

Bernanke, B. (2005), "The Global Saving Glut and the US Current Account Deficit," Board of Governors of the Federal Reserve System, Washington, DC.

——, Bertaut, C., DeMarco, L., and Kamin, S. (2011), "International Capital Flows and the Returns to Safe Assets in the United States, 2003–2007," International Finance Discussion Papers, no 1014.

Bosco, Sergi. (2009), "Globalization and Financial Development: A Model of the Dot-Com and the Housing Bubbles," mimeo, MIT.

Caballero, R. J., Farhi, E., and Gourinchas, P. O. (2008), "An Equilibrium Model of 'Global Imbalances' and Low Interest Rates," *American Economic Review*, 98(1): 358–393

Cheung, Y., Chinn, M. D., and Fujii, E. (2007), "The Overvaluation of Renminbi Undervaluation," *Journal of International Money and Finance*, 26: 762–785.

Clark, P., and MacDonald, R. (1998), "Exchange Rates and Economic Fundamentals: A Methodological Comparison of BEERs and FEERs," IMF Working Paper 98/67.

Cline, W., and Williamson, J. (2008), "Estimates of the Equilibrium Exchange Rate of the Renminbi: Is There a Consensus and, If Not, Why Not?" In M. Goldstein and N. R. Lardy, eds., *Debating China's exchange rate policy*. Washington, DC: Peterson Institute for International Economics: 131–154.

—— and ——. (2010a), "Notes on Equilibrium Exchange Rates," Peterson Institute for International Economics, Policy Brief PB10-2.

—— and ——. (2010b), "Estimates of Fundamental Equilibrium Exchange Rates," Peterson Institute for International Economics, Policy Brief 10-15.

Coudert, V., and Couharde, C. (2005), "Real Equilibrium Exchange Rate in China," CEPII Working Paper No. 2005-01.

Dooley, M., Falkerts-Landau, D., and Garber, P. (2004), "An Essay on the Revised Bretton Woods System," *INTERNATIONAL JOURNAL OF FINANCE AND ECONOMICS*, 9(4): 307–313.

Dunaway, S. (2009), "Global Imbalances and the Financial Crisis," Council on Foreign Relations Special Report, no 44.

Edwards, S. (2002), "Does the Current Account Matter?" In S. Edwards and J. A. Frankel, eds., *Preventing Currency Crises in Emerging Markets*. Chicago: University of Chicago Press: 21–69.

——. (2005a), "Is The US Current Account Deficit Sustainable? And If Not, How Costly Is Adjustment Likely To Be?" NBER Working Paper No. 11541.

——. (2005b), "The End of Large Current Account Deficits, 1970–2002: Are There Lessons for the United States?" NBER Working Paper No. 11669.

Fogli, A. and Perri, F. (2006), "The 'Great Moderation' and the US External Imbalance," NBER Working Paper No.12708.

Greenspan, A., and Kennedy, J. (2008), "Sources and Uses of Equity Extracted from Homes," *Oxford Review of Economic Policy*, 24(1): 120–144.

IIMA (Institute for International Monetary Affairs) (2007), "Toward Greater Financial Stability in the Asian Region: Exploring Steps to Create Regional Monetary Units (RMUs)," ASEAN+3 Finance Ministers Research Group.

——. (2008), "Toward Greater Financial Stability in the Asian Region: Measures for Possible Use of Regional Monetary Units for Surveillance and Transaction," ASEAN+3 Finance Ministers Research Group.

IMF (International Monetary Fund). (2006), "Private Consumption in Emerging Asia," In Regional Economic Outlook: *Asia and Pacific*. International Monetary Fund, Washington, DC: 49–62.

——. (2011), "People's Republic of China: 2011 Article IV Consultation," Country Report No. 11/192.

Kawai, M., E. Ogawa, and T. Ito (2004): "Developing a New Regional Financial Architecture: A proposal," mimeo, Tokyo.

Kawai, M. (2009a), "The Role of an Asian Currency Unit," in Koichi Hamada, Beate Reszat, and Ulrich Volz eds., *Towards Monetary and Financial Integration in East Asia*, Cheltenham: Edward Elgar Publishing: 304–322.

Kawai, M. (2009b), "An Asian Currency Unit for Regional Exchange-Rate Policy Coordination," in Duck-Koo Chung and Barry J. Eichengreen eds. *Fostering Monetary & Financial Cooperation in East Asia*, Singapore: World Scientific Publishing: 73–112.

Kuroda, H. and M. Kawai (2002) "Strengthening Regional Financial Cooperation," *Pacific Economic Papers*, 332: 1–35.

Kujis, L. (2005). "Investment and Savings in China." World Bank Policy Research Paper Series No. 3633, World Bank, Washington, DC.

Laibson, D., and Mollerstrom, J. (2010), "Capital Flows, Consumption Booms and Asset Bubbles: A Behavioral Alternative to the Saving Glut Hypothesis" NBER Working Paper No.15759.

MOON, W., Y. RHEE, and D. YOON (2006), "Regional Currency Unit in Asia: Property and Perspective," KIEP Working Paper, 06-03.

Obstfeld, M. and K. Rogoff (2003), "The Unsustainable US Current Account Position Revised," NBER Working Paper, 10869.

—— and ——. (2009), "Global Imbalances and the Financial Crisis: Products of Common Causes," Federal Reserve Bank of San Francisco Asia Economic Policy Conference Paper.

Ogawa, E. (2011), "Towards the Establishment of an Asian Currency Unit," ADBI Working Paper, forthcoming.

Ogawa, E., and Kudo, T. (2007), "Possible Depreciation of the US Dollar for Unsustainable Current Account Deficit in the United States," CESifo Forum, 8(4): 24–30.

Ogawa, E., and J. Shimizu (2005a), "A Deviation Measurement for Coordinated Exchange Rate Policies in East Asia," *RIETI Discussion Paper Series*, 05-E-017.

Ogawa, E., and J. Shimizu (2005b) "Risk properties of AMU denominated Asian bond," *Journal of Asian Economics*, 16(4): 590–611.

Ogawa, E. and T. Yoshimi (2010) "Analysis on β and σ Convergences of East Asian Currencies," *International Journal of Intelligent Technologies and Applied Statistics*, 3(5): 237–263.

Portes, R. (2009), "Global Imbalances," in M. Dewatripont, X. Freixas, and R. Portes (eds), Macroeconomic Stability and Financial Regulation: Key Issues for the G20. London: Centre for Economic Policy Research, 19–26.

Subramanian, A. (2010), "New PPP-Based Estimates of Renminbi Undervaluation and Policy Implications," Peterson Institute For International Economics Policy Brief 10-8.

Wang, Y., Hui, X., and Soofi, A.S. (2007), "Estimating Renminbi (RMB) Equilibrium Exchange Rate," *Journal of Policy Modeling*, 29(3): 417–429.

Weimer, C. (2008). "The Saving Story behind China's Trade Imbalance." Working Paper, National University of Singapore, Singapore.

Williamson, J. (1985), "The Exchange Rate System," 2nd ed., Institute of International Economics, Washington D.C.

CHAPTER 24

# REBALANCING OF THE WORLD ECONOMY AND ASIA

MENZIE D. CHINN AND HIRO ITO[1]

## 24.1 INTRODUCTION

IN the decade leading up to the global financial crisis of 2008, economists debated the causes and consequences of the expanding current account imbalances. The United States ran enormous deficits, while China, the rest of East Asia, and the oil exporting countries ran correspondingly large current account surpluses (Figure 24.1). It was therefore unsurprising that China and other East Asian economies received much attention; several policymakers and economists (Bernanke, 2005, Greenspan, 2005a,b, and Clarida, 2005) argued that excess saving in these countries financed and encouraged profligacy in the current account deficit countries, most notably the United States.

With the outbreak of the global financial crisis and ensuing recession, these current account balances reversed drastically, albeit incompletely. The proximity of the two events naturally leads to the question of whether the two phenomena are related or causal in nature.

With the resumption of growth in 2010, there was much speculation about whether the world economy would return to the precrisis situation where the United States (and other advanced economies in Europe) deficits are financed by China, Japan, and other East Asian economies. The possibility that large imbalances made the world economy vulnerable to the financial crisis reinforces the importance of understanding the origins of the precrisis situation. That concern is only heightened by the lack of substantial changes in East Asia's economic policy framework.

This paper focuses on the link between the rebalancing of the world economy and the contribution of the East Asian economies, especially China. We will examine the cross-country determinants of current account balances by applying a panel data analysis to both industrialized and developing countries for the last four decades. In order to

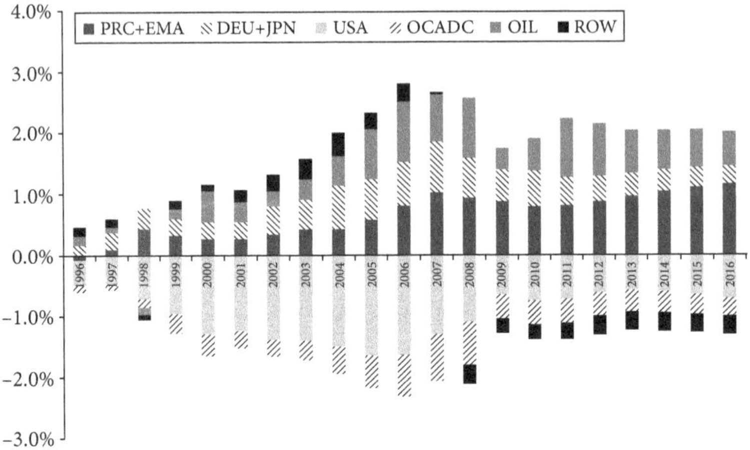


FIGURE 24.1 Current account balances as a share of world GDP.

*Notes:* 2010–2016 data are IMF projections. "PRC+EMA" is China plus other emerging countries in Asia, "DEU+JPN" is Germany plus Japan, "USA" is United States, "OCADC" is other advanced developed countries, "OIL" is oil exporting countries, and "ROW" is rest of the world.

*Source:* IMF, *World Economic Outlook*, April 2011.

project how the world economy will rebalance, it is important to know how the global imbalances developed. This exercise will also identify what is left as unexplained as the cross-country factors, that is, what is left as country-specific characteristics contributing to current account balances. Then, we devote special attention to China, the largest contributor to the global imbalances in East Asia, by reviewing the characteristics of its national saving and relevant policies.

Section 24.2 will briefly review competing hypotheses that explain the global imbalances. In Section 24.3, we discuss the results from cross-sectional analyses on the determinants of current account balances. We will focus on China in the last two sections of the chapter. In Section 24.4, we will review the characteristics of China's national saving on sectorial basis. Lastly, in Section 24.5 we will provide some prospects of rebalancing for the United States and China and also make concluding remarks.

## 24.2 Review of Competing Hypotheses

While global imbalances were troubling from a policy standpoint, the state of the imbalances has stirred debates in the academic community because no single standard theory or hypothesis appeared sufficient to explain the imbalances' unprecedented scales and persistency.

The rise of global imbalances has been explained in a variety of ways. These explanations include (1) trends in saving and investment balances, (2) the intertemporal approach, (3) mercantilist behavior, (4) the global saving glut, and (5) distortions in financial markets. Note that the explanations are not mutually exclusive.

## 24.2.1 The National Saving and Investment Approach

The saving-investment approach takes the perspective from the national saving identity, which states that the current account is equal to the budget balance and the private saving-investment gap. This is a tautology, unless one imposes some structure and causality.

One particularly simple variant of this approach relies upon assuming that the shocks primarily hit the government sector. Then changes in the budget balance are quasi-exogenous, and the current account consequently responds. The inspiration for this perspective is the mid-1980's experience with the Reagan era tax cuts and defense buildup. During that episode, the budget deficit and current account deficits both yawned to unprecedentedly large magnitudes, inspiring the term "the twin deficits."

Upon inspection, the simple interpretation of the twin deficits clearly does not hold, beyond the mid-1980s, and 2001-2004. Of course, other types of shocks perturb the economy, and once one allows for shocks to the other components of aggregate demand, or to the supply side, then no such positive correlation need hold at all times. However, that does not deny the validity of that view during the last decade.[2]

A systematic approach involves modeling the current account by explicitly focusing on the determinants of private investment and saving, and adding those variables to the budget balance. Chinn and Ito (2007, 2008a) find that the budget balance is an important determinant of the current account balance for industrial countries; the coefficient for the budget balance variable is 0.15 in a model controlling for macroeconomic and institutional variables. A series of robustness checks yield the results that a 1 percent point increase in the budget balance leads to a 0.1 to 0.5 percentage point increase in the current account balance.[3] For the United States, their analysis confirms the view that it is a saving drought—not investment boom—that is contributing to the enlargement of current account deficits, although there is some evidence of anomalous behavior in the 2001-2004 period.

## 24.2.2 The Intertemporal Approach

The intertemporal approach is the mainstay of the rigorous approach to explaining current account imbalances. In this perspective, consumption today is to equal a share of the present discounted value of future expected net output, or net wealth. Hence, changes in consumption are due solely to changes in either the interest rate or in expectations about future net output due to productivity shocks or reductions in investment and government spending.

The U.S. experience of the late 1990s can therefore be rationalized by an anticipation of a future productivity boom that induces an immediate increase in consumption, resulting in a current account deficit.[4] In the context of America in the 2000s, to consume more now means to import more and export less. The deficits leading up to the financial crisis of 2008-2009 are more difficult to fit into this approach. A large proportion of capital flowing to the United States takes place in the form of purchases of U.S. government securities—not purchases of American stocks or direct investment in its factories, as it did in the years leading up to 2000. Moreover, the heavy involvement of foreign central banks in purchasing U.S. assets suggests that the profit motive was not behind the ongoing flows to the United States.[5]

A formal test of the intertemporal approach, as applied to the recent U.S. experience, was conducted by Engel and Rogers (2006). They model the current account as a function of the expected discounted present value of its future share of world GDP relative to its current share of world GDP (where the world is the advanced economies). The key difficulty in testing this approach is in modeling expected output growth; using a Markov-switching approach, they find that the U.S. is not keeping on a long-run sustainable path.[6] However, using survey data on forecasted GDP growth in the G-7, Engel and Rogers's empirical model appears to explain the evolution of the U.S. current account remarkably well.[7]

### 24.2.3 The Mercantilist Explanation

Another prominent view attributes the East Asian surpluses to explicitly mercantilist behavior. From this perspective, the developing countries of East Asia have followed an export-led development strategy. That export-led strategy resulted in rapid growth; however, starting in the mid-1990's, current account surpluses evolved into current account deficits, as investment boomed in some of the Asian economies, especially those in Southeast Asia.

In the wake of the 1997 financial crisis, investment levels collapsed, while saving rates remained relatively high. Currencies depreciated sharply in the region; however, over time, East Asian central banks maintained their currencies at fairly weak levels and started increasing the amount of international reserves holding. Figure 24.2 illustrates China's experience; after 2004, the country's current account surplus persistently increased while its financial account did not fall into deficit, resulting in a pileup of international reserves (Figure 24.2). For some observers, this picture is worth a thousand words to explain that the relatively large and persistent current account surpluses in the region have been manufactured by currency manipulation. One difficulty with this explanation is that the export-led development path has been in place for decades, while the sharp rise in current account surpluses and international reserves holding broke out in the post-Asian crisis period.

Another difficulty with this argument is that while the model explains one half of the current account imbalances, it does not explain the other side—namely why it is that

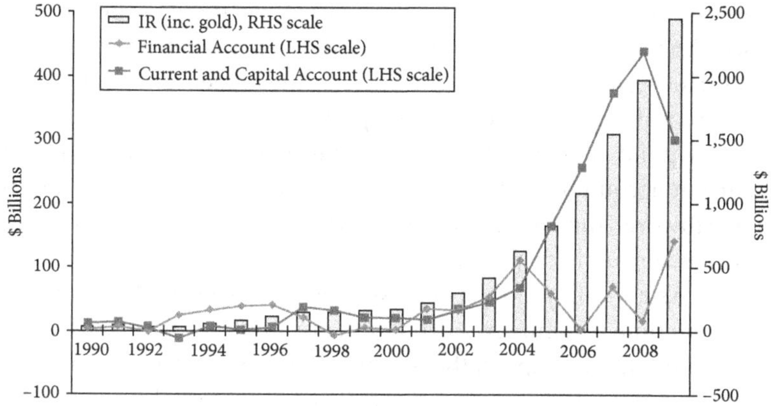


FIGURE 24.2 China's Current Account, Financial Account, and International Reserves Holding

*Source:* CEIC, World Development Indicators (WDI)

the United States, United Kingdom, and specific other developed countries ran substantial deficits. In a series of papers, Dooley, et al. (2003; 2008) interpret the U.S. current account deficit as the outcome of concerted mercantilist efforts by East Asian state actors. In this context, the financing of America's trade (and budget) deficit is an explicit quid pro quo for continued access to American markets. Their explanation argues that the government interventions are aimed at supporting exporting industries.

There are also problems with this thesis. Most notable is the mysterious aspect of timing: East Asian savings began flowing to the United States in 2003. Why not earlier, if the mercantilist impetus had been there all along? For a thorough critique, see Prasad and Wei (2005). On the other hand, for emerging markets, Gagnon (2010) shows that current account balances are highly correlated with central bank official intervention.

An alternative interpretation for the large-scale reserve accumulation has been attributed to the self-insurance or precautionary demand. Foreign exchange reserves can reduce the probability of an output drop induced by capital flight or sudden stop. This self-insurance motivation rose substantially in the wake of the East Asian crises; this point was verified by Aizenman and Marion (2003) and Aizenman and Lee (2007).[8]

## 24.2.4 The "Global Saving Glut" Hypothesis

The "global saving glut" explanation has been expounded by Bernanke (2005), Clarida (2005a,b), and Hubbard (2005). This argument views excess saving from Asian emerging market countries, driven by rising savings and collapsing investment in the aftermath of the financial crisis (and to a lesser extent Europe), as the cause of the U.S. current account deficit. More recently, the burgeoning surpluses of the oil exporters, ranging from the Persian Gulf countries to Russia, have moved to the fore as sources of excess saving. From this perspective, the U.S. external imbalance is a problem made abroad;

the lack of well-developed and open financial markets encourages countries with excess savings to seek financial intermediation in well-developed financial systems such as the United States. Hence, a solution may only arise in the longer term, as better developed financial systems mitigate this excess savings problem.[9]

The strongest point in favor of the saving glut hypothesis is the observation of a widening current account deficit in the United States, combined with low, real world interest rates. However, the saving glut versus twin deficits view is not an either-or proposition. An expansionary fiscal policy in the United States combined with an investment drought in East Asia would yield the observed increase in current account imbalances, while at the same time resulting in a drop in the real interest rate. Thus, a simple open economy macro model can explain the recent rise in U.S. current account deficits, East Asian current account surpluses, and the recent fall in global interest rates without resort to exotic demand for high quality assets, or the like (Chinn and Ito, 2008a).

In order to formally test the saving glut hypothesis, one can evaluate whether financial development and institutional development explain the pattern of imbalances. Using a structural model while controlling for the level of financial development and openness as well as institutional development, Chinn and Ito (2007) provide evidence against the argument that emerging market countries, especially those in East Asia, will experience lower rates of saving once these countries achieve higher levels of financial development and better developed legal infrastructure. In addition, more open financial markets do not appear to have any impact on current account balances for this group of countries.[10]

## 24.3 Estimations

One effective way of comparing the validities of these various arguments and hypotheses on the determinants of current account balances is to implement a systematic empirical exercise by using a reduced form of estimation and a large panel dataset that encompasses many countries and years.[11] In this section we estimate a simple analytical model of current account balances, as well as national saving and investment. In doing so we build on the work of Chinn and Prasad (2003) and Chinn and Ito (2007) and will estimate the following model.

Using the data from 23 industrial and 86 developing countries covering the four decades 1970-2008, we estimate the following regression equation:

$$\begin{aligned} y_{i,t} = \alpha + \beta_1 BB_{i,t} \\ &+ \beta_2 FD_{i,t} + \beta_3 LEGAL_i + \beta_3 KAOPEN_{i,t} \\ &+ \beta_4 (FD_{i,t} \times LEGAL_{i,t}) + \beta_5 (LEGAL_{i,t} \times KAOPEN_{i,t}) + \beta_6 (KAOPEN_{i,t} \times FD_{i,t}) \quad (1) \\ &+ X_{i,t}\Gamma + u_{i,t}\,. \end{aligned}$$

$y_{i,t}$ refers to three dependent variables: the current account balance, national saving, and investment, all expressed as a share of GDP. *FD* is a measure of financial development, for which private credit creation (*PCGDP*) is usually used; *KAOPEN*, the Chinn-Ito (2006) measure of financial openness; and *LEGAL* a measure of legal/institutional development—the first principal component of law and order (*LAO*), bureaucratic quality (*BQ*), and anti-corruption measures (*CORRUPT*).[12] $X_{i,t}$ is a vector of macroeconomic and policy control variables that include familiar determinants of current account balances such as net foreign assets as a ratio to GDP; relative income (to the U.S.); its quadratic term; relative dependency ratios on young and old population; terms of trade volatility; output growth rates; trade openness (= exports+imports/GDP); dummies for oil exporting countries; and time fixed effects.

Panels of non-overlapping five-year averages are used for all explanatory variables except when noted otherwise.[13] All the variables, except for net foreign assets to GDP, are converted into the deviations from their GDP-weighted world mean prior to the calculation of five year averages—net foreign asset ratios are sampled from the first year of each five-year panel as the initial conditions.[14] We regress current account balances, national saving, and investment on the same set of regressors separately for industrialized countries (IDC), developing countries (LDC), and emerging market economies (EMG).[15]

We report the estimation results in Tables 24.1 and 24.2. Note first that these are consistent with the twin deficits hypothesis: budget surpluses and current account surpluses move together, other things equal. A coefficient of less than one suggests, however, that they move together less than proportionately.[16] Larger net foreign assets, which should generate a stronger income account, affect the current account balance positively, as anticipated. The relative income terms, which tend to be jointly if not always individually significant, show that higher income countries generally have stronger current accounts ("capital tends to flow from higher to lower income countries"). Countries with higher dependency ratios (and, by the life-cycle hypothesis, lower savings rates) generally have weaker current accounts. Oil exporting countries have stronger current accounts, other things equal. All this is as expected.

The Caballero-Farhi-Gourinchas (2008) hypothesis that countries with more developed financial markets should have weaker currents accounts ("capital flows from China, with its underdeveloped capital markets, to the United States, which has a comparative advantage in producing safe financial assets") finds significant support in the full sample (left-most column in Table 24.1). Given that current account imbalances are more apparent between countries with different levels of income (e.g., the United States and China), the findings in the full sample can be informative.[17] The effect can be observed in the subsamples of industrialized countries and emerging market countries.

Together with the solo effect of financial development, its interactions with legal development and capital account openness are supportive of the Caballero et al. interpretation of global imbalances with statistically significant coefficients for the subsample of emerging markets; those with better developed financial markets and legal institutions or open capital accounts tend to have weaker current account balances, or

**Table 24.1 Current Account Regression with Institutional Variables**

| | Current Account | | | |
|---|---|---|---|---|
| | (1) | (2) | (3) | (4) |
| | Full | Industrial Countries (IDC) | Less Developed Countries (LDC) | EMG |
| Government budget balance | 0.295 | 0.289 | 0.279 | 0.094 |
| | [0.058]*** | [0.086]*** | [0.063]*** | [0.054]* |
| Net foreign assets (initial) | 0.037 | 0.078 | 0.028 | 0.026 |
| | [0.006]*** | [0.008]*** | [0.007]*** | [0.012]** |
| Relative income | 0.09 | 0.018 | 0.135 | 0.284 |
| | [0.018]*** | [0.022] | [0.022]*** | [0.093]*** |
| Relative income squared | 0.055 | 0.02 | 0.046 | 0.16 |
| | [0.018]*** | [0.094] | [0.017]*** | [0.081]* |
| Dependency ratio (young) | -0.033 | 0.004 | -0.029 | -0.029 |
| | [0.015]** | [0.025] | [0.017]* | [0.019] |
| Dependency ratio (old) | -0.019 | 0.057 | -0.022 | -0.068 |
| | [0.010]** | [0.021]*** | [0.011]** | [0.020]*** |
| Financial development (PCGDP) | -0.027 | -0.02 | 0 | -0.117 |
| | [0.014]* | [0.010]* | [0.029] | [0.038]*** |
| Legal development (LEGAL) | -0.008 | 0.015 | -0.015 | -0.018 |
| | [0.005]* | [0.005]*** | [0.007]** | [0.012] |
| PCGDP x LEGAL | -0.011 | -0.014 | -0.007 | -0.032 |
| | [0.008] | [0.012] | [0.008] | [0.014]** |
| Financial open. (KAOPEN) | 0.002 | 0.008 | -0.009 | -0.008 |
| | [0.005] | [0.004]* | [0.008] | [0.009] |
| KAOPEN x LEGAL | 0.003 | 0.012 | -0.001 | 0.004 |
| | [0.001]*** | [0.003]*** | [0.002] | [0.003] |
| KAOPEN x PCGDP | 0.002 | 0.028 | 0.003 | -0.02 |
| | [0.007] | [0.010]*** | [0.008] | [0.010]* |
| TOT volatility | 0 | 0.028 | -0.01 | 0.023 |
| | [0.023] | [0.047] | [0.024] | [0.025] |
| Avg. GDP growth | -0.097 | 0.178 | -0.09 | 0.072 |
| | [0.091] | [0.178] | [0.099] | [0.117] |
| Trade openness | -0.001 | -0.001 | -0.005 | 0 |
| | [0.006] | [0.011] | [0.010] | [0.012] |
| Oil exporting countries | 0.028 | – | 0.025 | 0.045 |
| | [0.013]** | – | [0.012]** | [0.016]*** |

**Table 24.1 Continued**

| | Current Account | | | |
|---|---|---|---|---|
| | (1) | (2) | (3) | (4) |
| | Full | Industrial Countries (IDC) | Less Developed Countries (LDC) | EMG |
| Dummy for 2001-05 | 0.025 | 0.015 | 0.033 | 0.041 |
| | [0.009]*** | [0.009]* | [0.015]** | [0.017]** |
| Dummy for 2006-08 | 0.017 | 0.002 | 0.032 | 0.019 |
| | [0.011] | [0.010] | [0.018]* | [0.022] |
| Observations | 621 | 174 | 447 | 250 |
| Adjusted R-squared | 0.5 | 0.63 | 0.52 | 0.46 |

*Note:* Time fixed effects are included in the estimation, but only those for the 2001–05 and 2006–08 periods are reported in the table.

experience the least tendency for capital to flow out. This is consistent with the saving glut hypothesis. When we look only at the industrial countries, however, these patterns are no longer evident.

Two dummy variables for the 2001-2005 and 2006-2008 subperiods look to the question of whether recent experience has been unusual.[18] Emerging market economies appear to have run unusually large surpluses in the 2001-2005 subperiod, consistent with the idea that they were fixated on minimizing financing vulnerabilities and accumulating reserves following the Asian crisis. Such behavior is not evident for emerging markets as a group in 2006-2008. We confirm this by adding a dummy variable for China in the post-2005 period and finding its coefficient significantly positive at the one per cent level. When a dummy is added for the emerging market group for the entire post-2001 period (instead of two five-year period dummies), its coefficient turns out to be zero, implying that the contribution of emerging markets to global imbalances can be a China story. A surprise is that we see the industrial countries as a group running larger surpluses in the same 2001-2005 period than their other characteristics would lead one to expect. Evidently the United States was an outlier in this respect.[19]

Table 24.2 then estimates the model for savings and investment separately. A few results of note are that government budget deficits affect primarily national saving (in the same direction as government saving, contrary to Ricardian equivalence stories), and that dependency ratios affect both savings and investment (as emphasized in Eichengreen and Fifer 2002).[20] As the saving glut proponents argue, further financial development would lessen the need for precautionary saving. If a country is equipped with better-developed legal systems, the negative impact of financial development on national saving can be even larger. Interestingly, the solo effect of financial development has a negative impact on national saving for emerging market countries, while it has

## Table 24.2 National Saving and Investment Regression with Institutional Variables

| | National Saving | | | | Investment | | | |
|---|---|---|---|---|---|---|---|---|
| | (5) | (6) | (7) | (8) | (9) | (10) | (11) | (12) |
| | Full | Industrial Countries (IDC) | Less Developed (LDC) | EMG | Full | Industrial Countries (IDC) | Less Developed (LDC) | EMG |
| Government budget balance | 0.432 | 0.476 | 0.419 | 0.2 | 0.033 | 0.304 | 0.022 | −0.011 |
| | [0.111]*** | [0.087]*** | [0.121]*** | [0.071]*** | [0.034] | [0.126]** | [0.033] | [0.061] |
| Net foreign assets (initial) | 0.022 | 0.072 | 0.017 | 0.053 | −0.007 | −0.014 | −0.003 | 0.012 |
| | [0.014] | [0.008]*** | [0.015] | [0.015]*** | [0.004]* | [0.010] | [0.005] | [0.013] |
| Relative income | 0.015 | 0 | 0.036 | −0.054 | −0.037 | −0.006 | −0.051 | −0.264 |
| | [0.034] | [0.027] | [0.044] | [0.093] | [0.018]** | [0.032] | [0.022]** | [0.075]*** |
| Relative income squared | 0.054 | −0.176 | 0.063 | −0.238 | 0 | −0.225 | 0.019 | −0.342 |
| | [0.035] | [0.116] | [0.031]** | [0.097]** | [0.018] | [0.155] | [0.018] | [0.071]*** |
| Dependency ratio (young) | −0.06 | −0.088 | −0.035 | −0.057 | −0.05 | −0.097 | −0.033 | −0.046 |
| | [0.017]*** | [0.025]*** | [0.022] | [0.020]*** | [0.013]*** | [0.026]*** | [0.014]** | [0.018]** |
| Dependency ratio (old) | −0.019 | −0.017 | −0.007 | −0.083 | −0.006 | −0.058 | 0.006 | −0.013 |
| | [0.015] | [0.021] | [0.017] | [0.020]*** | [0.009] | [0.020]*** | [0.010] | [0.019] |
| Financial development (PCGDP) | 0.02 | 0.017 | 0.073 | −0.091 | 0.037 | 0.026 | 0.073 | 0.046 |
| | [0.017] | [0.011] | [0.059] | [0.053]* | [0.008]*** | [0.012]** | [0.031]** | [0.043] |
| Legal development (LEGAL) | −0.012 | 0.011 | −0.019 | −0.034 | −0.002 | −0.01 | 0.007 | −0.015 |
| | [0.007]* | [0.006]* | [0.012] | [0.015]** | [0.004] | [0.006]* | [0.008] | [0.014] |
| PCGDP x LEGAL | −0.02 | −0.028 | −0.016 | −0.045 | 0 | −0.003 | 0.013 | 0.001 |
| | [0.008]** | [0.013]** | [0.014] | [0.018]** | [0.004] | [0.012] | [0.010] | [0.015] |

| | | | | | | | | |
|---|---|---|---|---|---|---|---|---|
| Financial open. (KAOPEN) | −0.004 | −0.004 | −0.013 | −0.001 | −0.011 | −0.01 | −0.016 | −0.006 |
| | [0.006] | [0.005] | [0.012] | [0.010] | [0.003]*** | [0.003]*** | [0.006]** | [0.007] |
| KAOPEN x LEGAL | −0.002 | 0.01 | −0.006 | 0.003 | −0.003 | 0.003 | −0.005 | −0.004 |
| | [0.001] | [0.003]*** | [0.004] | [0.004] | [0.001]*** | [0.005] | [0.002]** | [0.003] |
| KAOPEN x PCGDP | 0.007 | 0.009 | 0.012 | −0.011 | −0.001 | −0.003 | −0.004 | 0.002 |
| | [0.009] | [0.011] | [0.014] | [0.014] | [0.005] | [0.011] | [0.008] | [0.012] |
| TOT volatility | −0.024 | 0.314 | −0.051 | −0.066 | 0.017 | 0.252 | −0.003 | −0.052 |
| | [0.039] | [0.053]*** | [0.044] | [0.035]* | [0.022] | [0.045]*** | [0.025] | [0.031]* |
| Avg. GDP growth | 0.692 | 0.417 | 0.695 | 1.129 | 0.951 | 0.38 | 0.944 | 1.143 |
| | [0.165]*** | [0.252] | [0.190]*** | [0.169]*** | [0.094]*** | [0.268] | [0.097]*** | [0.127]*** |
| Trade openness | 0.021 | 0.033 | 0.024 | 0.033 | 0.02 | 0.023 | 0.025 | 0.035 |
| | [0.007]*** | [0.016]** | [0.013]* | [0.012]*** | [0.005]*** | [0.012]* | [0.008]*** | [0.009]*** |
| Oil exporting countries | 0.078 | – | 0.086 | 0.032 | 0.049 | – | 0.059 | 0.01 |
| | [0.018]*** | – | [0.020]*** | [0.017]* | [0.012]*** | – | [0.011]*** | [0.015] |
| Dummy for 2001-05 | 0.007 | −0.053 | 0.062 | 0.048 | −0.028 | −0.08 | 0.013 | −0.005 |
| | [0.013] | [0.012]*** | [0.017]*** | [0.020]** | [0.014]* | [0.021]*** | [0.014] | [0.018] |
| Dummy for 2006-08 | 0.027 | −0.041 | 0.097 | 0.045 | −0.011 | −0.058 | 0.031 | 0.014 |
| | [0.015]* | [0.012]*** | [0.023]*** | [0.026]* | [0.015] | [0.020]*** | [0.016]* | [0.020] |
| Observations | 621 | 174 | 447 | 250 | 621 | 174 | 447 | 250 |
| Adjusted R-squared | 0.46 | 0.63 | 0.49 | 0.57 | 0.35 | 0.46 | 0.39 | 0.5 |

a positive one on investment for industrialized countries. These findings suggest that increasing the level of financial development can have an overall negative impact on net saving, i.e., current account balances, although its channels can differ among different income levels of countries.

A number of alternative specifications yield very similar results.[21] One of interest involves adding foreign reserves as a percent of GDP, lagged one five-year period, as an additional explanatory variable. Lagging the reserves variable is designed to address the concern that the current account balance and contemporaneous reserves are simultaneously determined (positive shocks to the current account will translate into positive shocks to reserves). Reserve-adequacy arguments suggest that, other things equal, larger reserves should mean less incentive for reserve accumulation and a weaker current account. For the industrial countries, the coefficient on this variable is negative and significant, as hypothesized. For emerging market economies, it is insignificant.[22] For developing countries, it is positive and significant, contrary to the hypothesis.

However, one must be careful about this sort of exercise, especially if it is intended to examine the factors that led to the unique situation of the global imbalances on the eve of the crisis. Because the global crisis can be interpreted as a large-scale correction of the imbalances, some of the saving and investment behavior of countries, which contributed to the global imbalances, can only be interpreted as anomaly. If that is the case, there must be some portions of current account balances, or national saving or investment, that cannot be explained by cross-country variations of the explanatory variables.

In fact, Chinn et al.'s results suggest the possibility that current accounts may have behaved atypically in the 2006-2008 period, a period with global imbalances prior to the global crisis. Figure 24.3 shows the Kernel density estimates of the distribution of the prediction errors from the model estimation for the current account balances for the groups of industrialized countries and emerging market economies. Interestingly, for both groups, the distribution of the prediction errors from the regression estimation has become significantly wider in the 2006–2008 period. For the group of industrialized countries, the prediction errors are more skewed to the left and more widely distributed in 2006-2008. While industrialized countries seem to have experienced wide variation in the prediction errors in the 1980s and the 1990s as well as the last period, the wider variation in the global imbalances period stands out for the group of emerging market countries, suggesting a possibility of a regime shift in the current account balance series in this period.

As shown in Figure 24.4, the estimation model performs poorly for China and the United States as well. Figure 24.4b displays the implied current account balances for China along with 95 percent confidence intervals of prediction that are calculated using the estimation results. The figure shows that China's current account is well outside the confidence interval. The same kind of underperformance of the regression model is observed for the national saving estimation as well.

Chinn et al. (2011) also try to see if any factors, which are not included in the estimation model and which can be more prevalent in the global imbalances period than other period, can explain the unexplained portion of current account balances for the

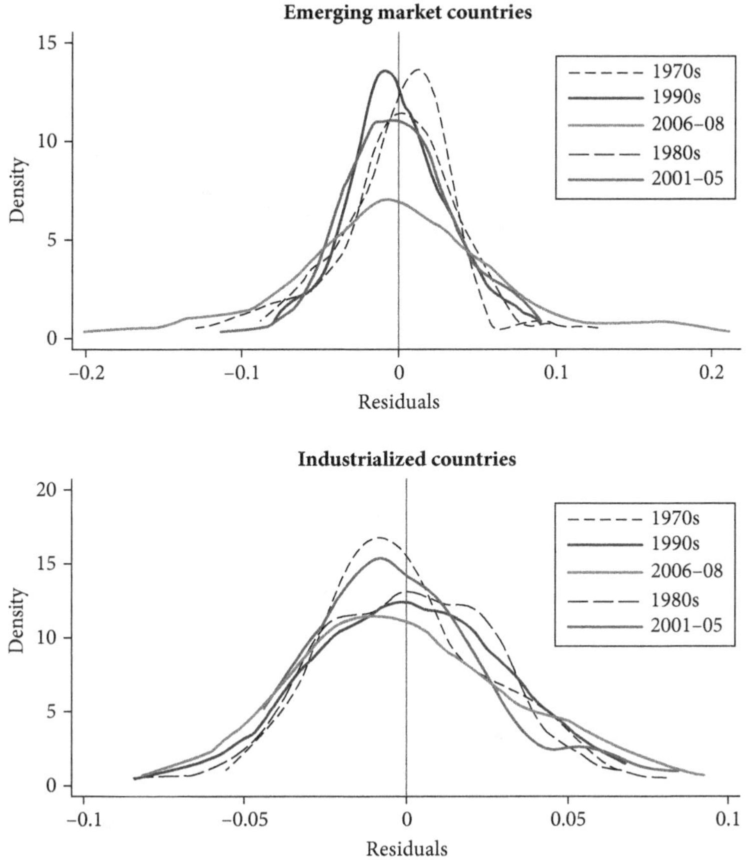


FIGURE 24.3 Kernel Distributions of Prediction Errors

*Source:* Chinn, Eichengreen, and Ito (2011)

countries. They test the variables that account for monetary or fiscal policy stance as well as the ones that represent the conditions of financial markets and most importantly, housing markets. While the boom in the financial markets and housing markets explain some portions of the current account balances that cannot be explained by the benchmark model, Chinn et al. find that there is still a large portion of current account balances for the countries with overly imbalanced current accounts, such as the United States, the United Kingdom, Greece, Iceland, and China.

These results indicate that these countries need to implement policies that are particularly tailored for their country-specific situations that affect the saving and investment decisions in order to guide themselves toward rebalancing. In the next section, we focus on the biggest contributor to the global imbalances in Asia and review the country's policies and socio-economic conditions that may have contributed to its unique saving and investment imbalances.

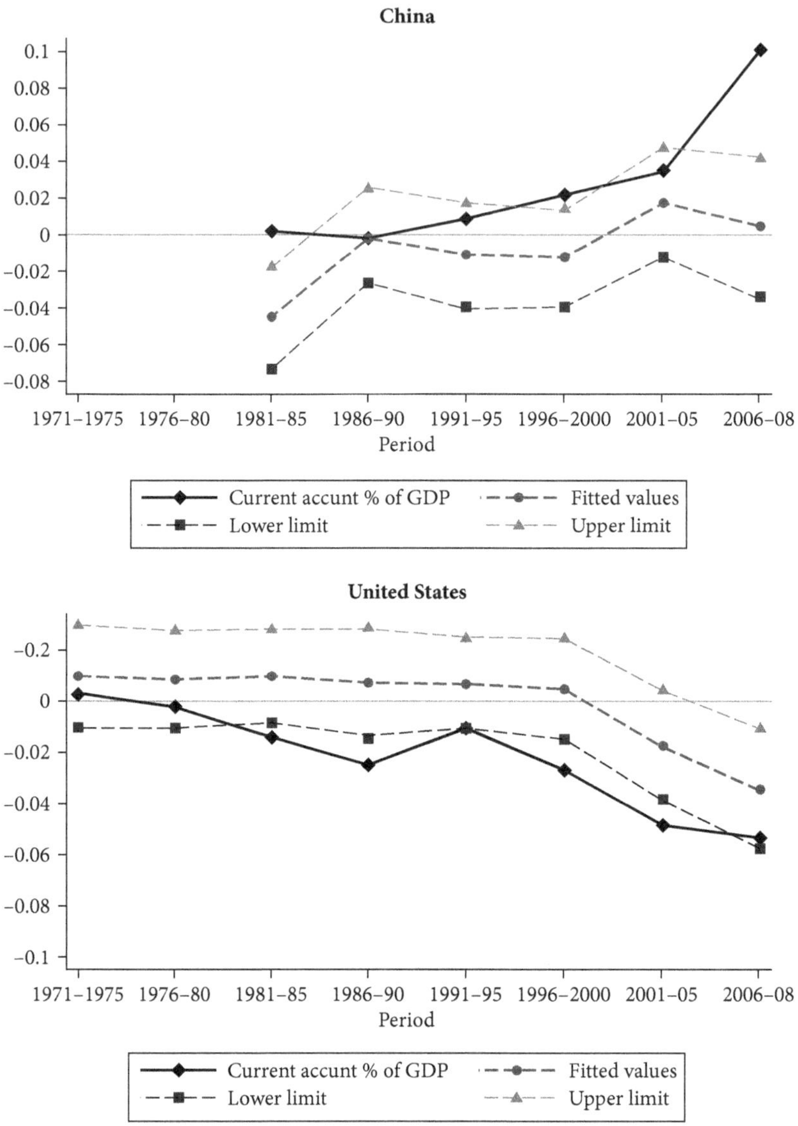


FIGURE 24.4 Predictions of Current Accounts

*Source:* Chinn, Eichengreen, and Ito (2011)

## 24.4 Explanations for China's High Saving Rate

To understand China's uniquely high saving rate, one of the main contributors to the global imbalances, we also need to discuss it in the context of the country's rapid, but unbalanced, growth. The first pertains to the wide income gap between industrial, high-growth coastal areas and agricultural, underdeveloped inland regions, which was essentially a result of the longtime emphasis on market-driven economic experimentation in the coastal cities. The second pertains to the gap between growth in the returns to capital versus labor. While the corporate sector profits, especially those of the manufacturing sector, have risen continuously throughout the 2000s, labor income has been declining in the same period. Both manufacturing-oriented industrialization and declining labor income have contributed to the third aspect of unbalanced growth, which is the rapid rise in savings, especially those of corporate and household sectors.

Figure 24.5 shows that, while the level of national investment of China has been fairly high in recent years, that of national saving has been even higher, the difference between the two accounting for the magnitude of the current account surplus. Hence, understanding the impact of financial globalization on China requires an examination of the growth imbalances that have contributed to China's unique saving behavior. For that purpose, we need to examine China's domestic savings from the perspective of the flow of funds.

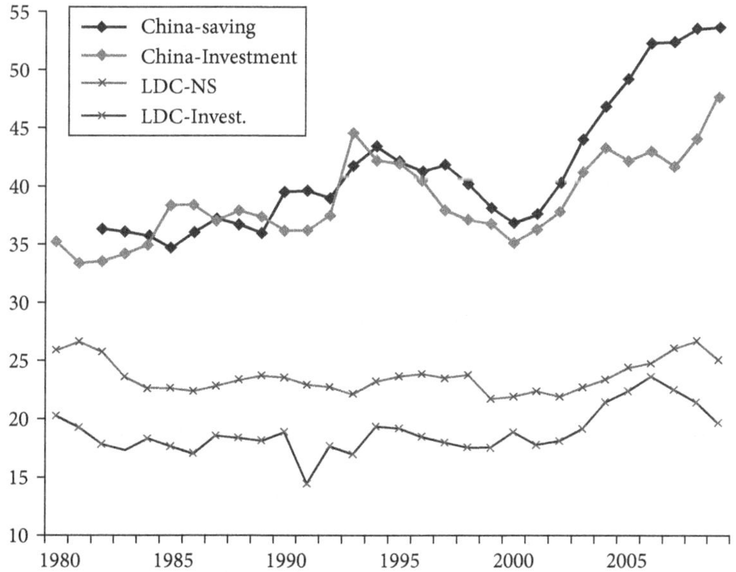


FIGURE 24.5 China's National Saving and Investment

*Source:* World Development Indicator

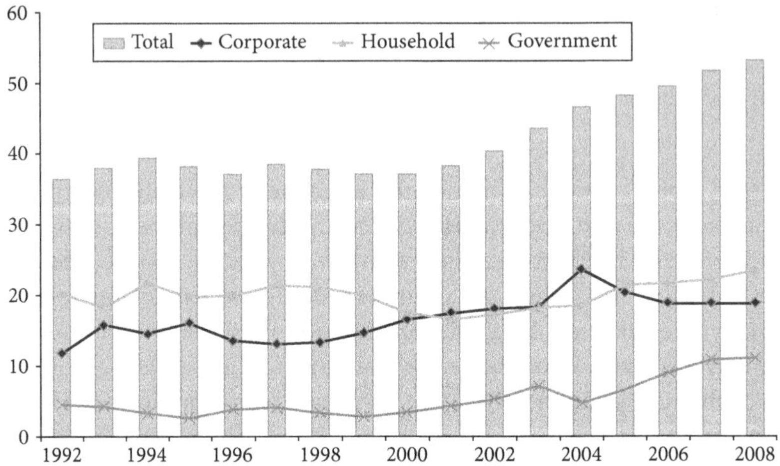


FIGURE 24.6 Compositions of China's National Saving (As a percentage of GDP)

*Source:* China National Bureau of Statistics

Figure 24.6 displays the development of national savings in three sectors: household, corporate, and government sectors. Since 2001, the level of aggregate national saving has been rising steadily through 2008. While household saving was the main contributor to the aggregate saving before 2000, both household and corporate savings have been the main contributors since then. During the last few years of the sample period, or the global imbalances years, household saving became the largest contributor again. However, it is also noteworthy that during the same period, government saving has been rising rapidly after having played a minor role for a long while.

Below, we only briefly review the types of economic and socio-economic factors and government policies that have contributed to the different paths of development for each of the three sectors' savings. For more in-depth analyses on China's saving behavior or the flow of funds, the reader should refer to Kuijs (2006), Ma and Yin (2010), Hung and Qian (2010), and Lin and Schramm (2009).

## 24.4.1 Financial Development and Corporate Finance in China

As was the case with other East Asian economies such as South Korea and Japan, China's rapid industrialization has been achieved through tight state controls on the financial system, that allowed (initially scarce) capital to be allocated to "strategically" important industries. In such financially repressed financial markets, the cost of capital would usually be artificially maintained low. The government, hoping to jump-start economic development with robust export growth, would encourage cheap capital to be allocated to capital intensive industries such as heavy and manufacturing industries that would produce tradable goods. While this sort of developmental strategy is typical among emerging market economies, what is unique about China's case is that 1) because of its communist past, the state-owned enterprises (SOEs) have played an important role in industrialization and export growth as well as in capital allocation process (to a much higher extent than Korea or Japan); 2) because of more direct government involvement in industrial policy and corporate finance (in contrast to more private-government collaborations in the case of Korea and Japan), the government policies have been much less responsive to market forces, resulting in overinvestment in certain industries; and 3) the lack of responsiveness to market forces meant that the country had little scheme to redistribute the benefits of capital intensive industrialization to workers in the forms of distribution of dividends.

Such a state-dominant financial system may have been effective in capital allocation, but has clearly been an obstacle to the marketization process in the financial sector, making financial development lag behind overall economic development. It is the gap between the impressive economic development and China's financial underdevelopment that has contributed to a rapid rise in corporate saving. That is, even after many corporations, including both state- and non-stated owned, improved profitability in the robust economy in the 2000s, the financial sector continued to be dominated by SOEs and failed to provide attractive financial instruments, to which corporate profits could have been invested. Also, until recently, the government did not create a scheme to force corporations to redistribute dividends to shareholders (that is the government in the case of SOEs). Furthermore, in such an environment, where financial resources are not allocated based on market signals, internal earnings functioned as an important alternative financing source for firms.

The inevitable consequence of all these conditions is a rise in corporate saving; due to the lack of financial development, corporate profits are neither effectively reinvested in financial instruments nor redistributed as dividends. For this sort of financial system, one could argue that one effective way to lowering China's high saving is to implement policies to allow corporate profits to be effectively reinvested or redistributed as dividends. However, that outcome is likely to occur only in the long term.[23]

## 24.4.2 Household Behavior

The peculiarities of China's economic and financial development have also affected households' saving behavior. The government's focus on capital intensive, tradable industries led to overconcentration of labor force in the manufacturing sector. The situation with labor surplus is worse in the urban areas due to constant migration from the rural areas, while the government's tight controls of labor unions has also discouraged workers' demand for higher wages. All these factors have contributed to a declining labor income share in the economy.[24] Furthermore, net interest income declined by about a half between 1992 and 2007, so did net transfers from the government mainly because of the increased contributions to pension funds and other welfare obligations (Ma and Yin, 2010).

While the household income share dropped, the average propensity to save (as a share to GDP) went up by 10 percentage points in the 2000s, resulting in a shrinkage of private consumption and a rise in household saving both as shares in GDP.

These changes in the household saving in China can be attributed to both macroeconomic factors as well as institutional factors. The life-cycle, permanent income hypothesis can be a good macroeconomic factor. Since 1980, the working-age share of the population rose from 60 percent to 74 percent in China, undoubtedly contributing to increasing the household saving rate. A combination of sluggish change in the consumption behavior and rapid output growth also contributed to a rise in the household saving rate, which is quite common among high-growth developing economies.

Furthermore, the restructuring and streamlining efforts as part of the marketization of the corporate sector after the 1990s, along with the large-scale influx of migrants from the rural areas, have made the labor markets highly fluid and led to a drastic shrinkage of the once comprehensive, "cradle-to-grave" social safety net, or "iron rice bowl." Many argue that these trends have motivated Chinese households toward precautionary saving.

Limited accessibility to mortgage financing despite increased private house ownership has been also argued to be a factor for the high household saving rate in China. According to Gao (2010), 82.3 percent of urban "registered city residents" (or city *hukou* holders) own houses. This figure has been growing rapidly nationwide. However, due to the lack of financial development as well as risk averseness of the government authorities and financial institutions, mortgage financing has been relatively limited, requiring a high down payment requirement and thus motivating Chinese people to save.[25]

## 24.4.3 Government Saving

As Figure 24.6 illustrates, government saving has been playing a minor role compared to the other two sectors. However, it has been rising rapidly in recently years and becoming a major contributor to the rise in China's national saving.

The rise in government saving is a reflection of a rapid rise in government income, which is also an outcome of rapid economic growth. As it has taken a while for the households to change their consumption behavior to catch up with the rapid economic growth, the same phenomenon has been in place for the government. Now the question is, why has the government consumption level been relatively stable and low, making its saving high, despite a rapid increase in its income?

The first reason for the recent rise in government saving is the government's emphasis on investment for infrastructure building and other growth-enhancing economic policies. This type of initiatives through active investment is a legacy of the communist style policy implementation. The central government also redistributes a share of fiscal revenue to less well-funded local governments or provide capital transfers to related state-owned enterprises to execute national growth-oriented policies (Kuijs, 2006).[26] Whether it is implemented at the central or local levels, this type of investment is not counted as government consumption, but counted as government saving.

Second, the pension system reform implemented in 1997 as a preparation for anticipated aging population has contributed to a rise in government saving. As a result of an increase in pension contributions, the government's holding of both financial and physical assets has increased in recent years, adding to government saving.

Thus, a strong emphasis on growth-oriented investment and preparation for future demographical changes (i.e., aging population) are the main contributors to the recent rise in government saving. However, these types of increase in government saving or investment will also mean that government consumption will have to rise in the future. That means government saving is to fall in the relatively near future, though probably not at the pace the critics of China's high saving in the rest of the world hope for.

## 24.5 Concluding Thoughts

### 24.5.1 The Prospects of Rebalancing

We now use the estimated relationships from the previous empirical exercise to forecast the prospects for global rebalancing out to the 2011-2015 period.[27] We make two types of forecasts: one type is the forecasts we make using data through 2008 and the other is the forecasts we make using data only through 2005. Given the possibility of a structural break in 2006, the forecasts made with data through 2005 can be interpreted as the projections of the current account countries may experience if their economic conditions revert to the pre-global imbalances period. Figure 24.7 presents forecasts of current account balances for several countries that contributed to the global imbalances. The forecasts made using data up to 2008 are shown in the grey line and the forecasts made using data through 2005 are shown in the light grey line. One standard deviation confidence intervals of forecast are also shown, that correspond to about 65 percent of probability of occurrence.

For the United States, the forecasts based on the data through 2008 in Figure 24.7a suggest modest movement in the direction of rebalancing. The forecasts with the data through 2005 suggest a more improved level of current accounts, but this level arises after experiencing a deterioration from the 2006-2008 level. Both models persistently underpredict U.S. current account deficits, suggesting that the United States is an outlier. In fact, when we reestimate current account balances for the full sample including the dummy for the United States, the coefficient on the country dummy is found to be significantly negative with a magnitude of 0.036 (i.e., −3.6 percent). This is consistent with the view that the United States has some special characteristic allowing it to run persistent current account deficits of some 3 percent of GDP, presumably as a result of its status as the issuer of the international vehicle currency.[28]

The UK's current deficit (as shown in Figure 24.7b) is projected to shrink over the 2011-2015 period based on the 2008 projection. However, in either the U.S. or U.K. case, the narrowing of current account deficits over the period is somewhat limited. The news for the surplus countries we consider—China, Japan, Germany, Singapore—(as shown in Figures 24.7c–7h) is even less reassuring. The forecasts suggest that their

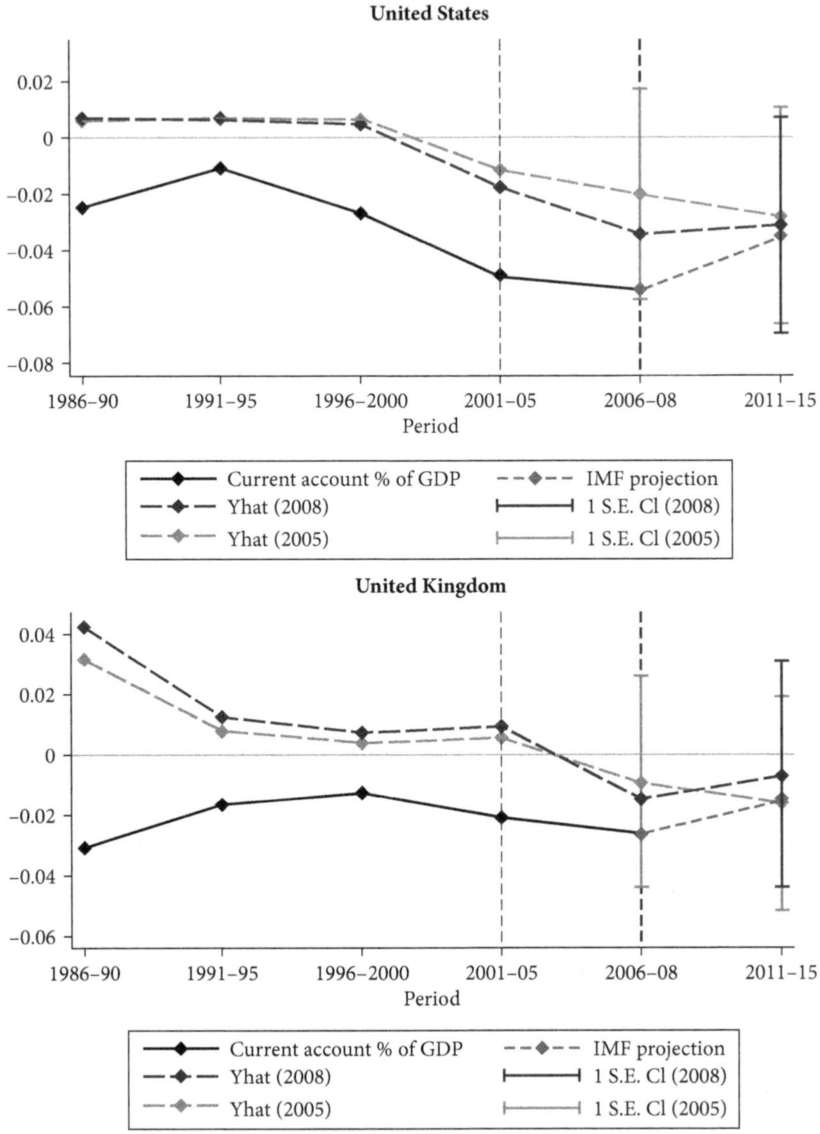


FIGURE 24.7 Forecasts of Current Account Balances for 2011–2015 using data up to 2008 or 2005

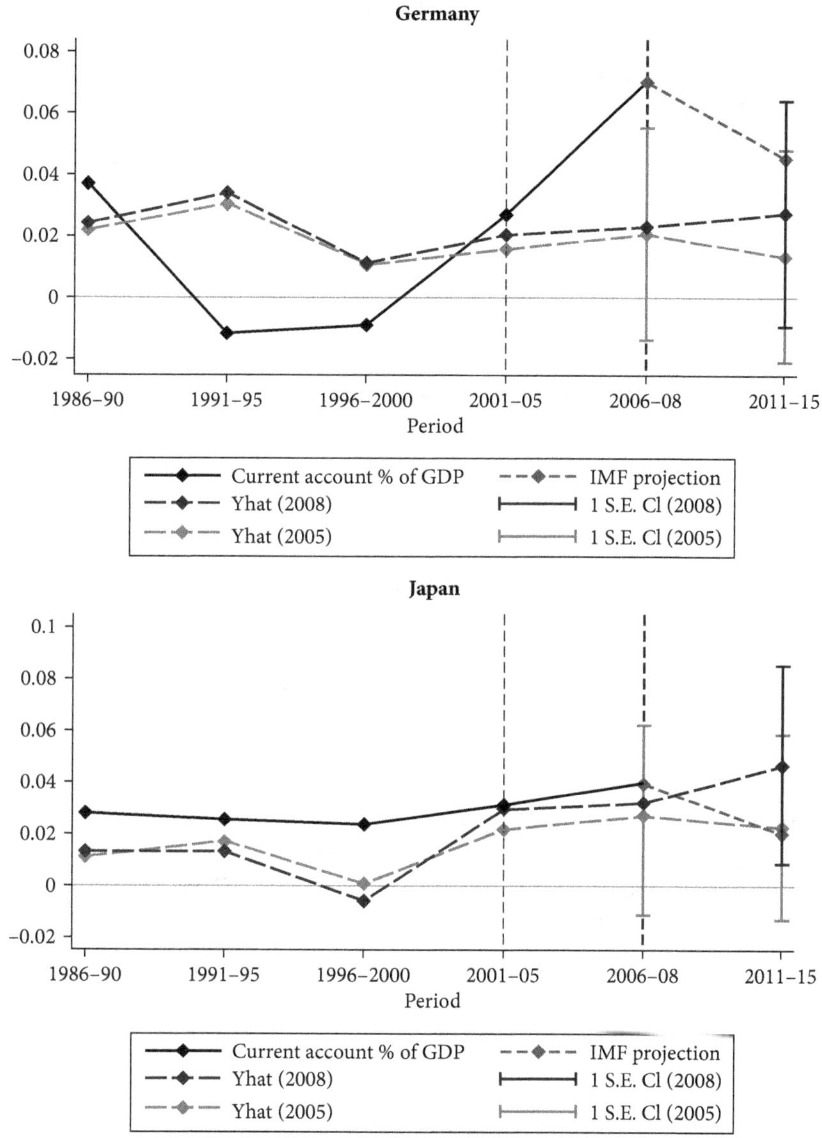


FIGURE 24.7 Continued

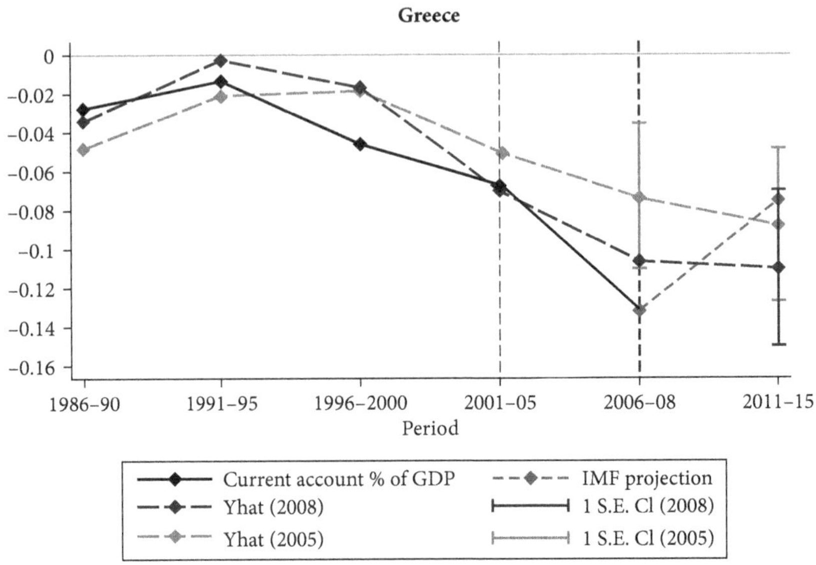


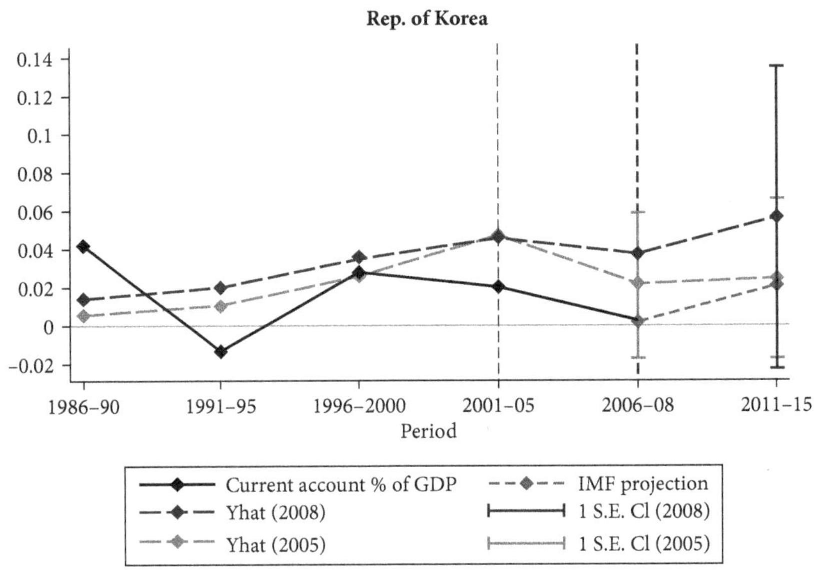


FIGURE 24.7 Continued

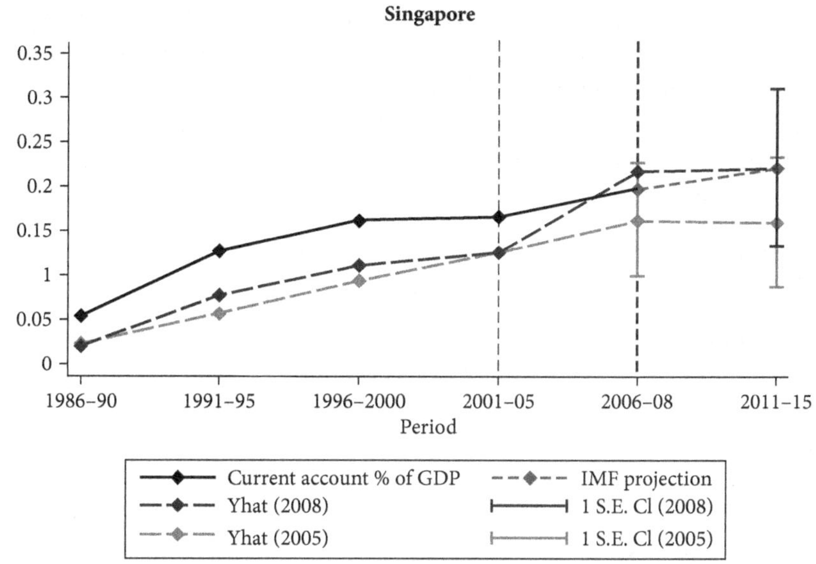


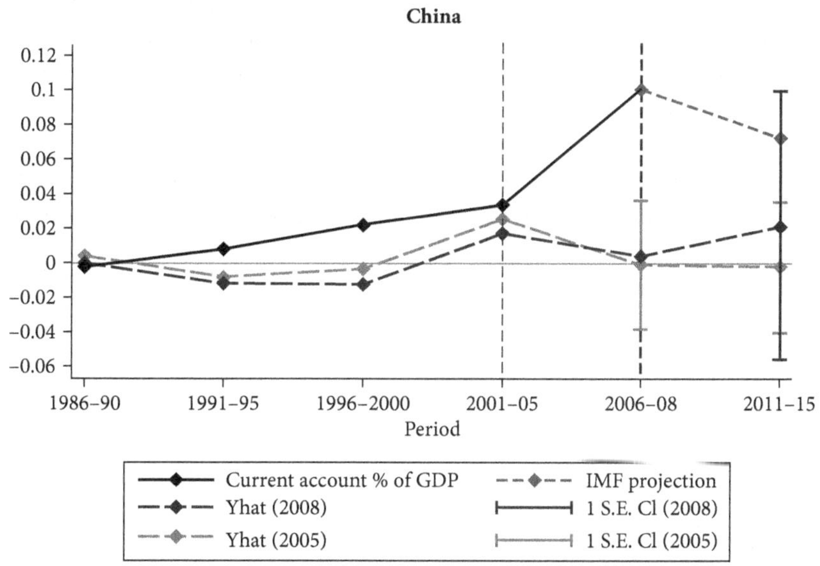


FIGURE 24.7 Continued

surpluses will remain stable or rise further, absent additional policy changes. One interpretation is that the circle will be squared by other countries that will run smaller surpluses and offset America's smaller deficits. A less reassuring interpretation is that the parts do not add up under current forecasts and that even partial rebalancing will require further policy changes. Either way, it seems clear that imbalances will persist.

### 24.5.1.1 *What Would Fiscal Consolidation Do to the United States?*

One of the big issues of macroeconomic management among advanced economies is fiscal consolidation. The industrial countries need to reduce budget deficits without nipping the green shoots of recovery. How will global imbalances evolve under different fiscal scenarios? Figure 24.8 presents different out-of-sample predictions for U.S. current account balances in the 2011-2015 period depending on the different scenarios about its budget balances, an optimistic scenario or a pessimistic one. The optimistic scenario is the case in which the average of the U.S. budget balances for the 2011-2015 period turns out to be higher than the average based on WEO projection (-6.5 percent of GDP) by three percentage points.[29] The pessimistic scenario is the case in which the 2011-2015 average is lower than the WEO projection by three percentage points.

Figure 24.8 shows that a 3 percentage point difference in the fiscal balance relative to the baseline scenario would change the current account balance by half a percentage point, suggesting that rebalancing cannot be accomplished through fiscal policy alone. If the shrinkage of budget deficits is coupled with overall economic recovery and consequent recovery in the financial markets, as in the optimistic scenario, this would in fact slightly drag down projected current account balances.[30]

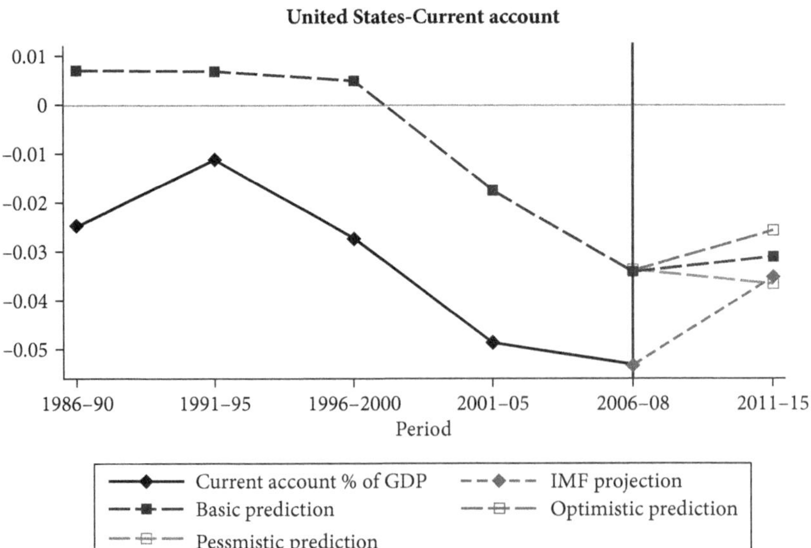


FIGURE 24.8 U.S. Current Account Projections for Optimistic and Pessimistic Scenarios

### 24.5.1.2 *What if China Liberalizes and Develops Its Financial Markets?*

We can similarly consider alternative scenarios for financial development and capital account liberalization in China (Figure 24.9). The figure shows, for comparison, the same projection as in Figure 24.8 with the dotted gray line. It also shows the forecast if China's level of financial openness increases moderately to the level of Thailand in 2008. In this case the current account surplus falls significantly, in line with the predictions of the proponents of the saving glut argument. The figure also shows what happens when financial liberalization proceeds to Brazilian and then Mexican levels.[31] Again, this leads to further declines in the current account surplus. Thus, financial liberalization may lead to an increase in net capital inflows and thereby to a deterioration of current account balances.[32]

Figure 24.10 makes alternative assumptions about financial development. Recall that this is measured by the average ratio of domestic credit to GDP, which fell, relative to the world average, between 2001-2005 and 2006-2008.[33] A modest assumption about Chinese financial development over the next five years is that this ratio returns to its 2001-2005 levels. If we place this assumption with Mexican levels of financial openness, this is enough to eliminate China's surplus. As a caveat, note that the model, based on average behavior in a cross-section of emerging markets, under-predicts the Chinese surplus in recent years. That the surplus *disappears* in 2015 under this scenario is at least as much an artifact of this under-prediction as it is a consequence of the financial liberalization and development. But the point remains: how quickly China narrows its surplus will be a function, in part, of how much progress it makes in financial liberalization and development. Furthermore, given that the return of PCGDP to the 2001-2005 level alone hardly changes the predicted current

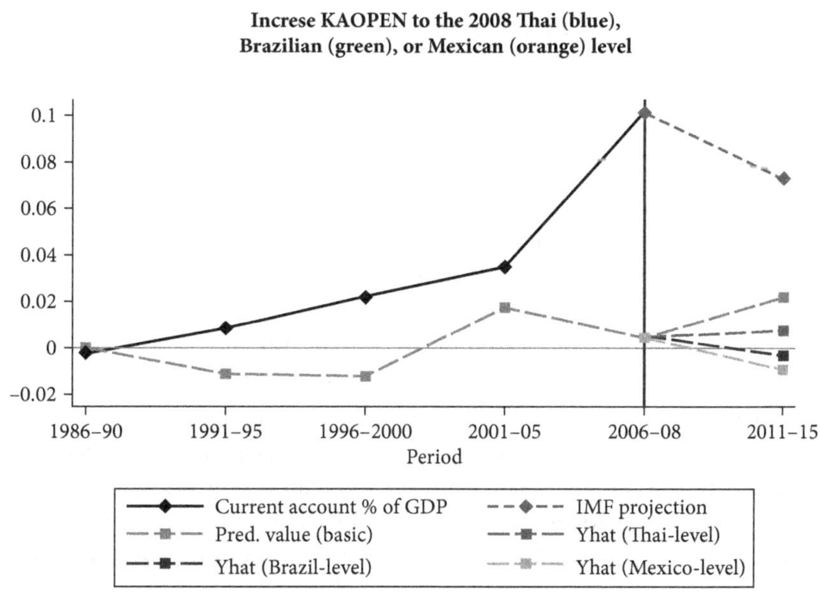


FIGURE 24.9 What if China Liberalizes Its Financial Markets

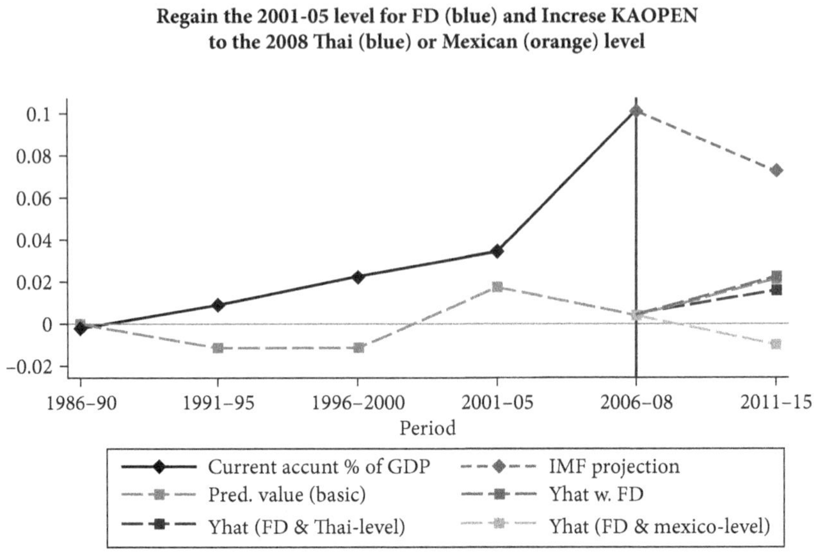


FIGURE 24.10 What if China both Develops and Liberalizes Its Financial Markets

account level, and that the predicted level declines only when financial development is coupled with financial liberalization, we surmise that financial liberalization would be more effective than financial development in reducing China's current account surplus.[34]

However, as we saw previously, our estimation model consistently underpredicts China's current account surplus. This indicates that, besides financial development and liberalization, other policies specific to China's situation, such as changing the rule about state-owned-enterprises' dividends, will be necessary to help reduce the enormous savings in all the three sectors of the country.

## 24.5.2 Conclusion

We examined the issue of rebalancing with primary focus on East Asia, particularly China. For that purpose, we undertook a empirical cross-country approach, augmented with an examination into the specific conditions facing China.

Empirically, we reexamined the determinants of current account balances, applying updated data to the framework based on Chinn and Ito (2007). The main purpose of this study is to examine whether the determinants of global current account balances changed during the period preceding the global crisis of 2008–2009, while inquiring into the prospects for the global imbalances in the post-crisis period. Based on our estimates, changes in the budget balance appear to be an important factor affecting current account balances for advanced current account deficit countries such as the United States. We also find evidence for the effect of the "saving glut variables" on current account balances for emerging market countries.

However, we also identified components of current account balances that cannot be explained by cross-country variation, but can be explained only by country-specific factors, suggesting that country-specific analysis is necessary to foresee the prospects of global rebalancing. For that purpose, we review the institutional aspects of China's development that has led to high saving in the country, particularly the factors that have contributed to high saving rates in all three of the public, corporate, and household sectors. We find that all these factors are the outcome of the country's growth strategies and intricately intertwined with each other. Also, because of the importance of past growth policies, the impact of policy reform on saving and investment behavior is likely to show up only after an extended period.

Looking forward, we found that for the United States, fiscal consolidation alone cannot induce significant current account deficit reduction. For China, financial development may help shrink its current account surplus, but only when it is coupled with financial liberalization.

These findings suggest that unless countries implement substantial policy changes, the global imbalances are unlikely to disappear. Merely changing the variables of "usual suspects" such as budget balances and the level of financial development or financial openness will not be sufficient to lead to drastic reductions in large current account imbalances.

## Notes

1. Acknowledgments: Chinn and Ito acknowledge the financial support of faculty research funds of the University of Wisconsin and Portland State University, respectively. We thank Xingwang Qian for providing data.
2. See for instance Chinn (2005). A dissenting view is Truman (2005).
3. Smaller estimates of the fiscal impact are reported by Bussiere (2005), Corsetti and Muller (2006), and Gruber and Kamin (2007).
4. See Pakko (1999) for an early interpretation in this vein. Note that the empirical evidence for the theoretical model underpinning this argument is weak. See Nason and Rogers (2006).
5. There are numerous ways in which to account for intertemporal effects in current account dynamics. Chinn and Lee (2009) apply a structural VAR approach, which allows for transitory and permanent shocks to drive the current account and the real exchange rate. Using the same approach as in Lee and Chinn (2006), they examine the United States, the Euro area and Japan, and find that a large share of the 2004–2007 U.S. current account is inexplicable using their model.
6. Engel and Rogers use data over the 1970–2004 period for one of their sustainability tests. The survey-based tests rely upon a shorter sample, 1994–2004.
7. Choi, Mark, and Sul (2008) allow for different rates of discount, and can replicate the pattern of imbalances in a two-country model.
8. Aizenman and Lee (2007) evaluated the relative importance of these of the various motivations by augmenting the conventional specifications for reserve holdings with proxy variables associated with the mercantilism and self-insurance/precautionary demand approaches. While variables associated with both approaches are statistically significant, the self-insurance variables play a greater economic role in accounting for recent trends. See also Jeanne and Ranciere (2005).
9. Caballero, Farhi, and Gourinchas (2008) model the saving glut explanation as a shortage of assets in the developing world. Mendoza, Quadrini, and Rios-Rull (2009) model financial development as the increase in the degree of enforcement of financial contracts.

10. Ito and Chinn (2009) examine whether their results are sensitive to the use of alternative indicators of financial development, namely measures of equity, bond, and insurance market activity, as well as different aspects of financial development such as the cost performance, size, and activeness of the industry. They find that credit to the private sector and stock market capitalization appear to be equally important determinants of current account behavior.
11. This section is mainly based on Chinn, Eichengreen, and Ito (2011).
12. *LAO*, *BQ*, and *CORRUPT* are extracted from the ICRG database. Higher values of these variables indicate better conditions.
13. The five-year panels are 1971–1975, 1976–1980, etc. However, the last panel is composed of only three years: 2006–2008. We can consider the last panel as the years of the global imbalances.
14. The variables for ToT volatility (*TOT*), trade openness (*OPN*), and legal development (*LEGAL*) are averaged for each country, i.e., they are time-invariant. Most of the economic variables are retrieved from the *World Development Indicators*, *International Financial Statistics*, and the IMF's *World Economic Outlook*.
15. The emerging market economies are defined as the economies classified as either emerging or frontier during 1980–1997 by the International Financial Corporation, plus Hong Kong and Singapore.
16. These estimates are very similar to those in Abbas et al. (2010), who find that the elasticity of the current account balance with respect to the fiscal balance is on the order of 0.2–0.3. Erceg et al. (2005) also show their simulation results yield the coefficient of the budget balance to be around 0.20.
17. Theoretically, the current account of the world must be zero, nullifying the validity of estimating for the full sample. But our "full" sample does not cover all the countries on the globe. Not to mention, there are usually expected to be measurement errors.
18. Time-fixed effects for all the five-year periods (except for the first five-year period) are included in the estimation, but only those for the 2001–2005 and 2006–2008 periods are reported in the table.
19. We confirm this by adding a dummy variable for the United States in the 2001-2005 subperiod; its coefficient is negative, and adding it does not eliminates the significant positive coefficient for 2001–2005 in the industrial-country column. Not surprisingly, when we include all countries (in the left-most column); these period dummy variables are insignificant, since by definition current accounts should sum to zero.
20. The Ricardian hypothesis predicts that any change in public saving would be offset by the exact same change but with the opposite sign in private saving, thus making the estimated coefficient of budget balances zero. The Ricardian framework can be extended to predict that public dissaving would not crowd out private investment, thus making public saving and investment uncorrelated.
21. Results not shown in the table.
22. This finding can be also interpreted as evidence that better current account balances are not driven by mercantilist currency interventions.
23. Recently, the Chinese government decided to require SOEs to distribute dividends (to shareholders, i.e., the government). However, decisions involving dividend distributions are a function of many factors such as corporate governance, shareholder protection, and portfolio management, all of which require much long-term managerial experience and know-how.
24. According to Ma and Yin, wages account for 80 percent of the Chinese household disposable income. Also, the "decline in the labour share accounts for some 60 percent of the observed decline in the household income share between 1992 and 2007."

25. A more novel argument (Wei and Zhang, 2010 and Du and Wei, 2010) is that the sex imbalance encourages saving by single men as a way of signaling their attractiveness as marriage partners. As a result of the one-child policy, the number of men outnumbers the number of women with the sex ratio of around 120 boys for each 100 girls as of 2007 (Wei and Zhang, 2009). In such an environment, men are motivated to save to attract marriage partners, as Du and Wei (2010) show using a simple overlapping generations model. Wei and Zhang (2010) argue that 60 percent of the actual increase in the household savings rate in the period from 1990 to 2007 can be explained by the increase in the sex ratio during this period.
26. These growth-enhancing projects are viewed importantly at all government levels because promotions of government officials are often measured by the performance of the economies under their jurisdiction. Furthermore, the tax reforms in the 2000s significantly reduced the amount of transfers from the central government, and that has made local governments prone for precautionary saving, adding to the government saving.
27. The forecasts start with 2011, omitting the crisis years 2009-2010, when behavior was unusual. The assumptions and the data for the out-of-sample projections are explained in Chinn et al. (2011). We use the separate estimates for industrial and emerging-market economies as the basis for our forecasts.
28. See Gourinchas and Rey (2007).
29. Three percentage points are equivalent to 1.5 standard deviations in the distribution of U.S. budget balances in the 1969–2008 period.
30. Consistent with the Caballero et al. effect.
31. The countries are ranked as Mexico (69.2 in the 100 scale), Brazil (58.8), Thailand (40.3), and China (16.1) in terms of the level of financial openness as of 2008. The average of KAOPEN for the LDC group as of 2008 is 50.2, whereas that for the EMG group is 60.9.
32. If capital account opening occurs while exchange rates are allowed to adjust more flexibly, the current account balance could also deteriorate through the price channel. Before the policy change of increasing the flexibility of the renminbi on June 19, 2010, it had been argued that one of the reasons for Chinese hesitation to allow greater exchange rate flexibility is that policymakers in Beijing are worried that financial liberalization may lead to further capital inflows, reinforcing the upward pressure on the currency.
33. Recall that in our empirical model all variables are normalized by the world average.
34. This conclusion relies upon our proxy of financial development, the ratio of private credit creation to GDP, accurately representing financial development. It would be preferable to use a broader measure of financial development, such as the composite bond/equity/bank indicators used in Ito and Chinn (2009), but the data are not yet available for that exercise.

## References

Abbas, SM Ali, J. Bouhga-Hagbe, A. Fatás, P. Mauro, and R. C. Velloso. 2010. "Fiscal Policy and the Current Account", CEPR Discussion Paper 7859.

Aizenman, J. and Marion, N. 2004. "International reserves holdings with sovereign risk and costly tax collection." *Economic Journal* 114: 569–591.

Aizenman, J. and Lee, J. 2007. "International reserves: precautionary versus mercantilist views, theory and evidence," *Open Economies Review*, 18(2): 191–214.

Bernanke, B., 2005. "The Global Saving Glut and the U.S. Current Account." Remarks at the Sandridge Lecture, Virginia Association of Economics, Richmond, VA, March 10.

Bussière, M., M. Fratzscher and G.J. Müller. 2005. "Productivity shocks, budget deficits and the current account," *ECB Working Paper* No. 509, Frankfurt: ECB.

Caballero, R., E. Farhi, and P. O. Gourinchas. 2008. "An Equilibrium Model of 'Global Imbalances' and Low Interest Rates," *American Economic Review*, 98(1) (March): 358–393.

Chinn, M.D. 2005. "Getting Serious about the Twin Deficits," *Council Special Report* No. 10 (New York: Council on Foreign Relations, September).

Chinn, Menzie, and Hiro Ito, 2006. "What Matters for Financial Development? Capital Controls, Institutions, and Interactions." *Journal of Development Economics*, 82: 163–192.

Chinn, M. D., B. Eichengreen, and H. Ito. 2011. A Forensic Analysis of Global Imbalances. NBER Working Paper Series, #17513 (October). Cambridge, MA.

Chinn, M. D., and H. Ito. 2007a. "Current Account Balances, Financial Development and Institutions: Assaying the World "Savings Glut," *Journal of International Money and Finance*, 26(4) (June):, 546–569.

Chinn, M. D., and H. Ito. 2007b. "Price-Based Measurement of Financial Globalization: A Cross-Country Study of Interest Rate Parity," *Pacific Economic Review* 12(4) (2007): 419–444.

Chinn, M.D. and H. Ito. 2008a. "Global Current Account Imbalances: American Fiscal Policy versus East Asian Savings". Review of International Economics, Volume 16, Issue 3, p. 479–498 (August).

Chinn, M. D., and H. Ito. 2008b. "A New Measure of Financial Openness." *Journal of Comparative Policy Analysis*, 10(3) (September): 309–322.

Chinn, M.D. and J. Lee. 2009. "Three current account balances: A 'Semi-Structuralist' interpretation," *Japan and the World Economy*, Elsevier, vol. 21(2), pages 202–212 (March).

Chinn, Menzie, and Eswar Prasad, 2003, "Medium-Term Determinants of Current Accounts in Industrial and Developing Countries: An Empirical Exploration," *Journal of International Economics* 59(1) (January): 47–76.

Choi, H., N.C. Mark, and D. Sul. 2008. "Endogenous Discounting, the World Saving Glut and the U.S. Current Account," *Journal of International Economics* 75(1) (May): 30–53.

Clarida, R. 2005. Some Thoughts on 'The Sustainability and Adjustment of Global Current Account Imbalances.' Speech given at the Council on Foreign Relations, March 28.

Corsetti, G. and G.J. Müller. 2006. "Twin Deficits: Squaring Theory, Evidence and Common Sense," *Economic Policy* 21(48) (October): 597–638.

Dooley, M., Folkerts-Landau, D., and Garber, P. 2003. "An Essay on the Revived Bretton Woods System," *NBER Working Paper* No. 9971 (September 2003).

Dooley, M., Folkerts-Landau, D., and Garber, P. 2008, "Direct Investment, Rising Real Wages, and the Absorption of Excess Labor in the Periphery," in Rich Clarida (editor), *G-7 Current Account Imbalances: Sustainability and Adjustment* (University of Chicago Press for NBER).

Du, Qingyuan, and Shang-jin Wei (2010), "A Sexually Unbalanced Model of Current Account Imbalances," NBER Working Paper no. 16000.

Eichengreen, Barry, and Molly Fifer (2002), "The Implications of Ageing for the Balance of Payments Between North and South," in Horst Siebert (ed.), *The Economics of Ageing Societies*, Tubingen: Mohr: 81–105.

Engel, C. and J. Rogers. 2006. "The U.S. Current Account Deficit and the Expected Share of World Output," *JOURNAL OF MONETARY ECONOMICS*, 53(5): 1063–1093.

Erceg, C. J., L. Guerrieri, and C. Gust. 2005. "Expansionary Fiscal Shocks and the US Trade Deficit," *International Finance*, 8, 363–397.

Gagnon, J. 2010. "Current Account Imbalances Coming Back," December revision of paper presented at the International Conference on Reshaping Global Economic Governance and the Role of Asia in the G-20, Seoul, Korea, October 26–27, 2010.

Gao, L (2010), "Achievements and Challenges: 30 years of Housing Reforms in the People's Republic of China," *ADB Economics Working Paper*, No 198, April.

Greenspan, A., 2005a. "Current Account." At Advancing Enterprise 2005 Conference, London, England, February 4.

Greenspan, A., 2005b. "Mortgage Banking." At American Bankers Association Annual Convention, Palm Desert, California, September 26.

Gourinchas, P. O. and H. Rey. 2007. "From World Banker to World Venture Capitalist: U.S. External Adjustment and the Exorbitant Privilege," In: *G7 Current Account Imbalances: Sustainability and Adjustment*, 11–66, National Bureau of Economic Research, Cambridge, MA.

Gruber, J., and S. Kamin. 2007. "Explaining the Global Pattern of Current Account Imbalances," *Journal of International Money and Finance* 26 (June): 500–522.

Hubbard, R. G., 2005. A Paradox of Interest. *Wall Street Journal*, June 23, page A12.

Hung, J. H., and R. Qian. 2010. "Why Is China's Saving Rate So High? A Comparative Study of Cross-Country Panel Data," Congressional Budget Office Working Paper Series 2010–07. Washington, D.C.

Ito, H. 2009. "U.S. Current Account Debate, with Japan then, with China Now," *Journal of Asian Economics*, 20(3) (May): 294–313.

Ito, H. and M.D. Chinn. 2009. "East Asia and Global Imbalances: Saving, Investment, and Financial Development". In Financial Sector Development in the Pacific Rim, edited by Takatoshi Ito and Andrew Rose, National Bureau of Economic Research-East Asian Seminar on Economics (NBER-EASE) Volume 18 (April).

Jeanne, O. and R. Ranciere. 2006. "The Optimal Level of International Reserves for Emerging Market Economies: Formulas and Applications," *IMF Working Paper* WP/06/229 Washington, D.C.: IMF(October).

Kuijs, L. 2006. "How Will China's Saving-Investment Balance Evolve?" World Banking Working Paper Series #3958.

Lee, J. and M.D. Chinn. 2006. "Current Account and Real Exchange Rate Dynamics in the G7 Countries." *Journal of International Money and Finance*, 25, 257–274.

Lin, G. and R. M. Schramm. 2009. "A Decade of Flow of Funds in China (1995–2006)," in Y.W. Cheung and K. Wang, ed. *China and Asia: Economic and Financial Interactions*, Routledge Studies in the Modern World Economy. New York, 26–43.

Ma, G., and Y. Wang. 2010. "China's High Saving Rate: Myth and Reality." BIS Working Paper No. 312 (June).

Nason, J.M. and J.H. Rogers. 2006. "The Present Value Model of the Current Account Has Been Rejected: Round Up the Usual Suspects," *Journal of International Economics* 68 (January): 159–187.

Mendoza, E.G., V. Quadrini, and J.V. Ríos-Rull. 2009. "Financial Integration, Financial Deepness and Global Imbalances," *Journal of Political Economy* 117(3): 317–416.

Pakko, M.R. 1999. "The U.S. Trade Deficit and the 'New Economy,'" Federal Reserve Bank of St. Louis Review 81(5): 11–20.

Prasad, E. and Wei, S.J. 2005. "The Chinese Approach to Capital Inflows: Patterns and Possible Explanations." IMF Working Paper No. 05/79 (April).

Wei, S. J. and X. Zhang. 2010. "The Competitive Saving Motive: Evidence from Rising Sex Ratios and Savings Rates in China." NBER Working Paper no. 15093.

CHAPTER 25

# CHINA'S FINANCIAL OPENNESS AND ASSET RETURN LINKAGES IN EAST ASIA

REUVEN GLICK AND MICHAEL HUTCHISON

## 25.1 INTRODUCTION

CHINA's pace of real economic growth and transformation into a global trading power over the past three decades has been unprecedented. However, development of its financial sector has been more gradual and irregular. Despite evident progress in the size and depth of the financial sector, state-controlled banks and institutions dominate financial markets, many asset prices are heavily managed, and a myriad of regulations and controls still affect international financial transactions. This uneven pattern of development raises the question of whether liberalization of China's financial sector and the "internationalization" of its currency, the renminbi, will ever catch up with the real side of the economy, allowing China to stand among other major economic powers as a world financial center.

"Internationalization" of a currency generally involves permitting its use by domestic and foreign agents in international trade and financial transactions both inside and outside of a country's borders. Full internationalization of the renminbi (rmb) is a tall order for a country that currently maintains numerous financial controls and heavily regulates domestic and cross-border financial transactions. Nonetheless, Chinese leaders have made concerted efforts to encourage greater international use of the rmb since the G-20 summit in November 2008 when Chinese President Hu Jintao called for "a new international financial order that is fair, just, inclusive, and orderly," and China subsequently began to encourage more use of its currency in international trade, swap arrangements between central banks, and bank deposits and bond issuances in Hong Kong.[1] Though

Prasad and Ye (2012) view the effects of these efforts on use of the rmb as modest in size so far, they regard them as symbolically important in signaling the shift in China's ambitions for the renminbi's future role in the global economy and international monetary system.

Views about the prospects for internationalization of the rmb vary. Some analysts (Ito, 2011) argue that an rmb currency bloc will soon emerge in Asia, within which the rmb would be used widely as a transactions currency for trade and finance, as well as treated as a reserve currency by other central banks. Other analysts predict a more gradual and slower pace for internationalization of the rmb in regional and global transactions. McCauley (2011), for example, maintains that the Chinese authorities have only just begun the process of permitting the rmb to become an international currency, in terms of allowing residents and non-residents alike to use the currency to trade, invest, borrow, and invoice outside of China. Prasad and Ye (2011) analyze the growing internationalization of the rmb through its use in the denomination and settlement of cross-border trade and financial transactions, the likelihood and timing of its convertibility, and the prospects for its greater utilization as a reserve currency. They also describe how rmb trade settlement in Hong Kong has expanded rapidly, the issuance of renminbi-denominated bonds both in Hong Kong and the Mainland is picking up, and signs that some central banks are holding rmb-denominated assets in their foreign exchange reserve portfolios. Nonetheless, they conclude that while internationalization of the rmb is steadily growing, it is a long way from attaining full convertibility or meeting other prerequisites for achieving reserve currency status.

Still others see relatively little internationalization of the rmb to date and are pessimistic about further developments, as it would undermine China's highly managed financial and monetary system. In this view, rmb internationalization cannot be undertaken without domestic financial reforms that more closely link the domestic financial system as well as domestic monetary and exchange rate policies to the international financial system.

A large body of literature has addressed various aspects of the policy challenges faced by China as it seeks to sequence capital-account opening and currency internationalization with other policies, such as exchange-rate flexibility and financial market development (see Girardin, 2011; Glick and Hutchison, 2010; IMF, 2011; Ma et al., 2011; Lee et al., 2011; Ma et al., 2011; Ogawa and Simizu, 2011; Pongsaporn and Unteroberdoerster, 2011). Less well-discussed is how the gradual process of financial liberalization and China's drive toward internationalization of the rmb has affected its East Asian regional neighbors. Given the sheer size and dynamism of China's economy, greater financial openness and internationalization of the rmb inevitably will have repercussions for the global economy, and of course even more so for its regional trade and financial partners in East Asia.

The objective of this chapter is to evaluate how changes in China's financial system, liberalization of capital controls, and the process of currency internationalization have affected financial markets in other East Asian economies. In particular, we examine the extent to which the financial market changes and openness in China have affected the cross-country links of financial asset returns within the region. We examine whether linkages have grown stronger over time, either because (i) capital account liberalization in China has permitted more financial capital flows and arbitrage and hence greater cross-country financial integration, or (ii) stronger real sector linkages, trade flows, and business cycle synchronization within the region as a result of China's emergence as an engine of economic growth have indirectly linked financial asset returns in the region even in the absence of financial capital flows and asset market arbitrage. We measure financial market integration by several metrics and, to the extent that we find such linkages, we attempt to determine whether they are generated by direct financial market connections or by indirect real economic linkages.

The main theme and conclusion of this chapter is that domestic financial development in China has been modest and internationalization of the currency and liberalization of capital controls to date very limited. As a result, substantial differences in some financial asset returns remain between China and its neighbors. In particular, we find that short-term financial asset returns, as measured by interbank interest rates, are essentially unlinked within the region, while only weak linkages may be detected in longer-term interest rates, as measured by five-year government bond rates. Much stronger linkages, however, appear in equity markets. We argue that the dominant factor linking equity markets in China with other East Asian economies is not equity market arbitrage working through capital markets, but rather strengthening trade relationships and synchronization of economic activity associated with the emergence of China as an engine of growth within the region.

The chapter is organized as follows. Section 25.2 summarizes recent steps China has taken to open its capital account. Section 25.3 reviews the empirical literature on financial linkages between China and its East Asian neighbors. Section 25.4 presents new empirical evidence on linkages between China and East Asia that analyzes short-run linkages between exchange rates, interest rate, and equity markets using regression analysis, as well as long-run linkages using cointegration analysis. We conclude with some general observations about policy implications of the analysis for East Asia countries and how they are likely to be influenced increasingly by China's financial policies in the coming years.

## 25.2 Capital Control Liberalization in China

China has pursued a cautious path toward greater financial openness. Although tax benefits and other incentives have been used to promote inward foreign direct investment, other forms of inflows, particularly portfolio capital and external debt, have been traditionally discouraged. Capital controls have also played a role in protecting the banking system from external competition by restricting the entry of foreign banks and by making it harder for capital to flow out of the country.

As China slowly liberalizes its capital account, it faces a key challenge of maintaining domestic monetary and price stability.[2] Large balance of payments surpluses through both the current and financial accounts have put upward pressure on the currency. To limit appreciation of the renminbi, Chinese monetary authorities have intervened in the foreign exchange market and accumulated massive amounts of foreign reserve. As a result, China's holdings of foreign reserves have risen from $140 billion in 1997 to over $3.2 trillion at the end of 2011.

This reserve buildup has raised concerns about monetary and inflation stability in China, as both money aggregates and prices have grown faster. A not-so-distant memory is the excessive expansion of the monetary base, money, and credit between 1991 and 1994—when these aggregates grew at times by over 40 percent per annum—resulting in high inflation, with CPI rising near 30 percent at its peak.[3] The foreign reserve boom over the past decade has similarly led to periods of very large increases in the monetary base, threatening at times a return of higher inflation (Glick and Hutchison, 2009).

As long as China continues to place a higher priority on exchange rate stability than on using monetary policy as a tool for macroeconomic control, China's scope for an autonomous monetary policy is constrained. Chinese monetary authorities have addressed this challenge by aggressive open-market sterilization operations as well as by raising reserve requirement ratios and employing window guidance measures.[4] As reserve accumulation continues, the conflict between monetary and exchange rate objectives will become increasingly harder to resolve, particularly as remaining controls on capital flow become more difficult to maintain.

Capital controls, which prevent money from moving in and out of an economy easily, have helped to insulate domestic monetary policy from balance of payments surpluses. Since the start of China's reform and open-door policies, foreign direct investment (FDI) inflows have been encouraged, while other inflows and capital outflows were initially heavily controlled.[5] Non-bank Chinese residents and institutions had been prohibited from directly investing in overseas securities, though banks were permitted to invest their own dollar assets in fixed income instruments

In recent years, China has liberalized controls on non-FDI capital flows very slowly. Authorized banks were allowed to transact cross-border to accommodate onshore non-bank depositors and borrowers wishing to deposit and borrow in foreign currency. China has sought to institutionalize the management of two-way portfolio flows through programs for so-called "qualified foreign institutional investors" (QFIIs) for portfolio inflows and "qualified domestic institutional investors" (QDIIs) for portfolio outflows.[6] Both programs involve pre-approval procedures, quota management, foreign exchange conversion rules, instrument restrictions, and intensive reporting requirements. With the introduction of the QDII plan in 2006, China opened an official channel for Chinese households and firms to gain access to global financial markets. Appreciation pressures on the rmb have led China to encourage outflows through other channels, for example, by relaxing restrictions on currency conversion by domestic residents.[7] In addition, firms and banks have been given flexibility to issue foreign-exchange denominated bonds in local markets and to raise their direct overseas investment.

Though China had tightly controlled portfolio flows and most external debts for a long time, there is evidence that these capital controls were leaky and had tended to become less effective over time even before the recent relaxation of capital controls.[8] The sheer magnitude of net and gross portfolio capital and "hot money" inflows clearly cast doubt on the effectiveness of China's capital control regime. Moreover, as the evidence presented in Glick and Hutchison (2009) and Ma and MacCauley (2007) illustrate, despite the existence of remaining capital controls, there are many indications that China's capital account flows respond to market conditions, suggesting limits to the effectiveness of these controls. "Hot money" flows have apparently been responsive to expectations of rmb appreciation. Similarly, foreign exchange deposits held by Chinese households and firms onshore with banks in China have tracked exchange rate expectations, rising as a share of total bank deposits when the rmb was expected to depreciate and falling when the rmb was expected to appreciate.

Although, as pointed out above, permitted cross-border flows have reduced the effectiveness of China's remaining capital controls, they have not been large enough to eliminate onshore/offshore rmb yield differences. For example, McCauley (2011) examines the growing role of offshore markets for the yuan in China's strategy for financial development, arguing that policymakers are seeking to internationalize the renminbi before fully liberalizing China's capital account. He argues that rmb are building up outside of Mainland China via "carefully drilled holes" in China's capital controls. However, currency, bond, and equity markets show that these controls nonetheless continue to bind. For example, the Chinese government in 2011 successfully issued rmb-denominated bonds in Hong Kong at rates lower than those offered onshore. The differential in the prices of Chinese shares between the mainland and Hong Kong also points to the effectiveness of capital controls.

Hutchison, Pasricha, and Singh (2011) measure the effectiveness of capital controls in China by covered interest parity deviations, using China's interbank offer rate (CHIBOR), the London Interbank Offer Rate (LIBOR for the dollar), the spot exchange rate, and the non-deliverable forward exchange rate (NDF). These parity deviations, shown in Figure 25.1, are frequently large and indicate that a lack of integration between China's domestic (short-term) financial markets and international financial markets. Other work also shows that sizable onshore-offshore yield gaps persist and provides evidence on the relationships between implied forward rates, interest rates, and equity prices that indicate Chinese capital controls have been effective in partly "decoupling" Chinese financial markets from those in the United States, Hong Kong, and elsewhere (see Cheung et al., 2006; Ma and McCauley, 2007; and Liu and Otani, 2005; McCauley, 2011; Prasad and Ye, 2012b).

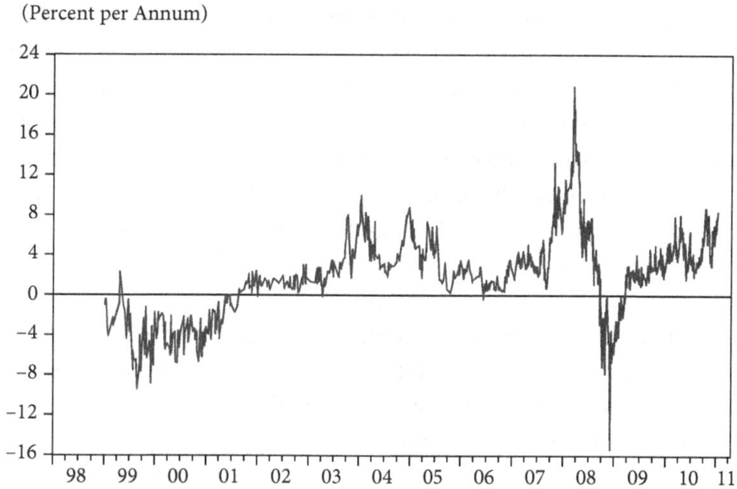


FIGURE 25.1 Covered Interest Parity Deviations (China Onshore less Offshore)

## 25.3 Empirical Literature on China's Financial Linkages with East Asia

China's growing role in global trade and financial markets has affected its East Asian regional neighbors. Given the sheer size and dynamism of China's economy, greater financial openness and internationalization of the rmb has repercussions for the global economy, and of course even more so for its regional trade and financial partners in East Asia. Several studies have investigated how these developments have affected asset price linkages in the region.

Jang (2011), for example, analyzes the degree of financial integration of China, Japan, Korea, and the United States by examining correlations of money and bond market rates as well as stock market changes using data from the early or mid 1990s through mid 2010. He finds that the correlations of monthly Asian money market rates with United States rates increased after the Asian financial crisis, though China's correlation is the lowest in the group. Correspondingly, the correlation of money rates of Japan and Korea with that of China,[9] which was negative before the Asian financial crisis, is now positive, as rates in the region have moved more closely with each other in recent years. He finds that the correlations of Japan and Korean government bond rates also increased with United States rates after the Asian financial crisis. In contrast, China's bond rate (with data available only since 2005) does not show a significant correlation with the United States after the crisis, though it does display positive correlations with Japan and Korea, particularly with the latter. In addition, he finds that stock markets in Japan, Korea, and China move more tightly with the U.S. stock market, though less so for China, after the

Asian financial crisis and also show positive correlations among themselves. The correlations in stock price indices in other East Asian countries also suggest a tighter interrelationship with the U.S. stock market following the Asian financial crisis. The relatively low correlations of U.S. and China asset price changes in recent years are consistent with their differences in economic recoveries and inflation concerns.[10] Jang concludes that in the last decade Asian countries have achieved remarkable progress in economic integration. However, the degree of financial integration lags significantly behind the degree of trade and real economy integration. Moreover, inter-regional links appear to be stronger than intra-regional links in East Asian countries.[11]

A number of papers focus on co-movements of exchange rates in region. For example, Balasubramaniam, Patnaik, and Shah (2011), following the methodology of Frankel and Wei (1994) and Frankel (2009), estimate the effects of changes in the dollar, euro, yen, and rmb on individual East Asian currencies over the period October 2005 to February 2011, using the Swiss Franc as the numeraire. They find that the effect of the rmb is significant only for Malaysia (from 2005 to 2007), Viet Nam (after 2009) and Taiwan (through the entire sample). (Somewhat ironically they find that the rmb mattered more outside of East Asia, including India and Pakistan as well as many countries in Africa.) These results suggest that while China has made strides in terms of achieving a major role for the rmb in international trade through the establishment of rmb settlement mechanisms and swap lines, there is relatively limited evidence of an independent effect of the rmb on exchange rate policies of neighboring economies.

Ma and McCauley (2010) argue that it is important to consider the frequency of the data when analyzing correlations. For example, they find that the co-movement of the renminbi with major currencies other than the dollar is greater at lower frequency, i.e., at weekly or monthly intervals rather than at a daily frequency. This suggests that the Chinese monetary authorities are trying to minimize currency fluctuations against the dollar on a daily basis, while managing the value of the rmb vis-à-vis a basket of currencies over the longer run, particularly during the period between mid-2006 and mid-2008.

## 25.4 China and East Asian Asset Returns: New Evidence

Our review of the literature on China's capital controls and increasing international financial integration suggests that its domestic financial development is proceeding slowly in tandem with some modest steps toward liberalization of the capital account and very limited exchange rate flexibility. Some authors have found that China's financial markets are becoming more integrated with its East Asian neighbors despite pervasive capital controls. Others argue that China's financial role in East Asia is minimal, not approaching its role in regional trade and importance as a regional source of economic growth.

## 25.4.1 Exchange Rates

Despite the binding nature of capital controls, financial market developments in China may still have an impact on asset prices in other East Asian economies. One factor that influences this linkage is the extent that exchange rates move together. Movements in the value of the rmb have been affected by several distinct phases of Chinese exchange rate policy since the early 1980s, as shown in Figure 25.2 and summarized in Table 25.1. We identify nine phases since 1981 (denoted in the figure by vertical lines at the break dates). China realigned its exchange rate and effectively devalued the rmb by about 50 percent against the dollar in January 1994 (from 5.8 to 8.7 rmb per dollar). Since that time, the rmb has been either fixed against the dollar (1995–2005 and for a period during 2008-2010) or allowed to gradually appreciate. As of March 2012, the rmb/dollar

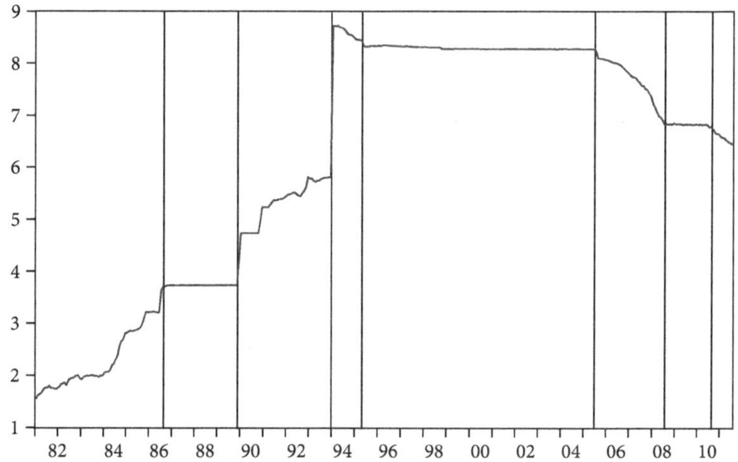


FIGURE 25.2 China RMB per US Dollar

**Table 25.1 China's Exchange Rate Regimes, 1981-2011**

| # | Time Range | Rate | |
|---|---|---|---|
| 1 | January 1981–August 1986 | 1.6 to 3.7 | substantial depreciation |
| 2 | August 1986–November 1989 | 3.7 | fixed rate, 3 years |
| 3 | November 1989–December 1993 | 3.7 to 5.8 | substantial depreciation |
| 4 | January 3, 1994 | 8.7 | sharp devaluation |
| 5 | January 1994–May 1995 | 8.7 to 8.3 | gradual appreciation |
| 6 | May 1995–June 2005 | 8.3 to 8.2 | fixed rate (narrow range), 10 years |
| 7 | June 2005–July 2008 | 8.3 to 6.8 | gradual appreciation |
| 8 | July 2008–June 2010 | 6.8 | fixed rate (narrow range), 2 years |
| 9 | June 2010–July 2011 | 6.8 to 6.4 | gradual appreciation |

rate stood at 6.3, implying a cumulative appreciation of 28 percent over the past 18 years (about 1½ percent per year). This implies that the value of the rmb has been relatively stable against the dollar by comparison with the currencies of other large economies.

Financial linkages between countries depend on exchange rates through interest parity. That is, the closer the currencies of other Asian countries are linked to China's exchange rate policies, the closer one would expect financial linkages between the domestic interest rates in these economies and China. Exchange rate developments in China and selected Asia countries are shown in Figure 25.3. (Normalized exchange rate developments are shown in order to allow comparative analysis.) The most striking

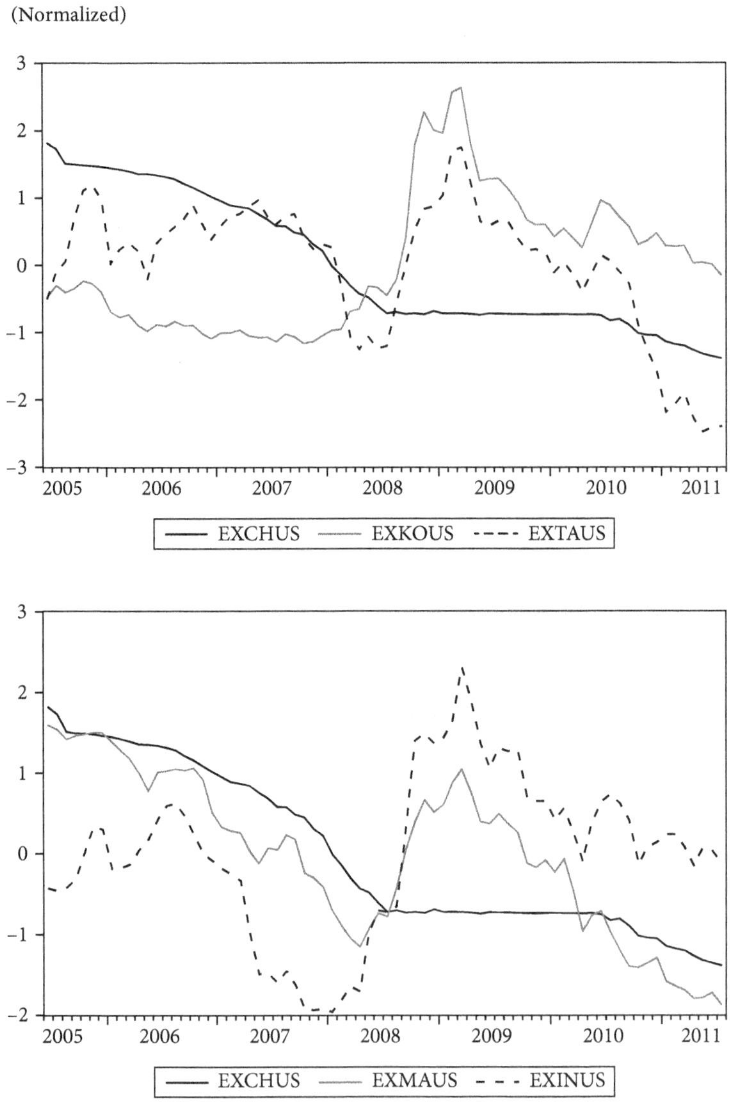


FIGURE 25.3 Exchange Rates (CH: China; KR: Korea; TW: Taiwan; HK: Hong Kong; MA: Malaysia; and IN: Indonesia.)

observation is that substantially greater exchange rate flexibility is observed in these countries compared to China. Only a weak correspondence between China's modest exchange rate movements and those elsewhere in Asia are evident, suggesting that financial linkages may also be relatively weak.

### 25.4.2 Broad Trends in Interest Rate and Equity Market Linkages

This sub-section analyzes co-movements between China's and East Asian financial asset returns. We investigate linkages for three financial assets—interbank interest rates,

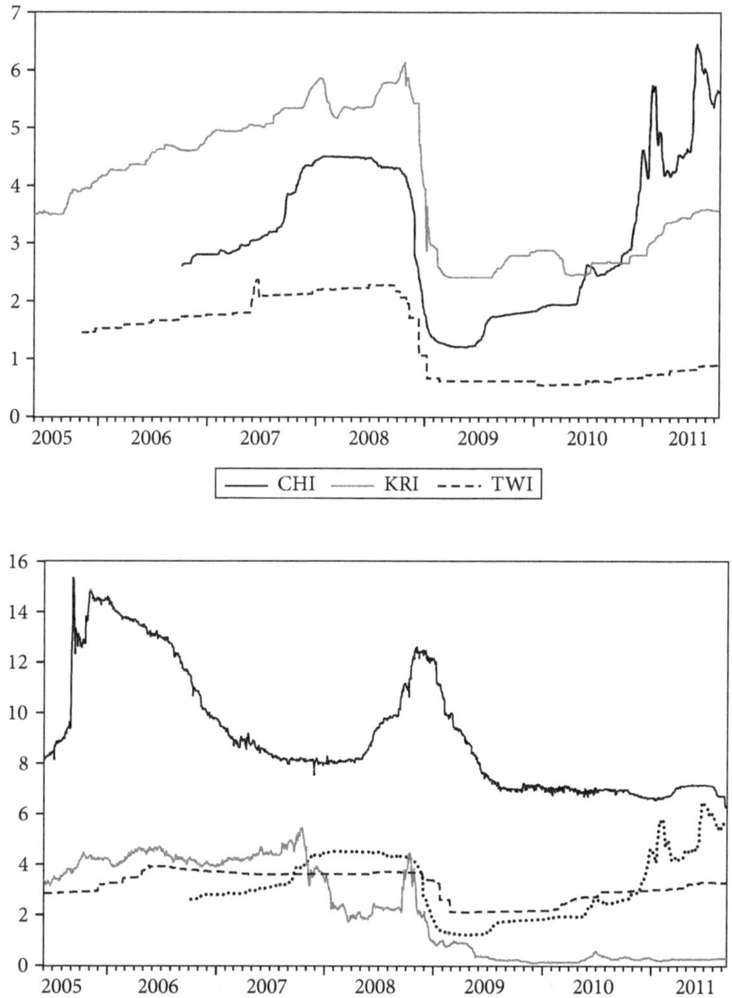


FIGURE 25.4 Interbank Interest Rates (CH: China; KR: Korea; TW: Taiwan; HK: Hong Kong; MA: Malaysia; and IN: Indonesia.)

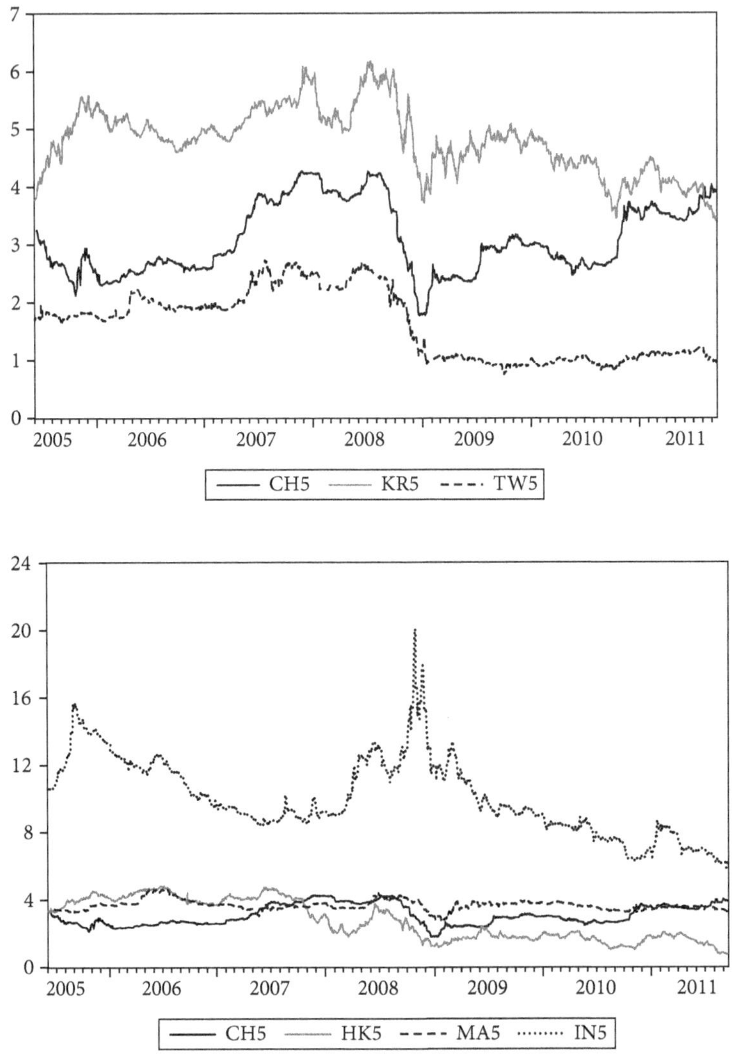


FIGURE 25.5 Five-year Government Bond Interest Rates

CH: China; KR: Korea; TW: Taiwan; HK: Hong Kong; MA: Malaysia; and IN: Indonesia.

five-year government bond interest rates, and equity prices—for Hong Kong, Korea, Taiwan, Malaysia, and Indonesia—using daily data. We consider the most financially open economy in the region, Hong Kong, as a "control" region since it is tightly linked to the U.S. dollar through its currency board arrangement, has no capital controls or other impediments to cross-border movement of capital, and is a world financial center. The other four countries are partially financially open and have developed financial sectors to various degrees, but it is not clear the extent to which China influences their domestic financial asset prices.

(Log Scale; Major National Indices)

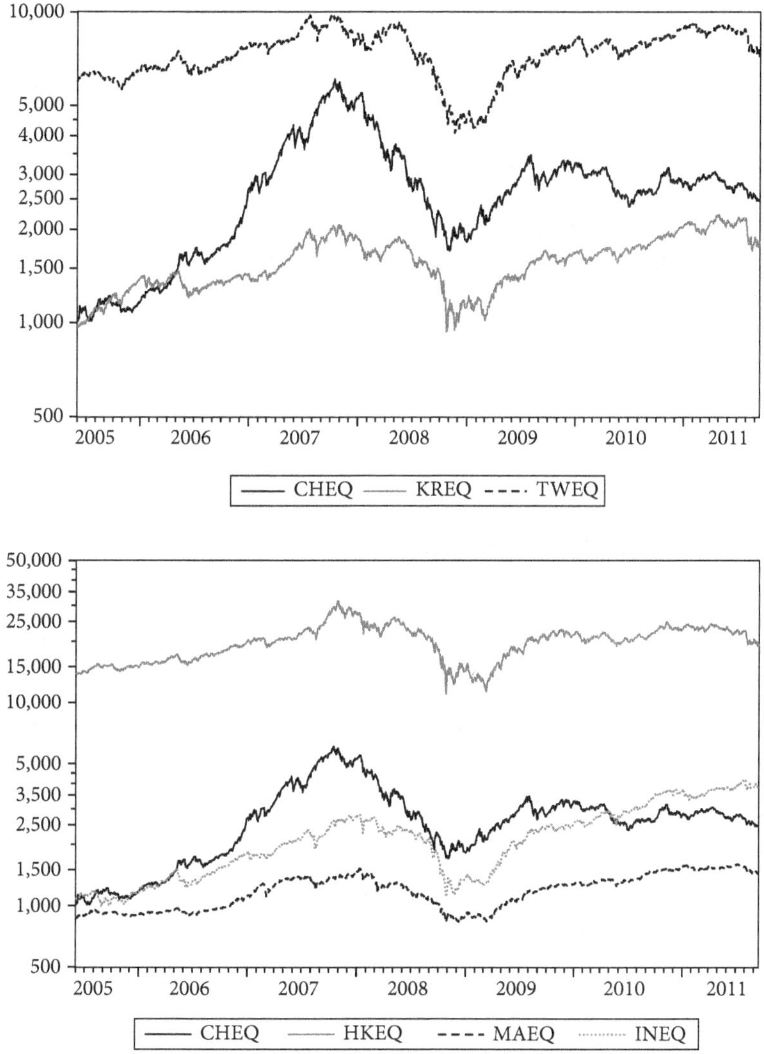


FIGURE 25.6 Equity Prices

(Log Scale; Major National Indices)CH: China; KR: Korea; TW: Taiwan; HK: Hong Kong; MA: Malaysia; and IN: Indonesia.

Our choice of asset price variables allows us to examine whether the degree of financial linkage with China varies across asset maturities and type. Interbank interest rates are at the shortest end of the maturity spectrum and are most directly influenced by the central bank's policy target rate. Evidence of tight linkage of interbank rates would indicate that China has significant short-run influence over domestic monetary policy in other countries. Five-year bond rates are "medium term" financial instruments, and evidence of linkage at this maturity would indicate that China has a significant effect on corporate and government costs of finance. Linkages among equity prices could represent either direct financial linkages or trade linkages—financial linkage through capital flows and arbitrage, and trade linkage by competition and interdependence through exports and imports.

The results are shown in Figure 25.4 for interbank interest rates), Figure 25.5 for five-year bond rates) and Figure 25.6 for equity market price levels (using a logarithmic scale). Figure 25.4 indicates that China's interbank interest rate developments display broadly similar movements with other East Asian economies over the long run, but also show substantial differences in the short run. Linkages among five-year bond rates, shown in Figure 25.5, indicate a similar pattern to that of interbank interest rates. The most dramatic linkages are shown in Figure 25.6 for equity prices (plotted using a log scale for comparison purposes). Equity prices for China and all the other East Asian countries are closely linked across time.

### 25.4.3 Daily Financial Market Linkages

To complement our graphical analysis, we analyze the daily linkages of financial asset prices of the same East Asian economies with China in a regression framework that controls for common shocks, represented by U.S. asset price fluctuations. Our object is to determine whether developments in China's financial markets significantly influence financial asset prices in the East Asia region, and whether the form of the exchange rate regime or degree of exchange rate flexibility in China influences the strength of the transmission mechanism. The full sample period is June 2, 2005, through September 16, 2011, with subperiods corresponding to the exchange rate episodes identified in the previous section as (1) June 2005–June 2008 (gradual appreciation), (2) July 2008–May 2010 (tight peg, narrow range), and (3) June 2010–September 2011 (very gradual appreciation). Note that China's desired degrees of exchange rate fixity is not independent of external conditions, as the second sub-sample corresponds with the global financial crisis.

The linkage regressions, reported in Table 25.2 for the interbank rates, Table 25.3 for the five-year bond rates, and Table 25.4 for the equity prices, regress each country's financial asset rate against the corresponding China–U.S. rates (the U.S. rate is lagged one day due to the time zone differences). All interest rate variables are in first differences, and the equity price is in log first-differences. (All of the variables in levels were non-stationary.) Regressions with additional lags of the China and U.S. asset prices were estimated, and are available from the authors upon request; the results were almost identical to estimation results reported in the tables.

The results are quite striking. Interbank rates in the four East Asian countries are not influenced by interbank rate movements in China, regardless of the sample period (i.e., exchange rate regime), except very marginally in one instance (Taiwan over the

**Table 25.2 Interbank Regressions**

| | | Hong Kong Interbank Rate | Korea Interbank Rate | Taiwan Interbank Rate | Malaysia Interbank Rate | Indonesia Interbank Rate |
|---|---|---|---|---|---|---|
| | U.S. Interbank Rate t-1 | 0.125*** | 0.012 | 0.016 | −0.004 | 0.005 |
| | | (0.028) | (0.018) | (0.013) | (0.013) | (0.034) |
| 6/2/05 - 9/16/11 | China Interbank Rate t | −0.008 | 0.047 | 0.047* | 0.010 | 0.008 |
| | | (0.057) | (0.041) | (0.028) | (0.029) | (0.073) |
| | Adj. R2 | 0.026 | 0.000 | 0.004 | −0.003 | −0.003 |
| | U.S. Interbank Rate t−1 | 0.048 | 0.010 | 0.014 | 0.000 | −0.025 |
| | | (0.050) | (0.009) | (0.014) | (0.002) | (0.047) |
| 6/2/05 - 6/27/08 | China Interbank Rate t | −0.477 | −0.015 | 0.017 | −0.018 | −0.443 |
| | | (0.404) | (0.071) | (0.112) | (0.016) | (0.356) |
| | Adj. R2 | 0.002 | −0.003 | −0.005 | −0.003 | −0.001 |
| | U.S. Interbank Rate t-1 | 0.179*** | 0.011 | 0.018 | −0.007 | 0.017 |
| | | (0.044) | (0.036) | (0.025) | (0.024) | (0.056) |
| 7/3/08 - 5/28/10 | China Interbank Rate t | −0.003 | 0.119 | 0.110 | 0.007 | −0.002 |
| | | (0.115) | (0.108) | (0.069) | (0.072) | (0.169) |
| | Adj. R2 | 0.056 | −0.003 | 0.004 | −0.007 | −0.008 |
| | U.S. Interbank Rate t-1 | 0.011 | −0.094 | −0.079 | −0.087 | 0.308 |
| | | (0.090) | (0.097) | (0.058) | (0.114) | (0.324) |
| 6/3/10 - 9/16/11 | China Interbank Rate t | −0.007 | −0.008 | −0.001 | 0.002 | 0.028 |
| | | (0.010) | (0.015) | (0.009) | (0.019) | (0.051) |
| | Adj. R2 | −0.009 | −0.005 | −0.001 | −0.009 | −0.005 |

*Notes:* First difference values for independent and dependent variables. Daily data. Standard errors in parentheses below. Significance levels: *10%, **5%, ***1%

**Table 25.3 5-yr Bond Regressions**

| | | Hong Kong 5 Yr Bond | Korea 5 Yr Bond | Taiwan 5 Yr Bond | Malaysia 5 Yr Bond | Indonesia 5 Yr Bond |
|---|---|---|---|---|---|---|
| | U.S. 5 Yr Bond t-1 | 0.488*** | 0.147*** | 0.088*** | 0.082*** | -0.196** |
| | | (0.017) | (0.027) | (0.015) | (0.017) | (0.098) |
| 6/2/05-9/16/11 | China 5 Yr Bond t | 0.030 | 0.201*** | 0.074*** | 0.029 | 0.526*** |
| | | (0.032) | (0.051) | (0.027) | (0.032) | (0.186) |
| | Adj. R2 | 0.481 | 0.049 | 0.052 | 0.029 | 0.012 |
| | U.S. 5 Yr Bond 1–1 | 0.549*** | 0.202*** | 0.119*** | 0.080*** | −0.033 |
| | | (0.028) | (0.035) | (0.022) | (0.024) | (0.072) |
| 6/2/05 - 6/27/08 | China 5 Yr Bond I | 0.077 | 0.094 | 0.124*** | 0.007 | 0.084 |
| | | (0.060) | (0.075) | (0.047) | (0.054) | (0.170) |
| | Adj. R2 | 0.485 | 0.078 | 0.093 | 0.025 | −0.004 |
| | U.S. 5 Yr Bond t-1 | 0.407*** | 0.089 | 0.032 | 0.091*** | −0.522** |
| | | (0.030) | (0.056) | (0.028) | (0.033) | (0.257) |
| 7/3/08 - 5/28/10 | China 5 Yr Bond | −0.010 | 0.300*** | 0.048 | 0.025 | 1.085** |
| | | (0.053) | (0.098) | (0.049) | (0.056) | (0.450) |
| | Adj. R2 | 0.409 | 0.035 | 0.001 | 0.022 | 0.030 |
| | U.S. 5 Yr Bond t-1 | 0.495*** | 0.120** | 0.104*** | 0.064*** | 0.133 |
| | | (0.025) | (0.052) | (0.021) | (0.024) | (0.111) |
| 6/3/10 - 9/16/11 | China 5 Yr Bond t | 0.015 | 0.121 | 0.015 | 0.082* | −0.054 |
| | | (0.041) | (0.088) | (0.033) | (0.047) | (0.176) |
| | Adj. R2 | 0.676 | 0.027 | 0.115 | 0.050 | −0.003 |

*Notes:* First difference values for independent and dependent variables. Daily data. Standard errors in parentheses below.

Significance levels: *10%, **5%, ***1%

**Table 25.4 Equity Regressions**

| | | Hong Kong Equity | Korea Equity | Taiwan Equity | Malaysia Equity | Indonesia Equity |
|---|---|---|---|---|---|---|
| | U.S. Equity t-1 | 0.429*** | 0.372*** | 0.361*** | 0.220*** | 0.368*** |
| | | (0.032) | (0.033) | (0.028) | (0.017) | (0.034) |
| 6/2/05 -9/16/11 | China Equity t | 0.326*** | 0.192*** | 0.163*** | 0.086*** | 0.143*** |
| | | (0.026) | (0.029) | (0.024) | (0.014) | (0.029) |
| | Adj. R2 | 0.328 | 0.198 | 0.229 | 0.227 | 0.171 |
| | U.S. Equity t-1 | 0.695*** | 0.554*** | 0.562*** | 0.406*** | 0.529*** |
| | | (0.055) | (0.059) | (0.054) | (0.039) | (0.070) |
| 6/2/05 - 6/27/08 | China Equity t | 0.213*** | 0.107*** | 0.129*** | 0.050** | 0.063* |
| | | (0.028) | (0.031) | (0.027) | (0.019) | (0.036) |
| | Adj. R2 | 0.370 | 0.211 | 0.266 | 0.237 | 0.138 |
| | U.S. Equity t-1 | 0.332*** | 0.298*** | 0.290*** | 0.168*** | 0.294*** |
| | | (0.055) | (0.057) | (0.046) | (0.024) | (0.054) |
| 7/3/08 - 5/28/10 | China Equity t | 0.494*** | 0.321*** | 0.213*** | 0.153*** | 0.257*** |
| | | (0.060) | (0.062) | (0.050) | (0.026) | (0.059) |
| | Adj. R2 | 0.344 | 0.218 | 0.217 | 0.304 | 0.205 |
| | U.S. Equity t-1 | 0.354*** | 0.352*** | 0.378*** | 0.177*** | 0.367*** |
| | | (0.048) | (0.064) | (0.054) | (0.028) | (0.059) |
| 6/3/10 - 9/16/11 | China Equity t | 0.341*** | 0.156** | 0.131** | 0.009 | 0.175** |
| | | (0.057) | (0.075) | (0.064) | (0.035) | (0.073) |
| | Adj. R2 | 0.398 | 0.193 | 0.256 | 0.199 | 0.246 |

*Notes:* First difference of log values for independent and dependent variables. Daily data. Standard errors in parentheses below. Significance levels: *10%, **5%, ***1%

full period, though not in any sub-sample period). This indicates that short-term bank funding costs and monetary policies in the region moved independently of China's financial markets developments.

By contrast, there is more support, albeit modest, of linkages with China for five-year bond rates. In particular, there is no five-year bond linkage in any sample with Hong Kong, but linkages appear in at least one sub-sample (or the full sample) for the other four economies. Linkage with Korea and Indonesia appears during the global financial crisis period, when China maintained a narrow pegged exchange rate against the dollar, and Korea's and Indonesia's exchange rates depreciated sharply. (The linkage during this sub-sample explains the significant linkage over the full sample.) No linkage is seen during the first and third sub-samples. Linkages with Taiwan are seen in the first sample period (carrying over to the full sample period) but not in the other two sub-samples. Linkages with Malaysia are only found in the last sub-sample.

Finally, equity market linkages between China and other East Asian economies are strong and consistent throughout the sample, regardless of the exchange rate regime. In particular, equity price movements in China are strongly correlated with equity price changes in every country and every sub-sample period, with a single exception (Malaysia in the last sub-sample). Moreover, in a number of cases, the strength of the linkage with China is stronger than the linkage with U.S. equity prices. More specifically, the link appears to be somewhat stronger during China's fixed rate peg period which corresponds with the Asian financial crisis.

Overall, these results suggest that China's capital controls are quite effective in "decoupling" financial markets in the region, at least in the short-term. The only consistently strong and robust linkage exists with equity price movements, and these very likely are more influenced by direct and indirect trade linkages as opposed to financial market linkages.

### 25.4.4 Long-Run Linkages

Despite our modest support for financial market asset price linkages between China and East Asian economies in the short run, it is possible that longer-run relationships may be identified. To this end, we consider the long-run linkage of five-year bond (shown in Figure 25.7) and equity prices between China and Korea, while controlling for fluctuations in U.S. asset prices. We chose Korea for this analysis since Korea is the largest economy in our group of East Asian economies investigated and, from the preceding section, probably has the strongest short-run linkage with China. We consider both nominal and real monthly bond interest rate and equity prices. The real bond interest rate is defined as the nominal rate less the 12-month inflation CPI inflation rate. The (log) real equity price is defined as the (log of the) nominal equity price divided by the CPI price index. Our sample period begins in June 2005, constrained by the availability of Chinese asset price data.

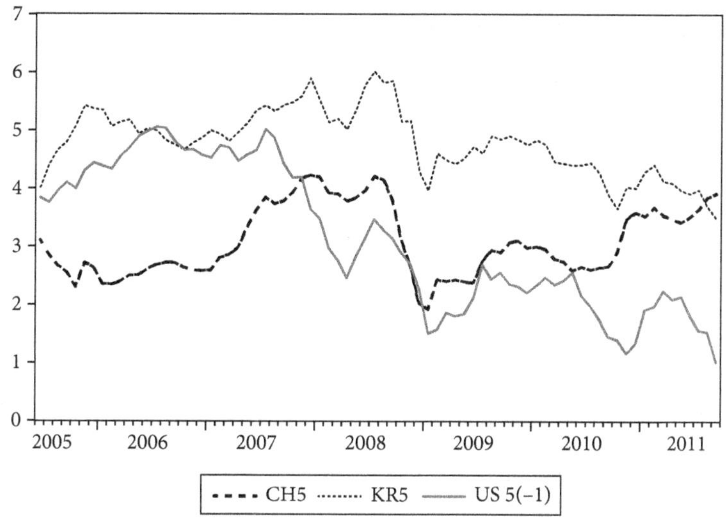


FIGURE 25.7 Five-year nominal bond interest rates in China, Korea and the United States

CH: China; KR: Korea; TW: Taiwan; HK: Hong Kong; MA: Malaysia; and IN: Indonesia.

We employ cointegration methodology to test whether asset prices demonstrate longer-run co-movement over time. Two variables are cointegrated if they move together over long periods, but perhaps deviate substantially over the short-term such as during business cycles. We employ two different cointegration tests—the Johansen (rank or trace test, and the eigenvalue test) system co-integration tests and the Engle-Granger single-equation cointegration test. These are standard tests of cointegration (Hamilton, 1994). We investigate the long-run linkage between China and Korea asset prices (as endogenous variables), while controlling for U.S. asset price fluctuations (treated as a deterministic common element).

The tests for nominal (real) five-year bond rate cointegration are reported in Table 25.5 (Table 25.6), and the tests for nominal (real) equity price cointegration are reported in Table 25.7 (Table 25.8). The left-hand-side of each table reports the Johansen tests, and the right-hand-side of each table reports the Engle-Granger cointegration tests.

We do not find cointegration between asset prices in China and Korea after controlling for U.S. asset prices movements. This is a robust result. The null hypothesis of "no cointegration" cannot be rejected in the system estimation (Johansen rank or eigenvalue test) or single-equation test (Engel-Granger test) at the 5 percent level or better for either nominal or real interest rates or equity prices. Moreover, further cointegration tests focusing on a system of three endogenous variables (Korea, China, and the United States) give similar results. China's bond rates do not apparently have a systematic long-term linkage with financial market prices in Korea. This result should be interpreted cautiously, however, due to the limited sample period in which Chinese financial market data is available (since 2005). This is a very short period to unveil "long-term" relationships. Nonetheless, it is suggestive that the ultimate financial

## Table 25.5 Nominal Five-Year Bond Rate

| Johansen System Cointegration Tests | Engle-Granger Single Equation Cointegration Test |
|---|---|
| Nominal Five-Year Bond Rate | |
| Sample (adjusted): 2005M09 2011M09 | Series: CH5 KR5 |
| Included observations: 73 after adjustments | Sample: 2005M06 2011M09 |
| Trend assumption: Linear deterministic trend | Included observations: 76 |
| Series: KR5 CH5 | Null hypothesis: Series are not cointegrated |
| Exogenous series: US5(−1) | Cointegrating equation deterministics: C US5(−1) |
| | Automatic lags specification based on Schwarz criterion (maxlag=11) |
| Lags interval (in first differences): 1 to 2 | |
| Unrestricted Cointegration Rank Test (Trace) | Dependent tau-statistic Prob.* z-statistic Prob.* |
| | CH5 −1.454738 0.9064 −6.453215 0.8161 |
| Hypothesized Trace 0.05 | KR5 −2.490964 0.4972 −11.06414 0.5103 |
| No. of CE(s) Eigenvalue Statistic Critical Value Prob .** | |
| | *MacKinnon (1996) p-values. |
| None 0.145861 11.98668 15.49471 0.1576 | |
| At most 1 0.006518 0.477389 3.841466 0.4896 | |
| Trace test indicates no cointegration at the 0.05 level | Intermediate Results: |
| *denotes rejection of the hypothesis at the 0.05 level | CH5 KR5 |
| **MacKinnon-Haug-Michelis (1999) p-values | Rho - 1 −0.058746 −0.147522 |
| | Rho S. E. 0.040383 0.059223 |
| Unrestricted Cointegration Rank Test (Maximum Eigenvalue) | Residual variance 0.031805 0.039113 |
| | Long-run residual variance 0.039113 |
| Hypothesized Max-Eigen 0.05 | Number of lags 1 0 |
| No. of CE(s) Eigenvalue Statistic Critical Value Prob.** | Number of observations 74 75 |
| : | Number of stochastic trends 2 2 |
| None 0.145861 11.50929 14.2646 0.1305 | |
| At most 1 0.006518 0.477389 3.841466 0.4896 | **Number of stochastic trends in asymptotic distribution |
| Max-eigenvalue test indicates no cointegration at the 0.05 level | |
| *denotes rejection of the hypothesis at the 0.05 level | |
| **MacKinnon-Haug-Michelis (1999) p-values | |

Notes: KR5, CH5 and US5 represent nominal five-year bond rates for Korea, China and the U.S., respectively.

The US is treated as a deterministic variable so tests of cointegraton are between Korea and China 5-year bond rates, controlling for a constant and US interest rates.

## Table 25.6 Real Five-Year Bond Rate

### Johansen System Cointegration Tests

Sample (adjusted): 2005M09 2011M08

Included observations: 72 after adjustments

Trend assumption: Linear deterministic trend

Series:KRR5 CHR5

Exogenous series: USR5

Lags interval (in first differences): 1 to 2

Unrestricted Cointegration Rank Test (Trace)

| Hypothesized No. of CE(s) | Eigenvalue | Trace Statistic | 0.05 Critical Value | Prob.** |
|---|---|---|---|---|
| None | 0.104277 | 10.80151 | 15.49471 | 0.224 |
| At most 1 | 0.039112 | 2.872602 | 3.841466 | 0.0901 |

Trace test indicates no cointegration at the 0.05 level

*denotes rejection of the hypothesis at the 0.05 level

**MacKinnon-Haug-Michelis (1999) p-values

Unrestricted Cointegration Rank Test (Maximum Eigenvalue)

| Hypothesized No. of CE(s) | Eigenvalue | Max-Eigen Statistic | 0.05 Critical Value | Prob.** |
|---|---|---|---|---|
| None | 0.104277 | 7.928912 | 14.2646 | 0.386 |
| At most 1 | 0.039112 | 2. 872602 | 3.841466 | 0.0901 |

Max-eigenvalue test indicates no cointegration at the 0.05 level

*denotes rejection of the hypothesis at the 0.05 level

**MacKinnon-Haug-Michelis (1999) p-values

### Engle-Granger Single Equation Cointegration Test

Series: KRR5 CHR5

Sample (adjusted): 2005M062011M08

Included observations: 75 after adjustments

Null hypothesis: Series are not cointegrated

Cointegrating equation deterministics: C USR5

Automatic lags specification based on Schwarz criterion maxlag=11)

| Dependent | tau-statistic | Prob.* | z-statistic | Prob.* |
|---|---|---|---|---|
| KRR5 | −2.127437 | 0.6789 | 11.29321 | 0.4944 |
| CHR5 | −2.261953 | 0.6138 | −9.607181 | 0.6079 |

*MacKinnon (1996) p-values.

Intermediate Results:

| | KRR5 | CHR5 |
|---|---|---|
| Rho - 1 | −0.110313 | −0.129827 |
| Rho S.E. | 0.051852 | 0.057396 |
| Residual variance | 0.16379 | 0.624692 |
| Long-run residual variance | 0.322125 | 0.624692 |
| Number of lags | 1 | 0 |
| Number of observations | 73 | 74 |
| Number of stochastic trends: | 2 | 2 |

**Number of stochastic trends in asymptotic distribution

*Notes:* KRR5, CHR5 and USR5 represent real five-year bond rates for Korea, China and the U.S., respectively.

The US is treated as a deterministic variable so tests of cointegration are between Korea and China 5-year bond rates, controlling for a constant and US interest rates. Real rates are the nominal rate less inflation over the previous 12 months.

## Table 25.7 Nominal Equity Prices

### Johansen System Cointegration Tests

Sample: 2005M06 2011M09

Included observations: 76

Trend assumption: Linear deterministic trend

Series: LOG(KREQ) LOG(CHEQ)

Exogenous series: LOG(USEQ)

Lags interval (in first differences): 1 to 2

Unrestricted Cointegration Rank Test (Trace)

| Hypothesized No. of CE(s) | Eigenvalue | Trace Statistic | 0.05 Critical Value | Prob.** |
|---|---|---|---|---|
| None | 0.118215 | 11.27631 | 15.49471 | 0.1951 |
| At most 1 | 0.022313 | 1.715018 | 3.841466 | 0.1903 |

Trace test indicates no cointegration at the 0.05 level

*denotes rejection of the hypothesis at the 0.05 level

**MacKinnon-Haug-Michelis (1999) p-values

Unrestricted Cointegration Rank Test (Maximum Eigenvalue)

| Hypothesized No. of CE(s) | Eigenvalue | Max-Eigen Statistic | 0.05 Critical Value | Prob.** |
|---|---|---|---|---|
| None | 0.118215 | 9.561293 | 14.2646 | 0.2424 |
| At most 1 | 0.022313 | 1.715018 | 3.841466 | 0.1903 |

Max-eigenvalue test indicates no cointegration at the 0.05 level

*denotes rejection of the hypothesis at the 0.05 level

**MacKinnon-Haug-Michelis (1999) p-values

### Engle-Granger Single Equation Cointegration Test

Series: LOG(KREQ) LOG(CHEQ)

Sample: 2005M06 2011M09

Included observations: 76

Null hypothesis: Series are not cointegrated

Cointegrating equation deterministics: C LOG(USEQ)

Automatic lags specification based on Schwarz criterion (maxlag=11)

| Dependent | tau-statistic | Prob.* | z-statistic | Prob.* |
|---|---|---|---|---|
| LOG(KREQ) | −1.144247 | 0.9524 | −3.498782 | 0.9499 |
| LOG(CHEQ) | −1.380522 | 0.9202 | −4.105315 | 0.9301 |

*MacKinnon (1996) p-values.

Intermediate Results:

| | LOG(KREQ) | LOG(CHEQ) |
|---|---|---|
| Rho - 1 | −0.050147 | −0.054738 |
| Rho.S.E. | 0.043825 | 0.03965 |
| Residual variance | 0.001851 | 0.009663 |
| Long-run residual variance | 0.001691 | 0.009663 |
| Number of lags | 2 | 0 |
| Number of observations | 73 | 75 |
| Number of stochastic trends: | 2 | 2 |

**Number of stochastic trends in asymptotic distribution

*Notes:* KREQ, CHEQ, USEQ represent nominal equity prices for Korea, China and the U. S., respectively.

The US is treated as a deterministic variable so tests of cointegraton are between Korea and China equity prices. All equity prices expressed in log values.

## Table 25.8 Real Equity Prices

### Johansen System Cointegration Tests

Sample (adjusted): 2005M06 2011M08

Included observations: 75 after adjustments

Trend assumption: Linear deterministic trend

Series: LKRREQ LCHREQ

Exogenous series: LUSREQ(–I)

Lags interval (in first differences): 1 to 2

Unrestricted Cointegration Rank Test (Trace)

| Hypothesized No. of CE(s) | Eigenvalue | Trace Statistic | 0.05 Critical Value | Prob.** |
|---|---|---|---|---|
| None | 0.100364 | 9.486957 | 15.49471 | 0.3222 |
| At most 1 | 0.020515 | 1.554615 | 3.841466 | 0.2125 |

Trace test indicates no cointegration at the 0.05 level

*denotes rejection of the hypothesis at the 0.05 level

**MacKinnon-Haug-Michelis (1999) p-values

Unrestricted Cointegration Rank Test (Maximum Eigenvalue)

| Hypothesized No. of CE(s) | Eigenvalue | Max-Eigen Statistic | 0.05 Critical Value | prob.** |
|---|---|---|---|---|
| None | 0.100364 | 7.932343 | 14.2646 | 0.3856 |
| At most 1 | 0.020515 | 1.554615 | 3.841466 | 0.2125 |

Max-eigenvalue test indicates no cointegration at the 0.05 level

*denotes rejection of the hypothesis at the 0.05 level

**MacKinnon-Haug-Michelis (1999) p-values

### Engle-Granger Single Equation Cointegration Test

Series: LKRREQ LCHREQ

Sample (adjusted): 2005M06 2011M08

Included observations: 75 after adjustments

Null hypothesis: Series are not cointegrated

Cointegrating equation deterministics: C LUSREQ

Automatic lags specification based on Schwarz criterion (maxlag=11)

| Dependent | tau-statistic | Prob.* | z-statistic | Prob.* |
|---|---|---|---|---|
| LKRREQ | −1.673709 | 0.8533 | −6.379997 | 0.8201 |
| LCHREQ | −1.490728 | 0.899 | −4.802817 | 0.9021 |

*MacKinnon (1996) p-values.

Intermediate Results:

| | LKRREQ | LCHREQ |
|---|---|---|
| Rho -1 | −0.088003 | −0.064903 |
| Rho S.E. | 0.05258 | 0.043538 |
| Residual variance | 0.001725 | 0.010586 |
| Long-run residual variance | 0.001749 | 0.010586 |
| Number of lags | 2 | 0 |
| Number of observations | 72 | 74 |
| Number of stochastic trends: | 2 | 2 |

**Number of stochastic trends in asymptotic distribution

*Notes:* LKRREQ, LCHREQ, LUSREQ represent (log) real equity prices for Korea, China and the United States, respectively

The United States is treated as a deterministic variable so tests of cointegraton are between Korea and China real equity prices.

effects of the emergence of China as a global economic power have not fully been realized.

## 25.5 Conclusion

This chapter evaluates how gradual changes in China's financial system, liberalization of capital controls, and the process of financial "internationalization" have affected financial markets in other East Asian economies. In particular, we examine how financial market changes in China's economy—whether driven by policy changes, market-driven developments, institutional changes, or the growing importance in the region—have influenced financial asset prices of its East Asian neighbors.

Our main conclusion is that domestic financial development in China as of early 2012 have been modest and internationalization of the currency and liberalization of capital controls has been very limited. Consequently, substantial divergences remain between the onshore and offshore prices of Chinese financial assets, as well as between the financial assets of China and its neighbors. Short-term financial asset prices, reflected in interbank interest rates, were essentially decoupled. Weak linkages were detected in longer-term interest rates (five-year bond rates). The strongest linkages, however, appeared in equity markets. We argue that equity market arbitrage working through capital markets was not the force driving these linkages between China and East Asia. Rather, the emergence of China as the clear regional economic power, the sheer size and dynamism of its economic activity and trading relationships, have played the dominant role in linking equity markets across the region.

## Notes

1. According to Mallaby and Wethington (2012), during the first six months of 2011, trade transactions settled in rmb totaled around $146 billion, a 13-fold increase over the same period during the previous year. By mid-2011, rmb deposits in Hong Kong equaled $85 billion, a roughly tenfold jump since Hu's 2008 statement. The yuan is already accepted as a form of payment in Mongolia, Pakistan, Thailand, and Vietnam. Chinese authorities have indicated that as soon as 2015, they want the yuan to be included in the basket of major currencies that determines the value of Special Drawing Rights.
2. For example, China in recent years has permitted limited expansion of portfolio capital flows through "qualified investment" programs. Moreover, unofficial flows into and out of China have grown over time.
3. This episode was also characterized by a sharp deterioration of asset quality, resulting in substantial increases in non-performing bank loans.
4. See Ma, Xiandong, and Xi (2011) for a detailed discussion of the use of reserve requirement changes as a tool of monetary policy in China.

5. The rmb has been convertible for current account transactions since December 1996, when China satisfied the IMF's Article VIII criteria for membership.
6. In December 2002, QFIIs were allowed to invest in A shares and other domestic securities, subject to requirements of at least $10 billion in assets under management and prior experience. Repatriation was limited by lock-up periods on stocks of as long as one-year. New rules in September 2006 lowered the asset under management criteria to $5 billion, reduced the lock-up period to three months, lessened experience requirements, and also raised the quotas for investment in Chinese equities. The QDII program, launched in July 2006, permitted qualified commercial banks, securities firms, and insurance companies in China to make limited offshore investments in foreign-currency denominated assets (restricted to fixed income securities in the case of banks and insurance companies). More recently, in response to concerns about increased capital outflows as the economy has slowed, China has accelerated its approval process to allow more capital inflows into its stock and bond markets via the QFII program.
7. In 2007 the PBOC raised to $50 thousand the ceiling on the conversion between rmb and foreign currency by Chinese individuals.
8. Prasad and Wei (2005a) provide an extensive chronology of capital controls over the period 1980–January 2005; Prasad and Ye (2012b) update the chronology into 2011. They document the increasing openness of China's capital account in both de jure and de facto terms through selective and cautious changes, consistent with the active promotion of the rmb as an international currency. However, in most cases, they argue that constraints on capital inflows and outflows have been merely relaxed rather than eliminated entirely.
9. The three-month deposit rate was used for China because the lack of alternative data.
10. He also examines deviations from uncovered interest parity, with the expected exchange rate change used in these calculations proxied by the previous period's actual change. For a related exercise analyzing real interest linkages among Pacific Basin countries, see Glick and Hutchison (1990).
11. Quantity-based measures include measurement of openness and restrictiveness in trade and financial transactions, cross-border movement of capital, output and consumption correlations, and savings-investment correlations. They yield similar conclusions; see Jang (2011).

## References

Balasubramaniam, Vimal, Ila Patnaik, and Ajay Shah (2011). "Who Cries about the Chinese Yuan?" National Institute of Public Finance and Policy, New Delhi, Working Paper 2011-89, May.

Frankel, Jeffrey. (2009). "New Estimation of China's Exchange Rate Regime," *Pacific Economic Review*, 14(3): 346–360.

Frankel, Jeffrey, and Shang-Jin Wei (1994). "Yen Bloc or Dollar Bloc? Exchange Rate Policies of the East Asian Countries," in *Macroeconomic Linkage: Savings, Exchange Rates and Capital Flows*, ed. by Takatoshi. Ito, and Anne Krueger. University of Chicago Press: 295–333.

Glick, Reuven, and Michael Hutchison (1990). "A Financial Liberalization in the Pacific Basin: Implications for Real Interest Rate Linkages," *Journal of the Japanese and International Economies*, 4(1): 36–48.

Glick, Reuven and Michael Hutchison (2009). "Navigating the Trilemma: Capital Flows and Monetary Policy in China," *Journal of Asian Economics* 20:(3) (May), 205–224.

Girardin, Eric (2011). "A De Facto Asian-Currency Unit Bloc in East Asia: It Has Been There But We Did Not Look for It," ADBI Working Paper No. 262 (January).

Hamilton, James (1994). *Time Series Analysis.* Princeton: Princeton University Press.

Hutchison, Michael, Gurnain Pasricha, and Nirvikar Singh (2011) "Effectiveness of Capital Controls in India: Evidence from the Offshore NDF Market" Bank of Canada Working Paper 2011-29, December.

International Monetary Fund (2011). IMF Country Report No. 11/192, People's Report of China, Article IV Consultation.

Jang, Hong Bum (2011). "Financial Integration and Cooperation in East Asia: Assessment of Recent Developments and Their Implications," Bank of Japan IMES Discussion Paper No. 2011-E-5.

Lee, Hyun-Hoon, Hyeon-seung Huh, and Donghyun Park (2011). "Financial Integration in East Asia: An Empirical Investigation," ADB Economics Working Paper Series No. 259 (May).

Ma, Guonan, and Robert N McCauley (2010). "The Evolving Renminbi Regime and Implications for Asian Currency Stability," BIS Working Papers No 32.1

Ma, Guonan, Yan Xiandong, and Liu Xi (2011). "China's Evolving Reserve Requirements," BOFIT Discussion Papers No. 30, Bank of Finland Institute for Economies in Transition.

Mallaby, S., and O. Wethington (2012). "The Future of the Yuan," *Foreign Affairs*, 91(1): 135–146.

McCauley, Robert. (2011). "Renminbi Internationalisation and China's Financial Development," *Bank for International Settlements Quarterly Review* (December), 41–56.

Ogawa, E., and J. Simizu (2011). "Asian Monetary Unit and Monetary Cooperation in Asia," Asian Development Bank Institute (ADBI) Working Paper No. 275 (April).

Pongsaparn, Runchana, and Olaf Unteroberdoerster (2011). "Financial Integration and Rebalancing in Asia," IMF WP/11/243.

Prasad, Eswar and Lei Ye (2012). "Will the Renminbi Rule?" IMF *Finance and Development* (March), 49(1): 26–29.

Prasad, Eswar, and Lei Ye (2011). "The Renminbi's Role in the Global Monetary System," forthcoming in R. Glick and M.M. Spiegel (eds.), *Asia's Role in the Post-Crisis Global Economy*, Federal Reserve Bank of San Francisco.

# CHAPTER 26

# THE OFFSHORE RMB MARKET IN HONG KONG AND RMB INTERNATIONALIZATION

YIN-WONG CHEUNG AND HUI MIAO

## 26.1 INTRODUCTION

AFTER the sovereignty change in 1997, Hong Kong has, by most measures, maintained its status as a renowned international financial center. The robust performance is usually attributed to the territory's proximity to and complex trade and financial links with China. The newly launched offshore renminbi (RMB) market is a milestone for the Hong Kong financial sector and for China's economic reform program.

In the last few decades, China has steadily expanded its presence in the global market and enjoyed substantial economic growth. As a major hub of the world production chain and the second largest trading country, China is quite closely integrated with the world economy via international trade channels. The integration of China trade into the world has substantially altered both the trade and production patterns around the globe. Compared with its trade network, China's financial linkages with the outside world, however, are quite limited. The launch of the offshore RMB market in Hong Kong represents a new chapter on China's efforts to promote the international use of its currency and foster its financial links with the rest of the world.

With its growing prominence in the global market, China's economic policies and activities are increasingly being scrutinized by the international community. The focus has drifted from issues pertaining to China's ability to attract foreign direct investment, to ballooning trade surplus, to staggering foreign exchange reserves, to exchange rate policy, to investments in other developing countries, and, more recently, to promoting the international use of the RMB. The shift in focus reflects the evolving role of China in the world. Specifically, with the recent measures to encourage the use of the RMB overseas, the world is rushed to reassess China's role in the international financial market and the global monetary architecture.

Coupled with its trade dominance, China's moves to boost the offshore use of RMB are widely believed to have substantial implications for the balance of the global economic and political powers. What are the intentions behind the policy of establishing an offshore RMB market? Are the policy measures introduced in the last few years motivated by economic pragmatism in the midst of dollar shortage, or parts of the ongoing modernizing process, or for building the international supremacy of RMB? A bigger question, of course, is: what are the implications for integrating China financial sector into the world economy?

It is not easy to answer these questions. In principle, there are both challenges and opportunities associated with China's move to integrate its financial markets with the global ones. The assessment of these challenges and opportunities is, however, beyond the scope of this chapter. To shed some insight on the subject matter, we discuss the development of the RMB offshore market in Hong Kong and the related implications for the internationalization of the RMB.

## 26.2 The Offshore RMB Market in Hong Kong

It is commonly perceived that Hong Kong, given its unique history, is China's designated experimental ground for liberalizing the RMB business. After Xiaochuan Zhou, the governor of the People's Bank of China, commented on the super-sovereign reserve currency and indirectly questioned the dominance of the US dollar in the global economy in the midst of the global financial crisis (Zhou, 2009), the offshore RMB market in Hong Kong has undergone a rapid growth in both transaction volume and the number of trading vehicles. Indeed, the HK offshore market accounts for a lion's share of the total overseas RMB transactions and its evolution is considered as a barometer of China's policy on internationalizing RMB.

Hong Kong is a special administrative region of China. Under the stipulation of the mini-constitution "The Basic Law of the Hong Kong Special Administrative Region," Hong Kong is allowed to maintain its own legal and financial systems. Specifically, Hong Kong has its own currency, the Hong Kong dollar, and imposes no capital controls.

Even before the transfer of sovereignty back to China in 1997, Hong Kong was already a renowned international financial center and a main entrepôt for China trade. Indeed, Hong Kong is widely considered as China's window to the rest of the world. After resuming its sovereignty over Hong Kong, China has maintained the "one country, two systems" policy that was originally envisioned by Xiaoping Deng and allowed Hong Kong to retain its own legal system. The differences in the legal and financial systems make it possible for China to use Hong Kong as a testing ground for its economic policies.

A noticeable example is the development of Hong Kong as a platform for the offshore RMB business. The policy of developing Hong Kong into a prime offshore RMB center was affirmed in China's 12th Five-Year Plan in 2011.

Notwithstanding Hong Kong is part of its territory, China treats Hong Kong as an offshore market in terms of RMB trading. It has instituted specific rules and procedures on cross-border RMB transactions between China and Hong Kong. Market practitioners see the RMB transacted in Hong Kong is different from the RMB in China; they coined the RMB traded in Hong Kong as CNH instead of the usual trading symbol CNY.

## 26.2.1 RMB Deposits in Hong Kong

The role of Hong Kong as a launch pad for offshore RMB transactions started in February 2004 when 32 banks in Hong Kong were authorized to accept RMB deposits and some selected RMB services. At the same time, individuals are allowed to convert up to RMB 20, 000 daily in Hong Kong. The daily RMB conversion and the RMB cash brought over by Chinese tourists are two main sources of initial RMB inflows to Hong Kong. The total CNH deposit at the end of February 2004 was only RMB 895 million. The evolution of CNH deposits is depicted in Figure 26.1.

Before 2008, the growth of the CNH deposit was quite slow. The market got a nudge in July 2007 when the first "Dim Sum" bond—a bond denominated in RMB and issued in Hong Kong—was issued by the China Development Bank, a Chinese policy bank that is under the direct jurisdiction of China's State Council. The total CNH deposit increased from RMB 27.9 billion in July 2007 to RMB 77.7 billion in May 2008.

The volume of CNH deposits began its steep ascent since the second half of 2010, after the expansion of the scheme for cross-border trade settlement in RMB in June 2010[1] and the signing of the Supplementary Memorandum of Co-operation between

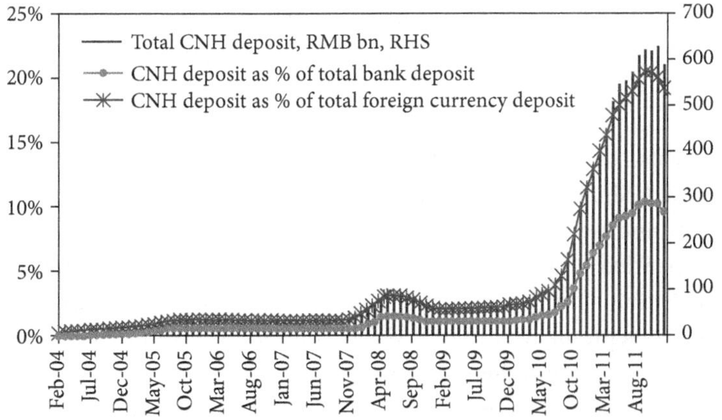


FIGURE 26.1 The RMB Deposit in Hong Kong

*Source:* CEIC.

the Hong Kong Monetary Authority and the People's Bank of China on RMB business in July 2010.[2] During the period from June 2008 to December 2011, the CNH deposit grew by 658 percent from the amount of RMB 77.6 billion to RMB 588.5 billion.

Undeniably, the RMB deposit market in Hong Kong has a relatively short history. Its growth is quite eye-opening and, in less than eight years, its size has increased by 656.6 times. The number of authorized institutions engaged in RMB business in Hong Kong is 133 as of December 2011, representing an increase of 101 (315.6 percent) from February 2004. As of December 2011, the CNH deposits represent about 7.7 percent of the total deposits and 15.2 percent of the foreign currency deposits in Hong Kong. If the stunning growth trend continues, the CNH could soon replace the US dollar—which accounts for 29.8 percent of the total deposits in Hong Kong as of December 2011—and become the most popular "foreign" currency in the Hong Kong market. In passing it is noted that, despite its phenomenal growth, the total amount of RMB deposits in Hong Kong is less than one percent of China's RMB deposit balance, which stood at the level of RMB 80.94 trillion as of December 2011.

The evolution of the CNH market is closely shaped by China's foreign exchange policies and their implications for the supply and demand of the offshore RMB. Besides the RMB cash brought into Hong Kong, the supply of offshore RMB is constrained by the daily RMB 2000 conversion rule and the net balance from the cross-border RMB trade settlement scheme.[3] On the demand side, the appreciation expectations could offer considerable support for the demand for RMB. Nonetheless, the demand for the currency could be seriously constrained by the absence of RMB-denominated investment opportunities beyond bank deposits.[4] With the expansion of the CNH deposit market, other assets priced in RMB are introduced. In the next section, we discuss the market for Dim Sum bonds.

## 26.2.2 The Dim Sum Bond Market

Dim Sum bonds are RMB-denominated bonds that are issued in Hong Kong. Prior to the issuance of Dim Sum bonds, most local Hong Kong banks offered an interest rate of 0.4 percent for CNH deposits and these deposits were deposited back to the People's Bank of China at the interest rate of 0.72 percent. The investment return from holding CNH deposits is very limited. Dim Sum bonds offer an investment alternative for the offshore RMB. Since the first issuance by the China Development Bank in 2007, the amount of outstanding Dim Sum bonds has steadily increased. The Dim Sum bond market has expanded quite quickly after the relaxation of rules on remitting offshore RMB back to China—for instance, the issuance jumped more than twentyfold from RMB 10 billion in September 2010 to RMB 212 billion by November 2011. The size of the Dim Sum bond market is graphed in Figure 26.2.

In the beginning, most of the Dim Sum bonds were issued by China's Ministry of Finance, China's policy banks (China Development Bank and Export-Import Bank of China), and state-own banks (Bank of China and China Construction Bank). Gradually, the list of issuers is expanded to include a) corporation issuers (for example, Hopewell Highway Infrastructure Ltd., the first corporate issuer), multinational corporations (for example, McDonald's and Caterpillar), and international institutions, including the World Bank and the Asian Development Bank. By 2011, 70 percent issuers are China-based entities such as the Ministry of Finance, policy banks, and commercial banks; more than 80 percent of issuers are deemed to be of investment grade, and 85 percent of bond tenors are below 3-years. The breakdown of the issuers is depicted in Figure 26.3.

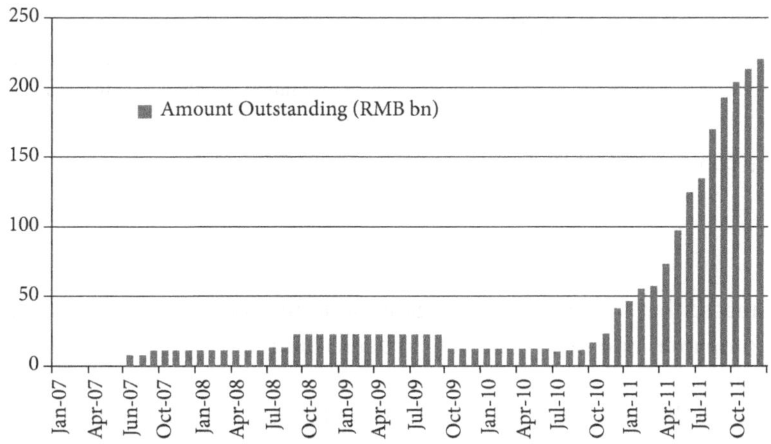


FIGURE 26.2 The Dim Sum Bond Market

*Source:* Deutsche Bank and Bloomberg

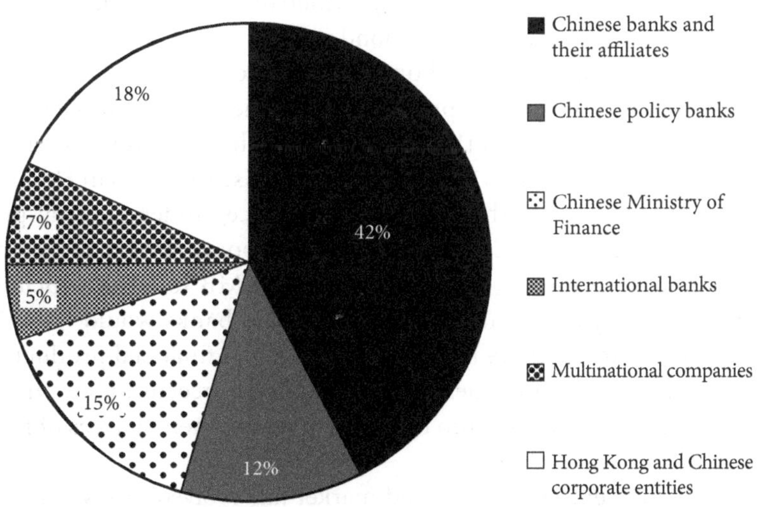


FIGURE 26.3 The distribution of Dim Sum Bond Issuers

*Note:* Because their sizes are relatively small, the issues by international institutions, including the World Bank and the Asian Development Bank, are included under the group of "international banks."

*Source:* Deutsche Bank and Bloomberg.

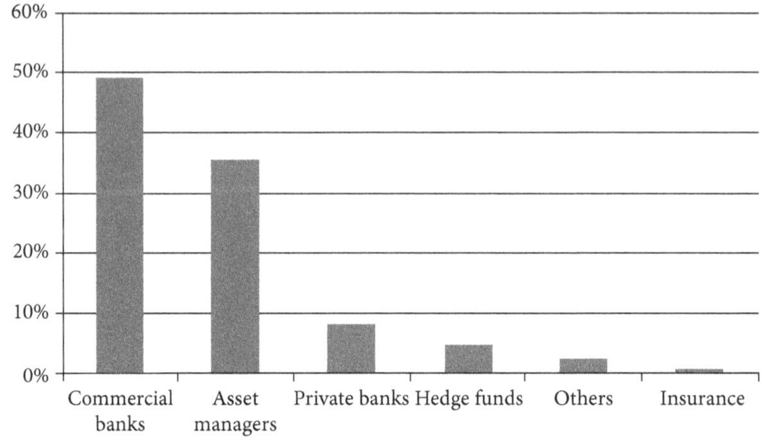


FIGURE 26.4 Dim Sum Bond Holders.

*Source:* Deutsche Bank and Bloomberg.

It is estimated that 85 percent of Dim Sum bond investors are from Asia. Asset management companies and local commercial banks are major buyers of Dim Sum bonds; see Figure 26.4.

The sovereign RMB bonds issued by China's Ministry of Finance have attracted considerable attention from the market. These sovereign issuances are usually large in size, ranging from the RMB 6 billion offer in September 2009 to the October 2011 offer of RMB 15 billion. These issuances cover a range of tenors up to 10 years. The long maturity offers are interpreted as efforts to provide a portfolio of medium-to-long term products and to set up a yield curve for the offshore bond market.

The motivation to issue Dim Sum bonds varies across issuers. Due to the relative scarcity of alternative investments priced in RMB, the CNH bond yield is typically 2 percent to 3 percent lower than the comparable onshore bond yield. The yield differential encourages borrowers with RMB assets to raise the RMB in Hong Kong and repatriate the proceeds for onshore uses. For instance, under the trial program of using RMB to fund FDI into China, the Dim Sum bond market represents a very attractive option. Nevertheless, remitting offshore RMB to China, including FDI, is subject to regulatory approval. Some international banks would issue Dim Sum bonds to raise CNH to facilitate trading of other CNH financial products. Further, some offshore Dim Sum bond issuers would swap the proceeds to the euro or the US dollar—these issuers using Dim Sum bonds to diversify their sources of funding at a reasonable rate.

Since 2007, the nascent Dim Sum bond market has evolved in several dimensions. A typical plain vanilla Dim Sum bond is denominated and traded in RMB. Shui On Land Ltd., a Hong Kong based property developer, in December 2010 issued a synthetic Dim Sum bond that is RMB denominated but is traded in the US dollar. Indeed, the bonds are sold in US dollars, will be redeemed for US dollars at maturity, and the coupons are paid in US dollars at prevailing exchange rates. Given the exchange rate component, the synthetic bond will appeal to investors who expect the RMB will appreciate against the US dollar during the holding period. From the issuer point of view, the US dollar proceeds from bond issuance could be remitted back to China following the existing procedure and, thus, avoid the uncertainty associated with RMB remittance, which has to be approved on a case-by-case basis.

In October 2011, Malaysia's sovereign wealth fund, Khazanah Nasional Berhad, issued the first sukuk in the Chinese currency RMB in Hong Kong. The first Dim Sum sukuk issuance had a relatively small size of RMB 500 million and a tenor of three years. For Hong Kong, the Khazanah Nasional Dim Sum sukuk issuance reassures its prominence status as an offshore RMB center and its potential role as an Islamic financing hub.

Despite its relatively short history, there are a few exchange traded funds (ETFs) devoted to the Dim Sum bond investment. Guggenheim Investments back in September 2011 launched the first US ETF that comprises Dim Sum bonds. The ETF's ticket symbol is unsurprisingly "RMB" and is designed to track the performance of a ruled-based index called the AlphaShares China Yuan Bond Index. Two other Dim Sum Bond EFTs are sponsored by the Invesco PowerShares (DSUM; based on the Citigroup Dim Sum Bond Index) and by the Van Eck Global (CHLC; based on the Market Vectors Renminbi Bond Index). Compared with existing Chinese RMB currency ETFs, these Dim Sim ETFs offer investors the potential for both investment income and currency appreciation. The introduction of these ETFs signifies the market potential of these RMB denominated bonds offered outside China

## 26.2.3 RMB Trade Settlement

Soon after the governor of the People's Bank of China commented on the super-sovereign reserve currency and implicitly challenged the dominance of the US dollar in the global economy in the midst of the recent global financial crisis (Zhou, 2009), China initiated the scheme to settle cross-border trade in RMB. In April 2009, the Chinese State Council approved a pilot scheme for cross-border trade settlement in RMB.[5] The scheme initially involved Shanghai and four other Chinese cities in the Guangdong Province, on the one hand, and Hong Kong on the other. The program was expanded to cover 20 of the 31 mainland Chinese provinces and to include companies that are domiciled in and outside Hong Kong in June 2010. After August 2011, the program is open to all of China.

The cumulative volume of trade settled in RMB was less than RMB 4 billion in 2009. After the expansion of the RMB trade settlement program in June 2010, the monthly volume of trade settled in RMB via Hong Kong has surged from the level of RMB 10 billion in July 2010 to RMB 239 billion in December 2011; an increase of 22 times within one and half years. Figure 26.5 presents the evolution of the RMB trade settlement activity.

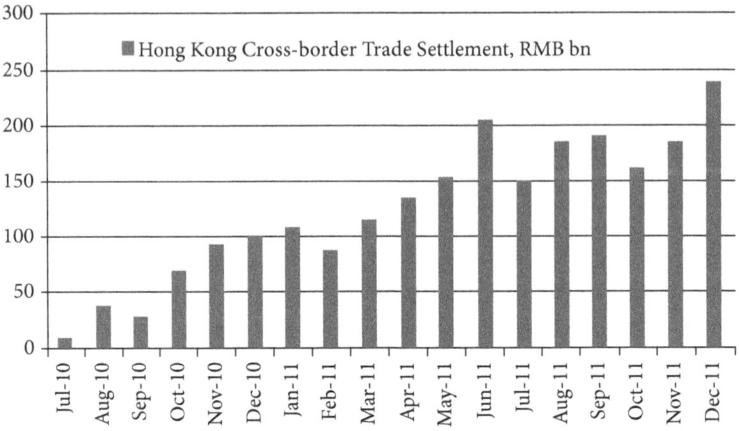


FIGURE 26.5 The volume of trade settled in RMB via Hong Kong

*Source:* CEIC.

The cross-border trade settlement in RMB program helps Chinese companies to manage exchange rate risk. The Chinese importers supply the offshore RMB by paying for their imports using the RMB. The foreign importers of Chinese goods demand the RMB to settle their trades. During the beginning phase of the program, the Chinese importers are the main users and, thus, lead to RMB outflows to the offshore market. One possible reason is that the foreign importers have to acquire RMB first before they could use the currency to pay for their imports from China. It is also perceived that when the CNH in Hong Kong is trading at a premium to the RMB in China, China's trading companies are willing to invoice their imports from their overseas associates in RMB and their overseas associates will convert the RMB into the US dollar in the CNH market at a better exchange rate to make the final payment. In a sense, such an arbitrage activity inflates the actual level of trade settled in RMB.

Despite its registered rapid growth, the amount of trade settled in RMB is relatively small. For instance, the value of RMB trade settlement in December 2011 is RMB 239 billion, which is far less than the prediction that one-third of China's exports could be invoiced in the RMB (Chen and Peng, 2007).[6] In passing, it is noted that Japan settles about at most 40 percent of its trade in the Japanese yen (Goldberg and Tille, 2008). Of course, whether the one-third stipulation is achievable or not depends on economic and political developments in both China and the global economy.

With China's robust strength in international trade, the market in general anticipates the RMB will gain its prominence in the area of trade settlement. However, due to inertia and network effect, the widespread use of RMB to settle China's trade will take some time to realize. For multinational corporations, they have to take the time to set up their internal systems, including the legal and risk management procedures, to handle RMB trade settlement. The scheme of cross-border trade settlement in RMB has jump-started the international use and acceptance of the RMB, and the positive network effect will encourage other corporations to use RMB to settle trade.

### 26.2.4 CNH Foreign Exchange (FX) Trading

Prior to the signing of the Supplementary Memorandum of Co-operation between the Hong Kong Monetary Authority and the People's Bank of China on RMB business in July 2010, there is no officially endorsed FX market for the RMB in Hong Kong. Among other things, the Supplementary Memorandum allows the trading of spot and forward RMB and RMB-linked structural products in Hong Kong.[7] Since then, the CNH could be essentially transacted like a convertible currency in Hong Kong. The Hong Kong daily trading in spot RMB has grown from almost nothing to an estimated average volume of US$ 400 million by the end of 2010, and to US$ 2 billion by the end of 2011.[8]

Due to the different supply and demand structures in Hong Kong and China and the presence of capital controls, the CNH in Hong Kong and the RMB (CNY) in the onshore China market are usually traded at different prices. Since the CNH money market in Hong Kong is relatively small, the CNH FX rate is largely driven by market expectations of the RMB appreciation potential and the global risk appetite.[9] The onshore rate, on the other hand, mainly follows the officially guided market rate. The persistence of price differentials attests to the effectiveness of capital control measures that separate the Hong Kong and China financial markets (Cheung and Qian, 2011; Ma and McCauley, 2008).

Figure 26.6 presents the premium of CNH over CNY. Before the sharp drop in September 2011, the CNH was traded at a premium up to 2.5 percent. After the drop CNH is traded at a discount to CNY. The swing in the premium is in accordance with the change of the 12-month RMB forward premium of 3 percent to 4 percent in January 2011 to the discount of 1.4 percent in December 2011. There is a speculation that the

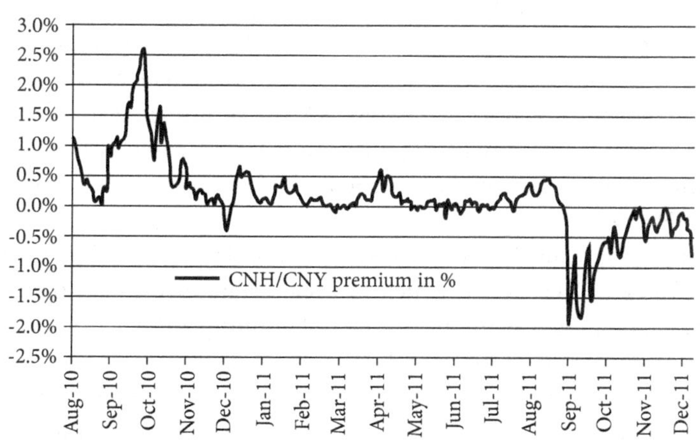


FIGURE 26.6 The CNH/CNY premium in percentages

*Source:* Bloomberg.

September 2011 drop is triggered by unwinding of CNH buying that was not backed by imports and exports trade activity and the possibility of the hard landing risk in China.

It is conceived that the price discrepancy between CNH and CNY contributes to the cross-border RMB movement. For instance, as described in the previous subsection, when CNH is trading at a premium to CNY, the Chinese importers are likely to invoice in RMB. It will then trigger RMB outflows to Hong Kong under the trade settlement channel. On the other hand, when CNH is trading at a discount to CNY, Chinese exports are likely to be invoiced in RMB, and such invoicing behavior will lead to the flow of the RMB back to China. Apparently, these export- and import-related arbitrage activities are small relative to investors' trading positions and, thus, the price discrepancy tends to persist.

There are a few groups of participants in the CNH FX market. The authorities endorse CNH trading derived from RMB trade settlements and the associated risk management activity. Indeed, a few months after signing the Supplementary Memorandum, the Hong Kong Monetary Authority (2010) issued guidelines regulating CNH trading and emphasizing trading should be connected to import and export, rather than speculative, activities. Despite the official intention, there are speculators and arbitragers who trade CNH to take advantage of the currency's appreciation trend and the differentials between on-shore and off-shore interest rates and exchange rates. The speculative and arbitrage activities have to bear the risk of sudden rate movements in a relatively thin market. As the market liquidity is improving over time, we expect the CNH market will gain in both depth and breadth, which will facilitate the price discovery process and pave the way for RMB convertibility.[10]

### 26.2.5 Other Products

The prospect of the offshore RMB market in Hong Kong depends on the menu of RMB-denominated assets and liabilities. On the one hand, Hong Kong has to accumulate a sizable amount of offshore RMB to support and sustain an active offshore market. On the other hand, the creation of offshore RMB-denominated investment products could promote the acceptability of the offshore market. In the last few years, several investment opportunities, beyond bank deposits and bonds, were introduced to expand the class of CNH assets.

In April 2011, Hong Kong had its first RMB-denominated initial public offering.[11] It was issued by the Hui Xian REIT, which is a real-estate investment trust backed by a major property in Beijing. Apparently, the lack of liquidity is the reason why retail investors are not too enthusiastic about this CNH asset.

Nonetheless, the potential for RMB equity listings in Hong Kong is huge. Indeed, in early 2012, it is reported that the Chinese securities regulators plan to revise rules on overseas listing and to encourage Chinese companies to issue RMB denominated stocks in Hong Kong. In recent years, Chinese companies have annually raised HK$ 200 to 300

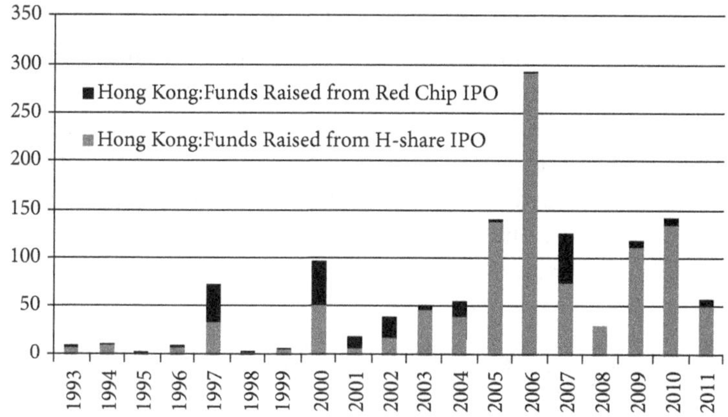


FIGURE 26.7 IPOs issued in Hong Kong by Chinese domiciled Company

*Source:* CEIC.

billion capital via IPO in the Hong Kong Exchange; see Figure 26.7.[12] The IPO proceeds are mostly used for RMB investments in China. For these companies, it makes a lot of sense to raise RMB directly in Hong Kong to reduce reliance on non-RMB funding and to manage exchange rate risk. With improvement in the clearing system of equity priced in RMB and market liquidity, one could expect more RMB denominated equity listings in Hong Kong.

Catching the trend of offering investment products in RMB, the century-old bullion house in Hong Kong, the Chinese Gold & Silver Exchange Society, has started trading a new product called "Renminbi Kilobar Gold" since October 2011. The Renminbi Kilobar Gold is quoted in RMB for one kilogram of gold. It requires settlement in RMB and physical delivery of specified gold bars. In February 2012, Hang Seng Bank offered the first RMB Gold ETF. Both products offer investors to deploy their offshore RMB holdings and promote the use of RMB outside China.

A natural place to deploy the offshore RMB is the onshore market in China. The obvious reason for developing investment products for offshore RMB is, because of capital controls, the remittance of RMB raised in Hong Kong back to China is not allowed without the Chinese authorities' approval. The launch of the RMB Qualified Foreign Institutional Investor (RQFII) scheme has significant implications for the offshore RMB market in Hong Kong and China's financial liberalization process.

The original Qualified Foreign Institutional Investor (QFII) scheme essentially allows authorized foreign entities to convert foreign currencies—mainly the US dollar—into RMB to invest in China. The RQFII program, in contrast, allows the offshore RMB to be invested through authorized overseas entities in China's local financial markets. It adds a significant channel for remitting CNH back to China under the capital account and, at the same time, is a step to internationalize China's financial market. The scheme definitely affirms China's commitment to develop the offshore market and is a boost to HK's status as a main offshore RMB center.

According to the joint announcement by the China Securities Regulatory Commission, the People's Bank of China and the State Administration of Foreign Exchange in December 2011, only Hong Kong subsidiaries of China's fund management companies and securities companies will be considered for the pilot RQFII scheme. The initial quota for the pilot scheme is RMB 20 billion, of which at least 80 percent are expected to be invested in fixed income products and the remaining could be in equities or equity investment funds. The market response is quite favorable. By early January 2012, various RQFII funds were approved and the RMB 20 billion quota was used up.

## 26.3 Looking Forward

The offshore RMB market is a landmark event for Hong Kong and for the global market. The anointment of Hong Kong as the offshore RMB market laboratory has reaffirmed and strengthened its position and prestige in the global financial market. The financial institutions in Hong Kong have enjoyed the first-mover advantages and grown along with the nascent offshore market. In the meanwhile, the global market is witnessing a grand experiment of creating an offshore market via mostly policy-driven initiatives. It is noted that, historically, offshore markets such as the euro-dollar market were sprung from and evolved according to market forces. China's policy driven approach to setup and nurture an offshore market is quite a venture by itself.

While the offshore RMB market in Hong Kong is gaining popularity, it is far from a fully fledged offshore market such as the euro dollar market. For instance, the offshore RMB market still lacks some basic features, including credit ratings of Dim Sum bonds and offshore RMB benchmark interest rates. In the early phase of the Dim Sum bond market, the issuers were mostly Chinese policy banks and large creditworthy corporations. The explosion of the Dim Sum bond market in 2011, for instance, comes with a considerable number of lower quality issuers. The presence of these issuers raises the concern about Dim Sum bonds that were issued without explicit clauses in their covenants to protect investors. As the market expands and evolves, investors—especially the sophisticated ones—would shift their attention from the opportunity to hold on and, possibly, benefit from the RMB's yield and appreciation potential to the creditworthiness of the issuers. Naturally, the availability of serious credit ratings and improved investor protection will foster the dynamic growth of the Dim Sum bond market.

For the nascent offshore RMB market, the Treasury Markets Association in Hong Kong posts CNH interbank offered rates from the Bank of China (HK), HSBC, and the Standard Chartered Bank on a daily basis. The maturity of the posted rates ranges from overnight to one year. However, a benchmark interest rate comparable to the well-known London interbank offered rate is lacking. It is conceived that a recognized offshore RMB benchmark interest rate could facilitate the growth of the offshore market by allowing banks and investors to better price the offshore RMB denominated loans, the borrowing costs and risk, and structural products, and this would help the development of new offshore RMB denominated products.

As part of China's policy to promote the international use of the RMB, Hong Kong would not be the only offshore RMB market. Indeed, Singapore started its offshore RMB business in early 2011. Another likely participant is the city of London, the world's dominating international financial center. In September 2011, after the fourth China-U.K. Economic and Financial Dialogue took place in London, both governments issued a joint statement on the intention to create an offshore RMB market in London. Despite the official endorsement, there is no concrete time table yet for launching the offshore RMB market in London at the time of writing.

Will the competition for offshore RMB businesses from other international financial centers threaten the status of Hong Kong? Even if the threat is not real in the near term, there is little doubt that the offshore RMB will migrate to, say, the London market. However, with its first-mover advantage and an officially designated offshore RMB clearing bank, Hong Kong is likely to be a major player in the global offshore RMB market.

Similar to its other economic reform policies, China has followed a measured strategy to experiment with the offshore RMB market. In creating a new offshore RMB market, the authorities have to work out the nitty-gritty of regulatory cooperation, in addition to the setting of clearing and settlement systems and market liquidity. From the policy point of view, a well-formulated offshore market helps to assess the implications of intermediating international transactions in the RMB without giving up capital controls outright (He and McCauley, 2012). Since Hong Kong is a special administrative region of China, it is relatively pliable. China could dictate both the growth and the evolution of the offshore market via necessary legislation. Thus, on the count of regulatory cooperation, Hong Kong has an insurmountable advantage over other international financial centers.

Despite its existing advantages, the eventual success of the offshore RMB market in Hong Kong depends on its growth in the global economy. It is not just the growth in the depth and breadth of the market but also in the availability of new and high-quality offshore RMB-denominated assets and liabilities. A productive development strategy for Hong Kong is to secure collaborations with other international financial centers to promote the offshore RMB business in the global market and, in the process, solidify its prominent role in the global offshore RMB market.[13]

## 26.4 The Offshore Market and the Internationalization of the RMB

Since the 2008 global financial crisis, the Chinese authorities have adopted an active, if not aggressive, policy to promote the international use of the RMB. Several initiatives, including the creation of the offshore RMB market in Hong Kong, are perceived as deliberated measures to assert the role of the RMB in the global market. Chen and Cheung (2011) note that these measures could be motivated by economic pragmatism in the midst of dollar shortage experienced during the crisis, could be parts of the ongoing modernizing process, or could be for developing the international supremacy of the RMB. Despite its motivation, the measures could drastically change the landscape of the international monetary architecture if they lead to an internationalized RMB.[14]

The role of the Chinese currency in the international market is disproportionately smaller than China's economic size. Throughout its phenomenal growth period, China has mainly relied on the US dollar to conduct its international transactions and has accumulated a large net long foreign currency (mainly the US dollar) position and, at the same time, a huge short domestic currency position. Such an imbalance in the currency composition presents China with a considerable exchange rate risk. If the Chinese RMB is a global currency and is widely used and accepted for international transactions, then China could replace its foreign currency claims on the rest of the world by domestic currency claims and, thus, reduce its exposure to exchange rate risk.

Cheung et al. (2011) acutely note that China's initiatives that promote the international use of the RMB could help normalize China's currency composition of international assets and liabilities. In addition to the offshore RMB markets, China has promoted the use of its currency by denominating its expanded official aid programs and outward direct investment in the RMB. Cheung et al. (2011) labeled the strategy of denominating China's claims on the rest of the world in RMB the "renminbisation" of China's foreign assets.

If normalizing China's currency composition of international assets and liabilities is a policy objective, then some commentators rightly alarmed a possible adverse policy effect of the offshore RMB market. As noted above, the RMB trade settlement in the offshore RMB market in Hong Kong is dominated by RMB payments for Chinese imports, while Chinese exports are still commonly settled using the US dollar. The process skews toward an accumulation of US dollar reserves for China. Nevertheless, the initial flow of the RMB to the offshore market is deemed to be inevitable because the rest of the world has to accumulate a sufficient amount of the currency before using the RMB to conduct trade and investment activities. When there is enough of an amount of the offshore RMB to meet its demand, the outflow will stop and even be reversed. The development seems not that discouraging, as the gap between the values of imports and exports settled in RMB is narrowed a bit and there is an increase in Dim Sum bonds issued by non-residents in 2011.

The prospect of the offshore RMB market hinges upon China's overall reform policy in general and its capital controls and exchange rate policy in particular. As repeated quite often in official statements, reform is China's predetermined policy. The doubts are about the speed and the extent of the reform. In February 2012, the Financial Survey and Statistics Department headed by SongCheng Sheng at the People's Bank of China issued a report in Chinese that outlines the process for opening up China's capital account and promoting the international use of the RMB.[15] The report suggests a three-stage approach. Specifically, the government could in one to three years relax restrictions on outward direct investments and promote the "Going Global" policy, in three to five years it could relax controls on trade and commercial credits and promote the international use of the RMB, and in five to ten years it could build up and strengthen financial markets and liberalize real estate, stock, and bond transactions.

While the proposed reform schedule is quite aggressive and is not in line with the usual gradual reform approach undertaken by China in the last few decades, it reflects the desire to continue the financial market reform and the RMB internationalization process. Against this backdrop, Hong Kong could leverage on its renowned financial market infrastructure and be a key component of the development plan for a well-functioning offshore RMB market, which would help intermediate international (trade and financial) transactions in the RMB and, hence, promote its acceptance.

Despite its head start, the success of the offshore RMB market in Hong Kong is not a foregone conclusion. While China's policy stance is a favorable factor at least in the short to medium term, the pace at which China pushes the international use of the RMB could prove crucial to the offshore market growth. As noted before, the RMB internationalization process is mostly dictated by policy measures rather than market forces. To become a fully fledged international currency, China has to develop a deep and efficient financial sector with prudent governance. Despite the usual hyperbolic rhetoric on how far and how fast China could liberalize its capital account and transform its financial sector, China has to take the time to put in place the hardware and, more importantly, the software that is required to establish and maintain a robust financial sector and the related regulatory framework.

Notwithstanding official policies and good intentions, the quality of the currency itself is not the sole factor determining the acceptance of the RMB in the global market. Beyond some fundamental structural changes in its financial sector, China has to convince other countries to conduct international trade and finance transactions in its currency. The persuasion, as attested by Japan's attempt to internationalize its currency in the late twentieth century (Ministry of Finance, Japan, 2003; Takagi, 2011), goes beyond economic reasoning. Political considerations, especially in East Asia, could play a non-negligible role in adopting an international currency. With the region's predominant antagonism toward hegemony, China's communist political structure, military buildup, and recent territorial disputes with its neighboring countries could be a drag on its effort to internationalize the RMB.

In addition to the uncertainty stemmed from the geopolitics about a global RMB, Hong Kong has to prepare for competition from other international finance centers. Arguably, London could be both a valuable partner and formidable competitor in promoting offshore RMB business in the near future. At the same time, one should not overlook the potential challenge from Shanghai, which is a city China has repeatedly indicated it plans to make a prime international financial center and RMB-trading hub.

Another growth factor is the quality of the new offshore RMB-denominated assets and liabilities. To be a true contender in the global monetary market, the offshore market has to offer a world-class asset category and related services. As noted above, the offshore RMB market in Hong Kong is still in its infancy. Despite its phenomenal growth, there is still substantial room for improvement. In passing, we note that, at the time of writing, both the value of RMB deposits in Hong Kong and CHN market activity experienced a slowdown in the last month of 2011 and the first month of the 2012. While one does not want to give too much weight to the figures of these two months, the circumstantial evidence hints at the possible non-monotonous evolution of the offshore market.

Given its efficient financial infrastructure and relative pliability, Hong Kong has the right elements to become the preferred base for experimenting with the international use of the RMB. The prospect of the offshore RMB market in Hong Kong depends, among other things, on both the geopolitics and economics surrounding the process of internationalizing RMB. Under the presumption that China will continue its liberalization process and adopt the necessary regulatory changes to promote the international use of the RMB, it is reasonable to be cautiously optimistic about the growth of the offshore RMB market in Hong Kong.

## Notes

1. See Section 26.2.3 for cross-border trade settlement in RMB.
2. The Supplementary Memorandum essentially allows a rich menu of RMB trading activities—including spot and forward RMB trading and RMB-linked structural products—in Hong Kong.
3. Another source is the bilateral currency swap arrangement between Hong Kong and China. The maximum value of the swap arrangement was doubled to RMB 400 billion in December 2011 and may be extended after its November 2014 expiration.
4. In July 2010, the CITIC Bank International issued the inaugural RMB denominated Certificate of Deposit (RMB CD) in Hong Kong targeting institutional investors. Now, RMB CDs for both institutional and retail investors are available.
5. The use of RMB to settle cross-border trade could be traced back to at least 2003. See, for example, the directives issued by China's State Administration of Foreign Exchange (2003a, b), in Chinese, on using the RMB in settling trade including "边境贸易外汇管理办法" and "关于境内机构对外贸易中以人民币作为计价货币有关问题的通知." Before 2009, the RMB trade settlement mainly occurred for trade taking place along China's borders with, say, Cambodia, Mongolia, Russia, and Vietnam. Data on these cross-border trade settlements are quite scant. The discussion in this subsection thus focuses only on the pro-2009 era.
6. For December 2011, China's imports and exports totaled US$ 332.92 billion
7. Before July 2010, non-deliverable RMB forwards instead of deliverable forwards were commonly traded in the market.
8. According to the Bank for International Settlements (2010) triennial central bank survey, the average RMB daily forex turnover in the *global* market surged from US$1.7 billion in the 2004 survey and US$14.6 billion in the 2007 survey to reach US$ 29.2 billion in the 2010 survey.

9. In passing, we note that the yield on Dim Sum bonds is also affected by the expectations of CNH movements.
10. The RMB forward, options, and structural markets are quite thinly traded; partly because of the absence of an established benchmark CNH interest rate (CNHIBOR). For instance, it is estimated that the daily RMB forward volume is around US$100 million.
11. The Hong Kong Exchange prepared the clearing system for RMB denominated listing of stocks and bonds back in September 2010.
12. These Chinese IPOs help make Hong Kong Exchange the world's leading exchange for new stock offerings in the past few years.
13. Indeed, the Hong Kong Monetary Authority and British Treasury planned a joint private-sector forum that will meet twice a year, with the first forum scheduled in May 2012, to promote cooperation between the two jurisdictions in developing offshore RMB businesses.
14. Some recent writings on the internationalization of the RMB are Ito (2011), McCauley (2011), and Wu et al. (2010).
15. The report in Chinese "我国加快资本账户开放的条件基本成熟" was published in the *China Securities Journal* online and is available at [http://www.cs.com.cn/xwzx/07/201202/t20120223_3253890.html].

## References

Bank for International Settlements, 2010, *Triennial Central Bank Survey: Foreign Exchange and Derivative Market Activity in 2010*, Basel: Bank for International Settlements.

Chen, Hongyi, and Wensheng Peng, 2007, "The Potential of the Renminbi as an International Currency," *China Economic Issues*, Number 7/07, Hong Kong Monetary Authority.

Chen, Xiaoli, and Yin-Wong Cheung, 2011, "Renminbi Going Global," *China & World Economy* 19, 1–18.

Cheung, Yin-Wong, Guonan Ma, Robert N. McCauley, 2011, "Renminbising China's Foreign Assets," *Pacific Economic Review* 16, 1–17.

Cheung, Yin-Wong, and XingWang Qian, 2011, "Deviations from Covered Interest Parity: The Case of China," Chapter 15, Yin-Wong Cheung, Vikkas Kakkar and Guonan Ma, editors, *The Evolving Role of Asia in Global Finance Frontiers of Economics and Globalization* Volume 9, Bingley, UK: Emerald Group Publishing Limited, pp. 369–386.

Goldberg, Linda S., and Cédric Tille. 2008. "Vehicle Currency Use in International Trade." *Journal of International Economics* 76, 177–192.

He, Dong, and Robert N. McCauley, 2012, "Offshore Markets for the Domestic Currency: Monetary and Financial Stability Issues," Chapter 10, Yin-Wong Cheung and Jakob de Haan, editors, "The Evolving Role of China in the Global Economy," Cambridge, MA: MIT Press; 301–337.

Hong Kong Monetary Authority, 2010, "Renminbi (RMB) Cross-Border Trade Settlement and Net Open Position," http://www.info.gov.hk/hkma/eng/guide/circu_date/20111223e1.pdf.

Ito, Takatoshi, 2011, "The Internationalization of the RMB: Opportunities and Pitfalls," CGS/IIGG Working Paper.

Ma, Guonan and Robert N. McCauley, 2008, "Efficacy of China's Capital Controls: Evidence from Price and Flow Data," *Pacific Economic Review* 13, 104–123.

McCauley, Robert N., 2011, "Renminbi Internationalization and China's Financial Development Model," CGS/IIGG Working Paper.

Ministry of Finance, Japan, 2003, "Study Group for the Promotion of the Internationalization of the Yen"—Chairpersons' Report, http://www.mof.go.jp/english/if/e20030123.htm.

State Administration of Foreign Exchange, 2003a,边境贸易外汇管理办法, http://www.safe.gov cn/model_safe/laws/law_detail.jsp?ID=80100000000000000,14&id=4.

State Administration of Foreign Exchange, 2003b, 关于境内机构对外贸易中以人民 币作为计价货币有关问题的通知, http://www.safe.gov.cn/model_safe/laws/law_detail.jsp?ID=80800000000000000,40&id=4.

Takagi, Shinji, 2011, "Internationalizing the Yen, 1984-2003: Unfinished Agenda or Mission Impossible?" Chapter 8, Yin-Wong Cheung and Gounan Ma, eds, *Asia and China in the Global Economy*, Singapore: The World Scientific Publishing Co. Pte. Ltd.; 219–244.

Wu, Friedrich, Rongfang Pan, and Di Wang, 2010, "Renminbi's Potential to Become a Global Currency," *China & World Economy* 18, 63–81.

Zhou, Xiaochuan, 2009, "Reform the International Monetary System," People's Bank of China, http://www.pbc.gov.cn/publish/english/956/ 2009/20091229104425550619706/20091229104425550619706_.html.

# AUTHOR INDEX

# SUBJECT INDEX